HANDBOOK OF
CONTEMPORARY
BEHAVIORAL
ECONOMICS

HANDBOOK OF CONTEMPORARY

BEHAVIORAL ECONOMICS

FOUNDATIONS AND DEVELOPMENTS

EDITED BY

MORRIS ALTMAN

M.E.Sharpe
Armonk, New York
London, England

Library of Congress Cataloging-in-Publication Data

Handbook of contemporary behavioral economics : foundations and developments
/ Morris Altman, [editor].
   p. cm.
 Includes bibliographical references and index.
 ISBN 13: 978-0-7656-1302-8 (hardcover : alk. paper)
 ISBN 10: 0-7656-1302-6 (hardcover : alk. paper)
 1. Economics—Psychological aspects. I. Altman, Morris.

HB74.P8.H363 2006
330'.01'9—dc22   2005022252

Printed in the United States of America

This book is dedicated to the memory and work of
Richard Cyert, Harvey Leibenstein, and Herbert Simon.

CONTENTS

LIST OF TABLES AND FIGURES

TABLES

FIGURES

INTRODUCTION

Morris Altman

The focus of this handbook is original papers by behavioral economists that expand on their own contributions to behavioral economics, providing in the process an insightful description and analysis of a particular and important aspect of behavioral economics. These are supplemented by a number of more conventional albeit critical surveys of the literature. Each contribution also provides extensive references. There are thirty-six original papers in this handbook, authored or co-authored by forty-seven scholars. Of particular importance in this handbook is giving voice not only to aspects of behavioral economics that have been most recently in the limelight, such as the issue of rationality in decision making, but also to original and significant contributions that are just beginning to make their mark. Moreover, we give voice to different perspectives in behavioral economics that can be quite inconsistent in results and approach. Too often texts in behavioral economics focus upon one perspective to the exclusion of all others.

Some critical underlying assumptions and thoughts made in designing this handbook are:

- Assumptions matter substantively for causal and predictive analysis.
- Assumptions can be of a psychological, sociological, or institutional type—it is not only psychology that is important to behavioral economics.
- There is no party line with regard to behavioral economics apart from appreciating the importance of modeling assumptions. We must remain open to different approaches. This was foundational to Herbert Simon's perspective on behavioral economics.
- Behavioral economists therefore can develop models that compete in their positive and normative dimensions.
- One aspect of behavioral economics is to determine the choices people make and how these choices are made, and to ascertain to what extent these deviate from the conventional wisdom.
- It is important to understand why people behave the way they do, with regard to both their cognitive abilities and their environmental constraints.
- Deviations from conventional norms, which exist aplenty, need not demonstrate irrationality in decision making.
- Related to this, neoclassical norms for rational behavior need not be ideal from a scientific perspective.
- It is important to understand how cognitive capacities, information flows, culture, learning, and institutions affect intelligent decision making.
- A critical component of behavioral economics is building models that better reflect actual behavior. Such behavior can be both rational and intelligent but not neoclassical.
- Nonmaximizing neoclassical behavior need not be irrational; it might simply be inefficient.

- What are the implications for economic theory if variables that are non-neoclassical (such as altruism) are important to choice behavior?
- Behavioral economics should not imply that economic theory as we know it should be junked.
- Behavioral economics does imply significant revisions to economic theory in areas where the conventional wisdom is deficient and even highly misleading.
- How might conventional theory be revised to incorporate insights from behavioral economics? For example:

  - Behavioral economics demonstrates not that individuals are insensitive to price and real income but that other variables can be of critical importance. This can yield starkly different analytical predictions and causal analyses.
  - Behavioral economics suggests that firms do not maximize output given inputs, that effort is a variable input, and that nominal wages are sticky downward over the business cycle. This implies not that individuals are unintelligent in choice behavior but rather that individuals behave differently than the neoclassical individual does. How would this modify our theories of the firm?
  - Behavioral economics has demonstrated that preferences are not consistent over time. Does this imply that individuals are irrational or that neoclassical theory does not correctly model the behavior of rational individuals? How would the theory of consumer behavior be affected by such behavioral findings?

What is critical to behavioral economics is the appreciation of the significance for economic analysis of the realism of one's modeling assumptions in terms of their behavioral and institutional dimensions. It is recognized that assumptions matter for both causal and predictive analyses. This one point critically distinguishes behavioral from mainstream economics, in that the latter pays little heed to the realism of assumption in model building and economic analysis. Nor is much attention paid to the institutional and sociocultural parameters that affect decision making and economic outcomes (Altman 1999; Friedman 1953; Leibenstein 1983; Reder 1982; Simon 1978, 1977).

With regard to the underlying importance of assumptions and the significance of the realism of modeling institutional and sociocultural constraints, some of Herbert Simon's thoughts are worth mentioning.

> Our predictions of the operations of markets and of the economy *are* sensitive to our assumptions about mechanisms at the level of decision processes. Moreover, the assumptions of the behavioral theories are almost certainly closer to reality than those of the classical theory. These two facts, in combination, constitute a direct refutation of the argument that the unrealism of the assumptions of the classical theory is harmless. We cannot use the *in vacua* version of the law of falling bodies to predict the sinking of a heavy body in molasses. The predictions of the classical and neoclassical theories and the policy recommendations derived from them must be treated with the greatest caution. (Simon 1979, 509)

Leibenstein makes a similar point, emphasizing that analytical prediction need not tell very much about causality given that there might be alternative modeling assumptions that generate the same prediction. Of course, if both the predictions and the assumptions are counterfactual, the extant theory is even more problematic.

I believe that counterfactual postulates are unlikely to lead to correct *coherent* explanations. If the postulates cannot be tested, then we are forced to consider only the implications. But we would believe there is something wrong if we had a theory whose postulates were known to be counter to fact but which lead to correct predictions...I do not believe that the only purpose of theory is as an engine for prediction, nor do I see that we should look at any particular set of methodological views as imposing decisive constraints on our scientific procedures at this stage in our knowledge. (Leibenstein 1983, 840)

Simon also points out that critiquing the conventional theories is beside the point unless one has a convincing alternative (or revision of the conventional narrative) that better explains the facts in terms of both causation and prediction.

Once a theory is well entrenched, it will survive many assaults of empirical evidence that purports to refute it unless an alternative theory, consistent with the evidence, stands ready to replace it. Such conservative protectiveness of established beliefs is, indeed, not unreasonable. In the first place, in empirical science we aspire only to approximate truths; we are under no illusion that we can find a single formula, or even a moderately complex one, that captures the whole truth and nothing else. We are committed to a strategy of successive approximations, and when we find discrepancies between theory and data, our first impulse is to patch rather than to rebuild from the foundations. In the second place, when discrepancies appear, it is seldom immediately obvious where the trouble lies. It may be located in the fundamental assumptions of the theory, but it may as well be merely a defect in the auxiliary hypotheses and measurement postulates we have had to assume in order to connect theory with observations. Revisions in these latter parts of the structure may be sufficient to save the remainder. What then is the present status of the classical theory of the firm? There can no longer be any doubt that the micro assumptions of the theory—the assumptions of perfect rationality—are contrary to fact. It is not a question of approximation; they do not even remotely describe the processes that human beings use for making decisions in complex situations. (Simon 1979: 509–10)

An important objective of many behavioral economists is to provide rigorous alternatives or revisions to the conventional wisdom.

Behavioral economists find that individuals, firms, particular markets, and economies all often behave differently than is predicted by the conventional wisdom. The manner in which individuals actually do behave critically depends on psychological, institutional, cultural, and even biological considerations that affect and constrain the choices individuals can and do make. In behavioral economics, the reality of behavior is foundational to developing new theories and revising the conventional ones, as are the insights of pioneers in behavioral economists such as George Akerlof, Richard Cyert, Harvey Leibenstein, James March, Herbert Simon, and Vernon Smith and "fellow travelers" such Gerd Gigerenzer, Daniel Kahneman, and Amos Tversky, as well as the findings of psychologists, sociologists, political scientists, legal scholars, and biologists, among others. This approach to the economics of everyday life has important ramifications for an understanding of economic behavior in, for example, labor markets, financial markets, the household, the economics of the environment, and ethics, and for economic methodology and empirical economics.

In all venues of economic analysis the clarion call of behavioral economics is that a coherent and intelligent understanding of the economic realm requires a solid foundation in the behavioral underpinnings of economic theory. The contributors to this handbook critically address and flesh out this simple but fundamentally important point from a variety of behavioral perspectives, touching on a wide array of economic and social questions. This is a major and comprehensive articulation of behavioral economics from the standpoint of some of its leading proponents at a time when both scholars and the public demand explanations and answers to key economic problems for which both conventional and heterodox approaches have so far met with failure.

In the first section of this handbook, "Inside the Economic Agent," there are contributions by Paul Albanese, Gerald· Cory, Roger Frantz, David George, Bruce Kaufman, and Gary Lynne. Albanese links the psychoanalytic approach to personality, consumer preferences, and analyses of consumer behavior. He thereby moves inside of the "black box" of the economic agent of traditional economic theory to better understand consumer behavior. Cory details research on the physiological reality of the brain and how this impacts and intersects with the social brain, which he argues is characterized by both self-interested and other-interested components that are critical to the social individual. The social brain has physiological roots, and the architecture of the brain has important implication for supply-and-demand analysis. Frantz focuses on intuition as a fundamentally important decision-making heuristic, especially in a world of uncertainty. Intuition is not fanciful or magical but has its roots in the physiological limits of our brain's conscious cognitive capabilities (bounded rationality) and in our development of tools to rationally deal with this reality. George examines the role that introspection—the individual's mental state as opposed to actual behavior—could play in economic analysis and discourse. He relates this to the analytical framework of metapreferences and unpreferred versus preferred preferences and the importance of this for normative analyses. Kaufman discusses the positive role that emotions play as a decision-making heuristic and overlaps with Frantz's analysis of intuition. Emotions are modeled as a critical component of rational individuals' decision-making toolbox, whose integration into economic modeling makes economic theory a more potent analytical tool. Lynne makes the case for the existence of subselves in the context of "metaeconomics" and explores how modeling decision making with this in mind, as opposed to the traditional single-self individual, will provide for a richer analyses of choice behavior. Lynne's "metaeconomics" is dialectically linked with Cory's narrative on the social brain.

In the second section, "Context and Modeling," we have papers by Morris Altman; Alexander Field; Alan James MacFadyen; Shlomo Maital; Jörg Rieskamp, Ralph Hertwig, and Peter M. Todd; Kevin Sontheimer; and John Tomer. Altman discusses the importance of introducing the more realistic behavioral assumption of effort variability, focusing on literature on efficiency wages and x-efficiency, and extensions to these theories. The conventional wisdom assumes that effort discretion does not exist. Behavioral models yield significantly different predictions with respect, for example, to the determinants of employment, economic efficiency, and the socioeconomic implications of real wages changes and levels, firm culture, and labor power. Field engages the selfishness-altruism debate in economics and in the social sciences in general. He defends a version of methodological individualism that incorporates recent advances in our understanding of the roles that reciprocity and evolution play in determining individual behavior in the economic realm. MacFadyen argues for incorporations of "beliefs" in the modeling choice behavior of rational individuals, finding that the absence of beliefs as an independent variable weakens the analytical power of conventional economic theory. His analysis ties into George's analyses of introspection. Maital makes the case that to become a more effective public policy instrument, economics needs to restore behavior and explicit values as central concerns, thereby rebuilding an ethical foundation of capitalism, akin to what Adam Smith attempted. Rieskamp, Hertwig, and Todd survey the fast-and-frugal heuristic approach to bounded rationality and decision making.

This is done in the context of the heuristics and biases approach, which has not had much exposure among economists and economic psychologists. The fast-and-frugal approach views individuals as intelligent in decision making, although often at odds with neoclassical predictions, whereas the latter approach suggests that deviations from the neoclassical "norm" represent, at best, gaps in intelligence. Sontheimer argues that in spite of the tensions between behavioral and neoclassical microeconomics, behavioral microeconomics is a generalization of the neoclassical theory, whereas neoclassical micro is a special case of behavioral microeconomics. He makes the case that behavioral economics enriches and enhances conventional microeconomic modeling. Tomer surveys the literature on the intangible aspects of human capital, specifically organizational and personal capital, which is largely ignored in the conventional literature. He makes the case that integrating intangible capital into economic modeling provides us with an improved understanding of the firm and of the economy at large.

In the third section, "Decision Making," we have chapters by Stephen Lea, Ellen K. Nyhus, and Paul Webley, Peter Lunt, Mark Pingle, and Hugh Schwartz. Lea argues that the sciences of ecology, economics, and psychology overlap significantly and that key questions can be answered only by somehow better integrating the analytical frameworks provided by these disciplines. Thus we need to go beyond the relative interdisciplinarity represented by behavioral economics or economic psychology to a more complex one that brings ecology to the table. Nyhus and Webley survey theoretical and empirical behavioral research on time preference, self-control, and saving, which includes a discussion of hyperbolic discounting. A critical concern is how individual differences in these variables are conceptualized, measured, and incorporated into economic theory. Lunt examines the intersection between economics, psychology, and sociology through the lens of a critical comparison of Gary Becker's social economics and Pierre Bourdieu's economic psychology and their efforts to relate the complexities of the economic and social aspects of life in the context of socioeconomic analysis. Pingle argues that deliberation cost is what distinguishes behavioral from neoclassical economics and explores how the introduction of deliberation cost into the neoclassical modeling of human agency makes for a more potent analytical tool. Deliberation cost flows from the reality of the brain's cognitive limitations, which is a key characteristic of Simon's bounded rationality. This essay overlaps with the contributions of Frantz and Kaufman. Schwartz examines the potential importance that in-depth interviews can have as an empirical heuristic for behavioral economics, where presently experiments are the critical focal point. He argues that appropriately designed interviews can play a critical role in gaining a handle on the decision-making process, wherein this serves to build more realistic and rigorous theories of firm decision making.

In the next section, "Experiments and Implications," the authors—Gerrit Antonides, Fergus Bolger, and Ger Trip; Werner Güth and Andreas Ortmann; Jack Knetch and Fang-Fang Teng; and Robert Oxoby—discuss different approaches to experimental economics and how they relate to behavioral economics and economic theory and public policy. Antonides, Bolger, and Trip discuss the role classroom experiments, as opposed to laboratory experiments, can have in informing economic theory and our understanding of the decision-making process. To this end, they survey some of the extant literature and their own experimental design and results, finding that classroom experiments serve as a useful heuristic in the analytical toolbox of behavioral economists. Güth and Ortmann present a detailed and a critical analytical survey of laboratory experiments designed to test conventional or canonical economic theory and the varied impact these experiments have had on the formation of economic theory and our understanding of the decision-making process. They emphasize the importance of experimental design and the need for experiments to map the incentive realities of real-world decision makers. In a review of the literature, Knetsch and Tang suggest that conventional assumptions about the stability of preferences, fungibility, and procedural invariance are misplaced. Rather, they argue, preferences often depend on the context or frame, or reference position. Their contributions bring to the fore Kahneman and Tversky's value function and framing effect and the need to modify theory to account for limitations of the canonical model. Oxoby critically evaluates the methods used by experimental economists and how often used methods can compromise their results. When experiments are not properly designed with regard to the hypotheses to be tested, one ends up with a "dirty test tube"—sullied results that do not properly test the hypotheses at hand. Keen attention must be paid to experimental design, with particular emphasis on appropriate context and incentives.

In the section "Labor-Related Issues," Nathan Berg and Lonnie Golden discuss the implications for labor economics of recent developments in behavioral economics. Berg surveys the literature in behavioral labor economics, where major contributions have been in the realm of theory building on the empirics of labor market behavior. This survey critically assesses the behavioral contributions in the context of neoclassical theory and argues that neoclassical labor is often taken as a subset of behavioral labor and that there remains much overlap between the two analytical approaches. Golden surveys the literature on hours of work and suggests revisions to the conventional economic model of hours of labor by incorporating into the standard model a variety of empirically based behavioral and social sources of constraints, preferences, and preference adaptation. A revised theory is required to better explain current patterns and changes in hours of work and to provide a normative heuristic for assessing revealed preferences for hours worked.

In the section "Gender and Decision Making," Nancy Folbre examines the significant implication of introducing the reality of gender conflict (differential gender-based objective functions) into the modeling of decision making at many levels. In the conventional model such conflict is assumed to be of no analytical consequence. Game-theoretical heuristics are employed to this end. Whose preferences dominate have significant implications for socioeconomic outcomes that cannot be captured in the conventional modeling of human agency. Erich Kirchler and Eva Hofmann critically examine the literature on household decision making in the context of differential preferences between men and women. They address the different empirical methodologies used to determine the decision-making process, with special attention to the use of diaries. Decision making in process and results tend to deviate from the predictions of the conventional economic wisdom.

In the section "Life and Death," the authors discuss decision making with regard to suicide and health-related issues. Bijou Yang and David Lester critically assess the empirical and theoretical literature on the socioeconomics of suicide, examining rational choice and behavioral models. They find that empirical results are often inconsistent as a consequence of the modeling of suicide. They argue for a broader modeling framework that incorporates psychological and sociological variables overcoming some of the limitations of simple rational choice models of suicide. Gideon Yaniv examines the literature on health-compromising behavior, apart from suicide, with special emphasis on such behavior in the context of rational choice theory. The rational choice approach emphasizes the role of incentives in remedying health-comprising behavior, as opposed to treatment, which is the derivative of the psychological (irrational) approach to this issue.

In "Taxation, Ethical Investment, and Tipping," chapters are contributed by Simon James; John Cullis, Philip Jones, and Alan Lewis; and Michael Lynn. James surveys the literature on taxation, contrasting neoclassical and behavioral approaches to the economics of taxation with special attention to the issue of compliance. He argues that our understanding of choice behavior with regard to taxation is much enriched by informing the general economic model, vested in narrow self-interested maximizing behavior, with behavioral variables such as social norms, morals, and perceptions of justice. These behavioral models are more rigorous and have significant implications for taxation compliance policy. Cullis, Jones, and Lewis survey the literature on ethical investment in the context of the determinants of choice behavior with regard to ethical investing. Special attention is paid to the relevance of instrumental and intrinsic motivations. They argue that a key determinant of ethical investment relates to the fact that individual choice is affected by the choices of others. This points to the importance of choice externalities in determining the level of ethical investment. Lynn critically surveys the literature on tipping with an eye toward identifying the determinants of tipping behavior and how such behavior sheds light on our understanding of the determinants of economic behavior and on our refinement of economic theory. To best understand tipping requires broadening the conventional economic model to incorporate psychological and sociological variables. Tipping is not simply a function of narrow materially maximizing behavior.

Hamid Hosseini, Tobias Rötheli, Erik Thorbecke, Thomas Ulen, and Tomasz Zaleskiewicz contribute to the final section, "Development, Behavioral Law, and Money." Hosseini examines the literature on economic development, arguing that development and behavioral economics can benefit from better integrating the concept of social capital into their modeling frameworks. By assuming away social capital, models of development bypass a critical component of the development process. Rötheli discusses the literature on monetary economics and examines the implications of behavioral economics for monetary economics. He argues that monetary economics has important behavioral dimensions, deviations from rational-expectation-type behavior being of particular importance. This has significant implications for our understanding of the real effects money can have on the real economy and for a better appreciation of the role of monetary policy. Thorbecke examines the development process in the context of the conventional wisdom's view of the causal role of income inequality. He finds that the conventional assumption that increasing inequality is a necessary condition for more growth and development is misplaced. Rather, the evidence would support modeling development as consistent with more relative income equality. This has far-reaching public policy implications. Ulen surveys the law and economics literature with a critical eye on how behavioral economics impacts the reliance upon rational choice modeling as the critical foundation for law and economic discourse and related public policy design. To the extent that people do not behave as rational choice theory predicts, one cannot develop policy that hinges upon the veracity of such analytical predictions. Zaleskiewicz examines the literature on behavioral finance and the psychology of investing in terms of how this can contribute better modeling and understand investment behavior. He argues that much investor behavior significantly differs from that of the suprarational investor of the canonical economic model. Introducing concepts such as overconfidence, emotions, bounded rationality, and home bias contribute toward building more effective models.

This project involved a considerable commitment of work and time, and I thank Louise Lamontagne, wife and colleague for over twenty-five years, for her advice and patience. Our eleven-year-old daughter, Hannah, has shown great tolerance for my wondering mind and impatience and has provided me with much joy and pride through her many achievements as a budding scholar, athlete, and mensch.

The successful completion of this exciting project required the cooperation, encouragement, and support of my superb editor at M.E. Sharpe, Lynn Taylor. In addition, this book benefited greatly from the diligent work of our editorial coordinator, Amenda Allensworth, from the assistance of our project manager, Eileen Chetti, and, finally, from the incredible copyediting of Susan Warga.

An edited volume such as this also requires the cooperation and dedication of its many contributing authors. Apart from penning excellent chapters, the authors were always prompt in their responses and patient with delays. I hope that this handbook lives up to their expectations.

REFERENCES

Altman, Morris. 1999. "The Methodology of Economics and the Survivor Principle Revisited and Revised: Some Welfare and Public Policy Implications of Modeling the Economic Agent." *Review of Social Economics* 57: 427–49.

Friedman, M. 1953. "The Methodology of Positive Economics." In *Essays in Positive Economics,* 3–43. Chicago: University of Chicago Press.

Leibenstein, Harvey. 1983. "Property Rights and X-Efficiency: Comment." *American Economic Review* 73: 831–42.

Reder, Melvin W. 1982. "Chicago Economics: Permanence and Change." *Journal of Economic Literature* 20: 1–38.

Simon, Herbert A. 1978. "Rationality as a Process and as a Product of Thought." *American Economic Review* 70: 1–16.

———. 1979. "Rational Decision Making in Business Organizations." *American Economic Review* 69: 493–513.

———. 1987. "Behavioral Economics." In John Eatwell, Murray Millgate, and Peter Newman, eds., *The New Palgrave: A Dictionary of Economics*. London: Macmillan.

PART 1

INSIDE THE ECONOMIC AGENT

CHAPTER 1

INSIDE ECONOMIC MAN

Behavioral Economics and Consumer Behavior

PAUL ALBANESE

The enigmatic title of this essay stems from the psychoanalytic approach to personality and consumer behavior—psychoanalytic object relations theory of the personality, to be precise. Object relations theory is what psychoanalytic theory became after more than a century of refinement of Freud's most fundamental insights. Object relations theory is an interpersonal theory of personality development that concentrates on the internalization of interpersonal relationships and the formation of the intrapsychic structure of the personality organization. The "inside" of the title refers to the intrapsychic structure of the personality organization. All that is left inside Economic Man of neoclassical ordinal utility theory is the scale of preferences of the individual consumer. The theoretical linkage between psychoanalytic object relations theory of the personality and neoclassical ordinal utility theory of the consumer is that the intrapsychic structure of the personality organization is reflected in the structure of the consumer's preferences.

While the scale of preferences is the last vestige of the consumer left in ordinal utility theory, the conception of rational Economic Man is the sine qua non for research on consumer behavior because it is the *only* theoretical conception of the individual consumer. To be rational, a consumer must have a transitive preference ordering. The mathematical property of transitivity can be translated in this context into a consumer who makes consistent choices. A consistent pattern of observable behavior is a surprisingly powerful postulate upon which to base a theory of consumer behavior. Thus the place to begin is the behavior of the individual consumer, whether we observe that behavior ourselves or draw upon the observations of others.

In this essay I intend to synthesize the essence of *The Personality Continuum and Consumer Behavior* (2002) for broadening the behavioral foundations of economic analysis and expanding the limits of applicability of economic theory. Broadening the behavioral foundations of economic analysis means including observable patterns of consumer behavior that do not fit into the neoclassical conception of the rational consumer. Expanding the limits of applicability of economic theory means that neoclassical ordinal utility theory can be modified to apply to these qualitatively different patterns of consumer behavior. In a positive way, the realistic limits of applicability of ordinal utility theory are being circumscribed and those limits are being expanded to include other qualitatively different patterns of observable consumer behavior.

The Personality Continuum is an integrative framework for the interdisciplinary study of consumer behavior. The Personality Continuum is divided into four discrete ranges representing qualitatively different levels of personality development that are hierarchically arranged in descending order from highest to lowest level: normal, neurotic, primitive, and psychotic. In object relations theory, personality development is a series of interpersonal achievements, and the level of personality development is defined by the level of intrapsychic structural formation achieved in the personality organization and the predominant defense used by the person against severe anxiety in interpersonal relationships. The importance of the Personality Continuum for the study of consumer behavior is that each level of personality development is reflected in a qualitatively different pattern of consumer behavior, and the Personality Continuum facilitates the comparison of these variations. Everything varies qualitatively with the level of personality development along the Personality Continuum.

The Personality Continuum was conceived as a one-page document befitting an integrative framework; because of page-size limitations, here it is reproduced as a table spread over four pages (Table 1.1), just as it was presented in *The Personality Continuum and Consumer Behavior* (though I have made some refinements since the 2002 publication of that book).[1]

I relate consumer behavior to personality because the personality provides a larger organizational framework that includes a person's pattern of behavior as a consumer and relates it to his or her pattern of behavior as a human being. The goal is a human understanding of consumer behavior. The focus here will be on consumer behavior; although I do intend to go into the substance of object relations theory on the internalization of interpersonal relationships and the formation of the intrapsychic structure of the personality organization, I cannot plumb the true depth in this essay and will leave it to the interested reader to see Albanese 2002. I will proceed by elaborating on the pattern of consumer behavior for each of the four qualitatively different levels of personality development, beginning with the normal range of the Personality Continuum and then descending downward to the neurotic, primitive, and psychotic ranges.

THE NORMAL RANGE OF THE PERSONALITY CONTINUUM AND CONSUMER BEHAVIOR

The crowning achievement of psychoanalytic object relations theory of the personality is the clear conception it provides of what it means to be a normal person—not as a rigid ideal of perfection, but as a realistic person who would simply be described as a mature human being (Albanese 2002). Psychoanalytic object relations theory of the personality grew out of the intense observation of the individual's behavior in the clinical situation by a trained psychoanalyst, and out of this situation has grown an interpersonal theory of personality development based upon the quality of interpersonal relationships (Fairbairn 1952, 34, 40). The portrait of the normal personality organization will be presented as a set of *human capacities,* from the basic to the highest, and *patterns of behavior,* from the general pattern of human behavior to an overall pattern of consumer behavior and then to a more specific pattern of consumption behavior.

A person with a personality organization at the normal level of personality development would have the capacity for concern for another person and oneself, the capacity to experience guilt for violating an internalized moral system, the capacity to fall and remain in love and to form intimate interpersonal relationships, the capacity for foresight and to plan realistically for the future, the capacity for genuine insight and the urge to change in meaningful ways, and a range of mature defenses against severe anxiety in interpersonal relationships (humor, sublimation, altruism, anticipation, and suppression) (Albanese 2002).

A person with a personality organization at the normal level of personality development would have a stable and consistent general pattern of human behavior. *Consistency* applies to a person's pattern of behavior at one point in time and *stability* refers to a consistent pattern of behavior over time. In object relations theory, the determinant of a consistent pattern of behavior is the interpersonal achievement of accepting both oneself and another person as both good and bad, and therefore as a whole and more realistic person (Kernberg 1984). This interpersonal achievement in personality development results in the integration of whole object relations, the most momentous development in the formation of the intrapsychic structure of the personality organization. In the course of personality development, interpersonal relationships are internalized continuously and the formation of the intrapsychic structure of the personality organization develops in levels that are hierarchically organized. The intrapsychic structure is the enduring part of the personality organization. In the beginning of personality development, good and bad interpersonal relations are internalized completely separately—in early infancy through introjection and in late infancy through identification—reflecting the inborn physiological capacity for positive and negative affective experience. In childhood, the good and bad introjections and identifications must be integrated to form whole object relations.

The integration of whole object relations signals the coming into existence of the ego. The outcome of the synthetic function of the ego is the formation of an ego identity as an integrated intrapsychic structure (Albanese 2002, 101–2, 104–5; Kernberg 1984, 31). The integration of whole object relations is the foundation for the human capacity for concern for another person and oneself, an ego capacity, and the human capacity for guilt, a superego capacity. The *prohibitive superego* is the intrapsychic structure that gives a person the human capacity for guilt. The contents of the *prohibitive superego* represent an internalized moral system that begins with the internalization of the more realistic parental prohibitions and demands. The formation of the prohibitive superego begins with the integration of whole object relations because good and bad must be juxtaposed for the person to be able to tell right from wrong. The integration of whole object relations is the foundation for a sense of *continuity of the self,* and it is the first precondition for an intimate interpersonal relationship: it gives the person the human capacity to fall in love.

In object relations theory, the determinant of a stable pattern of behavior is the interpersonal achievement of fully integrating satisfying genital sexual activity into an interpersonal relationship by successfully resolving the oedipal situation. In simpler terms, a person discovers the preferred pattern of genital sexual activity in a relationship with another person (Sullivan 1953, 297). This interpersonal achievement in personality development represents the second precondition for the human capacity for intimacy in an interpersonal relationship: it gives the person the capacity to remain in love. It is built upon the foundation of the integration of whole object relations (the first precondition for intimacy) and represents a higher interpersonal achievement in personality development. A person at the normal level of personality development would form stable and deep interpersonal relationships.

At the highest reaches of the normal level of personality development, a person would have a *protective superego,* an intrapsychic structure built upon the foundation of the prohibitive superego and the human capacity for guilt (Kernberg 1977). The formation of the protective superego at the normal level of personality development is the outcome of the interpersonal achievement in personality development: Sexual intercourse culminating in orgasm and the subjective experience of transcendence in an intimate interpersonal relationship form a new common social boundary around the couple, connecting the past, present, and future (Kernberg 1977). The subjective experience of transcendence involves crossing the boundaries of the self and momentarily becoming one with another person. The new common social boundary that forms around the couple is the protective superego, an intrapsychic structure that protects the couple from guilt for violating the more realistic parental prohibitions and demands internalized in the prohibitive superego—

many directed explicitly toward sexual behavior—and from the parents as well, who may still be around, making them feel guilty (Albanese 2002, 127; Kernberg 1977, 102–4).

The protective superego is the foundation for the human capacity for commitment and for a future orientation. A commitment by definition is made for the future. The contents of the protective superego represent an internalized value system shared with another person. Freud clearly recognized the lofty position of the protective superego and equated the value system with the culture: "Thus a child's super-ego is in fact constructed on the model not of its parents but its parents' super-ego; the contents which fill it are the same and it becomes the vehicle of tradition and of all time-resisting judgments of value which have propagated themselves in this manner from generation to generation" (Freud 1933, 67).

This is how the past, present, and future become connected. A value system is built on the foundation of a moral system, the contents of the prohibitive superego. A value system reflects the culture and represents a higher level of superego functioning involving more abstract concepts that inform the person's life and provide guidance for the future but remain realistic, flexible, and widely shared by other members of society (Albanese 2002, 134). The dominant value system of American culture would include the core values of individualism, freedom, democracy, capitalism, and success, at a minimum.

The protective superego represents the pinnacle of personality development. Thus far I have presented the portrait of the normal personality organization as the theoretically perfect person whose development was optimal (Fairbairn 1952). A more realistic portrait of the normal personality organization will emerge in the comparisons with personality organizations at the neurotic, primitive, and psychotic levels of personality development.

A Revision of Rational Economic Man

The economic conception of the consumer as rational Economic Man would occupy the normal range of the Personality Continuum. The general pattern of human behavior at the normal level of personality development must be stable and consistent. To be rational, a consumer need only make consistent choices at one point in time (reflecting a transitive preference ordering); stability requires that a consumer make consistent choices over time, and that goes beyond the requirement of a transitive preference ordering. A stable pattern of consumer behavior over time can be modeled dynamically. That is why a consistent pattern of observable behavior is such a powerful behavioral postulate upon which to base a theory of consumer behavior. The normal consumer would have a stable and consistent preference ordering, and the preferences revealed in the market would reflect all the human capacities of a person at the normal level of personality development, including the human capacity for concern, guilt, and intimacy.

Amartya Sen asked a prescient question in his classic "Rational Fools": "A person is given *one* preference ordering, and as and when the need arises this is supposed to reflect his interests, represent his welfare, summarize his idea of what should be done and describe his actual choices and behavior. Can one preference ordering do all these things? A person thus described may be 'rational' in the limited sense of revealing no inconsistencies in his choice behavior, but if he has no use for these distinctions between quite different concepts, he must be a bit of a fool. Economic theory has been much preoccupied with this *rational fool* decked in the glory of his one all-purpose preference ordering" (Sen 1977, 335–36).

One all-purpose preference ordering should reflect the distinctions between these quite different concepts. When given a choice between two bundles of commodities, a consumer must be able to say whether he or she prefers one bundle to the other or is indifferent, and from that datum the consumer's preference ordering can be constructed—that is all the consumer's scale of preferences represents. The personality organization of object relations provides the larger organizing framework that encompasses all of these distinctions and more, and by relating the economic conception of the consumer to the personality organization, we know precisely what human capacities should be reflected in the consumer's scale of preferences at each of the qualitatively different levels of personality development.

Equating the stable and consistent general pattern of human behavior at the normal level of personality development with the theoretical conception of the consumer of neoclassical ordinal utility theory strengthens the conception of rational Economic Man by adding the requirement of stability and a dynamic dimension. Reflecting the elevation of rational Economic Man to the normal range of the Personality Continuum, in this section I will refrain from using the archaic terminology of "Economic Man" and instead simply use the term "rational consumer" in all his or her glory.

The pattern of consumption behavior for the normal consumer would include self-control, delay of gratification, everything in moderation, and the prudent planning of consumption activities. A normal person would be self-reliant in the American transcendentalist sense, where self-reliance means economic independence, not social isolation and the absence of interpersonal relationships. The normal consumer would be predictable—not rigid, inflexible, routinized, mundane, bland, or boring, but simply displaying a stable and consistent pattern of human behavior.

Fundament of the Utility Function at the Normal Level of Personality Development

For someone with a personality organization in the normal range of the Personality Continuum, the preference structure is stable and consistent. The intrapsychic structure of the personality organization is reflected in the structure of preferences, and the form of the utility function must reflect the structure of preferences. The only modification necessary to ordinal utility theory at the normal level of personality development is in the fundamental conception of *utility* itself. Rather than being only satisfaction or pleasure, utility is the net outcome of good and bad consumption experiences. The interpretation of utility as both negative and positive is indicative of the separate inborn physiological capacities for positive and negative affective experience.

The utility function is $U = F(P, N)$
where N = negative introjections and identifications
P = positive introjections and identifications

At the normal level of personality development, after the integration of whole object relations, P is integrated with N. $P > N$, with a preponderance of P over N, $U > 0$.

Vindication of Adam Smith

It is a common misconception often thoughtlessly taught in introductory courses on economic theory that the rational consumer should pursue his or her self-interest selfishly. This selfish view of human nature is often attributed to Adam Smith and the "invisible hand" described in his *Wealth of Nations* (1776). But it is abundantly apparent to anyone who has ever read the opening sentence of his earlier *Theory of Moral Sentiments* that Adam Smith intended that a person pursue his or her own self-interest with sympathy for others and within the moral system of society: "How selfish soever man may be supposed, there are evidently some principles in his nature, which interest him in the fortune of others, and render their happiness necessary to him, though he derives nothing from it, except the pleasure of seeing it" (Smith 1759, 47).

Adam Smith based his view of human nature on the human capacity for sympathy for another person. Sympathy, as a human capacity, is synonymous with the human capacity for concern for another person and oneself in object relations theory: "Sympathy, though its meaning was, perhaps, originally the same, may now, however, without much impropriety, be made use of to denote our fellow-feeling with any passion whatsoever" (Smith 1759, 49). The interpersonal achievement in personality development that gives a person the capacity for concern is to accept both another person and oneself as both good and bad, and therefore as a whole and more realistic person. A person with a personality organization at the normal level of personality development would have the human capacity for concern. The following passage leaves no doubt about Adam Smith's exquisite view of human nature built on the capacity for sympathy: "And hence it is, that to feel much for others, and little for ourselves, that to restrain our selfish, and to indulge our benevolent, affections, constitutes the perfection of human nature; and can alone produce among mankind that harmony of sentiments and passions in which consists their whole grace and propriety" (Smith 1759, 71).

Along with the capacity for sympathy for another person and oneself, a person at the normal level of personality development would pursue his or her self-interest within the moral system of society. A person with a personality organization at the normal level of personality development has an integrated prohibitive superego, an internalized moral system, and the human capacity to experience guilt for violating the moral system of society. This is what Adam Smith intended, a theory of "moral" sentiments.

Smith believed that the individual should compete vigorously but fairly:

> In the race for wealth, and honours, and preferments, he may run as hard as he can, and strain every nerve and every muscle, in order to outstrip all his competitors. But if he should justle, or throw down any of them, the indulgence of the spectators is entirely at an end. It is a violation of fair play, which they cannot admit of. This man is to them, in every respect, as good as he: they do not enter into that self-love, by which he prefers himself so much to this other, and cannot go along with the motive from which he hurt him. (Smith 1759, 162–63)

Smith used the selfish individual—the individual in love with him- or herself, a phenomenon he aptly refers to as "self-love"—to make an invidious comparison to a person with the capacity for sympathy. This reflects Smith's clear understanding that these are qualitatively different patterns of behavior. The individual who pursues his or her self-interest selfishly hardly represents his perfection of human nature. It will be shown subsequently in the elaboration of the primitive level of personality development that the selfish individual violates the transitivity property and therefore does not fit the conception of the rational consumer.

Adam Smith intended that it be the *individual* who vigorously and fairly pursues his or her self-interest with sympathy for others and within the moral system of society. Smith's concept of the "invisible hand" has led to the overwhelmingly individual orientation of the neoclassical economic theory of consumer behavior. In America we do value individualism; the notion of rugged individualism is legendary. But what is relevant is not the individualism per se but the *nature* of the individual's pursuit of self-interest. At the normal level of personality development, the individual would pursue his or her self-interest with the human capacity for concern for another person and oneself and the capacity for guilt for violating an internalized moral system; at the highest level, the individual's pursuit of self-interest would be informed by an internalized value system. The individual must transcend his or her own selfish pursuit of self-interest to become a mature human being at the normal level of personality development.

Object relations theory grew out of the intense observation of individual behavior in the clinical setting, and this individual orientation represents a fundamental compatibility between object relations theory of the personality and neoclassical ordinal utility theory of the consumer. Further, because object relations theory is an interpersonal theory of personality development, linking it with the neoclassical economic theory of consumer behavior automatically overcomes the latter's overwhelmingly individual orientation.

THE NEUROTIC RANGE OF THE PERSONALITY CONTINUUM AND CONSUMER BEHAVIOR

The portrait of a person with a personality organization arrested at the neurotic level of personality development is complicated. There are a number of personality organizations in the neurotic range of the Personality Continuum—depressive, avoidant, dependent, obsessive, hysterical, and paranoid, in descending order. A person arrested at this level of personality development as a chronological adult has accepted both him- or herself and another person as both good and bad and therefore as whole and realistic people, but has failed at the interpersonal achievement in personality development that demarcates the normal range of the Personality Continuum: full integration of satisfying genital sexual activity in an interpersonal relationship by successfully resolving the oedipal situation. The failure to achieve the preferred pattern of genital sexual activity is an all-absorbing and all-frustrating preoccupation for the neurotic person (Sullivan 1953, 297). Thus while the integration of whole object relations has been accomplished and the neurotic person has an integrated ego identity and the human capacity for concern for another person and oneself, a prohibitive superego and the capacity for guilt, and the capacity to fall in love, he or she does not have the capacity to remain in love.

The general pattern of human behavior at the neurotic level of personality development is consistent under ordinary functioning but lacks stability under extraordinary functioning. There are three levels of functioning: ordinary, extraordinary, and high. *Ordinary functioning* involves the person functioning in everyday life at the level that had been achieved in personality development—in this case, a neurotic person functioning at a neurotic level of personality development. *Extraordinary functioning* involves interpersonal situations fraught with severe anxiety, resulting in a regression to a lower level of personality development and a return to earlier patterns of behavior—in this case, a neurotic person functioning at the primitive or lower psychotic level of personality development. *High functioning* involves fortunate interpersonal relations that elevate the person's functioning to a higher level of personality development—in this case, a neurotic person functioning at the normal level of personality development. Fortunate interpersonal relations that are relatively enduring can lead to favorable change in the level of personality development, because interpersonal relationships are continuously internalized in the formation of the intrapsychic structure of the personality organization throughout a person's life.

What is lacking in the pattern of behavior of a person at the neurotic level of personality development when compared to the normal person is *stability*. At one point in time, the neurotic person can be consistent under ordinary functioning, inconsistent under extraordinary functioning, or stable under high functioning. The *nature* of the unstable behavior of the person with a personality organization arrested at the neurotic level of personality development is merely inconsistent. Inconsistent behavior is the hallmark of all the personality organizations in the neurotic range of the Personality Continuum.

The neurotic consumer is inconsistent, indecisive, ambivalent, inhibited by feelings of guilt, and racked by cognitive dissonance. The indecisiveness, ambivalence, inhibitions, and cognitive dissonance of the neurotic consumer are a result of the relative balance of P and N. The pattern of consumption behavior of the neurotic person represents a continuous striving for consistent self-control, backsliding, and the use of precommitment devices to control behavior (Ainslie 1987). Although the neurotic person is inconsistent, there is a continuous striving for consistent self-control. As noted, the neurotic person has achieved the integration of whole object relations, and this contributes to the continuity of the self and to an integrated prohibitive superego. The prohibitive superego comes with an ego ideal, formed with the integration of whole object relations when the images of the ideal self and ideal object are brought together. Freud described this function of the prohibitive superego as "the vehicle of the ego ideal by which the ego measures itself, which it emulates, and whose demand for even greater perfection it strives to fulfill" (Freud 1933, 64–65). While backsliding does occur under extraordinary functioning, the continuous striving for consistent self-control means that the neurotic person will never give up trying to live up to the ego ideal—to get back on the wagon, so to speak. The use of precommitment devices— a bargain made with oneself—to shore up self-control represents the continuous striving for consistent self-control by the neurotic person (Ainslie 1987).

The implication for the limits of applicability of ordinal utility theory is that the theory would fit the behavior of the neurotic person under ordinary and high functioning but not under extraordinary functioning, where the transitivity property of the preference ordering would be violated by the inconsistent behavior. To the extent that the pattern of behavior of the neurotic person is consistent under ordinary functioning and there is a continuous striving for consistent self-control, the neurotic consumer does fit the conception of rational consumer of ordinal utility theory. Whether the neurotic person behaves consistently or inconsistently at one point in time or with stability over time depends on the quality of the person's interpersonal relationships. In Sullivan's interpersonal definition, personality is the relatively enduring pattern of recurrent interpersonal situations that characterizes a human life (Sullivan 1953, 110–11). The quality of this pattern of interpersonal relationships will determine the extent to which the neurotic person's pattern of behavior is consistent, inconsistent, or stable. What is missing in the person with a personality organization arrested at the neurotic level of personality development are the higher-level intrapsychic structures that would have brought stability if the person had not faltered at the interpersonal achievement in personality development that demarcates the normal range of the personality continuum.

Fundament of the Utility Function at the Neurotic Level of Personality Development

The modification that must be made to the fundament of the utility function at the neurotic level of personality of development is to capture the inconsistency of the neurotic consumer: the behavior is patterned and therefore can be modeled, but because the behavior lacks stability, it cannot be modeled dynamically. For personality organizations in the neurotic range of the Personality Continuum, preferences are *consistent* under ordinary functioning (and ordinal utility theory, mutatis mutandis, would apply) but *inconsistent* under extraordinary functioning (and the theory therefore would not apply). For the personality organization arrested at the neurotic level of personality development, whole object relations have been integrated; therefore, under ordinary functioning P is integrated with N, and $U > 0$. Although P is integrated with N, and $P > N$, P and N are relatively balanced in magnitude for the personality organizations arrested at a neurotic level of personality development when compared to the normal level. Life has been *just* good enough for the neurotic person; there has not been a preponderance of $P > N$, as in the normal range. At the point of demarcation between the neurotic and primitive ranges of the Personality Continuum, $P = N$. The integration of whole object relations is more tenuous and breaks down easily during extraordinary functioning, and hence the neurotic consumer's behavior becomes inconsistent. For movements up the neurotic range of the Personality Continuum, $P > N$ and varies continuously and increasingly within the range; thus for personality organizations higher up in the neurotic range of the Personality Continuum, the pattern of human behavior would be less inconsistent and more stable.

THE PRIMITIVE RANGE OF THE PERSONALITY CONTINUUM AND CONSUMER BEHAVIOR

The portrait of a person with a personality organization arrested at the primitive level of personality development is complex. There are a number of personality organizations in the primitive range of the Personality Continuum—borderline, infantile, narcissistic, antisocial, and schizoid, in descending order.

The person arrested at the primitive level of personality development has failed to accept both the self and another person as both good and bad and therefore as whole and more realistic person—the interpersonal achievement in personality development that demarcates the neurotic range of the Personality Continuum. The basic fault—the failure to integrate whole object relations—is the result of the intense frustrations that characterized the relatively enduring pattern of recurrent interpersonal situations in the early life of such a person. The integration of the good and bad aspects of another person—first and foremost the mother—threatens to contaminate or destroy what little good interpersonal experience the person actually had, because of the preponderance of negative over positive introjections and identifications.

To protect what little good interpersonal experience the person actually had early in life, the person arrested at the primitive level of personality development actively holds apart the good and bad aspects of another person and him- or herself in the primitive defense of *splitting*—an active and powerful defense against severe anxiety in interpersonal relationships and the predominant defense characteristic of all personality organizations in the primitive range of the Personality Continuum. The result of splitting is *primitive idealization:* to see oneself and others as unrealistically all-good, and to rigidly divide the world into all-good and all-bad with no middle ground, "you are either for us or against us." When the defense of splitting is working effectively, the person with a personality organization arrested at the primitive level of personality development is free from severe anxiety.

Sullivan has an interpersonal definition of anxiety: "Anxiety, as a phenomenon of relatively adult life, can often be explained plausibly as anticipated unfavorable appraisal of one's current activity by someone whose opinion is significant" (Sullivan 1953, 113). He argued that "the exclusively interpersonal origin of every instance of its manifestations . . . is the unique characteristic of anxiety" (Sullivan 1964, 238). For the person with a personality organization arrested at the primitive level of personality development, severe anxiety is sudden because the breakdown of the defense of splitting leaves the person defenseless, and it is intense and overwhelming because the breakdown of splitting represents a regression to a lower level of personality development and a return to earlier patterns of behavior. Sullivan likened the interpersonal experience of severe anxiety to a blow on the head: "When anxiety is severe, it has almost the effect of a blow on the head; one isn't really clear on the exact situation in which the anxiety occurred" (Sullivan

1953, 300). Severe anxiety is experienced as intolerable by the person with a personality organization arrested at the primitive level of personality development.

In contrast to the splitting that occurs at this level, at the neurotic and normal levels of personality development repression becomes the predominant defense against severe anxiety in interpersonal relationships. Repression is an unconscious defense that involves casting intolerable thoughts or feelings out of consciousness. When the defense of repression is effective, the unwanted thoughts or feelings do not occur, but the person is left feeling anxious as a warning signal (Freud 1915). In comparison, the primitive defense of splitting occurs within the consciousness of the person with a personality organization arrested at the primitive level of personality development.

The general pattern of human behavior for a person with a personality organization arrested at the primitive level of personality development is a chaotic pattern of alternating and contradictory behavior. The behavior is unstable—not merely inconsistent, as in the neurotic range, but contradictory, alternating in a chaotic way, and rigidly patterned. The chaotic pattern of alternating and contradictory behavior is a manifestation of the breakdown of splitting. The person with a personality organization arrested at the primitive level of personality development is already dealing with a high level of anxiety. The critical aspect of the lack of anxiety tolerance in such a person is the inability to tolerate any additional anxiety (to use the cherished terminology of neoclassical economic analysis, marginal anxiety). Any additional anxiety overloads the primitive defense of splitting, which then breaks down, leaving the person subject to severe anxiety.

The chaotic pattern of alternating and contradictory behavior is manifested under ordinary functioning by a person with a personality organization arrested at the primitive level of personality development. Under high functioning, with fortunate interpersonal relations, this person can function at the higher neurotic level; fortunate interpersonal relations that are relatively enduring can lead to favorable change in the level of personality development. Under extraordinary functioning, a person at the primitive level can regress to the lower psychotic level of personality development, in which a person fails to recognize him- or herself as separate from other—the interpersonal achievement in personality development that demarcates the primitive range of the Personality Continuum. When a person ordinarily functioning at the primitive level of personality development regresses to the lower psychotic level under extraordinary functioning, the boundary between oneself and other is lost—the ultimate psychopathological disaster for someone at this level (Fairbairn 1952).

The pattern of consumer behavior at the primitive level of personality development is compulsive (in the more extreme case, addictive) behavior—the dark side of consumer behavior. Such a person is driven by severe anxiety to engage in a compulsive or addictive pattern of consumer behavior in a desperate effort to restore the defense of splitting and once again be free from severe anxiety—at least temporarily, until the next episode of the breakdown of splitting. Someone with a personality organization arrested at the primitive level begins at a deficit because of the failure to integrate whole object relations and the preponderance of negative introjections and identifications. The compulsive or addictive pattern of consumer behavior represents compensatory or substitutive satisfactions that compensate the person for this deficit by restoring the defense of splitting.

The person with a personality organization arrested at the primitive level of personality development is driven by the return of bad objects—past all-bad internalized part-object relations—reactivated with the breakdown of splitting (Fairbairn 1952). These past internalized all-bad part-object relations that return to persecute the person with a personality organization arrested at the primitive level of personality development with severe anxiety constitute the *punitive superego,* an intrapsychic structure that represents the lowest level of superego functioning. Persecution by punitive superego produces the severe anxiety that drives the person to engage in compulsive or addictive consumer behavior in a *desperate* effort to restore the defense of splitting. This gives such behavior a frantic character. Fairbairn captured the persecution by the punitive superego in a chilling description: the person is "haunted by bad objects against the return of which all defenses have broken down, and from which there is no escape (except in death)" (1952, 166).

The person with a personality organization arrested at the primitive level of personality development does not have a prohibitive superego, the internalized moral system that provides the human capacity for guilt, and certainly does not have the higher-level protective superego and an internalized value system. Without a value or moral system, the person may rigidly adhere to a system of ideals that are not shared with another person and certainly are not widely shared with other members of society, and which will be pursued without concern for anyone else, or oneself, and without regard for the moral system of society (Albanese 2002, 116–17).

Personality organizations that occupy a higher relative position within the primitive range of the Personality Continuum (the borderline and infantile personality organizations in particular) are subject to a panoply of compulsive behaviors, and personality organizations that occupy a relatively lower position within the primitive range (particularly the narcissistic and antisocial personality organizations) are prone to addiction. The compulsive or addictive pattern of consumer behavior characteristic of the primitive range of the Personality Continuum is qualitatively different from the stable and consistent pattern of behavior of the rational consumer at the normal level of personality development and the inconsistent, indecisive, ambivalent, inhibited, and dissonant behavior of the neurotic consumer.

It is the primitive level of personality development, not the substance or the activity, that determines the person's predisposition toward compulsive or addictive behavior. This is crucial to a deeper understanding of compulsive and addictive behavior. A person at the primitive level can engage in a panoply of compulsive and addictive behaviors: certainly the ingestion of drugs and alcohol, and the ingestion of food as well, but also other behaviors such as frantic social interactions, sex, aggression, work, buying, exercise, and polymorphously perverse sexual behavior including masturbation and predatory sexual behavior (Kernberg 1985). While the list does include the ingestion of substances like drugs and alcohol, and food for that matter, it also includes many *activities* that do not involve ingesting any chemical substance, or any substance for that matter. Further, since the defense of splitting has broken down, it is the underlying level of intrapsychic structural formation of the personality organization that primarily determines the nature of the compulsive and more extreme addictive pattern of consumer behavior. The critical implication for the economic analysis of consumer behavior is that the nature of preferences is determined primarily by the level of intrapsychic structural formation that has been achieved.

The pattern of consumption behavior at the primitive level of personality development is characterized by the constant struggle with self-control and a selective lack of impulse control, the crude gratification of impulses, greed, ultimately self-destructive, myopic consumption behavior, present orientation and hyperbolic discounting. The immediate gratification of impulses without thought for future consequences represents myopic and ultimately self-destructive consumption behavior. The behavior of the addict, in particular, has a desperate and frantic character that is based in a strong present orientation (which in the extreme would be manifested in hyperbolic discounting) (Ainslie 1991).

Time preference varies qualitatively with the level of personality development. A person with a personality organization at the normal level of personality development has the human capacity for foresight and realistic planning for the future and the human capacity for commitment—a future orientation. Personality organizations at the neurotic level of personality development would continuously strive for a consistent plan for the future under ordinary functioning but under extraordinary functioning would backslide, behave inconsistently, and become more present-oriented. Personality organizations at the primitive level of personality development would be characterized by a rigid present orientation that is manifested in myopic consumption behavior or hyperbolic discounting. Personality organizations at the psychotic level of personality development are characterized by a strong past orientation.

The predictability of the person with a personality organization arrested at the primitive level of personality development is complex: depending on the interpersonal situation, it may manifest as oscillating, either/or behavior, as if the person had two selves. The two-selves hypothesis advanced by Schelling (1980) and Winston (1980)—that a person prone to addiction behaves as if he or she had two contradictory selves—is a behavioral manifestation of the primitive defense of splitting. For personality organizations in the primitive range of the Personality Continuum, the structure of preferences would be alternating and contradictory, reflecting the failure to achieve the integration of whole object relations. The unstable but rigid pattern of alternating and contradictory behavior of a person with a personality organization at the primitive level of personality development has been modeled mathematically by Winston (1980).

Fundament of the Utility Function at the Primitive Level of Personality Development

The person with a personality organization arrested at the primitive level of personality development begins at a deficit because of the failure to integrate whole object relations. The fundament of the utility function must reflect the deficit in personality development, $P < N$, representing the preponderance of negative over positive introjections and identifications, and it must account for the unstable but rigidly patterned chaotic, alternating, and contradictory behavior. For the consumer with a personality organization in the primitive range of the Personality Continuum, $P < N$, with a preponderance of $N > P$, and $U < 0$, represents the baseline level of ordinary functioning. For movements downward within the primitive range of the Personality Continuum, the difference between P and N varies increasingly and continuously.

The Selfish Pursuit of Individual Self-Interest

A person with a personality organization arrested at the primitive level of personality development would be characterized by the selfish pursuit of individual self-interest. If Economic Man of neoclassical ordinal utility theory were meant to be selfish, he would be arrested at the primitive level of personality development. But Economic Man cannot be meant to be selfish, because the alternating and contradictory preference structure of a person arrested at the primitive level of personality development—lacking in consistency and stability—violates the transitivity property under ordinary functioning.

When we do encounter a person in real life who behaves like the selfish misconception of Economic Man (and I do mean mainly *men* here), typically we find a person with a narcissistic personality organization arrested at the primitive level of personality development. The investigation of a particular personality organization goes beyond the Personality Continuum to delve more deeply into the richly detailed clinical case literature. The portrait of a person with a narcissistic personality organization would begin with being socially smooth and superficially charming, without concern or conscience, coldly calculating, ruthlessly exploiting others, and relentless in the selfish pursuit of individual self-interest. The narcissistic personality organization is characterized by the excessive self-reference that, as previously noted, Adam Smith called "self-love." The *grandiose self* is the central feature of the intrapsychic structure of the narcissistic personality organization. The fictional character James Bond has a classic narcissistic personality organization, going from conquest to conquest in a pattern of predatory sexual behavior but losing interest in the woman after the conquest is over.

The *Diagnostic and Statistical Manual of Mental Disorders: DSM-IV* of the American Psychiatric Association lists as diagnostic criteria for the narcissistic personality organization a grandiose sense of self-importance; a preoccupation with fantasies of unlimited success, power, brilliance, beauty, or ideal love; arrogant, haughty behaviors or attitudes; lack of empathy; interpersonally exploitative behavior; a sense of entitlement; a need for excessive admiration; envy of others or the belief that others are envious of him or her; and the belief that he or she is "special" and unique and can only be understood by, or should associate with, other special or high-status people (or institutions) (American Psychiatric Association 1994, 661). Envy is a motivation for materialism at the primitive level of personality development (Albanese 2002, 320–23). The basic character constellation of the person with a narcissistic personality organization comprises boredom, restlessness, and emptiness; devaluation, omnipotence, and withdrawal as primitive defenses against chronic intense envy; and an attitude of indifference in interpersonal relationships. The lack of continuity in the self contributes to the sense of boredom and restlessness because the self is fragmented into multiple selves—part-object relations lacking the integration of whole object relations—and the withdrawal into social isolation contributes to the subjective experience of emptiness.

The subjective experience of emptiness is pervasive in the narcissistic personality organization. The person with a narcissistic personality organization is prone to addiction as an escape from the pervasive experience of emptiness. The addictive behavior of the narcissistic personality organization restores the defense of splitting and refuels the grandiose self (Kernberg 1985, 222).

Adam Smith on the Dark Side of Consumer Behavior

The selfish (or, in the more extreme case, ruthless) pursuit of individual self-interest displayed by the person with a narcissistic personality organization arrested at the primitive level of personality development is hardly the epitome of the perfection of human nature so eloquently defined by Adam Smith (1759). It is American to pursue individual self-interest relentlessly, but that can be done vigorously and fairly within the moral system of society, with concern for others and oneself, and informed by a value system. Smith's appreciation of the higher side of life gave him a clear understanding of the darker side of life. He saw that what the ambitious man who pursues his individual self-interest ruthlessly is really pursuing is *honor,* albeit an honor ill understood:

> But, though they should be so lucky as to attain that wished-for greatness, they are always most miserably disappointed in the happiness which they expect to enjoy in it. It is not ease or pleasure, but always honour, of one kind or another, though frequently an honour very ill understood, that the ambitious man really pursues. But the honour of his exalted station appears, both in his eyes and in those of other people, polluted and defiled by the baseness of the means through which he rose to it. (Smith 1759, 131)

And there is no escape from dishonor because of the persistence of memory in oneself and others, according to Smith:

He invokes in vain the dark and dismal powers of forgetfulness and oblivion. He remembers himself what he has done, and the remembrance tells him that other people likewise remember it. Amidst all the gaudy pomp of the most ostentatious greatness; amidst the venal and vile adulation of the great and of the learned; amidst the more innocent, though more foolish, acclamations of the common people; amidst all the pride of conquest and the triumph of successful war, he is still secretly pursued by the avenging furies of shame and remorse; and, while glory seems to surround him on all sides, he himself, in his own imagination, sees black and foul infamy fast pursuing him, and every moment ready to overtake him from behind. (Smith 1759, 131–32)

The "avenging furies of shame and remorse" represent the severe anxiety produced by the punitive superego. Smith captures the sense of dread associated with it:

Such is the nature of the sentiment, which is properly called remorse; of all the sentiments which can enter the human breast the most dreadful. It is made up of shame from the sense of the impropriety of past conduct; of grief for the effects of it; of pity for those who suffer by it; and of the dread and terror of punishment from the consciousness of the justly-provoked resentment of all rational creatures. (Smith 1759, 164)

Remorse is not mere guilt over bad behavior, for which the person can make reparations for the harm done to another person. A person with a primitive personality organization—the narcissistic personality organization in particular—does not have the capacity to experience guilt. But such a person experiences persecution by the punitive superego, and this subjective experience of remorse—an admixture of shame, grief, pity, and terror—is far worse than guilt.

And there is no escape into solitude for the person who has done irreparable evil to another human being, because, according to Smith, solitude is still more dreadful than society:

Everything seems hostile, and he would be glad to fly to some inhospitable desert, where he might never more behold the face of a human creature, nor read in the countenance of mankind the condemnation of his crimes. But solitude is still more dreadful than society. His own thoughts can present him with nothing but what is black, unfortunate, and disastrous, the melancholy forebodings of incomprehensible misery and ruin. The horror of solitude drives him back into society, and he comes again into the presence of mankind, astonished to appear before them loaded with shame and distracted with fear, in order to supplicate some little protection from the countenance of those very judges, who know he knows have already all unanimously condemned him. (Smith 1759, 164)

This passage from the *Theory of Moral Sentiments* should leave no doubt that Adam Smith never intended that the individual pursue his or her self-interest selfishly. We can leave behind forevermore the misconception of Economic Man as selfish.

THE PSYCHOTIC RANGE OF THE PERSONALITY CONTINUUM AND CONSUMER BEHAVIOR

The arrest of personality development at the psychotic level is primarily the result of physiological problems and does not result from the quality of interpersonal relationships. The person with a personality organization arrested at the psychotic level of personality development has failed to recognize him- or herself as separate from other—the interpersonal achievement in personality development that demarcates the primitive range of the Personality Continuum—and, as a consequence, there is no boundary between self and other.

The person with a personality organization arrested at the psychotic level of personality development would display the absence of the capacity for reality testing, a changing and capricious (and hence unpredictable) general pattern of human behavior, an irrational pattern of consumer behavior, and the irrational pursuit of individual self-interest. The buying sprees in a manic episode of a person with a manic-depressive personality organization or bipolar disorder would represent an irrational pattern of consumer behavior. Unstable behavior at the psychotic level of personality development would be characterized as a changing and capricious general pattern of human behavior, which is qualitatively different from the chaotic pattern of alternating and contradictory behavior at the primitive level, the inconsistent pattern of behavior at the neurotic level, and the stable and consistent pattern of behavior at the normal level of personality development.

Fundament of the Utility Function at the Psychotic Level of Personality Development

For personality organizations in the psychotic range of the Personality Continuum, preferences are changing and capricious, representing the collapse of the intrapsychic structure of the personality organization. The pattern of consumer behavior is truly irrational. Thus the fundament of the utility function at the psychotic level of personality development cannot be defined. Ordinal utility theory does not apply to personality organizations in the psychotic range of the Personality Continuum. In contrast, at the primitive level of personality development, ordinal utility theory would not apply under ordinary or extraordinary functioning; at best, it would apply only under high functioning. At the neurotic level of personality development, ordinal utility theory would apply under ordinary and high functioning, but not under extraordinary functioning. At the normal level of personality development, ordinal utility theory would apply under ordinary and high functioning; with a stable and consistent general pattern of human behavior, that would be most of the time. Under extraordinary functioning, a person at the normal level of personality development will regress to a lower level of personality development and return to earlier patterns of behavior, including regression in the service of the ego. In a positive sense, this defines the realistic limits of applicability of ordinal utility theory over the ranges of the Personality Continuum.

THE RATIONAL-IRRATIONAL DICHOTOMY IN ECONOMIC ANALYSIS

In economics, only the extremes of "rational" and "irrational" have been considered, and any inconsistency in the consumer's behavior has been mislabeled as "irrational," but this dichotomy ignores the qualitatively different patterns of consumer behavior at the neurotic and primitive levels of personality development. Becker argued that irrational behavior at the individual level will not change the negative slope of the market demand curve: "Undue concentration at the individual level can easily lead to an overestimate of the degree of irrationality at the market level" (1962, 168). Becker's most important point is that the irrational individual will have to adapt realistically in the market: "Even irrational decision units must accept reality and could not, for example, maintain a choice that was no longer within their opportunity set"—that is, "irrational units would often be 'forced' by a change in opportunities to respond rationally" (1962, 167).

Leibenstein (1975) espoused a similar view with his conception of selective rationality: "it is sufficient that behavior at critical junctures be of a 'rational' type" (Leibenstein 1975, 3). Leibenstein's selective rationality describes the selective lack of impulse control characteristic of personality organizations in the primitive range of the Personality Continuum. The person with a personality organization arrested at the primitive level of personality development would adapt realistically to the market. The compulsive (or in the more extreme case addictive) pattern of consumer behavior characteristic of the complex personality organizations arrested at the primitive level of personality development would be manifested in highly price-inelastic behavior toward the commodities or activities for which the person has a selective lack of impulse control. When consumers in the market reveal a tendency toward compulsive and more extreme addictive consumer behavior, it will be reflected in a highly price-inelastic range of the market demand curve, but the demand curve will still be well behaved, with a negative slope, and the law of demand will operate.

Leibenstein's (1975) conception of selective rationality is significant because it fits the behavior of the personality organizations in the primitive range of the Personality Continuum. I believe that Becker (1962) is also largely describing behavior at the primitive level of personality, as opposed to irrational behavior. Truly irrational behavior is rare, manifested in a few million Americans at best, and fairly well documented, and it would not be enough to change the negative slope of the demand curve in any market.

PROBABILITY DISTRIBUTION OVER THE PERSONALITY CONTINUUM

Although the conception of the normal personality organization supports and strengthens the neoclassical conception of the consumer, it cannot simply be assumed that everyone will automatically reach the normal level of personality development, any more than an economist can automatically assume that the consumer's preference ordering will be stable and consistent. Behavioral economics should be based on the observation of economic behavior. In object relations theory, personality development is a matter of achievement, a series of interpersonal achievements in personality development. What proportion of the population has achieved the normal level of personality development? That is an open empirical question.

The behavioral foundations of economic analysis have been broadened to include the inconsistent pattern of behavior of the neurotic consumer, the chaotic pattern of alternating and contradictory behavior characteristic of the compulsive and addictive consumer arrested at the primitive level of personality development, and the changing and capricious pattern of consumer behavior of the truly irrational person at the psychotic level of personality development. What proportion of the population would occupy the neurotic, primitive, and psychotic ranges of the Personality Continuum? That is also an open empirical question.

A probability distribution is thereby formed over the Personality Continuum, demarcated by the four qualitatively different levels of personality development: normal, neurotic, primitive, and psychotic. Everything varies qualitatively with the level of personality development along the Personality Continuum. A third open empirical question is: What is the probability distribution over the Personality Continuum? Once the probability distribution has been defined, sampling should be stratified by the qualitatively different levels of personality development reflected in the ranges of the Personality Continuum. An individual difference or trait measure averaged over the qualitatively different levels of personality development would not reveal the qualitatively different patterns of consumer behavior representing the ranges of the Personality Continuum. Since everything is systematically related to everything else on the Personality Continuum, all of the relationships represent empirically testable hypotheses.

This is the challenge of the Personality Continuum: the open road for research on personality and consumer behavior and the opportunity to make progress on the journey toward a human understanding of consumer behavior.

NOTE

1. The Personality Continuum in its one-page format can be obtained by writing to the author or downloaded at www.personalitycontinuum.com.

REFERENCES

Ainslie, George. 1987. "Self-Reported Tactics of Impulse Control." *International Journal of Addictions* 22, 2: 167–79.

———. 1991. "Derivation of 'Rational' Economic Behavior from Hyperbolic Discount Curves." *American Economic Review* 81, 2: 334–40.

Albanese, Paul J. 2002. *The Personality Continuum and Consumer Behavior.* Westport, CT: Quorum Books.

American Psychiatric Association. 1994. *Diagnostic and Statistical Manual of Mental Disorders,* 4th ed. Washington, D.C.: American Psychiatric Association.

Becker, Gary S. 1962. "Irrational Behavior and Economic Theory." In *The Economic Approach to Human Behavior,* 153–68. Chicago: University of Chicago Press, 1976.

Fairbairn, W.R.D. 1952. *Psychoanalytic Studies of the Personality.* London: Routledge and Kegan Paul.

Freud, Sigmund. 1915. "The Unconscious." In *The Standard Edition of the Complete Psychological Works of Sigmund Freud,* ed. James Strachey, 14:159–215. London: Hogarth Press, 1957.

———. 1933. "The Dissection of the Psychical Personality." *New Introductory Lectures on Psycho-analysis.* In *The Standard Edition of the Complete Psychological Works of Sigmund Freud,* ed. James Strachey, 22:12–66. London: Hogarth Press, 1961.

Kernberg, Otto F. 1977. "Boundaries and Structure in Love Relations." *Journal of the American Psychoanalytic Association* 25: 81–114.

———. 1984. *Object-Relations Theory and Clinical Psychoanalysis.* New York: Jason Aronson.

———. 1985. *Borderline Conditions and Pathological Narcissism.* New York: Jason Aronson.

Leibenstein, Harvey. 1975. "The Economic Theory of Fertility Decline." *Quarterly Journal of Economics* 89, 1: 1–31.

Schelling, Thomas C. 1980. "The Intimate Contest for Self Command." *Public Interest* 60: 94–118.

Sen, Amartya. 1977. "Rational Fools: A Critique of the Behavioral Foundations of Economic Theory." *Philosophy and Public Affairs* 6: 317–44.

Smith, Adam. 1759. *The Theory of Moral Sentiments.* Indianapolis: Liberty Fund, 1976.

———. 1776. *An Inquiry into the Nature and Causes of the Wealth of Nations.* New York: Modern Library, 1937.

Sullivan, Harry Stack. 1953. *The Interpersonal Theory of Psychiatry.* New York: W.W. Norton.

———. 1964. *The Fusion of Psychiatry and Social Science.* New York: W.W. Norton.

Winston, Gordon W. 1980. "Addiction and Backsliding: A Theory of Compulsive Consumption." *Journal of Economic Behavior and Organization* 1: 295–324.

TABLE 1.1

Personality Continuum

PERSONALITY

RANGES	INTERPERSONAL ACHIEVEMENT IN PERSONALITY DEVELOPMENT	INTERNAL OBJECT RELATIONS	INTRAPSYCHIC STRUCTURAL FORMATION
NORMAL	Sexual intercourse culminating in orgasm and the subjective experience of transcendence in an intimate interpersonal relationship forms a new common social boundary around the couple connecting past, present, and future Full integration of satisfying genital sexual activity into an interpersonal relationship by successfully resolving the oedipal situation	Internalization of a value system shared with another person Depersonification, individuation, reshaping to resemble real person	Protective superego Continuous internalization of more realistic interpersonal relationships through selective, partial, sublimatory identifications, including a complementary sexual identification in harmony with individual identity formation
NEUROTIC	Accept another person, and oneself, as both good and bad and, therefore, a whole and more realistic person	Integration of whole object relations	Ego identity and prohibitive superego
PRIMITIVE	Recognize oneself as separate from other	Self differentiated from object, internalization of the role aspects of interpersonal relationships, modified and more diversified affect	Multiple good and bad selves and objects, part-object relations internalized through identification Punitive superego
PSYCHOTIC	Oneself same as other	Self undifferentiated from object, intense and overwhelming positive or negative affect	Separate all-good and all-bad objects internalized through introjection

CONTINUUM

PREDOMINANT DEFENSES	INTIMACY	PREFERRED PATTERNING OF SEXUAL BEHAVIOR	HUMAN CAPACITY
A range of mature defenses: humor, sublimation, altruism, anticipation, and suppression	Second precondition for intimacy	Passion in an intimate interpersonal relationship, intimacy makes sexual relations satisfying	Capacity for commitment and a future orientation Self-reliance, the capacity for foresight and to plan realistically for the future, trustworthiness, the capacity for genuine insight and the urge to change in meaningful ways, the capacity to remain in love and form intimate interpersonal relationships
Repression, intellectualization (isolation, obsessive behavior, undoing, rationalization), reaction formation, displacement (conversion, phobias, wit), dissociation (neurotic denial)	First precondition for intimacy	Failure to achieve preferred pattern of genital sexual activity is an all-absorbing and all-frustrating preoccupation	The capacity for concern for another person and oneself, the capacity to experience guilt for violating the more realistic parental prohibitions and demands internalized in the prohibitive superego, and the capacity to fall in love
Splitting, denial, projection (projective identification), fantasy (schizoid withdrawal, denial through fantasy), hypochondriasis, passive-aggressive behavior, acting out		Polymorphous perverse sexual behavior, predatory sexual behavior, intense infatuations mainly with body parts and not the whole person	The capacity for rage, jealousy and possessiveness, envy and materialism, mistrustfulness, the ruthless exploitation of others, varying degrees of immature dependence, and the incapacity to depend on another person
Denial of external reality, distortion, delusional projection		Sexual behavior unusual for the person	Absence of capacity for reality testing

(continued)

Table 1.1 *(continued)*

PERSONALITY

RANGES	GENERAL PATTERN OF HUMAN BEHAVIOR	PATTERN OF CONSUMER BEHAVIOR	PATTERN OF CONSUMPTION BEHAVIOR
NORMAL	Stable and consistent	Rational consumer	Dynamic pattern of consumption behavior that can be modeled over time Self-control, delay of gratification, everything in moderation, prudent planning of consumption activities
NEUROTIC	Consistent under ordinary functioning, but lacking stability under extraordinary functioning	Neurotic consumer is indecisive, ambivalent, inhibited by feelings of guilt, and racked by cognitive dissonance	Continuous striving for consistent self-control, backsliding, use of precommitment devices to control behavior
PRIMITIVE	Chaotic pattern of alternating and contradictory behavior	Compulsive and more extreme addictive consumer behavior, the dark side of consumer behavior	Constant struggle with self-control, selective lack of impulse control, crude gratification of impulses, greed, ultimately self-destructive, myopic consumption behavior, present orientation, hyperbolic discounting
PSYCHOTIC	Changing and capricious	Irrational consumer	Buying sprees in manic episode

CONTINUUM

INDIVIDUAL PURSUIT OF SELF-INTEREST	PREDICTABILITY	PERSONALITY ORGANIZATIONS
The individual pursuit of self-interest informed by a value system	Predictable	Normal
The individual pursuit of self-interest with the capacity for sympathy and within the moral system of society	Predictable under ordinary functioning, regression to earlier patterns of behavior under extraordinary functioning	Depressive Avoidant Obsessive Hysterical Paranoid
The selfish pursuit of individual self-interest	Depending on the interpersonal situation, oscillating, either/or behavior, as if the person had two selves	Borderline Infantile Narcissistic Antisocial Schizoid
The irrational pursuit of individual self-interest	Unpredictable	Manic-depressive Schizophrenic

CHAPTER 2

PHYSIOLOGY AND BEHAVIORAL ECONOMICS

The New Findings from Evolutionary Neuroscience

GERALD A. CORY JR.

The brain is a physiological organ. That is a fundamental fact of science. The gene-specified neural circuits or architecture constitute that fundamental physiology. And physiologically, the human brain is also a *social* brain. The emergence of the concept of the social brain, emphasizing both the self-preservational (self-interested) and affectional (other-interested) components necessary to social exchange, has been landmarked by the publication of two recent handbooks—*Foundations in Social Neuroscience* (Cacioppo et al. 2002) and *Handbook of Affective Sciences* (Davidson et al. 2003) (see also Cory and Gardner 2002). Earlier but still recent volumes include *Descartes' Error: Emotion, Reason, and the Human Brain* (Damasio 1994), *The Integrative Neurobiology of Affiliation* (Carter, Lederhendler, and Kirkpatrick 1997), and *Affective Neuroscience* (Panksepp 1998). This author's *The Reciprocal Modular Brain in Economics and Politics* (1999) and *The Consilient Brain: The Bioneurological Basis of Economics, Society, and Politics* (2004) represent efforts to tie these new findings graphically, algorithmically, and mathematically to behavioral economics. Recent years have thus brought great advances in detailing the many complex and interrelated pathways of brain's interactive social circuitry.

The social circuitry was forged over millions of years of evolutionary history in small kinship groups which required a cooperative interactive dynamic for survival. These dynamic social circuits motivate human social interaction and social exchange at all levels of our lives today. Like many other physiological processes—for example, blood pressure, body temperature, and glucose level—that mediate between our internal and external environments, these social circuits are homeostatically regulated (see Herbert and Schulkin 2002; Bloom, Nelson, and Lazerson 2001, esp. 167–206; Kandel, Schwartz, and Jessell 2000, 871–997; Nelson 2000, esp. 447–94; Lapeyre and Lledo 1994; Becker, Breedlove, and Crews 1992; Cannon 1932). In fact, the broader term *allostatic*, which means "adaptive," perhaps better describes the social circuitry's rather wide, variable, and modifiable set points and boundaries (see McEwen 2003; McEwen and Seeman 2002; Sterling and Eyer 1981).

THE EVOLUTIONARY BACKGROUND

Leading evolutionary neuroscientist Paul MacLean, longtime head of the Laboratory of Brain Evolution and Behavior of the National Institutes of Health, pioneered the study of the neural circuitry substrating the brain's social architecture. In his 1990 masterwork, *The Triune Brain in Evolution: Role in Paleocerebral Functions,* MacLean tells us that the primary function of the

24

Figure 2.1 **The Interconnected, Modular Tri-level Brain** (After MacLean)

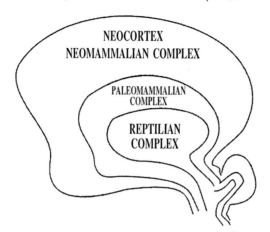

human brain is the preservation of the individual self and the human species. Although this may be said of the nervous system of any organism that must survive as an individual to reproduce, MacLean leads us to consider not just automatisms or tightly prewired instinctual mechanisms but the evolved social architecture or circuitry of the human brain upon which social choices are made. His concept of brain evolution, appropriately updated, provides the necessary conceptual platform for this undertaking. (For a detailed, documented critique and update of MacLean's concepts see Cory 1999, 2002a, 2004.) As represented here, the three brain divisions do not constitute distinct additions but rather modifications and elaborations of probable preexisting gene-based homologues reflecting phylogenetic continuity.

MacLean documents the human brain as an evolved three-level interconnected, modular structure (Figure 2.1). This structure includes a self-preservational component reflecting gene-based continuity from our ancestral reptiles, which split off from the dinosaur ancestral line during the Permian and Triassic periods about 250 million years ago. This is called the protoreptilian complex. Also included are a later modified and evolved mammalian affectional complex, and a most recently modified and elaborated higher neocortex representing the higher centers of the brain.

As brain evolution continued in the branching vertebrate line ancestral to humans, simple vertebrate or protoreptilian brain structure was not replaced but was modified and elaborated. The protoreptilian structure, then, provided the substructure and gene-based continuities (called homologues) for later brain development while largely retaining its basic character and function. The mammalian modifications and neocortical elaborations that followed reached the greatest development in the brain of humankind. Appreciating the qualitative differences of the three interconnected levels is important to understanding the dynamics of human social experience and exchange behavior.

The protoreptilian brain circuits function in humans, much as they did in our ancestral vertebrates, to govern the fundamentals, or the daily master routines, of our life-support operations: blood circulation, heartbeat, respiration, basic food-getting, reproduction, and defensive behaviors. These were functions and behaviors also necessary in the ancient ancestral reptiles as well as earlier amphibians and fishes. Located in what are usually called the hindbrain and the midbrain (i.e., the brain stem) as well as in certain structures at the base of the forebrain (i.e., the basal ganglia), this primal and innermost core of the human brain made up almost the entire brain in ancestral fishes, amphibians, and reptiles (although not necessarily their modern representatives, since they too have undergone further evolution).

The next developmental stage of our brain, which comes from rudimentary mammalian life and which MacLean called the paleo- or "old" mammalian brain, is identified with the structures designated collectively as our limbic system. Developing from gene-based continuities preexisting in the protoreptilian brain, these limbic circuits included significant elaboration of such physiological structures as the amygdala, hypothalamus, the hippocampus, the thalamus, the limbic cingulate cortex, and the orbital frontal cortex. Behavioral contributions to life from these modified and elaborated paleo-mammalian structures included, among other things, the mammalian features (absent in our ancestral reptiles) of warm-bloodedness, nursing, infant attachment, and parental care. These circuits became the basis of family life and our capacity for extended social bonding (e.g., Carter and Keverne 2002; Numan and Insel 2003). Without knowledge of neuroscience, such scholars as Bowlby (1969), Harlow and Harlow (1965), and Harlow (1986) earlier identified these behaviors as forming the basis of infant-mother attachment and affectional relations. These new characteristics were then neurally integrated with the life-support functional and behavioral circuitry of the protoreptilian brain circuitry to create the more complex life form of mammals.

The neocortex, which MacLean called the neo- or "new" mammalian brain, is the most recent stage of brain modification and elaboration. This great mass of hemispherical brain matter that dominates the skull case of higher primates and humans evolved by elaborating the preexisting continuities present in the brains of early vertebrates. The neocortex overgrew and encased the earlier (paleo-) mammalian and protoreptilian neural tissues, but essentially did not replace them. As a consequence of this neocortical evolution and growth, those older brain parts evolved greater complexity and extensive interconnected circuitry with these new tissue structures. In that way, they produced the behavioral adaptations necessary to humankind's increasingly sophisticated circumstances.

The unique features of our human brain were refined over a period of several million years in a mainly kinship-based foraging society where sharing or reciprocity was necessary to our survival (e.g., see Humphrey 1976; Isaac 1978; Knauft 1994; Erdal and Whiten 1996; Boehm 1999). Such sharing and reciprocity strengthened the adaptive evolution of the now combined mammalian characteristics of self-preservation and affection. Ego and empathy, self-interest and other-interest, are key features of our personal and social behavior deriving from these basic motivational circuits. To relate these to MacLean's concept we need a behavioral rather than neurophysiological vocabulary.

THE CONFLICT SYSTEMS NEUROBEHAVIORAL MODEL

The conflict systems neurobehavioral (CSN) model (Figure 2.2), developed by the author, uses computer-related vocabulary and assigns a dynamic to MacLean's clarified and updated conceptual platform as described above. This simplified cutaway representation of the brain shows the behavioral programs (or circuits) and the derivation of ego/self-interested and empathy/other-interested motives and behaviors. I should note that earlier models, such as Freud's (id, ego, and superego), postulated three-part conflictual models. Freud, however, was unable to tie his model to brain circuitry, and it remained ungrounded in neural science because brain research had simply not advanced to that point (Cory 1999, 2000a, 2000b, 2001a, 2001b, 2002a, 2002b, 2003, 2004).

Our self-preservation and affection programs are interconnected and motivated neural network circuits that *subjectively* generate and drive specific and *objectively* observable behaviors. These core motivational (and emotional) circuits are cognitively represented in the frontal regions of our neocortex as ego and empathy, respectively (e.g., see Berridge 2003). They

Figure 2.2 **The Conflict Systems Neurobehavioral (CSN) Model**

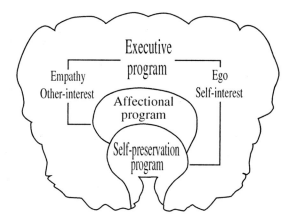

serve as dynamic factors of our behavior. That is, they are dynamically driven by our cellular as well as overall bodily processes of metabolism as mediated by hormonal, neurotransmitter, and neural architecture.

Each is an inseparable part of our makeup, because each is coded into our genes by the process of evolution. The degree of genome control seems to vary with the mechanism, however. Brain parts such as the hindbrain and parts of the limbic system, phylogenetically old and necessary for survival, seem to be more closely under gene control. Other, more recent tissues in the neocortex depend also on development and environmental experience. Neuroresearcher Antonio Damasio (1994, 1999) uses the terms *preset* and *preorganized* to avoid the implication of an overly deterministic prewiring or coding in some brain regions.

Behavioral conflict potentially exists, then, simply by virtue of the presence of these two large-scale dynamic modular program sets in our lives—up and running even prior to birth. Behavioral tension, which we may subjectively experience as frustration, anxiety, or anger, occurs whenever one of our two fundamental behavioral programs—self-preservation or affection—is activated but meets with some resistance or difficulty that blocks its satisfactory expression. This subjective tension becomes most paralyzing when both systems are activated and seek contending or incompatible responses *within a single situation.* Caught between "I want to" and "I can't"—for example, "I want to help him/her, but I can't surrender my needs"—we agonize. Whether this tension arises through the thwarted expression of a single impulse or the simultaneous but mutually exclusive urgings of two contending impulses, whenever it remains unresolved or unmanaged it leads to the worsening condition of behavioral stress.

The evolutionary process by which the two opposite promptings of self-preservation and affection were combined in us helped us to survive by binding us in social interaction and social exchange, thereby providing us with the widest range of behavioral responses to our environment. Our inborn conflicting programs are a curse, then, only to the degree that we fail to recognize them as a blessing. Our self-preservation and affection programs allow us a highly advanced sensitivity to our environment, keeping our interactive social exchange behaviors homeostatically within survival limits as well as enabling us to perceive and appreciate the survival requirements of others. Ironically, the accompanying behavioral tension—even the stress—is an integral part of this useful function, for it allows us to more immediately evaluate our behavior and the effect it is having on ourselves and others.

Figure 2.3   **The Major Ranges/Modes of Behavior**

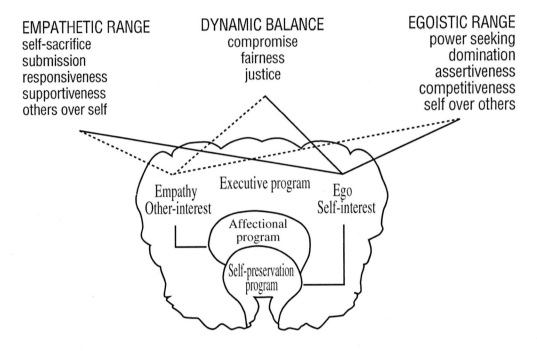

EMPATHETIC RANGE
self-sacrifice
submission
responsiveness
supportiveness
others over self

DYNAMIC BALANCE
compromise
fairness
justice

EGOISTIC RANGE
power seeking
domination
assertiveness
competitiveness
self over others

Empathy
Other-interest

Executive program

Ego
Self-interest

Affectional
program

Self-preservation
program

Behavioral tension serves as an internal emotional compass that we can use to guide ourselves through the often complicated and treacherous pathways of interpersonal exchange relations.

Behavioral stress tells us that we are exceeding safe limits for ourselves and others, and for our larger social, economic, and political structures.

Our executive programming or circuitry, seated in our frontal cortex (Pribram 1973, 1994; Fuster 1997, 1999; Miller and Cummings 1999; Goldberg 2001; Stuss and Knight 2002), cognitively represents the limbic and protoreptilian subcortical inputs (also see Berridge 2003), making what may be thought of as our *moral* as well as *rational* choices among our conflicting, impulsive, and irrational or nonrational motivations. This capacity to represent, generalize, and choose—accompanied, of course, with language—is what differentiates us from even closely related primate species and makes findings in primate behavior, although highly interesting and unquestionably important, insufficient in themselves to fully understand and account for human behavior.

THE MAJOR RANGES OF RECIPROCAL SOCIAL BEHAVIOR

The two master, inclusive circuits or programs of self-preservation and affection operate as global state variables (see Panksepp 2002; cf. Schulkin 2002, who refers to central motive states) to shape our social exchange behavior. They operate dynamically according to a set of *subjectively experienced* and *objectively expressed* behavioral rules, procedures, or algorithms.

The major ranges of the CSN model (Figure 2.3) illustrate the features of this ego-empathy dynamic. In the display, social behavior is divided from right to left into three main ranges, called the egoistic range, the dynamic balance range, and the empathetic range. Each range represents a varying mix of egoistically and empathetically motivated behaviors. The solid line stands for ego and pivots on the word *ego* in the executive program of our brain diagram. The broken line stands for empathy and pivots on the word *empathy* in the diagram. To simplify the graph, the three points are intended to mark the center points of each range, with varying mixes of ego and empathy on either side of each point. The graph thus intends to communicate not a zero-sum, either/or set of behavioral options or expressions but a spectrum of the increasing or decreasing (depending on direction of movement) proportions of ego and empathy in behavior. The graph represents only what may be thought of as central tendencies of interactive behavior and is far too simple to represent all the shadings of emotion and motivation.

The Egoistic Range

The egoistic range indicates behavior dominated by self-preservation programming. Since the two behavioral programs are locked in inseparable unity, empathy is present here, but to a lesser degree. Behavior in this range is self-centered or self-interested and may tend, for example, to be dominating, power-seeking, or even attacking, where empathy is less. When empathy is increased, ego behavior will become less harsh and may be described more moderately as controlling, competitive, or assertive. As empathy is gradually increased, the intersection of the two lines of the diagram will be drawn toward the range of dynamic balance. Ego behavior will be softened as empathy is added. But the defining characteristic of the egoistic, self-interested range is *self-over-others*. Whether we are blatantly power-seeking or more moderately assertive, in this range we are putting ourselves, our own priorities and feelings, ahead of others.

The Empathetic Range

The empathetic range represents behavior weighted in favor of empathy. Ego is present but is taking a backseat. When ego is present to a minimal degree, empathetic behavior may tend to extremes of self-sacrifice and submission. When ego is increased, empathetic behaviors become moderated and may be described as supportive, responsive, or any of a variety of "others first" behaviors. As the influence of ego is gradually added, empathetic behavior will approach the range of dynamic balance. In the empathetic range, the key phrase to remember is *others-over-self* or others first. Whether we are at the extreme of self-sacrifice or more moderately responsive, we are putting the priorities and feelings of others ahead of our own.

The Dynamic Balance Range

The range of dynamic balance represents a working balance between ego and empathy. At this point our behavioral programs are operating in roughly equal measure. I speak of "working," "rough," or "dynamic" balance because the tug and pull between the two programs continues ceaselessly. The dynamic nature of the circuitry means that "perfect" balance may be a theoretical point, unattainable in practice. Our more balanced behavior tends to be characterized by equality, justice, sharing, and other behaviors that show respect for ourselves and others. In fact, respect for self and others is the keynote of the range of dynamic balance.

Energy or Activity Level

The extent to which the programs of self-preservation and affection, ego and empathy, are out of balance, or pulling against each other, is a measure of behavioral tension. We experience this behavioral tension both internally and between ourselves and others in any relationship or interaction. Unmanaged or excessive tension becomes, of course, behavioral stress. But that's not all. Important also is the degree of energy we give to the interaction or the relationship. The amount of energy we put into any activity depends mostly upon how important we think it is or how enthusiastic we feel about it. In competitive sports or contests, qualitative differences in energy are easily observed. In intellectual contests, such as chess, the energy may be intense but less obvious.

THE RECIPROCAL ALGORITHMS OF SOCIAL BEHAVIOR

From the dynamic interplay of ego, empathy, and activity level come the following algorithmic rule statements:

> 1. Self-interested, egoistic behavior, because it lacks empathy to some degree, creates tension within ourselves and between ourselves and others. The tension increases from low to high activity levels. And it increases as we move toward the extremes of ego.
>
> Within ourselves, the tension created by the tug of neglected empathy is experienced as a feeling of obligation to others or an expectation that they might wish to "even the score" with us.
>
> Within others, the tension created by our self-interested behavior is experienced as a feeling of imposition or hurt, accompanied by an urge to "even the score."

We often see the dynamic of such behavior most clearly when children interact. Imagine two children playing on the living room floor. One hits the other, and the second child hits back, responding in kind. Or one child might call the other a bad name, and the second child reciprocates, kicking off a round of escalating name-calling. One child may eventually feel unable to even the score and will complain to a parent to intervene. Most of us have experienced such give-and-take as children and have seen it countless times in our own children and grandchildren. We even see similar behavior among adults—in husband-and-wife disputes, bar fights, hockey games, political campaigns, even the process of lawsuits. The rule operates not only in such highly visible conflict situations but also in very subtle interactions—in the small behavioral exchanges, the ongoing give-and-take of all interpersonal social exchange relations.

To express the underlying conflictual excitatory/inhibitory dynamic of the neural architecture, we can say that

> the reactions that build in ourselves and others do so potentially in proportion to the behavioral tension created by egoistic, self-interested behavior.

Behavior on the other side of the spectrum is described in the second rule statement:

> 2. Empathetic behavior, because it denies ego or self-interest to some degree, also creates tension within ourselves and others. This tension likewise increases as activity levels increase and as we move toward extremes of empathy.
>
> Within ourselves, the tension created by the tug of the neglected self-interest (ego) is experienced as a feeling that "others owe us one" and a growing need to "collect our due." This tension, especially if it continues over time, may be experienced as resentment at being exploited, taken for granted, not appreciated, or victimized by others.
>
> Within others, the tension created is experienced as a sense of obligation toward us.

The reactions that build in ourselves and others, again, are in proportion to the behavioral tension created. And again, the unmanaged or excessive tension is experienced as behavioral stress.

When we do things for others—give them things, make personal sacrifices for them—we can feel quite righteous, affectionate, loving. Nevertheless, we *do* want a payback. That's the tug of self-interest. The tug can be very slight, hardly noticeable at first. But let the giving, the self-sacrifice, go on for a while, unacknowledged or unappreciated (that is, without payback to the ego), and the tension, the stress, starts to show. We may complain that others are taking advantage of us, taking us for granted, victimizing us. Self-interest cannot be short-changed for long without demanding its due. We may eventually relieve the stress by blowing up at those we have been serving—accusing them of ingratitude, withdrawing our favor, or kicking them out of the house. Or we may wall up the stress, letting it eat away at our dispositions, our bodies.

On the other hand, when we do things for others, they often feel obliged to return the favor in some form to avoid being left with an uneasy sense of debt. Gift-giving notoriously stimulates the receiver to feel the need to reciprocate. We need only think of the times we received a holiday gift from someone for whom we had failed to buy a gift. Sometimes the sense of obligation prompted by the empathetic acts of others can become a nuisance.

The third rule statement describes the relative balance between the contending motives:

3. Behavior in the range of dynamic balance expresses the approximate balance of ego and empathy. It is the position of least behavioral tension. Within ourselves and others, it creates feelings of mutuality and shared respect.

Most of us find it satisfying to interact with others in equality, with no sense of obligation, superiority, or inferiority. When we work together in common humanity, in common cause, we experience behavioral dynamic balance. Certainly there are many versions of the experience of dynamic balance: the shared pride of parents in helping their children achieve, the joy of athletes in playing well as a team, the satisfaction of co-workers in working together successfully on an important project.

THE RECIPROCAL NATURE OF BEHAVIOR

These algorithms of behavior operate in the smallest interactions of everyday personal life. The dynamic of behavioral tension provides that for every interpersonal act, there is a balancing reciprocal. A self-interested act requires an empathetic reciprocal for balance. An empathetic act, likewise, requires a balancing self-interested reciprocal. This reciprocity goes back and forth many times even in a short conversation. Without the reciprocal, tension builds, stress accumulates, and either confrontation or withdrawal results. If not, and the relationship continues, it becomes a tense and stressful one of inequality or domination/submission, waiting and pressing for the opportunity for adjustment. These algorithms show how we get to reciprocity through conflict. They shape the conflict and reciprocity, the give-and-take, at all levels of our interactive, social lives.

Overemphasis on either self-interest or empathy, exercise of one program to the exclusion of the other, creates tension and stress in any social configuration—from simple dyadic person-to-person encounters up to and including social exchange interactions among members of the workplace, society at large, social groups, and entire economic and political systems.

VARIABILITY OF THE RECIPROCAL ALGORITHMS

The algorithmic rules of reciprocal behavior operate as *central tendencies* of behavior. They also show considerable individual variability. They cannot work as precisely as the laws of classical physics or even quantum mechanics because they are achieved through the process of organic evolution, which involves some random processes and natural selection. Gender, developmental, and experiential differences also contribute to variability (Cory 1999, 42–44). This variability and lack of absolute precision is generally true of biological algorithms (e.g., see Maynard Smith 2002).

RECIPROCITY: THE UNIVERSAL NORM

The norm of reciprocity expressing our social neural architecture has long been a major theme in anthropology and sociology (e.g., see Gouldner 1960; Baal 1975) and more recently in economics (e.g., Cory 1999, 2004; Fehr and Gachter 2000; Bowles and Gintis 1998, esp. ch. 17; Gintis 2000; Eckel and Grossman 1997). This universally observed norm, found in all societies, primitive and modern, has been accounted for, or shown to be possible, in evolutionary theory by such concepts as kin selection, inclusive fitness (Hamilton 1964), reciprocal altruism (Trivers 1971, 1981; Alexander 1987), and game theory (Axelrod and Hamilton 1981; Maynard Smith 1982). These efforts draw upon so-called gene-centered perspectives, which see such reciprocity as basically selfish. More recently, extensive reciprocity seen as based not upon selfishness but upon empathy has been reportedly observed in the behavior of rhesus monkeys (de Waal 1996). De Waal's approach is a welcome departure that tries to escape the selfishness of gene-centered approaches and looks to the implied motivational mechanisms. All these approaches, however, including de Waal's, have been based on the external observation of behavior. They have not attempted to identify or even speculate upon the neural mechanisms within the organism that must necessarily have been selected for by the evolutionary process to accomplish the functions of motivating, maintaining, and rewarding such observed reciprocal behavior.

According to the CSN model of our neural architecture, reciprocity through conflict is achieved in the range of dynamic balance, where behavioral tension operating freely tends to pull us. In dynamic balance, ego and empathy provide for the emergence of cooperation and fairness, trust and morality in interpersonal, social exchange activities. Taking the dynamic balance range to be approaching or approximating the equilibrium of ego and empathy as driven by behavioral tension, we can derive a formula that expresses this dynamic.

THE EQUATION OF SOCIALITY OR SOCIAL EXCHANGE

The reciprocal algorithms emerging from our social neural architecture have been illustrated graphically by the three major ranges of social behavior (refer back to Figure 2.3). They have also been written in plain English in the section describing their algorithmic interactive dynamic. I can now state them mathematically in the form of the equation of sociality or social exchange approaching equilibrium:

$$BT = \frac{Ego}{Emp} \ or \ \frac{Emp}{Ego} = \pm 1 \left(approx. \ equilibrium, \ unity, \ or \ dynamic \ balance\right)$$

In the above formula *BT* stands for behavioral tension and is a function of the ratio of ego to empathy or vice versa. Because of the physiological homeostatic nature of the dynamic, either ego or empathy can serve as the numerator or denominator as necessary to avoid the inconvenience of fractions and to more accurately reflect the magnitude of divergence or convergence. The degree of convergence or divergence is what is of interest.

This equation gives basic mathematical expression to the social exchange architecture of our evolved brain structure. As the conflicting modules of our social architecture approach equilibrium or dynamic balance—represented by the symbolic approximation to unity or dynamic balance, ±1—behavioral tension/stress are minimized. On the other hand, as the ratios diverge increasingly toward the extremes of ego or empathy, behavioral tension increases. That is, if we have an empathy magnitude of 8 and an ego magnitude of 4, or vice versa, we have a behavioral tension magnitude of 2. At a minimum the neural dynamic serves generally to keep our social behavior homeostatically within survival limits, which accounts for its Darwinian selection. On the other hand, at the level of optimal functioning, the algorithms, driven by behavioral tension, tend to move us toward dynamic balance of ego and empathy or self and other interest, that is, balanced reciprocity, or equality. The formula, therefore, is very simple, but deceptively so, because it can be quite variable and can ramify in many ways.

THE EVOLUTION OF THE MARKET

To understand the behavior of the modern-day free enterprise market as it is shaped by our inherited brain structure and behavior, it is helpful to go back to early times—to reconstruct as best we can the days before the market appeared. For a discussion and documentation in detail, see Cory 2004, 1999.

The Family or Group Bond

In those times, when people consumed what they produced, the excess that they shared with, gave to, or used to provide for the needs or demands of the family or community was in the nature of natural affection or empathy. The reward for the empathetic, supplying act was emotional—there was a diffuse, not specific, value assigned to it. It also had social effects—the givers or providers gained status in the group. Both the emotional and social effects were directly governed by the reciprocal algorithms of behavior.

Let us look more closely. The provider brought meat from the hunt or berries and fruits from the field, tanned skins, and so on to give to the family or group. The act of providing, giving, created behavioral tension in the giver, who, acting empathetically, denied ego to some degree and required a response of acknowledgment, gratitude, respect, affection, or some other reaffirmation of ego. This providing or giving also created behavioral tension in the receivers. It was a service to their ego, their needs or demands—to their own preservation—that created tension requiring an offsetting empathetic response, a thank-you, an expression of appreciation or respect. In any family or close group, even now, this dynamic flows constantly, even in the smallest activities. In the small group the rewards, the reciprocations of such social exchange, are largely not quantified but are diffuse. They become obligations—bonds—that hold the group together for protection or mutual survival. Nevertheless, they must achieve some approximation of balance or the unresolved tension will build within the group and become disruptive. Expressions for "thank you" and "you're welcome," found in all known human languages, reflect this reciprocity in social exchange activity.

The Gift

From these early, primitive behavioral exchanges, emerged the gift: an empathetic act of providing or serving that followed the same algorithmic behavioral rules that governed provision for survival. It created tension in the giver—an expectation of reciprocity—and tension in the receiver, who was bound to reciprocate. The rewards associated with the gift were diffuse, unspecified, unquantified—except by some subjective measure of feeling, emotion, or behavioral tension. A gift to a warrior or chief might vaguely obligate his protection. A gift to a prospective mate might vaguely obligate his or her attentions. The gift economy of so-called primitive peoples—an important theme in anthropology—operated in this way (see, e.g., Mauss 1925; Bohannon 1963; Cheal 1988; Godelier 1999; Gérard-Varet, Kolm, and Ythier 2000; Davis 2000; Fennell 2002).

From Gift to Transaction

From the gift evolved the transaction—namely, the gift with the reciprocal specified or quantified (e.g., see, Mauss 1925; Polanyi 1957; Sahlins 1972; Gregory 1982; Appadurai 1986; Seymour-Smith 1986, 44; Barfield 1997, 73; Hunt 2002; Osteen 2002). The transaction is the beginning of the contract, perhaps of the market itself. The transaction operates, however, by the same algorithms of behavior as the gift, except that it attempts to head off the residual, unresolved behavioral tension that creates a condition of obligation or bonding. After all, in the market, we may be dealing with strangers not to be seen again. Nevertheless, the transaction retains its essential mammalian characteristics as an act of empathy, of nurturing, which requires a balancing reciprocal act in payment to ego.

When we encounter its equivalent in the impersonalized market economy of today, how often do we feel the subjective experience of the transaction? We take our sick child to the physician, who empathetically and carefully applies the knowledge it took ten years and a fortune to gain. We pay the bill—that is, we make a return gift with money that represents a portion of our accumulated education and labor. The scenario is repeated in transactions with the plumber, the carpenter, the computer maker. The behavioral algorithms still apply, but the feeling, the subjective experience, has to a large degree been lost.

Behavioral Tension Yet Drives the Transaction

But wait! Let the transaction go wrong, the expected reciprocals not be forthcoming, and the behavioral tension becomes immediately and personally felt. The reality of the transaction—the market—reveals itself with clarity and intensity. No one likes to be cheated or shortchanged. And most will be motivated to take some action to correct the imbalance in expected reciprocity or harbor the behavioral tension indefinitely to be acted upon in the future. The dockets of our small-claims courts are filled with cases reflecting the tension of such unbalanced reciprocity.

The evolution of the transactional market (demand and supply) as shaped by neural architecture can be summarized in Figure 2.4.

METAECONOMICS AND THE DUALITY OF MOTIVES

From the transactional perspective, the CSN model also provides underpinning for what is called metaeconomics and the question of multiple motives or utilities (Lynne 1999, 2000;

Figure 2.4 **Evolution of Market Exchange Based on Dynamics of Neural Architecture**

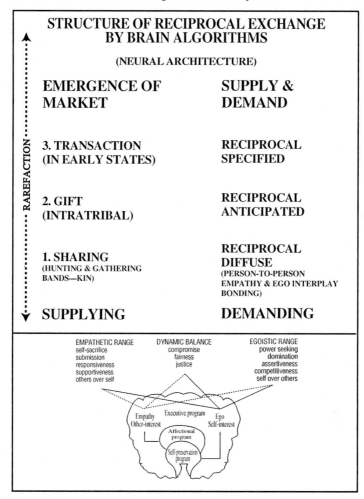

Lutz 1993; Etzioni 1986). The CSN model shows that the tug and pull between ego and empathy goes on constantly within us and between us as we interact socially. To the extent that our economic transactions or choices are social, and they inevitably are, they will involve the tug and pull of ego and empathy to some degree. The very nature of social or market exchange is transactional, give-and-take, or interpersonal. The idea that we make independent choices separate from interpersonal or social concerns is largely illusory. The transactional atom, when opened up, is shown to be composed of ego and empathy, mutual benefit, in a state of negotiated tension (Cory 1999, 77–78). There is therefore some degree of behavioral tension from the tug and pull of ego and empathy, a dual motive (or perhaps utility) on both sides in every social or market choice or transaction. The degree of tug and pull or behavioral tension will depend upon the triviality or significance of the transaction—something neoclassical theory does not distinguish. Adam Smith recognized clearly this essential mutual benefit nature of the market in the line quoted below, which immediately precedes the customarily quoted passage that traditionally has been wrongly taken to justify a sole self-interest motive.

Give me what I want, and you shall have what you want, is the meaning of every such offer. (Smith 1776, Book I, ch. 2).

In modern times we recognize the above quote on mutual benefit as *win-win*. The equal mutual benefit or balanced reciprocity position of win-win is reflected in the graph of the CSN model as dynamic balance and in the equation of social exchange as ±1.

THE SELF-REFERENCE FALLACY OF NEOCLASSICAL ECONOMICS

The confounding of *self-reference* with *self-interest* is a fundamental fallacy of the neoclassical approach. This logical fallacy allows the subsuming of all motives under the rubric of self-interest and obscures the roughly equal role of empathy. Taking the individual as the starting point, microeconomic theory mistakenly transforms this individual or self-referential *perspective* into an all-inclusive *motive* of self-interest. From this logically unwarranted transformation, any other motive is seen as proceeding from the self-interest motive. Therefore empathy (and its derivatives of cooperation and altruism, even love) can be trivialized as tastes or preferences indistinguishable in significance from coffee, tea, or milk. Nevertheless, the hidden duality of ego and empathy is seen in every demand curve and supply curve, especially when both are combined to show price equilibrium. The dual roles are always present implicitly if not explicitly. The supplier performs the empathetic role; the demander performs the egoistic role. (See Appendix 1 for examples of the hidden duality of ego and empathy within the customary self-referential neoclassical perspective.)

THE INVISIBLE HAND IN THE STRUCTURE AND BEHAVIOR OF THE MARKETPLACE

To understand the function of the invisible hand in the socioeconomic market, it helps to maintain a clear distinction between structure and behavior.

Structure

The invisible hand as the tug and pull of ego and empathy is expressed in the market structure as *demand* and *supply*. The reciprocal dynamic tends to work despite the unidimensional overemphasis on self-interest in classical economics by the fallacy of self-reference. This is because the very structure itself of the market is the institutionalized product of the ego/empathy dynamic of our evolved neural architecture. That is, as Adam Smith saw, when we enter into market exchange, we fundamentally agree to a give-and-take exchange that necessitates mutual benefit, reciprocity, and respect for self and others, or ego and empathy. Our self-survival ego *demands* are rooted ultimately in our ancestral protoreptilian or vertebrate neural complexes and represented in our higher frontal brain circuits as self-interest or ego. Contrastingly, the act of *providing* or *supplying* is fundamentally an act of mammalian nurturing—likewise represented in our higher frontal brain circuitry as other-interest or empathy. The market exchange system originated from and is sustained by this dynamic. The market could never have evolved or been maintained on the basis of ego or self-interest alone. Without empathy we would not know how to respond to the needs of others. Dinosaurs and crocodiles, as well as our ancestral vertebrates, never produced markets.

Behavior

Behavior, in individual choices and transactions within the above institutionalized structure, may vary considerably in the mix of ego and empathy motives on both the demand and supply sides. Nevertheless, even in the most ego-skewed (or self-interested) market behavior, the overall unobstructed tendency of the market will be toward a balance of ego and empathy. To survive in the market, individual and collective actors, whether seemingly motivated primarily by self-interest or not, will be compelled by the very evolved and institutionalized market structure itself to perform the structural equivalent of empathy. That is, under pressure of competition among providers, they will be required to provide (supply) a proper service or product to fill the needs (demand) of others. This is especially true of the idealized, purely competitive market envisioned by standard economic theory.

To the degree, however, that empathy is a consciously included and recognized behavioral motivational component within the market structure, the product or service provided may be enhanced in quality and the emergence of trust in market relationships will be facilitated. Conversely, the overemphasis on self-interest in the neoclassical paradigm tends to vitiate the development of quality and the emergence of trust in the market. Aside from the scientifically inaccurate concept of the market in neoclassical economics, this vitiation of quality and trust, adding to transaction costs, is one of its greatest drawbacks in practice.

Reciprocity through conflict is achieved in the range of dynamic balance where behavioral tension operating freely tends to pull us. In dynamic balance, ego and empathy provide for the emergence of cooperation and fairness, trust and morality in interpersonal, social, and economic exchange activities. Taking the dynamic balance range to be approaching or approximating the equilibrium of ego and empathy as driven by behavioral tension, again we call upon the previously derived formula:

$$BT = \frac{Ego}{Emp} \text{ or } \frac{Emp}{Ego} = \frac{Demand}{Supply} \text{ or } \frac{Supply}{Demand} = EP = \pm 1 \begin{pmatrix} \text{approx. equilibrium, unity, or} \\ \text{dynamic balance} \end{pmatrix}$$

The above equation—with either ego or empathy, demand or supply, as the numerator or denominator to accurately reflect the magnitude of behavioral tension—gives basic mathematical expression to the interaction of ego (demand) and empathy (supply). Appendices 2 and 3 clarify the effect of the above formula on the standard treatment in calculus for demand and supply and demonstrate its application more fully. As the two motives intersect freely in the marketplace, we tend to have equitable exchange. Or, in the case of specific products and services, we tend toward equilibrium price (EP) or fair price. Since the evolved algorithmic dynamic works imperfectly, I use the word *tend*.

The formula or equation proceeding from evolved neural network architecture thus provides the unifying linkage between brain physiology (or neuroscience) and economics or social exchange theory. The behavioral tension driving toward the proximate dynamic balance between demand and supply in the marketplace accounts for the motive force for the venerable invisible hand—that elusive dynamic previously accounted for variously by the hand of a deity, Newtonian mechanics, or other inappropriate physical processes (see Cory 2004, 1999, 92–95; Ingrao and Israel 1990).

The marketplace is thus clearly a product of the dynamic of our evolved neural architecture. The same dynamic formula can be shown to underlie not only market and social exchange but also power relationships, social stratification, and other relations of inequality

(Cory 2004). Kept free (by appropriate institutions) of the skewing effects of excessive wealth accumulation and the pressure of powerful special interests, both a democratic free enterprise economic system and a democratic political system will, in accord with the neural architecture, tend toward a dynamic equilibrium that minimizes economic and political inequalities.

On the other hand, the behavioral tension or inequality within a market system or a political system may be indexed by the same dynamic formula to the extent that it departs from dynamic equilibrium and the ratio begins to diverge increasingly.

CONCLUSION

In conclusion, the neural algorithms of our social brain function as competing or conflicting neural networks, both excitatory and mutually inhibitory, interacting with each other homeostatically within prescribed limits. Neural network models have been developed to express this ego/empathy dynamic (Levine and Jani 2002; cf. Leven 1994). They are thus a physiologically (homeostatically) regulated social mechanism like numerous other bodily functions—for example, blood pressure, blood sugar, and body temperature. Their interactive dynamic generally ensures that our social behavior stays within survival limits. At its optimum the dynamic tends toward equilibrium or dynamic balance, which promotes social harmony and cooperation. Over history, despite the emphasis on violence and war, the dynamic has worked successfully to achieve a human population of over six billion—creating, of course, new problems to be dealt with. In fact, one author has questioned whether the human species is not a suicidal success (Tickell 1993).

The interactive dynamic can be mapped onto mathematical operations or formulas identifiable with social stratification and inequality as well as the invisible hand of economic supply and demand. It is the convergence or divergence of the ratio that is of interest. As the ratio diverges from approximation to ± 1 or unity, it serves to index the behavioral tension and stresses among ourselves and within our economic, social, and political structures. The equations expressing their dynamic interactions approaching equilibrium or unity as reflected in exchange and political economy are as follows.

Neuroscience:

$$Behavioral\ Tension\ (BT) = \frac{Ego}{Empathy} \text{ or } \frac{Empathy}{Ego} = \pm 1 \left(\begin{array}{l} \text{approx. equilibrium, unity, or} \\ \text{dynamic balance} \end{array} \right)$$

Economics:

$$BT = Equilibrium\ Price = \frac{Demand}{Supply} \text{ or } \frac{Supply}{Demand} = \pm 1 \left(\begin{array}{l} \text{approx. equilibrium, unity, or} \\ \text{dynamic balance} \end{array} \right)$$

Political Economy:

$$BT = Political\ Tension = \frac{Domination}{Subordination} = \pm 1 \left(\begin{array}{l} \text{approx. equilibrium, unity, or} \\ \text{dynamic balance} \end{array} \right)$$

Figure 2.5 **The Demand Curve**

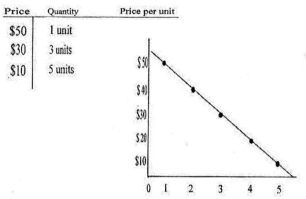

Price	Quantity
$50	1 unit
$30	3 units
$10	5 units

Invisible Hand
  of Economics:
  of Politics:

$$BT = \frac{Ego}{Emp} \ or \ \frac{Emp}{Ego} = \pm 1 \left(\begin{array}{l} \text{approx. equilibrium, unity, or} \\ \text{dynamic balance} \end{array} \right)$$

The CSN model, emerging from evolved neural architecture, anchors behavioral economics, equilibrium theory, and market and free enterprise theory firmly in the physiology of neuroscience and supports the introduction of the moral component of empathy into the rational calculus of economics, free enterprise theory, and other social sciences. The model supports ongoing efforts to introduce cooperation and fairness, trust and morality into the neoclassical calculus and definitively counters the long-prevailing, inaccurate, and troubling self-interested bias of received microeconomic and traditional business theory. The CSN model provides the basis for a new research program to develop and test the hypotheses proceeding therefrom and to explore the potential implications for rethinking aspects of contemporary economic, business, and political policy. It is particularly applicable to the challenges of global trade and business, which must be based on respect for self and others—the dynamic interplay of ego and empathy—if trade is to be conducted peacefully without the threat of military conflict.

APPENDIX 1: NEURAL ARCHITECTURE AND THE DUALITY OF THE MARKET

The demand, supply, and equilibrium curves that follow are presented in very simplified form. They nevertheless illustrate the essential features of all such curves.

I. The Demand Curve

The demand curve slopes downward because as price increases on the y-axis, the quantity people are willing and able to buy generally decreases (x-axis) (see Figure 2.5). Even the single-actor perspective of the demand curve shows the duality of exchange expressive of our neural architecture: Price = give = empathy; Quantity = take = ego. In other words, price is what we give, quantity is what we take. The demand curve, therefore, illustrates the reciprocal, give-and-take, empathy-ego social exchange relationship.

Figure 2.6 **The Supply Curve**

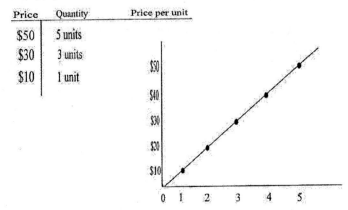

Price	Quantity
$50	5 units
$30	3 units
$10	1 unit

Figure 2.7 **Equilibrium in the Market**

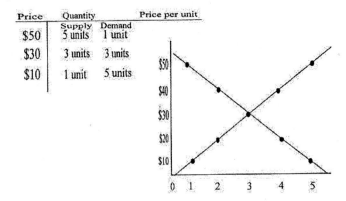

Price	Quantity	
	Supply	Demand
$50	5 units	1 unit
$30	3 units	3 units
$10	1 unit	5 units

II. The Supply Curve

The supply curve slopes upward because as price increases (y-axis) suppliers are willing and able to provide more units. (see Figure 2.6) The supply curve, like the demand curve, shows the duality of exchange expressive of our neural architecture. From this perspective: Quantity provided = give = empathy; Price = take = ego. Again, the supply curve illustrates a reciprocal, give-and-take, empathy-ego social exchange relationship.

III. Equilibrium in the Market

The duality of exchange expressive of our neural architecture is most clearly seen in the graph of demand and supply curves combined to show their equilibrium point (see Figure 2.7). The supplier performs the empathetic structural or institutional role; the demander performs the egoistic structural or institutional role. In standard economics the demand and supply curves are related only at the point of equilibrium.

The formula derived from our neural architecture provides a significant insight:

$$BT = (Equilibrium\ Price) = \frac{Demand}{Supply}\ or\ \frac{Supply}{Demand} = \pm1 \quad \left(\begin{array}{l} \text{approx. equilibrium, unity, or} \\ \text{dynamic balance} \end{array} \right)$$

In economics price is customarily treated as an exogenous, independent variable. That is, demand and supply curves are related only at the equilibrium price. Price as an exogenous, independent variable draws them together but remains essentially unexplained. The formula from neural architecture demonstrates the continuing relationship between demand and supply and the source of motivation for change that brings demand and supply into equilibrium—behavioral tension that motivates buyers and sellers to change their behavior. Thus, all points on the demand and supply curves that do not match the equilibrium point are indicators of behavioral tension. This effectively unifies the dynamics of neural architecture with economics.

The Problems with Empathy as a Preference or Taste

Currently economics proceeding from the self-reference perspective treats self-interest as the only primary motive. Empathy is treated as a taste or preference. The problems with such treatment are:

1. Empathy becomes optional. You may have such a taste or preference or not. This is distorting because empathy is not optional but a fundamental motive of our neural architecture roughly equal with self-interest or ego.
2. It trivializes empathy. Empathy as a preference or taste is indistinguishable from a taste or preference for Fords or Mercedes or for tennis shoes or sandals.
3. It distortingly forces a rational self-interested perspective.
4. It misconstrues the real nature of the market.
5. It obscures the dynamic shaping effect of the ego/empathy interplay in all social exchange.
6. It is not consilient with evolutionary neuroscience—a more fundamental science.

APPENDIX 2: CALCULUS IN PRICE THEORY

As represented in standard texts (e.g., Landsburg 1992; Lindsay 1984) on price theory, demand and supply are functions that convert prices to quantities.

$$D(P) = \text{Quantity demanded at price } P$$

$$S(P) = \text{Quantity supplied at price } P$$

Derivatives are expressed as follows:

The fact that the demand curve slopes downward is expressed by the inequality

$$D'(P) < 0 \text{ or } \frac{dQd}{dP} < 0$$

The fact that the supply curve slopes upward is expressed by the inequality

$$S'(P) > 0 \text{ or } \frac{dQs}{dP} > 0$$

Equilibrium price is the price at which

$$D(P) = S(P)$$

Equilibrium quantity is the common value.

Again, in this case as well as in the illustrations of the demand, supply, and equilibrium curves, when treated in the standard manner demand and supply are related *only* at the point of equilibrium—the equilibrium price. Price, again, is an exogenous, independent variable that brings them together but remains essentially unexplained. Demand and supply are treated separately prior to the equilibrium point. The calculus model used in economics as reflected above does not represent the relationship of behavioral tension that *exists at all other points.* The formula from neural architecture does this:

$$BT = EP = \frac{Demand}{Supply} \text{ or } \frac{Supply}{Demand} = \pm 1 \left(\begin{array}{l} \text{unity, approx. equilibrium, or} \\ \text{dynamic balance} \end{array} \right)$$

This reinforces or confirms the previous insight that all other points on the demand and supply curves are indicators of behavioral tension. Behavioral tension in equilibrium, then, equals price in equilibrium, and price or behavioral tension not in equilibrium is what motivates demanders and suppliers to alter prices or respond to them. Such is the essence of any negotiating process in the market, no matter how formalized. It is seen clearly in domestic flea markets and in many similar institutions (e.g., bazaars) around the world. Price thus becomes an endogenous variable, that is, one that we can explain or account for (Cory 2004, 2002a, 2002b; 2001a, 2001b).

APPENDIX 3: DEMONSTRATION OF APPLICATION OF THE BASIC HOMEOSTATIC EQUATION TO ECONOMICS

In applying the organic equation, units of change or the first order derivative must be used, rather than the actual numerical value. Solving for $EP \pm 1$, we go above or below the EP by an increment of 1. *Demand* and *Supply* as used in this demonstration, of course, refer to quantities demanded and supplied. Thus

$$BT @ EP + 1 = \$40. \text{ At } P \ \$40 \ \frac{Supply}{Demand} = \frac{4}{2} \text{ numerically or } \frac{2}{1} \text{ units of magnitude}$$

$$BT @ EP - 1 = \$20. \text{ At } P \ \$20 \ \frac{Demand}{Supply} = \frac{4}{2} \text{ numerically or } \frac{2}{1} \text{ units of magnitude}$$

Since we are representing an organic homeostatic algorithm (in contrast to a point reduction force vector of Newtonian mechanics) in which the opposing forces (circuits) constantly tug and pull against each other in countering deviations from homeostatic equilibrium, a decrement in one is counterbalanced by an increment in the other. Therefore, there is no change in magnitude of divergence or behavioral tension at equal increments above or below EP (see Figure 2.8).

Figure 2.8 **Demonstration of Application of the Basic Homeostatic Equation to Economics**

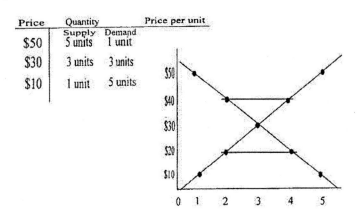

Price	Quantity	
	Supply	Demand
$50	5 units	1 unit
$30	3 units	3 units
$10	1 unit	5 units

The Constant Case

The previous example represents a special case chosen to demonstrate the application of the equation in easily understandable fashion. In this simple case both the unit of magnitude and numerical value have the same ratio. More complex applications require additional recourse to calculus and rely upon the units of magnitude of divergence. For example, in all cases where price and quantity increments or units are constant and the rate of change is constant, as represented by straight-line curves of demand and supply, the unit change between demand and supply will likewise remain constant. For each unit price change above or below *EP*, the unit change between demand and supply will be 2. Like two cars driving away from the same place in opposite directions at the same speed bound by an elastic counterforce, for each unit of time the distance increases by two units of distance.

This can be represented by the following elaboration of the basic equation to calculate divergence from balance and to derive values to be substituted into the original equation:

$$BT = \frac{d(D \leftarrow \rightarrow S) @ EP \pm X}{r(D \leftarrow \rightarrow S) @ EP} = ?$$

where *d* refers to the difference, differential, unit difference, or rate of change; $D \leftarrow \rightarrow S$ indicate that demand and supply are interconnected and the magnitude of their divergence is a fundamental measure of the homeostatic, self-correcting function of *BT* (behavioral tension) as one circuit acts to counter the other in deviations from homeostatic equilibrium. Thus, a value decrement in one is countered by a value increment in the other. No loss in magnitude of *BT* occurs. The unit magnitude of divergence between them is what is of interest as a measure of *BT*.

X represents the specific value of *EP* plus or minus; and
r denotes the ratio between demand and supply at *EP,* which by definition is unity or 1.

In simple terms, then, *BT* equals the unit differential between demand and supply or vice versa at values of *EP* ±1 or more, divided by the ratio between demand and supply or vice versa at *EP*, which is, by definition of equilibrium, unity or 1.

The constant rate of change can be expressed as a function. That is, $BT = f(x)$ @ $EP \pm$?; $f(x)$ is the unit differential between D and S, or S and D, or $f(x)$ is $d(D \leftarrow \rightarrow S)$, which represents an increment of 2 at every unit of price above or below EP as D and S increasingly diverge.

The following table results as divergence begins:

$$f(x) \text{ at } EP \pm 1 = 2$$

$$f(x) \text{ at } EP \pm 2 = 4$$

$$f(x) \text{ at } EP \pm 3 = 6$$

$$f(x) \text{ at } EP \pm 4 = 8$$

$$f(x) \text{ at } EP \pm 5 = 10$$

Substituting the values of the table into the elaborated equation:

$$BT @ EP = \frac{1}{1} = 1$$

$$BT @ EP \pm 1 = \frac{2}{1} = 2$$

$$BT @ EP \pm 2 = \frac{4}{1} = 4$$

$$BT @ EP \pm 3 = \frac{6}{1} = 6$$

$$BT @ EP \pm 4 = \frac{8}{1} = 8$$

$$BT @ EP \pm 5 = \frac{10}{1} = 10$$

Inserting values into the original basic equation approaching equilibrium:

$$BT = \frac{Demand}{Supply} \text{ or } \frac{Supply}{Demand} @ EP \pm 1$$

At equilibrium with no divergence:

$$BT @ EP = \frac{D}{S} \text{ or } \frac{S}{D} = \frac{1}{1} = 1$$

For positive values of EP above equilibrium, supply is the numerator.

To adequately represent the ratio, demand, then, is held constant at 1 as the units diverge between demand and supply

$$BT @ EP + 1 = \frac{S}{D} = \frac{2}{1} = 2$$

$$BT @ EP + 2 = \frac{S}{D} = \frac{4}{1} = 4$$

$$BT @ EP + 3 = \frac{S}{D} = \frac{6}{1} = 6$$

$$BT @ EP + 4 = \frac{S}{D} = \frac{8}{1} = 8$$

$$BT @ EP + 5 = \frac{S}{D} = \frac{10}{1} = 10$$

For negative values of *EP* below equilibrium, demand is the numerator.

To adequately represent the ratio, in the negative case, supply, then, is held constant at 1 as the units diverge between demand and supply.

$$BT @ EP - 1 = \frac{D}{S} = \frac{2}{1} = 2$$

$$BT @ EP - 2 = \frac{D}{S} = \frac{4}{1} = 4$$

$$BT @ EP - 3 = \frac{D}{S} = \frac{6}{1} = 6$$

$$BT @ EP - 4 = \frac{D}{S} = \frac{8}{1} = 8$$

$$BT @ EP - 5 = \frac{D}{S} = \frac{10}{1} = 10$$

The Nonconstant Case

When the conditions of constancy do not hold—rates of change are not constant—the determination of *BT* and the unit differences of demand and supply will require more complex mathematical operations, to include averaging processes. This, however, does not affect the validity of the organic equation's application to economics.

Interim Summary

Based upon the integration of the neural dynamic with demand and supply, we can conclude that all points on the demand and supply curves *not* at equilibrium represent points of behavioral tension. And it is this behavioral tension that *motivates* demanders and suppliers to change their behavior toward the equilibrium price.

Without such an organic motivating, self-correcting force the market could never come to equilibrium on its own except by accident or randomly.

At all prices, as long as the first order derivative, or rate of change is constant, or the slope is a straight line, and the units are of equal increments, the ratio between the unit differentials or demand and supply at $EP \pm 1$ will be 2:1 or a magnitude of divergence of 2. The ratio of divergence from EP will increase by an increment of 2 for each unit change of price. At $EP \pm 5$, for example, the unit differential between supply and demand, or vice versa, will be a magnitude of 10. This is the fundamental measure of behavioral tension.

When the rate of change is *not* constant, the determination of differential magnitudes will become more complex and will require an averaging process.

Price adds *significance* and acts as an amplifier of *BT*. As a general proposition, as price increments rise or fall, the magnitude of *BT* also rises or falls. That is: generally, buying a house or car carries more significance than a loaf of bread. Of course, this can vary subjectively with the situation of each party to the exchange.

Differences in Representing the Organic, Homeostatic Equation

Representing an organic, homeostatic algorithm, such as that of our social neural architecture, with a constant counterbalancing tug and pull of two forces or circuits requires some modification in mathematical representation. The magnitude of convergence or divergence from equilibrium is what is of interest, not the numerical value. Equal increments above or below the equilibrium point represent the *same* magnitude of behavioral tension because one force makes up for the other. That is why demand and supply may be inverted in the equation to represent the magnitude of divergence more accurately. This magnitude is the fundamental calculus of behavioral tension, amplified or diminished by *price* as an indicator of significance.

Extended Application of Organic Equation

Up to this point economics has lacked the conceptual apparatus to meaningfully and mathematically ask the question of sociobehavioral tension in the market. The very question of motivation for change toward equilibrium has been largely begged, brushed over simplistically, or left as an implicit assumption. The degree of sociobehavioral tension or stress in the market is, of course, of great importance to behavioral economics and socioeconomics as well as to sociology and political science in general. The organic social exchange equation provides a framework for addressing this important issue.

REFERENCES

Alexander, R. 1987. *The Biology of Moral Systems.* Hawthorne, NY: Aldine de Gruyter.
Appadurai, A., ed. 1986. *The Social Life of Things.* New York: Cambridge University Press.
Axelrod, R., and W. Hamilton. 1981. "The Evolution of Cooperation." *Science* 211: 1390.
Baal, J. van. 1975. *Reciprocity and the Position of Women.* Amsterdam: Van Gorcum, Assen.
Barfield, T., ed. 1997. *The Dictionary of Anthropology.* Oxford: Basil Blackwell.
Becker, J., S. Breedlove, and D. Crews, eds. 1992. *Behavioral Endocrinology.* Cambridge, MA: MIT Press.
Berridge, K. 2003. "Comparing the Emotional Brains of Humans and Other Animals." In R. Davidson, K. Scherer, and H. Goldsmith, eds., *Handbook of Affective Sciences,* 25–51. Oxford: Oxford University Press.
Boehm, C. 1999. *Hierarchy in the Forest: The Evolution of Egalitarian Behavior.* Cambridge, MA: Harvard University Press.

Bloom, F., C. Nelson, and A. Lazerson. 2001. *Brain, Mind, and Behavior,* 3rd ed. New York: Worth.

Bohannon, P. 1963. *Social Anthropology.* New York: Holt, Rinehart, and Winston.

Bowlby, J. 1969. *Attachment,* vol. 1. New York: Basic Books.

Bowles, S., and H. Gintis. 1998. *Recasting Egalitarianism.* London: Verso.

Cannon, W.B. 1932. *The Wisdom of the Body.* New York: Norton.

Cacioppo, J., G. Berntson, R. Adolphs, C. Carter, R. Davidson, M. McClintock, B. McEwen, M. Meaney, D. Schacter, E. Sternberg, S. Suomi, and S. Taylor, eds. 2002. *Foundations in Social Neuroscience.* Cambridge, MA: MIT Press.

Carter, C.S., and E. Keverne. 2002. "The Neurobiology of Social Affiliation and Pair Bonding." In D. Pfaff et al., eds., *Hormones, Brain, and Behavior,* 1: 299–337. New York: Academic Press.

Carter, C.S., I. Lederhendler, and B. Kirkpatrick, eds. 1997. *The Integrative Neurobiology of Affiliation.* New York: New York Academy of Sciences.

Cheal, D. 1988. *The Gift Economy.* London: Routledge.

Cory, G. 1999. *The Reciprocal Modular Brain in Economics and Politics: Shaping the Rational and Moral Basis of Organization, Exchange, and Choice.* New York: Plenum Press.

———. 2000a. "From MacLean's Triune Brain Concept to the Conflict Systems Neurobehavioral Model: The Subjective Basis of Moral and Spiritual Consciousness." *Zygon: Journal of Religion and Science* 35, 2: 385–414.

———. 2000b. *Toward Consilience: The Bioneurological Basis of Thought, Behavior, Language, and Experience.* New York: Kluwer Academic/Plenum.

———. 2001a. "Neural Network Theory and Neuroscience: Applications to Socio-Economic Theory." Paper presented at the 13th Annual Meeting on Socio-Economics, University of Amsterdam, June 28–July 1, 2001.

———. 2001b. "Transaction Costs, the Firm and Evolved Neural Architecture." Paper presented at the 76th annual conference of the Western Economic Association International, San Francisco, July 4–8.

———. 2002a. "Reappraising MacLean's Triune Brain Concept." In G. Cory and R. Gardner, eds., *The Evolutionary Neuroethology of Paul MacLean: Convergences and Frontiers,* 9–27. Westport, CT: Greenwood/Praeger.

———. 2002b. "Algorithms of Neural Architecture, Hamilton's Rule, and the Invisible Hand of Economics." In G. Cory and R. Gardner, eds., *The Evolutionary Neuroethology of Paul MacLean: Convergences and Frontiers,* 345–381. Westport, CT: Greenwood/Praeger.

———. 2003. "MacLean's Evolutionary Neuroscience and the CSN Model: Some Clinical and Social Policy Implications." In A. Somit and S. Peterson, eds., *Human Nature and Public Policy,* 161–80. New York: Palgrave Macmillan.

———. 2004. *The Consilient Brain: The Bioneurological Basis of Economics, Society, and Politics.* New York: Kluwer Academic/Plenum.

Cory, G., and R. Gardner, eds. 2002. *The Evolutionary Neuroethology of Paul MacLean: Convergences and Frontiers.* Westport, CT: Greenwood/Praeger.

Damasio, A. 1994. *Descartes' Error: Emotion, Reason, and the Human Brain.* New York: Grosset/Putnam.

———. 1999. *The Feeling of What Happens.* New York: Harcourt.

Davidson, R., K. Scherer, and H. Goldsmith, eds. 2003. *Handbook of Affective Sciences.* Oxford: Oxford University Press.

Davis, N. 2000. *The Gift in Sixteenth Century France.* Madison: University of Wisconsin Press.

de Waal, F. 1996. *Good Natured: The Origins of Right and Wrong in Humans and Other Animals.* Cambridge, MA: Harvard University Press.

Eckel, C., and P. Grossman, P. 1997. "Equity and Fairness in Economic Decisions: Evidence from Bargaining Experiments." In G. Antonides and W.F. van Raaij, eds., *Advances in Economic Psychology,* 281–301. New York: John Wiley.

Erdal, D., and A. Whiten. 1996. "Egalitarianism and Machiavellian Intelligence in Human Evolution." In P. Mellars and K. Gibson, eds., *Modelling the Early Human Mind,* 139–50. Cambridge: McDonald Institute.

Etzioni, A. 1986. "The Case for a Multiple-Utility Conception." *Economics and Philosophy* 2: 159–83.

———. 1988. *The Moral Dimension: Toward a New Economics.* New York: Macmillan.

Fehr, E., and S. Gachter. 2000. "Fairness and Retaliation: The Economics of Reciprocity." *Journal of Economic Perspectives* 14, 3: 159–81.

Fennell, L. 2002. "Unpacking the Gift." In M. Osteen, ed., *The Question of the Gift,* 85–101. London: Routledge.

Fuster, J. 1997. *The Prefrontal Cortex: Anatomy, Physiology, and Neuro-psychology of the Frontal Lobe,* 3rd ed. New York: Lippincott-Raven.

———. 1999. "Cognitive Functions of the Frontal Lobes." In B. Miller and J. Cummings, eds., *The Human Frontal Lobes,* 187–95. New York: Guilford Press.

Gérard-Varet, L.-A., S.-C. Kolm, and J. Ythier, eds. 2000. *The Economics of Reciprocity, Giving, and Altruism.* New York: St. Martin's Press.

Gintis, H. 2000. "Strong Reciprocity and Human Sociality." *Journal of Theoretical Biology* 206: 169–79.

Godelier, M. 1999. *The Enigma of the Gift.* New York: Polity Press.

Goldberg, E. 2001. *The Executive Brain: Frontal Lobes and the Civilized Mind.* New York: Oxford University Press.

Gouldner, A. 1960. "The Norm of Reciprocity; A Preliminary Statement." *American Sociological Review* 25: 161–78.

Gregory, C. 1982. *Gifts and Commodities.* New York: Academic Press.

Hamilton, W.D. 1964. "The Genetical Evolution of Social Behavior, I and II." *Journal of Theoretical Biology* 7: 1–16, 17–52.

Harlow, H. 1986. *From Learning to Love: The Selected Papers of H.F. Harlow,* ed. C. Harlow. New York: Praeger.

Harlow, H., and M. Harlow. 1965. "The Affectional Systems." In A.M. Schrier, H.F. Harlow, and F. Stollnitz, eds., *Behavior of Non-Human Primates,* 386–434. New York: Academic Press.

Herbert, J., and J. Schulkin. 2002. "Neurochemical Coding of Adaptive Responses in the Limbic System." In D. Pfaff, A. Arnold, S. Fahrbach, A. Etgen, and R. Rubin, eds., *Hormones, Brain and Behavior,* 659–89. New York: Academic Press.

Humphrey, N. 1976. "The Function of the Intellect." In P. Bateson and R. Hinde, eds., *Growing Points in Ethology,* 303–17. Cambridge: Cambridge University Press.

Hunt, R. 2002. "Economic Transfers and Exchanges: Concepts for Describing Allocations." In J. Ensminger, ed., *Theory in Economic Anthropology,* 105–18. New York: Altamira.

Ingrao, B., and G. Israel. 1990. *The Invisible Hand: Economic Equilibrium in the History of Science,* trans. I. McGilvray. Cambridge: Cambridge University Press.

Isaac, G. 1978. "The Food-sharing Behavior of Protohuman Hominids." *Scientific American* 238: 90–108.

Kandel, E., J. Schwartz, and T. Jessell. 2000. *Essentials of Neural Science and Behavior,* 4th ed. New York: McGraw-Hill.

Knauft, B. 1994. "Culture and Cooperation in Human Evolution." In L. Sponsel and T. Gregor, eds., *The Anthropology of Peace and Nonviolence,* 37–67. Boulder, CO: Lynne Rienner.

Landsburg, S.E. 1992. *Price Theory and Applications.* New York: Dryden.

Lapeyre, P., and P.-M. Lledo. 1994. "Homeostasis." In V. Ramachandran, ed., *The Encyclopedia of Human Behavior,* 517–28. San Diego: Academic Press.

Leven, S. 1994. "Semiotics, Meaning, and Discursive Neural Networks." In D. Levine and M. Aparicio, eds., *Neural Networks for Knowledge Representation and Inference,* 65–82. Hillsdale, NJ: Lawrence Erlbaum Associates.

Levine, D., and N. Jani. 2002. "A Neural Network Theory of the Triune Brain." In G. Cory and R. Gardner, eds., *The Evolutionary Neuroethology of Paul MacLean: Convergences and Frontiers,* 65–82. Westport, CT: Greenwood/Praeger.

Lindsay, C. 1984. *Applied Price Theory.* New York: Dryden Press.

Lutz, M. 1993. "The Utility of Multiple Utility: A Comment on Brennan. "*Economics and Philosophy* 9: 145–54.

Lynne, G. 1999. "Divided Self Models of the Socioeconomic Person: The Meta-Economics Approach." *Journal of Socio-Economics* 28: 267–88.

———. 2000. "A Metaeconomics Look at the Case for a Multiple-Utility Conception." Prepared for roundtable at the 12th annual meeting of the Society for the Advancement of Socio-Economics, London School of Economics, July 7–11, 2000.

MacLean, P. 1990. *The Triune Brain in Evolution: Role in Paleocerebral Functions.* New York: Plenum.

Mauss, M. 1925. *The Gift,* trans. W. Halls. New York: Norton, 1990.

Maynard Smith, J. 1982. "The Evolution of Social Behavior—A Classification of Models." In King's College Sociobiology Group, eds., *Current Problems in Sociobiology,* 28–44. Cambridge: Cambridge University Press.

———. 2002. "Equations of Life." In G. Farmelo, ed., *It Must Be Beautiful: Great Equations of Modern Science,* 193–211. London: Granta Books.

McEwen, B. 2003. "Protective and Damaging Effects of Stress Mediators." In J. Cappacio and G. Berntson, *Foundations in Social Neuroscience,* 1127–40. Cambridge, MA: MIT Press.

McEwen, B., and T. Seeman. 2003. "Stress and Affect: Applicability of the Concepts of Allostasis and Allostatic Load." In R. Davidson, K. Scherer, and H. Goldsmith, eds., *Handbook of Affective Sciences,* 1117–38. Oxford: Oxford University Press.

Miller, B., and J. Cummings, eds. 1999. *The Human Frontal Lobes.* New York: Guilford Press.

Nelson, R. 2000. *An Introduction to Behavioral Endocrinology,* 2nd ed. Sunderland, MA: Sinauer.

Numan, M., and T. Insel. 2003. *The Neurobiology of Parental Care.* New York: Springer-Verlag.

Osteen, M. 2002. "Gift or Commodity." In M. Osteen, ed., *The Question of the Gift,* 229–47. London: Routledge.

Panksepp, J. 1998. *Affective Neuroscience.* New York: Oxford University Press.

———. 2002. "Foreword: The MacLean Legacy and Some Modern Trends in Emotion Research." In G. Cory and R. Gardner, eds., *The Evolutionary Neuroethology of Paul MacLean: Convergences and Frontiers,* ix–xxvii. Westport, CT: Greenwood/Praeger.

Polanyi, K. 1957. *The Great Transformation.* Boston: Beacon Press.

Pribram, K. 1973. "The Primate Frontal Cortex—Executive of the Brain." In K. Pribram and A. Luria, eds., *Psychophysiology of the Frontal Lobes,* 293–314. New York: Academic Press.

———. 1994. "Brain and the Structure of Narrative." In D. Levine and M. Aparicio, eds., *Neural Networks for Knowledge Representation and Inference,* 375–415. Hillsdale, NJ: Lawrence Erlbaum Associates.

Sahlins, M. 1972. *Stone Age Economics.* Chicago: Aldine-Atherton.

Schulkin, J. 2002. "Hormonal Modulation of Central Motivational States." In D. Pfaff et al., eds., *Hormones, Brain, and Behavior,* 1: 633–57. New York: Academic Press.

Seymour-Smith, C. 1986. *Dictionary of Anthropology.* Boston: G.K. Hall.

Smith, Adam. 1776. *The Wealth of Nations,* ed. A. Skinner. London: Penguin Books, 1999.

Sterling, P., and J. Eyer. 1981. "Allostasis: A New Paradigm to Explain Arousal Pathology." In S. Fisher and J. Reason, eds., *Handbook of Life Stress, Cognition and Health,* 629–52. New York: Wiley.

Stuss, D., and R. Knight, eds. 2002. *Principles of Frontal Lobe Function.* Oxford: Oxford University Press.

Tickell, C. 1993. "The Human Species: A Suicidal Success." *Geographical Journal* 159: 219–26.

Trivers, R.L. 1971. "The Evolution of Reciprocal Altruism." *Quarterly Review of Biology* 46: 35–57.

———. 1981. "Sociobiology and Politics." In E. White, ed., *Sociobiology and Human Politics,* 1–44. Lexington, MA: D.C. Heath.

CHAPTER 3

INTUITION IN BEHAVIORAL ECONOMICS

ROGER FRANTZ

The purpose of this essay is to show the relevance of intuition in behavioral economics in the areas of knowing human nature, as a tool for decision making in general and with uncertainty in particular, and as a central component of heuristics. There is a large literature on intuition in business, the arts, and the sciences, which stands outside the scope of this chapter. A representative sample would include Agor 1984, 1989; Bastick 1982; Bergson 1946; Bishop 1967; Cobb-Stevens 1990; Comfort 1984; Davis-Floyd and Arvidson 1997; De Becker 1998; DePaul and Ramsey 1998; Dreyfus 1986; Falkenstein 1995; Fuller 1972; Hudson 1967; Levinas 1973; Noddings 1984; Parikh 1994; Piattelli-Palmarini 1994; Rehm 1990; Rowan 1986; Smyth 1978; Thomas 1999; Westcott 1968; Wilson 2000; and Yamaguchi 1969.

For purposes of discussion, intuitions may be said to be of four broad types. The first type is an insight gained by an expert in that field of inquiry after a period of study that appears to occur suddenly—the "eureka phenomenon." The eureka phenomenon is actually the last stage of an intellectual effort by an expert in the field. It involves thinking about a problem and then allowing it to slip into the subconscious while the conscious mind is focused on something else. After some time, be it seconds, hours, weeks, or months, the insight seems to occur suddenly, without a conscious, rational, step-by-step analytical process immediately preceding it. Sometimes intuition leads to a preanalytic "vision." The vision supplies the raw material for the subsequent analytical effort. How do we acquire our vision? Joseph Schumpeter says we acquire it "intuitively . . . This should be obvious" (Schumpeter 1954, 41).

The second type is expert judgments made on a daily or moment-by-moment basis. Intuitive diagnosis by a physician is an example of expert judgment on a daily basis. The play of chess grandmasters as discussed by Simon is an example of moment-by-moment expert judgment. Grandmasters report that chess is an intuitive activity in which they apply their professional judgment to the game at hand. Even under tournament conditions, grandmasters are said to usually decide on the best move in a matter of seconds, spending most of their time trying to verify their intuition (Simon 1982). Examples of the first two types of intuitions in the history of science are numerous and include the works of Jonas Salk (1983), Albert Einstein, August Kekulé, Henri Poincaré, and Pierre de Fermat (Hadamard 1945; Harmon and Feingold 1984; Medawar 1969; Miller 1996).

The third type is a (sudden) judgment that seems intuitive or obvious, regardless of the field and whether the person is an expert in that field. We may refer to this intuition as an axiom. These types of intuitions include a sense of danger, the intentions of others, the grammaticality of a sentence, the size of distant objects, the well-being of a friend at first glance. "We hold these truths to be self-evident" is another example of this form of intuition. John Locke was one of many seventeenth-century writers who spoke about intuition as an axiom. According to Locke, an intuition occurs when the mind perceives a relationship (or lack of one) between two ideas immediately, directly, and with a sense of certainty such that proof is not required. For example, he held it to be an intuition that $2 + 2 = 4$ or that a triangle has three sides. Economists are speaking about intuition as an axiom when they say, "It is intuitively obvious to the casual observer that . . ." Reasoning, on the other hand, is the mind perceiving a relationship (or lack of) between two ideas indirectly, that is, using intermediate ideas in order to do so. Reasoning is thus "indirect intuition." Locke believed that intuition is rapid reasoning (Locke 1894, 2:179) and is complementary to conscious reasoning. The fourth type includes "far-out" forms of ESP, but these will not be discussed here.

Intuition must be distinguished from *intuitionism*. Intuitionism is a philosophy that maintains that humans have an innate and infallible faculty for knowing right from wrong and, even more than that, for knowing the (self-evident) truth. I reject this in favor of intuition as a subconscious form of thinking, and allow for the fact that our intuitions may be incorrect. So U.S. Federal Reserve chair Alan Greenspan's intuition about future trends in interest rates should be taken more seriously than the intuitions on interest rates of a waiter at his favorite New York delicatessen. And the intuitions of Linus Pauling on organic chemistry should be taken much more seriously than my intuitions on that subject.

SOME DEFINITIONS AND EXAMPLES OF INTUITION

In *Intuition and Science* (1962) Mario Bunge states that intuition is a group of intellectual mechanisms that are difficult to define or analyze. The intellectual mechanisms Bunge cites include drawing inferences so quickly that reasoning seems to be absent, imagination, synthesizing disparate elements into a grand vision, and sound judgment. More common, everyday terms include "gut feeling," "educated hunch," "sixth sense," "picking up vibes," and the "eureka moment" or "aha experience." Peter Medawar, in *Induction and Intuition in Scientific Thought*, says that intuition means "perceiving logical implications instantly; seeing *at once* what follows from holding certain views," "the instant apprehension of analogy," and "thinking up or thinking out an experiment which provides a really searching test of a hypothesis . . . experimental flair or insight" (1969, 56–57). Daniel Kahneman and Amos Tversky, in their 1982 article "On the Study of Statistical Intuitions," define intuition as "an informal and unstructured mode of reasoning" (see also Hogarth 2001, 101). Herbert Simon says that intuition is analytical thinking "frozen into habit and into the capacity for rapid response through recognition of familiar kinds of situations" (Simon 1997, 139). The common element in all these descriptions is that intuition is a form of thinking, but not a conscious analytical (logical, sequential, step-by-step, and reasoned) process of thinking. Interestingly enough, relatively recent experiments by psychologists Amos Tversky and Daniel Kahneman and others have generally shown that heuristics or intuition often mimics the results of more analytically based judgments (Gigernzer, Czerlinski, and Martignon 2002). At the same time, the experiments show that the use of intuition can also lead to biases and errors in judgment.

Major economists in the history of economic thought, including Smith, Mill, Marshall, Keynes, Hayek, Schumpeter, and Simon, have written favorably about intuition, both explicitly and implicitly arguing that logic and intuition are complementary. In *The Making of an Economist* (1990) Klamer and Colander interview graduate students in economics from various departments throughout the United States, with the interesting insight that the students consider both mathematics and intuition to be important, and express an appreciation for the intuitive elements in the work of their professors.

Still, intuition has by and large taken a backseat in the mind of economists, who have stressed logical and analytical thinking both in doing economics and as the basis for the rational behavior of Homo economicus. This is the case even in research on behavioral economics, which has provided a theoretical alternative to orthodox neoclassical theory. This stress on logical and analytical thinking at the expense of other possibilities has led to complaints both within and from outside the profession about excessive theorizing and the use of mathematics. Perhaps as a result, it has become almost commonplace for an economist to state during a presentation, "The intuition behind the model [and/or result] is . . ." But in this context *intuition* means that an idea is easy to comprehend in plain and simple English.

THE BRAIN

Intuition may be said to be nothing less and nothing more than one way in which the human brain processes information. The human brain has two general ways to process information, intuitively and analytically, and hence has its own division of labor. Whereas Adam Smith's division of labor offers advantages to large firms, the brain's division of labor offers advantages for survival and progress. This division of labor is between the left and right hemispheres of the neocortex and has existed for at least a hundred thousand years (Ornstein 1997, 33). In 1960, Roger Sperry showed that each of the two hemispheres of the neocortex specialize, with the left hemisphere processing information in a logical, reasoned, step-by-step, sequential manner, and the right hemisphere processing information in a (complementary) nonverbal and intuitive way. In 1981 Sperry won the Nobel Prize in medicine for this work. Almost twenty-five hundred years before Sperry, Hippocrates, the founder of modern medicine, stated that the brain seemed to function in two distinct ways. He also believed that the brain, not the heart, was the source of pleasure and pain and judgment. Later research (Herrmann 1989) has shown that, like the neocortex, the left hemisphere of the limbic system also processes information logically. And, similar to the neocortex, the right hemisphere of the limbic system also processes information intuitively, accomplishing this in part by housing our ability for empathy (Taggart and Valenzi 1990), a term of importance to Adam Smith. Current psychological research on "spontaneous communication" is in fact referred to as "a conversation between limbic systems" (Buck and Ginsburg 1997, 23).

The fact is, the hemispheres interact in most of our decision-making and thought processes. It is also the case that both have their comparative advantage. Steve Sloman, in his article "Two Systems of Reasoning" (2002), says that we follow our "noses" but feel compelled to justify our behaviors with reasons. Sloman distinguishes what he calls the associative system of reasoning from the rule-based system. Forms of associative reasoning include intuition, imagination, and associative memory. Forms of rule-based reasoning are deliberation, formal analysis, and strategic memory. Sloman presents evidence from several studies showing that intuition and analysis often lead to similar judgments. In addition, he points out that analytically based judgments become more intuitive (commonsensical, or intuitively obvious to the casual observer) over time. Others have classified the dual processing system as experiential and rational (Epstein 1994), intuition and analysis (Hammond 1996), narrative and logical-scientific (Bruner 1986), and mystic and savant (Bergland 1985). Michael Polanyi refers to this duality as the intuitive and the formal (Polanyi 1974, 131). Frederick von Hayek discusses our "two types of mind" as two types of scientific thinking. One is "the perfect master of the subject" (Hayek 1978, 50), a person who has at his fingertips an apparently inexhaustible amount of facts and theories. The second consists of "puzzlers" or "muddlers" (ibid., 51). Puzzlers draw inspiration from "submerged" memories, process "wordless thought," "see" things they cannot put into words, and make discoveries that come as a "surprise" after a period of reflection (what has been referred to elsewhere as the "aha experience") (ibid., 53–54). Hayek describes himself as a puzzler. Although he never uses the word *intuition,* Hayek seems to be describing someone who makes extensive use of it.

The left hemisphere engages in step-by-step thinking. The right hemisphere makes an overall view of the environment, including others' intentions. The right hemisphere is also where our overall worldview or vision is generated and changed if need be to account for anomalies. The left hemisphere is more of a follower and indifferent to discrepancies. The left hemisphere assembles facts, while the right integrates the individual facts into an overall worldview. When we communicate, the left hemisphere processes the text, while the right hemisphere puts it within a context to create understanding. The right hemisphere holds various meanings of words, while the left hemisphere chooses the best. It is the right hemisphere that understands sarcasm, nonverbal communication, intentions, other people's state of mind, humor, proverbs, and metaphors.

If you tell an individual with damage to the right hemisphere that he needs to ground himself, he is likely to place his feet on the ground. If you tell such a person to clear her mind before choosing, she may put her head under a water tap. Ask people with this damage the meaning of the proverb "People who live in glass houses shouldn't throw stones" and they give you a literal meaning—if you throw something at a piece of glass, it may shatter. Because individuals with damage to the right hemisphere lack the ability to place things into context, they simply don't "get it."

The right hemisphere is essential in choosing rationally. Asked to explain a decision they've made, individuals with damage to their right hemisphere will rely exclusively on their left hemisphere. The left hemisphere will have an explanation that, regardless of how elaborate it may be, usually doesn't make much sense. The left hemisphere lacks the big picture, and so "the left hemisphere alone generally makes a mess of reality, not seeing the whole picture" (Ornstein 1997, 127). From the perspective of the brain's division of labor, arguing against intuition is arguing against the brain's normal functioning.

WHY WOULD BEHAVIORAL ECONOMICS BE INTERESTED IN INTUITION?

We Know Human Nature Intuitively

Let's start with Homo economicus. We assume that individuals are rational, calculating costs and benefits. Why do we calculate costs and benefits? We are *motivated* to do so. The concept of rationality is itself a "psychological interpretation" of observed behavior, hence the natural connection between economics and psychology. How do we know that humans are motivated, consciously or otherwise, to be rational? J.N. Keynes, in his book *The Scope and Method of Economics* (1955), says that the basic principles of economics, including the principle of rational behavior, are a priori. That is, we know them both before and independent of observing human behavior. The "facts of human nature," according to Keynes, are not directly observed; rather they were the result of "an *introspective* survey" of human motives (Lewin 1996, 1298). Economic laws, including the law of rational behavior, are thus derived from facts about human nature that are intuitive or obvious.

Max Weber argued that because we are human beings we understand the motives behind human behavior through our own introspections: "This verstehen, or intuitive understanding of human motivation, is what distinguishes the human sciences from the physical sciences" (cited in Lewin 1996, 1298). Verstehen is nothing more than Adam Smith's concept of sympathy. On the other hand, the majority opinion on this subject within the economics profession is that economics as a "science" has little need for verstehen or intuition, or concepts such as consciousness or understanding. Understanding, in fact, is a "meaningless pursuit," as science should limit itself to "observable empirical regularities" (ibid., 1305) and hence to describing these regularities. Slutsky, Hicks, Allen, and Samuelson were among the group preaching economics as a science approach. Slutsky focused on observable utility as expressed in price and quantity. Hicks and Allen continued this by replacing marginal utility with the marginal rate of substitution. Samuelson continued with revealed preferences (Schumpeter, 1954).

Behavioral economics assumes that cognitive activity—information processing—precedes behavior, serving as an intermediary between changes in the environment and changes in behavior. Human behavior is thus not mechanical, at least in the sense that it is variable. Understanding mechanical behavior requires an owner's manual, a calculator, a computer program, or perhaps only a well-defined production or cost function. Understanding nonmechanical behavior—unpredictable, untaught, capricious, variable—makes verstehen, or intuition, more important. In a changing environment, an individual must seek patterns or similarities with known environments and/or know another person's mind to predict how that person may behave. The fact is, human behavior comes in both mechanical and nonmechanical varieties. Robin Hogarth in his book *Educating Intuition* says that "humans have a variety of different information-processing systems that vary from the innate [intuitive] to the fully conscious, [and] that most of these systems operate continuously" (2001, 179).

In addition, none of the components of nonmechanical behavior may be motivated by utility maximization or psychological hedonism. William James rejected this one-motive approach to all human behavior, referring to it as unscientific and "narrow teleological superstition" (cited in Lewin 1996, 1299). Economists such as Keynes and Marshall understood that much is left out of economists' theory of human behavior, but that this is inescapable in our attempt to be scientific. Harvey Leibenstein's X-efficiency theory was based in part on the hypothesis that human behavior varies in the degree to which it exhibits rationality; he called this "selective rationality" (Leibenstein 1966). Herbert Simon referred to it as "bounded rationality" (Simon 1982).

The study of intuition may also yield significant payoffs because it is an ingredient in altruism. In *The Heart of Altruism,* Kristin Monroe states, "Early discussions of what contemporary scholars refer to as empathy and altruism utilize the term sympathy, Adam Smith being but one notable example" (1996, 243 n. 47). Furthermore, she reports that the word *empathy* comes from the German *Einfühlung,* meaning "the process of intuiting one's way into an object or event to see it from the inside" (ibid.). Collard (1978) and Ickes (1997) have also discussed altruism and its relationship with empathy, sympathy, and intuition.

Intuition Is a Tool for Decision Making Under Uncertainty

A classic statement about uncertainty is that of Frank Knight in *Risk, Uncertainty, and Profit* (1964). What is not well known is that in Knight's work, intuition plays a central part in dealing with uncertainty. According to Knight, perfect competition or an "imaginary society" is a "heroic abstraction." First, this imaginary society contains rational people. Rational people have "practical omniscience," and hence there is a lack of ignorance. Rational people know what they want; their motives are known consciously and are stable and consistent. Their responses are deliberate, and they know the consequences of their actions. Second, there is perfect mobility and no costs of adjustment. Third, there is costless intercommunication among people. Fourth, people make decisions independent of all others. Fifth, all activity is free and voluntary. These are the necessary conditions of perfect competition. Under perfect competition there is "general fore-knowledge of progressive changes" or knowledge of the "law of change." Under these conditions profits will move toward zero.

In real life, perfect intercommunication and hence perfect knowledge do not exist. In real life there is uncertainty, inertia, indifference, and habit, and hence the possibility of profit. Knight reviews literature associating profits with many factors, including a reward for risking capital, bargaining power stemming mainly from "superior knowledge and foresight" about the direction of change in an ever-changing environment, "frictions" created by uncertainty hindering the competitive process, and dynamic changes that lower costs. However, it is not change as such that creates profit, but ignorance of change, unpredictable change, or error.

In order to distinguish change from ignorance, or predictable change from change that is not predictable, Knight distinguishes risk from uncertainty. Risk refers to situations in which there is measurable randomness, while uncertainty refers to unknowable randomness—ignorance. Uncertainty about human behavior stems from Knight's belief that, unlike objects of the natural world, we are not unconscious mechanisms restricted to mechanistic behavior. We have consciousness and free will, feelings and emotions, and react to the same stimuli in various ways. We are motivated by love and hate, exhibit capriciousness, and are subject to persuasion. We are rational, deliberative, and purposive, but also emotional. Humans do not remain the same through time. We have memory and we adjust to experience. Unlike atoms, no two people are exactly the same, no two people react exactly the same to the same experience, and no two people experience the same "objective" environment exactly the same.

In Part 3 of *Risk, Uncertainty, and Profit* Knight examines the assumption of "practical omniscience." Knowledge begins with consciousness, or awareness. Consciousness is "forward-looking"—it anticipates the future, it sees things coming *before* they materialize. Knight says that the biological purpose of the nervous system is for adapting to the environment to better one's chances of survival, and this requires seeing ahead. Yet while Knight says that he is interested in the relationship between consciousness and knowledge and behavior, he also makes it clear that he is *not* interested in "the ultimate nature of reality or any other philosophical position."

The process of human inference is, in short, a nonmechanical process, a "fundamental mystery," and subject to error. Because of uncertainty we are forced to draw inferences about the meaning of a twinkle in another's eye, lines around the mouth, tone of voice. Following Adam Smith (see Frantz 2000), Knight says that it is consciousness that allows us to make inferences through "'sympathetic introspection' into what is going on in the 'mind' of the other person(s)." This ability is the "mysterious capacity of interpretation." Knight's theory of knowledge is not a theory of "*exact* knowledge" offered by logic. Knight is not sure that the world is understandable to any great extent, but if it can be understood, this is done through logical processes. Even the "ordinary decisions of life are made on the basis of 'estimates' of a crude and superficial character" and based on a process that is "very obscure." Hence logicians and psychologists have paid little attention to them. The obscurity, the subconscious nature, the apparent absence of logic, and the "mental rambling" nature of the process do not imply irrationality. This mental rambling is called judgment, common sense, and intuition. Knight considers intuition to be based on memory, association, and experience, a type of "unconscious induction," and made more valuable when combined with analysis. In these ways he is similar to other economists, notably Mill (see Frantz 2002) and Simon (see Frantz 2003). Intuitions are subject to error, but at the same time the ability to make correct judgments is the prime determinant of an individual's value and success in business.

Ronald Heiner in his 1983 paper "The Origin of Predictable Behavior" presents an interesting hypothesis: that uncertainty (caused by cognitive limits, the inability to make correct inferences from past experiences, and incorrect expectations) leads individuals to be cautious and follow rule-based behavior. Following rules, behavior becomes both predictable and more geared toward *satisficing* than maximizing. On the other hand, the lack of uncertainty leads individuals to "throw caution to the wind." This leads behavior to be less predictable and more geared toward maximizing than satisficing. Hence, maximizing behavior, made possible by the lack of uncertainty, leads to unpredictable behavior.

Standard theory attempts to explain choices based on the individual's competence (c) and the difficulty (d) of the decision, and assumes that $(c - d) \sim 0$. However, Heiner's point is that the $(c - d)$ gap creates uncertainty that leads to rule-based behaviors. The $(c - d)$ gap is generated by two broad classes of variables: environmental and perceptual. The former determine the degree of complexity faced, while the latter determine competence for dealing with complexity. Uncertainty increases as the former increases and/or the latter decreases. Uncertainty also increases the chance of making the wrong decision or the right decision at the wrong time. Choosing right or wrong is determined by "whether some process—conscious or not—will cause (or prevent) an 'alertness' or 'sensitivity' to information that might prompt selection of an action" (Heiner 1983, 565). Being alert to information is a developed skill, and greater uncertainty and a desire for making choices require more of the being-alert-to-information skill. Heiner makes use of the word *intuition* with phrases such as "intuitively measure" (ibid., 565), "intuitively interpret" (ibid., 566), "this intuitively means" (ibid., 567), and "as intuitively suggested" (ibid., 568). He also says that it is intuitive that without uncertainty, maximum flexibility of behavior—the ability to "loosen up"—yields the largest benefit (ibid., 563).

Intuition/Emotions as Well as Reason Is an Instrument in Decision Making

Yaniv Hanoch says, "Indeed people use reason to respond to . . . motivations, but they also use emotions. What sets the stage is our emotional mechanism, while one function of reason is to explore the possible paths to get there. That is, while ends cannot be determined logically by reason, once ends are determined, it is the role of reason to take us there" (Hanoch 2002, 3). Emotions interact with reason (rational thinking) in at least two important ways: by limiting the number of options considered and by limiting the aspects of the environment considered. This is contrasted with subjective expected utility (SEU) theory, which assumes that individuals make a thorough examination of all options and aspects of the environment until a probability about the future can be constructed. Being boundedly rational means having the ability to discriminate between different pieces or sets of information, focus on a subset of available information, produce alternative scenarios, gather facts about the environment, and draw inferences from these facts (ibid., 6). Emotions serve these functions. Emotions have been designed by evolution to assist us in being boundedly rational (ibid., 7).

In his book *Descartes' Error: Emotion, Reason, and the Human Brain* neurologist Antonio Damasio shows that intuition, emotions, and feelings play a positive role in rational decision making. A very important reason is that "the strategies of human reason probably did not develop, in either evolution or any single individual, without the guiding force of the mechanisms of biological regulation, of which emotion and feeling are notable expressions" (Damasio 1994, xii). Not all human decisions involve choosing and reasoning in the normal sense used by economists (conscious evaluation of the costs and benefits of various options). First, there are automatic bodily processes by which the body moves to a state of equilibrium. For example, a drop in blood sugar triggers physical changes in the body, leading to a state of hunger. We are neither conscious of nor have any control over these physical changes. Second, we engage in survival strategies that are automatic or instinctive. For example, when we see an oncoming car we auto-matically move away from it. We know that an oncoming car is dangerous and that the appropri-ate response or choice is to move. While we are conscious of what is going on, the movement away from the car is automatic. Third, there are many choices we make in our life—concerning career, family, friendships, recreation, vacations, saving, voting—that require us to reason and choose in the usual sense of the terms. These choices involve short- and long-run costs and ben-efits, all of which are shrouded by complexity and uncertainty. Descartes referred to the first two as being part of our "animal spirit," while the third is characteristic of our "human spirit" (ibid., 165–68). The third category of decisions are those traditionally believed to be optimized through logic or "rationality" and in the absence of emotions.

The difficulty with rational decision making is that calculating costs and benefits so as to maximize subjective expected utility will take too much time and is subject to too much error. Two reasons are offered: the human attention span is too short, and the capacity of our working memory is too small. Second, the strategy of eliminating emotion from decision making "has far more to do with the way patients with prefrontal damage go about deciding than with how normals usually operate" (ibid., 172). In other words, the economic theory of rational decision making is best illustrated by brain-damaged individuals. The real-world decision-making process of indi-viduals with normal brain functioning involves intuition. According to Damasio, the human mind at the beginning of a decision-making process is not a "blank slate" but contains numerous im-ages gleaned from experience. Depending upon the circumstances surrounding the decision, a subset of the available images will be automatically activated. Even before reasoning takes place, when the mind considers an option with a bad outcome, the individual experiences an unpleasant gut feeling in the body. If the option contains a positive outcome, the gut feeling is pleasant. Because the feeling is in the body, Damasio uses the term *somatic* (*soma* being the Greek word for "body"). The gut feeling in the body "marks" an image, hence the term *somatic marker*. Damasio says that somatic markers are an example of "*feelings generated from . . . emotions. Those emotions and feelings have been connected, by learning, to predicted future outcomes of certain scenarios*" (ibid., 174). Feelings and emotions are not identical. An emotion is a physical phenomenon with bodily correlates that are often automatic and prompted within the subcon-scious. For example, fear affects the heart rate and facial and/or other muscles. Emotions are often automatic and prompted by the subconscious.

The somatic marker creates a feeling in the body that "forces attention on the negative out-come to which a given action may lead, and functions as an automated *alarm signal* which says: Beware of danger ahead if you choose the option which leads to this outcome. . . . The automated signal protects you against future losses, without further ado, and then allows you *to choose from among fewer alternatives*" (ibid., 173). Somatic markers, having screened alternatives, allow any subsequent cost-benefit calculations to be more accurate, and allow the decision-making process to be more efficient. There are two important implications. First, somatic markers make use of both attention and working memory, but it is our *values* that drive the process. After all, pleasant and unpleasant gut feelings imply values or preferences. Second, there is an optimal level of emotion because emotions can be either beneficial or costly in the process of decision making. Third, emotion and logic (or intuition and analysis) are complements rather than substitutes. While Pascal said, "The heart has reasons that reason does not know at all," Damasio says, "*The organism has some reasons that reason must utilize*" (ibid., 200). We are not always conscious of somatic markers. Somatic markers also act subconsciously, affecting those parts of the brain that control our appetites. Thus, for no apparent reason we would feel drawn to or away from some particular behavior. He says, "This covert mechanism would be the source of what we call intuition, the mysterious mechanism by which we arrive at the solution of a problem *without* reasoning toward it" (ibid., 188).

Damasio reports the results of gambling experiments illustrating his somatic marker hypothesis. The experiment involves players turning over cards from four decks of cards. Some cards in decks A and B paid the player $100 (in play money), but others required payments in excess of $1,000. In decks C and D, some cards paid $50, while other cards required payments of less than $100 on average. Players without frontal lobe brain damage began by sampling cards from all four decks. Seeing high rewards from decks A and B, they showed a preference for these decks. As the game continued and they were forced to pay large sums by cards in decks A and B, they switched to decks C and D. Players with frontal lobe brain damage began by sampling cards from all four decks, then showed a preference for the high-reward decks, A and B. However, having lost large sums of money, they returned to their preference for decks A and B, lost all their money, and were forced to borrow more. Despite being attentive, risk-averse, and intelligent and possessing a preference to win, frontal-lobe-damaged individuals act "irrationally." Damasio's explanation is that people with frontal lobe damage lack somatic markers, thereby lacking an association between a stimulus and an appropriate somatic response. They act, therefore, as if they have an inappropriate preference for the present at the expense of the future. They have in Damasio's terms, a "myopia for the future" (ibid., 218). It is as if they do not retain what they learned through education or experience; they do not have a theory of their own mind.

In another article on the same topic the author, Gretchen Vogel, states, "Intuition may deserve more respect than it gets these days. Although it's often dismissed along with emotion as obscuring clear, rational thought, a new study suggests that it plays a critical role in humans' ability to make smart decisions" (Vogel 1997, 1269). Four neuroscientists from the University of Iowa College of Medicine studied patients with damage to their ventromedial prefrontal cortex. People with damage to this part of the brain score high on IQ tests and memory tests as often as non-brain-damaged persons. However, they tend to be more indecisive and make poor choices in real-life situations. Brain-damaged patients and a control group were given four decks of cards, two "good" decks and two "bad" decks. Each person was given $2,000, and each card listed an amount of money they won or lost. In the long run, choosing from the bad deck led to net losses, while the good deck led to net gains. The brain-damaged patients showed no emotion (measured by no physiological changes that accompany nervousness) as their net losses continued to increase and did not tend to switch to the good deck. Members of the control group showed signs of nervousness after a series of losses and switched to the good decks. They also began switching to the good decks even before they could articulate to the researchers that the good decks were a better long-term strategy. In other words, members of the control group had a hunch about which deck to choose from even before their conscious mind could formulate a reason. An explanation for the result is that the ventromedial prefrontal cortex is the part of the brain that stores memories of past rewards and punishments and creates an unconscious response to current rewards and punishments, which we call a hunch or an intuition. The brain-damaged patients lack this intuitive ability and hence make poor decisions.

Intuition as a Component of Heuristics

Intuition can be an expression or form of a heuristic because both usually bypass all conscious thinking processes. Why use a heuristic or intuition? Because in a world that contains much risk and uncertainty, objective measures of probability are not always available. Human cognition processes may be divided into two broad groups: intuition and reason. Humans use both because human cognition is a dual process. Adjectives used to describe the intuitive process include *automatic, effortless, rapid, parallel, affective, nonverbal,* and *experiential.* Adjectives used to describe reason include *analytical, deliberative, verbal, rational,* and *rule-based* (Slovic 2001, 4). Kahneman and Tversky (1982) refer to intuition as a "natural assessment," one with some advantages over reason. First, the intuitive process produces results faster than the analytical system. Second, under conditions of uncertainty, when objective measures of probability are not available, intuition becomes the best method for subjectively evaluating the probability of events. Third, because intuition is the product of a subconscious process, the conscious mind remains free to undertake other tasks and hence is more flexible. Fourth, in a complex environment, speed and flexibility are advantageous. In some sense, therefore, our intuitive system is more efficient than reason.

Evaluating intuitively based judgments implies a standard of comparison. One standard often used is how well intuitive judgments compare to those made by analytical methods such as the rules of probability. For example, the *extension rule* is a basic rule of probability and states that if $A > B$, then $P(A) = P(B)$. The extension rule can also be stated as the *conjunction rule,* $P(A \ \& \ B) = (B)$. For example, are there more seven-letter words ending in *-ing* (A) or seven-letter words whose sixth letter is *n* (B)? Since *-ing > -n-*, the correct answer is B. Yet surveys show that people's intuitions choose the former. Comparing actual intuitions to rules of probability creates a bias against intuitive judgments. In fact, rules of probability are statements of logic. Since nothing can be more logical than logic, intuitions can never be superior to the rules of probability. In any contest between intuition and logic, intuition's best outcome is a tie. The Tversky and Kahneman research agenda on biases and errors in judgment from using heuristics (intuition) shows that intuition is at best only as good as logic. And the emphasis is on the shortcomings of intuition.

The fact is that "people do not normally analyze daily events into exhaustive lists of possibilities or evaluate compound probabilities by aggregating elementary ones. Instead, they commonly use a number of heuristics" (Tversky and Kahneman 2002, 20). Hence, intuitive judgments are not made by listing possibilities and evaluating compound probabilities. In Kahneman and Tversky's prospect theory, intuitive judgments are shown to take many forms, including creating similarities or making associations between two or more events or people, perceptions of causality, and thinking about salient characteristics or archetypes of events or people. In each case, people are attempting to turn a difficult question into an easier one. In the example of *-ing* and *-n-* words, people can more easily remember the former, and thus they tend to believe that there are more of the former. During a hiring seminar a tenured faculty member is really trying to answer a difficult question: whether a candidate will remain intellectually active and is good enough to receive tenure. A simpler question is asked: how good is the candidate's presentation? In attempting to answer the difficult question of whether a particular person is a librarian or a salesperson, people answer an easier question: are the known characteristics of that person more similar to those of a librarian or those of a salesperson? People make intuitive judgments by creating mental images of their environment in which relationships and rules are obvious, even if less detailed. This means that intuition is the result of mental model building.

The mental model and the form of the intuition are dependent upon the question being answered. For example, in answering the question of what percentage of men who have suffered a heart attack are over age sixty, we ask ourselves to picture the typical heart attack victim (the exemplar or archetype) from memory of stories we have seen and/or read. This is known as the availability heuristic. If we are asked to choose an occupation for someone we do not know based only on a sketch of their personality, we look for similarities between the personality sketch and the representative personality of a person in a particular occupation. This is called the representative heuristic. If we are asked to make an assessment of something we know nothing about, such as the number of countries in the United Nations, we draw upon whatever data we are given. This is known as anchoring. Intuitions are a natural assessment or judgment mechanism of the human brain, and may be the best choice when no other means of judgment is available. No one expects models to be accurate and full of detail. In fact, the model-as-map analogy states that the power of a map or a model is that it does not have too much detail. In turning difficult questions into simpler ones and in building a generalized mental map of the environment, people would seem to be rational in using their intuition. Unfortunately, our mental images of the world and the real world are not always consistent with each other. And just as models don't always predict accurately, neither does intuition.

At the same time, when people attempt to think logically they often fail. It seems intuitive, therefore, that the true comparison should be between intuitive judgments and actual judgments when people are trying to be logical. If it's correct that "people are not accustomed to thinking hard" (Kahneman and Frederick 2002, 58), then perhaps one reason we use intuition is because we are lazy. At the very least, intuition may be a second-best way of making decisions. In their preface to *Heuristics and Biases,* Gilovich, Griffin, and Kahneman state, "The core idea of the heuristics and biases program is that judgment under uncertainty is often based on a number of simplifying heuristics rather than more formal and extensive algorithmic processing. These heuristics typically yield accurate judgments but can give rise to systematic error" (2002, xv). In other words, intuition can be accurate, often complementing analysis, but is subject to systematic error. At the same time, the series of experiments by psychologists Amos Tversky and Daniel Kahneman have been acknowledged by economists as demonstrating that human decision making deviates significantly from the predictions of economic theory. For example, in *Rethinking Intuition* (1998), Tamara Horowitz, a philosopher, argues that the results of the Tversky and Kahneman experiments demonstrates that people's intuitions produce decisions that are at odds with economic theory.

At the same time, what seems intuitively obvious to the casual observer today often turns out to be just plain wrong tomorrow. Once upon a time it was common sense that the earth was at the center of the universe. Once upon a time it was common sense that nature could not contain a vacuum. Once upon a time it was common sense that heavier objects fall faster than lighter objects. Galileo's thought experiments in his "mind's eye"—that is, his intuition—led to the new commonsense idea among physicists that all objects fall through a vacuum at the same speed. Once upon a time Newtonian physics was common sense among physicists. It was replaced by the common sense of Einstein's theory of special relativity. From Aristotle and the Greeks to Galileo, Newton, and Einstein is a movement from one commonsense idea to another (Miller 1996). In one respect, it is common sense that common sense changes as we evolve and gain understanding of the world. While it may seem counterintuitive that what we consider to be common sense changes, it actually is intuitively obvious that common sense changes!

Kahneman and Tversky emphasized the representative, availability, an anchoring heuristics. Paul Slovic introduced economists to the "affect heuristic" (Slovic 2001). While economists generally assume that decisions are the result only of cognition, Slovic argues that affect proceeds and influences cognition: affect "lubricates reason" (ibid., 3–4). Hence, the existence of "dual-process" theories of how we think, know, process information, and make decisions. These two processes are "intuitive, automatic, natural, non-verbal, narrative, and experiential," on one hand,

and "analytical, deliberative, verbal, and rational," on the other (ibid., 4). The intuitive system is affective in nature and is faster than the analytical system. The intuitive system is, therefore, also believed to be a more efficient way to interact with an uncertain, complex environment. The intuitive/affective system also relies on feeling states of which we may not be aware. In comparison, the analytical system relies on cognitions such as probabilities. There is a large body of research supporting the importance of affect in decision making. For example, we may have a positive feeling about strawberry Jell-O, but a negative feeling when hearing the name Bowl Championship Series.

While economists have focused on *anticipated* feelings such as regret and disappointment, psychologists have focused on *immediate* feelings and "visceral" or affective states occurring at the time of decisions (Lowenstein 2000; Slovic 2001). Visceral factors, or passions, include anger, fear, hunger, thirst, sexual desire, emotions, pain, and (drug) cravings. Unlike preferences, which are assumed to be stable and consistent in the short run, visceral states change quickly and are affected by the external environment and the condition of the body. Visceral states have long been assumed to be destructive of behavior, but they are essential to humans. They affect survival and reproduction and hence quality of life. They are essential in decision making, yet we tend to underestimate them, preferring instead to see our decisions as rationally formulated. Visceral factors are powerful enough to create an internal conflict in us between what we want to do and what we otherwise believe is the rational course of action. One example is that a visceral state such as fear can neutralize a rational evaluation of uncertainty (risk). Thus, utility maximization in the presence of visceral states, especially alternating "hot" and "cold" visceral states, is difficult. At high levels of visceral intensity we feel "out of control" and may be led to behave in ways contrary to what we believe to be our self-interest.

Affect affects our perception of risk. For example, the perception of risk from various hazards is positively correlated with feelings of danger about that hazard. Despite the fact that the benefits and costs of various hazards need not have any particular correlation, in laboratory studies people's perception of benefit and cost are negatively correlated with each other. That is, if people feel that the benefits of nuclear power or pesticide use in farming are high, then they tend to judge the risks as being low. And where the risks are said to be low, the benefits are perceived to be high (Slovic et al. 2002, 410–11). Studies of toxicologists asked about the risks of exposure to very low levels of various chemicals (1/100th of the exposure level warranting regulators' concern) show negative correlations between affect—the danger posed by the chemical—and perceived risk. Studies also show that people overpay for insurance when the object is beloved, regardless of its condition. Affective responses are part of almost every response or perception we have (Zajonc 1980). That is, we see a lovely sky, not a sky; a pretty face, not a face; an attractive house, not a house. Affect, therefore, affects preferences. In addition, the affective may be more important than is usually suggested when looking at the world through a cognitive or rational framework. Zajonc writes, "We sometimes delude ourselves that we proceed in a rational manner and weight all the pros and cons of the various alternatives. But this is probably seldom the actual case. Quite often, 'I decided in favor of X' is no more than 'I liked X'" (ibid., 155). The affective is considered part of our experiential system of thinking or information processing, as opposed to our analytical system. The experiential also includes intuition.

"Fast and frugal" heuristics are decision-making strategies that rely on cues. For example, are there more homeless people per million population in New York or Chicago? To answer this without researching the answer, you look for cues, such as the existence of rent control and public housing; unemployment, vacancy, and poverty rates; and average temperature. In the "minimalist" heuristic, you randomly select a cue; if you select rent control, since cities with rent control tend to have more homeless people, and since New York has rent control and Chicago does not, then you would choose New York as probably having more homeless people. In the "take the best" heuristic, you pick the most important cue. The "choosing by default" heuristic means choosing the first option you think about. This is a classic way of making decisions intuitively. Choosing by default is known as an "automated choice heuristic" (Frederick 2002).

In a review of fast and frugal heuristics, Gigerenzer, Czerlinski, and Martignon (2002) find that their performance is comparable with multiple regression and Bayesian networks. In 1992, Spencer Johnson, coauthor of *The One Minute Manager* (Blanchard and Johnson 1982), published a book, *"Yes" or "No": The Guide to Better Decision Making* (Johnson 1992), in which he described three questions you ask yourself when solving a problem: "Am I meeting the real need?" "Am I informing myself of options?" and "Am I thinking it through?" If your first thought about question 1 is yes, then you move on to question 2. If the answer to question 1 is no, then you begin analyzing what the real need is. When you get through with question 3, then you have made a better choice than you otherwise would.

Errors in judgment due to the use of intuition or heuristics are not limited to, say, undergraduates. Individuals of all levels of education and skill make such errors. Under- and overoptimism occur in predictions made by doctors, weather forecasters, lawyers, sports commentators, professional gamblers, economists, and stockbrokers (Koehler, Brenner, and Griffin 2002). Werner DeBondt and Richard Thaler studied the one- and two-year earnings-per-share forecasts by a group of professional forecasters. The result of their statistical analysis is that forecasters overreact and that earnings-per-share forecasts are unrealistically optimistic. The same overreaction has been reported in the literature for exchange rate and macroeconomic forecasts. DeBondt and Thaler conclude that the analysts surveyed are "decidedly human. The same pattern of overreaction found in the predictions of naïve undergraduates is replicated in the predictions of stock market professionals. Forecasted changes are simply too extreme to be considered rational. . . . When practitioners describe market crashes as panics, produced by investor overreaction, perhaps they are right" (2002, 685).

Herbert Simon's studies of MBA students and experienced business executives asked to analyze a situation show that the two groups come to similar conclusions. However, the experienced executives came to their conclusion in much less time, "with the usual appearance of intuition" (Simon 1997, 136). The work of the MBA students, on the other hand, "was done slowly, with much conscious and explicit analysis" (ibid.). The conclusion Simon reaches is that experience allows people to make decisions intuitively, that is, to make judgments "without careful analysis and calculation" (ibid.). In a study of decision making among physicists, Simon and Simon studied the protocols of two people solving a physics problem by recording them verbalizing what they were thinking while solving the problem. One of the persons was a novice at this type of problem solving, the other an expert. The expert solved the problem in less time, did not follow the reason-only steps, required fewer steps to solve the problem, spent less time per step, did not write down as many relevant facts or equations to solve, and expressed more confidence. In essence, the skilled person took a series of appropriate shortcuts. These shortcuts imply that the expert used what Simon calls physical intuition—intuition used by physicists. That is, the expert read the problem, created a mental representation, and created a set of equations based on that mental representation to solve the problem. While the expert's approach is more "physical" or "primitive" (Simon and Simon 1989, 224), the novice's approach is more algebraic. The conclusion that physical intuition "accounts for the superior ability of physicists to solve physics problem should occasion no surprise. Physicists and teachers of physics have been saying that for years" (Simon and Simon 1989, 230).

CONCLUSION

Taken separately, the importance of both behavioral economics and intuition should be intuitively obvious to the casual observer. Behavioral economics developed as a response to anomalies, empirical tests at odds with standard economic models of behavior. Behavioral economics has advanced our understanding of human behavior and increased the predictive power of our models. Intuition is a normal brain function, and by operating at a subconscious level, intuition leaves our conscious mind free for other uses. In other words, intuition is an efficient form of allocating our scarce mental resources, and major economists have discussed intuition as a tool in economics (Frantz 2005). In this essay I have tried to argue that intuition is part of several topics of interest to behavioral economists: understanding human nature, decision making under uncertainty, the role of emotion in decision making, and intuition as a heuristic. The role of intuition in decision making is also highlighted in the new field of neuroeconomics (Glimcher 2004). Behavioral economics and intuition as a tool of economic decision making will continue to gain importance within our profession.

REFERENCES

Agor, Weston H. 1984. *Intuitive Management: Integrating Left and Right Brain Management Skills.* Englewood Cliffs, NJ: Prentice-Hall.

———. 1989. *Intuition in Organizations: Leading and Managing Productively.* Newbury Park, CA: Sage Publications.

Bastick, Tony. 1982. *Intuition: How We Think and Act.* New York: Wiley.

Bergland, Richard. 1985. *The Fabric of Mind.* New York: Viking Penguin.

Bergson, Henri. 1946. *The Creative Mind.* New York: Philosophical Library.

Bishop, Paul. 1967. *Synchronicity and Intellectual Intuition in Kant, Swedenborg, and Jung.* Lewiston, NY: E. Mellen Press.

Blanchard, Ken, and Spencer Johnson. 1982. *The One Minute Manager.* New York: Morrow.

Bruner, J. 1986. *Actual Minds, Possible Worlds.* Cambridge, MA: Harvard University Press.

Buck, Ross, and Benson Ginsberg. 1997. "Communicative Genes and the Evolution of Empathy." In William Ickes, ed., *Empathic Accuracy,* 17–43. New York: Guilford Press.

Bunge, Mario. 1962. *Intuition and Science.* Englewood Cliffs, NJ: Prentice-Hall.

Cobb-Stevens, Richard. 1990. *Husserl and Analytic Philosophy.* Boston: Kluwer Academic Publishers.

Collard, D. 1978. *Altruism and Economy.* Oxford: Martin Roberston.

Comfort, Alex. 1984. *Reality and Empathy: Physics, Mind, and Science in the 21st Century.* Albany: State University of New York Press.

Damasio, Antonio. 1994. *Descartes' Error: Emotion, Reason, and the Human Brain.* New York: Avon Books.

Davis-Floyd, Robbie, and P. Sven Arvidson, eds. 1997. *Intuition: The Inside Story: Interdisciplinary Perspectives.* New York: Routledge.

De Becker, Gavin. 1998. *The Gift of Fear: Survival Signals That Protect Us from Violence.* New York: Dell Publishing.

DeBondt, Werner, and Richard Thaler. 2002. "Do Analysts Overreact?" In Thomas Gilovich, Dale Griffin, and Daniel Kahneman, eds., *Heuristics and Biases: The Psychology of Intuitive Judgment,* 678–85. Cambridge: Cambridge University Press.

DePaul, Michael, and William Ramsey, eds. 1998. *Rethinking Intuition: The Psychology of Intuition and Its Role in Philosophical Inquiry.* Lanham, MD: Rowman and Littlefield.

Dreyfus, Hubert L. 1986. *Mind Over Machine: The Power of Human Intuition and Expertise in the Era of the Computer.* New York: Free Press.

Earl, Peter. 1990. "Economics and Psychology." *Economic Journal* 100: 718–55.

Epstein, S. 1994. "Integration of the Cognitive and the Psychodynamic Unconscious." *American Psychologist* 49: 709–24.

Falkenstein, Lorne. 1995. *Kant's Intuitionism: A Commentary on the Transcendental Aesthetic.* Toronto: University of Toronto Press.

Frantz, Roger. 2000. "Intuitive Elements in Adam Smith." *Journal of Socio-Economics* 29, 1: 1–19.

————. 2002. "John Stuart Mill as an Anti-Intuitionist Social Reformer." *Journal of Socio-Economics* 31, 2: 125–36.

————. 2003. "Herbert Simon: Artificial Intelligence as a Framework for Understanding Intuition." *Journal of Economic Psychology* 32: 265–77.

————. 2005. *Two Minds: Intuition and Analysis in the History of Economic Thought.* London: Springer.

Frederick, Shane. 2002. "Automated Choice Heuristics." In Thomas Gilovich, Dale Griffin, and Daniel Kahneman, eds., *Heuristics and Biases: The Psychology of Intuitive Judgment,* 548–58. Cambridge: Cambridge University Press.

Fuller, R. Buckminster. 1972. *Intuition.* Garden City, NY: Doubleday.

Gilovich, Thomas, Dale Griffin, and Daniel Kahneman, eds. 2002. *Heuristics and Biases: The Psychology of Intuitive Judgment.* Cambridge: Cambridge University Press.

Gigerenzer, Gerd, Jean Czerlinski, and Laura Martignon. 2002. "How Good Are Fast and Frugal Heuristics." In Thomas Gilovich, Dale Griffin, and Daniel Kahneman, eds., *Heuristics and Biases: The Psychology of Intuitive Judgment,* 559–81. Cambridge: Cambridge University Press.

Glimcher, Paul. 2004. *Decisions, Uncertainty, and the Brain.* Cambridge, MA: MIT Press.

Hadamard, Jacques. 1945. *Essay on the Psychology of Invention in the Mathematical Field.* Princeton, NJ: Princeton University Press.

Hammond, K.R. 1996. *Human Judgment and Social Policy: Irreducible Uncertainty, Inevitable Error, Unavoidable Injustice.* New York: Oxford University Press.

Hanoch, Yaniv. 2002. "Neither an Angel Nor an Ant: Emotion as an Aid to Bounded Rationality." *Journal of Economic Psychology* 23: 1–25.

Harmon, Willis, and Howard Feingold. 1984. *Higher Creativity.* Los Angeles: Jeremy P. Tarcher.

Hayek, Frederick. 1978. *New Studies in Philosophy, Politics, Economics, and the History of Ideas.* Chicago: University of Chicago Press.

Heiner, Romald. 1983. "The Origin of Predictable Behavior." *American Economic Review* 73: 560–95.

Herrmann, Ned. 1989. *The Creative Brain.* Lake Lure, NC: Brain Books.

Hogarth, Robin. 2001. *Educating Intuition.* Chicago: University of Chicago Press.

Horowitz, Tamara. 1998. "Philosophical Intuitions and Psychological Theory." In Michael DePaul and William Ramsey, eds., *Rethinking Intuition: The Psychology of Intuition and Its Role in Philosophical Inquiry,* 143–60. New York: Rowman and Littlefield.

Hudson, W.D. 1967. *Ethical Intuitionism.* New York: St. Martin's Press.

Ickes, William. 1997. "Introduction." In William Ickes, ed., *Empathic Accuracy,* 1–16. New York: Guilford Press.

Johnson, Spencer. 1992. *"Yes" or "No": The Guide to Better Decisions.* New York: Harper Collins.

Kahneman, Daniel, and Shane Frederick. 2002. "Representativeness Revisited: Attribute Substitution in Intuitive Judgment." In Thomas Gilovich, D. Griffin, and Daniel Kahneman, eds., *Heuristics and Biases: The Psychology of Intuitive Judgment,* 49–81. Cambridge: Cambridge University Press.

Kahneman, Daniel, and Amos Tversky. 1982. "On the Study of Statistical Intuitions." *Cognition* 11: 123–41.

Keynes, J.N. 1955. *Scope and Method of Economics.* New York: Kelley and Millman.

Klamer, Arjo, and David Colander. 1990. *The Making of an Economist.* Boulder: Westview Press.

Knight, Frank. 1964. *Risk, Uncertainty, and Profit.* New York: A.M. Kelley.

Koehler, Derek, Lyle Brenner, and Dale Griffin. 2002. "The Calibration of Expert Judgment: Heuristics and Biases Beyond the Laboratory" In Thomas Gilovich, Dale Griffin, and Daniel Kahneman, eds., *Heuristics and Biases: The Psychology of Intuitive Judgment,* 686–715. Cambridge: Cambridge University Press.

Leibenstein, Harvey. 1966. "Allocative vs 'X-Efficiency.'" *American Economic Review* 56: 392–415.

Levinas, Emmanuel. 1973. *The Theory of Intuition in Husserl's Phenomenology.* Evanston: Northwestern University Press.

Lewin, Shira. 1996. "Economics and Psychology: Lessons for Our Own Day from the Early Twentieth Century." *Journal of Economic Literature* 34: 1293–323.

Locke, John. 1894. *An Essay Concerning Human Understanding.* Oxford: Clarendon Press.

Lowenstein, George. 2000. "Emotions in Economic Theory and Economic Behavior." *American Economic Review Papers and Proceedings* 90: 426–33.

Medawar, Peter. 1969. *Induction and Intuition in Scientific Thought.* Philadelphia: American Philosophical Society.

Miller, Arthur. 1996. *Insights of Genius: Imagery and Creativity in Science and Art.* New York: Springer Verlag.

Monroe, Kristin. 1996. *The Heart of Altruism.* Princeton, NJ: Princeton University Press.

Noddings, Nel. 1984. *Awakening the Inner Eye: Intuition in Education.* New York: Shore.

Ornstein, Robert. 1997. *The Right Mind: Making Sense of the Hemispheres.* New York: Harcourt Brace.

Parikh, Jagdish. 1994. *Intuition: The New Frontier of Management.* Cambridge, MA: Blackwell.

Piattelli-Palmarini, Massimo. 1994. *Inevitable Illusions.* New York: John Wiley.

Polanyi, Michael. 1974. *Personal Knowledge.* Chicago: University of Chicago Press.

Rehm, Jurgen. 1990. *Intuitive Predictions and Professional Forecasts: Cognitive Processes and Social Consequences.* New York: Pergamon Press.

Rowan, Roy. 1986. *The Intuitive Manager.* Boston: Little, Brown.

Salk, Jonas. 1983. *Anatomy of Reality: Merging of Intuition and Reason.* New York: Columbia University Press.

Schumpter, Joseph. 1954. *History of Economic Analysis.* New York: Oxford.

Simon, Herbert. 1982. *Models of Bounded Rationality: Behavioral Economics and Business Organization.* Cambridge, MA: MIT Press.

———. 1997. *Administrative Behavior.* New York: Free Press.

Simon, Herbert, and Dorothy Simon. 1989. "Individual Differences in Solving Physics Problems." In Herbert Simon, ed., *Models of Thought,* 2:215–31. New Haven, CT: Yale University Press.

Sloman, Steven. 2002. "Two Systems of Reasoning." In Thomas Gilovich, Dale Griffin, and Daniel Kahneman, eds., *Heuristics and Biases: The Psychology of Intuitive Judgment,* 379–96. Cambridge: Cambridge University Press.

Slovic, Paul. 2001. "Rational Actors or Rational Fools: Implications of the Affect Heuristic for Behavioral Economics." Paper prepared for the Nobel Symposium on Behavioral and Experimental Economics, Stockholm, December 4–6.

Slovic, Paul, M. Finucane, E. Peters, and D. MacGregor. 2002. "The Affect Heuristic." In Thomas Gilovich, Dale Griffin, and Daniel Kahneman, eds., *Heuristics and Biases: The Psychology of Intuitive Judgment,* 397–420. Cambridge: Cambridge University Press.

Smyth, Richard. 1978. *Forms of Intuition: An Historical Introduction to the Transcendental Aesthetic.* Boston: M. Nijhoff.

Taggart, William, and Enzo Valenzi. 1990. "Assessing Rational and Intuitive Styles: A Human Information Processing Metaphor." *Journal of Management Studies* 27: 149–72.

Thomas, James P. 1999. *Intuition and Reality: A Study of the Attributes of Substance in the Absolute Idealism of Spinoza.* Brookfield, VT: Ashgate.

Tversky, Amos, and Daniel Kahneman. 2002. "Extensional Versus Intuitive Reasoning . . ." In Thomas Gilovich, Dale Griffin, and Daniel Kahneman, eds., *Heuristics and Biases: The Psychology of Intuitive Judgment,* 19–48. Cambridge: Cambridge University Press.

Vogel, Gretchen. 1997. "Scientists Probe Feelings Behind Decision Making." *Science* 275: 1269.

Westcott, Malcolm. 1968. *Toward a Contemporary Psychology of Intuition: A Historical, Theoretical, and Empirical Inquiry.* New York: Holt, Rinehart, and Winston.

Wilson, James, Q. 2000. *Moral Intuitions.* New Brunswick, NJ: Transaction.

Yamaguchi, Minoru. 1969. *The Intuition of Zen and Bergson: Comparative Intellectual Approach to Zen, Reason of Divergencies Between East and West.* Tokyo: Enderle.

Zajonc, R.B. 1980. "Feeling and Thinking: Preferences Need No Inferences." *American Psychologist* 35: 151–75.

CHAPTER 4

INTROSPECTIVE ECONOMICS

Broadening Psychology's Reach

DAVID GEORGE

> Just as the planets lack inner lives but are fully explainable in terms of
> their "behaviors," so, from the point of view of economics as a natural science,
> individuals could lack inner lives and yet be fully explained by their "behaviors."
> *John B. Davis, The Theory of the Individual in Economics: Identity and Value*

> Consciousness is not just an important feature of reality. There is a
> sense in which it is *the* most important feature of reality because all other
> things have value, importance, merit, or worth only in relation to consciousness.
> *John R. Searle, Mind, Language and Society: Philosophy in the Real World*

The term "armchair theorists" well captures the image of early-nineteenth-century economists operating in the classical tradition of Adam Smith and David Ricardo and later-nineteenth-century economists operating in the marginalist tradition of Stanley Jevons and Alfred Marshall. By this interpretation of the development of economics, behavioral regularities were simple assumptions arrived at through casual reflection rather than through systematic observations in the field or in the laboratory. Assertions that people experienced diminishing marginal utility, that they were largely self-interested, and that they would avoid any activity whose cost exceeded its benefit were just commonsense generalizations arrived at based on simple introspection. It was not necessary to delve deeply into one's own experiences to find support for such psychological descriptions. One merely had to skim the surface of lived experience. An early proponent of an enriched psychological component for economics, George Katona, detected the simplistic state of psychological economics with his observation that "'economics with mechanistic psychology' might . . . be a more accurate phrase than 'economics without psychology'" (1951, 7).

"Behavioral economics"—the label that has been attached to economics having a connection to psychology—does not carry with it any deep commitment to the behaviorism that prevailed during the years when a very orthodox version of positivism was the rule. A look at the contributions to this growing field reveals numerous references to "motives," "perceptions," and other mainly mentalist constructs that someone raised on the behaviorism once prevailing in psychology would have had trouble allowing into the discussion just a few decades ago. Nonetheless, the focus on behaviors—whether as the main ultimate object of interest or as a necessary source of evidence—remains strong.

My intent here is to call into question the assumption that behaviors must occupy a privileged position in psychological economics relative to "mere thought." The first half of this essay offers a summary of the various meanings and significance attached to the terms *behavioral* and *behaviorism*. In addition, it considers the peculiar role that the cognitive revolution has played in simultaneously unseating and reinforcing different features of the behavioral tradition. The essay's second half summarizes some personal research experiences that have served to strengthen my belief that behavior can be grossly overrated both as an end and as the sole criterion for validation.

COMPETING RATIONALES FOR A FOCUS ON BEHAVIOR

There are three distinct justifications for placing behavior in a privileged position in relation to mere "consciousness." What follows spells out the particulars of each of these justifications as well as the connections between them.

Behaviorism as an Expression of Logical Positivism

There is first the well-known and self-described school of behaviorism that is usually associated with the works of B.F. Skinner but in fact predates his most well-known writings by several decades.[1] John Watson's classic 1913 paper represents something of a turning point in psychology with the claim, in the words of economist Shira Lewin, that "psychology must be reformulated so that it simply studies the laws of behavior, without discussing such vague concepts as 'consciousness'" (Lewin 1996, 1305). And as Lewin further points out, the spread of logical positivism was the source of the changed focus within the social sciences:

> According to logical positivism, science does not seek to help us to *understand* the nature of reality. That is the domain of metaphysics (a pejorative term). *Understanding* is, according to this view, a meaningless pursuit. The world simply consists of observable empirical regularities, and science should therefore restrict itself to *describing* these, in the form of objective, falsifiable propositions. (1996, 1395)

Just as the later writings of Skinner and others who followed in Watson's tradition came to be treated as the definitive word on behaviorism, so too did logical positivism undergo an extended incubation between the declarations of its early proponents within the economics profession and its eventual spread throughout the profession. We usually associate events of the 1930s with the rise of hard-core positivism in economics, as the writings of Lionel Robbins (1935) and Paul Samuelson (1938) substituted preferences that are "revealed" via behaviors for any mentalist talk of "utility." In fact, however, Vilfredo Pareto set the stage for these later pronouncements decades before, arguing that preferences ought to replace utility and that "the very discussion of motives was unnecessary and metaphysical" (Lewin 1996, 1309). The paradoxical nature of equating "behavioral economics" with "psychological economics" becomes apparent with Lewin's claim that "a behaviorist movement arose in economics, as theorists attempted to free economics of all psychological elements" (Lewin 1996, 1294).

To summarize this first (and most "official") meaning of *behavioral,* to be a strong positivist was to attach meaning only to the observable. Not only was behavioral evidence a necessary criterion for the validation of hypotheses, but in addition behaviors were treated as all that was really out there. Concepts without testable hypotheses, besides being nonobservable, were accorded no epistemic status. While this strong sense of *behavioral* has been in retreat for some time, there remain two other biases that favor observed behaviors over mental states and that remain largely unchallenged.[2]

Behavior as a Credibility Check

Neoclassical economics has been criticized for honoring in the breach the sort of hard-core behaviorism that has just been described. As already noted, the methodological revolution of the 1930s, associated most with the names of Robbins and Samuelson, sought to purge economics of all mentalist concepts. That it failed, and that those who believe themselves to be operating in that tradition still speak of "utility," does not lessen the fact that the rebellion has never been officially acknowledged by most practicing theorists.

The second type of behaviorism does not deny the existence of the nonobservable but is as procedurally insistent on behaviors as was its hard-core counterpart. As George Katona, often cited as an early pioneer in the field of psychological economics, has stated:

> Psychology is an empirical discipline. There is one, and only one, way to establish whether a psychological statement is correct, namely, by means of empirical evidence. . . . Statements not susceptible of empirical validation have no place in psychology. (1951, 29)

Yet just two pages later, a certain softening is detectable:

> Psychological principles and hypotheses must make use of intervening variables. Examples of such variables are the concepts of organization, habit, motive, attitude. Their manifestations—as, for example, verbal behavior, emotional behavior, differences and similarities in behavior—are susceptible to observation. (1951, 31)

While neither of these statements requires that only behavior be "real," the latter more than the former reveals acknowledgment of the very existence of nonbehaviors. Yet such nonbehaviors are assigned a second-class status, being treated as intervening variables that serve to link stimulus with the still privileged "response."[3]

An analogy with the notion of accountability in education may help to draw attention to a problem that this second rationale for granting priority to behavior represents. Requiring evidence directly observable to third parties is particularly necessary in social settings where trust is in short supply. Clearly, if every utterance was as believable as any replicable behavior, reliance on such behavioral evidence would lessen. In the spirit of accountability, writing requirements in higher education (and at lower levels as well) have likely increased over the same historical period that reading requirements have likely lessened. Reading is indirectly measurable, of course, but certainly not as concretely manifested as is writing. In a society that is built less on trust than on accountability, it is not surprising that the written word increases while the read word diminishes.[4]

Behavior as the Bottom Line

A still different sort of insistence on behaviors is strictly pragmatic in origin and in rationale. While distinct from the first behaviorism discussed (epistemic requirements) or the second (considerations of accountability), it is no less powerful and may indeed be more significant at the level of everyday activity. By this sort of rationale for granting behavior greater status than perceptions, motives, and affects, behavior is the proverbial bottom line—that which matters, relative to phenomena not manifested in action. Attributing higher status to action than to "mere thought" is a cultural attribute particularly associated with the United States, but the extent of the appeal of such thinking is complex and more than can be pursued further here.

This reason for respecting actions vis-à-vis thoughts, motivations, and attitudes may be justifiable to some extent if the subject of interest is on the supply side of the economy. The proverbial bottom line in such a setting is indeed a "product"—whether a good or service—that leaves the producer and is consumed by a purchaser. Since behaviors are a necessary condition of all production, to focus attention on behavior is understandable. The "intervening variables" are just that—namely, variables that are of interest to the extent that they help to determine the process between the act of combining resources and coming up with a product or service. Thought of differently, any single self-interested agent cares about actions emanating from other agents, since only actions have direct impacts on third parties. The butcher, baker, and brewer provide us with meat, bread, and beer, while their internal experienced state is out of our zone of awareness.

If, on the other hand, consumption is the locus of interest, the privileging of behavior is without much foundation. As often happens in economics, turning things on their heads is more than a mere metaphor, as roles truly do reverse, as does relative importance. How the consumer feels and what the consumer phenomenally experiences are the end that the consumption of a product or service contributes to determining. The product and the behavior to acquire the product are clearly the means, and the internal psychological state is the end. From a strongly narcissistic perspective, it may be true that only one affective state matters (one's own) and that it is ultimately only behaviors but not the internal states of others that affect one. Thus for an extreme pragmatist, behaviors do indeed "matter" more than internal states, as the latter are reduced to nothing more than one of many determinants of the former. But for economics understood in its broader role as a prescriptive pursuit concerned with overall human well-being, the experienced state of people is ultimately of the highest relative importance.

To sum up, of the three different rationales for according higher relative importance to behavior than to mental states, the first would argue that we are what we do and nothing else, the second would argue that we can discern what we are only through what we do, and the third would argue that what we do is inherently interesting and important relative to mental states.

COGNITIVE SCIENCE TO THE RESCUE?

On first consideration, it might seem as though there has been a very real counterforce at work going back at least fifty years that has served to calm down any possible excesses of a behavioral bias. Kenneth Boulding sought to draw attention to what he chose to call the "image"—the actual lived experience.

> Between the incoming and outgoing messages lies the great intervening variable of the image. The outgoing messages are the result of the image, not the result of the incoming messages. The incoming messages only modify the outgoing messages as they succeed in modifying the image. (1956, 29)

The pragmatic focus on behavior (captured as the "outgoing message") is present, but the reliance on the very word *image* reveals Boulding's desire to bring subjective states into the realm of the significant.

It is difficult to trace the extent to which the spread of interest in cognition among psychologists in the years since the above passage was written was helped along by the rise of the computer. What is clear, however, at least to two commentators on the subject—one an economist and one a psychologist—is that the dominance of the computer as the metaphor for cognition has come at a great price.

According to Jerome Bruner, while the intent of the cognitive revolution was to return the mind to the social sciences, "very early on . . . emphasis began shifting from 'meaning' to 'information,' from the *construction* of meaning to the *processing* of information" (1990, 4). While defending "folk psychology" and pointing out that "an obvious premise of our folk psychology . . . is that people have beliefs and desires" (1990, 39), Bruner does not see cognitive science as at all receptive to such constructs.

> Cognitive science in its new mood, despite all its hospitality toward goal-directed behavior, is still chary of the concept of agency. For "agency" implies the conduct of action under the sway of intentional states. So action based on belief, desire, and moral commitment is now regarded as something to be eschewed by right-minded cognitive scientists. (1990, 9)

As economist Philip Mirowski sees it, "the cognitive turn in economics has proved a debacle for the deliberative Self" (2002, 452). And in his historical sleuthing Mirowski manages to link certain constructs that are sometimes associated with behavioral economics to precisely this cognitive turn. Commenting on the rise of "multiple personality syndrome," Mirowski notes that "nothing more graphically calls into question the very existence of an integral Self than the spectacle of multiple warring personalities frantically fighting for control over a single human body" (2002, 447).[5]

Not all would agree with this characterization of the cognitive sciences. Roger McCain, for example, constructs a model built around the filtering capacity that plays such an important role in computer programming (1992, chaps. 5–8). Rather than anthropomorphizing the computer while attributing to it characteristics that are humanlike because computers operate "as if" they were people, projects such as this one engage in a certain sort of reverse anthropomorphism. People behave "as if" they are computers with filtering processes and the like.

In fairness to McCain, he is not at all eager to follow the clarion call of cognitive scientists such as Stephen Stich, who believes, according to Bruner, that "such commonsense terms as desire, intention, and belief . . . should . . . simply be ignored and not divert us from the grander task of establishing a psychology without intentional states" (Bruner 1990, 38), and whose book titled *From Folk Psychology to Cognitive Science* (Stich 1983) is described as being of such a nature that "no book published even in the heyday of early behaviorism could match [it for] antimentalist zeal" (Bruner 1990, 9). Quite to the contrary, McCain argues persuasively that the current prestige of economics relative to the other social sciences is in no small part due to the normative force of its claims (1992, chap. 11). Friedman's much cited methodological proclamations to the contrary notwithstanding (1953), many of those economists who are managing to import economic models into other realms of analysis hold appeal precisely because of their continual reference to free choice and their continual interest in welfare gains that require just such "folk psychological" concepts as desire and intent.[6]

A PERSONAL TALE: THE PERILS OF POSITIVISM

Spatial Orientation

In this section I will be offering my own experiences in moving out of psychology and into economics as an example of the damages that vestiges of the extreme behaviorism associated with logical positivism can cause. I majored in psychology as an undergraduate, enjoyed it immensely, and fully intended to go on for a doctorate. From the time of my graduation in 1969 up until late 1972, psychology was still very much on my mind. But after completing a paper on directional orientation—a truly intense personal interest—and managing to present the paper at a professional conference, I reluctantly came to the realization that the positivist grip was too strong ever to support the approach to psychological questions that I wanted to follow.

The insights that guided my intense interest in directional orientation were arrived at not from the observation of the behaviors of others but from examining what was going on inside my own mind—that is, from introspection or, perhaps more accurately, retrospection.[7] While the self-observation that I found most worth developing was far from economics, I beg the reader's indulgence in allowing me to briefly describe some of the particulars, for there are connections between this introspective experience and my later work in economics that bear comparison.

My initial insight was that whenever I re-created in my mind a particular place with which I was familiar, a particular directional orientation was a component of the experience. While often my orientations were consistent across space—what appeared to be "northward" while in my bedroom also appeared to be northward when in the kitchen just across the hallway—inconsistency was not at all uncommon. How I came to develop the ability to be aware of my orientation I cannot say, but aware of it I certainly could be. And with that came the ability to reverse orientations, to mentally take in my surroundings with a different orientation than normally prevailed. Such shifts were in the tradition of Gestalt perceptual psychology. My directional orientation could undergo a clean shift just as surely as the well-known Necker cube could undergo a perceptual shift. After spending some time playing around with this personal insight I began to be aware of systematic disorientations (or more correctly, inconsistent orientations). To take just two examples, I came to recognize that I located the screen of all movie theaters to the east of where I sat, and came to recognize that I mentally located my grandmother's house as though it were on the west side of a north-south street (the side on which my own, similarly constructed house was located) when it was actually on the east side.

Now, I might have been led to put these introspective and retrospective observations entirely to rest were it not for the fact that there was one observation that happened to have behavioral implications and was thus deemed legitimate to pursue in my undergraduate perceptual psychology class. I noted that the major streets near where I was raised in Detroit that did not conform to the prevailing grid system were still viewed by me as if they did. Grand River Avenue ran approximately northwest to southeast but "looked" to me to be exactly east-west when I was embedded on it. I was able to carry out an experiment that provided support for the hypothesis that others had perceptual habits similar to what I was aware of experiencing. By having subjects simply point to a distant known landmark, I was able to provide evidence that they perceived two successive 45-degree turns that just happened to be close to campus in Ann Arbor as two 90-degree turns and became disorientated by 90 degrees as a consequence of this.

After graduation I carried out an extension of this experiment while working with a professor of environmental design in Los Angeles (George 1973). But having already begun to experience serious doubts about the behavioral requirements that mainstream psychology was requiring, I sought in this second experiment to provide some indication of the severe limitations in seeking behavioral manifestations of perceptual constructs. I provided evidence in my experiment that behaviors could be very problematic guides to perceptions. While most subjects revealed that they were fully aware that the streets along which we walked were at odd angles to each other (i.e., they could draw maps that accurately reflected their relative positions), they also revealed through their pointing behavior that while actually embedded on each street they saw them as virtually parallel. In short, I carried out an experiment to demonstrate the potentially confounding nature of derived behaviors in seeking to explore a perceptual phenomenon.

At least as importantly from a personal standpoint, I came to the reluctant conclusion that going along with the behaviorist approach implicitly committed me to privileging behaviors over mere perceptions. A psychologist at the same university as the environmental design professor seemed concerned *only* with how inconsistent orientations would affect behaviors. I gradually realized that the most important implications of my introspection had nothing to do with behavior and would be nearly impossible to measure through behaviors. Returning to my earlier personal example, always orienting movie screens to the east simply had no behavioral ramifications. I never got lost in a theater and when I emerged I had no trouble imposing a different orientation on my surroundings. Existentially, I believed, the fact of my disorientation was significant. Behaviorally, it fell short by being untestable and, as significantly, by holding no implications for behavior.

Unpreferred Preferences

At around the same time that I realized academic psychology was too behavioral to accommodate my interests, my introspective energies moved in a different direction. My fairly regular patronization of fast-food places while simultaneously criticizing what I was buying simply made no sense. How could I both want a McDonald's burger and claim that I didn't want it? To say that I consisted of two selves that fought with each other wouldn't resolve the puzzle; having a reasonably developed identity, I felt that there was only one of me "there" and that this one self definitely wanted that burger (which is why I knowingly paid money to have it). What I came to realize was that I simultaneously had a preference of a very different sort, namely, a preference to be experiencing a different preference. This idea of a metapreference made sense of the conundrum of conflicted choice. While I would prefer to have a preference for say, a healthier sandwich, I was sort of stuck with the preference for the McDonald's burger, which I proceeded to act upon. It was just this ability to reflect on one's preferences to act that Harry Frankfurt (1971) isolated as the characteristic separating humans from nonhuman species. While animals have consistent preferences and meet the conditions that fulfill economists' rationality conditions, animals do not have the ability to reflect on and evaluate these preferences, while people do.

This is not the place to trace the path I have followed in the years since on the subject of metapreferences. Suffice it to point out that I did not originally turn to the work of psychologists interested in economic questions as a potential audience for my work. I was still wary of the orthodox behaviorism that prevailed in the late 1960s, and so my associational impulses led me more in the direction of philosophy and sociology. But were my concerns that a "serial introspector" would be unwelcome in the emerging field of behavioral economics unfounded?

In seeking to answer this, it will be necessary to keep in mind the earlier noted distinction between the strict behaviorism that prevailed in the 1930s (at the time of the transition from *utility* to *preference* as the word of choice in the theory of the consumer) and the more eclectic sorts of psychology that prevail today and which are receptive to the notion of mental states.

There is something slightly odd in the fact that the purging of the mental from the official lexicon of the economist resulted in the replacement of the word *utility* with *preference*. On first consideration this may seem to be a perfectly reasonable shift, for a preference is manifested in a behavior, but a level of cardinally measurable utility is not equivalently manifested. Thus it is understandable that an agent's voluntary choice of bundle A when both A and B are available can reveal that the agent "prefers" A to B but cannot tell us anything about how much better A is than B in any cardinally measurable sense.[8]

What makes the process slightly odd, at least from the standpoint of an introspection advocate, is that exactly such introspection makes preference a "concept with legs," whereas utility levels do not fare as well. While reliance on the direct awareness of my own preferences for things and my own preferences for preferences might make me venture into cardinality, this has not occurred. I have chosen to operate within the vocabulary of preferences and have steered clear of measurability.[9] In spite of this one sense in which metapreferences might appear to fit comfortably with prevailing neoclassical orthodoxy, such preferences about preferences differ markedly in two critical respects from their first-order counterparts. These differences will be considered in some detail in the remainder of this section.

A Weak Connection with "Choice"

First, while a first-order preference is revealed to the outside observer through the choice that an agent makes, a second-order preference is not. To illustrate, one who purchases a hamburger when a salad is also available expresses a preference for the former relative to the latter. The hamburger addict, however, need not make us aware that, were he able, he would have selected an internal motivational state different from the one he finds himself experiencing. This becomes especially apparent when the project of the early-twentieth-century positivists is taken into account. The goal of finding "a theoretical foundation for the transition . . . from a theory based on psychological motives, to one based on individual demand functions" (Lewin 1996, 1309) was very real. For mainstream economists this made all the more suspect the notion of a preference for preferences, since markets in which one could purchase a preference were nonexistent. (It was precisely on the basis of this fact that I built my argument that there is market failure in the production of our first-order preferences.)

As Amitai Etzioni notes, "Information about preference changes, neo-classicists assert, is 'ephemeral,' based on 'soft,' nonbehavioural data such as surveys of attitudes; further, preference changes involve non-observable states of mind" (1992, 14). While sympathetic to the recognition of metapreferences, this passage does not call into question the implicit assumption that only because of preference *changes* are metapreferences potentially of interest. The tradition of relying on behaviors to make us aware that an agent is unhappy with a preference has the effect of biasing us away from some very significant instances when no such behavior occurs. It is thus no surprise that attention has tended to focus on those cases when an agent's preferences actually do change as a result of deliberate measures and has tended to avoid focusing on cases in which agents are simply stuck with preferences that they would rather not be experiencing.

This behavioral bias, even while studying mental states, is captured well in Albert Hirschman's claim that "if . . . the two kinds of preferences are permanently at odds so that the agent always acts against his better judgment . . . this [second-order preference] cannot only be dismissed as wholly ineffective, but doubts will arise whether it is really there at all" (1985, 9). Such a bias has had the effect of steering attention away from the fact, most easily appreciated through plain old introspection, that altering a preference is no easy task. While it is important and interesting to consider strategies agents use to improve their preferences, what about instances when they are unable to do so? Yes, an agent may precommit to a salad for lunch tomorrow if able to do so today and may find that by doing so he not only will have the salad for lunch tomorrow but will prefer it to the hamburger.[10] But a more deeply seated bad habit may not be overcome by such a precommitment device. There are certainly drug users and smokers who will be in the grip of an unpreferred preference no matter how long the time between choice and actual consumption. For those still loyal to the orthodox behaviorist tradition, nothing will ever occur that will allow the conclusion to be reached that the agent was in the grip of an unpreferred preference.

At least as significantly, the loyalty to behaviors has likely clouded the sense of just how difficult the achievement of one's preferred preferences might be. By focusing on the changes in preferences, attention is drawn from the existential state of having to live with the conflict of choosing what one prefers while wishing one's preference were otherwise.

A Weak Connection with Verbal Reports

The first criticism derives primarily from an older sort of behaviorism that observes just nonverbal behaviors. Yet even when we allow for the acceptance of self-reports, the discovery of second-order preferences would have been unlikely indeed. Asking an unsuccessful smoker or dieter why he acts contrary to his apparent goal, one is likely to hear remarks such as "I just can't control myself," "I smoke even though I don't want to," or "Part of me wanted to and part of me wanted not to, but the first part won." For informal discourse, this will do just fine and may serve as a useful device for overcoming cognitive dissonance. Unfortunately, the two-self models that arose to account for such anomalies do little more than take people at their word.

As I have argued previously, to create two people where there appears to be one carries with it a normative paralysis, since it is impossible to say with any clarity that the self who wants not to smoke should be given more normative weight than the self who wants to smoke. Freudian notions of id, ego, and superego likely encouraged the peculiar notion of each person in fact consisting of "several selves." And as the psychologist Jerome Bruner notes, the possibility has been raised that the rise in multiple personality disorders in the United States has been a "pathology . . . engendered by therapists who accept the view that self is divisible and who, in the course of therapy, inadvertently offer this model of selfhood to their patients as a means of containing and alleviating their conflicts" (1990, 42).[11]

Two more recent historical trends, positivism from the 1930s through the 1960s and postmodernism over the past twenty years, have likely served to prop up this peculiar resolution of internal conflict. From Milton Friedman's methodological standpoint (1953), it matters not in the least whether theories are constructed on the assumption that an ostensibly single person is in fact two or more people. According to his instrumental methodological perspective, the issue is not the realism of assumptions but only their ability to lead to predictions that are supported by the empirical evidence. For postmodernists, such as Mihnea Moldoveanu and Howard Stevenson, "the self is not unitary—and the unitary self is an illusion" (2001, 297). Peculiar as such bedfellows might seem—clinical psychologists, libertarian positivists in the tradition of Friedman, and postmodernists—bedfellows they appear to be on the issue of the coherence of the person.[12]

Only by rejecting the easy claim that I was really two selves or that I really had no control over my burger eating was I able to come up with the idea of a second-order preference. My behaviors certainly didn't reveal such preferences, but my very real desire to have a different preference did. From the inside I recognized that my desire for the burger was similar in nature to my desire to desire to have a salad. The first I was able to act on directly, while the second was something I would have acted on if the choice had been that simple (and, accordingly, I then would have acted on a different first-order preference). Extensive observation of behaviors or verbal reports would not have brought this to my attention.

CONCLUSION

If there is any one contribution of economics that is likely to be universally respected, it is the very mundane point of trade-offs and the recognition that even when currency is not in the picture, actions are costly. Before the arrival of behavioral economics, a common observation was that the newly minted economics Ph.D.'s demonstrated rising levels of sophistication in mathematical proofs but stagnant or even falling levels of sophistication in "enlightened observation." The perspective of the intellectual was declining and being replaced by the perspective of the mathematically astute.

The influence that attention to what has come to be called "behavioral economics" has had and will continue to have on this state of affairs is by no means obvious. As I have argued here, there are risks that the movement will further strengthen the rise of the technical expert who can speak of engaging in the scientific method and of lifting economics from its prescientific legacy without even suffering pangs of doubt on exactly what this might entail. Such an expert will be trained in the testing of hypotheses but not in the art of introspection and related means of arriving at versions of reality that may or may not be subject to behavioral verification.

The movement of economists closer to psychology can be viewed in two different ways that have very different implications. There is, on one hand, the possibility of your average contemporary economist sharing ideas with your average contemporary psychologist, separated for years but each reflecting the "physics envy" that has caused the social sciences to turn their back on introspection as a tool for knowing and as an activity to be shared with others in the field. There is, on the other hand, the possibility of contemporary economists returning to the insights that psychology was able to offer before the positivist project came to dominate. Simply stated, do economists wish to welcome back the psychologists that they split from a century ago or the psychologists who also split from these psychologists?

NOTES

1. See Watson 1913 and 1930 and Hull 1951 for early pioneering arguments for behaviorism. For a strong and deliberately provocative position on the incoherence of nonbehavioral concepts, see Skinner 1971. For his own views on the forces behind his adoption of this position, see Skinner 1979. Assessments of the successes and shortcomings of behaviorism are voluminous. See, for example, Modgil and Modgil 1987, O'Donohue and Ferguson 2001, and Smith and Woodward 1996. For an assessment of the less than perfect link between behaviorism and logical positivism, see Smith 1986.

2. It is this first sort of behavioral bias that is critiqued in Kahneman, Wakker, and Sarin 1997.

3. Arguments such as Katona's have not convinced all economists. For a more recent attempt to persuade mainstream economists that mental states are worth studying, as long as they are manifested in behaviors, see Smith 1991. For a compelling account of the disappearance of consciousness from the mainstream economist's account of the individual, see Davis 2003.

4. Students are not the only group for whom writing requirements appear to be replacing reading requirements. I suspect that the output of faculty might be improved if professors were to write less and read more. Once again, however, the pragmatic behaviorists can measure the former far more easily than the latter.

5. I make a similar argument defending second-order preference models of internal conflict (George 2001, chap. 2). The odd counterintuitive connection between the cognitive sciences and postmodern thinking might also be noted. See, in particular, Moldoveanu and Stevenson 2001 for a postmodern attempt to bury the notion of a "self."

6. The movement away from such "folk psychological" concepts may help to shed some light on Berg's (2003) exploration of why behavioral economists have been reluctant to address normative questions.

7. It would be tempting but mistaken to equate introspection with intuition. The former, of course, treats one's own mental experiences as the object of study. The latter focuses on the means by which one draws conclusions from whatever is being studied. The object of study could be the behaviors of others or one's own mental experiences. While there is a temptation to classify introspection and intuition together and to suspect that advocates of one would be advocates of the other, they are in fact logically distinct concepts. One could, in principle, be a strong advocate of introspection while simultaneously placing little trust in intuition, and vice versa. For a close look at intuition's role in behavioral economics, see Frantz 2005.

8. This is not to say that the compatibility of behaviorism with revealed preference theory is altogether comfortable. As Shira Lewin notes, rationality travels closely with preference, and "rationality is a nonsensical concept if it is not motive-related, but only behavioral" (1996, 1293).

9. Something of an interesting compromise between ordinalism and cardinalism has emerged in studies of happiness. Common practice has been for agents to rank how happy they are ("very happy," "happy," etc.) or to assign a number between 1 and 10. Without going fully to cardinalism, such efforts are certainly a step in that direction. For a recent survey of the literature on happiness, see Frey and Stutzer 2002.

10. See Maital 1998 for one example of a justification of self-imposed constraints.

11. Bruner credits Nicholas Humphrey and Daniel Dennett (1989) with suggesting the connection between the rise in the disorder and the beliefs of therapists.

12. There are a variety of attempts to deal with the "present self" and the "future self" that might on the surface appear to speak of the simultaneous coexistence of more than one self. Most often, however, such projects do not rest on any assumption of a single self residing in a body at any moment in time. See, for example, Markus and Nurius 1986.

REFERENCES

Berg, Nathan. 2003. "Normative Behavioral Economics." *The Journal of Socio-Economics* 32, 4: 411–28.

Boulding, Kenneth E. 1956. *The Image.* Ann Arbor: University of Michigan Press

Bruner, Jerome. 1990. *Acts of Meaning.* Cambridge, MA: Harvard University Press.

Davis, John B. 2003. *The Theory of the Individual in Economics: Identity and Value.* New York: Routledge.

Etzioni, Amitai. 1992. "Socio-Economics: Select Policy Implications." In S.E.G. Lea, P. Webley, and B.M. Young, eds., *New Directions in Economic Psychology: Theory, Experiment and Application,* 13–27. Brookfield, VT: Edward Elgar.

Frankfurt, Harry G. 1971. "Freedom of the Will and the Concept of a Person." *Journal of Philosophy* 68: 5–20.

Frantz, Roger. 2005. *Two Minds: Intuition and Analysis in the History of Economic Thought.* London: Springer.

Frey, Bruno S., and Alois Stutzer. 2002. *Happiness and Economics: How the Economy and Institutions Affect Well-Being.* Princeton, NJ: Princeton University Press.

Friedman, Milton. 1953. *Essays in Positive Economics.* Chicago: University of Chicago Press.

George, David. 1973. "Frame Dependence in Directional Orientation." In Wolfgang Preiser, ed., *Environmental Design Research,* 2:210–17. Stroudsberg, PA: Dowden, Hutchinson, and Ross.

———. 2001. *Preference Pollution: How Markets Create the Desires We Dislike.* Ann Arbor: University of Michigan Press.

Hirschman, Albert O. 1985. "Against Parsimony: Three Easy Ways of Complicating Some Categories of Economic Discourse." *Economics and Philosophy* 1: 7–21.

Hull, Clark L. 1951. *Essentials of Behavior.* New Haven, CT: Yale University Press.

Humphrey, Nicholas, and Daniel Dennett. 1989. "Speaking for Ourselves: An Assessment of Multiple Personality Disorder." *Raritan: A Quarterly Review* 9: 68–98.

Kahneman, Daniel, Peter P. Wakker, and Rakesh Sarin. 1997. "Back to Bentham? Explorations of Experienced Utility." *Quarterly Journal of Economics* 112, 2: 375–405.

Katona, George. 1951. *Psychological Analysis of Economic Behavior.* New York: McGraw-Hill.

Lewin, Shira B. 1996. "Economics and Psychology: Lessons for Our Own Day from the Early Twentieth Century." *Journal of Economic Literature* 34, 3: 1293–323.

Maital, Shlomo. 1988. "Novelty, Comfort, and Pleasure: Inside the Utility-Function Black Box." In P.J. Albanese, ed., *Psychological Foundations of Economic Behavior,* 1–29. New York: Praeger.

Markus, Hazel, and Paula Nurius. 1986. "Possible Selves." *American Psychologist* 41, 9: 954–69.

McCain, Roger A. 1992. *A Framework for Cognitive Economics.* Westport, CT: Praeger.

Mirowski, Philip. 2002. *Machine Dreams: Economics Becomes a Cyborg Science.* New York: Cambridge University Press.

Modgil, Sohan, and Celia Modgil, eds. 1987. *B. F. Skinner: Consensus and Controversy.* New York: Falmer Press.

Moldoveanu, Mihnea, and Howard Stevenson. 2001. "The Self as a Problem: The Intra-Personal Coordination of Conflicting Desires." *Journal of Socio-Economics* 30, 4: 295–330.

O'Donohue, William, and Kyle E. Ferguson. 2001. *The Psychology of B. F. Skinner.* Thousand Oaks, CA: Sage Publications.

Robbins, Lionel. 1935. *An Essay on the Nature and Significance of Economic Science.* London: Macmillan.

Samuelson, Paul A. 1938. "A Note on the Pure Theory of Consumer's Behaviour." *Economica* 5, 17: 61–71.

Skinner, B.F. 1971. *Beyond Freedom and Dignity.* New York: Alfred A. Knopf.

———. 1979. *The Shaping of a Behaviorist: Part Two of an Autobiography.* New York: Alfred A. Knopf.

Smith, Laurence D. 1986. *Behaviorism and Logical Positivism: A Reassessment of the Alliance.* Stanford, CA: Stanford University Press.

Smith, Laurence D., and William R. Woodward, eds. 1996. *B. F. Skinner and Behaviorism in American Culture.* Bethlehem, PA: Lehigh University Press.

Smith, Vernon L. 1991. "Rational Choice: The Contrast Between Economics and Psychology." *Journal of Political Economy* 99, 4: 877–97.

Stich, Stephen P. 1983. *From Folk Psychology to Cognitive Science: The Case Against Belief.* Cambridge, MA: MIT Press.

Watson, John B. 1913. "Psychology as the Behaviorist Views It." *Psychological Review* 20, 2: 158–77.

———. 1930. *Behaviorism.* Chicago: University of Chicago Press.

CHAPTER 5

INTEGRATING EMOTIONS INTO ECONOMIC THEORY

BRUCE E. KAUFMAN

The emotions received only limited attention among psychologists until the mid-1980s, when research began to blossom. Emblematic is the publication of the first edition of the *Handbook of Emotions* in 1993. What was true of psychology was doubly so for economics. From the end of World War II to the late 1980s the topic of emotions was nearly invisible in mainstream economics and represented a niche area of research even among behavioral economists. Illustratively, the comprehensive (more than 600 pages) survey volume on economic psychology by Lea, Tarpy, and Webley (1987) not only did not have a chapter on emotions but did not even list the term in the index. Since then the tide has turned, albeit on a relatively modest scale. A harbinger of renewed interest in emotions among mainstream economists was Robert Frank's well-received book *Passions Within Reason* (1988), accompanied by a modest but increasingly visible flow of journal articles exploring various facets of emotion, such as happiness, envy, regret, trust, and fairness. Then the subject of emotion gained wider recognition in the discipline and a certain degree of official sanction when two survey articles appeared in top-line economics journals—by Elster in the *Journal of Economic Literature* (1998) and Loewenstein in the *American Economic Review* (2000).

I follow in the footsteps of these authors, albeit with more attention to the place of emotions in the corpus of economic theory and correspondingly lighter coverage of the relevant empirical literature. This chapter makes, in addition, three other contributions. The first is to include a number of studies published since the reviews by Elster and Loewenstein. The second is to introduce a more formalized model of the economic behavior process in order to better identify and highlight the conceptual linkages between emotions and economic theory. The third is to draw out from this literature review several important implications and conclusions regarding economic theory and the explanation of economic behavior.

THE PSYCHOLOGY OF EMOTIONS

Psychologists often distinguish between three fundamental constructs: motivation, cognition, and emotion. Motivation refers to the psychological process that directs behavior and determines its intensity and persistence, cognition represents the mental process of thinking and reasoning, and emotion is the domain of subjective feelings and reactions thereto. Although distinct, the three processes overlap and feed back into each other. Emblematic of these interrelations are the titles of two recently established psychology journals: *Cognition and Emotion* and *Motivation and Emotion*.

The concept of emotion is multidimensional and difficult to define in a short and precise manner. After a lengthy review of the history and contemporary literature on emotions, Oatley and Jenkins suggest this three-part definition:

1. An emotion is usually caused by a person consciously or unconsciously evaluating an event as relevant to a concern (a goal) that is important; the emotion is felt as positive when a concern is advanced and negative when a concern is impeded.
2. The core of an emotion is readiness to act and the prompting of plans; an emotion gives priority for one or a few kinds of action to which it gives a sense of urgency—so it can interrupt, or compete with, alternative mental processes or actions. Different types of readiness create different perceived relationships and opportunities with others.
3. An emotion is usually experienced as a distinctive type of mental state, sometimes accompanied by or followed by bodily changes, expressions, and actions. (Oatley and Jenkins 1996, 96)

One aspect of the multidimensionality of emotions is that they contain subjective, biological, purposive, and social components. For example, emotions are in part subjective feelings, such as the experience of anger, joy, or jealousy. Emotions also induce biological reactions and energy-mobilizing responses, such as the heightened pulse rate and increased mental and physiological arousal that go with, say, hatred or lust. Emotions are also purposive in that they direct (or redirect) attention and personal resources to deal with a specific event or concern, such as the fear induced by a threat to personal safety or shame caused by an inappropriate action toward others. And emotions are also social phenomena, since individuals use emotional indicators, such as an angry tone of voice or welcoming body language, as a means of interpersonal communication and social coordination.

A second part of the emotions' multidimensionality is that they can be a stimulus to behavior, an outcome of behavior, and/or a constraint on behavior. Pride and envy, for example, can stimulate people to work hard or say hurtful things when they otherwise would not. Likewise, pride and envy can be a consequence of behavior, such as when a person wins or loses a competitive event. And emotions, such as embarrassment and anxiety, can inhibit or constrain behavior by making people reluctant to pursue something they internally desire to do.

A third multidimensional aspect of emotions is with respect to their sheer number and differentiation. A widely held view, for example, is that some emotions are "primary" or basic (like colors) and are relatively common in definition and content across cultures, while numerous others are a derivative from or a permutation of the primary emotions and exhibit greater intercultural variation. The precise list of primary emotions differs among theorists, but typically six to ten are given, such as anger, fear, distress, joy, disgust, surprise, shame, guilt, interest, and contempt (Reeve 2001, 13). A primary emotion, such as anger, then has a family of associated emotions, including hostility, rage, hate, annoyance, frustration, and envy; alternatively, joy is a primary emotion that contains a cluster of closely associated emotions such as contentment, satisfaction, pride, amusement, and exhilaration. Altogether, researchers have identified more than 200 distinct emotions (Frijda 1999).

Yet another aspect of the emotions' multidimensionality concerns their relationship to reason and rational behavior. A viewpoint of ancient lineage is that emotions reflect the lower-order, primitive, and impulsive/irrational side of human beings (Hirschman 1977). Typically, when emotions are so viewed they appear to be a dangerous and disruptive force in human affairs and a potential source of folly and woe. Contrasted to emotion, in this schema, is reason and rationality, typically viewed as uniquely human and higher-order attributes that contribute to human progress through the power of logic, scientific discovery, and farsighted calculation of benefits and costs. The role of reason (the mind) from this perspective is to rule and control the passions (the heart). A contrasting point of view holds that emotions are central to effective human functioning and adaptation and in large part promote rather than subvert rationality (Isen 2000). From this perspective, emotions are cues that guide rational behavior by assigning priorities to alternative courses of action, alert the human agent to opportunities and threats in the environment, and mobilize action toward goal attainment. Rather than subverting rationality, in this view emotions are essential to rationality, at least as long as they do not take an extreme form.

Also multidimensional are the theorized causes of emotions. Common to nearly every theory of emotion is the idea that emotions are elicited or aroused by an external object or event, real or conjectured, that in some way affects a goal or desire of the individual. Theories then divide as to the process by which the emotion arises. One group of theorists hold that emotions are largely biological and neurophysiological phenomena that arise from ingrained or "hardwired" brain processes (Panksepp 2000). A second group of theorists maintain that most emotions arise from a human cognitive appraisal process in which the direction and content of the emotion is formed by a mental calculation (conscious or unconscious) regarding the meaning of the event for the goals of the person and attributions regarding who or what is responsible (Lazarus 1991). A distinct possibility is that both biological and cognitive theories are correct, with the former explaining certain primary emotions (often called "gut feelings") and the latter explaining more complex emotions.

A final form of multidimensionality is in the length, intensity, and scope of the emotional experience. Psychologists, for example, distinguish between emotion, mood, and affect (Frijda 1999). Emotion is the shortest and generally most intense experience and is typically directed at or elicited by a relatively well-defined object. A mood is a more generalized, lower-intensity, and longer-lasting sensation. A person may be in a sad or happy mood for days, weeks, or months, and the cause is generally diffuse and difficult to pinpoint. Finally, the term *affect* is often used to subsume all forms and states of emotional experience, thus giving it the broadest domain. In the remainder of this chapter I use the term *emotion* in the broad sense of affect.

EMOTIONS AND ECONOMIC THEORY: A CONCEPTUAL FRAMEWORK

Beginning with the ordinalist revolution in microeconomics in the 1930s and the ascendancy of the neoclassical paradigm after World War II, the dominant trend in the discipline of economics has been to formalize and axiomatize the model of the human agent, minimize the reliance on or reference to assumptions and theories in psychology, and always look first to differences in environmental states (budget constraints) rather than differences in tastes (indifference curves). As a result, by the mid-1980s psychology in any overt form had largely disappeared from economics discourse and most mainstream economists had concluded that predicting and understanding economic behavior could proceed psychology-free with little loss in explanatory power and considerable gain in parsimony (Stigler and Becker 1977). Rabin (1998, 41) characterizes the stance of economists toward psychology as "aggressive uncuriosity." Certainly most economists up to very recent times would have regarded the subject of emotions as being on the very fringe of the field and of little relevance for the main corpus of economic theory.

The peripheral, almost nonexistent role of emotions in economic theory is well illustrated by what is arguably the core theoretical model in microeconomics: the model of constrained utility

Figure 5.1 **Schematic Representation of the Human Behavioral Process
in Economic Models**

maximization. In the standard treatment, utility is simply an ordinal ranking; the wants and desires that create the preference relations in the indifference curves are taken as exogenous givens; preference relations are also individualistic and thus not influenced by actions or opinions of others; the economic agent is assumed to have unbiased perception and memory (information gathering and recall); optimization (information processing) is accurate and costless; and preference relations are independent of changes in the external environment (indifference curves are not affected by changes in the budget constraint).

In what follows I reexamine the model of constrained utility maximization and demonstrate two related propositions: (1) the model has a great deal of emotional content if one approaches the subject from an explicitly psychological perspective, and (2) a consideration of the emotional aspects of the model in nearly all cases adds new insights and in some cases suggests a fairly significant revision to the structure of the constrained utility maximization model and the nature of its predictions.

To help organize this discussion and give it greater conceptual coherence, a useful expository aid is to decompose the structure of the constrained utility maximization model into five discrete steps. This is done in Figure 5.1 (from Kaufman 1999b). The emotional content of each of these steps is then considered in the next section.

Starting on the left-hand side of the diagram, the first step in the behavioral chain is the assumed *goal* of the human agent. The goal is the objective or purpose the person seeks and is thus a central element of the motivational process (Locke and Latham 1990). In economics, as indicated above, the goal is assumed to be maximization of utility.

Since utility maximization is a global objective, the person must choose one course of action or behavior from among the available options (the opportunity set) in order to effectuate the goal. The choice process is shaped by the three factors represented in the second step of the diagram. These three factors are the *self, wants,* and the *environment.*

The self is the active agent in the decision-making process and is where the cognitive faculties necessary for decision making are located, such as perception and reasoning. The self is also where the emotions are experienced. As a psychological concept, the self gains significance and explanatory power to the extent the organism is endowed with consciousness.

Wants are desires for specific items or activities that provide satisfaction to the organism. Wants serve to both arouse and guide behavior in a specific direction in pursuit of the overall goal of utility maximization. Since wants are subjective feelings, they vary in intensity and valence across items and activities. In making choices, therefore, people have to establish a preference ordering among the wants, such as presumed in an indifference curve.

The final factor that influences behavior in this part of the behavioral chain is the environment external to the individual. The environment defines both the opportunities and constraints facing the human agent. Although possessing an objective external quality, the environment is inevitably perceived in subjective terms by the human agent due to the biased and incomplete nature of perception, information, memory, and mental calculation.

The next (third) step in the chain of behavior is *decision making*. Decision making is a cognitive process that takes place within the person (self) and involves the acquisition, interpretation, and processing of information for the purpose of helping the agent reach the utility maximization goal. As envisioned in standard economics, decision making is an instrumental process that seeks to determine the best means to reach a given end. In a broader model, decision making is also required to select and revise major life goals (the ends themselves).

The fourth step in the behavioral sequence is the initiation of overt *action*. Motivated by the desire to maximize utility, the person acts to attain the outcome that mental deliberation has determined to be optimal. Within the limits imposed by the environmental constraints and the probability distributions governing uncertain events, the utility maximization model typically assumes that the action undertaken by the agent will result in the desired outcome—that is, the equilibrium solution of the constrained maximization problem, albeit perhaps in terms of expected value or with a short-run lag in adjustment.

The final step in the behavioral chain is the *change in utility* resulting from the attainment of the optimal outcome. The change in utility may be either positive or negative, depending on whether the environment has become more accommodating or constraining, and thus reflects a flow variable that alters the stock of total utility existing at the beginning of the behavioral sequence. Reflective of the equilibrium nature of standard economic models, the net increment or decrement of utility experienced at this stage is typically assumed to lead to no further adjustments in behavior.

BRINGING EMOTIONS (BACK) INTO ECONOMICS

In this section I reexamine each of the five steps of the constrained utility maximization model illustrated in Figure 5.1 in order to demonstrate its emotional content and the implications thereof for economic theory and behavior. Given the expansiveness of the topic and relevant literature, the coverage is necessarily selective.

Utility Maximization

Although debate continues about the extent to which human behavior fits the canons of economic rationality, nearly everyone agrees that human behavior is purposive and goal-directed. But toward what goal(s)? Answering this question is the first step in any social science theory.

The answer given in mainstream economics is maximization of utility. The concept of utility was formalized by the nineteenth-century English philosopher Jeremy Bentham, although the concept goes back to the Greeks (Georgescu-Roegen 1968). According to Bentham (reprinted in Mack 1969, 86), "Nature has placed mankind under the governance of two sovereign masters, *pain* and *pleasure*. It is for them alone to point out what we ought to do, as well as to determine what we shall do. . . . They govern us in all we do, in all we say, in all we think." In the paragraph this quote comes from, Bentham equates utility with pleasure and disutility with pain—a theory of motivation frequently referred to as hedonism or hedonic psychology (Kahneman, Diener, and Schwarz 1999). Several paragraphs later, however, Bentham gives a broader statement: "By utility is meant that property in an object, whereby it tends to produce benefit, advantage, pleasure, good, or happiness (all of this in the present case comes to the same thing), or (what comes again to the same thing) to prevent the happening of mischief, pain, evil, or unhappiness to the party whose interest is considered." Thus, according to Bentham, the imperative that drives human beings in all they do is the quest to maximize the difference between positive utility and negative disutility, which can alternatively be construed as maximizing net pleasure, happiness, advantage, or some similar construct. For the purposes of this essay, it is important to note that the fundamental maximand in this theory is an emotion (pleasure), mood (happiness), or affective judgment (satisfaction). One could say, therefore, that in utility theory humans are indeed a "slave of their passions," although this slavery is exercised with a high degree of rationality.

Three issues surround Benthamite utility theory. The first is whether the goal of utility maximization is really what guides and energizes human behavior (Rabin 1998). Framed this way, the debate becomes one about alternative theories of human motivation. Motivation is not the subject of this chapter, so extended discussion of this matter cannot be given. Perusal of the literature on motivation suggests, however, that a utility theory of motivation is far from universally accepted. Some theories of motivation, for example, posit that human behavior originates from various internal physiological and psychological needs, instincts, and drives that "push" behavior in certain directions, as opposed to the "pull" exerted by the pursuit of pleasure or happiness (Reeve 2001). Other scholars argue that it is impossible to telescope all human goals into a single construct, such as pleasure or happiness, and thus multiple goals must be specified. Lane (2000), for example, argues that a better-specified model of the economic agent posits that people pursue three partially incommensurable goals: happiness, justice, and self-development. A third perspective is that utility theory is not so much an incorrect statement about human motivation as an empirically empty one, given its ability to rationalize any and all forms of behavior (e.g., suicide, charitable gift-giving, workaholism).

The second issue concerning Benthamite utility theory is the precise nature and specification of the utility construct. As indicated above, Bentham thought pleasure, happiness, goodness, and other such psychological variables could be used interchangeably. One branch of modern economics self-consciously restricts the utility concept to the notion of ordinal ranking, called by Kahneman, Wakker, and Sarin (1997) "decision utility." But often in modern economic discourse utility is also loosely and somewhat indiscriminately equated with satisfaction, happiness, welfare, well-being, and psychic income. Are these equivalent concepts? All represent what Kahneman, Wakker, and Sarin call "experience utility"—that is, a personally experienced affective state. Psychological research suggests, however, that these different utility variables are to some degree different behavioral constructs. For example, pleasure and pain tend to be relatively immediate sensations and most closely represent an emotion in the clinical meaning of that term. Happiness, on the other hand, is a more diffuse and longer-lasting mood (or "hedonic tone") that reflects a combination of positive affect (such as joy, optimism, and pride) and a cognitive evaluation that life is headed in a good direction. Last are satisfaction and its close equivalent, subjective well-being. Both concepts have a positive but considerably less than perfect correlation with pleasure and happiness, partly because they rest on a more reasoned and cognitive evaluation of objective life conditions (Argyle 2001).

A third issue concerns the measurability and interpersonal comparability of utility. Bentham thought utility could be measured and compared across people, although he did not specify how. After the late 1800s a growing number of economists and psychologists concluded that experience utility was inherently not quantifiable or comparable across people, and thus a cardinal measure of utility was impossible. When Pareto, Hicks, and other economists demonstrated that basic economic constructs could be derived using only ordinal utility, interest in a cardinal (measurable) form of utility nearly disappeared. In recent years, however, the subject has experienced a modest rebirth of attention. Psychologists have shown, for example, that people can clearly discriminate and report experienced levels of pleasure/happiness with ongoing life events or laboratory stimuli. Kahneman (1999) calls this ongoing stream of feelings "instant utility" and has explored whether discrete units of instant utility can be cumulated over a period of time to yield total utility. Another line of research, now proceeding for more than thirty years, is to ask people to self-report their happiness and satisfaction with life. Sometimes called "remembered utility," these self-reports allow researchers to make comparisons of utility across time, people, and countries (Schwarz and Strack 1999; Frey and Stutzer 2002). A recent example is the study "Money, Sex, and Happiness" by Blanchflower and Oswald (2004). They conclude, among other things, that people who are married and have sex more often are on average happier and that the average person rates an increase in sexual intercourse from once a month to at least once a week as being equivalent in happiness terms to $50,000.

During most of the twentieth century the great bulk of economists concluded that a Benthamite form of experienced utility was neither possible to construct nor of analytical value for economic theory, and thus ignored it in favor of ordinal utility. In the last decade or so, however, a very modest but discernible shift of opinion has occurred, spurred by new theoretical and empirical research by psychologists on utility and its empirical proxies and the pioneering research on theories and measurement of experienced utility by a small number of economists. Several interesting conclusions and implications have been found regarding economic theory and behavior.

One such implication is that happiness and subjective well-being have a strong relational component, suggesting the individualistic utility function specified in most economic models may be seriously incomplete (Elster 1998; Argyle 2001). Most emotions, as noted above, arise from an evaluative appraisal of the personal significance or consequence of some event, action, or object. But this evaluation is typically context-specific, and if the context changes, so does the emotion. For example, the amount of utility an individual derives from an annual salary of $V depends, in part, on whether $V is less than, equal to, or greater than the salary received by coworkers in a referent group. A person may receive a 4 percent salary increase and feel happy with this outcome, only to have happiness turn to bitterness when she learns a coworker received 6 percent. Another form of relative comparison is between goal and attainment (or aspiration and accomplishment). A standard neoclassical utility function implies that a worker's satisfaction increases with additional income above the current level, but everyday experience and psychological experiments reveal that a salary increase of, say, 4 percent may well lead to greater *un*happiness if the person had expected 6 percent. A more psychologically informed view of utility would thus suggest that economic models should include relational variables, such as relative income, target income, relative deprivation, and degree of norm adherence. An earlier generation of economists, such as Veblen (1899) and Duesenberry (1949), advocated this move, but for the most part mainstream economics continues to stay with independent utility functions. Encouraging signs of movement, however, are found in a number of recent studies on interdependent and endogenous preferences (e.g., Bagwell and Bernheim 1996; Postlewaite 1998; Bowles 1998).

A behavioral theory of utility contains a second major implication, in this case concerning the intertemporal determinants and behavior of utility. Research shows that emotional states, such as pleasure, happiness, and satisfaction, tend as a general statement to gravitate toward a zero point of affectivity at or near the average value of a stimulus (Parducci 1995). Thus Scitovsky noted in his pioneering book *The Joyless Economy* (1976) that despite the rise of affluence, many Americans reported no greater happiness with life, and some expressed growing unhappiness. His explanation was that emotional states such as pleasure and happiness are more closely tied to income flows than to stocks. That is, people become habituated to a certain level of income, and if income (the stimulus) remains unchanged over time, they come to feel neither significant pleasure nor displeasure but "comfort." If maintained long enough, however, comfort can degenerate into boredom (a negative hedonic state). The key to the experience of pleasure and happiness, there-fore, is an ongoing change in the stimulus above its average level, which in this example means a positive change in income.

The Self

Next consider the triad of the self, wants, and environment in Figure 5.1. Since the focus of this chapter is on the human agent, as well as for reasons of space, the environment is discussed no further.

Economic theory does not distinguish a specific psychological entity called the "self." Most economists would probably view the self as coterminous with "economic agent" and thus devoid of independent theoretical content. A smattering of articles has appeared, however, on the eco-nomics of self-control and the role of emotions as a regulatory mechanism in human behavior (e.g., Thaler and Shefrin 1981; Gifford 2002). In psychology, on the other hand, the self concept is the subject of extensive study and a sizable literature.

The self resides in each person's consciousness and embodies how we see, feel, and regard ourselves. The self concept is formed both from one's own subjective evaluation of personal at-tributes, capabilities, and actions and from the evaluations (real or imagined) made by other people (Banaji and Prentice 1994). Psychologically viewed, the self is the center of each person's universe and, according to Lane (1991), the self concept represents each person's most valued asset.

The self has numerous behavioral attributes. Economics gives a central place to one such attribute, self-interest, but typically ignores the others. A glance through psychology texts re-veals an opposite situation in that discipline. Self-interest is rarely mentioned, but given promi-nence are a variety of other self-concepts, such as self-actualization, self-awareness, self-confidence, self-efficacy, self-esteem, self-love, and self-worth. Arising from the various self concepts are, in turn, a variety of emotions, such as embarrassment, pride, respect, shame, and guilt. Greed and selfishness are sometimes treated as the emotional analog of self-interest, although they may be better thought of as an egoistic disposition or attitude. The negative emotions arise from an evaluation that the self has in some respect been inadequate or blame-worthy, while the positive emotions reflect an evaluation that the actions or behaviors of the self have been successful, praiseworthy, or well regarded. Pride thus reflects the emotional feeling from a "job well done," while embarrassment arises from a fumbling performance in front of others.

The concept of the self has several applications and implications for economics. An example is the origins of altruistic behavior. Critics of orthodox economics, while not denying a central role to self-interest, nonetheless contend that it errs by assuming that human beings are motivated *only* by self-interest. They cite, for example, many examples of what appear to be altruistic or other-regarding behaviors, such as tipping in restaurants, charitable gift giving, and saving people from fires and drowning at considerable personal risk. One response of mainstream economists is to argue that self-interest is compatible with other-regarding behavior once it is recognized that the performance of these acts not only increases the utility of the recipient but also increases the utility of the giver. But, respond the critics, this argument makes utility theory dangerously tauto-logical (i.e., whatever a person does must by definition increase utility), and furthermore, the essence of altruism is making self-sacrifice to help another person.

Incorporating emotions into the analysis provides a way to give firmer theoretical support to both perspectives. In the *Theory of Moral Sentiments,* for example, Adam Smith (1759) argued that sympathy leads people to move outside the bounds of narrow self-interest and take other-regarding actions. Sympathy, in effect, makes person B's welfare an argument in person A's utility function. In a similar vein, institutional economist John Commons (1919) cites patriotism as a reason why self-interested people would voluntarily give their lives in war for their country. Alternatively, one might also appeal to self-esteem to explain altruism. People internalize social norms and ethical precepts, such as helping blind people across the street and obeying the religious command not to steal, and violation of these norms frequently leads to feelings of shame, guilt, and loss of self-esteem. In such cases a purely individualistic calculation of benefits and costs nonetheless leads to other-regarding behavior since the person doing the act experiences positive marginal utility. But consideration of emotion also suggests a rationale for altruistic acts that confer no net benefit to the giver. Some emotions occur so quickly and strongly—what Loewenstein (2000) refers to as "visceral emotions" (gut feelings)—that they cause a person to act before any meaningful rational calculation of benefits and costs can be made. Thus, a passer-by may see a child in danger of drowning in a fast-moving river and instinctively swim to her rescue without regard for personal safety.

The self concept can also be used to explain other puzzling aspects of economic behavior. If economics has a core theorem, it is that behavior responds to changes in incentives. In this spirit, for example, Steven Landsburg remarks, "Most of economics can be summarized in four words: 'People respond to incentives.' The rest is commentary" (1993, 3). Typically, the incentives economists have in mind are external incentives, such as relative prices, incomes, and other budget constraint factors. In some cases, however, a change in budget constraints seems to lead to little if any change in behavior, while in other cases behavior is initiated and sustained independent of external rewards and punishments. The self concept and emotional reactions therefrom help explain both.

For example, one specific self concept is self-efficacy. Self-efficacy is a belief that one is competent and exercises considerable personal control over the direction of one's life and the events in it. People high in self-efficacy believe they can master most situations through personal initiative, while those low in self-efficacy believe they have little power to make a difference in various life events. Rotter (1966) has characterized the former group as having an "internal locus of control" and the latter group as having an "external locus of control." An interesting application of these concepts is to poverty reduction. The standard rational choice model of economics suggests that the way to move people from welfare to work is to change the implicit tax rates and guaranteed benefit levels, thus providing greater incentives to seek gainful employment. The negative income tax experiments revealed, however, that a change in financial incentives alone will lead to a disappointingly small movement from welfare to work (Munnell 1986). One explanation is that the people most likely to be on welfare are also those most likely to suffer from low self-esteem and low self-efficacy. Given this mind-set, a change in financial incentives elicits little response since welfare recipients feel ineffective and powerless to make their lives better even when given a positive inducement to do so. Psychologists call this condition "learned helplessness" (Seligman 1976; Peterson 1999), and it suggests that a successful poverty reduction program requires not only a change in incentives but also personal interventions to build self-esteem and self-efficacy (Foster 1993).

In other cases external incentives do not seem necessary to spur desired behavior and, indeed, can actually inhibit it. This is the case with behavior that is internally (intrinsically) motivated. Internally motivated behavior arises from a drive within the person and is performed for its own sake. The origin of the drive, according to Deci (1975), is the innate need of every person to feel competent and self-determining. This drive imparts a spontaneous origin, persistence, and dynamic growth that equilibrium, stimulus-response models of extrinsic motivation (as in economics) cannot easily explain. Thus, the standard assumption in economics is that work is a source of disutility and people must be bribed by the offer of wages to perform it. Likewise, unless closely supervised and given rewards or threatened with punishments, workers will shirk, call in sick, steal from the company, and in other ways act opportunistically. An alternative point of view is that if work can be made challenging and interesting, the employees given a significant degree of self-management, and a culture of fairness, respect, and team spirit established, then people will regard the work process as a positive source of utility, will feel pride in their work and love for their company, and will become internally motivated to perform as diligent and trustworthy employees (Kaufman 1999b). This idea is the behavioral linchpin of what is called in the modern management literature the "high-performance work system." Provocatively, some psychologists claim that the use of external rewards and punishments, such as a bonus for good attendance, can be self-defeating since it reduces intrinsic motivation, undermines trust, and is experienced by workers as a form of management control and manipulation (Kohn 1993).

Wants

The third part of the bracketed triad in Figure 5.1 is wants. Wants are desires for objects that, when consumed or experienced, yield the psychic form of pleasure that economists often refer to as utility or satisfaction. Wants are important in the economist's model of human behavior because they energize behavior and direct it toward specific ends. Satisfaction of wants is also frequently held up as the end goal of economic activity. Despite the importance of wants, mainstream economics has given them scant attention. Taylor remarks, for example, "Economists have avoided questions of wants. Wants are taken as fixed, and their origins left to psychology" (1988, 35).

Wants clearly have an emotional dimension, although they also arise from other physiological and psychological sources. A want for water, for example, arises when a person experiences the physiological condition of thirst, and the quenching of the "pain" of thirst with a drink of water produces a feeling of satisfaction or pleasure. In this case the emotion of pleasure is largely an outcome of satisfying the want, while the origin of the want arises in an unmet physiological need. In other cases an emotional state may also be causal to the origin and strength of a want. Marshall (1890), for example, argued that satisfaction of basic needs determines the structure of wants at a low income level but in more affluent societies wants endogenously emerge from new consumption experiences and the desire for novelty and distinction. Veblen (1899) gave particular emphasis to distinction and emulation as a source of wants, and Leibenstein (1950) and Becker (1991) have shown that status effects can be so powerful that they lead to upward-sloping demand curves. Wants are also created and structured by the marketing activities of business firms, and highly successful advertising and promotion campaigns can give rise to pronounced fads and fashions. The fact that much consumer advertising emphasizes sex appeal, social status, and pleasure enhancement over factual aspects of product performance and quality speaks directly to the role of emotions in want creation. While advertising creates new wants, moral and religious teachings restrict wants by attaching negative emotional consequences to their realization, such as guilt from stealing and shame from adultery. Certainly a long line of thought exists that unrestricted hedonism would lead to the degeneration and possible destruction of human society (Veenhoven 2003).

In mainstream economics, the position is generally taken that it is not the place of the economist to judge the meritoriousness of particular wants; rather, the task is to study the most efficient way to satisfy human wants whatever they may be. Thus, to the degree economists give attention to wants, it is not with regard to the wants themselves but with regard to the preference relations people have for the goods that satisfy the wants. Crucial to standard microeconomic theory is the assumption that preferences are "well-ordered." The reason is that the twin assumptions of maximization and well-ordered preferences constitute the core of the neoclassical rational choice model. Becker states, for example, "Everyone more or less agrees that rational behavior simply implies consistent maximization of a well-ordered function, such as a utility or profit function" (1976, 153). Well-ordered preferences rest, in turn, on properties such as transitivity, continuity, completeness, convexity, and nonsatiation.

An accumulating body of empirical research shows that these conditions are frequently violated, although debate continues over the causes of these violations and their seriousness for standard theory. These violations take particular forms and have become known as (among others) the "reflection effect, "endowment effect," "framing effect," "isolation effect," "status quo bias," "loss aversion," and "time-inconsistent" preferences (Kahneman and Tversky 2000). The reflection effect, for example, suggests that people have risk-averse preferences in the gain domain but risk-seeking preferences in the loss domain. An explanation for this phenomenon has become known as the status quo bias, which states that people assess prospective utility gain or loss in terms of the change in wealth relative to the status quo position (rather than absolute level of wealth). The endowment effect captures the observed tendency of people to place a higher value on a good once they possess it, while the framing effect describes the fact that people's valuation of an item changes with the context that frames the choice (e.g., a person's opinion of the value of a good differs depending on whether other people have expressed desire for or aversion to the item).

The preponderant portion of the literature has looked for a cognitive explanation for these violations of rational choice theory. Violations of transitivity, for example, have been attributed to the human brain's limited computational power, which forces people to rely on ad hoc and inconsistent decision heuristics and rules of thumb. Also, people often have only fuzzy and sometimes nonexistent information on all the possible items of choice, thus introducing errors into preference orderings. Another candidate is errors in perception: for example, the principle of diminishing sensitivity posits that the marginal effects in perceived well-being are greater for changes close to one's reference level than for changes further away (Rabin 1998).

A growing number of researchers, however, are also beginning to focus on the role of affect, either as an independent causal variable or as a mediating variable with cognition. The reflection effect, for example, gives rise to an S-shaped value function (plotting utility as a function of loss and gain around a status quo zero point). Kahneman and Tversky hypothesize that "the aggravation that one experiences in losing a sum of money appears to be greater than the pleasure associated with gaining the same amount" (2000, 33). The question is, why does the pain of a loss outweigh the pleasure of an equal-sized gain? One answer is that a loss gives rise to emotions that have greater negative intensity, such as fear, embarrassment, dread, and threatened loss of control, relative to the positive emotions of hope, joy, and security that go with a win (Mellers 2000).

Likewise, one explanation for the endowment effect is that ownership becomes invested with ego identification and enhancement. Thus Forgas states, "In modern industrial societies, the ownership of objects is heavily imbued with emotional meaning. . . . When many social relationships are superficial and are based on surface characteristics, the things we own may take on a greater emotional significance in defining and displaying our claimed status and social identity to others" (1998, 263). This affect-oriented explanation is complementary to a cognitive explanation that suggests ownership increases an object's value because people gain greater familiarity with it.

Other emotions economists have examined as an explanation for violation of well-ordered preference relations are regret, disappointment, and envy. Loomes and Sugden (1982) and Bell (1982), for example, develop regret theory to explain the reflection effect. They suggest that decision makers anticipate regret if their outcome is worse than that of another choice and joy if their outcome is better. The utility function is then modified so that the utility obtained from choosing item A is a composite of the utility of that item when considered in isolation from other choices (called "choiceless utility") and the prospective psychic gains or losses that come from regret or joy when item A is considered in relation to other possible choices. Josephs et al. (1992) extend regret theory by arguing that the degree of regret decision makers feel is negatively related to their strength of self-esteem.

In a later paper Loomes and Sugden (1986) take their basic model developed for regret theory and incorporate the emotions of disappointment and elation. While regret and rejoicing arise from the utility experienced when one good is chosen over another, disappointment and elation arise from the unexpected gain or loss of utility experienced for a single good relative to what was expected *ex ante* to choosing it. They use the model to show that it can account for empirically observed violations of the transitivity axiom of subjective expected utility theory. They reject the argument, however, that the resulting choices—even if intransitive—are either nonrational or evidence against rational choice theory. Rather, they argue that emotions should be incorporated into rational choice theory, thus broadening both the concept of rationality and the reach of the theory.

Another emotion that can disrupt well-ordered preference relations is envy. Envy is one of a larger class of emotions that arise from some form of interpersonal comparison. Mui (1995) gives numerous empirical examples of envy in action. A Chinese villager was well liked by his neighbors, for instance, until he began to get rich through various business ventures. The neighbors became envious of his success, and not only did their friendliness quickly turn to hostility but they also surreptitiously destroyed his property. Analytically, envy can be represented by including person B's resource endowment (or utility level) as an argument in person A's utility function, in effect making envy a form of negative externality for person A. Holding person B's endowment constant, well-ordered indifference curves for various goods can be generated for person A; an increase in person B's endowment, however, creates a condition of envy, and person A's indifference curves shift inward (showing that the utility associated with any combination of goods is now lower). Emotions can thus make preference relations unstable, albeit in predictable ways.

Decision Making

The fourth step in the behavioral chain represented in Figure 5.1 is decision making. In the previous step behavior has been motivated by the existence of needs and wants; now the organism must use its mental capabilities to choose the course of action that best satisfies these needs and wants, subject to the constraints imposed on choice by the environment.

Conventional neoclassical economic theory, as earlier noted, makes strong assumptions about the decision-making capacity of the human agent. In textbook models, the human agent is typically assumed to have complete and objective knowledge of the environment and the mental ability to effortlessly and costlessly calculate the behavioral choice that maximizes utility. More advanced models may relax certain of the assumptions by making outcomes probabilistic, such as in subjective expected utility theory, or by making the acquisition of information costly, such as in search theory. In most of mainstream economics, however, the core assumption that human agents have the mental ability and motivation to calculate optimal outcomes is seldom questioned or relaxed. The opposite side of the coin is that the theory almost completely neglects the role of emotion in decision making. The "economic man" in mainstream economics is very similar to

Mr. Spock in the *Star Trek* TV series—a completely dispassionate decision maker who makes choices solely based on logic and facts.

The model of man in rational choice theory has of course been the object of a long and spirited critique. Best known and most influential among the critics is Herbert Simon. Simon (1982) proposed that the "perfect rationality" of neoclassical economics be replaced with a model of "bounded rationality," in which behavior and choice are purposeful and reasoned but subject to biases, errors, and suboptimization due to cognitive and informational limitations. Simon gave little attention to emotions as a cause of bounded rationality, although bounded rationality was seen as having emotional consequences and implications. For example, Williamson's (1985) theory of new institutional economics makes use of bounded rationality to explain positive transaction cost and the origin of hierarchical business firms and other forms of economic organization. Because of bounded rationality, contracts are incomplete and market exchange becomes subject to a number of distortions and inefficiencies due to opportunism, moral hazard, principal-agent problems, and asymmetric information. To avoid these costs, economic agents sometimes find it advantageous to internalize market exchange by forming multiperson firms and using command and authority, rather than demand/supply and price, to coordinate economic activity. One of the advantages of internalization, according to Williamson, is that it promotes trust and cooperation and thereby efficiency—dispositions and outcomes undercut by negative emotions of fear, insecurity, and aggressive egoism that arise from human behavior in competitive, self-interested contexts.

In a recent article (Kaufman 1999a) I have suggested that Simon's concept of bounded rationality could be extended and enriched by a more explicit incorporation of emotions. I noted, first, that Simon drew part of his inspiration for the concept of bounded rationality from the work of institutional economist John Commons (1934) and, second, that Commons described the typical human condition to be one of purposeful behavior mixed with significant elements of "stupidity, passion, and ignorance" (p. 874). Simon's notion of bounded rationality thus corresponds to the two factors of "stupidity" (limited mental cognitive ability) and "ignorance" (limited knowledge) but largely omits the role of "passion" (human emotional states). This omission is unfortunate, I argue, for emotions are in several respects central to decision making and the quality of the choices that arise from it.

A traditional and still widely held view is that emotions are inimical to optimal decision making. Flin and colleagues state, for example, that "the traditional literature generally concludes that stress has a profoundly negative impact on decision making" (1997, 3). Certainly each reader of this essay has personally experienced making decisions that were substantially influenced by emotions and were later regretted, be it punching a wall in a fit of anger, engaging in unsafe sex in the heat of the moment, or impulsively buying a new car. These departures from rationality are real and will be discussed below; less well known and appreciated are the positive effect emotions have on decision making.

A growing body of evidence indicates that emotions are important to effective decision making and in many ways are functional for goal attainment. Perhaps the clearest evidence comes from studies of people with brain damage who had unimpaired cognitive abilities but suffered a complete loss of emotion. The speed of decision making noticeably degenerated as subjects spent hours deliberating over even relatively insignificant choices (what TV program to watch), while many of the choices they finally made (as in gambling experiments) were suboptimal (Damasio 1994). Also apropos is the recent literature on "emotional intelligence" (EQ), the major point of which is that success in life is materially helped by having the right portfolio of emotions and knowing how to skillfully manage them (Goleman 1995).

The degree to which emotions can enhance and impair decision making can be better understood with the concept of arousal. Arousal occurs when an organism is activated by a stimulus. The strength of activation (or energy flow) can range from very low to very high. Considerable evidence indicates that arousal has an inverted-U-shaped relation with the quality of task performance, a relationship often called the Yerkes-Dodson law. A well-known example is test taking (Ashcraft and Faust 1994). When arousal is low, the student taking the test is listless and uninvolved, and the test score is likely to be low; as arousal increases, so does the mental activity devoted to information processing, memory recall, and problem-solving, and the test score rises. But at a very high level of arousal the test score falls because excessive emotional charge inhibits lucid thinking, blocks memory and information processing, and leads to disruptive bodily reactions (a racing pulse, trembling hands). What is true for a specific mental task is also true, I argue, for decision making as a whole. Thus, three implications are derived: emotions can both hinder and enhance effective decision making; bounded rationality arises from not only limited human cognition and imperfect information but also extremes in emotional arousal; and the optimal level of emotion arousal for decision making is at an interior point on the arousal continuum.

In an interesting application of these ideas, Bardwick (1991) examined the influence of various levels of arousal and stress on the quality of management decision making in corporations before and after implementation of a downsizing/restructuring program. She concluded that these programs have both beneficial and harmful effects. The effects can be beneficial because the heightened stress and arousal level jolt managers out of a productivity-sapping sense of complacency and entitlement; they can be harmful because if the programs are sufficiently draconian, they unleash such rampant fear and insecurity that "the whole quality of decision-making suffers" (p. 34).

Action

The fourth step in the behavioral process depicted in Figure 5.1 is action—the initiation and completion of behavior to obtain the desired outcome. It is at this step that the psychological process of motivation becomes observable.

Emotions provide much of the fuel that energizes action. Emotions also shape and guide the direction of action. In some cases emotions lead to action that largely bypasses reasoned thought and calculation. The influence of high arousal has already been cited, but other reasons also exist. People sometimes take action that is largely emotion-driven, such as when fear motivates a person to stand back from the edge of a tall building or cliff even when a window or secure fence prevents falling. Actions that may not meet the norms of rationality also arise from emotions that result from blocked goal attainment, such as acts of violence committed by drivers suffering from the frustration of slow-moving traffic ("road rage"). A much larger class of human actions are more clearly the product of rational thought, although here again emotions are important to determining the direction and intensity of behavior. A popular theory of motivation, for example, is "expectancy × value" theory (Reeve 2001). It hypothesizes that the motivation to approach or avoid an object or event is the product of two factors: expectancy (the probability of success) and value (subjective attraction or aversion). Emotions thus influence motivation and action as they affect expectancy and/or value.

Several examples provide insight on the influence of emotions on human action in an economic context. The first concerns predicting stock prices and the time-series behavior of the stock market (Ackert, Church, and Deaves 2003). Based on the rational actor model and theory of competitive markets, financial economists have developed the efficient markets model of financial equities and the "random walk" theory of stock prices. The efficient markets model predicts that the price of corporate stocks will accurately reflect their underlying economic value, based on trading by large numbers of buyers and sellers with access to all currently available information relevant to future corporate earnings, while the random walk theory hypothesizes that future stock prices are unpredictable since their mean value already incorporates all known information and thus the only remaining source of price variation is a random error term. These theories thus preclude the existence of sustained bubbles in stock prices and suggest that it is impossible for individual traders to beat the market average in the long run.

In an early review, Eugene Fama remarked that "support of the efficient markets model is extensive, and (somewhat uniquely in economics) contradictory evidence is sparse" (1970, 416), while several years later Michael Jensen claimed that "there is no other proposition in economics which has more solid empirical evidence supporting it" (1978, 95). These positions have more recently been called into question, however. In his book *Irrational Exuberance,* for example, Robert Shiller claims that investors' emotional state "is no doubt one of the most important factors causing the bull market [of the late 1990s]" (2000, 57), while economic forecaster Donald Ratajczak states, "Emotions matter in investments, despite all attempts to put them aside" (1994, 17). Much earlier Keynes (1936) made much the same point when he identified "animal spirits" as an important influence on investment decisions.

Emotions may potentially affect investment decisions through several different channels. One is through the influence of optimism and pessimism. Katona (1975) was an early proponent of the view that part of the cause of business cycles is that in the early stage of an expansion consumers become more optimistic as jobs and income start to grow and their more upbeat mood causes them to increase spending more than otherwise, with the reverse process happening in downturns. For this reason, economic forecasters regularly include as an explanatory variable in the consumption function a measure of consumer sentiment. Swings in optimism and pessimism influence stock markets in much the same way; indeed, traders often explain upward or downward movements in stock prices as a reflection of shifts in buyer sentiment. Of course, buyer sentiment is itself a function of objective market conditions, but evidence indicates that emotions such as greed and fear that accompany optimism and pessimism also play a role, as they affect both the expectancy and value variables. Optimism and pessimism may also affect investor's degree of risk tolerance (Ackert, Church, and Deaves 2003).

A second channel through which emotions can affect investor buying decisions is called "herd behavior." Herd behavior arises because each investor has incomplete information and observes the behavior of other investors in the belief they may know something she doesn't. Herd behavior may get started, for example, when certain traders see another trader whom they believe to be especially well informed or prescient place a large purchase order, and they immediately follow suit. The actions of this group are observed by other traders, and they too place purchase orders, leading to a cascade of purchase orders and a sudden upward spike in the stock price. Models of herd behavior locate the cause of this phenomenon in information externalities (Banerjee 1992; Teraji 2003), but emotions of fear, greed, envy, and regret can accentuate herding behavior. In this respect, herding behavior is closely related to the bandwagon and snob effects in consumer demand identified by Leibenstein (1950).

A second example of how emotions affect economic action comes from bargaining theory. Some bargaining models imply, for example, that strikes are irrational acts because the company and union could both be better off if they agreed at the strike deadline to the poststrike wage settlement and thereby avoid the costs of striking. A behavioral perspective suggests, however, that this view may be overly simplistic. Cross (1969), for example, develops a bargaining model in which bargainers start the negotiations with overly optimistic expectations and then through a learning process converge toward a settlement. If the bargainers' expectations are significantly overly optimistic or their learning rate is slow, a strike will occur. But Kennan (1986) rejected Cross's explanation for strikes because, he claims, it rests on systematic overoptimism and is thus at odds with the theory of rational expectations. Kaufman (1999b) argues, however, that Cross's position is supported by what psychologists call the "fundamental attribution error"—the tendency of people to systematically overrate the influence and control they have over events in order to heighten their sense of self-efficacy and self-esteem.

Wheeler (1985) advances an alternative behavioral explanation for strikes that also provides a central role for emotions. The linchpin of his model is frustration-aggression theory. Frustration is an emotion that arises from blocked goal attainment due to the perceived obstruction or influence of a third party. Low to moderate levels of frustration can be functional in that the human agent is motivated to exert greater effort and thought to solving the problem. As frustration grows, however, emotional feelings increasingly cloud rational decision making until the person finally "loses it" and resorts to acts of violence and aggression against the person or thing blocking goal attainment. Wheeler hypothesizes that the frustration-aggression mechanism explains many strikes. Research shows, for example, that strikes increase during periods of inflation. A behavioral explanation is that the rank and file experience mounting frustration and anger as they see their real wages eroded by higher prices while their nominal wages are locked in by a multiyear contract, leading to a cathartic and not entirely rational (in dollar and cents terms) resort to strike action.

A third example of how emotions can affect the course of economic action comes from game theory. A central issue addressed in prisoner's-dilemma-type games is to discover the conditions that facilitate a movement to a cooperative outcome on the part of self-interested agents. One device is precommitment—a pledge by each agent to avoid opting for the outcome that maximizes short-run self-interest at the other's expense. Making a credible and enforceable precommitment in a market context can be difficult, however, because of frequent turnover among buyers and sellers and a legal ban on agreements that restrain trade. According to Frank (1988), one device that market participants use to establish a precommitment to a cooperative outcome is various emotional cues and signals. In the labor market, for example, companies proclaim to job applicants that they place great importance on honesty and fair dealing, while job applicants may send signals to employers about their cooperative intentions by emphasizing desire for a long-term employment relationship or involvement in other-regarding civic, charitable, or religious organizations.

Utility Change

The final step in the behavioral chain represented in Figure 5.1 is the change in utility that results from the action undertaken in the previous step. The change in utility may be either positive or negative, depending on whether the environment has become more accommodative or restrictive.

Standard economic theory treats the change in utility experienced by the economic agent as the end of the behavioral process. That is, behavior starts at the initial equilibrium position, an exogenous change takes place in the budget constraint, and—faced with a new incentive structure—the agent moves to a new equilibrium position. At this point matters rest until a new exogenous shock again changes the budget constraint.

Behavioral economics suggests the story is not quite so simple or easily worked out. The major amendment a behavioral perspective introduces is to note the existence of various feedback loops between changes in utility and earlier parts of the behavioral sequence. I will highlight two such loops and the role of emotions therein.

One feedback loop goes from change in utility to goal and wants. In the standard model the agent's tastes and preferences are independent of both the budget constraint and the experienced consumption bundle. But evidence from psychology suggests that human preferences and affective levels of happiness are, in fact, adaptive and endogenous (Frederick and Loewenstein 1999; Simon, Kraweczyk, and Holyoak 2004). One such route is explained by aspiration-level theory. Research shows that aspirations (targets) are not given but rise with success and fall with failure, thus causing indifference curves to change shape and possibly shift. A second route is explained by cognitive dissonance theory. Cognitive dissonance occurs when there is a disjunction between what one experiences and expects or believes; the larger the gap, the more unpleasant the hedonic sensation. Cognitive dissonance can be reduced by either changing one's beliefs and expectations to better fit experience or undertaking action so that experience better fits expectations and beliefs. Often the former is the easier option, implying a mental adjustment of preferences so they better align with the budget constraint. A third route is adaptation theory. As earlier noted, psychological research shows that the affective sensation derived from a repeated stimulus declines over time. An economic application is the concept of a *hedonic treadmill:* the notion that people initially experience pleasure from an improved circumstance (e.g., higher income) but then adapt to it over time until hedonic affect returns to a zero level (neither pleasant or unpleasant). Easterlin (2001), for example, has used this concept to explain the "paradox of happiness"—the fact that even as real income has increased significantly in the United States and other countries over several decades, people in national surveys nonetheless report stable or even declining levels of happiness.

A second feedback loop is from change in utility to action. This feedback loop arises from various interpersonal comparisons that are traditionally omitted from standard microeconomic theory. Assume an agent experiences an action and a consequent change in utility. If these are experienced in isolation, no further adjustment in action may arise. But, in general, people compare their outcomes with those of other people or situations, and these comparisons often precipitate a new round of action. In effect, utility functions are interdependent, and a utility change for person A leads to a consequent change in behavior for person B (Frank 1985). An important form such comparisons take is considerations of fairness and equity. Although equity is notoriously difficult to measure, conceptually it rests on two fundamental considerations: first, that an appropriate balance exists between inputs and outputs (for example, the pay is commensurate with the amount of work performed), and second, that the decision process used to determine the outcome is procedurally correct (Adams 1963; Sheppard, Lewicki, and Minton 1992). These twin dimensions of equity are often called *distributive justice* and *procedural justice.* If the action in step four of the behavioral chain violates an agent's conception of equity, his experienced utility change will decline and set off consequent reactions. If a pay increase is judged unfair, for example, an employee may quit, shirk, or form a union. Considerations of fairness, equity, and reciprocity have also been found to influence a wide range of other forms of economic behavior, such as altruism, cooperation, and public goods provision (Kahneman, Knetsch, and Thaler 1986; Fehr and Schmidt 1999).

CONCLUSION

The project of behavioral economics, as I see it, is to enrich standard economic theory with concepts and theories from psychology. One area of psychology that has until very recently received very little attention from economists is human emotions. Indeed, the main direction in years past has been to remove as much emotional content as possible from economic theory, epitomized by the emotionless rational actor model of modern mainstream economics.

As I have endeavored to indicate, a closer look at the rational actor model reveals that emotion, mood, and affect are still present within it, if perhaps disguised or emptied of behavioral content. I have also endeavored to indicate how this model can be modified and extended by incorporating the psychological concept of emotion. Toward this end, emotions were integrated into a five-step model of the human behavioral process. Although I hope this is of interest for its own sake, conventional economists will rightfully ask, "So what?" with respect to either economic theorizing or understanding and predicting economic behavior. Thus I have provided numerous examples throughout this chapter to demonstrate how consideration of emotions either suggests a revision of economic theory or sheds new light on economic behavior. With regard to economic theory, for example, taking emotions seriously strongly suggests that utility functions are interdependent and preferences are endogenous; with respect to human behavior, emotions explain a number of anomalies and puzzles, such as departures from the outcomes predicted by standard rational choice theory, acts of altruistic self-sacrifice, task performance done independent of external rewards, and the pervasive role of fairness in economic exchange.

Broadly viewed, perhaps the most interesting insight about emotions is that they play a role in human behavior very similar to prices in markets. That is, both people and markets can be viewed as a control/coordination system. To operate effectively, such a system needs a constant flow of information about changes in the environment and the status of goal attainment. Emotions are one way this information is provided to people, while prices serve the same purpose in markets. The interesting question for economists is to what extent emotions and prices effectively serve this coordination/control function. Mainstream economics has largely chosen to ignore the role of emotions and instead use models in which rationality and competition ensure prices alone effectively perform these tasks. The contribution of behavioral economics is to demonstrate that in real-world economies, where people and markets are imperfect and contracts are incomplete, emotions and other psychological factors also play an important coordination/control role. Frequently emotions, like prices, are a stabilizing element in human behavior and the market process and help both operate more effectively. In some cases, however, emotions are a destabilizing force and source of dysfunctional behavior—just as price movements sometimes destabilize markets and lead to inefficient outcomes. Exploring these parallels is an exciting but virtually untapped topic in economics.

REFERENCES

Ackert, Lucy, Bryan Church, and Richard Deaves. 2003. "Emotion and Financial Markets." *Economic Review—Federal Reserve Bank of Atlanta* 88: 33–41.

Adams, J. Stacy. 1963. "Toward an Understanding of Inequity." *Journal of Abnormal Psychology* 67: 422–36.

Argyle, Michael. 2001. *The Psychology of Happiness*. London: Routledge.

Ashcraft, H., and M. Faust. 1994. "Mathematics Anxiety and Mental Mathematics Performance: An Exploratory Study." *Cognition and Emotion* 8: 97–125.

Bagwell, Laurie, and Douglas Bernheim. 1996. "Veblen Effects in a Theory of Conspicuous Consumption." *American Economic Review* 86: 349–74.

Banaji, Mahzarin, and Deborah Prentice. 1994. "The Self in Social Contexts." *Annual Review of Psychology* 45: 297–332.

Banerjee, A.V. 1992. "A Simple Model of Herd Behavior." *Quarterly Journal of Economics* 107: 797–817.

Bardwick, Judith. 1991. *Danger in the Comfort Zone*. New York: AMACOM.

Becker, Gary. 1976. *The Economic Approach to Human Behavior*. Chicago: University of Chicago Press.

———. 1991. "A Note on Restaurant Pricing and Other Examples of Social Influence on Price." *Journal of Political Economy* 99: 1109–16.

Bell, David. 1982. "Regret in Decision-Making under Uncertainty." *Operations Research* 30: 961–81.

Blanchflower, David, and Andrew Oswald. 2004. "Money, Sex, and Happiness: An Empirical Study." NBER Working Paper 10499. Cambridge, MA: National Bureau of Economic Research.

Bowles, Samuel. 1998. "Endogenous Preferences: The Cultural Consequences of Markets and Other Economic Institutions." *Journal of Economic Literature* 36: 75–111.

Commons, John. 1919. *Industrial Goodwill.* New York: McGraw-Hill.

———. 1934. *Institutional Economics: Its Place in Political Economy.* New York: Macmillan.

Cross, John. 1969. *The Economics of Bargaining.* New York: Basic Books.

Damasio, Antonio. 1994. *Descartes' Error: Emotion, Reason, and the Human Brain.* New York: Putnam.

Deci, Edward. 1975. *Internal Motivation.* New York: Plenum.

Duesenberry, James. 1949. *Income, Saving, and the Theory of Consumer Behavior.* Cambridge, MA: Harvard University Press.

Easterlin, Richard. 2001. "Income and Happiness: Towards a Unified Theory." *Economic Journal* 114: 465–85.

Elster, Jon. 1998. "Emotions and Economic Theory." *Journal of Economic Literature* 36: 47–74.

Fama, Eugene. 1970. "Efficient Capital Markets: A Review of Theory and Empirical Work." *Journal of Finance* 25: 383–417.

Fehr, Ernst, and Klaus Schmidt. 1999. "A Theory of Fairness, Competition, and Cooperation." *Quarterly Journal of Economics* 114: 817–68.

Flin, Rhona, Eduardo Salas, Michael Strub, and Lynne Martin. 1997. *Decision Making Under Stress.* Brookfield: Ashgate.

Forgas, Joseph. 2000. "Affect and Information Processing Strategies: An Interactive Relationship." In J. Forgas, ed., *Feelings and Thinking: The Role of Affect in Social Cognition,* 253–82. New York: Cambridge University Press.

Foster, Michael. 1993. "Labor Economics and Public Policy: Dominance of Constraints or Preferences?" In W. Darity Jr., ed., *Labor Economics: Problems in Analyzing Labor Markets,* 269–94. Boston: Kluwer.

Frank, Robert. 1985. *Choosing the Right Pond.* New York: Oxford University Press.

———. 1988. *Passions Within Reason.* New York: Norton.

Frederick, Shane, and George Loewenstein. 1999. "Hedonic Adaptation." In D. Kahneman, E. Diener, and N. Schwarz, eds., *Well-Being: The Foundation of Hedonic Psychology,* 302–29. New York: Russell Sage Foundation.

Frey, Bruno, and Alois Stutzer. 2002. *Happiness and Economics: How the Economy and Institutions Affect Well-Being.* Princeton, NJ: Princeton University Press.

Frijda, Nico. 1999. "Emotions and Hedonic Experience." In D. Kahneman, E. Diener, and N. Schwarz, eds., *Well-Being: The Foundation of Hedonic Psychology,* 190–210. New York: Russell Sage Foundation.

Georgescu-Roegen, Nicholas. 1968. "Utility." In *International Encyclopedia of the Social Sciences* 16:236–67. New York: Macmillan.

Gifford, Adam. 2002. "Emotion and Self-Control." *Journal of Economic Behavior and Organization* 49: 113–30.

Goleman, Daniel. 1995. *Emotional Intelligence.* New York: Bantam.

Hirschman, Albert. 1977. *The Passions and the Interests.* Princeton, NJ: Princeton University Press.

Isen, Alice. 2000. "Positive Affect and Decision-Making." In M. Lewis and J. Haviland-Jones, eds., *Handbook of Emotions,* 2nd ed., 417–35. New York: Guilford Press.

Jensen, Michael. 1978. "Some Anomalous Evidence Regarding Market Efficiency." *Journal of Financial Economics* 6: 95–101.

Josephs, R., R. Larrick, P. Steele, and R. Nisbett. 1992. "Protecting the Self from the Negative Consequences of Risky Decisions." *Journal of Personality and Social Psychology* 62: 26–37.

Kahneman, Daniel. 1999. "Objective Happiness." In D. Kahneman, E. Diener, and N. Schwarz, eds., *Well-Being: The Foundation of Hedonic Psychology,* 3–25. New York: Russell Sage Foundation.

Kahneman, Daniel, Ed Diener, and Norbert Schwarz, eds. 1999. *Well-Being: The Foundation of Hedonic Psychology.* New York: Russell Sage Foundation.

Kahneman, Daniel, Jack Knetsch, and Richard Thaler. 1986. "Fairness as a Constraint on Profit-Seeking: Entitlements in the Market." *American Economic Review* 76: 728–41.

Kahneman, Daniel, and Amos Tversky. 2000. *Choices, Values, and Frames.* New York: Cambridge University Press.

Kahneman, Daniel, Peter Wakker, and Rakesh Sharin. 1997. "Back to Bentham? Explorations of Experienced Utility." *Quarterly Journal of Economics* 112: 375–405.

Katona, George. 1975. *Psychological Economics.* New York: Elsevier.

Kaufman, Bruce. 1999a. "Emotional Arousal as a Source of Bounded Rationality." *Journal of Economic Behavior and Organization* 38: 135–44.

————. 1999b. "Expanding the Behavioral Foundations of Labor Economics." *Industrial and Labor Relations Review* 52: 361–92.

Kennan, John. 1986. "The Economics of Strikes." In O. Ashenfelter and R. Layard, eds., *Handbook of Labor Economics,* 2:1091–137. New York: North-Holland.

Keynes, John. 1936. *The General Theory of Employment, Interest, and Money.* London: Harcourt Brace.

Kohn, Alfie. 1993. *Punished by Rewards.* New York: Houghton Mifflin.

Landsburg, Steven. 1993. *The Armchair Economist: Economics and Everyday Life.* New York: Free Press.

Lane, Robert. 1991. *The Market Experience.* New York: Cambridge University Press.

————. 2000. *The Loss of Happiness in Market Democracies.* New Haven, CT: Yale University Press.

Lazarus, Richard. 1991. *Emotion and Adaptation.* New York: Oxford University Press.

Lea, Stephen, Roger Tarpy, and Paul Webley. 1987. *The Individual in the Economy: A Textbook of Economic Psychology.* New York: Cambridge University Press.

Leibenstein, Harvey. 1950. "Bandwagon, Snob, and Veblen Effects in the Theory of Consumers' Demand." *Quarterly Journal of Economics* 64: 183–207.

Locke, Edwin, and Gary Latham. 1990. *A Theory of Goal-Setting.* Englewood Cliffs: Prentice-Hall.

Loewenstein, George. 2000. "Emotions in Economic Theory and Economic Behavior." *American Economic Review* 90: 426–32.

Loomes, Graham, and Robert Sugden. 1982. "Regret Theory: A Alternative Theory of Rational Choice Under Uncertainty." *Economic Journal* 92: 805–24.

————. 1986. "Disappointment and Dynamic Consistency of Choice Under Uncertainty." *Review of Economic Studies* 53: 271–82.

Mack, Mary. 1969. *A Bentham Reader.* New York: Pegasus.

Marshall, Alfred. 1890. *Principles of Economics.* London: Macmillan.

Mellers, Barbara. 2000. "Choice and the Relative Preference of Consequences." *Psychological Bulletin* 126: 910–24.

Mui, Vai-Lam. 1995. "The Economics of Envy." *Journal of Economic Behavior and Organization* 26: 311–36.

Munnell, Alicia. 1986. *Lessons from the Negative Income Tax Experiments.* Washington, DC: Brookings Institution.

Oatley, Keith, and Jennifer Jenkins. 1996. *Understanding Emotions.* New York: Blackwell.

Panksepp, Jaak. 2000. "Emotions as Natural Kinds Within the Mammalian Brain." In M. Lewis and J. Haviland-Jones, eds., *Handbook of Emotion,* 2nd ed., 137–56. New York: Guilford Press.

Parducci, Allen. 1995. *Happiness, Pleasure, and Judgment: The Contextual Theory and Its Applications.* Mahwah: Lawrence Erlbaum Associates.

Peterson, Christopher. 1999. "Personal Control and Well-Being." In D. Kahneman, E. Diener, and N. Schwarz, eds., *Well-Being: The Foundation of Hedonic Psychology,* 288–301. New York: Russell Sage Foundation.

Postlewaite, Andrew. 1998. "The Social Basis of Interdependent Preferences." *European Economic Review* 42: 779–800.

Rabin, Matthew. 1998. "Psychology and Economics." *Journal of Economic Literature* 36: 11–46.

Ratajczak, Donald. 1994. "Can Stock Markets Be Modeled?" *Journal of the American Society of CLU and ChFC* 48: 17–20.

Reeve, Johnmarshall. 2001. *Understanding Motivation and Emotion,* 3rd ed. New York: Harcourt.

Rotter, J. 1966. "Generalized Expectancies for Internal Versus External Control of Reinforcement." *Psychological Monographs* 80: 1–28.

Schwarz, Norbert, and Fritz Strack. 1999. "Reports of Subjective Well-being: Judgmental Processes and Their Methodological Implications." In D. Kahneman, E. Diener, and N. Schwarz, eds., *Well-Being: Foundations of Hedonic Psychology,* 61–84. New York: Russell Sage Foundation.

Scitovsky, Tibor. 1976. *The Joyless Economy.* New York: Oxford University Press.

Seligman, M. 1976. *Learned Helplessness and Depression in Animals and Man.* Morristown, NJ: General Learning Press.

Sheppard, Blair, Roy Lewicki, and John Minton. 1992. *Organizational Justice: The Search for Fairness in the Workplace.* New York: Lexington Books.

Shiller, Robert. 2000. *Irrational Exuberance.* Princeton, NJ: Princeton University Press.

Simon, Dan, Daniel Krawezyk, and Keith Holyoak. 2004. "Construction of Preferences by Constraint Satisfaction." *Psychological Science* 15: 331–36.

Simon, Herbert. 1982. *Models of Bounded Rationality*. Cambridge, MA: MIT Press.

Smith, Adam. 1759. *The Theory of Moral Sentiments.* London: A. Millar.

Stigler, George, and Gary Becker. 1977. "De Gustibus Non Est Disputandum." *American Economic Review* 67: 76–90.

Taylor, Lester. 1988. "A Model of Consumption and Demand Based on Psychological Opponent Processes." In P. Albanese, ed., *Psychological Foundations of Economic Behavior,* 35–58. New York: Praeger.

Teraji, Shinji. 2003. "Herd Behavior and the Quality of Opinions." *Journal of Economic Behavior and Organization* 32: 661–73.

Thaler, Richard, and H. Shefrin. 1981. "An Economic Theory of Self-Control." *Journal of Political Economy* 89: 392–406.

Veblen, Thorstein. 1899. *The Theory of the Leisure Class: A Study of Institutions.* New York: Macmillan.

Veenhoven, Ruut. 2003. "Hedonism and Happiness." *Journal of Happiness Studies* 4: 437–57.

Wheeler, Hoyt. 1985. *An Integrative Theory of Industrial Conflict.* Columbia: University of South Carolina Press.

Williamson, Oliver. 1985. *The Economic Institutions of Capitalism.* New York: Free Press.

CHAPTER 6

ON THE ECONOMICS OF SUBSELVES

Toward a Metaeconomics

GARY D. LYNNE

> When is it useful or not useful to look upon an individual as a single unit, a "Cohesive Self"? When is it useful or not useful to look upon any one as being constituted of many parts, each with an identity of its own? When is it more useful to see ourselves as part of the greater whole? I use the term "useful" rather than "true" since all are true—simultaneously and at all times.
> *(Beahrs 1982, 4–5, quoted in Rowan 1990, 190)*

> It is not so much that there is any real conceptual objection to the idea [of subselves or subparts] . . . nor is it the case that researchers are prejudiced against the notion . . . but rather that history has pushed people in the direction of ignoring or downplaying any such schema, and that for many years philosophy appeared not to give it house room.
> *(Rowan 1990, 191)*

> Researchers await a new theorist who will assimilate the old theories and present an integrated theory incorporating previous concepts and propositions. A cynical colleague of mine once said that such a task requires the services of someone in marketing because the ideas will not be new ones but merely old ones presented in new packaging.
> *(Lester 1995, 161)*

The idea that human nature is best characterized as having at least two subselves or tendencies goes back at least to Plato, who suggested the tripartite nature of humans in his metaphor of the charioteer and two horses: one horse is the prudent part, the other is the insolent part, and the third (the charioteer) the part that deals with the conflict (noted by Rowan [1990, 11], who also points to other historical traces of the idea of subselves in an extensive review of the subselves literature). Given the long history of the concept, economists need not be surprised by the suggestion that Adam Smith also engaged the idea in thinking about what drove the wealth of nations. The metaphor of the two horses has been recently revived in a slightly different context, that of searching for a core set of ideas for the emerging theory of ecological economics, by Hayes and Lynne (2004), wherein one horse is the egoistic self-interest, one horse is the empathetic other-interest, and the charioteer, oftentimes without sufficient will and discipline, and after some help from the outside, must resolve the inherent conflict between the horses. The result is going beyond both interests to the sum being larger than the parts and moving both economy and society to a higher plane. This metaphor also has a commonsense element to it: when asked, people typically indicate that they have within them two or more subselves, or tendencies, and experience conflict between them.

MOST INDIVIDUALS SEE MORE THAN ONE SUBSELF

How many subselves or tendencies? Empirical research by Lester (1992) shows a mean response of three and a half subselves, and each subself may be ideally suited to the role it plays (Lester 1998, 538). Rowan found a range of zero to eighteen subselves and argued that four to eight was the normal range (1990, 47). Berne (1961) posited the presence of five subselves: a Child (with the subsystems Adaptive Child and Free Child), a Parent (with the subsystems Nurturing Parent and Critical Parent), and an Adult (the rational agent in charge at least some if not most of the time). Boulding (1968, cited in Lester 1987, 606) pointed to several subsystems, with one moderating the decision-making process or executing the decisions. Margolis (1982) argued for a version with two selves, the selfish self and the self oriented to the group. Hirschman (1985) saw human behavior as far more complex than the mere pursuit of a single-minded self-interest. Etzioni (1986) pointed to two kinds of utility, the material and the moral, again suggesting two subselves or tendencies (the I and the We), both of which need to be represented in a new economic theory that includes the moral dimension (see Etzioni 1988). Khalil (1997) points to how economics as practiced is amoral because it focuses only on the rational-choice-based pursuit of self-interest narrowly defined to exclude the moral sentiments. In more philosophical terms, there is also Buber's (1922) notion of the "I-It" and the "I-Thou" in interrelationships among individuals, with I-Thou reflecting the integration of the two interests. This notion has recently been brought into the understanding of intrapersonal relatedness among subselves by Cooper (2003, 140), who suggests that a kind of "I-Thou" emerges within the self. Cooper refers to this as the "I-I," wherein one subpart within the self confirms another subpart, with conflicts within the self resolved. This is to say, the "I-I" relationship needs to be established within the unified self. The moral dimension is thus integrated with the hedonistic dimension within the self. Elster (1985) highlights the many kinds of selves identified in the literature, including the loosely integrated self, Faustian selves, hierarchical selves, successive selves, and parallel selves, as well as the Homo economicus and Homo sociologicus concepts of the private and public self, which really cannot be separated. There is also Elster's (1979) problem, conceived of in terms of the tale of Ulysses, of how to manage the instinct to unite with what is signified by "the sirens" while still serving the crew and protecting the ship. Schelling (1984) tells a similar story, noting that often one will manage the tendency to pursue hedonistic self-interest (e.g., drinking too much at a party) by asking others to intervene (e.g., giving one's car keys to a designated driver—ensuring an empathy-induced pursuit of a shared other-interest in road safety). Sober and Wilson (1998) see each individual as operating in both the egoistic-hedonistic domain and the empathetic-altruistic domain, likely at the same time, and suggest that simply facilitating individual expression in the latter domain may bring out that expression—that is, empathy-altruism is a kind of latent tendency that will be expressed if given the opportunity. Söderbaum (2000) offered the idea of a political-economic/social person as well as neoclassical economics' self-interest-seeking economic person residing within the same individual. Cory (1999, 2000a, 2000b, 2004) sees a more complex tripartite self, after the neuroscience notion of the triune brain (see MacLean 1990), with an egoistic self-interested part, an empathetic other-interested part, and a dynamic and rational balancer focused on resolving the inherent conflict. Lux (2003) points to the failure of monomotive theories, noting that people go beyond just seeking a self-interest-based profit.

TOWARD AN INTEGRATION OF IDEAS ABOUT SUBSELVES
INTO AN ECONOMIC FRAMEWORK

Building on these kinds of themes, I proposed an integrating framework, termed "metaeconomics" (see Lynne 1999), and supported the proposal through a series of empirical studies suggesting that a motive beyond self-interest was at work (Lynne, Shonkwiler, and Rola 1988; Lynne and Rola 1988; Lynne 1995; Lynne, Casey, et al., 1995; Lynne and Casey, 1998). I also drew heavily on Etzioni (1986, 1988) in suggesting that individuals pursue at least two utilities, represented in an "I-utility" and a "We-utility," with the conflict resolved by the Strict Father or through negotiation in a Nurturing Parent environment, in either case with discipline of some kind needed over these two subselves (Lynne 1999). The role of conflicting value systems in driving higher transaction costs had been already demonstrated empirically in Lynne, Shonkwiler, and Wilson 1991. In Lynne 2002, I shifted the terminology to be more in concordance with the conflict model of Cory (1999), speaking instead of self-interest and other-interest, and the rational (choice) balancer. Also, in Lynne 2002, I reemphasized the notion of possible incommensurability between the interests (Etzioni [1986] refers to this as the "irreducible" problem), at least for some economic actions, if not necessarily for all. The matter of whether these two utilities are commensurable or not is an empirical question that has yet to be answered. In Hayes and Lynne (2004), the terminology of self-interest and other-interest is fully integrated into the theory, while recognizing that the two interests are inherently in conflict and thus that an integrator/balancer is needed to resolve the conflict. A different kind of value theory is introduced, suggesting that value rationally emerges on a higher plane from the interaction and feedback between the two tendencies. This notion also seems consistent with the notion of "process rationality" (Altman 2004, 11), which is concerned with how the objectives and preferences evolve—a common theme in behavioral economics. It is also consistent with the old but solid idea from institutional economics that institutions matter (and which V. Smith's work has demonstrated empirically; see Smith 1991), that is, that the relationships matter. Yet rational value could not emerge during the decision-making process if the conflict could not be somehow resolved, which may not be accomplished easily, if at all (see Moldoveanu and Stevenson 2001), especially if the institution is not workable. Actually, as Lester (2003) notes, this may not be as difficult as they suggest. In fact, this conflict resolution process may be likened to the way conflict is resolved in small groups, with the group more often than not achieving an outcome qualitatively different from what any one individual can achieve alone (also see Lester 1985). We would have to assume that the underlying institution within the group and perhaps even within the individual—serving to network and integrate across the subparts—is workable.[1] The idea of rational value emerging during the decision-making process is not unrelated to the notion of emotions being at the base of all decisions, operating in the background (the subconscious), with the emergence of consciousness a main feature of human process, as demonstrated in our very evolution (see Damasio 1999, esp. 296). It is within the state of consciousness (or awareness, as empirically demonstrated in Kalinowski, Lynne, and Johnson, in press) that the cognitive process of rational choice can operate and the particular orientation of interests can emerge.

THE SUBSELVES IDEA IN ADAM SMITH'S TWO BOOKS

A key element of human nature is missing from microeconomics due to its exclusive focus on self-interest, as described in the Homo economicus version of human nature. We can trace the notion back to Adam Smith:

> It is not from the benevolence of the butcher, the brewer, or the baker, that we expect our dinner, but from their care for their own interest. We appeal not to their humanity but to their self-interest, and never talk to them of our own necessities, but of their advantages. (Smith 1776, Book I, Chapter 2)

But Smith also understood there was another element to human nature that needed to be included in the economic framework:

> How selfish soever, man may be supposed, there are evidently some principles in his nature, which interest him in the fortune of others, and render their happiness necessary to him, though he derives nothing from it, except the pleasure of seeing it. . . . That we often derive sorrow from the sorrow of others, is a matter of fact too obvious to require any instances to prove it; for this sentiment, like all the other original passions of human nature, is by no means confined to the virtuous and humane, though they perhaps may feel it with the most exquisite sensibility. The greatest ruffian, the most hardened violator of the laws of society, is not altogether without it. (Smith 1790 Part I, Section I, Chapter I, Paragraph 1)

As noted at the outset, this duality in human nature is even in economics, then, going back at least to Smith, suggesting "the Adam Smith problem" or the "two faces problem" (V. Smith 1998). As we will see, metaeconomics resolves the problem by seeing the two interests as arising jointly within the self.[2]

We seek a basis not only in the moral philosophy of Adam Smith but also in holistic psychology. Arguably offering the best holistic theory ever elaborated,[3] Angyal (1941) saw the dualistic (actually tripartite) nature of humans. He noted that the idea of the individual "merely as a participant in economic organization, the *homo economicus,* is only a fiction" (Angyal 1941, 184). Rather, Angyal sees two main tendencies: that toward the autonomous pursuit of self-interest, represented in the Homo economicus construct, and also that toward the homonomous pursuit of unity with others, causes, ideologies, and even places or things (homonomy is what modern literature refers to as "relatedness"; see Deci and Ryan 2000). Also, to achieve mental health and stability in an individual, each person needs to reconcile the two tendencies on this higher plane of neurosis- and depression-free living, suggesting the third part (see Angyal 1965). Perhaps what is true for the individual must also hold for the larger economy and society within which the person lives and contributes, and if so, it is this higher plane that gives hope for moving beyond a discordant society and depressed economy. At minimum, it remains intriguing why the construct of depression is used in standard economic parlance to describe a state of the economy when it is not working well. Yet microeconomics persists in solving the problem of depression by appealing only to the self-interest through such things as lowering interest rates, when in fact it takes far more attention to issues in the shared other-interest (e.g., extending unemployment benefits, which is an expression of empathy, of "walking in their shoes") as well.

Cory captures the essence of the issue:

> The trick or deception of assigning a self-interest motive to everything—even to the most empathetic or altruistic acts—is made plausible by the fact that the reciprocal is always there. There is always an egoistic reciprocal to any empathetic act; and, likewise there is always an empathetic reciprocal to any egoistic act. (Cory 1999, 52)

Drawing on neuroscience research, Cory tells a compelling story of how this dualistic, reciprocal nature is part of our evolutionary legacy, represented in our inherent instinct to be both egoistically self-interested and empathetically other-interested at the same time. The rational, cognitive third part of the brain works (at least in mentally healthy individuals and nondepressed economies) to resolve the inherent conflict between the two largely instinctual, mainly emotive tendencies, which is accomplished through reciprocity. (LeDoux [1996] sees emotion at a more fundamental level than cognition; this is also the message in Damasio 1999.) This reciprocity is ongoing not only among individuals but also within the self, as the subselves aspire to the higher plane in both conscious and unconscious ways. This notion of instinct, perhaps better described as emotion, is akin to Kahneman's (2003, 1451) "intuition," with both ego and empathy being fundamentally emotional instincts. Thus we may act on intuition (on our emotions) and/or we may act with a reasoned, rational-choice-based resolution of the conflict arising in our emotions, once we are consciously aware.

So we need to ask whether it is human nature to pursue an empathetic other-interest as well as an egoistic self-interest, at least if given the opportunity to do so. Sober and Wilson (1998), after an extensive review of the empirical literature, suggest the evidence does not support the proposition that we pursue only one interest in either the egoistic-hedonistic or the empathetic-altruistic domains; rather, it suggests that we have the inherent capability to pursue both, and often do. Gintis, too, argues that we already know human nature to be both selfish and altruistic, albeit "in complex and still to be fully revealed ways" (2000, xxiv), so testing for the two subselves is not the point; rather, what is sought is a better understanding of human nature's complexity. As Henrich and colleagues point out, literally hundreds of economic experiments suggest that people have social preferences and are willing to take action consistent with these preferences even at personal cost to themselves (2004, 8). This is to say that self-sacrifice is very real in day-to-day living, which metaeconomics acknowledges. Yet continued testing is important in that defenders of microeconomics generally want to be shown the power of the new framework. This is the challenge: not only must the framework be rigorously tested, but the metaeconomic analytical machinery offered as a substitute for the microeconomic machinery must be at least as powerful.

INDIFFERENCE CURVES, TWO FIELDS OF UTILITY, AND BUDGET CONSTRAINTS

In this spirit, metaeconomics chooses an approach similar to microeconomics, although microeconomics focuses attention on the household, starts with a single consumer within that household, and uses budget lines and indifference curves built upon the shared notion that this consumer may be sovereign (see Figure 6.1), at least when self-disciplined. As Kahneman, Wakker, and Sarin (1997, 397) have found in experimental testing, however, it may well be justified to apply outside (control) governance of individual consumers, due to their more common choice not to maximize utility, which suggests they may not know "what is good for them" (for example, ignoring the total maximum (dis)utility of being a drug addict and only going after the peak utility at the time of the "hit"). It has also become clear that individuals and firms often lack self-control in environmental actions, further putting in question the notion of consumer sovereignty (or producer sovereignty, in the case of pollution from business firms). Metaeconomics retains the fundamental hope that consumer (and producer) sovereignty can be honored, but it recognizes that the need for outside governance, such as environmental regulation or drug interdiction, is often legitimate when failures of self-control occur, and metaeconomics can model this (i.e., a failure in self-discipline to stay close to 0M may justify a regulation). In effect, the subselves idea and metaeconomics are a response to Leijonhufvad's call for dealing with the "constant criticisms (now ever more documented as legitimate with

Figure 6.1   **Jointly Egoistic Self-interest (I_G) and Empathetic Other-interest (I_M) Indifference Curves for q_2 and q_1**

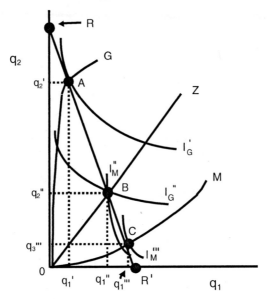

hard empirical evidence)" while recognizing that "neoclassical economics is the core of the subject. Instead of looking for an alternative theory to replace it, we should try to imagine an economic theory that might transcend its limitations" (2004, 5).

In addition to making the matter of self-control visible in the metaeconomic model, the individual consumer needs to be imagined as having at least two fields of utility, with a field in the egoistic-hedonistic, self-interested domain (I_G) and another field in the empathetic-altruistic, other-interested domain (I_M) (see Figure 6.1).[4] It is proposed there are potentially stable preferences arising within each field of utility, with substantive conflict and instability between the two fields. As a result, switching may occur. The breadth of rationality is also expanded; it may indeed be as rational to act mainly on emotional grounds in the I_M domain as it is to do so in the I_G domain, and in most cases it is rational to act mainly on what is emerging from these two emotional grounds in some complex integration after consciously cognitive consideration of both. The I_M domain, in turn, is what drives the underlying rules of the game in social and market interaction, the institution evolving from the shared other-interest learned through interaction and dialogue with others (i.e., the self in effect being defined by such dialogue; see Hermans, Kempen, and van Loon 1992), oftentimes passed down in stories from parent to child, with parent data (I_M) influencing child data (I_G).

The notion that the conflict between two subselves can be rationally resolved is consistent with Berne's (1961) widely accepted idea of an internal Parent, Child, and Adult, with the Adult providing the rationality. Rowan argues that Berne's theory must "obviously have a big part to play in any final synthesis that might be attempted" among the subselves theories (1990, 196). As noted earlier, Lester documents a range in self-reports of three to six subselves (2003, 502). This evidence is consistent with the suggestion in Berne-based transactional psychology for two ego-based childlike parts, two empathy-based parentlike parts, and one rational adultlike part, which yields five subselves easily accommodated within metaeconomics. Each individual, then, is like a small group of subselves having its own dynamic within a system. These subselves search for an "effective synergy" (Lester 1993/94, 318).

PEACE OF MIND AS THE ULTIMATE REASON FOR CHOICE

Given the idea of at least two subselves at work, the overall purpose of choice has changed from pursuing maximum satisfaction of the egoistic self to a focus on pursuing *peace of mind,* which we might use to characterize this effective synergy between the two main subselves.[5] Also, we could predict a dynamic at work within the self and within the markets until this peaceful equilibrium is achieved. This pursuit of maximum peace of mind is more like *satisficing* activity in the other domains (after Simon 1997), which is achieved on 0Z, in particular at point B (Figure 6.1).[6] This contrasts with only a maximizing activity in one domain, on 0G or 0M, achieved at either A or C. In fact, the internal conflict arises from the tendency to want to maximize each interest, which is inherently impossible in that one cannot choose both A and C.

The conflict generally has to be brought into consciousness for it to be resolved in a rational manner; that is, the two paths 0G and 0M, especially the latter, are more in the instincts (as suggested by Cory 1999) or the intuition (after Kahneman 2003), which is based in the emotions (LeDoux 1996; Damasio 1999). So, rational resolution first requires making the feelings explicit and subjecting them to rational thought and consideration. Yet, even if not made conscious, the tension between these two emotion-based tendencies may have been resolved, and at work in the background of the mind for each person operating in the market, and, thus, it follows, in the background of the market. This suggests that efficiency might be achieved and competitive markets might clear as though by magic (we might call it the invisible hand of the market at work) if the two tendencies have been fused within each individual who is active in the market, perhaps at a more unconscious level originating or having been put in place at some earlier time. The integration could arise due to interaction among individuals over many experiences in the market, through which the matter of what unifies them has emerged (e.g., the minimizing of costs and being progressive, both shared values in the modern market economy). These shared values in the other-interested I_M set may already have been fused with a self-interested I_G set on a path like 0Z. Many individuals sharing such a path could then arrive at a competitive equilibrium point B.

This also provides the theoretical basis for explaining the finding in experimental economics that the context or the rules of the game—the "institutions"—matter (again, see Smith 1991, esp. 878–80). The I_M set of rules represented in a shared other-interest gives rise to the institution—the kind of relatedness and unity one holds in common with others. We can also see why the standard economic result that Smith has sometimes found when individuals play the ultimatum and dictator games could arise if everyone thought it fair to have an unequal split, which would be revealed along 0G at point A.[7] This kind of standard economic fairness simply means the 0M path is identically located on top of the self-interest path 0G, so it is deemed fair to give an unequal split, in fact, to share nothing. We can now see, however, how the ultimatum and dictator games could also give quite different outcomes, while explaining why there is often substantive sharing, which would arise due to a path 0M down and away from the 0G path, causing a wide variety of sharing along alternative 0Z paths dependent upon the situation at hand. Every one of these outcomes is efficient, but only in the sense that it is influenced by the other-interest, which also lends support to the contention by V. Smith that markets tend to clear, but may clear somewhat differently depending upon the rules of the game—that is, upon the context, or the institution (shared other-interest) in place.[8]

This situation is represented in an objective function for a consumer constrained by income (y). (For the case of a production process and firm behavior, in addition to the model of consumer behavior presented herein, see Lynne in press.) The construction also suggests that the two utilities are commensurable only on a higher plane, if at all; that is, it is posited not that the two utilities can simply be added but rather that they interact in complex ways, leading to the real possibility of the sum being greater than the sum of the parts:

$$\Phi = V(I_G, I_M) + \lambda(y) \tag{1}$$

with the inherent jointness and conflict between self-interest (I_G) and other-interest (I_M) represented in

$$I_G = I_G(q_1, q_2) \tag{2}$$

$$I_M = I_M(q_1, q_2) \tag{3}$$

Notice these are not allocations of a good q_i, like a q_{iG} or a q_{iM} as presumed in microeconomics, such that one could form one utility function through summing across the allocations; rather, the two goods q_i are nonallocable between the two interests, jointly producing the two different kinds of utility at the same time, which need to be commensurated, if at all, on some higher plane.[9]

THE BUDGET CONSTRAINT CONTAINS SUBJECTIVE PRICES

A metaeconomics budget constraint also appears somewhat different, with the κ_i indicating an empathy element associated directly with expressions of price (which makes price and cost subjective in character, more like that proposed in Austrian economics), giving a budget constraint:

$$y = \kappa_1 p_1 q_1 + \kappa_2 p_2 q_2 \tag{4}$$

Generally in such a formulation (equations 1 through 4) we would assume the individual has the complete freedom to choose; there is no control, no governance (regulatory or cultural) outside the individual.

MODELING SELF-CONTROL, SELF-DISCIPLINE

This is to say, metaeconomics moves away from the mainly instinctual, intuitive, and emotional choice at A or C. It takes self-control (self-discipline) to avoid the extremes of acting almost completely hedonistically at A (e.g., maximizing an extreme form of hedonistic self-interest, such as in drug addictions) or almost completely altruistically at C (representing self-sacrifice, such as in the case of a soldier jumping on a grenade to save the commanding officer or a suicide bomber sacrificing his or her life for unity with a fundamentalist religious cause). Due to self-control, a synergistic and symbiotic joint combination of I_G and I_M is, instead, self-selected at B. Recall this is the result of having been to Adam Smith's (1790) third station, with one imagining being in the state of other(s) and then conditioning one's own internalized self-response accordingly.

RECOGNIZING THE NEED FOR REGULATION, OUTSIDE GOVERNANCE, AND CONTROL

In the real world, exerting self-control is not always that easy. People oftentimes do not manage it, acting on more fundamental egoistic or empathetic (often unconscious) emotions. This calls forth the need for everything from drug interdiction and environmental regulations to progressive taxes that produce money to support poverty-reduction programs. Metaeconomics recognizes the legitimate need to assert external control on individual consumer choice in such cases of lack of self-control. Frankfurt (1971), a legal scholar, in searching for a basis for law in the nature of what it means to be human, referred to this as the problem of not asserting "the Will," that is, the self-control to bring about good ends.

EMERGENT VALUE ON A HIGHER PLANE

The metaeconomic proposal that the value that precedes choice emerges as the two interests interact builds on a similar proposition by Khalil (1990, esp. 266), who observes that Adam Smith (1790) saw a "distinct entity" emerging "beyond self-interest and altruism" after an individual consulted the "impartial spectator" within, that part of the self who had a "fellow feeling (empathy)" toward others. This fellow feeling comes about through imagining what it might be like to be in that situation. The distinct entity emerged from having been at the "third station" where one strove to walk in the shoes of others—in other words, to empathize. Efficiency would also influence the character of the empathy, the imagining. The cause of the true wealth of a nation is the reciprocity between ego and empathy, self-interest and other-interest.

CONNECTING TO HOLISTIC PSYCHOLOGY

The psychology of metaeconomics goes back to the original work of Angyal (1941). In this theory, autonomy is a fundamental trend describing the pursuit of the self-interest, reflecting mastery and an attempt at an internalized self-control within the disciplined self. At the same time, homonomy is also a fundamental trend associated with the pursuit of the other-interest, reflecting the desire for unity or relatedness with others. Autonomy and homonomy are naturally in conflict until one manages to achieve the highest state of mental health, moving beyond all manner of neurosis (a main theme in Angyal 1965). Maslow (1954) referred to this as "fusing the dichotomies." Intriguingly, Maslow writes in strong support of Angyal's theory in the foreword to Angyal's 1965 book. Angyal's ideas have also made their way into modern psychology, as highlighted by Rowan (1990) and Lester (1995). After extensive reviews of the subselves literature, both give Angyal a prominent place in that historical development. As Sato argues in drawing on Angyal, eventually every culture needs to acknowledge the coexistence of "relatively balanced levels of relatedness . . . and autonomy" (2001, 118). Pursuing only one or the other is not desirable for the individual because it leads to neurosis and other mental problems (see Angyal 1965); it is also not desirable for the community, culture, economy, and society to which these individuals belong and within which they are embedded. Both need to be pursued at the same time in order to achieve both health and wealth at this larger scale.

Another intriguing part also included in metaeconomics is Angyal's heteronomy, which he defined as "government from the outside" (Angyal 1941, 39), emanating from the environment in which the individual operates. To operate in the autonomous state is to operate with "self-government," from within the self. In modern terminology, this distinction is akin to that between the "external locus of control" and the "internal locus of control" (see Ajzen 2002). Outside governance suggests consumer choice is to a large extent controlled by others within their own social and/or natural environment. Ironically, it is this very struggle by each individual to control his or her own situation that tends to lead to outside governance. In most of sociology, one would not even talk about people trying to control their own state in life, which explains Duesenberry's (1960) quip that "economics is all about how people make choices; sociology is all about how they don't have any choices to make" (cited in Granovetter and Swedberg 1992, 56). In metaeconomics, the degree of the perceived (and actual) level of internal control is an empirical question (e.g., see Lynne et al., 1995, wherein the role of control is tested).

Metaeconomics recognizes that consumers may prefer not having the complete freedom to choose, instead preferring a bounded choice. This idea is not unrelated to Simon (1997) and the "bounded rationality" problem, in that too much free choice leads to cognitive difficulties in arriving at a decision point.

ADDRESSING THE MICRO-TO-MACRO TRANSITION

As suggested in the experimental literature, it is often the case that isolated individuals are individually irrational, in the cognitively conscious sense usually presumed for markets, while collectively rational when interacting within the market. Vernon Smith (1991, 885) refers to this as a kind of "magic" at work. As noted earlier, this magic is really convergence, and emergence to a higher plane of value, due to empathy operating in the background to influence egoistic choices and ego influencing empathy, both working to yield a new path 0Z. It is the empathetic tendency and the resulting reciprocity with the egoistic tendency within each individual (and, as a result, among individuals who buy into a shared I_M, i.e., institutions matter) that produce the magic of market-clearing prices at a competitive equilibrium.

Adam Smith (1790) believed this to be the case. He wrote specifically of the need for "fellow feeling" (expressed, as noted earlier, in the "third station" of the "impartial spectator") in order that the true wealth of a nation could be realized. This is not interdependent utility within a monoutility function. If it were, everything could be expressed in self-interest, including one's fellow feeling for someone else. As Smith notes (following directly after his statement about how the fortune of others is also a part of our interest, and suggesting how to bring this other feature of the individual into economic thinking):

> As we have no immediate experience of what other men feel, we can form no idea of the manner in which they are affected, but by conceiving what we ourselves should feel in the like situation . . . it is by the imagination only that we can form any conception of what are his sensations. (Smith 1790, Part I, Section I, Chapter I, Paragraph 2)

It is not someone else's utility but rather our *imagination* of what it must be like to be in someone's situation that affects our utility. Smith provides twelve examples of this "fellow feeling" in *The Theory of Moral Sentiments* (Smith 1790, Part I, Section I, Chapter I, Paragraphs 2–13), which sets the stage for all that follows, including the notion of self-interest developed in his subsequent book, *The Wealth of Nations* (Smith, 1776), published some seventeen years after the first edition of the *Theory of Moral Sentiments,* which was first published in 1759. We now see that Smith (1776) and the notion of self-interest only make sense in the context of the *Moral Sentiments* book, which he not only published first, but continued working on (while he set the 1776 book largely aside) until releasing the sixth edition shortly before his death in 1790 (see Raphael and Macfie introductory comments, p. 1 in Smith 1790). One of the most direct examples is this:

Of all the calamities to which the condition of mortality exposes mankind, the loss of reason appears, to those who have the least spark of humanity, by far the most dreadful, and they behold that last stage of human wretchedness with deeper commiseration than any other. But the poor wretch, who is in it, laughs and sings perhaps, and is altogether insensible of his own misery. The anguish which humanity feels, therefore, at the site of such an object, cannot be the reflection of any sentiments of the sufferer. The compassion of the spectator must rise altogether from the consideration of what he himself would feel if he was reduced to the same unhappy situation, and, what perhaps is impossible, was at the same time able to regard it with his present reason and judgment. (Smith 1790, Part I, Section I, Chapter I, Paragraph 11)

Other examples Smith uses range from empathizing with someone "upon the rack" to projecting oneself into the grave of someone else. All require the imagination of being in that state or condition and have nothing whatsoever to do with interdependent utility of the monoutility kind, especially apparent with respect to the utility of the person in the grave, focusing on the utility that arises from putting ourselves in their situation—in this case their being dead, so they have no utility that could be interdependent with ours. Metaeconomics easily handles all twelve cases, with this imaginary projection represented in the I_M set of indifference curves. By placing I_M in the same space as I_G, we see that the "imagination" or "fellow feeling" is completely within the self, and it conditions and is joint with the self-interest, I_G. Intriguingly, Sen contends that Smith brings this fellow feeling to work through the impartial spectator to ensure economic justice: "The impartial spectator can place herself in different situations (without having to be present in any of them)" (Sen 2002, 46). It is through fellow feeling (of the kind displayed in the I_M set of Figure 6.1) that we bring justice to economic choices and true wealth to all nations, such as through the contemporary move to globalization.

There may be a multitude of other-interest indifference sets (as suggested by these twelve), all possibly in conflict with the self-interest set, arising from complex combinations of imagining about and actual interaction with others. As Sen would have it:

Furthermore, between the claims of oneself and the claims of all lie the claims of a variety of groups—for example, families, friends, local communities, peer groups, and economic and social classes. (Sen 1977, 318)

Sen notes the wide array of others with whom we may identify, based on such things as "class, gender, or other social convictions . . . [or] professional identities (such as being a doctor or educator)" (2002, 41). We may simply identify with being a human being. This pursuit for unity with (through identity with) goes well beyond identifying only with the nation-state to which each belongs. It also works in clarifying just who is the self or the "I" in the context of the other or the "We."

This idea that individuals interact with others (which also requires empathy) in defining self is also commonly found in various branches of modern psychology and social psychology. As Hermans and colleagues argue, individuals transcend individualism and rationalism through the process of dialogue with many different kinds of others, resulting in a "multiplicity of dialogically interacting selves" (Hermans et al. 1992, 23). Self-categorization theorists not only include other individuals in this dialogue but highlight the importance of intergroup interaction in helping define the individual. Onorato and Turner see substantive limits in the notion of a self-contained self, as though it were a central processing unit, not unlike a computer, that somehow can be on its own without the need to identify and connect with others and matters outside of itself. In drawing on self-categorization theory, Onorato and Turner argue that individuals often develop an identity that is socially shared with others (2002, 145, 146). As Turner and Oakes have noted, this is all about "the interdependence of individuality and shared, collective identity" (1989, 270, cited in Onorato and Turner 2002, 145).

There is then the real possibility of a kind of symbiotic sum, greater than the sum of the parts, as an outcome of this interaction and interdependence. This also suggests that the micro-to-macro transition problem can be solved by understanding this interdependence, arising from the imagination of the state of others, sometimes informed by actual contact/dialogue and sometimes not.

DEVELOPING THE ANALYTICAL MACHINERY

In contrast, standard microeconomics would suggest that the consumer represented in Figure 6.1 always tips the balance and orients the self along path 0G toward the autonomous, individuated, and isolated self-interest, choosing to maximize self-interest at A in Figures 6.1 and 6.2. It is presumed there is no other-interest, no substantive fellow feeling, shared or otherwise, and no interaction and interdependence, even though clearly there is, as demonstrated in Figure 6.1, a modest amount of other-interest, fellow feeling I_M at every point on 0G. This is the reason Adam Smith came back "channeled" in Wight's (2002) novel: economists need to consider and include the rest of the story they missed by not reading *The Theory of Moral Sentiments,* because there is always fellow feeling, just as there is always self-interest (the latter highlighted in *The Wealth of Nations*). In behavioral economic terms, someone choosing A is someone who scores high on a selfism scale (see Phares and Erskine 1984). This kind of personality is overly self-directed. Scoring high on an altruism scale would suggest a person is overly other-directed, although, as noted, some I_G curve passes through every point on 0M, including point C; even those with strong fellow feeling tendencies pursue a bit of the self-interest. We seek, instead, an overall integrated, symbiotic balance and orientation on a particular 0Z, with the possibility for several such 0Z paths representing a variety of other-interests. I already highlighted Sen's claims of many others. Onorato and Turner see the individual as having a rather fluid identity with "the self . . . as relatively interchangeable with other ingroup members, rather than as unique and individuated" (2002, 146). These "psychological groups" (Onorato and Turner 2002, 149) tug at the individual's path 0G, producing more than one path 0Z.

FINDING THE SYMBIOTIC EXPANSION PATH

The first order conditions leading to this 0Z path are:

$$\frac{\partial \Phi}{\partial q_1} = \frac{\partial V}{\partial I_G}\frac{\partial I_G}{\partial q_1} + \frac{\partial V}{\partial I_M}\frac{\partial I_M}{\partial q_1} - \lambda \kappa_1 p_1 = 0 \tag{5}$$

$$\frac{\partial \Phi}{\partial q_2} = \frac{\partial V}{\partial I_G}\frac{\partial I_G}{\partial q_2} + \frac{\partial V}{\partial I_M}\frac{\partial I_M}{\partial q_2} - \lambda \kappa_2 p_2 = 0 \tag{6}$$

$$\frac{\partial \Phi}{\partial \lambda} = y - \kappa_1 p_1 q_1 - \kappa_2 p_2 q_2 = 0 \tag{7}$$

The metaeconomically efficient path 0Z comes from this condition:

$$\frac{\dfrac{\partial V}{\partial I_G}\dfrac{\partial I_G}{\partial q_1} + \dfrac{\partial V}{\partial I_M}\dfrac{\partial I_M}{\partial q_1}}{\dfrac{\partial V}{\partial I_G}\dfrac{\partial I_G}{\partial q_2} + \dfrac{\partial V}{\partial I_M}\dfrac{\partial I_M}{\partial q_2}} = \frac{\kappa_1 p_1}{\kappa_2 p_2} \tag{8}$$

The path 0Z in Figure 6.1 from equation 8 is:

$$q_2 = q_2\left(\kappa_1 p_1, \kappa_2 p_2, q_1, I_G, I_M\right) \tag{9}$$

Note how the other-interest element I_M affects the location of the efficient path; this is to say that the fellow feeling, having been internalized, affects the economically efficient mix.

DEVELOPING THE SYMBIOTIC DEMAND FUNCTION

The demand function for q_1 is

$$q_1 = q_1\left(\kappa_1 p_1, \kappa_2 p_2, I_G, I_M, y\right) \tag{10}$$

along the path 0Z. Due to utility being an argument in the demand curve, we now see how framing (in the sense of Kahneman 2003, 1458–60) might affect the demand. For example, we might engage a consumer who is on the way into an office supply store about the problem of the destruction of old-growth forests and then ask about his or her intention to buy recycled paper. We might expect the effective synergy, and potentially the symbiotic integration, of the two interests to move the consumer's 0Z path toward the 0M path, with the consumer that day buying more recycled paper (q_1). Having a colleague engage the same consumer on another day about the finding that pens write better on regular paper (saying nothing about the impact on old-growth forests) would likely cause the consumer to edge his or her 0Z path toward the 0G path and tend to buy more regular paper (q_2). This suggests that framing is explained by which instinct, or emotion-based intuition, is stirred by the situation at hand and that preferences are oriented accordingly.

   We can also now see that institutions, defined as the way we relate to others in the transaction, do matter. Perhaps the consumer really likes to use fountain pens, which work much better on high-quality regular paper than on recycled paper, but realizes that the checkout clerk on duty that day is an old friend who is an environmentalist. We can reasonably predict that our consumer will purchase paper with at least some recycled content.

DERIVING THE EGO-EMPATHY FRONTIER

We can derive the joint utility "peace of mind" function used to draw the interests frontier in Figure 6.2 associated with staying on the budget constraint RR′ by solving equation 4 for q_1, obtaining

$$q_1 = \left(y - \kappa_2 p_2 q_2\right) / \kappa_1 p_1 \tag{11}$$

Figure 6.2   **Ego-Empathy Frontier Representing the Trade-off in the Joint Pursuit of the Egoistic Self-interest (I_G) and the Empathetic Other-interest (I_M)**

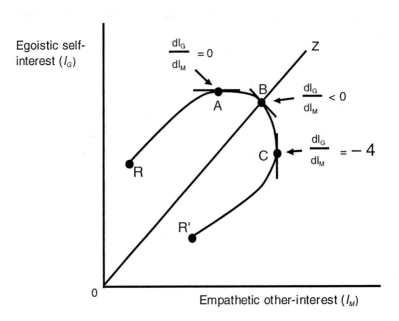

We then substitute equation 11 into $V(I_G, I_M)$,

$$V = V\{I_G[(y - \kappa_2 p_2 q_2)/\kappa_1 p_1, q_2], I_M[(y - \kappa_2 p_2 q_2)/\kappa_1 p_1, q_2]\} \tag{12}$$

Next, we substitute the economically efficient path equation (equation 9) and the demand function (equation 10) into equation 12,

$$V = V(I_G, I_M, \kappa_1 p_1, \kappa_2 p_2, y) \tag{13}$$

EXAMINING THE TRADE-OFFS BETWEEN THE INTERESTS

Notice that

$$dV = \frac{\partial V}{\partial I_G} dI_G + \frac{\partial V}{\partial I_M} dI_M + \frac{\partial V}{\partial p_1} dp_1 + \frac{\partial V}{\partial p_2} dp_2 + \frac{\partial V}{\partial y} dy \tag{14}$$

such that the case of $dp_1 = dp_2 = dy = dV = 0$ gives

$$\frac{dI_M}{dI_G} = TB_{MG} = \frac{\partial V}{\partial I_M} \bigg/ \frac{\partial V}{\partial I_G} \tag{15}$$

which represents the slope and the trade-off balance, T, of a frontier curve in Figure 6.2. Notice that a trade-off between the interests is possible in only the complex way of moving along a RR' constraint in Figure 6.1. The interests (and the associated utilities) are not separably traded off, in that every trade-off point now produces both utilities and satisfies both interests. It is far more complex than suggested by trading off playing a half day of golf mainly in the pursuit of self-interest with spending a half day with one's family mainly in the pursuit of the other-interest, when in fact we now see that both golfing and spending time with the family produce both kinds of utility and satisfy both interests. We might also reasonably posit that playing golf with the family could lead to a "sum greater than the sum of the parts," a higher plane arising in the symbiotic potential that now can be described.

CHARACTERIZING SYMBIOSIS IN THE EMERGENT VALUE

To address the matter of symbiosis, envision several ego-empathy curves in Figure 6.2 and the distances between them being of interest, in the sense of the symbiotic potential of reciprocal behavior. The symbiotic balance, S_{MG}, throughout the space from equation 13 is:

$$\frac{\partial^2 V}{\partial I_G \, \partial I_M} = S_{MG} \qquad (16)$$

We can now consider an empirical case to help illustrate the general outcomes above.

DEMONSTRATING TRADE-OFFS AND SYMBIOSIS

Consider a plausible V function representing equation 13 of the near quadratic form (holding everything else constant), including several parameters that serve to transform the utilities into V, the latter being a measure of the joint outcomes on the higher plane:

$$V = \iota (I_G)^2 + \tau (I_M)^2 + \gamma (I_G)(I_M) \qquad (17)$$

Assume for sake of discussion that $\iota, \tau > 0$. For this simple case, we would posit that a relatively large ι indicates an individual oriented toward the egoistic self-interest. A relatively large τ can be taken to mean an orientation mainly toward the empathetic other-interest.

A substantive g would indicate symbiotic interdependence, the possibility of symbiotic outcomes, and jointness (or symbiotic independence if it is 0) as between the two interests. We could find $\gamma = S_{MG} < 0$, which is the case of symbiotic complementarity illustrated in Figure 6.2. That is, $(\partial V / \partial I_G)$ decreases, indicating that I_G is increasing as I_M increases. The isocurves in Figure 6.2 become further apart as we move along some path 0Z.[10] This also means that $(\partial V / \partial I_M)$ decreases as the egoistic I_G increases, meaning that I_M is enhanced. In effect, the total arising from the orientation in the balance (and thus the bulge in the frontier in Figure 6.2) *is greater than the sum of the parts,* due to the symbiotic complementarity between I_G and I_M. As Cory argues, a kind of homeostasis is at work, with it being quite possible that it is symbiotic (2004, 35). This is also the only case wherein we could also observe the regions RA and R'C, wherein both of more kinds of utility can be gained together, suggesting another kind of complementarity at work.

When the interests are symbiotically competitive, then $\gamma = S_{MG} > 0$, and the ego-empathy curves in Figure 6.2 will become closer together as we move along some path 0Z. That is, $(\partial V/\partial I_G)$ increases as more I_M is pursued, implying that I_G is decreasing as I_M increases. The two interests are vying for expression within the self, not complementing each other. The sum is less than the sum of the parts. Intriguingly, the regions RA and R'C also vanish, and we only observe the competitive zone AC.

With $\gamma = S_{MG} = 0$, indicating symbiotic independence (no symbiosis), again, only AC will appear and the total is exactly the sum of the parts, with the ego-empathy curves equally spaced as we move out on 0Z. This is to say, egoistic pursuits do not affect empathy, and empathy does not affect egoistic pursuits. It might be expected that this kind of independence will not occur very often, although it is always presumed in standard microeconomics. Only in this case is the sum equal to the sum of the parts.

EMPIRICAL MEASUREMENT AND TESTING

Even though, as alluded to earlier, Gintis (2000), Henrich and colleagues (2004), and others (including Sober and Wilson 1998) have argued that it is obvious from both commonsense experience and empirical tests that individuals are both self-interested and altruistic in varying proportions in different times and situations, and even though Beahrs (1982) and Rowan (1990) declare it quite obvious that the subselves model of the unified self describes actual human nature, it still behooves us to keep testing for the existence of both subselves. Metaeconomics by its nature supports a continual testing of these declarations, in that one cannot now presume a priori that individuals only maximize self-interest or only seek relatedness and unity in a shared other-interest (the latter a common theme in sociology). Individuals may vacillate between the two interests, leading to a kind of switching behavior and the need to focus on the orientation in the behavior, both of which make generalizing more difficult. Analysis is more difficult in that it requires a shift to the continual collection of empirical data. What kind of data and evidence do we need?

The demand function in equation 10 points to the need to measure utility, in that I_G and I_M remain explicit. As Kahneman, Wakker, and Sarin (1997) argue in a somewhat different context, the focus needs to be put back on the kind of measurable utility that Bentham first visualized, as represented in the role of experienced utility in resolving the pain-pleasure calculus. Metaeconomics, in this sense, also goes back to Bentham. Experiments show that the disutility of physical pain can indeed be measured and compared across individuals (Kahneman, Wakker, and Sarin et al., 1997). Experiments also suggest that empathizing (and the emotional pain that goes with it) with someone else will fire the same part of the brain that recognizes physical pain (Singer et al., 2004), suggesting that pain is in the background of both pursuits of utility. Metaeconomics sees both the physical and emotional pain as commensurable on the cost side of the calculus, that is, the cost side of the pleasure outcome and the doing-the-right-thing outcome can be added into a common cost represented in a common budget or capital constraint line. Metaeconomics, then, is quite consistent with and supported by the experimental research on experienced utility. Metaeconomics differs, though, in showing there are two outcomes to every expression of cost, two ultimate sources of utility, *which may even be incommensurable in dollar terms*.[11] It follows that experimental efforts to measure utility must strive to measure both kinds of utility.

Experimental measurement needs to be supplemented with the more traditional survey-based approaches.[12] All of these approaches fit generally in the class of expectancy-value modeling (see Feather 1982). Experienced utility is measured by focusing on the attributes of the goods and the bundles of goods by measuring the beliefs about what the goods will do for the individual and the value the individual places on that outcome, and then multiplying these belief and value components as a proxy measure for the utility experienced from the good or action in question. Or one may just go after the multiplicand from the outset, as in measuring the "general attitude" or "general norm."

The subsequent econometric analysis then focuses on sorting out how the two proxies are balanced and oriented as indicators of how the individual is integrating the two kinds of utility (for an example, see Lynne and Casey 1998; for a summary of test results through 2004, see Hayes and Lynne 2004; for a recent test, see Kalinowski, Lynne, and Johnson in press). With few exceptions, the empirical evidence supports the contention that individuals do indeed integrate and orient toward either the self-interest or the other-interest, although we have mainly studied farmers and ranchers and their conservation (technology) decisions. We have also studied recycling behavior of households (see Kalinowski, Lynne, and Johnson in press) and the willingness to pay to keep green space (farmland) in urban areas (see Gustafson and Lynne 2003) with similar findings. At least for these subsets of the larger population, it appears the rational zone between 0G and 0M is very much the operating area for economic choice; it is the orientation within this zone that drives economic behavior. These kinds of phenomena have also been found in the study of behavior in the fishery industry (Kuperan and Sutinen 1998; Sutinen and Kuperan 1999); as Hayes and Lynne (2004) note, it is likely these kinds of findings will be confirmed in the study of most people in most situations most of the time.

MICROECONOMICS AND RENDITIONS FROM SOCIOLOGY AS THE DEFAULT CASE

Mainstream applications of microeconomic theory presume (generally without empirical test) that $\iota = 1$, $\tau = 0$, $\gamma = 0$, and we are at point A. There is the complete freedom to choose in reaching point A, with the preference for it also presumed. This also suggests the all-encompassing nature of metaeconomics. Even standard microeconomics is represented: *notice that the microeconomic prediction is the default case if we fail to reject the null hypotheses of no empathic influence/interest* (and also there is no evidence that individuals actually might prefer some outside regulation).

At the other extreme, which seems to be the view taken in mainstream sociology, a social- and community-oriented individual would, usually through outside community and social control (in that it is implicitly doubted that individuals have sufficient self-discipline and self-control to do this on their own) completely subdue the (selfish) self-interest. This individual purchases goods on the other-interest path 0M acting at point C in Figure 6.2 (maybe even choosing within R'C in an irrational pursuit of I_M). This prediction from sociology is the default *if we fail to reject the null hypothesis of no egoistic interest.* In metaeconomics, as with the other-interest, the degree to which the self-interest is a force—the orientation in the interests—is an empirical question.

LESS EXTREME OUTCOMES

Metaeconomics posits a less drastic outcome, offering that a disciplined and balanced person exercising self-control will operate in the region AC. It also empirically measures the extent to which the individual has and perceives substantive control and power over her or his own choices. We would also test for symbiotic complementary between ego and empathy, which would be indicated by $S_{MG} < 0$. If so, increasing either one tends to enhance the other, supporting this alternative value theory.

CRITIQUES OF METAECONOMICS AND OF MULTIPLE UTILITY THEORY GENERALLY

Etzioni created quite a stir in his 1986 paper, which led to an intriguing dialogue involving Brennan (1989) and Lutz (1993), centering on the need to add "moral utility" to the economic framework. As noted earlier, the overall suggestion that monoutility was too parsimonious (Etzioni 1986, 159) and that some provision for self-sacrifice (altruism) was needed in the economic model gave the major impetus for proposing the notion of I_M utility (as noted earlier, this was originally called "We-utility" in Lynne 1999). As metaeconomics has evolved, the I_M utility has been broadened from mere moral utility to representing the tendency to unity that becomes the main source of the content of the underlying institution and rules of the game. It also suggests why there are these rules and institutions. Metaeconomics now claims that I_M may or may not be irreducible (commensurable), depending on the good in question.

In addition, it is now clear that by proposing I_M as joint with I_G (i.e., both sets of indifference curves in the same space, as in Figure 6.1), true self-sacrifice could be represented in the utility model, which cannot be done with the interdependent utility approach, as critiques of metaeconomics more often than not suggest (for a response, see Lynne 2002, 421). As Etzioni (1986, 162, 177) notes, people pass judgment on their self-interested urges, and every choice is multifaceted, as depicted by an intersection of an I_M curve for every such urge at every point on the 0G path, and at every point on every I_G curve. Also, the joint utility model moves us away from the tautological claim that every economic action is an attempt to maximize satisfaction (as noted by Etzioni 1986, 163). Individuals represented in metaeconomics may also be trying to do the right thing along 0M while sacrificing I_G on 0G (Figure 6.1); this encompasses Etzioni's recognition that there are actions that individuals feel obligated to take, even if it results in true self-sacrifice, represented in the move to a lower level of I_G while moving to a higher level of I_M (Etzioni 1986, 167). Choosing some action in the direction of path 0M is to affirm or express a commitment through self-sacrifice, not unlike the kind of commitment that Sen (1977) has defined or that Frank (1988) highlights.

Brennan (1993) is not convinced. He argues that to claim that the monoutility theory is tautological is the pot calling the kettle black; multiple utility theory will also explain everything. I disagree, in that metaeconomics requires continual empirical testing for the integrative balance and orientation being struck in the utilities and interests instead of presuming there is only one self(ish)-interest, and not measuring the utility. Also, Brennan wants to think instead in terms of "I choose to restrain myself" as simply a constraint on the pursuit of a monoutility, rather than allowing that one could actually see doing the right thing in a moral utility as an ultimate end in itself (1993, 155). In fact, Brennan implicitly is concerned that using a multiple utility theory could somehow lead to limiting individual choice, so he rebels against it. He has a point. Perhaps such rebellion is not always good, however, as metaeconomics teaches about drug addiction or environmental destruction done in the uninhibited pursuit of a pleasurable self-interest. Also, by recognizing two subselves, this actually frees the choices: the individual can now choose between the pursuits, increasing the extent of the freedom to choose. The inner tension between altruistic and selfish acts (Brennan implicitly recognizes both exist) is a simple matter of opportunity costs (Brennan 1993, 157). Metaeconomics does not have a difficulty with this on the cost side of the equation, in that pain arises in both domains. The problem is that Brennan does not see the two fields of utility. Instead, he has inputs (costs and opportunity costs) and outputs (utilities) confused. In commenting on Brennan, Lutz (1993) helps the case for multiple utility theory by highlighting the possibility of appealing to the sense of social responsibility (embedded in the latent moral utility) to induce socially desirable outcomes, much like metaeconomics predicts. Also, Lutz points to the real possibility of disequilibrium, which metaeconomics highlights in the zone between and including 0G and 0M in Figure 6.1. Overall, and from the metaeconomics perspective, Brennan is the one that is not convincing. Many other specific criticisms of metaeconomics have also been answered (see Lynne 2002, 420–23).

ON TRADE-OFFS AND INFINITE SUBSTITUTABILITY

It is perhaps important to note that this kind of model leads to describing economic processes along expansion paths rather than along isocurves per se: trade-offs, substitutions, and options are really quite limited. This is to say that the consumer is quite limited in choices, leading to a kind of economics of limitative processes, much like Frisch (1965) developed in early versions of production economics. Unfortunately, the economics of limitative processes offered by Frisch never made a substantive showing in the mainstream of economics, which always favored total substitution and complete independence of free choices (like Friedman's "freedom to choose" notion) and generally assumed away all technically and symbiotically interdependent cases.

CONCLUSION

The presumptions about freedom of choice and the capacity for infinite substitutions (and thus essentially no limits within or from outside the individual) is fascinating enough. The question of why only the autonomous pursuit of the self-interest in an atmosphere of "anything goes" made its way into modern economics, to the exclusion of other-interest and the real possibility of limits to substitution and choice, needs to be pursued by an economic historian. One suspects there is an ideology at work here, subtly hidden in the equations, mathematics, and economic stories told involving allocable products, monoutility, and the presumed independence among consumers who face no limits. In contrast, an ideologically neutral metaeconomics not only would recognize the need for autonomy represented in the pursuit of self-interest but also would at least ask about homonomy (the need for unity with others and causes or ideas or places including the ecosystem/planet/universe itself), about heteronomy (the extent to which outside control is preferred), and about the potential for an associated symbiotic outcome. It would recognize Adam Smith's concern for empathy—that one would imagine oneself in the state of others, and that this projection would influence one's internal sense of peace of mind on the way to achieving economically efficient outcomes. The accuracy of this imagination in the state of others would be improved by dialogue and interaction with others. Efficiency, then, is really about symbiosis between the ego and the empathy, between self-interest and the (internalized) other-interest, with such symbiosis leading to better (efficient) choices for both the individual and society, and to the true wealth of a nation: We can now better understand its actual causes, in analytical terms, in effect making visible the magic of the market and the invisible hand. It would also acknowledge the reality of limits; that maximization, while an ideal, is not practical nor even possible in most cases; and that there are at best very limited substitutes for many things on the way to peace of mind.

NOTES

1. The latest rendition of metaeconomics continues to distance itself from dysfunctional institutions or dysfunctional relatedness within the self, as in the "multiplicity of selves" multiple personalities problem (Katzko 2003), or such things as "possession" or reincarnation (for a brief overview of these and other types

of subselves, see Lester 2004), which may be deemed something other than rational. Metaeconomics instead focuses on the interaction within the unified self, much as does Bogart (1994), and suggests that the internal conflict between the subselves is quite rational on the way to unity, at least for most people making economic decisions most of the time. Like Frick (1993, 123, 124), metaeconomics sees the matter of subselves more in terms of tendencies within the holistic self, as toward Berne's Parent, Child, or Adult, who are all part of a dynamic whole, in contrast to thinking of distinct, multiple personalities or selves. Yet while the holism perspective offered by Frick is perhaps desirable, there can also be legitimate switching as the frame changes, as between an orientation toward egoistic or empathetic tendencies, perhaps even vacillating, and appearing to be not unified. It is perhaps better to think in terms of a community of selves coordinated within the self, an idea reinforced by Bogart (1994, 83). As Katzko (2003) argues, there is an active "unity-multiplicity debate" in the literature; it cannot be fully resolved herein, albeit metaeconomics is resilient enough to handle most perspectives on it.

2. V. Smith (1998) also claims to have solved the problem by simply recognizing one behavioral tendency "to truck, barter, and exchange one thing for another." So, according to V. Smith (p. 3), the Adam Smith problem goes away by recognizing that individuals not only trade goods for goods but also trade "gifts, assistance, and favors out of sympathy." In both realms, humans relentlessly seek the "gains from trade." While perhaps reasonable within each realm, the danger with representing Adam Smith this way is that we are but one small step from suggesting trading between the two realms, which is commonly done (indeed, it has to be done in the monoutility framework) in microeconomics, as in the notions of trading goods (money) for doing the right thing or everything having a price (even, then, one's firstborn). As we will see, metaeconomics resolves the Adam Smith problem in a much more plausible manner by allowing a kind of trade-off between the realms that better captures the realms' true complexity. Also, some things, including one's firstborn, can be kept out of being monetized or commensurated in any terms other than achieving a higher sense of peace of mind from having done the right thing.

3. Lester (1995, 79) makes this claim, while pointing to the high esteem in which Maslow held Angyal and his theory; see also Maslow's foreword in Angyal 1965. Frick also notes that Angyal "presented the first systematic holistic theory of personality development" (1993, 126). As Lester argues, "Angyal proposed a holistic theory in much greater detail than any other scholar has done . . . [keeping the] theory at an abstract level" (1995, 79). It is this abstract level that makes it appealing as the psychological, holistic theory that can form the foundation of metaeconomics.

4. For background on the history of utility as field theory, see Mirowski 1989, in which the neoclassical claim about one field of utility is associated with the energy field theory of value from physics. The economists of the late 1800s adapted energy field theory to their needs, suggesting that all relative values rested in, and emerged from, this one self-interested field of utility. Metaeconomics stays close to this tradition but suggests there are two fields of utility and two kinds of value, with the true potential for achieving a higher plane of value from the interaction.

5. Wight argues that Adam Smith saw peace of mind from resolving this conflict between the two selves as the ultimate objective (2002, 32).

6. See Simon 1997, esp. 38–45, wherein altruism in introduced into his human behavior theory as a substantive part of the satisificing idea.

7. As highlighted in Altman 2004, 23, these games help us understand if people are truly "selfish materially-oriented maximizers" as standard economics presumes. Generally the games do not support the contention, indirectly lending credence to metaeconomic theory.

8. Figure 6.1 can also represent isoquants (see Lynne in press), now with I_G representing the maximum efficiency in producing more material output and I_M representing relations within the organization and industry, union influences, perhaps connections with the natural system, and other institutions and rules (shared in the other-interest) of the production game. All areas between and including the paths 0G and 0M are efficient in a general sense, but only those along 0G give maximum material output. So we see that the influence of the institutions and rules can produce any number of efficient paths 0Z, including 0Z being identically on top of 0G if the institution favors the maximum production (i.e., if 0M also lies identically on top of 0G). This seems to be the story being told by Leibenstein (1966) regarding "effort discretion," as highlighted in Altman 2004, 25–26. We could have economic efficiency with prices formed and a competitive equilibrium with firms producing I_G kinds of product throughout the whole spectrum of the AC zone in Figure 6.1, with a wide variety of x-efficiency and x-inefficiency, i.e., using the same amount of x represented on the RR' capital line, while producing over the range of I_G' to I_G''' (the latter not shown, but the I_G isoquant going through point C), dependent upon the influence of "industrial rela-

tions, bargaining power and cultural and social context" (terms used in Altman 2004, 25) represented in I_M for each firm in each industry.

9. Also, as suggested in note 8, these could be production functions (and equation 4 a capital constraint), with the argument being the *total amounts of input* (not the allocations), which gives rise to true jointness in production. See Lynne 1988, which builds on the arguably most useful notion of jointness as it relates to inputs in production (and as I have extrapolated it in this chapter to also address jointness in consumption) ever proposed but little used in the economic literature, as originally developed in Frisch 1965.

10. First suggested to me by Albert N. Halter, in the mid-1970s, who at that time was a professor in the Department of Agricultural Economics at Oregon State University, for the purpose of enhancing understanding of technical complementarity in production and cost; i.e., it is the changing distance across the production possibility frontiers that gives meaning to complementarity, competitiveness, and independence in joint production. This suggestion has led to the idea offered in this essay of symbiotic complementarity in consumption.

11. That is, while metaeconomics sees a kind of commensurable utility on a higher plane beyond both self-interest and other-interest (i.e., beyond altruism represented in self-sacrifice), represented in the idea of "peace of mind," it does not see it as necessarily either possible or desirable to convert the two kinds of utility into common dollars (or any other kind of unit). There may indeed be, as Etzioni (1986) claims, some things outside the economic domain, as in what price one would place on one's firstborn: This price is not commensurable even if it can be monetized, suggesting the underlying utility cannot be reduced to the same dollar terms as represented in the price of a new car.

12. Experienced utility, or proxies for it, can be measured through surveys. For methods, we can draw upon the social psychologists who have produced an impressive array of papers, many drawing back to Ajzen and Fishbein (1977) and more recently to Ajzen (1991), on how to measure the attitude construct, which in economic terms is to measure utility (after Vodopivec 1992; also, see Warsha and Dröge 1986). This survey and expectancy-value modeling approach, which focuses on measuring beliefs and values, has been used in the testing of metaeconomics. For ongoing work, see http://agecon.unl.edu/lynne/metapape.htm.

REFERENCES

Ajzen, I. 1991. "The Theory of Planned Behavior." *Organizational Behavior and Human Decision Processes* 50: 179–211.

———. 2002. "Perceived Behavioral Control, Self-Efficacy, Locus of Control, and the Theory of Planned Behavior." *Journal of Applied Social Psychology* 32: 1–20.

Ajzen, I., and M. Fishbein. 1977. "Attitude-Behavior Relations: A Theoretical Analysis and Review of the Empirical Research." *Psychological Bulletin* 84, 5: 888–918.

Altman, M. 2004. "The Nobel Prize in Behavioral and Experimental Economics: A Contextual and Critical Appraisal of the Contributions of Daniel Kahneman and Vernon Smith." *Review of Political Economy* 16: 3–41.

Angyal, A. 1941. *Foundations for a Science of Personality.* Cambridge, MA: Commonwealth Fund by Harvard University Press, 1967.

———. 1965. *Neurosis and Treatment: A Holistic Theory.* New York: Viking Press.

Beahrs, J.O. 1982. *Unity and Multiplicity: Multilevel Consciousness of Self in Hypnosis, Psychiatric Disorder and Mental Health.* New York: Brunner/Mazel.

Berne, E. 1961. *Transactional Analysis in Psychotherapy.* New York: Grove Press.

Bogart, V. 1994. "Transcending the Dichotomy of Either 'Subpersonalities' or 'An Integrated Self.'" *Journal of Humanistic Psychology* 34, 2: 82–89.

Boulding, K.E. 1968. *The Organizational Revolution.* Chicago: Quadrangle.

Brennan, T.J. 1989. "A Methodological Assessment of Multiple Utility Frameworks." *Economics and Philosophy* 5: 189–208.

———. 1993. "The Futility of Multiple Utility." *Economics and Philosophy* 9: 155–64.

Buber, M. 1922. *I and Thou,* trans. R.G. Smith. New York: Charles Scribner's Sons, 1958.

Cooper, M. 2003. "'I-I' and 'I-Me': Transposing Buber's Interpersonal Attitudes to the Intrapersonal Plane." *Journal of Constructivist Psychology* 16: 131–53.

Cory, G.A., Jr. 1999. *The Reciprocal Modular Brain in Economics and Politics.* New York: Kluwer Academic/Plenum.

———. 2000a. "From Maclean's Triune Brain Concept to the Conflict Systems Neurobehavioral Model: The Subjective Basis of Moral and Spiritual Consciousness." *Zygon* 35: 385–414.

———. 2000b. *Toward Consilience: The Bioneurological Basis of Behavior, Thought, Experience, and Language.* New York: Kluwer Academic/Plenum.

———. 2004. *The Consilient Brain: The Bioneurological Basis of Economics, Society and Politics.* New York: Kluwer Academic/Plenum.

Damasio, A. 1999. *The Feeling of What Happens: Body and Emotion in the Making of Consciousness.* New York: Harcourt.

Deci, E.L., and R.M. Ryan. 2000. "The 'What' and 'Why' of Goal Pursuits: Human Needs and the Self-Determination of Behavior." *Psychological Inquiry* 11: 227–68.

Duesenberry, J. 1960. "Comment on 'An Economic Analysis of Fertility.'" In Universities National Bureau for Economic Research, ed., *Demographic and Economic Change in Developed Countries.* Princeton, NJ: Princeton University Press.

Elster, J. 1979. *Ulysses and the Sirens.* New York: Cambridge University Press.

———. 1985. *The Multiple Self.* New York: Cambridge University Press.

Etzioni, A. 1986. "The Case for a Multiple Utility Conception." *Economics and Philosophy* 2: 159–83.

———. 1988. *The Moral Dimension: Toward a New Economics.* New York: Free Press.

Feather, N.T., ed. 1982. *Expectations and Actions: Expectancy-Value Models in Psychology.* Hillsdale, NJ: Lawrence Erlbaum Associates.

Frank, R. 1988. *Passions Within Reason: The Strategic Role of the Emotions.* New York: W.W. Norton.

Frankfurt, H.G. 1971. "Freedom of the Will and the Concept of a Person." *The Journal of Philosophy* 58: 5–21.

Frick, W.B. 1993. "Subpersonalities: Who Conducts the Orchestra." *Journal of Humanistic Psychology* 35, 2: 122–28.

Frisch, R. 1965. *Theory of Production.* Chicago: Rand McNally.

Gintis, H. 2000. *Game Theory Evolving.* Princeton, NJ: Princeton University Press.

Granovetter, M., and R. Swedberg, eds. 1992. *The Sociology of Economic Life.* Boulder, CO: Westview Press.

Gustafson, C., and G.D. Lynne. 2003. "Urbanization Pressures on Agricultural Land." *Focus* (Department of Agricultural Economics, University of Nebraska-Lincoln), fall/winter, 17–20.

Hayes, W.H., and G.D. Lynne. 2004. "A Centerpiece for Ecological Economics." *Ecological Economics* 49: 287–301.

Henrich, J., R. Boyd, S. Bowles, C.F. Camerer, E. Fehr, H. Gintis, and R. McElreath. 2004. "Overview and Synthesis." In J. Henrich, R. Boyd, S. Bowles, C. Camerer, E. Fehr, and H. Gintis, eds., *Foundations of Human Sociality: Economic Experiments and Ethnographic Evidence from Fifteen Small-Scale Societies,* 8–54. New York: Oxford University Press.

Hermans, H.J.M., H.J.G. Kempen, and R.J.P. van Loon. 1992. "The Dialogical Self: Beyond Individualism and Rationalism." *American Psychologist* 47: 23–33.

Hirschman, A.O. 1985. "Against Parsimony: Three Easy Ways of Complicating Some Categories of Economic Discourse." *Economics and Philosophy* 1: 7–21.

Kahneman, D. 2003. "Maps of Bounded Rationality: Psychology for Behavioral Economics." *American Economic Review* 93: 1449–75.

Kahneman, D., P. Wakker, and R. Sarin. 1997. "Back to Bentham? Explorations of Experienced Utility." *Quarterly Journal of Economics* 112: 375–405.

Kalinowski, C.M., G.D. Lynne, and B. Johnson. In press. "Recycling as a Reflection of Balanced Self-Interest." *Environment and Behavior.*

Katzko, M.W. 2003. "Unity Versus Multiplicity: A Conceptual Analysis of the Term 'Self' and Its Use in Personality Theories." *Journal of Personality* 71: 83–114.

Khalil, E.L. 1990. "Beyond Self-Interest and Altruism: A Reconstruction of Adam Smith's Theory of Human Conduct." *Economics and Philosophy* 6: 255–73.

———. 1997. "Etzioni Versus Becker: Do Moral Sentiments Differ from Ordinary Tastes?" *De Economist* 145: 491–520.

Kuperan, K., and J.G. Sutinen. 1998. "Blue Water Crime: Deterrence, Legitimacy, and Compliance in Fisheries." *Law and Society Review* 32: 309–37.

LeDoux, J. 1996. *The Emotional Brain: The Mysterious Underpinnings of Emotional Life.* New York: Simon and Schuster.

Leijonhufvad, A. 2004. "The Trento Summer School: Adaptive Economic Dynamics." In D. Friedman and A. Cassar, eds., *Economics Lab: An Intensive Course in Experimental Economics,* 5–11. New York: Routledge.

Leibenstein, H. 1966. "Allocative Efficiency vs. 'x-efficiency.'" *American Economic Review* 56: 392–415.

Lester, D. 1985. "Applications of the Principles of Group Behavior to Systems Theories of Personality." *Psychology* 22: 1–3.

———. 1987. "A Systems Perspective on Personality." *Psychological Reports* 61: 603–22.

———. 1992. "The Disunity of the Self." *Personality and Individual Differences* 8: 947–48.

———. 1993/94. "On the Disunity of the Self: A Systems Theory of Personality." *Current Psychology* 12: 312–26.

———. 1995. *Theories of Personality: A Systems Approach.* Washington, D.C.: Taylor and Francis.

———. 1998. "Phenomenological Description of Subselves Using George Kelly's Repertory Grid." *Perceptual and Motor Skills* 86: 537–38.

———. 2003. "Comment on 'The Self as Problem': Alternative Conceptions of the Multiple Self." *Journal of Socio-Economics* 32: 499–502.

———. 2004. "Subself Theory and Reincarnation/Possession." *Perceptual and Motor Skills* 99: 1336–8.

Lutz, M.A. 1993. "The Utility of Multiple Utility: A Comment on Brennan." *Economics and Philosophy* 9: 145–54.

Lux, K. 2003. "The Failure of the Profit Motive." *Ecological Economics* 44: 1–9.

Lynne, G.D. 1988. "Allocatable Fixed Inputs and Jointness in Agricultural Production: Implications for Economic Modeling: Comment." *American Journal of Agricultural Economics* 70: 948–49.

———. 1995. "Modifying the Neo-classical Approach to Technology Adoption with Behavioral Science Models." *Journal of Agricultural and Applied Economics* 27: 67–80.

———. 1999. "Divided Self Models of the Socioeconomic Person: The Metaeconomics Approach." *Journal of Socio-Economics* 28: 267–88.

———. 2002. "Agricultural Industrialization: A Metaeconomics Look at the Metaphors by Which We Live." *Review of Agricultural Economics* 24: 410–27.

———. In press. "Toward a Dual Motive Metaeconomic Theory." *Journal of Socio-Economics.*

Lynne, G.D., and L.R. Rola. 1988. "Improving Attitude-Behavior Prediction Models with Economic Variables." *Journal of Social Psychology.* 128, 1: 19–28.

Lynne, G.D., J.S. Shonkwiler, and J.R. Rola. 1988. "Attitudes and Farmer Conservation Behavior." *American Journal of Agricultural Economics* 70: 12–19.

Lynne, G.D., J.S. Shonkwiler, and M.E. Wilson. 1991. "Water Permitting Behavior Under the 1972 Florida Water Resources Act." *Land Economics* 67: 340–51.

Lynne, G.D., and C.F. Casey. 1998. "Regulation of Technology Adoption When Individuals Pursue Multiple Utility." *Journal of Socio-Economics* 27: 701–19.

Lynne, G.D., C.F. Casey, A. Hodges, and M. Rahmani. 1995. "Conservation Technology Adoption Decisions and the Theory of Planned Behavior." *Journal of Economic Psychology* 16: 581–98.

MacLean, P.D. 1990. *The Triune Brain in Evolution.* New York: Plenum Press.

Margolis, H. 1982. *Selfishness, Altruism, and Rationality: A Theory of Social Choice.* New York: Cambridge University Press.

Maslow, A.H. 1954. *Motivation and Personality.* New York: Harper and Row, 1970.

Mirowski, P. 1989. *More Heat than Light: Economics as Social Physics, Physics as Nature's Economics.* New York: Cambridge University Press.

Moldoveanu, M., and H. Stevenson. 2001. "The Self as a Problem: The Intra-Personal Coordination of Conflicting Desires." *Journal of Socio-Economics* 30: 295–330.

Onorato, R.S., and J.C. Turner. 2002. "Challenging the Primacy of the Personal Self: The Case for Depersonalized Self-Conception." In Y. Kashima, M. Foddy, and M.J. Platow, eds., *Self Identity: Personal, Social and Symbolic,* 145–78. Mahwah, NJ: Lawrence Erlbaum Associates.

Phares, E.J., and Erskine, N. 1984. "The Measurement of Selfism." *Educational and Psychological Measurement* 44: 597–608.

Rowan, J. 1990. *Subpersonalities: The People Within Us.* New York: Routledge.

Sato, T. 2001. "Autonomy and Relatedness in Psychopathology and Treatment: A Cross-Cultural Formulation." *Genetic, Social, and General Psychology Monographs* 127: 89–127.

Schelling, T.C. 1984. "Self-Command in Practice, in Policy, and in a Theory of Rational Choice." *American Economic Review* 74: 1–11.

Sen, A.K. 1977. "Rational Fools: A Critique of the Behavioral Foundations of Economic Theory." *Philosophy and Public Affairs* 6: 317–44.

———. 2002. "Justice Across Borders." In P. DeGrieff and C. Cronin, eds., *Global Justice and Transnational Politics: Essays on the Moral and Political Challenges of Globalization,* 37–51. Cambridge, MA: MIT Press.

Singer, T., B. Seymour, J. O'Doherty, H. Kaube, R.J. Dolan, and C.D. Firth. 2004. "Empathy for Pain Involves the Affective but Not Sensory Components of Pain." *Science* 303: 1157–62.

Simon, H.A. 1997. *An Empirically Based Microeconomics.* New York: Cambridge University Press.

Smith, A. 1790. *The Theory of Moral Sentiments.* 6th ed., ed. D.D. Raphael and A.L. Macfie. Indianapolis, IN: Liberty Classics, 1982. First published in 1759.

———. 1776. *An Inquiry into the Nature and Causes of the Wealth of Nations,* ed. E. Cannan. New York: Modern Library, 1937.

Smith, V. 1998. "The Two Faces of Adam Smith." *Southern Economic Journal* 65: 1–19.

———. 1991. "Rational Choice: The Contrast Between Economics and Psychology." *Journal of Political Economy* 99: 877–97.

Sober, E., and D.S. Wilson. 1998. *Unto Others: The Evolution and Psychology of Unselfish Behavior.* Cambridge, MA: Harvard University Press.

Söderbaum, P. 2000. *Ecological Economics.* London: Earthscan Publications.

Sutinen, J.G., and K. Kuperan. 1999. "A Socio-Economic Theory of Regulatory Compliance." *International Journal of Social Economy* 26: 174–93.

Turner, J.C., and P.J. Oakes. 1989. "Self-Categorization Theory and Social Influence." In P. B. Paulus, ed., *The Psychology of Group Influence,* 233–75. Hillsdale, NJ: Lawrence Erlbaum Associates.

Vodopivec, B. 1992. "A Need Theory Perspective on the Parallelism of Attitude and Utility." *Journal of Economic Psychology* 13: 19–37.

Warsha, P.R., and C. Dröge. 1986. "Economic Utility Versus the Attitudinal Perspective of Consumer Choice." *Journal of Economic Psychology* 7: 37–60.

Wight, J.B. 2002. *Saving Adam Smith: A Tale of Wealth, Transformation and Virtue.* Upper Saddle River, NJ: Prentice Hall.

PART 2

CONTEXT AND MODELING

CHAPTER 7

WHAT A DIFFERENCE AN ASSUMPTION MAKES

Effort Discretion, Economic Theory, and Public Policy

MORRIS ALTMAN

One of the most intriguing and important focal points of behavioral economics relates to research that falls under the analytical umbrella of efficiency wage and x-efficiency theories. Fundamental to these theories is the assumption of effort discretion—that individuals have some control over both the quality and quantity dimensions of the effort they put into the production process, and that this effort is maximized only under very special circumstances. Conventional economic theory assumes that effort is not a variable and that effort is maximized given the firm's production function and the economic agent's human capital endowment. For example, effort is assumed to be maximized in both its quantity and quality dimensions irrespective of market conditions or the firm's industrial relations system. In terms of modeling effort variability and its consequences, the assumption of effort variability dominates any of the other assumptions that are often part and parcel of the efficiency wage/x-efficiency narrative, such as irrationality, quasi-rationality, and imperfect product markets. Indeed, such assumptions, I argue, are subsidiary or secondary assumptions that are not necessary to modeling key economic scenarios in terms of effort variability.

This essay focuses upon the analytical importance and public policy consequences of introducing the behavioral assumption of effort variability and thereby effort discretion into the objective function of the individual and the firm. Special and critical attention is paid to the foundational contributions of Leibenstein and Akerlof and extensions to their modeling and analysis based on efficiency wage and x-efficiency theories. This review of the foundational efficiency wage/x-efficiency literature, as well as the revisions offered herein, builds to a large extent upon my own earlier contributions to the efficiency wage and x-efficiency literature. (See Berg's essay in this volume for an elaborate general discussion of this literature and Frantz 2004 for a comparison of the contributions of Akerlof and Leibenstein.) Implications of effort-variability-based theories for an understanding of involuntary unemployment, economic efficiency, economic convergence, globalization, economic efficiency, and altruism are briefly addressed, as is the overall sustainability of low- and high-wage firms and economies in the context of competitive markets. With regard to the latter, special attention is devoted to a critical appraisal of the reciprocity ultimatum game literature, which predicts the convergence toward relatively high-wage organizational forms.

This discourse on efficiency wage/x-efficiency theory is also placed in the context of the larger behavioral economics narrative. Related to this, I discuss a hypothesis that dominates much of contemporary behavioral economics: that individuals are fundamentally irrational in choice behavior. I argue that behavioral economics has little to do with irrationality, and this is certainly true of efficiency wage and x-efficiency theory, although leading proponents of both efficiency wage and x-efficiency theory embed their models and analytical frameworks in the context of irrational or quasi-rational individuals or economic agents.

BEHAVIORAL ECONOMICS

Research on efficiency wages and x-efficiency, both of which are critically concerned with the productivity of labor as this relates to effort variability, is integral to behavioral economics in terms of its concern for the realism of the underlying behavioral and institutional assumptions that underlie the theory of the firm. A good example of a behavioral approach to the economics of the firm is presented in Cyert and March 1963. On a general level, one of the pioneers of behavioral economics, Herbert Simon (1959, 1987), distinguishes behavioral economics from contemporary economic theory largely in terms of the analytical significance of behavioral assumptions to the construction of economic theory. As opposed to neoclassical economics, which assumes that the realism of behavioral assumptions are of no analytical consequence (Altman 1999; Friedman 1953; Reder 1982), in behavioral economics the realism of behavioral assumptions can be of fundamental analytical importance. Behavioral economics is therefore distinguished by its efforts to test the empirical validity of a theory's behavioral assumptions and to determine the analytical and policy-related significance of introducing more realistic assumptions into standard theories.

> Thus, behavioural economics is best characterized not as a single specific theory but as a commitment to empirical testing of the neoclassical assumptions of human behaviour and to modifying economic theory on the basis of what is found in the testing process. And not all of the economists who hold a behavioural point of view also hold a common theory, or are all preoccupied with examining the same parts of the economic mechanism. (Simon 1987, 221)

With regard to the importance of the social and institutional parameters of economic analysis as opposed to the psychological, which is the mainstay of contemporary behavioral economics, Simon writes:

> The principal forerunner of a behavioral theory of the firm is the tradition usually called Institutionalism. It is not clear that all of the writings, European and American, usually lumped under this rubric have much in common, or that their authors would agree with each other's views. At best, they share a conviction that economic theory must be reformulated to take account of the social and legal structures amidst which market transactions are carried out. . . . The name of John R. Commons is prominent—perhaps the most prominent—among American Institutionalists. (Simon 1978, 499)

The realism of assumptions—and they can be of the psychological, social, or institutional variety—matter in general for behavioral economics, given that they impact on the accuracy of one's analytical predictions and one's causal analysis. This, in turn, can have powerful consequences for public policy and can impact on choices individuals make.

Leibenstein makes similar methodological points that are fundamental to his x-efficiency approach to the firm. Leibenstein discusses the relationship between theory and facts, the connection between *ex ante* predictions and the *ex post* confrontation of theory with empirical results.

> But the *ex ante, ex post* distinction does not really get at the roots of the issue. If one is to test a theory by making a "prediction," then the result appears to be more convincing if the prediction is a consequence of an inference from the theory, and the result is not known when the prediction is made. This has to do with effect rather than scientific significance. There is room for much *ex post* analysis of data. Economic historians could hardly perform their tasks if they could not apply their theories to existing data. A major purpose of theory is to *account* for the facts, obtained either *ex ante* or *ex post.* However, a significant problem is to sufficiently constrain the use of "free" undetermined variables, that is, to be sensitive to the danger that a fit may be obtained by attributing values needed to one or more unmeasured, unspecified, or possibly hidden variables involved. (Leibenstein 1983, 840)

Related to this point, Leibenstein argues:

> On the F-twist methodological issue, I believe that counterfactual postulates are unlikely to lead to correct *coherent* explanations. If the postulates cannot be tested, then we are forced to consider only the implications. But we would believe there is something wrong if we had a theory whose postulates were known to be counter to fact but which lead to correct predictions. . . . I do not believe that the only purpose of theory is as an engine for prediction, nor do I see that we should look at any particular set of methodological views as imposing decisive constraints on our scientific procedures at this stage in our knowledge. (Leibenstein 1983, 840)

With regard to x-efficiency theory, what is critical to appreciate is that by counterfactually constraining effort to some unspecified maximum irrespective of behavioral or institutional context, one is omitting a key explanatory variable in productivity and related analyses and thereby misspecifying causality and often generating models with relatively poor predictive power. If effort is assumed to be maximized, one might assume that productivity is maximized when it is not, one might ignore an important source of productivity change (effort variability), or one might assume that the economic pie is fixed and unaffected by distributional issues when in fact that is not the case. Leibenstein argues that by building theory upon more realistic and relevant analytical assumptions, one will be better able to explain economic reality and predict the consequences of individual choice behavior and public policy.

With regard to contemporary efficiency wage theory and its connection with behavioral economics, George Akerlof writes: "My dream was to strengthen macroeconomic theory by incorporating assumptions honed to the observation of such behavior" (2002, 411). His rendition of macroeconomics has therefore a behavioralist foundation, since it

> incorporates realistic assumptions grounded in psychological and sociological observation, [and has] produced models that comfortably account for each of these macroeconomic phenomena . . . Instead of denying the very existence of involuntary unemployment, behavioral macroeconomists have provided coherent explanations. Efficiency wage theories, which first appeared in the 1970's and 1980's, make the concept of involuntary unemployment meaningful. These models posit that, for reasons such as morale, fairness, insider power, or

asymmetric information, employers have strong motives to pay workers more than the minimum necessary to attract them. Such "efficiency wages" are above market clearing, so that jobs are rationed and some workers cannot obtain them. These workers are involuntarily unemployed. (Akerlof 2002, 413–14)

Contemporary efficiency wage theory's raison d'être is to explain the existence of persistent involuntary unemployment based on realistic microeconomic assumptions. This is to correct for the arbitrary and unrealistic assumptions of the classical and new classical economists whose incorrect assumptions (according to the efficiency wage theorists) predict that all persistent unemployment must be voluntary.

CHOICE RATIONALITY

To situate one's modeling in the context of more realistic assumptions in no way implies that such behavioralist modeling presumes that economic agents need be irrational, although this is the sense one gets from much of contemporary behavioral economics (e.g., Kahneman and Tversky 1979; Tversky and Kahneman 1981; Kahneman 2003; Thaler 1992; for alternative behavioralist perspectives, see Altman 2003b; Gigerenzer 2000; Gigerenzer and Selten 2001; Goldstein and Gigerenzer 2002; Rieskamp, Hertwig, and Todd, this volume; Smith 2003, 2005; Todd and Gigerenzer 2003). For example, Kahneman writes:

> Our research attempted to obtain a map of bounded rationality, by exploring the systematic biases that separate the beliefs that people have and the choices they make from the optimal beliefs and choices assumed in rational-agent models. The rational-agent model was our starting point and the main source of our null hypotheses. (Kahneman 2003, 1449)

Deviations from the conventional norm imply, according to this perspective, errors and biases—the absence of rationality and even intelligence—in choice behavior. Given that the notion of individuals as fundamentally irrational is thought to be incompatible with general economic modeling, is this assumption of irrationality a necessary condition for behavioral economic theories, especially those related to the x-efficiency and efficiency wage discourse? Or is it simply the case that the conventional definitions of rationality are wanting from both descriptive and normative perspectives and need to be modified? In this case, one need not and should not drop the assumption of rational-intelligent economic agents. Behaving rationally, such as with regard to effort choice, may simply not be what the conventional wisdom presumes it to be. Indeed, behaving as a neoclassical rational agent in terms of effort choice might be the height of irrationality.

Herbert Simon argues that

> the term "rational" has long had in economics a much more specific meaning than its general dictionary signification of "agreeable to reason; not absurd, preposterous, extravagant, foolish, fanciful, or the like: intelligent, sensible." As is well known, the rational man of economics is a maximizer, who will settle for nothing less than the best. . . . It is this concept of rationality that is economics' main export commodity in its trade with the other social sciences. It is no novelty in those sciences to propose that people behave rationally—if that term is taken in its broader dictionary sense. Assumptions of rationality are essential components of virtually all the sociological, psychological, political, and anthropological theories with which I am familiar. What economics has to export then is not rationality, but a

very particular and special form of it—the rationality of the utility maximizer, and a pretty smart one at that. (Simon 1978, 2)

Simon also makes the case that

almost all human behavior has a large rational component but only in terms of the broader everyday sense of rationality, not the economists' more specialized sense of maximization [; moreover,] economics itself has not by any means limited itself to the narrower definition of rationality. [In addition,] economics has largely been preoccupied with the *results* of rational choice rather than the *process* of choice. (Simon 1978, 2)

From this perspective, deviations from the maximization assumption cannot be taken as evidence of irrational choice behavior.

More generally, Marsh argues:

Engineers of artificial intelligence have modified their perceptions of efficient problem solving procedures by studying the actual behavior of human problem solvers. Engineers of organizational decision making have modified their models of rationality on the basis of studies of actual organizational behavior. . . . Modern students of human choice behavior frequently assume, at least implicitly, that actual human choice behavior in some way or other is likely to make sense. It can be understood as being the behavior of an intelligent being or group of intelligent beings. (Marsh 1978, 589)

Therefore Marsh and Simon, amongst the founders of behavioral economics, argue that if one searches deep enough, one is likely to discover the rational underlying choice behavior even if this behavior is not maximizing in the traditional sense. More recently, Vernon Smith, the founding father of experimental economics, whose work ties into and overlaps with behavioral economics, has made a case for ecological rationality:

It is shown that the investor who chooses to maximize expected profit (discounted total withdrawals) fails in finite time. Moreover, there exist a variety of non-profit-maximizing behaviors that have a positive probability of never failing. In fact it is shown that firms that maximize profits are the least likely to be the market survivors. My point is simple: when experimental results are contrary to standard concepts of rationality, assume not just that people are irrational, but that you may not have the right model of rational behavior. *Listen to what your subjects may be trying to tell you.* Think of it this way. If you could choose your ancestors, would you want them to be survivalists or to be expected wealth maximizers? (Smith 2005, 149)

(On this point also see Gigerenzer 2002; Gigerenzer and Selten 2001; Goldstein and Gigerenzer 2002; Todd and Gigerenzer 2003.) Survival implies that economic agents have behaved sensibly and intelligently—that is to say rationally, if survival is a rational goal. Behaving neoclassically and not surviving would not be ecologically rational, nor is it how individuals actually behave, nor would one want such ecologically erroneous behavior to be recommended. Moreover, the ecological rationality perspective, referred to by Gigerenzer and associates as "fast and frugal heuristics," suggests that it is often the case that neoclassical rationality yields suboptimal results. From the perspective of economic efficiency, a rational neoclassical agent can be expected to perform less efficiently than an ecologically rational, "fast and frugal" economic agent. What are errors and biases for Kahneman and Tversky and fellow travelers are often optimal behavior from the benchmark of ecological rationality. If individuals behave neoclassically, they would be therefore behaving suboptimally with regard to economic efficiency, given their level of effort input.

Simon makes specific reference to theories of the firm in his discourse on rationality:

> The general features of bounded rationality, selective search, satisficing, and so on have been taken as the starting points for a number of attempts to build theories of the business firm incorporating behavioral assumptions [this includes Leibenstein's x-efficiency theory]. Characterized in this way, there seems to be little commonality among all of these theories and models, except that they depart in one way or another from the classical assumption of perfect rationality in firm decision making. A closer look, however, and a more abstract description of their assumptions, shows that they share several basic characteristics. Most of them depart from the assumption of profit maximization in the short run, and replace it with an assumption of goals defined in terms of targets—that is, they are to greater or lesser degree satisficing theories. If they do retain maximizing assumptions, they contain some kind of mechanism that prevents the maximum from being attained, at least in the short run. In the Cyert-March theory, and that of Leibenstein, this mechanism can be viewed as producing "organizational slack," the magnitude of which may itself be a function of motivational and environmental variables. (Simon 1978, 508–9)

The implications of deviating from the conventional maximization assumption can be of profound analytical significance, but many conventional economists find it disturbing. According to Simon:

> The presence of something like organizational slack in a model of the business firm introduces complexity in the firm's behavior in the short run. Since the firm may operate very far from any optimum, the slack serves as a buffer between the environment and the firm's decisions. Responses to environmental events can no longer be predicted simply by analyzing the "requirements of the situation," but depend on the specific decision processes that the firm employs. However well this characteristic of a business firm model corresponds to reality, it reduces the attractiveness of the model for many economists, who are reluctant to give up the process-independent predictions of classical theory, and who do not feel at home with the kind of empirical investigation that is required for disclosing actual real world decision processes. But there is another side to the matter. If, in the face of identical environmental conditions, different decision mechanisms can produce different firm behaviors, this sensitivity of outcomes to process can have important consequences for analysis at the level of markets and the economy. Political economy, whether descriptive or normative, cannot remain indifferent to this source of variability in response. (Simon 1978, 509)

This speaks to the notion of multiple equilibria, which is developed in some detail below in the discussion of a behavioral model of the firm.

In terms of a theory of the firm, here we have individuals who from the perspective of the firm deviate from maximizing behavior, which might take the form of not maximizing firm profit through organizational slack. Do such deviations from conventionally defined (in the economics literature) rational behavior imply that individuals are not behaving rationally or intelligently, and should we therefore define such deviant behavior as irrational or quasi-rational? With regard to efficiency wage and x-efficiency theory, does this then imply that if such deviancy (or biases and errors with regard to the conventional norm) is corrected, the economy would perform more efficiently? Or is it simply that rational behavior can yield economic inefficiency under normal circumstances and therefore that rational inefficiency need not be an aberration? In other words, if non-neoclassical behavior is intelligent given the circumstances faced by individuals and the substance of individuals' cognitive abilities, we must address the question of whether neoclassical efficiencies are realizable, and if they are, the circumstances under which they can be achieved. Both the efficiency wage and x-efficiency literatures suggest that economic efficiency can be achieved under reasonable circumstances.

Akerlof and Leibenstein and the modeling approaches that their contributions represent are quite sympathetic to the quasi-rational approach to economic agency because individuals deviate from neoclassical norms. However, Leibenstein's economic agents are certainly intelligent, as are Akerlof's. Leibenstein's agents simply do not conform to neoclassical behavioral norms with regard to maximizing effort input into the production process irrespective of circumstances. It is for this reason that Leibenstein refers to individuals as being quasi-rational—but this unnecessarily confounds the question of rationality with arbitrary neoclassical behavioral norms. Leibenstein also refers to neoclassical efficiency as his theoretical benchmark for ideal efficiency. But, once again, x-efficiency theory is all about a discourse on the necessary conditions for intelligent agents to perform optimally and to move the economy toward more efficiency in production. Also, in the efficiency wage literature agents are largely intelligent and rational, but given effort variability, real wages tend to be above their market-clearing values. But such behavior need not be inconsistent with utility maximization. Utility is not maximized by maximizing effort input. Quasi-rationality enters the picture as the solution to the market-clearing problem in terms of money illusion. And given how money illusion is defined in efficiency wage theory, related to the cognitive costs of computing and reacting to small decreases in real wages, it is not clear how such illusions are irrational even from a conventional neoclassical perspective.

I argue, in the traditional of Simon, March, Smith, and Gigerenzer, that economic agents can be modeled as rational or intelligent in behavior even if they do deviate from neoclassical norms. Thus individuals can be rational even if they do not maximize effort inputs under all circumstances. Indeed, individuals can be viewed as broadly rational:

> Individuals maximize utility in a consistent way, and . . . they consider the effect of their actions on future as well as present utilities . . . individuals are still assumed to make forward-looking, maximizing, and consistent choices. (Becker 1996, 22–23)

But in this modeling framework the individual's objective function is not specified. As Becker points out, rational individuals' preferences are influenced by circumstances inclusive of past experiences and social interactions.

Following from such an understanding of rationality, each individual can have a different objective function, and there is no a priori guarantee that objective functions are consistent across individuals. Rational agents might have conflicting preferences. There is no reason to expect a unitary objective function, nor that the dominant objective function with regard to decision making will be consistent with firms producing efficiently (effort maximization in terms of x-efficiency theory) or with an economy minimizing unemployment, which is the analytical focus of efficiency wage theory. I argue that the assumption of rationality, broadly defined and inclusive of maximizing individuals, is consistent with the realization of both economic efficiency and inefficiency as well as of either significant or marginal amounts of voluntary unemployment. At least the important efficiency wage/x-efficiency vein of behavioral economics can be effectively and efficiently mined and processed without reference to irrationality as a key causal variability. It is in fact quite telling that significant inefficiencies can be generated by the choices of rational individuals. In the behavioral model discussed below, persistent and significant rational ineffi- ciencies can be obtained even in a competitive environment. Survival does not imply efficiency. Being fit enough to survive as a firm can take on various organizational forms and economic results, only a subset of which need be consistent with economic efficiency. In this sense ecologi- cal rationality need not imply economic efficiency, where such efficiency is realizable only in particular environmental (institutional) settings.

EFFICIENCY WAGE THEORY AND EMPLOYMENT

Leibenstein's Foundational Modeling: Introducing Effort Variability

What is today dubbed efficiency wage theory was pioneered by Harvey Leibenstein (1957a, 1957b) to help resolve the apparent paradox of there being long-run surplus labor in less developed eco- nomics at positive real wages. Surplus labor can take the form of either hidden or actual unemploy- ment. All agents in his modeling framework are rational and maximizing with regard to profit (marginal cost equals marginal benefit) and utility. Leibenstein breaks with the conventional wisdom by intro- ducing the empirically based assumption that effort input varies positively with real wages since real wages affect the physiological ability of workers to work more intensively. Leibenstein assumes that the changing capacity of workers to work more or less hard will be translated into actual changes in effort input on the job. In the conventional modeling effort input remains constant in the face of change in real wages. Given the assumption of effort variability, cutting real wages in response to downward pressures on the labor market generated by surplus labor need not yield a profit-maxi- mizing solution to the firm, as it would in the conventional model. Thus, profit-maximizing rational firms will not cut real wages as they would in the conventional model, yielding surplus labor. In other words, long-term unemployment is a product of the downward stickiness of real wages, as it is in the pre-Keynesian classical world and in the more recent new classical rendition of the classical model. If only real wages could be cut, surplus labor would be employed. But Leibenstein maintains that rational firm owners attempt to form coalitions, often unstable, to prevent market forces from driving wages downward, since this would cut into profits, or else simply hire more workers than would be warranted by profit-maximizing conditions—they hire a subset of workers whose mar- ginal product exceeds their wage—to relieve downward market pressure on wages. This is, of course, a form of featherbedding.

By introducing effort variability into his modeling framework, Leibenstein posits that each real wage can be modeled as being related to a unique marginal product of labor curve and that where the wage equals the marginal product of labor there is a unique net profit accruing to the firm. Any cut in the wage rate shifts the marginal product of labor curve inward as compared to the conventional model, wherein a change in real wages simply results in movement along the marginal product curve. Therefore, with effort variability, cutting real wages could result in ei- ther the same or a lesser level of employment, instead of resulting in more employment. I would illustrate this basic argument in terms of Figure 7.1, where full employment is given by N_2, but current employment stands at only N_1 given the wage rate W_1, where the wage equals the mar- ginal product of labor at e^*. The wage W_1 yields marginal product curve MP_2. In the conven- tional model, market forces would force the real wage down, yielding full employment, N_2. But given effort variability, a cut in the real wages yields a lower marginal product curve, such as MP_3, where equilibrium is given at e_3 and employment is no higher than it was at the higher

Figure 7.1 **Labor Demand and Marginal Product**

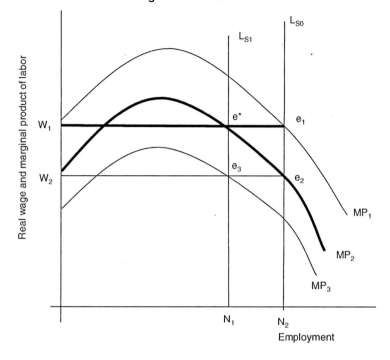

wage. Of course, employment could have fallen had the marginal product curve shifted inward any further as a result of the diminution in real wages.

Leibenstein takes this argument further, making specific assumptions about the shape and positioning of the marginal product of labor curve, illustrated in Figure 7.2, where the two marginal product curves are drawn in such a fashion that there is one point, e_2, where the curves are tangent. This would be at the point of full employment, N_2. In this scenario, the marginal product curve shifts inward from MP_1 to MP_3 with a cut in the real wage from W_1 to W_2. Moreover, given the shift in the marginal product curve as wages fall and the assumed shape of the marginal product curves, the area above the wage rate line W_1 for MP_1 is greater than the area above wage rate line W_2 for MP_2. Thus net profit is greater at the higher wage given effort variability. Given these assumptions, the firm maximizes profit at wage rate W_1, yielding a less than full employment level of employment, N_1. Full employment could be obtained at a lower wage, but this would be inconsistent with the firm maximizing its profit. And for this reason firms resist market pressure to pay workers a lower wage rate.

Another point made by Leibenstein and taken up by contemporary efficiency wage theorists is that there is one wage that yields optimal net profit. This argument is embedded in the implicit assumptions made by Leibenstein with regard to the elasticity of effort input with respect to changes in the real wage and the elasticity of productivity with respect to changes in effort input. Leibenstein assumes diminishing returns in the relationship between wage changes and changes in effort, and changes in effort and changes in productivity. For example, for any wage below the one that yields maximum profit, the elasticity of effort to wage changes is greater than 1, and above this wage the elasticity is less than 1. The unique wage that maximizes net profit is referred in the contemporary literature as the efficiency wage. This point can be illustrated in Figure 7.3,

Figure 7.2 **Labor Demand, Marginal Product, and Profits**

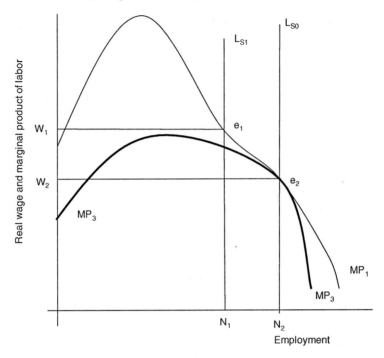

where optimal employment revenue is mapped along the vertical axis and employment along the horizontal axis. The concept of optimal employment revenue is derived from Leibenstein and refers to the maximum net revenue that is generated for any given real wage. Only one real wage yielding one level of employment maximizes net revenue, W_1 and N_1, respectively. This level of employment is less than full employment, where the latter can be achieved only at a lower real wage and at a lower net revenue or profit. There is an unambiguous trade-off between profit and higher levels of employment in this modeling framework. Thus, more employment is obtained here only if firms hire more workers than is warranted by maximum profits, such as occurs with featherbedding. Leibenstein argues that firms, independently and jointly, search for ways to hire more workers than can be justified by the criterion of profit maximization so as to relieve downward pressure on the labor market. And this makes sense as long as net profits remain greater than they would be at the market-clearing wage. However, each firm remains under severe pressure to pay lower real wages given the existence of surplus labor, thereby resulting in the efficiency wage being unstable. Alternatively, if workers could be made to accept lower wages without reducing effort inputs, more employment could be realized. But this could not come to pass if effort is strictly tied to real wage levels in a world where real income is so low that variations in real wages affect workers' capacity to generate more or less effort input.

A Behavioral Interlude to the Efficiency Wage Narrative

Prior to discussing contemporary efficiency wage theory it would be helpful to further elaborate upon the implications of efficiency wage theory on the cost side. Based on Altman 1992

Figure 7.3 **Labor Demand and Marginal Revenue**

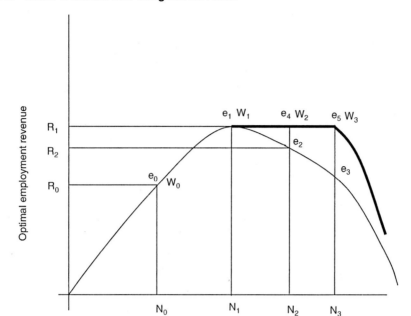

and 1996, we assume for simplicity that labor is the only factor input. Given this assumption, the cost dimension of efficiency wage narrative can be given by equations 1a and 1b and Figure 7.4.

$$MC = \frac{w}{\left(\dfrac{dQ}{dL}\right)} \qquad (1a)$$

$$AC = \frac{w}{\left(\dfrac{Q}{L}\right)} \qquad (1b)$$

where MC is marginal cost, w is the wage rate, (dQ/dL) is the marginal product of labor, AC is average cost, and (Q/L) is the average product of labor. In the efficiency wage narrative there is only one wage that minimizes marginal cost and average cost. Any downward deviation of the wage from the efficiency wage increases unit cost for example, just as it will reduce net profits. This point is further illustrated in Figure 7.4, where W_1 is the efficiency wage and cost is minimized at e_1. The efficiency wage is unique—cost increases if the wage rises or fall. This is given, it is critically important to note, by the assumed smooth convexity of the cost curve.

Figure 7.4   **Labor Demand and Production Costs I**

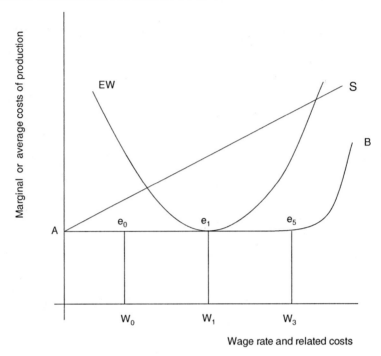

Contemporary Efficiency Wage Theory

Leibenstein's foundational efficiency wage narrative was finessed and enriched by a new line of scholars, exemplified by George Akerlof (Akerlof 1980, 1982, 1984, 2002; Akerlof and Yellen 1986, 1988, 1990; Akerlof, Dickens, and Perry 2000; Bewley 1999; Shapiro and Stiglitz 1984; Stiglitz 1987), whose objective was to provide a rigorous micro foundation for persistent involuntary unemployment. Indeed, Akerlof and Stiglitz were awarded the Nobel Prize in Economics in part for these efforts. Contemporary efficiency wage theory is not tied to the notion that effort variation is a function of the physiological capacity of workers to supply more or less effort input. Rather, it is argued that effort varies for sociological reasons such as fairness, which is tied to relative real wages. Workers retaliate against employers when they feel hard done by. The latter theme is developed in the ultimatum game and related reciprocity literature (see, for example, Fehr and Schmidt 1999; Fehr and Gachter 2000a, 2000b; Güth 1995; see also Güth and Ortmann, this volume).

This modeling of the labor market attempts to identify a rationale for the downward stickiness of real wages, which is out of the choice domain of workers. Firms refuse to cut real wages over the business cycle because they are quite aware of the fact that such wage cuts would only serve to reduce effort input on the part of their employees, thereby reducing profits and increasing unit cost. It is assumed that there is one wage, the efficiency wage, that serves to maximize profits and minimize unit cost. Thus workers are paid above the market-clearing wage, just as they are in Leibenstein's narrative. But unlike in Leibenstein's discourse, the efficiency wage is stable—individual firms have no incentive to pay a lower wage given the downward market pressures on the labor market. Surplus labor as manifested in involuntary unemployment is a stable equilibrium. Here we have the classical and new classical narrative revisited and refined such that workers bear no responsibility for the supply-side cause of persistent unemployment, as they must in the classical model of the labor market. Needless to say, the public policy metaphor is the same in both narratives—real wages must be cut if one wishes to secure more employment. The demand side might play a role in determining the level of employment, but supply conditions establish the micro priors for determining the extent to which more workers can be profitably employed. However, unlike Leibenstein, contemporary efficiency wage theorists, especially Akerlof, argue that is it quite possible for real wages to be cut over the course of the business cycle so as to secure more employment without unleashing the efficiency wage effect, which would make such a wage cut untenable from the perspective of profit-maximizing firms.

Critical to cutting real wages without workers retaliating by reducing effort input is the assumption that workers are subject to money illusion. If government adopts a mild inflationary policy, real wages fall, yielding more employment, without workers responding by reducing effort input. Thus real wages cannot be reduced by individual firms, since workers will reduce effort input in retaliation, but macro policy can certainly do the trick. Therefore, if workers are quasi-rational (some might say irrational), higher levels of employment can be secured. But such irrationality on the part of workers is strongly denied by the new classical economics, an assumption that Akerlof argues is fundamentally wrong. Akerlof argues with regard to the significance of efficiency wage theory for understanding the persistence of involuntary unemployment:

> A major contribution of behavioral macroeconomics is to demonstrate that, under sensible behavioral assumptions, monetary policy *does* affect real outcomes just as Keynesian economics long asserted. Cognitive psychology pictures decision makers as "intuitive scientists" who summarize information and make choices based on simplified mental frames. Reliance on rules of thumb that omit factors whose consideration have only a small effect on profit or utility is an implication of such cognitive parsimony. In the wage-price context, simple rules cause inertia in the response of aggregate wages (and prices) to shocks—the exact "sticky wage/price" behavior that New Classical economists had so scornfully derided. In the New Classical critique, the inertial wage behavior hypothesized in the "neoclassical synthesis" is irrational, costly for workers and firms, hence implausible. Behavioral economists have responded by demonstrating that rules of thumb involving "money illusion" are not only commonplace but also sensible—neither foolhardy nor implausible: the losses from reliance on such rules are extremely small. (Akerlof 2002, 416)

Akerlof elaborates on this point, relating his discourse to that of Kahneman-Tversky type behavioral economics:

> Keynes' assumption that workers resist nominal wage cuts was consistent with his intuitive understanding of psychology. The assumption also coincides with psychological theory and evidence. Prospect theory posits that individuals evaluate changes in their circumstances according to the gains or losses they entail relative to some reference point. The evidence suggests that individuals place much greater weight on avoiding losses than on incurring gains. Daniel Kahneman and Amos Tversky (1979) have demonstrated that many experimental results that are inconsistent with expected utility maximization can be rationalized by prospect theory. Downward wage rigidity is a natural implication of prospect theory if the current money wage is taken as a reference point by workers in measuring gains and losses. In support of this view, [Shafir, Diamond, and Tversky 1997] found in a question-

naire study that individuals' mental frames are defined not just in the real terms hypothesized by classical economists but also exhibit some money illusion. Numerous empirical studies document that money wages are, in fact, downward sticky. (Akerlof 2002, 420)

Thus, for Akerlof, the downward stickiness of wages applies specifically to money, not necessarily to real wages. Workers' cognitive limitations and the related costs of processing information, inclusive of the effects of low rates of inflation on real wages, open the door to the capacity of workers to be deluded into accepting lower real wages when this is a product of inflationary monetary policy.

Akerlof summarizes some of the empirics related to his argument that, contrary to the anti-Keynesian economists, monetary policy can have a permanent effect on employment:

At low inflation there is a long-run trade-off between output and inflation if there is aversion to nominal pay cuts. Unlike the Friedman-Phelps model, in which such a trade-off is transitory, long-term increases in inflation (if it is close to zero) result in significantly less employment and more output. The logic goes as follows. In both good times and bad, some firms and industries do better than others. Wages need to adjust to accommodate these differences in economic fortunes. In times of moderate inflation and productivity growth, relative wages can easily adjust. Unlucky firms can raise the wages they pay by less than the average, while the lucky firms can give above-average increases. However, if productivity growth is low (as it was from the early 1970's through the mid-1990's in the United States) and there is no inflation, firms that need to cut their real wages can do so only by cutting the money wages of their employees. Under realistic assumptions about the variability and serial correlation of demand shocks across firms, the needed frequency of nominal cuts rises rapidly as inflation declines. An aversion on the part of firms to impose nominal wage cuts results in higher permanent rates of unemployment. Because the real wages at which labor is supplied are higher at every level of employment when inflation is low, the unemployment rate consistent with stable inflation rises as inflation falls to low levels. Spillovers produce an aggregate employment impact that exceeds the employment changes in those firms that are constrained by their inability to cut wages. Thus, a benefit of a little inflation is that it "greases the wheels of the labor market." Simulations of a model with intersectoral shocks and aversion on the part of firms to nominal wage cuts suggests that, with realistically chosen parameters, the trade-off between inflation and unemployment is severe at very low rates of inflation, when productivity growth is low. For example, a permanent reduction in inflation from 2 percent per year to zero results in a permanent increase in unemployment of approximately 2 percentage points. (Akerlof 2002, 421)

Contemporary efficiency wage theorists, best exemplified in the work of Akerlof, not only recast Leibenstein's theoretical frame, such that it relates to developed economies where workers are paid well above physiological subsistence and efficiency wages are stable given their profit-maximizing function. They also make the case that it is possible to subvert the workers' tendency to reduce effort input when real wages are reduced. Thus Akerlof could argue that a solid theoretical basis has been established to demonstrate not only the reasonableness of the assumption of the downward inflexibility of wages but also why real wages can be cut in face of this inflexibility through sound monetary policy (for further details see Akerlof, Dickens, and Perry 1996, 2000).

It is important to note, however, that Keynes completely rejects the notion of money illusion, although he assumes that reductions in real wages are a necessary supply-side condition for increasing employment given the conventional assumption of diminishing returns to labor and therefore a downward-sloping marginal product of labor curve. Keynes argues:

> [Workers] do not resist reductions of real wages, which are associated with increases in aggregate employment and leave relative money-wages unchanged, unless the reduction proceeds so far as to threaten a reduction of the real wage below the marginal disutility of the existing volume of employment. Every trade union will put up some resistance to a cut in money-wages, however, small. But since no trade union would dream of striking on every occasion of a rise in the cost of living, they do not raise the obstacle to any increase in aggregate employment which is attributed to them by the classical school. (Keynes 1936, 14–15)

For Keynes, workers are not characterized by quasi-irrationality. They accept cuts in real wages up to some point, given their expectation of what this implies for increasing employment. This being said, the assumption that real wages must be cut for employment to be increased as an unequivocal derivative of efficiency wage theory requires some critical perspective given the policy implications of this assumption.

A BEHAVIORAL MODEL OF FIRM AND EFFICIENCY WAGE THEORY

One alternative narrative to conventional efficiency wage modeling stems from a behavioral model of the firm, which I've developed in some detail elsewhere (for example, Altman 1992, 1996, 1998, 1999, 2001b, 2002, 2003a, 2005). This modeling of the firm and economic agency also serves as a segue to my critical discussion of x-efficiency theory. Although effort is introduced into the short-run production function as a variable, unlike what is assumed in the traditional efficiency wage literature, in the behavioral model there exists some linearity with respect to the relationship between effort inputs and the wage rate, which, for simplicity, is assumed to embody the entire system of industrial relations within the firm. In this scenario, there is an array of wage rates consistent with a unique marginal, average cost, or net profit when productivity changes, brought about through effort input changes, just suffice to offset the cost impact that changes to the real wage might otherwise have. In the conventional efficiency wage view, there exists one unique wage that minimizes costs or maximizes profit.

These basic points can be illustrated in equations 1a and 1b, above, where labor is the only factor input. In this case, cost does not increase in the face of an increasing wage rate, nor does it fall when the wage rate falls if there exist corresponding and proportional changes in the marginal and average product, respectively. There is no one efficiency wage. It is important to note that productivity need not increase proportionally to increases in labor costs when labor is only one among many inputs into the production process, which is typically the case. When labor is not the only compensated factor input, labor productivity need increase less than proportionally to increases in labor costs so as to neutralize increases labor cost. This point is illustrated in equation 2:

$$\frac{dAC}{AC} = \left(\frac{dw}{w}\right) * \left(\frac{w*L}{w*L+NLC}\right) \tag{2}$$

where dAC is the change in average cost, dw is the change in the wage rate, and NLC is nonlabor costs. If, for example, the wage rate is increased by 10 percent (dw/w) and wage costs $(w*L)$

represent 100 percent of total costs, labor productivity must increase by 10 percent to compensate for what would otherwise be a 10 percent increase in average costs. However, if wage costs represent only 50 percent of total costs, labor productivity must increase by only 5 percent to compensate for what would otherwise be a 5 percent increase in average costs.

The implications of introducing some linearity to the wage productivity relationship are further illustrated in Figure 7.4, above. Line segments S, EW, and B refer to the assumed wage-cost relationship in the conventional, efficiency wage, and behavioral models, respectively. In the standard model, where effort is fixed, increasing wages increases costs, ceteris paribus. In the efficiency wage model there is one wage that minimizes cost. But in the behavioral model, there is an array of wage rates consistent with one unique unit cost, at least to W_3, after which output cannot be increased sufficiently to offset increasing wage costs—here we enter into the realm of diminishing returns. Introducing a degree of linearity into the wage-productivity relationship, with effort input as an intermediary variable, yields significantly different analytical predictions with regard to the impact wage changes have upon unit cost as compared to what is generated in either the standard or efficiency wage models. This point is further illustrated in Figure 7.3 above, where the relationship between wages, net profit, and employment is modeled. In this scenario, there is an array of wage rates and levels of employment consistent with one unique maximum net profit (optimal employment revenue). As the wage rate increases above W_3, net profit falls as increasing labor productivity related to increased effort input no longer suffices to compensate for the increases in the wage rate. This compares to the efficiency wage narrative, wherein only one wage rate corresponds to maximum net profit, and this at a less than full employment level of employment.

The behavioral model suggests that there exists a considerable degree of freedom with regard to possible real wages and employment combinations sustainable for a competitive profit-maximizing firm if effort discretion exists and there is no assumed mechanical (nonlinear) relationship posited between the level of real wages, effort input, and productivity. It is important to note that one can have some linearity in the wage-productivity relationship even if one assumes there exist eventually diminishing returns in the wage-effort input relationship. This point is illustrated in Figure 7.5, where effort input is mapped against total product in the right quadrant, yielding an effort-product curve (EP). This curve is constructed to reflect diminishing returns. The wage rate is mapped against total product in the left quadrant such that the wage rate equals total output in a one-factor input model. In this scenario, each percentage increase in total output equals the percentage increase in the wage rate, yielding constant unit cost. This diagram therefore addresses the question of the extent to which effort must increase if unit cost is to remain constant in face of wage rate increases, and how this is contextualized given diminishing returns to effort. Clearly diminishing returns to effort do not preclude linearity between wage rates and unit cost. Diminishing returns simply imply that effort input must increase at an increasing rate for every given change in the wage rate. Initially effort might have to increase much less than the proportional increase in the wage rate. But as the wage rate keeps increasing, effort will eventually have to increase much more than the proportional increase in the wage rate if unit cost is to remain constant. Eventually, effort input is maximized and increasing wages are matched by increasing unit cost, at point f along EP. Unit cost might also increase if economic agents will not increase effort input sufficiently to generate the productivity increase required to offset the impact of increasing wages. Thus unit cost can increase prior to point f. But there is no a priori reason to expect, in theory, that there will be one wage that will minimize unit cost when effort input is a variable in the production function. Much depends on how economic agents respond to changes in wages and this is an empirical question. The critical point here is that the assumption in efficiency

Figure 7.5   **Labor Demand and Production Costs II**

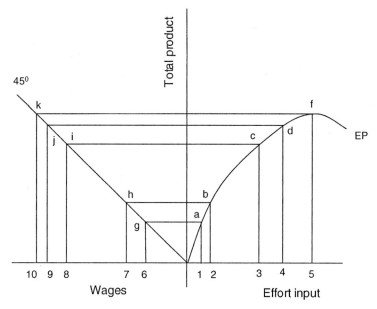

wage theory that relatively high wages yields excess unemployment due to their generating higher unit costs and lower net profits is simply an assumption, and it need not be the ideal one given the facts at hand.

Introducing some linearity into the wage-cost relationship is consistent with real wages being inflexible downward over the business cycle, as in the traditional efficiency wage narrative. Firm owners and managers have no incentive to reduce real wages if there is no perceived advantage in doing so and if there are short-term costs involved, such as worsening the labor-management relationship. This is especially true if it is perceived that real wages will be restored during the upswing in the business cycle. But the behavioral model suggests that relatively high real wages need not impede employment growth, given adequate aggregate demand, if such real wages are compensated for in terms of higher labor productivity. Moreover, in this case, increasing prices to reduce real wage, given that workers suffer from money illusion, is no longer a necessary condition to generate more employment (Altman 2006a).

In Figure 7.6, the increase in employment is illustrated using vertical supply curves wherein changes in employment are not affected by price changes. Holding the price level constant at P_0, employment increases from N_0 to N_1 as demand rises as a consequence of an outward shift of the marginal product of labor curve, which compensates for any increases in real wages required to induce the requisite increases in labor supply underlying increasing employment. This is reflected in the movement of the employment supply curve from S_2 to S_1. The employment supply curve is thus perfectly inelastic with respect to price, and employment becomes "full employment" once employment is at a maximum given the labor supply and production functions. In the short run, increasing demand from D_0 would simply increase price, given employment curve S_2. In the longer run, as the supply curve shifts outward to S_1, employment increases to N_1. An employment supply curve can be given by $P_0c_2c_1$. In this scenario, a price increase can accompany the increase in employment if the demand increases sufficiently, for example, to D_1. But unlike the Akerlof narrative, it is not the increase in the price level that actually causes the increase in

Figure 7.6 **Prices and Employment**

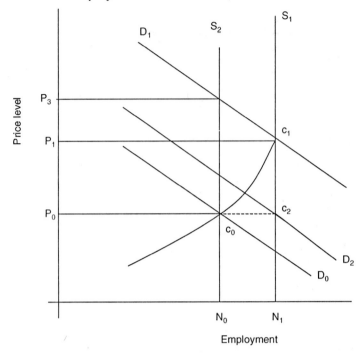

employment to N_1. Rather, it is an increase in aggregate demand in the context of the real-wage-rate-induced increase in labor productivity that is responsible for an increase in the level of employment. The supply curve shifts to the right for conventional reasons, which should incorporate extraordinary increases in efficiency as well as technological change induced by increasing real wages (Altman 2002). Cutting real wages by increasing demand and prices, on the other hand, would have the effect of shifting the supply curve to the left, yielding both higher prices and less employment. Thus if S_1 is the initial supply curve and demand is increased from D_2 to D_1, the price would rise first to P_1, cutting real wages. This would shift the supply curve to S_2, yielding a lower equilibrium employment at N_0 and a price of P_3. In this context, employment would be encouraged by efforts to promote increases in labor productivity and more aggressive demand management strategies designed to accommodate the resulting increase in aggregate output, as opposed to designing policy to cut real wages.

The behavioral model is consistent with the work of Blanchflower and Oswald (1995), who find, using an international sample population, that regions with low unemployment rates are systematically correlated with high wage rates and vice versa. The level of unemployment associated with a particular level of real wages critically depends on the elasticity of labor productivity to the wage rate and the responsiveness of macroeconomic demand-side variables to increasing output. The behavioral model also suggests that a positive empirical relationship between the price level (or the rate of inflation) and employment need not be a causal one. Inflation might simply be a reflection of an accommodating macroeconomic policy that allows for the absorption of the increasing output flowing from the increase in labor productivity. Inflation would here be a product of overshooting increases in aggregate demand in a world of uncertainty. In this sense, low rates of inflation are consistent with increasing the level of employment, although not the cause of such increases.

X-EFFICIENCY: A GENERAL FRAMEWORK

What Is X-efficiency?

Simon's remarks on why and how inefficiency can persist provides an informative context within which to discuss x-efficiency theory, wherein economically inefficient firms can survive in the long run. Simon argues, in the context of discussing the evolutionary argument with regard to firm survival, that unlike what is maintained in the neoclassical theory of the firm, where only the fittest—cost-minimizing or profit-maximizing—firms can survive, there is no good reason to expect that inefficient firms should be wiped out by market forces.

> In the biological world at least, many organisms survive that are not maximizers but that operate at far less than the highest achievable efficiency. Their survival is not threatened as long as no other organisms have evolved that can challenge the possession of their specific niches. Analogously, since there is no reason to suppose that every business firm is challenged by an optimally efficient competitor, survival only requires meeting the competition. In a system in which there are innumerable rents, of long-term and short-term duration, even egregious sub-optimality may permit survival. (Simon 1987, 223)

Inefficient firms can survive if they are not challenged by relatively efficient firms. Leibenstein makes the case that inefficiency persists because inefficient firms are protected from competitive forces. Critical to this protection is the existence of imperfect product markets, which provide firms with the capacity to produce at a higher unit cost than what can be achieved if firms produced optimally. Thus firms are typically not challenged, argues Leibenstein, by optimally efficient competitors.

Leibenstein's x-efficiency theory has two critical dimensions. Much of this theory is concerned with modeling persistent economic inefficiency as a product of suboptimal managerial performance. The other dimension, which is much less structured than the first, deals with economic inefficiency, which flows from economic agents having conflicting objective functions— the roots of economic efficiency here overlap with the narrative of how the firm is managed. X-efficiency theory, as presented by Leibenstein, models an economy in the context of imperfect product markets. Unlike what is predicted in the conventional model, Leibenstein argues that such an economy is not simply characterized by allocative inefficiencies, where the latter is typically of trivial empirical importance (Altman 1990; Frantz 2004; Leibenstein 1966). Rather, firms in imperfectly competitive markets embody what he refers to as x-inefficiencies, which cannot be identified in the conventional model given its assumption of effort being maximized and invariant (see Frantz 1997 for a survey of the empirics underlying the existence of x-inefficiency). Leibenstein, basing his argument on the extant empirical literature, holds that there exists a tremendous persistent diversity in productivity across like firms. This can be attributed to analogous diversity in effort inputs across firms where in a wide array of firms there exists a suboptimal (from a neoclassical perspective) level of effort inputs. Thus many firms operate in the interior of the neoclassical production possibility frontier as a consequence of effort not being maximized. The difference between the actual production possibility frontier and the ideal is one measure of x-inefficiency wherein the outermost frontier is the benchmark for x-efficiency in production. Leibenstein makes the case, however, that from a practical point of view, the best measure of x-efficiency is the most productive or relatively most x-efficient firm where the latter might be perfectly x-efficient with respect to some ideal benchmark. One should note that Leibenstein models x-efficiency in terms of both the quantity and quality of effort inputs. Thus productivity can vary holding the quantity dimension constant and simply varying the quality dimension— working smarter can affect productivity as much as, or even more than, working harder. Needless to say, critical to Leibenstein's model is the assumption of effort variability.

Leibenstein summarizes some of his key foundational points thusly:

> The assumptions about firms on which the theory rests are: (1) that labor contracts are vague and incomplete: (2) that detailed supervision of labor is impractical and or inefficient; hence, (3) there are normally many areas of choice open to managerial as well as other employees in determining how to fulfill their work roles. Legally, the firm makes contractual arrangements in its name, but the formal and informal contracts through which firms hire human inputs have significant gaps. The activities an individual is expected to carry out are rarely completely specified, and sometimes they are almost completely unspecified. Hence, it is necessary for individuals to interpret their jobs. (Leibenstein 1973a, 767)

Economic agents, therefore, have a considerable degree of freedom in terms of determining their effort input, where effort choice ultimately determines the extent of the firm's x-efficiency.

Unlike Leibenstein's foundational work on efficiency wage theory, x-efficiency theory applies to economies at any stage of the development process. Moreover, he delinks his x-efficiency narrative from any discussion of wages. Indeed, he assumes that the wage rate is constant and that effort input varies independently from variations in the real wage. Therefore, ceteris paribus, increases in effort input reduce unit cost, whereas reductions in effort serve to increase unit cost. This follows from equation 1b, where unit cost is determined by the wage divided by average product. Given that effort variation affects average product, effort variations drive changes in average cost. Average cost is minimized only when effort input is maximized. Unlike efficiency wage theory, there is no one wage (the efficiency wage) that minimizes unit cost or maximizes net profit, since here effort varies independently from changes in real wages. In this scenario, one measure of x-inefficiency is the difference in unit cost in the x-efficient and x-inefficient firms. X-inefficient firms are relatively high-cost producers, requiring some form of protection to survive, such as the degree of freedom with regard to pricing afforded by imperfect product markets. For this reason, Leibenstein makes the case that if one intensifies the degree of competitive pressure, firms become increasingly x-efficient. Under a perfectly competitive product market environment firms would be x-efficient. Economic agents would have no choice but to work as hard and as well as they can. Under a perfectly competitive regime the conventional and x-efficient models converge in terms of their predictions with regard to x-efficiency—firms operate along the maximum production possibility frontier, and unit cost is minimized across firms. Leibenstein argues that firm decision makers will actively invest in sheltering activities that provide protection to x-inefficient firms, such as tariffs, subsidies, cartels, and artificial monopolies. To the extent that firms can successfully shelter themselves from competitive pressures, society will be materially worse off. Indeed, Leibenstein argues that one critical determinant of per-person real incomes is a high degree of x-inefficiency and that a crucial determinant of growth, in terms of Solow's residual, is improvements in the extent of x-efficiency (Leibenstein 1966, 1973a, 1978, 1979, 1983).

Preference, Effort Variation, and X-efficiency

What drives effort variation, given imperfect product markets, are variations of managerial effort in both their quality and quantity dimensions. Leibenstein (1966, 1978) assumes that firm decision makers have a preference for working less hard and well. Although Leibenstein objects to the use of maximization-related concepts, in his model firm decision makers are in effect maximizing their utility in terms of an objective function that includes a preference for not working as hard as neoclassical theory assumes all economic agents should and do work. This is true for all economic agents. Leibenstein maintains that all individuals have objective functions that deviate from the neoclassical ideal of effort maximization. This relates to the personality of the typical individual and the relationship of the individual (personality), her or his peers, and external constraints.

> Personality is defined in terms of (b) a taste for responsiveness to opportunities and constraints within certain standards of behavior and (c) a simultaneous taste for "irresponsible" or unconstrained behavior. The standards of behavior include moral constraints reflected in attitudes toward trust, honesty, lying, altruism, group solidarity, sacrificing for group objectives, and so on, which play a role in behavior. The compromise between (b) and (c) that the personality makes leads to a most "comfortable" degree of internal pressure [(f)] which, if everything were in the person's control, would determine the degree of maximization deviation. . . . However, the economic context (e) in which the individual finds himself may impose a higher degree of external pressures [(d)] than desired internal pressure, and hence the interaction between (d) and (f) determines the actual degree of maximization deviation. That is, pressures from peers (horizontal relations) and authorities (vertical relations) within the firm determine a degree of selective rationality different from what the person would choose in the absence of such pressures. (Leibenstein 1979, 485; see also Leibenstein 1978)

The comfortable level of internal pressures yields an equilibrium level of what Leibenstein refers to as constraint concern, which yields the utility-maximizing level of effort input, absent external pressure. The neoclassical individual's equilibrium level of constraint concern yields x-efficient effort behavior even the absence of external pressure; not so in Leibenstein's modeling.

The relationship between constraint concern, external pressure, and the level of x-efficiency is illustrated in Figure 7.7, which builds upon the work of Leibenstein (1978, 1979). Leibenstein assumes a positive relationship between constraint concern and external pressure, with pressure as the independent variable, and between constraint concern and effort input, with constraint concern being the independent variable. There are diminishing returns to external pressure with respect to constraint concern and to constraint concern with regard to effort input. X-efficient effort input (j) can only be generated with sufficient constraint concern (c). In the neoclassical narrative the segment ce would best represent an individual's constraint concern function, wherein a level of constraint concern consistent with an x-efficient effort input prevails irrespective of the level of external pressure. In Leibenstein's narrative, CP_0 or CP_1 could represent an internally derived individual's constraint concern function, both of which yield a less than x-efficient effort input at zero or low levels of external pressure. For CP_0, n level of constraint concern is required to generate x-efficiency, whereas for CP_1, a lesser level of effort is required to generate x-efficiency. Constraint concern functions can shift upward as an individual becomes more internally motivated to contribute more effort to the production process independent of the level of external pressure. When it shifts to point c, one has effort behavior equivalent in results to the neoclassical individual.

For Leibenstein, x-efficiency is obtained only under high levels of external pressure, given individuals' assumed preference for less than x-efficient levels of constraint concern. Once such pressure is relaxed, ceteris paribus, the extent of x-inefficiency increases as the level of constraint concern and thereby effort input is reduced. Thus, an x-efficient scenario is highly unstable given that firm decision makers are not maximizing their preferred objective function if they are

Figure 7.7   **Constraint Concern, Pressure, and Effort**

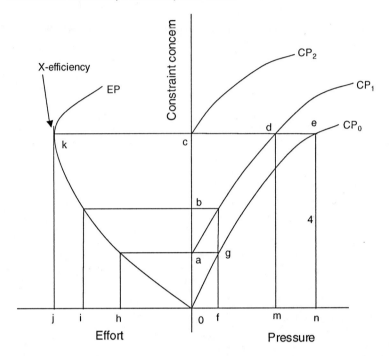

performing relatively x-efficiently. Given the assumed preference or objective function of the individual, there is an incentive for individuals to engage in sheltering activity, which provides firms with protection from competitive pressures allowing for higher and more preferred levels of x-inefficiency.

The instability of the x-efficient choice in terms of a utility-maximizing scenario is illustrated in Figure 7.8, where utility is mapped against effort input. The effort functions are concave and, as in Leibenstein's discourse, illustrate first increasing utility with increasing effort input and then diminishing utility for further increases (Leibenstein 1983, 834). X-efficiency is realized with D of effort input. Only an individual characterized by a utility function such as U_4 maximizes utility at an x-efficient level of effort input. For Leibenstein, the typical economic agent is characterized by a utility function that lies below U_4, such as U_3 and U_1. For example, if an individual with the U_1 utility function maximizes utility, only A of effort input is provided and the firm is x-inefficient. However, the individual might be forced into providing more effort input—that is, coerced into a higher level of constraint concern—by dint of competitive pressures. Indeed, these pressures might be so severe as to drive the individual into providing D of effort. In this case, the individual can be said to be maximizing her or his subutility function at P, yielding I of utility as compared to maximizing effort input at A, which would yield a higher level of utility of J. Any relaxation of market pressure provides the individual with the opportunity to move to her or his preferred equilibrium point, one consistent with x-inefficiency. Thus, in this scenario, with individuals of type U_1, x-efficiency is highly unstable in the sense that it is not a preferred equilibrium. Neoclassical theory assumes that individuals are characterized by preferences such as U_4. Relaxation of competitive pressures yields only trivial allocative inefficiencies, whereas for Leibenstein's economic agents the consequences of imperfect competitive pressures are much more severe.

Figure 7.8 **Effort Inputs and Utility**

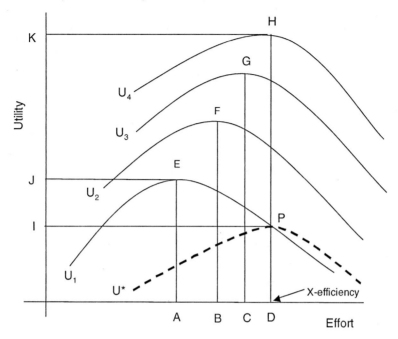

Given such x-inefficient preferences, the secret to significantly improving the level of society's material well-being lies in making an economy more competitive. In terms of public policy, if improving material welfare is an important objective, Leibenstein's theory is supportive of more competitive product markets given that they serve to improve the level of x-efficiency. Indeed, competitiveness has much more of an effect upon material welfare than conventional theory could predict. Conventional micro theory assumes that firm decision makers (indeed, all economic agents within the firm) maximize some objective function that is consistent with the firm minimizing unit cost—in other words, producing x-efficiently. The level of unit cost has no effect on effort input. In Leibenstein's model, the competitive unit cost has a recursive effect on effort choice. In other words, once the competitive unit cost is identified, economic agents are expected to choose the *minimum* effort input required to achieve this cost. This does not preclude the firm maximizing profit in the sense of behaving in a fashion consistent with equalizing marginal cost with marginal revenue, except that in the x-inefficiency narrative unit cost and marginal cost are higher than they would be in a world where x-efficiency prevails.

The Entrepreneur and X-efficiency

As Leibenstein builds his x-efficiency modeling framework his arguments become more nuanced, wherein he delves in more detail into the micro-micro (inside the firm) reasoning underlying the raison d'être of economic agents performing x-inefficiently. One important aspect of this refinement is Leibenstein's discourse on entrepreneurship, which relates to his focus on the importance of the behavior of managers and owners to the level of x-efficiency achieved by the firm. Entrepreneurs serve the opposite role of those engaged in sheltering activities; individuals who are rent seekers of one type or another. As part of his general x-efficiency theory, Leibenstein's theory of entrepreneurship assumes market imperfections. Given these imperfections, there is a role to be played by entrepreneurs.

> Consistent with X-efficiency theory we have to start with imperfect markets. Hence, our markets are characterized by gaps in input availabilities as well as obstacles that manifest themselves in less than equal access to inputs. Hence, in order to start a new firm, an entrepreneur must have the capacity to overcome the gaps and the obstacles in imperfect markets. He also has to be an input completer in the sense that less than the complete marshaling of inputs would not fulfill the entrepreneurial function. Obviously there are limits to the supply of gap fillers and input completers. (Leibenstein 1979, 490)

Leibenstein (1968, 74–76) adds that other important gap-filling roles of the entrepreneur include motivating firm members, providing leadership, and solving existing and potential crises. These roles are significant where economic agents have discretion over effort input. The concept of entrepreneurs as leaders and motivators speaks indirectly to seeing firms as multiagent entities, where productivity critically depends on the relationship between agents—an argument that Leibenstein eventually introduces into his modeling framework. Given a shortage of entrepreneurs that cannot be obviated by market forces alone, x-inefficiency can persist over time.

However, to the extent that this shortage can be overcome, Leibenstein argues that it would be possible for economic outcomes to mimic those of the neoclassical ideal, thereby generating an x-efficient economy.

> Our theory also allows for the special case in which entrepreneurship is so vigorous that it induces a very high degree of tightness, which in turn forces a degree of pressure so that firms either minimize costs or do not survive. However, we must note that this is a very special case, one not likely to exist in most industries. Thus the micro-micro theory enables us to distinguish the environmental micro-micro conditions for perfect competition as against what is probably the normal situation of some form of imperfect competition, and hence the case in which costs are not minimized. (Leibenstein 1979, 492)

Although Leibenstein (1968, 79–83) never develops a clearly specified model of the entrepreneur, he specifies relatively higher product price—and one would presume that this reflects relatively higher profits—as well as entrepreneurial-specific education, training and experience, and culture (related in part to personality types) as key determinants of supply. In addition, Leibenstein underlines the importance of institutional variables that affect the supply of entrepreneurship. Leibenstein argues that the "sociocultural and political constraints which influence the extent to which entrepreneurs take advantage of their capacities, and the degree to which potential entrepreneurs respond to different motivational states" are critical determinants of entrepreneurial supply (Leibenstein 1968, 78–79). Thus the supply curve of entrepreneurship is a positive function of relative price, training and experience, education, and culture. He maintains that there typically remains a persistent gap between the supply and demand for entrepreneurship, which appears to a large extent to be given by the assumption that individuals typically prefer less than x-efficient behavior or less than ideal effort input. Demand is given by the potential x-efficient level of output. In Leibenstein's model, the persistent gap between supply and demand assumes that product markets are sufficiently imperfect to allow for relatively x-inefficient high-priced production. However, in his model of entrepreneurship it is not at all clear why the deficiency in entrepreneurial supply would be eliminated simply as a product of more forceful competitive pressures given the multifarious nature of supply, so much of which is not directly related to market forces. More-over, in his narrative on entrepreneurship, competitive pressures critically depend on there being a sufficient supply of x-efficient-type entrepreneurs. There is a recursive relationship between competitive pressures and the supply of entrepreneurship.

The Multiagent Firm and Determinants of X-efficiency

One facet of Leibenstein's modeling of entrepreneurship is its effective highlighting of motivational issues in multiagent firms when effort discretion exists. Leibenstein discusses the potential significance of conflicting preferences among economic agents for determining the level of x-efficiency (Leibenstein 1978, 1979, 1982, 1983, 1984). Such conflict, if not resolved, can result in a prisoner's dilemma (or chicken, or mutual threat) game solution to the productivity problem, yielding a minimal level of productivity. In this narrative, unlike in the traditional x-efficiency narrative, economic incentives as determinants of productivity come into play, as they do in the efficiency wage discourse. Also of significance is the role of conventions in preventing a prisoner's dilemma solution from prevailing. Unlike in traditional x-efficiency theory, in this multiagent narrative the relationship of unit cost to productivity is no longer clear since productivity and labor compensation are implicitly linked. What is articulated in the prisoner's dilemma narrative, however, is that when effort discretion exists, a multiplicity of possible sustainable equilibrium solutions are available to the productivity problem based upon the effort conventions adopted in the firm. It is implicitly assumed that whatever the resulting unit cost, the market structure is such that it will provide protection to x-inefficient firms.

Why model the firm in terms of a prisoner's dilemma scenario?

> A basic criterion is that a prisoners' dilemma occurs wherever there are possibilities for adversarial behavior between the parties, and by all parties, which reduces the joint cooperative outcome. Now, it seems reasonable to presume that adversarial behavior between employees and the firm will usually decrease productivity, while cooperative behavior will increase it. This is certainly not the case in all types of games. But this is the case for the particular "game" set where productivity is the outcome. (Leibenstein 1982, 94)

But embedded in the prisoner's dilemma game is the potential for cooperative, relatively high-productivity solutions to the productivity problem. Leibenstein (1979, 493) argues that there are two components to the productivity problem: one relates to the determination of the size of the pie, while the second relates to the division of the pie. Looked upon independently, all agents can jointly gain by increasing the pie size, but optimal pie size is determined by the division of pie size, which involves winners and losers. However, Leibenstein writes, "the situation need not be a zero-sum game. Tactics that determine pie division can affect the size of the pie. It is this latter possibility that is especially significant" (1979, 493). Productivity is not determined independently of distribution, as it is in standard theory. Thus distribution also impacts upon the level of x-efficiency achieved by the firm—a point not discussed by Leibenstein.

Modeling the firm in terms of two types of agents, employees and employers, Leibenstein argues that employees can follow at one extreme the Golden Rule option and at the other a "maximization private satisfaction" option:

> Under the Golden Rule every employee acts in the best interest of the firm. He treats the firm as he would like the firm to treat him, and puts forth effort as if the enterprise was his

own. The alternative option is at the other extreme: the individual works as little as possible in the firm's interest and does other things (on the job) to pursue his own private interests. (Leibenstein 1982, 92–93)

The employer faces a symmetrical set of extreme options:

It could behave in a Golden Rule fashion in which it provides employees with the maximal conditions, salaries, and security, consistent with "sustainable profits"; it is as if the firm operates *almost* entirely in the interest of the employees. The other alternative is parametric maximization, which implies cost minimization. That is, the firm *attempts* to minimize working conditions and wages cost while trying to get the most effort from employees. (Leibenstein 1982, 93)

In terms of Leibenstein's payoff structure, the incentive exists for employees and employers to each choose strategically the private maximization option, in the hope that the other will choose the Golden Rule option and with full knowledge that if the other party also chooses the private maximization option he/she is better off doing the same. In the latter case one is simply minimizing one's losses. Agents expect the worst from each other (private maximization) given antagonistic labor-management relations. Agents are never actually better off when one chooses the private maximization option given that one's opposite make symmetrical choices. Only if, for example, employees choose the Golden Rule, either naively or in full knowledge that employers will maximize privately, will employers be better off than if all agents cooperate to achieve the Golden Rule productivity outcome. In a repeated game scenario, which Leibenstein does not explicitly discuss, it is unlikely that employees would repeat the Golden Rule choice if employers choose to maximize privately unless employees' utility is maximized by minimizing their own material well-being. Only if the Golden Rule option is chosen by all agents simultaneously (the cooperative solution) is pie size maximized, while the individual maximization option minimizes pie size.

Diagrammatically Leibenstein posits a mutual-gain diagonal joining the Golden Rule cooperative solution with the prisoner's dilemma individual maximization solution. In Figure 7.9 this is given by line segment ab. The Golden Rule cooperative solution is given by point a and the prisoner's dilemma solution by point b. The former requires more effort input than the latter. Also, as one moves from b to a, wages and profits both increase proportionally. The cooperative solution also represents maximum x-efficiency, whereas the private maximization solution (P-max) represents minimum x-efficiency, thus the highest degree of x-inefficiency. Employees and employers are better off, given adversarial relationships, if they select the private maximization (P-max) option, since each has a claim on 5 units of output, whereas if one party selected the Golden Rule and the other chose the P-max option, the cooperator would end up with only 3 units of output. If agents engaged in private utility maximization strategies give such payoffs, firms would be producing at minimum levels of x-efficiency.

But Leibenstein maintains that the prisoner's dilemma solution does not obtain for institutional reasons. Building upon the extant game-theoretical literature, conventions represent a potential solution to prisoner's dilemma problems, where the possibility exists of multiple equilibria that yield a range of outcomes, from one just greater than the prisoner's dilemma solution to the cooperative solution. Any of an array of possible conventions yields a productivity solution greater than what could be achieved in the absence of conventions when rational agents

Figure 7.9 **Prisoner's Dilemma and X-inefficiency**

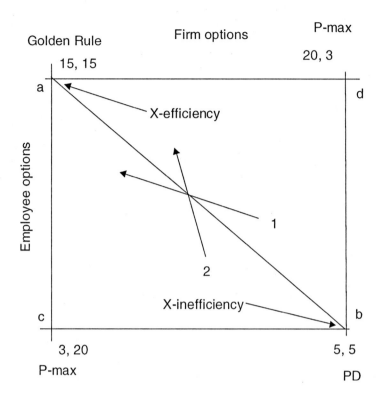

engage in private maximization. Conventions can yield solutions along the mutual benefit curve ab, where both employees and employers gain equally from productivity increases. But solutions can also be found along curve 1 or 2, where output increases but income is redistributed to labor along 1 and to the firm along 2. In both of these scenarios, both employees and employers are better off in absolute terms than under a less cooperative and less effort-intensive regime. But in the absence of conventions, employees and employers will revert to a private maximization prisoner's dilemma option.

> At any specific time the latent prisoners' dilemma possibilities are held in abeyance by conventions, institutions, and laws, involving trust, enforcement of contracts, etc. . . . If the adversarial portions are absent, then the mutual choice is the optimal position on the cooperative diagonal. Adversarial portions of the payoff table may be made essentially nonaccessible through nonmarket conventions, such as trust, honesty, fairness, legal recourse for misunderstanding or fraud, emphasis on reputation for fair dealings, etc. Thus, a convention of honesty in contractual relations eliminates adversarial behavior in which both sides attempt to cheat the other. Similarly, an effective low-cost system of laws which enforces contracts may minimize the inducement to use other types of adversarial behavior. (Leibenstein 1982, 96–97)

For this reason, "two countries with identical inputs, identical knowledge, identical capital accumulation, and the same level of employment, may yet produce significantly different outputs because production takes place on the basis of very different effort conventions" (Leibenstein 1982, 96).

Cooperative Determinants of X-efficiency

Related to this discourse, Leibenstein raises the importance of voluntary increases in effort input, as opposed to monitored or coerced increases in effort input in achieving x-efficient levels of output. He stresses that monitoring alone can backfire in terms of its productivity effect, given the existence of effort discretion:

> What fairly extensive monitoring essentially does is to set up something that approximates a mutual threat game. The firm stresses that if a minimal (or agreed upon) level of performance is not achieved, then the individual will be punished; for example, fired. The individual employee, and employees as a group, on the other hand, are in position to impose some damage to the firm by lowering effort, or strikes, and/or by contributing to labor turnover costs. (Leibenstein 1983, 838)

Leibenstein argues that x-efficiency can best be realized when firm members "interpret their jobs in such a way that they made effort choices which involved cooperation with peers, superiors, and subordinates, in such a way as to maximize their contribution to output" (1978, 206). Moreover:

> The main general point is that merely obtaining an acquiescent nonshirking effort is of limited value. Freely offered effort, inclusive of attentiveness and caring about the quality of effort, in return for what is viewed as a good deal (in the long run) is likely to result in higher productivity. (Leibenstein 1983, 838)

This involves a limited use of monitoring, "and instead resorts to other motivating forces, which in essence involve higher levels of trust and lower implicit adversarial relations. But such relations are likely to involve quite a bit of discretion on all sides" (Leibenstein 1983, 838). Thus, given effort discretion, effort input can move beyond prisoner's-dilemma-type outcomes only if agents develop conventions that are based on trust and which are therefore self-enforcing via peer pressure or constraint concern emanating from the individual her or himself. Just as Costa Nostra detainees need not succumb to the prisoner's dilemma option for reasons of fear and loyalty, which yield sufficient trust that the other party won't talk, cooperative labor-management relationships can have the same effect in the firm, keeping employees and employers from choosing relatively x-inefficient productivity options.

Leibenstein's narrative of the multiagent firm raises significant issues with regard to the determinants of x-inefficiency. Importantly, it raises the importance of incentives as a determinant of effort input, which is key to the various extant models of efficiency wages. But the connection between wages, effort input, unit cost, and net profit remains quite vague. Moreover, unlike in his foundational x-efficiency narrative, the connection between individual preferences, effort inputs, and the extent of competitiveness or environmental tightness is amorphous. What is clear from his multiagent narrative is that market forces remain significant in the background as increasing competitive pressures force agents to behave more x-efficiently—in this scenario by revising effort conventions—so as to maintain unit cost at a competitive level. But imperfect product markets provide the shelter behind which x-inefficiency can persist as equilibrium (albeit unstable equilibrium) behavior.

A BEHAVIORAL MODEL OF THE FIRM AND
X-EFFICIENCY THEORY

The behavioral model of the firm developed in Altman (1992, 1996, 1998, 1999, 2001b, 2002) and discussed above in the context of efficiency wage theory helps to fill some of the gaps contained in x-efficiency theory, providing a modeling framework to address significant paradoxes related both to the conventional wisdom and to x-efficiency theory itself. Common to the behavioral model, conventional x-efficiency, and efficiency wage theories, effort is assumed to be a variable input in the production function. Critical to the behavioral model is its joining of the concepts of the causal relationship between incentives and productivity contained in efficiency wage theories and that of the determinants of the level of x-efficiency.

Unlike in x-efficiency theory, where effort variability is discussed in the context of fixed levels of labor compensation, in the behavioral model, although effort can vary independent of material incentives, the latter can play a critical role in determining the extent of x-efficiency. Thus, unlike in x-efficiency theory, a direct causal link is explicitly posited between labor compensation, effort input, and labor productivity. This point is illustrated in Figure 7.10, where curves 1, 2, and 3 are wage x-efficiency curves that are assumed to be subject to diminishing returns. Wages are taken to represent the overall material incentive package of the firm. The level of x-efficiency is a positive function of the real wage. For each curve, the level of x-efficiency is given by the wage rate, such as W_0 or W_1. In contrast, in x-efficiency theory the level of x-efficiency is determined by the preferences of managers/owners. The level of x-efficiency can vary independent of the wage (though this argument is somewhat refined, but only vaguely in terms of modeling specificities, in Leibenstein's prisoner's dilemma scenarios). In the behavioral model the level of x-efficiency can be maximized only by providing economic agents (who can include managers) with an appropriate material incentive package, given by W_1 and wage x-efficiency curve 3. We have three such curves to reflect the reality, captured in the overall x-efficiency narrative, that nonmaterial incentives can affect the level of x-efficiency. Material incentives alone won't do the trick. Thus, maximizing the level of x-efficiency requires the appropriate mix of material and nonmaterial incentives, although material incentives are typically quite important. In the neoclassical framework the level of x-efficiency is always at a maximum, irrespective of the wages and preferences of economic agents.

Another feature of the behavioral model is illustrated in Figure 7.11, where the potential relationships between the level of x-efficiency and the level of unit cost are mapped. In the behavioral model, the possibility of the level of x-efficiency not affecting the level of unit cost is allowed for. This is given by the linear unit cost x-efficiency curves BM_0 and BM_1. Underlying differences in the level of x-efficiency are differences in the level of labor productivity, which in turn are driven by differences in the level and quality of effort input. X_M represents the maximum level of x-efficiency. Bear in mind that the level of x-efficiency is determined by the level of productivity. Thus, maximum x-efficiency is a product of productivity maximized with regard to effort input. Unit cost is inelastic with respect to changes in the level of x-efficiency if, in the background, productivity increases are just offset by changes in the level of input costs such as labor compensation. Therefore, a wide array of levels of labor compensation is consistent with some unique unit cost of production. Increasing wages, for example, need not increase unit cost, while cutting wages need not reduce unit cost. This refers back to the discussion surrounding equations 1a and 1b and Figure 7.4, above. In this case, neither maximizing nor minimizing the level of x-efficiency affects the level of unit cost and thereby the competitive position of the firm. The two unit cost x-efficiency curves reflect the possibility that firms can be characterized by different firm

Figure 7.10 **Wages and X-efficiency**

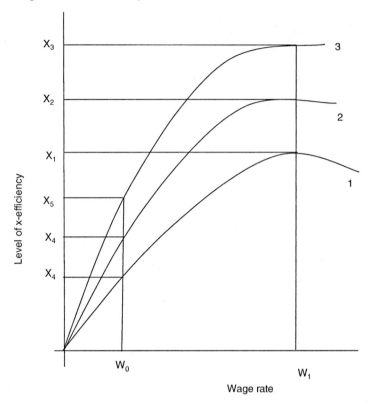

cultures such that the ratio of productivity to labor cost is greater in one firm than in another. At one extreme, at maximum x-efficiency, one firm might produce at a lower unit cost than another because firm members are more productive in one firm than in another at a lower wage. But this is sustainable only if the higher-cost firm is sheltered from competitive pressures.

The prediction derived from the traditional x-efficiency model that levels of x-efficiency are negatively related to unit cost is illustrated by unit cost x-efficiency curves XE_{W1} and XE_{W2}, where it assumed that the level of x-efficiency varies independently from wages. Relatively x-inefficient firms are less cost-competitive and can survive only when sheltered from competitive pressures. In the conventional neoclassical model, since all firms are assumed to be x-efficient at all times, it is differences in the rate of labor compensation that can have a determining effect on the firm's competitiveness. This is illustrated by points NC_{W0} and NC_{W1} in Figure 7.11, where firms are producing at maximum x-efficiency—there is no x-inefficiency—and differences in unit cost are driven by differences in the rate of labor compensation. In the behavioral model, unlike in the x-efficiency model, different levels of x-efficiency need not affect the state of a firm's relative competitiveness. And unlike in the conventional neoclassical model, in the behavioral model differences in the rate of labor compensation need not affect a firm's capacity to compete. High-wage firms need not be less competitive than low-wage firms.

A critical distinction between the behavioral model and x-efficiency theory is that in the behavioral model x-inefficiency can persist in a variety of product market structures, inclusive of a highly competitive one, since lower levels of x-efficiency need not translate into higher unit cost

Figure 7.11 **Unit Cost and X-efficiency**

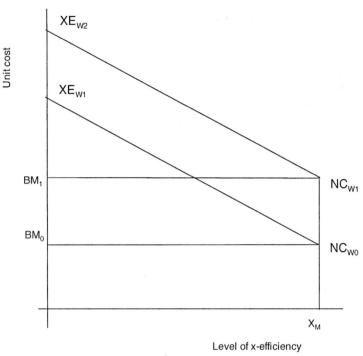

Level of x-efficiency

and higher levels of x-efficiency need not translate into lower unit cost. Firms characterized by high and low levels of x-efficiency can all be cost-competitive. Therefore, even perfect product market competition need not yield an x-efficient economy. On the other hand, x-efficiency can prevail even with highly imperfect product markets. In addition, in the behavioral model, the level of x-efficiency can be driven by production costs, of which labor costs are a critical component. Given market structure, the level of x-efficiency can be driven by differences in the level of labor compensation. Thus, high-wage firms or economies can be relatively x-efficient even if contained in a relatively sheltered product market environment. Also, unlike in efficiency wage theory, in the behavioral model there is no one wage (the efficiency wage) that is an equilibrium wage, one that minimizes cost and maximizes net profit. The behavioral model can also better explain the existence of multiple equilibria in terms of different levels of x-efficiency and also provide the underlying rationale for why superior x-efficient regimes can be rejected by firms even in light of competitive pressures—relatively x-efficient firms need not have a competitive advantage over relatively x-inefficient firms.

By explicitly linking material incentives to the determinations of levels of x-efficiency the behavioral model helps explain potential behaviors of economic agents and the incentives for producing more or less x-efficiently. In Leibenstein's multiagent modeling framework we are left with the impression that, given imperfect product markets, anything goes with regard to the level of x-efficiency, contingent upon the firms' work-related conventions. In the behavioral model, material incentives and work environment drive the level of x-efficiency, with explicit implications for cost and profit. In the behavioral model, to the extent that the Golden Rule and the prisoner's dilemma options yield the same unit cost and the same profit, both options are sustainable in either a competitive or noncompetitive environment. There is no Darwinian imperative driving the economy to any one option. Moreover, in this case, only labor benefits as one moves from the prisoner's dilemma to the Golden Rule option, since higher wages are required to enhance the level of x-efficiency. In this scenario, conventions can play an important role in determining the direction in which, with regard to the level of x-efficiency, the firm will move. Moreover, to the extent that firm decision makers prefer the prisoner's dilemma option—they don't materially benefit from the Golden Rule option and it requires more effort to achieve it—higher levels of x-efficiency are driven by the capacity of labor to achieve higher wages and improved working conditions in the context of the market economy. Once this capacity is diminished, one can expect that the firm would revert toward the prisoner's dilemma option.

This takes us back to our earlier discussion of the relationship between preferences and the level of x-efficiencies (Figure 7.8). When employees and employers have different objective functions—in this case, employees are willing to work relatively x-efficiently given the appropriate work environment, while employers would prefer less x-efficiency given workers' preferred environment—employers are maximizing only their subutility functions, as opposed to their preferred utility in the high-wage environment. This is an unstable Golden Rule equilibrium unless employer preferences change over time toward a preference for the higher-wage Golden Rule option. Thus, when employers do not clearly benefit from more x-efficiency—even if there is no zero-sum game involved—the behavioral model suggests that the extent of x-efficiency critically depends upon the power relations between employees and employers, the extent to which employers are sympathetic to the material and spiritual well-being of their employees, and, related to this, the capacity of the firm to build cooperative relationships between employees and employers. One should note that in the behavioral model there is no need to rely on notions of choice irrationality to generate any of its substantive analytical predictions. Agents can be maximizing their respective utility or subutility functions. But if individuals have conflicting objective functions or face severe constraints on their choice options, individuals' constrained utility-maximizing choices can be highly unstable, changing quite dramatically when individuals are afforded the opportunity. What is critical to this narrative of effort discretion are the determination and analysis of the preferred effort input under various circumstances, and the set of circumstances under which utility-maximizing individuals or groups of individuals would have stable preferences for x-efficient behavior.

In many of Leibenstein's multiagent scenarios (see Figure 7.9), all parties benefit as one moves toward the Golden Rule option, although it is possible for the increasing income to become more unequally distributed toward employees or employers. In the behavioral model, two distinct behavioral possibilities are suggested. One would be in the context of improvements in x-efficiencies, yielding no changes in unit cost. The other context would be when increases in x-efficiency yield not only increases in income to employers and employees, but also a reduction in unit cost. In both cases, increases in the level of x-efficiency can be provoked by increases in wages and improvements in working conditions that pressure firms into becoming more x-efficient. In the first case, however, rejection of or struggling against the Golden Rule option would incur a clear opportunity cost to employers—a loss of income or profit. Such a sacrifice could be made, although economists would expect that it would be a negative function of the level of increased income expected to accrue to employers with increases in the level of x-efficiency. As this expected income increases, one would expect the probability of engaging in such self-sacrifice to diminish, or the percentage of employers choosing such a sacrifice to diminish. But in this scenario competitive pressures per se cannot force firms into becoming more x-efficient. The preferences of employers and the bargaining power of employees play key roles in determining the level of x-efficiency.

In the second context, not only are employers sacrificing income, but firms are also producing at a higher unit cost when producing x-inefficiently. This scenario is most in line with Leibenstein's origin x-efficiency model. Economic agents—in particular, employers (inclusive of managers)—have a strong leisure preference. This yields x-inefficiency along with higher unit costs. Such firms can survive only when sheltered from competitive pressures. It is only this particular scenario that is consistent with the notion that increasing competitive pressures will drive firms into becoming more x-efficient. The behavioral model suggests that this scenario is only one of a variety of possible x-efficiency scenarios, especially when one gives proper attention to the connection between material incentives and overall working conditions and the level of x-efficiency.

The above scenario, which is a special case of the general framework of the behavioral model, is consistent in unit cost results with scenarios wherein effort varies irrespective of material incentives, which is the chief concern of Leibenstein's foundational x-efficiency narrative. Management drives the level of x-efficiency through its preference functions that lean toward x-inefficient behavior. It is assumed that the quantity and quality of effort input among all firm members is a function of managerial effort input or that variations in managerial effort input suffice to drive firm productivity. Thus, irrespective of the incentive system in place (inclusive of the system of industrial relations), firms can achieve x-efficiency in production as long as management has the will and the wherewithal to do so. In this case, ceteris paribus, one would expect that low-wage economies should dominate high-wage economies if there is a supply of sufficiently x-efficient managers and entrepreneurs, unless the relatively high-wage economies are sheltered from the competitive threat posed by the low-wage x-efficient economies. This must be the case if low-wage economies can achieve x-efficiency irrespective of how employees are rewarded and treated. It is here implicitly assumed, as it is in conventional neoclassical theory, that workers will work as hard and as well as they can, irrespective of wages and working conditions. Get rid of shelters and firms will be forced into becoming more x-efficient. However, even given Leibenstein's assumptions, competitive pressures yield x-efficiency only if the supply of x-efficient management and entrepreneurs is sufficient to generate the competitive pressures required to make all firms x-efficient, including those that have management with x-inefficient preferences. Competitive pressures alone are not enough.

As opposed to Leibenstein's foundational x-efficiency narrative, in the behavioral model, as is the case in Leibenstein's prisoner's dilemma narrative, at least implicitly, the level of effort input is a function of the incentive structure within the firm, inclusive of material rewards. In this scenario, increasing effort input and productivity are tied to higher input costs. Thus, increasing the level of x-efficiency might have no effect on unit cost, while reducing the level of x-efficiency, accompanied by lower input cost, might also have no effect on unit cost. Entrepreneurs, as gap fillers and input completers, can play a critical role in generating x-efficiency, in part by affecting the motivational structure within the firm. What is required for x-efficiency here is entrepreneurs who can contribute toward developing Golden Rule conventions in high-wage environments. But when increasing the level of x-efficiency is not accompanied by lower unit cost, increasing the supply of x-efficient entrepreneurs need not make the economy more competitive. Rather, they critically contribute to making firms and economies relatively more x-efficient irrespective of the extent of competitive pressures.

The behavioral model of the firm, which builds on the extant x-efficiency and efficiency wage literature, makes explicit the relationship between material incentives, x-efficiency, and unit cost. It thereby specifies the opportunity cost at different levels involved in remaining or becoming relatively x-inefficient. The behavioral model provides an analytical framework that allows for persistence of x-efficiency under different competitive environments as well for multiple equilibria in terms of levels of x-efficiency and in-firm conventions. Unlike in x-efficiency theory, in the behavioral model the level of x-efficiency is not largely driven by market imperfections and managerial preferences. And, unlike efficiency wage theory, it does not predict a high-wage efficiency wage equilibrium. Rather, the behavioral model of the firm provides a broad analytical framework that allows for conventional x-efficiency and efficiency predictions as special-case outcomes. More attention is paid to alternative scenarios that appear to be much consistent with realities of everyday economic life, past and present.

SOME CONTRIBUTIONS OF A BEHAVIORAL MODEL OF THE FIRM

I focus on five public-policy-related issues to highlight some of the potentially significant analytical contributions of a behavioral model. One relates to the question of convergence between low- and high-wage economies. Another issue relates to why superior work environments are not dominant. Connected to the above is the contention that globalization, in terms of more international trade, yields a race to the bottom with regard to wages and working conditions. I also briefly discuss the theory of the reciprocal firm, which predicts the dominance of relatively high-wage economies when effort discretion exists. Finally, I discuss the possibility of firms behaving ethically in competitive markets in the context of the behavioral model. The connection between levels of x-efficiency and technological change is touched upon.

Neoclassical theory predicts that convergence should take place between high- and low-wage economies in part given the cost advantage that low-wage firms have over high-wage firms in a world where all firms are assumed to be x-efficient. Such convergence has not taken place (Altman 2002; Baumol and Wolff 1988; DeLong 1988; Pritchett 1997). Rather, we've had convergence among the already high-wage economies, with some exceptions such as Japan, South Korea, and Taiwan. In the behavioral model, competitive pressures need not result in firms and economies converging in terms of wages and productivity, since differentials in wages and productivity can be offset by differences in productivity and wages, respectively. From the perspective of the behavioral model, one reason for the absence of convergence would be the low-level capacity of employees (workers and peasants) in low-wage economies to bargain for improved material benefits and standards of work that would, in turn, pressure firms into becoming more x-efficient. This raises the issue of the importance of power and institutions in the determination of economic results (Altman 2000; Rothschild 2002). Another reason for the absence of convergence consistent with the behavioral model as well as with both neoclassical and conventional x-efficiency theory is the sheltering of x-efficient firms. But the behavioral model suggests that reducing sheltering per se will not induce more x-efficiency in the absence of increased bargaining power on the part of employees and a sufficient number of x-efficiency-prone entrepreneurs. Moreover, in the behavioral model convergence would tend to take place dynamically, with the low-wage economies becoming high-wage economies as the low-wage economies catch up with the high-wage economies in terms of x-efficiency, as opposed to the high-wage economies converging downward in terms of wages and levels of x-efficiency. This model also has significant implications for understanding the implications of unions, minimum wages, unemployment insurance, and other institutional interventions on the market for economic efficiency and development (Altman 1992, 2001a, 2004).

There exist many alternative forms of industrial relationship with relatively high levels of x-efficiency, yet they do not dominate the marketplace. Neoclassical theory would predict that superior firms should rule the roost, whereas x-efficiency theory would predict that such firms should be producing at a lower unit cost and have a competitive advantage. The behavioral model makes analytical space for the reasonable scenarios wherein firms are superior in terms of their level of x-efficiency and in terms of providing employees with a preferred set of material benefits and work environment, yet fail to dominate their product markets. To the extent that superior firms are more costly to operate, their higher level of x-efficiency might serve to keep them competitive with the relatively low-input-cost x-inefficient "inferior" firms. In this case, there would be no reason to expect the superior firms to dominate, for they have no clear competitive advantage (Altman 2002). The extent to which superior firms make their presence felt becomes more a product of the bargaining power of employees and the preferences of employees and employers. Being superior need not provide firms with a competitive advantage (see also Ichniowski et al. 1996; Tomer 2001).

Both advocates and detractors of economic globalization often suggest a race to the bottom. For the former, economies have little choice but to make labor costs compatible with the new harsher competitive realities. This will yield higher levels of per capita output, which will somehow and sometime trickle down to the society at large. Opponents of economic globalization concur with the argument that in the first instance globalization will cause many to suffer economically and socially, and such suffering will persist into the future. There will be clear winners and even more losers in this zero-sum game. The behavioral model suggests that economic globalization generates significant benefits to employees under the appropriate institutional environment. To the extent that economic globalization increases the demand for labor and thereby the bargaining power of employees, this can have the effect of increasing wages and improving working conditions and thereby pushing economies into becoming more x-efficient. As labor market pressure intensifies along with product market competition, firms must become more x-efficient to remain competitive. In the absence of economic globalization, wherein the demand for labor is less, workers' bargaining power is reduced, reducing the pressure to improve wages and other labor benefits. Globalization can therefore serve to benefit labor and need not result to a race to the bottom (and can even have the opposite effect) if the basic democratic and related labor rights are in place, providing employees with the capacity to take advantage of increasing labor demand, which typically coincides with increased economic globalization. Globalization yields no improvement to workers' well-being only in the absence of such capacity-facilitating and -building rights, and if capabilities are created that allow employers to neutralize the advantages that increasing economic globalization tends to provide workers. Moreover, the behavioral model suggests that success in an increasingly global economy does not require a race to the bottom. A race to the top is quite consistent with increasing globalization (2006b).

A model of the reciprocal firm has been developed by Fehr and Gatcher (2000a, 2000b). Their model clearly and explicitly builds on efficiency wage theory and the ultimatum game experimental literature (Güth 1995). This model overlaps significantly with Leibenstein's prisoner's dilemma narratives. A key point made in this model that has received much critical acclaim is its prediction that, given imperfect labor contract and effort discretion, firms tend to pay workers relatively high wages, wages that exceed the opportunity cost of workers. Indeed, workers are paid an efficiency wage. This is a wage determined by the capacity of workers to retaliate (by reducing their effort input) against employers who pay them wages that are deemed to be unfair. In this context it is profitable for the firm to pay employees what would appear to be an excessively high wage. One would expect that firms should tend to pay workers such relatively high wages in both the short and long terms.

Both efficiency wage theories and the behavioral model are compatible with short downward inflexibility of real wage. In the behavioral model, although cutting real wages need not result in reduced net profit or increased unit cost, as it would in efficiency wage models, it also need not provide any persistent benefits in terms of higher net profit or reduced unit cost.

However, if firm decision makers view their capacity to reduce real wages as simply a product of the downward segment of the business cycle, which they expect will not last, cutting real wages might be viewed as engendering short-term costs in terms of loss of trust, increased labor-management conflict, and restructuring, which are not economically viable if real wages will have to be restored as economic conditions improve (Bewley 1999). The behavioral model, however, suggests that firms need not converge toward some high wage equilibrium, as is suggested by the model of the efficiency-wage reciprocal firm. In the behavioral model the possibility of multiple equilibria with regard to real wage rates, effort input, and levels of x-efficiency is highlighted. A low-wage equilibrium is a very real possibility even when effort discretion exists and workers thereby have the capacity for retaliating against employers for paying them an unfair wage. This is especially true when employers believe that their capacity to drive real wages down is not cyclical but is a product of long-run fundamentals. Thus if employers have a preference for low-wage workplace environments, they can be expected to pursue this option as long as it is consistent with competitive unit costs.

This modeling perspective is consistent with a positive empirical relationship between higher wages and higher levels of x-efficiency as well as with the simultaneous existence of low- and high-wage firms and economies plus a wide range of firm types in between these two extremes. This type of scenario is also much more consistent with the stylized facts of economic life. The existence of effort discretion and the capacity of workers to retaliate against unfair wages and working conditions need not result in employees being paid relatively high wages. Rather, in terms of the behavioral model, a key determinant of whether firms and economies are relatively high-wage is the institutional capacity of workers and peasants to bargain and pressure for higher wages in a world of effort discretion, where the latter allows firms to remain competitive in a high-wage environment. A similar point is made succinctly by Domar in his discussion of the evolution of serfdom and slavery (1970). If firms are constrained into paying an efficiency wage, one should expect convergence to take place between high- and low-wage firms as workers exercise their capacity to force employers to pay them at a fairer rate. Some optimal efficiency wage should be expected to dominate by dint of circumstances. Such does not appear to be the case. The determination of firm types is much more complex than either neoclassical or efficiency wage theories would have it, and this complexity is captured in part by the behavioral model.

Can firms behave ethically in a market economy? The standard argument is that to the extent that behaving ethically incurs higher unit costs, ethical behavior is not sustainable in a competitive economy. At best ethical firms must be sheltered and society at large must bear the economic cost of some economic agents realizing their particular ethical preferences. Even if economic agents (and firm decision makers in particular) prefer that their firms be ethical, such a preference cannot be realized over the long term within the framework of a competitive market economy. Ethical can mean different things to different folks, but there is some consensus that an ethical firm is consistent with a work environment where working conditions and benefits are relatively high and the industrial relations environment is relatively cooperative. Take this as an example of an ethical firm (see Altman 2001a for a discussion of sustainable ethical production from the perspective of "green" economies). Contrary to the conventional wisdom, the behavioral model suggests that the ethical firm need not have to produce at a higher unit cost, since higher input cost can be compensated for by a higher level and quality of effort input. There is an ethical dividend that can be expected when firms behave ethically. However, this dividend need not be large enough to lower unit cost or increase net profit. Rather, the ethical firm can be as cost-competitive and as profitable as the relatively unethical firm. For this reason, the behavioral model suggests that when effort discretion exists, firm decision makers actually do have some choice as to how ethical their firm will be. Market forces per se do not determine this choice for them, which would be the case from the perspective of the conventional wisdom. The behavioral model is therefore consistent with the simultaneous existence of both ethical and unethical firms (Altman 2005).

The focus of our discussion has been that of a world where technological change is being held constant so as to isolate the importance of effort variability for various economic issues. But technological change itself can be significantly affected by the level of x-efficiency (Leibenstein 1973b). And technological change is a critical driver of economic growth—as would be improvements in the level of x-efficiency both in the x-efficiency narrative and in the more general behavioral narratives. Technical change involves transformations to the process of production such that more output, controlling for quality, can be produced with fewer inputs. But as Leibenstein points out, new technologies need not be adopted if the associated increases in productivity require higher, or even x-efficient, levels of effort input and this is not within the preference domain of decision makers. In addition, if technological change requires increased effort inputs from employees who will not benefit from this change, the required effort inputs will not be forthcoming. "Best practice" technology from the perspective of conventional theory will not be adopted. More specifically, I develop elsewhere an induced theory of technological change, where technological change is induced by increases in factor input costs (Altman 2001b, ch. 6; 2005). High-wage firms, for example, are induced to adopt new technology that serves to keep unit cost competitive with the relatively low-wage firms. The high wages also induce economic agents to input the necessary effort required to make the new technology cost-effective. The relatively low-wage x-inefficient firms need not adopt the new technology if it will not serve to lower unit cost or enhance profit. This would be the case when the new technology requires higher levels of effort input, which in turn requires higher wage rates. This model helps explain why more productive technologies are often not adopted, especially in low-wage economies, even when competitive pressures are severe.

CONCLUSION

The introduction of effort discretion into the modeling of economic agency has had a profound impact upon economic theory, although the conventional wisdom remains dominated by theories that pay little to effort discretion. Once effort discretion is introduced as a choice variable, economic narratives that deal with the determination of employment, real wages, productivity, unit cost, and competitiveness take on a different meaning. Such narratives are not at all dependent upon assumptions of irrationality or the errors and biases narrative, which has received so much recent attention in the social science and public policy literature, often under the banner of behavioral economics. The assumption of effort discretion has given rise to a rich literature that falls most generally under the rubric of efficiency wage and x-efficiency theory. The focus of the latter is the relationship of material incentives to productivity as determined by the quality and quantity of effort input. The former focuses upon how preferences with regard to effort input, in the context of different sets of incentives, affect the level of economic efficiency.

Efficiency wage and x-efficiency theory are discussed in some detail, with special focus on their underlying assumptions and the implications of these theories for understanding the micro-micro economics of firm behavior and public policy. Critical attention is paid to the foundational work of Akerlof and Leibenstein. The efficiency and wage and x-efficiency narratives are critically appraised, and extensions and revisions are suggested in terms of a behavioral model of the firm developed by Altman as it bridges and extends the foundational argument of both theories. Fundamental to the behavioral model is that it allows for multiple equilibria with regard to the wage-effort-productivity relationship. Unlike efficiency wage theory, there need not be one unit-cost-minimizing and net-profit-maximizing wage, and involuntary unemployment need not be a product of real wages being too high. In other words, unemployment might be too high given demand-side problems and productivity being too low for marginal workers—such workers being too x-inefficient. Unlike x-efficiency theory, the behavioral model clearly links levels of x-efficiency to the material incentives that are one of the key determinants of the level of x-efficiency. The behavioral model suggests that key causal determinants of the degree of x-efficiency are real wages and working conditions. X-efficiency is not simply a function of preferences and the degree of competitiveness. The extent of institutional space provided to labor to bargain for improvements in their conditions is highlighted, as is the notion that given effort discretion, even under severely competitive markets, x-inefficiency is sustainable, as are both high- and low-wage firms and ethical and unethical firms.

In terms of the behavioral model, the existence of effort discretion provides individuals with a wide array of choices with regard to how firms and economies evolve. Choice is significantly affected by the institutional parameters within which choices are made, as well as how such parameters differentially affect the degree of freedom afforded to individuals and groups of individuals. Economic theory should be constructed to make allowance for the degree of choice that individuals actually do have in a market economy. Models incorporating effort discretion as a choice variable play an important role in this endeavor.

Future research can be expected to provide more nuanced models that incorporate the assumption of effort discretion and multiagent firms with preference functions, which deviate from neoclassical norms for good rational reasons. Such models can serve to better explain the economies in which we live. Needless to say, such models and their underlying assumptions must be tested using traditional data sets as well as through experiments and surveys. In the tradition of behavioral economics, theories should contribute to explaining the facts, with regard to both causality and analytical prediction. And this often involves introducing behavioral and institutional assumptions that are given little play in the conventional modeling narratives.

REFERENCES

Akerlof, George A. 1980. "A Theory of Social Custom, of Which Unemployment May be One Consequence." *Quarterly Journal of Economics* 94: 749–75.
———. 1982. "Labor Contracts as Partial Gift Exchange." *Quarterly Journal of Economics* 97: 543–69.
———. 1984. "Gift Exchange and Efficiency Wage Theory: Four Views." *American Economic Review, Papers and Proceedings* 74: 79–83.
———. 2002. "Behavioral Macroeconomics and Macroeconomic Behavior." *American Economic Review* 92: 411–33.
Akerlof, George A., William T. Dickens, and George L. Perry. 1996. "The Macroeconomics of Low Inflation." *Brookings Papers on Economic Activity* 1996, 1: 1–59.
———. 2000. "Near-Rational Wage and Price Setting and the Long-Run Phillips Curve." *Brookings Papers on Economic Activity* 2000, 1: 1–44.
Akerlof, George A., and Janet L. Yellen, eds. 1986. *Efficiency Wage Models of the Labor Market.* Cambridge: Cambridge University Press.
———. 1988. "Fairness and Unemployment." *American Economic Review, Papers and Proceedings* 78: 44–49.
———. 1990. "The Fair Wage Hypothesis and Unemployment." *Quarterly Journal of Economics* 105: 255–83.
Altman, Morris. 1990. "A Critical Appraisal of Corporate Bigness and the Transactions Cost Economizing Paradigm." In Roger Frantz, ed., *Handbook on Behavioral Economics,* 2A:217–32. London: JAI Press.
———. 1992. "The Economics of Exogenous Increases in Wage Rates in a Behavioral/X-efficiency Model of the Firm." *Review of Social Economy* 50: 163–92.
———. 1996. *Human Agency and Material Welfare: Revisions in Microeconomics and Their Implications for Public Policy.* Boston: Kluwer Academic Publishers.

————. 1998. "High Path to Economic Growth and Development." *Challenge: The Magazine of Economic Affairs* 41: 91–104.

————. 1999. "The Methodology of Economics and the Survivor Principle Revisited and Revised: Some Welfare and Public Policy Implications of Modeling the Economic Agent." *Review of Social Economics* 57: 427–49.

————. 2000. "Labor Rights and Labor Power and Welfare Maximization in a Market Economy: Revising the Conventional Wisdom." *International Journal of Social Economics* 27: 1252–69.

————. 2001a. "When Green Isn't Mean: Economic Theory and the Heuristics of the Impact of Environmental Regulations on Competitiveness and Opportunity Cost." *Ecological Economics* 36: 31–44.

————. 2001b. *Worker Satisfaction and Economic Performance.* Armonk, NY: M.E. Sharpe Publishers.

————. 2002. "Economic Theory, Public Policy and the Challenge of Innovative Work Practices." *Economic and Industrial Democracy: An International Journal* 23: 271–90.

————. 2003a. "Economic Growth and Income Equality: Implications of a Behavioral Model of Economic Growth for Public Policy." *Canadian Public Policy* 24: S87–S118.

————. 2003b. "The Nobel Prize in Behavioral and Experimental Economics: A Contextual and Critical Appraisal of the Contributions of Daniel Kahneman and Vernon Smith." *Review of Political Economy* 16: 3–41.

————. 2004. "Why Unemployment Insurance Might Not Only Be Good for the Soul, It Might Also Be Good for the Economy." *Review for Social Economy* 62: 517–41.

————. 2005. "Reconciling Altruistic, Moralistic, and Ethical Behavior with the Rational Economic Agent and Competitive Markets." *Journal of Economic Psychology* 26: 232–57.

————. 2006a. "Involuntary Unemployment, Macroeconomic Policy, and a Behavioral Model of the Firm: Why High Real Wages Need Not Cause High Unemployment." *Research in Economics* 60: forthcoming.

————. 2006b. "Economic Growth, 'Globalization' and Labor Power." *Global Business and Economics Review* 8: forthcoming.

Becker, Gary S. 1996. *Accounting for Tastes.* Cambridge, MA: Harvard University Press.

Bewley, Truman. 1999. *Why Wages Don't Fall During a Recession.* Cambridge, MA: Harvard University Press.

Baumol, William J., and Edward N. Wolff. 1988. "Productivity Growth, Convergence, and Welfare: Reply." *American Economic Review* 78: 1155–9.

Blanchflower, David G., and Andrew J. Oswald. 1995. "An Introduction to the Wage Curve." *Journal of Economic Perspectives* 9: 153–67.

Cyert, Richard M., and James C. March. 1963. *A Behavioral Theory of the Firm.* Englewood Cliffs, NJ: Prentice-Hall.

DeLong, Bradford J. 1988. "Productivity Growth, Convergence, and Welfare: Comment." *American Economic Review* 78: 1138–54.

Domar, Evsey D. 1970. "The Causes of Slavery or Serfdom: A Hypothesis." *Journal of Economic History* 30: 18–32.

Fehr, Ernst, and Simon Gachter. 2000a. "Reciprocal Fairness, Cooperation, and Limits to Cooperation." In Erich Holzl, ed., *Conference Proceedings: Fairness and Cooperation, XXV Annual Colloquium on Research in Economic Psychology and SABE 2000 Conference*, 1–7. Vienna: IAREP.

————. 2000b. "Fairness and Retaliation: The Economics of Reciprocity." *Journal of Economic Perspectives* 14: 159–81.

Fehr, Ernst, and Klaus M. Schmidt. 1999. "A Theory of Fairness, Competition, and Cooperation." *Quarterly Journal of Economics* 114: 817–68.

Frantz, Roger S. 1997. *X-efficiency Theory, Evidence and Applications.* Topics in Regulatory Economics and Policy 23. Boston: Kluwer Academic Publishers.

————. 2004. "The Behavioral Economics of George Akerlof and Harvey Leibenstein." *Journal of Socio-Economics* 33: 29–44.

Friedman, M. 1953. "The Methodology of Positive Economics." In *Essays in Positive Economics,* 3–43. Chicago: University of Chicago Press.

Gigerenzer, Gerd. 2002. *Adaptive Thinking: Rationality in the Real World.* Oxford: Oxford University Press.

Gigerenzer, Gerd, and Reinhard Selten. 2001. *Bounded Rationality: The Adaptive Toolbox.* Cambridge, MA: MIT Press.

Goldstein, Daniel G., and Gerd Gigerenzer. 2002. "Models of Ecological Rationality: The Recognition Heuristic." *Psychological Review* 109: 75–90.

Güth, Werner. 1995. "On Ultimatum Bargaining Experiments—A Personal Review." *Journal of Economic Organization and Behavior* 27: 329–44.

Ichniowski, Casey, Thomas A. Kochan, David Levine, Craig Olson, and George Strauss. 1996. "What Works at Work: Overview and Assessment." *Industrial Relations* 35: 299–333.

Kahneman, Daniel. 2003. "Maps of Bounded Rationality: Psychology for Behavioral Economics." *American Economic Review* 93: 1449–75.

Kahneman, Daniel, and Amos Tversky. 1979. "Prospect Theory: An Analysis of Decisions Under Risk." *Econometrica* 47: 263–91.

Keynes, John M. 1936. *The General Theory of Employment, Interest, and Money*. New York: Harcourt, Brace and Company.

Leibenstein, Harvey. 1957a. *Economic Backwardness and Economic Growth*. New York: J. Wiley and Sons.

———. 1957b. "The Theory of Underemployment in Backward Economies." *Journal of Political Economy* 65: 91–103.

———. 1966. "Allocative Efficiency vs. 'X-efficiency.'" *American Economic Review* 56: 392–415.

———. 1968. "Entrepreneurship and Development." *American Economic Review, Papers and Proceedings* 58: 72–78.

———. 1973a. "Competition and X-efficiency: Reply." *Journal of Political Economy* 81: 765–77.

———. 1973b. "Notes on X-efficiency and Technical Change." In E.B. Ayal, ed., *Micro-Aspects of Development*, 18–38. New York: Praeger.

———. 1978. "On the Basic Proposition of X-efficiency Theory." *American Economic Review, Papers and Proceedings* 68: 328–32.

———. 1979. "A Branch of Economics Is Missing: Micro-Micro Theory." *Journal of Economic Literature* 17: 477–502.

———. 1982. "The Prisoner's Dilemma in the Invisible Hand: An Analysis of Intrafirm Productivity." *American Economic Review* 72: 92–97.

———. 1983. "Property Rights and X-efficiency: Comment." *American Economic Review*. 73: 831–42.

———. 1984. "On the Economics of Conventions and Institutions: An Exploratory Essay." *Journal of Institutional and Theoretical Economics* 140: 74–89.

Marsh, James G. 1978. "Bounded Rationality, Ambiguity, and the Engineering of Choice." *Bell Journal of Economics* 9: 587–608.

Pritchett, Lant. 1997. "Divergence, Big Time." *Journal of Economic Perspectives* 11: 3–17.

Reder, Melvin W. 1982. "Chicago Economics: Permanence and Change." *Journal of Economic Literature* 20: 1–38.

Rothschild, Kurt W. 2002. "The Absence of Power in Contemporary Economic Theory." *Journal of Socio-Economics* 31: 433–42.

Shafir, Eldar, Peter Diamond, and Amos Tversky. 1997. "Money Illusion." *Quarterly Journal of Economics* 112: 341–74.

Shapiro, Carl, and Joseph E. Stiglitz. 1984. "Equilibrium Unemployment as a Worker Discipline Device." *American Economic Review* 74: 433–44.

Simon, Herbert A. 1959. "Theories of Decision Making in Economics and Behavioral Science." *American Economic Review* 49: 252–83.

———. 1978. "Rationality as a Process and as a Product of Thought." *American Economic Review* 70: 1–16.

———. 1987. "Behavioral Economics." In John Eatwell, Murray Millgate, and Peter Newman, eds., *The New Palgrave: A Dictionary of Economics*. London: Macmillan.

Smith, Vernon L. 2003. "Constructivist and Ecological Rationality in Economics." *American Economic Review* 93: 465–508.

———. 2005. "Behavioral Economics Research and the Foundations of Economics." *Journal of Socio-Economics* 34: 135–50.

Stiglitz, Joseph E. 1987. "The Causes and Consequences of the Dependence of Quantity on Price." *Journal of Economic Literature* 25: 1–48.

Thaler, Richard H. 1992. *The Winner's Curse: Paradoxes and Anomalies of Economic Life*. New York: Free Press.

Todd, Peter M., and Gerd Gigerenzer. 2003. "Bounding Rationality to the World." *Journal of Economic Psychology* 24: 143–65.

Tomer, John F. 2001. "Understanding High-Performance Work Systems: The Joint Contribution of Economics and Human Resource Management." *Journal of Socio-Economics* 30: 63–73.

Tversky, Amos, and Daniel Kahneman. 1981. "The Framing of Decisions and the Psychology of Choice." *Science* 211: 453–58.

CHAPTER 8

GROUP SELECTION AND BEHAVIORAL ECONOMICS

ALEXANDER J. FIELD

Economists reading Stephen Pinker's 2002 book, *How the Mind Works,* might be forgiven some surprise at finding their discipline lumped together with sociology and anthropology and accused of a common error. Pinker's assault on the tendency to treat the human mind as a blank slate at birth extended the attack on the standard social science model begun by John Tooby and Leda Cosmides (1992). To these scholars, social science is largely undifferentiated by discipline—a shock to economists, who have traditionally seen themselves standing to one side of a divide separating those approaching human behavior through the study of rational choice and others emphasizing the influence of such variables as culture and social structure. To be sure, institutionalists, economic historians, and development economists have straddled these two camps uneasily, but many rational choice theorists will find it astonishing to be accused of the same error as traditional sociologists and anthropologists. Surely something must be wrong here.

And something is wrong in the sense that Pinker and others, in their efforts to blunt the continuing influence of behaviorist psychology, have papered over important differences within the social sciences. One major difference is adherence to methodological individualism, a principle embraced by rational choice theorists and rejected by traditional sociologists and anthropologists. Another distinction missed is that although the latter disciplines have been generally hostile to Darwinian explanations of human behavior that emphasize the legacy of natural selection on human biology and action inclinations, economists have been more open to them.

The downside of this openness, however, has been that with a few important exceptions, economists' understanding of Darwinian evolutionary theory has tended to be superficial. Such theory is frequently adduced as support for the assumption of a narrow version of human selfishness: preferences or goals are individualistic in the sense that they are assumed to guide action aimed at efficiently advancing the material self-interest of the actor. This assumption has a long pedigree and is often treated as axiomatic. Over a century ago, Francis Edgeworth wrote that "the first principle of economics is that every agent is activated only by self interest" (1881, 16). The pursuit of self-interest *might* mean that since I am happier when you consume more, acting to benefit you would be selfish. As an empirical matter, however, that's not what it typically *does* mean, and the hardheaded realism of the behavioral assumptions often underlying "economic reasoning" have been part of what has attracted many students to the field.

What is the basis, however, for this first principle? When pressed for justification, the heavy guns of what is presumed to be Darwinism are often wheeled in for support: of course we're selfish, because our parents, our grandparents, and our great-grandparents were, and if they hadn't been, we wouldn't be here. Why? Had they been less selfish, the argument goes, they would have been at an evolutionary disadvantage and thus less likely to procreate.

This style of argument is one reason traditional sociologists and anthropologists, who tend to doubt that selfishness prevails in all realms of human action, want little to do with Darwinism, rational choice models, sociobiology, evolutionary psychology, or any type of thinking that even hints that genetics or biology might influence human behavior or cognition.

This chapter addresses controversial issues within the social and natural sciences. These controversies, which have implications for both major social scientific traditions, need to be considered if we are to make progress in understanding human behavior. I defend a version of methodological individualism against the emphasis on emergent properties of traditional sociology/anthropology, but at the same time I question the conclusions that many rational choice theorists have drawn about the implications of Darwinian thinking for human action inclinations.

ASSUMPTION OF SELFISHNESS

First and foremost, it is necessary to be clear about what rational choice theory does and does not claim. It is useful to think of such models as operating at one of three levels.[1] The first, level 1, simply asserts that people act in satisfaction of their desires. Analysis based on this approach may have a place in casual conversation but can have no claim to scientific standing, since there is no set of observations on human behavior that could contradict it.

Level 2 models, which represent the middle ground of economic theorizing, assume that preferences are stable and transitive. Without some stability over at least the short term, it is hard to conceive of humans engaging in sustained goal-oriented activity. Both observation and intuition suggest that we do so engage. Transitivity is justified by appeal to an evolutionary/money-pump argument. If you did in fact prefer A to B, B to C, and C to A, then, having given you C, I could get you to pay me successively to swap B for C, A for B, and finally C for A—thus inducing you to pay me three times for what I had originally given you for free. Presumably, it is argued, individuals with such preference structures would have been disfavored over time by evolutionary forces.

At least with respect to decisions of particular individuals, level 2 models are falsifiable. By presenting an individual with a sequence of binary choices, it is clearly possible for a person to choose B over C, A over B, and then C over A. If such a violation does occur, we must conclude that preferences lack either stability or transitivity. Level 2 models, however, do not require that preferences be self-interested in the sense in which Edgeworth intended it.

Level 3 models place the most restrictions on preferences. They assume, in addition to stability and transitivity, that the long history of natural selection has rendered humans, like other animals, behaviorally predisposed toward a particular version of selfishness: inclined toward actions that efficiently advance the material self-interest of the organism undertaking them.

Obviously, in many respects and many spheres of action, the assumption reflected in level 3 analysis—and the historical evolutionary explanation of why it is valid—have merit. Organisms that did not seek water when thirsty, food when hungry, or warmth when cold would have been more likely to perish before procreating, leaving those more inclined to such responses to contribute genes to future generations. In some circumstances, however, this assumption may imply behaviors different from those to which an organism predisposed to act in ways that fostered its inclusive reproductive fitness would be inclined.

In polite conversation, economists pursuing level 3 analysis will sometimes grant that "cultural influences" have here and there restrained such selfishness. Allowing restraint on selfishness to be explained in this manner represents an accommodation to the divide that the sociologist

Talcott Parsons (1937) and others tried to engineer. Parsons wished rational choice theory to focus on the choice of appropriate means to achieve given ends; sociology was to be about how human goals were socially determined or constructed. In less accommodationist moments, however, economists unambiguously reject the traditional sociological/anthropological approach, with its suggestion that culture and norms occupy a supraindividual realm, to be understood independently of the cognitions and behaviors of individuals whose activity they influence. In doing so, economists effectively reject as unscientific the concepts of culture and norms as used by sociologists and anthropologists because they violate the principles of methodological individualism (Field 1984).

This expression of disrespect for core disciplinary concepts is returned with accusations that economists are guilty of the sin of reductionism. Communication breaks down, and we are left pretty much where we have been for the last half century, if not longer. Traditional sociologists and anthropologists jealously guard such key concepts as culture and social norms, while the barbarian rational choice theorists take potshots from behind protected redoubts.

Culture is in fact a significant influence on human behavior, although critics have been right to insist that it not be treated as a superorganic force. Rational choice theorists, however, while rejecting superorganic interpretations of culture (and sometimes, wrongly, the importance of the concept itself), have nevertheless struggled to establish convincing explanations of the origins of human sociality from within a perspective based entirely on self-interested action.

There is in fact a large empirical literature documenting experimental and observational evidence at variance with this assumption. Whereas much of economists' interest in anomalies has focused on risky choices or the ways in which beliefs about the world are formed, my interest here is in simple choice situations where, from a wealth maximization standpoint, humans systematically choose less over more. I refer specifically, for example, to results in the ultimatum game, the trust game, the one-shot prisoner's dilemma, or voluntary contributions to public goods experiments (Kagel and Roth 1995; Fehr and Gächter 2000; Field 2001).

Sociologists and anthropologists have, as noted, tended to explain such behavior by appealing to norms, culture, or social structure, concepts that rational choice theorists have often viewed with suspicion. In considering culture, we need to reject both the idea that it is superorganic and the view that society is just the individual writ large. If we accept the merits of trying to understand culture—both its functioning and its origin—using a sophisticated version of methodological individualism, however, there remains the challenge of explaining human sociality. If we are to locate its origins in the characteristics of individuals, what should we assume about them? More specifically, if our social proclivities are ultimately rooted in a genetically mediated human nature, what are its characteristics? Economists have often insisted on trying to solve the problem using level 3 models. We need to understand why such models aren't up to the job.

WHY CAN'T LEVEL 3 MODELS WORK?

The basic problem of social organization has commonly and appropriately been modeled as a prisoner's dilemma. If we make level 3 behavioral assumptions, what we know from game-theoretic analysis can be easily summarized by considering the likelihood of nondefection outcomes in the indefinitely repeated game, the fixed- and known-duration (finitely repeated) game, and the one-shot game.

In the indefinitely repeated game, it is possible for mutual nondefection outcomes to emerge, although outcomes in which everyone defects are just as plausible: there are multiple equilibria, and we can't easily specify why one rather than another is selected. Once established, nondefection outcomes can be self-policing—sustained by self-interest alone—but there is no guarantee they will emerge in the first place. Indefinite repetition thus may be necessary but is not sufficient to guarantee a nondefection rational choice equilibrium outcome (Fudenberg and Maskin 1986).

In the fixed- and known-duration game, defection right from the start is the only rationalizable course for either party unless one believes that one's counterpart might be irrational.[2] Thus, using level 3 behavioral assumptions (wealth maximization), the only way one can rationalize a strategy other than continuous defection is by positing the absence of rational choice in one's counterpart—hardly a satisfying foundation on which to build a rational choice explanation of cooperation. In the finitely repeated two-player game, continuous defection by both parties is the only Nash equilibrium, although, in contrast with the one-shot case, the strategy is not strictly dominant.

In the one-shot game, defection is the only rationalizable strategy. Irrespective of the play of the counterpart, choosing rationally requires that one defect, because defection is strictly dominant. There is simply no way that cooperation in a one-shot prisoner's dilemma game can be philosophically justified, assuming the payoffs accurately reflect the benefits to the individuals associated with the different strategy profiles.

Within the context of a rational choice–game-theoretic framework, individuals must somehow transition from one-shot to indefinitely repeated games in order to have a chance at moving from an asocial state to social interaction. Yet it is clear that assumptions reflected in level 3 models would guarantee that this could not happen. To accommodate evidence of human sociality, then, we must either assume that the state of nature has "always" been one of indefinitely repeated interaction, and then try to explain why sociality equilibria have been selected (Binmore 1994), or modify the behavioral assumptions in level 3 models. In trying to explain sociality, rational choice theorists have been stuck between assuming indefinite repetition at the outset, which is unrealistic, and which in any event gets us only part of the way toward the intended objective because of the equilibrium selection problem, and an aversion to modifying behavioral assumptions because of the evolutionary argument that any behavior that systematically disadvantaged the organism practicing it would have been disfavored by natural selection.

Many people—particularly those wedded strongly to level 3 rational choice models—seem to feel that it is somehow unfair to raise the issue of origin, that it is akin to insisting that we explain what happened before the Big Bang. But the issues are quite different. Based on our knowledge of the fossil record and the biology of surviving organisms, we can be fairly certain that there was a time when there were no social animals, just as there was a time when there were no multicellular organisms, and before that a time when there were no nucleated cells. Real historical transitions occurred, and exploring the mechanisms of natural selection that enabled them, as well as the legacy of the most recent transitional experience on human predispositions, are legitimate endeavors.

The most plausible explanation of human sociality is that as a legacy of that transition, humans possess a genetically mediated behavioral inclination that predisposes us to "solve" one-shot prisoner's dilemmas, even when such action is at variance with that consistent with level 3 behavioral assumptions. This solution module, or primary sociality algorithm, enables pairings of humans some of the time to achieve a cooperate-cooperate profile at initial encounter. Such achievements, in turn, allow the interaction to go into extra innings.

Once continued interaction has been established, a set of secondary sociality algorithms inclines us to spend inordinate time scrutinizing third parties, discriminating among those who do and do not violate group norms (Cosmides and Tooby 1992), and engaging in costly punishment of those who do (Fehr and Gächter 2000). In order to understand how any of these inclinations might possibly have been favored by the operation of natural selection, we need to have a more sophisticated understanding of evolutionary theory.

THE GENE'S-EYE VIEW AND GROUP SELECTION

The preponderance of biological opinion today is that the ultimate locus of selection pressure is at the level of genes, not the cells, organs, or organisms that may contain them. To be sure, in many instances there is a mutuality of interest between the gene and the organism: if the organism does not survive, procreation may not take place, and thus in many cases genetically mediated behavioral predispositions that threaten the survival of the organism will be disfavored. Thus, again, it is no accident that organisms inclined to drink when thirsty are more likely to survive and procreate than those for some reason lacking this inclination.

But to say that this logic holds in most instances does not necessarily mean that it applies in all. Return to the economist's retort to those who might question level 3 behavioral assumptions. It is also true that if our great-grandparents hadn't altruistically sacrificed their material welfare to raise our grandparents, and our grandparents to raise our parents, we wouldn't be here either. Well, yes, comes the answer, but what we meant by selfishness was selfishness toward nonkin, not necessarily within the family. This allowance, however, grants a pretty important exception to the principle that natural selection makes us universally selfish. Let us further consider its logic.

Most economists accept the evidence (including that of our own behavior) that humans, along with many other animals, have a tendency altruistically to sacrifice their material welfare for their offspring. Since the late William Hamilton's work (1964) we have understood that genes so predisposing might be favored in spite of their threats to organism survival because children share half the genetic endowment of each parent.[3] If parental sacrifice, even sacrifice leading to premature death, enables several children to survive and procreate, then genes predisposing to such sacrifice might be favored. The logic and explanatory power of the inclusive-fitness calculus pioneered by Hamilton is now widely accepted by biologists and economists who have considered it.

Since humans may prefer their children's welfare to their own, we have established here a clear violation of the universal purview of level 3 behavioral assumptions, a violation based on a biologically and genetically mediated altruistic tendency that trumps the inclinations predisposing toward wealth maximization. What is happening here is that genes are "deviously" predisposing organisms (us) to self-sacrifice, because these behaviors have in the past resulted in an increase in the frequency of genes so predisposing. This example is an indication that the straitjacket natural selection places on assumptions about human behavioral inclinations is looser than a casual reading of Darwinism might suggest.

While the existence and explanation of altruistic tendencies toward kin is generally accepted, the question remains whether we might be biologically inclined, albeit at weaker levels, toward altruistic behavior toward nonkin. Is this possibility consistent with known mechanisms of natural selection? The straightforward and perhaps surprising answer is yes. As in the case of altruism toward kin, such a circumstance would require "devious" genes to incline an organism toward action potentially detrimental to the organism's material welfare, but nevertheless resulting in increasing frequencies of such genes in future generations. The rise from low to higher frequency of such genes would require a specific set of demographic conditions enabling the operation of selection above the level of the individual organism. This has historically been known as "group selection," although the term "multilevel selection" is often preferred today, as a means of emphasizing that current analysis is in no way inconsistent with a gene's-eye perspective.

It is important to understand both the logic and some of the intellectual history of this analysis in order to appreciate its implications for behavioral science. We begin by noting that the debate about the role of group selection in accounting for human sociality is one instance of a set of closely related debates surrounding several key evolutionary transitions. These include the origins of chromosomes, the transitions from prokaryotes to eukaryotes (cellular organisms) and subsequently to multicellular organisms, and the origin of sexual reproduction (Maynard Smith and Szathmáry 1995; Keller 1999). In each instance, appeal to how selection at a higher level overcomes selection pressures at a lower level is necessary in order to provide a coherent account of transition.

For example, with respect to sexual reproduction, parthenogenetically reproducing organisms would appear to have a twofold genetic advantage over those engaged in sexual reproduction, since the parent in the former case transmits 100 percent rather than 50 percent of genetic endowment to offspring. On the other hand, it is commonly accepted today that a system of sexual reproduction gives a species an advantage based on access to a larger pool of genetic variability in the face of rapidly evolving pathogens. But that advantage accrues to the group and could not have favored the origin of sexual reproduction if selection occurred no higher than the organism level.

The flashpoint has come when scholars both begin and end an explanation of a characteristic with reference to its function. Modern evolutionary theory insists that we specify how this equilibrium originated. Given that the ultimate locus of selection is at the level of the gene, not the organism, let alone the species, this means one must explore the operation of natural selection at multiple levels. It is uncontroversial that selection can take place at the gene level, the organism level, or levels intermediate. Virtually all biologists also admit the theoretical possibility of selection above the level of the organism. Because of a series of contentious intellectual debates that began four decades ago, however, the issue of the empirical importance of selection at this level remains the third rail of biological discourse. Fifteen years ago, even broaching the subject practically guaranteed electrocution. Today, the topic is again sometimes admitted into polite conversation, although many biologists engage in semantic contortions to avoid calling higher-level selection group selection.

Appeals to higher-level selection were common in the 1940s and 1950s among biologists such as Sewall Wright (1945), ethologists such as Konrad Lorenz (1966), and some social scientists who analogized social structures to organs of a body and "explained" them with reference to their function. But the empirical importance of group-level selection came under withering attack in the 1960s, in particular by George Williams (1966). In light of these attacks, the dominant position among biologists from the late 1960s on was that these processes were empirically unimportant in the evolution of humans and other species. Those who continued to consider or investigate its operation were marginalized, consigned in the disciplinary pecking order to a position slightly ahead of creationists (Wilson and Sober 1994, Sober and Wilson 1998).

The consensus position was based in part on the argument that a number of animal behaviors previously "explained" on the grounds that they benefited (were adaptive for) a group could now be shown to be favored by the forces of individual-level selection alone and were therefore not "altruistic" at all (Williams 1966). If behavioral predispositions benefited a group of nonkin, it was because they benefited these individuals *and* the actor (in other words, the behavior was mutualistic, not altruistic; to be favored by organism-level natural selection, the relative fitness of the actor still had to be improved). The apparent coup de grâce in the argument against group selection was the more systematic demonstration that traits that provided benefit to a group, provided they were initially widespread, could be sustained (protected from invasion by other strategies) by individual-level frequency-dependent selection alone (Maynard Smith and Price 1973).

For several reasons, group selection is now making a comeback in biology. First, there remains the set of critical evolutionary transitions, such as to sexual reproduction or to sociality, that are difficult to account for without allowing for the operation of selection at higher levels.

Second, models of group selection have moved away from the "islands" formulation associated with Sewall Wright to the structured deme approach pioneered by D.S. Wilson (a deme is a local community of potentially interbreeding individuals). Third, virtually all players today accept the necessity of a gene-centric approach. Finally, it is increasingly recognized that evolutionary game-theory models and the concept of an evolutionarily stable strategy (ESS) are tools for understanding and explaining how evolutionary equilibria are sustained, not necessarily how they originate. Third rail or not, a number of scholars both in and outside biology are saying that the rejection of the empirical likelihood of higher-level selection needs to be reexamined.

Sewall Wright recognized the fitness disadvantage experienced by altruists within each group. But he suggested that if groups were small enough and isolated enough, altruism might by chance— that is, through the mechanism of genetic drift—evolve to fixation within some groups, and that such groups could then outcompete others by persisting longer and colonizing new territories by contributing more dispersers. The conditions necessary for these "island" models to operate continue to be viewed by evolutionary biologists as unlikely to obtain. A major concern is that if there is enough dispersion to permit the colonization of new territories, there is also likely enough to permit dispersing nonaltruists from other groups, or islands, to invade existing altruist groups (Maynard Smith 1964; Wade 1978).

Because of these concerns, greater interest has focused in recent years on haystack or structured deme models, which depend on organisms separating or being separated into groups for part of a life cycle, or perhaps for a period of several generations, and then reentering a global population before again reassorting into groups. Genetic recombination, outcrossing, and infrequent mutation are sufficient to produce variability in individuals.[4] If the groups are small enough, average group predispositions toward altruistic behavior will vary, even where initial assortment into groups is done randomly (Cavalli-Sforza, Menozzi, and Piazza 1994, 13; Field 2003). Within each group, altruists will lose out in the competition for resources, and in particular the competition to pass on their genes to the next generation. Consequently, their share of each group will fall (or at best stay even in the unlikely event altruists completely dominate a group) throughout the period of time that the group has a distinct existence. But because the behavior of altruists differentially benefits groups in which their frequencies may be relatively higher, the proportion of altruists in the global population may rise in cases where the forces of group selection are stronger than the forces of individual selection.

Examples of circumstances favorable to group-level selection include the life cycle relationships between parasites and other disease vectors and their hosts. Suppose groups of a polymorphic virus with more and less virulent versions invade a number of host organisms, let us say rabbits. Among the rabbits, chance variation will result in varying mixtures of the two forms within each of them. Within each host, the more virulent versions enjoy a fitness advantage and increases in frequency. But organisms infected with high frequencies of the more virulent strain die quickly, before they can infect many other hosts. In contrast, hosts infected with less virulent mixtures live longer, more successfully spreading the disease. The longer-living hosts therefore exercise a greater weight in determining the frequencies of the two versions in subsequent time periods, and each of their "votes" carries a higher proportion of the less virulent strain. Paradoxically, the less virulent strain can be decreasing in frequency within every host, yet increasing over time within the global population.

In fact, such a scenario has been documented among rabbits in Australia in the early 1950s who were confronted by the myxoma virus, introduced by the government to control an exploding population. Initially mortality was very high, but gradually it declined, suggesting that the rabbits were acquiring resistance. Subsequent testing revealed two outcomes, one of which was surprising. First, the rabbits had indeed, on average, become more resistant to myxoma, which would be expected from individual-level selection operating through differential mortality within the rabbit population. The surprising and unexpected conclusion applied to the viral population. The virus itself became on average less virulent, as measured by extracting blood from rabbits in the wild and comparing samples so obtained with original viral samples stored in a laboratory. This outcome would not be expected if natural selection operated only at the level of the individual virus, as it indeed was within each host. The initial interpretation of this episode as reflecting the operation of group selection was controversial, but most evolutionary biologists, including George Williams, now accept it (Williams and Nesse 1991, 8; Williams 1992). The mechanism is essential to the burgeoning field of Darwinian medicine.

Wright's analysis of group selection relied on the evolution to fixation of altruistic traits within some groups, combined with interdemic competition. The structured deme approach does not require evolution to fixation in any group but emphasizes the necessity of periodic recombining of or migration between groups—called trait groups by D.S. Wilson—in order for group selection to occur. Altruists from the faster-growing more altruistic groups must periodically disperse throughout the global population (see Wade 1978 for discussion).

The possibility that altruists may be declining in frequency within every group and yet rising in frequency in the global population—an apparent contradiction—can be more easily understood with reference to the Simpson paradox (Simpson 1951). The paradox exists when a population divided into groups exhibits a population average that differs from the average of the group averages. A corollary is that under these conditions, changes in the average of the groups may differ from changes in the population average. A compelling example of this was an investigation at the University of California at Berkeley of alleged discrimination against women in admissions to graduate study in the 1970s. Aggregate data showed that admission rates for women were lower than for men. But when administrators looked at the data department by department they found no evidence of discrimination: in each department women were being admitted at approximately the same rate as men.

The explanation for the paradox was that the distribution of applicants by department was not the same for the two sexes. In particular, women were applying disproportionately to departments in which it was more difficult for an applicant of either sex to gain admission. This covariance meant that the averages of the departmental admission rates, roughly equivalent for men and women, differed from the global average admission rates, in which women did less well than men. What was true at the level of each individual group (department)—roughly equal admissions rates—was not true for the entire population of applicants (Dawes 1988, 297).[5] Similarly, in considering the fate of altruists, what is true for each individual group (altruists are losing out) may not be true for the global population, because groups in which altruists are differentially concentrated may grow more rapidly. The argument at first glance seems akin to the story of the retailer who lost money on every sale but made it up on volume. Upon careful examination, however, the Simpson paradox is not based on such an inherently contradictory claim.

THE ROLE OF GROUP SELECTION IN FOSTERING ALTRUISM TOWARD KIN AND NONKIN

Whereas the Hamilton inclusive-fitness logic as applied to altruism toward kin is broadly accepted, its application to the case of weaker altruistic predispositions toward nonkin, including restraint on first strike, remains controversial. Like Hamilton, recent proponents of group selection, such as D.S. Wilson, interpret the kin selection mechanism as an instance of multilevel selection, where the group is the family unit. They then proceed as if the phylogenies of altruism toward kin and altruism toward nonkin are similar in all fundamental respects. This, I argue, is a mistake because the biologically altruistic character of sacrifice for kin is largely independent of whether others in a group express similar behaviors. This is not necessarily true of the sociality algorithms, particularly the primary sociality algorithm, because of its role enabling reciprocity, upon which mutually beneficial exchange relations are based.

Certain behaviors expressed toward nonkin are clearly biologically altruistic (and, correspondingly, not rational for narrowly self-interested agents) upon first appearance. Lone cooperators in a sea of defectors harm themselves while benefiting others. If the result of a first encounter is death, it makes no difference what an organism may have been prepared to do should a continuing series of interactions have been initiated. All that matters is that she cooperated, to her detriment and to the advantage of another, on what turned out to be a one-shot game.

The fitness disadvantage of parental sacrifice for children is largely independent of whether such propensities are widely shared in a group. That is not so true of algorithms favoring cooperation among nonkin. The higher the frequency of nonkin cooperators in a population, the smaller the fitness disadvantage of cooperating (assume players are randomly paired to play one-shot prisoner's dilemma games). It is also, however, true that the fitness advantage of the remaining defectors rises with the frequency of cooperators—because a defector is now almost sure to be matched with a cooperator. That is why, if selection is only at the organism level and players play one-shot prisoner's dilemma games, the replicator dynamic will inexorably drive cooperators to extinction.

There is one condition under which cooperative strategies could be sustained by individual self-interest alone, and thus one condition under which populations not subject to selection above the level of the individual could be proof against direct invasion by defectors.[6] That condition is that players, instead of playing one-shot games with their counterpart, play a sequence of prisoner's dilemma games in which neither player knows in advance when the interaction will end. Under these conditions, it is possible to sustain contingently cooperative behavior as a self-policing rational choice equilibrium. If both parties were playing tit for tat, for example, with the right discount rate neither would have an incentive to deviate from her strategy, since each would be playing a best response to that of the other.

If one can assume indefinite interaction, then, one can tell a story in which group selection is necessary for contingently cooperative strategies to rise from low to higher frequencies, but in which the need for it disappears when such strategies have attained sufficiently high frequency. Indeed, a good deal of evolutionary game theory has been devoted to telling the second half of this story, neglecting, however, the fact that explanations of equilibrium maintenance are not necessarily the same as explanations of origin.

There is, however, an important weakness in this argument as it applies to the real world. In bilateral pairings, *either party typically has the option of terminating the interaction at any time.* Cohabitants can cease living together, long-term supplier-customer relationships can end, veteran employees can be fired, and military alliances can be and have been abrogated overnight. The assumption that the duration of the game is exogenous, while a convenient modeling convention, is as a practical matter unrealistic in the absence of third-party "umpires." If both players are strictly self-interested and know they can terminate at any time without third-party retribution, they will defect from the get-go, and there will be no continuing interaction.

Experimental results show that the human inclination to play cooperate in a one-shot prisoner's dilemma game with anonymity is in fact substantially greater than the Nash prediction of zero. This means that two players, selected at random, may, to their mutual benefit, be able to initiate and sustain a string of cooperative interactions. But such cooperation is fragile because the propensity to play cooperate is nowhere near 100 percent. Foraging algorithms reinforce a persisting temptation to play what remains, after all, a strictly dominant strategy.

Since freely chosen interactions cannot realistically be assumed to persist for indefinite durations beyond the control of the parties (even if this were so, this would only make self-interested cooperation possible, not guarantee it), the restraint of defection in a group requires more than the threat that a counterpart will match defection with defection. It requires a set of evolved secondary sociability algorithms that govern behaviors toward third parties. At least two of these have been well documented. First, humans devote remarkable amounts of energy to seeking out and identifying rule violators (defectors)—our obsession with this is so strong that it can distort our ability to think logically (Cosmides and Tooby 1992). Second, a high fraction of humans are prepared to engage in costly punishment of those who defect (Fehr and Gächter 2000). When present at sufficiently high frequency, these two algorithms serve to weaken the attractiveness of defecting in a prisoner's dilemma game. They may weaken it so much that even those so inclined find that the behavior is no longer a dominant strategy. In the limit, because of the threat of widespread third-party punishment, which reduces the net payoff to the defector in a defect/ cooperate profile, the prisoner's dilemma may, in fact, cease to be a prisoner's dilemma. That is why, when well established, reciprocal relations among nonkin (the precursor for exchange) appear to be mutually beneficial, and thus to have lost the altruistic character that the same contingently cooperative strategy, expressed within a sea of defectors, surely would have possessed.

Unfortunately, to the degree that the primary prisoner's dilemma may be approximately resolved in this fashion, a set of secondary dilemmas that are just as serious are created. Foraging algorithms, optimized for wealth maximization for the individual organism, counsel against being influenced by either of these secondary algorithms just as much as they counsel against an initial cooperative move in a bilateral pairing. The secondary sociality algorithms also involve action that benefits other group members at cost to self. Consequently they could have been reinforced by natural selection only if such selection occurred above the level of the individual organism.

Note that positing an inclination to punish those who fail to punish doesn't resolve the problem. It is always a strictly dominant strategy to let others punish rule violators, or to let others punish those who fail to punish, or to let others punish those who fail to punish those who fail to punish, and so on. As fast as one prisoner's dilemma is at least hypothetically resolved, another is created. Different societies have used different mechanisms to control defection, but none has eliminated the basic problem posed by the prisoner's dilemma, although some displace it to different levels.

So far I have not talked much about culture and socialization. The evidence is overwhelming that humans can be trained not only to master technologies (means) but also, within limits, to adopt certain ends. We are smart, but we also are apparently biologically prepared to accept indoctrination in group-reinforcing ideologies, particularly when we are young. With remarkable success parents are able to impart to their children not only their own language vocabularies and recipes for making cake but also their own religious or ethical beliefs and practices. This can be done for nonkin as well. It is an essential feature of military training that infantrymen are taught (learn) to throw themselves on a grenade to save other members of their squad. Organized political groups in the Middle East have been quite successful in recruiting and motivating suicide bombers.

The last two examples are particularly stark illustrations of the fact that humans can be taught (or learn through instruction or imitation) to express behaviors that from a level 3 game-theoretic standpoint are strictly dominated strategies. For many in the sociological/anthropological tradition, an appeal to culture or norms is all that is needed to explain human sociality. Cultural explanations, presume, however, that we have this capability to learn or be taught ends as well as means. But we must then ask how a capability to "learn" strictly dominated strategies ever could have evolved if selection occurred at no higher level than that of the individual.

The one-shot prisoner's dilemma is a source of great frustration for rational choice theorists. The cooperative profile, which can be attained only if each player plays a strictly dominated strategy, is clearly the most jointly attractive of the three efficient outcomes. The Nash equilibrium, on the other hand, is the only inefficient outcome. Economists often argue that the pursuit of individual self-interest also leads to social benefits. What economists are trying to say here is that behavior that looks as if it is selfish is really mutualistic from a biological standpoint.

But whereas voluntary exchange in an atmosphere where force and fraud are at low levels can be mutually beneficial, such exchange can persist only as the consequence of widespread secondary sociality algorithms whose operation continues to involve the play of strictly dominated strategies. So taking this more encompassing perspective, it is simply wrong to say that we can build a theory of social order based on level 3 rational choice models.

In a market economy, the sociability algorithms help establish a human environment in which individuals are able to pursue the counsel of their foraging algorithms in a context never anticipated by the forces of natural selection that honed them. The genius of markets is that in the limit they appear to turn games with people into games against nature, for which the foraging algorithms were originally selected. That limit is the purely competitive market where prices confront individuals as parametric.

But markets don't abolish the problem of the prisoner's dilemma. We may intone that crime doesn't pay. With sufficient third-party enforcement the statement may, at one level, become true. But at some other level it always pays. The appeal to the foraging algorithms to dissuade us from criminal behavior is ultimately destined to fail. That is why this claim is always paired with the nonconsequentialist argument that criminal acts are wrong. The fact that many humans are receptive to such arguments is, again, reflective of the fact that we can be trained—indoctrinated—to express in our behavior group-beneficial but strictly dominated strategies (to some degree these inclinations are hardwired at birth). Without being able to ensure indefinitely repeated interaction, one simply cannot have a self-policing rational choice equilibrium involving cooperation, even with frequency-dependent selection, and that is why the foraging algorithms alone are insufficient as a foundation for understanding political behavior.

Still, it is important to note that the effect of frequency-dependent selection can be a powerful influence on the relative fitness disadvantages of sociability algorithms in a way that is not true for sacrifice toward kin. The biologically altruistic character of sacrifice for kin is largely frequency-independent. Traits necessary for the development of sociality among nonkin have the property that as they rise in frequency within a population, the within-group selection becomes over time less negative. High frequencies of contingently cooperative behavior are preconditions for reciprocal relations, which enable mutually beneficial exchange.

Altruism toward kin is different in its phylogeny and in its game-theoretic character. Sacrifices for our children do not represent a solution to a prisoner's dilemma.[7] It is not really possible— even stretching—to interpret them as an instance of exchange over time (this is the idea behind the misnamed theory of reciprocal altruism; see Trivers 1971). The interaction of a parent with a helpless child lacks the strategic character of an encounter between two armed men, because the material payoff to the parent is unaffected by any action the baby takes. And finally, the genetic payoff to sacrificing for babies is largely independent of how widespread such inclinations may be among other parents in a group.

Whereas the kin selection mechanism has been relatively uncontroversial among evolutionary biologists,[8] the same cannot be said for group selection explanations of altruistic behavior toward nonkin. The initial Maynard Smith and Price work (1973) investigating restraints on intraspecific harm, and subsequent development of the concept of an evolutionarily stable strategy, explored the implications of frequency-dependent selection in equilibrium maintenance. Their great insight was to understand and explain how strategies that might benefit a group might be sustained in the absence of any selection at the group level. Initially, a number of theorists—perhaps even Maynard Smith and Price themselves—believed that this conclusion provided the explanation for the persistence *and* the emergence of altruistic behavior as the consequence of individual selection forces alone.[9] But this is an error that arises from confusing the explanation of forces that may sustain an equilibrium with those responsible for the evolutionary trajectory that led to it.

In human interactions behavior is influenced both by foraging algorithms and by the primary and secondary sociability algorithms augmented by cultural reinforcers. Whereas the foraging algorithms were always reinforced by selection at the level of the organism, the sociability algorithms required the operation of selection above that level. The development of predispositions to sacrifice for kin, particularly offspring, could not have been favored by natural selection operating no higher than the level of the organism. The same is true of the algorithms underlying cooperation among nonkin: the propensity to play cooperate in what might be a one-shot prisoner's dilemma, the inclination to search out rule violators, and the predisposition to engage in costly punishment of them.

Readers will observe the close analogues between rational choice game-theoretic analysis and evolutionary game theory, and the related roles played by indefinitely repeated interaction in the former and frequency-dependent selection in the latter. The assumption of indefinitely repeated interaction is necessary to provide a logically consistent account of how selfish actors might sustain a self-policing nondefection outcome. The assumption of frequency-dependent selection is necessary to explain how prosocial behavioral predispositions might be sustained in the absence of selection above the level of the organism. But in both cases there is a historical question left unanswered. In game theory, how could selfish actors ever have transitioned from one-shot to indefinitely repeated interaction? The obviously unsatisfactory answer is that they never had to (and never have to) because interaction is always indefinitely repeated.

In evolutionary game theory the challenge is to explain how prosocial behavioral predispositions ever could have transitioned from low to higher frequency without the operation of selection above the level of the organism. The equally unsatisfactory answer is that these traits are and have always been at sufficiently high frequency that we need not concern ourselves with problems of origin.

ECONOMISTS AND THE INTELLECTUAL HISTORY OF THE GROUP SELECTION DEBATE

The debate about the empirical likelihood of higher-level selection in human evolution and its likely legacy on our behavioral predispositions has profound implications for the conduct of social science. These are controversies that will benefit from interdisciplinary dialogue, not only within the social sciences but also between the social and natural sciences. For historical reasons, economists may be particularly well situated to contribute to this discourse. First, in comparison with sociologists or anthropologists, economists have been more favorably disposed toward considering biological/genetic explanations of human behavior and cognition. Second, to date only a very few have actually considered the mechanics and implications of the operation of selection pressures at different levels. Although this has resulted in superficial defenses of level 3 modeling as having an evolutionary justification, it may now be an advantage because, in contrast with biology, economics lacks a legacy of intellectual warfare in this area. It may be easier, consequently, to discuss the issue on its merits.

Although the number of economists aware of the debate has been small, those who have examined the issue have generally concluded that selection at higher levels must have been empirically important at some point in our history. A full-text JSTOR search for "group selection" among articles published in economics journals between 1890 and 1996 turns up just five hits that use the term in its evolutionary sense.[10] One is for an article by the biologist Edward O. Wilson in the *American Economic Review*. The other four hits included one for Paul Samuelson, one for Gary Becker, and two for the late Jack Hirshleifer. Each of these authors has written positively about the likelihood that group-level selection has operated at some time in our evolutionary past (Becker 1976, 284, 294; Hirshleifer 1977, 25; 1982, 30–33; Samuelson 1993).

To this list, which already includes two Nobelists, one should add a third. Although Friedrich Hayek's argument in *The Fatal Conceit* does not depend on the assumption that biological group selection played a role in human evolutionary history, he was clearly receptive to the likelihood that it did (1988, 25). His analysis is notable in turning the standard Hobbesian dilemma on its head.

Since 1996, other economists, including Herbert Gintis (2000) and Theodore Bergstrom (2002), have treated the likelihood of higher-level selection sympathetically in explorations of human sociality. I do not mean to suggest that all economists, particularly those who have more recently become aware of multilevel selection issues, have necessarily embraced the likelihood of higher-level selection. Indeed, a number, taking their lead from what has appeared to be the consensus view in biology, have not. But as a group economists have tended to be open-minded about the issue when presented with the logic and evidence in support of the hypothesis.

A case in point is Robert Frank. His influential 1988 book, *Passions Within Reason,* followed conventional biological wisdom and dismissed group selection as empirically unlikely. He then attempted to proceed within a modeling environment in which higher-level selection was out of bounds, resulting in a number of internal contradictions in his analysis (see Field 2001, ch. 4). Six years later, however, Frank acknowledged the limitations of his initial approach (Frank 1994, 620).

These data and citations are sufficient to establish two points: first, at least until recently, the number of economists who have considered or even been aware of the possibility of multilevel selection has been small. Second, in contrast to biology, the profession does not harbor a large cohort of individuals passionately prejudiced against the empirical likelihood of higher-level selection. Many remain unaware that it is a possibility, although this group has been shrinking.

As this has been happening, outside of economics Robert Boyd and Peter Richerson (see Richerson and Boyd 2004) have articulated an influential position that subtly undermines much of the progress that has been made to date in understanding the logic of group selection and its likely role in explaining some of the otherwise anomalous experimental results in behavioral economics. Richerson and Boyd argue that cultural group selection, reinforced by conformity norms and transmission through other than parent-to-child routes, has been an important influence on human development. At the same time, they maintain that there has never been any empirically important genetic/biological group selection, and thus there are no significant behavioral legacies of its operation. On this issue Richerson and Boyd essentially reendorse the position adopted by Williams in 1966, one that Williams has subsequently backed away from.

Richerson and Boyd are right to argue, contrary to some economists' prejudices, that cultural variation is an independent influence on behavioral outcomes, one that cannot be entirely swept back to environmental differences. Thus normative structures and behavior may differ in regions that share a similar resource base or access to similar technologies (see also Field 1991). There are, nevertheless, a number of difficulties with their rejection of an empirical legacy for biological group selection. These include the continuing need to account for prosocial inclinations prior to the development of cultural capabilities in humans, which Richerson and Boyd date from half a million years ago. Their position and its limitations are discussed in greater detail in Field 2005b and 2006.

CONCLUSION

As noted earlier, level 1 rational choice analysis, which assumes that people act according to their desires, can have no claim to scientific standing. Level 3 analysis, on the other hand (preferences are assumed stable, transitive, and strictly individualistic), is at variance with a broad range of experimental and observational evidence. There has sometimes been a reluctance to accept this evidence on the grounds that we must be universally selfish because Darwin told us so. One purpose of this chapter has been to undercut that argument. If we are to use rational choice as a general approach to building models of human behavior, and if these models are to have any chance of real predictive success, the action will have to be at level 2.

It is often said that economics is superior as a discipline to the other social sciences because it has a theory. If so, what are its essential features? If the distinguishing feature of economic theory is the assumption of universal selfishness, in the sense that in all realms we efficiently advance our material welfare, it is not a very good theory. There is abundant evidence that whenever people sacrifice for their children, exercise restraint on first strike in what might be a one-shot prisoner's dilemma, reject a positive offer in an ultimatum game, make voluntary contributions to a public good, engage in altruistic punishment, or enter the voting booth, we leave money on the table, literally or figuratively. Based on such evidence, traditional sociologists and anthropologists, and many economists, object to the assumption of universal selfishness reflected in level 3 models, and rightly so.

Level 2 models have their problems. To be sure, we face cognitive and computational problems in forming accurate beliefs about the world, and sometimes we do make choices that we would not have made if we had had stable and transitive preferences and maximized appropriately.[11] But the assumptions that humans are goal-oriented, that these goals don't change every minute, that our preferences are transitive, and that we try to do the best we can for ourselves, given these preferences and the constraints we face, is indeed a reasonable starting point. When spelled out in this way, it is hard to see anyone objecting to it as a first approximation. It is also difficult, however, to see people manning disciplinary ramparts in defense of the proposition that preferences are stable and transitive.

Selfishness, though, is another story entirely. The superiority economists secretly (and sometimes not so secretly) feel with respect to other social scientists is, I suspect, based less on the belief that we understand that preferences are stable and transitive while others don't, and more on the assumption that we understand that people are universally selfish while others don't. The hardheaded (apparent) realism of this assumption also helps account for some of the distaste, ambivalence, and envy those in other disciplines sometimes experience with respect to economics.

Still, there is unease within the profession: a significant number of economists may practice level 3 but will publicly defend level 2. Nevertheless, if we say that the core of economic theory rests on stability and transitivity, but what we mean is stability, transitivity, and selfishness, then we are ultimately forced to abandon what is *truly* distinctive about the rational choice approach: a commitment, to the degree scientifically possible, to explain collective phenomena with respect to the aggregated characteristics of constituent units. Only by firmly relinquishing the assumption of universal selfishness can behavioral scientists offer a coherent alternative to the traditional sociological and anthropological approaches to issues of human sociality.

As has been noted, the combination of methodological individualism with the assumptions of universal selfishness is a nonstarter in terms of explaining the origins of human sociality. If we insist on universal selfishness, we are forced to introduce culture as a supraindividual constraining force. If we relax that stricture, however, we are in a position to understand institutions, culture, or norms with reference to the aggregated properties of those individuals whose behavior they organize. These properties include behavioral and cognitive predispositions along with learned associations, conditional probabilities updated using Bayesian statistical methodologies, and the memory capabilities that facilitate this learning.

Language, for example, is broadly recognized as an important facilitative social institution. To understand its significance, however, we are not obliged to appeal to emergent properties. Its origin and operation can be understood entirely with reference to the aggregated properties of those individuals whose communication it organizes. Thanks to the work of Noam Chomsky and his followers, it is widely accepted today that we are born with a set of deep structural rules of grammar hardwired in our brain. This hardwiring explains a set of rules of universal grammar that all 5,000-plus known human languages obey. Vocabularies, on the other hand, vary widely: they are a learned cultural phenomenon. They represent shared expectations about how others will associate strings of phonemes with objects or concepts.

The analogy with respect to social organization is not exact. Shared vocabularies represent from a game-theoretic perspective the solution to a coordination problem. A particular language vocabulary can be viewed as a historically determined selection from a set of multiple equilibria. But it is not possible to fit all aspects of culture into this framework, especially those that are near universal. In addition to the oft-noted incest taboo, all known societies proscribe within-group murder and excessive within-group lying or cheating. Whether it has formal institutions of government or not, any group, if it is to survive or even form in the first place, must contain individuals who restrain their own potential use of force and fraud. Once sustained interaction is established, members must also be prepared to engage in costly punishment of others who don't. The challenge of surmounting the prisoner's dilemma in initiating interaction with nonkin, and of sustaining it once established, is universal, and because of its recurring character, the solution to it likely involves some genetic substrate.

Social solutions to coordination games are Nash, whereas social solutions to the one-shot prisoner's dilemma, the problem of voluntary contributions to public goods, or the problem of costly punishment of norm violators are not.[12] From an evolutionary perspective, some of the cognitive and behavioral machinery we bring to the tasks of dealing with other humans could not have evolved from low to higher frequency without the benefit of higher-level selection. Our historical and contemporary ability to "solve" these dilemmas is based on action inclinations sometimes at variance with those counseled by our foraging algorithms (those celebrated in traditional economic theory).

All social scientists, economists included, are susceptible to self-deception, which can involve projecting a level 3 rational choice interpretation on behavior that cannot possibly support it. There is no clearer instance of this than the goal-oriented rationalizations that obviously intelligent, logical individuals give for voting. The odds of influencing a national election through one's voting behavior are infinitesimal, and the act of voting is nearly impossible to defend using consequentialist reasoning (Field, 2005a).

Yet for many the urge to vote *and* the sense that they are rational level 3 maximizers are so powerful that they will simply cover their ears or otherwise indicate they do not wish to hear more "economist" arguments about the material benefit-cost ratio of the activity. There would be less discomfort were there greater understanding and acceptance of the proposition that in a number of important spheres of action we have hardwired dispositions to behave in ways contrary to our individual material well-being.

If we get "utility" from voting or from cooperating in prisoner's dilemma games where it is not in our material interest to do so, it is probably because we are biologically programmed to take pleasure in participating in some forms of collective action, an inclination that is apparently sufficiently strong to trump the logic of free riding and get more than 120 million voters to the polls in a national election in the United States. Socialization and education may explain some of the cross-sectional variation in such behavior, but the high participation rates in countries experiencing democratic elections for the first time suggest that this can be at best part of the story. An unavoidable conclusion is that activities such as voting are expressive, not goal-oriented, if goals are understood in the traditional terms of influencing outcomes. It may still make sense philosophically to adopt the principle of choosing as if our vote would decide the election, so long as we don't give the principle an instrumental rationale.

Similarly, when educated economists and mathematicians play cooperate in a one-shot prisoner's dilemma or in a fixed- and known-duration prisoner's dilemma, as did Armen Alchian and John Williams in the world's very first such experiment in 1950 (they played cooperate with increasing frequency as the game neared its end) (Poundstone 1992, 106–16), something must be trumping wealth maximization algorithms, even though this trumping may mean that the participants end up with more wealth. An appreciation of the richness and subtlety of evolutionary mechanisms and the operation of natural selection, in particular the possibility and likelihood of selection at multiple levels, is a necessary step in allowing us to advance behavioral science informed by a version of methodological individualism while at the same time avoiding the cul-de-sacs into which level 3 rational choice models have repeatedly led.

NOTES

This chapter was presented at the conference The Evolution of Preferences, April 5, 2003, University of California, Davis, at the Society for the Advancement of Behavioral Economics conference at Lake Tahoe, California, on July 29, 2003, at seminars at Brown and Emory universities on October 22 and 29, 2003, and at the Max Planck Institute, Jena, Germany, December 7, 2004. I am grateful to participants in these sessions and to Avinash Dixit, Herbert Gintis, and Bill Sundstrom for comments and discussion on earlier drafts.

1. I ignore here the elaborations necessary for a full treatment of decision making under uncertainty. Indeed, the focus here is on decisions that do *not* involve uncertain or risky choices or problems in forming correct beliefs about the world.

2. For example, if I believe my opponent is playing tit for tat, my best response as a strictly self-interested player is to cooperate at all stages save the last. But the resulting strategy profile is not Nash, since tit for tat is not the best response to the strategy just described.

3. The vast bulk of genetic endowment—over 98 percent—is identical for all humans. It ensures that we develop as *Homo sapiens,* not as a worm or an elephant. A relatively small fraction of our 3.1 billion base pairs may differ among us: they account for the genetic portion of human variation.

4. Genetic recombination occurs during the reproductive process in diploid species. Pairs of chromosomes trade segments before the final random assignment by meiotic division of one or the other of each recombined pair to produce germ cells (sperms or eggs). The latter process is sometimes referred to as outcrossing: the random selection of a single set of chromosomes from the mother (one from each recombined pair) and a single set of chromosomes from the father (one from each recombined pair) to produce a zygote.

5. Another example from the development economics literature: the capital-labor ratio in each sector may be dropping, but for the economy as a whole it may be rising if production is shifting to the more capital-intensive sectors. Thanks to Avinash Dixit for this example.

6. I ignore here the complication that, for example, a population of tit-for-tat players might be first invaded by the behaviorally indistinguishable all cooperate, for example, and would then be vulnerable to invasion by defectors.

7. Within political behavior I mean to include those economic interactions in which strategic considerations are relevant (in other words, the purview of game theory, as opposed to the analysis of purely competitive markets).

8. One might argue that human parents sacrifice for their children in anticipation of care during old age. Perhaps, but it is unlikely that other mammals who sacrifice for their young are making similar calculations. And humans have no rational (level 3) reasons for expecting anything other than default on these implied intergenerational obligations.

9. Its interpretation as an instance of group-level selection has been neither widely advertised (perhaps due to the group selection controversies) nor seriously disputed (it has, after all, been proposed by the originator of the mechanism).

10. Dawkins, for example, wrote, "There is a common misconception that cooperation within a group at a given level of organization must come about through selection between groups. . . . ESS theory provides a more parsimonious alternative" (1980, 360; cited in Sober and Wilson 1998, 79). According to Maynard Smith (1993), it is Dawkins who suffers from the misconception: ESS doesn't provide such an alternative because it addresses the stability of an outcome, not its origin.

11. JSTOR is an online archive for academic journals. A full-text search covers not just titles but also the text of the articles, including citations. Thus some of the hits may refer to articles that are not themselves included in the archive. Currently twenty-five of the most widely read economic journals are included.

12. If monotonic preferences are included within the maintained hypotheses underlying level 2 theorizing, then evidence that people leave money on the table also poses something of a problem for level 2.

REFERENCES

Becker, Gary. 1976. *The Economic Approach to Human Behavior.* Chicago: University of Chicago Press.

Bergstrom, Theodore. 2002. "Evolution of Social Behavior: Individual and Group Selection." *Journal of Economic Perspectives* 16: 67–88.

Binmore, Ken. 1994. *Game Theory and the Social Contract I: Playing Fair.* Cambridge, MA: MIT Press.

Cavalli-Sforza, L.L., Paolo Menozzi, and Alberto Piazza. 1994. *The History and Geography of Human Genes.* Princeton, NJ: Princeton University Press.

Cosmides, Leda, and John Tooby. 1992. "Cognitive Adaptations for Social Exchange." In Jerome H. Barkow, Leda Cosmides, and John Tooby, eds., *The Adapted Mind: Evolutionary Psychology and the Generation of Culture,* 163–228. New York: Oxford University Press.

Dawes, Robyn M. 1988. *Rational Choice in an Uncertain World.* San Diego: Harcourt Brace Jovanovich.

Dawkins, Richard. 1980. "Good Strategy or Evolutionary Stable Strategy?" In G.W. Barlow and J. Silverberg, eds., *Sociobiology: Beyond Nature/Nurture.* Boulder, CO: Westview Press.

Edgeworth, Francis Y. 1881. *Mathematical Psychics: An Essay on the Application of Mathematics to the Moral Sciences.* London: C.K. Paul.

Fehr, Ernst, and Simon Gächter. 2000. "Cooperation and Punishment in Public Goods Experiments." *American Economic Review* 90: 980–94.

Field, Alexander J. 1984. "Microeconomics, Norms, and Rationality." *Economic Development and Cultural Change* 32 (July): 683–711.

———. 1991. "Do Legal Systems Matter?" *Explorations in Economic History* 28: 1–35.

———. 2001. *Altruistically Inclined? Evolutionary Theory, the Behavioral Sciences, and the Origins of Reciprocity.* Ann Arbor: University of Michigan Press.

———. 2003. [Comment on Bergstrom, "Evolution of Social Behavior."] *Journal of Economic Perspectives* 17, 2: 209–10.

———. 2005a. "Dictatorship, Democracy, and Quasi-Magical Thinking." Paper presented at the Western Economic Association Annual Meetings, San Francisco, CA, July 5.

———. 2005b. Review article, "Foundations of Human Sociality: Economic Experiments and Ethnographic Evidence from Fifteen Small Scale Societies." *Quarterly Review of Biology* 80 (December): 453–59.

———. 2006. "Why Multilevel Selection Matters." *Journal of Bioeconomics* 8: forthcoming.

Frank, Robert. 1988. *Passions Within Reason: The Strategic Use of Emotions.* New York: W.W. Norton.
———. 1994. "Group Selection and "Genuine" Altruism." *Behavioral and Brain Sciences* 17: 620–21.
Fudenberg, Drew, and Eric Maskin. 1986. "The Folk Theorem in Repeated Games with Discounting or with Incomplete Information." *Econometrica* 54: 533–54.
Gintis, Herbert. 2000. *Game Theory Evolving.* Princeton, NJ: Princeton University Press.
Keller, Laurent, ed. 1999. *Levels of Selection in Evolution.* Princeton, NJ: Princeton University Press.
Hamilton, W.D. 1964. "The Genetical Evolution of Social Behaviour I, II." *Journal of Theoretical Biology* 7: 1–16, 17–52.
Hayek, Friedrich. 1988. *The Fatal Conceit.* Chicago: University of Chicago Press.
Hirshleifer, Jack. 1977. "Economics from a Biological Perspective." *Journal of Law and Economics* 20: 1–52.
———. 1982. "Evolutionary Models in Economics and Law." *Research in Law and Economics* 4: 1–60.
Kagel, John H., and Alvin E. Roth, eds. 1995. *Handbook of Experimental Economics.* Princeton, NJ: Princeton University Press.
Lorenz, Konrad. 1966. *On Aggression.* New York: Harcourt Brace and World.
Maynard Smith, John. 1964. "Group Selection and Kin Selection." *Nature* 201: 1145–7.
———. 1993. *The Theory of Evolution.* Cambridge: Cambridge University Press.
Maynard Smith, John, and George Price. 1973. "The Logic of Animal Conflict." *Nature* 246: 15–18.
Maynard Smith, John, and Eörs Szathmáry. 1995. *The Major Transitions in Evolution.* Oxford: Freeman.
Parsons, Talcott. 1937. *The Structure of Social Action.* New York: McGraw-Hill.
Pinker, Steven. 2002. *How the Mind Works: The Modern Denial of Human Nature.* New York: Viking.
Poundstone, William. 1992. *Prisoner's Dilemma.* New York: Doubleday.
Richerson, Peter J., and Robert Boyd. 2004. *Not by Genes Alone: How Culture Transformed Human Evolution.* Princeton, NJ: Princeton University Press.
Samuelson, Paul. 1993. "Altruism as a Problem Involving Group Versus Individual Selection in Economics and Biology." *American Economic Review* 83: 143–48.
Simpson, E.H. 1951. "The Interpretation of Interaction in Contingency Tables." *Journal of the Royal Statistical Society* B 13: 238–41.
Sober, Elliott, and David Sloan Wilson. 1998. *Unto Others: The Evolution and Psychology of Unselfish Behavior.* Cambridge, MA: Harvard University Press.
Tooby, John, and Leda Cosmides. 1992. "The Psychological Foundations of Culture." In Jerome H. Barkow, Leda Cosmides, and John Tooby, eds., *The Adapted Mind: Evolutionary Psychology and the Generation of Culture,* 19–136. New York: Oxford University Press.
Trivers, Robert. 1971. "The Evolution of Reciprocal Altruism." *Quarterly Review of Biology* 46: 35–57.
Wade, Michael J. 1978. "A Critical Review of Models of Group Selection." *Quarterly Review of Biology* 53: 101–14.
Williams, George C. 1966. *Adaptation and Natural Selection: A Critique of Some Current Evolutionary Thought.* Princeton, NJ: Princeton University Press.
———. 1992. *Natural Selection: Domains, Levels, and Challenges.* New York: Oxford University Press.
Williams, George C., and R.M. Nesse. 1991. "The Dawn of Darwinian Medicine." *Quarterly Review of Biology* 66: 1–22.
Wilson, David Sloan and Elliott Sober. 1994. "Reintroducing Group Selection to the Human Behavioral Sciences." *Behavioral and Brain Sciences* 17: 585–654.
Wright, Sewall. 1945. "Tempo and Mode in Evolution: A Critical Review." *Ecology* 26: 415–19.

CHAPTER 9

BELIEFS IN BEHAVIORAL AND NEOCLASSICAL ECONOMICS

ALAN JAMES MACFADYEN

In the most basic formulation of the rational choice model, which underlies neoclassical economics, an individual with given desires makes the optimal choice from among available opportunities. This suggests that individuals are cognitively active decision makers. However, for many behavioral economists, a major failing of neoclassical economics is the simplistic nature of its view of cognition. In line with this view, this chapter argues that conventional economics has failed to give adequate recognition to the concept of "beliefs." More extended discussions of rationality make explicit room for beliefs. Elster, for example, argues that a model of rationality requires more than "desires" and "opportunities"; desires themselves are subject to rational evaluation, and individuals must gather an optimal amount of information and utilize that information to form optimal beliefs (Elster 1989a, ch. 4). The critical importance of beliefs in models of human behavior has been widely recognized in philosophy (e.g., de Souza 1987, 19) and evolutionary economics (e.g., Robson 2002, 89) as well as in cognitive psychology. This essay contrasts the role given to beliefs in behavioral economics with the narrow, almost invisible part it plays in conventional neoclassical economics. It provides a brief discussion of why models of economic behavior can usefully incorporate the concept of beliefs, presents a brief overview of what a "belief" is, sets out a framework for incorporating the concept of beliefs in economic analysis, and provides specific examples of the importance of the concept of beliefs by examining the beliefs of neoclassical and behavioral economists.

WHY INCORPORATE BELIEFS?

It would seem commonplace to suggest that what we do must reflect what we believe, and that what we believe is, at best, a partial reflection of the complex reality of the world we inhabit, and often a severely biased depiction of that reality. For this chapter, it is useful to draw on Earl's suggestion (1983, 139–47) that economics could learn much from the "personal construct" theory of George Kelly (1955). Kelly argued that we are all "naïve scientists," constructing, testing, and modifying theories about the complicated and changing world we inhabit. Our personal constructs both interpret and limit our interpretations of the world and our behavior in it. Typically, we organize our concepts into structures that we apply to specific settings, and in any setting the concepts are usually applied sequentially; this ordinal view of the world is consistent with a lexicographic method of decision making in which alternatives are dismissed from consideration if they fail to meet the standards defined by specific concepts. Kelly argues that our concepts tend to be dichotomous, specifying both what is included and what is excluded; concepts are usually also range-limited.

Different situations will call forth different construct systems, and these systems may not be consistent with one another. Nor need specific concepts be applied in the same manner in different construct systems. For Kelly, construct systems act both to provide meaning to the world and also to allow exploration and learning; that is, they are simultaneously limiting, serving to buttress our current beliefs, and expansive, serving to increase our adaptability to new situations.

Kelly's approach is consistent with many other theories in the social sciences. Earl has argued that Kelly's personal construct theory can be tied to psychological models of cognitive dissonance. Festinger (1957) suggested that individuals are uncomfortable with incompatible beliefs and will engage in patterns of thinking that reduce the associated dissonance. This could be managed in a variety of ways, some of which would strike economists as rational (gathering more complete information and modifying beliefs in a considered manner), while others appear irrational (separating incompatible beliefs into separated construct systems, engaging in wishful thinking, or modifying beliefs arbitrarily to achieve consistency). Akerlof and Dickens (1982) have applied Festinger's theory to economic behavior, including examples of belief modification. That we see the world through assorted concept systems forms part of the psychology literature on mental models (Johnson-Laird 1983), categorization (McGarty 1999), children's ways of understanding the world (Gopnik and Meltzoff 1997), and the learning of concepts (Murphy 2002). Some neurologically based research on consciousness suggests that the brain has a variety of learning systems (Pfeifer and Scheier 1999), which fits well with the suggestion that we develop a number of somewhat separated belief systems, an idea that has also appealed to some philosophical analyses of beliefs (Joyce 1999, 70–71). From a decision-making point of view, some analysts have described our behavior as involving sequentially applied dichotomous criteria (Tversky 1972); others have emphasized framing effects, which could derive from the application of different construct systems in different contexts (Tversky and Kahneman 1986); and yet others have seen a dynamic aspect to belief systems as they evolve over time in response to changing environmental conditions (Nisbett and Ross 1980). Behavioral economists are familiar with the distinction Scitovsky (1976) makes between "comfort" and "joy," drawing on Berlyne's (1960) arousal theory of motivation; this can be related to the uneasy balance we try to establish between defensive reactions to maintain our existing construct systems and exploratory efforts to widen our horizons.

Two construct systems are of special interest: first, belief systems defining our view of how the world functions, and second, our beliefs about ourselves, who we are, what we value, and how we see ourselves in relation to other people. Bandura (1997) argues that we wish to view ourselves in positive terms and to believe that we can exercise some control in our lives. This could contribute to assorted biases such as attributing positive outcomes to ourselves and negative outcomes to outside forces (attribution bias); imagining approval from others, thereby increasing self-validity; self-serving beliefs that justify decisions undertaken; and the belief that our abilities are relatively higher than other people's (uniqueness bias). (Gilovich 1991, ch. 5, and Goethals and Klein 2000 provide useful reviews of such biases.)

Kelly's personal construct theory is compatible with the cognitive orientation of much of behavioral economics. There are exceptions. For example, some behavioral approaches are inclined to put more emphasis on reinforcement and habitual behavior (e.g., Alhadeff 1982; Foxall 1990; Lea, Tarpy, and Webley 1987). From an evolutionary perspective, questions can be raised about the value of emphasizing active, flexible cognition and choice; Gazzaniga (1998) refers to the "fictional self." Dennett's well-known work suggests that the reality of our consciousness lies in biology but that in order to understand it we should adopt an "intentional stance" in which we assume that people are goal-oriented problem solvers (Dennett 1987). For most behavioral economists, an understanding of how people visualize the world and make decisions is critical to any analysis of their behavior. These concerns are particularly apparent in the voluminous literature on individual decision making, including Busemeyer, Hastie, and Medin 1996; Camerer 1995; Dawes 1998; Goldstein and Hogarth 1997; Hastie 2001; Kahneman and Tversky 2000; Payne, Bettman, and Johnson 1992; and Starmer 2000. Also relevant are numerous studies designed to help individuals make better decisions, such as Gilovich 1991 and Hammond, Keeney, and Raiffa 1999.

WHAT ARE BELIEFS?

"Belief" will be defined as an idea, concept, or value that an individual holds, with some probability, to be true. Beliefs may be held with certainty, but the probabilistic nature of this definition is consistent with a Bayesian interpretation. A belief is subject to revision in light of new evidence. This may increase or decrease the probability with which the belief is held to be true, although this probability may not be a clearly defined number in the individual's mind. Nor is it argued that people are efficient Bayesians. In fact, most behavioral economists think that the failure of individuals to modify beliefs in a "rational" Bayesian manner has not been given sufficient weight by conventional economists.

Beliefs may refer to our understanding of how the world functions, what might be called beliefs "about" things. Belief also refers to what it is that we value, or our belief "in" something. In neoclassical economics this distinction has led to the division of analysis into "positive" and "normative" economics. We can make sense of the world only within various concept systems. It can be argued that the concepts we develop to describe the world (our positive beliefs) are inevitably influenced by what we value (our normative beliefs). A Marxist describes the world in terms of social classes; this concept does not play a role in neoclassical economics, but economic efficiency does. While this calls into question the independence of the positive and the normative, the distinction is still useful. Whether rationality should take values as given or be used to develop appropriate values is also a controversial issue (Elster 1989a, ch. 4; Viskovatoff 2001).

As discussed above in connection with Kelly's personal construct theory, we understand the world through assorted belief systems. It is useful to think of these in a methodological framework where some beliefs are of primary importance, forming a hard core that is sacrosanct and not open to debate. A variety of subsidiary beliefs surround the hard core and are seen as part of the belief system but not essential to it. It is important for the social scientist to understand which beliefs make up the hard core of a belief system and when an individual is willing to reassess subsidiary beliefs. Of particular interest are those rare occasions in which the individual questions the hard-core beliefs, and the belief system itself is significantly modified or begins to crumble.

Can the term *belief* be applied to something that lies hidden in the unconscious? (This is different from the extent to which beliefs may be formed unconsciously.) Clearly some of our behavior is motivated in largely unconscious ways. The issue is whether such behavior reflects beliefs in addition to factors such as instinct, pure emotion, conditioning, or habit. The relationships between conscious and unconscious influences on decision making have proved controversial (Smith and DeCoster 2000). Hastie (2001, 663) finds appeal in the argument that unconscious intuitive and conscious analytical procedures lie at either end of a continuum of decision-making processes, most decisions involving a mix of the two. It will often be useful to think in terms of what might be called "latent" or "hidden" beliefs (or, following Pettit 2000, "virtual" beliefs), which are unconscious beliefs that would be recognized as beliefs if brought to our attention. For the most part such beliefs remain hidden, but circumstances might lead an individual to reveal them. Thus, for instance, in discussion it might be pointed out that what an individual has said provides an insufficient basis for his argument, and the individual would then bring into the open a previously hidden belief. It seems likely that most belief systems include a number of such latent beliefs. Damasio (1999) suggests that many beliefs lie hidden in memory until accessed, and that the mechanisms that access the beliefs are largely unconscious. This notion of latent beliefs has some similarity to other concepts in the social sciences. Thus, for example, psychotherapy often aims at uncovering hidden memories, which lie unacknowledged by the conscious mind. Another example is offered by Pettit (2000) in his defense of narrowly selfish rational choice explanations of behavior. Pettit speaks of "virtual" self-regard, which is not ordinarily acknowledged but is nevertheless present; in a situation in which consciously acknowledged motives would lead to behavior strongly detrimental to the individual's narrow self-interest, a reaction is triggered, and narrow self-interest is brought into the conscious mind as a determinant of behavior.

The idea of latent or hidden beliefs helps to explain both habitual behavior and the power of incomplete belief systems. At the same time the very unconsciousness of these latent beliefs poses problems; it might be extremely difficult in practice, for instance, to separate a previously latent belief from a spur-of-the-moment justification or an after-the-fact belief that we acted in an intentional way. Rather than admitting the possibility of unconscious beliefs, one might insist that to be meaningful a belief must be conscious, and that unconscious motives to act must be treated as something other. While there is a certain fuzziness in the concept of latent beliefs, it seems incontrovertible that we often hold beliefs that we do not explicitly recognize but which we would immediately accept as a belief if brought to our attention. As discussed above, such latent beliefs are often a key part of a belief system and must be acknowledged if such systems are to be understood.

Our beliefs are formed, supported, and modified in many ways. For the purposes of this essay three aspects of these processes might be highlighted. The first is the incidental nature of much learning. If asked why we believe something, our initial reaction will not usually be a description of where the belief came from; rather, it will be an attempt to explain why it makes sense for us to believe this. Second, our beliefs are formed in a social context, heavily influenced both consciously and unconsciously by the words and behavior of those we love, like, and respect. In addition, beliefs, including latent unconscious beliefs, are strengthened by repetition. Third, beliefs often possess emotional valence. For example, a belief gained at an early age in the family context, or derived from social norms, typically has strong emotional overtones and is particularly rigid, as is often true of the deepest beliefs defining our value systems.

It is useful to think of beliefs as a kind of filter. This is illustrated in Figure 9.1, in which a belief filter is part of the information-screening process, which is postulated as lying between the individual (and that person's internal world) and the rest of the world (external to the person). The external world constantly emits a tremendous array of signals that are received by the information-processing screen. This screen is seen as comprising two main components, information-processing capacities and belief filters. The former refers to the inherent capabilities of the individual and the various external measurement instruments used. Belief filters give meaning to the information that is received, drawing on our existing beliefs. The arrows in Figure 9.1 represent bytes of information coming to us from the outside world. Three types of interaction are illustrated. The solid paths depict two extremes. Some signals pass through the screen directly and have an accurate perceived reality. Thus, a person can see a boulder on the path, or feel sunlight on skin and the sunburn that follows, or read the display sign that says oranges cost $2.00 a kilogram. Other signals are not acknowledged at all; instead, they bounce back off the information screen. Without the appropriate instrumentation and/or knowledge, people are unaware that the boulder is

Figure 9.1   **Belief Filters**

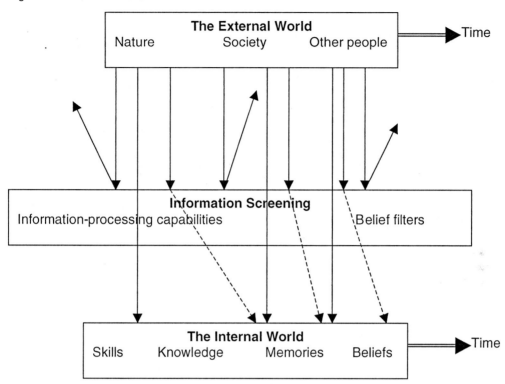

sandstone of Devonian age, or that sunlight contains ultraviolet rays, or that a fruit stand on the edge of town is selling oranges at $1.20 a kilogram. It is important to remember that accurate knowledge need not depend on direct personal perception. I cannot see ultraviolet light, but my schooling and reading of science lead me to accept its reality. Beliefs obviously play a role here: one reason for failing to receive a signal is that our current belief system holds no category to accept it, and therefore the potential signal is rejected entirely. Fernández-Armesto's (1997) discussion of truth is useful here. He argues that people find four different sources for truth: authority ("The High Priest says so," "Carl Sagan says so"), feeling ("I just know he loves me," "I can't believe anything else," "There is danger in high places"), empiricism and perception ("You can see that robins nest in trees, but loons don't," "Brand X costs more than brand Y"), and rationalism ("The world must have had a creator," "For us to understand the world and to acquire language so quickly, we must be born with certain fixed categories of thinking"). At any time our current beliefs will reflect a combination of these sources; the beliefs themselves and our receptivity to various sources form the belief filters discussed here.

In Figure 9.1 a number of the lines passing through the information screen are shown as bending to indicate that the meaning given to the external signal must be interpreted through our existing beliefs (both conscious and latent) and that this interpretation involves potential distortion. A belief filter might be seen as a complicated prism that sometimes refracts light away from us, sometimes lets it pass through unscathed, sometimes removes specific light waves while letting others through, and sometimes distorts the direction of flow. From a behavioral economics perspective, it is important to know how our existing beliefs function as filters of information and how beliefs will grow and be modified over time. Remember that modifications in belief may involve a change in the belief ("Interest rates will be lower next year, not higher as I thought last month") or a change in the certainty with which the belief is held ("I'm less certain than I was last month that interest rates will fall").

BELIEFS AND ECONOMIC BEHAVIOR

Behavioral economics builds on the premise that more useful economic models can be built through the explicit recognition of psychological concepts. There seems to be some division in the behavioral economics literature on whether this should be seen as requiring a new discipline as an alternative to neoclassical economics or whether it is largely a matter of adding psychologically relevant variables to conventional economic models. Two recent reviews by economists suggest that the latter approach is most productive. Mullainathan and Thaler argue that behavioral economics starts from conventional economic modeling: "The behavioral economics research program has consisted of two components: 1. Identifying the ways in which behavior differs from the standard model. 2. Showing how this behavior matters in economic contexts" (2002, 2).

Rabin says about behavioral economics that

> the underlying premise of this movement is far too compelling to consider it transitory: Ceteris paribus, the more realistic our assumptions about economic actors, the better our economics. Hence, economists should aspire to make our assumptions about humans as realistic as possible. . . .
>
> This research program is not only built on the premise that mainstream economic *methods* are great, but also that most mainstream economic *assumptions* are great. It does not abandon the correct insights of neoclassical economics, but supplements these insights with the insights to be had from realistic new assumptions. (Rabin 2002, 658–59)

The suggestion that the neoclassical framework is fundamentally a failure and must be replaced by an alternative, psychologically oriented approach is a much stronger claim. Not surprisingly, this suggestion has often come from psychologists who turn to consideration of economic behavior. It lies beneath much of the European work in economic psychology, as seen, for example, in the behavioral psychology orientation that informs much of Lea, Webley, and Tarpy 1987. Lewis, Webley, and Furnham (1995) adopt a social psychology perspective and suggest that the key distinction between behavioral economics and economic psychology is that the former works largely by incorporating economic concepts in economic models, while the latter studies economic behavior from a psychological framework outside the traditional economic framework. Early pioneers in the field, such as Katona (1975) and Simon (1955, 1982), also imply that economists should abandon the conventional rational choice optimization model. And prospect theory can be interpreted as a replacement model that is psychologically richer (Kahneman and Tversky 1979; Tversky and Kahneman 1992).

Rather than seeing these two approaches as contradictory, it is preferable to see them as convergent. Thus Rabin's recent (2003b) appreciation of Kahneman, on the occasion of his being awarded the Nobel prize, sees his work not as replacing conventional economic theories but as an outstanding example of a research program offering ways conventional economic models can be improved. This corresponds with March's suggestion that neoclassical economics claims to have "won the war," but only by building models that accommodate behavioral concerns (March 1978). Earl's survey is more eclectic but suggests that "economists who are willing to take on board the

Figure 9.2   **Economic Decision Making: A Behavioral Perspective**

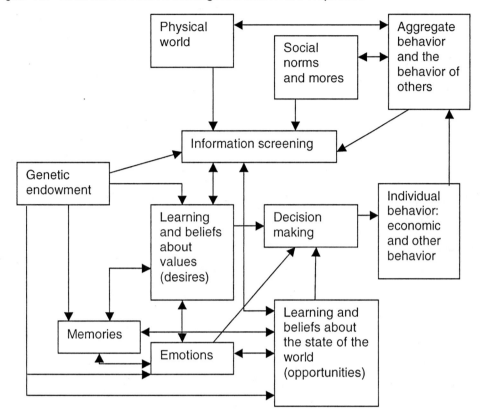

extra baggage of psychology may be able to enhance their predictive and explanatory capacities and thereby improve the quality of advice that they provide to policy makers" (Earl 1990, 750).

Most economists view human behavior as intentional or reason-based. That is, an individual acts because it is seen as being in the individual's interest; actions are judged by their expected ends, and the belief that the act will generate a positive result motivates it. This suggests two main avenues of extension to conventional economic analysis: first, the nature of desires, and second, cognitive limitations. Before exploring these in more detail, it will be useful to set out a more general framework. While some think of behavioral economics as the overall marriage of economics and psychology, the main emphasis has been on opening up the "black box" of decision making. Thus the strongest links have been with cognitive psychology. An emphasis on beliefs reflects this, as can be seen in Figure 9.2, which extends Figure 9.1 to allow a focus on economic behavior. The external world (the physical and social environment) is shown at the top of the figure, and the individual is at the bottom, with information screening as a link between the two. In this formulation, the social nature of external links is emphasized. We are responsive to a variety of social norms and often look to the behavior of others to guide our choices and help us to evaluate them. From a cognitive view, beliefs about the world and about what one values, as well as learning that modifies such beliefs, are key to understanding decisions.

Figure 9.2 incorporates three important internal influences on our behavior in addition to beliefs. The first is our genetic endowment, which imposes constraints on our capabilities. The second is memory, which is constantly triggered by our current situation. The third is our emotions. It seems clear that complex interdependencies tie memories, emotions, and beliefs together, and that much useful research remains to be done related to the relevance for economic behavior of these interconnections. In Figure 9.2 decision making is seen from a cognitive perspective as involving actions that have a deliberative underpinning; hence choices rely on beliefs and learning. Beliefs, learning, and information-screening processes are mutually interdependent. Information screening, in combination with the internal forces of genetic endowment, memory, and emotion, influences both beliefs and learning.

Beliefs, Genes, Memory, and Emotions

"Desires" and "opportunities" are not preexisting phenomena but dynamic grounds for behavior requiring their own explanations. As Elster (1989a) noted, there is an inconsistency in attempting to explain behavior with these as the two primary concepts, since desires are obviously subjective, while opportunities are external to the individual. However, as suggested by Figure 9.2, broadening this framework involves a complex mix of factors.

Sociobiology emphasizes genetic factors, likely developed in the hunter-gatherer phase of our development, but generalizing to new situations as they arise. Thus, for example, one might utilize a genetic explanation for the cognitive processing constraints that will be discussed below. It has been suggested that we may have evolved somewhat different decision-making propensities for different situations (Cosmides and Tooby 1996), which would be consistent with context-dependent decision making (Payne, Bettman, and Johnson 1992). Some economists have proposed inherited tendencies underlying our economic actions (e.g., Robson 2001, 2002). Robson is supportive of a biological basis for conventional rationality but suggests that "costs of complexity" might help explain why time preferences exhibit hyperbolic discounting, operating as an average of genetically induced impulses toward both immediate gratification and more careful consideration of the future (Robson 2001, 30). A number of simulation models of adaptation to changing environments have been used to assess how behavioral rules are used and could help us understand genetic evolution (e.g. Gigerenzer, Todd, and ABC Research Group 1999; Young 1998).

The beliefs that underlie our decisions are often drawn from memory (Damasio 1994, 1999). We tend to see our memory as a giant filing system recording all our past, but this is a misleading and simplistic view. Kahneman (2000a, 2000b) finds that the utility stored in memory is not identical to the utility associated with events as we live them. He suggests that analysis of behavior ought to distinguish among at least four forms of utility. "Decision utility" is inferred from the choices individuals make. "Predicted utility" refers to the expectation individuals have of the utility they will receive from an outcome. "Total utility" is the aggregate reported utility during an experience. "Remembered utility" is how previously experienced utility is recalled. Memories primarily reflect the strongest emotion felt and our feelings at the end of an experience, ignoring the total utility and duration of the experience. Mullainathan (2002) notes that both the salience of a memory and the frequency with which we recall it affect its accessibility, and suggests that these characteristics of memory contribute to several decision-making heuristics and biases. Also relevant is hindsight bias, where previous beliefs are falsely recalled as being consistent with actual events (Hawkins and Hastie 1990).

Zajonc (1980) is usually credited with the recent emphasis on the role of emotions in decision making. From an evolutionary basis, it might be argued that emotions are likely to be "rational" in the sense of being compatible with our general interests (Hanoch 2002), although Tranel, Bechara, and Damasio (2000) argue that either too little or too much emotion may hinder effective decision making. Thus emotions can be seen as simultaneously underlying our behavior and frustrating our ability to act optimally (Elster 1999; Helm 2001). A complication is that immediate visceral feelings differ from anticipated emotions, which we draw on as we assess possibilities (Gilbert and Wilson 2000; Loewenstein and Schkade 1999). A number of authors have seen emotions as helpful in economizing on costs of decision making (Hanoch 2002; Hastie 2001). One might also expect that more emotional experiences are more readily recalled, although the evidence on ties between emotions and memory may not be as strong as one might expect (Eagly et al. 1999). Finucane and colleagues suggest "that people use an *affect heuristic* to make judgments," where strength of affect influences which associations people draw on (2000, 3). Kahneman (2003) has also argued for consideration of affect, stressing the importance of "intuition" in many decisions, perhaps operating through "attribute substitution," where we replace some of the attributes of objects or tasks with other attributes ("heuristic attributes") that come more easily to mind (Kahneman and Frederick 2002); an attribute with strong affect would readily serve this purpose. Individuals may be subject to a negativity bias, where unpleasant information has more impact than pleasant information (Ajzen 2001, 35). The necessity of anticipating future desires may incorporate "projection biases" (Loewenstein, O'Donoghue, and Rabin 2003).

Beliefs and Desires

Hypotheses about the sources and structure of our desires have a long history in economics. For example, Menger envisioned a hierarchy of wants, and Veblen emphasized socially motivated consumption. More recently evolutionary psychology (Robson 2001, 2002) and the importance of social norms (Elster 1989b) have been incorporated into models of economic behavior. The structure of our desires raises the question of whether they have a hierarchical nature, as assumed by Maslow (1976) and many "humanistic" economists (Lutz and Lux 1979). Economists typically define utility functions in terms of levels, but Scitovsky (1976), for example, differentiated between "comfort" (derived from the level of consumption) and "joy" (stemming from the level of arousal or stimulation associated with changes in consumption). Prospect theory (Kahneman and Tversky 1979, Tversky and Kahneman 1992) argues that we evaluate options on the basis of changes from a reference point. It has also been suggested that our evaluations hinge on relative income and consumption in the form of social comparisons (our situation relative to others, as in Frank 1999). Social interaction effects, such as feelings of reciprocity, have been argued to be important (e.g., Fehr and Gächter 2000). In addition, desires and beliefs are responsive to repetition, which gives a "persuasion bias" (DeMarzo, Vayanos, and Zweibel 2003). Presumably many of our beliefs, and our feelings about ourselves, involve social acceptance and so are affected by social norms, widely accepted rules of behavior, and various feelings of social obligation (Akerlof and Kranton 2000; Goethals and Klein 2000).

The question of "sources" of desires has obvious links to psychological theories of motivation. MacFadyen and MacFadyen 1986 includes chapters illustrating how economic behavior could vary considerably depending upon whether based on instinct, reinforcement, social pressure, humanism, or existentialism. Some of these motivational forces are more easily understood in a cognitive framework, while others are primarily unconscious (MacFadyen 1986). One might also draw on personality theory to explore the nature of our desires (Albanese 2003).

In place of optimization, Simon (1955, 1982) suggested that desires are met by "satisficing." People express their desires not through a complete utility function but through a dynamic process of changing aspiration levels; given current aspirations, our behavior settles as soon as we find a satisfactory situation. This provides a plausible explanation for habitual behavior. In a continuously changing world, Heiner (1983) argued that predictable behavior reflects habits that ignore minor changes. The suggestion that desires are more labile than economists generally assume can be seen in models proposing that we have conflicting desires across time, which creates self-control problems (Thaler and Shefrin 1981), and advancing the idea that we should be viewed as possessing more than one utility function (but see Brennan 1989 in opposition).

The neoclassical economic model has taken desires and opportunities as given; moreover, desires are taken as complete (in the sense that every possible situation into which the individual might fall is readily comparable to other situations in utility terms) and unlimited (in the sense that there is always something else—more money, more time, or more of some good—that would raise utility). However, some of the work in behavioral economics casts doubt on the existence of a stable, complete utility function. For conventional economists, this is certainly one of the most troubling aspects of prospect theory, in which changes are always measured from a reference point and as gains or losses. As Kahneman and Tversky and many others have pointed out, this means that valuations are subject to framing effects, and the invariance of choice in the conventional economic model is lost. Identical choice alternatives may be ranked differently depending on how the information is presented.

It might be suggested that the modification to the conventional economic model required is relatively minor—for example, simply replacing the utility function in neoclassical economics with the prospect theory value function. However, some of the behavioral economics literature implies that the real problem is much more fundamental, calling into question the whole idea of any sort of reasonably well defined utility or value function. Rather, in many instances it has been suggested that coherent preferences simply do not exist. Even a naive psychological approach suggests a number of reasons why this might be the case. Preferences might be largely unconscious, called up only as needed and, because unconscious, not necessarily consistent with other preferences. They might be created anew by the individual as a result of experience. They might come into existence only when the individual is put into the position of having to cognitively think about what is valued (Fischhoff 1991; Kahneman 1994; Slovic 1995). Economists are not unacquainted with some aspects of this literature, as it has entered into the debate about whether the contingent valuation method (CVM) can be used to provide reasonable values for public policy analysis using benefit-cost analysis.

Another approach, this one with radical implications for conventional economics, argues that our beliefs and desires are conditioned almost entirely by our social setting, so all our actions are symbolic or ritualistic (Guerin 2003; Mason 2002). Instead of social outcomes being the aggregate of individual acts, individual actions become the product of the social setting. These models go beyond bandwagon or snob effects or models that include social norms. Instead, virtually all reference to any notion of individual rationality is dropped, and the relevant beliefs are "societal" beliefs (Bar-Tal 2000).

Cognitive Limitations

For most behavioral economists, information processing is an essential part of the decision-making process. This is founded in psychological literature emphasizing cognitive limits, such as the suggestion by Miller (1956) that we can manage "seven, plus or minus two" concepts, and has been well known in economics since Simon's development of the idea of "bounded rationality." (See Simon 1955, 1982; the recent survey of Simon's work in Earl 2002; and the special issue [vol. 24, no. 2 (2003)] of the *Journal of Economic Psychology,* as well as reviews of bounded rationality in Conlisk 1996 and Lipman 1995.) Bounded rationality may be seen in a rational choice framework, tied to Lopes's (1991) suggestion that the surprise is not that we are often irrational but that we are as rational as we are. Since belief formation is costly, constrained by limited time and information-processing capabilities, it can be seen as a traditional economic optimization problem, the solution of which might involve various decision-making heuristics. (For excellent overviews of these heuristics, see Gilovich, Griffen, and Kahneman 2002; Kahneman, Slovic, and Tversky 1982.)

An economic view of belief formation has interesting implications, including the suggestion that our beliefs may be particularly erroneous in situations in which the costs of forming rational beliefs are high (e.g., in complex and novel settings) and where the benefits derived are perceived as low (e.g., the consequences of the individual's single vote in elections or knowledge of the meaning of life). There are, however, logical inconsistencies in the suggestion that belief formation is but one example of a rational choice problem. On one hand, it poses an infinite regression problem, as suggested by Winter (1986); deciding how much information to gather to form a new belief is a rational choice problem that requires gathering information, which necessitates a decision on how much information to gather, and so on. On the other hand, if the decision-making heuristics are seen as having evolved as a way of economizing on decision-making costs, then it would seem that beliefs would not be formed rationally but would be subject to the various heuristics and biases that we are prone to use. From a behavioral economics perspective, this suggests that the view that beliefs are simply another part of the rational choice process is not convincing, and deeper exploration of decision-making heuristics and biases is necessary.

Less developed is a more general theory of when specific heuristics apply. (See Baars 1997 on unconscious context effects; Thaler 1999 on framing; Gigerenzer and Goldstein 1996 on cognitive algorithms; Heath, Larrick, and Wu 1999 on reference points; Griffen and Tversky 1992 on representations of probabilities and confidence judgments.) One link is ties to affect (emotion), as noted above. Some authors have applied simulation techniques to assess the effectiveness of alternative choice rules, often in an evolutionary setting with learning effects (e.g., Camerer 2003; Gigerenzer and Goldstein 1996; Gigerenzer, Todd, and ABC Research Group 1999; Rubenstein 1998; Samuelson 2002; and Young 1998). In consumer research, Bettman (1979) has developed a marketing theory based on information processing, and Rachlin (1989) combines behavioral and cognitive aspects into a theory of choice.

Certain heuristics and biases may be tied to our self-concept, which is one of our most important belief systems. Admitting that we have made errors may threaten our self-image and lead us to develop beliefs that are self-serving and self-deceptive (Dahl and Ransom 1999), including the restructuring of memories in our favor (Ross and Wilson 2001). Attempts to maintain our self-image and feeling of control could contribute to our resistance to radically new information (Camerer 1995, 595), which might lead to the well-known status quo bias, loss aversion, and sunk cost effects (Genovese and Mayer 2001; Samuelson and Zeckhauser 1988). Support of self-image could be linked to a number of the biases noted earlier, including hindsight (Christensen-Szalaski and Willham 1991), overconfidence (Benabou and Tirole 2002), the willingness to draw relatively firm beliefs from small samples (the "law of small numbers") (Rabin 2003a), the tendency to credit successes to our own actions, false hopes that we will be able to change our behavior (Polivy and Herman 2002), a belief that we are unusually skilled, and the well-known endowment effect (the tendency to increase the value of objects once we own them) (Kahneman, Knetsch, and Thaler 1991).

Expectancy Models

The suggestion that impulse toward action is directly correlated with a weighted average expectation is commonly invoked in the social sciences, as in the expected utility model (Savage 1954), which, because of its familiarity, allows economists to relate readily to other expectancy value models. The most prominent is prospect theory (Kahneman and Tversky 1979; Tversky and Kahneman 1992), which also incorporates information-processing heuristics. Marketing models such as the Fishbein and Ajzen (1975) model of "reasoned action" see attitudes toward commodities as the sum, across possible consequences of buying, of the products of beliefs about the nature of the consequence times the valuation of the consequence. Psychological models, going back at least as far as Tolman (1932), have a similar structure based on the expectation that a particular outcome will occur and its valuation (e.g., its emotional valence). In all these models the expected value reflects the beliefs of the individual. A criticism of expectancy value approaches is that they presume an excessive degree of calculation on the part of the decision maker: many decisions are not important enough to warrant much attention, and the models presuppose greater deliberation than is possible for most people.

BELIEF SYSTEMS OF NEOCLASSICAL AND BEHAVIORAL ECONOMICS

Beliefs "About": Positive Economics

Behavioral economists believe that our models should reflect how people are seen to behave, so heavy emphasis is placed on observations of individual behavior, and experimental studies are accorded high significance. Reliance on observation of behavior means that inductive methods are often used, and behavioral economists are not too concerned whether specific models are completely consistent with a broad overriding model.

Neoclassical economics operates on the broad general theory that individuals are rational decision makers. So it is highly deductive and ambivalent about the value of studying individual behavior. Many neoclassical economists argue that their prime interest is in aggregate economic behavior, particularly the operation of market mechanisms, and have accepted Milton Friedman's instrumental methodology. From this perspective the assumption that individuals are perfectly rational is useful because it generates results that correspond well with observed aggregate behavior; that is, we are wise to assume that people behave as if they were completely rational. Beyond this, some neoclassical economists argue that deviations from rationality are relatively small and random and so "cancel out." It has also been argued that a small group of rational individuals, or individuals who learn efficiently, will drive the market to the expected rational choice equilibrium. (For a behavioral view of these arguments see Rabin 1998, 2002).

The "as if" assumption is methodological, so the behavioral economic reaction to this must also be methodological: that some other assumption works better, or that we want to understand individual economic behavior as well as aggregate results. Most behavioral economists suggest that standard economic models can often be improved by adding behavioral elements, many deviations from rationality are not random, and rational marginal players do not necessarily drive economic systems to the result that would occur in a universe of rational individuals. A number of models have demonstrated that a subgroup of less than rational traders yields anomalies in market outcomes compared to the usual rational choice model (Akerlof and Yellen 1985; Haltiwanger and Waldman 1985; Russell and Thaler 1985). Camerer (1995), in his outstanding survey of experimental economic studies of individual economic decision making, returns repeatedly to this important issue. Learning as an avenue to rationality has also seemed unlikely to many behavioral economists, since naive new individuals continuously enter the economy, many major economic decisions are only undertaken once or rarely and so offer little chance for learning, and learning is subject to information processing. People seem to have some difficulty in generalizing situation-specific learning, and even experts often perform very poorly in decision-making tasks (Camerer and Johnson 1991).

Some of the communication problems between neoclassical and behavioral economists reflect differences in core beliefs. Thus, behavioral constructs shown to be consistent with a deductive model based on utility maximization are more likely to prove acceptable to a neoclassical economist. Behavior that is difficult to explain through the utility maximization model provides an obvious avenue for even committed neoclassical economists to consider alternative explanations. (See Thaler 1992, and the series of articles by him and various coauthors in assorted issues of the *Journal of Economic Perspectives* from the late 1980s, setting out numerous behavioral "anomalies.") Since construct systems have a social component, we are often reluctant to abandon the security of conventional construct systems, but there may be cascade effects as highly regarded practitioners adopt new ideas. Increasingly civil interactions among behavioral and neoclassical economists are common!

Beliefs "In": Normative Economics

Normative economics is necessarily more controversial than descriptive economics. Neoclassical "welfare economics" suggests that policies can be assessed in terms of their "efficiency" and "equity," where economists have particular interest in economic efficiency, which is often assessed through benefit-cost analysis. Efficiency is defined in terms of Pareto improvements. A pure Pareto improvement is a change that makes at least one person feel better off without making anyone feel worse off, while a potential Pareto improvement is one where parties who feel better off could still gain after potentially compensating those made to feel worse off. Efficiency relies on two widely accepted ethical judgments, which might be labeled "democracy" (all members of society are taken into account) and "nonpaternalism" (values are those individuals themselves associate with changes). The latter provides a link to descriptive neoclassical economics, since individuals who are effective utility maximizers will make choices (and impute values) that reflect their interests.

As a general foundation for ethics it is pretty thin gruel, as recognized in Sen's well-known dictum that only a "rational fool" would accept that a person's preferences, choices, happiness, and well-being are all the same thing (Sen 1977). A large literature demonstrates that correlations between measures of happiness and real income are low (Easterlin 2002; Frey and Stutzer 2002; Lane 2000; Seligman and Csikszentmihalyi 2000). Kahneman, Deiner, and Schwarz (1999) provide a variety of papers discussing what "well-being" and "happiness" mean, as do Ryan and Deci (2001). The tenuous link between measures of happiness and economic well-being have been credited to the likelihood that assessments of happiness hinge on our relative status (Frank 1999) or adaptation to higher consumption levels (Easterlin 2002), or that happiness scales measure our success in meeting aspiration levels rather than our well-being (Kahneman 2003). In general, if preferences are not well defined, the efficiency criterion loses its ready rationale (Bromley 1990; Cowen 1993).

Despite this, neoclassical economists are reluctant to abandon the belief construct of economic efficiency, since it provides a broadly applicable tool for policy analysis. Economists may come to accept its use in a somewhat more restrictive manner, as one to be applied along with a number of criteria such as "equity." Behavioral economics research may justify policies on efficiency grounds, as when Frank (1999) draws on the externalities associated with status effects and advocates a progressive consumption tax, with proceeds used to fund higher levels of public goods.

Before applying the efficiency criterion, one might ask whether underlying values are nonmalevolent, whether social comparison effects are pronounced, whether preferences seem to be clearly defined and stable, and so on. Paternalistic policies may be desirable in some circumstances, although most economists exhibit a degree of libertarianism as well (O'Donoghue and Rabin 2003; Thaler and Sunstein 2003).

Some behavioral economists are attuned to conventional economic policy analysis, but others have been attracted to greater behavioral "realism" primarily because of their strong normative interest in improving society. From this perspective the applicability of economic efficiency (as a valid criterion derived from utility-maximizing individual choices) is rejected. For example, Etzioni (1988) has founded an association for "socioeconomics" dedicated to the improvement of society; from a humanistic perspective, Lutz and Lux (1979) and Lutz (1998) suggest wide-ranging economic and social changes. Some analysts emphasize baser motives for our consumption, often grounded in socially influenced material values (Belk 1988; Dittmar 1992), which cuts the ground from the economic efficiency criterion. Many of these researchers have turned to psychological theories to find alternative criteria, which are often based on interpersonal or community values and assorted concepts of self-actualization.

CONCLUSION

The essence of the behavioral economics approach is that our science should be grounded in realistic depictions of the behavior of individuals. For most behavioral economists, this implies that the rational choice model of neoclassical economics should be expanded to incorporate more psychological realism. In this regard, cognitive psychology provides an obvious link, and, as this essay has argued, the concept of "beliefs" is critical. How we see the world, what we value, and how we act hinge to a significant degree upon our beliefs, and there is ample evidence (both in our observations of everyday behavior and in the research literature) that our beliefs are formed and applied in less than fully rational ways. Increasingly, economists are modifying their traditional models to include more realistic depictions of beliefs. One extension involves a more careful consideration of what it is that we believe "in": our underlying values and preferences. This can help us build better descriptive models (such as those that include relative income judgments, status effects, and concerns about reciprocity) and is essential as a basis for normative economic analysis. Recognition that our beliefs "about" the world will affect our decisions is also playing a more important role in economics, as more and more models examine the impacts of assorted decision-making heuristics and biases. It is gratifying to those who have been working in behavioral economics for some time to see the increased acceptance among neoclassical economists of concepts and research methods from behavioral economics. Recent surveys of behavioral economics (Mullainathan and Thaler 2002; Rabin 2002) have noted this trend and suggested that conventional economists will be increasingly willing to recognize that "the more realistic our assumptions about economic actors, the better our economics" (Rabin 2002, 658).

REFERENCES

Ajzen, Icek. 2001. "Nature and Operation of Attitudes." *Annual Review of Psychology* 52: 27–58.
Akerlof, George A., and William T. Dickens. 1982. "The Economic Consequences of Cognitive Dissonance." *American Economic Review* 72: 307–19.
Akerlof, George A., and Rachel E. Kranton. 2000. "Economics and Identity." *Quarterly Journal of Economics* 115: 715–53.
Akerlof, George A., and Janet Yellen. 1985. "Can Small Deviations from Rationality Make Significant Differences in Economic Equilibria?" *American Economic Review* 75: 708–20.

Albanese, Paul J. 2003. *The Personality Component of Economic Behavior.* Westport, CT: Quorum.

Alhadeff, David. 1982. *Microeconomics and Human Behavior.* Berkeley: University of California Press.

Baars, B.J. 1997. *In the Theater of Consciousness: The Workplace of the Mind.* New York: Cambridge University Press.

Bandura, Albert. 1997. *Self-Efficacy: The Exercise of Control.* New York: Freeman.

Bar-Tal, Daniel. 2000. *Shared Beliefs in a Society: Social Psychological Analysis.* Thousand Oaks, CA: Sage.

Belk, Russell. 1988. "Possessions and the Extended Self." *Journal of Consumer Research* 15: 139–68.

Benabou, Roland, and Jean Tirole. 2002. "Self-confidence and Personal Motivation." *Quarterly Journal of Economics* 117: 871–915.

Berlyne, D.E. 1960. *Conflict, Arousal and Curiosity.* New York: McGraw-Hill.

Bettman, J.R. 1979. *An Information Processing Theory of Consumer Choice.* Reading, MA: Addison-Wesley.

Brennan, Timothy J. 1989. "A Methodological Assessment of Multiple Utility Frameworks." *Economics and Philosophy* 5: 189–208.

Bromley, Daniel W. 1990. "The Ideology of Efficiency: Searching for a Theory of Policy Analysis." *Journal of Environmental Economics and Management* 19: 86–107.

Busemeyer, J., R. Hastie, and D.L. Medlin, eds. 1996. *Decision Making from a Cognitive Perspective.* San Diego: Academic Press.

Camerer, Colin F. 1995. "Individual Decision Making." In John H. Kagel and Alvin E. Roth, eds., *The Handbook of Experimental Economics,* 587–703. Princeton, NJ: Princeton University Press.

———. 2003. *Behavioral Game Theory: Experiments in Strategic Interaction.* Princeton, NJ: Princeton University Press.

Camerer, Colin F., and E.J. Johnson. 1991. "The Process-Performance Paradox in Expert Judgements: How Can Experts Know So Much and Predict So Badly?" In K.A. Ericsson and J. Smith, eds., *Toward a General Theory of Expertise: Prospects and Limits,* 195–217. Cambridge: Cambridge University Press.

Christensen-Szalaski, J.J., and C.F. Willham. 1991. "The Hindsight Bias: A Meta-Analysis." *Organizational Behavior and Human Decision Processes* 48: 147–68.

Conlisk, John. 1996. "Why Bounded Rationality." *Journal of Economic Literature* 34: 669–700.

Cosmides, L., and J. Tooby. 1996. "Are Humans Good Intuitive Statisticians After All? Rethinking Some Conclusions from the Literature on Judgement Under Uncertainty." *Cognition* 58: 1–73.

Cowen, Tyler. 1993. "The Scope and Limits of Preference Sovereignty." *Economics and Philosophy* 9: 253–69.

Dahl, Gordon B., and Michael R. Ransom. 1999. "Does Where You Stand Depend on Where You Sit? Tithing Donations and Self-Serving Beliefs." *American Economic Review* 89: 703–27.

Damasio, Antonio R. 1994. *Descartes' Error.* New York: Putnam.

———. 1999. *The Feeling of What Happens: Body and Emotion in the Making of Consciousness.* New York: Harcourt Brace.

Dawes, Robyn. 1998. "Behavioral Decision Making and Judgement." In D.T. Gilbert, S.T. Fiske, and G. Lindzey, eds., *The Handbook of Social Psychology,* 4th ed., 497–548. New York: McGraw-Hill.

DeMarzo, Peter M., Dimitri Vayanos, and Jeffrey Zweibel. 2003. "Persuasion Bias, Social Influence, and Unidimensional Opinions." *Quarterly Journal of Economics* 118: 909–68.

Dennett, Daniel. 1987. *The Intentional Stance.* Cambridge, MA: MIT Press.

de Souza, Ronald. 1987. *The Rationality of Emotion.* Cambridge, MA: MIT Press.

Dittmar, H. 1992. *The Social Psychology of Material Possessions: To Have Is to Be.* New York: St. Martin's Press.

Eagly, Alice H., Serena Chen, Shelley Chaiken, and Kelly Shaw-Barnes. 1999. "The Impact of Attributes on Memory: An Affair to Remember." *Psychological Bulletin* 125: 64–89.

Earl, Peter. 1983. *The Economic Imagination: Towards a Behavioral Theory of Choice.* Brighton: Wheatsheaf.

———. 1990. "Economics and Psychology: A Survey." *Economic Journal* 100: 718–55.

———, ed. 2002. *The Legacy of Herbert Simon in Economic Analysis.* Cheltenham, UK: Edward Elgar.

Easterlin, Richard ed. 2002. *Happiness in Economics.* Cheltenham, UK: Edward Elgar.

Elster, Jon. 1989a. *Nuts and Bolts for the Social Sciences.* Cambridge: Cambridge University Press.

———. 1989b. "Social Norms and Economic Theory." *Journal of Economic Perspectives* 3(4): 99–117.

———. 1999. *Alchemies of the Mind: Rationality and the Emotions.* Cambridge: Cambridge University Press.

Etzioni, Amitai. 1988. *The Moral Dimension: Toward a New Economics.* New York: Free Press.

Fehr, Ernst, and Simon Gächter. 2000. "Fairness and Reciprocity: The Economics of Reciprocity." *Journal of Economic Perspectives* 14(3): 159–81.

Fernández-Armesto, Filipe. 1997. *Truth: A History and a Guide for the Perplexed.* New York: St. Martin's.

Festinger, Leon. 1957. *A Theory of Cognitive Dissonance.* Stanford, CA: Stanford University Press.

Finucane, Melissa L., Ali Alhakami, Paul Slovic, and Stephen M. Johnson. 2000. "The Affect Heuristic in Judgments of Risk and Benefits." *Journal of Behavioral Decision Making* 13: 1–17.

Fischhoff, Baruch. 1991. "Value Elicitation: Is There Anything There?" *American Psychologist* 46: 835–47.

Fishbein, M. and I. Ajzen. 1975. *Belief, Attitude, Intention, Behavior: An Introduction to Theory and Research.* Reading, MA: Addison-Wesley.

Foxall, Gordon R. 1990. *Consumer Psychology in Behavioral Perspective.* London: Routledge.

Frank, Robert. 1999. *Luxury Fever: Why Money Fails to Satisfy in an Age of Excess.* New York: Free Press.

Frey, Bruno, and A. Stutzer. 2002. "What Can Economists Learn from Happiness Research?" *Journal of Economic Literature* XL: 402–35.

Gazzaniga, Michael S. 1998. *The Mind's Past.* Berkeley: University of California Press.

Genovese, D., and C. Mayer. 2001. "Loss Aversion and Seller Behavior: Evidence from the Housing Market." *Quarterly Journal of Economics* 116: 1233–60.

Gigerenzer, Gerd, and D.G. Goldstein. 1996. "Reasoning the Fast and Frugal Way: Models of Bounded Rationality." *Psychological Review* 103: 650–69.

Gigerenzer, Gerd, Peter M. Todd, and ABC Research Group. 1999. *Simple Heuristics that Make Us Smart.* New York: Oxford University Press.

Gilbert, D.T., and T.D. Wilson. 2000. "Miswanting: Some Problems in the Forecasting of Future Affective States." In *Feeling and Thinking: The Role of Affect in Social Cognition,* ed. J.P. Forgas, 178–97. Cambridge: Cambridge University Press.

Gilovich, T. 1991. *How We Know What Isn't So: Fallacies of Human Reason.* New York: Free Press.

Gilovich, T., Dale Griffen, and Daniel Kahneman eds. 2002. *Heuristics and Biases: The Psychology of Intuitive Judgement.* Cambridge: Cambridge University Press.

Goethals, George R., and William P. Klein. 2000. "Interpreting and Inventing Social Reality: Attributional and Constructive Elements in Social Comparison." In Jerry Suls and Ladd Wheeler, eds., *Handbook of Social Comparisons: Theory and Research,* 23–44. New York: Kluwer Academic.

Goldstein, W.M., and R.M. Hogarth. 1997. *Research on Judgment and Decision Making: Currents, Connections, and Controversies.* Cambridge: Cambridge University Press.

Gopnik, A., and A.N. Meltzoff. 1997. *Words, Thoughts and Theories.* Cambridge, MA: MIT Press.

Griffen, Dale, and Amos Tversky. 1992. "The Weighing of Evidence and the Determinants of Confidence." *Cognitive Psychology* 24: 411–35.

Guerin, Bernard. 2003. "Putting a Radical Socialness into Consumer Behavior Analysis." *Journal of Economic Psychology* 24: 697–718.

Haltiwanger, J., and M. Waldman. 1985. "Rational Expectations and the Limits of Rationality: An Analysis of Heterogeneity." *American Economic Review* 75: 326–40.

Hammond, J.S., R.L. Keeney, and Howard Raiffa. 1999. *Smart Choices: A Practical Guide to Making Better Decisions.* Boston: Harvard Business School Press.

Hanoch, Yaniv. 2002. "'Neither an Angel nor an Ant': Emotion as an Aid to Bounded Rationality." *Journal of Economic Psychology* 23: 1–25.

Hastie, R. 2001. "Problems for Judgment and Decision Making." *Annual Review of Psychology* 52: 653–83.

Hawkins, S.A., and R. Hastie. 1990. "Hind-sight Biased Judgments of Past Events After the Outcomes Are Known." *Psychological Bulletin* 107: 311–27.

Heath, C., R.P. Larrick, and G. Wu. 1999. "Goals as Reference Points." *Cognitive Psychology* 38: 79–109.

Heiner, Ronald. 1983. "The Origin of Predictable Behavior." *American Economic Review* 73: 560–95.

Helm, Bennett W. 2001. *Emotional Reason: Deliberation, Motivation, and the Nature of Value.* Cambridge: Cambridge University Press.

Johnson-Laird, P.N. 1983. *Mental Models: Towards a Cognitive Science of Language, Inference, and Consciousness.* Cambridge, MA: Harvard University Press.

Joyce, James M. 1999. *The Foundations of Causal Decision Theory.* Cambridge: Cambridge University Press.

Kahneman, Daniel. 1994. "New Challenges to the Rationality Assumption." *Journal of Institutional and Theoretical Economics* 150: 18–36.

———. 2000a. "Experienced Utility and Objective Happiness: A Moment-Based Approach." In Daniel

Kahneman and Amos Tversky, eds., *Choices, Values, and Frames*, 673–92. Cambridge: Cambridge University Press.

———. 2000b. "Evaluation by Moments: Past and Future." In Daniel Kahneman and Amos Tversky, eds., *Choices, Values, and Frames*, 693–708. Cambridge: Cambridge University Press.

———. 2003. "Maps of Bounded Rationality: Psychology for Behavioral Economics." *American Economic Review* 93: 1449–75.

Kahneman, Daniel, E. Diener, and N. Schwarz, eds. 1999. *Well-Being: The Foundation of Hedonic Psychology.* New York: Russell Sage Foundation.

Kahneman, Daniel, and Shane Frederick. 2002. "Representativeness Revisited: Attribute Substitution in Intuitive Judgement." In T. Gilovich, Dale Griffen, and Daniel Kahneman, eds., *Heuristics and Biases: The Psychology of Intuitive Judgement,* 49–81. Cambridge: Cambridge University Press.

Kahneman, Daniel, Jack Knetsch, and Richard Thaler. 1991. "Anomalies: The Endowment Effect, Loss Aversion, and the Status Quo Bias." *Journal of Economic Perspectives* 5: 193–206.

Kahneman, Daniel, Paul Slovic, and Amos Tversky, eds. 1982. *Judgment Under Uncertainty: Heuristics and Biases.* Cambridge: Cambridge University Press.

Kahneman, Daniel, and Amos Tversky. 1979. "Prospect Theory: An Analysis of Decision Under Risk." *Econometrica* 47: 263–91.

———, eds. 2000. *Choices, Values, and Frames.* Cambridge: Cambridge University Press.

Katona, George. 1975. *Psychological Economics.* New York: Elsevier.

Kelly, George A. 1955. *The Psychology of Personal Constructs.* New York: Norton.

Lane, Robert E. 2000. *The Loss of Happiness in Market Democracies.* New Haven, CT: Yale University Press.

Lea, Stephen E.G., Roger M. Tarpy, and Paul Webley. 1987. *The Individual in the Economy: A Textbook of Economic Psychology.* Cambridge: Cambridge University Press.

Lewis, Alan, Paul Webley, and Adrian Furnham. 1995. *The New Economic Mind: The Social Psychology of Economic Behaviour.* Hemel Hempstead, UK: Harvester Wheatsheaf.

Lipman, Barton L. 1995. "Information Processing and Bounded Rationality: A Survey." *Canadian Journal of Economics* 28: 42–67.

Loewenstein, George, Ted O'Donoghue, and Matthew Rabin. 2003. "Projection Bias in Predicting Future Utility." *Quarterly Journal of Economics* 118: 1209–48.

Loewenstein, George, and D. Schkade. 1999. "Wouldn't It Be Nice: Predicting Future Feelings." In D. Kahneman, E. Diener, and N. Schwarz, eds., *Well-Being: The Foundation of Hedonic Psychology,* 85–108. New York: Russell Sage Foundation.

Lopes, L.L. 1991. "The Rhetoric of Irrationality." *Theory and Psychology* 1: 65–82.

Lutz, Mark A. 1998. *Economics for the Common Good.* London: Routledge.

Lutz, Mark A., and Kenneth Lux. 1979. *The Challenge of Humanistic Economics.* Menlo Park, CA: Benjamin Cummings.

MacFadyen, Alan J., and Heather W. MacFadyen, eds. 1986. *Economic Psychology: Intersections in Theory and Application.* Amsterdam: North-Holland.

MacFadyen, Heather W. 1986. "Motivational Constructs in Psychology." In Alan J. MacFadyen and Heather W. MacFadyen, eds., *Economic Psychology: Intersections in Theory and Application,* 67–108. Amsterdam: North-Holland.

March, James G. 1978. "The War Is Over and the Victors Have Lost." *Journal of Socioeconomics* 21: 261–67.

Maslow, Abraham H. 1976. *The Farther Reaches of Human Nature.* New York: Penguin.

Mason, Roger. 2002. "Conspicuous Consumption in Economic Theory and Thought." In Edward Fullbrook, ed., *Intersubjectivity in Economics: Agents and Structures,* 85–104. London: Routledge.

McGarty, Craig. 1999. *Categorization in Social Psychology.* Thousand Oaks, CA: Sage.

Miller, George A. 1956. "The Magical Number Seven, Plus or Minus Two: Some Limits on Our Capacity for Processing Information." *Psychological Review* 63: 81–97.

Mullainathan, Sendhil. 2002. "A Memory-Based Model of Bounded Rationality." *Quarterly Journal of Economics* 117: 735–74.

Mullainathan, Sendhil, and Richard Thaler. 2002. "Behavioral Economics." NBER Working Paper 7948. National Bureau of Economic Research, Washington, DC.

Murphy, Gregory L. 2002. *The Big Book of Concepts.* Cambridge, MA: MIT Press.

Nisbett, R., and L. Ross. 1980. *Human Inference: Strategies and Shortcomings of Social Judgment.* Englewood Cliffs, NJ: Prentice-Hall.

O'Donoghue, Ted, and Matthew Rabin. 2003. "Studying Optimal Paternalism, Illustrated by a Model of Sin Taxes." *American Economic Review* 93, 2: 186–91.

Payne, W.J., J. Bettman, and E. Johnson. 1992. "Behavioral Decision Research: A Constructive Processing Perspective." *Annual Review of Psychology* 43: 87–131.

Pettit, Philip. 2000. "Rational Choice, Functional Selection and Empty Black Boxes." *Journal of Economic Methodology* 7: 33–57.

Pfeifer R., and C. Scheier. 1999. *Understanding Intelligence.* Cambridge, MA: MIT Press.

Polivy, Janet, and C. Peter Hermon. 2002. "If at First You Don't Succeed: False Hopes of Self-Change." *American Psychologist* 57: 677–89.

Rabin, Matthew. 1998. "Psychology and Economics." *Journal of Economic Literature* 36: 11–46.

———. 2002. "A Perspective on Psychology and Economics." *European Economic Review* 46: 657–85.

———. 2003a. "Inference by Believers in the Law of Small Numbers." *Quarterly Journal of Economics* 117: 775–816.

———. 2003b. "The Nobel Memorial Prize for Daniel Kahneman." *Scandinavian Journal of Economics* 105: 157–80.

Rachlin, Howard. 1989. *Judgment, Decision, and Choice: A Cognitive/Behavioral Synthesis.* New York: W.H. Freeman.

Robson, Arthur J. 2001. "The Biological Basis of Economic Behavior." *Journal of Economic Literature* 39: 11–33.

———. 2002. "Evolution and Human Nature." *Journal of Economic Perspectives* 16, 2: 89–106.

Ross, Michael, and Anne E. Wilson. 2001. "Constructing and Appraising Past Selves." In Daniel Schacter and Elaine Scarry, eds., *Memory, Brain, and Belief,* 231–58. Cambridge, MA: Harvard University Press.

Rubenstein, Ariel. 1998. *Modelling Bounded Rationality.* Cambridge, MA: MIT Press.

Russell, T., and Richard Thaler. 1985. "The Relevance of Quasi-Rationality in Markets." *American Economic Review* 75: 1071–82.

Ryan, Richard M., and Edward L. Deci. 2001. "On Happiness and Human Potential: A Review of Research on Hedonic and Eudaimonic Well-being." *Annual Review of Psychology* 52: 141–66.

Samuelson, Larry. 2002. "Evolution and Game Theory." *Journal of Economic Perspectives* 16, 2: 47–66.

Samuelson, William, and Richard Zeckhauser. 1988. "Status Quo Bias in Decision Making." *Journal of Risk and Uncertainty* 1: 7–59.

Savage, L.J. 1954. *The Foundations of Statistics.* New York: Wiley.

Scitovsky, Tibor. 1976. *The Joyless Economy: An Inquiry into Human Satisfaction and Consumer Dissatisfaction.* Oxford: Oxford University Press.

Seligman, Martin, and M. Csikszentmihalyi, eds. 2000. "Happiness, Excellence and Optimal Functioning." Special issue of *American Psychologist,* January.

Sen, A. 1977. "Rational Fools: A Critique of the Behavioral Foundations of Economic Theory." *Philosophy and Public Affairs* 6: 317–44.

Simon, Herbert A. 1955. "A Behavioral Model of Rational Choice." *Quarterly Journal of Economics* 69: 99–118.

———. 1982. *Models of Bounded Rationality,* vol. 2: *Behavioral Economics and Business Organization.* Cambridge, MA: MIT Press.

Slovic, Paul. 1995. "The Construction of Preference." *American Psychologist* 50: 364–71.

Smith, E.R., and J. DeCoster. 2000. "Dual-Process Models in Social and Cognitive Psychology: Conceptual Integration and Links to Underlying Memory Systems." *Personality and Social Psychology Review* 4: 108–31.

Starmer, Chris. 2000. "Developments in Non-Expected Utility Theory: The Hunt for a Descriptive Theory of Choice Under Risk." *Journal of Economic Literature* 38: 332–82.

Thaler, Richard H. 1992. *The Winner's Curse: Anomalies and Paradoxes of Economic Life.* New York: Free Press.

———. 1999. "Mental Accounting Matters." *Journal of Behavioral Decision Making* 12: 183–206.

Thaler, Richard H., and H.M. Shefrin. 1981. "An Economic Theory of Self-Control." *Journal of Political Economy* 89: 392–410.

Thaler, Richard H., and Cass R. Sunstein. 2003. "Libertarian Paternalism." *American Economic Review* 93, 2: 175–79.

Tolman, Edward C. 1932. *Purposive Behavior in Animals and Men.* New York: Appleton-Century-Crofts.

Tranel, Daniel, Antoine Bechara, and Antonio R. Damasio. 2000. "Decision Making and the Somatic Marker Hypothesis." In Michael S. Gazzaniga, ed., *The New Cognitive Neurosciences,* 2nd ed., 1047–61. Cambridge, MA: MIT Press.

Tversky, Amos. 1972. "Elimination by Aspects: A Theory of Choice." *Psychological Review* 79: 281–99.

Tversky, Amos, and Daniel Kahneman. 1986. "Rational Choice and the Framing of Decisions." *Journal of Business* 59: S251–78.

———. 1992. "Advances in Prospect Theory: Cumulative Representation of Uncertainty." *Journal of Risk and Uncertainty* 5: 292–323.

Viskovatoff, Alex. 2001. "Rationality as Optimal Choice Versus Rationality as Valid Inference." *Journal of Economic Methodology* 8: 313–37.

Winter, Sidney G. 1986. "The Research Program of the Behavioral Theory of the Firm: Orthodox Critique and Evolutionary Perspective." In Benjamin Gilad and Stanley Kaish, eds., *Handbook of Behavioral Economics,* vol. A: *Behavioral Microeconomics,* 151–88. Greenwich, CT: JAI Press.

Young, H. Peyton. 1998. *Individual Strategy and Social Structure: An Evolutionary Theory of Institutions.* Princeton, NJ: Princeton University Press.

Zajonc, R.B. 1980. "Feeling and Thinking: Preferences Need No Inferences." *American Psychologist* 2: 151–75.

CHAPTER 10

RECLAIMING MORAL SENTIMENTS

Behavioral Economics and the Ethical Foundations of Capitalism

SHLOMO MAITAL

> The economic welfare of a community of given
> size is likely to be greater the larger the share that
> accrues to the poor.
> —*A.C. Pigou (in Lekachman 1959, 384)*

> There is no way of comparing the satisfactions of
> different people.
> —*Lionel Robbins (in Lekachman 1959, 384)*

There is a fundamental paradox at the core of economics, its models and methods. Economics rules. But its practitioners, economists, are frequently reviled.

Like Alexander the Great, economics has conquered the world. Its core principle has swept over the world. Economics' central idea—the superiority of free open markets, in which individuals "vote" for products by buying them, the way people vote with ballots for candidates—has become the coin of the realm.[1] One can even mark the triumphal date: November 9, 1989, the day the Berlin Wall fell.

Capitalism is an economic system characterized by private ownership of property, open competition in free markets, and the desire to accumulate material goods and wealth. It has been embraced everywhere (except Cuba and Kazakhstan) as the central organizing principle of society. Capitalism's footprint, globalization—the creation of open, competitive, interconnected markets for goods, capital, technology, and information that span the world—is now irreversible.[2] Socialism, characterized by state ownership of property and state command over the economy, has been demoted from the organizing principle for more than a third of the world's inhabitants to a museum relic.

Arguably, economics now dominates such other disciplines as physics and biology. While those disciplines affect *parts* of our lives, economics pervades *all* of our lives, because economics now determines to a considerable degree the way we all live our lives.

With the victory of capitalism and its parent science, economics, one might reasonably expect that the esteem and stature of economists in the eyes of ordinary people should be commensurate with the ascendance of their discipline, on a par with judges and clergy. But this is far from the case. In surveys, economists consistently rank almost 20 points (out of 100) below lawyers in occupational prestige, significantly below political scientists, sociologists, and urban planners, and below sea level compared to doctors and judges (Survey and Documentation Analysis 1972–2002). Why?

I believe the answer is clear. Economists purposely and deliberately disqualified themselves from addressing the central debate confronting the world—the moral and ethical foundations of capitalism and globalization. Capitalism and globalization have brought enormous wealth to a few and prosperity to many. But they have brought poverty or stagnation to distressingly many others. And according to research, many of those who have become wealthier may not, overall, feel any better off. There is global instability, inequality, and anomie, and economists lack the tools to fix them. When policy makers throw down the gauntlet in their search for advice, economists cannot pick it up. And when business leaders voice their frustration with economists, there is no real defense.[3]

The core issues facing the world today affect everyone. They are moral in nature. They address the hard questions: What is good? What is right? What is fair? What is just? What is happiness? How *ought* we to live? Since Aristotle, these have *always* been the core questions. But seventy years ago, economists purposely expunged moral judgments—the word *ought*—from their discipline. Economics, a Greenpeace supporter once said, is a "morals-free zone." Therefore, economists have nothing to say about the core issues that society debates fiercely today and has always debated throughout history. As Dougherty (2002, 66) notes, in the divide between C.P. Snow's two cultures, the humanities and the sciences, "economics has fallen on the pocket calculator side," when in fact it could have been a lasting bridge between them.

Economists claimed to eliminate values and ethics, what ought to be, to make their discipline more scientific, more akin to physics, focused on what is. (In fact, economics was never truly value-free; a latent value—the primacy of the individual—always remained, as I will argue below.) The result was to make economists largely irrelevant. So economists' esteem in people's eyes rightly fell to a very low level. Those who brought globalization to the world do not appear to truly understand its implications or its vital issues. As a result, at the table where the burning issues related to global markets are debated, economics as a discipline has no seat.

In this essay, I will argue that economics as a discipline took several wrong turns, and I will propose how economics should get itself back on track, by restoring behavior and explicit values as central concerns, as they were for Adam Smith, in order to build the missing ethical foundations of capitalism.

The reader will quickly note that the previous sentence itself is an implicit value judgment. That is precisely the point. I reason that economics must put explicit discussion of values back at the center of its radar screen, where they once were, when economics was political economy. And the only way this can be done, I will claim, is by placing the close study of human behavior there with those values, side by side.[4]

In the early days of economics, values and behavior were at its heart. Adam Smith's *Theory of Moral Sentiments* (1759) preceded his *Wealth of Nations* (1776) by almost a whole generation. Over time, the legitimacy of studying human behavior disappeared from the economic agenda and was replaced by the abstract modeling of superhuman agents. Then moral principles too were banned. The result was the paradox of the universal embrace of economics' central idea and the social distaste for those who preach and teach it.

Unlike nearly all the other essays in this volume, which are creative surveys, this essay is polemic, subjective, and argumentative. Those who reject the fractious opening premise of this chapter may choose not to read further. In my defense, I plead that after my forty years of research, a single polemic essay may be allowed, as a period at the end of a long sentence. I deeply regret not having better understood and rejected the emptiness of conventional value-free economics at the start of my career rather than at the end of it. I hope young economists who read this will avoid the same mistake.

The first section of the essay reviews historically the wrong-turn process in which economics dumped overboard both moral sentiments and human behavior. The second section reviews research in two areas— rationality and happiness, or subjective well-being—and indicates why this research, done largely by noneconomists, reveals the bankruptcy of mainstream economics. Finally, the last section proposes how a new economics might be constructed to provide capitalism with strong moral foundations, built on the two pillars of ethics and behavior.

RECLAIMING MORAL SENTIMENTS

At a lecture by a leading prophet of globalization, an economist, I once heard the following argument:

> Capitalism is the only system that has generated sustained economic growth. Capitalism is based on greed. Socialism has far better ethics. Socialism is based on helping your neighbor. In times of crisis—9/11—people come together and help their neighbors. But this cannot be sustained over the long run. That is a fact. So only a system where people can be rewarded for hard work by becoming wealthy can create sustained hard work, and energy, and economic growth.

This view is widely held. It reflects a fundamental behavioral assumption about what drives human energy—the desire for wealth alone sustains hard work and growth. This is the foundation of capitalism. And it is, I am convinced, fundamentally and utterly erroneous.

As a witness, I call to the stand Adam Smith, the prophet of capitalism. Smith, born in 1723, studied moral philosophy at the University of Glasgow and Oxford and was appointed to a chair in this subject in 1751. His first book, *The Theory of Moral Sentiments,* was published in 1759. It was an instant hit. Smith remained a moral philosopher throughout his life and finished the sixth edition of *The Theory of Moral Sentiments* just before he died.[5]

Smith was not naive. He did not rest his moral system on what Lekachman calls "unalloyed kindness." Instead,

> he argued that we acted as we did out of a regard for the opinion of others. We shape our actions to please an impartial spectator . . . when we sympathize with a friend in trouble, our criteria are those we conceive will win the approval of this judicious soul . . . [T]hough he felt the softer of human emotions, [Adam Smith] expected human beings to pursue their own interest, in ways which violated no ethical canons. (Lekachman 1959, 78)

Before Smith, moral philosophers, like priests, imams, and rabbis, exhorted people to be more ethically high-minded. Smith changed direction. He cut right to the core, to the link between passions and interests. He showed how social institutions and market structures could make all of us better people. He based his whole theory on the idea that what matters to each of us is our own self-esteem, built in turn on the esteem of others. It was a brilliant insight, one that modern social psychologists have embraced and extended without attributing the idea to Smith (see, e.g., Bandura 1963). Everyone cites Smith's "passions and interests" passage. But they tend to ignore his key insight that we all have a passion for fulfilling the interests of others.

The thread that runs through all [Adam Smith's] works: how the market can be structured to make the pursuit of self-interest benefit consumers; how the passion for the approval of others can make us act more selflessly; how public institutions can be structured to ensure that they deliver the services they are mandated to provide. (Muller 1993, 6–7, cited in Dougherty 2002, 57)

It is clear that Smith refers to what Sen has called "obligation," a type of altruism generating advantage for someone whose welfare does not *directly* affect the agent's own well-being (see Mittone 2003). This is very far from Gary Becker's "rotten kid" altruism, in which selfish children behave outwardly selflessly toward family members because they inwardly expect from them a high return on their investment.

In rereading *Moral Sentiments,* I thought of the modern prophet of free markets and unbridled self-interest, Professor Milton Friedman. On winning the Nobel prize, Friedman was asked what he would do with the prize money. He would spend it, he said—a response consistent with his transitory-income consumption theory. But then he added that what really mattered to him was the respect and esteem of his peers, his fellow economists. Aha! I thought. Friedman *writes* like the character Gordon Gekko (played by Michael Douglas) in the movie *Wall Street:* greed is good, even essential. But Friedman *acts and thinks* like Adam Smith in *Moral Sentiments:* he seeks the esteem of his peers. And so, in the end, do I; so do most of us.

It is not socialism that is built on loving your neighbors like yourself and seeking their esteem. It is capitalism. Ask capitalism's prophet, Adam Smith.

Human beings are inherently unequal in the intellectual, physical, and financial assets they command. Capitalism and globalization allow people to freely leverage their assets to build more wealth. It is the nature of capitalism, baked into the cake, that the more assets and resources you have, the more you acquire of them, and the easier it is to do so. The less you have, the harder it is to build wealth. Inequality in the distribution of wealth and income is transmitted socially and fiscally from one generation to the next and, unless checked, tends to grow continually. Ultimately, the growing army of those who have nothing—either deprived groups within a country, or entire impoverished countries shut out of global markets—rises and out of desperation seeks some way to seize the wealth of those who have everything. The result is highly destructive to society. Winners and losers lose together.[6] This is not Marxism. It is reality.

The destruction caused by social strife is prevented by Smith's "moral sentiments"—by the strong desire of those who have wealth to achieve the esteem of those who lack it, by creatively redistributing their wealth in ways that do not destroy energy and industry among those who have wealth and want more, or have none and aspire to attain some. As the global distribution of wealth and income declines alarmingly, the importance of moral sentiments grows, as does the need for them to find practical and concrete expression.

Growing Inequality

Inequality both among countries and within countries has grown dramatically during the globalization process.

Between-Country Inequality

Only a minority of the world's population has benefited from global capitalism. This is the Achilles' heel of globalization. Consider these facts:

1. Of the world's 6.5 billion people, the poorest 40 percent (about 2.5 billion people) get only 3 percent of the world's GDP and have an annual per capita GDP of $430. The middle 44 percent of the world's population get 16 percent of the world's GDP, or $5,000 per capita GDP. The richest 16 percent, living in only about 25 countries and comprising fewer than 1 billion people, get 81 percent of the world's GDP and enjoy an average income of $26,510 a year (World Bank 2000, 2003).
2. People in the poorest 61 countries get only 6 percent of the world's GDP and have a per capita GDP of $2 a day or less (World Bank 2000, 2003). There, 90 of every 1,000 children die before age five, compared to 7 in 1,000 in the rich countries. An entire continent—Africa—has become deeply impoverished during the past generation.
3. Since 1970, the wealthiest 60 countries doubled their per capita income. The middle 60 and poorest 60 countries gained little or no ground.
4. Nothing is more symbolic than the twin problems of obesity and hunger. There are sufficient calories in the world to feed everyone. But a few have far too many, and many have far too few.
5. A billion people in the world are hungry. An equal number are obese. Both groups suffer even though on average the world's waistline is ideal. A transfer of calories from the fat to the thin would help both. (In the United States 66 percent of the population is overweight.)
6. In 1993, the Gini coefficient for world income distribution, measured in terms of GDP at purchasing power parity (reflecting the real buying power of national currencies), was 66, up from 62.5 only five years earlier (Wade 2002). This number means the world's income distribution is two-thirds of the way to perfect inequality (Gini coefficient of 100).
7. The share of world income going to the poorest 10 percent of the world's population fell in just five years, between 1988 and 1993, by over a quarter, whereas the share of the richest 10 percent rose by 8 percent (Wade 2001).

Within-Country Inequality

Inequality of wealth and income distribution in, for example, the United States, the world's largest economy, is large and growing.

- The richest 1 percent of Americans (2.8 million people) had more after-tax money in 2000 than did the bottom 40 percent (110 million people). In 1979, they had only half as much.
- The wealthiest 1 percent in America had the largest share of before-tax income for any year since 1929.
- After-tax income for the wealthiest 1 percent tripled between 1979 and 2000 and averaged $862,700; for the poorest 20 percent of households, their after-tax income rose only 9 percent between 1979 and 2000 and averaged $13,700, according to the Congressional Budget Office and the Center for Budget and Policy Priorities (Congressional Budget Office 2005; see also Browning 2003).
- For 1995, the richest 1 percent of U.S. households had average wealth of $7.75 million, and owned a third of all net worth; the next richest 10 percent owned another third; and the remaining households, 89 percent, had average wealth of $77,000 and owned the remaining third (Levy 1999, 169).

The good news is that globalization has created unprecedented wealth. The bad news is that only a small minority got it.

The issue is not whether to condemn or destroy globalization, but rather how to widen the circle of nations, families, and individuals who enjoy its fruits. *If globalization and the capitalist growth engine are to endure and prevail, ways must be found to make them more inclusive.*

The parallel between economic democracy and political democracy breaks down when closely examined. In political democracy, the guiding principle is "one person, one vote." In economic democracy, the principle is: "one dollar [or one baht, or one yuan], one unit of purchasing power." But the total amount of purchasing power individuals possess differs widely. And the prevailing global system of capitalism widens these gaps.

If we believe that wealth conveys political influence, then there is a fundamental contradiction between capitalism (economic democracy) and political democracy. When growing inequality of income and wealth distribution is tolerated, capitalism undercuts the equality of rights inherent in democracy. The argument that political democracy never exists without economic democracy is thus fallacious. Unchecked economic democracy is an enemy of true political democracy.

Pigou was right. Not only is greater equality an intrinsically good thing, it is also utilitarian (good because it leads to good consequences), because it ultimately preserves and strengthens the democratic process, which is itself a widely held value. Plato would say: equality is intrinsically right and also good, because it brings good results. But Pigou's insights are forgotten, because they were cast overboard shortly after they were published.

TWO WRONG TURNS

The path taken by a scientific discipline is always led by a handful of opinion leaders who define and create paradigm shifts. Several such shifts have occurred in economics. In each case, they represented a fork in economics' intellectual road. And in each case, economics took the wrong fork. The result is the current dead end.[7]

The First Wrong Turn

The first of economics' two wrong turns happened in 1890, when Cambridge professor Alfred Marshall defined economics with a daily-life-based spin.

> Economics is the study of people as they live and move and think in the ordinary business of life . . . for man's character has been molded by his every-day work and the material resources which he thereby procures, more than by any other influence . . . for the business by which a person earns his livelihood generally fills his thoughts during by far the greater part of those hours in which his mind is at its best; during them his character is being formed by the way in which he uses his faculties in his work, by the thoughts and feelings which it suggests, and by his relations to his associates in work, his employers or his employees. (Marshall 1936, 1)

But earlier, French-Swiss economist Leon Walras, in his *Elements d'Economie Politique,* regarded by many as "the towering achievement of all economics," had given economics a mathematical flavor by massaging the celestial mechanics he had studied as a (failed) engineering student (see Lekachman 1959, 155). He modeled people as if they were planets or electrons, in a system of equations modeled after the famous ones of Isaac Newton.

Economists applauded. It made their discipline much more like physics, giving it the illusion of precision. So economists picked Walras instead of Marshall. "We curtsy to Marshall," said Milton Friedman. "But we walk with Walras" (cited in Maital and Maital 1984, 58).

It seemed like a great decision for economics. But it was a terrible choice for economists. It replaced Marshall's behavioral, biological paradigm, in which society is a living, dynamic organism, with Walras's physical model. People became atoms. As a result, "economists neglected to examine the human costs of capitalist organization; they treated men like machines" (Lekachman 1959, 187, paraphrasing Hobson 1914). And ultimately this one wrong turn led to another.

The Second Wrong Turn

Physicists have values. But physics does not. So the next step in economics' road toward becoming scientific was inevitable.

Lionel Robbins's famous essay (1930) formally expunged all moral relevance from economics by asserting that "there is no way of comparing the satisfactions of different people." This was not Robbins's original idea; he simply validated what economists felt and thought at the time and had thought for some years. His objective clearly was "to free economics from value judgments" (Blaug 1962, 666). Saying that a dollar means more to a pauper than to a billionaire is positive, not ethical; saying the dollar should be transferred to the pauper is normative—and to most of us, ethically right. But if science deals only with positive, not normative, statements, as Robbins stated, then even the most basic of ethical notions is scrubbed out of the discipline. The inevitable result is capitalism with morality.

Robbins's logical positivism was a logical extension of Walras's mathematical purism. If you adopt the language of physics, you must also embrace its morals-free hygiene. And Robbins succeeded. A.C. Pigou's masterly *The Economics of Welfare* (1920), laden with value judgments, a rich bible of relevant policy applications of economics to the world's pressing issues, ultimately died in ignominy. Does even one economics student in a hundred read it today?

If you cannot clearly say that the world is a better place when the poor get money from the rich, what possible moral relevance can economics have? And if it has no moral relevance, then it has little to say about a part of our lives that is of great and growing significance, and nothing to say about the ethics of capitalism and the inequality it generates. So by dumping Marshall in favor of Walras, and dumping ethics in favor of scientific purity, economics shot itself in both feet, eschewing the study of behavior, discarding behavior-based issues, and opting out of the burning moral issues of the day. The attempt to rescue relevance through the compensation principle (if you *could* compensate the losers and still leave the winners ahead, then it is a good policy) is utterly vacuous. As a result, a value-free economic science has generated fundamentally bad science that delights in fitting data to curves, or often not even bothering, but stumbles when fitting solutions to real problems.

THE CONSEQUENCES OF TWO WRONG TURNS

Travelers know that one wrong turn in a strange city can lead to hours of wandering before their destination is finally reached. Economics, too, finds itself in a wasteland because of its wrong turns.

Pigou wrote about two goals of economics: "fruit" (policies) and "light" (understanding and insight, on which policies are based). No light, no fruit. The withered fruit of failed economic policies stems directly from the lack of light—the impossibly abstract and unreal view of human behavior that characterizes mainstream economics.

It is reasonable to state as economics' metaobjective the desire to improve the well-being of society. It is also reasonable to assume that the material wealth generated by capitalism improves well-being. But this assumption has been shown to be largely false. It is remarkable, yet little noticed, that economists have largely failed to examine this fundamental premise of capitalism, leaving the field to psychologists.[8] (Behavioral economists are an exception.) The empirically weak correlation between wealth and well-being is a major obstacle to building moral foundations for capitalism.

It is reasonable to assume that human beings are rational. Economists chose to define rationality in a highly abstract, unrealistic manner, using axioms shown by empirical research (again, done mainly by psychologists) to be false. As a result, the headlong dash to free markets is often destructive, owing to the lethal mixture of deregulation and nonrational behavior.[9]

There are key human behaviors that must be understood if economists are to build strong policies, yet which are generally ignored. I address only two of them: anomie (higher wealth and income without commensurate improvement in well-being) and nonrationality. There are many, many more.

Anomie

> "This lovely car has not brought us happiness.
> You agree, Morris? That is why I am thinking
> in terms of having the entire house recarpeted."
> —*New Yorker* cartoon

> If material well-being leads to happiness, why is it that neither capitalist nor socialist solutions seem to work? Why is it that the crew on the flagship of capitalist affluence is becoming increasingly addicted to drugs for falling asleep, for waking up, for staying slim, for escaping boredom and depression?
> —Csikszentmihalyi 1999, 822

The moral basis of capitalism could be framed as the following syllogism:

1. Capitalism and its ally globalization are engines of unprecedented power for building wealth.
2. Wealth, for those who possess it, leads to happiness.
3. Happiness is a good thing, perhaps *the* ultimate good.
4. Therefore, capitalism is morally good.

and a normative conclusion. If either of the factual premises is false, the conclusion does not logically follow. The first premise is probably true. The third premise is a widely accepted value judgment. But the second factual premise—the postulated link between material wealth and enduring happiness, is untrue.

Capitalism as Growth Engine

Consider capitalism as an extraordinary growth engine. We live in a truly incredible age. Humanity in its present form has existed for some 50,000 years. For nearly all that time, economic growth was *zero*.[10] The human race lived at subsistence levels.

In the Middle Ages, economic growth was probably negative. In fact, notes William Baumol, "many consumption choices available to . . . more-affluent Romans had long since disappeared by the time of the Industrial Revolution" (Baumol 2002, 3).

In stark contrast, during the past 150 years per capita incomes in free market economies have grown by between several hundred and several thousand percent! It was this fact, conveyed by television signals that leaped across walls, barbed wire, and border guards, that helped lead to the downfall of Communist regimes. People living under Communism wanted to share in the wealth that the growth machine of capitalism had delivered so generously to the capitalist world. Those who lived in East Germany wanted the same things that the West Germans had, as seen on television and which they knew with certainty that Communism could not, would not, ever bring them.

Capitalism, then, is very good at building wealth. But it is far less successful at spreading happiness. Wealth, apparently, does not lead to well-being. What follows is a survey of some of the evidence (see also Maital 2000).

Subjective Well-being

Richard Nixon ended his State of the Union speech in January 1970 by asking:

> In the next 10 years we will increase our wealth by 50 percent. The profound question is: does this mean that we will be 50 percent richer in any real sense. 50 percent better off, 50 percent happier? (Nixon in Campbell 1981, 4)

Researchers, mostly psychologists and behavioral economists, now have an answer to Nixon's question. They show we are richer but not happier. Between 1960 and 2000, Americans' inflation-adjusted per capita income tripled. Yet despite this, since the mid-1960s the percentage of Americans who state they are "very happy" has actually declined slightly, from 40 percent to just over 30 percent. Studies of self-reported subjective well-being show only a weak link, or no link at all, between happiness and wealth (Frey and Stutzer 2002; Blanchflower and Oswald 2000; Lane 1998; Myers 2000).

Yale political scientist Robert Lane observed that people are not very good judges of how to increase, let alone maximize, their happiness (Lane 2000). But when psychologists tell us we are not any happier than we once were, do they know what they are talking about? Are we really no happier today than we were in 1970? How do they know? And if we are not happier, what can we do about it?

There is no *objective* measure of happiness, no happiness voltmeter, because happiness is a state of mind. Psychologists claim that if you *believe* you are happy or unhappy, then you are. As leading happiness researchers David G. Myers and Ed Diener put it, "the final judge [of subjective well-being] is whoever lives inside a person's skin" (1995, 11). Psychologists use self-reporting measures that ask, "How satisfied are you with your life as a whole these days?" Or they ask people to choose one of three responses—"very happy," "pretty happy," "not too happy"— to the question "How are things?" No matter how you measure well-being and happiness, the result seems to be the same: the proportion of Americans who say they are "very happy" or "satisfied" with life has stayed more or less constant over long periods of time, while measures of wealth and income have risen strikingly.

Worldwide, the seventies were bleak in terms of wealth creation. But from mid-August 1982— that fateful Friday on which Paul Volcker signaled the start of the great bull market by slashing interest rates—America turned into a wealth-creating machine far beyond what Nixon imagined and for eighteen years unequaled in history.

In 1982 there were 13 American billionaires. By 1998 (adjusted for inflation) there were 189, with assets totaling $738 billion. But even the extremely rich are not immune to angst. A survey of people on *Forbes* magazine's list of the wealthiest Americans—those same 189 billionaires— found only slightly greater self-reported happiness than among average Americans, and three in eight were less happy than the average person (see, e.g., Reier 2000). (The link between wealth and happiness is asymmetric. *Loss* of wealth can generate great unhappiness, as the collapse of the stock market bubble that ended in March 2000 demonstrated.)

Most ordinary people firmly believe that if they had more money, they would be happier. In capitalism, this appears to be an article of faith. As Csikszentmihalyi observes, the supreme self-confidence of Western technological countries is based on the belief that the acquisition of wealth and consumer goods would be "the royal road to a happy life" (1999, 821). Surveys in the 1990s showed that 75 percent of Americans entering college believed that an "essential" or "very important" life goal was "being very well off financially"— almost double the 39 percent who said the same in 1970. Yet Brickman and Coates (1978), in a stunning study, show that lottery winners, who suddenly gained great wealth, were not happier than paralyzed accident victims, because they took less pleasure from mundane events.

Most of the over 1,000 studies of wealth and happiness show that while in poorer countries income is a good predictor of well-being, in wealthy nations it is self-esteem, not income, that is most closely linked with happiness. There is no doubt that grinding poverty is an enormous social ill and that escaping it greatly improves well-being, both for individuals and for entire countries. But as Myers and Diener observe, "once people are able to afford life's necessities, increasing levels of affluence matter surprisingly little" (1995, 17).

Why? One reason is that the hidden costs of acquiring wealth—destruction of families and relationships, for instance—are large and insidious. As psychologist Abraham Maslow observed, there is a hierarchy of needs. Once basic material needs are met, happiness is driven far more by "higher needs"—social support, love, esteem, respect of others, self-fulfillment. It is a tragedy of capitalism that the acquisition of wealth (basic needs) often destroys the achievement of higher needs—something many wealthy people discover late in life, and often too late to remedy. Moreover, the extrinsic (monetary) rewards characteristic of capitalism have been shown to destroy the intrinsic motivation (doing things for their own sake) that creates so much happiness and lasting fulfillment. Seligman, Petersen, and Maier (1993) trace epidemic levels of depression to impoverished social connections in the increasingly individualistic Western society, and the litany of social alienation in Robert Putnam's book *Bowling Alone* (2001) is truly distressing. It emerges that whom you love and who loves you is a far more powerful predictor of well-being than what you have.

In their book *Generations,* authors William Strauss and Neil Howe (1991) argue that the new generations now coming of age are beginning to reject the fervent materialism of their parents. It is beginning to dawn on the younger generation that their parents' wealth did not on the whole make their elders any happier. As a result, this generation may increasingly seek happiness in nonmaterial, spiritual activities and in human relationships.

Some psychologists argue that the happy life is one in which the best of whatever is experienced comes relatively often. Scitovsky (1976) and Maital (1988) disagree. They point to a happiness-destroying aspect of wealth. The more often we consume "the best of whatever is experienced," the less incremental enjoyment we derive, because we lose the enormous happiness inherent in novelty, or first-time joy. Happiness is often more dependent on our ability to constrain ourselves in creative ways than on our success in pushing budget constraints upward and outward (Maital 1986).

In truth, the best of what we experience often has little to do with money or markets. I believe this realization will be one of the foremost drivers of social and economic change in the United States and other wealthy countries during the next two decades. As the poorest five-sixths of the world continue to struggle to acquire more and better goods, the richest one-sixth will seek new ways to shape higher-quality lives that go beyond material affluence.

One must not be overly ingenuous. At a basic level, wealth and happiness are clearly and obviously linked. The Chinese peasants who migrate from the poor western provinces to Guangdong, find factory jobs, and work twelve-hour days at $1.20 an hour welcome the chance to earn money. They and their families are doubtless happier. And those jobs were made possible by capitalism and globalization. Hundreds of millions benefit. But the inescapable general conclusion, based on overwhelming evidence, is that above a basic threshold of income, happiness and wealth are not closely linked.

Nonrationality

Some twenty years ago, my wife, Sharone, and I surveyed the literature on behavioral economics (Maital and Maital 1984). We observed that the models and methods gap between psychology and economics was very wide. Despite considerable convergence since then, that gap remains large, especially in relation to how the two disciplines view the complex process of human reasoning and decision making under uncertainty (see, e.g., Maital 2004).

Mathematician and physicist John von Neumann was the patron saint of "unsolvable" problems, which he often tackled on the train ride between Princeton and New York. Behavior under uncertainty was an example. With his co-author Oskar Morgenstern, von Neumann wrote *The Theory of Games and Economic Behavior* (1944).

At first, the authors speak as behaviorists and warn against "shortcuts."[11] However, they immediately take one, because the exigencies of mathematical proof require it, and set up an axiomatic approach toward decisions under uncertainty. It was a shortcut because it did not take the route of empirically studying how people actually make decisions under uncertainty.

Their axiomatic shortcut gave birth to modern game theory and supplied expected utility theory, the underpinnings of the economics of finance. The problem is, all the basic axioms are consistently violated by actual choice behavior. Even when inconsistencies are noted and explained to subjects, the nonrationality in their behavior persists.

Every theory is based on assumptions that are not true. That is why it is called theory. What separates good and bad theory is the boundary defined by Einstein's version of Occam's razor: "Everything should be made as simple as possible—but not simpler." I believe the axiomatic version of Von Neumann and Morgenstern's expected utility theory was far too simple. Others seem to agree. Several Nobel prizes in economics have been awarded for research that repairs the superrationality underlying conventional economics. Nobel prizes were awarded to Simon for bounded rationality, the idea that cognitive capacity is limited and often prevents full optimization; to Ackerlof, Spencer, and Stiglitz for analyzing markets when some people know more than others; and to Kahneman for having integrated insights from psychological research into economic science, especially concerning human judgment and decision making under uncertainty.

We now know that human reasoning is imperfect, biased, emotion-ridden, and often impervious to prior experience or knowledge of probability. In their studies, Kahneman and Tversky often used subjects expert in probability, psychology, or statistics. They showed that judgment biases and heuristics are the same for experts as for laypeople. Once I and a colleague examined behavior toward risk among the most risk-savvy group we could find: pit bosses at a gambling casino. They exhibited the same nonrational biases as ordinary people (Maital and Paolucci 1990).

Addressing the issue of rationality, Kahneman wrote: "The time has perhaps come to set aside the overly general question of whether or not people are rational, . . . allowing research to be focused on more specific and more promising issues" (Kahneman 1994). He suggests that we ask instead, "What are the most important ways in which people fail to maximize their outcomes?" And how can this be changed?

One focus of behavioral economics is complexity and the human need to simplify. Confronting a complex, uncertain world, people look for ways to distill masses of information into understandable bites, to make the uncertain less so, to make complexity more simple, and to conserve the increasingly scarce cognitive resources on which a complex world places heavy demands. Who is to say that the Kahneman-Tversky heuristics, which characterize pervasive behavior toward uncertainty, are irrational if they in general serve our needs well, or at least serve them well enough? *Outcomes,* Kahneman observes, not *assumptions,* should be the acid test of what is regarded as rational or reasonable. In this, he lines up solidly with social psychologist Kurt Lewin. This outcome-based criterion applies not only to how people reason but also to how economists should measure the scientific validity of their own work.

TOWARD A NEW ECONOMICS

If social scientists truly wish to understand certain
phenomena, they should try to change them. Creating,
not predicting, is the most robust test of validity-actionability.
—Kurt Lewin, in Kaplan 1998, 89

You cannot solve a problem with the same
level of thinking that created it.
—Einstein 2000, 314

Twenty years ago, I wrote that economists are like police officers and armies: they are most successful when their services are needed least (Maital 1982, 3). Two decades later, there is supporting evidence for my claim, in two sad episodes: auctions for third-generation (3G) communications licenses, and Japanese deflation.

Economists used game theory to design revenue-maximizing auctions for 3G licenses. Near-universal embrace of these auctions was taken as proof, by economists, of economics' relevance and practicality. But the auction structure neglected "immoral sentiments"—the greed of telecom firms and governments alike. Telecoms overpaid and skated close to bankruptcy. Are economists to blame? If they are held to the standards of Lewin's law (successful intervention, not curve-fitting, is the true test of a theory) and required to build their interventions on a deeper understanding of behavior, then blame is legitimate.

Consider Japan, mired in recession since 1990. The Japanese have applied every macroeconomic theory and policy known to economists—more money, lower interest rates, bigger deficits. Nothing has worked. Nor will these policies work as long as the Japanese people remain fearful of the future and pessimistic.

To comply with Lewin's law, economics must address the core issues the world now faces. The world confronts two conflicting trends: on the one hand, capitalism, deregulation, and the impersonality of open free markets; on the other, noise, pollution, overcrowding, and, as a result, the ever-increasing impact individual decisions have on friends, neighbors, and strangers, and on society in general. These issues cannot be successfully tackled with the limited toolbox mainstream economics currently possesses. To become relevant, it will be necessary for economists to import the models and methods of philosophy, anthropology, sociology, and psychology. Nor can these disciplines be treated by economists like carpetbaggers or migrant workers. They must become *citizens*. They must be integrated into mainstream economics, becoming part of the essential training and required reading of every economist.

A.C. Pigou saw this eighty-four years ago. He put the distinction between individual and social well-being at the center of his research agenda and saw it as the core of economics.[12] But his agenda was rejected. When Miriam gains while John loses, there are two choices. Either we make an interpersonal comparison of utilities, which enables us to say something about whether Miriam's actions are good or bad, or we reject such comparisons, as Robbins did, which prevents economists from saying anything meaningful about inequality and lack of fairness, the issue that increasingly dominates and pervades our lives (though Altman's work [1996, 2001] is an important exception). Moreover, unless we enlist behavioral tools, we economists remain utterly at sea about how Miriam perceives John, about the role of John's well-being in Miriam's perceived well-being, and in general what it is that Miriam and John seek in life as they make their market-based decisions.

Were he alive today, Adam Smith would be a behavioral economist. In his time, he was. Today he could be nothing else. He would need behavioral tools to support his contention that individual self-esteem depends on what others think of us, and that we (imperfectly) internalize externalities where knowledge, cognition, and information permit. The mainstream economics of Walras and Robbins creates a mind-set that blinds us to the very existence of vital questions or forces abstention from even asking them. We should curtsy to Walras and Robbins but walk with Smith, Marshall, and Pigou.

In truth, there is no such thing as a value-free discipline. The attempt to make economics value-free was utterly doomed. The reason is simple. The view of capitalism, as espoused by Friedman and also by Hayek (1944), has an implicit value: that individual freedom is the ultimate value. One can agree or disagree. I personally would place well-being higher on the scale; individual freedom is one very important element in individual well-being, but there are others equally crucial. But one cannot say that the principle of free markets eliminates the moral biases of individual agents or policy makers. It simply selects its own value system and rejects those of others. As a result of its futile effort to become scientific, value-free, and objective, economics has thus succeeded in becoming both irrelevant and hypocritical, while remaining value-ridden.

More than a century and a half ago Thomas Carlyle called economists "Respectable Professors of the Dismal Science" (1850). The reason was economics' main contribution to the world: economist Thomas Malthus's bleak theory of permanent misery. Even if mankind got a few dollars ahead of subsistence, Malthus reasoned, this would dissipate through population growth, wars, and conflict over dwindling resources.

So far, Malthus has turned out to be wrong. But economics remains dismal. The reason is that economics brought a variety of capitalism to the world that purposely lacks moral foundations, because economics itself lacks explicit moral foundations, by choice, and has as a result become the old wine of dismal science in new bottles.

Society *is* perfectible. And so is the art of economics that seeks to understand and improve the well-being of ordinary people. There *are* "potent and remarkably salutary ways in which economics can transform the culture for the better" (Dougherty 2002, xiv).

Let us begin to transform the culture by redefining the ultimate goal of economics: to improve the well-being of those who live on the earth. Let us labor tirelessly to better understand what well-being is and what precisely creates, sustains, and improves it. Let us judge our theories by measuring their success at building policies that improve well-being. Let us state our values clearly and not hide or expunge them.[13] And let us above all anchor our work in the effort to grasp the richness and complexity of human behavior.

I urge young economists to make this worthy normative perspective the gold standard for their career research program.

NOTES

1. Free market advocates often link economic democracy (open competitive markets) with political democracy: "The free market is the only mechanism that has ever been discovered for achieving participatory democracy" (Friedman in Hayek 1944, xi). I will agree below that the growing distributional inequality inherent in economic democracy is inimical to political democracy.

2. A better definition of globalization: the shift from national markets to global ones in goods, services, technology, capital, and people, generated by deregulation, privatization, and the removal of barriers to the free flow of goods, people, and money; the ability to buy and sell anything, anywhere, anytime, from or to anyone.

Globalization is not new. A global trading system was built by the Greeks, then by the Romans, and later by the British Empire, which embraced much of the world and was as globally integrated, or more so, than today's world markets. See Standage 1999 for a fascinating argument that the nineteenth-century telegraph was as powerful an instrument for global communication as today's Internet.

3. As a *Business Week* journalist noted in a year-end summary in 2002, we know a lot less than we think we know about economic policy. The inability of economic theory to take decisive stands on key issues makes policy making highly partisan and value laden.

4. Berg (2003) makes a different but complementary argument for building behavioral foundations of economic policy: Behavioral approaches often lead to very different policy prescriptions than conventional economics do, and thus the risk of policy failure is diminished through a kind of policy portfolio diversification.

5. "Despite his decade of counting pins, tabulating tax rates, codifying the contents of his overcoat, and indulging in other such wonkish obsessions, Smith managed to remain the consummate moral philosopher" (Dougherty 2002, 56).

6. "The question is, how much more unequal world income distribution can become before the resulting political instabilities and flows of migrants reach the point of directly harming the well-being of the citizens of the rich world and the stability of their states" (Wade 2001).

7. Novelist and author John Gardner once said that societies that value philosophy, because it is philosophy, and degrade plumbing, because it is plumbing, will have neither pipes or theories that hold water.

8. Economist Bruno Frey is an important exception; see his fine book with Alois Stutzer (2002).

9. Norman Rothkopf, former Clinton administration official, has observed that while Wall Street financiers strongly favor free unregulated global capital markets, they would never dream of getting into an unregulated taxicab or brushing their teeth with "unregulated toothpaste." He was interviewed on *Frontline,* "The Crash" (PBS), 1999.

10. The proof that there had been no economic growth for at least two millennia is this: Suppose economic growth averaged only 0.2 percent yearly for 2,000 years. Then if average per capita GDP worldwide today is $1,000, in the year 1 it would have been $1,000/(1.002)^{2000}$ or only $18 a year, in today's prices. This is well below subsistence, so even 0.2 percent growth yearly could not have occurred.

11. "We believe that it is necessary to know as much as possible about the behavior of the individual" (von Neumann and Morgenstern 1944, 7).

12. By calling this phenomenon an "externality," a morally neutral term, economists downgraded its importance simply by the choice of language.

13. One of the best examples is Altman (1996), who argues that the "high road" of high wages and high productivity is welfare-improving compared with the "low road" of low wages and low productivity, based on an explicit value judgment that such a policy improves the distribution of wealth and income.

REFERENCES

Altman, Morris. 1996. *Human Agency and Material Welfare: Revisions in Microeconomics and Their Implications for Public Policy.* Boston: Kluwer.

———. 2001. *Worker Satisfaction and Economic Performance.* Armonk, NY: M.E. Sharpe.

Bandura, Albert. 1963. *Social Learning and Personality Development.* New York: Holt, Rinehart and Winston.

Baumol, William. 2002. *The Free-Market Innovation Machine: Analyzing the Growth Miracle of Capitalism.* Princeton, NJ: Princeton University Press.

Berg, Nathan. 2003. "Normative Behavioral Economics." *Journal of Socio-Economics* 32: 411–27.

Blanchflower, David G., and Andrew Oswald. 2000. "Well-Being over Time in Britain and the U.S." Working Paper #7487, National Bureau of Economic Research, Cambridge, MA.

Blaug, M. 1962. *Economic Theory in Retrospect.* London: Heinemann.

Brickman, Philip, and Dan Coates. 1978. "Lottery Winners and Accident Victims: Is Happiness Relative?" *Journal of Personality and Social Psychology* 36, 8: 917–27.

Browning, Lynnley. 2003. "US Rich Get Richer, and Poor Poorer, Data Shows." *International Herald Tribune,* September 25, 5.

Campbell, Angus. 1981. *The Sense of Well-Being in America: Recent Patterns and Trends.* New York: McGraw-Hill.

Carlyle, T. 1850. *Latter Day Pamphlets,* no. 1. London: Charles Scribner's, 1901.

Congressional Budget Office. 2005. *Historical Effective Federal Tax Rates, 1979–2002.* Washington, DC.

Csikszentmihalyi, Mihaly. 1999. "If We Are So Rich, Why Aren't We Happy?" *American Psychologist* 54, 10: 821–27.

Dougherty, Peter. 2002. *Who's Afraid of Adam Smith?* Princeton, NJ: Princeton University Press.

Einstein, Albert. 2000. *The Expanded Quotable Einstein,* coll. and ed. Alice Calaprice. Princeton, NJ: Princeton University Press.

Frey, Bruno, and Alois Stutzer. 2002. *Happiness and Economics.* Princeton, NJ: Princeton University Press.

Hayek, F.A. 1944. *The Road to Serfdom.* Chicago: University of Chicago Press, 1994.

Hobson, John. 1914. *Work and Wealth.* New York: Macmillan.

Kahneman, Daniel. 1994. "New Challenges to the Rationality Assumption." *Journal of Institutional and Theoretical Economics* 150: 18–36.

Kaplan, Robert. 1998. "Innovation Action Research: Creating New Management Theory and Practice." *Journal of Management Accounting Research* 10: 89–118.

Lane, Robert. 1998. "The Joyless Market Economy." In A. Ben Ner and Louise Putterman, eds., *Economics, Values and Organizations.* Cambridge: Cambridge University Press.

———. 2000. *The Loss of Happiness in Market Democracies.* New Haven, CT: Yale University Press.

Lekachman, Robert. 1959. *A History of Economic Ideas.* New York: Harper and Row.

Levy, Frank. 1999. "Rhetoric and Reality." *Harvard Business Review,* September-October.

Maital, Shlomo. 1982. *Minds, Markets and Money: Psychological Foundations of Economic Behavior.* New York: Basic Books.

———. 1986. "Prometheus Rebound: On Welfare-Improving Constraints." *Eastern Economic Journal* 12, 3: 337–44.

———. 1988. "Novelty, Comfort and Pleasure: Inside the Utility Function Black Box." In P. Albanese, ed., *Psychological Foundations of Economic Behavior.* New York: Praeger.

———. 2000. "The Pursuit of Happiness." *Barron's Financial Weekly,* May 1.

———. 2004. "Daniel Kahneman: On Redefining Rationality." *Journal of Socio-Economics* 32: 1–14.

Maital, Shlomo, and Sharone L. Maital. 1984. "Psychology and Economics." In M. Bornstein, ed., *Psychology and Its Allied Disciplines,* 55–88. Crosscurrents in Contemporary Psychology. Hillsdale, NJ: Lawrence Erlbaum.

Maital, Shlomo, and Cynthia Paolucci. 1990. "Subjective Probability Bias: Methodological Correction and Empirical Results for Risk-Experienced Subjects." In Leonard Green, ed., *Advances in Behavioral Economics,* vol. 2. Norwood, NJ: Ablex Publishing.

Marshall, Alfred. 1936. *Principles of Economics,* 8th ed. Macmillan: London.

Mittone, Luigi. 2003. "Ethical Altruism and Redistribution: An Experimental Approach." Department of Economics, University of Trento, Italy.

Muller, Jerry Z. 1993. *Adam Smith in His Time and Ours.* New York: Free Press.

Myers, David G. 2000. "The Funds, Friends and Faith of Happy People." *American Psychologist* 55, 1: 56–67.

Myers, David G., and Ed Diener. "Who Is Happy?" *Psychological Science* 6, 1: 10–18.

Pigou, A.C. 1920. *The Economics of Welfare*. London: Macmillan.

Putnam Robert. *Bowling Alone: The Collapse and Revival of American Community*. New York: Simon and Schuster, 2001.

Reier, Sharon. 2000. "You're Rich. What Do You Tell the Kids?" *International Herald Tribune,* January 24.

Robbins, Lionel. 1930. *An Essay on the Nature and Significance of Economic Science*. London: St. Martin's Press, 1969.

Scitovsky, Tibor. 1976. *The Joyless Economy*. New York: Oxford University Press.

Seligman, Martin, Christian Petersen, and Steven F. Maier. 1993. *Learned Helplessness*. New York: Oxford University Press.

Smith, Adam. 1759. *Theory of Moral Sentiments*. Oxford: Oxford University Press, 1984.

———. 1776. *The Wealth of Nations*. Amherst, NY: Prometheus Books, 1991.

Standage, Tom. 1999. *The Victorian Internet: The Remarkable Story of the Telegraph and the 19th Century's On-Line Pioneers*. New York: Berkeley Books.

Strauss, William, and Neil Howe. 1991. *Generations: The History of America's Future, 1584 to 2069*. New York: William Morrow.

Survey and Documentation Analysis. 1972–2002. General Social Survey Cumulative File, University of California, Berkeley. Available at http://sda.berkeley.edu.

von Neumann, John, and Oskar Morgenstern. 1944. *Theory of Games and Economic Behavior*. Princeton, NJ: Princeton University Press.

Wade, Robert. 2001. "Winners and Losers." *The Economist,* April 26.

World Bank. 2000. *World Development Report 1999/2000*. Washington, DC: World Bank.

———. 2003. *World Development Indicators*. Washington, DC: World Bank.

CHAPTER 11

BOUNDED RATIONALITY

Two Interpretations from Psychology

JÖRG RIESKAMP, RALPH HERTWIG, AND PETER M. TODD

Perhaps more than anybody else in economic theory, Herbert A. Simon stressed that individual decision makers have no choice but to make decisions under the constraints of limited cognitive resources (e.g., Simon 1978). On the basis of this indisputable truth about the human cognitive system, he challenged classical economic theory, which in his view projected an omniscient rationality assuming unbounded knowledge, computational capacities, and time. He also targeted Milton Friedman's (1953) famous defense of classic economic theory, "The Methodology of Positive Economics." Responding to the criticism that economic theory rests on unrealistic assumptions, Friedman argued:

> Complete "realism" is clearly unattainable, and the question whether a theory is realistic "enough" can be settled only by seeing whether it yields predictions that are good enough for the purpose in hand. (Friedman 1953, 41)

In Friedman's view, the purpose in hand is to account for aggregate behavior, that is, the behavior of firms, institutions, or, more generally, the market. Therefore, unrealistic assumptions and possible discrepancies between the predictions of the theories and individual choice behavior need not be detrimental to the fate of economic theory. Not without some smugness, Simon pointed out that "economists who are zealous in insisting that economic actors maximize [subsequently] turn around and become satisficers"—people satisfied with workable, if not optimal, solutions—"when the evaluation of their own theories is concerned," as in Friedman's good-enough criterion (Simon 1979, 495). Moreover, he argued that psychologically plausible theories of decision making, which assume realistic limits on the knowledge and computational abilities of the human agent, also lead to conclusions at the level of aggregate phenomena. Importantly, these conclusions are not always the same as those suggested by neoclassical theory, thus rendering possible crucial tests (Simon 1979). Simon's vision of a different rationality of economic behavior, *bounded rationality* (Simon 1956, 1990), has not only posed a challenge to economic theory but has also suggested a new research agenda revolving around the following key question: how rational are people, given their limited computational capabilities and their incomplete knowledge?

In psychology, two research programs have worked toward answering this question, and their answers are drastically different. One program is the heuristics and biases program instigated in the early 1970s by Daniel Kahneman and Amos Tversky; the other is the program on fast and frugal heuristics initiated by Gerd Gigerenzer and colleagues (e.g., Gigerenzer and Goldstein 1996; Gigerenzer, Todd, and the ABC Research Group 1999). Economists have typically been exposed to only one of psychology's views on bounded rationality, namely, that of the heuristics and biases program (e.g., Rabin 1998). The goal of this chapter is to introduce economists to the view of bounded rationality as espoused by the fast and frugal heuristics program. Specifically, we describe how differently the two programs have portrayed decision making under the constraints of limited cognitive resources, how differently they have interpreted the role of classic standards of rationality, and how divergent their implications for economic theory are. We first turn to the heuristics and biases program.

BOUNDED RATIONALITY AS IRRATIONALITY

The heuristics and biases program is undoubtedly the most influential psychological research program on human reasoning, judgment, and decision making over the past three decades. One key to this success is a brilliantly straightforward research strategy: first, participants in an experiment are presented with a reasoning problem to which there is, it is assumed, one unambiguous and normatively correct answer in terms of a rule from probability theory and statistics. Next, participants' responses are compared with the solution entailed by those norms, and the more-or-less inevitable (Hertwig and Todd 2000) systematic deviations that are found between the responses and the normative solutions are pronounced "biases," "fallacies," or "cognitive illusions." Finally, these biases are explained as the consequence of the use of some heuristic of reasoning.

Based on this strategy, the heuristics and biases program of Kahneman, Tversky, and others (e.g., Kahneman, Slovic, and Tversky 1982; Tversky and Kahneman 1974; Gilovich, Griffin, and Kahneman 2002) has produced two main results: (1) an extensive catalogue of norm violations such as the base-rate fallacy, the overconfidence bias, and the conjunction fallacy, and (2) explanations of these violations in terms of a small set of cognitive heuristics, of which the three most prominent are the availability, representativeness, and anchoring and adjustment heuristics. For illustration, consider base-rate neglect—from an economic perspective, a very significant error in probabilistic reasoning—and one of its explanations, the representativeness heuristic. When probabilities need to be updated to reflect new information, people are assumed to reason in a Bayesian way so as to maximize their benefit. In other words, people are assumed to be rational Bayesian expected utility maximizers. But are they really? Investigating people's reasoning in simple situations involving a binary predictor and criterion, Kahneman and Tversky concluded: "Man is apparently not a conservative Bayesian: he is not Bayesian at all" (1972, 450). They derived this conclusion from people's responses to reasoning problems such as the engineer-lawyer problem (Kahneman and Tversky 1973, 241). One group of participants read the following information:

> A panel of psychologists have interviewed and administered personality tests to 30 engineers and 70 lawyers, all successful in their respective fields. On the basis of this information, thumbnail descriptions of the 30 engineers and 70 lawyers have been written. You will find on your forms five descriptions, chosen at random from the 100 available descriptions. For each description, please indicate the probability that the person described is an engineer, on a scale from 0 to 100.

A second group received the same instructions, except the base rates were inverted (i.e., 70 engineers and 30 lawyers). All participants received the same personality descriptions, of which one read as follows:

Jack is a 45-year-old man. He is married and has four children. He is generally conservative, careful, and ambitious. He shows no interest in political and social issues and spends most of his free time on his many hobbies, which include home carpentry, sailing, and mathematical puzzles. The probability that Jack is one of the 30 engineers in the sample of 100 is _____%.

Although the likelihoods—p(description|engineer) and p(description|lawyer)—are not specified in this problem, it is still possible to use Bayes's theorem to compute the posterior probabilities by calculating the ratio of the odds in both groups, so that the likelihoods cancel out (see Kahneman and Tversky 1973). Bayes's theorem indicates that the posterior probabilities are different for the problems faced by the two groups of participants. In contrast to this norm, Kahneman and Tversky (1973) observed that the mean responses in the two groups, one receiving the base rate information 30 to 70, the other receiving 70 to 30, were for the most part the same. They concluded that "our subjects . . . failed to integrate prior probability with specific evidence. . . . The failure to appreciate the relevance of the prior probability in the presence of specific evidence is perhaps one of the most significant departures of intuition from the normative theory of prediction" (p. 243).

People's flawed intuition in the engineer-lawyer problem was explained by Kahneman and Tversky in terms of the *representativeness* heuristic. On this explanation, people determine the posterior probability by judging the similarity between the description of, say, Jack and the stereotype of an engineer. In other words, the degree to which the miniature bio is representative of (i.e., similar to) the stereotype shapes the probability assessment. In Kahneman and Tversky's view, reasoning abilities that reflect the laws of probability and logic are not part of the intuitive repertoire of the human mind. Instead, due to our limited cognitive capacities—the property of human information processing that Simon reminded economists about—adults need to rely on quick shortcuts, or heuristics such as representativeness, when we reason about unknown or uncertain aspects of real-world environments. But this use of heuristics leaves human reasoning prone to "severe and systematic errors" (Tversky and Kahneman 1974, 1124).

This portrayal of flawed human decision making under the constraints of limited cognitive capacities has shaped the bleak image that many psychologists have of human reasoning. In a recent critical review of research in the tradition of the heuristics and biases program in social psychology, Krueger and Funder (2004) described how lopsided in their view the social-psychological portrayal of human reasoning has become: human reasoning in the view of many psychologists is "ludicrous," "indefensible," and "self-defeating." This negative view has also extended to the concepts of heuristics and bounded rationality. Kahneman and Tversky's treatment of the terms *heuristics* and *biases* as more or less two sides of the same coin has created a connotation of irrationality that differs sharply from earlier usage of the heuristic concept in psychology and beyond (see Hertwig and Todd 2002). Though in Kahneman and Tversky's articles one finds only scant explicit references to Simon, they see their program as being inspired by his concern, namely, the investigation of "strategies of simplification that reduce the complexity of judgment tasks, to make them tractable for the kind of mind that people happen to have" (Kahneman, Slovic, and Tversky 1982, xii). By identifying this common ground with Simon's concept of bounded rationality, they also suggested a new interpretation of bounded rationality in terms of errors, biases, cognitive illusions, and, ultimately, human irrationality. This interpretation is the one that was adopted by key players in the field of behavioral economics early on and has been explicitly promoted since then. In the words of Richard Thaler:

Research on judgment and decision making under uncertainty, especially by Tversky and Kahneman (1974; Kahneman and Tversky 1996), has shown that such mental illusions should be considered the rule rather than the exception. Systematic, predictable differences between normative models of behavior and actual behavior occur because of what Herbert Simon (1957, p. 198) called "bounded rationality." (Thaler 2000, 270)

Indeed, much of today's behavioral economics and finance draws its inspiration and concepts from the heuristics and biases paradigm (e.g., Thaler 1993; Shiller 2000). There are excellent reasons for this attention, as systematic biases in individual decision making may have important economic implications that cannot or will not be remedied by the market. Camerer (1995, 594), for example, has conjectured that the well-documented high failure rate of small businesses may be due to overconfidence, one of the stock-in-trade examples of a cognitive illusion in the heuristics and biases program. Similarly, Odean and his collaborators have argued that overconfidence based on misinterpretation of random sequences of successes leads some (usually male) investors to trade too much (Barber and Odean 2000, 2001; Odean 1999). Shiller (2000) drew explicitly on the experimental findings of the heuristics and biases program to explain irrational exuberance in the stock market, and Hanson and Kysar (1999a, 1999b) argued that the reality of cognitive illusions has opened the door to systematic manipulation of consumer product markets. In what follows we analyze the notion of rationality endorsed by the heuristics and biases program and argue that the program's exclusive focus on human irrationality hinges critically on a narrow view of norms of sound reasoning.

Rationality Assumptions in the Heuristics and Biases Program

Most researchers of reasoning and decision making today share a vision whose roots trace back to the Enlightenment (see Chase, Hertwig, and Gigerenzer 1998). The original classical view held that the laws of probability and logic stem from, and indeed are equivalent to, the laws of human inference. For French astronomer Pierre Laplace, for example, probability theory embodied human intuition: "The theory of probability is at bottom nothing more than good sense reduced to a calculus" (1814, 196). Nineteenth-century German philosopher Theodor Lipps wrote that logic "is nothing if not the physics of thought" (1880, 530). So fundamental was the belief that the mind worked by the rules of probability and logic that when human intuition was observed to deviate from the current set of rules, the rules themselves were revised (Daston 1988). In short, many pre-twentieth-century thinkers believed that the psychological defines the rational.

Variants of the classical view have flourished in twentieth-century psychology. Many researchers maintain the belief that the laws of probability theory and logic at least approximately describe human inference. In the view of Cameron Peterson and Lee Beach, for example, "probability theory and statistics can be used as the basis for psychological models that integrate and account for human performance in a wide range of inferential tasks" (1967, 29). According to Jean Piaget, cognitive development culminates in a set of logico-mathematical abilities that essentially reflect the laws of probability and logic. More recently, psychologist Lance Rips (1994) has argued for the existence of "mental logic." Unlike their Enlightenment predecessors, however, these modern researchers see classical logical models as norms against which human reasoning can be evaluated rather than as codifications of that reasoning: when the two diverge, it is now concluded that there is something wrong with the reasoning, not with the norms.

The research program that perhaps most strongly emphasizes the divergence between laws of reasoning and laws of probability theory is the heuristics and biases program. The proponents of this program share with proponents of the neo-Enlightenment view, such as Peterson and Beach (1967), the conviction that rationality requires reasoning in accordance with the rules of probability theory. The problem is that people often fail to reason rationally in this way due to their limited resources. Indeed, in this view reasoning is error-prone to the extent that it is powered by quick-and-dirty cognitive heuristics. This premise is markedly different from Simon's view. Simon believed that investigations of bounded rationality would ultimately bring about new norms of rational decision making that, unlike the classical norms, rest on realistic assumptions about the human cognitive machine (Simon 1979, 499).

By pitting human behavior against classic norms of rationality, the heuristics and biases program has made good use of a simple and prolific research strategy. However, the research program relies on the premise that rationality requires reasoning in accordance with the rules of probability theory, statistics, and logic. This means that the broad conclusion that people do not behave rationally hinges on the assumption that these rules are the appropriate norms of rationality in the context of the tasks studied. As we next discuss, this assumption founders on the fact that there is often more than one applicable norm, and moreover, each norm may allow multiple solutions.

The Pretense of Unequivocal Norms

Violations of probability theory as documented by the heuristics and biases program have been called "cognitive illusions" (Tversky and Kahneman 1974). By using the illusion metaphor, an analogy is drawn between inference and perception or, more precisely, between errors in reasoning and errors in visual perception. This analogy is indeed supported by the similar research strategy in both fields: just as vision researchers construct situations in which the functioning of the visual system leads to incorrect inferences about the world (e.g., about line lengths in the Müller-Lyer illusion; see Figure 11.1), researchers in the heuristics and biases program select problems in which reasoning by cognitive heuristics leads to violations of probability theory (Lopes 1991). However, the conclusions the latter researchers draw from such designs often differ sharply from those drawn by researchers of perception. Vision scientists do not conclude from the robustness of the Müller-Lyer illusion, for instance, that people are generally poor at inferring object length. In contrast, many advocates of the heuristics and biases program conclude from the cognitive illusions found in laboratory tasks that human judgment is subject to severe and systematic biases, that these biases are the rule rather than the exception (Thaler 2000), and that they compromise the mind's general functioning (e.g., Piattelli-Palmarini 1994).

These forlorn conclusions are even more surprising given that the benchmarks for determining the accuracy of mental inferences are much more controversial than benchmarks for perceptual inferences. In research on visual illusions, the perceiver's judgment is compared to the physical dimensions of the object. For instance, in the Müller-Lyer illusion one can establish the correct judgment by measuring the lengths of the two horizontal lines. In contrast, in research on cognitive illusions, the reasoner's judgment will be compared to the rules of probability theory such as Bayes's rule. While there is in all likelihood little disagreement over the length of two lines (once they are measured in an agreed-upon way), there is substantive disagreement over how to use a normative inference standard such as Bayes's rule.

For one thing, no single conception of probability is shared by all statisticians and philosophers. Champions of different conceptions disagree on the applicability of the rules of probability theory to unique events, with some contending that they apply to unique events and others arguing that they apply only to classes of events (see Gigerenzer et al. 1989). For someone who interprets probability in the latter, strictly frequentistic sense, these rules are irrelevant to the

Figure 11.1 **Müller-Lyer Illusion**

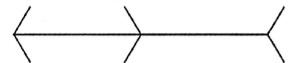

The line between the two arrows on the left is perceived as being shorter than the line between the two arrows at the right, although they are of identical length. Researchers in the heuristics and biases program have often drawn the analogy between illusions in perceptions and biases in reasoning. However, researchers in perception do not interpret the illusion as a demonstration of people's generally poor perception abilities.

many tasks involving unique events studied in the heuristics and biases program (such as the probability that Jack is an engineer). Because of these existing different conceptions of probability, Gigerenzer (1991, 1994) has argued that wherever a norm's applicability depends on the interpretation of probability, it seems unjustified to treat it as an unequivocal norm of sound reasoning (for a recent debate on this point, see Kahneman and Tversky 1996; Gigerenzer 1996; Vranas 2000; Gigerenzer 2001).

This debate is not merely of philosophical relevance. In many experimental tasks people are asked to make probability judgments, and their judgments are compared with solutions derived from probability theory. But different norms also imply different ways of describing decision tasks, and this has implications for how to help people reason more clearly. Specifically, many of the acclaimed reasoning errors can be reduced or even made to disappear when people are given frequency information (e.g., "908 of 1,000") rather than probabilities (e.g., "90.8%") and asked for frequency judgments instead of probability judgments. For example, the prominent "overconfidence bias" refers to the finding that people's average probability judgment is often higher than their percentage of correct answers. Gigerenzer (1994) and Gigerenzer, Hoffrage, and Kleinbölting (1991) showed that the overconfidence bias disappears when participants estimate the number of correct answers instead of the probability that a particular answer is correct (see also Juslin, Olsson, and Winman 1998). Koehler, Gibbs, and Hogarth (1994) reported that the "illusion of control," referring to people's greater confidence in their predictive ability when being personally involved in a judgment (Langer 1975), is reduced when the single-event format is replaced by a frequency format, that is, when participants judge a series of events rather than a single event. Hertwig and Gigerenzer (1999) showed that the "conjunction fallacy," which refers to erroneously judging the conjunction of two statements as more probable compared to one of the statements alone, is markedly reduced and sometimes completely eliminated when information is presented in frequencies instead of single-event probabilities (but see Mellers, Hertwig, and Kahneman 2001).

Finally, Bayesian reasoning, that is, judging conditional probabilities, improves in lay people (Cosmides and Tooby 1996; Gigerenzer and Hoffrage 1995) and experts (Hoffrage and Gigerenzer 1998; Hoffrage et al. 2000; Hertwig and Hoffrage 2002) when Bayesian problems are presented in natural frequencies (i.e., absolute frequencies obtained by natural sampling) rather than in a single-event probability format (see Figure 11.2). Natural frequencies have also proven very effective in training people to make conjoint and conditional probability judgments and Bayesian inferences (Kurzenhäuser and Hoffrage 2002; Sedlmeier and Gigerenzer 2001).

People's apparent violations of norms of rationality have also been reported frequently for their preferences among gambles. However, finding gold standards for evaluating preferences is at least as controversial as finding norms for people's probability judgments. Due to the subjec-

Figure 11.2 **Illustration of a Bayesian Reasoning Problem**

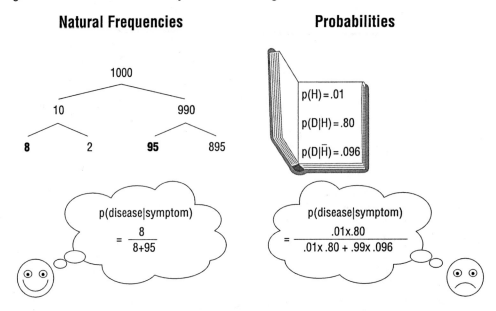

In a Bayesian reasoning problem involving symptoms and disease, conditional probability must be determined in order to assess the likelihood that someone with a particular symptom suffers from a given disease. The problem can be represented in either of two information formats: a single-event probability format or natural frequencies. The latter improves Bayesian reasoning.

tive character of people's preferences, it is common to evaluate those preferences by referring to consistency principles, including transitivity and procedural invariances such as preference reversals. Grether and Plott (1979) showed that when people are presented with two bets, one with a high probability of a low payoff (P-bet) and one with a low probability of a high payoff ($-bet), people prefer the P-bet when choosing between them, but when asked to provide a buying price for the two, they provide a higher price for the $-bet. Thus, the two procedures for eliciting preferences lead to a reversal of those preferences. One reason for these inconsistencies could be that people use different strategies for making choices compared to making price estimates (Billings and Marcus 1983). For instance, when choosing between gambles, strategies that compare the different aspects of the gamble step by step with each other might be applied. In contrast, when making price estimates, strategies might be used that evaluate the gambles independently of each other. These strategies can be rather efficient for making preference decisions, fulfilling a norm of adaptive behavior, but may sometimes violate the norm of preference consistency, again raising the question of which norms should be applied.

The Pretense of Unequivocal Solutions

As pointed out earlier, the research strategy of the heuristics and biases program is ingeniously simple: people are presented with word problems designed such that reasoning according to a normative principle (e.g., from probability theory or statistics) leads to the "correct" response. Reasoning according to other principles (e.g., using the representativeness heuristic) in these problems results in a qualitatively different and thus "incorrect" response. In this research strategy, the content of the word problems (e.g., the engineer-lawyer problem, the Linda problem, the cab problem) is largely irrelevant, because the content-blind normative principles are assumed to apply irrespective of the particular subject matter of the problems. The function of the content is merely decorative, to deliver the values or pieces of information that are to be mechanically plugged into the normative equation. In contrast to this mechanistic use of content-free norms, any realistic psychological modeling of rational judgment requires considering how people decide on which numbers (e.g., prior probabilities, likelihoods) should enter the equations, or on the particular information in a word problem that is relevant for the required judgment.

Take Birnbaum's (1983) thoughtful explication of a rational response to the cab problem, which, like the engineer-lawyer problem, was used to demonstrate that people are not updating probabilities according to Bayes's rule. It features a cab that is involved in a hit-and-run accident at night. The text provides the information that a witness identified the cab as being blue, along with information about the eyewitness's ability to discriminate blue and green cabs, and the base rate of blue and green cabs in the city. Rather than coming up with a normative solution by mechanically plugging these values into Bayes's formula, as is typically done in the heuristics and biases program, Birnbaum started with the content of the problem and made assumptions about various psychological processes witnesses may use. In terms of a signal detection model, for instance, witnesses may try to minimize some error function: if witnesses are concerned about being accused of incorrect testimony, then they may adjust their criterion so as to maximize the probability of a correct identification. If instead witnesses are concerned about being accused of other types of errors, then they can adjust their criterion so as to minimize those specific errors. Obviously, different goals will lead to different posterior probabilities (see Gigerenzer 1998 and Mueser, Cowan, and Mueser 1999 for the detailed arguments).

The lesson from Birnbaum's analysis is that "the normative solution to the cab problem requires the assumption of the theory of the witness, whether by the subject or the experimenter" (1983, 93). More generally, for many word problems there is often not one single "correct" solution (e.g., Hertwig and Gigerenzer 1999; Hertwig and Todd 2000). People make different assumptions about the pragmatically or semantically ambiguous information available in a given setting, and different assumptions may favor different solutions. Thus, depending on the content of problems and how this interacts with psychological processes, multiple "correct" responses may exist. The failure to recognize these interactions can lead reasonable responses to be misclassified as cognitive illusions (Kahneman and Tversky 1996; Gigerenzer 1996; Mellers, Hertwig, and Kahneman 2001).

Beyond the fact that the solution to a reasoning problem requires additional assumptions (e.g., a theory of the witness), there are other problems where we cannot practically determine the solutions. Consider the game of chess. It has long been known that there exists an optimal strategy for the game, but the strategy itself is unknown, and thus not surprisingly, chess masters may not move the pieces in accordance with it. But does that make them irrational? That would be an absurd position—after all, chess masters tend to outperform most other players. The imposition of norms of rationality on decision making is even more difficult outside of the clearly defined context of a board game: life seldom equips us with a strategy space as clearly defined as in chess. Instead we are typically faced with highly uncertain consequences of our decisions, and no possibility of finding an optimal solution. Therefore the only thing that humans can hope to achieve in such situations is to reach a good—not optimal—solution, just as Simon's satisficing approach proposed.

We now turn to the second view of bounded rationality that has emerged from research in psychology: the research program on fast and frugal heuristics initiated by Gigerenzer and colleagues (e.g., Gigerenzer and Goldstein 1996; Gigerenzer, Todd, and the ABC Research Group

1999). Unlike the heuristics and biases program, this view sees heuristics not as a problem but as *the* solution to decision making under conditions of limited time, limited knowledge, and limited computational capacities. The findings from this program suggest that boundedly rational heuristics can yield surprisingly adaptive decisions, choices, and judgments.

BOUNDED RATIONALITY AS ECOLOGICAL RATIONALITY

The research program on fast and frugal heuristics advocates a different interpretation of bounded rationality from that of heuristics and biases research—one that does not uncritically accept the normative standard of logic, statistics, and probability theory. In this view, psychological mechanisms such as heuristics are adapted to particular task environments, and this match between particular environment structures and heuristics can enable the reasoner to behave adaptively, that is, in a computationally fast, information-frugal, and comparatively accurate way in the face of environmental challenges. These real-world requirements fulfilled by the match between environment and cognition lead to a new conception of what proper reasoning is: ecological rationality. In other words, a heuristic is not just rational or irrational. Instead, it can be judged as rational only with respect to the environment in which it is used.

The notion of ecological rationality, that is, the tandem of cognition and environment, is highlighted in Simon's analogy between bounded rationality and a pair of scissors: "Human rational behavior . . . is shaped by a scissors whose two blades are the structure of task environments and the computational capabilities of the actor" (Simon 1990, 7). Just as one cannot understand the function of scissors by looking at a single blade, one cannot understand humans' cognition by studying either the environment or cognition alone.

Rationality Assumptions in the Program on Fast and Frugal Heuristics

The steps in the research rationale of the fast and frugal heuristics program are different from those in the heuristics and biases program. The latter selects a normative rule from probability theory, for instance, and then investigates whether human cognition deviates from it, thus moving from the abstract canon of rationality to the psychological. In contrast, the former program begins by analyzing the structure of a specific task environment people face, and then—based on the analysis—derives attributes of the cognitive models of reasoning that could fare well within the environment. This program thus moves from the environmental structures to the psychological structures, or in terms of Simon's metaphor from the environmental blade to the cognitive blade.

As an illustration, imagine an investment environment in which a resource has to be allocated repeatedly to different financial assets. The assets' returns may depend on the investments in the other assets, for instance, due to economy of scale effects. Thus, searching for the optimal allocation that produces the maximum payoff is not a trivial task. When the search space reflecting the underlying return function has a single peak, simple search strategies such as hill climbing will lead to the optimal allocation. But in an allocation environment with several peaks in the distribution of returns, a more systematic search strategy is required to find the global maximum and avoid local maxima (Rieskamp, Busemeyer, and Laine 2003). The point is that to understand which reasoning processes people might follow, and when and why these processes work well, one needs to explore the characteristics of the environment. This point was made over sixty years ago by Egon Brunswik (1943) and has been made by various psychologists since (e.g., Anderson 1991; Gibson 1979; Shepard 1990).

The cognitive blade of Simon's scissors analogy implies that models of people's reasoning should be psychologically plausible. That is, the cognitive processes proposed need to be realistic insofar as people need to be able to execute them given their computational capabilities. Simon (1956, 1990) repeatedly insisted that the cognitive constraints under which people make judgments and decisions have to be taken into account when modeling human behavior. Due to cognitive limitations, people cannot help but use "approximate methods to handle most tasks" (Simon 1990, 6). The strategy of taking both environmental structures and cognitive constraints into account winnows down the set of possible cognitive models that describe human decision making. Fast and frugal heuristics are suggested as one of the candidates for how humans actually make decisions. In this regard, Gigerenzer and colleagues' (1999) research program does not differ from the heuristics and biases tradition; the differences come in how each construes and assesses the heuristics they propose.

Owing to the focus on the task environment and the match between cognition and environment, the fast and frugal heuristics program does not compare people's judgments to mathematically defined norms of rationality with the explicit purpose of abstracting away from particular content domains and thus holding across a wide range of environments. Instead, it conceptualizes and measures human rationality in terms of performance criteria in the real world. Successful performance includes making accurate decisions in a minimal amount of time and using a minimal amount of information. In other words, this program of heuristics replaces the multiple coherence criteria (i.e., measures that evaluate the logical and mathematical consistency of decisions, stemming from the laws of probability theory and logic) with multiple correspondence criteria (i.e., measures that relate decision-making strategies to the external world and to success therein; Hammond 1996).

In what follows, we first illustrate the building blocks of ecologically rational heuristics and then describe one specific instance, the Take The Best heuristic, and show how it performs successfully while violating commandments that are often taken as characteristic of rational judgments.

Fast and Frugal Heuristics: How They Are Built and How Well They Perform

In stark contrast to the vague specifications of heuristics such as "availability," Gigerenzer and colleagues (1999) define heuristics as precise computational models that specify the steps of information gathering and processing involved in generating a decision. A heuristic consists of a search rule, a stopping rule, and a decision rule. Search rules specify how decision options are generated and how information about available options is gathered. Stopping rules define when the process of searching for options or information is terminated. These stopping principles themselves need to be simple (owing to the computational limitations of the human mind), such as the aspiration levels in Simon's notion of satisficing (Simon 1956, 1990). Finally, decision rules specify how decisions are made based on the information obtained. They, in turn, must also be simple and computationally bounded. For instance, a decision could be made based on only one reason or cue, regardless of the total number of cues retrieved during the information search.

To illustrate the application of a heuristic, consider the inference problem of choosing between two potential oil fields, one of them having a larger quantity of oil (Dieckmann and Rieskamp 2006). For this inference, different tests could be carried out: chemical analysis could determine the content of the organic matter in the bedrock, groundwater could be analyzed, or a seismic analysis could be done. Each test can have either a positive result, indicating a large quantity of oil, or a negative result, indicating a small quantity of oil. Each test has a specific validity, defined as the probability of an oil field with a positive result actually having a larger quantity of oil compared to a second oil field with a negative test result. But how should the test results be used

Figure 11.3 **Flow Diagram of the Take The Best Heuristic**

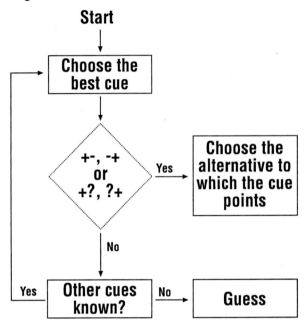

The Take The Best heuristic is used to infer which of two alternatives—each described by several cues—has a higher criterion value. The decision to stop or to continue to search for more cues (center diamond) is made based on the pair of values for the current cue (each of which can be – [negative], + [positive], or ? [unknown]).

to make an inference? Gigerenzer and Goldstein (1996) suggested a simple heuristic called Take The Best for solving the inference problem of choosing between two alternatives, each described by several cues—the one with the higher criterion value (see Figure 11.3). According to its search rule, Take The Best searches sequentially through cues in the order of their validity, defined as the conditional probability of making a correct inference given that the cue discriminates (i.e., one alternative has a positive and the other a negative cue value). According to its stopping rule, search is stopped as soon as one cue is found that discriminates between alternatives. Finally, Take The Best selects the alternative with the positive cue value, ignoring all other cues. (If no cue discriminates, Take The Best makes a random choice.)

At first glance, the Take The Best heuristic appears rather naive when compared with more sophisticated statistical techniques. For one thing, it is reasonable to expect that a heuristic that relies on only a small amount of information will be outperformed by a strategy taking more information into account. For another, many researchers adopt a cost-benefit perspective on strategy evaluation, assuming that a strategy's performance is positively correlated with its complexity. In this view, if an individual is aiming for high accuracy and is willing to invest high cognitive effort, she will select a more complex strategy rather than something as simple as Take The Best (Camerer and Hogarth 1999; Payne, Bettman, and Johnson 1988, 1993; Smith and Walker 1993). However, as we show next, the assumed correlation between a strategy's information use or complexity and its performance may be less pronounced than is often believed.

In many settings, Gigerenzer and colleagues have found that the one-reason decision-making approach of heuristics such as Take The Best performs surprisingly well when compared to more complex strategies that integrate available information. For instance, when the heuristic was applied to all pair comparisons of German cities with a population size of above 100,000 (e.g., is Braunschweig bigger than Bremen?), Take The Best achieved 74 percent correct decisions, thus matching the percentage correct made by a linear regression model that integrated all available information and took the correlations between cues into account (Gigerenzer and Goldstein 1996). Thus, a more complex mechanism did not guarantee better performance. At the same time, Take The Best achieved its good performance checking only a third of the cues that regression used before finding a discriminating cue and stopping its search; thus, the myth that more information is always better also falls (see also Hertwig and Todd 2003). This unexpectedly high performance of Take The Best was demonstrated across numerous environments, including inferring high house prices, car accidents, and automobile fuel consumption (see Czerlinski, Gigerenzer, and Goldstein 1999). For other tasks, such as estimating quantities, other simple heuristics have been proposed, and their good performance has been demonstrated (e.g., Hertwig, Hoffrage, and Martignon 1999).

What is the relationship between such successful heuristics and traditional normative principles of rationality? When considering the inference problem of choosing between two potential oil fields from a normative perspective, one could consider running a regression analysis that combines the three test results in a linear model to make a prediction, or one could consider building a Bayesian model that determines the posterior probability, given the three tests, that one oil field has a larger quantity of oil compared to the second oil field. However, these models do not represent psychological models of people's inferences, and they do not take the computational limits under which people make inferences into account. But what happens when we do apply a psychologically plausible mechanism such as Take The Best to making this inference about the oil fields?

Consider the three oil fields represented in Table 11.1, for which the test results are either positive, negative, or unknown. When comparing oil field A with oil field B, Take The Best first considers the highest-validity chemical analysis test. Since for oil field A the test is negative and for oil field B the test result is unknown, the second most valid test, groundwater analysis, is considered next, and that speaks for oil field A, which is therefore selected. When comparing oil fields B and C, the inference process leads to the selection of oil field B. Finally, when comparing oil fields A and C, Take The Best will lead to the selection of oil field C. Thus, the application of this fast and frugal heuristic leads to intransitive inferences (A > B, B > C, but C > A; see also Gigerenzer and Goldstein 1996). When evaluating it from a normative perspective, one would call the heuristic "irrational," because its inferences lead to violations of transitivity, and transitivity is often regarded as a cornerstone of rationality (Binmore 1994; Luce 2000). However, when considering Take The Best's performance in real-world environments, and thereby evaluating Take The Best by its ecological rationality (as done in the studies reported above), it does not appear less successful than other, more complex models such as linear regression. This does not mean that a heuristic always produces good solutions, and being intransitive can, in the long run, lead to severe losses. However, whether these losses actually occur will depend on the decision situation. For instance, one could build a money pump (see Cubitt and Sugden 2001; Davidson, McKinsey, and Suppes 1955) to exploit a person's intransitive choices. While we do not run into money pumps very often, if we did, we would probably learn to avoid them: experimental results show that building a successful money pump is not easy, because people typically recognize their losses and quickly change their behavior (Chu and Chu 1990). Thus, the argument that someone who makes intransitive choices by using an "irrational" simple heuristic can be exploited by a money pump holds little weight,

Table 11.1

Choosing Between Oil Fields the One with the Larger Quantity of Oil

Cue (validity)	Oil fields		
	A	B	C
Chemical analysis (0.80)	Negative	Unknown	Positive
Groundwater analysis (0.70)	Positive	Negative	Negative
Seismic analysis (0.60)	Positive	Positive	Negative

considering that the person will learn to change his or her behavior upon getting feedback that the intransitive choices led to large losses.

The study of heuristics is not limited to inference problems but has also been extended to preference and choice problems, such as choosing between apartments, cameras, or lottery tickets. Thorngate (1980) examined choices between gambles and demonstrated the good performance of heuristics that (partly) ignore the probability of outcomes. He concluded that "a wide variety of decision heuristics will usually produce optimal, or close to optimal, choices." Furthermore, people "may ignore or misuse probability information because the time or effort required to use it properly may be more costly than any decrease in payoffs associated with their occasional suboptimal choices" (Thorngate 1980, 223–24). In a similar vein, Payne, Bettman, and Johnson (1988, 1993) showed how well heuristics approximate the predictions of the expected value model.

Brandstätter, Gigerenzer, and Hertwig (2006) proposed a sequential heuristic, the "priority heuristic," to model the cognitive processes underlying choices between gambles. The heuristic first compares the gambles' minimum outcomes. If these outcomes differ by a substantial amount (10 percent of the maximum monetary amount offered in the gambles), the gamble with the larger minimum outcome is chosen; otherwise the probabilities of obtaining the minimum outcome are compared. If the probabilities differ by more than 10 percentage points, then the gamble with the lower chance of obtaining the minimum outcome is selected; otherwise the gamble's maximum outcomes are considered and the gamble with the larger maximum outcome is selected. Brandstätter and colleagues showed that the priority heuristic can predict violations of expected utility theory such as the Allais paradox, the certainty effect, and intransitive choices. They also showed that the heuristic predicted people's choices across a set of more than 250 gambles better than did, for instance, cumulative prospect theory.

What Makes Heuristics Work Well?

There are two main reasons why simple heuristics often perform so well in comparison with more complex strategies. First, many problems have "flat maxima," meaning the best solution does not differ substantially from other (e.g., heuristic) solutions. Second, heuristics can outperform other strategies in terms of generalization, that is, when applied to new situations.

Dawes and Corrigan (1974; see also Lovie and Lovie 1986) showed that if one uses a linear model for predicting a criterion, many sets of weights will lead to predictions that are similar to those made by optimal weights. In other words, around the model with maximum performance there are many other solutions with near-maximum performance—an example of the flat maximum phenomena. Likewise, Dawes (1979) showed that simply choosing unit (i.e., equal) weights for a linear model can lead to an accuracy similar to that of "proper linear models," which are models that use weights that optimally predict a criterion, such as a linear regression analysis. Flat maxima will especially occur when predictor variables (cues) are positively correlated with each other, so that different weighting schemes will nonetheless lead to similar predictions. This situation can be exploited by fast and frugal heuristics that base their decisions only on a subset of available information. The most extreme form of this is when a heuristic uses a noncompensatory weighting schema, so that basically only one single cue is employed for making a prediction (Martignon and Hoffrage 2002); even in this case, flat maxima can enable a simple heuristic to perform well.

The second advantage of these heuristics is their ability to generalize well. In many situations, the weights of "proper linear models" (or parameters of other models) are estimated on the basis of a sample. For instance, a policy to diagnose patients' diseases based on a number of symptoms could be developed by using a sample of past patients' records. But the sample might not accurately represent the population of future patients. In principle, the data of a sample can be thought of as consisting of two components: *structure* and *noise*. Although the structure is of primary interest, a relatively complex model will also increase its fit by adapting to (and trying to predict) the sample's noise. This leads to "overfitting," namely the problem that a model fits the data well but does poorly at predicting new data (see Browne 2000). When a complex model increases its sample accuracy by fitting noise, its performance will be relatively poor when applied to new independent data. In contrast, a relatively parsimonious, less flexible model—such as a simple heuristic—might perform worse when fitting the data but will often outperform the more general model when making predictions for a new sample. Thus, contrary to the cost-benefit perspective of strategy evaluation described above, the greater the complexity of a strategy, the greater the risk that it might perform poorly when applied to a new problem.

In sum, the decision maker can gain important advantages by selecting a simple heuristic for solving a new problem. First, a heuristic requires only a small amount of information, which is processed easily. Second, due to the flat maximum phenomenon and heuristics' robustness, heuristics can perform as well as, or even better than, more complex strategies, undermining the complexity–accuracy relationship that is usually assumed. Hence the belief that basing a decision on more information and computation will always lead to more accurate decisions—a belief that has dominated much research, including that in the heuristics and biases tradition (Gigerenzer and Murray 1987)—is a fiction.

Do People Use Simple Heuristics?

Empirical evidence for the use of simple heuristics such as lexicographic strategies (i.e., strategies that—like Take The Best—consider cues sequentially and where more important cues dominate less important cues) has been reported in several recent studies (e.g., Bröder 2000, 2003; Brandstätter, Gigerenzer, and Hertwig 2006; Bröder and Schiffer 2003; Newell and Shanks 2003; Newell, Weston, and Shanks 2003). Rieskamp and Hoffrage (1999, 2005) showed that under great time pressure, a lexicographic heuristic reached the highest fit in predicting participants' inferences. In a similar vein, Bröder (2000) showed that Take The Best predicted participants' inferences best in the presence of relatively high explicit information acquisition costs. Take The Best also predicted individuals' inferences well when the cue information had to be retrieved from memory (Bröder and Schiffer 2003). The use of simple heuristics also depends on the overall payoffs the heuristics produce, such that Take The Best is selected more frequently when it produces the highest payoff compared to other strategies (Bröder 2003). Newell and Shanks (2003) and Newell, Weston, and Shanks (2003) showed that the way people search for cues follows the search predicted by Take The Best under high information acquisition costs. Besides this recent work on inferential choice, there is a large body of research examining strategy selection for preferential choice, led by the contributions of Payne, Bettman, and Johnson (1988, 1993).

Can people learn to select strategies based on their fit to the structure of the current task environment? Rieskamp and Otto (2006) addressed the question of whether pure outcome feedback is sufficient for an adaptive selection of strategies. In their experiments, participants repeatedly had to choose the more creditworthy company from a pair on the basis of six cues. Participants received feedback on the correctness of their inferences. For one group of participants, an environment was presented in which a lexicographic heuristic reached the highest accuracy, whereas in another environment condition a strategy that integrates all available information reached the highest accuracy. The crucial question was whether participants would be able to intuitively adapt the selection of strategies to the feedback from the environments. This was the case: after some learning, the strategy that best predicted participant's choices in the particular condition was also the strategy that performed best in each environment. This result, along with those cited earlier, indicates that people not only use simple heuristics but also use them in the appropriate circumstances.

CONCLUSION

This chapter has given an overview of the two main views of bounded rationality from psychology. These two views relate very differently to the classical view of rationality typically found in economics, which defines rational behavior according to adherence to a strict set of normative mathematical principles. The first view of bounded rationality—expressed in the heuristics and biases program—accepts the normative standards of classical rationality. However, it argues that people systematically deviate from the norms and therefore do not behave rationally. The second view of bounded rationality—expressed in the fast and frugal heuristics program—does not take these normative standards at face value. Instead, it argues that unequivocal norms often do not exist, and that humans under the constraints of limited computational capacity and information can only strive to reach environmentally adaptive decisions.

One important contribution of the heuristics and biases program consists in challenging the view in economics that people follow the classical norms of rational behavior. However, since the program accepts the normative standards of rationality, violations are interpreted as "biases" or "fallacies," leading to a rather negative view of people's judgment and decision-making capacities. The implication is that to "help" people to overcome their "biases," they must be taught to follow the norms. The question is how helpful this will be. When people apply strategies that are well adapted to an environment, they might violate certain norms of rationality. If taught to obey the norms, they will need to give up the strategies that in general perform quite well in solving a task.

The program on fast and frugal heuristics leads to a rather different view of bounded rationality. The simple heuristics people use are adapted to particular task environments and perform well in solving decision problems in those specific environments, but they do not necessarily obey classical norms of rationality. While the application of a simple heuristic might often also lead to behavior that is consistent with the predictions from standard economic theory, this research approach offers a significant advantage over the "as if" optimizing approach typically adopted in mainstream economics. Because these heuristics are formulated and studied as precise cognitive mechanisms, they do not only provide deeper insight into how people make their decisions, but also allow better predictions of the conditions in which deviations from standard economic models will occur. In this way, the program on fast and frugal heuristics allows economic theory to be bound more closely to the reality of humans' thought.

REFERENCES

Anderson, J.R. 1991. "Is Human Cognition Adaptive?" *Behavioral and Brain Sciences* 14: 471–517.

Barber, B.M., and T. Odean. 2000. "Trading Is Hazardous to Your Wealth: The Common Stock Investment Performance of Individual Investors." *Journal of Finance* 55: 773–806.

———. 2001. "Boys Will Be Boys: Gender, Overconfidence, and Common Stock Investment." *Quarterly Journal of Economics* 116: 261–92.

Billings, R.S., and S.A. Marcus. 1983. "Measures of Compensatory and Non-compensatory Models of Decision Behavior: Process Tracing Versus Policy Capturing." *Organizational Behavior and Human Performance* 31: 331–52.

Binmore, K. 1994. *Game Theory and the Social Contract.* Vol. 1, *Playing Fair.* Cambridge, MA: MIT Press.

Birnbaum, M.H. 1983. "Base Rates in Bayesian Inference: Signal Detection Analysis of the Cab Problem." *American Journal of Psychology* 96: 85–94.

Brandstätter, E., G. Gigerenzer, and R. Hertwig. 2006. "The Priority Heuristic: Making Choices Without Trade-Offs." *Psychological Review* 113.

Bröder, A. 2000. "Assessing the Empirical Validity of the "Take-the-Best" Heuristic as a Model of Human Probabilistic Inference." *Journal of Experimental Psychology: Learning, Memory, and Cognition* 26: 1332–46.

———. 2003. "Decision Making with the 'Adaptive Toolbox': Influence of Environmental Structure, Intelligence, and Working Memory Load." *Journal of Experimental Psychology: Learning, Memory, and Cognition,* 29: 611–25.

Bröder, A., and S. Schiffer. 2003. "Take the Best Versus Simultaneous Feature Matching: Probabilistic Inferences from Memory and Effects of Representation Format." *Journal of Experimental Psychology: General* 132: 277–93.

Browne, M.W. 2000. "Cross-Validation Methods." *Journal of Mathematical Psychology* 44: 108–32.

Brunswik, E. 1943. "Organismic Achievement and Environmental Probability." *Psychological Review* 50: 255–72.

Camerer, C. 1995. "Individual Decision Making." In J.H. Kagel and A.E. Roth, eds., *The Handbook of Experimental Economics,* 587–703. Princeton, NJ: Princeton University Press.

Camerer, C.F., and R.M. Hogarth. 1999. "The Effects of Financial Incentives in Experiments: A Review and Capital-Labor-Production Framework." *Journal of Risk and Uncertainty* 19: 7–42.

Chase, V.M., R. Hertwig, and G. Gigerenzer. 1998. "Visions of Rationality." *Trends in Cognitive Sciences* 2: 206–14.

Chu, Y.-P., and R.-L. Chu. 1990. "The Subsidence of Preference Reversals in Simplified and Marketlike Experimental Settings: A Note." *American Economic Review* 80: 902–11.

Cosmides, L., and J. Tooby, 1996. "Are Humans Good Intuitive Statisticians After All? Rethinking Some Conclusions from the Literature on Judgment Under Uncertainty." *Cognition* 58: 1–73.

Cubitt, R.P., and R. Sugden. 2001. "On Money Pumps." *Games and Economic Behavior* 37: 121–60.

Czerlinski, J., G. Gigerenzer, and D.G. Goldstein. 1999. "How Good Are Simple Heuristics?" In G. Gigerenzer, P.M. Todd, and the ABC Research Group, *Simple Heuristics That Make Us Smart,* 97–118. New York: Oxford University Press.

Daston, L. 1988. *Classical Probability in the Enlightenment.* Princeton, NJ: Princeton University Press.

Davidson, D., J. McKinsey, and P. Suppes. 1955. "Outlines of a Formal Theory of Value." *Philosophy of Science* 22: 140–60.

Dawes, R.M. 1979. "The Robust Beauty of Improper Linear Models in Decision Making." *American Psychologist* 34: 571–82.

Dawes, R.M., and B. Corrigan. 1974. "Linear Models in Decision Making." *Psychological Bulletin* 81: 95–106.

Dieckmann, A., and J. Rieskamp. 2006. "Information Redundancy Influencing Probabilistic Inferences." Manuscript submitted for publication.

Friedman, M. 1953. *Essays in Positive Economics.* Chicago: University of Chicago.

Gibson, J.J. 1979. *The Ecological Approach to Visual Perception.* Boston: Houghton Mifflin.

Gigerenzer, G. 1991. "How to Make Cognitive Illusions Disappear: Beyond 'Heuristics and Biases.'" In W.S.M. Hewstone, ed., *European Review of Social Psychology* 2: 83–115. New York: Wiley.

———. 1994. "Why the Distinction Between Single-Event Probabilities and Frequencies Is Important for Psychology (and Vice Versa)." In G. Wright and P. Ayton, eds., *Subjective Probability,* 129–61. New York: Wiley.

———. 1996. "On Narrow Norms and Vague Heuristics: A Reply to Kahneman and Tversky." *Psychological Review* 103: 592–96.

———. 1998. "Ecological Intelligence: An Adaptation for Frequencies." In D.D. Cummins and C. Allen, eds., *The Evolution of Mind*, 9–29. New York: Oxford University Press.

———. 2001. "Content-Blind Norms, No Norms, or Good Norms? A Reply to Vranas." *Cognition* 81: 93–103.

Gigerenzer, G., and D.G. Goldstein. 1996. "Reasoning the Fast and Frugal Way: Models of Bounded Rationality." *Psychological Review* 103: 650–69.

Gigerenzer, G., and U. Hoffrage. 1995. "How to Improve Bayesian Reasoning Without Instruction: Frequency Formats." *Psychological Review* 102: 684–704.

Gigerenzer, G., U. Hoffrage, and H. Kleinbölting. 1991. "Probabilistic Mental Models: A Brunswikian Theory of Confidence." *Psychological Review* 98: 506–28.

Gigerenzer, G., and D.J. Murray. 1987. "Thinking: From Insight to Intuitive Statistics." In G. Gigerenzer and D.J. Murray, eds., *Cognition as Intuitive Statistics*, 137–81. Hillsdale, NJ: Erlbaum.

Gigerenzer, G., Z.G. Swijtink, T.M. Porter, L. Daston, J. Beatty, and L. Krueger. 1989. *The Empire of Chance: How Probability Changed Science and Everyday Life*. Cambridge, MA: MIT Press.

Gigerenzer, G., P.M. Todd, and the ABC Research Group. 1999. *Simple Heuristics That Make Us Smart*. New York: Oxford University Press.

Gilovich, T., D. Griffin, and D. Kahneman, eds. 2002. *Heuristics and Biases: The Psychology of Intuitive Judgment*. New York: Cambridge University Press.

Grether, D.M., and C.R. Plott. 1979. "Economic Theory of Choice and the Preference Reversal Phenomenon." *American Economic Review* 69: 623–38.

Hammond, K.R. 1996. "Upon Reflection." *Thinking and Reasoning* 2: 239–49.

Hanson, J.D., and D.A. Kysar. 1999a. "Taking Behavioralism Seriously: The Problem of Market Manipulation." *New York University Law Review* 74: 630–749.

———. 1999b. "Taking Behavioralism Seriously: Some Evidence of Market Manipulation." *Harvard Law Review* 112: 1420–572.

Hertwig, R., and G. Gigerenzer. 1999. "The 'Conjunction Fallacy' Revisited: How Intelligent Inferences Look Like Reasoning Errors." *Journal of Behavioral Decision Making* 12: 275–305.

Hertwig, R., and U. Hoffrage. 2002. "Technology Needs Psychology: How Natural Frequencies Foster Insight in Medical and Legal Experts." In P. Sedlmeier and T. Betsch, eds., *Etc. Frequency Processing and Cognition*, 285–302. New York: Oxford University Press.

Hertwig, R., U. Hoffrage, and L. Martignon. 1999. "Quick Estimation: Letting the Environment do the Work." In G. Gigerenzer, P.M. Todd, and the ABC Research Group, *Simple Heuristics That Make Us Smart*, 209–34. New York: Oxford University Press.

Hertwig, R., and P.M. Todd. 2000. "Biases to the Left, Fallacies to the Right: Stuck in the Middle with Null Hypothesis Significance Testing. Commentary on Krueger on Social Bias." *Psycoloquy* 11(028). http://www.cogsci.ecs.soton.ac.uk/cgi/psyc/newpsy?11.028.

———. 2002. "Heuristics." In V.S. Ramachandran, ed., *Encyclopedia of the Human Brain*, 2:449–60. New York: Academic Press.

———. 2003. "More Is Not Always Better: The Benefits of Cognitive Limits." In D. Hardman and L. Macchi, eds., *Thinking: Psychological Perspectives on Reasoning, Judgment and Decision Making*, 213–31. Chichester, UK: Wiley.

Hoffrage, U., and G. Gigerenzer. 1998. "Using Natural Frequencies to Improve Diagnostic Inferences." *Academic Medicine* 73: 538–40.

Hoffrage, U., S. Lindsey, R. Hertwig, and G. Gigerenzer. 2000. "Communicating Statistical Information." *Science* 290: 2261–62.

Juslin, P., H. Olsson, and A. Winman. 1998. "The Calibration Issue: Theoretical Comments on Suantak, Bolger, and Ferrell (1996)." *Organizational Behavior and Human Decision Processes* 73: 3–26.

Kahneman, D., P. Slovic, and A. Tversky, eds. 1982. *Judgment Under Uncertainty: Heuristics and Biases*. Cambridge: Cambridge University Press.

Kahneman, D., and A. Tversky. 1972. "Subjective Probability: A Judgment of Representativeness." *Cognitive Psychology* 3: 430–54.

———. 1973. "On the Psychology of Prediction." *Psychological Review* 80: 237–51.

———. 1996. "On the Reality of Cognitive Illusions." *Psychological Review* 103: 582–91.

Koehler, J.J., B.J. Gibbs, and R.M. Hogarth. 1994. "Shattering the Illusion of Control: Multi-Shot Versus Single-Shot Gambles." *Journal of Behavioral Decision Making* 7: 183–91.

Krueger, J.I., and I. Funder. 2004. "Towards a Balanced Social Psychology: Causes, Consequences and Cures for the Problem-Seeking Approach to Social Behavior and Cognition." *Behavioral and Brain Sciences* 27: 313–27.

Kurzenhäuser, S., and U. Hoffrage. 2002. "Teaching Bayesian Reasoning: An Evaluation of a Classroom Tutorial for Medical Students." *Medical Teacher* 24: 516–21.

Langer, E. 1975. "The Illusion of Control." *Journal of Personality and Social Psychology* 32: 311–28.

Laplace, P.S. 1814. *A Philosophical Essay on Probabilities.* New York: Dover, 1951.

Lipps, T. 1880. "Die Aufgabe der Erkenntnistheorie und die Wundt'sche Logik I." *Philosophische Monatshefte* 16: 529–39.

Lopes, L.A. 1991. "The Rhetoric of Irrationality." *Theory and Psychology* 1: 65–82.

Lovie, A.D., and P. Lovie. 1986. "The Flat Maximum Effect and Linear Scoring Models for Prediction." *Journal of Forecasting* 5: 159–68.

Luce, R.D. 2000. *Utility of Gains and Losses.* Mahwah, NJ: Erlbaum.

Martignon, L., and U. Hoffrage. 2002. "Fast, Frugal, and Fit: Simple Heuristics for Paired Comparison." *Theory and Decision* 52: 29–71.

Mellers, B., R. Hertwig, and D. Kahneman. 2001. "Do Frequency Representations Eliminate Conjunction Effects? An Exercise in Adversarial Collaboration." *Psychological Science* 12: 269–75.

Mueser, P.R., N. Cowan, and K.T. Mueser. 1999. "A Generalized Signal Detection Model to Predict Rational Variation in Base Rate Use." *Cognition* 69: 267–312.

Newell, B.R., and D.R. Shanks. 2003. "Take the Best or Look at the Rest? Factors Influencing 'One-Reason' Decision Making." *Journal of Experimental Psychology: Learning, Memory, and Cognition* 29: 53–65.

Newell, B.R., N. Weston, and D.R. Shanks. 2003. "Empirical Tests of a Fast and Frugal Heuristic: Not Everyone "Takes-the-Best." *Organizational Behavior and Human Decision Processes* 91: 82–96.

Odean, T. 1999. "Do Investors Trade Too Much?" *American Economic Review* 89: 1279–98.

Payne, J.W., J.R. Bettman, and E.J. Johnson. 1988. "Adaptive Strategy Selection in Decision Making." *Journal of Experimental Psychology: Learning, Memory, and Cognition* 14: 534–52.

———. 1993. *The Adaptive Decision Maker.* New York: Cambridge University Press.

Peterson, C.R., and L.R. Beach. 1967. "Man as an Intuitive Statistician." *Psychological Bulletin* 68: 29–46.

Piattelli-Palmarini, M. 1994. *Inevitable Illusions: How Mistakes of Reason Rule Our Minds.* New York: Wiley.

Rabin, M. 1998. "Psychology and Economics." *Journal of Economic Literature* 36: 11–46.

Rieskamp, J., J.R. Busemeyer, and T. Laine. 2003. "How Do People Learn to Allocate Resources? Comparing Two Learning Theories." *Journal of Experimental Psychology: Learning, Memory, and Cognition* 29: 1066–81.

Rieskamp, J., and U. Hoffrage. 1999. "When Do People Use Simple Heuristics, and How Can We Tell?" In G. Gigerenzer, P.M. Todd, and the ABC Research Group, *Simple Heuristics That Make Us Smart,* 141–67. New York: Oxford University Press.

———. 2006. "The Use of Simple Heuristics: Inferences and Preferences Under Time Pressure." *Journal of Experimental Psychology: General* 135.

Rieskamp, J., and P.E. Otto. 2006. "SSL: A Theory of How People Learn to Select Strategies." Manuscript submitted for publication.

Rips, L. 1994. *The Psychology of Proof: Deductive Reasoning in Human Thinking.* Cambridge, MA: MIT Press.

Sedlmeier, P., and G. Gigerenzer. 2001. "Teaching Bayesian Reasoning in Less than Two Hours." *Journal of Experimental Psychology: General* 130: 380–400.

Shepard, R.N. 1990. *Mind Sights: Original Visual Illusions, Ambiguities, and Other Anomalies, with a Commentary on the Play of Mind in Perception and Art.* New York: W.H. Freeman.

Shiller, R.J. 2000. "Measuring Bubble Expectations and Investor Confidence." *Journal of Psychology and Financial Markets* 1: 49–60.

Simon, H.A. 1956. "Rational Choice and the Structure of the Environment." *Psychological Review* 63: 129–38.

———. 1957. "A Behavioral Model of Rational Choice." In H.A. Simon, ed., *Models of Man: Social and Rational,* 241–60. New York: Wiley.

———. 1978. "Rationality as Process and as Product of Thought." *American Economic Review* 68: 1–16.

———. 1979. "Rational Decision Making in Business Organizations." *American Economic Review* 69: 493–513.

———. 1990. "Invariants of Human Behavior." *Annual Review of Psychology* 41: 1–19.

Smith, V.L., and J.M. Walker. 1993. "Monetary Rewards and Decision Cost in Experimental Economics." *Economic Inquiry* 31: 245–61.

Thaler, R.H., ed. 1993. *Advances in Behavioral Finance.* New York: Russell Sage Foundation.

———, 2000. "Toward a Positive Theory of Consumer Choice." In D. Kahneman and A. Tversky, eds., *Choices, Values, and Frames,* 269–87. New York: Cambridge University Press.

Thorngate, W. 1980. "Efficient Decision Heuristics." *Behavioral Science* 25: 219–25.

Tversky, A., and D. Kahneman. 1974. "Judgment Under Uncertainty: Heuristics and Biases." *Science* 185: 1124–31.

Vranas, P.B.M. 2000. "Gigerenzer's Normative Critique of Kahneman and Tversky." *Cognition* 76: 179–93.

CHAPTER 12

BEHAVIORAL VERSUS NEOCLASSICAL ECONOMICS

Paradigm Shift or Generalization?

KEVIN SONTHEIMER

> In the 1940s and 1950s I undertook to apply to questions in economics the
> concept of bounded rationality and the related concept of satisficing. . . . These
> proposals were received by most mainline economists with something less than
> unbounded enthusiasm. In fact, they were largely ignored as irrelevant for economics
> (and as probably wrong) for many years. . . . Classical and behavioral economics have
> stood apart, eyeing each other nervously and suspiciously. They have put off the
> synthesis that we shall need to fully grasp the economic world around us.
> —*Simon 1997, 269, 275–76*

This essay explores the tension that exists between behavioral microeconomics and microeconomic theory as developed within the neoclassical framework. The tension between the two streams of work is sometimes seen from the behavioralist side as due to a paradigm shift and from the neoclassical side as the result of unsophisticated theorizing and anomalous empirical findings by behavioralists. It is argued here that neither side correctly views the other. Behavioral microeconomics does not constitute a paradigm shift, at least not yet; it is not a result of unsophisticated analysis; nor does it provide only anomalous data. The developing field of behavioral microeconomics is in fact a generalization of the neoclassical framework—alternatively, neoclassically based microeconomics is a special case of behavioral microeconomics.

Features that distinguish behavioral economics from neoclassical economics as it is practiced are (1) the unabashed dominating commitment of the behavioral economists to empirical research, (2) an insistence on maintaining an intimate linkage between empirical facts and economic theory, and (3) a focus on procedural rationality rather than substantive rationality. Neoclassical economists, on the other hand, have followed a path of development that has allowed for both empirical research and for theoretical modeling but has been tolerant of theorizing that sometimes has had weak links to empirical reality. Also, the focus of neoclassical economics has been on substantive rationality, not procedural rationality.

A standing assumption in the body of research of both behavioral microeconomics and neoclassical economics is that individual human economic behavior is purposeful behavior. That is, individual human economic behavior is goal- or objective-oriented, and reason is used in pursuit of the goal or objective.[1] But purposeful behavior is not necessarily optimizing or maximizing behavior. It also is not necessarily rational behavior in the sense of being consistent behavior. For example, purposeful but nonoptimizing behavior is the benchmark for models of bounded rationality, and a lack of rationality as consistency in individual decision making is central in the investigations into the phenomenon of preference reversals, where the purposefulness of the individual research subjects is not called into question. Similarly, behavioral economics does not necessarily characterize organizations, such as firms, as optimizing or maximizing decision centers. In particular, it does not restrict its perception of firms to the narrow category of profit-maximizing organizations. But neoclassical economics does, for the most part, view consumers as preference- or utility-maximizing agents and firms as profit-maximizing organizations. Also, the neoclassical view of behavior is typically even more restricted in that individual agents are taken as employing selfish preferences or utility functions in their maximization decisions. Thus the scope of purposeful behavior is much narrower or more restricted in the neoclassical research stream than it is in the behavioral economic research stream.

The two streams of thought have coexisted uneasily because applied microeconomic researchers of both dispositions could view circumstantial or field data to be consistent with their respective views. Since field data are not gathered under controlled conditions, both sides could discern situations (data sets) that seemed to be consistent with their perspective. The ambiguity of field data gathered at different times and under different conditions makes it difficult to conclusively reject the proposition that people optimize, or to prove decisively that they engage in nonoptimizing behavior. Thus a stand-off developed between adherents of the alternative perspectives. But with the advent of controlled human-subject experiments, first in psychology and then in economics, the weight of the evidence is tipping in favor of the behavioral perspective, and the uneasy coexistence might be coming to an end.

The new evidence, by itself, could support a blunt "we won and you lost" attitude and a disregard of the body of results built within the neoclassical framework.[2] But one theme of this essay is that a different ending to the uneasy coexistence is appropriate. It is argued here that a graceful integration of the two schools of thought ought to take place. The reason for an optimistic view of reconciliation and integration is not because the weight of evidence is in favor of the behaviorist perspective, but because the neoclassical perspective is a special case of the behavioral perspective. Thus behavioralists should use the special case as a benchmark and test as they pursue further theoretical developments along with more empirical evidence, and neoclassicists should take greater cognizance of additional constraints on individual and organizational behavior and types of economic problems than has been the case. Neoclassicists can be proud of their heritage while they become behavioralists (and they are), and behavioralists can respect and at times use the best of the results of neoclassical thought.

BEHAVIORALISM VERSUS NEOCLASSICISM

With regard to information and information processing, neoclassical theory employs a framework that incorporates both full information and unlimited information-processing capacity. Neoclassical consumers and firms are assumed to have all the information relevant to their decisions and all the processing capacity required to achieve their maximization goals. On the other hand, behavioral economic research sees limited information to be a common problem confronting human agents. It also recognizes that economic agents typically have limited capabilities to process information. Consequently, behavioral economics recognizes that even if the purposeful goal of agents was to maximize some interest, such as utility or profits, either limitations on information, limitations on processing capacity, or both could obstruct maximization. So information and information-processing limits can induce or cause nonmaximizing behavior within the behavioral framework.

The two streams of research and theory sometimes also differ with regard to the structural complexity of decision problems. Neoclassical economics is concerned with decision problems that are structurally simple, and behavioral economics is concerned with decision problems that are often but not always structurally complex. A structurally simple decision problem is one wherein the individual decision maker's choice is restricted by fixed environmental parameters that are not consciously determined by any other particular individual or group of individuals and the decision maker can make any choice consistent with the parametric restrictions. For example, cases in which consumers are price takers, or the firm is a price taker, or a monopolist confronts a given and fully known demand curve are structurally simple problems. Anything else is a structurally complex problem—for example, problems of strategic interaction between two or more firms, between consumers with a measure of monopsony power and firms with a measure of monopoly power, between agents for owners and agents for employees, and so on.

One reason that structural complexity is of interest is that it bears on information issues from the opposite side than information limits or processing limits. Structurally simple problems might be solvable in an optimizing sense even though there are limits on information and/or processing capabilities. If the latter restrictions are not binding, they are not relevant. But solving a problem might require large amounts of data and large processing capacity, which might make information availability and processing capacities limits relevant. Structural complexity drives the demand for information and processing capacity, whereas cognitive endowments can limit processing capacity (supply) and data-gathering costs can limit information availability (supply).

For example, structural complexity can reflect interests or motivations of decision makers that go beyond their narrow and selfish interests with respect to income, profit, or commodity consumption. The decision makers' interests or motivations induce altruistic or punishing behavior toward others, and the information or information-processing capacity required for optimally calculated behavior can be excessively large relative to the information or processing capacity available.

Time limits can also play a role in inducing nonoptimizing behavior. Whether a given information-processing capacity is binding can depend on the time allowed for decision making. If a decision must be made or is otherwise desired, the context or environment in which the decision problem is set involves a time limit, and the information-processing capacity is not sufficient relative to the time limit for an optimizing decision, then an alternative resolution of the decision problem must be resorted to. That is, if information processing takes time, then whether a given information-processing capacity constraint will be binding will depend on the time allowed. So time constraints also are relevant to inducing nonoptimizing behavior.

Part of the view offered here is that which underlies the concept of bounded rationality and Simon's theory of satisficing behavior: that human decision making will deviate from optimizing decisions because of limitations of information, limits on analytical processing capacity, time limits, or all three. But this also means that human decision making in situations that are simple enough (i.e., do not have burdensome time and information and/or processing capacity requirements) will be optimizing decisions. A given decision maker can be an optimizer in one situation and a nonoptimizer (behavioralist) in another situation. Whether a purposeful decision will be an optimizing one or deviate from optimal behavior depends on whether or not there are burdensome information requirements, burdensome processing capacity requirements, or binding time, effort, or other cost limits.

Simon's basic view was that individuals often do not optimize because they can't. The implication of his view is that if there are no problematic limitations, then individuals will optimize. Stating the reasoning more broadly, if individuals do not optimize because of constraints, then when the constraints are not binding they will optimize. That there is this flip side to Simon's basic view should not be a matter of controversy, and the flip side exposes the generalization-specialization link between behavioral and neoclassical microeconomics.

Fundamentally, the tension that exists between the two streams of work stems from the limited empirical detail and specification employed within the neoclassical framework. The neoclassical framework has been centered on a description of reality that is structurally simple and does not account for many limitations that human beings often have to deal with. The neoclassical framework lacks much empirical detail, some of which can be safely ignored, but some of which is important in many circumstances; neglecting it limits the reach of neoclassical theory.

Despite the simplifications of the neoclassical framework, the findings generated within the neoclassical framework have not been without useful and fruitful applications. For example, the law of demand, the law of supply, neoclassical models of international trade, competitive industry equilibrium, the comparative statics of competitive industry equilibrium, and general competitive equilibrium theory have proven to be useful for some policy purposes. Decision theory in general is an outgrowth of neoclassical theory and perhaps is its greatest product.[3] The role of the economist as a business or market engineer, as in the development of optimal portfolio theory and the subsequent designing of security trading programs, is based on applying principles of neoclassical microeconomic theory. Yet another example is the neoclassically based public choice theory, which has shed beneficial light on political behavior and other public sector phenomena. So it is important that the baby not be thrown out with the bathwater. Indeed, it would not be consistent with the goal of behavioral economics to disregard tools widely used in policy analyses even though the tools might not fully describe reality. Using competitive market models in many policy applications is itself an example of bounded rationality.

THE CONNECTION

One way in which people are purposeful is that they typically do not make random or arbitrary decisions.[4] Individuals typically do not choose using probabilistic or random devices. Decision environments are often marked by risk or uncertainty, but people's decision processes are not typically probabilistic or random. For example, individual human decision making is not characterized by a random walk. This assessment is implicit in the agreement mentioned by Simon (see note 1).

It should not be controversial to assert that in simple nonstrategic binary decision problems, individuals will choose the most preferred alternative (alternatively, they will maximize their utility). For example, imagine a teenager and mother driving through the middle of the Arizona desert on a hot day. Desiring some ice cream, they stop at a remote gas station staffed by complete strangers. It is highly unlikely that they would have difficulty choosing for themselves from an option set restricted to vanilla or chocolate ice cream. It is further difficult to imagine that their choices would not be their preferred option (at that time and place and for the other given circumstances) for each of them. Both behavioral economists and neoclassical economists, if they knew the preferences of the mother and teenager, would not hesitate to predict choices consistent with the selfish preferences and maximizing behavior. The recognition of the empirical validity of decision making characterized by selfish preference maximizing is not foreign to either behavioral economic or neoclassical research under some (simple) circumstances.

Now consider a simple and familiar problem. The problem is to maximize a nonnegative valued function $f(x, y)$ that is defined over the nonnegative quadrant and strictly concave, and subject to a constraint $g(x, y) = 0$ defined for the same values of x and y. For example, let $f(x, y)$ be a utility function and let $g(x, y) = p_x x + p_y y$ where p_x and p_y are nonnegative parameters (prices). It is clear in this familiar problem that the unconstrained maximization problem is a special case of the constrained maximization problem. That is, if p_x and p_y take on the special values $p_x = 0$ and $p_y = 0$, the constraint is not binding, and the constrained maximization problem becomes an unconstrained problem. This result is valid even if the unconstrained problem does not have a maximum.

Additional constraints do not change the nested nature of the problem structure. For example, let utility be a function not just of the quantities of N commodities, but also of leisure time and the effort allocated to leisure, where utility is increasing with respect to both the time and effort devoted to leisure. In addition, recognizing that acquiring goods requires time and effort, there are constraints that relate quantities of the goods acquired to the time and effort devoted to doing so. The problem is formulated as follows:

$$\max\ U(x_1, \ldots, x_N, L, e_L)$$

Subject to:

$$\begin{align}
\sum_i p_i x_i &= I \tag{1} \\
L + T_s &= K \tag{2} \\
T_s &= t_s{}^* + \sum_i t_{si} x_i \tag{3} \\
e_L + \sum_i e_{si} x_i &= 1 \tag{4}
\end{align}$$

In this formulation there are $i = 1, 2, \ldots, N$ commodities in quantities x_i, L denotes leisure time, T_s is the time spent shopping or acquiring the various quantities of the several commodities, t_{si} represents the time required to gain a unit of commodity i, and K is a positive number (the total time available). The symbol $t_s{}^*$ is a nonnegative constant that allows for the fact that acquiring goods might entail a fixed time component. The nonnegative effort devoted to leisure is e_L, and e_{si} is a nonnegative number representing the effort required to gain a unit of commodity i, $i = 1, 2, \ldots, N$. Constraint 4 says that the total effort expended acquiring goods must sum with e_L to unity.[5] Constraint 1 is the usual budget constraint. So this problem adds to the conventional consumer's problem the fact that acquiring goods might require not just financial resources but also scarce time and effort. But the formulation also clearly shows that for the special case where the parameters $t_s{}^*$, t_{si}, and e_{si} are all equal to zero, the problem reduces to the usual constrained maximization problem with only the conventional budget constraint. So the usual consumer's maximization problem is nested in the problem above, and the unconstrained problem is nested within the usual budget-constrained problem.

Clearly, if we added information and information-processing constraints to the problem above, we would still retain the usual neoclassical consumer problem as a special case. Now much of the content of behavioral economics comes from the existence not only of a budget constraint but also of other constraints that are binding in decision problems, in particular constraints on information per se and/or constraints on the capacity for processing information. That is the essential story of Simon's conception of *bounded rationality*. The above argument shows that the neoclassical consumer's problem is a special case of the bounded rationality characterization. The same reduction holds for profit maximization problems. So the neoclassical utility maximization and profit maximization characterizations can be seen to be special cases of the bounded rationality behavioral economic characterizations.

It also should be noted that while selfish preferences or utility functions are commonly assumed in many neoclassically based analyses, and sometimes in behavioral analyses, there is nothing inherent in either theoretical base that requires selfishness. Other-regarding preferences are empirically relevant and integral to many problems that can and have been approached using both frameworks. Neoclassical optimization remains a special case of the bounded rationality framework even with nonselfish preferences.

SATISFICING AND THE ADAPTIVE TOOLBOX

The intuition supported by the above argument is limited in that the objective function is not affected by changing values of the parameters in the constraints. The problem was to optimize (e.g., maximize) the fixed or given objective function whatever the specific values of the constraint parameters within the wide range of allowable values. This means that another essential aspect of behavioral economics generally, and the theory of bounded rationality in particular, is not captured in the above argument. The missing and essential aspect is the view that when the information and/or processing capacity constraints are binding, people can convert the immediate decision problem from optimizing to some other type of problem, such as satisficing. The essential aspects of the alternative types are that they do not involve direct optimization.

Satisficing

Satisficing is a decision process that does not involve any direct optimization and involves some sequential procedure of searching and deciding (testing, consuming, or operating) at different aspiration levels. The procedure of satisficing can take several forms (Simon 1997, 295–98), including converting an optimization problem into a sequence of problems, each of which consists of simply finding the boundary of a constraint set, where the constraint set satisfies all the constraints of the original problem, if any, plus one or more constraints *added* that characterize a satisfactory alternative or aspiration level (interim solution).[6] The satisficing procedure calls for possibly solving similar and subsequent problems, each of which involves finding subsequent and improved options by raising or lowering the aspiration level(s) and therefore the standards of what is "satisfactory," based on the difficulties or costs of further searching, calculating, and so on.[7]

It should be noted that the original objective function in the optimization problem has not necessarily disappeared from the procedure; it might only have slid into the background and still play a role. If, for example, the first satisficing choice was easily found and further search is assessed as being desirable and feasible, then the true objective function, if fully known, can inform the selection of a new and higher aspiration level(s). And if the search process does ultimately allow the full original constraint set to be searched, the constrained maximum will be reached. So Simon's form of satisficing in fact reduces to the neoclassical optimization problem when the information, information-processing capacity, and time and effort constraints become nonbinding. That is, the neoclassical decision problem is a special case of satisficing if the neoclassical problem itself is well defined, which entails having a well-defined objective function.[8]

How the various aspiration levels are chosen is an open problem. If they are not chosen arbitrarily or randomly, it is hard to see any explanation that does not rely on some notion of preference, well-being, or other similar characterization of purpose for consumers. The same issue exists for satisficing as a description of firm behavior. The choosing of aspiration levels is an important area of behavioral economics that has not been well explored but merits serious attention.

It should be noted that by defining decision problems as entailing both possible limits on information and possible limits on information processing, different types of problems can arise such that neoclassical optimization might not be achievable (at least in one step). In one type of problem information-processing capacity is not limiting but information about alternatives is deficient (e.g., computing power is ample but the data are not adequate for the optimization problem). Another type is that the set of alternatives might be fully known but the ability to make comparative assessments is deficient. Composites of both types also can occur.

Another form of satisficing has been offered by Hogarth (1980). Hogarth's approach involves both deliberately reducing the constraint set to a feasibly searched and assessed subset and using aspiration levels to determine acceptable choices. Subsequent steps in the procedure involve expanding the searchable and assessable subset and adjusting the aspiration levels as search and/or calculation proves to be worthwhile. The true objective function remains in the background, and if the information, processing capacity, and time and effort constraints become nonbinding, the process leads to the constrained optimum. So again the neoclassical decision problem is a special case.

In many economic decision problems Hogarth's formulation is similar to Simon's satisficing. It is implicit in Simon's satisficing that the entire original constraint set is not searched in any single step, that is, the constraint set to be searched is a subset of the full constraint set. But Hogarth's approach can also work for finding satisfactory results for decision problems where the neoclassical case does not apply. Simon noted that Hogarth's approach can be applied to problems where the problems involve differing goals or aspirations of incommensurable dimensions.[9]

It should be noted that Hogarth's approach to satisficing does not necessarily require replacing the original objective function. In particular, if the problem is that the full set of options cannot be reasonably searched and/or evaluated, whether because of a too limited processing capacity or too large a set of alternatives (these are relative assessments), or insufficient information, or time and effort limits, the actual objective function can be consulted to select the best alternative from a reduced and manageable subset of alternatives. Again, as the information, processing capacity, and time and effort constraints become nonbinding, the neoclassical decision problem emerges as a special case if incommensurability is not present.

For example, changing the option set from two to forty-two different flavors of ice cream in the example above would not change the nature of the neoclassical economist's prediction. He or she would still predict a selection of the most preferred flavors in accordance with selfish preferences. But for behavioral economists, circumstances can influence behavior, and therefore advance a more cautious characterization of the choice. The larger choice set might make it difficult for both the teenager and the mother to sample all the unfamiliar alternatives in order to determine their respective best choices in the time available. Or they might not be able to consistently rank the many choices because they do not have sufficiently vivid recall of their past assessments of all alternative flavors and do not have time to sample them all. In either case they might opt to subjectively and deliberately shrink the option set to a familiar and good enough subset, à la Hogarth, and choose the preferred flavor from that subset, even though the selection might not be the most preferred among forty-two options in the fully informed or reflected situation.[10]

Other efforts have been put forth to advance the theory of satisficing. Selten (1998, 2001) has offered an approach that also allows for incommensurable goals and aspirations (in which case preferences can only provide a partial ordering of the decision space).[11] The approach provides a detailed specification for the process of adapting aspirations. The approach has a natural interpretation in the case where the goal variables are discrete. However, for continuous goal variables or mixed continuous and discrete goal variables, the approach suffers along with all other contributions in that it does not provide an explanation of how and why the selected aspiration levels are what they are; the same is true for the adaptations of aspiration levels.

The Adaptive Toolbox

The term *adaptive toolbox* is a metaphor for a collection of decision rules or heuristics as opposed to a general-purpose decision-making algorithm. The rules or heuristics are parts of models or theories of bounded rationality. The collection of rules or heuristics share two key characteristics: (1) they are "fast, frugal, and computationally cheap rather than consistent, coherent, and general," and (2) they are ecologically rational, that is, particular rules or heuristics are appropriate only for particular decision environments (Gigerenzer and Selten 2001, 9). The rules or heuristics are not intended or expected to yield optimizing decisions and outcomes. They are more like rules of thumb for specific situations. The adaptive toolbox is not a theory of bounded rationality. The yet-to-be-completed theory of bounded rationality is taken to eschew optimization (Gigerenzer and Selten 2001, 3; Selten 2001, 16, 34; Gigerenzer 2001, 40). But the meaning of optimization within the context of their efforts to construct a theory of bounded rationality is often not clear, not unambiguous (Klein 2001, 104–8). What the collectors of tools for inclusion in the adaptive toolbox seem to have in mind in using the word *optimization* is the literal calculation of first- and second-order conditions and their literal use in decision making (Gigerenzer 2001, 40). But if optimizing means selecting the most preferred option from a set of options by whatever practicable means, as opposed to resorting to only mathematical programming, then eschewing optimization is a mistaken strategy.

There are several reasons why eschewing optimization as a possible goal in decision making is a mistake while developing a theory of bounded rationality. First, a theory of bounded rationality must be about *how* people make decisions, including in situations that are simple enough that people do choose their preferred option. Second, there is evidence that people want to try to optimize in various situations. For example, the use of elaborate computer routines for calculating efficient portfolio frontiers, and calculating arbitrage opportunities and strategies, demonstrate a desire and effort to optimize, including the use of formal reasoning.[12] Third, optimizing can and should be viewed as a boundary case of a theory of bounded rationality. Fourth, even boundedly rational people make marginal calculations of the type defined by the necessary first-order conditions of optimization problems—for example, in relatively simple arbitrage opportunities. Fifth, simple models based on optimizing behavior are used by both professional and political policy makers in motivating and reaching policy decisions in response to their boundedly rational circumstances.

So in developing a theory of bounded rationality, it undoubtedly should be the case that major attention ought be paid to determining the various fast, frugal, computationally cheap, and ecologically rational procedures that are actually used by people and are effective, and therefore belong in the adaptive toolbox. But on the other hand, no tool that is actually used by people to choose in a purposeful, reflective, and effective way in some circumstances, even if it is an optimizing tool, should be left out of the adaptive toolbox.

EMOTIONS, FEELINGS, NEUROBIOLOGY, AND BEHAVIOR

Satisficing is a plausible and useful characterization of humans' decision process for various situations. Likewise, the adaptive toolbox, containing a variety of decision tools that are helpful in various situations, is a realistic and useful approach from both descriptive and prescriptive perspectives. But both perceive the decision maker in the same basic manner as in the neoclassical framework. In all three cases the decision maker is taken to be purposeful, but unemotional and unfeeling.

Maintaining the model of a purposeful but unemotional and unfeeling decision maker has not caused a paradigm shift in microeconomic theory. Moreover, it is hard to see how such a maintained approach could do so. The maintained hypothesis is a constraint on the research agenda.

Behavioral economists should be sensitive to the fact that people are emotional and feeling actors. And contrary to the neoclassical or satisficing or adaptive toolbox perspectives, emotions and feelings might matter in decision making.[13] So if there is a paradigm change in the offing, it might well arise by studying emotional and feeling decision makers. Fortunately, research by neuroscientists into the workings of the brain and the mind are leading to greater understanding of human behavior, including human decision making. In particular, it appears to be the case that emotions and feelings are not mere background noise for decision makers, even those who try to be purposeful. Rather, they affect the behavior of most everyone, not just abnormal people, and are often critical parts of consciously purposeful decision processes.

Early work in biology and more recent work in neurobiology construct a picture of humans that is different from but quite congenial to some of the basic premises of microeconomics.[14] For example, at the level of emotions and supporting biological processes, "the goal of the homeostasis endeavor is to provide a better than neutral life state, what we as thinking and affluent creatures identify as wellness and *well-being*."[15] Indeed, the human organism reacts to changes in its internal or external environments that might affect it so as to "create the most beneficial situation for its own self-preservation and efficient functioning" (Damasio 2003, 35). That is, there seems to be an internal drive toward an optimal stasis.[16] Also, in a neurobiological tip of the hat to the early utilitarians, the feelings that follow emotions have pleasure or pain as a *necessary* component (Damasio 2003, 85, 123).

Feelings can have an independent claim to affect behavior because they intimately involve the mind. Damasio explains a feeling as "the perception of a certain state of the body along with the perception of a certain mode of thinking and of thoughts with certain themes." In brief, the essential content of feeling is the mapping of a particular body state; the substrate of feelings is the set of neural patterns that map the body state and from which a mental image of the body state can emerge. A feeling in essence is an idea—an idea of the body and, even more particularly, an idea of a certain aspect of the body, its interior, in certain circumstances. A feeling of emotion is an idea of the body when it is perturbed by the emoting process (Damasio 2003, 86, 88).

Feelings—the ideas, the body maps—are retained and are recallable from memory, as are the associations between emotions and feelings and the associations between causes of emotions (emotionally competent stimuli, in the language of Damasio [2003]) and the emotions. Functionally, the stored ideas, body maps, and associated emotions and emotionally competent stimuli are seen to normally serve to enhance the efficiency and quality of decision making. When a familiar stimulus appears (is sensed), the appropriate emotions and body maps are almost immediately available, and the response too can be almost immediate; or, if the response need not be almost immediate, the reasoning process prior to response can be both informed and made more efficient by the focused information. On the other hand, as noted earlier, neurobiology and a lot of historical experience tell us that some emotions can be triggered under circumstances in which they are maladaptive.

Emotions, and emotional reactions, have a long evolutionary history. "Emotions are built from simple reactions that easily promote the survival of an organism and thus could easily prevail in evolution" (Damasio 2003, 30). Feelings trail emotions in the evolutionary sequence because feelings require a nervous system and brain capable of producing and retaining the neural body maps necessary for feelings. In evolutionary terms, survival and well-being are the goals of organisms. Pain (or discomfort or distress) is the sensory signal of a threat to survival, while pleasure is the sensory signal of well-being, that is, survival is not threatened and an efficiently functioning biological state is to a greater or lesser extent achieved.

The complex emotion apparatus comes to us largely as built-in equipment. However, learning and experience over time do influence the release or restraint of emotional responses, in particular social emotions such as jealousy, admiration, indignation, sympathy, and others (Damasio 2003, 34–49). The body maps that are an essential component of feelings are also hardwired. Some of the wiring comes built-in at birth, while other portions are strung in place with experience and learning.

So how might recognition of emotions and the feelings to which they give rise help in the further development of behavioral economics? Fortunately, Amos Tversky, Daniel Kahneman, and others have already blazed part of the intellectual trail via their investigations into the processes of decision making. The concept of intuition, as used in the architecture of cognition described by Kahneman (2003a, 1450–52), has a strong intersection with Damasio's conception of emotion (see Damasio 2003, 53). Not surprisingly, then, emotion has a "central role" in the concept of intuition (Kahneman 2003, 1470). Damasio sees emotions as involving automatic and rapid responses to external or internal, actual or mental, stimuli. The purpose and result of the responses are to put organisms, including people, in states conducive to survival and well-being. In human beings with normal uninjured brains and nervous systems, emotions give rise to feelings that reflect the state of the body. For Kahneman (2003a, 1451) and others, intuition consists of cognitive processes that are "fast, automatic, effortless, associative, and often emotionally charged; they are also governed by habit, and are therefore difficult to control or modify."[17] Both concepts are part of two visions of solving various problems. For Damasio the "problems" are stimuli of any type to which the organism can or must respond for the purposes of survival and/or survival with well-being. For cognitive psychologists and economists the problems are decisions, deductions, or inferences that often have emotional components or associations and often are related to achieving more or less well-being but are commonly not connected to immediate or short-term threats to survival.

While cognitive psychologists such as Kahneman and Tversky and various economists are aware of the interplay between emotions and decisions, they have not delved deeply into it. In particular, they have not explored the emotional foundations of decision making. What follows are some examples of how the developing knowledge generated in neurobiology connects to, and might provide an explanation for, some significant patterns of behavior of particular interest to economists. The purpose of the examples is to indicate that recent developments in neurobiology suggest there are fundamental biological and neurological causes for economic behaviors that presently are considered anomalies. The laboratory and theoretical research in neurobiology provides a basis for instead seeing the behavior as normal and regular, and therefore a basis of support for behavioral economists' challenge to the neoclassical perspective. The first example will be the phenomenon of loss aversion.

Loss Aversion

The related phenomena known as loss aversion, the status quo effect, and the endowment effect now will be considered. But first a result from neurobiology will be taken up. The result is indicative but not dispositive for the phenomenon of loss aversion. The amygdala is an important portion of the brain for registering stimuli, especially auditory and visual, and setting emotions in response. This is particularly true for the emotions of fear and anger. Interestingly, research shows that significantly more neurons in the amygdala are connected or receptive to disturbing stimuli than to attractive or pleasing stimuli (Damasio 2003, 60; Oya et al. 2002). This is suggestive of a broader and stronger emotional response to negative stimuli than to positive stimuli. Since losses and prospective losses are negative stimuli, and gains and prospective gains are attractive or pleasing stimuli, the neural connection counts suggest a stronger response to losses or prospective losses than to gains or prospective gains, that is, loss aversion.

Another neural site that triggers emotions is the ventromedial prefrontal cortex. At this site more neurons respond to disturbing visual stimuli, and respond differently, than to attractive or pleasing stimuli. Moreover, the disproportionate sensitivity to negative stimuli is more pronounced in the right region than in the left (Damasio 2003, 62; Kawasaki et al. 2001) This finding too can be taken as indicative that negative stimuli such as losses or other prospects of harm induce stronger responses in people than do equal strength gains or prospective gains, but they are not dispositive.

Consider an organism in the lower levels of the tree of evolution. Imagine the organism is in the vicinity of a predator and aware of the predator, but at a distance such that an attack by the predator is not imminent. The organism is in a state of tension but not fully threatened, that is, not engaged in fight or flight, but alert and watching. Now further consider that the predator makes one of two moves: either it moves toward the organism and reduces the distance separating them by 50 percent, or it moves away by an equal distance. As the predator approaches, the prospect of loss is total and the fight-or-flight reaction kicks in. But if the predator moves away, the state of alert diminishes, that is, the organism moves from a state of less than full relaxation to a state of greater relaxation, perhaps even full relaxation. In the approach movement, the threat of loss is total. In the receding movement of the predator, the gain is marginal. It makes sense that nature would be more attuned to threats to survival (loss) than to gains within the state of survival.

Now consider that the organism is an early hominid. There is no reason to imagine a different response scenario. Nor is there a reason to suspect a different response scenario if the organism was an early *Homo sapiens*. What this suggests is that loss aversion, as it is known in economics, is hardwired into people and arises from the biological drive for survival. At root it is an emotional response, related to the fight-or-flight response that is maintained in the tree of evolution.

The phenomenon of loss aversion has been known in economics for some time and exhibited in controlled experiments. What has been missing in economics is an understanding of why and how the behavior comes about. What is argued here is that the recent findings of neuroscientists, connected to the earlier findings by Darwin and other biologists and combined with the theorizing of Damasio (2003), provide a picture of how and why loss aversion appears in human behavior, and in economic behavior in particular. The view of loss aversion as being hardwired into the human being also means that it is not an anomaly but a regularity. Loss aversion is an anomaly only from the neoclassical perspective. Loss aversion from the neurobiological perspective is a conservative, evolutionarily persistent trait in a predatory world. Translated into economic terms, where entry is possible and exit could be a firm's fate, a price-making firm might perceive that in its market situation it could raise its price and significantly raise its short-term profits, but doing so also might entice rival firms into the industry and result in a lowering of long-term profits to below its current profit level. Such a firm might forgo short-term profits to protect market position, as in contestable markets. Loss aversion can be a sustaining trait in economics as well. The evidence for hardwiring suggests that the impulse to avoid pain is stronger than the impulse to achieve pleasure. It suggests a neurobiological explanation for economic behavior in which people forgo larger potential gains to avoid smaller potential losses.

A hardwired and disproportionate reaction to potential loss as compared to equal-strength potential gain also provides an explanation for phenomena such as status quo bias (Knetsch and

Sinden 1984) and endowment effects (Thaler 1980). A move away from an established status quo or endowment point by giving up something of value might be resisted unless a quid pro quo of clearly superior value is available.

Framing Effects

The phenomenon of framing effects is well known and deeply disturbing to any claim of descriptive veridicality for the neoclassical model of decision making. But how and why framing effects arise is not known. However, the same neurobiological findings that potentially illuminate the phenomenon of loss aversion also potentially offer an explanation of how and why many kinds of framing effects are observed.

Consider the well-known Asian disease example provided by Tversky and Kahneman (1981). The example involves losses versus gains, in particular survival versus nonsurvival of other persons. The latter evokes the social emotions of sympathy and empathy, which are connected to the fundamental feelings of pain and pleasure (Damasio 2003, 45–49). The case involves presenting two substantively equivalent decision problems to two different sets of randomly selected subjects (Kahneman 2003a). The first version of the decision problem is:

> Imagine that the United States is preparing for the outbreak of an unusual Asian disease, which is expected to kill 600 people. Two alternative programs to combat the disease have been proposed. Assume that the exact scientific estimates of the consequences of the programs are as follows: If Program A is adopted, 200 people will be saved. If Program B is adopted, there is a one-third probability that 600 people will be saved and a two-thirds probability that no people will be saved. Which of the two programs would you favor?

A clear majority of subjects presented the above version selected program A, which is the risk-averse option.

The second version of the decision problem was presented to the second set of subjects. It used the same opening scenario, but with differently worded alternatives: If Program A is adopted, 400 people will die. If Program B is adopted, there is a one-third probability that nobody will die and a two-thirds probability that 600 people will die. In the second presentation a clear majority favored the probabilistic alternative, which is the risk-taking alternative.

Why the difference? Clearly both presentations of the substantively identical choice problem are emotionally loaded. Both evoke the emotions of sympathy and/or empathy. But the first version presents the choice as between alternative gains (pleasing) in the form of lives saved, and the second presents the choice as between alternative losses (pain) in the form of lives lost. While the survival of the subjects themselves was not threatened, and correspondingly their lives were not to be saved, their social emotion set must have been activated. In the first version the emotionally competent stimuli in the two options are gains and therefore connected to the basic feeling of pleasure. In this instance the smaller set of neural receptors should be activated, and so provide a relatively weaker neural response. In the second version, the emotionally competent stimuli in the two options are losses and therefore connected to the basic feeling of pain. In this latter instance the larger set of neural receptors should be activated, and provide a relatively stronger neural response, which is seen in choosing the risk-taking, probabilistic program. It also should be noted that the risk-taking alternative also is the cognitively more demanding choice.

The same explanation can be applied to framing effects in many other contexts so long as they involve substantively equivalent choice problems involving alternative presentations translatable or interpretable as gains or losses. The framing effect provided by McNeil and colleagues (1982) and cited by Kahneman (2003b) is a case in point. The latter case involves a choice problem with alternative therapies (surgery versus radiation) and emotion-stimulating alternative outcomes presented in terms of either survival rates (gains) or mortality rates (losses). Other examples of framing effects are available with less emotionally charged options. Framing effects also are found in other economic domains, for example, the examination of relative fairness judgments with respect to the behavior of firms by Kahneman, Knetsch, and Thaler (1986) in relation to conflating nominal (money) wages and prices with relative prices and real wages (money illusion).

Neural Processes

The foregoing explanation for loss aversion and framing effects might be overly simple. While nature must have a reason for the disparity in neuron counts, using neural counts as an indicator or explanatory variable for the relative strength of emotions and feelings and resultant behavior might be too crude a tool to explain the neural processes that yield decisions.

A recent study by Gonzalez and colleagues (2003) suggests that it is too simple. The researchers employed notions of alternative cognitive costs. One notion was the cognitive-effort cost of computing, and in the framing type of problems the computation is taken to be the computing of the expected value of the probable outcomes. This would be a cost at the level of system 2 (reasoning) for Kahneman (2003a), and could be labeled C_2. The other notion of cost is a cognitive-emotional cost. This is a cost involving the base level and systems 1 and 2 for Kahneman and might be labeled C_1.

Gonzalez and colleagues used functional magnetic resonance imaging (fMRI) to study the levels of activity in various regions of the brains of ten subjects while the subjects considered and made decisions in a variety of framed problems. The use of fMRI evidence puts the analysis at the level of the neural processes involved in deciding. It brings new and additional evidentiary data into the analysis, as opposed to having only the data of the problem posed and the decision made, as in economic laboratory experiments. The specific data gained were information about the areas of the brain that were activated (used) in dealing with the framing problems, the levels of activation, and the reaction (decision) times. The findings were mixed relative to a priori expectations (hypotheses).

First, the mean reaction time was greater for the negative-reference frames than for the positive-reference frames, and this comparison held even when comparing certain (risky) choices to certain (risky) choices across frames. This result is suggestive of a greater reaction to the negative-reference frames than to the positive-reference frames, which would be consistent with the implication taken above from the neuron count data. But when the activation data were examined, the researchers did not find similar support for stronger reactions to the negative-reference frames. In fact, while the activation was marginally higher in the negative-reference frame for nineteen out of thirty-two regions assessed, the differences in activation levels were not statistically significant for any of the thirty-two regions. The activation readings were taken by Gonzalez and colleagues as more direct evidence of brain activity than of reaction time, and the finding of no statistically significant differences in activity between positive- and negative-referenced frames was taken as more dispositive than the reaction time results. That is, the conclusion drawn by Gonzalez and colleagues was that there was no significant difference in brain activity found between consideration of positive-referenced problems and negative-referenced problems in any of the thirty-two regions of interest. Their findings, to the extent that brain activation is taken to be an indicator of cognitive costs, do not support the phenomenon of loss aversion. But this implication of the activation results cannot be considered conclusive. While the results do not affirm loss aversion, they do not disprove it. In fact, the activation results highlight the reaction time data. The reaction time data were consistent with loss aversion, and the activation data were not supportive but also not directly contradictory. The combined results tilt in the direction of loss aversion. The systematic reaction time data must reflect something about the cognitive impact of the choices. Attention span is not a trivial matter. Indeed, it might be that the integral of the activation over the reaction interval is the appropriate indicator of cognitive cost.

The inconsistent indications from the activation and reaction time data raise two important questions for neurobiologists. First, what exactly do activation levels indicate? This question will be drawn out below. Second, what does reaction time or attention span indicate?

Further consideration of the activation data by Gonzalez and colleagues did reveal differences between the activations for the risky choices and the activations for certain choices in the gain or positive-reference frames. Statistically significant differences were found, with higher activation in the right-side dorsolateral prefrontal cortex and the right-side posterior precentral sulcus for the positive-frame risky or probable choices than for the corresponding certain choices. But this result did not obtain in the loss or negative-reference frames. In the latter cases, there were no statistically significant differences between the activations for the probable or risky choices versus the certain choices. These results suggest that risk aversion in situations of prospective gain is stronger than risk seeking in situations of prospective loss (Gonzalez et al. 2003, 15).

The researchers offer a plausible theoretical explanation for the latter suggested conclusion. Their explanation is modified here to account for the positive (pleasure) aspect of gain and the pure emotional cost of loss (C_3). In the positive frame, "the risky choice is more costly than the certain option because it involves more effort to calculate the expected value and a greater emotional response due to the uncertainty of the rewards" (Gonzalez et al. 2003, 16).[18] The cost of the larger emotional response due to the uncertainty of the rewards is here taken to be C_1. In addition to the two mentioned costs, there is still the fact that the costs are related to the consideration of gains, and so there would be activation of neurons associated with positive stimuli. The certain-gain alternative, on the other hand, does not require the computation cost (C_2) of expected value, nor an emotional cost related to contemplating the uncertainty of outcome (C_1), but there would be activation of neurons due to the stimulus of contemplation of the certain gain. Presumably the statistically significant difference in activation is due to the difference in costs between the alternative choices outweighing any difference in activation between contemplation of the probable gain and contemplation of the certain gain. The usual clear tendency to choose the certain-gain outcomes is thus seen as a choice taking the lower cognitive cost option. In the negative-reference frames the risky choice again involves cognitive costs associated with computing the expected loss (C_2), a cognitive and emotional cost associated with the uncertainty of the outcome (C_1), and a cognitive and emotional cost (C_3) or negative gain ($-g$) associated with contemplating loss rather than gain. But in this frame there is also the emotional cost of the certain-loss alternative, which is presumed to be high (Gonzalez et al. 2003, 16). The lack of a statistically significant difference in activation between the risky and certain choices in the negative-reference frames presumably means the emotional cost associated with the certain loss is approximately the same as the sum of the costs ($C_1 + C_2 + C_3$) in the uncertain-loss choice. So the fact that the risky choice option is nonetheless the tendency in negative-reference frames is taken to mean that there is a difference between the costs along another (qualitative?) dimension and that "people are more willing to accept computational than emotional cost" (Gonzalez et al. 2003, 17).

The theoretical explanation offered to explain the conclusion that there is greater risk aversion in gain or positive-reference-framed choices than there is risk seeking in loss or negative-reference-framed choices again raises the question of what activation levels reflect. In the explanation activation levels are a composite result. They reflect at least two kinds of costs, according to Gonzalez and colleagues.[19] And in the risky choice of the positive-reference frame, not only can the activation be taken to reflect two kinds of cognitive costs being incurred, but there also must be a reflection of the positive nature of the potential gain. So the activation level should be reflecting at least three variables, C_1, C_2, and g ($g = -C_3$). The idea that "people are more willing to accept computational than emotional cost" adds yet another dimension, something like a cost-specific type of loss aversion (within loss aversion?).

Consider instead the following simple four-variable model. Let C_1, C_2, and C_3 be defined as above. Also let g represent the emotional cognitive realization of gain (instead of defining $g = -C_3$). Assume that measured activations are proportional to the emotional-cognitive realizations C_1, C_2, C_3, and g, where the proportionality parameters α^n and α^p are positive numbers determined by the number of neurons that are tuned to negative and positive stimuli, respectively, including cognitive costs. That is, the activation related to a cost level C_2 is $\alpha^n C_2$, and the activation level associated with a gain g is $\alpha^p g$.

In this model, then, the higher activation connected to the risky or probable alternative in the positive frame, and the related risk-averse choice, means that the following inequality would hold:

$$\alpha^p g^c < \alpha^n(C_1^P + C_2^P) + \alpha^p g^r \Rightarrow \alpha^p g^c - \alpha^p g^r < \alpha^n(C_1^P + C_2^P) \qquad (1)$$

where the superscripts ^{P}, ^{c}, and ^{r} refer to the positive frame, the certainty choice, and the risky choice, respectively. The latter inequality can be expressed alternatively as:

$$g^c - g^r < (\alpha^n/\alpha^p)(C_1^P + C_2^P) \qquad (1')$$

So for risk aversion to obtain in the positive-reference frame, the difference between the activation due to the perceived certain gain and the activation due to the perceived probable or expected gain must be less than the sum of the activations due to the costs C_1^P and C_2^P. Inequality 1 restates the risk-averse selection as due to the difference in the stimuli from the perceived gains being smaller than the weighted sum of the cognitive-emotional costs. The weight factor is related to the relative numbers of neurons that are tuned to positive versus negative stimuli, and taken to be greater than 1 on the basis of indications that negatively sensitive neurons are more numerous than positively sensitive ones.[20] The weight factor being greater than 1 is consistent with the notion that cognitive-emotional costs are weighed more heavily than cognitive-emotional gains in the positive-reference frame.

In order for risk-seeking behavior to be reflected in the activation data, the following inequality would have to hold in the negative-reference frame:

$$\alpha^n(C_1^N + C_2^N + C_3^N) < \alpha^n(C_3^c) \qquad (2)$$

where the superscript N refers to the negative-reference frame. This latter alternative can be rewritten as:

$$(C_1^N + C_2^N) < (C_3^c - C_3^N) \qquad (2)$$

So for risk seeking to obtain in the negative-reference frame, the difference between the perceived certain loss and the perceived probable or expected loss must be positive and greater than the sum of the cognitive cost C_2^N and the cognitive-emotional cost C_1^N. That is to say, in negative-reference frames, risk seeking requires that the "certain option involves a high emotional cost" (Gonzalez et al. 2003, 16).

But what the researchers find is that the activation data correspond to

$$(C_1^N + C_2^N) \cong (C_3^c - C_3^N) \qquad (3)$$

even though the subjects mostly choose the risk-seeking option. That is to say, the certain option involves a high, but not excessively high, emotional cost relative to the emotional cost attached to contemplating the probable or expected cost in the risky choice.

What the paper by Gonzalez and colleagues shows is both the promise of neurobiological research for illuminating the internal structure of decision processes and the need for further development within neurobiology itself. The promise it offers for decision science will not be realized until issues such as whether there are different types of neurological costs and gains within emotional and cognitive categories are clarified. The promise also will not be realized until the different costs can be separately assessed in relation to activation data.

Perhaps the fMRI research needs to take a step back. For example, fMRI experiments involving the contemplation of pure and certain gifts and losses could be assessed for their neurological profiles and activation levels. Similarly, problems computationally identical to calculating expected values but without using the concept of probability and emotionally charged interpretations could be used to assess the neurological profile of the pure computation process. Such experiments and others might provide data that would allow for breaking the kinds of measurement done by Gonzalez and colleagues into the hypothesized components and provide a sharper focus on the mental processes related to phenomena such as loss aversion, framing effects, and other reputed anomalies. Additional information about the relative abundance of positively sensitive neurons and negatively sensitive neurons in the various regions of interest in the brain, and the connection between abundance and activation data, would be useful. Further, consideration of the significance (or the lack thereof) of reaction times should be informative and helpful, especially with regard to the finding of no statistically significant difference in activation data between the certain and risky choices in the negative-reference frames. In this last regard, it also needs to be considered whether the activation data and the reaction times are compounding indicators.

CONCLUSION

The aversion that most economists exhibited toward the concept of bounded rationality that Herbert Simon noted was never justified. It certainly did not reflect a scientific approach to economic research. The issue that separated Simon and colleagues from their neoclassical counterparts was always an empirical one. The stubbornness of the neoclassical economists that prevented them from conducting the empirical tests, or taking seriously the empirical testing of the behavioralists, reflected more of an emotional reaction than a thoughtful and reflective response. Perhaps it was (and to some extent remains) due to vested interest.

The aversion to considering the concept of bounded rationality seriously was not sensible not only because of its insensitivity to empirical facts but also because it reflected a blindness to logic. Simon and others were not rejecting the neoclassical model lock, stock, and barrel but instead were proposing a more general and empirically detailed model of decision making that incorporated the neoclassical utility and profit maximization model as a special case. The aversion and unreasoned rivalry were wholly unnecessary, unjustified, and a waste, and remain so.

Fortunately, the waste seems to be coming to an end as increasing resources are devoted to behavioral research in economics and finance.

If the aversion and rivalry are cast aside, what research paths appear to have priority in the quest to better understand human decision making relative to economic behavior? Several paths demand attention, and not only from economists. One path is to try to understand how and why people change an optimization problem into a differently structured problem, such as a satisficing problem or the use of a simple heuristic. It is all well and good to seek to catalogue heuristics, rules of thumb, and responses to varieties of cues and to ascertain their ecological rationality, but the questions of how and why are important for greater understanding. In addressing the question of how, economists might well take a page from psychology and other more historical laboratory sciences and devote more resources to gathering data on how people actually do make decisions before trying to test alternative hypotheses. Laboratory data ought to inform the specification of alternative hypotheses. Also, as tools in the decision toolbox are identified, it will be important to ascertain whether they are learned, hardwired, or some combination thereof. Further, the how and why issues also raise the questions of whether the choice of strategy changes as the bounds on rationality change, and how the bounds on rationality and changes in the bounds on rationality interact with ecological niches. In turn, these questions relate to how and when people switch from optimizing in simple cases to nonoptimizing methods as the decision problem becomes more difficult; that is, what determines the boundary, as well as how and why people switch from one process or heuristic to another?

Within the specific category of satisficing as a decision procedure, the issues of how people do determine aspiration levels and how they ought to determine them is an open area. To the extent that satisficing describes a significant amount of behavior or is used in a significant variety of decision problems, the value of better prescriptive procedures or rules should correspondingly be significant.

The recognition by economists that decision makers are emotional and feeling beings as well as purposive beings is the second and perhaps richest path to explore. Whether the tools in the adaptive toolbox and their rational niches are only the result of experience, and maybe evolutionary experience, is an appropriate topic to explore. If the tools are simply the result of experience, are the associations between particular tools and ecologically appropriate occasions hardwired together in the brain via the emotions (though perhaps needing to be initiated by example [Damasio 2003, 47]) and resulting feelings? If so, then along this path is the force for a paradigm shift in economic analysis. The long list of anomalies that have been identified, and specifically addressed in the *Journal of Economic Perspectives,* are perhaps simply awaiting explanation to be seen as regularities. Since the neoclassical framework cannot explain the so-called anomalies, perhaps the inclusion of emotions and feelings, possibly mixed with some purely cognitive learning, can provide the explanations.

Neurobiological research seems to be suggesting that regularities such as loss aversion, framing, and other effects might have their origin in the hardwiring of the human mechanism. It also raises the question of whether economic decision making should be characterized as being wholly and always rational. For example, one notion of rationality is as consistency in decision making. But framing effects yield inconsistent choice. If framing effects arise due to emotions, which supports the notion of regularity, then the idea of decision makers as rational in the sense of consistency might have to be relaxed. Neurobiological research also begs the question of whether the notion of rationality in the sense of decisions being in the best interest of the actor is an appropriate assumption. There is good reason to assess some hardwired emotion-feeling-response mechanisms as being maladaptive in various settings in modern societies. If traits such as loss aversion are hardwired, then the question arises as to whether these traits can be and are operative in situations where they are inappropriate. If so, then the assumption that economic actors pursue their best interest is shaky. It might well be that further neurobiological and psychological research related to economic behavior will require that economists relax their presumptions of rationality as either consistency or best-interest-serving choice. Nonetheless, greater knowledge of how and why such effects arise will be useful in guiding social policies and decisions and in the analysis and guiding of personal behavior.

Since the fundamental issues are the how and why of decision making, the increasing ability of neuroscientists to observe and measure some aspects of decision processes *as they occur* offers an important path for increasing the understanding of economic decision making in particular. Clearly this path leads to a better understanding of how the emotions, feelings, and cognitive processes are intertwined and combine in the creation of behavior generally, and the creation of economic behavior in particular. But interested economists are going to have to work in close cooperation with neuroscientists and psychologists to ensure that the data that are produced focus increasingly on the detail and structure of economic decisions. And in doing so neuroscientists are going to have to look for finer neurological structure than is captured in activation data. The result of such collaborative work might well give rise to a paradigm shift in economic theory and analysis.

NOTES

1. This point has been emphasized by Simon (1997, 367) in the context of comparing the use of the concept of rationality in economics versus its use in psychology. "One point should be set immediately outside dispute. Everyone agrees that people have reasons for what they do. They have motivations, and they use reason (well or badly) to respond to these motivations and reach their goals." His emphasis applies at least as strongly in a comparison between behavioral microeconomics and neoclassically based microeconomics.

2. For an excellent exposition of much of the relevant experimental evidence, and an extensive bibliography of original sources, see Camerer 2003.

3. I am indebted to Herb Gintis for this observation.

4. The behavior of people with severely damaged or impaired neurological functions is not being described here, just as it has not been characterized in neoclassical theory or behavioral economics to date.

5. Since the marginal utility of effort devoted to leisure is positive, total effort expended will be 100 percent in any solution, or sum to 1.

6. Care needs to be exercised here. An information constraint might mean that the full, true choice set is not and cannot be known at once (e.g., the full constraint set must be uncovered by search), and therefore an aspiration level can be chosen only with respect to what is known about the choice set. An information-processing constraint might mean that only finite adjustments, and only a finite number of finite adjustments, can be considered. Because the variety of bounded rationality problems is immense, the description of satisficing must correspondingly be described with care.

7. Selection of the first aspiration level might be somewhat arbitrary, or it might correspond to the value of a default option. An example of a somewhat arbitrary option would be if there is knowledge of the type "more is preferred to less," in which case the first selection might be an arbitrary choice among all the options defined by the upper boundary of the constraint set, if it is known.

8. That the intimate linkage between neoclassical microeconomics and bounded rationality, and in particular satisficing, has not been well noted before is not easy to explain. Certainly the connection should have been in clear view. In a reduced-form model of elegant simplicity, Day (1967) showed that for a monopoly firm for which more profits were preferred to less, the satisficing process converged to the neoclassical profit maximum solution in the limit. In the context of this chapter, ". . . in the limit" can be restated as meaning that the information, information-processing, and time constraints became nonbinding. Day was more focused on illuminating the role of learning, and satisficing as a learning process, than on examining the inherent structural relationship between satisficing and the neoclassical monopoly profit problem. He did remark that "the unity between the behavioral and rational approaches is illustrated" via the proof of convergence. But he did not note that, for well-behaved underlying functions, the convergence is guaranteed because of the nested nature of the neoclassical and bounded rationality problems. What is surprising is that

the intimate structural linkage was never picked up and remarked upon by his readers or other subsequent researchers. Apparently the not fully rational attachment to neoclassical marginal analysis (as exemplified by marginalist approaches to information problems, as in Stigler 1961 and elaborated by optimal search theory) was too strong.

9. See Simon 1997, 297. The difficulty presented by incommensurable dimensions that are part of the objectives or purpose of a problem represents a boundary for the principle being advocated here.

10. Given enough time to consider and reflect on all the pairwise choices, and perhaps sample some unfamiliar flavors, the teenager and mother could move to a most preferred option, which would be the neoclassical economist's outcome.

11. Selten cites the seminal source of the approach as a German-language paper by Sauermann and Selten (1962).

12. The use of aids such as computers and software in searching for optimal solutions demonstrates not only a desire but also an effort to choose optimally and even sometimes use formal mathematical and statistical methods. But Sadrieh and collaborators make the observation that such computer aids also offer evidence of bounded rationality (Sadrieh et al. 2001, 88–89). Their point is that the design and construction of the interface between the user and the routine incorporates concessions to the bounded rationality of the user. That may be, but some such artifacts might also only be time-saving innovations. If time is valuable whether a person is boundedly rational or unboundedly rational, then both more efficient computer routines and more efficient interfaces are desirable. Either way, the use of such decision aids demonstrate a desire to optimize and the use of formal decision rules.

13. That emotions might have potentially rich implications for economics has been noted before, most explicitly by Jon Elster (1998) and Robert Frank (1988). But neither accounted for feelings as distinct from their antecedents, emotions. That emotions (not to mention feelings) have been neglected by economists was pointed out vividly by Elster in noting that there was no mention of emotions in an article by Matthew Rabin (1998) published jointly with Elster's.

14. This section draws heavily from the work of Antonio Damasio, in particular his excellent monograph *Looking for Spinoza: Joy, Sorrow, and the Feeling Brain* (2003), and on the works of his co-authors and numerous other researchers cited in his extensive references. The borrowing and interpretations contained herein, however, do not come close to providing an adequate sense of the depth and elegance of the work of Damasio or other original sources.

15. Emphasis in the original. "Wellness" here fundamentally includes survival.

16. On the other hand, "the deployment of some emotions in current human circumstances may be maladaptive" and the emotions themselves "are terrible advisors," and learning may be required to suppress them (Damasio 2003, 39–40).

17. Intuition for Kahneman (2003a, 1450–2) is one stage or system with a three-part cognitive system. The base system is that of perception, the next is intuition (system 1), and the third is reasoning (system 2). Damasio's framework would integrate perception and intuition. He also would seem not to make a sharp distinction between reasoning and the lower systems à la Kahneman, but presumably envisions a more intimately integrated system. Damasio's theory of the brain and mind is more cognizant of evolutionary considerations than that of Kahneman and other cognitive psychologists.

18. Presumably, since the subject is taken to calculate the expected value, "the uncertainty of the rewards" has to do with a subject's realization that the expected value is not a feasible outcome if the probabilities are not 0 and 1. There is some ambiguity as to the nature of the second cost since elsewhere the second cost is described as "possible emotions decision makers might experience with the expectation of losses and gains" (Gonzalez et al. 2003, 15), which seems to refer to the expected value as opposed to the uncertain (but feasible) outcomes. This ambiguity suggests further ambiguity about how the subjects are perceived to be actually making decisions. If subjects are perceived to be maximizing expected value (utility), then in the positive-reference frame there would only be one cost, that of calculating the expected gain, and two (positive) emotional reactions, that of contemplating the expected gain and that of contemplating the certain gain. If there are two costs in the positive-reference frame, then the decision process must be different. Perhaps in these one-shot decisions the alternative has the subject computing the expected value as an indicator or aid in choosing between the options, and the computation is costly, but she is still cognizant of the fact that the actual outcomes will be different from the expected value, and that gives rise to another sense of cost related to the uncertainty of rewards. Instead of maximizing expected value, subjects might be selecting another tool from the adaptive toolbox. Perhaps the subjects who do not exhibit both risk aversion in the frame of gains and risk seeking in the frame of losses are deciding on some basis other than expected value. Or perhaps they are just lousy calculators.

19. The cost C_3 was added in this paper.

20. That this might be so generally across regions of the brain would seem to be consistent with evolutionary changes. The drive for survival can be taken to be fundamental whatever the level of well-being of an organism, whatever the sensory mechanism, and whatever the stage of evolutionary development. In the simple model used here it is assumed that the proportion of negatively sensitive neurons relative to positively sensitive neurons does not vary across regions of the brain, which need not be the case.

REFERENCES

Camerer, Colin F. 2003. *Behavioral Game Theory.* Princeton, NJ: Princeton University Press.

Damasio, Antonio. 2003. *Looking for Spinoza: Joy, Sorrow, and the Feeling Brain.* New York. Harcourt.

Day, Richard H. 1967. "Profits, Learning and the Convergence of Satisficing to Marginalism." *Quarterly Journal of Economics* 81: 302–11.

Elster, Jon. 1998. "Emotions and Economic Theory." *Journal of Economic Literature* 36: 47–74.

Frank, Robert H. 1988. *Passions Within Reason.* New York: Norton.

Gigerenzer, G. 2001. "The Adaptive Toolbox." In G. Gigerenzer and R. Selten, eds., *Bounded Rationality: The Adaptive Toolbox,* 37–50. Cambridge, MA: MIT Press.

Gigerenzer, G., and R. Selten. 2001. "Rethinking Rationality." In G. Gigerenzer and R. Selten, eds., *Bounded Rationality: The Adaptive Toolbox,* 1–12. Cambridge, MA: MIT Press.

Gonzalez, C., J. Dana, H. Koshino, and M. Just. 2003. "Framing Effects on Risky Decisions: Examining the Choice Process with fMRI." Draft paper, Carnegie Mellon University.

Hogarth, R.M. 1980. *Judgement and Choice: The Psychology of Decision.* New York: Wiley.

Kahneman, Daniel. 2003a. "Maps of Bounded Rationality: Psychology for Behavioral Economics." *American Economic Review* 93: 1449–75.

———. 2003b. "A Perspective on Judgement and Choice: Mapping Bounded Rationality." *American Psychologist* 56: 697–720.

Kahneman, D., J.L. Knetsch, and R.H. Thaler. 1986. "Fairness as a Constraint on Profit Seeking: Entitlements in the Market." *American Economic Review* 76: 728–41.

Kawasaki, H., R. Adolphs, O. Kaufman, H. Damasio, A. Damasio, M. Granner, H. Baaken, T. Hori, and M.A. Howard. 2001. "Single-Unit Responses to Emotional Visual Stimuli Recorded in Human Ventral Prefrontal Cortex." *Nature Neuroscience* 4: 15–16.

Klein, G. 2001. "The Fiction of Optimization." In G. Gigerenzer and R. Selten, eds., *Bounded Rationality: The Adaptive Toolbox,* 103–21. Cambridge, MA: MIT Press.

Knetsch, Jack L., and John A. Sinden. 1984. "Willingness to Pay and Compensation Demanded: Experimental Evidence of an Unexpected Disparity in Measures of Value." *Quarterly Journal of Economics* 99: 507–21.

McNeil, B.J., S.G. Pauker, H.C. Sox, and A. Tversky. 1982. "On the Elicitation of Preferences for Alternative Therapies." *New England Journal of Medicine* 306: 1259–62.

Oya, Hiroyuki, Hiroto Kawasaki, Matthew Howard, and Ralph Adolphs. "Electrophysiological Responses Recorded in the Human Amygdala Discriminate Emotion Categories of Visual Stimuli." *Journal of Neuroscience* 22: 9502–12.

Rabin, Matthew. "Psychology and Economics." *Journal of Economic Literature* 36: 11–46.

Sadrieh, A., W. Guth, P. Hammerstein, S. Harnad, U. Hoffrage, B. Kuon, B.R. Munier, P.M. Todd, M. Warglien, and M. Weber. "Group Report: Is There Evidence for an Adaptive Toolbox?" In G. Gigerenzer and R. Selten, eds., *Bounded Rationality: The Adaptive Toolbox,* 83–102. Cambridge, MA: MIT Press.

Sauermann, H., and R. Selten. 1962. "Anspruchsanpassungtheorie der Unternehmung." *Zeitschrift für die gesamte Staatswissenschaft* 118: 577–97.

Selten, R. 1998. "Aspiration Adaptation Theory." *Journal of Mathematical Psychology* 42: 191–214.

———. 2001. "What Is Bounded Rationality?" In G. Gigerenzer and R. Selten, eds., *Bounded Rationality: The Adaptive Toolbox,* 13–35. Cambridge, MA: MIT Press.

Simon, Herbert A. 1997. *Models of Bounded Rationality,* vol. 3. Cambridge, MA: MIT Press.

Stigler, George J. 1961. "The Economics of Information." *Journal of Political Economy* 69: 213–25.

Thaler, Richard H. 1980. "Toward a Positive Theory of Consumer Choice." *Journal of Economic Behavior and Organization* 1: 39–60.

Tversky, A., and D. Kahneman. 1981. "The Framing of Decisions and the Psychology of Choice." *Science* 211: 453–58.

CHAPTER 13

ORGANIZATIONAL CAPITAL AND PERSONAL CAPITAL

The Role of Intangible Capital Formation in the Economy

JOHN F. TOMER

Mainstream economists accept the basic idea of human capital. At least they accept its more tangible aspects, for example, the parts related to education and training. However, there is still much resistance to accepting the intangible aspects. Hence my writing on intangible capital has been aimed at providing explanations that overcome this lack of appreciation and understanding. In two books and a fair number of articles, I have developed the concept of organizational capital, and recently I have written a number of articles dealing with personal capital. The purpose of this essay is to provide an overview explanation of how intangible capital is important for understanding the functioning and growth of the economy. In doing this, it integrates more than two decades of my writing on these topics.

To understand intangible capital, it is useful to start with a very general definition of capital as a "lasting productive capacity that is produced and, subsequently, used by economic entities to achieve their purposes" (Tomer 1999a, 1049). Practically all economists today realize there are important sources of productive capacity other than tangible assets such as factories and equipment. The general definition of capital helps us to understand how intangible factors may legitimately be considered a type of capital. With the increasing recognition of the role of intangibles as sources of economic growth, the term *capital* has more and more been extended to these intangible aspects of human capital in which productive capacity is embodied not only in individuals but in the relationships among them.

ORGANIZATIONAL CAPITAL BASICS

Investment in *organizational capital* uses up resources in order to bring about lasting improvements in productivity, worker well-being, or social performance through changes in the functioning of the organization (Tomer 1987, 24).[1] It involves changing the formal and informal social relationships and patterns of activity within the enterprise, changing individual attributes important to organizational functioning, or accumulating information useful in matching workers with organizational situations. Organizational capital is embodied in organizational relationships, particular members of organizations, the organization's repositories of information, or some combination of these. Pure organizational capital provides the best contrast with standard human capital because it is vested entirely in the relationships among workers, not in the workers themselves. It is these relationships—for example, particular organizational structures—that enable desired worker behavior to be evoked or fostered, thereby enabling higher economic and social performance than without it.

Since organizational capital is embodied in humans, it is a type of human capital; it is also a type of social capital. The term *social capital* has been developed largely by sociologists, most notably James Coleman (1988, 1990). During the 1990s, the concept of social capital, with widely differing definitions, was employed by many sociologists but little used by economists. Klaus Nielsen (2003, 3) provides a very useful definition that is generally consistent with the definitions of capital and organizational capital given here: "Social capital is a set of norms and social relations embedded in the social structure that a single subject (for instance, an entrepreneur or a worker) or a collective subject (either private or public) can make use at any given moment to achieve desired goals." In general, sociologists have emphasized that social capital enables a variety of actors, not just business entities, to accomplish more than would be possible in its absence. In this view, social capital is often created as a by-product of activities engaged in for other reasons, in contrast to organizational capital, which is generally created intentionally by people who view it as an investment from which they hope to profit.

ORGANIZATIONAL CAPITAL'S ROLE IN THE FIRM

The Firm as a Human Entity

To fully appreciate the role of organizational capital in improving the economic and social performance of the firm, it is necessary to consider the firm as a human entity rather than as the machinelike conception of neoclassical economics (Tomer 1999b, 1–6; Tomer 2002, 101–4). The neoclassical firm is machinelike in that it responds to market and regulatory incentives in an unfailingly maximizing mode. In contrast, the human firm is human in two important senses: (1) its behavior may reflect the highest human potential, the qualities of mentally and physically healthy people who have attained a high degree of competence, and (2) its behavior may reflect two ordinary human failings: to accomplish what could be accomplished and to be what we could be. Further, the human firm, unlike the neoclassical firm, contains not only hard but soft aspects of reality.

> Hard attributes are tangible, physical, measurable, capable of being expressed in mathematical relationships, visible and explicit. Soft attributes are the opposite to the above and involve less definite, immeasurable and holistic aspects of the world. The right hemisphere of the brain is said to be better at appreciating the softer aspects, and the left hemisphere is better equipped for dealing with the hard aspects. Financial relationships, ownership and organizational structure (hierarchy) are relatively hard, whereas enthusiasm, fairness, kindness, harmony and compassion are relatively soft. (Tomer 1999b, 3)

The human firm is a socioeconomic organization in the sense of its embeddedness in society. More accurately, it is partially embedded in society in that it responds in part to economic incentives and in part to social influences (Granovetter 1985). "Such firms respond to the expectation of profit but also act in accord with moral values, commitments to community, and other social bonds and influences depending on the web of socio-economic-political relationships in which they are involved" (Tomer 1999b, 6). To the extent that human or socioeconomic firms invest in different types of social capital, creating a variety of social connections both within the firm and outside it, the firm's actors can be expected to respond more favorably to particular types of social influences. Clearly, these actors are not the detached economic maximizers of neoclassical theory. Using these created organizational connections, the firm's actors can be expected to choose actions leading to greater productivity and social responsibility than if these investments had not been made. The following sections provide a variety of perspectives on the role of these organizational investments in firms.

The Reality and Potential of the Firm

As Harvey Leibenstein labored to explain, a firm's actual output is typically much less than its potential output. That is, internal inefficiency or X-inefficiency is the usual state of affairs. This inefficiency reflects such things as low worker effort and best business practices not being used. When worker efforts are low or misdirected, this in turn likely reflects the state of the firm's organization and management. In regard to these organizational considerations, the firm's capacity is a result of the amount and quality of its investment in organizational capital. When a firm makes appropriate investments in organizational capital, it raises its productivity because it lowers its X-inefficiency. The kind of organizational investments that raise X-efficiency and worker effort include improving the organizational structure, improving the overall pattern of work supervision, creating clear and meaningful goals for jobs and the organization, developing a favorable implicit psychological contract between employer and employees, creating worker career paths with positive long-term incentives, and developing a system that matches workers with tasks that are both accomplishable and challenging. Inevitably, many viable investments in organizational capital are not made, and thus some degree of inefficiency is a fact of life.

When a firm makes good investments in organizational capital, this raises its internal organizational capabilities, the key determinants of how a firm responds to the special opportunities and incentives confronting it. Among these are the firm's capability for rational organizational decision making, socially responsible behavior, entrepreneurial behavior, and organizational learning.

> The ideal (or Z-) firm is the socio-economic (SE) firm that has developed all these internal organizational capabilities as much as possible, thereby reaching its highest human potential. The Z-firm is thus both highly competitive and highly responsible. It is not only outstanding in responding to competitive challenges related to its basic business activities, but it has also found fully responsible ways to deal with its external and internal stakeholders and society as a whole. To put this in perspective, the Z-firm is on the ideal of a continuum of actual SE firms. Actual firms rarely come very close to this ideal either because of insufficient human and organizational investments or because of discouragement from their external environments. Actual firms, therefore, ordinarily manifest some degree of inefficiency and irresponsibility. (Tomer 1999b, 9)

Because Z-firms are oriented to the long term, vision, and relationships, firms approximating these Z attributes should be well adapted to survive and prosper in any socio-political-economic conditions that emerge. The Z-firm ideal may not be more attainable than the neoclassical ideal, but it is more human and, in my view, more desirable.

Organizational Capital and Cooperation

Lack of cooperation among employees and groups within firms is an important source of X-inefficiency (Leibenstein 1987, chaps. 5–7; Tomer 1987, chap. 5). Employees cooperate when they work harmoniously toward common ends and when they engage in behavior helpful to other employees. Given the uncertainty, complexity, and interdependence that generally accompany division of labor, efficient task completion inevitably depends on employees helping one another on their respective work assignments. If workers are self-interested egoists rewarded only for accomplishment on their own work assignments, the reciprocal helpfulness of cooperative egoism can easily break down. As illustrated by the prisoner's dilemma model, there is an underlying conflict between such employees that could cause competition to trump cooperation, winding up with an outcome unfavorable to both parties rather than the mutually cooperative and favorable one. For the organization, lack of cooperation means either lower output than possible or more resources used than necessary. If employees do not help, tasks do not get accomplished, or if they do get accomplished, it is only with the help of greater managerial resources, adding to cost.

Because of the costs associated with noncooperation, organizations have a direct stake in maintaining and developing cooperative employee relationships, and organizations have come to understand that they can influence the cooperative outcome by promoting organizational features conducive to cooperation.

> If cooperative behavior is desired, the essence of the organization's task is to manage its implicit psychological contract with employees so that strong, reliable encouragements to cooperative behavior are provided and opportunistic tendencies are attenuated. . . . Second, organizations should develop considerate supervisors and encourage collective decision making and employee participation in order to foster strong work-group norms consistent with organization goals. Third, organizations should foster employees' latent altruistic tendencies. This might be done by emphasizing service to others and harmonious relationships. Fourth, financial and other extrinsic incentives could be used to reward employees' cooperative behavior, effectively changing their payoffs. (Tomer 1987, 66)

In general, cooperative effort will be encouraged when organizational factors attenuate opportunism, foster trust, encourage open communication, and promote the acceptance of common purposes and values. Obviously, to create these features associated with a highly cooperative organization will require a substantial investment in organizational capital.

Strategy and Structure

The hierarchical firm (H-firm) incorporates strategy and structure in the manner of the dominant operating mode of the large Western corporation during much of the second half of the twentieth century. The flexible integrated firm's (FI-firm) mode of operation represents tendencies present in high-performance global companies around the beginning of the twenty-first century, particularly as these companies have been understood by leading managerial thinkers (Tomer 1999b, chap. 5). There are many reasons to believe that the strategy and structure of the FI-firm allow it to be both more flexible, in the sense of not being rigid and being quick to adapt to environmental novelty, and better integrated, in the sense of being well coordinated and of having attained a unity among the different elements of the organization. FI-firms are distinguished by the following:

1. Are horizontal in nature, not hierarchical
2. Discourage opportunism and rely on trust and long-term understandings
3. Involve integration of thinking and doing

4. Incorporate learning and problem solving at the lowest levels
5. Provide synergistic linkages among product activities
6. Involve coordination of adjacent production activities through various forms of quasi-integration (Tomer 1999b, 97)

Based on a careful comparison of a number of the different structural and strategic differences, and given the rapidly changing, global nature of today's competition, the FI-firm is arguably better adapted than the H-firm to survive and prosper in today's competitive environment (Tomer 1999b, 86–97). The FI-firm's features are embodied in its corporate strategy, organizational structure, culture, organizational procedures, and so on. When firms use resources to develop these features, they are investing in the kind of organizational capital that many believe is crucial to successful performance in the global economy.

Organizational Capital and Joining Up

A pervasive organizational problem is the tendency for employees' efforts to be suboptimal, that is, employees typically devote too little effort on behalf of the organization. This inadequacy in organizational citizenship can be remedied if firms create the right kind of bonds between the organization and their members in the joining-up process (Williams and Anderson 1991, 601–2; Tomer 1999b, ch. 3). Joining up refers to the process by which an individual and an organization form a relationship shaping their future interactions. Joining up has two stages, selection and socialization, both designed to produce a good fit between the person and organization. Selection involves assessing the applicant's characteristics, which include developed skills and abilities, intelligence, knowledge and experience, values, and so on (Chatman 1991, 461). Socialization is the process by which a newly selected organization member comes to learn the values, norms, required behavior, expectations, and social knowledge essential to participation in the organization (Schein 1988, 54). If the process goes as well as possible and a strong mutual bond (organizational commitment) is created between the individual and the organization, the new employee will have been granted full membership in the organization (O'Reilly 1989, 17; Tomer 1999b, 44–45; Schein 1978, 111). It is expected that this new organizational citizen, who has a strong identification with and commitment to the organization, will not skimp on organizational efforts. Of course, it is possible that the joining-up process will leave the employee psychologically unattached, in which case the employee is unlikely to make the kind of efforts on behalf of the organization that an organizational citizen would. In the former case, where employees strongly identify with the organization and share its goals and values, they will in a sense benefit, even if not directly, from their efforts that benefit the organization. As a consequence, these employees will not want to be free-riding shirkers. To achieve this desirable result, the organization must devote resources to developing its joining-up process. This investment in organizational capital can be expected to have a significant payoff to the organization in higher employee citizenship efforts and thus higher productivity.

Japanese Management

The success of many large Japanese companies has led some researchers to inquire whether the critical factor in their success is the nature of Japanese management (Pascale and Athos 1981). Upon careful examination, there are many reasons for believing that J-management, the essence of the Japanese management ideal, is associated with greater X-efficiency than is the case for typical American management (A-management) (Ouchi 1981; Tomer 1987, chap. 7). The essence of J-management is:

1. Lifetime employment ideal is effective in practice.
2. Strong corporate culture and philosophy provide for implicit control of employees who internalize these values, in contrast to A-management's emphasis on explicit control mechanisms.
3. Community or family relations characterize relations among employees, and holistic rather than pure economic relations predominate.
4. Decision making and responsibility taking are collective in nature; the decision-making process emphasizes consensus formation.
5. Careers are characterized by slow evaluation and promotion and by nonspecialization. (Tomer 1987, 71)

The implicit psychological contract (IPC) of a firm is its relationship between employees and the organization. The IPC relates to a set of mutual expectations concerning performance, roles, trust, and influence, and it specifies what each should contribute to a relationship and what each should get out of it (Tomer 1987, 74). The IPC of J-organizations differs from that of A-organizations in that J-employees' tenure is long ("lifetime"), J-employees are members of a community and make commitments far beyond their economic contribution, J-employees share the organization's goals and share in decision making, J-employees are subject to implicit control through internalization of goals and values, and so on (Tomer 1987, 74–76). Because of these IPCs, J-organizations experience lower labor market transaction costs, the costs associated with contracting for labor. Also, these IPCs are associated with greater cooperation among employees, and thus lower costs of noncooperation.

The superiority of J-management is also due to its positive influence on worker motivation. Utilizing a modified version of Leibenstein's (1976, chap. 6) analysis of work effort choice, it can be shown that J-management leads workers to choose higher effort compared to what their effort choice would be in A-management. The analysis focuses on the present value of the future steam of utility that workers experience as a consequence of their effort decisions.

> The essence of the argument is that J workers, as compared to A workers have reason to expect higher increments in current and future utility from extra current effort, are likely to discount future utility at a lower rate, and are likely to direct more of their efforts toward organization goals. In other words, workers in J organizations are believed to find that the extra satisfactions afforded by working more responsibly, cooperatively and innovatively, with more attention to quality and organizational goals, etc., substantial and certain enough to motivate them to adopt higher effort positions. (Tomer 1987, 80)

In addition, higher work effort is expected because the time horizon in J-organizations is longer, because J-management allows workers to satisfy more of their higher human needs, and because J-workers apply a lower discount rate to future satisfactions from effort due to the lower personal risk involved and the lower rate of time preference (Tomer 1987, 81–82). There may also be lower monitoring costs and less organizational inertia in J organizations.

In any case, it is a nontrivial task to accumulate the kind of organizational capital necessary to create a J-organization.

High-Performance Work Systems

High-performance work systems (HPWS) are organizations that utilize a fundamentally different approach to managing than the traditional hierarchical approach associated with mass production/scientific management. At the heart of this emerging approach is a radically different employer-employee relationship (Tomer 2001). The essential characteristics of HPWS are:

1. Employment security
2. Selective hiring of new personnel
3. Self-managed teams and decentralization of decision making as the basic principles of organizational design
4. Comparatively high compensation contingent on organizational performance
5. Extensive training
6. Reduced status distinctions and barriers, including dress, language, office arrangements, and wage differences across levels
7. Extensive sharing of financial and performance information throughout the organization (Pfeffer 1998, ch. 3)

The main idea of HPWS is to create an organization based on employee involvement, commitment, and empowerment, not employee control (Lawler 1992). The particular set of managerial practices will vary from company to company. This distinction between the traditional control-oriented approach and the involvement-oriented approach associated with HPWS is critically important. In the former, workers at the lowest levels are unthinking agents of owner/manager principals. In contrast, in HPWS, workers are to a large degree self-controlled and self-managed. HPWS workers have shed the mentality of agents; they have become owners in their outlook (Tomer 2001, 64–65).

A number of studies have investigated whether firms utilizing a significant group of HPWS practices have achieved higher levels of performance than traditionally managed firms. In general, these empirical studies show that these systems of innovative HRM practices are strongly and positively associated with higher worker productivity as well as substantially improved financial performance (Tomer 2001, 65–67; see, for example, Huselid 1995 and Ichniowski, Shaw, and Prennushi 1997).

Theories from mainstream organizational economics have not helped to understand the performance superiority of HPWS because its concepts are designed to understand control-oriented organizations in which there is a clear principal-agent relationship (Tomer 2001, 67). Thus, mainstream organizational economics is concerned with *agent motivation* (where agents are controlled by external rewards and penalties), not the *deep owner motivation* of workers in involvement-oriented organizations.

> Deep owner motivation is the motivation experienced by employees who are not an agent of anybody and who are "owners" of the organization in much more than the financial/legal sense. Employees motivated in this way experience high psychological energy when their organizations provide them with the opportunity for self-actualization. . . . [It] arises when the employee is connected with or bonded with the organization in a deep and meaningful way, sharing a common destiny, mission, core values, and spirit. (Tomer 2001, 70)

When a business transforms its organization by installing the managerial practices and organizational features known as HPWS, it is making a very significant investment in organizational capital (Becker et al. 1997). Presumably a good part of the payoff to that investment is the improved performance deriving from the enhanced deep owner motivation. Although the payoffs may be high, this kind of investment can be complex and often involves a profound change from past practices. Thus diffusion of HPWS has been slow, as many managers have been understandably reluctant to make more than hesitant steps toward it.

Leadership

Mainstream economics' model of the firm is the production function. This machine model includes only hard factors, no soft elements or holism. Unfortunately, this model fails to help us understand why some firms achieve greatness and why others fail miserably (Tomer 1999b, chap. 6). To appreciate such differences, a holistic human model of the firm is needed. In the holistic model, two essential soft ingredients are the key: spirit and leadership. Spirit, according to Jack Hawley, relates to our deep inner self. It

> is the *us* beyond all the things [physical body, five senses, mind, feelings, innate tendencies, etc.] we usually think are the real us. . . . Spirit . . . refers to our (and our organizations') aliveness . . . [It] is the vitality that dwells in our body, . . . the very source of that energy. . . . Spirit refers to our other reality, our real reality, our higher reality—the one which at some inner level we know exists but at times forget that we know. (Hawley 1993, 16–17)

According to Peter Vaill,

> All true leadership is indeed spiritual leadership. . . . The reason is . . . leadership is concerned with bringing out the best in people. As such, one's best is tied intimately to one's deepest sense of oneself, to one's spirit. My leadership efforts must touch that in myself and in others. (Vaill 1990, 224)

The most important function of leaders in tapping this energy is to establish a collective vision for the organization. When organization members are fully enrolled in the highest purposes of the organization, they will work with powerful motivation, inspiration, and focus.

> Besides establishing the firm's vision, the other important role of leaders is to design and maintain the soft structures that channel creative energies toward desired results. The soft structures are the organizational features that facilitate and guide member behavior, as contrasted with the hard structures put in place by managers, that tend to control member performance. First on the list of soft structures is organizational culture, which involves shared values, sensitivities and attitudes; other soft structures include habits, belief structures, an understanding of the firm's core competencies, and the firm's mission. . . . When leaders identify the firm's existing core competencies and how these need to evolve, and link these to the organization's culture and mission, organization members' energies become powerfully focused. Thus in a variety of ways, the soft structures created by leaders represent very important intangible productive capacity; they are a type of organizational capital. (Tomer 1999b, 108–9)

If the firm's leaders do a great job creating the vision and appropriate soft structures, the intermediate soft outcome will be a combination of high energy and vitality and members who are fully aligned with the organization's mission and purpose. If the firm's managers also do a great job, they create intermediate hard outcomes, essentially intangible hard structures providing coordination and control. When these two intermediate outcomes are in exactly the right balance with each other, the firm is able to realize its highest potential; it has become a high-performance or Z-firm (Tomer 1999b, 109–11).

The Social Responsibilities of Firms

From the standpoint of pure neoclassical economics, firms' only role is an economic one, producing goods and services in response to prevailing economic incentives. In this view, firms have no obligation to society. Increasingly, at least in the eyes of many heterodox economists and noneconomist social scientists, the firm is being viewed as a socioeconomic entity that is embedded in society and has responsibilities and obligations to society. And increasingly, firms are being judged not just on their economic performance but also on their social performance. According to the doctrine of corporate social responsibility, corporations as social institutions should adopt policies and actions that are in conformity to the norms and goals of society (Tomer 1999b, chap. 7). Thus, corporations should voluntarily exercise self-control, aligning their efforts with the common good in the long term rather than simply allowing the market or government or even pressure groups to control them (Bowen 1978, 116–17). To become socially responsible, corporations have to discipline themselves in order to be in harmony with their external and internal stakeholders as well as society as a whole (Jones 1980, 65). The key to this discipline is decision making that reflects a highly ethical orientation and patience. The capacity for socially responsible behavior is one that inheres in the organization; it is one that can be improved through investment in organizational capital. The doctrine of corporate social responsibility implies the existence of a "social contract" between the corporation and society. As society's preferences change, this means a redefining and thus a renegotiating of the social contract.

As mentioned earlier, the ideal (Z-) firm is one that not only is outstanding in responding to competitive business challenges but also has learned how to respond to societal challenges in a fully responsible manner.

> Due to its highly ethical orientation, the Z-firm will seek win-win relationships with its external stakeholders. Due to its patience, it will be willing to sacrifice current profit for the prospect of future gain, even if uncertain. Because of its innovativeness and ability to learn, it will be able to discover and take advantage of opportunities that enable it to gain economically while pursuing an ethical, socially harmonious course of action. This . . . provides a solution to the negative externality problem. It is not that the Z-firm's behavior will be expected to have only positive impacts on others; it is that the Z-firm's self-regulated behavior will have no socially unacceptable negative impacts. (Tomer 1999b, 10)

Summing Up

In sum, in the human firm, there are many important capabilities that can be developed via investment in organizational capital. Firms may not choose to realize these potentials, but it is important to understand what these inherent capabilities are.

PERSONAL CAPITAL BASICS

Personal capital is a kind of human capital because it relates to capacity embodied in individuals. However, personal capital differs from standard human capital in that the human capacity involved is not the type developed by academic education or by the usual types of job-related training. The personal capital capacities are fundamentally different from cognitive intelligence or intellectual knowledge. Personal capital relates to an individual's basic personal qualities and reflects the quality of an individual's psychological, physical, and spiritual functioning. Further, it mirrors one's internal biochemical balance, physical health and conditioning, psychological strengths and weaknesses, and purpose in life. An individual's stock of personal capital is partly a product of genetic inheritance, partly a result of life-shaping events, and partly an outcome of individual efforts to mature and to grow in nonintellectual ways. Thus, it is in part produced intentionally. These personal capital capacities make possible expanded achievement possibilities (Tomer 2003, 456).

A very important component of personal capital that has received much recent attention is the human capacity called emotional intelligence (EI). My use of the concept draws heavily upon Daniel Goleman's (1995, 1998) writings, especially his second book, which focuses on the important contribution that organization members' EI makes in the workplace.

> "Emotional intelligence" refers *to the capacity for recognizing our own feelings and those of others, for motivating ourselves, and for managing emotions well in ourselves and in our relationships.* It describes abilities distinct from, but complementary to, academic intelligence, the purely cognitive capacities measured by IQ. (Goleman 1998, 317)

Emotional intelligence has five elements: self-awareness, motivation, self-regulation, empathy, and adeptness in relationships (Goleman 1998, 24). These determine one's potential for mastering the twenty-five emotional competencies, the more specific human capacities essential for success in the workplace.

It is important to note that different kinds of emotional competence are required by different industries, organizations, and jobs (Goleman 1998, 28–29). Thus, individuals who improve their EI and emotional competence in ways that match the demands of their work situation can be expected to raise their job performance. Spending time and effort on such improvements is the essence of what successful, performance-related investment in personal capital involves. Each and every occupation has a unique profile of emotional competencies that, along with cognitive intelligence, education, training, mentoring, and supervising, would be necessary for excellent performance. Because of the relative importance of emotional competencies in successful job performance, it makes sense for companies to assess jobs to determine their emotional competence requirements and to recruit employees with these competencies or to help existing organization members develop the needed competencies. Increasingly, this is being done in systematic ways. "Assessing the competencies that make someone outstanding at a particular job has become something of a mini-industry, with practitioners using a range of well-validated methods to tease out the ingredients of star performance" (Goleman 1998, 251, 259–62, quote on 260). Consider strategic planners. It has always been thought that the key ingredient of their success is "analytical and conceptual thinking," that is, cognitive ability.

> It turns out there's more to success as a planner than brainpower. Emotional skills are essential as well.
> Studies reveal that the *outstanding* strategic planners are not necessarily superior in their analytic skills. Instead the skills that raise them above the crowd are those of emotional competence: astute political awareness, the ability to make arguments with emotional impact, and high levels of interpersonal influence. (Goleman 1998, 259)

Presumably businesses with the aid of this kind of assessment can be more successful in their recruiting and developing efforts, and thus, can be more successful in adding to their firm's stock of personal capital.

PERSONAL CAPITAL'S ROLE IN THE FIRM

Personal Capital as Preorganizational Capital

In Tomer (1999b, 46–48), the term *preorganizational capital* is used to refer to certain human qualities providing productive capacity in that they are a necessary antecedent to an individual's successful joining-up with an organization. Preorganizational capital is a kind of personal capital, the kind that determines a person's capability for being successfully joined to an organization. Individuals with the appropriate endowments of personal capital can be expected

> to develop a more effective psychological contract with the organization, develop more cooperative, trusting and efficacious relationships with other organization members, and make deeper commitments that integrate their own purposes with those of the organization than do others with comparatively low endowments. To the extent that developing strong individual-organization attachments is important for productivity, it follows that a society's endowment of this capital provides real economic capacity. (Tomer 1999b, 47)

It is believed that workers possessing such virtues as loyalty, honesty, trust, discipline, an ethical orientation, and cooperativeness are more likely to develop commitment towards, and otherwise favorable bonds with, their organization (Tomer 1999b, 47).

> Different societies invest in or develop different pre-organizational qualities. For example, in Japanese schools, . . . janitors are not required because children clean and otherwise service their classrooms with relatively little overt supervision. From this experience, Japanese children acquire favorable attitudes regarding work cooperation, cleanliness and responsibility, attitudes which undoubtedly contribute to the productivity of their future workplaces. Similarly, many societies utilize sports activities to impart important cultural attitudes. Young athletes acquire a sense of disciplined intensity, teamwork and sportsmanship or ethics, among other things, that surely carries over to their work life. (Tomer 1999b, 48)

The Relationship Between Personal Capital and Social Capital

In some situations, personal capital and social capital are complements; in other situations, they are substitutes. When successful social capital formation requires that the individuals involved possess certain types of personal capital (the case of preorganizational capital, explained above), personal capital can be considered a complement to social capital (Tomer 2003, 465). There are two senses in which personal capital and social capital can be substitutes. First, suppose the organizational capital formation has gone very well and the organizational relationships developed provide plenty of structure, focus, and comfort to participants. Such relationships are likely to have the effect of calming people's negative emotions that might otherwise be a contaminant to organizational efforts. It is in this sense that strong social capital substitutes for the personal capital deficiencies of organization members. Second, suppose the organization's workers have strong personal capital qualities and have a low likelihood of manifesting any negative, contaminating emotion. With these workers, there is less need for the kind of social capital that calms and structures their interactions because these workers are more likely to cooperate and coordinate their efforts spontaneously. Thus, their strong personal capital is able to substitute to an extent for investment in social capital (Tomer 2003, 466).

Investments in Personal Capital

It is only recently that some firms have begun to pay significant systematic attention to personal capital capacities such as EI, and thus to make the kind of efforts necessary to raise their competitive performance through investments in personal capital.

> Firms, for example, are using psychological testing to identify the EI of prospective employees and employing search firms that explicitly screen job candidates for desired types of EI. Earlier, there was little or no effort to incorporate these considerations in the firm's joining-up process or the human resource development process. It is also important to note that more and more people on their own are making efforts to recognize their strengths and weaknesses and, as a consequence, are making personal capital investments in themselves through formal and informal experiences that develop their desired personal qualities. In some cases, people are correcting EI deficiencies (for example, overcoming addictions, attachments, psychological hang-ups, and so on). In other cases, they are seeking various kinds of personal growth or maturity. (Tomer 2003, 461)

Some of the self-help activities involved are targeted carefully to improve job capabilities; some are not. The specific activities involved range widely and may include going to seminars and workshops, reading books and listening to tapes, or engaging in psychotherapy. In any case, what in the past was either not done or done in a hit-or-miss way is increasingly being done in a big way and systematically. Now that firms and people are devoting significant resources to personal capital formation and that personal competence has become recognized as critical to successful business performance, neither economists nor anyone else can afford to ignore personal capital formation.

Personal Capital and the Z-Firm

Recall the Z-firm ideal, a firm that has developed its internal organizational capabilities, especially through organizational capital investments, to the point where it has reached its highest human potential in terms of competitiveness and responsibility. The Z-firm has another dimension, one related to personal capital, that has not been previously considered: it has invested very highly in the personal capital of its employees and encouraged its employees to make many of their own investments in personal capital. Assuming these are well-targeted investments in personal capital, a Z-firm with this dimension can be even more competitive and more socially responsible than one without it.

INTANGIBLE CAPITAL AND ECONOMIC GROWTH

Intangible Capital and Growth Accounting

If, as indicated above, investment in organizational capital and personal capital adds in a variety of ways to the productivity of business organizations, this same investment ought to contribute to the nation's productivity growth, and thereby its economic growth. In other words, when organizations grow and change and when people become more capable because, for example, they are more emotionally intelligent, this ought to raise the economy's productive capacity. To investigate this, it is useful, following neoclassical economists, to view the economy as an aggregate production function. From this standpoint, growth in the output of goods and services is made possible by growth in inputs, notably capital and labor, as well as by technological change. Recall that capital is defined here in a very general way to accommodate its very heterogeneous nature, including both tangible and intangible types. It follows that the growth of intangible types of capital such as organizational and personal capital contribute to economic growth just as the more tangible types do. Based on the production function concept, Edward Denison (1974) and other economists have used "growth accounting" methods to estimate the sources of economic growth. In particular, they have used data on the growth of certain inputs and output in order to estimate how much of the output growth is accounted for by the growth of these different inputs. The unaccounted-for growth, the residual, is a measure of the amount of technological change as well as the effect of the unmeasured influences and mismeasurement (Maddison 1995, 40–46). The residual is thus a measure of our ignorance (Abramovitz 1993, 218; Tomer 2003, 453).

In seeking to explain or account for a larger proportion of economic growth (and decrease the residual), economists have more and more included intangible inputs in their analyses. Most importantly, they have included human capital deriving from education and training. Although the use of these standard human capital measures has enabled economists to account for a greater amount of economic growth, a significant residual remains. For the most part, economists have been reluctant to consider inputs more intangible than standard human capital. The more intangible factors have received less attention in part because they frequently do not lend themselves to measurement; a related reason is the strong positivistic research tradition in mainstream economics. Despite this lack of attention, there is good reason to believe that these intangible sources of growth are much more important now than they were formerly (Abramovitz 1993). Below a few examples of the contribution to economic growth made by different types of intangible capital are considered.

The Organizational Capital Contribution

To measure the annual contribution of organizational capital formation to economic growth, it is necessary to measure the annual growth of the stock of organizational capital. Measuring the annual investment in organizational capital is no different in principle from measuring the annual investment in tangible capital. The measure is simply the real annual cost of these capital goods, the dollar cost adjusted for price change (Tomer 1987, 38–39). Note that in addition to explicit outlays, an important component of the cost of organizational capital is the opportunity cost associated with the value of the firm's output not produced because members of the firm were devoting their efforts to organizing work rather than their regular work, which presumably would contribute to current output. Using Denison's methods and estimates of the annual organizational investment due to management consultants' efforts in client firms, I have estimated that the growth of organizational capital input resulting from management consultants' efforts in client firms from 1929 to 1969 accounts for 2.79 percent of the residual growth in output over this period (Tomer 1987, 39–45). While this estimate cannot be considered a precise one, it does indicate how the organizational capital contribution to economic growth might be measured.

Another approach that can provide interesting evidence of organizational (or social) capital's contribution to economic growth utilizes cross-country empirical analyses. The basic approach is to regress countries' rates of growth of real GDP per capita over long periods of time on a variety of explanatory variables, including one or more relating to the type of intangible capital being investigated. Knack and Keefer (1997), for example, find that two social capital variables, trust and civic cooperation, have a strong positive and significant association with the rate of growth of per capita income for a sample of twenty-nine countries, controlling for education-related human capital and tangible capital investment.

The Personal Capital Contribution

There is some interesting evidence from a number of cross-country empirical analyses that bears on the personal capital contribution to economic growth, even though none of the variables used explicitly reflect personal capital or emotional intelligence.

> Barro's (1997) analysis, for example, is notable for using a life expectancy variable reflecting health status and the general quality of human capital and three regional variables for two low growth areas (sub-Saharan Africa and Latin America) and one high growth area (East Asia). Barro (1997) and Barro and Lee (1994, 43) find that although school attainment contributes to growth, it is a less important contributor than life expectancy. Life expectancy's strong positive relation to growth is apparently because it reflects not only good physical health but desirable behavior owing to good work and personal habits and other competencies (p. 18). It would not be surprising, therefore, if life expectancy was picking up some personal capital elements. Barro's regional variables might also pick up some personal capital aspects. This would be the case if there were, say, emotional intelligence patterns common to regions. (Tomer 2003, 462)

One obvious difficulty involved with measuring the personal capital contribution to economic growth is identifying the best measures of investment in personal capital and obtaining data on these. It would be most desirable to have one or two overall personal capital measures. However, this is problematic because, for example, emotional intelligence alone has five main elements, with twenty-five specific associated emotional competencies.

One intriguing study focuses on the key noncognitive personal characteristics of organization and efficiency, as operationalized by data on the cleanliness of a worker's dwelling. The argument is that "keeping a clean and organized home reflects an overall ability and desire to maintain a sense of order in a wide range of life activities" (Dunifon, Duncan, and Brooks-Gunn 2001, 150). Controlling for socioeconomic status and including cognitive ability, completed schooling, and other factors, the authors find a highly significant relationship between the cleanliness/organization variable and workers' wages twenty-five years later. For example, they find that "a one-standard-deviation increase in the clean-home measure is associated with a 13-percent increase in average hourly earnings 25 years later, which is slightly larger than the estimated impact of an additional year of schooling" (Dunifon, Duncan, and Brooks-Gunn 2001, 153).

Personal capital (and social capital) are also important for understanding whether less developed countries are likely to achieve sustained economic growth. Some less-developed countries (LDCs) may have the kind of culture that fosters the development of the types of EI critical to initiating the economic growth process; others may not.

> According to Fidelis Ezeala-Harrison (1995), "human factor depravity" deriving from past colonial economic exploitation and current lack of leadership is an extremely important

reason why so many LDCs remain underdeveloped. For satisfactory economic and social development, the basic human factor attributes such as "honesty, respect for the rule of law, individual innate self-discipline, accountability, and commitment to patriotic and selfless efforts" must be present (p. 3). "*Human factor depravity* . . . occurs as society fails to instill such ideals as honesty, respect for the rule of law, individual innate self-discipline, and social accountability into the basic training and development of its human resources" (p. 4). (Tomer 2003, 467)

Human factor depravity can be understood as a deficiency of a number of personal capital (and perhaps social capital) capacities. Thus, a key part of overcoming LDCs' economic underdevelopment is making the appropriate investments in personal and social capital.

THE GOVERNMENT ROLE WITH RESPECT TO ORGANIZATIONAL AND PERSONAL CAPITAL: INDUSTRIAL POLICY

Economists holding mainstream conceptions of the firm almost inevitably advocate that government should perform a regulatory role in the sense that there should be laws, along with government agency regulations, that serve to correct problematic (or inefficient) firm behavior. Rather than the government as regulator, an alternative approach that is more consistent with the socioeconomic conception of the firm is the government as coach. Charles Hampden-Turner (1988, 44) has asked: "Is it possible . . . for capitalist free enterprise to be 'coached' to greater humanity and success?" His answer (and my answer as well) is a resounding yes. Firms' socioeconomic performance can be raised through appropriate coaching. Coaching makes sense when we conceive of firms as organisms that learn, not only compete but cooperate, and are involved in complex social networks. Further, the coaching approach follows when we conceive of firms as fully human, socioeconomic entities whose learning (and cooperation) can be nurtured, facilitated, prodded, and otherwise encouraged. It is through such means that the human firm's capacity for competitiveness and responsibility can be raised and, thereby, the economic failure addressed. In contrast to the regulatory approach, the emphasis in coaching is *not* to get the firm to do the opposite of what it would naturally do but to provide the firm with plenty of opportunity and a conducive environment that will enable it to realize its highest potential in its relationship with society.

The government as coach, à la industrial policy, is oriented to developing the economy's capacity, and this generally means developing the capacity of human firms. Consider some of the specific roles of the government coach. First, an economy suffering from lack of competitiveness might be the result of firms in which organizational learning is deficient. Government might be able to provide the critical help necessary to enable firms to overcome the obstacles to the needed learning (Reich 1983; Johnson 1984). If this aid is successful, the targeted firms would gain competitive advantage, and the nation's productivity would rise. Second, poor performance of the economy might be related to firms that lack flexibility and integration, the organizational procedures necessary for rational decision making, the right kind of leadership, and so forth. Conceivably, the government as coach might be able to diagnose these problems and supply the kinds of assistance that would enable such firms to boost their competitiveness. If the government succeeded in these efforts, this would develop the nation's intangible collective human capacities, especially its organizational capital and personal capital, and would thereby enable the country to avoid deindustrialization and reach its economic growth goals.

The government coaching role need not be limited to dealing with the problem of competitiveness. Another major role for the government qua coach is developing firms', and thus the economy's, capacity for responsible behavior. This would address the kinds of economic failure that stem from irresponsible behavior. As indicated earlier, it is possible for firms to find socially responsible solutions to negative externality situations that obviate government's use of regulatory incentives. The policy implication is that the government as coach can help firms achieve these highly responsible solutions to externality-related failure situations through actions designed either to assist firms in improving their internal capabilities or to improve the external social influences on firms. Other situations may require the government coach to provide critical knowledge or to reduce undesirable and unintended regulatory influences.

CONCLUSION

Economists too easily lose sight of the economy's human nature. Firms and economies do not perform in the strict machinelike manner depicted in neoclassical theory. To understand fully the functioning and growth of the economy, one must appreciate the economy and its productive organizations as human entities with very important intangible aspects. In particular, organizational capital and personal capital, two important types of intangible capital, provide a very substantial part of human firms' productive capacity. Humans' soft capacities include social and noncognitive aspects of human behavior. This essay has explored the nature and importance of many of these intangible capacities and whether government attention to them is needed. Because these intangible capacities are essential to determining the economic performance of business enterprises and the growth of the nation's output, economists can no longer afford to ignore them.

More particularly, this essay has focused on the contributions that organizational capital and personal capital make directly to firms and to economic growth overall. Firms making investments in organizational capital can expect the returns to be realized as higher productivity (reduced X-inefficiency), more socially responsible behavior, better decision making, improved organizational learning, greater employee cooperation, greater flexibility and integration, greater organizational commitment, higher worker motivation, greater creativity, better alignment of workers with the organization's purposes, and so on. Firms making investments in their members' personal capital can expect higher returns because their employees will then have the specific intangible competencies required for successful performance of their organizational tasks. With respect to economic growth, the perspective of growth accounting is useful as a way to conceive of the overall contribution of investments in organizational capital and personal capital over time. There is good reason to believe (and some evidence to support the view) that growth in this accumulated intangible capital is now contributing substantially to the economic growth rate of countries throughout the world, whether advanced industrial ones or less developed ones. In light of the importance of this contribution, it is imperative that governments give consideration to whether the processes giving rise to these intangible capacities require encouraging via industrial policy. If so, the government as coach may need to take responsibility for their continuing development.

NOTE

1. The concept of organizational capital was first developed in my 1973 Ph.D. thesis (Rutgers University) and later in an article and book (Tomer 1981, 1987).

REFERENCES

Abramovitz, Moses. 1993. "The Search for the Sources of Growth: Areas of Ignorance, Old and New." *Journal of Economic History,* June, 217–43.

Barro, Robert J. 1997. *Determinants of Economic Growth: A Cross-Country Empirical Study.* Cambridge, MA: MIT Press.

Barro, Robert J., and Jong-Wha Lee. 1994. "Sources of Economic Growth." *Carnegie-Rochester Conference Series on Public Policy* 40: 1–46.

Becker, B.E., M.A. Huselid, P.S. Pickus, and M.F. Spratt. 1997. "HR as a Source of Shareholder Value: Research and Recommendations." *Human Resource Management* 36, 1: 39–47.

Bowen, Howard R. 1978. "Social Responsibility of the Businessman—Twenty Years Later." In Edwin M. Epstein and Dow Votaw, eds., *Rationality, Legitimacy and Responsibility: The Search for New Directions in Business and Society.* Santa Monica, CA: Goodyear.

Chatman, Jennifer A. 1991. "Matching People and Organizations: Selection and Socialization in Public Accounting Firms." *Administrative Science Quarterly* 36: 459–84.

Coleman, James S. 1988. "Social Capital in the Creation of Human Capital." *American Journal of Sociology,* 94 (supplement): 95–120.

———. 1990. *Foundations of Social Theory.* Cambridge, MA: Belknap Press.

Denison, Edward F. 1974. *Accounting for United States Economic Growth, 1929–1969.* Washington, DC: Brookings Institution.

Dunifon, Rachel, Greg Duncan, and Jeanne Brooks-Gunn. 2001. "As Ye Sweep, So Shall Ye Reap." *American Economic Review* 91, 2: 150–54.

Ezeala-Harrison, Fidelis. 1995. "Human Factor Issues in the History of Economic Underdevelopment." *Review of Human Factor Studies,* June, 1–25.

Goleman, Daniel. 1995. *Emotional Intelligence.* New York: Bantam Books.

———. 1998. *Working with Emotional Intelligence.* New York: Bantam Books.

Granovetter, Mark. 1985. "Economic Action and Social Structure: The Problem of Embeddedness." *American Journal of Sociology* 91: 481–510.

Hampden-Turner, Charles. 1988. "Three Images of Government: The Referee, the Coach, and the Abolitionist." *New Management* 6, 2: 43–49.

Hawley, Jack. 1993. *Reawakening the Spirit in Work: The Power of Dharmic Management.* San Francisco: Berrett-Koehler.

Huselid, M.A. 1995. "The Impact of Human Resource Management Practices on Turnover, Productivity, and Corporate Financial Performance." *Academy of Management Journal* 48, 3: 635–72.

Ichniowski, C., K. Shaw, and G. Prennushi. 1997. "The Effects of Human Resource Management Practices on Productivity: A Study of Steel Finishing Lines." *American Economic Review* 87, 3: 291–313.

Johnson, Chalmers, ed. 1984. *The Industrial Policy Debate.* San Francisco: Institute for Contemporary Studies.

Jones, Thomas M. 1980. "Corporate Social Responsibility Revisited, Redefined." *California Management Review* 22: 59–67.

Knack, Stephen, and Philip Keefer. 1997. "Does Social Capital Have an Economic Payoff? A Cross-Country Investigation," *Quarterly Journal of Economics* 112, 4: 1251–88.

Lawler, Edward E. 1992. *The Ultimate Advantage: Creating the High Involvement Organization.* San Francisco: Jossey-Bass.

Leibenstein, Harvey. 1976. *Beyond Economic Man: A New Foundation for Microeconomics.* Cambridge, MA: Harvard University Press.

———. 1987. *Inside the Firm: The Inefficiencies of Hierarchy.* Cambridge, MA: Harvard University Press.

Maddison, A. 1995. *Monitoring the World Economy 1820–1992.* Paris: Organization for Economic Cooperation and Development.

Nielsen, Klaus. 2003. "Social Capital and the Evaluation of Innovation Policy." *International Journal of Technology Management,* 26, 2–4: 205–25.

O'Reilly, Charles. 1989. "Corporations, Culture, and Commitment: Motivation and Social Control in Organizations." *California Management Review* 31: 9–28.

Ouchi, William G. 1981. *Theory Z: How American Business Can Meet the Japanese Challenge.* Reading, MA: Addison-Wesley.

Pascale, Richard T., and Anthony G. Athos. 1981. *The Art of Japanese Management: Applications for American Executives.* New York: Simon and Schuster.

Pfeffer, Jeffrey. 1998. *The Human Equation: Building Profits by Putting People First.* Boston: Harvard Business School Press.

Reich, Robert. 1983. *The Next American Frontier.* New York: New York Times Books.

Schein, Edgar H. 1978. *Career Dynamics: Matching Individual and Organizational Needs.* Reading, MA: Addison-Wesley.

———. 1988. "Organizational Socialization and the Profession of Management." *Sloan Management Review* 30: 53–65.

Tomer, John F. 1981. "Organizational Change, Organizational Capital and Economic Growth." *Eastern Economic Journal* 7: 1–14.

———. 1987. *Organizational Capital: The Path to Higher Productivity and Well-Being.* New York: Praeger.

———. 1999a. "Social and Organizational Capital." In Phillip Anthony O'Hara, ed., *Encyclopedia of Political Economy,* 2:1049–51. London: Routledge.

———. 1999b. *The Human Firm: A Socio-Economic Analysis of Its Behavior and Potential in a New Economic Age.* London: Routledge.

———. 2001. "Understanding High-Performance Work Systems: The Joint Contribution of Economics and Human Resource Management." *Journal of Socio-Economics* 30, 1: 63–73.

———. 2002. "The Firm Is Human: It Is Not a Neoclassical Machine." *Indicators* 1, 3: 101–15.

———. 2003. "Personal Capital and Emotional Intelligence: An Increasingly Important Intangible Source of Economic Growth." *Eastern Economic Journal* 29, 3: 453–70.

Vaill, Peter B. 1990. *Managing as a Performing Art: New Ideas for a World of Chaotic Change.* San Francisco: Jossey-Bass.

Williams, Larry J., and Stella E. Anderson. 1991. "Job Satisfaction and Organizational Commitment as Predictors of Organizational Citizenship and In-Role Behaviors." *Journal of Management* 17, 3: 601–17.

PART 3

DECISION MAKING

CHAPTER 14

HOW TO DO AS WELL AS YOU CAN

The Psychology of Economic Behavior and Behavioral Ecology

STEPHEN E.G. LEA

This essay seeks to locate the emerging discipline of behavioral economics by setting out a general point of view about the relationships between three disciplines. It is not primarily a summary or an introduction to the literature of a particular part of behavioral economics, but it does provide samples of research literature that illustrate its general theme.

The point of view expounded in this essay is simple. It is that the sciences of ecology, economics, and psychology overlap more than has been realized; that there are problems, important in both scientific and social terms, that can be solved only by using psychological analysis along with economic analysis, ecological analysis, or both; and that if we are to make progress with this kind of interdisciplinary approach, we need paradigms different from those currently most often used.

In part of its argument, at least, this essay stands in the mainstream of other contributions to this handbook. All the present essays share, in one way or another, the view that psychology and economics have something important to do with each other. But this essay is about the meeting of three disciplines, not two, and its arguments about the relation between psychology and ecology will have less supportive context in the rest of the book. They may perhaps be less immediately persuasive, especially as they refer as much to animal psychology as to human psychology. It should be recognized at once that the essay is making the implicit assertion that there is some psychological unity across species, although of course it also recognizes the essential psychological differences between humans and other animals.

Since this essay is written by someone who is, by training, a psychologist, psychological analysis may tend to take pride of place here. But that is not to say that it is in any way more important, or more fundamental, than the ecological or economic approach. The thrust of the argument is the need for more interdisciplinary work, and that will not be furthered by mere disciplinary imperialism—trying to pretend that psychology could "take over" economics, or vice versa.

It might be expected that a balanced presentation of the relations between three disciplines would be structured as a triangle, with each discipline relating to the other two. In practice, however, this essay largely discusses the relations between psychology, on one hand, and ecology and economics, on the other: the structure of the discussion is illustrated by Figure 14.1. It is a key part of the argument that psychology relates to both ecology and economics in essentially the same way, while the relation between ecology and economics is rather different. However, at the end of the essay, that third side of the triangle is briefly reviewed.

Figure 14.1   **Relations Between the Disciplines of Psychology, Ecology, and Economics**

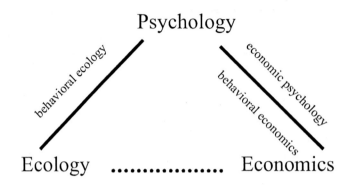

This essay shares its title with the Lister Lecture given by the author in 1983 to the British Association for the Advancement of Science, the foremost public showcase for science in the United Kingdom. Returning to that title more than twenty years later provides an opportunity to reexamine themes expounded in the lecture and see how they have progressed after two decades—a period that has seen crucial developments both in behavioral economics and in behavioral ecology, with those two interdisciplinary areas moving strongly toward the main-stream. In 1983 it seemed necessary both to demonstrate and to justify an upsurge in interdisciplinary activity that was beginning to involve psychology in both economic and ecological analyses—to point to both intellectual and institutional developments, as well as events in the world, that were making economic psychology and behavioral ecology active research areas and familiar concepts. Now, and especially in the context of the present volume, that argument scarcely needs making.

However, it remains worth asking why interdisciplinary research areas develop. Do they arise at times when the mainstreams of traditional disciplines are running dry of research openings, forcing the ambitious to the fringes? In the middle of the twentieth century a standard biochemistry textbook offered a cynic's definition of biochemists as men who talk about chemistry to biologists, about biology to chemists, and about women among themselves. It is not just the sexist humor that has dated irreversibly: the subsequent history of biochemistry has triumphantly refuted the author's skepticism about his own discipline. By 1948, when that book was first published, both chemistry and biology had reached a stage of development where, for further progress in certain well-defined directions, they needed each other, and half a century later we have seen how the new science of biochemistry has transformed our understanding of life and of human society.

The argument of the present essay is that by about 1975 a similar point had been reached in the relations of psychology with both economics and ecology. Some of the traditional concerns of psychology, particularly in the areas of instrumental behaviors (human and animal), could no longer be tackled without using the kind of approach characteristic of economics or ecology. And some of the traditional concerns of economics and ecology, such as the response of consumers to changes in price and income, and of foraging animals to the availability of food, were ripe for the sort of empirical input about the attitudes and behavior of individuals that only a psychological approach could provide. A quarter of a century further on, it is possible to look at the progress that has been made in forging interdisciplinary links.

PSYCHOLOGY AND ECONOMICS, PSYCHOLOGY AND ECOLOGY

Before considering the substance of interdisciplinary work, however, it is necessary to look a little more systematically at the nature of the relationships between the three disciplines with which this essay is concerned—at least in their traditional, monodisciplinary forms.

Two things mark off psychology from either economics or ecology: a difference of subject matter and a difference of approach. At first glance, it might seem that the really fundamental difference is that of subject matter. If we are interested in individual behavior and mental life, that makes us psychologists. If we are interested in the movements of scarce resources, of money and goods, around whole social systems, that makes us economists. If we are interested in the interactions of whole species of animals with the other species that constitute their biological environment, that makes us ecologists.

A second glance makes it clear that these differences are relatively superficial. On one hand, societies and species are made up of individuals, so the behavior of economies or species are products of individual behavior, and the leading theories in both fields attempt to derive the behavior of aggregates from the behavior of individuals. On the other hand, the prevailing economic or ecological situation has an important influence on every individual within it. Consequently, long before the institutions of economic psychology and behavioral economics came into existence, there were areas in which both economists and psychologists were taking an interest. The motivation and incentive for work behavior is an obvious example. Similarly for psychology and ecology: both have a long-standing interest in feeding behavior, for example. What makes an approach to a problem ecological or economic rather than psychological is not the problem under consideration but the framework within which the problem is viewed.

That framework is partly a matter of the other problems that form the context for looking at any one particular problem. An economist approaching the incentive to work sees employment as one more situation in which a commodity is bought and sold, so it can be compared with the purchase and sale of goods and services. A psychologist sees it as one more situation in which people enter into social relations, so the workplace can be compared with the family, the neighborhood, and other scenes of interpersonal interaction. Similarly with feeding behavior: an ecologist might see it as one way in which the numbers and fitness of animals of one species are acted on and act upon the numbers of other species, to be compared with competition for space or the spread of disease. A psychologist, on the other hand, might see it as one variety of motivation or reinforcement, to be compared, perhaps, with sexuality or curiosity.

Much more important, however, is the theoretical lens through which any problem is viewed. Psychologists, by and large, are low-level theorists. Faced with a new phenomenon, or a new area of study, our first inclination is to collect some data. When we have a fair amount of data in hand, we usually try to produce a descriptive generalization rather than interpreting the data in terms of any wide-ranging theory. When we do carry out a theory-driven investigation, the theory in question is normally quite specific, not part of some grand general approach to the whole of psychology. One psychologist might inquire, for example, whether Maslow's (1970) hierarchical theory of motivation applies to the employment situation, but another could regard Maslow as wholly irrelevant to the problem without thereby ceasing to be a psychologist.

Both economists and ecologists behave very differently. Each discipline has its grand theory, which is part of, and characteristic of, an economic or ecological approach to any problem whatever. In the case of economics, it is the theory of rational decision making; in the case of ecology, it is Darwin's theory of the evolution of species by natural selection. There are differences, both in substantive content and in logical status, between these two theories. But in terms of their relations to psychology, both say somewhat the same thing. They say that individuals—animal or human—will do the best they can. Economists tend to describe this as behaving "rationally," ecologists as behaving "optimally," but each discipline has powerful reasons for expecting it to happen.

So when either an ecologist or an economist approaches a new phenomenon or a new problem area, his or her first urge is not to set up a study and collect some data. It is to apply the grand theory and find out what ought to happen. That "ought" has two senses. In the first sense, it asks what the predictions of the grand theory are. In the second, it asks how the individual animal or person should behave if he, she, or it is to do as well as possible in the given situation. That is not to say that either ecologists or economists do not collect data. No one would ever have supposed that of ecologists, but a reader of elementary economics textbooks might be forgiven for thinking it of economists. Most elementary treatments of the discipline, and even some of its most prestigious research, pay no attention to the huge masses of econometric data that are constantly being collected and analyzed, charting the effects of changes in prices, incomes, and other conditions on important economic behaviors such as hours worked, amounts of goods and services bought and sold, and amounts of money saved. One of the major changes over the past twenty years, however, has been that economics has become an empirical discipline in an additional sense, through the rapid development of a lively subdiscipline of experimental economics, crowned in 2002 by the award of the Nobel prize to Vernon Smith "for having established laboratory experiments as a tool in empirical economic analysis, especially in the study of alternative market mechanisms."

But though both ecology and economics are genuinely empirical disciplines, they are both theory-driven in a sense that psychology is not. It is possible to ask, "What does economic theory say about this question?" and obtain a coherent answer. If you then ask, "And what does psychological theory say?" the only reasonable answer would be "Which psychological theory?" This fact imposes an asymmetry on the relationship between the disciplines; it has also led to the tacit adoption of a paradigm for behavioral investigation of economic questions that has frequently been unhelpful.

THE PITFALL OF THE RATIONALITY QUESTION

The fact that economics and ecology as disciplines are unified by a coherent theory sets a snare in the path of the psychologist who becomes interested in the sorts of questions studied by ecologists or economists. All too readily, psychologists see themselves as able to produce the data by which the assumption of rationality or optimality can be tested, so that the role of psychology is testing (and probably refuting) that assumption. Most psychologists believe that humans or animals faced with real economic or ecological problems will not, in fact, do as well as they can. Data from other situations, and any one of the numerous low-level theories psychology can muster, make this seem obvious.

Twenty years ago, it was necessary to spend a good deal of time clearing the issue of the rationality question out of the way. At that point it still virtually formed a paradigm, in the sense in which Kuhn (1962) used that term. When economic psychology approached a new research area, the tendency was to marshal ideas, theories, and data into those that support rationality and those that oppose it. All too often the result looked like a contest between psychology and economics, or between psychology and ecology. Increasingly, however, economic psychologists have taken the view that this way of looking at the area is fundamentally misguided (e.g., Lea 1994). Not only does a pro- and anti-rationality paradigm tend to set up oppositions between disciplines when what is needed is collaborative effort, but it rests upon a misconception about the nature and role of the rationality or optimality assumption in the first place.

Part of the problem is the multitude of different things we might mean when we say that behavior is rational. For the present essay, a particularly important distinction is between descriptive and procedural rationality (Simon 1978). If we are using rationality as a description, we describe a behavior as rational if it is the one that would be performed by an ideally logical decision maker, armed with all the available information, and able to calculate from it what the best thing to do is—what Gigerenzer and Goldstein (1996) call a "Laplacean demon." But if we are using rationality to define a procedure, we would mean that the person taking the decision was or was seeking to be such an ideally logical decision maker, that is, that the person used rational forethought in coming to a decision: there is then no commitment as to how successful the decision maker has been. It is obvious that descriptive rationality and procedural rationality do not entail each other. On one hand, the kind of cognitive limitations that Simon has constantly pointed out means that people who are seeking to be rational will almost necessarily fail to equal the performance of the Laplacean demon. On the other hand, we can envisage that entirely mechanical processes, such as could be conferred on animals by the evolution of instincts, might produce optimal behavior in particular situations without any need or possibility of reflective forethought (cf. Lea 1978).

Ecologists have always been perfectly clear about the status of rationality (more usually called optimality in the ecological context) within their theorizing. The theory of natural selection leads them to expect that optimality will hold, more or less, at the descriptive, behavioral level. It makes no prediction whatever about the mechanism underlying that behavior. Ecologists will readily agree that even if an animal's foraging behavior agrees with an optimal model, it is still unlikely that the animal is consciously working out the best possible way to get food. It is much more likely that some mechanism other than rational forethought is responsible for producing rational behavior. In other words, the word *rationality* confuses two things that biologists have learned, by painful experience, to keep separate: functional explanations and mechanistic explanations. When we have specified the function of some organ or piece of behavior, we have indeed explained it in one important sense. We have provided what is often called an ultimate explanation—an explanation within the terms of evolutionary theory. But we have not provided a proximate explanation until we have also specified the mechanism by which the function is exercised. As an aside to the present argument, we should note that we also need a third sort of explanation, a developmental account, specifying how the individual organism develops from not having that organ or behavior as an embryo to possessing it in the full adult form. Behavioral economics also needs its developmental arm, and the attempt to discover the socialization processes that underlie adult economic behavior has been one of the more fruitful avenues for interdisciplinary research (cf. Harbaugh, Krause, and Berry 2001; Webley 2004).

Compared with ecology, mainstream economic thinking has in general not been so clear about the distinction between ultimate and proximate causation. It has used the human capacity for rational forethought as a guarantee that rationality will provide an appropriate descriptive account of behavior, and that argument is unsound. It is not in doubt that humans can use rational forethought. But the fact that I have feet does not mean that I necessarily stand up all the time, nor does the capacity for rational forethought mean that all behavior will be governed by it. And even when I do think rationally, I may not be able to mobilize all the information that the ideal decision maker would use, or to process it in the time available—to return to Simon's fundamental point about the external and internal bounds for rationality.

Of course, within economics there are alternative arguments according to which human economic behavior can be expected to be rational at the descriptive level. In the case of firms rather than individuals, competition processes will impose a kind of selection not unlike that spurring genetic evolution in animals: firms that behave optimally will be more likely to survive in such a climate than suboptimal firms, which will be bankrupted, so the remaining firms will all behave in ways that seem fairly rational (Hirshleifer 1977). However, as Cyert and March (1963) point out, such competitive pressures are often ineffective outside periods of dire financial stringency, and the recent history of the dot-com boom and the behavior of firms such as Enron shows how very far from optimality firms' behavior can get—even if in the longer run a competitive nemesis is waiting for them.

Such arguments show some awareness of the distinction between proximate and ultimate causation. Furthermore, within economics there have always been dissident voices, arguing for a more nuanced concept of rationality (e.g., March 1978). But still one can find economics and psychology being set up as rival systems for explaining behavior, one assuming rationality and the other denying it. To economic psychology, such contests are or should be wholly irrelevant. What matters to an economic analysis is to characterize the rational behavior in a given situation. What matters to a psychological analysis is the mechanism producing rational behavior, or (more usually) something like it, or (unusually) something quite unlike it. The two questions are almost entirely independent. This is one reason why asking whether or not observed performance is rational is a poor way to approach the psychological foundations of economic behavior.

However, the most important reason for rejecting "testing rationality" as a paradigm for interdisciplinary research is that mainstream economics treats the assumption of rationality in a rather special way. When it discovers some aspect of economic behavior that is manifestly irrational, it does not reject the assumption; instead, it changes the definition of rationality. For example, all authorities agree that people are too much inclined to accept present gain at the cost of future loss. One simple way in which this "excessive time preference" (in economic terms) or "failure to delay gratification" (in psychological terms) can be made consistent with rationality is simply by specifying a subjective discount rate that is different from the objective rate at which an abstractly rational decision maker would discount the future (e.g., Friedman 1963), or, if no single subjective discount rate will do the job, a subjective discount function different from the exponential decay function implicit in standard rationality (for example, the hyperbolic form proposed by Ainslie 1992). Psychologists sometimes feel there is something unsatisfactory about this tinkering with rationality. On the contrary, it is simply a device to enable the apparatus of economic theory to work, to produce descriptive accounts of the sense in which behavior is rational.

According to this formalist view, rationality within economics is not a theory to be tested. It is a framework within which behavior can be described and smaller-scale theories about it tested. A psychological approach that sets itself to test rationality is therefore doomed to irrelevance within an interdisciplinary perspective (Lea 1994).

Everything that has been said here about the relation between psychology and economics applies with equal force to the relation between psychology and ecology. But in this respect, at least, one is preaching to the converted in the case of ecology; the status of the optimality assumption within ecology is much better understood by both psychologists and ecologists than the status of the rationality assumption within economics.

ALTERNATIVE FRAMEWORKS FOR ECONOMIC PSYCHOLOGY

If we cannot organize a fruitful interdisciplinary discussion around the rationality question, what structure can we use? Are there any alternative paradigms? Much of the rest of this essay is taken up with the discussion of two possibilities, which are complementary rather than competing.

First, we could opt for a division of roles between psychology and economics. We give to economics its traditional role of describing behavior in terms of rationality: of finding rational models that are consistent with at least the gross facts of observed behavior (or, in other words, of finding how the simple assumption of rationality must be modified and fleshed out if it is to be a valid description of behavior). We then give to psychology the task of discovering the mechanism and the process of development that gives rise to more or less rational behavior. This is very much the solution that has been adopted in the ecological case. This will be referred to below as the "function/mechanism" or "ultimate/proximate explanation" paradigm.

Within this paradigm, it is very plain that psychology can and should tell you *how* to do as well as you can. Economics or ecology will tell you what the best thing to do is; psychology will furnish the mechanism by which to produce this rational or optimal behavior, or the nearest approach to it that you can manage with the cognitive resources you have. It will do so whether we are talking about the immediate mechanism of one small instance of behavior or the process of lifetime development that produces the behavioral tendencies that in turn solve problems in the optimal way.

The second alternative refers back to the point made earlier in this essay, that disciplines are separated not by their subject matter but by the manner in which they approach it. Psychology focuses on the individual. Economics and ecology both focus on the structured whole, the society within which the individual must live. Within the social sciences generally, there have always been two ways of seeking to understand both individuals and societies. One is the atomistic approach, which starts from the individual and attempts to understand the entire society as the aggregation of the knowable behaviors of individuals. The alternative is the organic approach, which starts from the entire society, treating it as an entity with behavior of its own and laws of its own governing that behavior, and attempts to understand the individual as a product of the knowable behavior of the society he or she lives in. Applying these two broad approaches to the narrower context of economic behavior, it is evident that we can either start from the choice behaviors of individuals and try to aggregate them so as to understand the entire economy, or we can start from the behavior of the economy as a system and try to deduce individuals' economic behavior. It is important to recognize that though psychology focuses on the individual while economics focuses on the system, it is not the case that psychology is atomistic while economics is organic. True, there are tendencies in those directions. But Anglo-American economics, at least, is almost as atomistic in its general trends as Anglo-American psychology; microeconomic theory is the field par excellence of the analysis of system-level economic phenomena in terms of individual choice behaviors. The doctrine of "consumer sovereignty" means nothing else but that the entire behavior of the economy can be predicted from the choice behavior of individual consumers: in the words of the 1990s Ford Europe slogan lifted from a Queen lyric, "Everything we do is driven by you."

A more radical proposal for a framework within which to study economic psychology, therefore, involves accepting that atomistic and organic approaches to society both have validity—that they are complementary rather than competing—and furthermore that both economics and psychology make use of both. In other words, there is a dual causation both of individual economic behavior and of large-scale economic phenomena. Both are caused partly by processes operating at the level of the entire economy and partly by processes operating at the level of the individual. Lea, Tarpy, and Webley (1987) developed this approach more fully. We called it the "dual causation paradigm"; it is in many ways a simplified version of the basic model for economic psychology set out by Van Raaij (1981) in the first issue of the *Journal of Economic Psychology*.

This might seem a modest proposal, since it simply recognizes some obvious realities. In practice, however, it is quite radical, because rejecting the assumption of unidirectional causation means accepting a range of methodological difficulties. Once we accept that economic behavior is embedded within a social system, we have to accept that many investigations of economic behavior are likely to give inconclusive or misleading results. Dual causation implies circular causation, that is, feedback processes. Where social feedback is negative, causal processes that have been discovered in isolated systems (e.g., the laboratory) will often fail to have any effect when we study them in their original societal context. Even more unsettling, where social feedback is positive, effects may occur for which there is very little apparent cause. Biochemists must constantly make the distinction between in vitro and in vivo behaviors of reagents; behavioral economists need to draw the same distinction—and, like biochemists, not reject laboratory results because they cannot be reproduced on the societal scale. It is impossible to understand a social process without understanding the individual processes that make it up, even if in the social context those individual processes do not reach the same logical end points as they do in the laboratory.

Everything that has been said in this essay so far has been abstract. The remainder of the essay reviews the use of both these alternative frameworks in three specific, concrete areas where psychology overlaps with economics and ecology. In terms of their nonpsychological content, the first belongs purely to ecology, the second is a hybrid of ecological and economic questions, and the last is purely economic. Each of them is examined with the aid of the two paradigms just discussed. It will quickly become apparent that the two approaches are by no means mutually exclusive. It is especially important to realize that they are not alternative theories to be tested against one another. Even the rationality-question paradigm, which we earlier rejected as a general key to understanding, will turn out to have some place in the ensuing discussions.

THE PSYCHOLOGY OF FORAGING

As an ecological example, we shall consider the case of foraging for food and, more particularly, of optimal foraging theory.

This case is particularly easily analyzed within the function/mechanism paradigm. Ecology has always been interested in feeding, for food availability is one of the major factors with the potential to limit the numbers of any animal species. MacArthur and Pianka (1966) first stated clearly a very simple idea that has been immensely influential. Each animal species, they argued, has been produced by natural selection. The efficiency of foraging—hunting for food, whether animal or vegetable—will have a powerful influence on the fitness of any animal, that is, on the number of descendants it manages to leave. Natural selection implies that any behavior that increases foraging efficiency, so as to give one animal a competitive edge over its neighbors, will be selected for strongly. In fact, this selection pressure is likely to be so strong that all the animals in the species will end up as optimal foragers within their own particular environment: they will become so efficient that no further improvement is possible. At any rate, there will be no way an individual can improve without changing radically the sort of animal it is.

This idea is a special case of the general claim that natural selection will produce descriptively rational behavior. It forms the core of what has become known as optimal foraging theory. That theory is only interesting, however, because we can add substantially to that core. It proves to be possible to specify the optimal foraging "strategy" in a number of environments that are at least reasonable approximations to the infinitely complex real environment in which real foragers live. For example, we can consider an environment that contains a number of different kinds of prey, differing both in their food value and the time it takes to eat them; the general optimal foraging theory is then specialized to provide an optimal diet model. Or we can consider an environment that contains perceptible patches within which some food is to be found, but between which there is only barren land across which the forager must travel to get from patch to patch; we then generate a patch selection theory (Charnov 1976). Or we can consider an environment that contains a central "home," where the forager feeds its young or stores food for later consumption, and more or less distant feeding grounds, and develop a theory for the central-place forager (Orians and Pearson 1979).

The obvious move is then empirical: go out into the field, study some real animals' foraging behavior, and see whether it is as optimal foraging theory suggests that it should be. In the years following MacArthur and Pianka's paper, there have been almost innumerable studies doing just that, either in wholly natural situations or in reasonable approximations to them arranged in the laboratory. An early example was Goss-Custard's extensive studies of redshank feeding in the mud of English estuaries. Goss-Custard (1977) found that redshanks' selection between different kinds of prey was much more affected by the availability of the better kinds of prey than by the availability of the worse kinds (this is one of the more surprising predictions of optimal diet models). On the other hand, the redshank occasionally sampled all kinds of prey, whereas theory predicts that, provided they are present in sufficient density, only the better kinds will be taken.

Initially, optimal foraging theory was almost wholly an affair for behavioral ecologists. But then psychologists began to take an interest. A number of people asked themselves whether the predictions of optimal foraging theory would hold for animals working in the quite unnatural, abstract conditions of the psychological laboratory, as well as under more natural circumstances. Using rats and pigeons and the conventional apparatus and procedures of the operant conditioning laboratory, it was quickly demonstrated that there was nothing special about the natural environment. Collier and Rovee-Collier (1981) showed that optimal foraging theory provided a good prediction for the behavior of rats in a Skinner box when choices were structured to resemble those facing natural foragers; Lea (1979) obtained the same result from pigeons and extended the experiment to various situations in which laboratory animals are known to behave suboptimally from the point of view of maximizing the rate of food intake; and Abarca and Fantino (1982) brought these experiments within the context of a general mechanistic approach to animal choice, delay-reduction theory.

All empirical tests of optimal foraging theories are, in one sense, raising the question of the validity of rationality assumptions. But the general trend has been away from questions of optimality as such, toward a much healthier concentration on the mechanism by which either optimal or nearly optimal behavior is produced. This is a question to which psychologists have a great deal to contribute, because that mechanism must necessarily involve some learning, and animal learning is one topic on which psychologists have gathered a great many data and a great many ideas.

Even the simple kinds of foraging problem described above require some level of learning. Optimal behavior varies according to the densities of different kinds of prey in different places, and in a changing environment these must be learned from day to day and even from minute to minute. The operant psychology that emerged from B.F. Skinner's analysis of instrumental learning provided simple tools by which the learning of such parameters could be studied (cf. Dow and Lea 1987; Killeen et al. 1996). Conversely, the general need of animals to forage optimally provided a much-needed ecological and evolutionary context and anchoring for the principles of operant psychology, which had previously seemed a wholly artificial creation.

However, consideration of the needs of foraging animals has contributed a great deal more to the study of animal learning than just providing an adaptive rationale for the well-understood principles of classical and operant conditioning. In the final quarter of the twentieth century, the psychological study of animal learning was dominated by a new approach, usually referred to as "animal cognition" (Pearce 1997; Vauclair 1996): instead of trying to derive everything from a bottom-up analysis of behavior, psychologists have been taking cognitive analyses and concepts that are effective in the study of human mental life and seeing whether they can be applied effectively to other animals. Part of the thrust of this approach is to consider why and how human cognitive capacities may have evolved. A particularly powerful way to do this is to consider species that have unusual foraging needs and to investigate whether these are matched with unusual cognitive capacities.

So, for example, in seeking to investigate memory processes in animals, psychologists and zoologists have turned their attention to species that cache food in times of abundance and recover their caches in times of scarcity. From the point of view of memory, the most interesting cachers are those that make a large number of small hoards, because (for obvious reasons to do with preventing cache robbery) such caches cannot be marked in any way, nor can they be placed where they could be discovered by smell or other public cues. The animals must rely on a private cue to take them back, sometimes months later, to the cache sites, and the only obvious candidate is pure memory. The memory load this implies can be severe, because the caches that some animals make are very numerous: Clark's nutcracker, a bird of the American West, has been calculated to cache 20,000 to 100,000 seeds each autumn, in caches containing between one and fourteen seeds each (Vander Wall 1990, 300–5), while in England the gray squirrel needs to hide and recover around 3,000 nuts each year in order to survive the winter (Macdonald 1997). Here the ecology of foraging sets a problem, and comparative psychologists have set themselves to solve it by seeking to find out the cognitive mechanisms (e.g., Kamil, Balda, and Olson 1994) and even the brain structures (e.g., Basil et al. 1996) underlying these exceptional performances. It turns out that scatter-caching species do have exceptional memories when compared with otherwise similar animals that do not cache, and that these abilities are mirrored in an enlarged hippocampus, a part of the brain that in birds and nonhuman mammals seems to have a specialized function as a spatial memory store.

From an evolutionary point of view the most interesting cognitive adaptations are those that we find in the animals most closely related to ourselves, and which might therefore pave the way for the emergence of human intelligence. Here a good example would be some recent work on food processing techniques in chimpanzees and gorillas (Byrne, Corp, and Byrne 2001; Corp and Byrne 2002a, 2002b). One might expect the great apes, as the most intelligent animals in their environments, to have a wide choice of food sources. In fact they do not: Byrne and colleagues show that they survive thanks to their ability to exploit foodstuffs that other species can make no use of, such as thistles and *Saba florida* fruits, because the apes alone have the manual dexterity and learning ability that enable them to prepare for eating plants that are well protected by their structure against less intelligent predators.

So far our study of foraging has given us plenty of evidence of the way in which ecology specifies the optimal behavior, and psychology looks for evidence of how individual animals forage as well as they can. The function/mechanism paradigm for economic psychology or behavioral ecology has been well to the fore. But is there any place for the second alternative, the dual causation paradigm? Clearly there is. At the broadest level, the evolution of specialist brain structures and cognitive mechanisms, as in squirrels or great apes, changes the range of behaviors that an individual can emit. But there are also top-down, societal influences that are important on the much shorter time scale of an individual forager's lifetime. What is optimal for a given individual depends on the qualities and quantities of prey present and the skills that the individual has acquired in the course of its development, but it does not depend only on these individual and environmental factors: it also depends on the society in which the individual lives. Goss-Custard, Cayford, and Lea (1998) showed that early in the autumn, juvenile oystercatchers feeding on the mussel beds of the River Exe estuary could make a substantial contribution to their food intake by robbing other birds of mussels those birds had already opened; by October, however, the victims of such kleptoparasitism became sharply more aggressive, shifting the juvenile birds' balance of advantage toward foraging for themselves (at which they were in any case becoming more adept).

Just as social processes affect foraging, so the foraging situation may affect social structure. An early study was carried out in the laboratory by Goldstein, Johnson, and Ward (1989), using rats in a large arena that contained eight operant conditioning setups, each with a lever and a food dispenser, as in a conventional Skinner box. The cost of food at different places in the environment could be controlled precisely by setting up schedules of reinforcement to determine when food would be delivered. The rats could move freely from one lever/dispenser combination to another. The researchers were therefore able to study the number of rats feeding at any one station, and show that the distribution of animals depended on the schedules of reinforcement used and their parameters—for example, the more presses required to obtain each pellet, the more dispersed the rats tended to be. This is a demonstration at a small scale, and on a moment-to-moment basis, of something that is almost certainly critical on the large scale and over the evolutionary time frame: the differences of social structure between species within related groups are probably best understood in terms of differences in their characteristic prey distribution (Clutton-Brock and Harvey 1977; Wrangham 1979).

In the study of animals' foraging behavior, we have seen a most fruitful collaboration between psychologists and ecologists, psychological analysis and ecological analysis. If psychologists had confined themselves to trying to prove that foraging behavior was not optimal and ecologists had confined themselves to defending optimal foraging theory at all costs, very little progress would have been made. What, though, of human foraging, and how it might have impacted on our cognitive evolution?

It is taken for granted among evolutionary psychologists that the evolution of modern humans took place within a hunter-gatherer economic system. Ethnographers have shown that standard optimal foraging theory provides a good basis for describing the foraging of modern hunter-gatherers (e.g., Winterhalder and Smith 1981). The repeated, small-scale decisions of gathering will therefore have had the opportunity to shape the course of human cognitive evolution. Gigerenzer and Goldstein (1996) argue that evolution will tend to produce decision-making heuristics that compensate for the inevitable bounds on our rationality by allowing us to make nearly optimal decisions nearly all the time. It is in the demands of early human foraging that we should look for the details of the selective pressures that have produced those heuristics.

HOARDING AND SAVING

The second example of an overlap area involves both ecology and economics. It starts not very far from optimal foraging theory but ends in one of the most central areas of modern economic theory.

Anyone who has ever kept a golden hamster will know that these charming little creatures, though generally excellent pets or laboratory subjects, do have a number of irritating habits. Chief among these is their tendency to remove their food supply to some place of their own finding. This is not the scatter hoarding of squirrels, considered in the last section, but larder hoarding—the establishment of a large single store of food, usually in the animal's nest. Hamsters' capacity for transporting and hoarding food is astonishing and famous. Lanier, Estep, and

Dewsbury (1974) report that the local name for the golden hamster in its native Syria translates as "father of saddlebags," and that hamster nests have been found containing sackfuls of grain. Similar behavior is shown by the other species of hamster—for example, the English name for these animals comes from the verb *hamstern*, which in Germanic languages means "to hoard," and this was first applied not to the golden hamster but to the similar but larger European black-bellied hamster. All species of hamster are anatomically adapted for hoarding—the food pouches in their cheeks can carry several grams of food, and when they depouch a load it is difficult to tell that the food has even been touched.

It is not hard to guess at some potential ultimate explanations of the behavioral and anatomical traits that result in larder hoarding. Presumably, the tendency to hoard enables hamsters to forage more efficiently. When food is in good supply, they can gather as much as they can carry and store it in their nests. When food is hard to find, they need not forage at all, but can consume their hoards. This will work whether the variations in food supply occur from day to day or from season to season. Over a year or a lifetime, a hoarding animal can manage with spending only a fraction of the time above ground that a nonhoarder would have to spend, and for a slow-moving, burrow-nesting, fat, succulent animal such as a hamster, time spent foraging means time above ground, during which the hamster is all too likely to fall victim to some predator animal's foraging efforts.

The effects of hoarding on hamsters' behavior are fairly startling. For example, unlike other animals of similar size and generally similar environment, hamsters are only weak hibernators: since they can live off their hoards during the winter, they have no need to minimize energy consumption or to build up internal food stores in the form of fat. Furthermore, unlike almost all other animals that have been studied, golden hamsters do not respond to an enforced fast by eating more on recovery days, so that their weight remains low for several days after a single day's deprivation of food (Silverman and Zucker 1976). But if the opportunity to hoard is available, Siberian hamsters respond to food deprivation by adding to their hoards (Bartness and Clein 1994).

This second finding gives us a hint that the mechanisms controlling food intake may be very different in hamsters from those familiar to psychologists from their work with rats. At once our alternative paradigm for economic psychology or behavioral economics is activated. It is fairly clear that hoarding is a special way in which hamsters come near to doing "as well as they can" in terms of getting food out of the environment. Have we here another situation where psychology can ask how the animal does as well as it can.

But hamsters' hoarding is not just a problem in the interaction of psychology and ecology. There is in fact a considerable psychological literature on the hoarding behavior of rats, stemming from a paper by Wolfe (1939). Rats do not hoard anything like as much or as spontaneously as hamsters (Waddell 1951), but they can be persuaded to do so—for example, by current or previous food deprivation, by low temperatures, or by providing food in the form of inconveniently large pellets (Whishaw and Tomie 1989). The early work on hoarding came, in fact, from the heyday of rat psychology, and its authors saw themselves as not merely investigating rats: they were seeking a model of human saving behavior and general possessiveness. Although the belief in that kind of applicability of animal data to human psychology is now thoroughly and rightly unfashionable, it is not so unreasonable in this particular case. Economists trying to account for saving behavior usually include in the list of motivations to save something like "pure miserliness" (Keynes 1936)—in other words, the mere instinct to hoard. If we want to know what a hoarding instinct looks like, the behavior of hamsters seems a promising place to start.

In an effort to get a grip on the simultaneously ecological, psychological, and economic questions posed by hamsters' hoarding behavior, we carried out a series of experiments in which we manipulated the cost of food to hamsters (Lea and Tarpy 1986). The hamsters lived in Skinner boxes, where they could always earn food by pressing on a lever, and they had a little nesting box in which they slept and where they could make a hoard. We varied the cost of food by varying the number of responses the hamster had to make to earn each pellet of food. If you do that systematically, you end up being able to plot a curve of the number of food pellets taken against the cost per pellet, which is what an economist would call a demand curve (see also Hursh 1980; Lea 1978, 1981). In one of our experiments, we varied the price from a fairly low value (six presses per pellet) up to the point where the hamsters virtually stopped pressing the lever (usually twenty-four or forty-eight presses per pellet). Each day we observed how many pellets had been taken, and by counting those hoarded in the nest box, we knew how many had been eaten. But we also stole the hamster's entire hoard—in economic terms, we imposed a 100 percent daily wealth tax. We got three very interesting results.

Unlike other animals, as the price of food went up, hamsters did not greatly increase the amount of work they did, so the number of pellets they earned declined. However, the number of pellets actually eaten was not greatly affected by price. What fell off (and it fell off very dramatically) was the number of pellets hoarded. Similar results were obtained, with different experimental procedures, by Day and Bartness (2003) in Siberian hamsters: making food more expensive to get sharply reduced the amount hoarded. On the other hand, we found that our "wealth tax" did not affect hoarding in the slightest, and the hamsters did not respond to the theft of their hoards by hoarding less. Indeed, Phillips, Robinson, and Davey (1989) found that artificially depleting golden hamsters' hoards led them to hoard more rather than less.

That last finding clearly shows that the hamsters' behavior was not optimal (and the detailed data relating to the other results confirmed this). But to make much of this fact, as the rationality-question paradigm would lead us to, would be to miss the most interesting points. The hamsters' indifference to the "wealth tax" shows that their hoarding is, indeed, largely instinctive. Presumably, hamsters must lose some of their hoards under natural conditions, but the loss must be sufficiently regular for there to be no adaptive advantage for a hamster in taking account of the rate of loss. It does not always pay to be too clever—it may not be optimal for an animal to be equipped to deal with every contingency. If the environment is sufficiently reliable, then an instinctive response to some of its stimuli will be more certain and often quicker than a more comprehensive response that depends upon learning.

Furthermore, the first two findings show that even under the drastic and quite unnatural manipulation of daily total hoard loss, the hoarding behavior was still functional. When food costs increased, the hamsters were able to maintain food intake more or less intact without increasing their work output, even without being allowed to feed from their hoards, just by sacrificing the hoarding behavior. An economic psychologist is reminded of some of the results of Cyert and March (1963) on behavior within firms and other organizations. When financially hard times come around, firms ensure their survival by dropping procedures and laying off staff that are not strictly necessary, such as personal secretaries for executives. This is not to say either that hoarding has no function for hamsters or that executives have no need of secretaries. It is just that these luxuries can be dispensed with temporarily, and it is adaptive to do so in difficult times. They form a kind of behavioral buffer against environmental variation.

Once again we have seen how ecological considerations can tell us the function of a behavior, psychological considerations can throw light on the mechanisms that produce it, and both disciplines stand to gain from an interdisciplinary approach. And in this case, the economic dimension is also present. I would not wish to push the golden hamster very far as a model of human savers.

Its indifference to the "wealth tax," though, recalls the fact that, at least with single-figure inflation, individuals in the economy normally regard inflation as a sign of hard times and respond to it by increasing their saving behavior (Katona 1975, ch. 9). Both these trends are against received economic wisdom, according to which mild inflation is a normal accompaniment of economic growth, while increases in inflation make it more worthwhile to spend than to save. Katona explained these "irrationalities" by saying that people treat a reserve of savings almost like a consumer durable good: it is one of the things, like kitchen machinery and cars, that we aspire to own as we grow more affluent. Thus people dislike inflation, because it devalues their savings, but save more during it, so as to maintain their savings' value. But suppose we are, just a little, merely instinctive savers like the hamster. Might we not then continue to save anyway, no matter what the slings and arrows of outrageous macroeconomics might do to our hoard? It is not clear that there are any data that could demonstrate that this account is any less satisfactory than Katona's.

All this discussion of hoarding has been in terms of the function/mechanism paradigm. But saving has its social dimension too, as the last paragraph reminded us. Human beings are not hamsters. Katona was interested in saving precisely because of its potential macroeconomic impact: if a sufficient number of consumers increase or decrease the proportion of their income that they save, that has a deflationary or expansionary effect on the entire economy. But economic psychology has now gathered a very considerable amount of data on the individual processes underlying saving and the factors that affect them (Wärneryd 1999). We know that if inflation, or wealth tax, goes to extremes, we will change the way we save, or stop saving altogether, and inflation and taxes are properties of the economy as a whole. Dual causation is virtually axiomatic in the study of saving.

PSYCHOLOGY AND MONEY

In the third illustration that we shall consider, the social dimension becomes paramount, and we shift definitively from considering behavioral ecology to economic psychology and behavioral economics proper.

For most of the first century of academic psychology, few psychologists took any interest in money. Yet psychologically speaking, it is fascinating stuff—and not only for those few unfortunates who develop a pathological attraction to it. Anthropologists have found that a wonderful variety of objects can be used as money: everyone has heard of cowrie shells, and cows and bales of cloth make a sort of sense; but what about two-meter granite boulders, or woodpecker scalps? In present-day society, most forms of money are utterly valueless in themselves, and many forms (e.g., entries in the memories of bank computers) are utterly abstract. Yet we rely on money totally and unthinkingly for day-to-day purposes, and only with great reluctance do we rely on anything else for year-to-year purposes (one of the most unpopular features of high inflation is the way it requires people who merely want to maintain the purchasing power of their savings to think about investment strategy). And, to take an example that will be developed more fully below, we resist any attempt to interfere with it. There are interesting macroeconomic arguments as to whether or not it would be to the United Kingdom's advantage to join the euro zone, and no doubt they have some influence on the government, but it is beyond doubt that the key issue in the public debate is the British public's almost visceral attachment to the pound sterling (Routh and Burgoyne 1998). This has led to the different outcome of the political question about the euro in the United Kingdom as compared with most other European Union states, where the macroeconomic background is not very different but the emotional context certainly is (Müller-Peters 1998). We have recently reviewed some of the oddities of human behavior toward money and concluded that they are so odd that we have to consider money as functioning, in part, as a drug, not just as a neutral tool (Lea and Webley in press).

Over the past twenty years, the rise of economic psychology as an organized interdisciplinary study has filled some of the gaps in a psychological study of money, to the point where it is possible to have a serious textbook devoted to the subject, written by two of the United Kingdom's most prolific and eminent social psychologists (Furnham and Argyle 1998). However, there is still much work to do, and the study of the psychology of money is a good illustration of the danger of naive thinking about other disciplines. In terms of the simplest possible economic analysis, modern money is valuable to an individual only as a means of exchange or a store of value. Its only use is to be got rid of as soon as possible, in exchange for real goods or services, or to be saved for a specific purpose. In reality, money is itself an economic good, something that is only available in restricted amounts: there is a demand for money, a supply of money, and a market in money. Here a naive concentration on the rationality question would easily lead psychologists astray: we might find the demand for money and the desire to possess money irrational, and imagine that we had scored a point against economic theory. In practice, the concept of economic rationality is quite rightly adjusted to allow for the need to hold money stocks.

The alternative paradigms we have proposed prove to be much more fruitful. Consider first the distinction between function, on one hand, and mechanism and development, on the other. The very oddness of modern money as a phenomenon has led quite a number of psychologists to ask how children come to learn how to use it. One of the classic questions in the study of economic socialization has been the way concepts of money develop, and this is readily posed within the framework of Piaget's general approach to cognitive development (e.g., Danziger 1958). These studies are quite illuminating, and could in principle be of practical use to parents trying to educate their children in the effective management of money—a subject on which there is a huge self-help literature (e.g., Whitcomb 2000) but still almost no academic research, or at least none that has given rise to reliable positive results. But these early studies of children's understanding of money missed an important point, which is brought to light more clearly within the dual causation paradigm (see Lea, Tarpy, and Webley 1987, 325–26). The Piagetian psychologists of money treat money as a given, almost the way they treat aspects of the physical universe. But money is actually a social creation. Its continued existence depends upon the way individuals behave to and with it. The "cognitive equilibrium" that the Piagetians see as the end of development need not, in principle, be found within existing institutions. In terms of the dual causation paradigm, the Piagetians are being, Continental-fashion, too organicist. They are giving too little weight to the fact that individuals not just are determined by the economic whole but also help to determine it.

To illustrate how individuals can determine economic institutions we can return to the example of people's resistance to new forms of money, and to one specific example, the effects of the replacement of notes by coins. Hussein (1985) investigated what happened in the United Kingdom when the £1 note was replaced with a coin in 1983. She was interested in the possibility that, because it was a coin, it would be spent faster than £1 notes—a process Duncan (1975) suggested might contribute to inflation. To this end, Hussein rewarded volunteers in an irrelevant experiment with a payment of £1, made either by coin or note, and marked all the coins and notes with an ultraviolet pen. She then recalled the volunteers the next day and checked the contents of their purses and wallets. Sure enough, everyone's £1 coins disappeared in less than a day, while the majority of those who had received a £1 note still had it; in another study, Hussein found that the lifetime of a £1 note in purse or wallet averaged 1.1 to 4.0 days. At the time, however, it hardly required this degree of sophistication to tell us that the £1 coins were psychologically different from notes and that people's attitudes toward them were strong enough to affect the economic processes. When the coins were first introduced, many people simply refused to take them when they drew money from banks or got change in shops, with the result that six months after their introduction, less than a third of those minted were in circulation. In the United States, an attempt to introduce a dollar coin in 1979 essentially failed, and the coins simply did not circulate (Caskey and St. Laurent 1994); by the late 1990s, the only large-scale use of this coin, the Susan B. Anthony dollar, was to pay fares on a few urban transit systems, as in Chicago—coins that were intended as legal tender had fallen to the status of special-purpose tokens. The U.S. Mint introduced a new "golden" dollar coin in 2000 but has felt it necessary to mount a strong propaganda campaign to persuade people to use it: there is even a "Coin Coalition" that has been set up to advocate for wider use of the new coin, joining together major commercial and public corporations from the New York City Transit Authority to the International Carwash Association. At the time of writing (2005), the circulation of the golden dollar appears to be minimal.

The reasons for people's odd behavior in the face of currency changes are surely open to psychological investigation. It is often said that £1 coins did not initially seem valuable, or that the Anthony dollar was confusable with the quarter. But new coins nowadays are carefully researched before production (e.g., Bruce et al. 1983), so these objections seem more likely to be rationalizations of less superficial objections. Economic psychological research has thrown some light on those deeper processes. In the first place, though the rejection of new coins seems odd, it is not necessarily irrational: Caskey and St. Laurent (1994) showed there are real costs in using new forms of money, especially when few other people are doing so, so there are economic reasons why take-up may be slow at first and can fail if a critical level of usage is not reached. Second, both pound and dollar are the defining units of their national currencies, so perhaps changes affecting them are particularly susceptible to interference from factors of national pride, which Müller-Peters (1998) showed to be a key factor in attitudes toward the introduction of the euro. The detailed psychological analysis that has been carried out, Europe-wide, in connection with this particular currency change (see Pepermans, Burgoyne, and Müller-Peters 1998) goes much further than dismissing any difficulties as "irrational"; by recognizing that behavior toward money is both a product of and a cause of the societal phenomenon of money, it becomes possible to understand it.

CLOSING THE TRIANGLE: ECOLOGICAL AND ENVIRONMENTAL ECONOMICS

What, though, of the third possible relation between our three disciplines, that between economics and ecology? The very similarity of the words suggests that there must be a relationship; according to the *Oxford English Dictionary,* the word *ecology* was coined in imitation of *economy,* and we can see how its nineteenth-century inventors would have wanted to parallel the economy of nature against the national and international economy, seeing both as systems in which huge numbers of elements and processes were held in an equilibrium that was relatively resistant to disruption but subject to continual progressive forces.

Whatever the derivation of the words, however, ecology is not a derivative or subset of economics, but rather the reverse, in two important senses. From the point of view of individual people, economics is just human ecology: it is the economy that specifies how we gain access to resources and how we impact on our environment. But at the macro level, the human economy is embedded in the planetary ecology, dependent, on it and impacting on it.

Two subtly different disciplines have sprung up to study the relations between the two, environmental economics (e.g., Field and Field 2001) and ecological economics (e.g. Söderbaum 2000). The distinction is not hard and fast, but as a general rule academics and practitioners calling themselves environmental economists are likely to be found assessing the environmental impact of proposed economic developments, on the large or small scale, or alternatively the economic impact of proposed environmental developments such as the designation of national parks. They would tend to see the environment as a scarce resource that can be studied through the methods of economics, the science of scarce resources. This leads to an attempt to follow a value-neutral approach, setting out ecological and economic costs and benefits of different courses of action, often with a leaning toward market solutions or at least toward minimizing interference with the market. Those calling themselves ecological economists, on the other hand, would be more likely to be pursuing a normative, policy-oriented approach, driven by the belief that economic developments must be sustainable within the planetary ecology, and considering the Earth as a single economic and ecological system whose productive capacity is limited and needs to be understood. For example, Costanza et al (1997) argued that the contribution of the planet to economic production should be recognized, and calculated that at a conservative estimate, the economic value of ecosystem services was around U.S. \$33 trillion, twice the total of the world's gross national products. Ecological economists thus tend to take a nonstandard, critical approach to conventional economics, and their approach has some points in common with that of economic psychologists (Lea 2001).

CONCLUSION

We have seen that psychologists interested in interacting with either economics or ecology face the difficulty of getting a data-driven discipline to interface with one where theory, and in particular a single all-pervading theory, plays a larger role. We have also seen that there are ways in which that difficulty can be overcome: many essays in the present book give evidence that it is being overcome successfully in the case of economics, and in this essay we have reviewed some of the ways it which it is being overcome successfully in the case of ecology. It might be thought that psychologists interested in interacting with both economics and ecology face a double difficulty, but in fact the links that exist between the two disciplines open up both a specialized possibility and a general one. From a specialized point of view, psychologists have a contribution to make to the study of the human behaviors through which the economy interacts with the planetary ecology. Individual preferences underlie the choice between technologies or activities that are relatively benign or relatively damaging to the environment, and economic psychologists have consistently shown an interest in areas such as green consumption (see the survey by Beckmann 1999) and ethical investment (see, for example, Lewis et al. 1998), where such preferences can be studied.

More generally, however, we need to realize that if economics is human ecology, the sorts of considerations that govern behavioral ecology will also govern economic psychology. The parallels I have been seeking between these two interdisciplinary endeavors are not accidental. All animals are adapted to behave in ways that enable them to survive in their ecological niches, and the human economy is our ecological niche. It has changed so fast in the past 10,000 years that no genetic adaptation process could keep up: to a significant extent we all have to deal with the Internet-age economy using Stone Age psychology. Perhaps our difficulties with money are in part a result. But I would argue that the differences between a natural economy and a modern one are more superficial than fundamental. What is fundamental is that we are immersed in a network of flows of scarce resources, more or less in equilibrium, which we both influence and are influenced by. Within that network, rational or optimal behavior will provide a rough prediction of actual behavior; we have to understand psychology, however, if we are to know the limits of that prediction, and the mechanisms through which animals or humans, in their different environments, do as well as they can.

NOTE

An earlier version of this essay formed a keynote address at the September 2003 conference of the International Association for Research in Economic Psychology, Christchurch, New Zealand. It is a reflectively updated form of a paper of the same title given as the Lister Lecture to the British Association for the Advancement of Science, Brighton, United Kingdom, August 1983. The writing was completed while the author was a visiting scholar in the Department of Psychology of the University of California, Berkeley, United States, and thanks are due to Dr Lucia Jacobs for facilities there.

REFERENCES

Abarca, N., and E. Fantino. 1982. "Choice and Foraging." *Journal of the Experimental Analysis of Behavior* 38: 117–23.
Ainslie, G. 1992. *Picoeconomics.* Cambridge: Cambridge University Press.
Bartness, T.J., and M.R. Clein. 1994. "Effects of Food-Deprivation and Restriction, and Metabolic Blockers on Food Hoarding in Siberian Hamsters." *American Journal of Physiology* 266: R1111–7.
Basil, J.A., A.C. Kamil, R.P. Balda, and K.V. Fite. 1996. "Differences in Hippocampal Volume among Food Storing Corvids." *Brain Behavior and Evolution* 47: 156–64.
Beckmann, S.C. 1999. "Ecology and Consumption." In P.E. Earl and S. Kemp, eds., *The Elgar Companion to Consumer Research and Economic Psychology,* 170–75. Cheltenham: Elgar.
Bruce, V.G., D. Gilmore, L. Mason, and P. Mayhew. 1983. "Factors Affecting the Perceived Value of Coins." *Journal of Economic Psychology* 4: 335–47.
Byrne, R.W., N. Corp, and J.M.E. Byrne. 2001. "Estimating the Complexity of Animal Behaviour: How Mountain Gorillas Eat Thistles." *Behaviour* 138: 525–57.
Caskey, J.P., and S. St. Laurent. 1994. "The Susan B. Anthony Dollar and the Theory of Coin/Note Substitutions." *Journal of Money, Credit and Banking* 26: 495–510.
Charnov, E.L. 1976. "Optimal Foraging: The Marginal Value Theorem." *Theoretical Population Biology* 9: 129–36.
Clutton-Brock, T.H., and P.H. Harvey. 1977. "Primate Ecology and Social Organization." *Journal of Zoology* 183: 1–39.
Collier, G.H. and C.K. Rovee-Collier. 1981. "A Comparative Analysis of Optimal Foraging Behavior: Laboratory Simulations." In A.C. Kamil and T.D. Sargent, eds., *Foraging Behavior,* 39–76. New York: Garland.
Corp, N., and R.W. Byrne. 2002a. "Leaf Processing by Wild Chimpanzees: Physically Defended Leaves Reveal Complex Manual Skills." *Ethology* 108: 673–96.
——— 2002b. "The Ontogeny of Manual Skill in Wild Chimpanzees: Evidence from Feeding on the Fruit of *Saba florida.*" *Behaviour* 139: 137–68.
Costanza, R., R. D'Arge, R. DeGroot, S. Farber, M. Grasso, B. Hannon, K. Limburg, S. Naeem, R.V. O'Neill, J. Paruelo, R.G. Raskin, P. Sutton, and M. Van Den Belt. 1997. "The Value of the World's Ecosystem and Natural Capital." *Nature* 387: 253–59.
Cyert, R.M., and J.G. March. 1963. *A Behavioral Theory of the Firm.* Englewood Cliffs, NJ: Prentice-Hall.
Danziger, K. 1958. "Children's Earliest Conception of Economic Relationships." *Journal of Social Psychology* 47: 231–40.
Day, D.E., and T.J. Bartness. 2003. "Fasting-Induced Increases in Food Hoarding Are Dependent on the Foraging-Effort Level." *Physiology and Behavior* 78: 655–68.
Dow, S.M., and S.E.G. Lea. 1987. "Foraging in a Changing Environment: Simulations in the Operant Laboratory." In M.L. Commons, A. Kacelnik, and S.J. Shettleworth, eds., *Quantitative Analyses of Behavior,* vol. 6: *Foraging,* 89–113. Hillsdale, NJ: Erlbaum.
Duncan, D.C. 1975. "Psychology and Inflation." *New Behaviour,* July 26, 436.

Field, B.C., and M.K. Field. 2001. *Environmental Economics,* 3rd ed. New York: McGraw-Hill.

Friedman, M. 1963. "Windfalls, the 'Horizon,' and Related Concepts in the Permanent Income Hypothesis." In C.F. Christ et al., eds., *Measurement in Economics.* Stanford, CA: Stanford University Press.

Furnham, A., and M. Argyle. 1998. *The Psychology of Money.* London: Routledge.

Gigerenzer, G., and D.G. Goldstein. 1996. "Reasoning the Fast and Frugal Way: Models of Bounded Rationality." *Psychological Review* 103: 650–69.

Goldstein, S.R., P. Johnson, and G. Ward. 1989. "Schedules of Reinforcement as Regulators of Dispersion Patterns." *Behavioural Processes* 20: 177–88.

Goss-Custard, J.D. 1977. "The Energetics of Prey Selection by Redshank, *Tringa tetanus* (L.), in Relation to Prey Density." *Journal of Animal Ecology* 46: 1–19.

Goss-Custard, J.D., J.T. Cayford, and S.E.G. Lea. 1998. "The Changing Trade-Off Between Food Finding and Food Stealing in Juvenile Oystercatchers." *Animal Behaviour* 55: 745–60.

Harbaugh, W.T., K. Krause, and T.R. Berry. 2001. "GARP for Kids: On the Development of Rational Choice Behavior." *American Economic Review* 91: 1539–45.

Hirshleifer, J. 1977. "Economics from a Biological Viewpoint." *Journal of Law and Economics* 20: 1–52.

Hursh, S.R. 1980. "Economic Concepts for the Analysis of Behavior." *Journal of the Experimental Analysis of Behavior* 34: 219–38.

Hussein, G. 1985. "An Examination of the Psychological Aspects of Money." M.Phil. dissertation, University of Exeter.

Kamil, A.C., R.P. Balda, and D.J. Olson. 1994. "Performance of Four Seed-Caching Corvid Species in the Radial-Arm Maze Analog." *Journal of Comparative Psychology* 108: 385–93.

Katona, G. 1975. *Psychological Economics.* New York: Elsevier.

Keynes, J.M. 1936. *The General Theory of Employment, Interest and Money.* London: Macmillan.

Killeen, P.R., G.-M. Palombo, L.R. Gottlob, and J. Beam. 1996. "Bayesian Analysis of Foraging by Pigeons *Columba livia.*" *Journal of Experimental Psychology: Animal Behavior Processes* 22: 480–96.

Kuhn, T.S. 1962. *The Structure of Scientific Revolutions.* Chicago: University of Chicago Press.

Lanier, K.L., D.Q. Estep, and D.A. Dewsbury. 1974. "Food Hoarding in Muroid Rodents." *Behavioural Biology* 11: 177–87.

Lea, S.E.G. 1978. "The Psychology and Economics of Demand." *Psychological Bulletin* 85: 441–66.

———. 1979. "Foraging and Reinforcement Schedules in the Pigeon: Optimal and Non-Optimal Aspects of Choice." *Animal Behaviour* 27: 875–86.

———. 1981. "Animal Experiments in Economic Psychology." *Journal of Economic Psychology* 1: 245–71.

———. 1994. "Rationality: The Formalist View." In W. Güth and H. Brandstätter, eds., *Essays in Economic Psychology,* 71–89. Berlin: Springer-Verlag.

———. 2001. "Economic Psychology and Ecological Economics: Two Unconventional Approaches to the Future of Economics." *World Futures* 56: 15–29.

Lea, S.E.G., and R.M. Tarpy. 1986. "Hamsters' Demand for Food to Eat and Hoard as a Function of Deprivation and Cost." *Animal Behaviour* 34: 1759–68.

Lea, S.E.G., R.M. Tarpy, and P. Webley. 1987. *The Individual in the Economy.* Cambridge, UK: Cambridge University Press.

Lea, S.E.G., and P. Webley. In press. "Money as Tool, Money as Drug: The Biological Psychology of a Strong Incentive." *Behavioral and Brain Sciences.*

Lewis, A., C. Mackenzie, P. Webley, and A. Winnett. 1998. "Morals and Markets: The Case of Ethical Investing." In P. Taylor-Gooby, ed., *Choice and Public Policy.* London: Macmillan.

MacArthur, R.H., and E.R. Pianka. 1966. "On the Optimal Use of a Patchy Environment." *American Naturalist* 100: 603–9.

Macdonald, I.M.V. 1997. "Field Experiments on Duration and Precision of Grey and Red Squirrel Spatial Memory." *Animal Behaviour* 54: 879–91.

March, J.G. 1978. "Bounded Rationality, Ambiguity, and the Engineering of Choice." *Bell Journal of Economics* 9: 587–608.

Maslow, A.H. 1970. *Motivation and Personality,* 2nd ed. New York: Harper and Row.

Müller-Peters, A. 1998. "The Significance of National Pride and National Identity to the Attitude Toward the Single European Currency: A Europe-Wide Comparison." *Journal of Economic Psychology* 19: 701–19.

Orians, G.H., and N.E. Pearson. 1979. "On the Theory of Central Place Foraging." In D.F. Horn, ed., *Analysis of Ecological Systems,* 155–77. Columbus: Ohio State University Press.

Pearce, J.M. 1997. *Animal Learning and Cognition,* 2nd ed. Hove, UK: Psychology Press.

Pepermans, R., C.B. Burgoyne, and A. Müller-Peters. 1998. "Editorial: European Integration, Psychology and the Euro." *Journal of Economic Psychology* 19: 657–61.

Phillips, J.H., A. Robinson, and G.C.L. Davey. 1989. "Food Hoarding Behaviour in the Golden Hamster (*Mesocricetus auratus*): Effects of Body-Weight Loss and Hoard-Size Discrimination." *Quarterly Journal of Experimental Psychology* 41B: 33–47.

Routh, D.A., and C.B. Burgoyne. 1998. "Being in Two Minds About a Single Currency: A UK Perspective on the Euro." *Journal of Economic Psychology* 19: 741–54.

Silverman, H.J., and I. Zucker. 1976. "Absence of Post–Fast Food Compensation in the Golden Hamster *Mesocricetus auratus*." *Physiology and Behavior* 17: 271–85.

Simon, H.A. 1978. "Rationality as a Process and as a Product of Thought." *American Economic Review* 68, 2: 1–16.

Söderbaum, P. 2000. *Ecological Economics.* London: Earthscan.

Vander Wall, S.B. 1990. *Food Hoarding in Animals.* Chicago: University of Chicago Press.

Van Raaij, W.F. 1981. "Economic Psychology." *Journal of Economic Psychology* 1: 1–24.

Vauclair, J. 1996. *Animal Cognition.* Cambridge, MA: Harvard University Press.

Waddell, D. 1951. "Hoarding in the Golden Hamster." *Journal of Comparative and Physiological Psychology* 44: 383–88.

Wärneryd, K.-E. 1999. *The Psychology of Saving: A Study on Economic Psychology.* Cheltenham, UK: Edward Elgar.

Webley, P. 2004. "Children's Understanding of Economics." In M. Barrett and E. Buchanan-Barrow, eds., *Children's Understanding of Society,* 43–67. Hove, UK: Psychology Press.

Whishaw, I.Q., and A. Tomie. 1989. "Food-Pellet Size Modifies the Hoarding Behavior of Foraging Rats." *Psychobiology* 17: 93–101.

Whitcomb, J.E. 2000. *Capitate Your Kids: Teaching Your Teens Financial Independence.* Milwaukee, WI: Popcorn.

Winterhalder, B., and E.A. Smith. 1981. *Hunter-Gatherer Foraging Strategies.* Chicago: University of Chicago Press.

Wolfe, J.B. 1939. "An Exploratory Study of Food-Hoarding in Rats." *Journal of Comparative Psychology* 28: 97–108.

Wrangham, R.W. 1979. "On the Evolution of Ape Social Systems." *Social Science Information* 18: 335–68.

CHAPTER 15

DISCOUNTING, SELF-CONTROL, AND SAVING

ELLEN K. NYHUS AND PAUL WEBLEY

Establishing the causes of saving has occupied scholars since Aristotle (384–322 B.C.), who considered whether the accumulation of wealth was laudable or objectionable. In the two past centuries in particular, household saving has been subject to extensive theoretical and empirical research. This is due, in part, to its increasing importance for national economies. In spite of this we only have a partial understanding of households' motivations for saving. We know some variables that might be used as predictors for household saving, such as income and age, but the underlying psychological processes governing the choice between saving and spending are still not well understood.

Saving or dissaving during a period of time is a product of several decisions of varying significance, such as whether to buy a cheap or expensive product, whether to spend now or later, and whether to borrow or save. Saving is a result of continuous intertemporal decisions, where outcomes (payments and consumption of goods) appear at different points in time. When studying saving we have to assume that consumers have some awareness of their overall economic situation when they make spending or saving decisions and also some expectations about their future economic situation. We must also assume that they make a judgment of the consequences of the decisions and that some factors will play a part across the majority of these decisions. Studies of saving involve identifying such factors. Only these factors will serve as useful determinants and predictors of saving over extended periods and have a potential for being useful for analyses at the aggregate level.

In this essay, we will review research on two of the psychological concepts that have been considered important in the savings literature: time preference and self-control. First we will briefly review the ideas of the creators of the concept of time preference to explicate the psychological processes assumed to govern intertemporal decisions. We will then proceed to review the findings from empirical tests of time preference and its determinants. Next we will discuss the consequences of hyperbolic discounting and the role of self-control before we examine the empirical findings concerning the relationship between saving and time preference. After that we will review and evaluate the saving models that incorporate hyperbolic discounting and self-control. Finally, we will discuss challenges for future research and suggest some concepts that can serve as alternatives to time preference.

THE CONCEPT OF TIME PREFERENCE

The first models of saving focused on the intertemporal choice between consuming now or later and on factors that may influence this choice. Although several economists in the nineteenth century had discussed similar ideas, Böhm-Bawerk (1889) and Fisher (1930) are considered the creators of the concept and theory of time preference.[1] They were concerned with why interest rates exist and how they are formed. They tried to answer the question of why people want rewards for saving money by lending it to others and why they are willing to pay compensation in order to borrow money. The core of their theories is the trade-off between spending and investing, the choice between immediate enjoyment and possible greater deferred enjoyment. By focusing on this intertemporal dilemma, they point to a central problem of human life: giving up immediate pleasures in order to obtain long-term goals. They recognized that saving and investing are results of how people handle this intertemporal conflict.

Fisher introduced the concept of time preference, which he explains as reflecting a person's impatience for consumption. In his model, time preference is an important determinant of saving. He formally defined the rate of time preference (also called the subjective discount factor or the rate of impatience) as "the (percentage) excess of the *present* marginal want for one more unit of *present* goods over the *present* marginal want for one more unit of *future* goods" (1930, 62). The rate of time preference is a derivative of marginal desirability, that is, the preference for present over future goods. With this definition, Fisher also stressed the importance of discounting, as it is the *present* want for future goods that is assumed to form the basis for decisions. Future costs or benefits must be discounted into present equivalents in order to enable meaningful comparisons and choices.

Fisher's theory of time preference included factors that will explain differences both between *and* within individuals. Individuals may have different discount rates in different situations or at different points in time. These individual differences are seldom included in economic models of intertemporal choice, as Fisher suggested that they would be harmonized in the capital market. He argued that at the macro level, the real interest rate reflects the aggregate time preference of all individuals in the society. People who derive high utility for increased consumption and therefore are impatient to spend (that is, who have a high rate of time preference) will borrow money from those who are less impatient (who have a lower rate of time preference). He also assumed decreasing marginal utility from consumption. For each extra unit the impatient people could consume, the lower the marginal utility for extra consumption and the less compensation they would be willing to pay in order to consume even more. This was illustrated with the following demand schedule:

> For each successive one hundred dollars added to his present income, assuming that income is stable and certain, a certain prospective borrower is willing to pay out of next year's income, as follows:
>
> For the first $100, $120, with an impatience rate of 20%.
> For the second $100, $115, with an impatience rate of 15%.
> For the third $100, $110, with an impatience rate of 10%.
> For the fourth $100, $106, with an impatience rate of 6%.
> For the fifth $100, $105, with an impatience rate of 5%.
> For the sixth $100, $104, with an impatience rate of 4%. (Fisher 1930, 97)

Likewise, the less the patient people consume in the present, the higher the marginal utility for extra forgone consumption and the more compensation they will demand in order to give up further consumption. Consequently, in a perfect capital market with no liquidity constraints, the process of lending and borrowing will continue until the compensation offered and the compensation demanded for extra units of consumption are equal. That is, it will continue until every person in the society has the same marginal rate of impatience. This process of harmonizing rates of time preference, which show the opposing forces between the motivation to spread consumption over time due to diminishing marginal utility and the motivation to concentrate consumption in the present due to a positive time preference, describes the formation of the interest rate in a society. At the macro level, the aggregate degree of impatience of all individuals determines the rate of interest. At the individual level, the relationship is opposite. For individuals (each having a negligible influence on the market interest rate) the interest rate will be fixed, and it is their individual rate of impatience that varies and determines their tendency to lend or borrow. A person is assumed to harmonize his or her rate of time preference with the market interest rate. Therefore, the real interest rate in the market is often used as a proxy for time preference. This rate is therefore also considered to represent all the different motives underlying intertemporal choice. The same rate of time preference is assumed to apply to all forms of consumption.

Fisher also formulated his theory in mathematical terms. In the part of his 1930 book that is devoted to this, little of the psychological insight that characterized the first part of the book is on display. The assumptions about the formation of the market interest rate as described above are taken for granted, so the economic models of intertemporal choice rely on the assumption of the individual rate of time preference being equal to the market real interest rate. Thus, intertemporal choices can be described by using the apparatus of indifference curves (or Fisher curves).

Fisher's theory of interest (as formulated in the stylized mathematical version) formed the basis for the discounted utility (DU) model, which was formally developed by Samuelson (1937), Koopmans (1960), Lancaster (1963), and Fishburn and Rubinstein (1982). This model, built on strict axioms concerning preferences and utility functions, describes how rational individuals with rational preferences will distribute consumption between the present and the future. Although even the inventors of the DU model realized it lacked mundane realism (see Frederick, Loewenstein, and O'Donoghue 2002; Loewenstein 1992), the model has been the most powerful tool to date for analyzing intertemporal decisions, including saving decisions.

EMPIRICAL RESEARCH ON TIME PREFERENCE

In the past decades, empirical research has found that the DU model is a poor descriptor of intertemporal choice. First, the general conclusion that can be drawn from numerous empirical studies is that the assumption that all individuals have the same time preference is not supported. This has been demonstrated in studies using hypothetical choice situations and in those where real-world behavior is observed. In general, the time preference rates found in empirical studies exceed market interest rates. For example, Hausman (1979) studied actual purchases of air conditioners and derived subjective discount rates ranging between 5.1 and 89.0 percent (the mean discount rate was 26.5 percent). Gately (1980) reported discount rates between 45 and 300 percent in a similar study of refrigerator purchases. Houston (1983) found a mean discount rate of 22.5 percent in an experimental study of choice of an "untried energy-saving durable good." Thaler (1981) found median discount rates as high as 345 percent over a one-month horizon, while Benzion, Rapoport, and Yagil (1989) found mean discount rates as high as 59.8 percent among university students responding to hypothetical choice situations.[2] Samwick (1998) estimated time preference rates from wealth data and found a median annual rate of time preference equal to 7.63 percent. One-quarter of the time preference rates were below 2.93 percent and another quarter were above 14.66 percent, with 14 percent above 20 percent.[3] Odum and Rainaud (2003) showed that discount rates differed significantly between different substances, with money being less steeply discounted than alcohol and food. For example, $100 delayed by one year was worth $47.50 now, whereas $100 worth of food was worth only $22.50 now. Several similar examples can be found in Frederick, Loewenstein, and O'Donoghue 2002.

The discount rates found in empirical studies tend to be very high. This means that the future is given less, and sometimes very much less, weight than the present. This is contrary to the assumptions of the rational model. Some discounting of the future is appropriate (because of the possibility of death, default, or unanticipated events), but it should be relatively low, as the probability of these events is itself low. The rational model requires the decision maker to be able to predict future tastes, and some recent research indicates that this is not the case. It seems that most people have a general tendency to devalue future events either because of a lack of imagination or because of the way the brain is constructed. Ross and Newby-Clark have conducted several studies in order to compare people's views of their pasts and futures, which turn out to be qualitatively different. They have found that the variation in evaluations of personally significant episodes is much higher for the past than for the future. Respondents report both positive and negative events in the past, while they typically anticipated a homogeneously ideal future. They further reported that people needed more time to anticipate negative future events than positive future events, and they also needed more time to respond when asked to judge how likely they thought the negative events were compared to the positive events (Ross and Newby-Clark 1998; Newby-Clark and Ross 2003).

Loewenstein, O'Donoghue, and Rabin's (2003) review of the literature on taste change suggests that people understand qualitatively the direction in which their future tastes will change but systematically underestimate the magnitude of these changes. This has been found true for people waiting for a kidney transplant when predicting what their quality of life would be one year later (Jepson, Loewenstein, and Ubel 2001) and cigarette smokers when asked to predict their own risk of becoming addicted (U.S. Department of Health and Human Services 1994, cited in Loewenstein, O'Donoghue, and Rabin 2003). People have also been found to exaggerate the degree to which their future tastes will be like their current tastes. Read and Van Leeuwen (1998) asked hungry and satiated respondents to choose between healthy and unhealthy snacks to be received one week later either after lunch or in the afternoon. Respondents who were hungry at the point of the interview but expected not to be when receiving the snack the next week (after lunch) correctly predicted the direction in change in taste but underestimated its magnitude. This failure to predict future feelings may result in overconsumption in the present relative to the consumption level that would maximize intertemporal utility if the future tastes had been predicted correctly.

Discount rates have also been found to vary considerably between individuals. These differences could be attributed to an imperfect capital market, as the latter was an important underlying assumption in Fisher's argument. Another interpretation is that factors other than time preference might be playing an important role in intertemporal choices and so distort people's estimates of subjective discount rates.

Either way, the results suggest that Fisher (1930) assumed too much temporal consistency. He did suggest that individuals differ in their time preference, and he argued that individuals' time preference might change when one of the factors determining time preference changed. For example, he suggested that the rate of time preference could change as an individual ages, as has recently been supported in research by Read and Read (2004).[4] Nevertheless, it seems that he expected a person at any given moment to use the same rate of time preference across all intertemporal choice situations. The results from the empirical studies reported below show that this is not the case. In fact, decision-specific factors seem to be the most important determinants of rates of time preference found in empirical studies.

Loewenstein and Prelec (1993) reported results from experiments indicating that people generally like sequences of events that improve over time and dislike sequences that deteriorate (where the individual events making up the sequence are the same). This means that the discount rate is not necessarily positive but in some situations it may be negative. Hence, the discount rate used in a particular intertemporal decision may depend on whether the decision maker perceives the decision as a single event or as a decision in a sequence of events. Prelec and Loewenstein (1998) also find a form of debt aversion in some settings. When people are asked if they would like to pay for a holiday before or after the holiday has taken place, the majority answer that they want to pay before. Similar experiments show that this sort of debt aversion occurs where debt is construed as either consuming something before paying for it or getting advance payment for future work. Prelec and Loewenstein discuss two different mechanisms that may motivate people to prepay for a product. One is the anticipation of enjoying the product without having to think about the payment, as "the pain of paying" may reduce the utility of consuming the product. The other is to avoid paying for consumption that has already been enjoyed. Then the pain of paying is not being buffered by the joy of consumption. This debt aversion does not, however, apply to all products. When asked about the preferred timing for paying for, say, a washing machine or Internet access, the majority preferred paying after receiving the product. This is in line with the findings by Hirst, Joyce, and Schadewald (1992), who reported the results of a series of experiments that revealed a preference for matching the duration of a loan with the life of the durable. The way consumers are asked to pay for a certain product may therefore influence the decision to buy.

Findings from several studies suggest that individuals react very differently to situations involving receipt of money compared to those involving paying money, and to speed-ups as opposed to delays (Benzion, Rapoport, and Yagil 1989; Loewenstein 1988; Nyhus 1997; Shelley 1993). These results have been attributed to shifts in reference points. Loewenstein (1988) and Shelley (1993) argued that the effects of outcome sign (receipt versus payment) and question framing (delay versus speed-up) should be combined when the results are interpreted. They defined delay of reward and speed-up of payment as "immediate losses" because these situations involve a worsening of present well-being. Likewise, speed-up of reward and delay of payment were defined as "immediate gains," because these situations involve an improvement in present well-being. They argued that the present state is used as a reference point. The sign of the change for the present situation determines whether a situation is considered a gain or a loss. This theory has much in common with prospect theory (Kahneman and Tversky 1979), which proposes that the value function for losses is steeper than that for gains. It also holds that outcomes are evaluated in terms of deviations from reference points instead of absolute values. However, the intertemporal reference point model also suffers from the same weakness as prospect theory: our knowledge about which reference point a consumer uses and how it is formed or chosen is very limited. In situations outside the laboratory, where the researcher cannot manipulate the reference point, we know very little about whether a particular outcome is perceived as a gain or a loss.

Nyhus (1997) found that people not only change their discount rate from one situation to another but also change their impatience levels relative to others. She investigated the consistency in answers to twelve time preference questions using responses from a Dutch sample of over 4,000 individuals. She found that, in general, correlations between answers to different time preference questions were low, but they were higher for questions involving the same framing (i.e., high between items involving delaying receipt of money and between items that involved delaying payment). This suggests that not only does the size of the discount rates used for different situations change, but also that people change their relative position in the distribution of responses when the situations are framed differently. A person who appears to be the most impatient in one situation may be among the more patient in another.

All the results reviewed above suggest that there are fundamental measurement problems in empirical studies of time preference. In many studies people are faced with hypothetical choices between money now or in the future, and it is not clear that such hypothetical choices reflect actual choices and therefore real time preferences. Even when real money is used in experiments, the amounts involved are small, which makes generalization difficult. Studies of real-world choices (which do involve substantial sums of money) are contaminated by uncontrolled variables. And different combinations of present and future gains and losses give rise to alternative measures of time preferences, which are likely to result in different estimates of the discount rates. Frederick, Loewenstein, and O'Donoghue have provided the most extensive review of the empirical studies of time preference, and conclude: "In contrast to estimates of physical phenomena such as the speed of light, there is no evidence of methodological progress; the range of estimates is not shrinking over time" (2002, 377).

Knetsch (2000) argues that the methods used in most time preference studies are likely to produce biased estimates. In most studies, people are asked to choose between two gains (do you prefer $1,000 today or $1,000 + x in one month?) or two losses (do you prefer to pay $1,000 today or pay $1,000 + x in one year?). He suggests that questions combining gains and losses (how much would you be willing to give up today in order to get $1,000 in one month, or how much would you demand today in order to accept a loss of $1,000 in one year?) will provide more realistic answers, as these kind of choices are more often encountered in everyday life. They also correspond more to most cost-benefit analyses. So far, this way of asking questions to identify time preference has been little used.

Another important finding from empirical research on intertemporal choice is that an individual's rate of time preference tends to change as a function of time (being high for the present and immediate future and lower for periods in the future). The findings suggest that instead of discounting future events with a constant discount rate (which can be illustrated by exponential curves), individuals use higher discount rates for the near future than for the remote future (which can be illustrated by hyperbolic curves). The curves found in experimental designs differ in their specific forms, but they share this common hyperbolic characteristic. Thaler (1981) described the phenomenon with the following example: most people prefer two apples in one year and one day to one apple in one year, but when asked to choose between one apple today and two apples tomorrow, most people will want an apple today. This means that their discount rate for the future apples is much lower than for the apples available in the present or near future. The result is a change in tastes over time and time-inconsistent behavior.

Figure 15.1a (from Ainslie 1992) illustrates an individual's preferences and behavior under stable time preferences. The graphs illustrate the present value assigned to the two alternatives after discounting it to the present value. At T_0 the individual prefers alternative B, which is larger but is available at a later point in time than alternative A. As T_n approaches, alternative B is still considered superior because the decision maker uses the same discount rate when evaluating the alternatives. The preference curves are exponential and proportional to each other. They never cross. The decision maker waits for alternative B, which is available at T_{n+1}. Figure 15.1b shows the preferences and behavior under hyperbolic discounting. At T_0, the individual prefers alternative B to A. However, as the time of availability for A approaches, the decision maker starts using a higher discount rate, which causes a shift of preferences. When the two alternatives are discounted with a much higher rate, the alternative closest in time has the highest present value. The change in discount rates produces more curved preference curves, and the curves cross. Alternative A is chosen, in spite of the preference for alternative B when choosing from a more remote temporal distance.

Figure 15.1   **Effects of Exponential and Hyperbolic Discounting**

15.1a: Exponential discount rates:
stable preferences

15.1b: Hyperbolic discount rates:
preference reversal

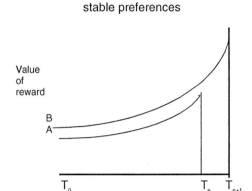
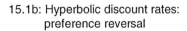
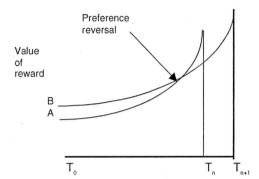

Ainslie (1975) reviewed numerous studies of this kind of inconsistent behavior, which he denotes "impulsivity." Impulsive behavior has been found among birds, animals, children, and adults. Preferences for two goods available at two different points in time are better described by hyperbolic curves than by exponential ones. The effects of overvaluation of the present were theoretically outlined by Strotz as far back as 1956. He showed that if time preference changes as a function of time, the result is dynamically inconsistent behavior. A conflict will occur between today's preferences and tomorrow's preferences. People do things they would not have done if they had made the decision to act from a remote perspective, and they do not follow their own plans.

At least five explanations for this apparently dynamic inconsistent behavior have been put forward. Some of them argue that the observed behavior is not inconsistent at all, while others try to model internal inconsistent preferences. Loewenstein (1996) argued that the economic theory of intertemporal choice is misspecified because it does not include "visceral" factors (or "passions"). He points to the weakness of the theory of changing discount rates, which fails to explain why inconsistent behavior is only induced in some situations and not in others. He attributed "inconsistent behavior" to the role of visceral factors, which he described as important dimensions of human reality such as hunger, thirst, mood, emotion, drive, desire, physical pain, and so on. The traditional economic man has no passions in the sense of yearning or craving, and for this reason every deviation from deliberative and stable preferences is left unexplained by the economic models. They are interpreted as a change in tastes and irrational time-inconsistency. Loewenstein's (1996) point was that if the role of visceral factors is included in models of choice over time, impulsive behavior will not be viewed as an irrational shift in preferences.[5] The preferences remain stable, but other factors that interact with them in determining behavior must be taken into account when predicting behavior.

Hoch and Loewenstein (1991) and Loewenstein (1996) claimed that visceral factors can explain why some types of behavior are associated with impulsive behavior and others are not. Hoch and Loewenstein argued that shifts in reference points are important for impulsive behavior. Reference points might change because of physical and temporal proximity that makes not consuming painful. Or it might change through unfavorable social comparisons with peers or others. They defined consumer self-control as a struggle between the two psychological forces of desire and willpower. In their model, self-controlling strategies were divided into two classes: attempts to directly reduce desire, and willpower tactics that seek to overcome desire. Loewenstein (1996), on the other hand, argued that impulsive behavior is caused not so much by the immediate availability of the events, goods, or outcomes as by the immediacy and intensity of visceral factors. At high levels of intensity, passions gain complete control, and perceptions of self-interest become unable to influence behavior. As the level of intensity increases, an individual will focus his attention and effort on the present and on himself as opposed to other points in time and other people. Loewenstein further argued that passions are more systematic in their effects than previously supposed, so it is possible to model the interaction between interests and passions.

Empirical studies support some of the aspects of Loewenstein's (1996) theory. Some buying is a result of tempting situations (immediacy of goods). Research in prepurchase processes suggests that there are substantial differences among consumers in the amount of prepurchase deliberation (e.g., Rogers and Shoemaker 1971). According to a review of household prepurchase decision making by Olshavsky and Granbois (1979), 20–25 percent of durable goods and clothing purchases, up to 50 percent of supermarket purchases, and 33 percent of transactions in variety stores and drugstores are "impulsive purchases" in the sense that shoppers do not state intentions to buy these items in store entrance interviews. Indirect support for the role of visceral factors is also provided by the fact that for decades marketers have investigated how to stimulate impulsive buying by manipulating the atmosphere, smell, structure, and display of products in shopping centers and supermarkets.

Metcalfe and Mischel (1999) have proposed a "hot-cool" model based on knowledge of biological predispositions in the human brain. It is to some extent similar to Loewenstein's model of visceral influences but is more detailed in terms of describing the processes at work in the brain. They propose a model consisting of two interactive systems. The "cool" system is an emotionally neutral "know-system": cognitive, complex, slow, and contemplative. It consists of a network of informational cool nodes that are interconnected to each other and generate rational and planful behavior. The activation of the cool system increases with age, except under high stress levels that may reduce the system's effect. The emotional "hot" system, on the other hand, is a "go-system," specialized for quick emotional processing. It is simple and fast, consisting of relatively few representations or "hot spots" that trigger reflexive actions. The hot system develops early in life and is dominant in young infants. Both the hot and cool systems are heavily influenced by biological dispositions, learning, and maturation. The way the hot and cool systems are assumed to interact is that both are activated by external referents. The hot spots and cool nodes that have the same external referent are linked to one another and thereby link the two systems. Hot spots can therefore be evoked by activation of the corresponding cool nodes and vice versa. Self-control problems typically arise if hot spots do not have, or cannot access, the corresponding cool representation, so that the cool system regulation of hot impulses is nonexistent. The child's increased ability to delay gratification as it grows older is explained by the developmental lag between the two systems. The hot system is present at birth, whereas the cool system develops with age. Stress seems to reduce access to the cool system, making the individual unable to divert activity away from the hot system.

An alternative perspective on inconsistent behavior is to model an economic man with two selves similar to Freud's theory of the ego and the id (Schelling 1978; Thaler and Shefrin 1981). This framework attributes observed time-inconsistent behavior not to changing tastes but to a short-sighted self gaining more control of behavior than a long-sighted self. Thaler and Shefrin (1981) modeled the internal conflicts between short-term and long-term preferences (e.g., eating versus losing weight) as a principal-agent problem. They argued that there is a constant conflict between the "planner" (the self that maximizes long-term utility) and the "doer" (the myopic self that maximizes only present utility). Ainslie (1992, 1993) advocated a similar perspective under the label "picoeconomics." He modeled the intrapersonal struggle as a repeated prisoner's dilemma and argued that the two (or more selves) are continuously bargaining.

George (2001) put forward yet another model to resolve the observed paradoxes in behavior and stated preferences, arguing that we have two sets of preferences: first-order and second-order (see also George's essay in this volume). The first-order preferences are preferences about things. The second-order preferences are preferences about the first-order preferences, that is, alternatives in a choice set are allowed to be preference rankings of things rather than themselves things. An example would be the choice between a healthy meal (H) and a burger meal (B). Time-inconsistent behavior is a result of the simultaneous occurrence of a regular, or first-order, preference for B (B > H) and a second-order preference for H [(H > B) > (B > H)]. Hence, a felt or experienced first-order preference can be a preference one would have rather not felt. This model differs from the multiple-self (or multiple-utility) models in one important way. The multiple-self models retain the assumption of one ranking per agent at a single moment while also treating an agent as in fact two, three, or more agents, each having its own ranking. Instead, this model allows agents to have preferences about preferences, and the assumption about complete preference orderings and comparable alternative actions need not be relaxed. George uses this model to explain unhealthy eating, gambling, credit, entertainment, and sexual behaviors.

Finally, Gifford (2002) has put forward a biology-based model of choice as an alternative to these approaches. Gifford claims that time inconsistencies in behavior are simply a specific example of the kind of inconsistencies that occur when people make choices between alternatives that differ in their level of abstraction. If you are choosing between a piece of one kind of cake that is physically present and another that is represented only by a printed word on a piece of paper, you are likely to choose the type of cake that is present. Change which kind is present and you get a reversal of choices. Gifford's view is that since the future is always abstract, choices between present and future consumption will often be choices of this type. Underlying Gifford's approach is the idea that humans have essentially two systems for making choices. One is based on emotional and motivational systems that have evolved to enhance inclusive fitness, and incorporates a high discount rate that is shared by nonhuman animals. The other rests on our cognitive ability and depends on the fact that we can think symbolically. This incorporates a lower discount rate that has been acquired culturally. Which system dominates will depend on the situation and on an individual's ability to inhibit particular responses.

TIME PREFERENCES AND SAVING BEHAVIOR

Fisher (1930) argued that time preference was the most important determinant of saving, as it captured the interaction effects of socioeconomic and personality factors. However, only a few empirical studies have focused on the impact of time preference on saving and borrowing behavior, and the results so far are ambiguous. Antonides (1988) found differences in the discount factors between people who saved and people who did not save. The average monthly discount factor of the savers was 1.4 percent, while it was 2.6 percent for the nonsavers. Ritzema (1992) found that time preference was significantly related to the likelihood of having financial problems and to total debt. Webley and Nyhus (2001) found that people with debt problems had higher time preferences (measured by delayed payment scenarios) than those with mild or nonexistent debt problems. Donkers and van Soest (1999) found a negative relationship between time preference and the probability of owning a house, while they found a positive relationship with the probability of holding risky assets. Daniel (1994), on the other hand, using the same data, did not find a significant relationship between time preference and five different measures of saving behavior.

The lack of conclusive results concerning the relationship between time preferences and saving behavior might be the consequence of the measurement problems involved when estimating time preference. A second reason may be that most studies are cross-sectional. If we think about the way time preference is supposed to work, we have to take diminishing marginal utility into account as well. In a panel study, we may expect to find that high time preference in one period is associated with lower saving or increased borrowing in the next period. In a cross-sectional study, it is not as straightforward to say anything about the relationship between time preferences and financial behavior. One usual expectation would be to expect that high debt is associated with high time preference. However, if we also consider the existence of diminishing marginal utility, high debt could equally well be associated with low time preference, since credit-financed consumption may have made the consumer less impatient to consume more. This will depend on the consumer's aspiration level with respect to consumption. It is therefore a mistake to expect a particular relationship between saving and borrowing and time preference at a certain point in time. Time preference should be used to predict future behavior, and its effect should be studied using longitudinal data. A third reason may be that time preference is not the only factor that influences intertemporal choices. For example, Julander (1975), studying the effect of bookkeeping on saving, reported that both an index intended to measure lack of impulse control and an index intended to measure ability to delay gratification correlated with some of his saving measures. A person governed by visceral sensations will have problems with rational planning due to the tendency to form temporary preferences. But most people manage their financial affairs satisfactorily to the extent that they avoid debt problems, usually get up in the morning, do their duties at school and work, and resist most consumption temptations exposed in shopping centers and supermarkets. Not all situations involving intrapersonal conflicts of interest produce time-inconsistent behavior. Mechanisms other than impatience and temptation must be playing an important role. In some way, people must be able to follow their long-term plans by committing themselves to them. The applied techniques have been called self-controlling strategies, impulse control (Ainslie 1992, 2001), or "tricks we play on ourselves to make us do the things we ought to do or to keep us from the things we ought to forswear" (Schelling 1978, 290).

SELF-CONTROL

Concepts such as self-control and thrift have been linked to saving at least since Adam Smith included a chapter on self-command in *The Theory of Moral Sentiments* (see Loewenstein 1992; Wärneryd 1989, 1999). The theories that incorporate the role of self-control implicitly recognize that refraining from pleasure can be difficult. Within this perspective, behavior is a result not only of the experienced intensity of the temptations but also of the ability to exercise self-control in situations where there is a conflict between short-term and long-term goals. Self-control may be defined as those efforts made by the individual to avoid or resist behaving inconsistently, or it may be defined as a deliberate choice to accept pain in order to gain something (Schelling 1984). When Strotz (1956), Elster (1979), and Ainslie (1992, 1993) discussed the problem of nonexponential discounting and intertemporal inconsistency, they used the story from Homer's *Odyssey* about Ulysses and the Sirens as an example of how inconsistent behavior can be avoided.[6] The story neatly demonstrates two main techniques for controlling impulses and resisting temptations: prior commitment and avoiding exposure. Ulysses precommitted himself by letting others tie him to the mast so that he could not execute any change in the ship's direction. He controlled his crew by preventing their exposure to the harmful Siren song. In Loewenstein's (1996) terms, Ulysses used techniques to overcome impulses to act upon visceral sensations. By controlling his actions through precommitment, he acted in accordance with his more stable preferences.

Strotz (1956) suggested that future actions might be controlled by precommitment and the strategies of consistent planning. Using strategies of consistent planning means that an individual should choose the best of the plans that she believes it is possible to follow. Similar techniques have been proposed by Ainslie (1992, 1993), who argues that the process underlying impulse control can be modeled as a repetitive, intertemporal prisoner's dilemma. He argues that one choice will set precedents for later ones. Since a person wants to act rationally in her future choices, she might act rationally in the present too, since she believes that it will serve as an example of future behavior. "If she makes an impulsive choice, she will have little reason to believe she will not go on doing so, and if she controls her impulse, she has evidence that she may go on doing that" (Ainslie 1992, 336). According to Ainslie's framework, self-control is most likely to be observed for choices that will be repeated (i.e., that are one in a series of similar choices). Elster (1979) proposed many ways of precommitting oneself by invoking social mechanisms. By making (side) bets with others, people exaggerate the negative aspects of failing to achieve their long-term goals. Another self-controlling strategy is to punish oneself when one behaves myopically. Thaler and Shefrin (1981) compared intrapersonal conflicts with the conflicts described in principal-agent theories. Following the suggestions about how principals might control agents, they suggest that one's future actions can be controlled by altering incentives (monitoring available resources) or altering rules (by establishing self-imposed rules of thumb, habits, and routine). In this way, it will be in the shortsighted self's interest to behave in accordance with the longsighted self's preferences.

Both Katona (1975) and Bernheim (1995) reported that people say they save less than planned or that they would like to save more, which give some indication of self-control problems with respect to saving and spending. Romal and Kaplan (1995) report that savers have a higher score on Rosenbaum's Self-Control Schedule than spenders. Some empirical evidence suggests that self-controlling strategies can be found in economic management. Examples of such strategies are fixed saving arrangements, deliberate overpayment of income tax (Cox and Plumley 1988), participation in Christmas clubs or other saving clubs, and even installment buying, since this produces a stream of obligations to pay (Caplovitz 1963).[7] Other research suggests that people use mental budgets, so that a moment of weakness that leads to an impulsive purchase is compensated for by decreased expenditure on other things (Heath and Soll 1996). Self-controlling techniques and methods used to accommodate deviations in original plans might therefore be important for saving. In spite of this, the extent and role of self-controlling strategies in economic affairs have not yet been subject to much empirical testing. For example, methods for monitoring one's own time preferences by avoiding exposure have received very little attention from researchers. Such techniques could be not going to shopping malls or avoiding mail and telephone marketing. Webley and Nyhus (2001) found that people experiencing debt problems used the technique of not going shopping more often than others, and Sonuga-Barke and Webley (1993) report that in an experimental saving game some children will avoid going into a sweet shop. Other techniques could involve the choice of friends and neighborhood, as exposure to other peoples' possessions can give rise to desires for the same lifestyle and products (Duesenberry 1949; Schor 1998). The delay of gratification experiments carried out on children support the idea that avoiding exposure enhances ability to delay gratification. The children participating in the experiments tried to wait for the delayed larger rewards by avoiding thinking about the immediate available awards. They distracted themselves by singing, playing games, and even sleeping. Distraction from the available rewards was found to be an important factor in waiting behavior (Mischel and Ebbesen 1970).

BEHAVIORAL SAVING MODELS

Alongside the development of theories of time preference and self-control, a number of behavioral saving models have been developed. Three models, two of which are firmly rooted in behavioral economics, will be described and evaluated below.

The Behavioral Life Cycle Model

The most influential economic theories assume that the prime motive for saving today is so that one can consume tomorrow; in other words, people are simply making choices between spending now and spending later. Most theoretical effort has been concentrated on the issue of how individuals deal with variations in income across their life span. The best-known of these theories is the life cycle hypothesis (LCH) developed by Modigliani and Brumberg (1954). They started off with an assumption that people want to have a stable consumption (or utility) across all periods in their remaining lifetime (due to diminishing marginal utility) and an observation of the most common income profile of a worker over his or her working life. Further, they suggested that people are rationally determining how much they can consume over the remainder of their life by taking their assets and all future earnings into account and that in any given year the difference between this level of consumption and income will be the amount saved (or the amount borrowed). Young people borrow to pay for consumption, the middle-aged save for retirement, and the old spend those savings (the so-called hump-shaped age/saving profile). The model assumes quite a substantial decision-making capacity and knowledge about the future, as pointed out by Thaler: "The essence of the life-cycle theory is this: in any year compute the present value of your wealth, including current income, net assets, and future income; figure out the level annuity you could purchase with that money; then consume the amount you would receive if you in fact owned such an annuity" (1990, 193–94).

Friedman's (1957) permanent income hypothesis is similar to the LCH. Friedman claimed that people have a notion of what their mean permanent income will be across a time period and aim to consume a fixed proportion of it during that time. Their actual income and consumption may well vary from the permanent income, and saving or borrowing will take up the slack. One important difference between this and the life cycle hypothesis is that the permanent income is not the same as expected lifetime earnings. Friedman recognized that individuals make calculations based on a time horizon that does not necessarily extend to their deaths.

Although the LCH has been modified in order to make it more realistic since it was first proposed (e.g., by including a rising income profile, uncertainty with respect to future income, and length of life) it still relies, in the majority of studies, on strict assumptions about time preferences. The model assumes that time preference is adjusted to expected lifetime resources. This means that the model would not predict overspending. The marginal utility of extra consumption in the present is assumed to never be so high that overspending occurs. However, many reports on behavior in our Western consumer society suggest that it does (see, for example, Schor 1998). New models of saving and consumption have therefore been developed so as to adapt the theory to observations such as a general decline in saving in Western countries (Maital and Maital 1994; Parker 1999) and a growing number of cases of personal bankruptcy (Stavins 2000).

In 1988, Shefrin and Thaler, who had completed several studies of self-control, launched the behavioral life cycle model (BLCH). The incorporation of self-control reflects recognition that refraining from consumption is difficult. In the LCH framework, it is not considered a problem for the consumer to distribute her income over the life span. However, as discussed previously, research on intertemporal decision making has revealed that such a model appears too simplistic. Although people have preferences for saving in order to have a smooth consumption stream, they also have preferences for immediate gratification. Therefore, as previously noted, Shefrin and Thaler (1988) modeled saving and consumption decisions as an internal conflict between two mutually inconsistent personalities, one concerned with the long run (the "planner") and one with the short run (the "doer"). They argued that modeling these two competing forces is consistent with findings from brain research and that it corresponds to the interaction between the prefrontal cortex and the limbic system. Apart from the use of sheer willpower (which is effortful), the planner controls the doer's expenditures by introducing rules of thumb and so-called mental accounts. The purpose of mental accounts is that each is associated with different levels of spending temptation, which means that also the fungibility assumption underlying the LCH is relaxed. Shefrin and Thaler (1988) propose that three mental accounts are useful in studies of saving: current income, current assets, and future income.[8] They argue that the temptation to spend from these accounts varies, so the propensity to consume from the different accounts also varies. The temptation to spend is assumed greatest for current income and least for future income, and the self-control needed to refrain from spending is higher for current income than for wealth (past income) and future income. This contrasts with the LCH framework, in which such mental labeling of money is absent.

An implication of this theory is that the propensity to consume from income is dependent on which mental account it is put into or how the income is viewed. If, for example, a windfall is entered into the "wealth account," the propensity to consume the windfall would be lower than if it is entered into the "present income account." For this reason, Shefrin and Thaler (1988) argued that lump sum bonuses are treated differently than increases in regular income. The saving rate can be affected by the way increments to wealth are described. Another important implication of the BLCH framework is that saving would be inadequate without social security and pensions. This opinion was reiterated by Maital and Maital (1994) when they criticized the deregulation of the credit markets. Adopting the doer-planner framework of the BLCH, they pointed to the fact that externally imposed restrictions as well as self-imposed constraints on spending and debt have been weakened in the past decades. They attributed the general decline of saving in the West to this weakened precommitment and argued that saving will not increase again until precommitment mechanisms are reestablished. It is increasingly easy to borrow money, and automatic teller machines provide easy access to savings. Some banks even offer automatic loans if a consumer overdraws his bank balance.

The BLCH has been only partially tested, but it is supported by some empirical findings. Shefrin and Thaler (1988) presented some results from a small survey designed to study the differences in propensity to consume from an increase in regular payments ($200 in twelve months), a lump sum payment ($2,400), or a future payment ($2,400 plus interest in five years). They found that although the total amount of the payments was identical, the students in their sample would use more of the regular payments than of the lump sum payment. Most of the respondents claimed that they would not increase their present consumption based on a promise of money five years on. This was interpreted as support for the assumption of the existence of mental accounts and that people have different propensities to consume for different mental accounts.

In addition, Shefrin and Thaler (1988) derived ten predictions from their theory:

1. Changes in discretionary saving from a change in pension saving is less (absolutely) than 1.0 and declines sharply as age falls.
2. The change in discretionary saving from a change in pension saving increases with income or wealth.
3. Without sufficiently large compulsory schemes, postretirement consumption is less than preretirement consumption.
4. The saving rate increases with permanent income.
5. Holding wealth constant, consumption tracks income.
6. The marginal propensity to consume bonus income is lower than that for regular income.
7. For (non-negligible) windfalls, the marginal propensity to consume is less than the marginal propensity to consume regular income but greater than the annuity value of the windfall. The marginal propensity to consume out of windfall income declines as the size of the windfall increases.
8. Holding lifetime income constant, home ownership increases wealth at retirement.
9. The marginal propensity to consume inheritance income will depend on the form in which the inheritance is received.
10. The marginal propensity to consume dividend income is greater than the marginal propensity to consume increases in the value of stock holdings.

To find support for these predictions, Shefrin and Thaler (1988) reviewed numerous studies in which investigators have distinguished between different types of wealth and incomes, and they found support for the ten predictions derived from the BLCH. In addition, Shefrin and Thaler found that results from studies of the effect of pension saving and social security wealth on saving supported the BLCH. Finally, they reported findings that support the assumption that the propensity to save increases with income.

Levin (1998) carried out the first study designed to test the BLCH using a large panel data set (the Retirement History Survey). He conducted a comparative study to investigate which of the two models (the LCH or the BLCH) could best explain variation in consumption. He tested the effects of level of wealth as well as the form of the wealth on the expenditures on ten different goods. The results are strongly in favor of the BLCH, as they reject the fungibility assumption, they support a different propensity to consume for different wealth components, and they show that the labeling of income (into which mental account it is entered) affects spending. These results were valid both for liquidity-constrained subjects and for unconstrained subjects. However, Levin did not find support for the assumption that the marginal propensity to consume past (illiquid) wealth was higher than that for future wealth. Levin explained this finding by the increase in the value of social security in the period of the data collection. The increase in one period might have influenced the confidence that it would continue to rise in the future.

Other studies have been conducted in order to test some of the underlying assumptions of the BLCH. For example, Heath, Chatterjee, and France (1995) found support for the existence of mental accounting principles.[9] Heath and Soll (1996) found that people do apply mental budgeting and that these mental budgets affect our consumption. People use resources differently depending on how they are labeled. They found evidence that consumers earmark money for certain product categories and that labels affect expenditures within the categories in predictable ways. In particular, they found that the mental budgets were quite inflexible. Karlsson, Gärling, and Selart (1999) found that willingness to buy was greater when the subjects in their experiments were asked to imagine they received a temporary income increase as opposed to a temporary income decrease (holding total assets equal). They also found support for the existence and use of mental accounts in specific buying decisions. Webley and Plaisier (1998) found some evidence for mental accounts in eight- to twelve-year-old children, who spent money from different sources (pocket money, holiday money, birthday money) quite differently. In a rather different study, Selart, Gärling, and Karlsson (1997) analyzed data from a nationwide Swedish sample (996 individuals) and a student sample (277 randomly selected undergraduate students) in order to replicate the results of Shefrin and Thaler. In this study, they found that subjects expected to consume more when they were asked to imagine that an income increase would be received as an immediate lump sum than when the income increase would be received as future monthly increments. Selart and colleagues interpreted this as being contrary to the predictions of the behavioral life cycle hypothesis. There is, however, a possibility that the respondents perceived the alternative, including monthly increments, also as future income, and the findings are then in accordance with the BLCH in that people were more willing to spend money from current assets than from future income.

Prelec and Loewenstein (1998) elaborated the idea of mental accounting and suggested a "double-entry" mental accounting theory in which the pain of paying as well as the thought of paying was taken into account. They introduced a mental accounting theory in which one set of entries records the net utility of consumption (which means that the disutility of associated payments are subtracted) and the other set of entries records the net disutility of payments (after subtracting the utility of associated consumption). An underlying assumption of their theory was that prepaid consumption can be enjoyed as if it were free and that the pain associated with payments made prior to consumption (but not after) is buffered by thoughts of the benefits financed by the payment. They conducted several experiments to investigate this assumption, and they found that people are debt-averse: they prefer to pay before consuming and to be paid after finishing work. They also found that the degree to which consumption calls to mind thoughts of payments is important.

Graham and Isaac (2002) used a survey-based data set in order to test whether consumers could solve the optimization problems as assumed by the life cycle model. They asked university faculty members to choose to receive a nine-month (academic year) salary either over nine months or over twelve months. According to neoclassical theory, respondents should prefer the nine-month option, since this alternative is more valuable in a present-value sense (assuming a positive interest rate). They found that the behavior of even highly educated consumers deviates considerably from the neoclassical predictions in that they prefer to postpone the receipt of income (76 of the 109 respondents). Graham and Isaac interpret this as evidence that many consumers believe that a smooth income stream helps them to control spending. While a preference for income smoothing is a difficulty for the neoclassical model, it is consistent with the predictions of the behavioral life cycle model.

The behavioral life cycle hypothesis does a good job of accounting for the (limited) data and is explicitly behavioral. The two-self model is naive, but it is one step on a road to creating a behavioral economic model. This approach is still firmly based on the idea of rational action: both the doer and the planner "act" rationally according to their preferences. The ideas about the effect of framing also suffer from the same weaknesses as prospect theory (Kahneman and Tversky 1979) and the reference point model (Loewenstein 1988): since we know little about how reference points are formed, we know little about how different people will frame a certain payment, and therefore it will be difficult to predict behavior. Shefrin and Thaler (1988) noted that people might differ in their mental accounting practices, but did not elaborate on how these differences can be identified so that they can be taken into account when testing the model. The framing of a lump sum payment might, for example, depend on the ratio between the present income and the size of the lump sum, so that high-income people will have a greater tendency to put lump sum payments into the present income account than people with low income. Alternatively, the effect of the size of the lump sum might interact with saving motives. Many possible factors that might influence the framing of an income component need to be explored. Moreover, the theory should be elaborated in order to incorporate factors that influence the marginal propensity to spend from the different accounts. Although this model is based on ideas about human decision making that are more realistic, we know little about the extent to which these assumptions correspond more to actual behavior than those of the LCH.

The Buffer Stock Model

Inclusion of a precautionary motive is the principal innovation of the LCH in the past decade (Browning and Lusardi 1996). Being pessimistic or uncertain about future income will obviously affect the financial decisions that people make. Those who face greater income uncertainty will consume less. One implication of the existence of this motive is that the path of consumption is not necessarily independent of the path of income. If the future variability of income increases, saving for the future will increase too. Likewise, an agent facing higher income uncertainty will also save more (Carroll and Samwick 1997; Hubbard, Skinner, and Zeldes 1995). The magnitude of the effect depends on the level of current assets and income relative to expected future income.

The precautionary motive alone cannot explain why so many households have very little wealth. Deaton (1992) and Carroll (1997) therefore proposed inclusion of a competing factor. They attributed low saving to so-called buffer stock behavior, which implies that there is an upper limit for precautionary saving. The assumptions underlying buffer stock models are that people are impatient (have a high rate of time preference) and fear the possibility of having no consumption opportunities in the future (the precautionary motive). Carroll (1997) argued that people therefore have a (typically small) wealth/income ratio target for their saving. If wealth is below the target, prudence dominates, as people are afraid of destitution in later periods. If wealth is above this level, impatience dominates and the available resources will be consumed. Carroll (1997) suggested that it is the possibility of poverty later in life that stops people from borrowing when they are young. The more uncertainty that is associated with future income, the higher the buffer stock saving. The interaction between precautionary saving motives and impatience is that consumption will track income in the early part of life, while (significant) saving will only be observed in later years. Carroll (1997) and Carroll and Samwick (1997) found empirical support for the buffer stock model. Gourinchas and Parker (2002) found that it is young people who engage in buffer stock saving, while older people (older than forty-two years) accumulate liquid assets for retirement in line with the standard LCH. Similarly, Zhou (2003) found that young households in Japan were more likely to save for precautionary purposes than were older households. Gourinchas and Parker interpreted these findings as being a result of the life cycle profile of expected income, which causes saving motives to change over the life cycle. Samwick (1998) reported findings suggesting that households save only to maintain a buffer stock until retirement is only a few years away.

Hubbard, Skinner, and Zeldes (1995) tested a buffer stock model (assuming a rate of time preference of 10 percent and a consumption floor of $1,000) against a model with lower time preference rates (3 percent) and incorporation of the asset-based means testing of welfare programs used in the United States. The latter model fit the data better than the buffer stock model. In particular, it provided a better explanation of why many households showed a strong persistence in low levels of wealth: saving while receiving transfers is discouraged, as higher wealth is a disqualification for receiving further transfers. The buffer stock model predicts that households will have a strong motive to rebuild their buffer stock at all levels of income and wealth. The buffer stock model therefore failed to explain why 56 percent of the households that had assets worth less than $1,000 in 1984 still had less than $1,000 total wealth in 1989. Carroll and Samwick (1997) argued that they found evidence of the buffer stock model performing better than the model of Hubbard, Skinner, and Zeldes (1995). Consumers facing greater income uncertainty held more wealth. In particular, they found that buffer stock saving is important for consumers younger than fifty years of age. After this age, people engage in retirement saving. Furthermore, they reported that sensitivity to uncertainty decreased with rising time preferences.

There is other evidence that is consistent with the buffer stock model. Dunn (2003) has shown that income uncertainty has an important effect on the timing of home purchases. Consistent with the buffer stock model, households that face greater income uncertainty buy a new home when the ratio of the value of their existing home to permanent income is lower than the ratio for similar households with less uncertain incomes.

The buffer stock model of saving is one example of how the opposing forces of impatience and a precautionary saving motive can be incorporated into the LCH framework.

The Golden Eggs Model

Building on work by Strotz (1956) and Phelps and Pollak (1968), Laibson (1997) introduced hyperbolic discount functions to the LCH framework and elaborated and tested the model in several studies (e.g. Laibson, Repetto, and Tobacman 2003; Angeletos et al. 2001). The result is the so-called golden eggs model, in which the theory of hyperbolic discounting is transformed from a psychological peculiarity into a tool that can be used in macroeconomic analyses.

Laibson (1994) proposed a model assuming a declining discount rate between the present period and the next, and a constant discount rate in the following periods. He used this model to explore the consequences of hyperbolic discounting for consumption and saving behavior. In two successive papers (Laibson 1997, 1998) he explored the effects of illiquid assets ("golden eggs") on saving behavior. He regarded illiquid assets (such as a house), whose sale must be initiated one period before the sale proceeds, as a commitment technology that will limit overconsumption. Illiquid wealth will prevent the consumer from smoothing the consumption stream in periods with low income. The model can explain the observation of household consumption flows tracking household income too closely compared to what the LCH would predict. The model also explains why consumers have asset-specific marginal propensities to consume, but with an explanation different from Shefrin and Thaler's mental account theory. An implication of the model is that new financial innovations that have increased liquidity (e.g., instantaneous credit) and eliminated commitment opportunities are responsible for the ongoing decline in U.S. savings rates. Laibson also suggested that the changes in financial markets may reduce welfare by providing "too much" liquidity.

In three other papers, Laibson and his collaborators compared the performance of models assuming exponential and hyperbolic discount functions, respectively, with a special focus on the so-called debt puzzle (Angeletos et al. 2001; Harris and Laibson 2001; Laibson, Repetto, and Tobacman 2003). The debt puzzle was identified by Gross and Souleles (2002) using a large panel data set of thousands of credit card accounts from several different card issuers. They found a substantial coexistence of credit card debt with illiquid assets in addition to a coexistence of credit card debt with liquid assets. Two-thirds of United States households had credit cards by the end of 1998, and more than half of these revolve debt on their cards. Still, a large fraction of this group holds a substantial sum of liquid assets. This behavior, which also breaks with the assumption of money being fungible, cannot be explained by the LCH assuming exponential discount functions. By simulating and comparing the savings and asset allocation choices of households with exponential and hyperbolic preferences, respectively, Laibson, Repetto, and Tobacman (2003) showed that the hyperbolic consumption model can explain this anomaly. They found that a "hyperbolic household" would borrow more frequently in the revolving credit market, hold relatively more illiquid wealth and relatively less liquid wealth, exhibit greater consumption-income co-movement, and experience a greater drop in consumption than an "exponential household." The psychological ideas underlying the hyperbolic model are that a person's current willingness to accumulate for retirement is greater in the present than the willingness he or she expects to have at a later state in his or her life. For this reason, the person will accumulate illiquid assets for retirement so that he or she imposes restrictions on the spending of future selves, who are likely to act impatiently. Since the simulated behavior of the hyperbolic households matches observed consumption data better than that of the exponential households, the model seems to be capable of accounting for a wide range of apparent LCH anomalies, such as (1) variation in time preference over the life cycle, (2) consumer self-reports of "undersaving," (3) disproportionate retirement accumulation in illiquid assets, (4) marginal propensities to consume that are specific to particular assets, and (5) declining national savings rates in developed countries. The model also supports the notion of mental accounts in the sense of people having asset-specific marginal propensities to consume. Bertaut and Haliassos (2002) set out to solve the same puzzle and proposed that self-control consideration can be a likely explanation.

CHALLENGES FOR FUTURE RESEARCH

It is clear that our understanding of discounting, self-control and saving has developed considerably since the pioneering work of Fisher. We now have a much more sophisticated understanding of the psychological processes that underpin saving decisions, and this knowledge has been used to produce macroeconomic theories that are predictive. This development of the economic theories of saving and consumption is an excellent example of how psychology and economics can be fruitfully linked. Although the intertemporal conflict between present enjoyment and future profit was identified by Adam Smith and has been acknowledged by many economists since, it has taken a long time for this psychological insight to be incorporated into economic models of saving. Psychologists, and some economists, have for decades studied behavior associated with ability to delay gratification, willpower, and hyperbolic discounting, and the large body of evidence of behavior that challenged the assumptions of the neoclassical model was, in the end, difficult to ignore. The most recent models of saving incorporate both impatience and self-control in such a way that the standard analytic tools in economics can still be used.

However, we believe that further progress is necessary in four main directions. First, we need to start analyzing how people think about time, to explore how they conceive of things available in the future. Second, the difficulties involved in measuring both time preference and self-control must be overcome. Third, the relationship between time preferences and related concepts such as time perspective and future orientation and length of planning horizon needs to be resolved. Existing psychological scales for measuring these concepts may well tap the concept of time preference and may be used instead of time preference measures, and the psychological theories that underpin these concepts may then have a role to play in theory development. Fourth, we need to have a much better understanding of how saving, self-control, and discounting develop during childhood, adolescence, and adulthood. Only in this way will we know how we can influence saving behavior in the long term.

How Do People Think About the Future?

One of the striking things about theoretical development in this area over the last few years is that while considerable effort has been put into analyzing the agent (e.g., decomposing her into a planner and a doer), time itself has been seen as unproblematic. So under both exponential and hyperbolic discounting, time is a smooth continuous variable. But if we think back to Thaler's (1981) example of most people preferring two apples in one year and one day to one apple in one year, we can see that a simple explanation is that the two periods—one year, and one year and one day—are seen as equivalent. If people segment time (now, tomorrow, next week, next year, etc.) and think of it as a discontinuous variable, we would not expect to find the kind of neat curves displayed in Figure 15.1.

Even if people do see time as continuous, they may think about the future in different ways. Atance and O'Neill (2001), for example, proposed that there are two kinds of ways people can think about the future. In episodic future thinking, people project themselves into the future to preexperience an event, whereas semantic future thinking is more generalized and script-based (and so depends on an understanding of how a particular event *generally* unfolds). This raises the question of whether the way in which people think about the future has an impact on the steps they take in the present: does a tendency to think about the future in episodic ways encourage people to save, for example?

Time may also change the way people think about the same events, an idea pursued by Trope and Liberman (2003). Trope and Liberman have put forward "construal-level theory." This suggests that how far away in time events or decisions are changes the way people mentally represent those events or decisions. The farther away in time an event is, the more likely that it will be represented in terms of high-level abstract features. Conversely, an event near in time will be more likely to be represented in a concrete and low-level way. So reading a novel in a year's time might be construed as "broadening my horizons," whereas the same activity carried out this afternoon might be seen as simply "flipping pages." This difference in the way people think about events depending on when they occur clearly has relevance for how they evaluated alternatives. In one of Trope and Liberman's studies, they explored the effect of temporal distance on the evaluation of two radio sets: one had poor sound and a good built-in clock, the other had good sound but a poor clock. As predicted, the relative preference for the latter was greater the further in the future the options were rated. Construal-level theory also provides an alternative explanation for the results of delay of gratification experiments. If amount is central (and so a high-level feature) and delay peripheral (and so a low-level feature), then people would choose according to amount in the far future more than they do in the near future—which is the standard finding. Note that this also suggests that if, for a particular individual making a particular kind of choice, delay is a more central feature, the results might be reversed.

Trope and Liberman's approach has the potential to help us understand the impact of time on people's choices. Leaving aside the merits of their particular approach, however, we clearly need more theorizing on the conceptualization of time.

Measurement of Time Preference and Self-Control

One important parameter in all saving models is the discount rate people use when making saving decisions. Some of the challenges associated with measuring time preference have been considered previously in this chapter and are discussed at considerable length by Frederick, Loewenstein, and O'Donoghue (2002). They provide a thorough review of empirical studies in this domain, which reveal what they characterize as "spectacular" disagreements. The variability in estimates of discount rates is tremendous (from –6 percent to infinity), though there is a predominance of high rates, which are well above market interest rates. Their view is that this variability is a result of measurement techniques that confound time preference with other factors (such as uncertainty about the future reward and visceral factors). This not only creates variability but may also account for the high discount rates, as most of the confounding factors would tend to push rates upward. The researchers provide a helpful distinction between time discounting and time preference. They define time discounting as any reason for caring less about a future consequence, including factors that diminish the expected utility generated by a future consequence, such as uncertainty or changing tastes. Time preference, on the other hand, refers more specifically to the preference for immediate utility over delayed utility. Time preference in this sense will necessarily be difficult to estimate, as the researcher needs to control for all the other reasons for discounting the future. While this is difficult, it is not impossible. Of more concern is whether time preference is actually a unitary concept—that is, whether it is stable, predicts behavior across a range of situations, and has measures that intercorrelate. Frederick, Loewenstein, and O'Donoghue are agnostic on this: "in our view the cumulative evidence raises serious doubts about whether there is, in fact, such a construct—a stable factor that operates identically on, and applies equally to, all sources of utility" (2002, 392).

Self-control is also not straightforward to measure, though it is clearly highly relevant to saving. Part of the problem is the difficulty of distinguishing self-control achieved through willpower (resisting temptation takes energy) from self-control resulting from the exercise of skill (using techniques such as precommitment). Baumeister and Vohs (2003) have shown that while willpower is a folk concept, it also captures some important properties of self-control. Their studies suggest that people have a limited pool of resources that they can use, so successfully resisting one temptation makes it less likely that an immediately following temptation can be resisted. Precommitment means that one avoids the need to use willpower. Though it is clearly very relevant to the kind of saving that Katona (1975) labeled "contractual saving," we do not know if people differ in their ability to use precommitment techniques. On the spending side, while it is possible to identify a wide range of money management techniques (such as withdrawing a fixed amount of cash before entering a supermarket, thereby limiting the amount that is spent), and people are able to describe their own approach quite successfully, to date it has not proved possible to devise a reliable questionnaire-based measure of these techniques (Webley and Nyhus 2001).

Time Preference and Related Concepts

As we said at the outset, saving models must include variables that are likely to affect the majority of consumption and spending decisions. Results from empirical investigation suggest that although the subjective discount factor fits the bill theoretically, the discount factors found in both experiments and field studies seem to be more influenced by situational factors than by individual characteristics. However, the notion that people vary in their evaluation of the future is plausible. We suggest that it might be appropriate to use other concepts from the psychological literature as substitutes for discount rates, such as length of planning horizon or future orientation.

Empirical studies indicate that people differ with respect to how far into the future they think and plan. While some people plan years ahead, others limit their planning to weeks. Most empirical studies have found a positive relationship between time horizon and saving (e.g., Alessie,

Lusardi, and Kapteyn 1995; Nyhus 2002; Julander 1975, Wärneryd 2000). Moreover, those with debt problems have been found to have a shorter time horizon than mild debtors and nondebtors (Lea, Webley, and Walker 1995; Webley and Nyhus 2001).

Nyhus (2002) used a crude measure of time horizon and found that it correlated significantly with many different definitions of wealth, for example, with financial wealth ($r = .190, p < .01$) and total wealth ($r = .256, p < .01$). Regression analyses showed that this positive relationship also is present in multivariate analyses where socioeconomic and other psychological variables were controlled for. Further, Nyhus found that the longer the time horizon, the lower the probability that a household has debt.

Only a few studies have looked at the relationship between time horizon and time preference. By definition, consumption beyond the time horizon is given the value of zero and is not discounted. The time horizon can then be elicited by identifying the discount rate used. For example, Landsberger (1971) found discount rates between 17 and 45 percent and concluded that people's horizon is between two and six years. Alternatively, the discount rate can be inferred from the time horizon people use. For example, Lusardi (1998) used a self-reported planning horizon as an index for time preference. Samwick (1998) compared his estimates of time preference rates with the respondents' self-reported most important planning horizon with respect to saving and spending decisions, in order to validate his time preference estimates. He found that average values of time preference rates decline steadily with the planning horizons that ranged from "the next few months" (average rate = 10.43 percent) to "ten years or more" (average rate = 5.91 percent). This suggests that measures of time horizon may help validate time preference measures.

Future orientation, on the face of it, seems likely to be very closely linked to time preference. Strathman et al. (1994), for example, produced a "concern for future consequences" scale and found that those who were more concerned about the future smoked and drank less than others and engaged in more environmentally concerned behavior (such as recycling glass). Similar results were found by Ebreo and Vining (2001). Likewise, Keough, Zimbardo, and Boyd (1999) reported that those having a more present time perspective are more likely to report using alcohol, drugs, and tobacco. Hodgins and Engel (2002) showed that pathological gamblers had significantly shorter time horizons than social gamblers. However, Zimbardo's approach to time perspective (see Zimbardo and Boyd 1999) should give us pause. Zimbardo's time perspective inventory (ZPTI) has five valid and reliable factors. These are past-negative, past-positive, present-fatalistic, present-hedonistic, and future orientation. While future orientation correlates highly with Strathman's consideration of future consequences scale (and with conscientiousness), Zimbardo and Boyd pointed out that the assumption that scoring low on a scale of future orientation is equivalent to scoring highly on a scale of present orientation or that not being present oriented is the same as being future orientated is false. So it is possible to score highly on future orientation and, for example, also on present-hedonism (which includes such items as "taking risks keeps my life from becoming boring" and "I do things impulsively").

Future orientation does have the desirable characteristics that Frederick, Loewenstein, and O'Donoghue (2002) identified: that is, it is stable and does predict behavior across a range of situations. However, close inspection of the items that make up the scale suggests to us that it might be better to think of this as a measure of future planfulness (one typical item "I believe that a person's day should be planned ahead each morning"). It is clearly possible to plan time use (whether for the day or the month) while valuing the future significantly less than the present, so this is not the same concept as time preference. We suspect that it will prove to be a good empirical predictor of saving: the difficultly is how one can incorporate broader psychological concepts such as this into economic theory.

THE FORMATION OF TIME PREFERENCE AND SELF-CONTROL

The question of how saving, self-control, and discounting develop during childhood, adolescence, and adulthood is a crucial one for Western governments, which are concerned with the decline in saving rates and encouraging individuals to save for their pensions. It should also be of great interest to behavioral economists, though most to date have followed the lead of mainstream economists and ignored children and developmental issues.

Fisher proposed that upbringing might have an important effect on time preference and this idea receives some empirical support. For example, Mischel (1958) found that children from the Trinidadian black subculture, in which immediate self-reward was the prevailing gratification pattern, displayed a greater preference for immediate rewards than children of Trinidadian Indians, who more often exhibited self-denying delayed-gratification behavior.

These differences in ability to delay gratification when young are predictive over the long term. Mischel, Shoda, and Rodriguez (1992) carried out experiments on a group of four-year-olds' ability to delay gratification and compared the results with the children's achievements more than ten years later. They found that children who could defer gratification longer than others when they were four years old were later described as being more successful in school and coping better with frustration and stress than those who were not able to wait. Those who delayed longer at four had significantly higher education levels at age twenty-eight (Ayduk et al. 2000).

Maital and Maital (1977) also suggested that socioeconomic factors have an important influence on delay-of-gratification behavior. Their evidence points to time preference patterns being firmly established for life by adolescence. They further argued that differences in time preference among individuals play an important role in determining both the distribution of income at a particular point in time and the transmission of economic inequality from one generation to another. However, we cannot tell from this work whether the ability to delay gratification in childhood is relevant for saving behavior in adulthood (though it seems likely). And the studies mentioned above do not directly imply that the *time preference* of the children varied—it may be that they have simply learned better techniques for self-control.

A more recent study by Bernheim, Garrett, and Maki (2001) suggests that the teaching of self-controlling techniques is important. They studied the influence on asset accumulation in adulthood of taking courses in household financial decision making in high school. These courses covered topics such as budgeting, credit management, balancing checkbooks, and compound interest. Some states never adopted these consumer educational programs, while others adopted them at different times, making it possible to compare subsequent saving across states and over time. Bernheim, Garrett, and Maki found that asset accumulation was higher in the states that had adopted these educational programs than in those that did not. Moreover, those who as children had been encouraged to save using a bank account saved more than others as adults. Similarly, those who characterized their parents as having saved more than average saved more than others.

While children are assumed to adopt the time preferences and ability to delay gratification of their parents, there is, in fact, very little conclusive evidence on this issue (see Wood 1998 for a review). Seginer, Vermulst, and Shoyer (2004) have studied the link between perceived parenting style and adolescents' motivation to engage in future thinking, the cognitive representation of the future, and future-related behaviors. They looked at the domains of work and career and marriage and family. They found that autonomous-accepting parenting was indirectly linked to future orientation (via self-evaluation). Pursuing a similar line of investigation, Webley and Nyhus (2006) have recently investigated the idea that the behavior of parents (particularly that related to intertemporal choice) influences the economic behavior of their children. They used Dutch panel data to compare the future orientation, conscientiousness, and saving of children ages sixteen to twenty-one with those of their parents. Their results show that parental behavior (such as discussing financial matters with children) and parental orientations (conscientiousness, future orientation) have a weak but clear impact on children's economic behavior as well as on economic behavior in adulthood. Hence, we can see evidence of an overall economic orientation being passed down through the generations, though the exact mechanisms through which this is achieved remains obscure.

CONCLUSION

We have tried in this essay to give a balanced account of behavioral economic (and economic psychological) work in the linked areas of time preference, self-control, and saving. It is our belief that considerable strides have been made in recent years in these areas, both theoretically and empirically, and that over the next few years there will be further fruitful developments. Our main concern is how individual differences can be conceptualized, properly measured, and incorporated into economic theory (in saving and in other areas). Time preferences can clearly be incorporated into theory, but they show too much situational variance to be a good individual difference measure. Future orientation, as conceived of by Zimbardo, is a good individual difference measure, but it is hard to see how to use it in a formal model. Reconciling these very different approaches will be a major challenge for the future.

ACKNOWLEDGMENTS

The first author acknowledges financial support from the Norwegian Research Council (project number 135090/510). The work for this chapter was carried out while the second author was a research visitor at the School of Management, Agder University College. He is very grateful for their financial support and hospitality.

NOTES

1. See Frederick, Loewenstein, and O'Donoghue 2002, Loewenstein 1992, and Wärneryd 1999 on the writings of early economists such as Rae, Senior, Mills, and Jevons.
2. The mean discount rates in these studies varied with the characteristics of the questions used to measure them. The mean rate given here is from the question with the lowest amount and the shortest time period.
3. Samwick (1998) also found the rate of time preference of 5.32 percent of the sample to be lower than −15 percent. He attributes all findings of negative rates to a strong bequest motive or inheritance. Inclusion of inheritance (or initial wealth) gives higher estimates of the rate of time preference.
4. Read and Read (2004) measured discount factors for several contexts and delays in people of various ages. They reported systematic but complex relationships between age and discounting. The major trends were for the elderly to discount the most and for the middle-aged to discount less than either the elderly or the young. Hence patience increases until middle age and decreases thereafter.
5. According to Loewenstein (1996) there are three important differences between preferences and visceral factors: (1) Visceral factors change more rapidly than preferences because they are correlated with external circumstances such as stimulation and deprivation. Consequently, it is more difficult to defend oneself against them. (2) Visceral factors draw

on different neuropsychological mechanisms than preferences do. Neurological research has found that the core of the brain (the limbic system) uses chemical regulation to control body functions, and different configurations of these chemicals are experienced as hunger, thirst, sleepiness, elation, depression, and so on. The role of this part of the brain is also critical in the regulation of behavior. Preferences, on the other hand, consist of information stored in memory concerning the relative desirability of different goods and activities. (3) We have a limited ability to imagine hunger, pain, anger, or other passions when we are not experiencing them. Human memory is not suited to storing information about visceral sensations. For example, we can recognize pain when we reexperience it, but we cannot recall pain at will by reexperiencing it in our imagination. Often we might regret and feel ashamed about behavior induced by visceral factors, since we cannot remember the intensity of the pain, hunger, or arousal in later periods. Similarly, it will be difficult to consider visceral sensations when planning future behavior.

6. Ulysses, preparing for a sea voyage, was warned by Circe that he would be tempted by the irresistible song of the Sirens, which would so enchant him that he would never get home. In other words, he was warned about the possibility that he would act in a dynamically inconsistent way. Still, wishing to sail his ship past the Sirens and finish his voyage, Ulysses prepared himself: he had his men bind him to the ship's mast before he came within earshot of the Sirens so that he could not yield to the temptation. He plugged the ears of his crew with wax so that they would not hear the song and be tempted themselves. This way, Ulysses managed to both enjoy the Sirens' song and to finish his journey.

7. Christmas clubs are organizations that help people save for the extra expenditures many have before Christmas (e.g., presents). Money is paid (sometimes regularly) by members into an account, no interest is earned on the accumulated assets, and the account cannot be drawn on until a specified date (e.g., December 1). Since saving in a regular interest-bearing savings account is a better alternative, it must be the labeling of the account (as "Christmas spending") as well as the inability to withdraw the money before the set date that are the attractive characteristics.

8. Shefrin and Thaler (1988) admitted that the rules applied by households will differ from one household to another and might be context specific. Winnett and Lewis (1995) have suggested a different tripartite classification (liquidity, windfall/regular, capital/labor), and Kojima and Hama (1982) have found that Japanese housewives have nine "psychological purses" (see Webley 1995). However, Shefrin and Thaler argue that there are some common elements that can be used for aggregate predictions, which are the three mental accounts they propose.

9. A review of evidence of physical labeling of money can be found in Zelizer 1993. People have been found to use sets of envelopes, china pitchers, tin cans, and so on for dedicating different parts of their income to particular expenses.

REFERENCES

Ainslie, George. 1975. "Specious Reward: A Behavioral Theory of Impulsiveness and Impulse Control." *Psychological Bulletin* 82: 463–96.
———. 1992. *Picoeconomics: The Strategic Interaction of Successive Motivational States Within the Person.* New York: Cambridge University Press.
———. 1993. "Picoeconomics: A Bargaining Model of the Will and Its Lapses." Paper presented at the Marcus Wallenberg Symposium, Will and Economic Behavior, Stockholm School of Economics, Stockholm, Sweden.

———. 2001. *Breakdown of Will.* Cambridge: Cambridge University Press.

Alessie, Rob J.M., AnnaMaria Lusardi, and Arie Kapteyn. 1995. "Saving and Wealth Holdings of the Elderly." *Ricerche Economiche* 49: 293–315.

Angeletos, George-Marios, David Laibson, Andrea Repetto, Jeremy Tobacman, and Stephen Weinberg. 2001. "The Hyperbolic Consumption Model: Calibration, Simulation, and Empirical Evaluation." *Journal of Economic Perspectives* 15: 47–69.

Antonides, Gerrit. 1988. "Scrapping a Durable Consumption Good." Doctoral dissertation, Erasmus University, Rotterdam, The Netherlands.

Atance, Christina M., and Daniela K. O'Neill. 2001. "Episodic Future Thinking." *Trends in Cognitive Science* 5: 533–39.

Ayduk, Ozlem, Rodolfo Mendoza-Denton, Walter Mischel, G. Downey, Philip K. Peake, and Monica Rodriguez. 2000. "Regulating the Inter-Personal Self: Strategic Self-Regulation for Coping with Rejection Sensitivity." *Journal of Personality and Social Psychology* 79: 776–92.

Baumeister, Roy F., and Kathleen D. Vohs. 2003. "Willpower, Choice, and Self-Control." In George Loewenstein, Daniel Read, and Roy F. Baumeister, eds., *Time and Decision,* 201–16. New York: Russell Sage Foundation.

Benzion, Uri, Amnon Rapoport, and Joseph Yagil. 1989. "Discount Rates Inferred from Decisions: An Experimental Study." *Management Science* 35: 270–84.

Bernheim, B. Douglas. 1995. "Do Households Appreciate Their Financial Vulnerabilities? An Analysis of Actions, Perceptions, and Public Policy." In *Tax Policy and Economic Growth,* 1–30. Washington, DC: American Council for Capital Formation.

Bernheim, B. Douglas, Daniel M. Garrett, and Dean M. Maki. 2001. "Education and Saving: The Long-Term Effects of High School Financial Curriculum Mandates." *Journal of Public Economics* 80: 435–65.

Bertaut, Carol C., and Michael Haliassos. 2001. "Debt Revolvers for Self-Control." HERMES Center Working Paper 01–11. Department of Economics, University of Cyprus, Greece.

Böhm-Bawerk, Eugen von. 1889. *Capital and Interest.* South Holland, IL: Libertarian Press, 1959.

Browning, Martin, and AnnaMaria Lusardi. 1996. "Household Savings: Micro Theories and Micro Facts." *Journal of Economic Literature* 34: 1797–855.

Caplovitz, David. 1963. *The Poor Pay More: Consumer Practices of Low-Income Families.* New York: Free Press of Glencoe.

Carroll, Christopher D. 1997. "Buffer-Stock Saving and the Life Cycle/Permanent Income Hypothesis." *Quarterly Journal of Economics* 112: 1–56.

Carroll, Christopher D., and Andrew A. Samwick. 1997. "The Nature of Precautionary Wealth." *Journal of Monetary Economics* 40: 41–71.

Cox, Dennis, and Alan Plumley. 1988. "Analysis of Voluntary Compliance Rates for Different Income Source Classes." Washington, DC: Internal Revenue Service, Research Division.

Daniel, Teresa R. 1994. "Time Preference and Saving: An Analysis of Panel Data." VSB-Center Savings Project Progress Report No. 2. Center for Economic Research, Tilburg University, The Netherlands.

Deaton, Angus S. 1992. *Understanding Consumption.* Oxford: Clarendon Press.

Donkers, Bas, and Arthur van Soest. 1999. "Subjective Measures of Household Preferences and Financial Decisions." *Journal of Economic Psychology* 20: 613–42.

Duesenberry, James S. 1949. *Income, Saving and the Theory of Consumer Behavior.* Cambridge, MA: Harvard University Press.

Dunn, Wendy. 2003. "The Effects of Precautionary Saving Motives on (S,s) Bands for Home Purchases." *Regional Science and Urban Economics* 33: 467–88.

Ebreo, Angela, and Johanne Vining. 2001. "How Similar Are Recycling and Waste Reduction? Future Orientation and Reasons for Reducing Waste as Predictors of Self-Reported Behavior." *Environment and Behavior* 33: 424–48.

Elster, Jon. 1979. *Ulysses and the Sirens. Studies in Rationality and Irrationality.* New York: Cambridge University Press.

Fishburn, Peter C., and Ariel Rubinstein. 1982. "Time Preference." *International Economic Review* 23: 677–94.

Fisher, Irving. 1930. *The Theory of Interest as Determined by Impatience to Spend Income and Opportunity to Invest It.* New York: Macmillan.

Frederick, Shane, George Loewenstein, and Ted O'Donoghue. 2002. "Time Discounting and Time Preference: A Critical Review." *Journal of Economic Literature* 15: 351–401.

Friedman, M. 1957. *A Theory of the Consumption Function.* Princeton, NJ: Princeton University Press.

Gately, Dermot. 1980. "Individual Discount Rates and the Purchase and Utilization of Energy-Using Durables: Comment." *Bell Journal of Economics* 11: 373–74.

George, David. 2001. *Preference Pollution: How Markets Create the Desires We Dislike.* Ann Arbor: University of Michigan Press.

Gifford, Adam Jr. 2002. "Emotions and Self-Control." *Journal of Economic Behavior and Organization* 49: 113–30.

Gourinchas, Pierre-Olivier, and Jonathan Parker. 2002. "Consumption over the Lifecycle." *Econometrica* 70: 47–90.

Graham, Fred, and Alan G. Isaac. 2002. "The Behavioral Life-Cycle Theory of Consumer Behavior: Survey Evidence." *Journal of Economic Behavior and Organization* 48: 391–401.

Gross, David B., and Nicholas S. Souleles. 2002. "An Empirical Analysis of Personal Bankruptcy and Delinquency." *Review of Financial Studies* 15: 319–47.

Harris, Christopher, and David Laibson. 2001. "Dynamic Choices of Hyperbolic Consumers." *Econometrica* 69: 935–57.

Hausman, Jerry A. 1979. "Individual Discount Rates and the Purchase and Utilization of Energy-Using Durables." *Bell Journal of Economics* 10: 33–54.

Heath, Chip, and Jack B. Soll. 1996. "Mental Accounting and Consumer Decisions." *Journal of Consumer Research* 23: 40–52.

Heath, Timothy B., Subimal Chatterjee, and Karen R. France. 1995. "Mental Accounting and Changes in Price: The Frame Dependence of Reference Dependence." *Journal of Consumer Research* 22: 90–97.

Hirst, Eric D., Edward J. Joyce, and Michael S. Schadewald. 1992. "Mental Accounting and Outcome Contiguity in Consumer Borrowing Decisions." *Organizational Behavior & Human Decision Processes* 58: 136–52.

Hoch, Stephen J., and George F. Loewenstein. 1991. "Time-Inconsistent Preferences and Consumer Self-Control." *Journal of Consumer Research* 17: 492–507.

Hodgins, D.C., and A. Engel. 2002. "Future Time Perspective in Pathological Gamblers." *Journal of Nervous and Mental Disease* 190: 775–80.

Houston, Douglas A. 1983. "Implicit Discount Rates and the Purchase of Untried, Energy-Saving Durable Goods." *Journal of Consumer Research* 10: 236–46.

Hubbard, R. Glenn, Jonathan Skinner, and Stephen P. Zeldes. 1995. "Precautionary Saving and Social Insurance." *Journal of Political Economy* 103: 360–99.

Jepson, Christopher, George Loewenstein, and Peter A. Ubel. 2001. "Actual Versus Estimated Difference in Quality of Life Before and After Renal Transplant." Working Paper, Department of Social and Decision Sciences, Carnegie Mellon University.

Julander, Claes-Robert. 1975. "Sparande Och Effecter av Ökad Kunskap om Inkomstens Använding" [Saving behavior and the effects of increased knowledge of income use]. Doctoral dissertation, Stockholm School of Economics.

Kahneman, Daniel, and Amos Tversky. 1979. "Prospect Theory: An Analysis of Decision Under Risk." *Econometrica* 47: 363–91.

Karlsson, Niklas, Tommy Gärling, and Marcus Selart. 1999. "Explanations of Effects of Prior Outcomes on Intertemporal Choices." *Journal of Economic Psychology* 20: 449–63.

Katona, George. 1975. *Psychological Economics.* New York: Elsevier.

Keough, Kelli A., Philip G. Zimbardo, and John N. Boyd. 1999. "Who's Smoking, Drinking, and Using Drugs? Time Perspective as a Predictor of Substance Use." *Basic and Applied Social Psychology* 21: 149–64.

Knetsch, Jack L. 2000. "Environmental Valuations and Standard Theory: Behavioral Findings, Context Dependence, and Implications." In Tom Tietenberg and Henk Folmer, *The International Yearbook of Environmental and Resource Economics, 2000/2001: A Survey of Current Issues,* 267–99. Cheltenham, UK: Edward Elgar.

Kojima, Sotohiro, and Yasuhisa Hama. 1982. "Aspects of the Psychology of Spending." *Japanese Psychological Review* 24: 29–38.

Koopmans, Tjalling C. 1960. "Stationary Ordinal Utility and Impatience." *Econometrica* 28: 287–309.

Laibson, David I. 1994. "Self-control and Savings." Doctoral dissertation, Massachusetts Institute of Technology, Cambridge, MA.

———. 1997. "Golden Eggs and Hyperbolic Discounting." *Quarterly Journal of Economics* 112: 443–77.

———. 1998. "Life-Cycle Consumption and Hyperbolic Discount Functions." *European Economic Review* 42: 861–71.

Laibson, David I., Andrea Repetto, and Jeremy Tobacman. 2003. "A Debt Puzzle." In Philippe Aghion, Roman Frydman, Joseph Stiglitz, and Michael Woodford, eds., *Knowledge, Information, and Expectations in Modern Macroeconomics: In Honor of Edmund S. Phelps*. Princeton, NJ: Princeton University Press.

Lancaster, Kelvin. 1963. "An Axiomatic Theory of Consumer Time Preference." *International Economic Review* 4: 221–31.

Landsberger, Michael. 1971. "Consumer Discount Rate and the Horizon: New Evidence." *Journal of Political Economics* 79: 1346–59.

Lea, Stephen E.G., Paul Webley, and Catherine M. Walker. 1995. "Psychological Factors in Consumer Debt: Money Management, Time Horizons and Consumer Behavior." *Journal of Economic Psychology* 16: 681–701.

Levin, Laurence. 1998. "Are Assets Fungible? Testing the Behavioral Theory of Life-Cycle Savings." *Journal of Economic Behavior and Organization* 36: 59–83.

Loewenstein, George. 1988. "Frames of Mind in Intertemporal Choice." *Management Science* 34: 200–14.

———. 1992. "The Fall and Rise of Psychological Explanations in the Economics of Intertemporal Choice." In George F. Loewenstein and Jon Elster, *Choice over Time*, 3–34. New York: Russell Sage Foundation.

———. 1996. "Out of Control: Visceral Influences on Behavior." *Organizational Behavior and Human Decision Processes* 65: 272–92.

Loewenstein, George, Ted O'Donoghue, and Matthew Rabin. 2003. "Projection Bias in Predicting Future Utility." *Quarterly Journal of Economics* 118: 1209–48.

Loewenstein, George, and Drazen Prelec. 1993. "Preferences for Sequences of Outcomes." *Psychological Review* 100: 91–108.

Lusardi, AnnaMaria. 1998. "On the Importance of the Precautionary Saving Motive." *American Economic Review* 88: 449–53.

Maital, Shlomo, and Sharone L. Maital. 1977. "Time Preference, Delay of Gratification and the Intergenerational Transmission of Economic Inequality: A Behavioral Theory of Income Distribution." In Orely C. Ashenfelter and Wallace E. Oates, eds., *Essays in Labor Market Analysis: In Memory of Yochanan Peter Comay*, 179–99. New York: Wiley and Sons.

———. 1994. "Is the Future What It Used to Be? A Behavioral Theory of the Decline of Saving in the West." *Journal of Socio-Economics* 23: 1–32.

Metcalfe, Janet, and Walter Mischel. 1999. "A Hot/Cool-System Analysis of Delay of Gratification: Dynamics of Willpower." *Psychological Review* 106: 3–19.

Mischel, Walter. 1958. "Preference for Delayed Reinforcement: An Experimental Study of a Cultural Observation." *Journal of Abnormal Psychology* 56: 57–61.

Mischel, Walter, and Ebbe B. Ebbesen. 1970. "Attention in Delay of Gratification." *Journal of Personality and Social Psychology* 16: 329–37.

Mischel, Walter, Yuichi Shoda, and Monica L. Rodriguez. 1992. "Delay of Gratification in Children." In George Loewenstein and Jon Elster, eds., *Choice over Time*, 147–64. New York: Russell Sage Foundation.

Modigliani, Franco, and Richard Brumberg. 1954. "Utility Analysis and the Consumption Function: An Interpretation of Cross-Section Data." In Kenneth K. Kurihara, ed., *Post-Keynesian Economics*, 388–438. New Brunswick, NJ: Rutgers University Press.

Nyhus, Ellen K. 1997. "On the Measurement of Time Preferences and Subjective Discount Rates." In *Proceedings of the XXII International Colloquium of Economic Psychology*, 1095–111. Valencia: University of Valencia.

———. 2002. "Psychological Determinants of Household Saving Behavior." Doctoral dissertation, Norwegian School of Economics and Business Administration, Bergen.

Newby-Clark, Ian R., and Michael Ross. 2003. "Conceiving the Past and Future." *Personality and Social Psychological Bulletin* 29: 807–18.

Odum, Amy L., and Carla P. Rainaud. 2003. "Discounting of Delayed Hypothetical Money, Alcohol, and Food." *Behavioral Processes* 64: 305–13.

Olshavsky, Richard W., and Donald H. Granbois. 1979. "Consumer Decision Making—Fact or Fiction?" *Journal of Consumer Research* 6: 93–100.

Parker, Jonathan A. 1999. "Spendthrift in America? On Two Decades of Decline in the US Saving Rate." In Ben S. Bernanke and Julio Rotemberg, eds., *NBER Macroeconomic Annual 1999*, 317–70. Cambridge, MA: MIT Press.

Phelps, E.S., and R.A. Pollak. 1968. "On Second-Best National Saving and Game-Equilibrium Growth." *Review of Economic Studies* 35: 185–99.

Prelec, Drazen, and George Loewenstein. 1998. "The Red and the Black: Mental Accounting of Savings and Debt." *Marketing Science* 17: 4–28.

Read, Daniel, and Barbara van Leeuwen. 1998. "Predicting Hunger: The Effects of Appetite and Delay on Choice." *Organisational Behavior and Human Decision Processes* 76: 189–205.

Read, Daniel, and N.L. Read. 2004. "Time Discounting over the Lifespan." *Organizational Behavior and Human Processes* 94: 22–32.

Ritzema, J. 1992. *An Extended Behavioral Life-Cycle Model.* Department of Economic Sociology and Economic Psychology, Erasmus University, Rotterdam, The Netherlands.

Rogers, Everett M., and F. Floyd Shoemaker. 1971. *Communication of Innovations: A Cross-Cultural Approach.* New York: The Free Press.

Romal, Jane B., and Barbara J. Kaplan. 1995. "Difference in Self-Control Among Spenders and Savers." *Psychology: A Journal of Human Behavior* 37: 8–17.

Ross, Michael, and Ian R. Newby-Clark. 1998. "Constructing the Past and Future." *Social Cognition* 16: 133–50.

Samuelson, Paul A. 1937. "A Note on Measurement of Utility." *Review of Economic Studies, 4:* 155–61.

Samwick, Andrew A. 1998. "Discount Rate Heterogeneity and Social Security Reform." *Journal of Development Economics* 57: 117–47.

Schelling, Thomas C. 1978. "Egonomics, or the Art of Self-Management." *American Economic Review* 68: 290–94.

———. 1984. "Self-Command in Practice, in Policy and in a Theory of Rational Choice." *American Economic Review* 74: 1–11.

Schor, Juliet B. 1998. *The Overspent American.* New York: Basic Books.

Seginer, Rachel, Ad Vermulst, and Shirli Shoyer. 2004. "The Indirect Link Between Perceived Parenting and Adolescent Future Orientation: A Multiple-Step Model." *International Journal of Behavioral Development* 28: 365–78.

Selart, Marcus, Tommy Gärling, and Niklas Karlsson. 1997. "Self-Control and Loss Aversion in Intertemporal Choice." *Journal of Socio-Economics* 26: 513–24.

Shefrin, Hersh M., and Richard H. Thaler. 1988. "The Behavioral Life-Cycle Hypothesis." *Economic Inquiry* 26: 609–43.

Shelley, Marjorie K. 1993. "Outcome Signs, Question Frames, and Discount Rates." *Management Science* 39: 806–15.

Sonuga-Barke, Edmund J.S., and Paul Webley. 1993. *Children's Saving.* Hillsdale, NJ: Erlbaum.

Stavins, Joanna. 2000. "Credit Card Borrowing, Delinquency, and Personal Bankruptcy." *New England Economic Review,* July/August: 15–30.

Strathman, Alan, Faith Gleicher, David S. Boninger, and C. Scott Edwards. 1994. "The Consideration of Future Consequences: Weighing Immediate and Distant Outcomes of Behavior." *Journal of Personality and Social Psychology* 66: 742–52.

Strotz, R. H. 1956. "Myopia and Inconsistency in Dynamic Utility Maximization." *Review of Economic Studies* 23: 163–80.

Thaler, Richard H. 1981. "Some Empirical Evidence on Dynamic Inconsistency." *Economic Letters* 8: 201–7.

———. 1990. "Saving, Fungibility, and Mental Accounts." *Journal of Economic Perspectives* 4: 193–205.

Thaler, Richard H., and Hersh M. Shefrin. 1981. "An Economic Theory of Self-Control." *Journal of Political Economy* 89: 392–406.

Trope, Yaacov, and Nira Liberman. 2003. "Temporal Construal." *Psychological Review* 110: 403–21.

U.S. Department of Health and Human Services. 1994. *Preventing Tobacco Use Among Young People: A Report of the Surgeon General.* Washington, DC: U.S. Government Printing Office.

Wärneryd, Karl-Erik. 1989. "On the Psychology of Saving: An Essay on Economic Behavior." *Journal of Economic Psychology* 4: 297–317.

———. 1999. *The Psychology of Saving: A Study on Economic Psychology.* Cheltenham, UK: Edward Elgar.

———. 2000. "Personality: Future-Orientation, Self-Control and Saving." Paper presented at the 27th International Congress of Psychology, Stockholm, Sweden.

Webley, Paul. 1995. "Accounts of Accounts: En Route to an Economic Psychology of Personal Finance." *Journal of Economic Psychology* 16: 469–75.

Webley, Paul, and Ellen K. Nyhus. 2001. "Life-Cycle and Dispositional Routes into Problem Debt." *British Journal of Psychology* 92: 423–46.

———. 2006. "Parents' Influence on Children's Future Orientation and Saving." *Journal of Economic Psychology* 27: 140–64.

Webley, Paul, and Zarrea Plaisier 1998. "Mental Accounting in Childhood." *Children's Social and Economics Education* 3: 55–64.

Winnett, Adrian, and Alan Lewis. 1995. "Household Accounts, Mental Accounts and Savings Behavior: Some Old Economics Rediscovered?" *Journal of Economic Psychology* 16: 431–48.

Wood, Michael. 1998. "Socio-Economic Status, Delay of Gratification, and Impulse Buying." *Journal of Economic Psychology* 19: 295–320.

Zelizer, Viviana A. 1993. "Making Multiple Monies." In Richard Swedberg, ed., *Explorations in Economic Sociology,* 193–212. New York: Sage.

Zhou, Yanfei. 2003. "Precautionary Saving and Earnings Uncertainty in Japan: A Household-Level Analysis." *Journal of the Japanese and International Economies* 17: 192–212.

Zimbardo, Phillip G., and John N. Boyd. 1999. "Putting Time in Perspective: A Valid, Reliable Individual Differences Metric." *Journal of Personality and Social Psychology* 77: 1271–88.

CHAPTER 16

RATIONAL CHOICE THEORY VERSUS CULTURAL THEORY

On Taste and Social Capital

PETER LUNT

There is, quite justifiably, a great deal of excitement and interest in the achievements and the potential for interdisciplinary collaboration between economics and psychology. In this essay, while not wishing to detract from these developments at all, I will consider a potential area for collaboration that remains relatively unexplored: the intersection between economics, social psychology, and sociology. The dominant approaches to the intersection between psychology and economics are applications of ideas from cognitive psychology to problems in economics. Psychologists have offered alternatives to economic accounts of behavior and decision making in positive contributions to understanding bounded rationality (Kahneman, Slovic, and Tversky 1982), economic decisions as games (Camerer 1997), emotions (Loewenstein 2000), mental accounting (Thaler 1992), and the behavioral life cycle (Shefrin and Thaler 1988). I would not go as far as Fine (2001), who argues that these developments are less collaboration than appropriation of the psychological by an imperialistic economics, but I would say that the collaboration is only on certain terms. What has proved most fruitful in interdisciplinary writing between economics and psychology is the application of cognitive principles to anomalies in economic theories. In contrast, social psychological theories and findings are largely ignored (Lunt 1995, 1996), and this may be partly because although cognitive psychologists are critical of economics, particularly of the rationality assumptions of economic analysis of consumer behavior, they nevertheless have many things in common with economists in the focus on choice and decision making, in the focus on individual cognitive processes, and in the assumption that abstract principles of decision theory are the best explanation of economic behavior.

In contrast, social psychological analysis of economic behavior (Lunt and Livingstone 1992; Dittmar 1992) has also developed in recent years but has not so directly addressed the agendas of economic theory and analysis. However, there is an approach within economics that engages with sociological and social psychological themes: the social economic theory propounded by Gary Becker (1991, 1993, 1996; Becker and Murphy 2000). In this essay I will juxtapose Becker's social economics with the social psychology of social influence and economic sociology as represented by Pierre Bourdieu (1977, 1984, 1990, 1993).

In their long and distinguished careers both Becker and Bourdieu have worked on questions of taste, analyzed the family as a productive unit in the economy, have had an enduring and fruitful interest in education, have an interest in discrimination and social class, and have developed concepts of social capital. There are clear overlaps in the substantive research agendas of these two brilliant scholars, motivated by the inadequacy of treating the family and education as black boxes irrelevant to understanding the economy and a focus on the difficulties of drawing the distinction between social and economic policy in contemporary pluralized societies. However, there are also important differences in approach to theory, empirical research programs, and normative projects between Becker and Bourdieu. Having checked most of both of these authors' work, I could not find any direct references to each other despite the fact that they both worked on the same topics and were exact contemporaries. This has partly to do with the unfortunate consequences of disciplinary horizons, but I do think it extraordinary that these positions proceed in glorious isolation from each other. However, there is an indirect connection between their work in that Becker has often acknowledged the influence of Coleman's work, particularly *Foundations of Social Theory* (Coleman 1990), in which Coleman refers briefly to Bourdieu. Coleman also co-edited a collection with Bourdieu (Bourdieu and Coleman 1991). However, even that collaboration was work in parallel rather than an attempt at integration or cross-fertilization (Coleman wrote the introduction and Bourdieu the epilogue, and neither refers to the other's work).

Becker takes inspiration from Coleman's (1990) social theory, but his main focus is on developing an economic perspective that incorporates the interaction between agents and their social environment. In contrast, Bourdieu, rather exceptionally, combines an extended corpus of work on social theory with an interest in substantive sociological questions related to consumption. It is important, in this context, to be careful when comparing Becker and Bourdieu. It would be wrong to take Becker's work as primarily a contribution to social theory, whereas much of Bourdieu's work is precisely that. My approach, therefore, is to compare the social theories of Bourdieu (1977, 1984, 1990, 1993) and Coleman (1990), followed by a critical examination of the social psychological and social theoretical assumptions of Becker's work. In all this I owe a debt to Fine's (2001) juxtaposition of Becker's and Bourdieu's accounts of social capital as a way of challenging what he sees as the intellectual imperialism of economics, and also to his more general critique of the concept of "social capital."

THE SOCIAL THEORY BACKGROUND

In this section I will outline some of the main features of Coleman's and Bourdieu's work and place them in their intellectual context (rational choice theory and the sociology of culture, respectively). Both of these writers are original, and both respond to the changing nature of societies (increasing complexity, pluralism, and more open systems) in order to overcome what they see as the manifest limitations of the traditions in which their work is located. As Abell (1996) suggests, Coleman (1990) is an important part of a movement to rejuvenate rational choice theory within sociology in the face of widespread critique. Bourdieu, for his part, was part of a generation attempting to rejuvenate historical materialism in the context of rapidly changing social, economic, and political conditions.

Weber's Social Theory

In their interest in the relation between economy and society and in the central role that each gives to the analysis of agency, both Coleman and Bourdieu trace their social theory heritage back to Weber (1930, 1968). Weber reflected on the methodological issues that emerged in his substantive historical and sociological writings. Ritzer (1996) locates these methodological reflections in the background debates in Germany over the status of historical theory and knowledge (see also Burke 1992). The debate was polarized between the positivists, who argued for a scientific history oriented toward developing general laws of history, and those who proposed an idiographic approach focusing on concrete actions and events. Weber aimed to overcome this polarization through the development of ideal types, which are abstract characterizations of social processes, grounded in the study of concrete cases such as bureaucracy. The resulting arsenal of ideal-typical concepts forms an analytic framework that can be used to interpret empirical historical data in order to rank social factors in terms of their causal significance. However, Weber understood this application of sociological concepts to historical data as a process of interpretation. He was trying to take the best of both nomothetic and idiographic methods and to combine them in a historical sociology that included both interpretation and causal analysis. To Weber, interpretation was just as systematic and no more subjective than causal analysis. *Verstehen* is an attempt to grasp the meaning of action in a social context, not an intuitive grasp of the meaning of a specific action or event. This is important because it means that the interpretive activities of sociology are not an attempt to do psychology, to understand the motives and thoughts of social actors, but rather an attempt to interpret action by understanding its meaning in a given social context. Action is understood to make visible the categories and processes of culture, not the motives for behavior.

Both Coleman and Bourdieu would agree with much of this perspective. Both are interested in social action in relation to economic life, and both seek to relate subjectivist and objectivist accounts of economic behavior, but they take different views on the depth of analysis that explanation requires at the level of action. Coleman takes the view, common in rational choice theory, that social analysis, although grounded in the analysis of individual action, should follow the principle of adopting the simplest possible model of human action. In contrast, the cultural sociology of Bourdieu aims for a rich, contextual interpretation of human action. Another continuity between Coleman and Bourdieu is the requirement that causal explanation should focus on understanding the interrelations among a multiplicity of factors in the interaction between complex systems. However, they take fundamentally different positions on the relationship between agency and social environment. Coleman adopts the view that there are determinable relations between the environment, the characteristics of the agent, decisions, and outcomes. His focus is on the constraints on and conditions for personal choice and the unintended consequences of these choices in the constitution of the social environment. In contrast, Bourdieu adopts a different view of the relation between structure and agency. He sees the social environment as cultural, offering guidelines for action rather than constraints on resources for action.

The Social Theory of Action

To some extent these differences reflect the indeterminacies in Weber's formulation of action. Cohen (1996) suggests that we understand Weber's account of action as three interconnected assumptions. The first is to concentrate on actions that are oriented toward others (social action). Now, as Cohen (1996) and others have pointed out, this is a very general commitment in Weber's account of action and does not pin down the range of social phenomena that are included in this definition of action. Is action oriented toward other individuals, groups, communities, institutions, or ancestors? A critical difference between Bourdieu and Coleman is that the former takes an inclusive notion of the social environment and the latter a narrower position. Coleman regards the social environment as aggregated behavior or complex forms of exchange, whereas Bourdieu interprets it as a complex intersection between rules, roles, and dispositions.

The second assumption in Weber's analysis of action is that actors orient their actions to one another's understanding. Here again an apparently simple definition disguises a great deal of variation that can be interpreted as consensus or aggregate or as a more contingent negotiation of positions. Rational choice theorists adopt aggregated or consensual models, whereas cultural theorists such as Bourdieu emphasize the contingent and strategic aspects of action.

The third assumption that Weber makes is that action can be oriented toward large-scale institutional orders. This formulation has many advantages in that it stays within the purview of self-interpreting action but allows for the specification of institutional rationality and relatively stable, macro structures as strong orienting features of social action. Weber attempted to keep these considerations of stable social structures within a theory that includes an account of agency. There has been considerable controversy over this final assumption in Weber's theory, but for our purposes again the statement of this principle can be interpreted in divergent ways, as exemplified by Coleman and Bourdieu. These differences are expressed as different positions on rationality and on the character of the social environment. Coleman takes the view that rationality should be defined exclusively in terms of means/end calculations expressed through individuals' choices as part of utility maximization. In contrast, Bourdieu falls into the tradition of the analysis of praxis, which recognizes different forms of rationality, distinguishing between means/end rationality, orientation toward others (social group membership), and rationality oriented toward macro social structures (positions on religious codes, bureaucratic or legal constraints, and social norms).

Parsons's Structural Functionalism

One of the reasons why more recent rational choice theorists have pushed the principle of adopting minimal presuppositions about individuals and social action was the relative failure of Parsons's (1951) systematic sociology. In Parsons's early work (1937) he offered a systematic analysis of the action system, and in his later work he attempted to develop a similar systematic account of the social system. He is regarded as having achieved much in his account of action, but his later work on social systems is seen as deeply problematic. The insight of contemporary rational choice theorists is that these two things are related: developing a rich account of social action is inimical to developing a powerful, formal theory of the social system. Abell (1996) contrasts the difficulties Parsons was having in the 1950s developing and gaining acceptance for a systematic account of the social system at a time when neoclassical economics was rapidly developing an account of the economic system based on the thinnest of assumptions concerning rational economic actors. Rational choice theorists take the view that the success of the macroeconomist can be reproduced in social theory by a similar device of adopting minimal assumptions about agency and social action. Linking rich descriptions of action with systematic descriptions of social and economic systems is regarded as too difficult, leading to ad hoc elaboration and a lack of elegance at both levels. These are among the reasons why rational choice theorists adopt minimal presuppositions about action, but this squarely puts the theory in conflict with approaches that focus on the complexity, contingency, and richness of action, here represented by Bourdieu.

BOURDIEU'S SOCIAL THEORY

Theory of Practice

As a social theorist, Bourdieu is in many ways the antithesis of rational choice theory. From his earliest published works, he has been concerned with the problems that accrue in attempts to separate out issues of culture and economy. In his earliest work, *Outline of a Theory of Practice*, Bourdieu (1977) presents the fruits of a social anthropological study of the Kabyle of Algeria. His ethnography is broad-ranging and attempts to depict the various kinds of ways that social practices are organized among the Kabyle. His theoretical orientation was against the prevailing trends of Marxist analysis of political economy, with its tendency to separate out culture and economy, and structural anthropology, with its reduced conception of human agency that looked to explain social behavior as the expression of rigidly structured codes and symbolic rules (Connor 1996, 359).

In contrast, Bourdieu offers a dynamic conception of the structuring of practice using two central concepts: habitus and cultural capital. By habitus, Bourdieu means the dispositions or propensities of a given social group that organize rather than govern practice. Social influence is not imposed on the individual from above but is enculturated in the individual through socialization and education and expressed through cultural practices such as consumption. Bourdieu complemented this conception of social influence with an emphasis on nonmaterial forms of value. Cultural capital is the expression of social position through cultural practice, and social capital refers to social contacts and relations available to the individual. Access to these forms of capital is an expression of symbolic power. Bourdieu does not reduce cultural value to economic value, but he accepts that nonmaterial forms of capital are organized as a system of exchange. In his excellent empirical study of taste, *Distinction: A Social Critique of the Judgement of Taste* (1984), Bourdieu offers a detailed examination of the tastes, preferences, and cultural judgments of French society in the late 1960s. Bourdieu sought to demonstrate the fusion of economic and symbolic value through the way that practice fuses the forms of rationality related to economic and social value (or use value and cultural value). Bourdieu linked this analysis of the culture of consumption to social structure and power, arguing that taste is not some abstracted criterion of aesthetic judgment but is an expression of cultural capital that plays a central role in legitimating social difference. Cultural capital is understood as constitutive of social class and power rather than as reducible to economic resources. Bourdieu exploits the indeterminacies in the relations between different forms of capital. The relationship between social position and nonmaterial forms of capital is indeterminate because it is mediated by social reproduction (socialization and education) and because expressions of taste take the form of practices rather than judgments (as in rational choice theory). Two ideas are important here. First, the meaning of expressions of taste in consumption is their ability to symbolize social background through cultural practice, educational qualifications, and social contacts. Second, acts of consumption are inserted into appropriate contexts to enroll social capital to realize material advantages.

Cultural Theory and Social Structure

Bourdieu links this account of the culture of consumption to social class. He argues that the dominant social class appropriates the cultural field as a sphere for the symbolic expression of difference that simultaneously constitutes and justifies social and material inequality. Bourdieu developed these themes in his analysis of the cultural reception of modern art in *The Field of Cultural Production*. In this work, Bourdieu adopts a classic Marxist mode of ideology critique. He analyzes the production and reception of cultural production as a series of interlinked ideologies. In modern culture industries the creative genius of the artist is constructed as the fount of production, and a naturalistic account of reception as critical judgment is developed. This pairing of production and consumption is "masked" by the marketing of cultural objects as appealing to a natural preference. In *Distinction*, Bourdieu (1984) documents fine-grained cultural distinctions between social class fragments, for example, between the petit bourgeoisie and those with "old money." He then links these distinctions to different expressive orders. Petit bourgeois culture takes the form of rigid self-discipline, in contrast to the preference for imaginative disorder among those with higher cultural capital (Fowler 1997, 45). The relaxed attitude of the cultural elite is played out subconsciously as practice in the context of everyday culture. This focus on embodied performance in a social context is in direct contrast to the cognitive orientation of the ideology of production as the output of creative imagination and consumption as aesthetic judgment. Central to this is the way that socialization and education encode these different attitudes toward the culture of consumption. Bourgeois culture is exemplified by the application of apparently abstract, idealized, and individual judgments of taste to everyday consumption decisions in a way that reproduces and legitimates social class differences. Taste is a public practice that functions to display and legitimate social class distinctions, and this is an important component of the symbolic value of consuming a given good or service. As Slater (1997) points out, the resulting taste systems (as opposed to the hierarchy of emulation implied by Becker) are threefold: those belonging to legitimate culture, those that can potentially be legitimized, and the remainder, which by default fall into the sphere of personal choice. In contrast, Becker empties goods of their meaning in his focus on personal choice.

Habitus and Field

There is much more to say about Bourdieu, but I will conclude this exposition with a schematic account of his theory of practice. Bourdieu valorizes social structure, but he is conscious of the need to contextualize this in an account of the cognitive and practical knowledge of social actors, which he does not reduce to either social determinism or rule following (Thompson 1991). He hoped to achieve this through adopting a specific account of action as practice, for which he used the concept of habitus. By this, Bourdieu refers to the disposition to act, understand, and orient toward the world in relatively stable, regular ways, but not according to conscious control or by following rules. Bourdieu understood these dispositions to be cultivated through a process of socialization that reflects a particular social milieu. This is a mutually reinforcing cycle because people share a habitus and their nonreflective actions create the conditions under which their actions make practical sense and fit with their corporeal orientation to the world. The link between the habitus and the concepts of capital in Bourdieu's work result from his view of the interaction between habitus and context, which he articulates through the concept of "field" or "game," reflecting Wittgenstein's (1958) notion of "language games." Such games depend upon the pragmatic agreement of agents, and Bourdieu concentrates on commitment to the rules of the game and an agreement as to what is at stake or of value in the game. The field is a site of struggle over the appropriate form of capital for the game being played. As we have seen, Bourdieu uses the language of exchange to understand the field. Although most fields are social or cultural rather than economic, they are similar to markets in the sense that they are oriented toward some form of capital or profit. Agents enroll (invest) their resources in their actions in social contexts in order to gain a return in terms of sequences of actions or outcomes that result in augmentation of capital or profitable "exchange."

The critical move here is the way that fields act as contexts for the exchange of different forms of capital, including economic capital, so that social, cultural, and symbolic capital can (in the appropriate context) be cashed in provided the right actions are taken or qualifications obtained. Thompson (1991) gives the example of buying extra oxen for the purposes of increasing symbolic capital so as to enhance marriage prospects. Economic capital is used in an appropriate way (which requires cultural capital or "know-how") so as to enhance symbolic power (in this case the ritual expression of economic capital) in order to enhance the prospects of increased social capital by making a good marriage, which potentially creates the conditions for both economic rewards and social reproduction. We can see that in this trajectory there are complicated transfers of value across different forms of capital in a particular field (the marriage market). As a sociologist interested in social inequality, Bourdieu relates this cultural analysis to the background of social class differences. Social situations on this reading are a creative interaction between three different sources of value: cultural expression, accumulated capital (material and nonmaterial), and social context (field). It is the task of analysis to separate out these different sources of value for a given practice.

We can see that the underlying social theories of Coleman and Bourdieu have some intriguing continuities and discontinuities. First, both are grounded in traditional debates in sociology and political economy. Both are also attempting to develop theories of social action. Both offer homage to Weber, and both challenge the structural functionalism of Parsons. They are both aware of the problem for social theory of specifying the relation between micro and macro levels of social analysis. Methodologically, Coleman seeks to resuscitate agent-based approaches on the assumption that what matters are behaviors with structural consequences. He accepts the limitations of methodological individualism but moderates this by considering objective social conditions. In contrast, Bourdieu cautiously adopts a structuralist position moderated by accounting for the practices of everyday life.

BECKER'S SOCIAL ECONOMICS

Background Assumptions

I will now make a comparison between Becker's social economics and Bourdieu's work. I will use Becker's recent summary of his interests in *Social Economics* (Becker and Murphy 2000) as my focal text, and I will work through some of the arguments and presuppositions in this book and criticize it from the point of view of cultural studies of consumption, as exemplified by Bourdieu's work. I will also make a variety of criticisms from the point of view of the social psychology of social influence, which is the practical context within which Becker develops his account of social economics.

In the spirit of Coleman's (1990) *Foundations of Social Theory,* Becker seeks to extend economic analysis to include social phenomena. Becker acknowledges that his project is radical, since economists typically make the assumption that individual behavior is not influenced by the actions of others. Becker claims that economic analysis can be flexible enough to include social influences on behavior, and he seeks to extend the scope of economic analysis while retaining the advantages of abstraction and explanatory power that he claims are the exclusive domain of economic analysis within the social sciences. Becker does not offer a scholarly critique of the relevant sociological and anthropological literature; instead he waves a dismissive hand in the direction of the other social sciences. Nor does he blame economists for ignoring social science research on social influence "because these other fields have not developed powerful techniques for analyzing social influences on behavior" (Becker and Murphy 2000, 3).

It is important to be clear about these claims because they set the style and the substance of Becker's engagement with the other social sciences. Essentially Becker means that social scientists have not delivered variables with the appropriate specification for economic modeling. Although Becker is radical in economic terms because of his engagement with social variables, he takes a normative stance on the nature of economic theory and modeling and makes no attempt to meet social scientists halfway or to challenge the broad approach of economics. Becker is offering not a rapprochement with other social sciences but rather a way of managing a formal characterization of social influence that might be useful to the economic analysis of social behavior.

Becker places so strong an emphasis on the formal character of economic theory that he does not consider the scope of explanation of his social economics. He fails to appreciate that social scientists give analytic priority to the validity and the scope of their theories. Put simply, there is a trade-off between formal specification and scope in explaining complex social phenomena. The potential problems for Becker are evident when he gives examples of the kinds of social behavior that he seeks to explain. He acknowledges that a wide range of social processes must be included (culture, norms, and social structure) and that these are implicated in a wide variety of social phenomena:

> Popular restaurants and books are determined in good part by what is considered "in"; a teenager's propensity to take drugs and to smoke is very much affected by whether his peers do; a person's preference for political candidates is affected by polls stating who is more popular; whether an unmarried mother applies for welfare is influenced by whether many women in her neighborhood are collecting welfare; the popularity of particular types of clothing, designer watches, painting and architectural styles. (Becker and Murphy 2000, 3–4)

An economic theory is a theory of choice, and Becker gives examples of the choices that are influenced by the level of adoption among the relevant social group (the social environment), which thereby creates peer pressure:

> drinking in bars, smoking and eating at parties, playing tennis and other sports, attending the theater . . . attending school, praying and socializing at churches, visiting museums, working in teams or groups . . . searching for marriage mates at social gatherings, caring for lawns visible to neighbors . . . driving on one or the other side of roads. (Becker and Murphy 2000, 4)

This conceptual level in Becker's theory refers to agents and outcomes, which are the proximal cause and consequences of rational choice. In sympathy with rational choice theory, therefore, Becker conceptualizes social influence as underlying processes (culture, norms, and social structure), wide-ranging features of the social environment (expressed as the degree of aggregation of particular social behaviors), and choices (agent and consequences).

THE SOCIAL PSYCHOLOGY OF SOCIAL INFLUENCE

Conformity

Social psychologists and other social scientists draw different conceptual distinctions from those implied by the separation into abstract social processes, features of the social environment and choices (agent plus outcome). I will focus on Bourdieu as an exemplar of a social scientist with a very different approach to these phenomena, but first I want to draw a comparison between Becker and the standard treatment of social influence within social psychology. One only has to look at any textbook of social psychology to see that a wide range of social influences is theorized and subject to empirical research (e.g., Hogg and Vaughan 2005). Social psychologists identify various forms of social influence, such as conformity, obedience, compliance, imitation, conversion (minority influence), and persuasion. There are important differences among these different types of social influence. Some are explicit and others implicit; they vary depending on whether the source of influence is present or diffuse and in the mode of address (e.g., command, request). Some of these social influence processes affect public behaviors, whereas others influence private beliefs and behaviors.

Becker's formulation of social influence as peer pressure quantifiable in terms of the proportion of the reference group adopting the target behavior picks out particular values on each of these dimensions. Social pressure is implicit, based on visible normative behaviors; it affects public behaviors, and the underlying process is one of conformity. Becker is careful in his anecdotal choice of illustrative behaviors, but there are others that are better explained in terms of the operations of institutions, authority, or obedience, as well as those primarily concerned with private behaviors.

Another feature of the social psychology of social influence is that although a particular process may be the focus of the research (conformity, obedience, compliance, etc.), much of the empirical work explores the mediating influence of social context on such processes. Variables such as the visibility and proximity of the source of social influence are typically examined. What is interesting is that most studies record relatively low levels of conformity, and the experiments demonstrate how fragile conformity processes are when other contextual variables are in operation. For example, in Asch's (1952) classic studies of conformity to a group norm in a social judgment task (the social influence paradigm closest to Becker's characterization), conformity affects only 37 percent of judgments. Many subjects displayed very low levels of conformity, and when the consensus of the reference group was softened, conformity levels dropped dramatically, to around 9 percent of judgments. None of the studies of conformity in social psychology provides evidence that implicit social influence is a strong phenomenon even in laboratory settings with relatively carefully controlled experimental procedures. Becker does not refer to the literature on social influence, but it may be that he has in mind experiments such as the famous electric shock studies of obedience by Milgram (1974), where most of the subjects showed high levels of obedience. However, obedience to authority is a form of social influence very different from implicit conformity to group norms based on the kinds of social comparison processes that Becker seems to have in mind. What this suggests is that the kinds of effect imagined by Becker would require an institutionalized form of explicit social influence that operates on psychological processes such as norm conflict (the explanation suggested by Milgram). Becker, therefore, makes questionable assumptions about the power and simplicity of social influence processes. Relating this back to the formulation of rational choice theory as being opposed to social or cultural explanations of social behavior, Becker takes the side of simple assumptions about environments and agents. Yet the social psychology of social influence suggests a more complex relation between agent and context if the kinds of effect assumed by Becker are to operate.

Minority Influence

Within social psychology, the debate about levels of and conditions of social influence has broadened to include questions related to the differences between majority and minority social influence (Moscovici 1976). Working within the area of conformity, Moscovici understood that social psychologists had assumed that all social influence processes involve a majority influencing a minority. This is also one of Becker's assumptions because he focuses on the impact of group norms as a feature of the social environment that influences individual decision making. Moscovici, Lage, and Naffrechoux (1969) conducted a fascinating experiment, reversing the conditions of the Asch experiment, in which a minority group of confederates influence the judgments of a larger group. The results demonstrate that minority influence is a low-power effect that takes time and operates by converting the private beliefs of individuals provided that they attribute competence to the minority. Moscovici interprets this kind of social influence as akin to conversion, in contrast to the combination of public compliance and private resistance that typifies conformity to group norms. The importance of these findings is that social influence can operate, if the conditions are appropriate, in a manner opposite to that suggested by Becker, and these processes are likely to be important in producing social innovation. It does not necessarily work through emulation, with the individual fitting her public behavior to group norms. Minority influence operates strategically through the attribution of competence or expertise when presented with a consistent manner but with a flexible negotiating or presentation style.

Fashion

Becker also suggests that the influence of fashion can be understood as conformity to group norms. However, in cultural analysis of fashion (e.g., McRobbie 1999) fashion is analyzed as a trickle-down of emulated styles, which are refreshed from innovations in everyday clothing styles, formalized in haute couture, and then marketed, first as fashion, then as high street style. It is difficult to see how Becker could accommodate the dynamic qualities of either the powerful minority or the circulation of styles in the production of fashion because neither operates simply through the aggregation of public behaviors. Similar difficulties occur in accounting for the role of advertising in social economics resulting from Becker's formalization of influence as conformity to peer pressure and the treatment of sources of social influence as aggregates of individuals.

Becker's Analysis of Social Economic Behavior

So far we have been testing the foundational assumptions of Becker's social economics against social and psychological theories of influence. But Becker goes beyond discussing the theoretical foundations of his subject to offer economic models of social behavior. With great creative insight, Becker expresses the normative influence of aggregate normative behavior as a term in the utility function, which he expresses as stocks of social capital. For a given choice an important determinant of utility is how much the target behavior is spread among the relevant reference group. This concept of social capital is the most important moment in the translation of the theoretical background that we have considered thus far into a formulation that potentially has a role in the utility function. It is here that Becker's focus on conformity becomes important because the notion of social capital as a force can be equated with the commonality of a given choice within the relevant reference group. The more people make a particular choice within the relevant social group, the more social capital accrues in making that choice. Consuming a particular good or service that has high social capital gets an added value in consumption by conferring the benefits of group membership.

Becker addresses the apparent conceptual contradiction inherent in an analysis of choice in behaviors where conformity pressures are strong. His argument is that conformity is not a contradiction of the principle of choice, since choosing to follow the norm can increase utility. This involves the assumption that the sanctions for nonconformity are always equivalent to the loss of utility gained through conformity. In contrast, social psychologists have been careful to separate social influence from sanctions.

Another kind of social influence comes into play when Becker discusses strong complementarities between behavior and social capital such as driving on the right-hand side of the road. Becker treats such examples as cases in which strong complementarity between behavior and social capital are necessary conditions for utility (how else could we enjoy the pleasures of driving?). He does not deny that social interaction can lead to information gain, nor that similarities in behavior can result from the influence of particular technological constraints. His point is that these mechanisms cannot account for some of the market effects of social forces that go beyond information exchange and technical bias. The problem I have with this is that it seems important to distinguish between conformity and compliance in explaining these different cases of social influence. As a social psychological phenomenon, driving on the right-hand side of the road is a case of compliance rather than conformity. When the mechanism of social influence takes the form of a request (or, in this case, a rule backed by law), then the issue is not one of how many people are behaving in a particular way. Going against conformity involves breaking a norm, whereas not complying means breaking a rule, and each receives a different sanction—social disapprobation in the first case, compared with getting a ticket for traffic violation.

The Social Economics of Demand

Becker takes forward his assumptions into his formal economic analysis, beginning with an analysis of the relations between social interactions and demand. His demand analysis is exemplified by the case of selective exposure resulting in differential neighborhood characteristics. Agents choose which social pressure to succumb to (since presumably they have to succumb to some social pressures), choosing the social pressure with positive effects on the choices that reflect their preferences. Becker uses this account of choices as responses to social pressure as a way of replying to criticisms that the logic of normative social influence (whether institutional or interpersonal) works as a social logic with no relation to choice within markets. He is particularly keen to assert that the social influence process works through the incentives provided by the impact of conformity on utility in the context of the choices that individuals make. He is precisely arguing against the idea that there is always a clear boundary between the logic of markets and the logic of social integration. Here he aligns himself with the neo-Durkheimian work of Mary Douglas (Douglas and Isherwood 1978), quoting her insistence that in making their consumption choices people choose their associates and ways of living.

There is a very important slippage here in Becker's argument. Douglas conceives of the social environment as being structured along the twin dimensions of rule following and social affiliation such that social environments vary in how closely they constrain social behavior and how much they bind people through association. Becker locates choice at the center (as perhaps an economist should), but Douglas, by contrast, works with an important distinction from Durkheimian sociology, that between ritual as a mechanism that produces social solidarity because it reflects institutional structures and power relations in society, and the forms of association that emerge through cultural practice. Bourdieu is equally against the dominance of social structure and wants to avoid giving too much power to the agent (he therefore wants to include social influence but not social determinism). Although the agent provides the link between the social and the economic, Bourdieu has a quite different view of the mechanisms involved. For Bourdieu, the mechanisms are socialization and education, along with social status and connections in the habitus. In contrast to Becker, Bourdieu conceives of social forces not in a mechanical way but as rules (guiding principles) operating in a taste system (a system of cultural capital) mediated by social contacts (social capital).

The Social Economics of Supply

Becker complements this analysis of social influences on demand with an analysis of the interaction with supply, for which he uses a basic framework of social emulation based on a social hierarchy encoded as better neighborhoods, more attractive partners, or friendship with the rich and famous—the very things that produce positive effects on utility for the person who "chooses" to conform. Becker assumes that there is similarity of preferences across a heterogeneity of agents, this being the source of competition for socially valued goods and services. For Bourdieu, in contrast, the social environment is divided into different cultural fields that offer a context within which social groups of different kinds can play the different games of life. In Bourdieu's formulation the link between consumption behavior and social hierarchy is complex and indirect because the habitus affords a context for the expression of difference, articulated as naturalistic "taste," resulting in the consolidation of social position in both material and cultural benefits. The field also creates the potential for the exchange of different capitals, with culture (in the shape of the habitus and fields) mediating economic exchange. For Becker social hierarchy has economic effects because it affords an enhancement of utility. There is no equivalent of Bourdieu's cultural capital, habitus, and field in this account.

CONCLUSION

We can see that Becker's social economics is grounded in a series of assumptions, of which some are social theoretical, some relate to the empirical phenomena of social influence, and some relate to conceptual and methodological issues concerning the interface between economics and the other social sciences. The social theoretical assumptions are derived largely from Coleman's revival of rational choice theory, and these were compared to the social theory of Bourdieu. This comparison helps to clarify a range of assumptions in the background of Becker's work. Comparisons were also drawn between the social psychology of social influence and Becker's assumptions, leading to a question of the scope of his explanations: he focuses on conformity (although at various points Becker considers compliance); he conceives of the social environment as aggregate behavior (as opposed to institutional forces and other kinds of collective social forces); and his analysis focuses on the environment, agent, and outcomes of choices as opposed to Bourdieu's focus on socialization, cultural capital, collective processes, ritual, and practice.

Becker also makes a variety of assumptions about reference groups but does not consider the complexities of the role of such groups in social influence. Proximity (in time and space), abstraction (taxonomic versus collective groups), and institutional status (friendship groups/locale/institution/social collective) all mediate the impact of reference group conformity. Becker implicitly engages with a range of theoretical distinctions through the examples he considers, but these are not clearly specified in his analysis, and he adopts a very generalized conception of aspiration linked to shared preferences. In contrast, Bourdieu allows for a consideration of a wider range of social distinctions. Becker and Bourdieu also have different notions of social capital. For Becker social capital is something that is realized within the idealized economic agent (as part of the utility function) as a consequence of aligning with normative behavior under social pressure. In Bourdieu, social capital is understood by contrast to economic, symbolic, and cultural capital (with the focus on cultural capital) as part of a social process through which value is realized.

On a more abstract level, Becker and Bourdieu offer different accounts of the relation between economy and society and have different conceptions of agency. However, it is what they see as constituting the social that most clearly distinguishes their approaches. For Becker, the social environment is an emergent property of mass group behavior, not consensus, public opinion, ritual, or the formation of collective or institutional processes. In contrast, Bourdieu sees in the practices of agents a reflection of their past (socialization and education), which in turn reflects social position and is constituted as cultural practice. Social environments are represented as fields of cultural practice with a variety of sources of nonmaterial value.

There are some other important differences in the specification of agency in Becker and Bourdieu. Becker focuses on decision making in the context of social emulation, whereas Bourdieu is more concerned with broader processes of socialization and enculturation, and so his account of agency is focused on practice, not choice. There are also differences in their concepts of value—the value of belonging to a group, living in a nice neighborhood, and mixing with beautiful and rich people are immanent for Becker. Value is understood to result from widely shared preferences, but for Bourdieu value takes the form of a variety of nonmaterial capitals that are potentially exchanged through the cultural practices of consumption.

The social psychology of social influence and Bourdieu's cultural theory of consumption clearly highlight a variety of issues in Becker's social economics. One temptation is to assert the radical incommensurability of economic and social science approaches to consumption. However, perhaps the features of the social environment, social influence, and agency identified in social and cultural theory could, in principle, be handled within economic theory. In Becker's work, these aspects of social influence, considered so important in the work of sociologists, anthropologists, and social psychologists, are repudiated because they do not conform to the assumptions of rational choice theory, not because they cannot in principle be specified for economic analysis. But that would be to challenge the assumptions of rational choice theory and the normative project of economics.

Finally, these theoretical issues have a particular purchase at the moment because of the increasing attention given to social capital in analyses of civic participation (Putnam 2000), analyses of economic policy (Dasgupta and Serageldin 1999), and recent analyses of related social phenomena in economic decision making such as trust (Glaeser, Laibson, and Scheinkman 2000; Sobel 2002). The theoretical differences between Becker and Bourdieu and the implicit debate over how to relate social and cultural phenomena to economics reflect some of the issues in rationalizing the rich but multifaceted concept of social capital. Although profoundly different in their approaches, both Becker and Bourdieu have shown a strong commitment to the importance of as well as the complexities involved in relating social to economic life.

REFERENCES

Abell, Peter. 1996. "Sociological Theory and Rational Choice Theory." In Bryan S. Turner, ed., *The Blackwell Companion to Social Theory,* 252–77. Oxford: Blackwell.
Asch, Solomon E. 1952. *Social Psychology.* Englewood Cliffs, NJ: Prentice Hall.
Becker, Gary S. 1991. *A Treatise on the Family.* Cambridge, MA: Harvard University Press.
———. 1993. *Human Capital: A Theoretical and Empirical Analysis, with Special Reference to Education.* Chicago: University of Chicago Press.
———. 1996. *Accounting for Tastes.* Cambridge, MA: Harvard University Press.
Becker, Gary S., and Kevin M. Murphy. 2000. *Social Economics: Market Behavior in a Social Environment.* Cambridge, MA: Harvard University Press.
Bourdieu, Pierre. 1977. *Outline of a Theory of Practice.* Cambridge: Cambridge University Press.
———. 1984. *Distinction.* London: Routledge.
———. 1990. *The Logic of Practice.* Cambridge: Polity Press.
———. 1993. *The Field of Cultural Production.* Cambridge: Polity Press.
Bourdieu, Pierre, and James S. Coleman, eds. 1991. *Social Theory for a Changing Society.* Boulder: Westview Press.

Burke, Peter. 1992. *History and Social Theory.* Cambridge: Polity.

Camerer, C. (1997). Progress in behavioral game theory. *Journal of Economic Perspectives* 11, 4, 167–8.

Coleman, James S. 1990. *Foundations of Social Theory.* Cambridge, MA: Harvard University Press.

Cohen, Ira J. 1996. "Theories of Action and Praxis." In Bryan S. Turner, ed., *The Blackwell Companion to Social Theory,* 111–42. Oxford: Blackwell.

Connor, Steven. 1996. "Cultural Sociology and Cultural Sciences." In Bryan S. Turner, ed., *The Blackwell Companion to Social Theory,* 340–68. Oxford: Blackwell.

Dasgupta, Partha, and Ismail Serageldin, eds. 1999. *Social Capital: A Multifaceted Perspective.* Washington, DC: World Bank.

Dittmar, Helga. 1992. *The Social Psychology of Material Possessions: To Have Is to Be.* Hemel Hempstead: Harvester Wheatsheaf.

Douglas, Mary, and Baron Isherwood. 1978. *The World of Goods: Towards an Anthropology of Consumption.* Harmondsworth: Penguin.

Fine, Ben. 2001. *Social Capital Versus Social Theory: Political Economy and Social Science at the Turn of the Millennium.* London: Routledge.

Fowler, Bridget. 1997. *Pierre Bourdieu and Cultural Theory: Critical Investigations.* London: Sage.

Glaeser, Edward L., David Laibson, and Jose A. Scheinkman. 2000. "Measuring Trust." *Quarterly Journal of Economics* 115: 811–41.

Hogg, Michael, and Graham Vaughan. 2005. *Social Psychology.* Harlow: Pearson.

Kahneman, Daniel, Paul Slovic, and Amos Tversky. 1982. *Judgment Under Uncertainty: Heuristics and Biases.* Cambridge: Cambridge University Press.

Lunt, Peter. 1995. "Psychological Approaches to Consumption." In Daniel Miller, ed., *Acknowledging Consumption,* 238–63. London: Routledge.

———. 1996. "Rethinking the Relation Between Psychology and Economics." *Journal of Economic Psychology* 17: 275–87.

Lunt, Peter, and Sonia Livingstone. 1992. *Mass Consumption and Personal Identity.* Buckingham: Open University Press.

Loewenstein, George. 2000. "Emotions in Economic Theory and Economic Behaviour." *American Psychological Review* 90, 2: 426–32.

McRobbie, Angela. 1999. *In the Culture Society: Art, Fashion and Popular.* London: Routledge.

Milgram, Stanley. 1974. *Obedience to Authority.* New York: Harper and Row.

Moscovici, Serge. 1976. *Social Influence and Social Change.* London: Academic Press.

Moscovici, Serge, Elizabeth Lage, and Michel Naffrechoux. 1969. "Influence of a Consistent Minority on the Responses of a Majority in a Color Perception Task." *Sociometry* 32: 365–79.

Parsons, Talcott. 1937. *The Structure of Social Actions.* New York: McGraw-Hill.

———. 1951. *The Social System.* Glencoe, IL: Free Press.

Putnam, Robert. 2000. *Bowling Alone.* New York: Simon and Schuster.

Ritzer, George. 1996. *Classical Sociological Theory.* New York: McGraw-Hill.

Shefrin, Hersh M., and Richard Thaler. 1988. "The Behavioral Life-Cycle Hypothesis." *Economic Inquiry* 26, 4: 609–43.

Slater, Don. 1997. *Consumer Culture and Modernity.* Cambridge: Polity.

Sobel, Joel. 2002. "Can We Trust Social Capital." *Journal of Economic Literature* 40: 139–54.

Thaler, Richard. 1992. *The Winner's Curse: Paradoxes and Anomalies of Economic Life.* New York: Free Press.

Thompson, John B., ed. 1991. "Editor's Introduction." In Pierre Bourdieu, *Language and Symbolic Power.* Cambridge: Polity.

Weber, Max. 1930. *The Protestant Ethic and the Spirit of Capitalism.* London: George Allen and Unwin.

———. 1968. *Economy and Society.* 3 vols. Totowa, NJ: Bedminster Press.

Wittgenstein, Ludwig. 1958. *Philosophical Investigations.* Oxford: Blackwell.

CHAPTER 17

DELIBERATION COST AS A FOUNDATION FOR BEHAVIORAL ECONOMICS

MARK PINGLE

> Once one introduces into the subjective expected utility maximization Eden the
> snake of boundedness, it becomes difficult to find a univocal meaning of rationality,
> hence a unique theory of how people will, or should, decide. Economics, and the
> social sciences generally, will never have the certainty of natural science.
> —*Simon 2000, 250*

What is behavioral economics? Why is the word *behavioral* necessary? Why is the word *economics* not sufficient? So much research could fall under the umbrella of behavioral economics that the description may not have much meaning. What distinguishes behavioral economic research? The thesis explored here is that *deliberation cost* is a distinguishing feature upon which behavioral economics can be founded as a useful field of economics.

In his Nobel lecture, Gary Becker describes the "rational choice model" as the "economic way of looking at behavior." He emphasizes that the rational choice model is an analytical method, as opposed to being a behavioral postulate. People may be modeled as "selfish, altruistic, loyal, spiteful, or masochistic." What is fundamental to the method is the assumption that "individuals maximize welfare as they receive it" (Becker 1993, 386). The maximization assumption greatly simplifies the analysis, for it allows one to ignore as inconsequential the process the decision maker uses to find the maximum. In the rational choice model, behavior is an outcome (the choice), not a process. Explaining behavior involves delineating how changes in the decision environment affect the optimal choice, and this has proven to be useful.

In the rational choice model, resource scarcity is a central feature. It is resource scarcity that creates trade-offs and therefore costs. Economic analysis often amounts to examining how changes in various environmental factors influence the allocation of the scarce resource. If we abstract from reality and assume resources are not scarce, then most of economics goes away because no choices need be made. Recognizing that resources are scarce is fundamental to economics, and one way to distinguish economic analysis from other social science analysis is to say that economics examines the implications of resource scarcity.

One might think moving beyond the rational choice model to examine the decision-making process is to move beyond economics. However, examining the decision process can be motivated by the desire to recognize and explore the implications of cognitive scarcity, and doing so is not outside the realm of economics. Cognitive scarcity forces a decision maker to decide how to allocate cognition, and this implies that a deliberation cost is incurred when a set of alternatives is evaluated. (See Simon 1990 for a discussion of how human cognition is limited by physiology.) If we abstract from reality and assume cognition is not scarce, we are in the world of the rational choice model. There is no reason to examine the decision process, for unlimited cognition ensures that the optimal outcome is obtained. However, once we recognize cognitive scarcity and the deliberation cost it elicits, the economist is forced to examine the process of decision making, not just the outcome. It is possible, therefore, to distinguish behavioral economics as the field of economics that explores the implications of cognitive scarcity, with the goal of better understanding decision-making processes.

Modeling decision making as an optimization problem has become a tradition so ingrained in economics that attempts to do otherwise may be labeled "ad hoc." The belief that people desire to maximize is reasonable. However, this belief should lead economists to recognize that rational choice theory also deserves the ad hoc label in the world where deliberation is costly, for some mode of decision behavior could be more effective than one involving the evaluation of all alternatives.

As indicated by the opening quote from Simon, in the world of behavioral economics, where cognitive resources are scarce, there is no method for framing a decision problem that is independent of the context. If you slip and start to fall off a cliff, which branch do you grab to try to save yourself? Do you consider all alternatives? Do you take the time to decide how to decide? Do you apply a preconceived "falling off cliff" rule of thumb? The context not only influences the set of alternatives, as in rational choice theory, but also influences the extent to which deliberation is costly, which will tend to affect how a choice is made.

Concluding his Nobel lecture, Becker claims that "the rational choice model provides the most promising basis presently available for a unified analysis of the social world" (1993, 385). This may be true, but it is not likely that psychologists and sociologists will ever embrace the rational choice model because they spend so much of their time examining the decision-making process. By forcing economics into the realm where the process of making the choice must be considered, recognizing deliberation cost more closely associates economics with its social science cousins. Consequently, there is reason to think that what may ultimately do much to unify the social sciences is a behavioral economics research agenda focused on the implications of deliberation cost.

A CANONICAL DECISION PROBLEM

Suppose a decision maker's choice x from the set of alternatives X results in the outcome from y among the set of possible outcomes Y. Assume that the relationship between x and y is functional so that $y=f(x,a)$, where the function $f(\bullet,\bullet)$ maps the set of alternatives X onto the set of outcomes Y for the given decision-making environment described by the parameter a. For each given environment a in the set of possible environments A, assume that the function $f(\bullet,\bullet)$ reaches a unique maximum value $\bar{y}(a)$ at the choice $\bar{x}(a)$. Assume that the decision maker has perfect knowledge of how choices affect outcomes, or that the function $f(\bullet,\bullet)$ is known. Behaviorally, assume the objective of the decision maker is to make an optimal choice. That is, the decision maker's goal is to find $\bar{x}(a)$ from among the alternatives X so that outcome $\bar{y}(a)$ is experienced when environment a is the context.

NONBEHAVIORAL CHOICE THEORY

If there is no cost to sorting through the set of alternatives X, then the decision maker can formulate the decision problem as a mathematical programming problem. By assumption, the problem can be solved. The solutions are $\bar{x}(a)$ and $\bar{y}(a)$. Different functional forms for the function $f(\bullet,\bullet)$ will generate different optimal choice and outcome functions $\bar{x}(a)$ and $\bar{y}(a)$.

Except for the assumption that people seek an optimal choice, there is little in this choice theory that can be described as behavioral. The assumption that the decision maker can search through the set of alternatives without cost greatly simplifies the analysis by allowing one to entirely abstract from the process used to evaluate the alternatives. All decision processes are costless and all lead to the same outcome, so the decision maker must be indifferent to all decision processes. Ironically, economic behavior is modeled in a manner that abstracts from the economizing process itself.

However, this nonbehavioral choice theory is not trivial because the functions $\bar{x}(a)$ and $\bar{y}(a)$ relate the decision environment a to the decision maker's choice $\bar{x}(a)$ and outcome $\bar{y}(a)$. In practice, economists typically use this choice theory in one of two ways. First, the researcher may specify a particular functional form $f(\bullet,\bullet)$ believed to be relevant to a decision-making situation of interest. Then, using the functional form $f(\bullet,\bullet)$, the predictions $\bar{x}(a)$ and $\bar{y}(a)$ are derived by the researcher and offered as predictive descriptions of how the decision maker's choice and outcome experienced will be related to the environment. Second, the researcher may construct the relationships $\bar{x}(a)$ and $\bar{y}(a)$ from data observations, and then use these relationships to make inferences about the functional form $f(\bullet,\bullet)$. That is, the researcher can make inferences about the decision maker's preferences or objectives, given the choices and environments actually observed. The predictive power of this theory and the ability to use this theory to infer preferences each depends upon the assumption that people make optimal choices.

BEHAVIORAL CHOICE THEORY

Behavioral choice theory, as defined here, arises from the fact that deliberating is costly because cognitive resources are scarce.

The production possibilities frontier is a familiar tool used to examine the implications of resource scarcity. If cognition is a valuable, then it must produce something. While cognition may be an input in the production of every good, Figure 17.1 is presented under the assumption that some goods require cognition and other goods do not. The horizontal axis measures the production of goods that require cognition. Assume point A represents an outcome in a world where deliberation is free. In this world, the optimal point A can be found without sacrificing any goods that require the application of cognition. Now, consider a world where a fixed amount of cognition must be applied to evaluate the set alternatives. The deliberation cost is the loss of cognitive goods that could be produced with the cognition that must be applied to evaluating the set of alternatives. This shifts the production possibilities frontier to the left, as shown in Figure 17.1. The deliberation cost reduces the size of the production possibilities set and makes the new best choice point B.

Of course, point B does not yield as much satisfaction as point A. Moreover, in the shaded area above and to the right of point B, there are points in the old production possibilities set in addition to point A that yield more satisfaction than point B. It is apparent that the size of this shaded area depends upon the size of the deliberation cost. If the deliberation cost is very small, then point B is very near point A. In this case, the deliberation cost is rather inconsequential, for the outcome B yields satisfaction close to outcome A. However, the deliberation cost becomes more consequential as it grows larger. As more cognitive resources must be expended to evaluate the set of alternatives, the choice (point B) will be further from the choice (point A)

Figure 17.1   **Recognizing Cognitive Scarcity and Deliberation Cost**

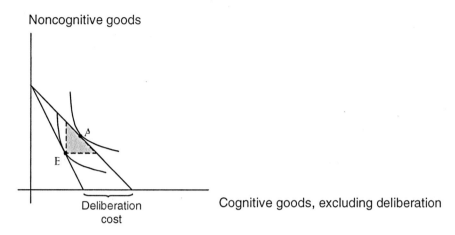

that would be made if deliberation were costless, and the outcome experienced by the decision maker becomes less satisfying.

The general point is that cognitive scarcity binds rationality, and the effectiveness of rationality as a process of thought is directly related to the size of the deliberation cost that must be expended to completely evaluate the set of alternatives. Conlisk succinctly makes this point when he says, "To say optimization cost is positive is to say rationality is bounded" (1988, 214). Models of bounded rationality can therefore be thought of as descriptions of how humans cope with the deliberation cost that arises from cognitive scarcity.

Nonbehavioral rational choice theory could still be applied if one could easily construct a model of bounded rationality by folding the deliberation cost into the decision maker's optimization problem so as to fully account for it. Baumol and Quandt (1964) speak of an "optimally imperfect" decision, where one sets the marginal cost of "more refined calculation" equal to its "gross yield." However, they do not present an optimization problem that folds in optimization cost, and the logical difficulty with writing one down is that the higher-order problem would also be costly to solve. The inability to formulate an optimization problem that folds in the cost of its own solution has become known as the "infinite regress problem," with Savage (1954) appearing to be the first to use the regress label. (For other discussions of the regress issue see Raiffa 1968; Radner 1968, 1975; Winter 1975; Johansen 1977; Gottinger 1982; Conlisk 1988, 1995; Smith 1991; Lipman 1991; Day and Pingle 1991.) The presence of a deliberation cost is responsible for the infinite regress problem, and the infinite regress problem is what spawns the need for a behavioral choice theory that goes beyond rational choice theory.

Frank Knight was one of the first (if not the first in print) to recognize that the presence of a deliberation cost motivates the use of methods of choice that do not involve evaluating all alternatives: "It is evident that the rational thing to do is to be irrational, where deliberation and estimation cost more than they are worth" (1921, 67). That is, the use of nonrational modes of decision making can be explained as behaviors people choose so as to economize on the use of scarce cognitive resources. There is a niche for behavioral economics to explain how people "decide how to decide."

THE AS-IF HYPOTHESIS

While Knight recognized that deliberation tends to be costly, he argued that the rational choice model would nonetheless be adequate for many purposes because maximization is the decision maker's goal. Friedman's (1953) "as-if hypothesis" has become the definitive statement of this perspective. The hypothesis is that while any of a myriad of decision methods might be used to find the optimal choice, the rational choice model gains its predictive power from the fact that the decision process does lead the decision maker to the optimum. The decision maker behaves "as if" he evaluates all alternatives with zero deliberation cost, even though he may not. Using the terminology of Simon (1978), we would say the decision maker is "substantively rational," so the degree to which the process is "procedurally rational" is of no consequence.

In a panel discussion, Herbert Simon commented, "The expressed purpose of Friedman's principle of unreality (or as-if hypothesis) is to save Classical theory in the face of the patent invalidity of the assumption that people have the cognitive capacity to find a maximum." He went on to say that the "unreality of premises is not a virtue in scientific theory but a necessary evil—a concession to the finite computing capacity of the scientist." Ironically, we researchers use simplifying assumptions because of our limited cognitive capacity but often do not expect that the decision makers we create in our models will do the same. Simon proposed that we should replace the as-if hypothesis with the "principle of continuity of approximation," which recognizes that "if the conditions of the real world approximate sufficiently well the assumptions of the ideal type, the derivations from these assumptions will be approximately correct" (Archibald, Simon, and Samuelson 1963, 236).

The as-if hypothesis implies that the decision maker can so effectively cope with cognitive scarcity that the deliberation cost is near zero. This potentially testable hypothesis may or may not represent reality. The principle of continuity of approximation indicates, as shown in Figure 17.1, that the rational choice model will be effective when the decision maker can effectively make cognitive scarcity a nonbinding constraint. In this case, behavioral economics can contribute by explaining how this is accomplished. Alternatively, if the deliberation cost prevents the rational choice model from being a useful approximation, then behavioral economics can contribute by offering another model that explains how the decision maker will procedurally cope with the deliberation cost in the given context.

TRANSACTIONS COSTS AND DELIBERATION COSTS: A PARALLEL

When transactions can occur without cost, institutional form is insignificant in terms of determining the allocation of resources and economic efficiency. North (1994) gives Coase (1960) credit for extending neoclassical theory by recognizing that institutions matter when it is costly to transact. North presents this fact as the foundation for a theory that explains the existence of institutions and their forms as responses to the fact that it is costly to transact.

Analogously, the notion that it is costly to deliberate can be considered a fundamental fact, and this fact can be used to extend neoclassical theory. When a set of alternatives can be considered without cost, then there is no need to consider the procedural behavior of the decision maker. However, once we recognize that it is costly to deliberate, the method used to make a decision matters. A theory of decision making can therefore be constructed that explains the existence and forms of particular modes of decision making as responses to the fact that it is costly to deliberate.

MODELS OF BOUNDED RATIONALITY

Models of bounded rationality describe individual decision making in a way that recognizes the fact that it is costly to deliberate.

Conlisk's Deliberation Technology

One approach to recognizing deliberation cost is to introduce it at one level but ignore it at a higher level. This approach is suggested by Conlisk (1988, 1995, 1996). While ignoring deliberation cost at any level can be considered ad hoc, the advantage of this approach is that classical optimization methods can still be used.

As presented by Conlisk (1995), a deliberation technology allows the decision maker to develop the approximation $X(T)$ to the unboundedly rational choice $X*$ if the cognition level T is applied. At one extreme lies the approximation $X(0)$ that results from some rule of thumb (e.g., randomly choose from the set of alternatives) that can be applied without expending any cognition. As more cognition is applied, the approximation improves, with the assumption that $X(\infty) = X*$, or that unlimited cognition yields optimality.

The outcome experienced by the decision maker is $\Pi(X(T))$. Assuming that marginal deliberation cost is the constant C and is measured in the same units as the outcome, the problem for the decision maker is to maximize $\Pi(X(T)) - CT$ by choosing the level of cognition T to apply to the problem. The optimal level of cognition to apply is the level $T*$ that equates the marginal benefit of cognition with the marginal cost. That is, $\Pi'(X(T*)) = C$.

The model can be used to examine how the optimal allocation of scarce cognition will affect the location and quality of the choice. The degree of substantive rationality can be measured by the distance $|X(T*) - X*|$, and it is determined endogenously when the optimal level of cognition $T*$ is chosen. Under standard assumptions, one would expect a decline in the marginal deliberation cost C to increase the optimal level of cognition $T*$, which would improve the approximation $X(T)$. Besides examining the impact of the deliberation cost, the influences of other context factors may be examined by modeling their impact as changes in either the objective function $\Pi(\cdot)$ or in the approximation function $X(\cdot)$. Conlisk (1996) applies this deliberation technology to explain market fluctuations.

To not ignore deliberation cost at some level, one must abandon optimization to some degree. Conlisk (1995) notes that the standard alternative to closing a model by assuming costless optimization is to close it by assuming that some adaptive rule of thumb determines the choice. This suggests that *observed adaptive behavior can be explained as a response to the fact that people cannot costlessly optimize.* Whereas the deliberation cost binds the decision maker from the optimum in a "one-shot" decision, adaptation gives the decision maker the opportunity to approach the optimal choice over time because of its lower cost of implementation, as the following models illustrate.

Simon's Behavioral Model of Rational Choice

Herbert Simon took on the task of "replac[ing] the global rationality of economic man with a kind of rational behavior that is compatible with the access to information and computational capacities that are actually possessed" (1955, 101). His approach was to look at how humans actually make decisions. Simon identifies the traditional "global model of rational choice" as the description of the ideal "economic man," and a defining characteristic of this model is the assumption that all alternatives are evaluated before a choice is made. In contrast to this model, Simon claims actual human decision making typically involves the sequential examination of alternatives.

The contrasting views of decision making described by Simon can be associated with optimum-seeking "search plans" that mathematicians have defined. Wilde (1964) describes a "simultaneous" search plan as one that specifies the location of every "experiment" before any results are known, whereas a "sequential" search plan permits future experiments to be based upon the observed outcomes of past experiments. The global model of rational choice implies a comprehensive simultaneous search plan, whereas Simon's claim is that humans tend to use sequential search plans.

Once one recognizes that cognitive scarcity elicits a deliberation cost, it is not difficult to understand why humans would choose to utilize sequential search methods. A basic result of mathematical search theory is that sequential search is more effective than simultaneous search because the information obtained from past outcomes allows one to strategically choose the next experiment. Effectiveness is commonly measured by the size of the "region of uncertainty" that contains the optimum after a given number of experiments. When there is no cost to applying the search plan, which is true for the ideal economic man, the efficiency of the search plan is of no concern. However, the prevalence of sequential search among humans testifies to the existence of a deliberation cost.

If we accept that human decision making can be modeled using a sequential search algorithm, we must also accept that people apply some kind of "stopping rule" to determine which alternative is ultimately accepted as the choice. Simon (1955) introduced the "aspiration level" concept as the stopping rule. Behaviorally, the assumption is that people set a goal for their satisfaction level and stop searching when the goal is achieved. The sequential search algorithm together with a stopping rule can be called a decision process. Such a decision process is analogous to what engineers and computer programmers call a "solution," a design or method that achieves a certain desired end even though it may not be ideal.

When it is costly to search, stopping sooner is better, but not if significant benefits from further search are forgone. Thus a search algorithm will be more effective if it can somehow effectively estimate the marginal benefit of an additional experiment so that it can be compared to the marginal cost. Simon (1955) addressed this problem by suggesting that the decision maker's aspiration level might change as feedback from the search was obtained. In particular, he suggested that the aspiration level would rise when satisfactory alternatives are easy to find and would fall when satisfactory alternatives are hard to find.

Day's Recursive Programming

Recursive programming (Day 1963; Day and Cigno 1978) provides an alternative explanation for how people with cognitive limitations economize, or evaluate a set of alternatives. The behavioral premise is that people do maximize, but cognitive scarcity leads the decision maker to simplify a more complex problem by decomposing it into a sequence of simpler problems. The form of the problem at each stage in the sequence is conditioned by past decisions and by observed changes in the decision environment. Solutions at each stage are optimal. However, because each stage examines only a fraction of the available set of alternatives, the decision sequence need not converge to a global optimum. In fact, recursive programming models tend to display rich patterns of behavior, including the oscillation and "phase changes" often observed in reality.

A recursive program consists of three components: a "data operator," an "optimizing operator," and a "feedback operator." The optimizing operator determines the values of the choice variables based upon the "objective" of the decision maker, the set of alternatives defined by the "constraint functions," and the "data" or parameter values of the model. The optimizing operator could be a linear programming algorithm or some nonlinear programming method. The data operator defines how the data entering the decision maker's objective function, and constraint functions depend on the decision maker's current state. The data operator can be used to model cognitive scarcity because it can narrow the size of the set of alternatives to any desired degree. The feedback operator specifies how the succeeding state of the system depends upon the current optimal decision variables, the data, and the previous state.

The degree of rationality present in a recursive program can be varied. At one extreme, the decision maker does not evaluate alternatives at all, and decisions are made using some rule of thumb. In this case, the model can be considered a system dynamics model of the Forrester (1961) type. Even though there is no rationality in a system dynamics model in the form of a conscious evaluation of alternatives, effective adaptation rules can lead the decision maker to a high-quality choice over time.

Bounded rationality disappears and unbounded rationality appears as the decision maker's cognitive capacity increases, so the recursive program approaches a dynamic program that is optimally controlled. Bellman's principle of optimality tells us that an optimal choice must be made at each stage in a dynamic program in order for the dynamic sequence of choices to be optimal overall. The unboundedly rational decision maker has the cognitive capacity to look forward and solve the dynamic program using backward induction. That is, the unboundedly rational thinker can effectively anticipate how present choices will affect the future. The unboundedly rational decision maker using a recursive program would optimally choose the optimizing and data operators. Recursive programs typically represent bounded rationality because the data and optimizing operators are fixed and can be thought of as the simplifying and adaptive rules of thumb used by the decision maker.

Lippman and McCall's Search Model and Bayesian Updating

Any economist who examines Figure 17.1 can readily identify the optimal choice. It is the point where one finds an indifference curve tangent to the set of alternatives. However, if one takes away the indifference mapping, it is no longer obvious where to find the best point in the triangle of alternatives. In the real world, it is unlikely that decision makers formulate indifference mappings, if not for any other reason than that the cost of doing so would likely exceed the benefit. Suppose a decision maker knows his preferences in the sense that the ordinal value of any alternative can be ascertained, but suppose an indifference mapping cannot be readily constructed. How might the decision maker compare alternatives?

After sampling one alternative, the decision maker will not know whether or not the next alternative sampled will be better. Thus, accepting the first sample as the choice involves chance. Because it is unlikely that the decision maker knows the distribution of outcomes associated with the set of alternatives, accepting any sample alternative as a choice is not just risky, it is uncertain. If comparing alternatives were not costly, there would be no uncertainty, for any number of samples could be taken to help identify the best choice. The uncertainty arising in this basic choice problem arises because deliberation cost precludes unlimited sampling. That is, *in the world where deliberation costs are present, all decision making is under uncertainty.*

Savage's (1954) subjective expected utility framework is the traditional model for how a decision maker with unbounded rationality will behave under uncertainty. In Savage's model, the decision maker subjectively creates an outcome distribution. This distribution provides probability weights to each of the possible outcomes, which allows the decision maker to construct an expected utility maximization problem. The model is attractive because a change in the decision maker's subjective estimate of the form of the outcome distribution will change the predicted choice in a reasonable way. A problem with this framework, however, is that the presence of a deliberation cost may prevent its application.

An alternative that allows one to recognize a deliberation cost is to assume that the decision maker draws sequentially from the set of alternatives, using some stopping rule to determine when the choice is made. If the distribution of outcomes is known, if the draws are independent, and if the cost of making one draw is constant, then an optimal search strategy exists (see Lippman and McCall 1976). The optimal strategy for a risk-neutral searcher is to continue searching as long as the expected marginal benefit of another search exceeds its expected marginal cost. A "reservation" outcome comparable to Simon's (1955) aspiration level is implied. The decision maker should stop once an alternative is found that exceeds the reservation outcome, meaning there should be no desire to "recall" a draw made previously and accept it as the choice.

Experimental studies designed to examine human subject behavior in this basic search model find that the model has predictive power (e.g., Schotter and Braunstein 1981; Harrison and Morgan 1990; Offerman and Sonnemans 1998). However, there is also evidence that subjects search too little, that subjects do want the option to recall a previous draw, and that they do choose previously examined alternatives (Schotter and Braunstein 1981; Kogut 1990). In an environment like this, Sonnemans (1998) examined the search strategies used by individuals. He found that most subjects did not use reservation prices, as suggested by the optimal strategy, but rather used strategies that combined a focus on earnings (such as bounded rational satisficers would do) and a focus on the last or best alternative (as optimizers would). He also observed "remarkable" individual differences in subject behavior.

One might not expect a model using a stable distribution of outcomes to perform well because the subjective form of any distribution used by real-world decision makers is likely to change as additional sample draws provide information. Indeed, the term *learning* is often used in the economics literature to describe updating the form of a perceived probability distribution. Bayesian updating is optimal under a variety of circumstances. Offerman and Sonnemans (1998) present an experiment where learning from one's own experience is compared to Bayesian updating. They find that subjects do learn from their own experience but fall significantly short of ideal Bayesian updating.

Another complicating feature of real-world decision making is that it is unlikely that any decision maker would sample alternatives at random. If a decision maker knows that his preferences are transitive and exhibit continuity, this information can be used to narrow the search region. Also, mathematical search theory (Wilde 1964) indicates that random search can be outperformed by other methods in a wide variety of circumstances. Thus, while it is clear that the presence of deliberation cost makes any decision uncertain, it is not clear how to model choice under uncertainty when the decision maker is not restricted to random draws.

Roth and Erev's Reinforcement Learning

Recent theoretical and experimental research in game theory has examined the roots of decision behavior. Game theory predicts the behavior of "players" in "strategic" situations, where the outcome of an action depends upon the behavior of one or more other players. At one end of the modeling spectrum are traditional models where the predicted behavior is equilibrium behavior associated with un-bounded rationality and self-interest. At the other end of the modeling spectrum are evolutionary game theory models where behavior evolves (in disequilibrium) as it arises over time from a selection process, and there need not be any conscious comparison of alternatives involved.

Much recent research has focused on explaining why people do not exhibit the rational behavior predicted by equilibrium game theory models. For example, because something is better than nothing, the responder in Guth, Schmitberger, and Schwartz's (1982) one-shot ultimatum bargaining game should accept any offer received, but responders regularly reject offers that significantly favor the proposer. One explanation for such nonrational behavior is that the decision maker is optimizing but is not purely self-interested (e.g., Bolten and Ockenfels 2000). However, much of the "learning literature" is motivated by the premise that observed behavior is disequilibrium behavior exhibited because the decision maker does not have the cognitive capacity to solve the optimization problem. By obtaining feedback from these disequilibrium choices, a decision maker with an effective learning algorithm can move toward the equilibrium behavior predicted by unbounded rationality.

Roth and Erev (1995) introduced a "reinforcement learning" model and have shown it has predictive power. They consider learning models as lying between traditional models that assume unbounded rationality and the evolutionary models that rely upon selection. They develop their model using two basic principles in the psychological learning literature: the law of effect (Thorndike 1898) and the power law of practice (Blackburn 1936). The law of effect is the notion that more successful behavior is more likely to be repeated. The power law of practice holds that the learning curve is steep initially and then flattens as practice or experience is obtained.

Because it was developed for the game theory context, the decision maker in the Roth and Erev model chooses a strategy for play. Each player is parameterized by an initial probability distribution defined over the available set of strategies. In a case where there is a discrete number of strategies, the strategy k would be adopted with initial propensity q_k. Each player has a probabilistic choice rule $P_k(t)$ that determines the probability that strategy k will chosen at time t. The reinforcement of receiving a payoff x is given by an increasing reinforcement function $R(x)$. The heart of the model is the updating of the probability choice rule, which occurs after a choice is experienced. A player choosing strategy k and experiencing reinforcement of $R(x)$ will update the probabilistic choice rule $P_k(t)$ for each strategy in a manner that respects the law of effect. The functional forms used also ensure that the power law of practice is obeyed. The single parameter in the most basic model is a measure of the speed of learning, and this parameter can be estimated by fitting simulations of the model to available data.

An important alternative to reinforcement learning is "belief learning." Belief learning can be considered a higher form of rationality in that the belief learner tries to learn the strategies of others so as to better anticipate their play, whereas the reinforcement learner makes decisions based only upon own experience. Beliefs are typically based on a weighted average of previous observations of what other players have done. The beliefs are then used to compute the expected payoffs associated with different strategies. Erev and Roth (1998) stress that the pure belief learning model is deterministic, not probabilistic. Subjective expected utility maximization determines the choice, not a probabilistic draw from the set of strategies, as in reinforcement learning. Roth and Erev favor probabilistic choice because they claim it is more consistent with the law of effect, and they also note that the maximization and information-gathering requirements of belief learning imply that belief learning forces the use of more cognitive resources.

Erev and Roth (1998) show that even a one-parameter reinforcement learning model can describe and predict decision behavior better than static equilibrium models that assume decision makers have the cognitive capacity to evaluate all possible strategies prior to play. This is true for both aggregate behavior and for the individual decisions of each player. For the data they examine, Erev and Roth conclude that a "higher-rationality" belief-based model did not appear to have an advantage over "lower-rationality" reinforcement models. Camerer and Ho (1999) find that their "experience-weighted attraction" model, which combines reinforcement learning and belief learning, can explain decision behavior better than either reinforcement learning or belief learning alone.

EXPLAINING OBSERVED DECISION PROCESSES AS RESPONSES TO DELIBERATION COST

Pingle (1992) experimentally demonstrates how the introduction of a deliberation cost can change choice behavior. A group of human subjects who could costlessly use trial and error to sort through a set of alternatives used twenty times more decision time and considered eight times the number of alternatives as another group that faced a deliberation cost. A measure of decision-making quality indicated that the average choice made by subjects not facing a deliberation cost was 2.8 times better than the average choice made by subjects facing a deliberation cost. The presence of a deliberation cost also substantially increased the variability of decision performance. The standard deviation of the decision quality measure was thirty times higher when a deliberation cost was present.

How do people respond to the fact that deliberation cost tends to reduce the quality and increase the variability of decision performance? An adaptive perspective suggests that decision modes will arise that consistently produce quality decisions while economizing on deliberation cost. The models of bounded rationality discussed above are decision processes that economize on deliberation cost while still giving decision makers the ability to progress toward a high-quality choice. Below some other important modes of decision making are recognized.

Heuristics and Habit

A decision-making heuristic is any device that reduces the search necessary to find a solution to a choice problem (Schwartz 1998, 66). The simplest heuristic is a habit that links a specific context to a choice: "When in situation A, make choice B." Beyond this, heuristics tend to take three forms: a device for simplifying preferences, a device for simplifying the information set, or a device for simplifying the process of evaluating alternatives. Cognitive scarcity is the standard explanation for the use of heuristics. As Simon explains:

> If . . . we accept the proposition that both the knowledge and the computational power of the decision maker are severely limited, then we must distinguish between the real world and the actor's perception of it and reasoning about it. That is to say we must construct a theory (and test it empirically) of the process of decision. Our theory must include not only the reasoning processes but also the processes that generated the actor's subjective representation of the decision problem, his or her frame. (Simon 1986, 27)

Payne, Bettman, and Johnson (1988, 1993) emphasize that there tends to be a trade-off between the accuracy of a heuristic and the effort required to implement it. They find that people can recognize this trade-off as it relates to different tasks and contexts, adapting their decision strategy, though often imperfectly. As an alternative to conscious decision, Martignon and Hoffrage suggest that simple heuristics "owe their fitness to their ecological rationality, that is, to the way in which they exploit the structure of their task environments" (2002, 33). The notion that heuristics owe their existence to evolution rather than conscious choice offers an explanation for how decision makers might effectively skirt deliberation cost.

Gigerenzer, Todd, and the ABC Research Group show that "simple heuristics make us smart" because they take less time, require less knowledge, and less computation. They perceive the mind as being "equipped with an adaptive toolbox of fast, frugal, and fit heuristics" (1999, 9). *Simple* is defined so as to exclude any calculation of probabilities or utilities, with the single-attribute lexicographic rule being especially attractive. Martignon and Hoffrage (2002) compare lexicographic, linear, and Bayesian decision heuristics, varying the computational complexity of each from minimal to simple to sophisticated. They demonstrate that simple models fit in a variety of contexts and often generalize to new data.

Kahneman, Slovic, and Tversky (1982) illustrate that heuristics can introduce biases in decision making. As described by Payne, Bettman, and Johnson (1992, 1993), behavioral decision research has since emerged as a subdiscipline of psychology that tests the descriptive accuracy of heuristics, or normative theories of judgment and choice. The notion that decision makers adaptively apply a toolbox of heuristics is an alternative to the rational choice model, one that has deliberation cost at its foundation and simultaneously explains the decision process and ultimate choice.

Imitation

Conlisk (1980) theoretically demonstrated that imitation can complement optimizing in an economic system when there is a deliberation cost. When optimizing is more expensive to apply than imitation, imitation and optimizing can coexist. The comparative advantage of optimizing is its ability to find an improved choice, while the comparative advantage of imitation is its ability to economize on deliberation cost.

Gale and Rosenthal (1999) examine a social system with less rationality by combining imitation and experimentation. An experimenter exhibits trial-and-error behavior, adopting the new behavior if it yields an improvement and reverting to the old behavior if improvement is not obtained. Imitators adjust their action in the direction of the average agent. Under reasonable assumptions the system converges to an equilibrium where all agents behave as predicted by the model that assumes unbounded rationality.

Pingle (1995) experimentally examined an environment where human subjects could choose to make a choice either via imitation or via experimentation. The tendency to imitate was greatest when it was first made possible, and it decreased as the same decision environment was experienced repeatedly. Environmental change prompted increased imitation. The introduction of the opportunity to imitate into an environment where experimentation had been the only available choice method increased a decision-making efficiency measure by more than one-third. Imitation was especially effective when an inexperienced "apprentice" could learn by watching a more experienced decision maker. As explained by Day and Pingle (1996), the niche for imitation is in relatively unfamiliar situations, while the niche for experimentation is finding an improved choice when imitation is not an option or when imitating others is not effective at obtaining improvement.

Offerman and Sonnemans (1998) also compare learning from own experience to learning through imitation, but they examine how subjects learn the form of a probability distribution that represents beliefs about an uncertain situation. They find that subjects learn both ways, but learning through imitation is more effective in that the results are closer to the ideal Bayesian updating. Less successful subjects choose to imitate more often, and more successful subjects are more often imitated.

Submission to Authority

People often submit to the instructions of authorities. Why do people submit? An obvious explanation is that the authority wields power. However, Arrow argues that power "cannot be the sole or even the major basis for acceptance of authority" because the cost of obtaining the required power would outweigh the benefits (1974, 17). Simon notes that "intense interdependence is precisely what makes it advantageous to organize people instead of depending wholly on market transactions" (1991, 27). Both the new institutional analysis of Williamson (1985) and the principal-agent analysis of Grossman and Hart (1983) are based upon the interdependence of subordinates and authorities. While the forms of organizations have been explained as responses to transaction costs, an information problem, or a public goods problem, little recognition has been given to the possibility that organizations with authority-subordinate relationships form in particular ways so that authorities can transmit decision-making rules of thumb to subordinates to minimize deliberation cost.

Pingle (1997) experimentally examined an environment where human subjects could make a choice via experimentation but received a recommended choice from an "authority" (the computer). In one experiment, subjects in different groups were given prescribed choices of different qualities. Because the prescribed choice turned out to be an anchor for the typical subject's experimentation, the quality of the authority's prescribed choice significantly affected the quality of decision making. In a second experiment, where the quality of the authority's prescribed choice was poor, it was demonstrated that a severe penalty for disobedience is not necessary to obtain compliance. Poorer decision makers will tend to comply because they are unable to make disobedience pay by finding improved choices that can offset even a small penalty. In a third experiment, the prescribed choice evolved in that it was the best choice of the previous decision maker. While the choice of the second subject was far from optimal, the prescribed choice was near optimal by the tenth subject, allowing succeeding subjects to experience near-optimal choices.

DELIBERATION COST, ORGANIZATION, AND SOCIAL INTERACTION

Both North (1994) and Simon (2000) stress the need to develop better theories of learning in order to develop better theories of organization. Simon comments, "As human beings are adaptive organisms and social organisms that can preserve bodies of learning. . . . , studying their behavior will not return us to permanently invariant laws, for human learning and social influence will continue to change people's ways of making rational decisions" (2000, 252). Social interaction enhances opportunities to reduce deliberation cost through imitation and though submission to authority.

An evolutionary perspective suggests that organizations and social relationships will evolve into forms that reduce deliberation cost. Simon (2002a) notes that all living systems share the feature of near decomposability, meaning a more complex system can be decomposed into smaller, relatively independent subsystems. The biological explanation for decomposability is that it contributes to fitness relative to a single complex system with a large number of highly interrelated components. Simon argues that "modern business firms and government organizations derive much of their efficiency from conforming to these biological principles, while inefficiency may be related to a complex (bureaucratic) system that is not readily decomposable" (2002a, 595). Decomposition in organizations allows independent subsystems to specialize in the solving of specific problems, which would reduce deliberation costs.

Simon (2002b) discusses the fact that people identify with groups, for example, families, tribes, gangs, corporations, government organizations, ethnicity, religion, linguistic groups, and nations. Group bonding and social ties in general can be explained as a response to deliberation costs. The experience of group members may provide rules of thumb that can reduce deliberation costs for those who submit to the group, making independent living relatively inefficient. Fernandes and Simon find that "identification based on professional, ethnic or other characteristics can cause individuals to apply problem-solving strategies that match the goals or norms of the group identified with" (1999, 226).

Simon refers to docility as "the tendency to depend upon the suggestions, recommendations, persuasion, and information obtained through social channels as a major basis for choice." He goes on to say that "being docile contributes to fitness because we obtain advice (on what to choose) that is for our own good and obtain information that is better than if we gathered it on our own" (1993, 160). In an unboundedly rational world, why should a person be sociable? In the world of behavioral economics, to be more sociable is to be more fit if the people you socialize with anchor your choices in the neighborhood of an optimum. Alternatively, exceptionally poor life experiences can be explained as being anchored to choices that are far from optimal by socializing with the wrong people.

CONCLUSION

Once a deliberation cost is recognized, the rational choice model is no less ad hoc than many others that might be proposed. The principle of continuity of approximation indicates that the rational choice model will be more useful when deliberation cost is low. Paradoxically, if people optimize when deliberation is costly, it is because they do not think or reason. Optimal choice is made possible by very effective rules of thumb. When deliberation cost is present, all choice is uncertain. If an optimal choice is made, the decision maker cannot know it, for knowing it requires that all choices be compared.

Decision making in the face of a deliberation cost may be pursued independently or in a social context. Models of bounded rationality typically describe how an independent decision maker copes with deliberation cost. One approach is to limit the comparison of alternatives by satisficing, which involves defining "good enough" in advance and searching up to that point. A second approach is suboptimization, where a set of alternatives is comprehensively evaluated, but the set is small relative to the set that could be examined. A final approach is to adapt, which implies that no comparison of alternatives is made prior to choice but that the method effectively compares successive choices in a similar environment, so improvement can be made over time.

Boundedly rational choice theories are economic theories because it is cognitive scarcity that motivates them. However, because optimization is costly, a decision maker facing deliberation cost cannot optimally choose a choice method. Ultimately, optimization must be abandoned to fully explain the choice methods people use. Adaptive and evolutionary theories are the obvious alternatives. From this perspective, the heuristics people use are fit responses selected in an evolutionary process that proceeds because of the presence of deliberation cost. Adaptation allows improved choices to be found when optimization is not possible.

The presence of deliberation cost also can also be used to explain socialization and organization. The perspective suggests that people will organize and socialize in a way that makes decision making easier. The observed decomposition of social and organizational units into related but largely independent subunits can be explained as an evolutionary development that has facilitated the development of improved decision-making heuristics. Social interaction, group bonding, and loyalty can each facilitate imitation and the transmission of good heuristics through authorities, meaning deliberation cost may well motivate their existence and forms.

REFERENCES

Archibald, G.C., H.A. Simon, and P. Samuelson. 1963. "Discussion." *American Economic Review* 53, 2: 227–36.

Arrow, K.J. 1974. *The Limits of Organization.* New York: Norton.

Baumol, W.J., and R.E. Quandt. 1964. "Rules of Thumb and Optimally Imperfect Decisions." *American Economic Review* 54, 1: 23–46.

Becker, G.S. 1993. "Nobel Lecture: The Economic Way of Looking at Behavior." *Journal of Political Economy* 100, 3: 385–409.

Blackburn, J.M. 1936. "Acquisition of Skill: An Analysis of Learning Curves." IHRB report no. 73.

Bolten, G.E., and A. Ockenfels. 2000. "ERC: A Theory of Equity, Reciprocity, and Competition." *American Economic Review* 90: 160–93.

Camerer, C., and T.H. Ho. 1999. "Experience Weighted Attraction Learning in Normal Form Games." *Econometrica* 67: 827–73.

Coase, R. 1960. "The Problem of Social Cost." *Journal of Law and Economics* 3, 1: 1–44.

Conlisk, J. 1980. "Costly Optimizers Versus Cheap Imitators." *Journal of Economic Behavior and Organization* 1: 275–93.

———. 1988. "Optimization Cost." *Journal of Economic Behavior and Organization* 9, 3: 213–28.

———. 1995. "Why Bounded Rationality." *Journal of Economic Literature* 34: 669–700.

———. 1996. "Bounded Rationality and Market Fluctuations." *Journal of Economic Behavior and Organization* 29, 2: 233–50.

Day, R.H. 1963. *Recursive Programming and Production Response.* Amsterdam: North-Holland.

Day, R.H, and A. Cigno. 1978. *Modeling Economic Change: The Recursive Programming Approach.* Amsterdam: North-Holland.

Day, R.H., and M. Pingle. 1991. "Economizing Economizing." In R. Frantz, H. Singh, and J. Gerber, eds., *Behavioral Decision-Making: Handbook of Behavioral Economics,* 2B:509–22. Greenwich, CT: JAI Press.

———. 1996. "Modes of Economizing Behavior: Experimental Evidence." *Journal of Economic Behavior and Organization* 29: 191–209.

Erev, I., and A.E. Roth. 1998. "Predicting How People Play Games: Reinforcement Learning in Experimental Games with Unique, Mixed Strategy Equilibria." *American Economic Review* 88, 4: 848–81.

Fehr, E., and K. Schmidt. "A Theory of Fairness, Competition, and Cooperation." *Quarterly Journal of Economics* 114: 817–51.

Fernandes, R., and H.A. Simon. 1999. "A Study of How Individuals Solve Complex and Ill-structured Problems." *Policy Sciences* 32: 225–45.

Forrester, J. 1961. *Industrial Dynamics.* Cambridge, MA: MIT Press.

Friedman, M. 1953. "The Methodology of Positive Economics." In *Essays in Positive Economics,* 3–43. Chicago: University of Chicago Press.

Gale, D., and R.W. Rosenthal. 1999. "Experimentation, Imitation, and Stochastic Stability." *Journal of Economic Theory* 84: 1–40.

Gigerenzer G, P.M. Todd, and the ABC Research Group. 1999. *Simple Heuristics That Make Us Smart.* Oxford: Oxford University Press.

Gottinger, H.W. 1982. "Computational Costs and Bounded Rationality." In W. Stegmuller, W. Balzer, and W. Spohn, eds., *Philosophy of Economics,* 223–38. Berlin: Springer-Verlag.

Grossman, S., and O. Hart. 1983. "An Analysis of the Principal-Agent Problem." *Journal of Political Economy* 51: 7–45.

Guth, W., R. Schmitberger, and B. Schwartz. 1982. "An Experimental Analysis of Ultimatum Bargaining." *Journal of Economic Behavior and Organization* 3: 367–88.

Harrison, G.W., and P. Morgan. 1990. "Search Intensity in Experiments." *Economic Journal* 100: 478–86.

Johansen, L. 1977. *Lectures on Macroeconomic Planning. Part 1: General Aspects.* Amsterdam: North-Holland.

Kahneman, D., P. Slovic, and A. Tversky. 1982. *Judgment Under Uncertainty: Heuristics and Biases.* Cambridge: Cambridge University Press.

Knight, Frank H. 1921. *Risk, Uncertainty, and Profit.* New York: Sentry Press, 1964.

Kogut, C.A. 1990. "Consumer Search Behavior and Sunk Costs." *Journal of Economic Behavior and Organization* 14: 381–92.

Lipman, B., 1991. "How to Decide How to Decide How to . . . : Modeling Bounded Rationality." *Econometrica* 59, 4: 1105–25.

Lippman, S.A., and J.J. McCall. 1976. "The Economics of Job Search: A Survey—Part I." *Economic Inquiry* 14: 155–90.

Martignon, L., and U. Hoffrage. 2002. "Fast, Frugal and Fit: Heuristics for Pair Comparison." *Theory and Decision* 52: 29–71.

North, D. 1994. "Economic Performance Through Time." *American Economic Review* 84, 3: 359–68.

Offerman, T., and J. Sonnemans. 1998. "Learning by Experience and Learning by Imitating Successful Others." *Journal of Economic Behavior and Organization* 34, 4: 559–75.

Payne, J.W., J.R. Bettman, and E.J. Johnson, 1988. "Adaptive Strategy Selection in Decision Making." *Journal of Experimental Psychology* 14, 3: 534–52.

———. 1992. "Behavioral Decision Research: A Constructive Processing Perspective." *Annual Review of Psychology* 43: 87–131.

———. 1993. *The Adaptive Decision Maker.* Cambridge: Cambridge University Press.

Pingle, M. 1992. "Costly Optimization: An Experiment." *Journal of Economic Behavior and Organization* 17: 3–30.

———. 1995. "Imitation Versus Rationality: An Experimental Perspective on Decision-Making." *Journal of Socio-Economics* 24, 2: 281–315.

———. 1997. "Submitting to Authority: Its Effect on Decision-Making." *Journal of Psychology* 18: 45–68.

Radner, R. 1968. "Competitive Equilibrium Under Uncertainty." *Econometrica* 36, 1: 31–58.

———. 1975. "Satisficing." *Journal of Mathematical Economics* 2, 2: 253–62.

Raiffa, H. 1968. *Decision Analysis: Introductory Lectures on Choices Under Uncertainty.* Reading, MA: Addison-Wesley.

Roth, A.E., and I. Erev. 1995. "Learning in Extensive-Form Games: Experimental Data and Simple Dynamic Models in the Intermediate Term." *Games and Economic Behavior* 8, 1: 164–212.

Savage, L.J. 1954. *The Foundations of Statistics.* New York: Wiley.

Schotter, A., and Y.M. Braunstein. 1981. "Economic Search: An Experimental Study." *Economic Inquiry* 19: 1–25.

Schwartz, H. 1998. *Rationality Gone Awry? Decision Making Inconsistent with Economic and Financial Theory.* Westport, CT: Praeger.

Simon, H.A. 1955. "A Behavioral Model of Rational Choice." *Quarterly Journal of Economics* 69, 1: 99–118.

———. 1978. "Rationality as a Product and Process of Thought." *American Economic Review Papers and Proceedings* 68: 1–16.

———. 1986. "Rationality in Psychology and Economics." In R.M. Hogarth and M.W. Reder, eds., *Rational Choice: The Contrast Between Economics and Psychology,* 25–40. Chicago: University of Chicago Press.

———. 1990. "Invariants of Human Behavior." *Annual Behavioral Psychology* 41: 1–19.

———. 1991. "Organization and Markets." *Journal of Economic Perspectives* 5, 2: 25–44.

———. 1993. "Altruism and Economics." *American Economic Review* 83, 2: 156–61.

———. 2000. "Review: Barrier and Bounds of Rationality." *Structural Change and Economic Dynamics* 11: 243–53.

———. 2002a. "Near Decomposability and the Speed of Evolution." *Industrial and Corporate Change* 11, 3: 587–99.

———. 2002b. "We and They: The Human Urge to Identify with Groups." *Industrial and Corporate Change* 11, 3: 607–10.

Smith, H. 1991. "Deciding How to Decide: Is There a Regress Problem?" In M. Bacharach and S. Hurley, eds., *Foundations of Decision Theory,* 194–217. London: Basil Blackwell.

Sonnemans, J. 1998. "Strategies of Search." *Journal of Economic Behavior and Organization* 35, 3: 309–32.

Thorndike, E.L. 1898. "Animal Intelligence: An Experimental Study of the Associate Process in Animals." *Psychological Monographs* 2, 8.

Wilde, Douglass J. 1964. *Optimum Seeking Methods.* Englewood Cliffs, NJ: Prentice-Hall.

Williamson, O. 1985. *The Economic Institutions of Capitalism.* New York: Free Press.

Winter, S. 1975. "Optimization and Evolution in the Theory of the Firm." In R.H. Day and T. Groves, eds., *Adaptive Economizing Models,* 73–118. New York: Academic Press.

CHAPTER 18

IN-DEPTH INTERVIEWS AS A MEANS OF UNDERSTANDING ECONOMIC REASONING

Decision Making as Explained by Business Leaders and Business Economists

HUGH SCHWARTZ

Most economic analyses of decision making are based on data from experimental economics laboratories or on aggregate macro or micro data. In both types of cases what is reflected is the *result* of decision-making processes. Studies by economists based on interviews with or observations of decision makers that attempt to ferret out the reasoning underlying business decisions date back more than half a century, but there have been few of them. Several have been published since the late 1980s, however. Increasingly, these go beyond the use of systematic questionnaires aimed at establishing statistical tendencies and employ open-ended, in-depth exchanges aimed at better understanding decision-making processes. They have a number of objectives, but primarily they seek to draw attention to the most promising among the available hypotheses about decision making and, in a few cases, to suggest more realistic theories of economic behavior.

Two recent studies based on personal contacts have been essentially in the tradition of household surveys and have asked the same set of questions of all respondents. Recanatini, Wallsten, and Xu 2000 reported on surveys prepared by the World Bank over the course of a decade. The second of the survey-based analyses, by Alan Blinder, the former vice chairman of the Federal Reserve Board, and several associates, sought to determine which of many available theories best explained the stickiness of prices (Blinder et al. 1998). Differing from that approach, Bromiley 1986 provided an analysis based on highly structured but open-ended interviews with a small number of enterprises. Later, Bewley, an economist known for his work in econometrics and general equilibrium theory, undertook open-ended interviews with business and labor leaders aimed at understanding the downward stickiness of wages in recession (Bewley 1999). At present he is analyzing interviews with a large number of enterprises in an effort to explain price formation. In addition, there is the work of this author, whose focus has been primarily on industrial development (Schwartz 1987, 1998, 2004). Those studies have included interviews with business economists as well as enterprise leaders and have attempted to capture the essence of the reasoning processes employed in several types of decisions. Finally, there is the work of Shlomo Maital, who has authored or co-authored a number of papers based on in-depth interviews. Most are confidential in-house case studies prepared in conjunction with executive education programs for training global leaders, but it is possible to cite Sweetman and Maital 2003 as well as Maital et al.

2002. Maital et al. 2002 is included in Boshyk 2002, which contains several other essays that depend in part on in-depth interviews.

THE WORLD BANK STUDIES

The World Bank studies have attempted to bring greater consistency to the enterprise-level surveys for the various countries, providing data for policy analyses and World Bank operations. An overriding theme has been the importance of microeconomic data underlying macroeconomic phenomena. Recanatini, Wallsten, and Xu 2000 urges the use of standard questions of firm performance to get consistent data on output, profitability, and productivity. It recommends the estimation of production functions to determine if financially constrained firms are less productive than those that are not so affected. The overview discusses the coverage of corporate governance, human capital, technology, market structure, transaction analysis, the role of the state, and the micro foundations of macroeconomics, particularly with respect to the relationship of growth and investment. It observes that the coverage of these topics has varied from survey to survey, as has the reliability of a number of the response categories. The surveys queried respondents about their attitudes toward various issues and their recollection of past events. Recanatini, Wallsten, and Xu recommend that attention be paid in such surveys to avoid inappropriate and ambiguous wording, multipurpose questions, manipulative information, inappropriate emphasis, emotional words and phrases, and questions that can be answered differently by people with the same opinion, as well as questions that can be answered identically by people with opposite opinions.

The report discusses problems related to response scales, the order effect, "don't know" responses, filters and branching, context effects (in particular, the sequencing of specific and general questions), and the use of sensitive questions. It notes the importance of pretests and offers a list of lessons learned, but, except for a general question at the end as to how to check for data quality, the report does not consider the use of ex post audits to gauge the order of accuracy of the various categories of information (although the World Bank does undertake ex post project evaluations). Without such guidelines it is difficult to know whether certain categories of data should be used in analyses that are intended to explain economic relationships and provide guidelines for World Bank policy. The importance of this is underscored by follow-up questioning undertaken by the author of this chapter, the responses to which conflict with a World Bank finding regarding the perceived importance of a factor cited as one of the most serious obstacles to investment in a particular country and raise serious questions about another. The interviewers who carried out some of the World Bank surveys were encouraged to employ follow-up in-depth questioning where it seemed advisable to do so, but time constraints, the large number of topics usually covered, and the unfamiliarity of most of the questioners with such an approach made that generally infeasible. This is not to deny that the usefulness of firm surveys would be improved were they to take the points raised in this evaluation of the surveys into account.

THE BLINDER PROJECT ON PRICE RIGIDITY

The Blinder project was based on interviews that began in 1990 and ended in 1992. (Some respondents were reached during the last months of a business upturn and others during periods when the economy was in recession, which may have affected the results somewhat.) The justification for resorting to a survey in which business leaders would be asked not only for factual information but also for assessments of what they had done was twofold. First, the study maintained that traditional econometric inquiries had failed to resolve which theory or theories best explained the stickiness of prices. Second, it was believed that decision makers ought to recognize the chain of reasoning that goes through their minds. It was acknowledged that to the extent that the true reasons for price stickiness were buried deep in the subconscious, interviews would be unlikely to uncover them, and the study defended itself against the contention that interviews might be unreliable, outlining cross-checks that were undertaken while also noting limitations of the more common econometric exercises. The study is forthright in indicating many response problems and acknowledges that at least some could have been mitigated by use of free-form interviews.

Twelve theories of price stickiness were selected for consideration, one of which was suggested by businesspeople in a pretest of the questionnaire. A few theories that might have been plausible candidates were eliminated because they might have induced respondents to give evasive answers or because they were too difficult to formulate in a manner easily comprehended by many businesspeople. The theories initially considered were based on the nature of costs, demand, contracts, market interactions (most of which were omitted because they might have involved collusion), and imperfect information. Also included was a theory based on the hierarchical structure of large firms. Respondents were asked if any important factors had not been considered, and none was suggested—though that response may have been influenced by the presentation of so many theories, the absence of any specific follow-up questions, and the relatively short time period (forty-five to seventy minutes for a large number of questions).

The manner in which the Blinder study was carried out was influenced by the team's review of previous survey research on pricing. Eleven studies were considered, seven of which involved personal contact with the business leaders: Hall and Hitch 1939; Kaplan, Dirlam, and Lanzillotti 1958; Lanzillotti 1964; Fog 1960; Haynes 1962; Nowotny and Walther 1978; and Gordon 1981. The Hall and Hitch study was characterized as the only one to have had a major impact on the thinking of economists. While it was cited as having a number of methodological shortcomings, it was acknowledged to have contributed four possible explanations for sticky prices. Initially Blinder sought free-form interviews with about twenty companies, believing that the questions should be tailored to each respondent company. However, a decision was made to expand the number to two hundred companies and to aim for a random survey sample of GDP in order to achieve statistically meaningful conclusions on a national level. In shifting to a larger number, the study was obliged to use several interviewers. The latter, all graduate students in economics, while not experienced in the task at hand, were trained and rehearsed, and a variety of controls was introduced. It was maintained that the result was more objective than would have been the case with a single interviewer. A few questions had structured follow-up points, and though some respondents did elaborate on various matters, that material was deemed to be statistically unusable and did not influence the final study's conclusions. The questionnaires (there were minor variations for the versions directed, respectively, at manufacturing, wholesale and retail trade, and the services) translated technical economics into plain English and were pretested. That pretesting led to the addition of one theory and to the elimination of another. The questionnaire contained two parts, the first of which dealt with basic data about the enterprise, its customer base, the firm's contacts with customers, its cost structure, and basic pricing practices. The second part examined twelve theories that might explain price stickiness. For those theories that depended upon a particular hypothesis, questions were asked about the validity of the premise. Of the companies contacted, 61 percent agreed to be interviewed. In the case of smaller companies, the interview was usually with the CEO, while in the larger firms, it was ordinarily with a leading executive other than the CEO.

The study first ascertained that prices are in fact sticky: 78 percent of GDP was repriced quarterly or less frequently and half of GDP was repriced only once a year. This was during a period of relatively low inflation. Nearly a quarter maintained that to change prices would antagonize or cause difficulties for their customers. Competitive pressures, the cost of changing prices, and the fact that their own costs did not change more often than that were each cited by just under 15 percent. No evidence was found for the general belief that price adjustments are more rapid upward than downward, nor for the belief that firms respond more rapidly to cost than to demand shocks. Large firms stated that they changed prices somewhat more frequently than their smaller colleagues indicated. The frequency of price adjustments varied greatly from one sector to another. Half of the firms contended that they never took the general level of inflation into account, and although many were unaccustomed to think in terms of elasticity responses, nearly half seemed to think that their demand was insensitive to price. Most thought that they could gauge marginal costs well, but in fact difficulties were revealed in distinguishing between fixed and variable costs. Almost 50 percent replied that they produced under conditions of constant marginal costs, and 40 percent responded that they produced under conditions of declining costs, casting doubt on the textbook U-shaped cost curves. Rankings were indicated for the twelve theories explaining price stickiness. The one that received greatest support was coordination failure, described briefly as "Firms hold back on price changes, waiting for other firms to go first."[1] Although only a tenth of the firms declared that coordination failure provided the basic explanation of price stickiness, more than 60 percent of the firms did judge the phenomenon to be at least moderately important in explaining the speed of price adjustment. The second most popular theory was that of cost-based pricing—that a firm's prices respond with a lag to costs—and the third most popular was nonprice competition, which is given little attention by economists. Another theory supported as relatively important in explaining price stickiness involved the use of implicit contracts. The study concluded that the theories do a better job of explaining upward than downward price stickiness, contrary to general expectations.

Each of the twelve theories and the findings relating to them are set out in individual chapters. These chapters explain the theories in some detail and then present the findings, taking note of results that are troubling and that it would have been good to have understood better. Only two publications that might be characterized as behavioral economics are cited in the text, and only two more in the bibliography. The main relation to behavioral economics is in the discussion of fairness in the context of a theory of implicit contracts. In addition, the discussion of the theory of psychological pricing points refers to the "folklore of marketing." In the concluding chapter, "What Have We Learned," Blinder and his colleagues state that the standard investigative tools of economics, theory, and econometrics, have been unable to discriminate among alternative theories of price stickiness and that interviews might provide a more promising route. The authors discuss implications of their findings for macroeconomic theory and policy.

These questions along with the findings of the study provide fertile ground for follow-up in-depth interviews. Perhaps there is a better list of theoretical explanations for price stickiness. If one is to deal with the matter of upward price adjustment, for example, one should take account of price movements or their lack in markets in which there is a dominant firm that has achieved "pricing power." Many firms seek to cultivate one or more products in which they enjoy pricing power. Where there is such pricing power and the firm in question is truly the strong price leader there may well be price rigidity (including the failure of prices to decline nearly as much as technological change would seem to allow), but it is not as likely to be explained by coordination failure. Beyond that, globalization and increasing new supply even in the absence of price increases, as from other international sources (such as from major developing countries), also limit price increases in some product markets, especially those of low-to-intermediate-level technology. Instead of coordination failure, perhaps businessmen should be confronted with a broader array of theoretical alternatives as to why prices are upwardly rigid, one that includes a spectrum of competitive responses. Surveys of enterprises might well be preceded by in-depth interviews as much as by pretests of questionnaires. The use of in-depth interviews would ensure that consideration of the new-supply theme would emerge, provided only that one or more firms in some of the affected high-, intermediate-, or low-technology industries were included (or one or more of the relatively simple service activities in firms of high-technology industries).

BROMILEY'S INTERVIEWS WITH A SMALL NUMBER OF ENTERPRISES

Bromiley 1986 incorporates data from interviews undertaken between 1979 and 1982, in addition to the results of simulation and econometric studies. In the foreword, Herbert Simon states:

> First, he has added substantially to our knowledge of how the bounded rationality of executives, limited by knowledge and ability to compute complex consequences, is actually employed in making decisions. Second, he enriches our methodology for carrying out empirical studies of this kind, for many more will be needed before we have the picture of managerial behavior comprehensive enough to provide a firm foundation for our microeconomic theories. Third, he shows us how the picture that emerges from his empirical studies can be related to the contemporary classical theory of investment, to provide it with both the numerical parameters and the modifications it needs in order to fit the realities of the industrial world. (Simon in Bromiley 1986, x)

The study is based on multiple interviews with each of four Fortune 500 companies, one of which is named and the other three of which are not, in accordance with anonymity agreements. In addition, acknowledgment is given to four other companies, also unnamed, whose data were not included in the study. The basis for selecting the four key companies or the four others is not explained. Qualitative data from interviews and other company information, quantitative as well as qualitative, relating to a wide range of matters were used. The objectives were to understand the corporate planning and implementation processes related to investment, to generate a model based on the planning process in one of the firms, and to use that model to make econometric estimates of investment, using data from the other three firms interviewed. The study concludes with a conceptual framework for the determinants of capital investment. It recommends further interviews to check hypotheses and the use of large samples in subsequent research.

The study begins with an exposition of the orthodox theory of capital investment and then raises a number of strategic considerations. Bromiley conducted more than thirty interviews in the four firms, ranging from first-line supervisors to vice presidents. Some were taped. The book includes a substantial number of excerpts from the interviews.

Chapter 2 provides an intensive examination of Copperweld, a Pittsburgh manufacturer of welded and seamless tubing and other steel products. Short-term profit plans were found to influence annual capital expenditures more than longer-range plans. A breakdown of the profit planning process is offered, revealing its bottom-up nature. The sales forecasts include inputs from econometric services and trade associations. A great deal of judgment is involved. The revised sales forecasts are given to industrial engineers who plan production, using a number of rules of thumb. The nature of the rules is explained briefly, with some note of the biases involved but no indication as to whether those rules might be evolving over time. Auxiliary costs are then taken into account in deriving a first forecast of income. Allowance is taken for productivity increases in estimating the capital investment to be undertaken, but with the use of rules of thumb that are characterized as not necessarily consistent. A series of iterations is undertaken, followed by a review at divisional headquarters that sometimes leads to further efforts to improve income forecasts. An aggregation of division plans follows, and then final corporate-level planning. These stages reveal concern with factors such as financial ratios and market interest rates but involve some judgments without clear rules, particularly in determining the trade-offs between capital investment and changes in corporate debt. Implementation of the profit plan is described with the aid of a number of quotations from those interviewed. All this leads to the development of a basic model.

The next chapters deal with the interviews of the other three firms and the application of the model developed for Copperweld to the data of the other three corporations. The structure of planning is used to generate forecasts of operations, funds available, investments desired, and the implications of those for changes required in the level of debt. The level of capital investment forecast by the model for the second corporation using the interview data tended to exceed somewhat that actually undertaken. Nonetheless, the interview data are said to have provided a more satisfactory explanation of the direction of causality with respect to debt-dividend-investment than traditional, aggregate statistical techniques. The third corporation assigns more weight to strategic, longer-term plans than the other companies and employs top-down as well as bottom-up approaches to planning. Econometrics plays a more important role in forecasting sales. The company's economists change their forecasts more slowly than public forecasters do, with the bias representing an attempt to take account of longer-term considerations (but also to compensate for biases of lower-level estimators). In the interviews with the fourth firm, Bromiley suggested more of the interview topics than he did with the other enterprises. The strategic planning process in that firm was held to function as a communication tool rather than as a target-setting or control mechanism. The connections between long-range plans and budgets are less well defined than in the other companies and the author concluded that it was necessary to respecify the equations for determining dividends, working capital, and investment capital.

Bromiley summarizes his empirical findings regarding the capital investment process (the result of aggregate planning, project approval, and implementation considerations), the cash flow equations (as a fundamental consideration that periodically constrains capital investment), the changes in hurdle rates (never changed more often than once every five years), the limits on debt (not always determined by sophisticated analysis), corporate forecasts (often not the forecaster's best guess), asymmetries (with the response of capital expenditures to sales or income less than forecast, differing in accordance with corporate strategy), constraints on investment (with the operative constraint varying over time), intertemporal differences (with changing parameters due to causes not well determined), interfirm differences, and research strategy (with inferences based on interview data supported by the quantitative results). His conceptual framework is that planning involves the desire for investment, the ability to implement, and financial constraints. Bromiley compares the relation of his explanation of corporate investment with those of standard economic theories. His "multi-constraint" framework uses many of the same variables as the standard models, but he contends that the variables need to be combined in a very different manner. Bromiley maintains that there may be substantial, systematic interfirm and intertemporal variations in the determinants of investment between firms, and he suggests the implications of those differences for corporate practice and research about corporate management, and for public policy. He concludes, "This research raises the question of how to manage the ties between corporate and financial planning systems. . . . Managers handle a complex planning process usually characterized by biased information, multiple interconnecting systems, caring about totals but also parts (e.g., projects), varying analytical products, and political and managerial concerns" (1986, 159). While

Bromiley's conceptual framework captures the details of the planning process well enough to predict investment satisfactorily, at least for the handful of firms he worked with, he does not attempt to indicate where the differences between the corporate practice he observed and the decisions that traditional economic models would call for reflect rules of thumb that are as close to the best that can be obtained in the circumstances (being improved over time, moreover) and where they represent a less nearly optimal decision-making process.

THE STUDIES OF TRUMAN BEWLEY

Bewley's studies have provided a major breakthrough in revealing the potential of in-depth interviews. Preliminary reports of the first study were published in 1995 and 1998, and the final version appeared in 1999.

Consider first his remarks that draw on the study of prices in progress as well as on the book dealing with downward wage rigidity (Bewley 2002). "An obvious way to learn about motives, constraints, and the decision making process is to ask decision makers about them," Bewley begins (p. 343). An obstacle, he observes, is that many categories of decisions are considered to be highly confidential, and though providing confidentiality prevents perfect replication, others can undertake similar studies employing the same general method. Given that networking might have led to a certain bias in the wage study, a large number of potential respondents were approached without any intermediary or reference. On the other hand, in the study of pricing, where greater sensitivity is involved, reliance has been placed entirely on networking. Note that release of confidential information, either directly or without the permission of the companies involved, can close off the investigator's access to a wide range of business entities and impede the access of other investigators as well. There is an additional reason for encouraging discretion in the use of any confidential information that is offered even though not sought: "Judicial authorities can require an academic investigator to testify in court." "Whatever the method of sampling," Bewley adds, "it is vital . . . to achieve as much variety as possible . . . because without it you cannot see the connections between responses and the circumstances of various types of respondents" (p. 345).

"If the objective [of interviewing] is to test given theories, you should be sure to cover the questions relevant to those theories. If the objective is to understand the shape of a general phenomenon with a view to formulating new theories, then the style should be less structured in the hopes that the respondent will come up with unexpected descriptions and arguments" (p. 346). Bewley concluded that while systematically following a fixed list of questions led to more inconsistencies and contradictions, this could be offset to a degree by broaching important issues at several separated times and in different ways. Use of a looser, more relaxed discussion "was more consistent with the overall logic of their remarks and probably reflected their views more accurately" (p. 346). Bewley adds that "it is wise to keep the discussion as concrete as possible, by requesting specific examples and by confining the discussion to the realm of the informant's experience. Abstractions should be avoided, because they lead from matters learned by experience to speculations that may reflect only passing thoughts. For the same reason, I avoid discussion of economic theories" (p. 346).

In order to sustain the interest of busy interviewees, Bewley stresses the importance of eye contact and the desirability of not looking down at a list of notes. His comment that people enjoy being provoked in a humorous tone (and not only, as he states, if they are dodging questions) is well taken. Telephone interviews may have an advantage in studies in which multiple sessions with respondents are sought, I would add; business exigencies often make scheduled interview times inconvenient, while if the interviews are by phone, they can be postponed more easily to a time that is better for the respondent. On the other hand, if an on-site interview is scheduled in another city, the respondent may be more hesitant to change the arrangement but may be more inconvenienced—and, as a result, may be less willing to accept follow-up sessions (or as many of them) because they might constrain his or her activities (or make the participant uneasy about any inconvenience caused for the interviewer).

Bewley notes, "There are certain necessary background questions, such as the nature of a company and the informant's function within it. The main questions have to do with the person's decision problem; its objectives, the possible actions, the constraints on them, the decisions made, how they are arrived at, and how they change with circumstance. Finally, you might ask how respondents acquired their knowledge; were they educated by experience or business culture" (p. 347). Bewley did not use a tape recorder because he was concerned that it might inhibit respondents, but in his (more sensitive) study of pricing, he has done so and few have been bothered by it. I would add, though, that the interviewer should be ready to turn the recorder off at times, and not just when the interviewee requests.

Bewley recommends organizing the transcripts or notes of the interviews into two kinds of documents, one a set of spreadsheets and the other lists of quotations, and he provides suggestions on how to go about this. He observes, "It is especially important to look for the relation between the circumstances informants face and what they say, for this can reveal the factors in the environment that influence decisions" (p. 347). Bewley provides an example—which is reinforced by recent work on heuristics (see especially Gigerenzer and Selten 2001)—that stresses the degree to which heuristics of successful decision making are tied to context or domain.

"My experience has been that there is a surprising amount of uniformity among the explanations of informants in similar circumstances," Bewley observes. "It is impossible to say whether the uniformity is due to the logic of the circumstances or to the culture of the business community or of particular industries. . . . Disagreement usually reflects ambiguity as to what the correct decisions are. Because the economic world is full of imponderables, it is not always clear how to maximize profits or best to protect the interests of a business." As for candor, Bewley concedes, "The most you can hope for . . . is to see a coherent story of the interaction of motivation and constraints that leads to decisions" (pp. 348–49).

One should not accept what people say about their actions at face value, and Bewley suggests that actions should be observed if it is possible to do so. With respect to the view that interview data should not be trusted because this leads to an emphasis on irrational behavior, whereas rationality is the common thread that holds economic theory together, he observes that "interviewing reveals rationality as well as irrationality" (p. 350). The author rebuts the well-known argument of Milton Friedman regarding the irrelevance of a theory's assumptions, maintaining that a deeper understanding is required for successful prediction if conditions change or if one wants to interpret phenomena for policy purposes. He gives a convincing example with respect to an intertemporal substitution theory of cyclical unemployment. Bewley concludes that we should supplement existing standard statistical sources with "a kind of main street economics" such as that provided by interviews (p. 352).

Bewley 1999 has four objectives. Most important, he offers the results of 336 interviews with business leaders, union officials, employment counselors, and business consultants in the northeastern United States (principally Connecticut) during the recession of the early 1990s, dealing not only with wage rigidity, the overriding concern, but also with a host of factors regarding employment—company risk aversion, internal and external pay structure, hiring generally and the pay of new hires in what he terms the primary and secondary sectors, in particular, raises, resistance to pay reduction, layoffs, severance benefits, voluntary turnover, the situation of the unemployed, labor negotiation, and (directly as well as indirectly) morale. He maintains that it is necessary to understand the mechanisms creating unemployment because they are critical for discovering how to reduce it. Second, the book offers arguments for and against the type of less structured, open-ended, approach of basically just listening to firms with only a memorized list of questions and concerns, not all of which are necessarily to be asked of all those interviewed. The approach eschewed statistical analysis of that data but the overall study introduced the results of many other statistical analyses to set the framework and help assess the interview findings. Third, the book provides a careful description as well as a critique of the leading theories that have been advanced to explain wage rigidity and evaluates those theories in the light of the evidence of the respondents and other evidence more generally available.

The conclusion is that only one theoretical explanation seems to be consistent with the evidence uncovered—that dealing with the importance of morale and the decisions of managers in response to their perception of the likely effects of morale factors. The other theories, Bewley suggests, lead to conclusions that are not supported by the evidence, and he attributes this shortcoming to their reliance on unrealistic assumptions. The analysis then attempts to deal with the rather imprecise concept that is morale and to build upon existing theories emphasizing morale, drawing on the interview data but also on introspection. Finally, Bewley 1999 offers suggestions on what might be done next. This includes the use of additional surveys and tests of existing theories and his reinforced theory of wage rigidity. Throughout, he provides extended quotations from the interviews and refers to numerous empirical and theoretical analyses of others concerning employment.

Bewley states that his interview findings support only those economic theories of wage rigidity that emphasize the impact of pay cuts on morale. "Other theories fail in part because they are based on the unrealistic psychological assumption that people's ability do not depend on their state of mind. . . . Wage rigidity is the product of more complicated employee behavior, in the face of which manager reluctance to cut pay is rational" (p. 1). He adds, "A model that captures the essence of wage rigidity must take into account the capacity of employees to identify with their firm and to internalize its objectives" (p. 2). He points to the models of Solow (1979), Akerlof (1982), and Akerlof and Yellen (1988, 1990), maintaining that pay rates have a positive effect on productivity through their impact on morale.

He states, "The implications of rationality depend on the conditions constraining decision makers" (p. 7). Bewley discusses problems with surveys and notes that he has compared the information he has obtained with official data, as well as econometric and other studies. He observes that motives may be unconscious—people may not be aware of the principles governing their behavior—and he cites implicit contracting as an example of this. He comments that in the course of the study he learned that cutting pay would have almost no effect on employment, that hiring new workers at reduced pay would antagonize them, that reducing the pay of existing workers would affect worker attitudes, and that the advantage of layoffs over pay cuts is that it gets misery out the door. None of the employers he spoke with stated that they offered a choice between layoffs and lower pay. The interviews revealed that labor is in excess supply during recessions (contrary to the reasoning of some prominent macroeconomic models), that employers avoid hiring overqualified workers, and that to the extent that there is some downward wage flexibility it is in secondary markets that are characterized by heavy turnover and relatively more part time work.

The recession under consideration lasted from the summer of 1990 through the spring of 1991, and the interviews were held during 1992 and 1993, the last ending in the spring of 1994. The initial interviews were arranged through the New Haven Chamber of Commerce and personal connections, but the majority came through references from those sources and from cold calls. Bewley aimed for a varied sample but looked particularly for companies that had experienced large layoffs.

He observed that there was a trade-off between randomness and interview quality. He changed the focus of the interviews over time, moving from an initial emphasis on wage and salary structures to a greater emphasis on questions of morale and overqualification. He undertook all of the interviews personally (usually an hour and a half to two hours) and made some telephone follow-ups. He concluded that the sessions with a fixed list of questions were less successful than those that were more free-flowing. The focus was on the experience of the companies interviewed, and his questions avoided economic jargon, with any theoretical queries reserved for the end of the sessions. He emphasized factual matters and did not ask direct questions about interpretive issues. As noted above, he relied entirely on notes. Whereas Blinder and colleagues (1998) interviewed only sellers of goods and services, Bewley spoke with buyers as well, and he did not attempt to avoid discussions that might be considered to be frightening (such as those bearing on collusion), as the Blinder study did. He avoided gathering precise quantitative data, however.

Bewley found that managers believed morale to be vital for productivity, recruitment, and retention. He defined good morale as characterized by a common sense of purpose consistent with company goals (not unlike what Simon 1990, 1992, and 1993 referred to as a variant of altruism—selfish altruism, in Simon's terms), cooperativeness, happiness or tolerance of unpleasantness, zest for the job, moral behavior, mutual trust, and ease of communication (p. 41). In discussing what affects morale, he noted a sense of community, an understanding of company actions and policies, and a belief that company actions are fair, along with an employee's emotional state, ego satisfaction from work, and trust in co-workers and in company leadership. His respondents indicated that poor morale led to low productivity, poor customer service, high turnover, and recruiting difficulties. There is no specification of any trade-offs that might be involved in the role of the various factors in contributing to morale, in the precise impact of morale on productivity, or in the precise role of that morale-based productivity in keeping wages relatively rigid.

A chapter on company risk aversion contributes to the discussion, as do the chapters on the external and internal pay structure, the latter of which is held to be important to internal harmony and morale, job performance, and turnover. The results indicate that the rigidity of the pay of new hires in the primary sector stems from considerations about the internal pay structure. The findings on salary increases reveal that beyond what is required by contracts, managers view raises as important in providing incentives and motivation. They are driven by the same factors in recession as in good times, he found: profits, the cost of living, raises in other firms, product market competition, and the competition for labor. Raises are not delayed because of concern about turnover of key employees. Managers resist reducing pay during a recession for fear of its effect on morale and the effect of that on productivity, along with concern for turnover of the best employees—those factors are much more important than any pressure from labor unions.

Layoffs are preferred to pay cuts not only because the latter are felt to affect the morale and productivity of the remaining workforce more but also because labor costs were estimated to be a small part of total costs (and so would facilitate only small reductions in prices) and demand was often held to be relatively inelastic. Layoffs also were preferred to pay cuts where it was not felt that competitors would match price cuts or where competition was based on more than price. Layoffs were favored as well where it was concluded that sales levels in the overall industry were lower, because of financial difficulties in the firms involved (which would not be alleviated much by wage reductions because of the level of benefits also available to employees), because of considerations of technological change, because of the opportunity to reorganize operations and eliminate organizational slack, and because of the possibility of increasing the work of the remaining employees. Bewley found that most severance pay obligations were not high (because it was believed that there was a lack of employee interest in them). It was uncommon to replace employees with cheaper labor because it was felt that the company would lose in terms of skill and morale. Managers acknowledged that those laid off were dealt a heavy blow, but they concluded that the psychological impact did not extend to the remaining workforce.

Interviews with labor officials indicated that the information asymmetries assumed in some theoretical explanations of wage rigidity were not of much significance. Similarly, the shirking theory, which assumes that workers are paid more than necessary and are dismissed if they do not meet certain standards, was rejected as an explanation of wage rigidity, as were all efficiency wage theories.

The principal critique of the existing theories is given in Chapter 20. The first section deals with the labor supply theories in which wages are downwardly rigid because people withdraw their labor when wages fall, with real business cycle theories, and especially with the intertemporal substitution theory of Lucas and Rapping. Interview and other data indicated that voluntary quits did not increase but rather decreased sharply during recessions. The few pay cuts that were made led to little turnover. Firms found it easier to recruit. The attitudes of the unemployed were not consistent with their having chosen leisure over work, and indeed, some workers who were able took on second jobs to maintain their income.

Worker bargaining theories in which workers' bargaining power causes downward rigidity also were rejected. The monopoly union model was rejected in large measure because of the low percentage of companies that were unionized and because the first line of resistance to pay cuts was almost always from management. The seniority rights model received limited support in the interviews. The "insider-outsider" model did not correspond to observations inasmuch as few nonunion employers bargain with their employees, even implicitly, and there is usually no conflict between insiders and outsiders over pay cuts.

In reviewing the evidence on the theories based on market interaction, consideration was given to those models dealing with search—market misperception theories and theories involving the transactions approach—and those relating to the holdup problem as well as to Keynes's relative wage theory. Two other groups of theories were examined: the theories attributing wage behavior to firms' behavior and theories of recessions as reallocators of labor. The first include implicit contracts (the implicit insurance contract model and the moral obligation implicit contract model), the efficiency wage theories (the turnover and flat labor supply model and the dual labor market model), models assuming asymmetric information, the adverse selection model, the menu cost theories, and the stigma-of-unemployment explanation. All of these are seriously criticized on both logical and empirical grounds, but available morale models and the fair wage model are judged to come closest to explaining the downward wage rigidity. With respect to the morale theory, Bewley states, "The theory is correct in emphasizing morale but errs to the extent that it attaches importance to wage levels rather than to the negative impact of wage cuts" (p. 415). The fair wage theory is termed correct in part but incorrect insofar as the fair wage is supposed to depend on wages at other firms and on labor market conditions. With respect to the reallocation explanation of wage rigidity he comments, "My observations were hard to reconcile with Hamilton's . . . idea that unemployment is the consequence of shifting labor from declining to expanding sectors and of people's choosing to consume leisure while waiting for jobs to reopen in their own sector" (p. 422). Bewley's objection to these models is not with the findings themselves but with their interpretation.

Finally, Bewley presents his extension of a morale-based theory of wage rigidity. Before doing so he states:

> Crucial aspects of the theory are that productivity depends on employees' mood that workers with good morale internalize their firm's goals, and that pay cuts impair both mood and identification with the employer. None of these aspects is closely connected with rational-

ity, which, in economist's usage, has to do with striving to achieve given objectives rather than with the selection of objectives or with the psychological capacity to accomplish them, matters central to morale. Nor does there seem to be a useful way to discuss formally the choice of objectives. I propose . . . a choice theoretic theory of mood that does not glaringly conflict with rationality. (430)

He then summarizes the evidence from his interviews which he terms the morale theory and notes some distinctive implications of that theory. Later, before presenting his formal model, he adds, "I believe it is general human experience that capacities to act and perceptions of pain or pleasure adapt to our circumstances" (p. 443). He then presents a model that "preserves the utility maximization principle used in economics." That model includes unconsciously as well as consciously felt mental and physical goals and costs. He closes with indications of applications to macroeconomic policy. The closing chapter, "Whereto from Here?" suggests further studies and tests of theoretical hypothesis that might be undertaken and raises a number of questions that might best be answered with the aid of the kind of data collection possible only in direct personal interviews.

Bewley 1999 is a seminal work, but a few words of caution are in order. First, Bewley begins by affirming the existence of wage rigidity and by citing evidence from his interviews supporting that during the period covered (as Blinder and associates did with respect to price rigidity). At the same time he acknowledges that wages are more downwardly flexible in firms in financial difficulty, particularly where employees recognize the situation (often the case). This raises the question whether wage rigidity is not tempered or even eliminated if a recession lasts long enough (was this true for Japan during the 1990s or for the United States during the Great Depression?) or if the general adversity is great enough for entire industries or regions or economies from the outset (consider Japan again, but even more so, consider Argentina and Uruguay since 1999—two relatively industrialized "developing" countries that have had a long tradition of strong labor unions and which experienced widespread wage cuts of 20 to 50 percent in real terms, often following layoffs and then followed by more layoffs). The long decline of traditional industries such as textiles and garments in those two countries seems to have been accompanied by major wage cuts as well as layoffs, and something similar occurred for low-skilled and semiskilled labor in New England for several decades as industries moved south or out of the country. The same phenomenon seems to have taken place in other regions with automobile assembly workers, with machinists, and recently with service employees of various skill levels even in a number of high-tech industries—witness the phenomenon of outsourcing to India and China. There seems to be a point at which wage rigidity does break down, and the seeds of that breakdown are captured in some of the responses Bewley notes.

A second consideration is that while the evidence from interviews coupled with that of available econometric and other studies provides ample grounds for rejecting the ability of most of the theoretical explanations of wage rigidity, and the unrealistic assumptions of those theories seems to underlie their inadequacy, the morale-based theoretical efforts seem to be an exception. This leads Bewley to offer an extension of the morale-based theories, but one that seems rather speculative, depending on the unconscious as well as conscious reasoning of managers. This may capture enough of what really matters, but the interview data do not appear to provide the entire basis for the conjecture. Nor is it clear how some aspects of the theory might be tested. Nonetheless, this chapter, however interesting and even potentially important, is not the most significant contribution that Bewley 1999 makes. The most notable contribution is that interviews can uncover data about decisions and the assumptions concerning the motivations of others that help explain those decisions—data that not only are rich in detail but also differ in part from the introspection of economists.

Bewley characterizes the information gathered from interviews as uncovering motives, constraints, and an understanding of the decision-making process. He acknowledges the uncertain reliability of some interview responses (and indicates efforts to detect and deal with inconsistencies), but one might hope that his current study of prices would specify how much time passed between the events and the recording of the information that took place in those events. Most observers might want to assign less weight to responses that are less recent unless strong arguments were offered for not doing so. Even where the information about intent and the general underlying motives is accurate, the actual reasoning processes employed in making some decisions may involve other considerations, and these may not be recalled with ease after even a few months, particularly where circumstances lead decision makers to deviate from their customary guidelines. In dealing with responses referring to events that are more distant in time, it may be necessary to add supporting material, perhaps consistent actions or reasoning taken at the same time.

THE SCHWARTZ AND MAITAL STUDIES

Schwartz 1987 involved interviews with metalworking enterprises in several regions each of the United States, Mexico, and Argentina in an effort to understand decision-making processes in a particular group of industries. Two rounds of interviews and a limited number of follow-up observation visits were made in 1976–77 and notes taken. (No tape recorder was used, and a significant portion of the note taking was based on recall immediately after the sessions.) Schwartz 1998 dealt with a broader range of industries in a single country but focused on a narrower set of issues; thirty-six firms were interviewed, with the principal emphasis on the decision making of Uruguayan manufacturers in preparation for the forthcoming increased economic integration of their country with Brazil, Argentina, and Paraguay. It followed a larger but more open-ended survey undertaken (largely by mail) in 1994. Schwartz 2004 involved repeated interviews with each of a dozen business economists. The principal objective was to discern how frequently those economists deviate from traditional optimizing calculations in preparing their analyses for management, the rules of thumb they select when they do so, and the extent to which they make efforts to allow for biases or improve the heuristics. Notes were taken, sessions were taped, and there were extensive e-mail exchanges with two respondents.

Schwartz 1987 involved interviews with 113 metalworking firms and nine trade associations in three regions of three countries between September 1976 and June 1977. The enterprises were recommended by the trade associations in response to the request for "well-regarded and financially successful companies." The response rate of the requests for interviews was more than 80 percent. Nearly all of the firms were interviewed a second time, and ten (all of those asked) agreed to observation sessions. Most of the interviews lasted from two to four hours. The observation sessions lasted from three hours to three days. The author conducted all of the sessions but was aided in one of the countries by substantial materials prepared in advance by an economist and an engineer. The industries selected had the following characteristics: relatively stable technology, only moderate economies of scale (derived principally from length of production run), and relatively little market power in most product lines. Preparation for the study involved extensive readings on the industries in question, a short course in metal stamping at an engineering college, tutoring on other metal fabrication activities, and discussions with three psychologists working on decision making and two specialists in social science interviewing. Anticipated findings were understatement of profit maximization objectives when speaking in broad terms, but a revealed behavior toward optimization in resolving problems. I defined economic perception as the process by which economic agents confronted with technological, market, and public policy data "read" those data, assigning quantitative or qualitative values to them. Economic judgment was defined as the process of assessing the probable economic consequence of perceived technological, market, and public policy data and included formal optimization techniques, systematic heuristics, and unique, even presumably "seat-of-the-pants" responses.

Most of the preliminary findings and hypotheses fell into three categories: overall findings, those concerning economic perception, and those concerning economic judgment.

The overall findings and hypotheses: (1) Most small differences at the margin are not well perceived; much greater differences are required in order to be taken into account (I call this the principle of the just noticeable difference). (2) Businesspeople often fail to recognize that small samples do not have the properties of larger ones; in particular, there is a failure to detect regression toward the mean, and there is frequent reliance on the anchoring and adjustment heuristic. (3) There is a diminishing entrepreneurial response to incentives (both market incentives and those from public policy). In the case of those emanating from public policy, extraordinarily large incentives actually can lead to negative responses (in anticipation of a reaction of the community that leads to the withdrawal or substantial reduction of the incentives).

Preliminary findings and hypotheses concerning economic perception:

1. Decision makers reveal differences in their ability to perceive the various categories of data; the asymmetry of perceptions can be important. This was noted for a new metal-working technology and also for the cost of inputs, for the price differential between domestic and imported goods, and for equipment costs. In the case of the last of these (and to a degree in the case of the price of imported goods) asymmetries in perception were a factor along with informational asymmetries. A prime example of a tendency to perceive certain categories of data imperfectly—and differently in the case of different individuals—is illustrated by examples of money illusion.
2. The differing perception of economic data is explained in part by differences in professional background and the frequency of exposure to similar data, as well as by institutional factors (such as a long tradition of historical cost accounting).

Findings and preliminary hypotheses concerning economic judgment:

1. Enterprise estimation of demand at prices other than those recently charged is not common.
2. The imperfect perception of some input prices combined with limited record keeping leads to limited variation in the degree to which enterprise estimation of costs reflects opportunity costs, and this is accentuated in periods of rapid inflation.
3. The enterprises interviewed did not determine the composition of output by careful calculation and doubted that the prevailing product mix was the most profitable. Most enterprises continued to produce more inputs in-house than could be justified by profit-maximizing considerations (at least in the late 1970s).
4. The anchoring and availability heuristics are important determinants of inventory determination.
5. The reasons cited for not undertaking second or third shifts in small firms and those run by managers without a business administration background were refutable more often than not. Assessment of defective production was generally made by use of a heuristic rather than careful calculation, particularly for components not sold but used in-house. Efforts to improve operational efficiency were undertaken primarily in response to adversity or anticipated adversity, in accordance with the slack thesis of Cyert and March (1992).

6. Responses to special depreciation or investment allowances and to decisions about the sources of financing suggested hypotheses that were consistent with much traditional economic literature for most of the firms.

Principal finding and hypothesis on the acquisition and processing of information:

The enterprises elected *not* to receive a considerable amount of information that was readily available and inexpensive to obtain, often counter to the interests of their profitability, though this tendency was reduced as market structure became more competitive. To some extent the decision to receive less of such information is related to the way in which data was processed, which had not changed much from what it had been two decades before. While some of this was rational enough, overall it reflected a good deal of suboptimality.

Principal finding and hypothesis regarding enterprise objectives and motivation:

High profits (the stated objective of more than two-thirds of the firms, including most of the larger ones) did not mean consistently maximizing behavior. Differences were revealed between stated and revealed objectives, due in part to failure to pursue a maximizing process, but also to difficulties in realizing objectives. However, in some cases, better perception of economic data enabled firms to record higher returns even in the context of reduced profits objectives.

Conclusions: Decision makers sometimes fail to perceive data accurately, and hence they address themselves to problems that are variants of the ones they actually confront. Heuristics are often employed, and they can lead to results that differ from those of standard economic analysis. The objectives of decision makers are often more complicated than simple profit maximization (or simple revenue maximization or satisficing, for that matter). The findings are grouped into three categories: those largely consistent with standard economics, those inconsistent with standard economics but of limited consequence, and those inconsistent and of major consequence. Among the implications is that in order to obtain the necessary insights about producer behavior, for many matters it is essential to go directly to the individuals involved, preferably in their own environment; it is not enough to rely on how they say they behave or on the evidence of how they behave in laboratory settings.

Schwartz 1998 deals with decision making in 1994 in thirty-six Uruguayan manufacturing enterprises in a wide array of industries. Two-thirds of the firms were Uruguayan-owned and the remainder were international. More than two-thirds of the firms exported, but only ten thought that they would be able to compete in the emerging integration scheme with Argentina, Brazil, and Paraguay without substantial difficulties, sixteen concluded that they might be able to do so, and ten viewed their situation as highly unfavorable. The study sought to provide preliminary verification and somewhat fuller specification of behavioral hypotheses that could be used to design policies capable of promoting more efficient responses of enterprises to the changing incentives of increased economic liberalization and integration. Most of the interviews were carried out by an individual with a recent M.A. in economics who had worked for twenty years as an accountant. The study sought to delve into the reasoning processes underlying decision making, giving attention to the importance of framing in doing so. It sought to acknowledge traditional economic reasoning and to note any alternative, behavioral lines of reasoning.

The principal findings that lend themselves to hypotheses to be tested further are as follows:

1. The reasoning of decision makers usually involved heuristics rather than careful calculation, among the most common being reasoning by analogy from a past experience. The heuristics used by most firms to determine which alternatives to examine more carefully and the amount of information to gather in doing so do not appear to be consistent with optimization and profit maximization.
2. Competitive pressures influence the degree to which profit maximization was found to be the principal objective of the enterprises and was critical to fostering the implementation of cost minimization and profit maximization among those enterprises that had such objectives.
3. Even those firms that sought to maximize did not always employ implementation procedures consistent with that objective, particularly in the search for information.
4. Loss aversion and attitudes toward risk and return in dynamic contexts varied somewhat from the results found by experimental economics.
5. Problems in perceiving data accurately were almost as important as the lack of data. Increased coordination within the enterprises succeeded in overcoming some of the most serious problems of economic perception. Further intra- and interfirm coordination may further reduce data perception problems.
6. Some of the conflict that the private sector had with the government with respect to the overvaluation of the peso might have been resolved had the government given more attention to measures that would have aided productivity in the private sector—had its perceptions in this regard been more accurate and had its judgments been better.
7. An understanding of the way in which businesspeople respond to what they perceive as obstacles is as important as the identification of the obstacles themselves in determining the most effective means of alleviating the adverse consequences and of designing policies.

Schwartz 2004 analyzes ongoing interviews over a year with a dozen business economists, eleven employed in or recently retired from Fortune 1000 companies in manufacturing and construction and one who spent his career consulting with leading financial institutions. As many as twelve interviews were held with each respondent, initially on four subjects but ultimately on a broad range of topics. The objective was to ascertain the extent to which business economists used the kind of maximization techniques that the profession has developed, and the degree to which they employed less formal heuristics. Where the latter was the case, the effort was to determine how those heuristics were developed and their biases taken into account. The elimination of two-thirds of the economics positions in the firms interviewed during the 1990s gave the economists who remained a strong incentive to provide analyses and advice that contributed to higher profits.

The interviews revealed that the business economists, all of whom expressed their conviction about the efficiency of the market and regarded themselves as neoclassical in orientation, nonetheless employed some of the approaches of behavioral economics. They often included heuristics (rules of thumb, in their terminology) in their analyses along with more traditional techniques. They were obliged to do so, they maintained, by the pressure of time, the lack of data (or the cost in obtaining the necessary data), technological change, and what some of them characterized as the need for alternative frameworks at turning points. In most cases they conceded that the heuristics they used were not consistent with Bayesian analysis, though it should be noted that they almost never employed several common (and usually more biased) heuristics often identified in consumer or public policy decision making. Many of the respondents believed that what they did reflected what Simon termed procedural rationality. This is most clearly true of the participants who insisted on the multiple character of rationality, incorporating not only economic but also social rationality and rational behavior with respect to different personality types. The last two elements reflect considerations of fairness and of the role of emotional states.

Even in these private enterprises, the information most sought from the economists was macro- rather than microeconomic. Much microeconomic analysis was left to noneconomists, who varied greatly in the degree to which they made decisions as if they were taking the principles of economics into account, and the economists varied, in turn, in the extent to which they attempted to help make the as-if assumption more nearly a reality among their colleagues. While most of the economists recognized that their companies had problems of slack, reflecting other than the most efficient use of resources (even when allocated to the most indicated activities), they were not generally close enough to the activities in question to help much, nor did they propose guidelines to aid others in reducing slack. Indeed, most of these very large companies employed so few economists that slack reduction would have to have been a second-order priority. While most economists recognized the inconsistencies of certain accounting conventions with economic principles, they were not active in efforts to alleviate the problem, such as by contributing to the development of activity-based accounting. They spoke against the sunk cost fallacy but sometimes lagged in efforts to overcome the problem. The economists reported on productivity trends ex post and included assumptions about them in projections but did not develop criteria for cost reduction and ongoing productivity improvement. With a few exceptions they did not participate in the preparation of corporate approaches to risk management. While most of the hurdle rate heuristics used in assessing investment projects seemed to make sense, some raise questions.

There was a tendency for many business economists not to press an economic point of view when it was known that this would go against strong preferences of the CEO or other key leaders and it was felt that such an effort would lead to reduced effectiveness of the economist in other areas in which more weight was given to objective analysis. Three seemed quite strong in their defense of economic principles, but nine conceded that they were less assertive. Finally, while most of the economists combined heuristics with traditional maximization calculations, they generally did not record the context of the heuristics or the dimensions of the biases involved, both of which might have enabled better results in future analyses, beginning with the possible improvement of the heuristics employed. The business economists, although clearly seeking to improve company profits, cannot be said to have been attempting to maximize in most cases. Rather, they tended to operate in a quasi-rational manner. Thus, the kind of economy-wide cost of substantial but incomplete enterprise maximization demonstrated by Akerlof and Yellen 1985 may be quite large. One of the strongest recommendations of the business economists was that university courses in economics give more attention to applications of the theoretical concepts and logical demonstrations, and to communicating economic concepts to noneconomists. Several indicated that the most effective means of implementing economic reasoning would be by emphasizing such applied approaches in the basic MBA economics courses that an increasing number of corporate leaders take—and that this would be even more effective than increasing the number of economists. This would be a means of making the as-if assumption more nearly valid—particularly, I would add, if those courses included discussions of how to increase profitability with the use of heuristics when circumstances require something other than standard calculation techniques.

Sweetman and Maital 2003, prepared for the Action Learning and Executive Development portion of the annual Global Forum on Business, summarizes the use of proprietary case studies that have been used internationally in at least half a dozen schools of business administration. After reviewing the merger between Bell Atlantic and GTE into Verizon, the paper maintains that "when the objective is to induce change, you must heed the proven psychological principle that positive reinforcement (success) is far more powerful than negative reinforcement (failure)" (p. 13). The authors maintain that successes are far more powerful if the goal of the stories and cases is to generate motivation, incentives, and role models that drive change. "While it is widely assumed in business schools that failure is more instructive than success because failure demands action while success demands only more of the same, in today's rapidly changing global markets, success also demands action because 'more of the same' is a recipe for future failure" (p. 13). There is a need to find solutions that are significantly better than the status quo, the authors insist, and "it is better to spend our time understanding what works than what doesn't" (p. 14). Sweetman and Maital also contend, "The less clear the solution and the harder the struggle to find the right answer, *the more valuable the self-discovered learning.* When investigating the case, find out more than what happened. Also find out what *didn't* happen—the choices that were not made, the courses of action that were rejected (or simply neglected)" (p. 22). The authors affirm, "What grips the participants and motivates discussion is the creative tension in the false starts, near misses, and internal struggle of the protagonist as he or she works in new ways towards a solution" (p. 15).

While much of the material considers alternatives that the enterprises were confronted with and why they chose one rather than the others, I would maintain that it is important to understand certain less successful choices, particularly when those choices lead to the demise of a company. Maital et al. 2002 explains the incorporation of proprietary case studies in the "action learning programs" (programs that emphasize learning by doing) of the executive education arm of Technion, Israel's science and technology university.

CONCLUSION

In-depth interview-based analyses usually require more time than other types of studies and, subject as they are to a number of limitations, they have tended to be ignored by most economists. Consider, though, their potential.

First, studies allowing for open-ended responses can reveal the inadequacy of theoretical assumptions that are manifestly poor indicators of the reasoning processes that underlie decision making and thus can enable us to do away with a wasteful use of resources in testing those theories.

Second, while it is true that a reasonable number of interview-based studies may be necessary to provide a firm foundation for new hypotheses about economic behavior, even isolated efforts may uncover explanations that economists have overlooked, leading to the formulation of better hypotheses about economic behavior. These may derive directly from the interview responses, or those responses may facilitate the construction of the new hypotheses. Moreover, case studies that reflect an improved understanding of decision making may motivate more successful economic behavior among those to whom they are disseminated.

Third, interview-based studies may help us to improve our understanding of (and our ability to modify) behavior that inhibits successful decision making.

Fourth, by focusing on reasoning processes in real life contexts, the in-depth interview-based studies may enable us to develop hypotheses of how best to implement the recommendations that emanate from good analyses (or how to do so relatively successfully, in any event), something that many economists do not really concern themselves with.

Fifth, in-depth interview-based studies may enable us to understand how to better take the biases associated with the use of heuristics into account, how to adapt heuristics to different contexts, and, more generally, how to improve performance when lack of time, lack of data, uncertain technological change, or other dynamic factors simply prevent calculation of what would be optimal.

NOTE

1. Blinder and colleagues note, "Coordination failure can lead to price rigidity if each firm would adjust its price if it expected other firms to do so, but also would hold prices fixed if it expected other firms not to change their prices" (2001, 269).

REFERENCES

Akerlof, George A. 1982. "Labor Contracts as Partial Gift Exchange." *Quarterly Journal of Economics* 97: 543–69.
Akerlof, George, and Janet L. Yellen. 1985 "Can Small Deviations from Rationality Make Significant Differences to Economic Equilibria?" *American Economic Review* 75, 4: 708–20.
———. 1988. "Fairness and Unemployment." *American Economic Review, Papers and Proceedings* 78: 44–49.
———. 1990. "The Fair Wage-Effort Hypothesis and Unemployment." *Quarterly Journal of Economics* 105: 255–83.
Bewley, Truman F. 1995. "A Depressed Labor Market, as Explained by Participants." *American Economic Review* 85: 250–54.
———. 1998. "Why Not Cut Pay?" *European Economic Review* 42, 2–3: 459–90.
———. 1999. *Why Wages Don't Fall During a Recession.* Cambridge, MA: Harvard University Press.
———. 2002. "Interviews as a Valid Empirical Tool in Economics." *Journal of Socio-Economics* 31, 4: 343–53.
Blinder, Alan S., Elie R.D. Canetti, David E. Lebow, and Jeremy B. Rudd. 1998. *Asking About Prices: A New Approach to Understanding Price Stickiness.* New York: Russell Sage Foundation.
Boshyk, Yury, ed. 2002. *Action Learning Worldwide: Experiences of Leadership and Organizational Development.* Houndmills, UK: Palgrave Macmillan.
Bromiley, Philip. 1986. *Corporate Capital Investment: A Behavioral Approach.* Cambridge: Cambridge University Press.
Cyert, Richard M., and James G. March. 1992. *A Behavioral Theory of the Firm.* 2nd ed. Oxford: Blackwell.
Fog, Bjarke. 1960. *Industrial Pricing Policies: An Analysis of Pricing Policies of Danish Manufacturers.* Amsterdam: North-Holland.
Gigerenzer, Gerd, and Reinhard Selten, eds. 2001. *Bounded Rationality: The Adaptive Toolbox.* Cambridge, MA: MIT Press.
Gordon, Robert J. 1981. "Output Fluctuations and Gradual Price Adjustment." *Journal of Economic Literature* 19: 493–530.
Hall, R.L., and C.J. Hitch. 1939. "Price Theory and Business Behavior." *Oxford Economic Papers.* 2: 12–45.
Haynes, W. Warren. 1963. *Pricing Decisions in Small Business.* Westport, CT: Greenwood Press.
Kaplan, A.D.H., Joel B. Dirlam, and Robert F. Lanzillotti. 1958. *Pricing in Big Business: A Case Approach.* Washington, DC: Brookings Institution.
Lanzillotti, Robert F. 1964. *Pricing, Production, and Marketing Policies of Small Manufacturers.* Pullman, WA: University of Washington Press.
Maital, Shlomo, Sherri Cizin, Galit Gilan, and Tali Ramon. 2002. "Action Learning and National Competitive Strategy: A Case Study on the Technion Institute of Management." In Yury Boshyk, ed., *Action Learning Worldwide: Experiences of Leadership and Organizational Development.* Houndmills, UK: Palgrave Macmillan.
Nowotny, Ewald, and Herbert Walther. 1978. "The Kinked Demand Curve—Some Empirical Observations." *Kyklos* 31: 53–67.
Recanatini, Francesca, Scott J. Wallsten, and Lixin Colin Xu. 2000. "Surveying Surveys and Questioning Questions: Learning from World Bank Experience." World Bank Policy Research Working Paper #2307, World Bank, Washington, DC.
Schwartz, Hugh H. 1987. "Perception, Judgment and Motivation in Manufacturing Enterprises. Findings and Preliminary Hypotheses from In-Depth Interviews." *Journal of Economic Behavior and Organization* 8, 4: 543–65.
———. 1998. "A Case Study: Entrepreneurial Response to Economic Liberalization and Integration." In

Rationality Gone Awry? Decision Making Inconsistent with Economic and Financial Theory. Westport, CT: Praeger.

———. 2004. "The Economic Analysis Underlying Corporate Decision Making: What Economists Do When Confronted with Business Realities—and How They Might Improve." *Business Economics* 39, 3: 50–59.

Simon, Herbert. 1990. "A Mechanism for Social Selection and Successful Altruism." *Science* 250: 1665–8.

———. 1992. "Altruism and Economics." *Eastern Economics Journal* 18, 1: 73–83.

———. 1993. "Altruism and Economics." *American Economic Review* 83, 2: 156–61.

Solow, Robert M. 1979. "Another Possible Source of Wage Stickiness." *Journal of Macroeconomics* 1: 79–82.

Sweetman, Kate, and Shlomo Maital. 2003. "Harnessing Change from Within: Proprietary Case Studies as Tools for Inducing Diagnosis and Stimulating Action." Paper presented at the Eighth Annual Global Forum on Business-Driven Action Learning and Executive Development, Amsterdam, May 20–23.

PART 4

EXPERIMENTS AND IMPLICATIONS

CHAPTER 19

CLASSROOM EXPERIMENTS IN BEHAVIORAL ECONOMICS

GERRIT ANTONIDES, FERGUS BOLGER, AND GER TRIP

Economic experiments have been popular ever since they were instrumental in the discovery of some famous economic paradoxes, such as the Allais, Ellsberg, and St. Petersburg paradoxes. Later experiments have been extended to problems outside the area of risk and uncertainty. Also, current economic experiments tend to involve real money or products, rather than hypothetical choices.

Economic experiments have become a tool for educational purposes. The earliest classroom experiments were conducted by Edward Chamberlin (1948), who studied market equilibria for buyers and sellers of hypothetical goods. Modern versions of Chamberlin's experiments are reported in Smith 1962, Holt 1996, and Fels 1993. Classroom experiments are but one type of experiment. Nowadays, several experimental setups can be distinguished, including laboratory experiments, classroom experiments (DeYoung 1993), and Internet experiments (Anderhub, Müller, and Schmidt 2001). Also, software is easily available for use in economics classes (e.g., Charles Holt's Web page, http://www.people.virginia.edu/~cah2k/home.html), and even a textbook for teaching economics by conducting experiments exists (Bergstrom and Miller 1999).

Experimental economics has become an industry. Laboratories for experimental economic research exist around the globe; the *Journal of Experimental Economics* has existed since 1998; and a *Handbook of Experimental Economics* has appeared (Kagel and Roth 1995). A good overview of activities, names, and Web sites in the industry is provided on Alvin Roth's Web page (http://www.economics.harvard.edu/~aroth/alroth.html).

There is a difference in focus between experimental and behavioral economics. Experimental economists usually test economic theories in market environments (i.e., auctions, rent seeking, provision of public goods, etc.). Several Web sites offer experimental setups as illustrations of economic theory (e.g., how to elicit a demand curve in class). Experimental economics aims at using insights from experiments to change market conditions in order to achieve efficient outcomes (Varian 2002). Behavioral economics refers more to the individual behavior of economic agents and subsequent research into the determinants of anomalous behavior, that is, behavior that is left unexplained by neoclassical economics. Our essay is more in line with behavioral economics.

The authors teach classes in the areas of economics, consumer behavior, and psychology. We use classroom experiments to illustrate the development of theories in these areas. We believe that students will be more interested and remember the courses better if they have personal experience with the working of the theories considered. Some of our classroom experiments were also used as pilot experiments for scientific research.

When we conduct experiments for research, we may have to use other than our own classes for two reasons. First, our own classes may be "framed" because they already may know something about the theories we are interested in, possibly leading to demand effects (Orne and Scheibe 1964). Second, our own classes usually are too small for experiments including different groups. Sometimes splitting a larger class into different groups is not feasible either—for example, if one group should not be aware of the experimental manipulations in the other group. In the laboratory, we usually assign the participants to different groups randomly, in order to avoid selection bias. When we have to use different classes we pay attention to the type of students in each. However, sometimes classes are formed according to the alphabetic order of the students' names. Such classes are ideal for use as random groups in an experiment.

Sometimes the types of student vary across different classes. In such cases there is the probability of selection affecting our results. For example, it is known that game theoretic classes may behave differently than social science classes in experiments on cooperative behavior (Frank, Gilovich, and Regan 1993). Some other factors that may selectively influence our results are gender, age, income, intelligence, ethnicity, and residence. Some of these variables may be included as co-variates in the analysis of results to assess their possible influence.[1]

Yet another type of classes we use are from Dutch secondary schools. Partly as a promotion for Wageningen University, mobile laboratories on economics, physics, chemistry, agriculture, and food are taken to secondary school classes, where pupils participate in the experiments. Since in this essay we report on several experiments from the mobile economics laboratory, we provide a brief overview of this project next.

MOBILE LABORATORY ON ECONOMICS

Wageningen University has developed several mobile laboratories for education in secondary schools in the Netherlands, including physics and chemistry laboratories. In 2002 the idea of creating a mobile laboratory in economics came up. The objectives of the project were twofold: stimulating scientific interest in economics and promoting Wageningen University. The basic idea was that by presenting interactive experiments derived from behavioral economics pupils would experience the richness of the economic discipline. Active participation of pupils was stimulated by using real products and real money. A provocative title—"Adam Smith Was Wrong"— was chosen, mainly to attract the attention of the teachers (most pupils do not know who Adam Smith was). This title was derived from the movie *A Beautiful Mind* about the life of John Nash. A clip of this movie was actually included in the laboratory.

In the academic year 2003–4 the economics laboratory was presented in approximately eighty classrooms all over the Netherlands. Each laboratory was presented by two students of Wageningen University, who were trained for two weeks and then went out touring for six weeks. Then the next pair was trained and went out to the schools.

The final form of the mobile economics laboratory consisted of a ninety-minute program. In exceptional cases, part of the program could be presented within a forty-five-minute framework. The full program was as follows: introduction, ultimatum game, framing experiment, endowment experiment, beauty contest (i.e., guess-the-number game), prisoner's dilemma experiment, and conclusion. The clip of the movie *A Beautiful Mind* shows four young men—one of them John Nash—who meet five young women in a café, one being blond and her friends being dark-haired. The young men prefer the blonde, but Nash makes clear that if they all go for the blonde they "will block each other," and after the men are rejected by the blonde, the dark-haired women will also lose interest "because nobody likes to be second choice." So some form of cooperation is needed to achieve the common goal, which is finding a girl for the night.

The main theme of the laboratory is the concept of economic rationality. If economic rationality is defined as a short-term maximization of own profit, regardless of the interests of others, then what can be concluded from the experiments in this laboratory? The pupils are invited to think about this key question, maybe inventing and elaborating their own experiment. Some lessons from the mobile laboratory that the pupils should take into account are that people do care about the interests of others, people behave inconsistently, and even if one is fully rational it is wise to take into account the irrationality of others. These lessons are well known from the behavioral approach to economics but have not reached the regular introductory textbooks. In the words of Kahneman: "A search through some introductory textbooks in economics indicates that if there has been any change, it has not yet filtered down to that level: the same assumptions are still in place as the cornerstones of economic analysis" (2003a, 162). The cornerstones Kahneman refers to are selfishness, rationality, and unchanging tastes (or consistency).

ENDOWMENT EFFECT

An important topic in behavioral economics is the idea that utility is not derived from total assets and levels of consumption but rather from changes with respect to these entities (Kahneman 2003b). Kahneman and Tversky's work on prospect theory (1979, 1992) points to the asymmetric evaluation of changes in the current state of affairs. The current state of affairs serves as a reference point for evaluating the changes. In particular, positive changes are evaluated less positively than negative changes are evaluated negatively. This has led to the popular credo that losses loom larger than gains. Because of this result, people in general are more eager to avoid losses than to acquire gains, which is called loss aversion.

Loss aversion has been investigated in different contexts. In finance, it has been observed that investors realize their gains too early and are reluctant to take their losses (Shefrin and Statman 1985; Odean 1998). In consumer behavior, people dislike product alternatives that in some respect deviate negatively from the products they currently use (Tversky and Kahneman 1991; Johnson et al. 1993). This phenomenon appears so strong that people in general seem to prefer the status quo over alternatives (Samuelson and Zeckhauser 1988). For example, when trading in their cars, consumers value a high trade-in price for their old car more than a discount on the new car, indicating loss aversion for their old car (Purohit 1995). Also, the sunk cost effect—that is, taking into account past investments when making current decisions—points to the psychological importance of lost assets or past expenses (Thaler 1980).

Probably the strongest illustration of loss aversion is the endowment effect, basically implying that goods in one's possession are valued higher than before they were possessed (Knetsch and Sinden 1984; Knetsch 1995). Ownership of a good seems to change the value placed on the good. The Coase theorem in standard economic theory claims that the value of a good should be independent of one's entitlement to the good (Coase 1960). The endowment effect is easily shown by randomly distributing two different goods, say A and B, among a number of people (Knetsch and Sinden 1984). Standard economic theory assumes that people would prefer either A or B or are indifferent. Hence, the standard assumption is that about half of the people have obtained the nonpreferred good and would be willing to exchange it for the other good. However, when asked for their willingness to exchange, in fact only 10 percent of the people want to exchange. This result substantially deviates from the standard economic expectation. Similar results were obtained by asking nonowners of a good for their willingness to pay (WTP) for the good. Kahneman, Knetsch, and Thaler (1990) report an average WTP of $2.21 for a mug. Likewise, owners of the good were asked for their willingness to accept (WTA) the loss of the good in exchange for a monetary compensation. The average monetary compensation required (WTA) was $5.78. The WTA was 161 percent higher than WTP, indicating the effect of loss aversion for the owners of the good.

How can we know that the endowment effect is due to loss aversion rather than "acquisition aversion" (resulting in lower WTP)? Kahneman, Knetsch, and Thaler (1990) compared product valuations of three groups: buyers, choosers, and sellers. Buyers' average WTP for a mug amounted to $2.87, whereas sellers' average WTA was $7.12. The WTA/WTP ratio of 2.5 clearly shows the endowment effect. Choosers neither owned a mug nor were asked to pay for the mug. They indicated for a number of different cash amounts whether they preferred the mug or cash. The amount at which choosers were indifferent between the mug and cash, $3.12 on average, indicated their value of the mug. Since the choosers' valuations were very close to the buyers' evaluation, the WTP/WTA disparity can hardly be explained by reluctance to pay for the mug but should be explained from loss aversion.

A number of other factors appear to influence the size of the endowment effect, including:

1. Reduction of the cognitive dissonance created by possible incompatibility between one's prior opinions concerning a good and the ownership of the good
2. Mere exposure, i.e., repeated exposure to a good tends to increase one's liking for the good
3. Mere possession, i.e., possessing a coupon or gift certificate for a good increases preference for the good
4. Mere ownership, i.e., people tend to judge their own possessions as more attractive than the possessions of others
5. Attachment, i.e., relatively high evaluation of products consistent with one's self-image, and products obtained by one's own effort rather than by chance
6. Transaction demand, i.e., the eagerness to buy or sell may reduce the endowment effect
7. Duration of ownership, i.e., the longer one owns a good, the stronger the endowment effect tends to be
8. Product-related factors: substitutability of goods tends to reduce the endowment effect and hedonic goods seem to be preferred in a forfeiture task, whereas functional goods seem to be preferred in an acquisition task (DeGroot 2003)

In our own research into factors influencing the endowment effect we frequently use classroom experiments. Our research shows how classroom experiments can be used both to replicate the endowment effect and to design relevant variations of the classical experiments.

Classroom Experiments on the Endowment Effect

Cognitive Dissonance Effect

Above we mentioned cognitive dissonance as a factor contributing to the endowment effect. Cognitive dissonance theory predicts that attitudes and opinions that are inconsistent with the actual situation will be changed in accordance with the situation (Festinger 1957; Cooper and Fazio 1984). For example, students who had to debate an issue (e.g., abortion) from a standpoint opposite to their own developed a more positive attitude toward the issue than before (Scott 1957). In this case, the situation was the actual defense of the opposite standpoint. In the case of the endowment effect, the situation is the legal entitlement to the good. So being endowed with a good might change one's attitude toward the good.

We conducted several experiments in which students randomly received one of a pair of goods. In one study, we used rolls of Top Drop or Top Gum (two types of licorice); in another study, we used Toblerone or Milka chocolate bars. We told the students that the product they had received was theirs to keep. When the students were offered the possibility of exchanging their good for the alternative, less than 20 percent wanted to trade (thus showing the endowment effect). Then we asked all students to justify their decisions.[2] Of those who did not want to trade, a large majority stated that they preferred the candy they had in their hand to the alternative, even though the initial distribution had been random. Clearly, simply receiving some candy had the effect, for many people, of making it their "most preferred."

Type of Good

Substitutability. The type of good may influence the size of the endowment effect. Hanemann (1991) suggested that substitutability of the goods would increase the willingness to trade. Chapman (1998) offered owners of a good the opportunity to trade their goods for both identical goods and similar goods (not exactly identical). Only part of the sample was willing to trade identical goods. Similar (not identical) goods were traded somewhat more easily when her participants received a small compensation (5 cents) for exchange, but only for those participants who were willing to trade the identical goods. In other circumstances the willingness to trade hardly differed across similar and dissimilar goods. Van Dijk and Van Knippenberg (1998) found even less willingness to trade wines from different countries than wines from the same country. In this particular case, similar goods were exchanged more than dissimilar goods. Our experience with a variety of snacks, pens, mugs, and postcards is that the endowment effect usually is quite strong, even for similar goods.

Evaluability. Hsee (1996) developed the idea that the ease of evaluating a good may influence a consumer's willingness to pay for the good under different circumstances. Easy-to-evaluate product attributes (e.g., broken dinnerware or damaged book covers) were found to be more important in situations where the good was evaluated in isolation. Product attributes that were hard to evaluate in isolation (e.g., number of entries in a dictionary) turned out to be more important when comparisons with similar goods were possible. The willingness to pay for (or the willingness to exchange) a hard-to-evaluate product may be lower than for an easy-to-evaluate good, leading to a larger endowment effect for the former than for the latter. We tested this hypothesis in a classroom setting.[3]

We randomly distributed Pentel fine-line pens and opaque drinking glasses among a group of twenty-nine law and economics students. Each student rated both products with respect to ease of evaluation and stated both WTA for the good in possession and WTP for the alternative good. Then a random price was drawn and transactions were made. For the pen, the average WTP was €0.53 and the average WTA was €0.92; for the glass, the average WTP was €0.74 and the average WTA was €1.13. The differences between WTA and WTP were significant for both goods ($p < .01$), in agreement with the endowment effect. The effect of the product was not significant, and neither was the product × price interaction effect. Despite higher ratings of evaluability for the glass than for the pen, the nonsignificant interaction effect indicated that the size of the endowment effect was not affected by evaluability.

Hedonic versus functional goods. Since hedonic goods can be defined as providing affective and sensory experiences of aesthetic or sensory pleasure, fantasy, and fun (Hirschman and Holbrook 1982), these goods may lead to more psychological attachment than functional goods, whose consumption is more cognitively driven and goal-oriented and which accomplish a functional or practical task (Strahilevitz and Loewenstein 1998). Hence the willing-

Table 19.1

Willingness to Exchange Different Goods and Money (%)

	Hedonic goods	Functional goods	Money
Mobile laboratory: peppermints, pens	22	47	
Knetsch 1989: mugs, chocolate	10	11	
Knetsch 1995: mugs, pens, money		10	16
Dhar and Wertenbroch 2000: M&Ms, glue sticks	15	85	

ness to exchange may be lower for hedonic than functional goods. Further, since money is supposed to lead to even less psychological attachment, willingness to exchange money will be higher than for goods.

In the mobile laboratory we studied the endowment effect for a hedonic good (peppermint) versus a functional good (pen). It appeared that willingness to exchange the hedonic goods was lower than for the functional good. However, Knetsch (1989) found hardly any difference in willingness to exchange across the two types of good. Knetsch (1995) used goods versus goods and goods versus money. It appeared that money was exchanged more easily than goods, although the result was not significant. Dhar and Wertenbroch (2000) found a strong difference in choices for giving up M&Ms or glue sticks when individuals were endowed with both goods. The willingness to give up the glue stick was far greater than for the M&Ms.[4] The size of the endowment effect for different types of goods is shown in Table 19.1.

If we accept WTA as the measure of willingness to exchange, endowment effects appear even larger than in goods exchanges. In a class of fifteen Ph.D. students, participants could buy or receive a box of chocolates and a flashlight (retail price €3.50 each). The average WTP was €6.15 for chocolates and €3.10 for flashlights, while the average WTA was €2.55 and €0.69, respectively. The endowment effect was significant ($p < .01$), and chocolates were valued higher than flashlights ($p < .01$) despite equal retail prices. However, no significant interaction effect occurred, so the endowment effect appeared about equally strong for chocolates as for flashlights.

Endowment effect for imagined transactions. The endowment effect also worked when students just imagined that they could acquire or relinquish an object. We used an elementary economics class of fifty students, half of whom were told that a plant would be given to one of them as a gift. Each member of this group had to state the minimum WTA in case the plant was given to him or her. The other half of the class stated their maximum WTP for the plant in order to buy it from the owner of the plant. Then one student from each group was drawn randomly. If WTP of the buyer exceeded the WTA of the new owner of the plant, the plant would change hands; otherwise the owner took the plant home.

The average WTP for the plant was €2.55; the average WTA was €4.31 ($p < .05$), thus showing the endowment effect for an object that was not really owned and which could be obtained with only a very small chance.

PRISONER'S DILEMMA

The prisoner's dilemma is a cooperation game frequently studied in the social sciences. The game deals with a district attorney who wants two prisoners to confess their joint crime. The district attorney tells each prisoner: "If you both confess, you will each go into jail for three

Table 19.2

Payoff Table of a Prisoner's Dilemma

		Prisoner II	
		Deny	Confess
Prisoner I	Deny	(−1, −1)	(−10, 0)
	Confess	(0, −10)	(−3, −3)

years. If you both deny, you will each go into jail for one year. If only you confess, you will be free and the other person will get ten years in prison." Communication between the prisoners is not allowed. Regardless of the other prisoner's behavior, it is always better to confess, as is shown in the payoff matrix in Table 19.2. The matrix shows the outcomes of the prisoners' choice combinations (left entries between parentheses for prisoner I, right entries for prisoner II). For "confess" the outcomes for prisoner I (0 or −3) are better than for "deny" (−1, −10, respectively), and vice versa for prisoner II. This makes both prisoners confess, leading to a worse outcome than under mutual denial. Denial is indicated as the cooperative strategy, confession as the defective strategy.

By systematically varying the payoffs, different motives for playing the game can be investigated. For example, by changing player I's payoffs while keeping player II's payoff constant, the effect of player I's individualistic motive can be shown. By changing player II's payoff while keeping constant player I's payoff, player I's altruistic motive can be shown. Competition can be shown by changing the payoff difference between players I and II. Charness and Rabin (2002) showed the existence of both cooperative motives and a motive for avoiding very low outcomes of the other player.

The prisoner's dilemma can be extended to multiple players in different ways. Variations of prisoner's dilemma games and free rider problems in public economics can be found in, for example, Kagel and Roth 1995. Dawes (1980) considers the "take some game," in which each player can either choose to receive $1 (cooperative choice) or choose to receive $3, in which case everyone is fined $1 for that choice (defective choice). If everyone cooperates, each player will receive $1. If everyone defects, each player will receive $3 minus $1 times the number of players.

In the "give some game" (Dawes 1980) each player may choose either to keep $8 received from the experimenter (defective choice) or give $3 from the experimenter to each of the players (cooperative choice). If everyone cooperates, each player receives $3 times the number of players. If everyone defects, each player will receive $8.

Another variation of the multiple-player prisoner's dilemma game that was used in the mobile laboratory on economics is the "disappearing lottery prize," taken from Hofstaedter 1983 and Bazerman 1998. In this game, the pupils could submit up to six lottery tickets to win a prize. However, the prize was divided by the total amount of tickets that were submitted. The cooperative choice of the players is to submit only one ticket each. In this case, the prize is maximal while the chances of winning are equal for all players. However, the temptation of defective choice is strong. If one player submits six lottery tickets, the chance of winning is six times the chance of winning under cooperative choice. However, if everyone plays six lottery tickets, chances of winning are equal but the prize is six times as small as under cooperative choice. We wanted to test two hypotheses: (1) both sexes behave equally cooperatively and (2) both sexes expect the other sex to behave equally cooperatively. The results are given below.

Disappearing Lottery Prize Experiment

The experiment is best explained by following its instructions:

> *The next experiment is not just fun, it will also be used for scientific research. During this research you are not allowed to talk or discuss. If this happens we have to stop the experiment and there will be no winner. We will play two rounds. In the meantime: be quiet. No questions can be raised during the experiment. It will take approximately 5 minutes.*
>
> *In this classroom there are N pupils. Therefore the maximum amount to win will be N × 5 euros. Each pupil in the classroom will receive a sheet of paper. On this sheet you can indicate how many lottery tickets you want to play, minimum 0 and maximum 6. All sheets will be collected and one of the participating tickets will be the winner. The winning prize depends on the total number of participating lottery tickets. Make sure nobody sees how many tickets you play.*
>
> *In the instruction you will see an example: Suppose a classroom with four pupils. A plays 3 tickets, B plays 2 tickets, C plays 0 tickets, and D plays 3 tickets. Now the average number of playing tickets is 2 and the total amount to win is 8 euros. The ones who play the highest number of tickets have the biggest chance of winning; however, the higher the total number of lottery tickets played by the whole classroom, the lower the prize. In this example the maximum prize could have been 4 × 5 = 20 euros, but the actual prize will be 20 ÷ 8 = 2.50 euros. Now we will distribute the sheets of paper. The exact procedure can be read on the sheets, as a reminder.*

So the actual prize equaled the maximum possible prize divided by the number of participating tickets. After the lottery sheets from the first round were collected, a second round was played immediately thereafter. In this round boys and girls played as two subgroups, each for its own prize. The prize for the winner among the boys depended upon the total amount of lottery tickets played by the boys, and likewise for the girls. This experimental design was employed to study differences in behavior of the sexes when they played against their own sex or against the other sex.

Apart from choosing the amount of lottery tickets to participate in the lottery, the pupils also had to predict the expected average amount of lottery tickets played by the whole group (round 1), played by the boys (round 2), and played by the girls (round 2). In total, five items were gathered for each participant: the number of lottery tickets played in round 1, the expectation about average behavior in round 1, the number of lottery tickets played in round 2, the expectation for boys' behavior in round 2, and the expectation for girls' behavior in round 2.

One additional remark that was written on the answer sheet and not given in the general instructions was what would happen if everyone played 0 tickets. This situation, although being a hypothetical case, had to be addressed in order to avoid any misunderstanding, and also to prevent giving an alibi for not playing cooperatively. The solution to this was: "If everyone plays with zero lottery tickets, one pupil will be randomly drawn and will receive 10 euros. So the bonus for (everyone) playing 0 is higher than for (everyone) playing 1 ticket, since in that case the prize would be 5 euros."

Results from the Disappearing Lottery Prize Experiment

The results from twenty schools visited during autumn 2003 were analyzed.[5] The experiment was conducted in the highest classes of the secondary schools that prepare for university. The

Table 19.3

Distribution of the Number of Lottery Tickets Played

	Boys (N = 148)	Girls (N = 136)	Total (N = 284)
Round 1			
0 tickets	2	1	3
1 ticket	31	46	77
2 tickets	41	65	106
3 tickets	28	19	47
4 tickets	7	1	8
5 tickets	1	0	1
6 tickets	38	4	42
Mean	3.09 (1.91)[a]	1.92 (1.00)	2.53 (1.65)
Round 2			
0 tickets	1	0	1
1 ticket	29	53	82
2 tickets	38	50	88
3 tickets	25	26	51
4 tickets	10	0	10
5 tickets	4	2	6
6 tickets	41	5	46
Mean	3.28 (1.93)	1.99 (1.15)	2.67 (1.72)

[a]The figure in parentheses is the standard deviation.

age of most pupils was approximately 17 years. The average size of the classes was 22.1 pupils; the smallest class had 14 and the largest class 34. The total number of pupils was 442: 235 boys and 207 girls.

A statistical analysis was conducted for the respondents who filled out all five items: the number of lottery tickets played in round 1, the expectation about average behavior in round 1, the number of lottery tickets played in round 2, the expectation for boys' behavior in round 2, and the expectation for girls' behavior in round 2. Quite often expectations were not filled out, probably because these questions were stated at the end of the sheet. For 284 pupils, however, 148 boys and 136 girls, a complete record was obtained.

The distribution of number of lottery tickets played is shown in Table 19.3. Most of the time 1, 2, or 3 tickets were played; 0, 4, or 5 tickets were played rarely. Boys quite often chose to play all 6 tickets; girls did this seldom. On average boys played slightly more than 3 tickets, while girls played slightly less than 2 tickets. The difference (1.18) was highly significant ($p < .001$) (see Table 19.4). The difference in behavior between the two rounds was small. Both the boys' and the girls' subgroups played slightly more tickets, but the difference with the first round was not statistically significant.

So there was in fact a large difference in behavior between boys and girls. The next question to address is whether it was foreseen by the participants. Participants indeed predicted more tickets played by boys than by girls. They expected the boys to play on average approximately 0.5 tickets more than the girls. Since the difference in reality was larger (more than 1.0), they underestimated the level of difference in behavior. Although both sexes gave accurate predictions of their own group behavior, boys underestimated the level of cooperative behavior of girls, and girls overestimated the level of cooperative behavior of boys.

Table 19.4

Average Number of Lottery Tickets Played

	Boys (N = 148)	Girls (N = 136)	Difference Boys − Girls
Round 1	3.09 (0.16)[a]	1.92 (0.09)	1.18[b] (0.18)
Round 2	3.28 (0.16)	1.99 (0.10)	1.29[b] (0.19)
Difference (Round 2 − Round 1)	0.19 (0.10)	0.07 (0.09)	

[a] The number in parentheses is the standard error of the mean.
[b] $p < .001$.

Finally, we tested whether participants played tactically. If someone plays with more tickets than he or she predicts for the whole group, that person is deliberately trying to take advantage of the cooperative behavior of others for his or her own benefit. If someone plays with less tickets than he or she predicts for the whole group, that person is deliberately playing for the benefit of the group, despite his or her self-interest. A variable, *tact,* defined as the number of lottery tickets played minus the average number of lottery tickets predicted for the whole (sub)group, was taken as a measure of tactical playing. Boys obtained scores higher than zero, indicating that they played tactically for their own self-interest (round 1). Girls obtained scores lower than zero, indicating tactical play for the group interest (round 1). In round 2, boys continued this behavior in their own subgroup, whereas girls played the same number of lottery tickets as they expected for the whole subgroup.

DUAL PROCESSING AND EVALUATION OF GOODS

There is a long tradition of thinkers ranging from Aristotle to Freud and on to modern-day writers such as Epstein (1973) and Sloman (1996) who have argued for two (or more) systems involved in thought. For example, Epstein (Denes-Raj and Epstein 1994) proposes that there are two inter-active parallel systems of cognition: rational and experiential. The former is a verbally mediated and primarily conscious analytic system that functions by a person's understanding of logic and evidence. The experiential system operates in an automatic, associational, and holistic manner. While generally adaptive in natural situations, it is often maladaptive in unnatural situations that cannot be resolved on the basis of generalizations from past experience but instead require logical analysis and an understanding of abstract relations.

One dual-process model that is of particular relevance to understanding economic behavior is the one proposed by Mittal (1988). The relevance of Mittal's model stems from two sources. First, it is specifically a model of consumer choice: many of the recent dual-process models are concerned with social-psychological processes more generally, for example, attitude change or social perception (see Chaiken and Trope 1999). Second, it directly addresses the relationship between processing mode and type of good, which we discussed above in relation to the endowment effect. In Mittal's model, choices can be made by means of either an *information processing mode* (IPM) or an *affective choice mode* (ACM). In IPM, product attributes are evaluated, then combined into an overall choice by means of some cognitive algebra. In contrast, in ACM, a property of the product as a whole, such as its hedonic impact or social image, determines choice. It is proposed that products can be purely functional or have both utilitarian and expressive properties to varying degrees. The *expressiveness* of a product refers to its ability to fulfill various psychosocial goals such as pleasing the senses and bolstering the ego. The more expressive a product is, the more affective processing there is. In addition, products can be more or less *involving;* in other words, there can be a greater or lesser motivation for the consumer to make the right choice (see, e.g., Mitchell 1981; Park and Mittal 1985). The more involving the product, the more information processing will take place. Finally, the reasons for choices made by affective processing are much harder to express than those for choices made by information processing.

Mittal (1988, 1994) sought empirical support for his model through two experiments. In each study participants were asked to make choices between products, then complete a questionnaire designed to assess the amount of involvement with the chosen product and the perceived expressiveness of that product, as well as the degree to which information processing and affective choice modes were used in product selection. Structural equation modeling was then used to test the relations between constructs predicted by the model. The results provide broad support for Mittal's model in that there is confirmation of the major constructs—involvement, expressiveness, ACM, and IPM—and for the proposal that ACM is positively related to expressiveness and IPM is positively related to involvement. Unfortunately, some of the predicted paths are quite weak or insignificant, some nonpredicted paths are significant, the overall model fits are far from perfect, and ACM is reported as being poorly measured. Further, the first study posed hypothetical choices (in the form of scenarios), so the external validity of the results of this study is questionable (see the methodological considerations below). Although the second study overcomes this problem by giving participants a real choice between products, which they were then subsequently allowed to keep, there is a confounding of the information given about each product and its anticipated expressiveness. For instance, products expected to be high in expressiveness were described to the participants in terms of their social and hedonic properties, whereas products low in expressiveness were described in terms of their functional and utilitarian properties. It is therefore not possible to determine whether the pattern of responses given by participants was due to their perceptions of the expressiveness of products, due to the product information, or both.

Classroom Experiments on Dual Processing

Two of us have conducted a number of classroom studies investigating the effects of processing mode. Our starting point was to conduct a partial replication of Mittal's experiments in which we tried to rectify the methodological problems outlined above (i.e., we gave participants real choices, removed the confound between product descriptions and their expressiveness, and included more measures of ACM). Despite these changes, we obtained equivocal results similar to Mittal's. We therefore decided to try a new experimental method whereby we attempted to directly manipulate processing mode, then examine the effects of this manipulation on product valuation within a choice setup. In particular, we measured the size of the endowment effect for a chosen product when the choice was made under either IPM or ACM. For reasons similar to those given above with regard to hedonic versus functional goods, we hypothesized that the endowment effect would be greater when choice of product was made under ACM than under IPM.

One hundred forty-five first-year economics undergraduates from Erasmus University Rotterdam took part during their normal classes. All participants took away with them from the experiment either a pen worth about €1.00 or a small amount of money (between €0.25 and €2.50). A two-by-two factorial design of processing by task was employed, which resulted in four independent groups of participants of approximately equal size: IPM-WTP, IPM-WTA, ACM-WTP, ACM-WTA. The products used in this experiment were two types of pen. The processing manipulation in the IPM condition was a list of ten features whereby the two pens could be differentiated: color, form, materials, form of clip, nib type, nib protection, ink color, ink permanence, writing comfort, and weight. The instructions were to rate each attribute for each pen on a five-point scale where 1 was an extremely negative evaluation and 5 a strongly positive evaluation. In the ACM condition twenty-one adjectives were provided that might be used to describe the pens in a global, emotional way, the approximate English equivalents being *eye-catching, boring, pretty, exciting, practical, nice, mundane, chic, functional, different, amusing, cheap, attractive, novel, "me," comfortable, unusual, "not me," quality, ugly,* and *ordinary*. The participants were instructed to select as many of these as they thought were appropriate to describe each pen (with a minimum of one adjective for each pen). In both conditions the participants were asked finally to select which of the two pens they preferred.

Each of the four experimental groups was a different class of a first-year course in marketing. The classes were composed in a random way at the beginning of the year. Each class was verbally informed as a whole that they were being asked to participate in a study of consumer choice and that this would involve them making evaluations of two different brands of pen. They were also urged that they should attempt to make these evaluations on an individual basis. Next the products were distributed along with the processing manipulation: everyone within a group received the same processing manipulation (i.e., either IPM or ACM), and each group was randomly split into acquisition and forfeiture subgroups. After everyone had made his or her evaluation and indicated a preference, either all the products were collected (WTP condition) or the nonchosen product was collected (WTA condition). As a manipulation check, participants were next asked to complete a questionnaire designed to measure the amount of ACM and IPM. After everyone had returned the questionnaire they were asked to state either the sum of money they would be willing to accept in return for giving up their chosen pen (WTA) or the amount of money that they would need to receive such that it would be preferred to receiving their chosen pen (WTP). This question and the random price mechanism (see below) that was to be used in order to elicit true valuations were explained to them both verbally and in writing on the response sheet. After everyone had indicated a price, one of the participants was invited to draw a chip out of a group upon which were written prices from €0.25 to €2.50 in 25-cent increments. Finally money or pens were awarded to the participants on the basis of the result of the draw: those stating WTA prices equal to or lower than the drawn price got the drawn amount of money, otherwise they kept the pen, whereas those stating WTP prices *higher* than the drawn price received the drawn amount, otherwise they kept the pen.

Unfortunately, the hypothesis that the endowment effect would be greater for those evaluating products under ACM than IPM was not borne out. However, there was a significant main effect of processing ($F(1,141) = 5.918$, $p = .016$) such that people on average indicated that they would pay €0.19 more for the pens in the ACM condition than the IPM condition. It seems likely that this difference in valuation of the products due to processing mode led to a ceiling effect under ACM, which meant that an endowment effect was not observed for this type of processing (i.e., participants could not value these products any more in the WTA condition than WTP since their WTP amounts were already at a maximum price for these products).

Another experiment with classes of Ph.D. and undergraduate students produced similar results. Here processing mode was manipulated by letting the participants evaluate a product either on scales consisting of affective adjectives or on scales concerning attributes of the product. It was intended that affective scales would elicit ACM, whereas the rating scales would elicit IPM. The product evaluated was a candle lamp. After evaluating the candle lamp, students were required to state their WTP. Then one student was selected at random and for this student the candle lamp was auctioned by using the random price mechanism. The average WTP under ACM was €1.69, whereas under IPM processing it was only €0.95 ($p < .05$).

The effect of processing mode may be subtle. The manipulation we used can easily fail if the participants have time to evaluate the product in a different way after completing the questionnaire. In a large class of Danish students, WTP did not differ across conditions, possibly because we waited until every student had completed the questionnaire. By that time, the students might have been thinking about the product in different ways, thus destroying the experimental manipulation. To avoid different ways of thinking after completing the questionnaire, either we walked around in class to present the students with WTP questions immediately after they completed the questionnaire or the students were given the WTP question in an envelope that was opened immediately after completing the questionnaire.

In some more recent experiments we have abandoned the use of the discrepancy between WTP and WTA as a measure of the endowment effect in favor of the swapping paradigm used by Knetsch and Sinden (1984), mentioned above. In one experiment, 102 high school students (ages fifteen to seventeen) and 66 undergraduate students took part. Again a two-by-two design of processing by choice was employed, which resulted in four groups of participants: ACM-Retain, ACM-Switch, IPM-Retain, IPM-Switch. There were eighty-five participants in the IPM group and eighty-three in the ACM: whether participants were in the Retain or Switch group was their own decision and was, in fact, our dependent variable. The products used in the experiment were two different kinds of confectionary: a bag of Autodrop licorice and a bag of Chupa Chups lollipops. These two products cost about the same amount, €1.42 and €1.19, respectively. Moreover, according to a supermarket manager, they were equally popular among the teenagers in the sample.

The processing manipulation consisted of a list of ten product attributes/features of either Autodrop or Chupa Chups to be evaluated on five-point bipolar scales. In the IPM condition, participants were asked to rate functional attributes of each product separately, for example, size, weight, energy, and shelf life. In the ACM condition the products were evaluated on hedonic attributes, for example, taste, brand quality, attractiveness, and ability to satisfy. Each of the four groups at each of the two locations was verbally informed as a whole that they were being asked to participate in a study on consumer behavior. This would involve evaluating the bags of Autodrop and Chupa Chups. The participants were urged to make these evaluations on an individual basis. Next either the Autodrop or the Chupa Chups were distributed along with the processing manipulation—either ACM or IPM—and an envelope to be opened directly after finishing the questionnaire. The envelope asked participants whether they wanted to keep the product they had been given or switch to the other product. The participants could keep or acquire their preferred product. After having made their choice to retain or to switch, participants were asked to estimate the prices of the two products.

The results were in line with the hypothesis that the endowment effect would be stronger for ACM than IPM. Of the 46 participants in the ACM group endowed with Autodrop, only two (4 percent) switched to Chupa Chups. In contrast, in the IPM group, 15 out of 40 (37.5 percent) traded in the licorice for the lollipops. Of the 37 participants in the ACM group endowed with Chupa Chups, just five (13.5 percent) participants switched to Autodrop, whereas in the IPM group 13 out of 45 (29 percent) made the switch. A probit analysis shows that the endowment effect was statistically significant (one-tailed $p < .01$). The expected interaction of processing mode by choice was also significant (one-tailed $p < .05$). There was therefore an endowment effect in both conditions, and it was greater for ACM, as predicted.

SUBJECTIVE DISCOUNTING

Discounting refers to valuing present outcomes higher than equal future outcomes (Fishburn and Rubinstein 1982). Usually in economics exponential discounting is assumed, implying an equal discounting rate in each future period. For example, if someone values $100 today as equal to $110 in one year (discount rate of 10 percent), then according to these assumptions $121 in two years will also be valued equally. However, the standard assumption is not realistic in the area of consumer behavior. It appears that consumers frequently use higher discount rates in the near future and lower discount rates in the distant future (e.g., Thaler 1981). An alternative discounting function has therefore been proposed (Loewenstein and Prelec 1992; Ahlbrecht and Weber 1995) that reflects the idea of changing discount rates over time. This is called hyperbolic discounting.

It is quite easy to demonstrate hyperbolic discounting in class, and we have reported several experiments elsewhere (Antonides and Wunderink 2001). For example, one may ask students for future amounts they are willing to accept in order to forgo $1.50 payable on the same day. Future dates may vary between one week and one year. Hyperbolic discounting will be evident from the data by decreasing amounts per time period for periods of one week ($3), two weeks ($4.50, or $2.25 per week), ten weeks ($8, or $0.80 per week), and fifty weeks ($30, or $0.60 per week).

Hyperbolic discounting may lead to preference reversals. For example, viewed from today, an amount of $1,000 in two years may be preferred to an amount of $800 in one year because both outcomes occur in the future. However, after one year, the situation is receiving $800 the same day or receiving $1,000 in one year. At that moment, cashing in the $800 may be more likely because it has become a present outcome. Likewise, a pregnant woman who is asked six months before the event may prefer delivering the baby naturally to delivery under anesthesia, because natural delivery has larger long-term benefits than the short-term benefits of anesthesia. However, when the labor starts, she may prefer the immediate, smaller benefits of anesthesia (Christensen-Szalanski 1984).

Also, different types of good may be associated with different discount functions. For example, for healthful items such as fruit the benefits may be perceived as higher in the long run than for less healthful snacks. Hence, one may prefer an apple to a less healthful snack to be consumed in one week (Read and Van Leeuwen 1998). However, after one week consumption can take place immediately and many people change their preference in favor of the less healthful snack.

Another distinction related to time preference is between hedonic and utilitarian goods. Gattig (2002) showed that time preference is higher for hedonic items (e.g., CD or television set) than for functional items (e.g., computer diskette or washing machine). Hence, the participants in his studies preferred advancing the delivery of hedonic goods to advancing the delivery of utilitarian goods. However, when monetary compensation was given to postpone the delivery of the goods, no significant differences were found between advancement choices for hedonic and utilitarian goods. It seems that adding monetary aspects to the choices made people decide more rationally.

EXPERIMENTS ON THE EFFECT OF SITUATION ON CONSUMER BEHAVIOR

The effect of situation in consumer judgment has become of interest to marketers because volatile consumer behavior can only partly be explained on the basis of personal characteristics, income, attitudes, and social norms. Situational effects can be demonstrated easily with a questionnaire asking for preferences for goods in different situations. For example, it can easily be shown that an ice cream is preferred to an apple on a hot beach, whereas the reverse is true after lunch. Likewise, the probability of consumption differs across social situations (Belk 1974; Lutz and Kakkar 1975).

Also, the situation may affect preferences for the same good. Thaler (1980) asked his students for their willingness to pay for a beer under two different conditions: when the beer was purchased from a fancy resort hotel or when the beer was purchased at a run-down grocery store. In both cases, the beer was to be consumed at the beach. WTP appeared to be higher when the beer

Table 19.5

Classified Reactions to Receiving Each of the Social Resources

Student's reaction	Money	Product	Service	Love	Status	Information
Other's gift						
Money	11	4	20	4	3	0
Product	1	19	7	0	1	0
Service	0	8	22	0	0	5
Love	0	7	13	18	1	0
Status	0	0	0	1	15	0
Information	0	14	6	1	3	2

was to be purchased at the hotel than at the grocery store. The different WTP could only be due to the nature of the point of sale. Thaler (1980) assumed the existence of two different kinds of utilities: acquisition and transaction utility. Acquisition utility is derived from the product itself, whereas transaction utility is derived from the purchase environment. Although acquisition utility was the same for the beer from the hotel and the beer from the grocery store, the transaction utilities differed across the two points of sale.

Framing is just another instance of a situational effect. Framing refers to a particular description of a good that may be considered as an information situation. For example, Levin and Gaeth (1988) found that preference for a steak that was "50 percent fat free" was higher than for a steak that "contained 50 percent fat."

The type of item appears to influence its suitability in mutual exchange for another item, which is considered another situational effect. Foa (1971) developed a theory explaining the likelihood of exchange for different "resources," including goods, services, money, information, status, and love. In the original experiment participants were asked which of a pair of resources was most appropriate in return for a particular resource given to another person. For example, participants were asked: "What is the proper compensation you wish to receive in exchange for giving information to a person? Money or a good?" Since there are fifteen possible combinations of the six resources, participants were presented with fifteen pairs of choices. Information was most likely to be exchanged for status and money and less likely to be exchanged for love and services. This procedure was repeated six times for each resource, amounting to ninety pairs of choices. It appeared that personalized resources such as love, status, and services generally were not preferred in exchange for general resources such as cash, information, and goods. Also, abstract resources, such as status and information, were not preferred in exchange for concrete resources such as goods and services.

Foa's idea can be replicated rather easily in class. First we gave students an overview of the kind of resources that one may use in social exchange. Then we asked students about the most appropriate reaction to each of six situations: (1) someone who gave you money (500) when you needed it, (2) someone who gave you a product to be used in your room, (3) someone who helped you clean your room for one day, (4) someone who gave you emotional support when you had a difficult time, (5) someone who praised you about your good exam results in the presence of other people, and (6) someone who gave you information about a job vacancy (you got the job). Students formulated their answers themselves (in contrast with Foa's original research), which were then coded into the resource categories. An overview of the answers is shown in Table 19.5. The results are by and large in agreement with Foa's theory: most reactions fell within the same category as the resource that was given (numbers on the diagonal of the matrix in Table 19.5).

Also common were reactions including resources that in Foa's theory were close to the resource that was given (numbers around the diagonal). Other reactions were less common (numbers away from the diagonal). Services appear as a quite popular resource given in exchange for another person's gift.

METHODOLOGICAL CONSIDERATIONS

Incentives

One important way in which the experimental methods of psychologists and economists differ is in the use of incentives. Many economists strongly believe (see, e.g., Binmore 1987; Hertwig and Ortmann 2001) that experimental participants must be given large external incentives that are performance-related if they are to be adequately motivated to give responses with external validity (i.e., that will be generalizable to situations outside the laboratory). Meanwhile, psychologists tend to regard participants as being motivated by many factors other than external financial reward, which renders financial incentives either at best unnecessary or at worst counterproductive (see, e.g., Loewenstein 1999; Rakow 2001). For example, Roth (2001) points out that the endowment effect never would have been observed if only the valuation of monetary amounts had been investigated. This debate remains to be resolved empirically, although at least one metastudy suggests that providing financial incentives does not have any significant effect on the reliability of data, which is an indication that the effort made by participants is not necessarily contingent on external reward (Camerer and Hogarth 1999). Whatever the eventual outcome of this debate, by the nature of the field of inquiry, there will still be many classroom experiments in behavioral economics that require some money or goods to pass from the experimenter(s) to the participant(s): for instance, participants have to be endowed with a good in endowment-effect experiments and should receive a payout commensurate with their performance in a prisoner's dilemma game.

In an ideal world there would be no issue: classroom experimenters would be able to ensure external validity by giving sizable incentives to participants in all cases where it was deemed advantageous to do so. Further, they would always use products or sums of money that ensured high involvement (i.e., the degree to which a participant feels it is important to give a correct or truthful response; see the discussion of involvement above in relation to dual processing for more details). Unfortunately, in the real world, classroom experimenters will usually find themselves funding their experiments out of very restricted budgets (or, indeed, their own pockets; the same arguments apply to projects run by students, but to an even greater degree). Although a certain amount of expenditure of this sort might be considered worthwhile on the basis that it both provides potentially useful pilot data and is a valuable teaching tool, ways of minimizing one's expenditure as an experimenter are, we are sure, to be welcomed. We will therefore now briefly provide some suggestions regarding this aspect of classroom experimentation.

In some cases it may be possible to get good results without any cost at all to the experimenter. For example, we have managed to obtain significant effects of framing, mental accounting, time discounting, and satiation, as well as sizable (and statistically significant) reversals of preference, money illusions, overconfidence, sunk costs, and certainty effects, using purely hypothetical situations. Although the use or otherwise of hypothetical rather than real situations is a hotly debated issue in its own right (e.g., Roth 1995) that we do not wish to get involved in here, we suggest that as far as the classroom experiment goes, the use of hypothetical situations is perfectly justifiable if it is solely for demonstration purposes. However, one would be advised to stick to phenomena with relatively large and frequently replicated effects, such as those listed above.

In other instances, products used or the amount of financial incentive given can be fairly small and still produce significant effects. For example, strong endowment effects have been obtained with inexpensive products such as chocolate bars and coffee mugs, while small sums of money can be sufficient to produce the expected results in experimental games such as the ultimatum bargaining game. Where larger inducements are required—for instance, where effects might be quite small—then alternative procedures exist. A common technique is to use some random allocation of a subset of the participants to the prizes: this may be done by giving participants raffle tickets as payment, or by selecting one or more winners of a prize by drawing from a hat (a variation on this latter procedure is that these winners are then rewarded on the basis of performance on the experimental task). To give a couple of specific examples: one of the authors has had a student endow participants with ten raffle tickets each to win a (relatively) expensive product A, and later give them the chance to swap some or all of their tickets for raffle tickets for a chance to win an equally expensive product B. At the end of the experiment, all tickets are put into a hat and two tickets are drawn, one for each product. The winners are notified by e-mail. The number of tickets retained for product A (or B; whichever is selected is arbitrary) is a measure of the endowment effect and, as a measure, has the advantage over the frequencies obtained by the usual swapping method (see above) in terms of the range and power of statistical analyses that can be applied. It also has an advantage over the random price mechanism (see below) in terms of transparency to the participant (it also seems to work, but it should be noted that there may be some disadvantages, for instance, in the interpretation of the phenomenon that is being measured by this procedure, i.e., is it really the endowment effect?). Another example is that of the ultimatum bargaining game. Here one of us has randomly allocated students to roles, paired them up, then asked them to make their allocations with the understanding that one of the pairs would be selected, also at random, to make the transaction for real.

An alternative approach that can be used in experiments with multiple trials—such as an iterated prisoner's dilemma or market entry game—is to pick one or more trials at random and allocate the rewards according to performance on that particular trial. Thus in an iterated ultimatum bargaining game with six trials, one of the trials can be chosen to be played for real using dice. If in the selected trial the proposer had offered only 10 percent of the stake and the receiver had refused this proposal, then neither player would receive any money (even if proposals had been accepted in all the other five trials).

Both these procedures are variations on what is known as the random lottery incentive scheme. Although there are some who argue against the use of such schemes (e.g., Holt 1986), these criticisms can be largely ignored if one is simply running an experiment for pedagogical reasons. There are also good counterarguments to the criticisms (see Cubitt, Starmer, and Sugden 1998), and since this procedure is rather widespread in the literature, a paper almost certainly would not be barred from publication for employing it.

A further way of minimizing costs is by having a small sample size. In classroom experiments one usually has little control over sample size, and often the size is not optimal (i.e., either too big or too small) for one's purposes, an issue we will come to in a moment. In the United Kingdom at least, classroom experiments in economic psychology or behavioral economics will most commonly be conducted with undergraduates in their final year or with postgraduates. In either case, the classes will be rather small, and it will be not expense so much as experimental power that will be the greatest and most common problem. When sample sizes are small, power can be increased by using repeated-measures designs. In the extreme, taking a large number of measurements (or fewer but very rich measurements) from participants can allow the sample size to be reduced to one, as in psychophysical experiments (or in case studies). It follows, then, that where one does have control over sample size but one's budget is tight, expense may be kept down by using a small number of participants in a repeated-measures design.

Repeated-measures designs cannot, however, always be used because of learning and other carryover effects, or contamination, from one condition to another. As a specific example, let us consider an experiment to test whether choosing the product one wishes to be endowed with leads to a stronger endowment effect than when one is given no choice, but that this only works when the products are evaluated under IPM, not ACM (note that this is a hypothesis constructed for illustrative purposes only). This proposal could be operationalized by presenting participants with two products, getting judges to evaluate these products under either IPM or ACM (see above), then either giving them one of the products at random or allowing them to choose which one to keep. It is obviously going to be difficult to manipulate choice versus no choice within subjects, as the expectations from the first trial are going to be carried over to the second trial (i.e., the expectation being that if one chooses a product the first time one will choose again the second time, and so on; if one attempts to dispel these expectations through instructions, then the participants may be disgruntled), and these expectations may interfere with the evaluation (processing) of the second pair of products. In contrast, there is no particular reason to believe that the type of processing evoked in the first trial will be carried over to the second trial (as we have already seen, the effects of the processing manipulation appear rather short-lived), so this could potentially be manipulated within subjects. However, even if one believes that there should not be any carryover effects in one's experiment, it is necessary to counterbalance the order of presentation of the within-subjects conditions (in the above example, half the participants should be asked to evaluate the products analytically first and holistically second, the other half holistically first and analytically second). One can then check that there is no difference between the two orderings to ensure no (or negligible) carryover effects.

One problem with providing incentives in classroom experiments that one probably would not anticipate is that student participants can be reluctant to accept the prizes or sums of money offered, or to take them seriously. This can occur for at least three reasons. First, incentives that are very small might be rejected purely on the basis that they are too trivial. Second, and more commonly, incentives are rejected because they are perceived as both too trivial to receive individually and rather costly to the experimenter in the aggregate (there can also be an element of embarrassment about receiving "gifts" from the teacher). Third, if the prizes or monetary amounts are rather large, then there may be disbelief that they will actually be awarded. Obviously there is a problem if incentives are not wanted in some way or are disbelieved, because then they are not really acting as incentives. If one is intending to run a series of experiments with the same class, then one can "train" students in the acceptance of incentives. The first class where incentives are used is therefore something of a loss leader: the students get used to the idea of incentives being awarded, with the data collected being of little use. Henceforth there should be no significant problems so long as the experimenter is conscientious about giving out the rewards as stated, even if they are protested against by the recipients. Conscientiousness on the part of the experimenter is very important in order to build trust and positive reputational effects, an issue we will return to later. It should additionally be noted that some rewards are more acceptable to students than others, with chocolate bars being a generally safe bet in terms of acceptability (although there will always be someone who is not that interested in chocolate; a savory snack such as potato chips can be used as a complementary alternative, and the two together will generally cater to everyone's tastes).

A last brief comment on monetary incentives is that there may also be religious or cultural objections to their use, so some care should be taken if one is conducting experiments in a country of which one is not a native, or with culturally heterogeneous participants. For example, many Muslims find gambling unacceptable, so using monetary payoffs in experimental setups that may be interpreted as gambling situations (as is the case with many tests of economic axioms) may not be possible in Islamic countries or where there are a number of Muslim students in the class unless these tasks are heavily disguised.

Random Price Mechanism

An important methodological issue is how to elicit true preferences, or prices, from participants. This is related to the issue of incentives in that highly motivated and involved participants are likely to try to respond as accurately as possible; however, there are some other factors that also influence the reliability and validity of participants' responses. There is not the space here to discuss all the arguments regarding the obstacles to eliciting true preferences or all the means that have been devised to try to overcome these obstacles (see Bateman et al. 1997 for a discussion and comparison of several different elicitation techniques). Rather, we shall focus our attention on one procedure—the random price mechanism (Becker, DeGroot, and Marschak 1964)—that we have used frequently in our classroom experiments (and is therefore mentioned in several places above). When attempting to elicit prices—for instance, WTP and WTA—there may be a number of reasons participants may not give their true prices. The most serious of these reasons would be that the participants do not actually have a single true price to state, but, assuming for pragmatic reasons that they do, they may reasonably wish to reduce their WTP to a minimum that they think they can get away with, while similarly attempting to maximize their WTA. The random price mechanism essentially seeks to punish people who do not state their best price by potentially making them pay more than their true WTP or receive less than their true WTA. This is usually done by informing participants that a price (within a set range) will be drawn at random. If this random price is smaller than participants' stated WTP or greater than their WTA, then they pay (receive) the random price; otherwise they pay (receive) their stated price. If we take WTP as an example, imagine the quoted price range of a good is between 1 and 11. If one's true WTP is 6 but one states the minimum price of 1, then there is a high likelihood that the random price will be greater than one's stated price (thus one will have to pay it) and an even chance that it will be greater than one's true WTP. With the random price mechanism, there is thus a disincentive to state prices that are different from one's true price, for if one does, one stands a chance of paying more than one would ideally like to obtain a product or receiving less than one ideally wants in order to part with a product. A variation of the random price mechanism used for the endowment effect involves swapping an endowed product for money or trading potential ownership of a product for a sum of money. In this case, if one does not state one's true price, then one may end up parting with the product for too little money or "buying" it for too much.

This is all very well, but the random price mechanism can be difficult to administer in practice, particularly within the constraints of the classroom experiment. One problem is that by giving a range of values one provides an anchor for an estimation of the "objective" value of the product (i.e., the price one could obtain it for in the store). Thus in the above example, participants might be drawn toward the price of 6, the midpoint of the range provided. Another problem that some of us have experienced is that logic of the procedure can be difficult to explain to participants, and if they do not understand it fully, then the procedure is unlikely to achieve its desired effects. This problem can be alleviated by careful wording of the instructions, examples, and practice trials, but all this can be rather time-consuming: in general, it is a good idea to pilot any instructions and other materials with a similar group of participants, if at all practicable, in order to ensure as smooth a running of the classroom experiment as possible. A rather more mundane problem with the random price mechanism is that if one has to do the draw individually for many participants, it can also be very time-consuming: a solution to this is to select one student to draw the random price and apply it to everyone. A third, even more mundane problem, but real nonetheless, is that with the random price mechanism the experimenter is never sure how much he or she will have to pay out. This means one has to prepare for the worst in terms of the amount of money to hand out (and goods, if appropriate). This also applies to many other random lottery incentive schemes. The obvious solution to this problem would be to rig the random lottery, but we strongly advise against doing that (see the section on use of deception below).

Sample Size

Returning to the issue of sample size, if sample sizes are small, then there will be a number of experiments that simply are not possible. For example, some effects are fairly small and will only reliably show up in large samples (e.g., some of the effects of dual processes; see above). In other cases, data might be such that one needs lots of observations to reveal even moderate effects, as is the case, for example, with frequencies and much categorical (or nominal) data (i.e., one does not get much out of each participant, and the methods of analysis available are not very sensitive). Further, as already mentioned, complex experimental designs with several different conditions will obviously not be possible with small sample sizes, so it would not be possible to answer certain research questions.

Although big sample sizes are desirable from the viewpoint of experimental power, they also can be problematic to the classroom experimenter in logistic terms. In particular, a large class may be difficult to manage without assistance. For example, if the class has to be split up into two or more experimental groups requiring separate instructions, then this will be difficult to do unless one has help (although not necessarily impossible). Separate rooms might also be required if there are experimental manipulations that cannot be conducted on paper (e.g., a mood manipulation using film or music).

If one is attempting to run a study single-handed, then a questionnaire might be the best bet for a large group, although this is not totally without difficulties either. For example, if one has a class of more than a hundred, then it can take quite a few minutes to distribute a questionnaire. Our experience therefore suggests that one should not permit students to start answering the questionnaire as soon as they receive it because the first students to receive the survey may well have finished before the last students to receive it have even started. As a general rule, it is not good to have large numbers of students idle while others are busy, as it will be difficult to keep noise levels down and/or participants become bored and unmotivated. It can also be difficult to regain control of the class after the questionnaire is completed if many people are talking. One strategy to deal with this problem is to allow students to leave as soon as they have finished (and possibly reconvene later), although this too creates a disturbance and tends to reward those who are least diligent in their responses. Another strategy is simply to make sure that one provides enough tasks to keep everyone occupied during the available time, but with the least important tasks toward the end.

Another common problem with classroom experiments, and one that is exacerbated by large sample sizes, is the provision of feedback about the results. For pedagogical reasons it is desirable to get the results back as soon as possible; ideally the feedback should be given within the session where the data is collected. Three ways of dealing with this are to have an assistant calculate some preliminary results while one is doing something else with the students, calculate the results oneself during a break, and get the students themselves to calculate the results. In each case the calculations should be fairly simple (i.e., not require sophisticated analyses), for example, mean prices or counts of number of exchanges. Getting the students themselves to do some analysis can be a good ploy, as in addition to speeding things up and reducing one's workload it can help the students gain insight into the experiment. An alternative to doing the analysis on the spot is to do the classroom experiment some time in advance of the lecture when one wishes to make use of the results. This is obviously a less desirable option, since it reduces immediacy and continuity, but it may be necessary if some complex analysis is required; if the delay between data collection and feedback is fairly short (no more than a week), then any undesirable effects should not be great. An additional strategy for providing feedback is to do so via a Web page. This way detailed information about the rationale for the classroom experiment, the procedure, the results, and their interpretation can be provided. We recommend, where possible, providing rough results on the spot and then more detailed feedback on the Web as soon as possible thereafter.

One way of running complex classroom experiments single-handedly is to use computers. Networks of computers that can be used for teaching purposes are common today, and software for running experiments is widely available (e.g., ELSE G4 software for running experimental games [Tomlinson 2002]; the downloadable software package z-Tree from the Institute for Empirical Research in Economics, University of Zürich; the experiments available at http://veconlab.econ.virginia.edu/admin.htm). Computers can be made to do the hard work of coordinating the activities of many students simultaneously, collecting their responses, analyzing them, and providing rapid feedback. For example, computers are ideal for running experiments with repeated trials of varying types such as a market entry game with different market capacities varied randomly over trials. Computers are not, however, a panacea. First, it can take a great deal of effort to program the experiment: even with good software a number of iterations of development will be required, and there is also the time required to learn the software. Second, in our experience, computers and their software have an uncanny knack for failing at crucial moments, so a good amount of piloting is recommended. Third, there will be a limited number of machines in a classroom, which rules out most large classes unless students double up (which creates its own problems). Fourth, computer labs may not be the most conducive places for doing whatever else one wants to do with students, such as give a lecture or do group work.

Deception

We started this discussion of methodological issues in classroom experiments by examining one way in which psychologists and economists differ with regard to experimentation: the use of incentives. To conclude this section we want to briefly discuss another major methodological difference between the experiments of psychologists and economists, the use of deception. Economists are very strongly against the use of deception (see, e.g., Ortmann and Hertwig 1997), whereas psychologists, especially social psychologists, regard deception as an essential tool for the investigation of certain research questions (e.g., Baron 2001; Davis and Durham 2001; Goodie 2001; Hilton 2001). The economists argue that the use of deception leads to a breakdown in trust between experimenters and participants, which produces undesirable reputational effects for researchers. In other words, once participants learn that they are likely to be deceived by researchers, they no longer trust them: this results in, at best, attempts to divine the "true purpose" of the experiment, which can lead to an increase in error variance, a deliberate lack of cooperation, or even sabotage, which can destroy the validity of experimental findings. Psychologists' response to this is that deception of some sort is often necessary in order to conceal the true nature of the experiment and remove compliance and demand effects; they argue that the negative reputational effects can be removed by a thorough debriefing. As is the case with the use of incentives in experiments, the "truth" about the effects of the use of deception is far from clear. For one thing, there are several degrees of deception: is deception by omission to be regarded as negatively as deception by commission? If so, we would always have to inform our participants of our experimental hypotheses, which we doubt is what most economists have in mind (and see, e.g., McDaniel and Starmer 1989; Hey 1989). Also, the effects of deception are likely to be different for different people. Psychology students, for instance, tend to become poor participants as a result of cynicism arising out of overexposure to psychologists' methods, including deception. Other groups who may act as participants rather infrequently may well never learn to mistrust researchers. Returning to classroom experiments, if one makes experimentation a regular feature of one's class, then one's student participants are going to be very susceptible to reputational effects, so it is particularly important that one does not use deception. In addition, one should ensure that one's reputation as an experimenter is spotless in other respects too, for instance, promptly providing promised incentives and/or feedback.

CONCLUSION

We have presented our experiments as behavioral economic experiments. This implies that the behavior of the participants may be, and frequently is, different from what standard economic theory would predict. This comes as no surprise to psychologists and sociologists, as well as people from marketing and many other disciplines. However, to a number of economists the results of our experiments may be unacceptable for several reasons.

Since we considered classroom experiments, the behavior of participants was less under control than in economic laboratories. Hence the results may be influenced by random error, type of participants, social influences, and systematic error due to classroom settings, logistic difficulties, and lack of attention, among other things. Rather than viewing the lack of control as a disadvantage, we believe that the results indicate the robustness of the phenomena studied. Stated differently, when standard economic theory is considered the null hypothesis in our experiments, we believe that we make a correct decision by rejecting it.

Other reasons for rejecting results from economic classroom experiments are similar to those that have been mentioned in relation to behavioral economic research in general (Thaler 1986):

- The use of small incentives in experiments (however, see our discussion on incentives above).
- Negligibility of heterogeneous preferences in aggregate predictions (Musgrave 1981). However, many aggregate predictions, seem to be false and heterogeneous preferences may be systematically related to personal characteristics and contextual circumstances.
- Negligibility of unstable preferences in long-run predictions. However, unstable preferences may also be systematic (e.g., in the case of hyperbolic discounting).
- In practice, learning may lead to more rational behavior than in one-shot experiments. However, experiments on melioration (Herrnstein and Prelec 1991) and overconfidence (Fischhoff, Slovic, and Lichtenstein 1977; Barber and Odean 2000) show that learning may not prevent anomalous behavior. Furthermore, in many practical situations learning opportunities are absent.
- In practice, irrational behavior is weeded out because of arbitrage and competition. However, markets do not always eliminate error (see, for example, Odean 1998 on loss aversion in financial markets).

We believe that the standard economic model should not be abandoned but needs to be adapted by including insights from behavioral experiments. In this respect we agree with Thaler, who offered two false statements: "1. Rational models are useless. 2. All behavior is rational" (1986, S283).

NOTES

1. Such effects may also occur when the same class is divided into groups. One of the authors has run a classroom experiment on donations to charity organizations, several of which were introduced briefly in class. The class was divided into those sitting in the front and those sitting in the back. The two groups were given different anchors for their donations. The front group was given a high anchor by being asked: "Would you donate more or less than 10 euros?" The back group was given a low anchor (1 euro). Then all students donated money. Although we hypothesized that the high-anchored students would give more than the low-anchored students, the reverse result was obtained. Why? In the discussion afterward, it turned out that the front group consisted mostly of foreign students who were not familiar with the charity organizations mentioned in the introduction. For this reason, they donated less.

2. This variation was suggested by Daniel Read, who was also involved in carrying out the experiment.

3. Together with Alessandra Arcuri.

4. Formally, this is not a test of the endowment effect since nothing had to be given up in order to acquire something.

5. We thank Tjeerd van den Berg for computing the results of this experiment.

REFERENCES

Ahlbrecht, M., and M. Weber. 1995. "Hyperbolic Discounting Models in Prescriptive Theory of Intertemporal Choice." *Zeitschrift für Wirtschafts- und Sozialwissenschaften* 115: 535–68.

Anderhub, V., R. Müller, and C. Schmidt. 2001. "Design and Evaluation of an Economic Experiment via the Internet." Merit-Infonomics Research Memorandum Series, Maastricht, the Netherlands.

Antonides, G., and S.R. Wunderink. 2001. "Time Preference and Willingness to Pay for an Energy-Saving Durable Good." *Zeitschrift für Sozialpsychologie* 32, 3: 133–41.

Barber, B.M., and T. Odean. 2000. "Trading Is Hazardous to Your Wealth: The Common Stock Investment Performance of Individual Investors." *Journal of Finance* 55: 773–806.

Baron, J. 2001. "Purposes and Methods." *Behavioral and Brain Sciences* 24: 403.

Bateman, I., A. Monroe, B. Rhodes, C. Starmer, and R. Sugden. 1997. "A Test of the Theory of Reference-Dependent Preferences." *Quarterly Journal of Economics* 112: 479–505.

Bazerman, M. 1998. *Judgment in Managerial Decision Making.* New York: John Wiley.

Becker, G.M., M.H. DeGroot, and J. Marschak. 1964. "Measuring Utility by a Single-Response Sequential Method." *Behavioral Science* 9: 226–32.

Belk, R.W. 1974. "An Exploratory Assessment of Situational Effects in Buyer Behavior." *Journal of Marketing Research* 11: 156–63.

Bergstrom, T.C., and J.H. Miller. 1999. *Experiments with Economic Principles.* New York: McGraw-Hill.

Binmore, K. 1987. "Experimental Economics." *European Economic Review* 31: 257–64.

Camerer, C.F., and R.M. Hogarth. 1999. "The Effects of Financial Incentives in Experiments: A Review and Capital-Labor-Production Framework." *Journal of Risk and Uncertainty* 19: 7–42.

Chaiken, S., and Y. Trope. 1999. *Dual Process Theories in Social Psychology.* New York: Guilford Press.

Chamberlin, E.H. 1948. "An Experimental Imperfect Market." *Journal of Political Economy* 56, 2: 95–108.

Chapman, G.B. 1998. "Similarity and Reluctance to Trade." *Journal of Behavioral Decision Making* 11: 47–58.

Charness, G., and M. Rabin. 2002. "Understanding Social Preferences with Simple Tests." *Quarterly Journal of Economics* 117: 817–69.

Christensen-Szalanski, J.J.J. 1984. "Discount Functions and the Measurement of Patients' Values: Women's Decisions During Childbirth." *Medical Decision Making* 4: 48–57.

Coase, R.H. 1960. "The Problem of Social Cost." *Journal of Law and Economics* 3: 1–44.

Cooper, J., and R.H. Fazio. 1984. "A New Look at Dissonance Theory." In L. Berkowitz, ed., *Advances in Experimental Social Psychology* 17:229–66. New York: Academic Press.

Cubitt, R.P., C. Starmer, and R. Sugden. 1998. "On the Validity of the Random Lottery Incentive System." *Experimental Economics* 1: 115–31.

Davis, H.P., and R.L. Durham. 2001. "Economic and Psychological Experimental Methodology: Separating the Wheat from the Chaff." *Behavioral and Brain Sciences* 24: 405–6.

Dawes, R.M. 1980. "Social Dilemmas." *Annual Review of Psychology* 31: 169–93.

DeGroot, I.M. 2003. "Product Trials: The Effects of Direct Experience on Product Evaluation." Ph.D. thesis, Tilburg University.

Denes-Raj, V., and S. Epstein. 1994. "Conflict Between Intuitive and Rational Processing: When People Behave Against Their Better Judgment." *Journal of Personality and Social Psychology* 66: 819–29.

DeYoung, R. 1993. "Market Experiments: The Laboratory Versus the Classroom." *Journal of Economic Education* 24: 335–51.

Dhar, R., and K. Wertenbroch. 2000. "Consumer Choice Between Hedonic and Utilitarian Goods." *Journal of Marketing Research* 37: 60–71.

Epstein, S. 1973. "The Self-Concept Revisited, or a Theory of a Theory." *American Psychologist* 28: 404–16.

Fels, R. 1993. "This Is What I Do, and I Like It." *Journal of Economic Education* 24: 365–70.

Festinger, L. 1957. *A Theory of Cognitive Dissonance.* Evanston, IL: Row, Peterson.

Fischhoff, B., P. Slovic, and S. Lichtenstein. 1977. "Knowing with Certainty: The Appropriateness of Extreme Confidence." *Journal of Experimental Psychology: Human Perception and Performance* 3: 552–64.

Fishburn, P.C., and A. Rubinstein. 1982. "Time Preference." *International Economic Review* 23: 677–94.

Foa, U.G. 1971. "Interpersonal and Economic Resources." *Science* 171: 345–51.

Frank, R.H., T. Gilovich, and D.T. Regan. 1993. "Does Studying Economics Inhibit Cooperation?" *Journal of Economic Perspectives* 7: 159–71.

Gattig, A. 2002. "Intertemporal Decision Making: Studies on the Working of Myopia." Ph.D. thesis, University of Groningen, the Netherlands.

Goodie, A.S. 2001. "Are Scripts or Deception Necessary When Repeated Trials Are Used? On the Social Context of Psychological Experiments." *Behavioral and Brain Sciences* 24: 412.

Hanemann, W.M. 1991. "Willingness to Pay and Willingness to Accept: How Much Can They Differ?" *American Economic Review* 81: 635–47.

Herrnstein, R.J., and D. Prelec. 1999. "Melioration: A Theory of Distributed Choice." *Journal of Economic Perspectives* 5: 137–56.

Hertwig, R., and A. Ortmann. 2001. "Experimental Practices in Economics: A Methodological Challenge for Psychologists." *Behavioral and Brain Sciences* 24: 383–451.

Hey, J. D. 1998. "Experimental Economics and Deception: A Comment." *Journal of Economic Psychology* 19: 397–401.

Hilton, D.J. 2001. "Is the Challenge for Psychologists to Return to Behaviorism?" *Behavioral and Brain Sciences* 24: 415–16.

Hirschman, E.C., and M.B. Holbrook. 1982. "Hedonic Consumption: Emerging Concepts, Methods and Propositions." *Journal of Marketing* 46: 92–101.

Hofstaedter, D. 1983. "Metamagical Themas." *Scientific American* 248: 14–28.

Holt, C.A. 1986. "Preference Reversals and the Independence Axiom." *American Economic Review* 76: 508–15.

———. 1996. "Trading in a Pit Market." *Journal of Economic Perspectives* 10: 193–203.

Hsee, C.K. 1996. "The Evaluability Hypothesis: An Explanation for Preference Reversals Between Joint and Separate Evaluations of Alternatives." *Organizational Behavior and Human Decision Processes* 67: 247–57.

Johnson, E.J., J. Hershey, J. Meszaros, and H. Kunreuther. 1993. "Framing, Probability Distortions, and Insurance Decisions." *Journal of Risk and Uncertainty* 7: 35–51.

Kagel, J.H., and A.E. Roth. 1995. *Handbook of Experimental Economics.* Princeton, NJ: Princeton University Press.

Kahneman, Daniel. 2003a. "A Psychological Perspective on Economics." *American Economic Review* 93: 162–68.

———. 2003b. "Maps of Bounded Rationality: Psychology for Behavioral Economics." *American Economic Review* 93: 1449–75.

Kahneman, D., J.L. Knetsch, and R.H. Thaler. 1990. "Experimental Tests of the Endowment Effect and the Coase Theorem." *Journal of Political Economy* 98: 1325–48.

Kahneman, D., and A. Tversky. 1979. "Prospect Theory: Analysis of Decisions Under Risk." *Econometrica* 47: 263–91.

———. 1992. "Advances in Prospect Theory: Cumulative Representation of Uncertainty." *Journal of Risk and Uncertainty* 5: 297–324.

Knetsch, J.L. 1989. "The Endowment Effect and Evidence of Nonreversibility of Indifference Curves." *American Economic Review* 79: 1277–84.

———. 1995. "Asymmetric Valuation of Gains and Losses and Preference Order Assumptions." *Economic Inquiry* 33: 134–41.

Knetsch, J.L., and J.A. Sinden. 1984. "Willingness to Pay and Compensation Demanded: Experimental Evidence of an Unexpected Disparity in Measures of Value." *Quarterly Journal of Economics* 99: 507–21.

Levin, I.P., and G.J. Gaeth. 1988. "How Consumers Are Affected by the Framing of Attribute Information Before and After Consuming the Product." *Journal of Consumer Research* 15: 374–78.

Loewenstein, G. 1999. "Experimental Economics from the Vantage Point of Behavioral Economics." *The Economic Journal* 109: F25–34.

Loewenstein, G., and D. Prelec. 1992. "Anomalies in Intertemporal Choice: Evidence and an Interpretation." *Quarterly Journal of Economics* 107: 573–97.

Lutz, R.J., and P. Kakkar. 1975. "The Psychological Situation as a Determinant of Consumer Behavior." *Advances in Consumer Research* 1: 439–53.

McDaniel, T., and C. Starmer. 1998. "Experimental Economics and Deception: A Comment." *Journal of Economic Psychology* 19: 403–9.

Mitchell, A.A. 1981. "The Dimensions of Advertising Involvement." In K.B. Monroe, ed., *Advances in Consumer Research*, 25–35. Ann Arbor, MI: Association for Consumer Research.

Mittal, B. 1988. "The Role of Affective Choice Mode in the Consumer Purchase of Expressive Products." *Journal of Economic Psychology* 9: 499–524.

———. 1994. "A Study of the Concept of Affective Choice Mode for Consumer Decisions." *Advances in Consumer Research* 21: 256–62.

Musgrave, A. 1981. "Unreal Assumptions in Economic Theory: The F-Twist Untwisted." *Kyklos* 34: 377–87.

Odean, T. 1998. "Are Investors Reluctant to Realize Their Losses?" *Journal of Finance* 53: 1775–98.

Orne, M.T., and K.E. Scheibe. 1964. "The Contribution of Nondeprivation Factors in the Production of Sensory Deprivation Effects: The Psychology of the Panic Button." *Journal of Abnormal and Social Psychology* 68: 3–12.

Ortmann, A., and R. Hertwig. 1997. "Is Deception Acceptable?" *American Psychologist,* July, 746–47.

Park, C. W., and B. Mittal. 1985. "A Theory of Involvement in Consumer Behavior: Problems and Issues." In J.N. Sheth, ed., *Research in Consumer Behavior,* 1:201–31. Greenwich, CT: JAI Press.

Purohit, D. 1995. "Playing the Role of Buyer and Seller: The Mental Accounting of Trade-ins." *Marketing Letters* 6: 101–10.

Rakow, T. 2001. "Theorize It Both Ways?" *Behavioral and Brain Sciences* 24: 425–26.

Read, D., and B. Van Leeuwen. 1998. "Predicting Hunger: The Effects of Appetite and Delay on Choice." *Organizational Behavior and Human Decision Processes* 76: 189–205.

Roth, A.E. 1995. "Introduction to Experimental Economics." In J.H. Kagel and A.E. Roth, eds., *The Handbook of Experimental Economics.* Princeton, NJ: Princeton University Press.

———. 2001. "Form and Function in Experimental Design." *Behavioral and Brain Sciences* 24: 427–28.

Samuelson, W., and R. Zeckhauser. 1988. "Status Quo Bias in Decision Making." *Journal of Risk and Uncertainty* 1: 7–59.

Scott, W.A. 1957. "Attitude Change Through Reward of Verbal Behavior." *Journal of Abnormal and Social Psychology* 55: 72–75.

Shefrin, H.M., and M. Statman. 1985. "The Disposition to Sell Winners Too Early and Ride Losers Too Long." *Journal of Finance* 40: 777–90.

Sloman, S.A. 1996. "The Empirical Case for Two Systems of Reasoning." *Psychological Bulletin* 119: 3–22.

Smith, V.L. 1962. "An Experimental Study of Competitive Market Behavior." *Journal of Political Economy* 70, 2: 111–37.

Strahilevitz, M., and G. Loewenstein. 1998. "The Effects of Ownership History on the Valuation of Objects." *Journal of Consumer Research* 25: 276–89.

Thaler, R.H. 1980. "Toward a Positive Theory of Consumer Choice." *Journal of Economic Behavior and Organization* 1: 39–60.

———. 1981. "Some Empirical Evidence on Dynamic Inconsistency." *Economics Letters* 8: 201–7.

———. 1986. "The Psychology and Economics Handbook: Comments on Simon, on Einhorn and Hogarth, and on Tversky and Kahneman." *Journal of Business* 59, 4: S279–84.

Tomlinson, C.D. 2002. "Specification for the 4th Generation of ELSE Experimental Software." ESRC ELSE Centre Internal Report, University College, London.

Tversky, A., and D. Kahneman. 1991. "Loss Aversion in Riskless Choice: A Reference Dependent Model." *Quarterly Journal of Economics* 106: 1039–61.

Van Dijk, E., and D. Van Knippenberg. 1996. "Buying and Selling Exchange Goods: Loss Aversion and the Endowment Effect." *Journal of Economic Psychology* 17: 517–24.

Varian, H.R. 2002. "Observe, Theorize, Measure, Test and Don't Overlook What Goes Wrong: Nobel Experiments." *New York Times,* October 24.

CHAPTER 20

A BEHAVIORAL APPROACH TO DISTRIBUTION AND BARGAINING

WERNER GÜTH AND ANDREAS ORTMANN

Canonical game theory (as codified in textbooks such as Kreps 1990a, 1990b and Mas-Colell, Whinston, and Green 1995) requires unlimited cognitive and information-processing capabilities. It is obvious that these requirements are at odds with what humans are equipped with or typically have at their disposal.[1] Cowan (2001), updating the message of a famous paper by Miller (1956), has summarized the available evidence and argues that people can remember on average about four chunks of information. Given such cognitive capacity constraints, only a very small set of games can be analyzed ("solved") in accordance with canonical game theory by real people.

Canonical game theory's solution concepts for a given class of games—for example, the class of finite games in normal form or extensive form—is largely based on invariance or covariance with respect to certain sets of transformations, and thus partitions the class of games into *equivalence classes*.[2] Two games from the same equivalence class are said to be strategically equivalent. Most solution concepts, for example, allow for positively affine utility transformations. Experimentally, one can try to induce such transformations by scaling up or down the monetary payoffs ("stakes") appropriately. These changes, which according to canonical game theory ought to be irrelevant, can nevertheless change participant behavior quite dramatically (e.g., Smith and Walker 1993; Hertwig and Ortmann 2001a, 2001b, 2003; see also Laury and Holt 2002 and Harrison et al. 2005 for studies that make a similar point regarding decision making).

Even if we do not transform a game at all but present (or frame) the same game differently, behavior may still react to the change (presentation/framing effects). Consider, for instance, the prisoner's dilemma game, played once or repeatedly, which has been a dominant paradigm of experimentation (Colman 1982, 1995) because it captures succinctly the possibility that individual rationality might contradict social welfare, at least for one-shot or finitely repeated games. This, of course, stands in sharp contradiction to Smith's famous dictum "It is not from the benevolence of the butcher, the brewer, or the baker, that we expect our dinner, but from their regard to their own interest" (Smith 1976, 22).

In the prisoner's dilemma game, if defection always leads to the same payoff advantage when compared to the cooperative strategy (i.e., regardless of what the other player chooses), one can decompose the same game in infinitely many ways by describing for each individual choice how much it grants to the other and how much the individual player assigns to himself. (Unlike a transformation, a decomposition does not change the game.) This leads to a one-parameter family of decomposed prisoner's dilemma games that do not question that the same prisoner's dilemma game is played. Nonetheless, average cooperation rates react quite dramatically to decomposition (Pruitt 1967).

For closely related public good provision problems, Andreoni (1995a) has demonstrated that their positive or negative framing can affect cooperation rates dramatically. Andreoni (1995b) has furthermore demonstrated, also for public good provision games, that what looks like kindness is often, and to a significant degree, subject confusion. McCabe, Smith, and LePore (2000) and Cooper and Van Huyck (2003), building on earlier results (e.g., Schotter, Weigelt, and Wilson 1994), have demonstrated for a variety of games that presenting a game in normal form or extensive form can make a significant difference.

Note that, strictly speaking, in an experiment a commonly known finite upper bound for the number of repetitions cannot be avoided and should be commonly known. If one accepts this reasoning, folk theorems do not apply, and pervasive mutual defection, induced by backward induction, is the solution proposed by canonical game theory (e.g., Mas-Colell, Whinston, and Green 1995 proposition 9.B.3) in repeated prisoner's dilemma games, and in fact in all kinds of social dilemma games such as public good provision or common pool exploitation problems.[3] The same result applies also to asymmetric games of the principal-agent or gift exchange variety (e.g., Fehr, Kirchsteiger, and Riedl 1998).

The robust results, however, of many experiments are that players *cooperate in most rounds,* even when the final round is known and does not have to be inferred, although they defect toward the end (e.g., Selten and Stöcker 1986). Since many participants try to avoid being preempted (meaning that their partner terminates cooperation earlier), they seem to be aware of the backward induction idea. Because of its detrimental consequences, however, they do not follow its recommendations but rather account for it only when the end of interaction is near. Not relying on canonical game theory can be a good idea.

Since folk theorems do not apply in games that are finitely repeated (in some commonly known way; see Neyman 1999), these results have posed quite a puzzle for game theorists and have inspired the innovative *reputation approach* (or "crazy perturbation"; see Kreps et al. 1982).[4] The basic idea is to allow for (a little) incomplete information concerning another player's type: in repeated prisoner's dilemma games he or she may be an unconditional cooperator (i.e., a bit "crazy"). In this way one can try to build up the impression (the other's posterior probability) of an unconditional cooperator. Furthermore, the a priori probability of the other person being "crazy," necessary to justify initial cooperation, can be small when the number of iterations is large.

Although the reputation approach has been rather successful (in the sense of inspiring a large literature), some qualitative aspects of reputation equilibria are supported only poorly, if at all, by experimental data (e.g. McKelvey and Palfrey 1992; Anderhub, Engelmann, and Güth 2002). These include the possibly gradual decline in the probability of cooperation, leading to certain defection in the last period (some participants, for instance, cooperate in the last round), and the specific mixing (the change of mixed strategies over time).

Nevertheless, reputation equilibria illustrate how canonical (game) theory can be enriched by paying attention to robust experimental findings. Reputation equilibria do not question rationality itself, only the idea that rationality is clearly expected in participants. Other applications concern trust, bargaining, and signaling games and, most of all, the classic paradigms of the industrial organization literature.

EXPERIMENTAL RESULTS IN DISTRIBUTION GAMES

Following decades of experimental research on prisoner's dilemma and public good provision problems (much of it done by psychologists, as documented in Colman 1982), in the early 1980s researchers became concerned with deceptively simple models of distribution. Just as in the earlier experiments on prisoner's dilemma and public good provision problems, the experimental results of these simple models of distribution stood in stark contrast to the predictions of canonical game theory, especially in those cases where the predicted distribution was considered unfair. One of these games, the so-called ultimatum game, "is beginning to upstage the PDG in the freak show of human irrationality" (Colman 2003, 147). It is probably no coincidence that this new workhorse of experimental research is a sequential (and asymmetric) game rather than a simultaneous (and symmetric) game.

In ultimatum experiments (Güth, Schmittberger, and Schwarze 1982; see Güth 1976 for an earlier discussion) a positive sum p of money, the "pie," can be distributed by first allowing the proposer to decide on his or her offer o with $0 \leq o \leq p$ to the responder, who can then either accept the offer o (so that the proposer gets $p - o$ and the responder o) or reject it (in which case both players get nothing).

The solution of canonical game theory (assuming that both players care only about their own monetary payoff) predicts that the proposer offers 0 (or the smallest positive monetary unit) and that the responder accepts all (positive) offers. Typical experimental findings (see Camerer 2003, chaps. 1 and 2, for a recent survey), however, are that responders reject even substantial positive offers o in the range $0 < o < p/2$, which they apparently regard as unfair, and proposers shy away from excessively low offers o; the most frequent (modal) offer is usually the equal split $o = p/2$.

These results are quite robust along a number of dimensions such as the financial incentives that subjects face and demographic variables such as gender, race, academic major, and age (Camerer 2003, chap. 2, especially Tables 2.3 and 2.2); they even seem robust across countries and cultures (see Roth et al. 1991, but see also Henrich et al. 2001, which documents exceptions claimed to be due to individual heterogeneity, noise, and culture-specific socialization; for a critique of the experimental procedures employed in that research, see Ortmann 2005). To justify the offer $o = p/2$ instead of $o = \varepsilon$ (with ε denoting the smallest positive unit of money), the proposer must be extremely risk-averse or the responder probably irrational or "crazy," e.g., in the sense of infinite inequity aversion.

A similar challenge, for experimentalists and theorists alike, is provided by the results of so-called dictator games, which were earlier and much more adequately studied in social psychology as reward allocation experiments guaranteeing entitlements (see Shapiro 1975; Mikula 1973). In dictator game experiments (e.g., Forsythe et al. 1994), a positive sum p of money, the "pie," can be distributed by allowing a dictator to decide on his or her offer o with $0 \leq o \leq p$ to the recipient. Here the recipient is just that. He or she cannot veto the proposer's allocation, effectively eliminating the strategic interaction of the ultimatum game. Strictly speaking, the dictator game is not a game.

The solution of canonical game theory for this allocation problem (assuming that the dictator cares only about his or her own monetary payoff) predicts that the dictator offers 0. Importantly, the outcome of canonical game theory for this allocation problem thus coincides with the prediction for the ultimatum game. Typical experimental findings (Camerer 2003, chap. 2, especially Table 2.4), however, find dictators making significant allocations in the range $0 < o < p/2$, although offers on average are clearly lower than in the ultimatum game. Specifically, the equal split $o = p/2$ is no longer the modal offer.

Allocations in the dictator game (as already indicated in Forsythe et al. 1994; see the pay versus no-pay conditions, or the different results elicited by the stakes) have been less robust. Two studies stand out. Hoffman, McCabe, and Smith (1996) studied how social distance (in the form of various anonymity conditions) affected allocation and found that social distance is inversely related to the generosity of offers. In a double-blind treatment meant to control for experimenter effects, the modal response coincided with the prediction of canonical game theory, with about 40 percent, however, still sharing some of the wealth that was bestowed on subjects through the experimenter. More recently, Cherry, Frykblom, and Shogren (2002) demonstrated that the very nature of the wealth—whether it was handed down as manna from heaven, as is typical for almost all (economic but not psychological reward allocation) experiments, or had to be earned—dramatically affects allocation. When wealth had to be earned, 80 to 95 percent of dictators—dependent on the degree of anonymity—followed the game-theoretic prediction. This is a remarkable result because the prediction of canonical game theory for the dictator game is a boundary point that does not allow for noise in the form of subject confusion. While with the benefit of hindsight (e.g., calling back into memory the results of Harrison and McCabe 1985, or Güth and Tietz 1986) this result is not that surprising, it is troubling given standard experimental practices. The key question is whether indeed, as Cherry, Frykblom, and Shogren (2002) claim, their procedure gives us more external validity than the one currently used. If indeed these authors' claim is true, then it would constitute a very damaging critique of the literature on dictator games as well as related literatures such as that on public good provision experiments (e.g., Ledyard 1995, on the verdict of which, regarding the alleged failure of hard-nosed game theory, Cherry, Frykblom, and Shogren 2002 seems to allude to with its title).

A related study for ultimatum games (List and Cherry 2000) was concerned with learning in low- and high-stakes environments and a critique of an earlier high-stakes ultimatum experiment (Slonim and Roth 1998). It did find a downward shift in offers compared to other studies in both conditions (but not nearly as much as the downward shift in dictator game). That seems to have been a rational decision of sorts on the part of proposers, as proportionally smaller offers were rejected more often than larger offers in both in the low- and high-stakes environment. A closer look at the design and implementation suggests that the nature of the earned income was not common knowledge. In fact, responders were simply told that proposers had "earned an amount of money by participating in a previous session." This description must have left open many questions in the responders' minds about how much proposers had to work for their wealth, doubts that proposers very likely anticipated to some extent. It would be interesting to see how the distributions of offers and rejections would shift if indeed the nature of the task—a quiz consisting of seventeen questions taken from the sample section of the Graduate Management Admissions Test—would be common knowledge. More fundamentally, entitlement in the proper sense would have to be based on contributions relevant to the role in the game, similar to the practice of reward allocation experiments. Güth and Tietz (1986) have tried to guarantee this by auctioning the positions in a game.

Apart from testing the robustness of aspects of the experimental design and implementation that according to canonical game theory should not play a role, researchers have also chosen to study related or richer game models hoping that their experimental results add to our understanding of the reasons why proposers usually offer rather fair shares and responders are unwilling to accept meager offers.

One can generalize, for example, the ultimatum game by assuming that nonacceptance of the offer o implies the conflict payoff $\rho\,(p-o)$ for the proposer and λo for the responder with $0 \leq \rho$, $\lambda \leq 1$. The ultimatum game corresponds to $\rho = 0$ and $\lambda = 0$, whereas $\rho = 1$ and $\lambda = 1$ represent dictatorship (the responder has lost all veto power). Similarly, one can study $\rho = 1$ and $\lambda = 0$, the so-called impunity game (for experimental studies of "corner-point games" see Bolton and Zwick 1995 as well as Güth and Huck 1997) but also "interior games" such as $0 < \rho = \lambda < 1$ (see

Suleiman 1996) or $0 < \rho = 1 - \lambda < 1$ (see Fellner and Güth 2003). One general conclusion from this research is that behavior strongly depends on how efficiently the responder can punish the proposer.

One can also combine aspects of ultimatum bargaining and dictatorship. If one includes, for instance, a dummy player in addition to the proposer and the responder, an ultimatum proposal would consist of two offers, o_R and o_D with $o_R, o_D \geq 0$ and $o_R + o_D \leq p$, meaning that the proposer offers o_R to the responder R and o_D to the dummy D and wants to keep $p - o_R - o_D$ and that rejection by R implies 0-profits for all (for experimental studies, see Güth and van Damme 1998; Brandstätter and Güth 2002; Güth, Schmidt, and Sutter forthcoming). The fact that (according to the results of Güth and van Damme 1998) o_D was usually much smaller than o_R and no rejection by R could be attributed to an embarrassingly low asymmetric o_D alone seems to suggest that neither proposers nor responders have a strong intrinsic concern for fairness (see also Bolton and Ockenfels 1998, which explains this by inequity aversion).

Another interesting twist on ultimatum bargaining and dictatorship has been provided by so-called trust experiments. The quickly exploding literature on the trust (or investment) game was initiated by Berg, Dickhaut, and McCabe (1995).[5] In the game (for an early discussion see Kreps 1990a) a proposer makes an initial investment that, on its way to a responder, gets multiplied by a factor greater than 1. The responder then decides how much of what he or she receives—this is the dictatorship aspect of the trust game—will be sent back to the sender (proposer). The prediction of canonical game theory is that the proposer—correctly anticipating that the responder would not return anything—would not invest a thing. The trust game thus predicts an extreme form of underinvestment due to the holdup problem (see Malcolmson 1997).

Experimental results, however, have shown significant investments and returns, with the modal investment being about half of the original endowment and the average return being about what has been invested (but not much more). This result has been shown to be rather robust under a variety of experimental manipulations (Ortmann, Fitzgerald, and Boeing 2000; see Camerer 2003, ch. 2, for a good review of that literature, revealing a striking heterogeneity of subject behavior, and Bolle and Kaehler 2003 for a methodological critique of parameter selection in trust games).

Very recently Cox (2004) has provided a fundamental critique of this research program by pointing out that trust (on the part of the proposer) and reciprocity (on the part of the responder) are not the only candidates for explanation of the fairly robust experimental results in trust games (and the theory developments these results have spawned). Let us define "other-regarding preferences" as preferences that are altruistic (e.g., Andreoni and Miller 2002), inequality-averse (Bolton and Ockenfels 2000; Fehr and Schmidt 1999), quasi-maximin (Charness and Rabin 2003), or maybe even malevolent (Kirchsteiger 1994). Then the behavior of the responder may be reciprocal (i.e., the responder may react to an investment of a proposer), or it may be altruistic, inequality-averse, or whatnot. Anticipating such responder motivations, a proposer may then invest an amount even if he or she has no other-regarding preferences whatsoever. Such investment behavior would reflect trust, or at least the rational expectation that on average other-regarding behavior of responders is likely not to make a reasonable amount of investment a losing proposition.[6] As a matter of fact, that seems about true (see, e.g., the review in Bolle and Kaehler 2003).

Using a triadic design (i.e., comparing giving behavior in the first stage of the trust game with that in a dictator game meant to control for unconditional other-regarding behavior of first movers, and comparing giving behavior in the second stage of the trust game with that in a dictator game meant to control for unconditional other-regarding behavior of second movers), Cox (2004) attempts to separate reciprocity from altruism or inequality aversion, and trust from altruism. He finds significant amounts of trusting behavior and reciprocating behavior but also significant amounts of altruism and/or inequality aversion. Regarding the first stage of the trust game, trust explains about 60 percent of the investment behavior that Cox finds in his study, while other-regarding behavior might explain the rest. Regarding the second stage of the trust game, reciprocity explains about 60 percent, with the rest possibly being explained by other-regarding behavior. Of course, given that the prediction of canonical game theory is a corner-point solution, other explanations (e.g., subject confusion, or curiosity of subjects about what happens if they invest small amounts) are possible.

The experimental results of the very elementary bargaining procedures captured by ultimatum bargaining and the trust game provoked a lively debate among game theorists as to whether or not canonical game theory is just a normative exercise that has little value in application. The simplicity of the tasks suggests that cognitive limitations are not the problem.[7] Putting aside legitimate questions about the implementation of experiments (e.g., the question of earned assets), it seems that the game-theoretic concept of subgame perfect equilibrium points is not descriptively satisfying. As in decision tasks, the question is whether rationality explains experimental behavior (at least by experienced participants) or whether canonical game theory has to be supplemented by a behavioral theory. A premier candidate for a satisfying explanation seems to be social preferences.[8] Such an explanatory strategy, however, poses the question of how such idiosyncratic other-regarding preferences can ever become commonly known (at least probabilistically).

EXPERIMENTAL RESULTS IN (ALTERNATING OFFER) BARGAINING GAMES

One typical reaction to striking experimental findings is to ask how the results would change when the theoretical and experimental setup is enriched. In the case of ultimatum bargaining, it has been argued that fairness may matter less when parties are not limited to only one negotiation round for reaching an agreement. The guiding model for this line of experimental research is that of alternating offer bargaining (e.g., Rubinstein, 1982). In odd rounds t player 1 offers and player 2 responds; in even rounds t the roles are reversed. Agreement is achieved if an offer is accepted. Otherwise one proceeds to the next round (except in the last round, when nonacceptance means conflict, implying zero payoff). Assume, for example, that T, the number of the last round, is a large odd integer (player 1 is the last proposer) and that the same pie p can be divided, regardless of the round $t = 1,...,T$ in which an agreement is achieved (the closest approximation seems to be Güth, Levati, and Maciejovsky 2005). The solution outcome is, of course, the same as in the case $T = 1$. In an experiment, however, participants might learn from unsuccessful offers in earlier periods $t < T$ how issues of fairness matter. Yet the usual assumption in experimental studies has been that delaying agreement is costly (i.e., there are risks posed by a shrinking pie).

There are now several experimental studies of alternating offer bargaining (see Roth 1995 for a survey) that vary the time preferences involved (for example, in the form of equal or unequal discount factors) and the horizon (the maximum number of rounds). The latter is, of course, finite, although one study (Felsenthal, Weg, and Rapoport 1990) tries to create an illusion of an infinite horizon. Other studies (Güth, Ockenfels, and Wendel 1993; Anderhub, Güth, and Marchand 2004) assume that every periodic proposer can declare his or her offer to be an ultimatum, and that the pie p is either increasing or decreasing or even varying nonmonotonically. As in a centipede experiment, both participants here may gain by trusting (i.e., by not terminating early). The explanation of the centipede results in terms of (expected) altruism (in the tradition of reputation equilibria; see McKelvey and Palfrey 1992) cannot account, for instance, for the increasing pie results.

More recently, Johnson, Camerer, Sen, and Rymon (2002) have provided us with an intriguing study that addresses both cognitive limitations and social preferences in insightful ways. The game that they study is a three-round bargaining game where the initial subgame perfect equilibrium offer was $1.25 and the equal split ("fair") solution was $2.50. The study is remarkable both for the various treatments that try to insulate the relative contributions of cognitive limitations and social preferences and for the technology used (Mouselab). This technology (which has recently also been used to study normal form games and depth of reasoning, e.g., Costa-Gomes, Crawford, and Broseta 2001) allows the researchers to track the patterns of information acquisition and then to make inferences about the thought process (e.g., to what extent and under what conditions subjects engage in backward induction). The authors study four treatments. The first is a baseline treatment meant to assure the reader that there is nothing about the subject pool of the implementation that is idiosyncratic. Indeed, in this baseline treatment offers average $2.11, with offers below $1.80 being rejected half the time. These results replicate earlier results. The Mouselab data make it very clear that subjects do not tackle the problem in a way that would please a game theorist (i.e., by thinking through the problem from the back). In the second treatment, the authors turn off social preferences and let subjects play against robots that they know are programmed in the way that would please a traditional game theorist. While average offers are lower ($1.84), they remained way off the prediction of canonical game theory, as did the frequent (especially in the first couple of rounds) rejections. In a third treatment, the authors taught their subjects about backward induction, which caused them to make offers to robots that essentially coincided with the prediction of canonical game theory. Of course, providing such commonly known behavior may have made it look like an indoctrination test. In a final treatment, Johnson and his colleagues let untrained and trained subjects fight it out, with this tug-of-war resulting in meeting roughly halfway.

Whereas the models underlying these experimental tests rely on asymmetric bargaining rules, among the symmetrical bargaining models the so-called demand game (Nash game) has received the most attention (Nash 1950, 1953). Here all parties simultaneously choose their demands, which are what they obtain whenever the vector of demands is feasible; otherwise they receive their conflict payoffs. An interesting study (Roth and Malouf 1979) applies the binary lottery technique when studying demand bargaining (allowing, however, for several rounds of simultaneous demands). Parties can earn individual positive monetary prizes and bargain only about the probability of winning their prize (with complementary probability, the other party wins its prize). What is varied systematically is the information available about the other's prize. When prize information is completely private, parties usually agree on equal winning probabilities. If both prizes are generally known, parties often choose winning probabilities that equate their monetary expectations. This, of course, contradicts the axiom of independence with respect to affine utility transformations.

Due to the usually large number of strict equilibria (all efficient vectors of demands exceeding conflict payoffs), participants in the demand game face an additional coordination problem that might justify introducing preplay communication or more strategic possibilities. The main findings are that the (Nash) bargaining solution maximizing the product of agreement dividends must be focal (e.g., as a corner point of a piecewise linear utility frontier) to be selected and that the (Nash) axioms, although normatively convincing, are behaviorally questionable. Experimentally, the monotonicity axiom (Kalai and Smorodinsky 1975) is better supported.

CHARACTERISTIC FUNCTION EXPERIMENTS

Experimental game theory, like game theory, was dominated at first by characteristic function models. A characteristic function for a cooperative game describes for every nonempty subset—that is, coalition C of the player set $N = \{1, \ldots, n\}$ of, say market participants—the sum of profits of the members of C if side payments are possible. A good example for a coalition is a more or less complete cartel, for example, on a market.

It is not at all clear a priori how to implement a given characteristic function as an experiment (it is not, after all, a strategic game). The usual procedure is to permit free face-to-face communication and to let coalitions announce payoff agreements, which become binding if no coalition member withdraws within a certain number of minutes.

Given the usual heterogeneity in individuals' behavior, value concepts were rarely used, although they may become important in accounting experiments; among these, reward or cost allocation experiments (Mikula 1973; Shapiro 1975) may offer early but (too) simple precedents. But in most studies (see Sauermann 1978a, 1978b) the well-known set solutions, such as the core, internally stable, and externally stable (von Neumann and Morgenstern 1947) solution sets or the various bargaining sets, were tested, or new related concepts developed.

Robust results (see Selten and Uhlich 1988; Sauermann 1978a, 1978b) are that:

- Players in the same coalition obey the power structure (by granting a more powerful coalition member at least as much as a less powerful one).
- Equal payoff distributions are frequently proposed and often are used as counterproposals when trying to argue against a previous proposal.
- Coalitions smaller than the grand coalition are formed, even when they are inefficient.

Characteristic function experiments were performed not only by game theorists but also by (social) psychologists. A typical situation is to rely on majority voting games $(w_1, \ldots, w_n; m)$ where w_i with $0 \leq w_i \leq 1$ and $w_1 + \cdots + w_n = 1$ denotes the voting share of player $i = 1, \ldots, n$ and m with $\frac{1}{2} \leq m \leq 1$, mostly $m = .5$, the majority level which a winning coalition S with $\sum_{i \in S} w_i > m$ must obtain. The characteristic function $v(\cdot)$ allowing for side payments assumes $v(S) = 1$ if S is winning and $v(S) = 0$ otherwise. In case of $n = 3$, $m = .5$, and $w_1 = .49$, $w_2 = .39$, $w_3 = .12$, one has $v(\{i\}) = 0$ for $i = 1, 2, 3$, and $v(S) = 1$ for any coalition S with at least two members. Thus the power structure, as reflected by the winning coalitions, is completely symmetric despite the large differences in voting shares. In such a situation, experimentally observed payoff distributions are often influenced by both the power structure and the voting shares (see Komorita and Chertkoff 1973).

Due to the dominance of strategic models in the industrial organization literature, characteristic function experiments became a less popular research topic. Since strategic models seem to account for every possible result without any serious restrictions on what to assume (see the discussion of repairs, below), there may, however, be a revival of characteristic function experiments for special situations where cooperative solutions are informative, for example, in the sense of a small but nonempty core. The main advantage would be that such informative solutions do not depend on subtle strategic aspects that are behaviorally irrelevant but crucial for the noncooperative solution. An example is the sequential timing of moves in ultimatum bargaining, whose characteristic function is, however, symmetrical in the sense of $v(\{i\}) = 0$ for both players i and $v(N) = p$ for the grand coalition N consisting of both players.

EXPERIMENTS ON (DE)CENTRALIZATION IN WAGE BARGAINING

Several experiments on wage bargaining are concerned with the problem of centralization in bargaining. These experiments were motivated by the empirical results of Calmfors and Driffill (1988), which seem to show that the degree of centralization of wage bargaining procedures in an economy has an impact on macroeconomic performance: Countries with a low level of centralization (e.g., the United States and Canada) or a high level of centralization (e.g., Austria and Sweden) are characterized by low wage levels, while countries with a moderate level of centralization (e.g., Germany) have high wage rates. The opposite relation holds for the degree of centralization and the unemployment level. Up to now a satisfactory theoretical explanation of this phenomenon has been missing. In experiments on centralized versus decentralized bargaining (Berninghaus et al. 2001; Berninghaus, Güth, and Keser 2003) it was investigated whether a tendency to centralized bargaining can be observed at all when trade unions have the choice to centralize.

Berninghaus, Güth, and Keser (2003) assume three players, X, Y, and Z. These players can negotiate either in a decentralized way or collectively. In decentralized bargaining, X negotiates with Z about the allocation of a pie P_{XZ}, and, independently, Y negotiates with Z about the allocation of a pie P_{YZ}. In the case of collective bargaining, X and Y merge into a new player, XY, who then bargains with Z about the allocation of the total pie $P_{XYZ} = (P_{YZ} + P_{XZ})$. Whatever XY earns is shared by X and Y. Let i and j denote one of the two bargaining parties; that is, (i, j) is either (X, Z) or (Y, Z) or (XY, Z). A modified Nash demand game is applied: Each of the two parties $k = i, j$ chooses a demand D_k and a bottom line B_k with $P_{ij} \geq D_k \geq B_k \geq C_k$, where C_k (≥ 0) denotes the conflict payoff of party k. Given the vector (D_i, B_i, D_j, B_j) of bargaining choices and the size of the pie P_{ij}, a demand agreement is reached if $D_i + D_j \leq P_{ij}$. A bottom-line agreement is reached in case of no demand agreement and $B_i + B_j \leq P_{ij}$. While both parties $k = i, j$ obtain their demand D_k in case of a demand agreement, their profits are determined by their bottom lines B_k in case of a bottom-line agreement. If neither of these two agreements is achieved, the two parties end up in conflict, with conflict payoffs C_k.[9]

Conflict payoffs C_k depend on the pairing (i, j); therefore, we write $C_k(i, j)$. It is assumed that $C_Y(Y, Z) > C_X(X, Z)$ holds, that is, Y is stronger than X.

To solve this game theoretically, note that the acceptance borders are the (only) essential strategic variables. Obviously, in an efficient equilibrium the bargaining parties must choose $B_i + B_j = P_{ij}$. To select a unique efficient equilibrium outcome as a benchmark solution, one relies on the Nash bargaining solution, which maximizes the product of the dividends $(B_k - C_k)$ for $k = i, j$. For example, for the pair $(i, j) = (X, Z)$ we maximize $(B_X - C_X(XZ)) (B_Z - C_Z(XZ))$ subject to $B_X + B_Z = P_{XZ}$. Since the stronger party Y has no interest in forming XY, condition $B^*_Y > B^*_{XY}/2$ had to be satisfied by the solution choices. Of the three players only X has positive incentives for centralizing. The benchmark solution thus predicts decentralized bargaining. However, the experimental results suggest that centralization helps. This might reflect a common experience or belief that one gains in strength by merging, based on factual or expected synergy. This sometimes finds expression in phrases such as "Unity is strength" or, in German, "*Einigkeit macht stark.*" Players also might view (the choice of) centralization as signaling "I am tough."

CONCLUSION

We have documented various reactions to the sometimes striking results of experimental tests of the sharp predictions of canonical game theory for simple distribution and bargaining games. Roughly, these reactions can be classified as follows.

First, researchers have extended their study of deceptively simple games such as dictator and ultimatum games to somewhat more complicated games such as trust or alternating offer games. These studies, as the examples of Cox (2004) and Johnson and colleagues (2002) demonstrate in an exemplary manner, have inspired interesting new questions about the importance of cognitive limitations and the impact of social preferences. The Johnson and colleagues study (2002) is of particular interest, as it introduces economists to a noninvasive technique that allows us to better understand (through comparison for look-up patterns of information in various treatments) the reasoning process of subjects. In a related study, Costa-Gomes, Crawford, and Broseta (2001) have applied this technique to identify reasoning types and processes in normal form games. This, in turn, has generated interesting new theorizing attempts for situations that match asymmetrically endowed players (Crawford 2003).

Second, researchers have tried to "repair" the representation of the experimental situation ("game fitting"), for example, by assuming that utilities depend not only on profits but also on their distribution, on a desire for reciprocity, or on what one participant thinks is expected by other(s). These repairs do not question rationality. Since nearly all results can be "saved" in this way, repairs should be at least reasonable and intuitive. For instance, it is obvious that we often care about the distribution of rewards, but when and why we do so is currently poorly understood. Consider, for instance, models of social preferences (e.g., Bolton and Ockenfels 2000; Fehr and Schmidt 1999) that are meant to incorporate what the experimental studies seem to suggest: that people not only are considering own payoffs but also react to what others get. Such concerns are very obvious in close interaction situations (e.g., work teams) but very unlikely when shopping in a supermarket. What is thus required is a kind of cognitive switch that (does not) trigger(s) other-regarding concerns. The same applies to models of intentionality (Charness and Rabin 2003; Dufwenberg and Kirchsteiger 2004; Falk and Fischbacher 2001).

Other researchers (e.g., McKelvey and Palfrey 1995, 1998; Goeree and Holt 2001; Camerer, Ho, and Chong 2004; see also Reny 1992) allow for noise in decision behavior partly in the sense that we rationally anticipate such noise (which might be trembles or indeed altruism) and react optimally to it. While these new models enrich our understanding of cognitive limitations and social preferences, no model addresses successfully where social preferences come from and how boundedly rational decision makers take them into account. Rather, they are just postulated to exist. There exists, however, a rich literature on preference evolution, usually employing the indirect evolutionary approach (see Samuelson 2001 and the collection of articles in that special issue of the *Journal of Economic Theory*), providing some underpinning for which social concerns can be expected to evolve in certain environments.

Third, researchers have tried to understand whether features of standard experimental procedures have contributed to these results. Three developments deserve particular attention. One troubling aspect, as illustrated by the study of Cherry, Frykblom, and Shogren (2002) but also by the tradition of reward allocation experiments in psychology (e.g., Mikula 1973; Shapiro 1975), is the question of the external validity of subject payments that are bestowed on subjects like manna from heaven. Another troubling aspect, as illustrated by Hoffman, McCabe, and Smith (1996) but also by a huge literature in social psychology on expectancy effects (e.g., Rosenthal and Rubin 1978; Rosenthal and Rosnow 1991, 119–25, 128–33; Ortmann 2005), is the potential of experimenter effects. These concerns are of differential importance for various classes of games: they are not likely to play a role, for instance, in guessing games (Nagel 1995), but they warrant concern in distribution and bargaining games. The studies just mentioned, as well as innovative studies such as the one by Johnson and colleagues (2002) go a long way toward a better understanding of the impact of experimental design and implementation and why we see sometimes dramatic deviations from the predictions of canonical game theory.

Yet another troubling aspect is experimental economists' urge to get rid of social context in most of their experiments. There is mounting evidence that this experimental practice, which originally was meant to increase control, often does just the opposite (Ortmann and Gigerenzer 1997). Very simply put, the abstract nature of experimental goods and environments often does not allow subjects to access the inference machines that typically allow them to navigate their "habitats" just fine (e.g., Cosmides and Tooby 1996; Gigerenzer, Todd, and the ABC Research Group 2000). Of course, introducing field referents in various forms in the design and implementation of experiments runs the risk of prompting associations and interpretations of the experimental situation that may be incorrect, a risk that accounted for the usual practice in experimental economics. The advantages and disadvantages of each of these methods are currently poorly understood, although economists can surely learn a thing or two from similar debates that took place in psychology decades ago. A well-known example is memory research, where much of traditional laboratory research initially followed Ebbinghaus (1885) in conducting tightly controlled experiments using even nonsense syllables in an attempt to enhance control. This research paradigm was eventually questioned (e.g., Neisser 1978; Koriat and Goldsmith 1996a; see also Koriat and Goldsmith 1996b, which is of particular interest to experimental economists and psychologists). Closely related to the issue of what subjects bring to the laboratory and what they learn in the laboratory is the progress in developing software packages for computerized experiments. It has inspired a new experimental tradition: participants play the same base game (e.g., a 2-by-2 bimatrix game) repeatedly with randomly changing partners. This research tradition is too recent to permit any general conclusions about how people adapt to past experiences and how such path dependence is combined with undeniable strategic deliberation. One rather robust result is that behavior in two-person coordination games converges to strict equilibria, but not necessarily to the payoff-dominating strict equilibrium (see Camerer 2003). It is striking, however, to observe how closely theoretical exercises of adaptive dynamics and experimental studies are related to each other (e.g., Costa-Gomes, Crawford, and Broseta 2001). If the same simple game is played very frequently, boredom might lead players to seek variety. In studies of robust learning (see Güth 2002 for a selective account), where participants confront repeatedly a variety of related games instead of just one such game, this seems less likely, however.

The present authors disagree on the relative importance of what the experimental evidence tells us. Güth sees them as having established a persuasive case for a descriptive theory. Ortmann argues that more attention ought to be paid to experimental design and implementation issues and the question of the external validity of the (sometimes admittedly striking) laboratory results of distribution and bargaining experiments. That paying attention to experimental design and implementation is a worthwhile enterprise is, to Ortmann's mind, superbly documented in the controversy over the epistemic value of the heuristics and biases program, which reigned supreme in psychology for decades before serious questions were asked about the way the alleged biases had been produced and the heuristics had been formulated (e.g., Gigerenzer 1991; Gigerenzer 1996; Gigerenzer et al. forthcoming; Koehler 1996; Krueger and Funder 2004; Ortmann and Ostatnicky 2004). Ortmann sees in the results of Hoffman, McCabe, and Smith (1996), Cherry, Frykblom, and Shogren (2002), and Johnson and colleagues (2002) and in the emerging debate over the artificiality of our laboratory settings (e.g., List 2004; Harrison and List 2004; Carpenter, Harrison, and List 2005) evidence of methodological problems that warrant more attention than economists have accorded them so far. He also believes that there is a good chance that many of the striking results documented in the literature may be laboratory artifacts in that they are striking only when measured against the predictions of canonical game theory. Ortmann and Hertwig (2000) have pointed out that these striking deviations are overwhelmingly found in social dilemma games of various makes and that their outcomes can be easily rationalized in models that do not assume one-shot or finitely repeated game interactions. The question, then—and it is the question that Ortmann and Hertwig (2000) and others (e.g., Binmore and Samuelson 1994) before them have asked—is whether subjects bring to the laboratory the rules of thumb that serve them just fine in their daily lives and which can be interpreted as series of intertwined indefinitely repeated games.

The present authors agree that the three developments sketched above—the study of more complicated games, the attempts at theory generation, and the questioning of experimental methods—have been fruitful, especially to the extent that they acknowledge that *Homo sapiens* is, at best, rational within limits. Even if one is convinced that humans behave in ways other than those predicted by canonical theory, it is possible to learn a great deal from reasonable refinements of canonical game theory that do not in principle question rationality ("neoclassical repairs"). When a situation is relatively simple, so that even a boundedly rational participant can easily understand it, the neoclassical repairs will often reflect how participants derive their decisions. The tradition of enriching models (fitting games, in particular with assumptions about—far too often commonly known—risk aversion, social preferences, and the like) to match earlier experimental results and testing their solutions with new experiments will therefore continue.

We also agree that much work remains to be done regarding the incorporation of cognitive limitations into our models. We conjecture that, even for relatively simple games, many subjects transform games in simplified decision situations by looking, for example, in gift exchange games at the maximum gain and loss and the likelihood of them occurring.

The basic problem of the rational choice approach is that it assumes all the evaluation problems to be solved, whereas in actual life one often does not know the decisive decision alternatives (in an ultimatum experiment one does not usually consider all offers but focuses attention on a few previously selected ones, such as $1/2$, $1/3$, or $1/4$ of the pie) and how to evaluate them (if I offer only $1/3$ of the pie in an ultimatum experiment, what are the chances that this offer will be accepted, and how do I feel if it is accepted?).

Weakening the assumptions of normative decision theory—such as is done by theories of nonadditive utility, regret theories, and prospect theories (see Starmer 2000)—does not help much, since these new theories also rely on given evaluation functions. What all this literature neglects are the dynamics of decision making, even in one-person games where just one decision maker first generates a few choice alternatives that he or she then seriously considers.

A more realistic picture of human decision making would have to incorporate the basic stages of such decision dynamics as checking one's own and others' experiences for guidance as to what one might do and how successful these alternatives have been, and possibly by relying on routines developed for the problem (this allows for path dependence but requires, of course, some theory of qualitative and quantitative resemblance or similarity); developing a cognitive representation of the decision environment that one faces, either by comparing it with previously experienced decision problems or by mentally modeling the basic causality structures (bounded rationality denies perfect rationality but not forward-looking deliberation altogether); generating a few choice alternatives and measures of success (e.g., in an ultimatum experiment, an aspiration level when being the proposer or the responder, and—as the proposer—an aspiration for how likely one's offer should be accepted, e.g., "certainly" when offering $1/2$, "almost certainly" when offering 4/10, and "not sure" when offering only $1/3$ of the pie); applying some choice procedure, such as by claiming that one of the success measures should be decisive (e.g., the chances of having one's offer in an ultimatum experiment accepted); and evaluating one's choice ex post, if possible in the light of feedback information, in order to update's one behavioral repertoire.

Process models of dynamic decision emergence that are rich enough easily become rather complex (for a simpler process see Güth 2000; Deutsch and Strack 2004; Güth and Ortmann 2006). These models do not yet offer ready algorithms for generating choice behavior but rather present a general frame on how to combine the various aspects of human decision-making processes. Like neoclassical economics (which only suggests choices when putting in all evaluative judgments like utilities, probabilities, structural assumptions, etc.), an algorithm needs much more information. This, however, should not prevent us from trying hard(er) to develop such algorithms.

NOTES

1. The same can be said of canonical decision theory, i.e., expected utility theory, whose descriptive merits have been questioned (e.g., Camerer 1995; Starmer 2000; but see Myagkov and Plott 1997; List 2004).

2. Since the early nineties an interesting literature has emerged that departs from the heroic rationality and knowledge assumptions of canonical game theory and tries to explain the outcomes (equilibria) of games "evolutively" through dynamic models rather than "educatively." A path-breaking paper in this tradition was Friedman 1991, which established that Nash equilibria, under fairly weak conditions, are the fixed points of dynamic models that incorporate various forms of bounded rationality and limited knowledge. Note, however, that learning and evolution usually demand (indefinitely) repeated interaction. Similar to a tradition in general equilibrium theory, stability of behavior is defined partly by dynamic stability concepts (rest points) and partly by static concepts, e.g., evolutionarily stable strategies. Among noteworthy recent monographs addressing the former are Weibull 1995; Vega-Redondo 1996, 2003; Samuelson 1998; a good introductory text addressing the latter is Hammerstein and Selten 1994. Below we will discuss these developments only in passing, although they do speak to the issue of (the emergence of) social preferences.

3. The authors disagree on this point. Ortmann argues that we might then as well dispute the possibility of indefinitely repeated games during one's lifetime. Surely all of us know that in this life we will reach an endpoint. Güth argues that the neglect of termination is best explained by boundedly rational reasoning, e.g., in a forward induction way ("let's start to cooperate and think about how to terminate when the end is near").

4. Finitely repeated games with multiple equilibria can allow for folk-theorem-like results since they allow for punishing by switching equilibria (e.g., Benoit and Krishna 1985).

5. Binary trust games (where one usually decides between not trusting at all and full trust), which have a somewhat longer tradition, especially in social psychology (see, for instance, Snijders 1996 and the literature review there), are neglected here.

6. The basic idea of this argument is well known (e.g., Reny 1992) and, in fact, goes back at least to Ellsberg's (1956, 1959) critique of a key solution concept proposed by Von Neumann and Morgenstern (1947), the maximin.

7. Although Henrich (2000) reports that several of his subjects, even after thirty minutes of individualized instruction and numerous examples, had to be dismissed because they could not answer control questions. On the other hand, Takezawa, Gummerum, and Keller (2004) report no problem in implementing dictator and ultimatum games with German children ages eleven and thirteen.

8. The authors strongly disagree on this, with Güth viewing this more as a reformulation of the question "Why prosocial behavior?" by asking "Why prosocial preferences?"

9. The reason for splitting up the bargaining choice into demand and bottom line is that although game theory does not account for this, it seems to help the parties to coordinate more easily on how to split the surplus. Behaviorally speaking, demands can aim at an efficient allocation, whereas bottom lines can be seen as a way to avoid conflict. Participants can also try to reach their higher aspirations by high demands and play safe by using more modest bottom lines. A positive difference $D_k - B_k$ might be interpreted as a concession.

REFERENCES

Anderhub, V., D. Engelmann, and W. Güth. 2002. "An Experimental Study of the Repeated Trust Game with Incomplete Information." *Journal of Economic Behavior and Organization* 48: 197–216.

Anderhub, V., W. Güth, and N. Marchand. 2004. "Early or Late Conflict Settlement in a Variety of Games— An Experimental Study." *Journal of Economic Psychology* 25: 177–194.

Andreoni J. 1995a. "Warm-Glow Versus Cold-Prickle: The Effects of Positive and Negative Framing on Cooperation in Experiments." *Quarterly Journal of Economics* 110: 1–21.
———. 1995b. "Cooperation in Public Goods Experiments: Kindness of Confusion." *American Economic Review* 85: 891–904.
Andreoni, J., and J.H. Miller. 2002. "Giving According to GARP: An Experimental Test of the Consistency of Preferences for Altruism." *Econometrica* 70: 737–53.
Benoit, J.P., and V. Krishna. 1985. "Finitely Repeated Games." *Econometrica* 53: 905–22.
Berg, J.E., J.W. Dickhaut, and K.A. McCabe. 1995. "Trust, Reciprocity, and Social History." *Games and Economic Behavior* 10: 122–42.
Berninghaus, S.K., W. Güth, R. Lechler, and H.-J. Ramser. 2001. "Decentralized Versus Collective Bargaining: An Experimental Study." *International Journal of Game Theory* 30: 437–48.
Berninghaus, S.K., W. Güth, and C. Keser. 2003. "Unity Suggests Strength: An Experimental Study of Decentralized and Collective Bargaining." *Journal of Labour Economics* 10: 465–79.
Binmore, K., and L. Samuelson. 1994. "An Economist's Perspective on the Evolution of Norms." *Journal of Institutional and Theoretical Economics* 190: 45–63.
Bolle, F. and J. Kaehler. 2003. "Is There a Harmful Selection Bias When Experimenters Choose Their Experiments?" Discussion Paper 189, Europa Universität Viadrina Frankfurt.
Bolton, G., and A. Ockenfels. 1998. "An ERC-Analysis of the Güth-Van Damme Game." *Journal of Mathematical Psychology* 42: 215–26.
———. 2000. "ERC: A Theory of Equity, Reciprocity and Competition." *American Economic Review* 90: 166–93.
Bolton, G., and R. Zwick. 1995. "Anonymity Versus Punishment in Ultimatum Bargaining." *Games and Economic Behavior* 10: 95–121.
Brandstätter, H., and W. Güth. 2002. "Personality in Dictator and Ultimatum Games." *Central European Journal of Operations Research* 3: 191–215.
Calmfors, L., and J. Driffill. 1988. "Bargaining Structure, Corporatism and Macroeconomic Performance." *Economic Policy* 6: 14–61.
Camerer, C.F. 1995. "Individual Decision Making." In J.H. Kagel and A.E. Roth, eds., *Handbook of Experimental Economics,* 587–703. Princeton, NJ: Princeton University Press.
———. 2003. *Behavioral Game Theory: Experiments in Strategic Interaction.* Princeton, NJ: Princeton University Press.
Camerer, C.F., T.-H. Ho, and J.-K. Chong. 2004. "A Cognitive Hierarchy Model of Games." *Quarterly Journal of Economics* 119: 861–98.
Carpenter, J., G.W. Harrison, and J.A. List, eds. 2005. *Field Experiments in Economics.* Greenwich, CT: JAI Press.
Charness G., and M. Rabin. 2003. "Understanding Social Preferences with Simple Tests." *Quarterly Journal of Economics* 117: 817–69.
Cherry, T.L., P. Frykblom, and J.F. Shogren. 2002. "Hardnose the Dictator." *American Economic Review* 92: 1218–21.
Colman, A.M. 1982. *Game Theory and Experimental Games: The Study of Strategic Interaction.* Oxford: Pergamon.
———. 1995. *Game Theory and Its Applications in the Social and Biological Sciences,* 2nd ed. Amsterdam: Butterworth-Heinemann.
———. 2003. "Cooperation, Psychological Game Theory, and Limitations of Rationality in Social Interaction." *Behavioral and Brain Sciences* 26: 139–98.
Cooper, R.W., and J. Van Huyck. 2003. "Evidence on the Equivalence of the Strategic and Extensive Form Representation of Games." *Journal of Economic Theory* 110: 290–308.
Cosmides, L., and J. Tooby. 1996. "Are Humans Good Intuitive Statisticians After All? Rethinking Some Conclusions from the Literature on Judgment Under Uncertainty." *Cognition* 58: 1–73.
Cox, J.C. 2004. "How to Identify Trust and Reciprocity." *Games and Economic Behavior* 46: 260–81.
Costa-Gomes, M., V. Crawford, and B. Broseta. 2001. "Cognition and Behavior in Normal-Form Games: An Experimental Study." *Econometrica* 69: 1193–235.
Cowan, N. 2001. "The Magical Number 4 in Short-term Memory: A Reconsideration of Mental Storage Capacity." *Behavioral and Brain Sciences* 24: 87–114.
Crawford, V.P. 2003. "Lying for Strategic Advantage: Rational and Boundedly Rational Misrepresentation of Intentions." *American Economic Review* 93: 133–49.

Deutsch, R., and F. Strack. 2004. "Reflective and Impulsive Determinants of Social Behavior." *Personality and Social Psychology Review* 8: 220–47.

Dufwenberg, M., and G. Kirchsteiger. 2004. "A Theory of Sequential Reciprocity." *Games and Economic Behavior* 47: 268–98.

Ebbinghaus, H. 1885. *Memory: A Contribution to Experimental Psychology.* New York: Dover.

Ellsberg, D. 1956. "Theory of the Reluctant Duelist." *American Economic Review* 46: 909–23.

———. 1959. "Rejoinder." *Review of Economics and Statistics* 41: 42–43.

Falk, A., and U. Fischbacher. 2001. "Distributional Consequences and Intentions in a Model of Reciprocity." *Annales d'Economie et de Statistique* 62: 112–29.

Fehr, E., G. Kirchsteiger, and A. Riedl. 1998. "Gift Exchange and Reciprocity in Competitive Experimental Markets." *European Economic Review* 42: 1-34.

Fehr, E., and K. Schmidt. 1999. "A Theory of Fairness, Competition and Cooperation." *Quarterly Journal of Economics* 114: 817–68.

Fellner, G., and W. Güth. 2003. "What Limits Escalation? Varying Threat Power in an Ultimatum Experiment." *Economics Letters* 80: 53–60.

Felsenthal, D.S., E. Weg, and A. Rapoport. 1990. "Two-Person Bargaining Behavior in Fixed Discounting Factor Games with Infinite Horizon." *Games and Economic Behavior* 2: 76–95.

Festinger, L. 1957. *A Theory of Cognitive Dissonance.* Stanford, CA: Stanford University Press.

Forsythe, R., J. Horowitz, N. Savin, and M. Sefton. 1994. "Replicability, Fairness and Play in Experiments with Simple Bargaining Games." *Games and Economic Behavior* 6: 347–69.

Friedman, D. 1991. "Evolutionary Games in Economics." *Econometrica* 59: 637–66.

Gigerenzer, G. 1991. "How to Make Cognitive Illusion Disappear: Beyond Heuristics and Biases." In W. Stroebe and M. Hewstone, eds., *European Review of Social Psychology.* New York: Wiley.

———. 1996. "On Narrow Norms and Vague Heuristics: A Reply to Kahneman and Tversky." *Psychological Review* 103: 592–96.

Gigerenzer, G., R. Hertwig, U. Hoffrage, and P. Sedlmeier. Forthcoming. "Cognitive Illusions Reconsidered." In C.R. Plott and V.L. Smith, eds., *Handbook of Experimental Economics Results.* New York: Elsevier.

Gigerenzer, G., P.M. Todd, and the ABC Research Group 2000. *Simple Heuristics That Make Us Smart.* Oxford: Oxford University Press.

Goeree, J.K., and C.A. Holt. 2001. "Ten Little Treasures of Game Theory and Ten Intuitive Contradictions." *American Economic Review* 91: 1402–22.

Güth, W. 1976. "Towards a More General Study of v. Stackelberg Situations." *Zeitschrift für die gesamte Staatswissenschaft* 4: 592–608.

———. 2000. "Boundedly Rational Decisions Emergence—A General Perspective and Some Selective Illustrations." *Journal of Economic Psychology* 21: 433–58.

———. 2002. "Robust Learning Experiments." In F. Andersson and H. Holm, eds., *Experimental Economics: Financial Markets, Auctions, and Decision Making, Interviews and Contributions from the 20th Arne Ryde Symposium.* New York: Kluwer Academic Publishers.

Güth, W., and S. Huck. 1997. "From Ultimatum Bargaining to Dictatorship—An Experimental Study of Four Games Varying in Veto Power." *Metroeconomica* 48: 262–79.

Güth, W., M.V. Levati, and B. Maciejovsky. 2005. "Deadline Effects in Sequential Bargaining—An Experimental Study." *International Game Theory Review* 7: 117-135.

Güth, W., P. Ockenfels, and M. Wendel. 1993. "Efficiency by Trust in Fairness? Multiperiod Ultimatum Bargaining Experiments with an Increasing Pie." *International Journal of Game Theory* 22: 51–73.

Güth, W., and A. Ortmann. 2006. "Decision Making: When Deliberation? And When Routines? And How to Get to the Latter from the Former?" Max Planck Institute, Jena, Germany.

Güth, W., C. Schmidt, and M. Sutter. Forthcoming. "Bargaining Outside the Lab—A Newspaper Experiment of a Three-Person Ultimatum Game." *Economic Journal.*

Güth, W., R. Schmittberger, and B. Schwarze. 1982. "An Experimental Analysis of Ultimatum Bargaining." *Journal of Economic Behavior and Organization* 3: 367–88.

Güth, W., and R. Tietz. 1986. "Auctioning Ultimatum Bargaining Positions—How to Act if Rational Decisions Are Unacceptable." In R.W. Scholz, ed., *Current Issues in West German Decision Research*, 173–85. Frankfurt: P. Lang.

Güth, W., and E. van Damme. 1998. "Information, Strategic Behavior, and Fairness in Ultimatum Bargaining: An Experimental Study." *Journal of Mathematical Psychology* 42: 227–47.

Hammerstein, P., and R. Selten. 1994. "Game Theory and Evolutionary Biology." In R.J. Aumann and S. Hart, eds., *Handbook of Game Theory,* 2:928–93. Amsterdam: Elsevier.

Harrison, G.W., E. Johnson, M.M. McInnes, and E.E. Rutstroem. Forthcoming. "Risk Aversion and Incentive Effects: Comment." *American Economic Review.*

Harrison, G.W., and J. List. 2004. "Field Experiments." *Journal of Economic Literature* 42: 1009–55.

Harrison, G.W., and K.A. McCabe. 1985. "Experimental Evaluation of the Coase Theorem." *Journal of Law and Economics* 28: 653–70.

Henrich, J. 2000. "Does Culture Matter in Economic Behavior? Ultimatum Game Bargaining Among the Machiguenga of the Peruvian Amazon." *American Economic Review* 90: 973–79.

Henrich, J., R. Boyd, S. Bowles, C. Camerer, E. Fehr, H. Gintis, and R. McElreath. 2001. "In Search of Homo Economicus: Behavioral Experiments in 15 Small-Scale Societies." *American Economic Review* 91: 73–78.

Hertwig, R., and A. Ortmann. 2001a. "Experimental Practices in Economics: A Methodological Challenge for Psychologists?" *Behavioral and Brain Sciences* 24: 383–403.

———. 2001b. "Money, Lies, and Replicability: On the Need for Empirically Grounded Experimental Practices and Interdisciplinary Discourse." *Behavioral and Brain Sciences* 24: 433–44.

———. 2003. "Economists' and Psychologists' Experimental Practices: How They Differ, Why They Differ, and How They Could Converge." In I. Brocas and J.D. Carrillo, eds., *The Psychology of Economic Decisions.* Oxford: Oxford University Press.

Hoffman, E., K.A. McCabe, and V.L. Smith. 1996. "Social Distance and Other-Regarding Behavior in Dictator Games." *American Economic Review* 86: 653–60.

Johnson, E., C.F. Camerer, S. Sen, and T. Rymon. 2002. "Detecting Failures of Backward Induction: Monitoring Information Search in Sequential Bargaining." *Journal of Economic Theory* 104: 16–47.

Kalai, E., and M. Smorodinsky. 1975. "Other Solutions to Nash's Bargaining Problem." *Econometrica* 43: 513–18.

Kirchsteiger, G. 1994. "The Role of Envy in Ultimatum Games." *Journal of Economic Behavior and Organization* 25: 373–89.

Koehler, J.J. 1996. "The Base Rate Fallacy Reconsidered: Descriptive, Normative, and Methodological Challenges." *Behavioral and Brain Sciences* 19: 1–53.

Komorita, S.S., and J.M. Chertkoff. 1973. "A Bargaining Theory of Coalition Formation." *Psychological Review* 80: 149–62.

Koriat, A., and M. Goldsmith. 1996a. "Memory Metaphors and the Real-Life/Laboratory Controversy: Correspondence Versus Storehouse Conceptions of Memory." *Behavioral and Brain Sciences* 19: 167–28.

———. 1996b. "Monitoring and Control Processes in the Strategic Regulation of Memory Accuracy." *Psychological Review* 106: 490–517.

Kreps, D.M. 1990a. *A Course in Microeconomic Theory.* Princeton, NJ: Princeton University Press.

———. 1990b. *Game Theory and Economic Modeling.* Oxford: Oxford University Press.

Kreps, D.M., P. Milgrom, J. Roberts, and R. Wilson. 1982. "Rational Cooperation in the Finitely Repeated Prisoner's Dilemma." *Journal of Economic Theory* 27: 245–52.

Krueger, J.I., and I. Funder. 2004. "Towards a Balanced Social Psychology: Causes, Consequences, and Cures for the Problem-Seeking Approach to Social Behavior and Cognition." *Behavioral and Brain Sciences* 27: 313–76.

Laury, S.K., and C.A. Holt. 2002. "Further Reflections on Prospect Theory." Working Paper, Department of Economics, University of Virginia.

Ledyard, J.O. 1995. "Public Goods: A Survey of Experimental Research." In J.H. Kagel and A.E. Roth, eds., *The Handbook of Experimental Economics.* Princeton, NJ: Princeton University Press.

List, J.A. 2004. "Neoclassical Theory Versus Prospect Theory: Evidence from the Marketplace." *Econometrica* 72: 313–76.

List, J.A., and T.L. Cherry. 2000. "Learning to Accept in Ultimatum Games: Evidence from an Experimental Design That Generates Low Offers." *Experimental Economics* 3: 81–100.

Malcomson, J. 1997. "Contracts, Hold-Up, and Labor Markets." *Journal of Economic Literature* 35: 1916–1957.

Mas-Colell, A., M.D. Whinston, and J.R. Green. 1995. *Microeconomic Theory.* New York: Oxford University Press.

McCabe, K.A., V.L. Smith, and M. LePore. 2000. "Intentionality Detection and 'Mindreading': Why Does Game Form Matter?" *Proceedings of the National Academy of Sciences* 97: 4404–9.

McKelvey, R.D., and T. Palfrey. 1992. "An Experimental Study of the Centipede Game." *Econometrica* 60: 803–36.

———. 1995. "Quantal Response Equilibria for Normal Form Games." *Games and Economic Behavior* 10: 6–38.

———. 1998. "Quantal Response Equilibria for Extensive Form Games." *Experimental Economics* 1: 9–41.

Mikula, G. 1973. "Gewinnaufteilungsverhalten in Dyaden bei variiertem Leistungsverhältnis." *Zeitschrift für Sozialpsychologie* 3: 126–33.

Miller, G.A. 1956. "The Magical Number of Seven, Plus or Minus Two: Some Limits on Our Capacity for Processing Information." *Psychological Review* 63: 81–97.

Myagkov, M., and C.R. Plott. 1997. "Exchange Economies and Loss Exposure: Experiments Exploring Prospect Theory and Competitive Equilibria in Market Environments." *American Economic Review* 87: 801–28.

Nagel, R. 1995. "Unraveling in Guessing Games: An Experimental Study." *American Economic Review* 85: 1313–26.

Nash, J.F. 1950. "The Bargaining Problem." *Econometrica* 18: 155–62.

———. 1953. "Two-Person Cooperative Games." *Econometrica* 21: 128–40.

Neisser, U. 1978. "Memory: What Are the Important Questions?" In M.M. Gruneberg, P.E. Morris, and R.N. Sykes, eds., *Practical Aspects of Memory*, 3–24. San Diego: Academic Press.

Neyman, A. 1999. "Cooperation in Repeated Games When the Number of Stages Is Not Commonly Known." *Metroeconomica* 67: 45–64.

Ortmann, A. 2005. "Field Experiments in Economics: Some Methodological Caveats." In J. Carpenter, G.W. Harrison, and J.A. List, eds., *Field Experiments in Economics*. Greenwich, CT: JAI Press.

Ortmann, A., and G. Gigerenzer. 1997. "Reasoning in Economics and Psychology: Why Social Context Matters." *Journal of Institutional and Theoretical Economics* 153: 700–10.

Ortmann, A., J. Fitzgerald, and C. Boeing. 2000. "Trust, Reciprocity, and Social History: A Re-Examination." *Experimental Economics* 3: 81–100.

Ortmann, A., and M. Ostatnicky. 2004. "Proper Experimental Design and Implementation Are Necessary Conditions for a Balanced Social Psychology." *Behavioral and Brain Science* 27: 352–53.

Ortmann, A., and R. Hertwig. 2000. "Why Anomalies Cluster in Experimental Tests of One-shot and/or Finitely Repeated Games: Suggestive Evidence from Psychology and Neuroscience." Paper presented at ESA Meetings, New York, NY. Available at http://home.cerge-ei.cz/ortmann.

Pruitt, D.G. 1967. "Reward Structure and Cooperation: The Decomposed Prisoner's Dilemma Game." *Journal of Personality and Social Psychology* 7: 21–27.

Reny, P. 1992. "Rationality in Extensive Form Games." *Journal of Economic Perspectives* 6: 103–18.

Rosenthal, R., and R.L. Rosnow. 1991. *Essentials of Behavioral Research: Methods and Data Analysis*, 2nd ed. New York: McGraw-Hill.

Rosenthal, R., and D.B. Rubin. 1978. "Interpersonal Expectancy Effects: The First 345 Studies." *Behavioral and Brain Sciences* 1: 377–415.

Roth, A.E. 1995. "Introduction to Experimental Economics." In J.H. Kagel and A.E. Roth, eds., *Handbook of Experimental Economics*, 3–109. Princeton, NJ: Princeton University Press.

Roth, A.E., and M.W.K. Malouf. 1979. "Game Theoretic Models and the Role of Information in Bargaining." *Psychological Review* 86: 574–94.

Roth, A.E., V. Prasnikar, M. Okuno-Fujiwara, and S. Zamir. 1991. "Bargaining and Market Behavior in Jerusalem, Ljubljana, Pittsburgh and Tokyo: An Experimental Study." *American Economic Review* 81: 1068–95.

Rubinstein, A. 1982. "Perfect Equilibrium in a Bargaining Model." *Econometrica* 50: 97–110.

Samuelson, L. 1998. *Evolutionary Games and Equilibrium Selection*. Cambridge, MA: MIT Press.

———. 2001. "Introduction to the Evolution of Preferences (Symposium)." *Journal of Economic Theory* 97: 225–30.

Sauermann, H. 1978. *Bargaining Behavior: Contributions to Experimental Economics, Vol. 7*. Tübingen: Mohr.

———. 1978a. *Coalition-Former Behavior: Contributions to Experimental Economics, Vol. 8*. Tübingen: Mohr.

Schotter, A., K. Weigelt, and C. Wilson. 1994. "A Laboratory Investigation of Multiperson Rationality and Presentation Effects." *Games and Economic Behavior* 6: 445–68.

Selten, R., and R. Stöcker. 1986. "End Behavior in Sequences of Finite Prisoner's Dilemma Supergames: A Learning Theory Approach." *Journal of Economic Behavior and Organization* 7: 47–70.

Selten, R., and G.R. Uhlich. 1988. "Order of Strength and Exhaustivity as Additional Hypotheses in Theories for Three-Person Characteristic Function Games." In: Bounded rational behavior in experimental games and markets: Proceedings of the Fourth Conference on Experimental Economics (Bielefeld, West Germany, September 21–25 1986), R. Tietz, W. Albers, R. Selten (eds.), *Lecture Notes in Economics and Mathematical Systems* 314, Berlin: Springer, 235–50.

Shapiro, E.G. 1975. "Effects of Future Interaction in Reward Allocation in Dyads: Equity or Equality." *Journal of Personality and Social Psychology* 31: 873–80.

Slonim, R.L., and A.E. Roth. 1998. Learning in High Stakes Ultimatum Games: An Experiment in the Slovak Republic." *Econometrica* 66: 569–96.

Smith, A..1776/1976. "An Inquiry into the Nature and Causes of the Wealth of Nations." Vol. I. Oxford: Oxford University Press.

Smith, V.L., and J.M. Walker. 1993. "Monetary Rewards and Decision Cost in Experimental Economics." *Economic Inquiry* 31: 245–61.

Snijders, C. 1996. "Trust and Commitments." Ph.D. dissertation, Utrecht University.

Starmer, C. 2000. "Developments in Non-Expected Utility Theory: The Hunt for a Descriptive Theory of the Choice Under Risk." *Journal of Economic Literature* 38: 332–82.

Suleiman, R. 1996. "Expectations and Fairness in a Modified Ultimatum Game." *Journal of Economic Psychology* 17: 531–54.

Takezawa, M., M. Gummerum, and M. Keller. 2004. "A Social World for the Rational Tail of the Emotional Dog: Roles of Moral Reasoning in Group Decision Making." Available from take@mpib-berlin.mpg.de.

Vega-Redondo, F. 1996. *Evolution, Games, and Economic Behaviour.* Oxford: Oxford University Press.

———. 2003. *Economics and the Theory of Games.* Cambridge: Cambridge University Press.

Von Neumann, J., and O. Morgenstern. 1947. *Games and Economic Behavior,* 2nd ed. Princeton, NJ: Princeton University Press.

Weibull, J.W. 1995. *Evolutionary Game Theory.* Cambridge, MA: MIT Press.

CHAPTER 21

THE CONTEXT, OR REFERENCE, DEPENDENCE OF ECONOMIC VALUES

Further Evidence and Some Predictable Patterns

JACK L. KNETSCH AND FANG-FANG TANG

The available empirical evidence is frequently at odds with the stability of preferences, fungibility, and procedural invariance assumptions of standard theory and economic practice. The findings indicate that instead of according with the usual axioms, people's preferences commonly depend on the context, or the reference position, in which valuations are made. The numerous recent reports of such discrepancies reflect both the ease of demonstrating them and the consistency of results across a range of search methods.

> By focusing attention on particular axioms such as independence and transitivity, we have overlooked an even more fundamental assumption, which most economists seem to take for granted, but which is almost certainly false: namely, that people come to problems armed with a clear and reasonably complete set of preferences, and process all decision tasks according to this given preference structure. (Loomes 1999, F37)

The purposes here are to provide further evidence of the wide extent of the context dependence of valuations and to demonstrate that, rather than being isolated observations having little relationship to each other, these new results, as well as previously reported findings, fall into some predictable patterns in which valuations vary depending on the influence of different context variables.

THE CONTEXT OF GAINS AND THE CONTEXT OF LOSSES

The most well-documented context, or reference, dependence is doubtless the pervasive finding that people value a loss from a reference state more, and often much more, than an otherwise commensurate gain to it—what has become known as the endowment effect or, less often, the reference effect. This disparity between the valuation of a gain and a loss is also illustrative of the implications of other forms of context dependence.

The usual assumption of standard theory, which is the basis for nearly all economic explanations and analyses, predictions, and prescriptions, is that the value or well-being associated with an entitlement increases at a decreasing rate with larger quantities of a good (consumer goods, money, environmental quality, safety, or whatever). It then follows that for nearly all practical matters the value of incremental increases in quantity is taken to be equal to the value of a commensurate decrease in quantity. While a popular notion, at least among economists and economic analysts, it is not one that seems to match most people's usual behavior and the way they make decisions.

> The idea that decision makers evaluate outcomes by the utility of wealth positions has been retained in economic analyses for almost 300 years. This is rather remarkable because the idea is easily shown to be wrong. (Kahneman 2003b, 704)

The earliest reported findings of a disparity between people's valuation of gains and losses involved responses to hypothetical survey questions. For example, a sample of bird hunters in the United States said they would be willing to pay, on average, $247 to preserve a marsh area important to the propagation of ducks, but would demand a minimum of $1,044 to agree to its loss—a difference so large, and so inconsistent with the assumptions of standard theory, that the investigators initially attributed it to respondents' misunderstanding of the questions (Hammack and Brown 1974).

Some questioning of the relationship between quantity of a good or money and people's well-being or valuations, assumed in the tenants of standard theory, began some time ago. For the most part, this questioning either was speculative—on the basis of the conventional view not appearing to explain feelings associated with changes in quantities of goods (Markowitz 1952)—or accompanied further reports of observed differences between people's valuations of gains and losses (Gordon and Knetsch 1979; Thaler 1980).

Like the earlier questioning, increasing accumulations of empirical findings that were inconsistent with the conventional views of economists had little impact on how economics was discussed, and even less on how economics was done. When more serious attention to the disparity issue came, it followed, in large part, the work of Daniel Kahneman and Amos Tversky, which "integrated insights from psychological research into economic science," as was noted in the citation for the 2002 Nobel prize for economic science, given to Daniel Kahneman. This work more clearly showed why the commonly observed disparity between people's valuations of gains and losses should not be regarded as a surprising anomaly but instead should be taken as a fully expected outcome.

Kahneman and Tversky suggested that the relationship between quantities of a good and people's level of well-being has been largely misspecified by the assumptions of standard theory. In particular, they pointed to three important characteristics of this relationship that would more accurately describe people's preferences and be more consistent with observed behavior (Kahneman and Tversky 1979).

The first is that people value changes in the quantity of a good or an entitlement in terms of additions or subtractions from a reference state rather than in terms of differences between two end states, as in conventional views. Second, people value losses from the reference state more, and often much more, than gains to it—a characteristic of preferences they termed loss aversion. And third, people register decreasing sensitivity to larger gains or larger losses—the difference between 10 and 20 seems more important than the difference between 210 and 220, for example.

Taken together, these three differences point to a relationship between well-being and quantity of a good, as illustrated in Figure 21.1—a function kinked at the reference state and steeper in the domain of losses than in the domain of gains, rather than one represented by a smooth curve increasing at a decreasing rate over the whole range of gain and loss outcomes, as assumed in standard theory.

Figure 21.1 **Value of Gains and Losses from Reference State**

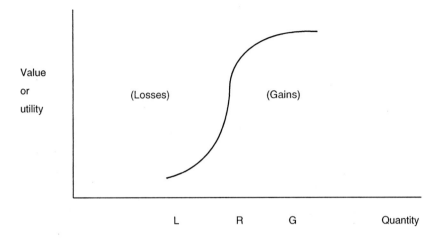

The consequences of loss aversion for the trade-off of gains and losses can also be illustrated, ignoring the curvature of the utility function for gains or losses, with a simplified version of a function linking quantity of some x with its value $v(x)$, proposed by Tversky and Kahneman (1992):

$$v(x) = x, \qquad x \geq 0$$
$$= \lambda x, \qquad x < 0 \tag{21.1}$$

with loss aversion implied by having $\lambda > 1$.

While many of Kahneman's studies and his earlier work with Tversky have had very significant implications for economics, it is almost certain that the single contribution most responsible for his being awarded the Nobel prize for economics was the 1979 paper, co-written with Tversky, on prospect theory, which outlined the reasons for the relationship illustrated in Figure 21.1, and led to later empirical verifications.[1] The choices and behavior suggested by the Kahneman-Tversky formulation have been confirmed by many replicated laboratory and field studies carried out by numerous investigators using a wide variety of methods and entitlements (see summaries in, for example, Kahneman, Knetsch, and Thaler 1990; Rabin 1998).[2]

Many of the earlier tests for differences in valuations of gains and losses, as noted earlier, were based on responses to hypothetical survey questions. For example, Thaler (1980) found that the minimum compensation people demanded to accept a 0.1 percent risk of sudden death was higher by one or two orders of magnitude than the amount they were willing to pay to eliminate the identical risk. In a widely cited study of changes in risks associated with the consumer use of pesticides, individuals in a large sample of consumers were found to demand nearly nine times more to accept a small increase in risk of injury than they would be willing to pay for a commensurate decrease in this risk (Viscusi, Magat, and Huber 1987).

More direct experimental tests for an endowment effect involving real exchanges of money and goods, as opposed to hypothetical ones, began some twenty years ago (Knetsch and Sinden 1984). Participants in this initial real exchange experiment demanded a minimum of four times as much money to give up a lottery ticket than the maximum sum they were willing to pay to acquire one. One of many later simple demonstrations of this disparity is provided by the results of an even more persuasive within-subject experiment, also involving real exchanges of money and lottery tickets. In this experiment the *same* individuals were asked for both the maximum amount they would be willing to pay to acquire (i.e., gain) an entitlement to a 50 percent chance to win $20 and, when they already had such an entitlement, the minimum sum they would require to give it up.[3] The easy assumption of conventional theory, that "we shall normally expect the results to be so close together that it would not matter which we choose" (Henderson 1941, 121), which was apparently formulated without benefit of any explicit empirical test, was clearly contradicted by the result. Rather than the predicted near equivalence, these individuals were willing to pay an average of $5.60 to gain the chance to win $20 but on average demanded $10.87 to give it up—they valued the loss about twice as much as the fully commensurate gain (Kachelmeier and Shehata 1992). Other such studies have demonstrated that the valuation disparity is pervasive, usually large, persistent over repeated trials, and not a result of income effects, wealth constraints, or transaction costs (Kahneman, Knetsch, and Thaler 1990).

In a recent review of forty-five tests of the valuation differences, Horowitz and McConnell (2002) found the mean ratio of WTA values over WTP values to be over 7. Further, they found that these differences "do not appear to be experimental artifacts" (p. 442) and that they are generally larger for nonmarket goods than for ordinary private goods.

Several questions have been raised about the validity of the numerous results of valuation experiments and the extent to which they should be taken seriously. These have included the suggestion that the stakes in experimental markets are not sufficient to motivate people to make well-considered decisions; another is that people need experience of repeated trials to learn both their own valuation of an entitlement and how to express this in what is usually an unfamiliar venue and format of an economic experiment. A further suggestion is that while naive participants may well often act in ways inconsistent with standard theory, such as valuing losses more than gains, experienced and well-motivated traders would not (List 2003). Thus far a limited amount of empirical evidence has been provided that appears to show some support for each of these criticisms. However, the weight of all of the current evidence appears to support the behavioral findings.

It is very likely true, for example, that merchants do not consider a sale of a stock item as a loss—that presumably being the point of their enterprise. Such individuals are unlikely to exhibit an endowment effect, at least with respect to buying and selling goods, although they may well show the same inclination in other business dealings. But the absence of an endowment effect in such circumstances has long been recognized—"there is no reason in general to expect reluctance to resell goods that are held especially for that purpose" (Kahneman, Knetsch, and Thaler 1990, 1344)—and quite clearly is a special case.

It is also sometimes the case that repeated trials do result in people changing their valuations of gains and losses such that the usual valuation disparity is reduced or even eliminated. However, in nearly all such demonstrations the evidence has come from experiments using a second-price Vickrey auction, in which the highest bidder buys at the second highest bid, and the lowest offerer sells at the second lowest offer. While this institution has been thought to lead to truthful revelations of value for all participants, as noted below, the results of explicit tests of the demand-revealing properties of second-price Vickrey auctions are very much in doubt. Consequently, even the limited experimental evidence showing convergence of buying and selling prices seems, at a minimum, open to serious question.

Further studies of the endowment effect have also been carried out on the basis of field data recording how people make everyday decisions. While not conclusive by themselves because of the usual lack of the stringent controls that mark most economic experiments that are carefully designed for the purpose, they do overcome some of the alleged weaknesses of hypothetical survey and experimental studies.

The results of studies of people's ordinary behavior on the whole provide strong support for the results of the experimental studies. People generally have been found to value losses and reductions of losses substantially more than gains and opportunity costs. For example, a greater sensitivity of investors to losses is apparent in their observed reluctance to realize a loss by selling, leading to smaller volumes of sales of securities that have declined in price relative to those for which prices have increased (Shefrin and Statman 1985). This same asymmetry was evident in an extensive study of the trading records of 10,000 individuals over seven years, which found that not only did taxation and other institutional reasons explain very little of the observed trading behavior, but the stocks that had gone up in price and were sold would have returned an average of 3.4 percent more over the following year than the losing stocks that were not sold (Odean 1998). The strong reluctance to give up a default automobile insurance option when an otherwise more attractive choice is readily available (Johnson et al. 1993), the greater sensitivity to losses in judgments of fairness (Kahneman, Knetsch, and Thaler 1986), and the stronger legal protection accorded to losses over forgone gains in judicial choices (Cohen and Knetsch 1992) are further examples of the difference in people's valuation of gains and losses.

A perhaps even more compelling example is provided by the dramatic change in employee contributions to their retirement savings resulting from provision of a new alternative that recognized the disparity in valuations (Thaler and Benartzi 2004). As is the case with most firms, new employees in a large U.S. company were asked how much of their wages or salaries they would like to have deducted from their pay and put into their pension scheme. This choice frames the contribution as a loss of income, which, because of the usual heavier weighting of losses, discourages agreeing to large deductions. The consequence was an unsatisfactorily low rate of contribution. Thaler and Benartzi's suggestion was to offer employees the opportunity to make pension contributions from future wage and salary increases, thereby framing the payment as a much less aversive forgone gain. The result was that employees increased their private pension plan contribution rate from 3.5 percent to 11.6 percent.

The results of the many studies of people's valuations of gains and losses appear consistent with most people's intuition about the relative weight of gains and losses. This was explicitly noted more than a century ago by the American jurist Oliver Wendell Holmes:

> It is in the nature of man's mind. A thing which you have enjoyed and used as your own for a long time, whether property or an opinion, takes root in your being and cannot be torn away without your resenting the act and trying to defend yourself, however you came by it. The law can ask no better justification than the deepest instincts of man. (1897, 477)

It was similarly remarked on even earlier by the same Adam Smith so often championed by defenders of more conventional views of standard economic theory:

> We suffer more . . . when we fall from a better to a worse situation, than we ever enjoy when we rise from a worse to a better. (1759, 213)

This seems to be a very general view of most noneconomists, to the point of their wondering why economists should think otherwise.

It is also notable that the findings of large differences between people's valuations of the gain

Figure 21.2   **Combinations of Gains and Losses and Differing Valuations of a Mug (CAD$)**

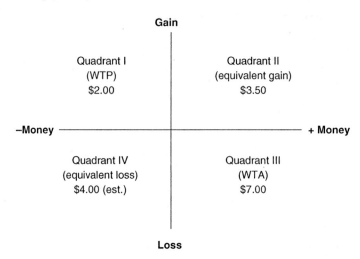

and the loss of a good or entitlement, which have been demonstrated in so many behavioral economics experiments, would not have been apparent in economic experiments that relied on induced values. Induced value experiments have been used extensively, especially for empirical tests of alternative auction rules and market institutions (Smith 1994). However, these experiments are carried out by, essentially, assigning specific values to tokens, as items of trade, and having participants exchange entitlements to these tokens on the basis of these assigned values and the rules governing the exercise.[4] For example, a person holding a token that can be cashed in at the end of the experiment for $5 is motivated to sell it to another person who is told that the token can be cashed in for $10. The value of an entitlement (a token) is prescribed, or a given, in these experiments; values are not ascribed to the entitlement by each participant. It is only when participants in an experiment are given the opportunity to value a good or an entitlement depending on whether the individual is facing its gain or loss that differences in valuations can be exhibited.

PATTERNS OF GAINS AND LOSSES

An illustrative example of the differing valuations of an otherwise identical entitlement is provided by the results of a real exchange experiment in which different groups of participants valued a coffee mug but did so in different ways (Kahneman, Knetsch, and Thaler 1990). Individuals in one group valued the mug in terms of the amount of money they would give up to gain the mug. This is a loss from the reference level of money and a gain to the reference state of mugs, and is the trade-off in Quadrant I of Figure 21.2 (with the gain or loss of the entitlement indicated by the vertical axis and the gain or loss of money by the horizontal). As a gain of an entitlement (a mug for this group) is expected to be worth less than its loss, and a loss of money is valued more than the gain of an equal sum, these individuals would presumably be willing to pay (WTP) relatively less for the good. This low valuation is confirmed by the average WTP of only CAD$2.00. In analogous fashion, the minimum amount they are willing to accept (WTA) (Quadrant III), in which individuals valued the mug in terms of money gained to give up the mug, yielded the expected highest monetary valuation, $7.00. Another group of individuals valued a mug in terms

Figure 21.3   **Proportion of Individuals Preferring £0.80 to Four Cans of Cola**

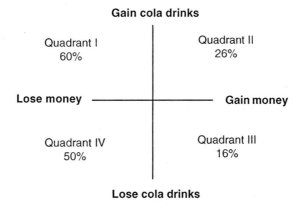

of a choice between a gain of a mug and a gain of money (Quadrant II), resulting in $3.50 being judged equivalent to the gain of the mug, a value predictably intermediate between the gain (WTP) and loss (WTA) values. A fourth value is provided by the choice between the loss of a mug and the loss of money, the willingness to pay to avoid a loss (Quadrant IV). This equivalent loss valuation was not included in the mug experiment, but a reasonable estimate (based on the ratios of QI to QII values and QII to QIII values) would be around $4.00.

The disparity between people's valuations of gains and losses is responsible for the predictable pattern of different values evident in the results of the mug experiment (and displayed in Figure 21.2). The mug did not have a single and invariant value; it had a different value depending on the context of the valuation. The opportunity cost of forgoing an entitlement was not valued the same as the real cost of giving it up, for example, and a gain was seen as being worth less than avoiding a loss. The difference in valuations of gains and losses can be expected to give rise to similar patterns in other cases as well, although the extent of the differences will vary for different entitle-ments and different valuation contexts. While specific tests for such patterns have been limited, the evidence that is available strongly suggests that this predictable pattern appears over a wide array of examples and circumstances.

Bateman and colleagues (1997), for example, asked people to value a common good, four cans of cola drinks, using different reference positions similar to those used in the mug experi-ment noted above. Arraying the proportions of individuals preferring £0.80 to the cola, which they report in similar quadrant fashion (Figure 21.3), reveals the same predicted pattern of valuations. The aversion to giving up this sum of money to gain the cola drinks, relative to the reverse of losing the cola drinks to gain money, is evident in the 60 percent who valued money more than cola in the first case (Quadrant I) and the minimal 16 percent who did so in the second (Quadrant III). The equivalent gain (Quadrant II) and equivalent loss (Quadrant IV) measures are predictably between the others, with their relative valuations presumably reflect-ing the strength of the loss aversion of the good (cans of cola, in this case) relative to that of the numeraire (money, in this case).

The same pattern is also evident in another test involving choices between two goods, rather than between money and a good. In this case, three different groups of participants valued a coffee mug relative to a chocolate bar (Knetsch 1989). Individuals in one group were initially given a chocolate bar and then offered an exchange involving giving up the chocolate bar to gain a mug. Those in a second group were given a choice of gaining either one of the two goods.

Figure 21.4   **Proportion of Individuals Preferring a Mug to a Chocolate Bar**

Figure 21.5   **Proportion of Individuals Preferring 0.5 Percent Change in the Risk of an Accident to CAD$700**

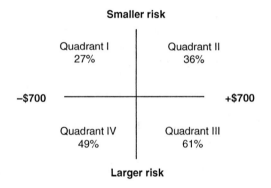

People in the third group were first given a mug and then offered a chocolate bar in exchange. As individuals in all three groups could easily select their preferred good, the standard stability-of-preferences assumption offers the clear prediction of equal proportions across the three groups. However, as indicated in Figure 21.4, the proportion of individuals preferring a mug to a chocolate bar varied from 10 percent (Quadrant I) to 89 percent (Quadrant III). The equivalent gain measure (Quadrant II) was predictably between the other measures (at 56 percent).

The expected pattern has also been found for valuations of risks. In one examination, respondents in a random Toronto household telephone survey were asked one of four valuation questions involving a choice between a CAD$700 change in annual income and a 0.5 percent change (from either 0.5 to 1 percent, or from 1 to 0.5 percent) in the chance of having "to be admitted to hospital in any given year as a result of a car accident, a work injury, a fall, or some other mishap" (Figure 21.5).

A further test involved time preferences. Just as people are willing to pay less for a present gain than they are willing to accept for a commensurate present loss, they can also be expected to pay less now for a future gain than they demand now to accept a future loss. As the sums they are willing to pay and willing to accept are then the present values of these future outcomes, the

Figure 21.6   **The Present Value, in Days, of 11 Days of Vacation Five Years in the Future**

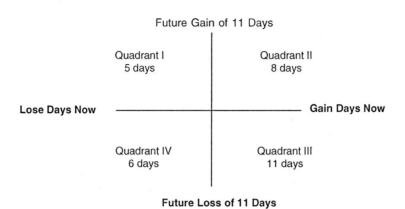

differences between them imply that people use different rates of discount for future gains and future losses.

This again predictable pattern was found when people were asked to indicate how they would trade off the number of days of vacation given by their employers in the current year and in the future. Four groups of respondents were asked to value the gain or the loss of eleven days of vacation time five years in the future in terms of receiving added days, or giving up days, of vacation time in the present year. The results indicate that people used different rates to discount the value of the future outcomes, with the rates predictably dependent on the particular gain or loss context of the valuation. People were willing to give up relatively few present days to gain eleven days in the future, suggesting a small present value and higher discount rate in this context. They demanded a significantly ($p < 0.01$) larger number of days now to accept a future loss, indicating a large present value and low discount rate for the future loss (Figure 21.6). The equivalent gain and equivalent loss rates, as expected, fell between and were not significantly different from each other ($p = 0.3383$).

Over all of these examples of varied exchanges—money for goods, goods for goods, risk changes, and the trade-offs between present and future outcomes—the patterns of varying rates were similar and, importantly, predictably so. While all of these results violate the preference stability assumptions, each of the variations is in accord with the predicted impact of the single-context variable of a change being a lower-valued gain or a higher-valued loss.

OTHER CONTEXT VARIABLES: VALUATIONS IN SECOND- AND NINTH-PRICE VICKREY AUCTIONS

A further series of experiments was carried out to test for not only the impact of gains and losses on valuations but also the impact of a different form of context dependence—the different evaluations of attributes of an entitlement that vary between two forms of Vickrey auctions. This preference-revealing mechanism is widely believed to have "the remarkable property that each bidder should announce his true willingness to pay for the auctioned object as a dominant strategy" (Laffont 1987, 268) and is widely used in experimental and behavioral economics research studies. The empirical studies reported here were parts of a series carried out in Canada, Singapore,

Table 21.1

The Median Maximum Amount Individuals Would Pay to Buy a Mug and Median Minimum Amount Individuals Would Accept to Sell a Mug: Canada Sample
(CAD$, $N = 20$ for each manipulation)

Trial	1	2	3	4	5	6	All
WTP to buy							
Second-price auction	4.50	5.00	4.88	5.03	5.52	5.15	5.01
Ninth-price auction	3.45	2.63	2.08	1.70	1.60	1.00	2.97
WTA to sell							
Second-price auction	5.00	4.75	4.75	5.00	4.75	5.00	4.83
Ninth-price auction	9.00	10.00	10.50	10.25	10.75	10.75	10.07

and the People's Republic of China, and thereby also provide some evidence of possible cultural impacts—or lack thereof—on this limited form of economic behavior.

Canada Data

The first test was a between-subject comparison of the valuation of a simple good in a real, not hypothetical, exchange Vickrey auction by Canadian undergraduate students (each of whom was paid CAD$10 for participating). All participants, in groups of ten, valued a coffee mug in one of four versions of a Vickrey auction. Two versions—a second-price auction and a ninth-price auction—elicited values in terms of the maximum sum each individual was willing to pay for a mug. In the other two versions—again, a second- and ninth-price Vickrey auction—the valuation of a mug was in terms of the minimum amount each would accept to give up a mug (Knetsch, Tang, and Thaler 2001). Each auction was repeated six times for each group, with the winning price posted between rounds and the trial that was used as the basis for the actual exchanges selected by random draw after the last round was completed.

In a second-price auction, the buyer willing to pay the highest sum buys the good at the second-highest price, and the seller willing to sell at the lowest price sells it at the second-lowest price. In the ninth-price auction, eight of the ten individuals in each group buy a mug at the ninth-highest price, and eight sell a mug at the ninth-lowest price. If preferences are stable over contexts, in accord with the conventional assumption, this manipulation should have no effect on the bids and offers made by these individuals—they should reveal equal values in either the second- or ninth-price version (as well as indicate the same buying and selling valuations).

The actual results were very different from those expected with the stability assumption of procedural invariance (Table 21.1). The identical good—a mug—was systematically valued differently in the context of an auction in which buying or selling one mug was on offer than in the context of an auction in which eight mugs were bought or sold ($p < 0.001$ for t-test of individual bid medians, for both buying and selling). There was little evidence of a disparity between buying and selling prices in the second-price auctions—a result fully consistent with the results reported by Shogren and colleagues (1994). The patterns were very different for the ninth-price auction, where a large difference was evident in the first valuation round (a median buy value of $3.45 and a median sell value of $9.00). The difference grew even larger over successive trials ($1.00 versus $10.75 in the final trial). Clearly, not only did the different context of a gain or loss of a mug lead to different valuations, but the context of a second- or ninth-price auction also influenced the resulting values.

Table 21.2

The Median Maximum Amount Individuals Would Pay to Buy a Mug and Median Minimum Amount Individuals Would Accept to Sell a Mug: Singapore Sample
(S$, N = 20 for each manipulation)

Trial	1	2	3	4	5	6	All
WTP to buy							
Second-price auction	3.00	3.00	2.60	2.50	2.00	2.50	2.60
Ninth-price auction	2.00	1.00	1.26	1.00	1.00	1.00	1.00
WTA to sell							
Second-price auction	3.40	2.25	3.00	2.00	2.00	2.00	2.50
Ninth-price auction	5.00	8.00	10.00	10.00	11.00	12.50	9.00

Singapore Data

The comparison of second- and ninth-price Vickrey auction valuations was repeated in a second real (not hypothetical) exchange experimental study carried out in Singapore. The Canadian study used a between-subject design in which the valuations of participants in a second-price auction were compared to the valuations of those taking part in a ninth-price auction. The Singapore study used a within-subject design, in which the same individuals named both a second and a ninth price in each of the six rounds. Participants were told the auction would be conducted in one of two ways, with the rule that counts to be decided later by a flip of a coin, and that they would therefore need to name two prices, which "can be the same or different." The Singapore participants were not paid a fee for taking part in the experiment, but all of the other details of the experimental tests in Singapore and Canada, including the actual exchanges of mugs and money, were essentially the same.

The results of the Singapore test (Table 21.2) were very comparable to those from the study in Canada (Table 21.1). Again, the significantly different valuations in the second- and ninth-price auctions were apparent both in the sums demanded to give up a mug and in the amounts people were willing to pay to acquire a mug ($p < 0.001$ for individual bid medians for both buying and selling). The median sum over all trials that participants were willing to pay to acquire a mug was $2.60 in the second-price auctions and $1.00 in the ninth-price auctions; the comparable median sum they demanded to give up a mug was $2.50 in the second-price auctions and $9.00 in the ninth-price auctions. Again, no differences between gain and loss values were evident in the second-price auction, and large differences in the initial trial that increased over successive rounds were exhibited in the ninth-price auctions.

It seems clear in the results of both the Canada and Singapore experiments that individuals valued a common good, a coffee mug, differently depending not just on its gain or loss but on other particulars of the context in which the valuations were made—in this case whether a second- or ninth-price auction was used. This was true for both between-subject comparisons (the Canada data) and within-subject comparisons (the Singapore data), and for both acquiring a mug (the maximum willingness to pay) and giving up a mug (the minimum compensation demanded).

OTHER CONTEXT-DEPENDENT VALUATIONS

People's valuations of entitlements can vary not just on the basis of their being gains or losses or the nature of an auction used to elicit values but because of other context variables as well. Different contexts appear to give rise to varying valuations, at least in part by altering the prominence of particular attributes of an entitlement. This effect of shifting attention to different characteristics of a good was demonstrated by Hsee in a series of joint versus separate valuations (1998). In one experiment, participants seeing only a small cup overflowing with ice cream were willing to pay significantly more for it than other individuals were willing to pay for a partially filled large cup, even though the large cup contained far more ice cream than the smaller one. When a third group was offered both cups together, the participants had no difficulty seeing the difference in the size of the servings and priced them accordingly. This reversal of preference apparently occurred because when they were offered one cup at a time there was little reference for judging whether the serving was large or small. Individuals therefore tended to ignore this quantity characteristic and instead gave undue prominence to the nominally irrelevant factor of how much of the cup was filled with ice cream. Because of this, they valued the serving in the small cup more highly. However, when the two cups were offered together, the comparison provided a ready reference for judging the quantity dimension and the relative attractiveness of the two servings, resulting in their ignoring cup size and placing a higher value on the larger serving.

An example of a similar role of context influencing people's views of the importance of an attribute was provided by people rating a lottery offering a 7/36 chance to win $9 and a 29/36 chance to lose $0.05 to be significantly more attractive than others' rating of a lottery offering only the same chance to win $9 without the possibility of a loss (Slovic et al. 2002). Even though the offer to the first group is slightly inferior to the other, because of the possibility of losing $0.05, people in the second group had little basis for judging their offer to be very attractive. The introduction of the small loss to the first group provided a reference, or basis, for judging, and they immediately saw the chance to win $9 and only lose $0.05 to be a good deal.

The differing contexts of choosing or rejecting may also shift the focus of attention among different attributes and give rise to different preferences (Shafir 1993). People tend to increase their weighting of positive dimensions of goods when asked to choose between them and to weigh negative characteristics more when asked to reject one of them. Consequently, there often is a tendency to prefer one good over another in the context of choosing and to prefer the other in the context of rejecting.

These and many other examples suggest that different attributes of a good or object often appear to be more or less salient depending on the circumstances, or context, of the valuation (Kahneman, Ritov, and Schkade 1999). Increasing the focus on more salient attributes seems to increase the prominence or weight people give to these characteristics. This both increases the significance of these attributes in the final choice or judgment and inhibits the processing of information about other attributes, thereby further decreasing their importance. As well, this initial valuation reaction is likely to effectively create an anchor from which adjustments may be inhibited. All of this often leads to some attributes being given greater weight than warranted by conventional views of economic values, and other characteristics being given less importance.

DEGREES OF CONTEXT DEPENDENCE

The evidence suggests that the value an individual places on an entitlement, in the usual sense of a willingness to sacrifice, will likely be a function of the context variables that are relevant to the particular valuation.[5] That is, the value will vary depending on, for example, whether it is in terms of a gain or a loss, whether it is in a context that provides a choice or one that provides little or no reference guidance, and whether it is for a present or future outcome. The sensitivity to these context variables can be expected to vary for different goods, in a manner perhaps analogous to the different sensitivities of market goods to price and the incomes of potential buyers. Some goods have a higher price elasticity of demand than others, some have a higher income elasticity, and some have higher cross-price elasticities of demand. While some characteristics of goods are known to influence these elasticities—goods with more substitutes will tend to have a larger price elasticity of demand than ones with fewer, for example—determining the coefficients of elasticity for individual goods remains largely an empirical matter.

The available findings indicate that much the same may be expected for the impacts of context on values; some context variables are likely to have the same sorts of impacts on different valuations, but determinations of particular influences seem also to be largely an empirical matter. Analogous to coefficients of elasticity, what might be thought of as context-dependent coefficients seem likely to be functions of particulars of the valuations.

An illustration of differences and possible patterns in the impact of context variables on valuations was provided by a further series of Vickrey auction experimental studies. In this case each included a variation in the size of the group taking part in the auction to either buy or sell a good. The impact of changes in the number of bidders has been the subject of several studies, mainly tests of the prediction that increased numbers would lead to more aggressive bidding and higher prices (a review is provided by Kagel 1995).

Singapore Data

One real exchange study, carried out in Singapore as part of the earlier series, involved a large number of entitlements to be gained or lost, comparable to the ninth-price auction of the earlier comparisons. Participants again took part in groups of ten. After explanations of the nature of the auctions and how payouts would take place, sellers were informed (with analogous instructions for buyers), "For each round, the auction will be conducted in one of two ways. The one that counts will be determined later by a flip of a coin." One rule was that the auction would involve all ten individuals, with eight selling at the ninth-lowest price. The other rule was that the group would be divided randomly into two groups of five, with three of the five in each small group selling at the fourth-lowest price. They were then instructed to make two offer prices, one for each group size eventuality.

As in the earlier ninth-price auctions, large differences between WTA and WTP values are again evident in the results. The valuations, however, indicate less, and inconsistent, sensitivity to the size of the group (Table 21.3). There was a small, and not significant, difference between the valuations of large and small groups for WTP valuations ($p > 0.30$ for t-test of individual bid medians). The differences between median WTA values for small and large groups were significant, though of modest size ($p < 0.01$).

China Data

A further real exchange test of the influence of group size on valuations was carried out at Chongqing University in the People's Republic of China, with senior computer and architecture students taking part. While the essentials of the experiment mirrored those of the group size experiment conducted in Singapore, this second test included second-price auctions for both large and small groups, as well as ninth-price auctions for large groups and fourth-price auctions for small groups. As mugs were not available, comparably priced graduation photo albums were used in this experiment.

The China results were consistent with those from the earlier tests conducted in Canada and Singapore in several important ways (Table 21.4). There was again a large difference in WTA

Table 21.3

The Median Maximum Amount Individuals Would Pay to Buy a Mug and Median Minimum Amount Individuals Would Accept to Sell a Mug in Small and Large Groups: Singapore Sample (S$, *N* = 20 for each manipulation)

Trial	1	2	3	4	5	6	All
WTP to buy							
Small group (fourth price)	4.00	2.50	2.25	2.25	2.05	2.00	2.50
Large group (ninth price)	5.00	3.00	2.00	2.25	2.00	1.35	2.00
WTA to sell							
Small group (fourth price)	5.00	5.75	5.80	5.75	6.00	6.00	6.00
Large group (ninth price)	6.00	7.50	7.00	8.00	9.00	9.25	8.00

Table 21.4

The Median Maximum Amount Individuals Would Pay to Buy an Album and Median Minimum Amount Individuals Would Accept to Sell an Album, by Group Size and Varied Price Auctions: China Sample (¥, *N* = 20 for each manipulation)

Trial	1	2	3	4	5	6	All
WTP to buy							
Second-price auction							
Small group	4.50	3.96	3.79	3.72	3.70	3.85	3.92
Large group	4.33	4.21	3.93	3.89	3.96	4.12	4.07
Fourth- and ninth-price auction							
Small group (fourth price)	2.09	2.14	2.59	2.57	2.50	3.40	2.55
Large group (ninth price)	2.27	2.58	3.02	2.88	2.84	3.70	2.88
WTA to sell							
Second-price auction							
Small group	7.04	6.04	4.46	4.15	3.49	3.52	4.78
Large group	6.98	5.56	3.92	3.43	2.87	3.04	4.30
Fourth- and ninth-price auction							
Small group (fourth price)	11.72	12.09	11.39	11.15	11.68	10.55	11.44
Large group (ninth price)	13.90	13.98	14.70	14.17	14.55	13.99	14.22

and WTP values in the ninth-price auctions, but little in the second-price auctions. The size of the group also had a smaller and less consistent impact on valuations. As with the Singapore results, there was no significant difference between the fourth- and ninth-price WTP values for small and large groups ($p = 0.259$), but there was a significant, though relatively modest in absolute size, difference between the fourth- and ninth-price WTA values of small and large groups ($p = 0.0075$). There were smaller, and marginally nonsignificant, differences between the small and large groups using second-price WTP and WTA valuations ($p = 0.0691$ and $p = 0.0763$, respectively).

There was some suggestion, at least in this data set, that the number of entitlements being bought or sold may be an important context variable. When only one album was to change hands, participants seemed to give greater prominence to this variable and to give less weight to the gain or loss attribute, thereby giving rise to the lack of significant differences between WTA and WTP values in second-price auctions. With more albums changing hands in the ninth-price auctions for large groups and fourth-price ones for small groups, more prominence was given to whether a gain or a loss was at issue—consistent with the finding of large differences in the ninth-price auctions.

In all, the results demonstrate that different context variables vary in the magnitude of their impact on preferences and valuations. They also indicate that variables such as the size of the group are likely to have a far smaller impact on valuations than the context variables of gain or loss and second- or ninth-price auctions.

CONCLUSION

There appears to be little evidence that people hold stable preferences in the common textbook sense. The preferences that are revealed in the real choices in the experiments reported here, and in other studies, are context-dependent rather than stable and invariant to valuation procedures.[6] Further, the results of these studies suggest that some context variables, such as the gain or the loss of an entitlement, impart a very predictable influence on preferences and valuations. However, there appear to be many other context variables that have varying, and sometimes dramatic if less obviously predictable, impacts—the large difference between second- and ninth price-valuations in Vickrey auctions seems to be such a case.

To the extent that context variables change the prominence or importance of different attributes of entitlements, the same good may take on the character of becoming essentially different goods in different contexts. That is, the loss dimension becomes a prominent attribute of the good in the context of a loss, and the gain dimension becomes one in the context of a gain. This might help explain, for example, the seemingly low correlations observed between people's buy and sell prices in several within-subject experiments (Borges and Knetsch 1998). A reasonable presumption would seem to be that individuals valuing a good more would be willing to both pay more to obtain it and demand more to give it up, and that those valuing it less would be willing to both pay less for it and demand less for its loss—giving rise to high buy and sell correlations. However, the limited evidence on this suggests correlation coefficients in the range of 0.25 to 0.40. While there may be other explanations, such low correlations seem consistent with people viewing a good in the context of a loss as being in some essentials a different good from that in the context of a gain—and there would then be little more reason to expect high buy and sell correlations for the nominally same good than there would be to expect them when people are buying and selling completely different entitlements.

Context-dependent preferences would presumably include stable preferences as a special case—one that might arise with, for example, near-perfect substitutes valued in identical contexts. Viewing context dependence as a more general class would appear to offer better explanations of a wider range of economic behavior, to include, for example, a wide range of what are now commonly taken to be preference reversals.

In much the same way, the context-dependent way in which gains and losses are differently weighed gives rise to the observed lack of complete reversibility of indifference curves as individuals demand more to give up one good than they are prepared to exchange for another (Knetsch 1989). Similarly, the gains from trade are likely to be overstated by analyses based on standard theory (Borges and Knetsch 1998), and nearly all standard preference order assumptions are commonly violated by people's actual behavior (Knetsch 1995).

Nearly all comment on the observed discrepancy between people's behavior and that suggested by standard models of rational economic choice suggests that such differences are due to either some broadly defined forms of transaction costs, including the effort necessary to think through the implications of options, or human limitations of not being able to accurately discern all of the implications and consequences of all alternatives (bounded rationality). Both of these traditional explanations no doubt account for many of the disparities.

However, the evidence is also consistent with people's behavior and choices not being

hampered by transaction costs or bounded rationality but instead reflecting their real preferences—preferences that are not accurately modeled by the standard economic theory of rational choice.

While economics texts have long proclaimed that people's valuations of gains and losses should
be equivalent (except for an income or wealth effect), there seems to be little reason for accepting
this empirically unsubstantiated behavioral assertion as an accurate description of people's actual
preferences and therefore the standard of how they should behave. The empirical evidence suggests when people demand a higher sum to give up a good than they are willing to pay to acquire
the identical entitlement, they are not making mistakes and they are not displaying the inability to
foresee the consequences of their actions. This is not to suggest that human limitations implied by
bounded rationality are not important. But it is to suggest that this is not likely the whole of the
matter, and may not even be the more interesting part of it.

NOTES

This research was supported in part by the U.S. Forest Service through a cooperative agreement with Simon
Fraser University.

1. It is also nearly certain that Amos Tversky would have shared the prize had it not been for his early
death in 1996. Kahneman and Tversky's decision to publish their 1979 paper on prospect theory in
Econometrica, one of the most notable international journals in all of economics, was made not because of
"a wish to influence economics" but instead largely on the grounds that this "just happened to be the journal
where the best papers on decision-making to date had been published, and we were aspiring to be in that
company" (Kahneman 2003a, 13). It is, and has been for many years, by far the most often cited paper ever
published in *Econometrica,* and one of the most cited in all of economics—a testament not only to its
importance but to the wide range of the implications of their findings.

2. Many of the most notable studies and detailing of implications of these findings have been collected
in Kahneman and Tversky 2000.

3. The order of the two transactions was reversed for half of the participants to eliminate any order
effects on the valuations.

4. This is usually done by having the experimenter stand ready to redeem the token at whatever price is
specified.

5. The variability of valuations demonstrated by the many reported examples has prompted the suggestion that preferences might better be thought of as being "constructed" or "assembled" during the decision
process, rather than revealed by it (Payne, Bettman, and Johnson 1992; Slovic 1995). However, it seems
more accurate to describe most economic preferences as being "rather imprecise, organized (perhaps fairly
loosely) around certain very basic principles" (Loomes 1998, 478), perhaps more akin to being context-
dependent, the term used here.

6. While a very limited test for any cultural differences, the results indicate similar behavior among the
participants in Canada, Singapore, and China. Given what seems to be little empirical evidence relative to
the large numbers of speculations and assertions of the likely impacts of such differences on economic
behavior of the sort examined here, results of further tests might be of considerable interest.

REFERENCES

Bateman, Ian, Alistair Munro, Bruce Rhodes, Chris Starmer, and Robert Sugden. 1997. "A Test of the
    Theory of Reference-Dependent Preferences." *The Quarterly Journal of Economics* 92: 479–505.
Borges, Bernhard F.J., and Jack L. Knetsch. 1998. "Tests of Market Outcomes with Asymmetric Valuations
    of Gains and Losses: Smaller Gains, Fewer Trades, and Less Value." *Journal of Economic Behavior and
    Organization* 33: 185–93.
Cohen, David, and Jack L. Knetsch. 1992. "Judicial Choice and Disparities Between Measures of Economic
    Values." *Osgoode Hall Law Journal* 30: 737–70.
Gordon, Irene M., and Jack L. Knetsch. 1979. "Consumer's Surplus Measures and the Evaluation of Re-
    sources." *Land Economics* 34: 1–10.

Hammack, Judd, and Gardner M. Brown. 1974. *Waterfowl and Wetlands: Toward Bio-Economic Analysis.* Baltimore: Johns Hopkins University Press.

Henderson, A.M. 1941. "Consumer's Surplus and the Compensation Variation." *Review of Economic Studies* 8: 117.

Holmes, Oliver Wendell. 1897. "The Path of the Law." *Harvard Law Review* 10: 457–78.

Horowitz, J.K., and K.E. McConnell. 2002. "A Review of WTA/WTP Studies." *Journal of Environmental Economics and Management* 44: 426–47.

Hsee, Chris M. 1998. "Less Is Better: When Low-Value Options Are Valued More Highly than High-Value Options." *Journal of Behavioral Decision Making* 11: 107–21.

Johnson, E.J., J. Hershey, J. Meszaro, and H. Kunreuther. 1993. "Framing, Probability Distortions, and Insurance Decisions." *Journal of Risk and Uncertainty* 7: 35–51.

Kachelmeier, Steven J., and Mohd. Shehata. 1992. "Examining Risk Preferences Under High Monetary Incentives: Experimental Evidence from the People's Republic of China." *American Economic Review* 82: 1120–40.

Kagel, John H. 1995. "Auctions: A Survey of Experimental Research." In John H. Kagel and Alvin E. Roth, eds., *Handbook of Experimental Economics,* 501–85. Princeton, NJ: Princeton University Press.

Kahneman, Daniel. 2003a. "Daniel Kahneman—Autobiography" (available at http://nobelprize.org/economics/laureates/2002/kahneman-autobio.html).

———. 2003b. "A Perspective on Judgment and Choice: Mapping Bounded Rationality." *American Psychologist* 58: 697–720.

Kahneman, Daniel, Jack L. Knetsch, and Richard H. Thaler. 1986. "Fairness as a Constraint on Profit Seeking: Entitlements in the Market." *American Economic Review* 76: 728–41.

———. 1990. "Experimental Tests of the Endowment Effect and the Coase Theorem." *Journal of Political Economy* 98: 1325–48.

Kahneman, Daniel, Ilana Ritov, and David Schkade. 1999. "Economic Preferences or Attitude Expressions? An Analysis of Dollar Responses to Public Issues." *Journal of Risk and Uncertainty* 19: 136–53.

Kahneman, Daniel, and Amos Tversky. 1979. "Prospect Theory: An Analysis of Decisions Under Risk." *Econometrica* 47: 263–91.

———. 2000. *Choices, Values, and Frames.* New York: Cambridge University Press.

Knetsch, Jack L. 1989. "The Endowment Effect and Evidence of Nonreversible Indifference Curves." *American Economic Review* 79: 1277–84.

———. 1995. "Asymmetric Valuation of Gains and Losses and Preference Order Assumptions." *Economic Inquiry* 33: 134–41.

Knetsch, Jack L., and John A. Sinden. 1984. "Willingness to Pay and Compensation Demanded: Experimental Evidence of an Unexpected Disparity in Measures of Value." *Quarterly Journal of Economics* 99: 507–21.

Knetsch, Jack L. Fang-Fang Tang, and Richard H. Thaler. 2001. "The Endowment Effect and Repeated Market Trials: Is the Vickrey Auction Demand Revealing?" *Experimental Economics* 4: 257–68.

Laffont, J.J. 1987. "Revelation of Preferences." In John Eatwell, Murray Milgate, and Peter Newman, eds., *The New Palgrave: A Dictionary of Economics,* 170–71. London: Macmillan.

List, John A. 2003. "Does Market Experience Eliminate Market Anomalies?" *Quarterly Journal of Economics* 118: 47–71.

Loomes, Graham. 1998. "Probabilities vs Money: A Test of Some Fundamental Assumptions About Rational Decision Making." *Economic Journal* 108: 477–89.

———. 1999. "Some Lessons from Past Experiments and Some Challenges for the Future." *Economic Journal* 109: F34–45.

Markowitz, Harry. 1952. "The Utility of Wealth." *Journal of Political Economy* 60: 151–58.

Odean, Terrance. 1998. "Are Investors Reluctant to Realize Their Losses?" *Journal of Finance* 53: 1775–98.

Payne, John W., James R. Bettman, and Eric Johnson. 1992. "Behavioral Decision Research: A Constructive Processing Perspective." *Annual Review of Psychology* 43: 87–132.

Rabin, Matthew. 1998. "Psychology and Economics." *Journal of Economic Literature* 36: 11–46.

Shafir, Eldar. 1993. "Choosing Versus Rejecting: Why Some Options Are Both Better and Worse than Others." *Memory and Cognition* 21: 546–56.

Shefrin, H., and M. Statman. 1985. "The Disposition to Sell Winners Too Early and Ride Losers Too Long: Theory and Evidence." *Journal of Finance* 40: 777–90.

Shogren, Jason F., Seung Y. Shin, Dermot J. Hayes, and James B. Kliebenstein. 1994. "Resolving Differences in Willingness to Pay and Willingness to Accept." *American Economic Review* 84: 255–70.

Slovic, Paul. 1995. "The Construction of Preference." *American Psychologist* 50: 364–71.

Slovic, Paul, M. Finucane, E. Peters, and D.G. MacGregor. 2002. "The Affect Heuristic." In T. Gilovich, D. Griffin, and D. Kahneman, eds., *Heuristics and Biases: The Psychology of Intuitive Judgment.* Cambridge: Cambridge University Press.

Smith, Adam. 1759. *The Theory of Moral Sentiments.* Indianapolis: Liberty Press, 1982.

Smith, Vernon L. 1994. "Economics in the Laboratory." *Journal of Economic Perspectives* 8: 113–31.

Thaler, Richard H. 1980. "Toward a Positive Theory of Consumer Choice." *Journal of Economic Organization and Behavior* 1: 39–60.

Thaler, Richard H., and Shlomo Benartzi. 2004. "Saving More Tomorrow: Using Behavioral Economics to Increase Employee Saving." *Journal of Political Economy* 112: S164–87.

Tversky, Amos, and Daniel Kahneman. 1992. "Advances in Prospect Theory: Cumulative Representation of Uncertainty." *Journal of Risk and Uncertainty* 5: 297–323.

Viscusi, W. Kip, Wesley A. Magat, and Joel Huber. 1987. "An Investigation of the Rationality of Consumer Valuations of Multiple Health Risks," *Rand Journal of Economics* 18: 465–79.

CHAPTER 22

EXPERIMENTS AND BEHAVIORAL ECONOMICS

ROBERT J. OXOBY

Experimental methods are now considered an important part of economic research. This should come as no surprise: for a field so closely aligned with psychology in its interest in individual behavior, experimental methods are a natural (and some would argue necessary) tool. Concurrently, the "second wave" of research in behavioral economics (Rabin 1998, 2002) has brought recognition to the value of incorporating psychological insights into economic theory. The implications of these insights are becoming increasingly important in enriching (and invigorating) economic theory and informing policy debates.

As a result, economists have been actively using experimental methods, the traditional methodology of psychologists. Following the reasoning of others (e.g., Lazear 2000), the strength of economists' theoretical methodology provides the opportunity and ability to pursue research questions traditionally considered outside the purview of economics. Indeed, methodological individualism and mathematical formalism provide economics with an advantage over other social sciences in tractably identifying the assumptions that underlie human behavior. These advantages make economics, in many ways, an ideal realm for experimental methods. The clear definition of assumptions provides researchers with formal refutable hypotheses that can be directly tested in laboratory environments.

That said, the rapid growth in the application of experimental methods in economics and the increasing focus on behavioral issues brings a strong need to reevaluate experimental methodology as applied in economics (and other disciplines, for that matter). In this chapter, we review some of the basic elements of the experimental methods employed in economics and critically examine how economists conduct experiments. Our attention here is on how the research conducted by behavioral economists may be compromised by some of the experimental methods currently employed in economics. Thus our intent is not to develop a manual of how to conduct an experiment (interested readers are referred to Friedman and Sunder 1994; Davis and Holt 1993; Aronson, Wilson, and Brewer 1998). Rather, we raise a series of issues that economists (whether theorists, experimentalists, or policy makers) should bear in mind regarding the application of experimental methods in economics, particularly when exploring behavioral aspects of decision making. Specifically, we focus our attention on the issues of validity and realism as applied to the use of experiments in research in behavioral economics.

EXPERIMENTAL METHODS IN ECONOMICS

While there does not appear to be a well-specified set of professional standards for conducting economics experiments, there is general agreement on the necessary components for a good experiment (for example, see Davis and Holt 1993; Friedman and Sunder 1994; Roth 1988; Smith 1987). Violating these guides may result in experiments conducted in "dirty test tubes" (Binmore 1999) and results that inadequately test the hypotheses in question.

First and foremost, participants in an economics experiment must face adequate incentives. Given economists' focus on the application of cost-benefit analysis in decision making, the provision of adequate and salient incentives is a necessary condition for observing economic decision making in the laboratory. Second, most economists agree that the problem faced by participants in an experiment must not be too complex and must be framed in a manner simple enough for participants to understand. Third, if we are interested in decision making, experiments must allow participants to make good, effective decisions. Thus, deception is inappropriate (and potentially damaging) for economics experiments.[1] Finally, many experimental economists believe that time for trial and error must be allowed for participants to learn the workings of an experiment (i.e., how to "play the game"). Many of the experimental games used in economics are abstract or foreign to day-to-day decision making. Thus, repetition might be in order to allow participants to make trial-and-error adjustments. Given these guidelines, our interest is in how these aspects of an economics experiment influence the validity and realism of experimental results for research questions in behavioral economics.

In the discussion of validity and realism in experiments, it is useful to have an example to illustrate various concepts. Throughout this chapter we will make use of the ultimatum game as an example. In the ultimatum game, a proposer is allocated an endowment ω of which she must choose an amount $x \in [0, \omega]$ to offer a responder. The responder can then either accept or reject the offer. If the offer is accepted, the responder receives a payoff of x and the proposer receives a payoff of $\omega - x$. If the offer is rejected, each participant receives a payoff of zero.

As economics folklore has it, the ultimatum game was first proposed to Werner Güth (Güth, Schmittberger, and Schwarze 1982) by Reinhardt Selten as an example of a game in which there would be consistent deviations from the subgame perfect Nash equilibrium (Selten 1975). Given preferences over own wealth, subgame perfection implies that the responder will accept any non-negative offer and, given this, the proposer will choose $x = 0$. On the other hand, ultimatum game experiments indicate that responders typically reject offers of less than 30 percent of the endowment, and proposers offer between 30 and 50 percent of the endowment. This game has been widely studied and experimental results are strikingly robust across incentive amounts, cultures, and elicitation methods (Henrich et al. 2001; Oxoby and McLeish 2003; Roth et al. 1991; Slonim and Roth 1998; see Camerer 2003 for a thorough review of this literature and results). As a result, the ultimatum game is often used in the motivation of theoretic models of fairness, reciprocity, and other forms of concern for others (e.g., Bolton and Ockenfels 2000; Charness and Rabin 2002; Fehr and Schmidt 1999).

EXPERIMENTAL VALIDITY

One of the primary advantages of experiments is the degree of control one obtains in identifying the causal relationships between dependent and independent variables. Ideally, one would like to conduct experiments in the field (i.e., natural or field experiments; see Harrison and List 2004) in which individuals make real decisions. However, experiments in the field are plagued by various forms of heterogeneity and "noise" that reduce one's ability to infer causal relationships. Economists, perhaps more than other social scientists, recognize the important trade-offs that exist between experimental control and outside realism.

In this section, we focus on these trade-offs by examining the types of validity experiments can provide for behavioral economists. Cook and Campbell (1979) identify three types of validity that may be used to interpret experimental results: internal validity, external validity, and construct validity.[2]

Internal Validity

Internal validity refers to the structure of an experiment itself and the degree with which one may infer causal relationships from the results. Internal validity asks the question, "To what extent are the independent (treatment) variables the sole source of the distribution of dependent variable?" The key in assessing internal validity is to examine the experiment to identify aspects of the decision environment, beyond the treatment variable, that could influence the experimental results. A good experiment makes use of the ability to observe behavior and decision making in a controlled environment, controlling the variation between experimental treatments to ensure that participants receive the same stimuli and experience the same conditions. As a result, the differences in observed behavior can be attributed to the differences participants encounter in the experimental treatments (i.e., the independent variables). The internal validity of an experiment is often questioned when there is noise in the experimental protocol or there are uncontrolled stimuli affecting participants' decisions in the experiment.

As an example, consider an experimental ultimatum game in which internal validity is compromised. A growing literature has examined the extent to which the threat of negative reciprocity in the ultimatum game (i.e., responders rejecting strictly positive offers) is subject to found-money effects.[3] Consider an ultimatum game experiment designed to identify the extent to which the distribution of offers is subject to the origin of the endowment used in bargaining. Thus the treatment variable is the source of the endowment used in bargaining. In the control treatment, participants play the ultimatum game following standard protocols (e.g., Güth, Schmittberger, and Schwarze 1982) in which the endowment is determined and provided by the experimenter. In the second treatment, the source of the endowment is altered. We will consider two potential sources for the endowment. In treatment T1, the endowment is provided not by the experimenter but rather by the proposers. That is, individuals assigned the role of proposer must provide an endowment from their own resources when they arrive at the experiment (cf. Clark 2002). In treatment T2, proposers must earn the endowment by engaging in some task.[4]

Consider the comparisons of experimental results between the control treatment and either treatment T1 or T2. Which of the treatment sessions (T1 or T2) provides stronger evidence of how robust behavior in the ultimatum game is to found-money effects? That is, is there greater internal validity in a comparison of the results from the control against results from treatment T1 or against results from treatment T2? Many would answer that there is greater internal validity in comparing the results from the control treatment with those from treatment T2, since between session T2 and the control session only one aspect of the decision environment has been altered (the mechanism used to allocate the endowments) and the experimenter can accurately observe how the endowment was determined. A similar difference exists between the control session and session T1, but the relationship between the source of the endowment and behavior is muddied, as the experimenter has no control or information regarding the determination or source of the money participants bring to the experiment—it could have been earned through the participants' employment, received as a gift, or unexpectedly found. Note that the latter two cases are examples of "found money" and precisely what the experimenter is trying to avoid in having participants provide their own endowments.

The key to obtaining internal validity is taking advantage of an experiment's ability to eliminate confounding factors that affect behavior and limit the differences between treatments to only one (or a selected number) of independent variables. In this way, the experimenter can neatly identify the effect of the independent variable(s) on decision making in the absence of confounds presented by other mitigating factors.

In addition to correctly choosing the independent variables in an experiment, a critical tool for achieving internal validity is random assignment. That is, if individuals are randomly assigned to each treatment in an experiment, then ex ante heterogeneity among the population of participants is controlled for insofar as there are no other factors (e.g., age, gender, level of education) that may directly differ between the treatments. Thus, given a properly designed experiment in which only the independent variables differ across treatments, random assignment solves the problem of internal validity. For example, there is ample evidence that individuals' personal and demographic characteristics have a strong influence on behavior. Eckel and Grossman (1998) find that women donate almost twice as much as men in anonymous dictator games. Similarly, Carter and Irons (1991) and Kahneman, Knetsch, and Thaler (1986) find that economics and business majors offer significantly less in ultimatum games.[5] Random assignment implies that the populations of participants in each treatment have similar distributions of personal characteristics (e.g., gender, education). Thus these (potentially unobservable) characteristics do not account for differences in the distribution of results between treatments.

In economics experiments, random assignment is often only partially implemented. In ideal circumstances, participants in an experiment would be assigned to different treatments and participate in the experiment at the same time. Thus, the population characteristics of the subject pool, differences in the communication of instructions, and temporal events that may affect participants in a similar manner (e.g., returning from a long weekend, lunch) are controlled.[6] While there may be no reason to think that these (seemingly minor) events could have an effect on behavior, neither is there any a priori reason to think that they will not affect behavior.[7]

In economics, we often observe comparisons between experimental results conducted at different times, with different participant pools, and administered by different experimenters. In such cases there is always the potential that the results may be attributable to events occurring in the period between the sessions, differences between the participant pools, or differences in the characteristics of the administrating experimenter (e.g., personality or demographic differences). To the reader seeking to inform theory or develop policy based on experimental results, one should always cautiously ask how much of the experiment's results may be attributable to such differences. For behavioral economists who are interested in using experiments to elucidate and explore psychological phenomena and processes in economic contexts, there is a rich literature demonstrating how these factors can influence participants' behavior in experiments (see Aronson, Wilson, and Brewer 1998).

Note that there may often be practical reasons for conducting the treatments of an experiment at different times or different places. For example, different treatments may require different continuances or facilities, which precludes conducting treatments at the same time. In such circumstances, the importance of random assignment in the initial phases of the experiment (i.e., recruiting) is heightened. This, along with the collection of demographic information to analyze the results for fixed effects, can help strengthen the internal validity of such experiments.

As a final note, psychologists typically regard within-subject designs as preferable to between-subject designs when it comes to maintaining internal validity. In within-subject designs, each subject participates in the experiment under each treatment. As such, each participant serves as her own control, thereby identifying individual-level differences that might otherwise be treated as errors in the analysis of a between-subject design. In many economics experiments, however, particularly when money is used as an incentive and where income effects may engender different types of behaviors, within-subject designs may actually introduce greater confounds. In such environments there is an implicit trade-off between the internal validity obtained from within-subject design and the internal validity obtained by controlling for wealth effects or other economic phenomena affecting decision making.

External Validity

While issues of internal validity may challenge the causal relationship inferred from an experiment's results, *external validity* addresses the extent to which the causal relationship identified in the experimental setting can be generalized to other contexts, places, times, and people (e.g., Andersen et al. 2004). Questions of external validity often revolve around the context or participant pool used in the experiment. More subtly, external validity refers to the particular causal relationship gleaned from an experiment and the extent to which this relationship is robust in other environments. For example, experiments of ersatz labor markets conducted with university students may be subject to the criticism of the subject pool involved, the characteristics of which may or may not be representative of the population actively involved in the labor market (Sears 1986). As such, the results from the experiment may not translate into policy that can be implemented in real labor markets.

A particularly difficult challenge to the external validity of experiments in behavioral economics is that of context. Economists are very wary of establishing context in their experiments. In public goods games, instructions typically avoid use of the words "public good," and labor market experiments refer to the artificial employers and employees as "type A" and "type B" participants. However, most of the decisions people make are viewed by the decision maker as being within a given context and accompanied by a particular history that influences the understanding of events. For experimentalists, establishing a little bit of context can go a long way: there are strong differences between the way participants play the "community game" and the "Wall Street game" even when these two games are identical variations of the prisoner's dilemma game (Loewenstein 1999).[8] Given the influential work of Kahneman and Tversky on framing effects and reference dependency (Kahneman and Tversky 1979, 1988), it is clear that contextual issues play an important role in determining individual and group decision making.

In some sense, the problem of context is particularly difficult for behavioral economists. Many of the very insights they seek to incorporate into economics (ideas of fairness, emotions, reciprocity) are founded on the contextual aspects of a decision environment. For example, while experiments with the ultimatum game have led to advances regarding theories of fairness and reciprocity (e.g., Charness and Rabin 2002; Dufwenberg and Kirchsteiger 2004), the game itself is usually conducted in the absence of any context. Rather, participants are assigned roles and no "story" is given as to why the proposer/responder relationship develops or exists. As such, participants look for a decision-making strategy to employ in this environment. Although participants may also look for such strategies when a context is established by the experimenter, the absence of context concedes control over interpreted context to the participant, thereby reducing the experimenter's control in the laboratory. The tension created between self-interest and rules of thumb such as 50-50 may explain the observed results of offers ranging from 30 to 40 percent and rejection of offers below 30 percent.

While there is little doubt of the robustness of ultimatum game results (Camerer 2003), let us consider how important context is in this experiment. First, we may think behavior in this game will be strongly influenced by norms (e.g., 50-50). As such, when playing this game without context, participants opt to implement a commonly understood norm of behavior. However, if the game is repeated, one may think of a context endogenously arising (at least in the minds of participants) and influencing behavior. For example, Binmore and colleagues (1993) find evolution toward the theoretic prediction in the distribution of offers and acceptance rates in a repeated ultimatum game.[9] This evolution may be evidence of the import of context: once participants have had an opportunity to experience the game, a new context may develop in which a new norm may come into being. The fact that we do not observe evolution to the subgame perfect Nash equilibrium should not come as a surprise: norms are strikingly robust, and when a norm is adhered to by a majority, transgressing it may be difficult.[10] Norms evolve slowly but systematically. The fact that we observe any evolution in the experimental environment developed by Binmore and colleagues (1993) should be taken as evidence that repetition can change the context of an experiment, thereby changing the rule of thumb or norm employed by participants.

A more important question of external validity arises when one considers the policy implications of an experiment. With the wider acceptance of incorporating behavioral insights into economics, economists conducting behavioral research are increasingly being asked questions that relate to economic policy (Camerer et al. 2003; Thaler and Sunstein 2003). While one might agree that results from experimental ultimatum games should inform economic theory, it is difficult to say precisely how these results should inform economic policy. Experimental results indicate that individuals take into account the payoffs of others in determining behavior, but how should such a finding influence policy regarding welfare programs, the provision of public goods (e.g., school choice initiatives or the funding of public schools), labor market regulation, or redistributive taxation? This is a trickier question, as individual decision making in the face of economic policy is rife with context. In bargaining environments, individuals are not proposers and responders but employers and employees, unions and firms, parents and children. The context created by these titles alone may significantly change the way in which others' payoffs are incorporated into one's utility function and how reciprocity or kindness are construed.

That said, it is worth asking how important external validity is to behavioral economics. In some sense, research in behavioral economics has been founded on the desire to develop a richer theory of decision making, one building on the neoclassical model but incorporating insights from research in psychology and sociology. Thus, many of the experiments in economics were devised to test existing theory and models rather than to make generalizations that might inform policy debates (e.g., Güth, Schmittberger, and Schwarze 1982). Indeed, much of the "first wave" of behavioral research in economics was characterized as anomalies against existing economic theory (see Thaler 1992). There is a definite benefit in theory testing, and experiments are an effective method toward this end.[11] Further, insofar as theory informs policy, so should experiments help in policy analysis and design. To borrow an analogy from Laver and Shepsle (1996), while experimental analysis and policy analysis are apples and oranges, they are both fruit. As such, one can certainly (although perhaps cautiously) inform policy analysis with the behavioral insights gained from experiments.

Construct Validity

As with external validity, *construct validity* challenges neither the internal consistency of an experiment nor the causal relationship between the dependent and independent variables inferred from the experiment's results. Rather, construct validity explores how these variables are measured in an individual's decision making and looks at the underlying relationship between these variables. A natural way to think of construct validity is in terms of how the dependent and independent variables are factored into an individual's decision calculus.

As an example of the import of construct validity in the ultimatum game, there have been several papers developing theoretical models explaining the large offers and rejection of strictly positive offers observed in experiments. For example, Fehr and Schmidt (1999) develop a model based on inequity aversion (extended to include efficiency concerns and reciprocity by Charness and Rabin 2002). Bolton and Ockenfels (2000) develop a similar model based on relative payoffs. Rabin (1993) models a "kindness function" that yields cooperation with or punishment of others' acts, and Dufwenberg and Kirchsteiger (2004) extend this to describe reciprocity in extensive form games. Each of these models differs in important ways that implicitly point to different psychological underpinnings of how the variables in the ultimatum game influence decision making. This issue of construct validity in the ultimatum game focuses on which of these models is "correct" in the way in which it characterizes decision making in that environment.

In a similar spirit, Rubinstein (2001) addresses the issue of construct validity using anomalies in intertemporal choice, demonstrating that both quasi-hyperbolic discounting (Laibson 1996) and a procedural decision rule based on canceling similar events (e.g., Tversky 1977) describe the same anomalies. Again, construct validity asks which of these models most accurately captures the fundamental psychological process that is at work in intertemporal decision making.

The construct validity of an experiment can be challenged in several ways. The complexity of the decision environment may compromise the contextual validity of an experiment by muddying the relationship between the treatment (independent) variable and the theoretic variable or issue of interest. Similarly, the context (or lack thereof) of an experiment may distort the extent to which the treatment variable appropriately represents the theoretical process and variables employed in decision making. The key to fostering construct validity is the proper choice of an independent variable and sufficient treatment conditions to allow the experimenter to identify the behavioral insight and process actually at work.[12]

REALISM

Most experimentalists agree that many of the experiments they conduct lack what would be casually referred to as realism. Due to the conditions of an experiment and the desire to control for outside influences on behavior, experiments (save for natural experiments) often lack realism in that the circumstances individuals are encountering are unlikely to arise in the real world (they are often referred to as lacking *mundane realism;* see Aronson, Wilson, and Brewer 1998). From the perspective of behavioral economics, mundane realism may not be the most important aspect of an experiment. Rather, in the interest of bringing psychological insights into the realm of economic analysis, economists conducting experiments should be concerned with *experimental realism* and *psychological realism.*

Experimental realism is often defined as the degree to which the situations constructed in the experiment actively engage participants. On the other hand, psychological realism (as defined by Aronson, Wilson, and Akert 1994) refers to the degree to which the psychological processes occurring in an experiment are comparable with the psychological processes occurring in ordinary decision making.

With respect to experimental realism, economists have often been critical of experiments in psychology and hypothetical studies (e.g., hypothetical contingent valuation studies) in which individuals' behaviors and decision making are not motivated by adequate incentives or deception was employed. In the eyes of economists, the results obtained from experiments with insufficient incentives may be suspect, as individuals were not able to "put their money where their mouth is" and their decisions had no consequences. In game-theoretic jargon, the behavior observed in these experiments may be only cheap talk and an inadequate reflection of what individuals would do if real incentives or costs were involved. This is not to say that experiments with hypothetical consequences have no value or cannot inform theory and empirical economics; rather, we should not expect these experiments to engage participants in the same way as experiments with real consequences (Binmore 1999; Holt 1995). Similarly, if participants believe they may be deceived in an experiment, they have no reason to try to make an optimal choice. Given that participants may be wary of the decision environment in the experiment, deception may imply that they do not even know how to make an optimal choice in that environment.

With respect to incentives, Smith (1987) presents a conceptual framework with two sufficient conditions for a valid controlled experiment: saliency and nonsatiation. Formally, saliency requires that for a given outcome x, individuals' rewards are linked to the outcome via a function mapping outcomes onto rewards: $\pi = f(x)$. Nonsatiation requires that the utility function defined over rewards be strictly increasing (the utility function is an increasing monotone function): if $\pi > \pi'$ then $u(\pi) > u(\pi')$.

Given these conditions, experimental economists usually insist on the use of adequate incentives in experiments, and these incentives are usually in the form of monetary payments. As argued by Smith, economists should "use a monetary reward function to induce utility value on the abstract accounting outcomes of an experiment" (1987, 245). Thus, the offers and rejections observed in an ultimatum game played with real money are considered more "valid" and a truer reflection of individuals' preferences than those obtained from an ultimatum game played with hypothetical money.

In a large sense, this type of thinking is right. However, as Loewenstein (1999) states, "experimental economists should not deceive themselves into believing that the use of such rewards allows them to control the incentives operating in their experiments." This is particularly true for experiments in behavioral economics. Many times the phenomena we are interested in studying (e.g., other-regarding behavior or decision-making heuristics) are motivated by nonmonetary incentives associated with conformity or maintaining one's self-esteem. Further, many of the decisions we make in real life are not motivated by monetary payments.

There has been active research on the effect of monetary incentives on decision making in experiments. In tests of expected utility theory, Loomes and Beattie (1997) and Loomes (1998) find that providing incentives to participants changes little the extent to which behavior violates the axioms of expected utility. In his experiences conducting experiments, Rubinstein (2001) found little difference between experiments conducted with no money and results published using real money. Similarly, Henrich and colleagues (2001), Oxoby and McLeish (2003), Roth and colleagues (1991), and Slonim and Roth (1998) find striking robustness in ultimatum game results across cultures, sizes of incentive, and elicitation methods. On the other hand, Blumenschein and colleagues (1997), Forsyth and colleagues (1994), Kruse Brown and Thompson (2001), and McClintock and McNeel (1967) find significant effects of incentives in experimental games. Thus, results on the importance of monetary incentives are mixed. The presence of these mixed results is supported by the review of Smith and Walker (1993): in some experiments the size of financial incentives matters little, while in others financial incentives reduce the deviations from theoretic predictions. These findings are consistent with the view expressed by Camerer: "The effect of paying subjects is likely to depend on the task they perform" (1995, 635).

Thus, even with the use of financial rewards, there may be questions regarding the extent to which experimental realism holds in an experiment. It may be not the nature of the monetary incentives per se that influences the realism of an experiment, but the context in which those incentives are provided. As a striking example, consider the research of Cherry, Frykblom, and Shogren (2002), Oxoby and Spraggon (forthcoming), and Ruffle (1996) on the influence of found-money effects. In these experiments, senders in dictator games allocated significantly more to themselves when they had "earned" the endowment and significantly more to receivers when they perceived the receiver as having "earned" the endowment. This should not be surprising: casual empiricism and research on found-money effects (Arkes et al. 1994; Thaler 1999) suggest that the source of an endowment of money plays a large role in how decisions are made over that money. These results indicate that one potential source of experimental realism is the legitimacy of assets in an experiment. As argued by Cherry, Frykblom, and Shogren, "just as rewards must be salient . . . the assets in a bargain must be legitimate to produce a rational result" (2002, 1220).

These results also point to a potential problem with experiments in behavioral economics regarding psychological realism. Taking the dictator game (or the ultimatum game, for that matter) as an example, there are very few circumstances in which a person may find herself in a real-world situation similar to the dictator game. Thus the game may lack external validity. While this may not be a major concern (see Mook 1983 and the preceding discussion), the fact that the endowments in a standard experiment are delivered by the experimenter may alter the way individuals think in the experiment. The results of Cherry, Frykblom, and Shogren (2002) provide a profound illustration of this: legitimizing assets on the part of dictators resulted in 95 percent support for the theoretic prediction. Thus, the standard dictator or ultimatum game may lack psychological realism in that the type of decision making participants display in the experiment may be very different from that employed in real-world situations.

The problems of psychological realism may be greater for behavioral economists given the standardized use of monetary incentives. There may be strong interactions between nonpecuniary motives and financial motives. Frey (1997) argues that the presence of monetary incentives may undermine or strengthen (depending on the decision-making environment) the intrinsic motivations of individuals. As a result, experiments that use financial rewards may be testing not the actual behavioral phenomena but rather how these phenomena are altered by monetary concerns. To the extent that these monetary concerns are absent in the context-dependent environments individuals encounter, the psychological processes individuals utilize may be different and yield different behaviors. Indeed, the interaction between monetary incentives and personal or social motivations is poorly understood.

One of the more interesting findings along this line of research is that of Gneezy and Rustinchini (2000) and Gneezy (2003), namely, that the effect of incentives is nonmonotonic and that small (inadequate) incentives may result in poorer performance than no incentives at all. As Gneezy (2003) argues, extrinsic motivation (i.e., monetary incentives) might change the way participants perceive an activity and (along the lines of Frey 1997) destroy the intrinsic motivations to act when there is no explicit reward from the activity. Related evidence shows how monetary incentives (more specifically, the structure of those incentives) influences the way individuals make decisions and perceive the behavior of others. Oxoby (2005) finds that the use of a decision-making heuristic (the proportion heuristic from Silvera, Josephs, and Giesler 2001) is heavily influenced by the type of incentive mechanism used to ostensibly motivate behavior. Similarly, Oxoby and Friedrich (2002) find that behavior in a trust game is strongly affected (and in a nonintuitive way) by whether the money used in bargaining was earned using joint or relative performance evaluations (i.e., team or tournament-style contracts).[13] Given that the psychological processes employed by experimental participants may be influenced by an experiment's constructs, caution should be used when interpreting these results as directly testing the psychological processes utilized in decision making taking place beyond the laboratory.

With respect to the use of deception in experiments, economists typically view deception as taboo (Hey 1998; McDaniel and Starmer 1998). First, deception dilutes the perceived incentives individuals face, thus compromising experimental realism. This can occur even with the hint of deception, thus making it important that deception *never* be employed lest it taint the pool of potential participants.[14] Second, and perhaps more important, we cannot expect individuals to make "normal" decisions when they believe they may be being deceived. Casually, we know that we make different types of decisions when we think we may have been misled; we should expect the same from participants in our experiments. If we are interested in studying decision making, the experiments we employ must give participants accurate (although maybe not all) the information necessary for engaging in good decision making. The presence of deception significantly changes the behavior of participants, confounding the inferred relation between the independent and dependent variables and compromising the psychological realism of the experiment.

CONCLUSION

Research in behavioral economics is founded on an interdisciplinary approach to understanding human behavior. As such, interested researchers should make use of all the available methodologies in their pursuits. The benefits of incorporating these methods have yielded a richer description of economic man and have provided researchers with greater insights into human decision making. In turn, these gains allow policy makers to design economic and social policies grounded in a more accurate theory of individual decision making.

For those interested in understanding psychological phenomena, experiments are an invaluable tool when brought together with the economic methodology used to understand behavior. However, the application of experimental methods in economics poses particular challenges, particularly for behavioral economists interested in incorporating psychological insights into the realm of economic analysis. For example, economists' focus on incentives and cost-benefit decision making dictates an experimental method that uses salient rewards to motivate decision making. However, behavioral phenomena such as altruism and heuristic-based decision making may be strongly influenced not only by the mere presence of incentives but also, more profoundly, by the context and inferred intentions these incentives create. Thus, designing experiments with strong (internal and external) validity and clear testable hypotheses becomes of paramount importance to experimenting economists.

For behavioral economists, there is ample evidence that the psychological phenomena at work in decision making are heavily influenced by the context and implicit incentives people face. As a result, behavioral economists face an additional challenge in the design of experiments: attention must be paid not only to internal and external validity but also to the construct validity and psychological realism of experiments and theories. It is with these guides that behavioral economics draws its power in informing neoclassical economics of the important details inherent in individual decision making.

As behavioral economics "goes mainstream," more attention will be paid to the policy implications and normative import of behavioral research. This implies that we must pay close attention to the methods employed in empirically testing these new and emerging theories.

NOTES

1. For a lively debate on the role, and lack thereof, of deception in experimental economics, see Bonetti 1998; Hey 1998; McDaniel and Starmer 1998.

2. Other researchers have defined other types of validity that should be accounted for in experiments and, more generally, behavioral research. For example, Sommer and Sommer (2002) define, in addition to those above, content validity, criterion validity, concurrent validity, and predictive validity.

3. See Thaler 1980; Arkes et al. 1994. Recent experiments in this area include Cherry 2001; Cherry, Frykblom, and Shogren 2002; Oxoby and Spraggon forthcoming; Ruffle 1996.

4. Previous experiments in which participants have had to earn the endowments include taking exams (Ruffle 1996) and cracking walnuts (Fahr and Irlenbusch 2000).

5. Similarly, Spraggon and Oxoby (2003) find that "sophisticated" participants (defined as those having taken an undergraduate course in game theory) are more likely to choose Nash-type behaviors in public goods games.

6. A friend recounted a story regarding a series of bargaining experiments (ultimatum and trust games). One treatment was conducted a week prior to the terrorist attacks of September 11, 2001; the control sessions were conducted several weeks after the attacks. Although the results from the first and second sessions differed, he was unsure as to how much of the difference may be attributable to the events of September 11 and the emotional impact they had on people.

7. As an example of the way in which the hunger experienced before lunch can influence individuals' projection of future preferences, see Read and van Leeuwen 1998.

8. Relatedly, Charness, Frechette, and Kagel (2004) find that the presence of a payoff table significantly affects the way in which individuals behave in a gift-giving game. The presence of such a table may not only facilitate participants' calculations of payoffs but also change the way they approach the interactions occurring during the experiment.

9. Similar results are obtained in the two-period ultimatum game of Binmore, Shaked, and Sutton (1985).

10. In the Quentin Tarantino film *Reservoir Dogs,* the opening scene depicts the difficulty one may have violating a simple tipping norm. Oxoby 2003 documents the evolution and development of social and cultural norms over the 1990s.

11. This point is eloquently argued by Mook (1983).

12. In the context of identifying the relationship between outcome- and intention-based reasons for other-regarding behavior, good examples of experiments with strong internal and construct validity include Cox 2004 and McCabe, Rigdon, and Smith 2003.

13. These results indicate that team-based incentives resulted in *less* observed trust and trustworthiness when those contributing less to the team's output were assigned the role of proposer. Under tournaments, losers assigned the role of proposer displayed significantly more trust than did winners assigned the role of proposer.

14. Hey (1998) argues against the use of deception in experiments. He eloquently discusses the difference between the use of deception and "partial information" in experiments.

REFERENCES

Andersen, Steffen, Glenn W. Harrison, Morten I. Lau, and E. Elisabeth Rustrom. 2004. "Preference Heterogeneity in Experiments: Comparing the Field and Lab." Working paper, Department of Economics, University of Central Florida.

Arkes, Hal R., Cynthia A. Joiner, Mark V. Pezzo, Karen Siegel-Jacobs, and Eric Stone. 1994. "The Psychology of Windfall Gains." *Organizational Behavior and Human Decision Processes* 59, 3: 311–47.

Aronson, Elliot, Timothy D. Wilson, and R.M. Akert. 1994. *Social Psychology: The Heart and the Mind.* New York: HarperCollins.

Aronson, Elliot, Timothy D. Wilson, and Marilynn B. Brewer. 1998. "Experimentation in Social Psychology." In Daniel T. Gilbert, Susan T. Fiske, and Gardner Lindzey, eds., *The Handbook of Social Psychology,* 99–142. New York: McGraw-Hill.

Binmore, Ken. 1999. "Why Experiment in Economics." *Economic Journal* 109: F16–F24.

Binmore, Ken, A. Shaked, and J. Sutton. 1985. "Testing Non-Cooperative Game Theory: A Preliminary Study." *American Economic Review* 75, 5: 1178–80.

Binmore, Ken, J. Swierzsbinski, S. Hsu, and C. Proulx. 1993. "Focal Points and Bargaining." *International Journal of Game Theory* 22, 4: 381–409.

Blumenschein, Karen, Magnus Johannesson, Glenn C. Blomquist, Bengh Liljas, and Richard M. O'Conor. 1997. "Hypothetical Versus Real Payments in Vickery Auctions." *Economics Letters* 56, 2: 177–80.

Bolton, Gary E., and Axel Ockenfels. 2000. "ERC: A Theory of Equity, Reciprocity, and Competition." *American Economic Review* 90, 1: 166–93.

Bonetti, Shane. 1998. "Deception and Experimental Economics." *Journal of Economic Psychology* 19, 3: 377–95.

Camerer, Colin. 1995. "Individual Decision Making." In John H. Kagel and Alvin E. Roth, eds., *Handbook of Experimental Economics*. Princeton, NJ: Princeton University Press.

———. 2003. *Behavioral Game Theory*. Princeton, NJ: Princeton University Press.

Camerer, Colin, Samuel Issacharoff, George Loewenstein, Ted O'Donoghue, and Matthew Rabin. 2003. "Regulation for Conservatives: Behavioral Economics and the Case for Asymmetric Paternalism." *University of Pennsylvania Law Review* 151: 1211–54.

Carter, John, and Michael Irons. 1991. "Are Economists Different, and if So, Why?" *Journal of Economic Perspectives* 5, 2: 171–77.

Charness, Gary, Guillaume Frechette, and John Kagel. 2004. "How Robust Is Laboratory Gift Exchange?" *Experimental Economics* 7, 2: 189–203.

Charness, Gary, and Matthew Rabin. 2002. "Understanding Social Preferences with Simple Tests." *Quarterly Journal of Economics* 117: 817–69.

Cherry, Todd L. 2001. "Mental Accounting and Other-Regarding Behavior: Evidence from the Lab." *Journal of Economic Psychology* 22, 5: 605–15.

Cherry, Todd L., Peter Frykblom, and Jason Shogren. 2002. "Hardnose the Dictator." *American Economic Review* 92, 4: 1218–21.

Clark, Jeremy. 2002. "House Money Effects in Public Good Experiments." *Experimental Economics* 5, 3: 223–31.

Cook, Thomas D., and Donald T. Campbell. 1979. *Quasi-Experimentation: Design and Analysis Issues for Field Settings*. Chicago: Rand-McNally.

Cox, James. 2004. "How to Identify Trust and Reciprocity." *Games and Economic Behavior* 46, 2: 260–81.

Davis, Douglas D., and Charles A. Holt. 1993. *Experimental Economics*. Princeton, NJ: Princeton University Press.

Dufwenberg, Martin, and Georg Kirchsteiger. 2004. "A Theory of Sequential Reciprocity." *Games and Economic Behavior* 47, 2: 268–98.

Eckel, Catherine C., and Philip J. Grossman. 1998. "Are Women Less Selfish Than Men? Evidence from Dictator Experiments." *Economic Journal* 108: 726–35.

Fahr, René, and Bernd Irlenbusch. 2000. "Fairness as a Constraint on Trust in Reciprocity: Earned Property Rights in a Reciprocal Exchange Experiment." *Economics Letters*, 66, 3: 275–82.

Fehr, Ernst, and Klaus Schmidt. 1999. "A Theory of Fairness, Competition, and Cooperation." *Quarterly Journal of Economics* 114: 817–68.

Forsythe, Robert, Joel L. Horowitz, N.E. Savin, and Martin Sefton. 1994. "Fairness in Simple Bargaining Games." *Games and Economic Behavior* 6, 3: 347–69.

Frey, Bruno S. 1997. *Not Just for the Money: An Economic Theory of Personal Motivation*. Brookfield, VT: Edward Elgar.

Friedman, Daniel, and Shyam Sunder. 1994. *Experimental Methods: A Primer for Economists*. New York: Cambridge University Press.

Gneezy, Uri. 2003. "The W Effect of Incentives." Working paper, Graduate School of Business, University of Chicago.

Gneezy, Uri, and Aldo Rustichini. 2000. "Pay Enough or Don't Pay at All." *Quarterly Journal of Economics* 115: 791–810.

Güth, Werner, K. Schmittberger, and B. Schwarze. 1982. "An Experimental Analysis of Ultimatum Bargaining." *Journal of Economic Behavior and Organization* 3: 367–88.

Harrison, Glen, and John A. List. 2004. "Field Experiments." *Journal of Economic Literature* 42: 1009–55.

Henrich, Joseph, Robert Boyd, Samuel Bowles, Colin Camerer, Ernst Fehr, Herbert Gintis, and Richard McElreath. 2001. "In Search of Homo-Economicus: Behavioral Experiments in 15 Small-Scale Societies." *American Economic Review* 91, 2: 73–78.

Hey, John D. 1998. "Experimental Economics and Deception: A Comment." *Journal of Economic Psychology* 19, 3: 397–401.

Holt, Charles A. 1995. "Psychology and Economics." Discussion paper presented at the annual meeting of the Allied Social Science Association, San Francisco.

Kahneman, Daniel, Jack Knetsch, and Richard Thaler. 1986. "Fairness and the Assumptions of Economics." *Journal of Business* 59, 4: S286–S300.

Kahneman, Daniel, and Amos Tversky. 1979. "Prospect Theory: An Analysis of Decision Under Risk." *Econometrica* 47, 2: 263–91.

———. 1988. "Rational Choice and the Framing of Decisions." *Journal of Business* 59, 4: S251–S278.

Kruse Brown, Jamie, and Mark A. Thompson. 2001. "A Comparison of Salient Rewards in Experiments: Money and Class Points." *Economics Letters* 74, 1: 113–17.

Laibson, David. 1996. "Golden Eggs and Hyperbolic Discounting." *Quarterly Journal of Economics* 112, 2: 443–77.

Laver, M., and K. Shepsle, eds. 1996. *Making and Breaking Governments: Cabinets and Legislatures in Parliamentary Democracies.* New York: Cambridge University Press.

Lazear, Edward. 2000. "Economic Imperialism." *Quarterly Journal of Economics* 115, 1: 99–146.

Loewenstein, George. 1999. "Experimental Economics from the Vantage-Point of Behavioral Economics." *Economic Journal* 109: F25–F34.

Loomes, Graham. 1998. "Probabilities vs Money: A Test of Some Fundamental Assumptions About Rational Decision Making." *Economic Journal* 108: 477–89.

Loomes, Graham, and Jane Beattie. 1997. "The Impact of Incentives upon Risky Choice Experiments." *Journal of Risk and Uncertainty* 14: 149–62.

McCabe, Kevin, Mary Rigdon, and Vernon Smith. 2003. "Positive Reciprocity and Intentions in Trust Games." *Journal of Economic Behavior and Organization* 52, 2: 267–75.

McClintock, C.G., and S.P. McNeel. 1967. "Reward and Score Feedback as Determinants of Cooperative and Competitive Game Behavior." *Journal of Personality and Social Psychology* 4: 606–13.

McDaniel, Tanga, and Chris Starmer. 1998. "Experimental Economics and Deception: A Comment." *Journal of Economic Psychology* 19, 3: 403–9.

Mook, Douglas G. 1983. "In Defense of External Invalidity." *American Psychologist* 38, 4: 379–87.

Oxoby, Marc. 2003. *The 1990's.* Westport, CT: Greenwood Publishing Group.

Oxoby, Robert J. 2005. "How Much Does Size Matter? The Proportion Heuristic and the Structure of Incentives." Working paper, Department of Economics, University of Calgary.

Oxoby, Robert J., and Colette Friedrich. 2002. "Trust and the Structure of Incentives." Working paper, Department of Economics, University of Calgary.

Oxoby, Robert J., and Kendra N. McLeish. 2003. "Specific Decision and Strategy Vector Methods in Ultimatum Bargaining: Evidence on the Strength of Other-Regarding Behavior." *Economics Letters* 84, 3: 399–405.

Oxoby, Robert J., and John Spraggon. Forthcoming. "Yours, Mine, and Ours: The Effect of Ersatz Property Rights on Outcome Based Fairness and Reciprocity." Technical Paper 041012, Institute for Advanced Policy Research, University of Calgary.

Rabin, Matthew. 1993. "Incorporating Fairness into Game Theory and Economics." *American Economic Review* 83, 5: 1281–302.

———. 1998. "Psychology and Economics." *Journal of Economic Literature* 36, 1: 11–46.

———. 2002. "A Perspective on Psychology and Economics." *European Economic Review* 46, 4–5: 657–85.

Read, Daniel, and Barbara van Leeuwen. 1998. "Predicting Hunger: The Effects of Appetite and Delay on Choice." *Organizational Behavior and Human Decision Processes* 76, 2: 189–205.

Roth, Alvin E. 1988. "Laboratory Experimentation in Economics: A Methodological Overview." *Economic Journal* 98: 974–1031.

Roth, Alvin E., Vensa Prasnikar, Masahiro Okuno-Fujiwara, and Shmuel Zamir. 1991. "Bargaining and Market Behavior in Jerusalem, Ljubljana, Pittsburg, and Tokyo: An Experimental Investigation." *American Economic Review* 81, 5: 1068–95.

Rubinstein, Ariel. 2001. "A Theorist's View of Experiments." *European Economic Review* 45, 4–5: 615–28.

Ruffle, Bradley J. 1996. "More Is Better, but Fair Is Fair: Tipping in Dictator and Ultimatum Games." *Games and Economic Behavior* 23, 2: 247–65.

Sears, Donald O. 1986. "College Sophomores in the Laboratory: Influences of a Narrow Data Base on Social Psychology's View of Human Nature." *Journal of Personality and Social Psychology* 51, 3: 515–30.

Selten, Reinhardt. 1975. "Reexamination of the Perfectness Concept for Equilibrium Points in Extensive Games." *International Journal of Game Theory* 4, 1: 25–55.

Silvera, David H., Robert A. Josephs, and R. Brian Giesler. 2001. "The Proportion Heuristic: Problem Set Size as a Basis for Performance Judgments." *Journal of Behavioral Decision Making* 14, 3: 207–21.

Slonim, Robert, and Alvin Roth. 1998. "Learning in High Stakes Ultimatum Games: An Experiment in the Slovak Republic." *Econometrica* 66: 569–96.

Smith, Vernon L. 1987. "Experimental Methods in Economics." In J. Eatwell et al., eds., *The New Palgrave Dictionary of Economic Theory and Doctrine.* London: Macmillan.

Smith, Vernon L., and James M. Walker. 1993. "Monetary Rewards and Decision Costs in Experimental Economics." *Economic Inquiry* 31, 2: 245–61.

Sommer, Robert, and Barbara Sommer. 2002. *A Practical Guide to Behavioral Research,* 5th ed. New York: Oxford University Press.

Spraggon, John, and Robert J. Oxoby. 2003. "Can We Train Students to Be Nash Payoff Maximizers?" Working paper, Department of Economics, Lakehead University. Mimeo.

Thaler, Richard H. 1980. "Towards a Positive Theory of Consumer Choice." *Journal of Economic Behavior and Organization* 1, 1: 39–60.

———. 1992. *The Winner's Curse: Paradoxes and Anomalies of Economic Life.* Princeton, NJ: Princeton University Press.

———. 1999. "Mental Accounting Matters." *Journal of Behavioral Decision Making* 12, 3: 183–206.

Thaler, Richard H., and Cass R. Sunstein. 2003. "Libertarian Paternalism." *American Economic Review* 93, 5: 175–79.

Tversky, Amos. 1977. "Features of Similarity." *Psychological Review* 84, 4: 327–52.

PART 5

LABOR-RELATED ISSUES

CHAPTER 23

BEHAVIORAL LABOR ECONOMICS

NATHAN BERG

Behavioral economics has in recent decades emerged as a prominent set of methodological developments that have attracted considerable attention both within and outside the economics profession. The time is therefore auspicious to assess behavioral contributions to particular subfields of economics such as labor economics. With empirical validity among its chief objectives, one might guess that behavioral economics would have made its clearest mark in data-driven subfields such as labor economics. Theoretical subfields, however, have led much of the recent behavioral movement, drawing on laboratory data for its empirical basis as opposed to the large panels of field observations common in labor economics.

Motivated in part by the question of why labor economics has been a relatively slow adopter of behavioral theory, this essay surveys a wide range of behavioral studies that address core labor issues. The objective of the survey is to construct a map of areas within labor economics where behavioral methods have already produced new insights, in hope that the existing literature (and the gaps therein) will suggest new directions for future applications of behavioral concepts. Comparison and contrast of neoclassical versus behavioral methods and the consequences of those methodological differences provide the map's relief, bringing high and low points of the current labor literature's coverage into sharper focus.

One finding of this survey worth pointing out at the outset is that, rather than two disjoint bodies of work, the relationship between behavioral and neoclassical economics appears to be that of superset and subset. Instead of rejecting neoclassical concepts such as self-interest, maximization, and equilibrium, behavioral economists' methodological agenda proves to be one of expansion and generalization. This suggests a possible explanation for why the influence of behavioral economics in labor economics has been less dramatic than in other subfields. It seems that neoclassical practitioners in labor economics have been unusually frank in exposing the empirical problems with standard labor market theory and unusually creative in considering the complexity of labor market decisions and their psychological dimensions. Therefore, the gap between traditional and behavioral labor economics is less dramatic than in other subfields of economics. Thus, the survey aims to describe contrasts between behavioral and neoclassical approaches to labor economics while revealing how fuzzy the boundary separating the two actually is. Kaufman (1989, 1999) in his essays on the behavioral foundations of labor economics similarly argues that the behavioral approach is, in principle, an expansion upon rather than a departure from the psychological foundations of neoclassical economics. In practice, however, the behavioral/neoclassical distinction represents a real boundary. In spite of abundant evidence that psychological factors play a critical role in labor market decisions, Kaufman reports that only two papers in the *Journal of Labor Economics* from 1992 to 1997 adopted expanded or modified models of man that considered psychological processes (i.e., models that include decision-making elements other than narrow self-interest, maximization, and fixed preferences).

Regarding the fixity of preferences, Kaufman acknowledges the concern of Gary Becker that models that admit psychological complexity and preference change run the risk of overexplaining observed economic decision making. Kaufman illustrates his counterposition in favor of dynamic preferences with the much studied problem of explaining the reduction of annual work hours in the United States over the period 1900–1980. The neoclassical explanation for this pattern is that a large income effect in response to rising real wages resulted in increased consumption of leisure and fewer hours on the job. The fixed preference paradigm posits that the average worker in 1900 would have made the same labor/leisure choice as today's average worker if the real wage in 1900 had been what it is today. Since 1980, however, the trend has reversed. The real wage in the United States has continued to rise but annual hours on the job have increased. If the neoclassical story has trouble matching the facts, Kaufman asks, why not consider cultural, sociological, and psychological variables, including hypotheses that link observed patterns to systematic changes in preferences? Of course the validity of new explanations is not immediately obvious, and subjecting them to empirical and theoretical tests is an important part of the behavioral agenda. The point, however, is that in addition to falsifying existing theories there is a role in economic science for the synthesis of new ideas.

The collection of material reviewed below focuses broadly on behavioral studies that adopt models of man consistent with the recommendations in the Kaufman essays. The survey provides cause for optimism that attempted realism is worth its cost in terms of forgone theoretical parsimony. In fact, the price of realism is quite low when the next best alternative fails to deliver the predictive power positivists claim in favor of as-if theory. When the price is as low—as it is, for example, in the case of the falsified income-effect explanation of labor-supply trends in the United States—it is easy to predict that consumers of economic thought will increasingly buy behavioral in years to come.

The survey is divided into sections covering worker effort, labor supply and income tax policy, heterogeneity in labor markets, reciprocity and trust, and finally labor contracts, unions, and the scheduling of work. The last section summarizes the resulting map of behavioral labor economics and suggests five priorities for future research.

EFFORT

It is common in neoclassical economics to assume that effort is constant, and therefore that the cost of employing a particular quantity of effective labor is linear in time spent on the job. The assumption that effort is impervious to physical weariness, opportunities to find work elsewhere, the wages of other workers, and even the absolute level of the worker's own real wage derives from an analogy based on physical capital. This analogy supports the constant-effort assumption by noticing, for instance, that a well-functioning meat grinder's capacity to transform inputs into outputs does not vary in its second versus ninth hour of use, with the machine's price, or with management's decisions about whether and for how much to rent other machines.

Were it easy to observe, monitor, and measure effort, we might expect firms to contract with workers for levels of effort in addition to quantities of labor hours. Alternatively, one might argue that the widespread practice of paying wages in exchange for time, with effort levels left unspecified, implies that approximation error resulting from the constant-effort assumption is minor relative to the costs of quantifying and contracting for effort. However, to Adam Smith, the variable nature of effort was important enough to write, "Where wages are high, accordingly, we shall always find the workmen more active, diligent, and expeditious, than where they are low" (quoted in Altman 1999a). Evidently Smith saw some psychological regularity underlying workers' supply of variable effort.

Arguing in favor of building richer psychological content into economic models, some have since wondered whether the economists of Smith's day understood human psychology better than economists do today (Gilad and Kaish 1986; Lewin and Strauss 1988; Schwartz 2002). The articles reviewed in this section are based on the premise that the constant-effort hypothesis is incomplete, and that by studying the determinants of variable effort, new insights into the real-world practices of firms and their employment of labor may emerge.

Efficiency Wages, Psychology, and Unemployment

The efficiency wage models of the 1980s reintroduced to mainstream economics the idea of an effort function that depends on real wages. This modification fit within an otherwise neoclassical framework of maximization and competition while producing involuntary unemployment as an equilibrium outcome. Motivated largely by the failure of neoclassical macroeconomic models to satisfactorily explain real wage rigidity in the United States and elsewhere, some economists turned to more complicated models of the psychology of work, models that implied variable levels of effort (Akerlof 1982; Shapiro and Stiglitz 1984).

Assuming that effort increases as a function of the real wage, with convex and then concave regions, there exists a unique point on the effort curve that maximizes effort per dollar of real wage. Under quite general conditions, profit maximization implies that firms choose that point, referred to as the efficiency wage. Thus, firms choose to pay the efficiency wage no matter what labor supply conditions are, and the wage gets stuck there, above the level that would otherwise clear the labor market.

The basic efficiency wage model implies that, so long as the effort curve is fixed, the real wage paid by firms is absolutely rigid and does adjust downward during recessions or when there is excess labor supply. The reason that unemployed workers cannot bid the wage down is that firms, although they would be happier to pay less when hiring additional workers, anticipate higher costs associated with shirking, the result of reduced effort in response to a lower wage. Because the efficiency wage already optimally trades off the savings of shirking costs against additional cash wage outlays, agreeing to low-wage offers by unemployed workers is unattractive to firms: the costs of increased shirking outweigh the savings on wages.

The psychology underlying effort curves reflects assumptions about worker motivation and the need for there to be a noticeable gap between workers' satisfaction with their jobs and being unemployed. Otherwise the threat of dismissal is ineffective in eliciting effort, according to efficiency wage theory. At lower wages, workers are nearly indifferent between working and being unemployed, and therefore have little incentive to work hard. Workers may also feel the wage is unfair if it is perceived as being low relative to wage expectations, providing a rationale for firms to fire workers instead of lowering wages, in an effort to preserve high levels of effort among the employed. In contrast, at higher wages, the psychology of gift exchange becomes relevant, as workers supply additional effort to reciprocate for the employer's willingness to pay more than the minimum possible.

Critics have pointed to flaws in the efficiency wage theory having to do with its incomplete account of effort and firms' strategies in eliciting the desired level of it. Carlin (1989) observes that many firms permit certain forms of shirking without firing workers. Carlin points out that firing can be costly and that the degree of shirking varies across firms, variation that is not adequately explained by efficiency wage theory. In his game-theoretic model of effort supply and incentive design on the part of firms, asymmetric information is required to deter shirking, implying that workers' uncertainty about the consequences of shirking may be an important part of what motivates them.

Other critics suggest that maximizing effort per dollar of wages may not be a wise objective for firms. Assuming workers derive positive utility from shirking, permissive managerial stances can serve as a cheaper alternative to cash compensation. Another reason why firms may find it in their interest to allow workers the discretion to shirk is that doing so provides the firm with valuable information. Observing who among workers shirks and who voluntarily exhibits discipline can help guide promotion decisions, especially in identifying prospects for future managerial positions (Ireland 1989).

Apart from the theoretical possibility that positive levels of shirking serve a useful economic function, analysts with direct evidence of worker-firm relations and the wage-setting process raise doubts as to whether shirking is an important consideration in the first place. In U.S. and Swedish samples of managers and labor negotiators, shirking rarely surfaces as a major concern (Bewley 1999; Agell and Lundborg 2003). Instead, these studies point to factors such as workplace morale and the psychological dynamics of discouragement and unemployment as the relevant considerations for those directly responsible for setting wages.

Research with a more explicitly psychological bent has uncovered interesting patterns among psychometric measures of workers' mental states and objective measures of productivity. Such work has led to more intricate theories of unemployment in which psychological well-being and joblessness are endogenously determined (Darity and Goldsmith 1996). The basic idea is that unemployment hurts workers' productivity. Lower aggregate productivity, in turn, depresses labor demand, which, in a self-reinforcing cycle, begets further unemployment. The process by which unemployment damages a worker's psychological well-being can be differentiated by psychometric criteria into categories such as self-esteem, learned helplessness, loss of practice and skills, and depression (Feather 1990; Goldsmith and Darity 1992; Korpi 1997).

The dynamics of employment and psychological well-being imply that path dependence and multiple equilibria are important to consider. For example, when a severe spell of unemployment leads to psychological depression, from that point on, future bouts of psychological depression are more likely, even if future economic downturns are less severe, because the availability of depressive episodes in the brain's memory heightens susceptibility to its recurrence. Thus, steady-state levels of unemployment and psychological distress are tied to history, and the contrast between low-employment/high-mental-health equilibria and inferior equilibria featuring high unemployment is stark.

The Darity and Goldsmith perspective advocates that labor economics rely more on quantitative attitude measures. Their emphasis on psychological health brings out implications that contrast sharply with the assumptions of efficiency wage theory. In efficiency wage theory, the threat of dismissal is a primary motivator that leads employees to supply high levels of effort. (Recall that, according to efficiency wage theory, firms are hypothesized to set wages above the market-clearing level so that the opportunity cost of job loss is high enough to induce high effort.) In contrast, Darity and Goldsmith's work cautions that the threat of unemployment is itself a stressful event, one that can potentially reduce productivity. While acknowledging that fears of job loss may motivate some workers to provide additional effort, Darity and Goldsmith emphasize instead that on-the-job effort can be compromised when workers spend effort seeking alternative employment opportunities, experience "survivor guilt" following a round of layoffs, or suffer from poor concentration as a result of the emotional toll of job insecurity.

Another implication of the hypothesis that unemployment harms worker productivity is that employers may rationally use a worker's unemployment history as a basis for predicting productivity and making hiring decisions. This points to yet another theoretical cause of hysterisis. A bout of unemployment shrinks the pool of workers with unbroken employment histories, and therefore shrinks the pool of workers regarded as having desirable work histories. Thus, unemployment itself reduces the supply of desirable workers, reducing the number of hires, leading to another round of increased unemployment. The idea that employers take cues from workers' employment histories also implies the existence of multiple equilibria. High-employment, high-output steady states are possible, just as low-employment, low-output steady states are. Thus, there is scope for policy to intervene and guide the economy away from less desirable paths. Path dependence and the multiplicity of equilibria, in many economists' eyes, provide a rationale for policies aimed at reducing unemployment and maintaining the psychological health of the temporarily unemployed.

Gender asymmetries are another consideration in analyzing the gap between wages and levels of effort. Those who study the well-documented male marriage premium, widely reported in the empirical labor literature, suggest that the anomalous premium may actually serve to compensate spouses who supply productivity-enhancing inputs that improve the husband's performance at work (Grossbard-Shechtman 1986). Another behavioral hypothesis relating to marriage is that firms value certain "virtues" that they believe are positively correlated with marital status (Grossbard-Shechtman 1988). Students of gender issues in the workplace have, however, found surprising uniformity across male and female workers in survey-based measures of workplace stress and other attitudinal variables (Allen and Fry 1987). If wage asymmetries involving gender and marriage could be explained in terms of productivity, then one might expect to see these asymmetries reflected in survey data measuring stress, intensity of work, and attitudes toward employers.

The economics of effort literature has also investigated the concept of stress and the possibility that excessive effort causes problems for workers and their employers. Although high-stakes incentive structures can temporarily boost output by eliciting "workaholic" behavior from employees, such structures frequently prove to be unsustainable, ending in costly burnouts and highly uncooperative worker dispositions (Camerer 1998). Although there is abundant evidence that increased rewards do indeed elicit greater effort, the efficacy of effort becomes problematic when effort is taken to excess, as when athletes "overthink" their actions and choke under pressure, or when performance-based rewards, such as bonuses or sales competitions, wind up harming morale because they are perceived as unfair (Wiesenfeld and Brockner 1998).

Employing an otherwise neoclassical framework, Kantarelis (forthcoming) shows that maximizing profit and maximizing output are conflicting goals. The profit-maximizing level of workplace stress is, as one would expect, less than the level that maximizes output. Screening for stress and labeling it as an affliction can itself cause stress, leading to higher levels of absenteeism (Westman and Gafni 1988).

Another question regarding the economic analysis of stress is whether it should be explicitly included in cost-benefit studies of project proposals in both private industry and the public sphere. Although cost-benefit studies rarely attempt to account for psychic costs of stress and the resulting dollar costs arising from its physiological manifestations, Schechter (1988) makes the case that psychic costs of stress and anxiety should be explicitly figured into studies of certain environmental impact studies. Although this debate is relatively recent, and far from being resolved, there is at least some consensus on the characteristics of risk that consumers and workers find most distressing: those that are involuntary, are uncontrollable, or have delayed consequences (Pieters and Verplanken 1988).

X-Efficiency

Effort variability and the interdependency of workers' effort supply are central components of Harvey Leibenstein's theory of X-efficiency (Leibenstein 1986; Altman 1992). Because workers dislike being monitored by managers and tend to respond to the distrust it signals by shirking (i.e., supplying a lower level of effort along any dimension over which the worker enjoys discretion), there is scope for a mutually beneficial exchange: reduced monitoring in return for higher voluntary levels of effort. According to X-efficiency theory, as monitoring and sanctions against low-effort behavior increase, two opposing results follow. First, the minimum feasible level of effort (chosen by workers with antagonistic feelings toward management or other reasons to shirk) rises because the threshold at which monitors intervene and sanctions go into effect is set to be more sensitive to shirking. All else equal, this pushes workers to supply increased levels of effort. The second result, which pushes worker behavior in the opposite direction, is a decrease in voluntary effort chosen by workers from within their discretionary bounds. This is a reciprocal response to managers who signal distrust by stepping up monitoring, delegating less, and restricting the range of discretion in employee hands.

According to Leibenstein, most workers do not bump up against workplace sanctions frequently enough to be fully aware of what they are or where the thresholds lie that trigger disciplinary responses from management. Another aspect of Leibenstein's framework is the general idea of inertia within bounds combined with discrete responses at the boundaries. In terms of worker behavior, this means there is typically a wide range of effort levels over which no response from management is forthcoming—no change in wage, no disciplinary response, no feedback at all. Thus, factors such as the attitudes of other workers and the degree to which participatory modes of decision making are implemented as workplace norms determine whether high or low levels of effort are chosen from within workers' discretionary bounds.

Leibenstein and other analysts of X-efficiency emphasize the importance of interaction between patterns of production and worker morale, suggesting that conventional measures of economic efficiency fail to identify unrealized opportunities for both higher wages and increased output per wage dollar. Whenever a given level of effort at a given level of monitoring could be supplied voluntarily under an alternative managerial policy, the firm has not attained X-efficiency. In effect, there is a prisoner's dilemma in which high monitoring and low effort are the dominant strategies. According to Leibenstein, the individually rational yet collectively unwise Nash equilibrium can be improved upon by means of consensual procedures and effort conventions that attain high-effort, high-wage/good-work-condition outcomes.

Although Leibenstein tied X-inefficiency to market imperfections, which allow firms with suboptimal management to survive, subsequent research has shown that even under perfect competition, X-efficiency is not guaranteed so long as effort is a function of the real wage (Altman 1996). That competition fails to ensure X-efficiency poses an important problem for studies of labor market discrimination. Given X-inefficiency, lower pay that was caused by discriminatory animus will at some point lead to lower productivity. At that point, disentangling discrimination from productivity differentials becomes more complicated.

Neoclassical discrimination studies, based on the premise that the expected wage function in a discrimination-free environment should depend exclusively on factors tied to worker productivity, may fail to detect discriminatory outcomes (Altman 1995). The discriminated-against worker who responds to an unfairly low wage by withholding effort appears to be paid fairly when viewed through the neoclassical lens.

Frantz (1986) provides empirical evidence of widespread X-inefficiency. He describes a psychological basis in terms of id and ego for the quadratic-shaped relationship between managerial pressure and effort/performance. Sometimes referred to as the Yerkes-Dodson law in psychology, the arc-shaped relationship between pressure and performance is a key implication of X-efficiency theory.

Organizational theory takes on added importance within the X-efficiency framework. If particular patterns of work and managerial techniques elicit higher effort with lower monitoring costs, then one would hope for a prescriptive theory explaining how to organize production and create high-effort X-efficient firms. Empirical studies of work structure and managerial practices reveal a surprising degree of variation, even among longtime rivals in competitive industries (Altman 2002). This suggests that competition does not necessarily produce convergence across firms in the structure and style of work. Either there exist many profit-maximizing management strategies or X-inefficiency is a common problem that is difficult for owners and managers of firms to solve.

A number of essays have been published with prescriptive recommendations aimed at achieving X-efficiency. Recommendations have focused on areas such as effort-augmenting organizational capital (Tomer 1986), recruitment and job redesign (Filer 1986), the interface between workers and the acquisition of new physical capital (Evangelista 1996), and techniques for improving relations among workers (Frantz and Green 1982). Policies intended to improve working conditions have also been analyzed in connection with X-efficiency, as a means for enabling firms to switch away from low-effort/low-wage equilibria to superior high-wage/high-effort outcomes. Such policies include minimum wage legislation (Altman 1992), restrictions on child labor (Altman 2001a), and expanded negotiating rights for organized labor (Altman 2000). The potential for these interventions to help the economy achieve a superior equilibrium follows from the multiple-equilibria implication of X-efficiency theory. In contrast, the single-equilibrium neoclassical approach almost always concludes that these same policies are inefficient, at least by the Pareto criterion.

Relative Position

One of the most widely discussed issues at the frontier of labor economics is social hierarchy and the role that coworkers' incomes play in determining a worker's satisfaction with his or her own income. More and more economists accept the idea, for example, that workers typically would prefer to earn $90,000 at a firm where the average worker earns $50,000 over a salary of $100,000 at a firm where the average is $200,000. Frank (1987) refers to goods such as labor income, whose relative quantities, in addition to absolute levels, affect utility, as positional goods. By specifying preferences with utility representations that depend on the consumption levels of others, as well as one's own consumption, Frank's generalization of the neoclassical utility framework formalizes an idea found in Duesenberry (1949), Veblen (1899), and Adam Smith's *Theory of Moral Sentiments:* that social hierarchy is a crucial element that any general theory of choice must address.

The notion of other-regarding preferences leading individuals to seek relative position in hierarchical systems can be justified in evolutionary terms, as a hardwired feature of human decision making (Gintis 2000), or as the result of competitive pressures in present-day decision-making contexts such as the mutual fund industry (Berg and Lien 2003). Complementing such theoretical arguments that seek to provide a rationale for the prevalence of other-regarding preferences, the psychological literature on motivation provides abundant experimental evidence in support of the idea that relative consumption can be just as important as absolute consumption (Baxter 1988).

Lazear's (1995) *Personnel Economics,* while critical of Frank's theory of positional goods, develops innovative arguments more closely rooted in neoclassical theories of asymmetric information and commitment problems in strategic settings, ultimately arriving at similar conclusions: that economics must take account of emotions and relative comparisons in order to understand many important features of contemporary labor markets.

Clearly, more empirical detail is needed to disentangle the many determinants of effort. Extant empirical work in this area verifies that effort and productivity are indeed highly variable, even over short stretches of time when wages are fixed (Boddy, Frantz, and Poe-Tierney 1986; Filer 1987). It is also well established that quantitative attitude measures help explain variation in effort (Norsworthy and Zabala 1990) and that effort supply rests on a deep sociological foundation (Akerlof and Yellen 1990). Innovation in the measurement and empirical analysis of effort will almost surely continue as a focus in behavioral labor economics.

LABOR SUPPLY, INCENTIVES, AND TAXES

Behavioral Analyses of Labor Supply

One of the most famous of recent labor-supply findings concerns New York City cab drivers (Camerer et al. 1997), who reportedly work fewer hours on days when customers are plentiful and longer when paying customers are difficult to find. This pattern of behavior implies that cabbies' daily supply of hours is negatively correlated with their wage, the return on an hour spent in the cab. Because cab drivers choose their own hours, and day-to-day wages are transitory rather than permanent (the result of factors such as weather, the scheduling of conventions, and subway breakdowns), the cab driver data appear to offer a clean test of whether intertemporal substitution decisions adhere to standard life-cycle theory.

The standard theory predicts that as long as a worker's time horizon is longer than a day, workers should work longer on high-wage days and rest when the cash wages forgone are low, that is, on slow days. New York City cab drivers' behavior is inconsistent with that prediction. Instead, their behavior appears to be consistent with a one-day time horizon and a simple income-targeting rule: work until the daily earnings target is reached and then stop. Subsequent work has questioned the income-targeting interpretation of the cab driver data, raising the possibility that other factors better account for the negative wage-hours correlation, including errors in reported hours or physiological constraints (Fehr and Goette 2002; Farber 2003). Nevertheless, strong psychological evidence in favor of reference points and the bracketing of decision problems into smaller units (e.g., focusing on daily rather than weekly or lifetime earnings) makes plausible the income-targeting hypothesis and helps account for its extensive track record in economics (Sharir 1976; Altman 2001b).

Another prominent instance of economists drawing on experimental evidence rooted in the psychology literature to put forth an alternative model of decision making is the concept of loss aversion. Loss aversion is a preference specification in which a particular reference-point level of consumption plays a dominant role. Relative to the reference point, a one-unit reduction in consumption generates loss of utility with a magnitude that exceeds the utility gain from a one-unit increase. Thus, the utility function, an increasing function of consumption as in standard utility models, is kinked, and its slope is flatter to the right of the kink. In addition, loss-aversion theory frequently assumes risk-loving behavior over losses, implying convexity to the left of the kink, and risk aversion, or concavity, to the right. The loss-aversion utility specification is based on the observation that decision makers who exhibit risk aversion over positive outcomes often prefer to gamble over negative outcomes rather than accept a certain loss.

Loss aversion is used to account for a wide variety of apparent anomalies in economics, and Dunn (1996) applies it to explain the puzzling observation that many workers choose to work just until overtime pay rates are about to start, quitting for the day just when wage rates jump to higher overtime levels. This behavior appears to be inconsistent with standard neoclassical models of labor supply, which imply that workers work up to the point where the wage just offsets the marginal disutility of the last hour or minute of work. Assuming that disutility of work (frequently assumed to equal the utility of leisure) is twice differentiable, then the marginal disutility of work should increase smoothly and no discrete jumps in the worker's psychic costs of work are possible.

Under these assumptions, the observed stopping behavior does not make sense. Because the worker agrees to work the last hour at the lower regular wage, we infer that the disutility of the eighth hour is less than the regular wage. When the worker quits for the day instead of working one overtime hour, we infer that the disutility of the ninth hour overwhelms even the larger overtime wage in magnitude. This implies a dramatic jump in the disutility of work, whereby the psychic cost of the ninth hour is dramatically higher than that of the eighth. But this is inconsistent with the smoothness assumptions already made about the utility function.

Thus, with neoclassical smoothness assumptions in place, the observed behavior is not rational. However, assuming that the relevant reference point is the eight-hour workday, then the kinked utility function implied by loss-averse preferences is consistent with observation. Accepting the regular wage to work the eighth hour while refusing a higher overtime wage for the ninth hour is consistent because the utility-of-consumption function is relatively flat to the right of the eight-hour-day reference-point level of consumption, effectively discounting the value of additional consumption financed with the higher overtime wage.

Animal studies have explored a number of behavioral hypotheses about labor supply and the theory of choice (Kagel, Battalio, and Green 1995), discovering remarkable consistency with reported findings in human populations. Income-compensated variations in relative prices demonstrate negative substitution effects. And in terms of labor supply, strong income effects give rise to rapidly backward-bending labor supply curves. Violations of the expected utility axioms have been reported, as well as evidence consistent with loss-averse preferences.

As alluded to in the introduction, behavioral economists looking at labor supply trends through time have identified problems with neoclassical explanations of fluctuations in the level of employment. Standard explanations for such trends typically rely on factors such as population size, the real wage, human capital, and fertility trends. Behavioral research has expanded upon such analyses by considering macro-level cultural trends and the possibility of preference change. For example, Altman (1999b) attributes the shortening of the workweek in Canada from 1880 to 1930 to shifting preferences. And Romme (1990), analyzing increasing trends in the labor supply of females in Holland, explicitly rejects the connection between real wage and labor supply in favor of cultural variables and dynamic preferences.

Another segment of the labor supply literature working to extend neoclassical models to include a wider set of behavioral variables is that focused on the problem of estimating wage premiums associated with risky jobs. One goal related to this problem is to decompose the wages of occupations such as firefighters, pilots, and waste disposal personnel into separate terms reflecting human capital and compensation for bearing risk. Such studies require a delicate quantification of risks, however, which has forced economists to conceive of risk in greater detail than the traditional risk-is-variance approach would suggest. Whether risks are voluntary, controllable, or delayed registers strongly with most workers' preferences. Saliency also plays a role, wherein easy-to-conjure or highly vivid risks (such as airplane crashes) are overweighted relative to the prescriptions of expected utility theory. Small risks that may seem less dramatic (such as skin cancer due to sun exposure) also appear to be systematically underweighted. Reber, Wallin, and Chhokar (1984) attempt to apply these results and produce behaviorally informed normative guidelines aimed at helping modify workplace behavior and improve safety.

Although many interesting empirical estimates have emerged regarding workplace risks and compensation, there is considerable pessimism about their reliability because of numerous auxiliary assumptions that are required (Dickens 1990). Hedonic wage regressions that use human capital controls to absorb variation due to nonrisk factors rest on the assumption that wage data are observed in states of competitive equilibrium and that the risk factors are correctly (i.e., rationally) priced. Lack of competition in labor markets, together with the difficulty workers face in learning about possible negative outcomes and their rare-event distributions, make it unlikely that job-risk coefficients from wage regressions have the desired interpretation, as willingness-to-pay for risk avoidance.

Entrepreneurship and Innovation

Perceptions of and attitudes toward risk are fundamental to understanding variation in rates of innovation and business creation. Thus, behavioral economics has a comparative advantage in studying entrepreneurship. The study of innovation and entrepreneurship from a behavioral perspective has much in common with the economic subfield of Austrian-school analysis and the intellectual tradition of Schumpeter and Hayek (Gilad, Kaish, and Ronen 1988). Shared priorities, aimed at relaxing the neoclassical methodological norms of perfect rationality and equilibrium, bring together a remarkably wide range of political orientations under the umbrella of behavioral economics (Berg 2003). It should not be surprising, however, that ideology and political orientation recede as secondary concerns in behavioral economics, which touts empiricism as its unifying theme.

The Schumpeterian tradition asserts that economics can produce analytical insights without the assumptions of maximization and equilibrium (Helmstadter and Perlman 1996), focusing instead on expectation formation and the creative process underlying the synthesis of new ideas, products, and firms. This Austrian-style behavioral literature analyzes a number of interesting policy debates that hinge on the question of economic rewards, the disincentivizing effects of redistribution using income taxes, and the social disruptiveness of technological innovation. Shen's (1996) Schumpeterian simulation study illustrates these points, defying ideological tradition by finding that a progressive income tax, which discourages entrepreneurial activity to a certain degree by lowering the return on risk taking, may be socially optimal.

The study of innovation in behavioral economics overlaps with the analysis of how firms are managed and the search for organizational schemes that nurture creativity, discoveries, and economic growth. In this spirit, Schwartz (1987), based on in-depth interviews, provides prescriptive guidelines for managers to help reduce inefficiency resulting from decision-making pitfalls such as failing to gather technological information, unreasonable resistance to change, nominal/real interest rate confusion, overreliance on outsourcing, and unfounded assumptions about quality-price correlation when purchasing inputs. Drawing on multiple methodological traditions, Langowitz (1991) constructs a complementary list of organizational suggestions focused on improving interactions between firms and their workers. And O'Higgins (1988) documents the importance of matching managers to particular kinds of tasks according to their relative strengths in entrepreneurial thinking versus cost-minimizing analysis.

Taxes and Income Redistribution

Income tax policy is a controversial topic, in part because difficult-to-verify behavioral assumptions deeply affect the conclusions and policy implications of competing theoretical models, especially models of labor supply and savings decisions. The relationship between labor supply and marginal income tax rates is crucial in analyzing how income taxes affect economic output. In the tax policy literature, the label "behavioral" is often used to signify simply that a particular model allows for labor supply adjustment in response to changes in tax rates (Duncan and Weeks 1997).

As far as the empirical record goes, correlations and structural estimates of labor supply elasticities with respect to income tax rates are notably small. According to Krueger (2003), the best estimates from the vast labor supply literature imply that a tax cut that raises take-home income by 10 percent would expand labor supply by only 1 percent among men and 3 percent among women. Such small magnitudes rule out (Hausman and Poterba 1987) the claims by some that tax cuts would pay for themselves, at least through the labor supply channel.

Behavioral tax analyses tend to bring in additional empirical detail often suppressed in representative-consumer neoclassical studies of tax policy and taxpayer behavior. Apps and Rees (1996) find that introducing household production and intrafamily welfare distributions can reverse the policy implications of empirical income tax studies. Thus, the requirements that members of households have identical objectives and that consumption is distributed evenly within the household are not innocent assumptions.

Another assumption that substantively influences conclusions about optimal tax and income-redistribution policies concerns whether workers' labor supply responses take the form of adjustment along the extensive (entering the labor force or not) or intensive (adjusting effort or hours of work) margin. When labor force participation is the dominant mode of response, the optimal policy, according to Saez (2002), is one that provides a low level of guaranteed income and negative income tax rates over low income levels, as with the earned income tax credit. When effort/hours adjustment is more pronounced, however, the preferred policy provides a larger minimum level of income and a more rapid phasing out of transfers as income increases.

Another tax-related topic of interest to behavioral economics is charitable giving and the interaction of altruistic sentiments and tax policy. Although some policy analysts have expressed optimism that tax incentives might be used to stimulate private charitable giving and reduce government transfers without reducing overall support for the needy, Barrett, McGuirk, and Steinberg (1997) estimate that reducing taxes on charitable giving by $1 raises charitable giving by only 40 cents.

Another behavioral question about income redistribution concerns non-labor-supply responses to income maintenance programs. In an overview of reported outcomes from income maintenance experiments in the United States, Hanushek (1986) provides several encouraging observations. He finds that children of transfer recipients spend less time at work and more time studying. Also, based on comparisons of average consumption before and after transfer programs were begun, it does not appear that recipient families binge on extra consumption, as some feared they might.

WORKER HETEROGENEITY

Part of what makes behavioral economics stand apart from the neoclassical approach is its interest in describing the particularity of special groups. Deviations from the average become the object of study rather than a nuisance to be dispensed with en route to the application of representative agent theory. Thus, descriptive studies detailing heterogeneity and its consequences enjoy a well-established home in the behavioral literature. In contemplating the underlying causes of heterogeneity, it is interesting to consider the tremendous variation in preferences reported in animal studies, e.g., taste for income, or risk aversion—despite strict laboratory controls over gene pools and environmental conditions (Kagel, Battalio, and Green 1995).

Descriptive labor studies are common to behavioral economics, sociology, and other disciplines within the social sciences. Beyond common demographic categories such as race, gender, age, and geography, the behavioral labor literature provides comparative descriptions of other kinds of special groups as well, sometimes based on distinct types of preferences, disease (Kahn 1998), or job type (Sorenson 1990). Gender is an especially important and frequently analyzed dimension of heterogeneity.

Gender

There is a strong link between behavioral economists' analyses of gender and neoclassical studies of household behavior, both of which deal with the problem of aggregating the choices of household members and the possibility of conflicting interests within households. Stiglitz's (1988) analysis of productivity differences and household decision making demonstrates that gender can be brought into the neoclassical framework while maintaining assumptions such as negative marginal utility of effort, constant preferences, and the fixity of cultural and sociological norms. Phipps and Burton (1995), on the other hand, critique the limitations of neoclassical household analysis, preferring instead to quantify social/institutional variables that describe cross-country heterogeneity, checking observed correlations against reduced-form implications from more complex theoretical models.

Empirical research into gender heterogeneity points to the importance of jointly specifying labor supply and fertility decisions (Di Tommaso and Weeks 2000) in econometric studies of female labor supply. Another complication is that couples do not make labor supply decisions independently. One component of the joint labor supply problem is scheduling work so that leisure hours overlap, which imposes constraints on the jobs and hours couples choose (Chenu and Robinson 2002). Case studies of executives and other relatively successful workers at a particular rank and level of income reveal that female career trajectories into leadership roles are noticeably different, in general requiring more time, on-the-job experience, and family sacrifices from women (Martin and Morgan 1995).

Unequal distribution of consumption within the household gives rise to another kind of gender asymmetry, one that can make real household income a poor measure of household well-being (Altman and Lamontagne 2003). Women in households with highly unequal distributions may be relatively deprived, despite belonging to a well-off household. Thus, without knowledge of within-household distributions of resources, measurement of well-being requires consumption data disaggregated from the household down to the individual level.

Explaining Heterogeneity

Beyond describing particular segments of the labor market and their special characteristics, behavioral economics is also concerned with the underlying causes of heterogeneity. Henrich and colleagues (2001) conduct ultimatum-game experiments in fifteen small-scale societies from twelve different countries, uncovering tremendous variety in the degree of reciprocal behavior. Rejecting the self-interest/zero-reciprocity model in all groups studied, and noting that individual demographic variables fail to explain variation in individual levels of reciprocity, the study provides an alternative environmental explanation. Using quantitative measures of the degree to which different groups' techniques of production and patterns of exchange require interaction and cooperation, the authors link group-level environmental variables to variation in reciprocity. This widely discussed finding implies that the rational self actor model should be enlarged to include a moderate degree of reciprocity and that preferences are systematically shaped by economic environments rather than exogenously determined.

Other single-population studies have, in the absence of good data on variation of the environment, found that demographic variables such as age, earnings, race, and gender do help predict reciprocity, as measured by proposed divisions of the pie and rates of rejection in ultimatum game experiments (Eckel and Grossman 2001). Thus, the role of individual demographic characteristics in explaining different propensities to reciprocate remains an open question. The fascinating issue of explaining preferences in terms of economic environments promises to be an area worthy of more investigation, despite the high costs of cross-cultural studies such as that of Henrich and colleagues (2001) and the requirement of anthropological expertise.

A variety of other forms of heterogeneity have been studied using conventional regression analysis. For example, workers in more competitive industries report higher levels of happiness, possibly suggesting that competitive pressures lead firms to improve working conditions (Tiemann and Veglahn 1979). In an efficiency study of farmers in India, those who are older, own large or geographically fragmented land holdings, or have subsistence needs in addition to raising cash crops appear to be less efficient (Ali, Parikh, and Shah 1996). Attempting to explain racial/ethnic differences in workers' propensity to cross picket lines during a strike, Gramm and Schnell (1994) find that minority participation in the 1987 National Football League strike depended significantly and positively on the minority status of each team's union representative. Explaining why Turkish immigrants choose to immigrate to Germany, Waldorf, Esparza, and Huff (1990) report a wide variety of motives, many of which are not financial, ranging from perceived lifestyle benefits to the expressed desire to reunite with family members.

Heterogeneity in entrepreneurs' closeness to government is documented in a study of Israeli entrepreneurs (Lerner 1989), which finds that variables such as risk tolerance, interest in foreign trade, and industry type strongly condition the probability of receiving state-subsidized capital. And research on heterogeneous preferences and their connection to labor/leisure choices (based on differential desires for income) suggests that these sources of variation are correlated with marital status (Grossbard-Shechtman and Neuman 1988) and with attitudinal measures of "family orientation" (Cappelli, Constantine, and Chadwick 2000). Thus, the marriage premium puzzle may be a consequence of heterogeneous preferences, measures of which are generally absent in wage regressions, which, because they are correlated with marriage, would therefore lead to spurious marriage-on-wage effects.

SOCIAL NORMS AND TRUST

One way to model externalities is to include agent i's consumption in agent j's utility function. This is simply a formalization of the idea that people care about the choices of others, which in itself does not imply that they are altruistic or inclined toward reciprocity. A simplification of this approach is to specify preferences that, in addition to one's own consumption, depend on the population's average level of consumption. This framework provides a nice explanation for the existence of the modern welfare state. With a small amount of altruism (reflected by positive utility from increased levels of average consumption) or risk aversion toward aggregate income shocks, Lindbeck (1997) shows that the most preferred tax-transfer policy provides a moderate minimum income guarantee using progressive taxation.

Arguments in favor of other-regarding behavior are by now numerous: a small propensity to cooperate can be an adaptive trait that enhances the fitness of groups competing for resources (Gintis 2000); in a robust class of evolutionary games, reciprocators who punish those deviating from social norms can invade populations of nonreciprocators (Sethi and Somanathan 2001, 2003); honesty, even when dishonesty is feasible, can increase a firm's profitability (Cialdini 1996); and firms with prosocial corporate cultures save on labor costs when hiring workers with a particular level of human capital (Frank 1996). The welfare-enhancing role of social norms in favor of trust or concern with the least well-off members of the group are documented in small-scale societies (Onyeiwu 1997; Heinrich et al. 2001), informal credit markets (Yotopoulos and Floro 1992), and modern economic environments such as the agribusiness industry (Wilson 2000).

Skeptics worry, however, that social norms favoring in-group cooperation may be too weak to offset individual gains from noncooperation, while, in other settings, excessive in-group cooperation may lead to undesirable forms of discrimination against nongroup members. Loewenstein (1996) paints an extremely bleak picture for the possibility of managerial altruism. He points out that the experimental evidence on altruism suggests that such sentiments are typically weak and transient. According to studies he cites, most individuals find it easy to discount negative consequences borne by others, especially when there is no face-to-face interaction with victims. Loewenstein warns that future reputational benefits, which some have suggested might lead to prosocial behavior among firms and managers, tend to be overwhelmed by immediate benefits. He cautions that decision-making biases do not seem to self-correct and that unequal gains are easily rationalized by the recipients of those gains. The potentially discriminatory consequences of favorable in-group sentiment in the labor-market context are illustrated by models of reputational cascades (Kuran 1998), social conventions (Kaneko and Kimura 1992), and the psychology of "inappropriate helpfulness" (Brewer 1996).

LABOR CONTRACTS AND THE STRUCTURE OF WORK

More than fifty years ago, Simon (1951) posed a fundamental question concerning labor contracts: why is it more common that such contracts stipulate the exchange of wages for time rather than the completion of a particular task? Simon points out that because workers remain interested in how employers use their labor even after work contracts are agreed to, rental contracts offer a better, although still imperfect, analogy for labor than do sales contracts. Simon's analysis demonstrates that uncertainty over which actions will be most effective in accomplishing the employer's objectives makes it desirable for the employer to purchase an option on the employee's time rather than contracting for piecework.

According to Simon's model, workers have ranges of accepted behaviors that can agreeably be asked of them. The more indifferent workers are over the elements within this range, the cheaper workers will sell an option on their time (i.e., the lower the wage). Simon emphasizes that, apart from the domain of negotiable job characteristics, other elements of work remain entirely under the discretion of workers and thus susceptible to varying levels of effort, an idea that overlaps with the ideas of Leibenstein described in an earlier section. A wide range of economic and multidisciplinary research exists analyzing various aspects of labor contracts and the structure of work. The following sections cover areas that stand out in terms of the role that behavioral techniques have played in providing new insights, in the tradition of Simon and beyond.

Absenteeism, Overtime, and the Structure of the Workweek

Neoclassical analyses suggest that compressing the workweek (e.g., from five eight-hour days to four ten-hour days) should reduce absenteeism and discourage workers from taking too many high-wage overtime hours. The four-day 40-hour workweek discourages absenteeism because the cost of missing a day's work is ten hours of lost wage income instead of eight. Overtime is less attractive with the four-day workweek because the marginal disutility of the eleventh and twelfth hours exceeds that of the ninth and tenth hours. Since the psychic cost of overtime is higher, due to both physical and mental exhaustion after ten hours on the job, workers are predicted to choose less of it (Yaniv 1986).

Similar cost savings as well as reductions in transportation congestion costs have been attributed to the idea of flextime (labor contracts that give employees flexibility in setting their own work hours). Although survey evidence suggests that flextime is popular with workers, the empirical evidence on its capacity to provide cost savings is weak (Moss and Curtis 1985). Golden (1996, 1998) emphasizes that one must consider flows of potential benefits associated with time on the job that are not included in the standard neoclassical model in order to theoretically model flexibility of hours worked. Golden (2001) reports that access to flexible work hours increased dramatically from the mid-1980s through the early 1990s, with nearly one in three workers reporting some ability to set their own hours in 1997, but that the increasing trend came to a halt, leaving a static, highly nonuniform distribution of access to flexibility across job types and worker ethnicity and gender. Behavioralists working with cultural and attitudinal measures have suggested links between those variables, workplace flexibility, and rates of absenteeism (Kaiser 1998).

Worker Participation and Control

Worker participation in production decisions and control over hours, wages, and other workplace issues typically under the purview of managers and corporate boards brings with it both costs and benefits. Behavioral economics has devoted considerable attention to the question of how those costs and benefits compare and to the normative issue of whether U.S. firms employ an optimal mix of worker versus managerial and board control. Tomer (1988) argues that there exists a maximally X-efficient participative ideal, that is, an organizational scheme for distributing control among workers, owners, and managers. Using this ideal as a benchmark, several behavioral analysts conclude that superior organizational schemes are indeed available and that firms and perhaps governments should actively promote workplace decentralization, promising significant improvements in both profits and workers' well being (Wiendieck 1988).

Case studies illustrate the immense potential for innovative control structures to produce impressive levels of efficiency. Hattwick's (1987) study of the Woodward Governor Company tells the story of how a one-worker/one-vote democratic decision-making procedure helped that company survive the Great Depression. Faced with steep losses, the company asked workers whether they preferred layoffs or hours reductions. Workers negotiated and voted on a deal that offered reduction to half-time hours in exchange for a commitment to avoid layoffs for as long as possible. Managers wound up taking out loans against their personal assets to make good on their commitment to avoid layoffs.

Eventually, Woodward Governor turned profitable again and emerged as a successful Fortune 100 firm. The atmosphere of mutual trust and appreciation that came out of those challenging times persisted for decades, as did the participatory mode of decision making. As the firm grew, decisions such as whether to invest in new production facilities were put to firmwide employee votes. Management voluntarily provided health insurance and paid workers to stay home when ill, which, managers claimed, helped prevent the spread of illness among workers. In designing its pension plan, the firm provided identical retirement packages for all employees, from top managers to entry-level employees. The relatively modest pension plan reflected the owners' complex beliefs, which valued self-reliance while rejecting paternalistic or welfare-state managerial models, always placing a high value on equality and participation in the decision-making process.

Studies of the grievance process through which workers present their requests to corporate decision makers demonstrate that differences in management styles consistently predict grievance outcomes, with the implication that friendly and participative structures of control are better for all parties involved (Bemmels 1994). Skeptics point out, however, that in spite of the benefits from worker participation and shared control, worker-controlled firms may never be able to compete and gain a foothold in the business world. One important reason for such pessimism is the possibility that, because workers generally lack the political connections (and perhaps managerial expertise) that owners have, worker-controlled firms may face higher borrowing costs. All else equal, unless the benefits of nonstandard control systems offset their elevated costs of investment financing, even X-efficiency-superior control systems, may never get off the ground (Putterman 1992).

Unions

Walton and McKersie (1991) detail four distinct functions of bargaining in labor negotiations. Zero-sum bargaining over wages and other financial benefits is probably the most obvious function of unions. However, in addition to adversarial, fixed-pie negotiation, bargaining can also serve a so-called integrative function, aimed at increasing mutual benefits and expanding the size of the pie. Third, because workers and managers generally care about the worker-manager relationship itself and its impact on quality of life during work hours, so-called attitudinal bargaining serves to expand nonfinancial benefits stemming from on-the-job social interaction. Finally, because there are other stake holders in the outcomes considered in many labor negotiations, bargaining sometimes focuses on the interests of third parties, a function referred to as intraorganizational. Statistical studies of actual negotiations and outcomes tend to support Walton and McKersie's claim that negotiations have both distributive (zero-sum) and integrative components (Peterson and Tracy 1977).

When put to empirical econometric tests, neoclassical theories of strikes have trouble explaining the available data (Freeman 1997). Both theoretical and experimental studies of reciprocity (Fehr, Gachter, and Kirchsteiger 1997) suggest that the integrative aspect of bargaining, missing from many neoclassical analyses, is an important part of why the standard theory on the subject is incomplete.

Among those patterns that have proven difficult to explain are the following. The mere availability of the strike option, restricted by law for some public employees in certain states, appears to raise teacher salaries by as much as 10 percent (Delaney 1983). Also, unionized workers are more likely to have pension benefits than nonunion workers (Gustman and Steinmeier 1986).

Some analysts suggest, however, that the union/nonunion distinction is fuzzy, with many unionlike options, such as slowdowns and sabotage, available to nonunion workers as well (Ulman 1990). In explaining the strengthening and subsequent decline of union strength in the United States, Piore (1995) argues that cultural trends, social forces, and collective emotions are the most important causes. Debate about the functions and consequences of unions is likely to continue.

CONCLUSION

This survey demonstrates that behavioral labor economics is pursing a path of generalization rather than revolution. In many instances, its methods include or overlap with neoclassical methods that deal with the same problems. Concerning the connection between behavioral methodology and policy, the studies cited here clearly demonstrate that empiricism trumps ideology. Behavioralists show themselves to be empiricists principally, elaborating and testing theory based on assumptions that accord with observation.

Critics sometimes raise the concern that behavioral economics' openness to the possibility of decision-making imperfections also opens the door to theories that favor paternalistic economic policy. However, the existence of policies that lead to improvements over decentralized markets in no way follows from the existence of decision-making imperfections (see Smith 2003). Virtually all the behavioralists whose works are cited above acknowledge this point in some way. Some even suggest that the existence of micro-level imperfections underscores the need for free markets and competition—to effectively aggregate information, make that information public, and coordinate behavior in the absence of centralized control. While some papers reported on here call for policy interventions to help steer the economy along an improved path, this is by no means the general case.

The survey documents an impressive accumulation of contributions to long-standing labor questions such as fluctuations in real wages, hours worked, the participation rate, and the economic impact of labor unions. While these questions will no doubt continue to attract the attention of behavioral economics in years to come, five research and data collection priorities stand out: (1) better empirical measures of effort and study designs that make effort easier to observe, (2) survey data sets that include psychometric measures of mental health and attitudinal variables along with traditional labor variables such as earnings, hours, and demographics, (3) macro labor models with preference change that make falsifiable predictions, (4) normative analysis of the potential for efficiency improvements from greater flexibility in the scheduling of work, and (5) anthropological techniques for collecting better descriptive accounts of economic environments and the preferences of labor market participants.

Because behavioral labor is rooted in empiricism, the five priorities listed above concentrate on the development of new measures, the collection of new data, and the construction of theories with explicit empirical implications. Many of the existing behavioral analyses of effort, unemployment, and worker psychology point directly to the need for better data. Better data are also required for behavioral theory to prove its worth in the domain of policy analysis. The existing literature makes definite strides down that path. Improved data with variables designed for testing psychological theories and models of preference change will ultimately help sort out good results from those that turn out merely to be good tries.

REFERENCES

Agell, Jonas, and Per Lundborg. 2003. "Survey Evidence on Wage Rigidity and Unemployment: Sweden in the 1990s." *Scandinavian Journal of Economics* 105: 15–29.

Akerlof, George A. 1982. "Labor Contracts as Partial Gift Exchange." *Quarterly Journal of Economics* 97: 543–69.

Akerlof, George A., and Janet L. Yellen. 1990. "The Fair Wage-Effort Hypothesis and Unemployment." *Quarterly Journal of Economics* 105: 255–83.

Ali, Farman, Ashok Parikh, and Mir Kalan Shah. 1996. "Measurement of Economic Efficiency Using the Behavioral and Stochastic Cost Frontier Approach." *Journal of Policy Modeling* 18: 271–87.

Allen, R. Douglas, and Fred L. Fry. 1987. "An Investigation of Sex as a Moderator of the Relationship Between Occupational Stress and Perceived Organizational Effectiveness in Formal Groups." *Journal of Behavioral Economics* 16: 9–15.

Altman, Morris. 1992. "The Economics of Exogenous Increases in Wage Rates in a Behavioral/X-Efficiency Model of the Firm." *Review of Social Economy* 50: 163–92.

———. 1995. "Labor Market Discrimination, Pay Inequality, and Effort Variability: An Alternative to the Neoclassical Model." *Eastern Economic Journal* 21: 157–69.

———. 1996. *Human Agency and Material Welfare: Revisions in Microeconomics and Their Implications for Public Policy.* Boston: Kluwer Academic Publishers.

———. 1999a. "Labour Market and Market Power." In Phillip O'Hara, ed., *Encyclopedia of Political Economy,* 643–45. London: Routledge.

———. 1999b. "New Estimates of Hours of Work and Real Income from the 1880s to 1930: Long Run Trends and Workers' Preferences." *Review of Income and Wealth* 45: 353–72.

———. 2000. "Labor Rights and Labor Power and Welfare Maximization in a Market Economy: Revising the Conventional Wisdom." *International Journal of Social Economics* 27: 1252–69.

———. 2001a. "A Revisionist View of the Economic Implications of Child Labor Regulations." *Forum for Social Economics* 30: 1–23.

———. 2001b. "Preferences and Labor Supply: Casting Some Light into the Black Box of Income-Leisure Choice." *Journal of Socio-Economics* 30: 199–219.

———. 2002. "Economic Theory, Public Policy and the Challenge of Innovative Work Practices." *Economic and Industrial Democracy: An International Journal* 23: 271–90.

Altman, Morris, and Louise Lamontagne. 2003. "On the Natural Intelligence of Women in a World of Constrained Choice: How the Feminization of Clerical Work Contributed to Gender Pay Equality in Early Twentieth Century Canada." *Journal of Economic Issues* 37, 4: 1045–74.

Apps, P.F., and R. Rees. 1996. "Labor Supply, Household Production and Intra-Family Welfare Distribution." *Journal of Public Economics* 60: 199–219.

Barrett, Kevin Stanton, Anya M. McGuirk, and Richard Steinberg. 1997. "Further Evidence on the Dynamic Impact of Taxes on Charitable Giving." *National Tax Journal* 50: 321–34.

Baxter, J.L. 1988. *Social and Psychological Foundations of Economic Analysis.* New York: Simon and Schuster.

Bemmels, Brian. 1994. "The Determinants of Grievance Initiation." *Industrial and Labor Relations Review* 47: 285–301.

Berg, Nathan. 2003. "Normative Behavioral Economics." *Journal of Socio-Economics* 32: 411–27.

Berg, Nathan, and Donald Lien. 2003. "Tracking Error Rules and Accumulated Wealth." *Applied Mathematical Finance* 10, 2: 91–119.

Bewley, Truman. 1999. *Why Wages Don't Fall During a Recession.* Cambridge, MA: Harvard University Press.

Boddy, Raford, Roger Frantz, and Barbara Poe-Tierney. 1986. "The Marginal Productivity Theory: Production Line and Machine Level by Work-Shift and Time of Day." *Journal of Behavioral Economics* 15: 1–23.

Brewer, Marilynn B. 1996. "In-Group Favoritism: The Subtle Side of Intergroup Discrimination." In David M. Messick and Anne E. Tenbrunsel, eds., *Codes of Conduct: Behavioral Research into Business Ethics,* 160–70. New York: Russell Sage Foundation.

Camerer, Colin. 1998. "Behavioral Economics and Nonrational Organizational Decision Making." In Jennifer Halpern and Robert Stern, eds., *Debating Rationality: Nonrational Aspects of Organizational Decision Making,* 53–77. Ithaca, NY: Cornell University Press.

Camerer, Collin, Linda Babcock, George Loewenstein, and Richard Thaler. 1997. "Labor Supply of New York City Cabdrivers: One Day at a Time." *Quarterly Journal of Economics* 112: 407–41.

Cappelli, Peter, Jill Constantine, and Clint Chadwick. 2000. "It Pays to Value Family: Work and Family Tradeoffs Reconsidered." *Industrial Relations* 39: 175–98.

Carlin, Paul S. 1989. "Why the Incidence of Shirking Varies Across Employers." *Journal of Behavioral Economics* 18: 61–73.

Chenu, Alain, and John P. Robinson. 2002. "Synchronicity in the Work Schedules of Working Couples." *Monthly Labor Review* 125: 55–63.

Cialdini, Robert B. 1996. "Social Influence and the Triple Tumor Structure of Organizational Dishonesty." In David M. Messick and Anne E. Tenbrunsel, eds., *Codes of Conduct: Behavioral Research into Business Ethics,* 44–58. New York: Russell Sage Foundation.

Darity, William A., and Arthur H. Goldsmith. 1996. "Social Psychology, Unemployment and Macroeconomics." *Journal of Economic Perspectives* 10: 121–40.

Delaney, John Thomas. 1983. "Strikes, Arbitration, and Teacher Salaries: A Behavioral Analysis." *Industrial and Labor Relations Review* 36: 431–46.

Dickens, William T. 1990. "Assuming the Can Opener: Hedonic Wage Estimates and the Value of Life." *Journal of Forensic Economics* 3: 51–60.

Di Tommaso, Maria L., and Melvyn Weeks. 2000. "Decision Structures and Discrete Choices: An Application to Labour Market Participation and Fertility." Cambridge Working Papers in Economics 2000-9, University of Cambridge.

Duesenberry, James S. 1949. *Income, Saving and the Theory of Consumer Behavior.* Cambridge, MA: Harvard University Press.

Duncan, Alan, and Melvyn Weeks. 1997. "Behavioral Tax Microsimulation with Finite Hours Choices." *European Economic Review* 41: 619–26.

Dunn, L.F. 1996. "Loss Aversion and Adaptation in the Labor Market: Empirical Indifference Functions and Labor Supply." *Review of Economics and Statistics* 78: 441–50.

Eckel, Catherine C., and Philip Grossman. 2001. "Chivalry and Solidarity in Ultimatum Games." *Economic Inquiry* 39: 171–88.

Evangelista, Rinaldo. 1996. "Embodied and Disembodied Innovative Activities: Evidence from the Italian Manufacturing Industry." In Ernst Helmstadter and Mark Perlman, eds., *Behavioral Norms, Technological Progress, and Economic Dynamics: Studies in Schumpeterian Economics,* 199–221. Ann Arbor: University of Michigan Press.

Farber, Henry S. 2003. "Is Tomorrow Another Day? The Labor Supply of New York City Cab Drivers." National Bureau of Economic Research Working Paper 9706, Cambridge, MA.

Feather, N.T. 1990. *The Psychological Impact of Unemployment.* New York: Springer-Verlag.

Fehr, Ernst, Simon Gachter, and Georg Kirchsteiger. 1997. "Reciprocity as a Contract Enforcement Device: Experimental Evidence." *Econometrica* 65: 833–60.

Fehr, Ernst, and Lorenz Goette. 2002. "Do Workers Work More if Wages Are High? Evidence from a Randomized Field Experiment." Institute for Empirical Research in Economics Working Paper 125, Zurich.

Filer, Randall K. 1986. "People and Productivity: Effort Supply as Viewed by Economists and Psychologists." In Benjamin Gilad and Stanley Kaish, eds., *Handbook of Behavioral Economics,* A:261–88. Greenwich, CT: JAI Press.

———. 1987. "Joint Estimates of the Supply of Labor Hours and the Intensity of Work Effort." *Journal of Behavioral Economics* 16: 1–12.

Frank, Robert. 1987. *Choosing the Right Pond: Human Behavior and the Quest for Status.* New York: Oxford University Press.

———. 1996. "Can Socially Responsible Firms Survive in a Competitive Environment?" In David M. Messick and Anne E. Tenbrunsel, eds., *Codes of Conduct: Behavioral Research into Business Ethics,* 86–103. New York: Russell Sage Foundation.

Frantz, Roger S. 1986. "X-Efficiency in Behavioral Economics." In Benjamin Gilad and Stanley Kaish, eds., *Handbook of Behavioral Economics,* A:307–23. Greenwich, CT: JAI Press.

Frantz, Roger S., and Lou Green. 1982. "Prejudice, Mistrust and Labor Effort: Social Influences on Productivity." *Journal of Behavioral Economics* 11: 101–31.

Freeman, Richard B. 1997. "In Honor of David Card: Winner of the John Bates Clark Medal." *Journal of Economic Perspectives* 11: 161–78.

Gilad, Benjamin, and Stanley Kaish, eds. 1986. *Handbook of Behavioral Economics.* Greenwich, CT: JAI Press.

Gilad, Benjamin, Stanley Kaish, and Joshua Ronen. 1988. "The Entrepreneurial Way with Information." In Shlomo Maital, ed., *Applied Behavioral Economics,* 2: 480–503. New York: New York University Press.

Gintis, Herbert. 2000. *Game Theory Evolving: A Problem-Centered Introduction to Modeling Strategic Interaction.* Princeton, NJ: Princeton University Press.

Golden, Lonnie. 1996. "The Economics of Worktime Length, Adjustment and Flexibility: Contributions of Three Competing Paradigms." *Review of Social Economy* 54: 1–44.

———. 1998. "Working Time and the Impact of Policy Institutions: Reforming the Overtime Hours Law and Regulation." *Review of Social Economy* 56: 525–44.

———. 2001. "Which Workers Get Flexible Work Schedules?" *American Behavioral Scientist* 44: 1157–78.

Goldsmith, Arthur H., and William Darity. 1992. "Social Psychology, Unemployment Exposure and Equilibrium Unemployment." *Journal of Economic Psychology* 13: 449–71.

Gramm, Cynthia L., and John F. Schnell. 1994. "Difficult Choices: Crossing the Picket Line During the 1987 National Football League Strike." *Journal of Labor Economics* 12: 41–73.

Grossbard-Shechtman, Shoshana Amyra. 1986. "Marriage and Productivity: An Interdisciplinary Analysis." In Benjamin Gilad and Stanley Kaish, eds., *Handbook of Behavioral Economics,* A:289–302. Greenwich, CT: JAI Press.

———. 1988. "Virtue, Work and Marriage." In Shlomo Maital, ed., *Applied Behavioral Economics,* 1:199–211. New York: New York University Press.

Grossbard-Shechtman, Shoshana Amyra, and Shoshana Neuman. 1988. "Women's Labor Supply and Marital Choice." *Journal of Political Economy* 96: 1294–302.

Gustman, Alan L., and Thomas L. Steinmeier. 1986. "Pensions, Unions and Implicit Contracts." Working Paper 2036, National Bureau of Economic Research, Cambridge, MA.

Hanushek, Eric A. 1986. "Nonlabor Supply Responses to the Income Maintenance Experiments." In Alicia H. Munnell, ed., *Lessons from the Income Maintenance Experiments: Proceedings of a Conference Held at Melvin Village, New Hampshire,* 106–21. Boston: Federal Reserve Bank of Boston.

Hattwick, Richard E. 1987. "Democratizing the Workplace: The Case of Irl C. Martin and the Woodward Governor Company." *Journal of Behavioral Economics* 16: 69–77.

Hausman, Jerry A., and James M. Poterba. 1987. "Household Behavior and the Tax Reform Act of 1986." *Journal of Economic Perspectives* 1: 101–19.

Helmstadter, Ernst, and Mark Perlman, eds. 1996. *Behavioral Norms, Technological Progress, and Economic Dynamics: Studies in Schumpeterian Economics.* Ann Arbor: University of Michigan Press.

Henrich, J., R. Boyd, S. Bowles, C. Camerer, E. Fehr, H. Gintis, and R. McElreath. 2001. "In Search of Homo Economicus: Behavioral Experiments in 15 Small-Scale Societies." *American Economic Review Papers and Proceedings* 91: 73–78.

Ireland, Thomas R. 1989. "How Shirking Can Help Productivity: A Critique of Carlin and the 'Shirking as Harm' Theory." *Journal of Behavioral Economics* 18: 75–79.

Kagel, John H., Raymond C. Battalio, and Leonard Green. 1995. *Economic Choice Theory: An Experimental Analysis of Animal Behavior.* Cambridge: Cambridge University Press.

Kahn, Matthew E. 1998. "Health and Labor Market Performance: The Case of Diabetes." *Journal of Labor Economics* 16: 878–99.

Kaiser, Carl P. 1998. "Dimensions of Culture, Distributive Principles, and Decommodification: Implications for Employee Absence Behavior." *Journal of Socio-Economics* 27, 5: 551–64.

Kaneko, M., and T. Kimura. 1992. "Conventions, Social Prejudices and Discrimination: A Festival Game with Merrymakers." *Games and Economic Behavior* 4: 511–27.

Kantarelis, Demetri. Forthcoming. "Occupational Stress: Some Microeconomic Issues." *International Journal of Management Concepts and Philosophy.*

Kaufman, Bruce E. 1989. "Models of Man in Industrial Relations Research." *Industrial and Labor Relations Review* 43: 72–88.

———. 1999. "Expanding the Behavioral Foundations of Labor Economics." *Industrial and Labor Relations Review* 52: 361–92.

Korpi, Tomas. 1997. "Is Utility Related to Employment Status? Employment, Unemployment, Labor Market Policies and Subjective Well-Being Among Swedish Youth." *Labour Economics* 4: 125–47.

Krueger, Alan. 2003. "Why Tax Cuts Will Not Pay Off." *New York Times,* June 26.

Kuran, Timur. 1998. "Ethnic Norms and Their Transformation Through Reputational Cascades." *Journal of Legal Studies* 27: 623–59.

Langowitz, Nan S. 1991. "Motivations for Innovation in Firms: Economic Insight into the U.S. Competitive Stance." *Journal of Socio-Economics* 20: 251–62.

Lazear, Edward. 1995. *Personnel Economics.* Cambridge, MA: MIT Press.

Leibenstein, Harvey. 1986. "Intra-firm Effort Decisions and Sanctions: Hierarchy Versus Peers." In Benjamin Gilad and Stanley Kaish, eds., *Handbook of Behavioral Economics,* A:213–31. Greenwich, CT: JAI Press.

Lerner, Miri. 1989. "Paternalism and Entrepreneurship: The Emergence of State-Made Entrepreneurs." *Journal of Behavioral Economics* 18: 149–66.

Lewin, David, and George Strauss. 1988. "Behavioral Research in Industrial Relations: Introduction." *Industrial Relations* 27: 1–6.

Lindbeck, Assar. 1997. "Incentives and Social Norms in Household Behavior." *American Economic Review* 87: 370–77.

Loewenstein, George. 1996. "Behavioral Decision Theory and Business Ethics: Skewed Trade-Offs Between Self and Other." In David M. Messick and Anne E. Tenbrunsel, eds., *Codes of Conduct: Behavioral Research into Business Ethics,* 214–27. New York: Russell Sage Foundation.

Maital, Shlomo, ed. 1988. *Applied Behavioral Economics.* 2 vols. New York: New York University Press.

Martin, Linda R., and Sandra Morgan. 1995. "Middle Managers in Banking: An Investigation of Gender Differences in Behavior, Demographics, and Productivity." *Quarterly Journal of Business and Economics* 34: 55–68.

Moss, Richard Loring, and Thomas D. Curtis. 1985. "The Economics of Flextime." *Journal of Behavioral Economics* 14: 95–114.

Norsworthy, J.R., and Craig A. Zabala. 1990. "Worker Attitudes and the Cost of Production: Hypothesis Tests in an Equilibrium Model." *Economic Inquiry* 28: 57–78.

O'Higgins, Eleanor R.E. 1988. "Innovation, Entrepreneurship, Efficiency and Strategy-Manager Fit in Irish Agricultural Cooperatives." In Shlomo Maital, ed., *Applied Behavioral Economics,* 2:458–79. New York: New York University Press.

Onyeiwu, Steve. 1997. "Altruism and Economic Development: The Case of the Igbo of Southeastern Nigeria." *Journal of Socio-Economics* 26, 4: 407–20.

Peterson, Richard B., and Lane Tracy. 1977. "Testing a Behavioral Theory Model of Labor Negotiations." *Industrial Relations* 16: 35–50.

Phipps, Shelley A., and Peter S. Burton. 1995. "Social/Institutional Variables and Behavior Within Households: An Empirical Test Using the Luxembourg Income Study." *Feminist Economics* 1: 151–74.

Pieters, Rik G.M., and Bas Verplanken. 1988. "The Joy of Thinking about Nuclear Energy." In Shlomo Maital, ed., *Applied Behavioral Economics,* 2:537–49. New York: New York University Press.

Piore, Michael. 1995. *Beyond Individualism.* Cambridge, MA: Harvard University Press.

Putterman, Louis. 1982. "Some Behavioral Perspectives on the Dominance of Hierarchical over Democratic Forms of Enterprise." *Journal of Economic Behavior and Organization* 3: 139–60.

Reber, Robert A., Jerry A. Wallen, and Jagdeep S. Chhokar. 1984. "Reducing Industrial Accidents: A Behavioral Experiment." *Industrial Relations* 23: 119–25.

Romme, A. Georges L. 1990. "Projecting Female Labor Supply: The Relevance of Social Norm Change." *Journal of Economic Psychology* 11: 85–99.

Saez, Emmanuel. 2002. "Optimal Income Transfer Programs: Intensive Versus Extensive Labor Supply Responses." *Quarterly Journal of Economics* 117: 1039–73.

Schechter, Mordecai. 1988. "Incorporating Anxiety Induced by Environmental Episodes in Life Valuation." In Shlomo Maital, ed., *Applied Behavioral Economics,* 1:529–36. New York: New York University Press.

Schwartz, Hugh. 1987. "Perception, Judgment, and Motivation in Manufacturing Enterprises: Findings and Preliminary Hypotheses from In-Depth Interviews." *Journal of Economic Behavior and Organization* 8: 543–65.

———. 2002. "Herbert Simon and Behavioral Economics." *Journal of Socio-Economics* 31, 3: 181–89.

Sethi, Rajiv, and E. Somanathan. 2001. "Preference Evolution and Reciprocity." *Journal of Economic Theory* 97, 2: 273–97.

———. 2003. "Understanding Reciprocity." *Journal of Economic Behavior and Organization* 50, 1: 1–27.

Shapiro, Carl, and Joseph E. Stiglitz. 1984. "Equilibrium Unemployment as a Worker Discipline Device." *American Economic Review* 74: 433–44.

Sharir, Shmuel. 1976. "Work Choices Under an Earnings Target: The Case of Multiple Jobholding." *Journal of Behavioral Economics* 5: 93–118.

Shen, T.Y. 1996. "Schumpeterian Competition and Social Welfare." In Ernst Helmstadter and Mark Perlman, eds., *Behavioral Norms, Technological Progress, and Economic Dynamics: Studies in Schumpeterian Economics,* 51–70. Ann Arbor: University of Michigan Press.

Simon, Herbert A. 1951. "A Formal Theory of the Employment Relationship." *Econometrica* 19: 293–305.

Smith, Adam. 1759. *Theory of Moral Sentiments.* Oxford: Oxford University Press, 1984.

Smith, Vernon L. 2003. "Constructivist and Ecological Rationality in Economics." *American Economic Review* 93: 465–508.

Sorensen, James E. 1990. "The Behavioral Study of Accountants: A New School of Behavioral Research in Accounting." *Managerial and Decision Economics* 11: 327–41.

Stiglitz, Joseph. 1988. "Economic Organization, Information, and Development." In H. Chenery and T.N. Srinivasan, eds., *Handbook of Development Economics,* 94–160. New York: Elsevier.

Tiemann, Thomas K., and Peter A. Veglahn. 1979. "Market Concentration: The Relationship to Job Satisfaction." *Journal of Behavioral Economics* 8: 137–50.

Tomer, John. 1986. "Productivity and Organizational Behavior: Where Human Capital Theory Fails." In Benjamin Gilad and Stanley Kaish, eds., *Handbook of Behavioral Economics,* A:233–55. Greenwich, CT: JAI Press.

———. 1988. "Worker Participation: Paths to Higher Productivity and Well-Being." In Shlomo Maital, ed., *Applied Behavioral Economics,* 2:637–49. New York: New York University Press.

Ulman, Lloyd. 1990. "Labor Market Analysis and Concerted Behavior." *Industrial Relations* 29: 281–99.

Veblen, Thorstein. 1899. *The Theory of the Leisure Class.* New York: Macmillan.

Waldorf, B.S., A. Esparza, and J.O. Huff. 1990. "A Behavioral Model of International Labor and Nonlabor Migration: The Case of Turkish Movements to West Germany, 1960–1986." *Environment and Planning A* 22: 961–73.

Walton, Richard E., and Robert B. McKersie. 1991. *A Behavioral Theory of Labor Negotiations: An Analysis of a Social Interaction System.* 2nd ed. Ithaca, NY: ILR Press.

Westman, Mina, and Amiram Gafni. 1988. "Hypertension Labeling as a Stressful Event Leading to an Increase in Absenteeism: A Possible Explanation for an Empirically Measured Phenomenon." In Shlomo Maital, ed., *Applied Behavioral Economics,* 2:507–27. New York: New York University Press.

Wiendieck, Gerd. 1988. "Quality Circles and Corporate Identity—Towards Overcoming the Crisis of Taylorism." In Shlomo Maital, ed., *Applied Behavioral Economics,* 2:620–36. New York: New York University Press.

Wiesenfeld, Batia, and Joel Brockner. 1998. "Toward a Psychology of Contingent Work." In Jennifer Halpern and Robert Stern, eds., *Debating Rationality: Nonrational Aspects of Organizational Decision Making,* 195–215. Ithaca, NY: Cornell University Press.

Wilson, Paul N. 2000. "Social Capital, Trust, and the Agribusiness of Economics." *Journal of Agricultural and Resource Economics* 25: 1–13.

Yaniv, Gideon. 1986. "Absenteeism, Overtime, and the Compressed Workweek." *Journal of Behavioral Economics* 15: 211–19.

Yotopoulos, Pan A., and Sagrario L. Floro. 1992. "Income Distribution, Transaction Costs and Market Fragmentation in Informal Credit Markets." *Cambridge Journal of Economics* 16: 303–26.

CHAPTER 24

HOURS OF LABOR SUPPLY

A More Flexible Approach

LONNIE GOLDEN

Why do people work as much as they do? What causes their hours of work to climb, recede, or shift in timing? Initial insights may be gained from applying behavioral economic perspectives regarding the root sources of why people work for pay generally (e.g., Wolfe 1997; Kaufman 1999; Kelloway, Gallagher, and Barling 2004). The particular question in this chapter is, once an individual decides to devote time and energy to work in the paid labor force, what is the process that determines how many hours and which hours he or she actually works? In addition, in what sense can someone be working "too much"? Finally, what inhibits the spread of alternative hours-of-work options and flexibility that might better match workers' preferences with those of employers'?

The purpose of this chapter is to expand the conventional economic model of hours of labor by incorporating the various behavioral and social sources of constraints, preferences, and preference adaptation. The directions for expansion are consistent with the behavioral economic program of explaining real-world observations based on generalizations that accord with empirical evidence, but beyond those that currently overlap with neoclassical approaches (see Berg, this volume). A broader economic model of the processes that determine hours of labor is needed to better understand and predict developments regarding how much and which time people devote to work. Specifically, a model of labor hours should entail how preferences may be adaptable under social influences and how inflexibility in the workplace may often prevent individuals from getting their desired timing of work and/or a reduced number of hours. The extent of such inflexibilities puts at risk the long-term sustainability of labor as a productive resource. In a world where preferences are becoming more diverse, more prone to change over one's life cycle, a year, or even each week, and perhaps ever more likely to deviate from required hours and schedules of work, a more flexible, dynamic approach is needed. Indeed, the notion of flexibility itself deserves more direct attention in models of hours-of-labor supply and demand. This chapter is in part an answer to Berg's call (in this volume) for revised models with empirical roots that prioritize work effort, variable preferences, mental health, social interdependency, and normative analysis of labor market rigidities, particularly the potential for more flexible arrangements to provide efficiency improvements beneficial to both firms and employees.

The conventional microeconomic model of labor supply provides a parsimonious yet powerful foundational starting point to understand the relationship between hours of work, preferences, and individual well-being. The wholly separate model of firm labor demand also creates the groundwork for understanding the role of employers in determining work hours of their employees. The demand side may place constraints on some employees to often work hours and schedules that deviate from their preferred number and timing of work hours. However, by portraying humans' behavior as a two-dimensional world, centered mainly on the market wage rate, the minimalism of the conventional labor supply and demand approach renders it less and less useful in understanding the realm of worker behavior in a world where individuals increasingly have multiple and interconnected roles and jobs.

Several trends present in most advanced economic societies are raising the stakes in the process of how individuals' work hours and schedules are determined. This includes the well-established stylized facts of more multiple-earner households, a higher employment-to-population ratio (particularly among mothers of young children), longer average work hours per household unit (Mishel, Bernstein, and Allegretto 2005), a greater proportion of the workforce working long (fifty or more) weekly hours (Kuhn and Lozano 2004), longer average overtime hours in industry (Hetrick 2000), perceptions of greater job insecurity, working for more employers over a career, the shift of leisure time over the life cycle toward retirement years, the dissolving of the standard eight-hour-day and forty-hour-week norms, the potential for more work to be performed at home as work becomes more portable and products intangible, and so on.

CONVENTIONAL MODELS OF HOURS OF LABOR SUPPLY

Once workforce participation is decided, the conventional model of labor-leisure choice portrays optimizing individuals as setting and adjusting their hours of labor supply toward their preferred number per week, to maximize their utility level. The model assumes that workers form their desired number of work hours based on their market wage rate, nonlabor income sources, and innate preferences for work and leisure. The pure neoclassical conception of the hedonic labor market assumes the quantity of labor desired by employers must, in the long run, equate with the quantity of labor desired by workers. The wage rate, the only factor common to both functions, serves as the equilibrating force to align the quantity of labor demand and supply. Workers and firms are assumed to sort themselves in ways that match up desired and required hours of work. The labor supply side approach rests on the three-legged stool of utility maximization behavior, equilibrating markets, and stable preferences (Humphries 1998). Workers maximize their utility by adjusting their hours until the unique point where the marginal rate of substitution (MRS), the relative preference for an hour of leisure vis-à-vis work, exactly equals the equilibrium market wage rate. At that point, the wage for the last hour worked is just sufficient to compensate workers for the disutility caused by that last hour of forgone leisure. Individuals are assumed to possess their own unique, inherent taste or distaste for work. In virtually all textbook treatments of labor supply, the focus is placed mainly on the opposing income and substitution effects of wage rate changes. The net effect reveals the slope (wage elasticity) of their labor supply curve, which may contain a point at which the curve begins to bend backward as wage rates reach relatively higher levels.

The standard utility function is $U(X, L)$; $T = H + L$ where T is total time endowment (per day or week), L denotes hours of leisure, and H is hours of paid work. Utility is increasing and concave in both arguments X and L, strictly concave in at least one and twice differentiable. Income from working at an hourly wage of w is wH or $w(T - L)$. The individual decides optimal labor supply after knowing w and nonlabor income, N. The budget constraint on consumption of goods and services is total income (Y): $Y = wL + N$. To maximize utility, an individual chooses a level for H. The first-order condition is $U_H - wU_X = 0$, where subscripts denote partial derivatives. The sufficient second-order condition is $U_{HH} + 2wU_{XH} + w2U_{XX} < 0$, to satisfy the assumption of concavity. An increase in nonlabor income is always positive on utility and negative on desired labor supply.

THE NEED TO AMEND THE MODEL OF LABOR SUPPLY AND UTILITY

Even most neoclassical approaches recognize there is a potential divergence of optimally desired hours of labor supply from the hours of labor demand of employers, jobs, or relevant labor markets. Thus, most workers will at some point face exogenous, binding constraints of their actual labor supply. Employers often establish fixed shift lengths, particularly in the presence of continuous-production technology. They also tend to set minimum hours per employee, stemming from quasi-fixed costs of labor. The fixed costs of adding employees tend to increase with the skill requirements and thus human capital investment in jobs, as well with the increased cost of contributions to employee benefits because such contributions are commonly structured as fixed per employee rather than per hour worked (Hart 2004; Contensou and Vranceanu 2000).

Conventional labor supply models have been modified further to incorporate the various cost incentives for employers, in the vein of either the principal-agent or efficiency wage type models, that preclude downward adjustment of work hours for many workers (e.g., Landers, Rebitzer, and Taylor 1996; Lang and Kahn 2001). If workers would be willing to give up some income to reduce their hours of work burden but lack that option at their current job, they are in a state of overemployment, in which a worker is not able to optimize (see Appendix 24.1). Conversely, if they are unable to get as many hours of work and income as they would prefer at their current job, that is, if they would be willing to give up some hours of nonwork time for additional income, they are experiencing underemployment.

The standard labor supply model has proven itself versatile in that it has been expanded to integrate many contributions rooted in behavioral labor economics. This includes the literatures that examine: incentives created by taxation to vary labor supply or effort, workers' relative positioning behavior, labor contracts with social norms, trust and reciprocity, and worker heterogeneity (see Berg chapter, this volume; Goldsmith et al. 2004). Pertaining to work hours, Berg suggests there is still much room to develop the concepts emphasized in the current chapter, including differential desires for income, worker participation and control, synchronization of schedules to maximize leisure with other people, and the impact on absenteeism of the structure of the workweek, including overtime and a compressed workweek.

The key insight of Becker (1985) was to amend the utility function to include unpaid household production (P) as a distinct, third argument in the utility function. Household production entails self-produced goods and services, such as cooking and caregiving, that substitute for those market-produced and paid for. Because these activities have elements of both work and leisure, it may be regarded as a separate argument in the utility function: $U = f(Y; L; P)$.

Nevertheless, each one of the conventional model's three legs is too simplistic. First, worker welfare increasingly depends on more than just the standard determinants of income (Y) and leisure (L)—even when the model is expanded to Becker's third component of time allocation, self-directed time for self-producing household goods and services. Second, the labor market may indefinitely diverge from equilibrium, with extended periods of unemployment, underemployment, and overemployment existing simultaneously. Even when labor markets do equilibrate, the result may be suboptimal for workers, in part because of negative spillover costs on others in the family, household, or public. Third, preferences for income and leisure are not necessarily stable but are naturally adaptive. They are not only determined by individuals or even by the family but may be heavily influenced by the surrounding workplace and culture.

With the rise of dual-earner households, rather than a division of labor, the importance of *combining* market work and unpaid work activities on a daily basis has become elevated. Thus, a separate and distinct contributor to individuals' well-being has become the timing or scheduling (S) of work activities. For a given duration of work hours (H) and leisure time (L), a worker's well-being may be influenced by work schedule fit (see Barnett, Gareis, and Brennan 1999). Utility is positive in the degree to which the timing is the schedule that is preferred by the worker: $U = f(Y; L; P; S)$.

RISING IMPORTANCE OF WORK SCHEDULING

The importance of S to individual well-being arguably has been increasing. Not only workers with direct care responsibilities but also younger and older workers seem to be placing a higher value on having the ability to stagger work schedules or synchronize with others. Synchronization is more likely to occur with workplaces that institute practices such as flextime, compressed workweeks, teleworking, and generally more autonomy in determining the timing and location of work. The value of flexible scheduling lies in the improved capacity to coordinate competing activities, such as reducing the frequency, size, or risk of time gaps around daily caregiving responsibilities. For example, there is more tag-team parenting and nontraditional shift work among parents (e.g., Presser 2003). As the complexity of household production activities grows with more time spent in the paid workforce, it increases the value of having the ability to adjust not only the number but the scheduling of work hours, in response to either unanticipated or anticipated changes in preferences, and the ability to transition seamlessly between income earning, caregiving, and leisure activities over the course of the day or the life cycle. Those lacking flexibility are likely to become more prone to multitasking. Overlapping activities are quite common and not only cut into leisure time but also cause stress (Floro and Miles 2003; Hamermesh and Lee 2004; Ruuskanen 2004). Indeed, the value of scheduling coordination is reflected in the fact that workers with flexible daily starting and ending times seem prepared to make sacrifices in the form of either leisure time or average compensation, since flexible schedules are associated with working excessively long hours or being employed part time (Golden 2005).

The *timing* of work and nonwork activity, in addition to the volume of nonwork time, matters for worker well-being. The daily and weekly scheduling of work (e.g., shop, office, school, class, or store hours) as well as leisure and nonwork responsibilities is often outside the direct control of the individual. To the extent that the scheduling of a given number of hours of work interferes or conflicts with workers' ability to execute their other responsibilities—particularly when these change unexpectedly, with little notice—the scheduling of work itself influences well-being. The scheduling of work may lengthen or shorten commuting times, hinder or facilitate attendance in formal classes, or inhibit or facilitate social, family, and couples interaction. The ease with which schedules allow individuals to transition between work and nonwork activities is often a highly valued feature of a job (Galinsky and Bond 1998).

The independent importance of work timing has not gone entirely unnoticed among more conventional models (e.g., Weiss 1996; Hamermesh 1999; García and Vázquez 2005). In the conventional economists' model, a smoothly operating labor market guarantees that employers will eventually move to accommodate a growing preference among workers for more flexible schedules, so long as workers are willing to accept a lower wage in return or make other concessions that save on costs (see Gunderson and Weiermair 1988). However, evidence points not only to a chronic excess demand for more flexible work schedules, at least among some workers (see, e.g., Galinsky and Bond 1998; Golden 2005), but to the absence of a compensating wage differential for the inconvenient timing of work (e.g., Ehrenberg and Schumann 1984; Altonji and Paxson 1988; Gariety and Shaffer 2001; McCrate 2002; Gagne 2003). Conventional economists have so far devoted too little attention to the adverse welfare effects of mismatches between employers' assigned schedules and workers' desired schedules.

THREE DEGREES OF FLEXIBILITY: FROM THE TIMING TO DURATION DIMENSIONS OF HOURS

The term *flexibility* is generally amorphous. However, to workers, the concept of flexible hours connotes an ability to better fit work around other, competing demands on their time, reducing or eliminating otherwise recurring time conflicts. In actual workplaces, the degree of flexibility afforded workers in their work hours varies. Thus, the welfare gain workers receive from more flexible working arrangements clearly is also a matter of degree. While flexibility certainly occurs along a continuum, we may identify three distinct degrees along that spectrum. Welfare is likely to increase linearly with the amount of discretion to influence both the timing and number of work hours across the work day or workweek.

First-degree flexibility would exist if a worker's workplace features a set daily work schedule for employees but at least periodically allows the employee, if approved, to start or leave somewhat earlier or later than the usual fixed daily schedule. First-degree flexibility characterizes most flextime practices, formal workplace programs that permit employees to vary their starting and ending times in a range or band around a required core set of hours each day, such as starting anytime between 7 a.m. and 10 a.m. and leaving between 3 p.m. and 6 p.m. It may also reflect more informal flexible schedule arrangements, those that allow employees to vary their starting and/or ending times of their typical workday if it can be arranged with a supervisor and/or co-workers.

Second-degree flexibility goes further, providing workers the discretion, either at the onset or during the course of employment, to set and adjust to preference their own timing of work, across either the day or the week. Second-degree flexibility consists of more than just marginal changes in the daily starting and ending times with a predetermined set of core hours. For example, if there were no core hours at all on at least some days, this offers workers the option of compressing the required workweek over a worker's preferred days (e.g., off on Friday or Wednesday) or moving the location of work to the site most preferred by the employee, perhaps at home. Compressed workweeks allow employees to concentrate their standard workweek in fewer than five days per week, sometimes also around a core set of days. The second type of flexibility surely improves welfare potentially more than the first. Note that welfare does not depend on whether a schedule is flexible because of a formal workplace program or an informal arrangement with supervisors or fellow employees (informal is actually more common among those with flexible daily schedules; see Golden 2005).

Both the first and second degrees involve providing a given volume of daily or weekly work hours. Third-degree flexibility allows employees to adjust not only the timing but the duration of their work hours across a week or year. Such flexibility includes the ability to turn down overtime work when it is requested by the employer, or to reduce the length of the workday or the number of workdays per week (presumably with a commensurate reduction in compensation). The latter may involve going to part-time job status for a period of time when less work is preferred. While discretion at the margins of the work day is surely valued by employees, autonomy and outright control of work time are likely to be valued even more. The third degree thus is more welfare-improving than the most basic form of flextime. Indeed, the latter may not improve welfare much at all for those workers who prefer boundaries and borders in their work-life integration efforts (Kossek, Lautsch, and Eaton 2005).

A SIMPLE MODEL OF SCHEDULE FLEXIBILITY AND UTILITY

A simple framework shows that workers usually have some preferences regarding the precise time slot or interval (I) for work, the block of time in the course of a day over which work is scheduled. Even if their actual hours (H) and desired hours (H^*) are identical in each week over an entire time period, utility cannot be *maximized* unless a worker's actual I is equal to his or her desired interval (I^*) each day. Workers presumably are not indifferent to the time slot over which their total number of hours of work are scheduled. Workers might have some preferred interval (I^*) of daily hours, from some shift start time (0) to a particular finishing time (n). For example, a worker may prefer a regular, predictable, traditional 9 a.m. to 5 p.m. daily schedule of eight hours each work day. Yet the worker's time may be scheduled on an inconvenient eight-hour evening or night shift that creates time conflicts with other required activities, such as parental or student responsibilities, or with natural circadian rhythms. Alternatively, a worker may be on a fixed daily schedule (I) where the starting (I_0) and ending (I_n) times deviate from the worker's preferred work schedule times, denoted by I^*:

$$\begin{array}{ccccccc}
| & \downarrow & & \downarrow & & | \\
\emptyset & I_0 & & I_n & & T \\
& (9am) & & (5pm) &
\end{array}$$

$$\tag{24.4}$$

$$\begin{array}{cccccc}
& I^*_0 & & I^*_n & & \\
| & | \quad \downarrow & & | \quad \downarrow & & | \\
\emptyset & I_0 & & I_n & T \\
& (7am) & & (3pm) &
\end{array}$$

at starting times 0 and n. As an illustration, suppose $H = H^* = 8$ for all five days of the workweek, but the worker's preferred daily schedule changes to 7 a.m. to 3 p.m.

The general degree of schedule flexibility can be represented by the expression

$$\Delta I_t = \gamma (I^*_t - \overline{I_{t-1}}), 0 \leq \gamma \leq 1. \tag{24.5}$$

The term γ captures the degree of responsiveness of the actual daily I slot, e.g., fixed at 9 a.m. to 5 p.m., toward the preferred daily schedule I^* in the case when I^* changes and thus deviates from $\overline{I}$. If γ is 1.0, a worker has second-degree schedule flexibility, accommodating his or her preferred timing.

The degree of inconvenience experienced each day by a worker who is not provided a fully flexible schedule is $(I^*_0 - I_0) + (I^*_n - I_n)$. Summing these differences would reflect the detriment to worker welfare if the work schedule is entirely inflexible, unresponsive to the worker's desired starting time (0) and ending time (n), requiring that the worker be at the work site at time slots during which he or she experiences the need to be elsewhere, or that the worker remain off the work site at times when he or she would be most willing to be at work.

The utility impact of scheduling (S) flexibility is captured by the expression $U = U[Y, L; \gamma]$ assuming : $dU/dY, dU/dL, dU/d\gamma > 0$. Thus, to attain more flexibility in the scheduling (S), workers would be willing to trade off at least some leisure time (more work hours) or income. Moreover, as the absolute difference between I and I^* gets larger, utility is likely to diminish at an exponential rate, assuming large gaps matter proportionately more than small gaps. A worker may be willing to tolerate inflexible or unpredictable schedules if these also involve relatively short workweeks. Conversely, a worker may accept long average workweek lengths if the daily timing is more open to workers' discretion. Consequently, utility functions are amended to include an argument, S, that recognizes that workers may be trading off the volume of hours for better timing or vice versa. This trade-off may be subject to the usual concavity assumption (see Appendix 24.2). It also means that if the worker sacrifices either leisure time or income to get the flexibility, the employer can be induced to offer it (see Appendix 24.3). Given that flexible schedules are available more frequently at fifty hours or more and at thirty-four or fewer average hours per week, workers' indifference curve may be a more complex link of various indifference curves at different numbers of weekly or daily hours (see Appendix 24.4).

Evidence abounds that scheduling flexibility increases worker well-being in a variety of forms, at least under certain conditions. It clearly reduces the otherwise negative impact of work hours on workers' ability to balance work and nonwork commitments (Hill et al. 2001; Bond et al. 2002). At any level of work hours, employees whose work schedules are different from what they preferred are more disengaged, distracted, and alienated at work than are their counterparts who are working their preferred schedules (Barnett, Gareis, and Brennan 1999; Clarkberg 2001). In addition, flexible scheduling improves workers' satisfaction with and commitment to their jobs and organization (Christensen and Staines 1990; Scandura and Lankau 1997; Baltes et al. 1999). Workers' control over scheduling, independent of shift times, contributes to their general health and psychological well-being (Martens et al. 1999; Krausz, Sagie, and Bidermann 2000; Fenwick and Tausig 2001). However, the positive effects of flextime on job satisfaction may be either not very long-lasting (Baltes et al. 1999) or offset by resulting dissatisfaction due to inflexibility of nonwork (home) obligations (Kraus and Freibach 1983).

CHRONIC EXCESS DEMAND FOR SCHEDULE FLEXIBILITY

Despite marked growth in availability of flexible daily scheduling to about 28 percent of the workforce, such schedules are not available for use on a daily basis and remain quite skewed in their distribution (Hamermesh 1999; Presser 2003; Golden 2001; McCrate 2002). Overall, about 80 percent of workers would like more flexibility in their schedule (Bond et al. 2002). Among several scheduling options, compressed workweeks and flextime were more than twice as popular as the standard workweek (Ahmadi, Raiszedeh, and Wells 1986; Bond et al. 2002). The likelihood of having a flexible daily schedule depends significantly on an individual's demographic characteristics, number of weekly hours devoted to work, and type of job. Specifically, women have somewhat less access than men to flexible daily work schedules. This is mainly because they have considerably less access to informal-type arrangements, which is the dominant form of flexible scheduling arrangements in the United States. In addition, flexible schedules are generally no more available to married workers but are somewhat more available for parents with young children. Moreover, workers with either part-time hours or long weekly hours get greater access to flexible schedules, particularly informally arranged flexibility. Workers in most managerial, professional, and sales positions have more flexibility in schedules than other workers. The distribution supports the notion that flexible hours tend to be adopted more because of employer preference than to meet the demand of particular workers who would most benefit from it.

THIRD-DEGREE FLEXIBILITY: ADJUSTING DURATION OF HOURS
AND OVEREMPLOYMENT

A third level of flexibility involves having discretion over the number of work hours in a day, week, or year. This is in addition to the inherent change in daily work schedule that this will entail. A wholly distinct dimension of people's working time is the extent to which some hours are worked involuntarily. An individual's actual hours worked can exceed desired hours if, for example, there is unwelcome but mandatory overtime, no opportunity to cut back hours to part time, or inadequate vacation time in a job. While there are well-documented adverse welfare effects stemming from long work hours per se (e.g., Sparks and Cooper 1997, Spurgeon, Harrington, and Cooper 2001; Farris 2002; Caruso et al. 2004; Dembe et al. 2005), there are also documented add-on negative effects on indicators of worker well-being of working required overtime hours (Spurgeon, Harrington, and Cooper 1997; Institute of Workplace Studies 1999; Fenwick and Tausig 2001; Dollard and Winefield 2002; Golden and Wiens-Tuers 2005).

A worker is experiencing overemployment when he or she is employed beyond the desired number of hours of work and is willing but unable to sacrifice either income or imminent raises for reduced hours at the current job (illustrated in Appendix 24.1). The source of overemployment must be either (1) an underlying inflexibility of work hours imposed by the employer that sanctions workers, explicitly or implicitly, for realizing a new preference for working fewer hours than the expected norm of the workplace or job, or (2) an unanticipated, indefinite increase in the employer's hours demanded, beyond the number in the original wage-hour bundle agreed to by the worker, without an explicit or implicit right of refusal. Exogenously fixed hours create a kinked budget constraint, driving a wedge between the market wage and a worker's marginal rate of substitution at the optimally preferred number of hours. Actual hours worked can exceed workers' desired hours as an equilibrium but suboptimal state, with workers settling for a longer than optimal workweek. Such settling may occur because switching to a shorter-hours job is too costly, either in terms of a transition to a new career or because compensation losses associated with part-time status, such as less benefit coverage, are considerably more than proportional to the hours reduction. Thus, while individuals might not alter either their employment or hours—that is, it may be considered rational to remain overemployed—the inability of a sizable segment of the workforce to obtain their optimally desired hours is well recognized by virtually all labor supply models (e.g., Stewart and Swaffield 1997; Feather and Shaw 2000; Altonji and Oldham 2003; Boheim and Taylor 2004) and the sociologically based literature (Jacobs and Gerson 2001; Bielinski, Bosch, and Wagner 2002; Reynolds 2004; Messenger 2004).

The existence of overemployment has long been recognized by economic historians. The highly competitive, unregulated market for labor in the nineteenth century contributed to long hours of work per week that left workers' desire for a shorter workday unfulfilled (Altman 1999; Bourdieu and Reynaud 2001; Atack, Bateman, and Margo 2003). Overemployment is recognized today as both an economic and social problem, not only because it leads to suboptimal worker utility but also as a well-documented source of costly worker absenteeism, tardiness, or excessive on-the-job leisure (Moss and Curtis 1985; Dunn and Youngblood 1986; Drago and Wooden 1992; Yaniv 1995; Thierry and Jansen 1998; Barnett, Gareis, and Brennan 1999; Brown 1999; Kaufman 1999, Burawoy et al. 2001; Major, Klein, and Ehrhart 2002; Lamberg 2004). In the extreme case, the worker quits or suffers burnout that results in labor force withdrawal.

Two major weaknesses persist in applying the conventional labor supply model toward understanding trends in work hours. One is its inability to explain sufficiently the level and timing of changes in the average hours per worker over the twentieth century (Altman 2002). The other is its discounting of hours mismatches that can result in sustained overemployment or underemployment in the labor market. Conventional models have not adequately explored the reasons why the rate of overemployment—as a share of the workforce—may rise or fall over time. In part this is so because the percentage of workers who are overemployed tends to pale in comparison to the proportion who are underemployed, particularly in the United States. Estimates of the overemployment rate range widely, not only between countries but within the United States, from as little as 6 percent to as much as 50 percent (Shank 1986; Kahn and Lang 1995; Galinsky and Bond 1998; Schor 1999, Feather and Shaw 2000; Stier and Lewin-Epstein 2003; Reynolds 2004; Golden 2004; Scacciati 2004; Messenger 2004). Even the most plausible estimates vary greatly, largely because of the way the question is posed about the willingness to trade income for time. The most reliable estimates are that 13 and 23 percent of the workforce is in the state of overemployment, assuming that stated preferences match revealed preferences. Estimates are generally lower than this range if the survey includes an alternative to greater income through more hours of work. Estimates are higher than this range if respondents are presented exclusively with various options for reductions, such as the willingness to accept a 10 percent cut in pay, 20 percent cut, and so on to get proportionally lower hours.

MODEL OF HOURS FLEXIBILITY

At the microeconomic labor supply level, the degree of flexibility in the duration of hours can be portrayed as the term δ in the equation $\Delta H_t = \delta (H_t^* - H_{t-1})$ $0 \leq \delta \leq 1$. Thus, actual hours (H) and desired hours (H^*) will be synchronized only in the event an employer sets and adjusts hours according to employees' desires or, alternatively, hires only those workers whose preferences do not deviate from management's preference. The impact of all working time dimensions on worker utility (U) is now captured by $U = U[Y, L; \gamma, \delta]$. Thus, worker well-being increases not only in income (Y) and leisure time (L) but in the speed with which H adjusts toward changes in desired hours (H^*), as well as the daily schedule (I^*). Suboptimal utility occurs anytime actual hours are slow to adjust toward either temporary or permanent changes in H^*. Note again that overemployed workers receive some form of a forced trade-off of greater than originally preferred income and/ or greater flexibility in schedule (see Golden 1996).

ENDOGENOUS LABOR SUPPLY AND THE DYNAMICS OF OVEREMPLOYMENT

By focusing on work hours preferences primarily as a reflection of changes in wages that generate opposing income and substitution effects, the conventional model of labor supply has paid insufficient attention to the importance of preference formation (see Nyland 1989). The factors that shift the entire labor supply curve are typically relegated to the status of exogenous changes in innate preferences or constraints. This oversimplification is unfortunate not only because knowing the source of labor supply shifts is important for understanding recent trends but also because some of the shifts may be endogenous.

Under the assumption that preference formation may be adaptive rather than static, one possible response of overemployed workers is to eventually adjust upward their number of preferred hours of work. Indeed, surveys reveal a much stronger preference for hours reduction in the more distant future than in the current period (Hart and Associates 2003). A greater aversion to income loss than the benefit from an equivalent income gain can be aptly explained by modified neoclassical labor supply models (Dunn 1996; Goette, Huffman, and Fehr 2004). However, less explored is the potential dynamic process by which an individual may start out being overemployed and later no longer prefer shorter work hours, without any reduction in their hours (Altman and Golden 2004). A truly rich model would explain not only lengthening work hours but the rise and fall of overemployment over time. Such an approach would apply the social and behavioral psychology basis of labor supply decisions to explain why workers' desired hours may rise commensurately with hours demanded and why initial preferences for shorter hours may eventually dissipate.

INDIVIDUAL LABOR SUPPLY SHIFTERS: WHY PREFERRED WORK HOURS MAY RISE

Besides the net substitution effect of rising wages, or even the net income effect of falling wages (Sharif 2000; Prasch 2001), desired work hours may rise not only because of changes in a worker's family or household context, which is well recognized by neoclassical analyses, but also because of the influence of social reference groups and culture and diminishing institutional constraints such as government regulation or labor unions.

Relative Positioning in the Workplace and Income Spectrum

Rising job and income insecurity may lead workers currently to prefer longer hours in order to build up savings to serve as a buffer against expected future job or income losses. Also, if workers believe their employer is screening before a downsizing or reorganization, they may view longer hours as an inoculation against the risk of future job loss, income loss, or demotion (Landers, Rebitzer, and Taylor 1996; Bluestone and Rose 1998). Moreover, the incentives of workplaces, occupations, and the labor market have heightened the economic motivation to strive for promotion. Working longer hours becomes a way to signal promotability to employers, who interpret the "presenteeism" as an indication of an employee's level of effort and commitment. A greater dispersion of earnings among occupations and industries as well as between racial groups has served to incentivize workers to work relatively longer hours. The wider the gap between pay grades, the larger the motivation to engage in such positive signaling tactics (Bell 2001; Bowles and Park 2005). Workers may attempt to equal or perhaps exceed the hours worked by their co-workers. Among those who expect to be in managerial positions, there is a clear positive empirical relationship between the number of work hours they prefer and the actual work hours of their co-workers (Eastman 1998; Brett and Stroh 2003). Similarly, there are negative signaling effects for workers requesting shorter hours (Rebitzer and Taylor 1995). Those expressing a wish to reduce work hours may be passed up for hiring, in an adverse selection model of hiring decisions. There is a rising presence of professions, including law and consulting, that reward and valorize long hours, which promotes a "rat race" with workers increasing their own work hours for reasons of long-term relative status (Landers, Rebitzer, and Taylor 1996; Haight 1997; Yakura 2001).

However, with the apparent rising amenities of the workplace relative to household work, from on-site day care to a more stimulating, more rewarding, and less stressful environment, the office has a growing allure relative to the household (Hochschild 1997). More amenable working conditions, which make jobs less hazardous or unpleasant, may reduce the resistance to long hours, particularly among the more highly educated (Gramm 1987; LaJeunesse 2004). If work activity is becoming more intrinsically rewarding, stimulating, safer, discretionary, and autonomous, then this implies something much different than if work is becoming more stressful, anxiety-producing, onerous, routinized, and alienating. Work time might be yielding less disutility than it had historically (Wisman 1989).

Relative Positioning in the Household

The member in the household with relatively greater earnings may attain a relative bargaining power advantage within the household, owing to his or her superior income. Such leverage is not symmetrically derived from bringing home more "leisure" time. The individual with relatively greater income gains leverage in household decision making, increasing the relative weight his or her preferences receive in decisions such as consumption purchases, leisure time use, and allocations among sons versus daughters (see Winkler 1998).

Relative Positioning in Consumption

Veblen effects in consumption mean that individuals may compete for higher status by acquiring or accumulating social-status-conferring goods and services. Individuals seek to emulate the consumption patterns of the rich in order to enhance their own relative status. In the context of rising income inequality, this requires that less well-off individuals work more hours in order to gain income to sustain their relative position in consumption levels (Rima 1984; Altman 2001; Pingle and Mitchell 2002). Indeed, as the top income bracket pulls away, those left behind, even with greater absolute income, may be no better off in welfare terms.

Intensified marketing and advertising arguably create tastes for more and more market goods and services. Wants may escalate over time, as they have over the past centuries, moving the income target ever further out, so that it is never actually reached or reachable (George 1997; Fraser and Paton 2003). Workers may start with metapreferences for a shorter working time, but the cumulative effects of intensifying promotional efforts for products eventually leads workers to prefer more income to purchase these now familiar products or services. Bandwagon effects and the interdependent utility function suggest that individuals derive satisfaction from consuming goods and services that others are consuming (see Altman 2001). As new commodities are introduced, new bandwagon effects are triggered, and what was once considered a luxury or amenity item gradually becomes a necessity, a new want to satisfy. Moreover, the steady increase in debt-financed consumption, which recently has led to record increases in consumer debt-to-income ratios and consumer-debt servicing on relatively high-interest-rate credit cards, makes longer work hours an option to avoid high-interest balances or risk of personal bankruptcy. This debt might, of course, be a product of an increasing target income.

Income-Targeting Behavior

Income-targeting behavior suggests that individuals first assume a predominant identity or role, leading them to seek market work sufficient to support their preestablished goals regarding unsatisfied consumption wants and nonmarket time (Altman 2001). Goals reflect a hierarchical ordering of their physiological and unsatisfied needs. The positional effects suggest that individuals seek work hours in order to enhance their relative status in at least three spheres: consumption, the workplace, and the household. What restrains desired hours from escalating ever upward is that there is a hierarchy of needs, which includes the need for nonmarket time. But there may be a sequence of decision making, with individuals prioritizing the achievement of their income target, then adjusting future preferences or behavior in order to seek their targeted amount of nonmarket time.

Endogenous Labor Supply Preferences

Suppose hours demanded by the employer rise above those preferred by an individual, creating a spell of overemployment. This creates a feeling of time scarcity in the household. This scarcity in turn will lead a household to eventually change its preferences from self-produced goods and services (P) to those that are more market-produced, which requires income (Y). The household may also shift from time-*using* goods and services toward the more time-*saving* type. This shift requires more income. In addition, households are likely to shift preferences from time-intensive to income-intensive leisure activities. Together, these effects ratchet upward individuals' targeted consumption levels and gradually dissipates the initial desire for shorter work hours (Rothschild 1982). Overall, these various motivations yield the same predicted outcome—workers may be choosing to work longer than predicted by a model that assumes that individuals decide their hours in isolation from others, in a static climate. Moreover, actual hours worked might be greater than predicted by a model of income-leisure choice that neglects the interpersonal aspects of decision making and the importance of hierarchy of wants as core determinants.

OVEREMPLOYMENT AT THE MACROECONOMIC LEVEL

Labor-leisure models portray overemployment as an individual labor-market phenomenon, but it can also be viewed from a macroeconomic perspective. Categorization of the contributing sources of overemployment can be treated as analogous to the categorization of sources of unemployment. There are three distinct types: cyclical, structural, and frictional. *Cyclical* overemployment occurs during periodic booms as aggregate demand (orders, customers) surges, leading to longer hours demanded per worker by employers. Demand for hours may be rising faster than workers' desired hours (e.g., induced by rising wage rates if the substitution effect on labor supply is dominant). *Structural* overemployment occurs because of the existence of structural incentives inherent in labor market institutions and work organization. Labor market institutions include the inherently fixed costs of employment faced by employers. Their sources may be increasing skill shortages and escalating employee benefit premiums, which facilitate an upward push in demand for hours of work per employee or the imposition of minimum-hours constraints. Such institutional practices also include the degree of willful compliance with and government enforcement of Fair Labor Standards Act (FLSA) overtime regulations. It also includes the recent exemption of many jobs from the purview of the FLSA, and these jobs tend to be more prone to uncompensated, extended hours (Hamermesh 2000; Cherry 2004). Finally, *frictional* overemployment occurs due to the bundling of wages and hours in employment contracts and incomplete markets and information. A lack of knowledge among employers about their employees' preferences and among worker applicants about job requirements leads to mismatches. Lack of accessibility and barriers to full information regarding alternative jobs and work hours arrangements can be one source. Because such frictions cannot be entirely removed (like unemployment), it is unrealistic to expect that overemployment can ever reach a rate of zero. However, it would be socially optimal if overemployment declined toward zero, or if overemployment spells could be made very short-lived.

CONCLUSION

The purpose of this essay has been to broaden the theoretical conception of labor supply so as to understand the economic importance of flexible work arrangements that facilitate a desired reduction in hours of labor supply or shift in work schedule. Existing labor supply models should be enhanced to incorporate the behavioral microeconomic and macroeconomic forces that account for the incidence of either inflexible schedules or overemployment. Because of the spillover costs of inflexibility and spillover benefits of flexibility, there is a strong public goods case for subsidizing both firms and workers to promote policies that minimize overemployment and prevent the dynamic process that ratchets upward desired work hours to the point where they threaten to become socially counterproductive.

Future research should develop further the extent and nature of the trade-offs workers incur for more flexible schedules or hours, the adverse welfare effects of inflexible schedules and overemployment irrespective of the duration of their actual hours, the role of competitive market and consumerist forces in producing ever-longer desired hours instead of the more socially optimal expansion of options for workers and firms to moderate hours, and the specific policies that reward firms for creating such options and reward workers for availing themselves of these options.

ACKNOWLEDGMENT

The author acknowledges support from the Alfred P. Sloan Foundation, Workplace, Workforce and Working Families Program, Grant #2004-5-32.

REFERENCES

Ahmadi, Mohammed, Farhad Raiszedeh, and William Wells. 1986. "Traditional vs. Non-Traditional Work Schedules: A Case Study of Employee Preference." *Industrial Management* 28, 2: 20–23.

Altman, M. 1999. "New Estimates of Hours of Work and Real Income from the 1880s to 1930: Long Run Trends and Workers' Preferences." *Review of Income and Wealth* 45: 353–72.

———. 2001. "Preferences and Labor Supply: Casting Some Light into the Black Box of Income-Leisure Choice." *Journal of Socio-Economics* 30: 199–219.

———. 2002. "Economic Theory, Public Policy and the Challenge of Innovative Work Practices." *Economic and Industrial Democracy* 23: 271–90.

Altman, M., and L. Golden. 2004. "Alternative Economic Approaches to Analyzing Hours of Work Determination and Standards." In M. Oppenheimer and N. Mercuro, eds., *Law and Economics: Alternative Economic Approaches to Legal and Regulatory Issues*, 286–307. Armonk, NY: M.E. Sharpe.

Altonji, Joseph G., and Jennifer Oldham. 2003. "Vacation Laws and Annual Work Hours." *Economic Perspectives* (Federal Reserve Bank of Chicago), fall, 19–29.

Altonji, Joseph, and Christina Paxson. 1988. "Labor Supply Preferences, Hours Constraints, and Hours-Wage Trade-Offs." *Journal of Labor Economics* 6, 2: 254–76.

Atack, J., F. Bateman, and R. Margo. 2003. "Productivity in Manufacturing and the Length of the Working Day: Evidence from the 1880 Census of Manufacturers." *Explorations in Economic History* 40, 2: 170–94.

Baltes, B., T. Briggs, J. Wright, and G. Neuman. 1999. "Flexible and Compressed Workweek Schedules: A Meta-Analysis of Their Effects on Work-Related Criteria." *Journal of Applied Psychology* 84, 4: 496–513.

Barnett, R., K. Gareis, and R. Brennan. 1999. "Fit as a Mediator of the Relationship Between Work Hours and Burnout." *Journal of Occupational Health Psychology* 4: 307–17.

Becker, G. 1985. "Human Capital, Effort, and the Sexual Division of Labor." *Journal of Labor Economics* 3, 1 (part 2): S33–S58.

Bell, L. 2001. "The Incentive to Work Hard: Differences in Black and White Workers' Hours and Preferences." In L. Golden and D. Figart, eds., *Working Time: International Trends, Theory and Policy Perspectives*, 106–26. New York: Routledge.

Bielinski, H., G. Bosch, and A. Wagner. 2002. *Europeans' Work Time Preferences*. Luxembourg: European Foundation for the Improvement of Living and Working Conditions.

Bluestone, B., and S. Rose. 1998. "Macroeconomics of Work Time." *Review of Social Economy* 56: 425–41.

Böheim, René, and Mark Taylor. 2004. "Actual and Preferred Working Hours." *British Journal of Industrial Relations* 42, 1: 149–66.

Bond, James T., Cindy Thompson, Ellen Galinsky, and David Prottas. 2002. *Highlights of the 2002 National Study of the Changing Work Force*. New York: Families and Work Institute.

Bourdieu, Jérôme, and Bénédicte Reynaud. 2001. "Externalities and Institutions: The Decrease in Working Hours in Nineteenth Century France." Laboratoire d'Economie Appliquée, Research Unit Working Paper 00–01, Paris.

Bowles, S., and Y. Park. 2005. "Emulation, Inequality, and Work Hours: Was Thorsten Veblen Right?" *Economic Journal* 115, 507: F397–F412.

Brett, J., and L. Stroh. 2003. "Working 61 Plus Hours a Week: Why Do Managers Do It?" *Journal of Applied Psychology* 88, 1: 67–78.

Brown, S. 1999. "Worker Absenteeism and Overtime Bans." *Applied Economics* 31: 165–74.

Burawoy, M., N. Fligstein, A. Hochschild, J. Schor, and K. Voss. 2001. "Roundtable Discussion: Overwork: Causes and Consequences of Rising Work Hours." *Berkeley Journal of Sociology* 45: 180–96.

Caruso, Claire, Edward Hitchcock, Robert Dick, John Russo, and Jennifer Schmit. 2004. *Overtime and Extended Work Shifts: Recent Findings on Illnesses, Injuries and Health Behaviors.* Cincinnati, OH: National Institute for Occupational Safety and Health.

Cherry, M. 2004. "Are Salaried Workers Compensated for Overtime Hours?" *Journal of Labor Research* 25, 3: 485–94.

Christensen, K., and G. Staines. 1990. "Flextime: A Viable Solution to Work/Family Conflict?" *Journal of Family Issues* 11: 455–76.

Clarkberg, Marin. 2001. "Understanding the Time-Squeeze: Married Couples' Preferred and Actual Work-Hour Strategies." *American Behavioral Scientist* 44: 1115–36.

Contensou, F., and R. Vranceanu. 2000. *Working Time: Theory and Policy Implications.* Cheltenham, UK: Edward Elgar.

Dembe, Allard, J.B. Erickson, R.G. Delbos, and S.M. Banks. 2005. "The Impact of Overtime and Long Work Hours on Occupational Injuries and Illnesses: New Evidence from the United States." *Occupational Environment Medicine* 62: 588–97.

Dollard, Maureen, and Anthony Winefield. 2002. "Mental Health: Overemployment, Underemployment, Unemployment and Healthy Jobs." *Australian e-Journal for the Advancement of Mental Health* 1, 3.

Drago, R., and Wooden, M. 1992. "The Determinants of Labor Absence: Economic Factors and Work Group Norms." *Industrial and Labor Relations Review* 45: 34–47.

Dunn, L.F. 1996. "Loss Aversion and Adaptation in the Labor Market: Empirical Indifference Functions and Labor Supply." *Review of Economics and Statistics* 78: 441–50.

Dunn, L.F., and Stuart Youngblood. 1986. "Absenteeism as a Mechanism for Approaching an Optimal Labor Market Equilibrium: An Empirical Study." *Review of Economics and Statistics* 68, 4: 668–74.

Eastman, W. 1998. "Working for Position: Women, Men, and Managerial Work Hours." *Industrial Relations* 37: 51–66.

Ehrenberg, R., and P. Schumann. 1984. "Compensating Wage Differentials for Mandatory Overtime." *Economic Inquiry* 22, 4: 460-78.

Farris, David. 2002. "Are Transformed Workplaces More Productively Efficient?" *Journal of Economic Issues* 36, 3: 659–70.

Feather, P., and D. Shaw. 2000. "The Demand for Leisure Time in the Presence of Constrained Work Hours." *Economic Inquiry* 38: 651–62.

Fenwick, R., and M. Tausig. 2001. "Scheduling Stress: Family and Health Outcomes of Shift Work and Schedule Control." *American Behavioral Scientist* 44, 7: 1179–98.

Floro, M.S., and M. Miles. 2003. "Time Use, Work and Overlapping Activities: Evidence from Australia." *Cambridge Journal of Economics* 27: 881–904.

Fraser, Stuart, and David Paton. 2003, "Does Advertising Increase Labour Supply? Time Series Evidence from the UK." *Applied Economics* 35, 11: 1357–68.

Gagne, Lynda. 2003. "Family Friendly Employee Benefits: Incidence and Relationship with Wages." University of Victoria, Canada.

Galinsky, E., and J.T. Bond. 1998. *The 1997 National Study of the Changing Work Force.* New York: Families and Work Institute.

García Sánchez, Antonio, and María Del Mar Vázquez Méndez. 2005. "The Timing of Work in a General Equilibrium Model with Shiftwork." *Investigaciones Económicas* 29, 1: 149–79.

Gariety, Bonnie, and Sherrill Shaffer. 2001. "Wage Differentials Associated With Flextime." *Monthly Labor Review* 24, 3: 68–75.

George, D. 1997. "Working Longer Hours: Pressure from the Boss or from Marketers?" *Review of Social Economy* 55, 1: 33–65.

Goette, Lorenz, David Huffman, and Ernst Fehr. 2004. "Loss Aversion and Labor Supply." *Journal of the European Economic Association* 2, 2–3: 216–28.

Golden, L. 1996. "The Economics of Worktime Length, Adjustment and Flexibility: Contributions of Three Competing Paradigms." *Review of Social Economy* 54: 1–44.

———. 2004. "Overemployment in the US Labor Market." *2004 Annual Proceedings of the Industrial Relations Research Association.* Urbana, IL: Industrial Relations Research Association, 19–29.

———. 2005. "The Flexibility Gap: Access to Flexible Work Schedules." In I. U. Zeytinoglu, ed., *Flexibility in Workplaces: Effects on Workers, Work Environment and the Unions,* 1–19. Geneva: IIRA/ILO.

Golden, L., and B. Wiens-Tuers. 2005. "Mandatory Overtime Work: Who, What and Where?" *Labor Studies Journal* 30, 1: 1–23.

Goldsmith, A., S. Sedo, W. Darity, and D. Hamilton. 2004. "The Labor Supply Consequences of Perceptions of Employer Discrimination During Search and On-the-Job: Integrating Neoclassical Theory and Cognitive Dissonance." *Journal of Economic Psychology* 25: 15–39.

Gramm, W. 1987. "Labor, Work and Leisure." *Journal of Economic Issues* 21: 167–88.

Gunderson, M., and K. Weiermair. 1988. "Labor Market Rigidities: Economic Analysis of Alternative Work Schedules Including Overtime Restrictions." In G. Dlugo, W. Doron, and K. Weiermair, eds., *Management Under Differing Labour Market and Employment Systems,* 154–63. Berlin: Walter de Gruyter.

Haight, A.D. 1997. "Padded Prowess: A Veblenian Interpretation of the Long Hours of Salaried Workers." *Journal of Economic Issues* 31: 29–38.

Hamermesh, Daniel. 1999. "The Timing of Work Over Time." *Economic Journal* 109, 452: 37–66.

———. 2000. "12 Million Salaried Workers Are Missing." *Industrial and Labor Relations Review* 55: 649–75.

Hamermesh, Daniel, and Jung-Min Lee. 2004. "Stressed Out on Four Continents: Time Crunch or Yuppie Kvetch?" Working Paper #10186, National Bureau of Economic Research, Cambridge, MA.

Hart, Peter, and Associates. 2003. *Imagining the Future of Work.* New York: Alfred P. Sloan Foundation.

Hart, R. 2004. *The Economics of Overtime Working.* Cambridge: Cambridge University Press.

Hetrick, Ronald. 2000. "Analyzing the Upward Surge in Overtime Hours. *Monthly Labor Review,* February, 30–33.

Hill, E.J., A. Hawkins, M. Ferris, and M. Weitzman. 2001. "Finding an Extra Day a Week: Positive Influence of Perceived Job Flexibility on Work and Family Balance." *Family Relations* 50, 1: 49–58.

Hochschild, A. 1997. *The Time Bind: When Work Becomes Home and Home Becomes Work.* New York: Metropolitan Books.

Humphries, Jane. 1998. "Toward a Family-Friendly Economics." *New Political Economy* 3, 2: 223–40.

Institute of Workplace Studies. 1999. *Overtime and the American Worker.* New York State School of Industrial and Labor Relations, Cornell University, Ithaca, NY.

Jacobs, J., and K. Gerson. 2001. "Who Are the Overworked Americans?" In L. Golden and D. Figart, eds., *Working Time: International Trends, Theory, and Policy Perspectives,* 89–105. New York: Routledge.

Lang, Kevin, and Shulamit Kahn. 2001. "Hours Constraints: Theory, Evidence and Policy Implications." In G. Wong and G. Picot, eds., *Working Time in a Comparative Perspective,* vol. 1. Kalamazoo, MI: Upjohn Institute for Employment Research.

Kaufman, B. 1999. "Expanding the Behavioral Foundations of Labor Economics." *Industrial and Labor Relations Review* 52: 361–92.

Kelloway, K., D. Gallagher, and J. Barling. 2004. "Work, Employment and the Individual." In B. Kaufman, ed., *Theoretical Perspectives on Work and the Employment Relationship.* Urbana, IL: Industrial Relations Research Association.

Kossek, E., B. Lautsch, and S. Eaton. 2005. "Flexibility Enactment Theory: Implications of Flexibility Type, Boundary Management and Control for Work-Family Effectiveness." In E. Kossek and S.J. Lambert, eds., *Work and Life Integration: Organizational, Cultural and Individual Perspectives.* Mahwah, N.J.: Lawrence Erlbaum Associates.

Krausz, M., and N. Freibach. 1983. "Effects of Flexible Working Time for Employed Women upon Satisfaction, Strains and Absenteeism." *Journal of Occupational Psychology* 2: 155–59.

Krausz, M., A. Sagie, and Y. Bidermann. 2000. "Actual and Preferred Work Schedules and Scheduling Control as Determinants of Job-Related Attitudes." *Journal of Vocational Behavior* 56: 1–11.

Kuhn, Peter, and Fernando Lozano. 2005. "The Expanding Workweek? Understanding Trends in Long Work Hours Among U.S. Men, 1979–2004." NBER Working Paper 11895, December.

LaJeunesse, Robert. 2004. "An Institutionalist Approach to Work Time." In D. Champlin and J. Knoedler, eds., *The Institutionalist Tradition in Labor Economics.* Armonk, NY: M.E. Sharpe, 159–74.

Lamberg, Lynne. 2004. "Impact of Long Working Hours Explored." *Journal of the American Medical Association* 292: 25–26.

Landers, R., J. Rebitzer, and L. Taylor. 1996. "Rat Race Redux: Adverse Selection in the Determination of Work Hours in Law Firms." *American Economic Review* 86: 3229–48.

Major, V.S., K. Klein, and M. Ehrhart. 2002. "Work Time, Work Interference with Family and Psychological Distress." *Journal of Applied Psychology* 87: 427–36.

Martens, M., F. Nijhuis, M. Van Boxtel, and J. Knottnerus. 1999. "Flexible Work Schedules and Mental and Physical Health: A Study of a Working Population with Non-Traditional Working Hours." *Journal of Organizational Behavior* 20, 1:35–46.

McCrate, E. 2002. *Working Mothers in a Double Bind.* Briefing Paper, Economic Policy Institute, Washington, DC.

Messenger, Jon, ed. 2004. *Working Time and Workers' Preferences in Industrialized Countries: Finding the Balance.* Geneva: ILO Conditions of Work and Employment Programme.

Mishel, L., J. Bernstein, and A. Allegretto. 2005. *The State of Working America, 2004–05.* Washington, DC: Economic Policy Institute.

Moss, R.L., and T.D. Curtis. 1985. "The Economics of Flexitime." *Journal of Behavioral Economics,* summer, 95–114.

Nyland, Chris. 1989. *Reduced Working Time and the Management of Production.* Cambridge: Cambridge University Press.

Pingle, M., and M. Mitchell. 2002. "What Motivates Positional Concerns for Income." *Journal of Economic Psychology* 23: 127–48.

Prasch, R. 2001. "Revising the Labor Supply Schedule: Implications for Work Time and Minimum Wage Legislation." In L. Golden and D. Figart, eds., *Working Time: International Trends, Theory, and Policy Perspectives,* ch. 10. New York: Routledge Press.

Presser, Harriet. 2003. *Working in a 24/7 Economy: Challenges for American Families.* New York: Russell Sage Foundation.

Rebitzer, J., and L. Taylor. 1995. "Do Labor Markets Provide Enough Short-Hour Jobs? An Analysis of Work Hours and Work Incentives." *Economic Inquiry* 33: 257–73.

Reynolds, J. 2004. "When Too Much Is Not Enough: Actual and Preferred Work Hours in the United States and Abroad." *Sociological Forum* 19, 1: 89–120.

Rima, I. 1984. "Involuntary Unemployment and the Re-Specified Labor Supply Curve." *Journal of Post Keynesian Economics* 6: 540–50.

Rothschild, K. 1982. "A Note on Some of Economic and Welfare Aspects of Working Time Regulations." *Australian Economic Papers* 21: 214–18.

Ruuskanen, Olli-Pekka. 2004. "More than Two Hands: Is Multi-Tasking the Answer to Stress?" Paper presented at the annual conference of the International Association for Time Use Research, October 27–29, Rome.

Scacciati, Francesco. 2004. "Erosion of Purchasing Power and Labor Supply." *Journal of Socio-Economics* 33: 725–44.

Scandura, T., and M. Lankau. 1997. "Relationships of Gender, Family Responsibility and Flexible Work Hours to Organizational Commitment and Job Satisfaction." *Journal of Organizational Behavior* 18, 4: 377–91.

Schor, J. 1999. *The Overspent American: Upscaling, Downshifting and the New Consumer.* New York: Basic Books.

Schuetze, H.J. 2001. Topic 2.2b: Fixed Hours Constraints, Economics 370 (available at http://web.uvic.ca/~hschuetz/econ370/topic2_2b.pdf).

Shank, S. 1986. "Preferred Hours of Work and Corresponding Earnings." *Monthly Labor Review* 109: 40–44.

Sharif, M. 2000. "Inverted 'S'—The Complete Neoclassical Labor Supply Function." *International Labor Review* 139: 409–35.

Sparks, Kate, and Cary Cooper. 1997. "The Effects of Hours of Work on Health: a Meta-Analytic Review." *Journal of Occupational and Organizational Psychology* 70: 391–408.

Spurgeon, A., J.M. Harrington, and C.L. Cooper. 1997. "Health and Safety Problems Associated With Long Working Hours: A Review of the Current Position." *Occupational and Environmental Medicine* 54: 367–75.

Stewart, M.B., and J.K. Swaffield. 1997. "Constraints on the Desired Hours of Work of British Men." *Economic Journal* 107: 520–35.

Stier, H., and N. Lewin-Epstein. 2003. "Time to Work: A Comparative Analysis of Preferences for Working Hours." *Work and Occupations* 30, 3: 302.

Thierry, H., and B. Jansen. 1998. "Work Time and Behavior at Work." In H. Thierry and P.J.D. Drenth, eds., *Handbook of Work and Organizational Psychology,* vol. 2, *Work Psychology,* 2nd ed. Hove, UK: Psychology Press, 89–119.

Weiss, Y. 1996. "Synchronization of Work Schedules." *International Economic Review* 37: 157–79.

Winkler, Anne E. 1998. "Earnings of Husbands and Wives in Dual-Earner Families." *Monthly Labor Review* 121, 4: 42–48.

Wisman, J. 1989. "Straightening Out the Backward Bending Supply Curve of Labour: From Overt to Covert Compulsion and Beyond." *Review of Political Economy* 1: 94–112.

Wolfe, A. 1997. "The Moral Meaning of Work." *Journal of Socio-Economics* 26, 6: 559.

Yakura, E. 2001. "Billables: The Valorization of Time in Consulting." *American Behavioral Scientist* 44, 7: 1076–96.

Yaniv, G. 1995. "Burnout, Absenteeism, and the Overtime Decision." *Journal of Economic Psychology* 16, 2: 297–309.

Appendix 24.1 Conventional Model of Suboptimal Utility with Overemployment

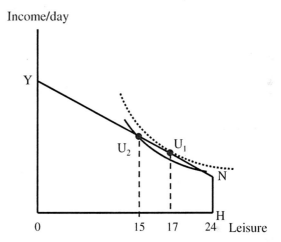

• If an individual is free to choose the number of hours of work, he or she chooses point U_1, with 17 hours of leisure and 7 hours of work . . .

• If the individual is **constrained** to work a standard workday of 9 hours or not at all, he or she will choose point U_2, lower than optimal utility level, overemployed by 2 hours per day.

Income/day

Y

U_2 U_1

N

H

0   15   17   24   Leisure

Appendix 24.2 Trade-off Between the Duration and Flexibility Dimensions of Hours: Willingness to Trade Off Some Leisure Time or Income to Attain Schedule Flexibility

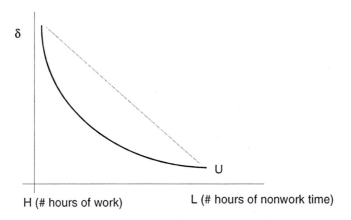

δ

U

H (# hours of work)   L (# hours of nonwork time)

δ = Flexibility to supply hours on worker's preferred schedule

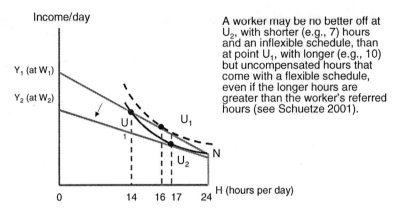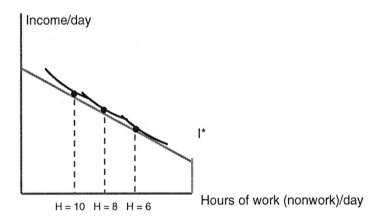

Appendix 24.3   **A Firm Providing Flexible Schedule Induces Workers to Accept a Lower Wage Rate Per Hour**

Income/day

Y_1 (at W_1)

Y_2 (at W_2)

U_1

U_1

U_2

N

0   14   16 17   24   H (hours per day)

A worker may be no better off at U_2, with shorter (e.g., 7) hours and an inflexible schedule, than at point U_1, with longer (e.g., 10) but uncompensated hours that come with a flexible schedule, even if the longer hours are greater than the worker's referred hours (see Schuetze 2001).

Appendix 24.4   **Nonlinear Indifference Curve If Longer and Shorter Than Standard 8-Hour Days Comes with More Schedule Flexibility**

Income/day

I^*

H = 10   H = 8   H = 6   Hours of work (nonwork)/day

PART 6

GENDER AND DECISION MAKING

CHAPTER 25

CHICKS, HAWKS, AND
PATRIARCHAL INSTITUTIONS

NANCY FOLBRE

> Cooperation occurs only in the shadow of conflict.
> —*Jack Hirshleifer (2001, 11)*
>
> Conflict lies at the heart of sexual reproduction.
> —*J.R. Krebs and N.B. Davies (1981, 134)*

The notion that conflict between men and women plays a central role in the evolution of hierarchical social institutions has a long intellectual history. In the nineteenth century William Thompson, Friedrich Engels, and August Bebel, among others, insisted that collective male efforts to consolidate control over women helped explain the origin of the state. Gerda Lerner lent historical substance to this argument with her study of ancient Mesopotamian and Hebrew societies, *The Origin of Patriarchy* (1986). Yet institutional economists pay scant attention to gender conflict.[1] They tend to focus on property rights relevant to the market or the state, rather than the family. They often accept the predominant economic assumption (formalized in a joint utility function) that mothers, fathers, and children share common preferences. And they seldom entertain the possibility that men and women have different collective identities and interests.

The intellectual division of labor within the academy has contributed to uneven development of feminist theory. Scholars within more qualitative (and also generally more "feminine") disciplines of history and anthropology have been more intrigued by gender conflict than those within the more quantitative ("masculine") sciences of economics and biology. As a result, arguments concerning the impact of gender conflict on social institutions have often been expressed in narrative, rather than analytical form. In this essay I make an explicit effort to translate narrative arguments into game-theoretic models in order to clarify their structure and encourage interdisciplinary discussion.

I begin with a brief review of three areas of research that help explain the genealogy of my perspective. From behavioral ecology, I take the claim that natural selection for different levels of parenting and mating effort between males and females leaves an imprint on preferences that can influence behavior. From political economy, I take the claim that coalitions engage in collective actions that serve their interests, ranging from violent coercion to establishment of advantageous property rights or political rules. From feminist theory, I take the claim that coalitions based on gender can shape social institutions and influence the level of male domination within groups, with implications for intra-group competition and conflict.

The second section builds on this interdisciplinary literature to outline my general approach to an institutional "battle of the sexes." Evolutionary biologists emphasize that males and females of a given species co-evolve within a specific ecological niche; I emphasize that a social process of bargaining over institutions governing human reproduction represents an analogous form of cultural evolution. Important strategic interactions take place between individual men and women, between gender-based coalitions within groups, and between strongly male-dominated groups and more gender-egalitarian ones. Small initial differences in gender-based endowments and preferences lead to the emergence of patriarchal social institutions that favor males. However, technological and social change may alter bargaining environments in ways that improve the relative position of females.

The next section focuses on individual decisions regarding investments in children, criticizing the standard neoclassical economic model of parental investments. The model I develop translates the insights of behavioral ecology into language more familiar to economists, showing that parents face different budget constraints that lead fathers to prefer child quantity over quality. The potential impact of differences in parental preferences is illustrated by a discussion of the noncooperative game popularly known as Chicken.

The following sections turn to more explicit consideration of the evolution of patriarchal institutions in early hunter-gatherer societies. A graphical analysis of the implications of different fallback positions for males and females in "autarkic promiscuity" illustrates the relative gains to parental collaboration formalized by rules of marriage. Specific conditions may lead to the emergence of patriarchal marriage rules that are more advantageous to males than females.

The essay concludes with explicit consideration of group selection, suggesting that male domination of political decision making (like male domination of household decision making) will shift investments toward child quantity rather than child quality. The logic of a Hawk-Dove game in which the costs and benefits of aggression are defined in terms of child quantity/quality outcomes shows why male domination may increase a group's propensity to adopt Hawk-like strategies of military aggression. This argument, foreshadowed by Plutarch's account of the rape of the Sabine women, is consistent with anthropological research on "woman stealing" and lends support to Gerda Lerner's (1986) historical analysis of the relationship between patriarchy and slavery.

A THEORETICAL MÉNAGE À TROIS

What do individuals want and how do they go about getting it? Evolutionary biology suggests that the forces of natural selection reward those who maximize their reproductive fitness. Economic theory suggests that individuals consciously seek to maximize their own happiness or utility. These two suggestions are not inconsistent: a species with utility functions that did not provide psychological reinforcement for fitness-improving behaviors would be unlikely to last for very long (Bergstrom 1996). Yet there are obvious tensions between these two models of optimization, related to the longer time horizon of natural selection and the rapid pace of environmental and institutional change, which may lead to long periods of disequilibrium. Cultural evolution provides humans with greater flexibility through the establishment of norms and rules that may, in turn, modify or at least modulate individual preferences (Boyd and Richerson 1985).

Both biology and economics are riven by controversies over the relative importance of individual versus group dynamics. Biologists critical of so-called group selection (e.g., Dawkins 1976) often invoke arguments similar to those wielded by economists skeptical of the role of collective action (e.g., Olson 1971). Yet some scholars in both disciplines are now emphasizing multilevel selection, rather than focusing exclusively on one or the other (Sober and Wilson 1998; Bowles 2003). Kin-based altruism and family life represent an arena of human interaction intermediate between the individual and the larger society. Feminist emphasis on the potential for both cooperation and conflict within the family promises some intriguing insights.

A full exploration of these interdisciplinary issues would require a superhighway. This essay carves a narrower trail of reasoning from biological differences to implications for collective decision making in households and social groups. Social institutions lead to stronger forms of male domination than biological differences alone are likely to generate. The combined impact of technological and social change, however, can lead to significant improvements in women's relative bargaining power.

Behavioral Ecology

Evolution plays tricks that most human cultures would describe as cruel. On one hand, individuals who fail to reproduce fail to replicate their genes, which are consequently less well represented in the gene pool. On the other hand, those who do reproduce are subjected to a tug of war between the interests of potential and actual offspring, which plays out in conflict between the interests of parents (who must survive in order to produce future potential offspring) and the interests of current offspring. Robert Trivers (1972) provides the classic formulation of this conflict and points to the biological basis for conflicts of interest between mothers and fathers.

Differences in the size and quantity of gametes males and females produce, combined with the physiological cost of gestation, nursing, and prolonged nurturance, have significant implications. Mothers have more invested in individual offspring and more to lose (in terms of reproductive fitness) from loss of a child. Women also lose their reproductive capacity at a much younger age than men. Mothers bond more closely and more quickly with offspring than fathers do (Hrdy 2000). As a result, fathers are in a stronger position than mothers to make a credible threat to abandon offspring.

The biology of gender differences implies that a different set of evolutionary pressures operates on males and females. Natural selection rewards males who improve their mating effort, increasing their sexual access to females. But natural selection rewards females who increase their parenting effort, improving the likelihood that their offspring will successfully reach maturity (Daly and Wilson 1983). Female parenting effort may take the form of bargaining with males for increased support of offspring (Low 2000).

These evolutionary pressures may also have implications for the broader development of male and female capabilities and preferences. Physical strength becomes an advantage for males in competition with other males. Selection for mating effort tends to place males in "winner-take-all" games that reward risk-taking behavior. If they fail to mate, their long-term success helping nurture offspring becomes irrelevant. Selection for parental effort places females in strategic environments more likely to reward cooperation. Rather than facing a shortage of potential partners, they face substantial long-term risks of being unable to raise highly dependent offspring to maturity (Low 2000). Evolutionary psychologists note that gender-based differences in preferences are likely to influence the relative social and economic position of men and women (Buss 1996). They have less to say about the social institutions that may emerge as a result of (or alter the implications of) these gender differences.

Economic Theory

Neoclassical economists following Gary Becker's lead (1981) devote considerable attention to family decision making. Contradicting their own commitment to methodological individualism, they generally begin from the assumption that family members share a joint utility function, which implies no significant differences in preferences or interests. An emerging literature on bargaining within the family draws from both cooperative and noncooperative game theory, emphasizing conflicts of interest over the distribution of goods and leisure time (Lundberg and Pollak 1993; Katz 1997). This literature focuses almost entirely on individual decisions, setting aside issues of collective action.

Some institutionalist economics, notably Sam Bowles (2003) and Herb Gintis (2000), develop multilevel analyses of individual and social bargaining in an evolutionary context. They focus on the emergence of strong reciprocity and relatively egalitarian social institutions. Another evolutionary economic perspective, represented by Jack Hirshleifer (2001) and Stergios Skaperdas (2002), places more emphasis on collective conflict and physical violence. Unfortunately (and, one hopes, temporarily), both these perspectives largely ignore issues of gender conflict. The exception is an important but often overlooked article by Stephen Cheung (1972) that explains the mutilation of Chinese women's feet as a way of enforcing patriarchal property rights.

Institutionalist economic reasoning provides a framework for understanding exchange, conflict, and the development of social institutions. The difficulties of enforcing contracts and solving coordination problems, combined with information and transaction costs, require the development of social institutions such as rules, laws, and norms (Bowles 2003). Groups devise ways of overcoming free-rider problems to pursue their collective interests. The so-called technology of conflict determines the relative payoffs to conflict and exchange (Hirshleifer 2001). Strong groups may gang up on weak ones.

Although both individuals and groups may seek to optimize, they are often able to reach only local optima, or may be required to choose among a variety of Pareto-efficient outcomes. Outcomes may reflect a complex interaction among random variation, explicit optimization efforts, and coordination problems that create substantial inefficiencies. Individuals participate in a complex strategic environment of overlapping games; cooperation with one group may aid them in conflict with another. Individual preferences may influence which social institutions are feasible, but institutions in turn tend to influence preferences (Gintis 2000; Bowles 2003). This dialectic is particularly relevant to the issue of gender-linked preferences. Social institutions may reinforce the gender differences that influence their genesis. At the same time, however, technological change and collective bargaining may lead to institutional changes that reconfigure preferences.

Feminist Theory

Biological reasoning has often been used to justify institutionalized gender inequalities (Tavris 1992). It is hardly surprising, therefore, that many feminist social theorists express deep skepticism regarding so-called sociobiological explanations of gender differences. In recent years feminist scholars in anthropology and biology have bridged that skepticism by offering evolutionary interpretations that insist on the "context-dependent nature" of women's biological and behavioral responses (Lancaster 1991, 1) and emphasize "behavioral flexibility, cross-cultural variability, and possibilities for future change" (Smuts 1995, 1).

Evolutionary biology has traditionally emphasized the selection pressures at work on males, emphasizing their competition among each other for females. A growing literature, however, emphasizes the selection pressures at work on females. Among species in which offspring are dependent on maternal nurturance and protection for a prolonged period, females are selected not merely for maternal altruism but also for the intelligence, resourcefulness, and strategic thinking required to help offspring reach maturity (Hrdy 1999). Males may be selected for their ability to manipulate and control females, but females are, likewise, selected for their ability to minimize the adverse effects of such manipulation on their own reproductive fitness (Gowaty 1997, 2003). Female primates often form coalitions designed to protect themselves and their offspring from male violence (Smuts 1992).

Feminist theorists in the social sciences have much to gain from more serious consideration of evolutionary biology. Gowaty's emphasis on the co-evolution of male and female strategies of maximizing reproductive fitness suggests a direct parallel with gender-based collective bargaining over social institutions. Feminist political scientists often use the term "sexual contract" to refer to social institutions that seem to reflect the interplay of coercion and negotiation between men and women (Pateman 1988). This approach extends the liberal metaphor of the social contract to the realm of family life and sets the stage for an analysis of collective bargaining over social institutions. It rejects the common presumption that the social/sexual contract generally evolves toward egalitarian solutions or 50/50 sharing rules (Skyrms 1996).

As suggested by the earlier reference to Stephen Cheung's seminal essay on patriarchal property rights, institutionalist analysis can be extended to inequalities based on gender. Restrictions on women's rights to own or accumulate property independently of fathers and husbands often have conspicuous economic implications (Braunstein and Folbre 2001). Moreover, feminist theory insists that the concept of property rights must be extended to include "reproductive rights" such as those pertaining to custody of children and access to contraception and abortion. Indeed, reproductive rights can be construed as a kind of property right over the production and maintenance of human capital.[2] In many societies, men enjoy greater sexual freedom and less responsibility for the care of dependents than women. The emergence of these asymmetric rights and responsibilities through the institutionalization of marriage rules predates the emergence of rights to private property in livestock or land.

A feminist approach to institutional economics also calls attention to the rules of collective governance and larger structures of constraint (Folbre 1994). Why have women so often been excluded from participation in institutions of inherited power (such as kingships) as well as from voting? What are the possible causes and consequences of such exclusion? What are the links between patriarchal control over women within the family and by the state? Evolutionary theories of social institutions should pose such questions. Game theory provides a useful analytical framework for answering them.

GENDER GAMES

Institutionalist economists are critical of neoclassical or Walrasian assumptions that economic transactions always represent simple, costless forms of mutually advantageous exchange. Sexual intercourse between men and women provides an excellent example of a complex, multidimensional, risky transaction. It may represent the reciprocal exchange of physical pleasure or the violent coercion of rape. Its reproductive outcome is often uncertain. An agreement to collaborate in raising offspring is even more complex. Women typically offer childbearing and child-rearing services and implicit or explicit guarantees of paternity in return for economic assistance. This contractual relationship lasts for a long period of time and is difficult to enforce. It seems likely that the costs of monitoring female sexual fidelity are lower than the costs of enforcing male economic commitments.

In terms of reproductive fitness, females offer a good—the ovum—that is scarcer than the good offered by males, the sperm. Males are forced to compete with one another for access to this good. But once the ovum is fertilized, the higher costs of losing it put females in a weaker position. Fathers enjoy a first-mover advantage. If they violate a contractual agreement to provide support, they can be fairly confident that mothers will provide for offspring. In the Greek myth dramatized by Euripedes in the fourth century BC, Jason announces that he is sending his first wife, Medea, and their two sons into exile in order to marry another woman, the daughter of a powerful king. Medea realizes that she cannot retaliate without hurting herself as well: "What point in racking their father's heart," she asks, "if I break my own twice over?" (Euripedes 2002, 31). Still, she chooses revenge over love, and murders not only the new bride but also her own children. Few mothers are willing to engage in such drastic and costly retaliation. They become, in a sense, prisoners of love.

The "battle of the sexes" that enjoys standard treatment in most game-theory texts is often described as a trivial coordination problem. A husband would prefer to go to a prize fight, while his wife would prefer to attend the opera, yet both would prefer one another's company. The quality/quantity trade-off regarding investments in children represents a far more profound issue. Even if fathers and mothers prefer to collaborate, they may have different preferences concerning the terms of their collaboration. They are players in a noncooperative game in which they may both gain from social coordination. But they are also players in a cooperative game in which they may conspire to develop forms of social coordination that work to their advantage.

The following three sections provide simple illustrations of gender games between individual men and women, between and among groups of men and women, and between "fiercely patriarchal" and more egalitarian groups.

INDIVIDUAL BARGAINING OVER QUANTITY/QUALITY OF OFFSPRING

The insights of evolutionary biology can be translated into terms more familiar to economists through their application to standard utility maximization and to simple game theory.

The Quantity-Quality Trade-Off

The standard neoclassical economic analysis of fertility starts with a married couple that maximizes a joint utility function and faces a budget constraint that represents a trade-off between number of children and expenditures per child or "child quality" (Becker 1981). A series of indifference curves represent their preferences for child quality relative to child quantity. The optimal combination is represented by the point of tangency between the budget line and the indifference curve farthest from the origin (see Figure 25.1).[3]

From an evolutionary point of view, the indifference curves could also represent isoquants that represent combinations of quantity and quality that offer equivalent levels of reproductive fitness. This would imply that environmental factors influencing fitness remain stable over a sufficiently long period of time to select for the optimal preferences within the population. One could argue that husbands and wives in monogamous relationships share common preferences for quantity versus quality (independent of costs) precisely because they both seek to maximize their reproductive fitness.

Even under this restrictive assumption, however, reproductive biology suggests that the budget constraints for mothers and fathers are different. The biological maximum of children for women is much lower than that for men. Even under rules of monogamy, men are more likely to remarry and raise additional children after the death of their spouse. Fathers can com-

Figure 25.1   **Parental Investments in Quantity/Quality Assuming a Common Budget Constraint**

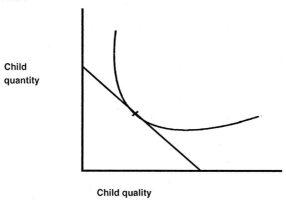

Child quantity

Child quality

Figure 25.2   **Maternal and Paternal Investments in Quantity/Quality Assuming Different Budget Constraints**

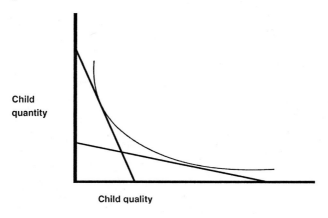

Child quantity

Child quality

pensate mothers for some of the physiological costs of childbearing by transferring resources to them. The biological stresses, strains, and risks of motherhood, however, cannot be fully compensated. Investments in child quality are more fungible but also lack perfect substitutability. A mother's milk, for instance, is superior to most substitutes. For mothers, the costs of child quantity are costlier in terms of quality than those for fathers, as reflected in the flatter of the two budget constraints in Figure 25.2. As the same figure illustrates, the optimal choice for mothers differs from the optimal choice for fathers, even assuming they face identical indifference curves.

How will the couple reconcile this difference? In principle, it could be resolved through exchange. The father could offer a side payment to the mother to have more children; likewise, the mother could offer a side payment to have fewer. But the terms of this exchange, and indeed the larger process of negotiation, can be affected by coercion, contracting problems, and strategic maneuvers. In the language of institutional economics, it represents a "holdup problem" that may be affected by differences in the physical strength of men and women or the "technology of conflict." It may also be affected by differences in maternal and paternal preferences.

Figure 25.3   **Traditional Chicken**

		Teenage boy 2	
		Wimp (swerve)	Macho (don't swerve)
Teenage boy 1	Wimp (swerve)	2, 2	1, 3
	Macho (don't swerve)	3, 1	0, 0

Gendered Preferences

The notion that gendered preferences can be described in terms of a Chicken game is widely appreciated in evolutionary biology (Trivers 1972; Smith 1982; Low 2000). Economists, however, have yet to fully acknowledge this point. In many game theory texts, the Chicken game is described as a contest between two teenage males, designed to show who is the most Macho.[4] They drive their hot rods toward each other. The one who swerves first is a chicken or a Wimp. If neither swerves, both are killed (the worst outcome). If both swerve, both are revealed as cowards, and humiliated. The best outcome for either individual is for the other to swerve. As the payoff matrix in Figure 25.3 suggests, there are two pure-strategy Nash equilibria. Each player strictly prefers the equilibrium in which the other player backs down.

Given these payoffs, individuals fare best if they play a mixed strategy, choosing to swerve 50 percent of the time and incurring significant costs (since a fatal crash will occur 25 percent of the time). In an evolutionary setting, with a population of Machos and Wimps, the Machos do best in a population dominated by Wimps, and vice versa; with the payoff matrix above, we expect an evolutionarily stable strategy with a population equally divided between the two types. If the two types are easily observable to one another (e.g., one wears blue, the other pink), further efficiency gains can be expected. A "correlated convention" may emerge. Blues will never swerve when playing with Pinks, and Pinks will always swerve when playing with Blues. Norms that help shape and signal risk aversion based on gender could offer social benefits.

The game of Chicken also describes collective action problems concerning the supply of effort to projects that offer public benefits. In this context, the payoffs resemble those described above, but the actions differ. Instead of Wimps who swerve, we have Suckers who devote effort. Instead of Machos who don't swerve, we have Opportunists who shirk. If both players provide effort, some inefficient duplication occurs. Each player would prefer the other to provide effort, but the worst possible outcome is one in which neither provides effort (Bowles 2003).

Parental effort devoted to children can be described in these terms (Folbre and Weisskopf 1998). If mothers and fathers care equally about their offspring but parental effort is costly, they will prefer that the other parent provide high effort, while they provide only low effort. If neither parent provides a high level of effort, the offspring will suffer. However, behavioral ecology suggests that payoffs to fathers and mothers of child welfare are asymmetric, as in Figure 25.4. Assume that mothers value the extra benefits of high effort for children more than fathers do, by some amount x. Likewise, they are more averse to the costs of low effort, by the amount $-x$.

This remains a Chicken game, in the sense that each parent would prefer to choose the opposite of what the other parent chooses. The possibility of a low-effort/low-effort outcome remains,

Figure 25.4   **Caring Chicken with Asymmetric Payoffs**

Effort Devoted to Children with Differing Parental Altruism

		Father	
		High effort	Low effort
Mother	High effort	2 + x, 2	1 + x, 3
	Low effort	3 + x, 1	−x, 0

but the risk is lower, since the optimal mixed strategy for mothers to provide high effort becomes $(1 + x) / (x + 2)$. It is greater than 50 percent as long as x is positive, and approaches 100 percent as x increases. The payoffs to this game may be further modified if one assumes "warm glow" altruism or endogenous preferences (see Appendix 25.1).

In sum, the insights of evolutionary biology suggest that mothers and fathers face different costs in the production of child quality and child quantity even if they share a common preference for the optimal quality of offspring. In a bargaining context, mothers are likely to be more risk-averse than fathers, and also to devote more effort to children. These outcomes do not inevitably lead to patriarchal institutions. But these outcomes are likely to affect the outcomes of decentralized forms of repeated collective action and the collective bargaining power that coalitions of men and women can exercise over the formation of social institutions such as marriage rules.

COLLECTIVE BARGAINING OVER MARRIAGE RULES

Monogamy is widespread among bird species, and human beings may also be behaviorally predisposed to it. But such predispositions are apparently inadequate coordination devices. Most societies institutionalize strict marriage rules that range from strict monogamy to polygamy and polyandry and also govern obligations for the care of dependents. I argue that such rules are typically shaped by processes of collective as well as individual negotiation. Gender, like class, race, or nation, represents a form of collective identity that is conducive to coalition formation.

The Potential Gains from Monogamy

Evolutionary biologists studying nonhuman species and historians and anthropologists studying humans concur that monogamy is most likely to emerge in circumstances in which it improves reproductive fitness. By constraining males to the number of offspring one female can provide, monogamy better aligns the reproductive interests of males and females. Yet monogamy can take many different forms. Sexually exclusive partnerships between males and females may last for a week, a breeding season, or a lifetime. They may also involve different degrees of cheating by concealing intercourse with another partner. One implication of this variation is that social rules of monogamy may favor one gender over another.

Monogamy is often described as a metaphorical bargain in which males provide more assistance to females in rearing offspring in return for greater assurance of paternity.[5] In environments in which offspring are unlikely to survive without care from both parents, monogamy offers distinct evolutionary benefits (Krebs and Davies 1981). But it is important to note that the overall

Figure 25.5 **Large Potential Gains in Reproductive Fitness from Parental Cooperation**

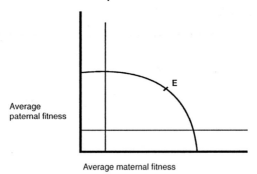

Average
paternal fitness

Average maternal fitness

(Straight lines represent fallbacks in the absence of cooperation; curved line
represents trade-offs between paternal and maternal fitness)

gains from monogamy do not require egalitarian or gender-neutral rules. This point can be illustrated with the Nash-bargaining approach that economists use to explain gains from marriage (McElroy 1990) using a metric of reproductive fitness rather than utility or income. In Figure 25.5 the reproductive fitness frontier (drawn to resemble a utility frontier or a production possibilities curve) represents the potential combinations of male and female reproductive fitness resulting from the parental cooperation, which can take the form of polygamy, polyandry, monogamy, or combinations thereof.

The vertical line represents the female fallback and the horizontal line the male fallback of reproductive fitness that would result from absence of collaboration in parenting effort. This might be termed the "autarkic promiscuity" fallback. For the purpose of simplicity, imagine a situation in which all males randomly meet and mate with all females; all females become pregnant and raise children without any assistance from men or from one another. Fallbacks for males and females would be symmetric.[6] (I will shortly explore a more realistic assumption.)

In Figure 25.5, the large area to the northeast of the intersection of the fallback positions but still within a feasible set represents the large potential gains from cooperative agreements between mothers and fathers, or marriage. These gains are not necessarily equally shared. Polygamous rules of cooperation allocate several women to one man, excluding some males from mating. Such rules increase the average reproductive fitness of men who acquire wives but may also lower the average reproductive fitness of females, who must compete with one another for resources from one husband. Still, women will benefit as long as their reproductive fitness is at least as high as it would be in autarkic promiscuity. Only with "perfect" monogamy, defined as neither partner reproducing with another (even after the death of the original partner), would mothers and fathers have equal reproductive fitness, represented by point E on the frontier.

Very different circumstances are depicted in Figure 25.6. There, parental collaboration offers potential gains to each partner, but there is no distribution of the gains in reproductive fitness that leaves both the mother and father better off than they would be in autarkic promiscuity. There are no points to the northeast of the intersection of the fallbacks within the feasible set. In these circumstances parental collaboration is unlikely. In between these two extremes of equal fallbacks with large gains and equal fallbacks with no gains lies a more interesting alternative: asymmetric fallbacks combined with large gains from collaboration.

Several possible factors could lead to asymmetric fallbacks for men and women.

Males have the physical strength and physiological capacity to rape females who fail to gain

Figure 25.6 **No Joint Gains from Parental Cooperation**

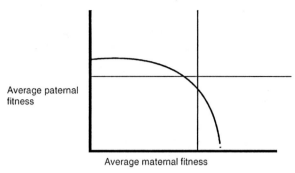

Average paternal
fitness

Average maternal fitness

(Straight lines represent fallbacks in the absence of cooperation; curved line
represents trade-offs between paternal and maternal fitness)

Figure 25.7 **Unequal Joint Gains from Parental Cooperation**

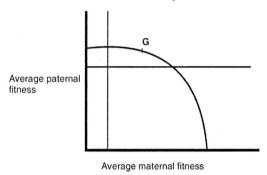

Average paternal
fitness

Average maternal fitness

(Straight lines represent fallbacks in the absence of cooperation; curved line
represents trade-offs between paternal and maternal fitness)

protection from another male, thus restricting their choice of mates or the timing of their reproductive commitments. Some anthropologists suggest that females opt for marriage as a way of gaining protection from unwanted copulations (Jones et al. 2000). If the strongest males are able to exclude other males from mating and all females are impregnated, fathers will enjoy higher average reproductive fitness than mothers.[7] This, in turn, creates an incentive for females to mate only with dominant males, rejecting those who are subordinate. Female choices could lead to further psychological differentiation between males and females (Buss 1996).

Stronger fallback positions for fathers would also result from a situation in which initially monogamous males who abandon females with offspring can mate with other females, while initially monogamous females with offspring are unable to find males willing to help provide for their current or future offspring. These circumstances are consistent with first-mover advantage and the "caring chicken with asymmetric payoffs" scenario described above. Because fathers are more willing to abandon offspring than mothers, their fallbacks within collaborative relationships are stronger.

Figure 25.7 illustrates fathers' stronger fallback positions. Even if both mothers and fathers gain from collaboration, perfect monogamy is an unlikely outcome and fathers enjoy a distinct advantage in relative fitness, because the range of feasible outcomes on the fitness frontier is well above the point at which reproductive fitness of both partners is equal (Medea would have ended up within that range of outcomes had she accepted exile).[8] In most areas of the world negative sanctions imposed on women having intercourse outside of marriage have traditionally been much harsher than those imposed on men (Daly and Wilson 1983, 291). This result does not depend on any specific bargaining rule, such as a Nash solution. Rather, it follows simply from the asymmetric fallbacks: even if men agree to the feasible collaborative outcome that favors them the least, they will still fare better than women.

Coalitions and Collective Bargaining

In hunter-gatherer societies, it is men who tend to exchange women, rather than the other way around (Lévi-Strauss 1969). Rules of marriage tend to be formulated by men, rather than by women, and to offer men more favorable terms.[9] Such rules could emerge in at least three different ways. They could result from a decentralized process of collective action and gradually become institutionalized. Alternatively, men could get together around the campfire, discuss the rules of marriage they would prefer, and make women an offer. Women would then make a counteroffer. A final possibility is that men simply choose the rules they prefer without explicitly bargaining with women, but taking potential contract enforcement or principal-agent problems into account.

What evidence supports the claim that collective gender bargaining might take place? Evolutionary biology offers strong support for the relevance of gender coalitions. The threat of violence is particularly effective when carried out (or simply condoned) by large groups of males (Smuts 1992; Wilson, Daly, and Scheib 1997). Among primates, as well as other animal species, male invaders often kill the young offspring of other males (Hrdy 1999). Male strategies can also include affiliative control—rules regarding whom females are allowed to come in contact with and under what terms (Gowaty 1997). Studies of bonobos and rhesus monkeys show that females can form coalitions that mitigate male violence and encourage intrafemale cooperation in the care of offspring (Smuts 1992, 1995). Females who develop systems of "allomothering" improve their collective fallback position (Hrdy 1999).

Gender coalitions in human societies are even more conspicuous, and they are likely to influence the formation of social institutions (Folbre 1994). As Daly and Wilson put it, "men strive to control women and to traffic in female reproductive capacity" (1983, 290). The establishment of marriage rules represents a social institution that probably predates the establishment of property rights over land and livestock, and could help explain why many hunter-gatherer societies exclude women from collective governance.

Attention to gender coalitions does not preclude attention to coalitions based on other dimensions of collective identity. Indeed, it strengthens a larger theory of collective action and coalitional bargaining. It has been suggested that subordinate males form coalitions in order to challenge polygamous rules and establish rules of monogamy that lead to greater equality among men (Alexander 1987). A coalition between subordinate males and females would be even more likely to succeed in this respect. On the other hand, coalitions based on class or race tend to cross gender lines and often reinforce gender inequalities. Several accounts of the emergence of foot binding and genital mutilation suggest that mothers' gains from ensuring their daughters' marriageability to higher-status males exceed the losses imposed by such actions (Dickemann 1979; Mackie 1996). As these examples suggest, the outcomes of gender-based coalition formation and collective bargaining also have important implications for group selection.

GENDER INEQUALITY AND MILITARY AGGRESSION

A number of factors could explain why males typically have more influence than females over the collective governance of hunter-gatherer societies. Under technological conditions in which physical strength has a significant positive impact on productive potential and ability to coerce others, females operate at a disadvantage. The typically male activity of hunting may be conducive to the formation of strong male alliances. Patterns of patrilocality in which women marry out of the group and are less likely to reside with biological kin may weaken their ability to form coalitions. Specialization in child rearing itself may weaken women's bargaining power through the prisoner-of-love dynamics described above.

A Hawk-Dove Scenario

Could differences in male and female preferences for child quality affect the success of strongly patriarchal groups relative to those in which women have a stronger voice? If this were the case, the emergence of strong male political dominance could result from a process of group selection in which patriarchies prevail over matriarchies, or in which "fierce" patriarchies outcompete "gentle" ones.

Most historical discussions of group warfare focus on underlying economic capabilities that shape military technology (Diamond 1999). However, in the hunting and gathering societies characteristic of much of human history, the technology of conflict had distinctly different consequences for fathers than for mothers. The primary cost of war was the high mortality of young adult males, and the primary benefit of war was the capture of young females (Lévi-Strauss 1969; Chagnon 1983).

Stealing women allows a group to increase child quantity. Capture of new females benefits males directly by increasing their pool of potential mates. However, it benefits females in the tribe only indirectly if it increases the fitness of the group as a whole. It may actually lower their reproductive fitness by encouraging substitution away from quality toward quantity, or diluting the resources available to their own offspring. Indeed, the loss of young male warriors who have not yet fulfilled their reproductive potential represents a reduction in child quality that is costlier to warriors' mothers than to their fathers.

The payoffs of a Hawk-Dove game help explain the impact of systems of group governance on the probability of adopting an aggressive strategy. When two Hawks meet they fight, paying costs but enjoying some positive probability of benefits. When Hawks meet Doves, they consume them at no cost. When Doves meet Doves, they share equally and avoid conflict. As shown in the payoff matrix in Figure 25.8, V refers to the value of the resource gained, and C to the cost of aggressive behavior. In an individual choice model, individuals choose a Hawk or Dove strategy. In an evolutionary model, different individuals in the population represent Hawks or Doves, and their interactions determine the composition of the population.

Here I apply the model to a specific form of group selection. Different groups choose to act as Hawks or Doves based on explicit calculation of the potential benefits. What determines their choices? Assume, for the purpose of simplicity, that a Hawk group has a 50 percent chance of winning against another Hawk group. The dynamics of the game depend on the relative sizes of V and C. If $V > C$, the game becomes a prisoner's dilemma and Hawks invade and take over even though this is not the socially most efficient outcome. If $V < C$, the game resembles Chicken. Hawks prefer to meet Doves, but there is no pure strategy equilibrium. I expect a polymorphic population of groups.

Figure 25.8   **A Standard Hawk-Dove Game**

		B	
		Hawk	Dove
A	Hawk	$(V-C)/2, (V-C)/2$	$V, 0$
	Dove	$0, V$	$V/2, V/2$

Assume further that the relevant costs and benefits are those facing decision makers, not those facing the group as a whole (alternatively, one could argue that decision makers simply place a disproportionate weight on their own costs and benefits). Decision makers in patriarchal groups face costs C_p that are lower than the costs C facing decision makers in other groups. Similarly, the resources gained through conflict offer greater benefits V_p to decision makers in patriarchal groups than the benefits V facing decision makers in other groups.[10]

Under these assumptions, Hawk becomes a more attractive strategy for patriarchal groups than for others, because $V_p - C_p > V - C$. Even if $V_p < C_p$, leading to a mixed strategy, patriarchal groups will adopt this strategy more frequently than others. As mentioned, their decision makers may also be less risk-averse than those of other groups. Will they be able to successfully invade and dominate society as a whole? The answer depends on the relative size of V and C as well as V_p and C_p. But since the optimal strategy depends on the proportion of Hawks within the stable polymorphic population, the emergence of patriarchal groups could lead to a tipping phenomenon. If the ratio of V_p to C_p is greater than 1, Hawk strategies become completely dominant among patriarchal groups, which could in turn make Hawk strategies dominant for other groups. Furthermore, the advantages of adopting a Hawk strategy could encourage patriarchal governance.

A Hawk-Chicken Scenario

The scenario above depends on certain assumptions regarding the technology of conflict. The outcomes would obviously be different if groups sent young women to fight and captured young men as potential slaves (perhaps this is what the Amazons originally had in mind). This technology of conflict is obviously influenced by biological differences between men and women. In hand-to-hand combat, men make better warriors than women. In a world of high desired fertility, women represent a more valuable reproductive asset than males. Also relevant are the differences in male and female preferences described in the Chicken game above.

Women are more easily domesticated by capturing groups because maternal altruism holds them hostage. Once impregnated by their captors, they have much to gain from cooperation with them in order to promote the welfare of their children. When a band of men first founded the city of Rome, they found it difficult to obtain sufficient women to start families of their own. They resorted to trickery, inviting the neighboring Sabines to bring their daughters to a festival, then seizing the women. The Sabine men retreated, and by the time they had mustered sufficient military force to demand their daughters' return, many of the women were pregnant with Roman children.

In a dramatic gesture famously narrated by Plutarch, the Sabine mothers ran onto the battlefield and pleaded with their fathers and husbands not to fight, essentially saying that it was too late:

You did not come to vindicate our honour, while we were virgins, against our assailants; but do come now to force away wives from their husbands and mothers from their children, a succour more grievous to its wretched objects than the former betrayal and neglect of them. Which shall we call the worst, their love-making or your compassion? (Plutarch 1992, 33).

The scene has been painted by some of the most influential painters of Western civilization, including Poussin, David, and Picasso. Rape and forced marriages are also a central image in biblical warfare (Low 1992).

A stronger version of this overall approach to Chickens and Hawks would allow for the possibility that no explicit calculation is made, and an evolutionary process selects among groups that have randomly chosen to be Hawks or Doves, and to seize either males or females (or both) from other groups. In this case, the benefits to the group as a whole would be more relevant than the benefits to the governing gender. In future work, I hope to model this interaction in more detail. In the meantime, however, I suggest that explicit calculations by governing coalitions are relevant to a consideration of the dynamics of collective conflict. And I would be delighted by evidence that patriarchal strategies of group aggression might, in the long run, prove less than evolutionarily stable.

CONCLUSION

Bargaining is a form of cooperation that takes place in the shadow of conflict. Its outcomes are determined not only by exogenous factors but also by noncooperative outcomes and endogenously determined social institutions. Individual men and women bargain over the terms of their collaboration as parents. Coalitions of men and women bargain over the establishment of marriage rules that influence more general rules of political governance. Groups with different rules of political governance compete with one other for resources. Thus, small initial differences in gendered endowments and preferences may be amplified by the development of social institutions and the process of group selection.

Much of this essay has focused on possible explanations for the emergence of patriarchal institutions of marriage and collective governance. However, I believe that an even greater strength of this approach is the potential ability to explain factors that may increase women's bargaining power and lead to the weakening of patriarchal institutions. The process of economic development is generally associated with processes of technological change that reduce the relative importance of physical strength, leading to a reduction of male physical advantages in both production and coercion. More important, it is associated with increases in women's ability to restrict child quantity and exercise more direct control over reproductive decisions. In most of the developed countries, women have dramatically improved their economic and political position relative to men.

The increased demand for child quality (specifically, high levels of education) that is also associated with economic development has more contradictory effects. On one hand, it helps align the interests of mothers and fathers, who realize that they must collaborate effectively in order to ensure their children's success. On the other hand, when combined with increased female potential for economic independence, the high costs of raising children may increase fathers' temptations to default on their commitments. Cross-national differences in the degree of public support for child rearing are significantly influenced by coalitions based on class and race (Folbre 1994). A better understanding of the dynamics of individual and coalitional conflict could improve our collective well-being.

NOTES

1. The "institutionalist" economists we have in mind here include Bowles (2003), North (1981), Olson (1982), and Hirshleifer (2001). The exceptions to this generalization include Cheung (1972), who developed a pioneering analysis of patriarchal property rights, and Akerlof and Kranton (2000), who emphasize the importance of gender as a form of identity.

2. Most of the traditional literature on human capital defines it narrowly in terms of cognitive skills acquired in school or on the job. But the biological and social substrate for such knowledge also represents capital and has been treated as such by scholars as diverse as Irving Fisher (1930) and John Kendrick (1976). This was also the approach taken by Cheung (1972).

3. Becker makes the additional assumption that child quality will be constant across all children, an assumption that offers a more complex interpretation of the trade-off between quality and quantity than a simple linear budget constraint would imply. Biologists will recognize that this assumption is inconsistent with the principle of parent-offspring conflict. We set this issue aside here because it has no direct bearing on the argument at hand.

4. For a more direct application of family politics to parenting effort, see Gintis 2000, 81.

5. Human females, unlike those of many related species, do not physiologically signal their fertile periods and indeed may be unaware of them. Does this trait have adaptive significance?

It has been speculated that intelligent females could have learned to avoid copulation during fertile periods, lowering their reproductive fitness compared to less intelligent females; inability to identify fertile periods preempts this strategy (Barkow and Burley 1980).

6. At first glance it might seem that males would have a higher fallback position simply because they are willing to settle for a lower ratio of quality to quantity per child than females. But the aggregate reproductive fitness of males must equal the aggregate reproductive fitness of females.

7. Note how this argument differs from the more traditionally neoclassical model developed by Willis (1999), which assumes that in equilibrium married and unmarried males must be equally well off.

8. An alternative interpretation of the bargaining asymmetry would suggest that, holding reproductive fitness constant for both sexes, wives pay a higher price for that fitness in terms of their own level of consumption and leisure. This is the outcome more commonly described in the economic household bargaining literature.

9. For a discussion of marital property rights within the Anglo-American tradition, see Braunstein and Folbre 2001.

10. Note that one could argue, in a parallel fashion, that matriarchal societies would be governed by individuals who place too low a benefit on group aggression.

REFERENCES

Akerlof, George A., and Rachel E. Kranton. 2000. "Economics and Identity." *Quarterly Journal of Economics* 115, 3: 715–53.

Alexander, Richard D. 1987. *The Biology of Moral Systems.* Hawthorne, NY: Aldine de Gruyter.

Barkow, J.S., and N. Burley. 1980. "Human Fertility, Evolutionary Biology, and the Demographic Transition." *Ethology and Sociobiology* 1: 163–80.

Becker, Gary. 1981. *A Treatise on the Family.* Cambridge, MA: Harvard University Press.

Bergstrom, Theodore C. 1996. "Economics in a Family Way." *Journal of Economic Literature* 34, 4: 1903–34.

Bowles, Samuel. 2003. *Microeconomics: Behavior, Institutions, and Evolution.* Princeton, NJ: Princeton University Press.

Boyd, Robert, and R.J. Richerson. 1985. *Culture and the Evolutionary Process.* Chicago: University of Chicago Press.

Braunstein, Elissa, and Nancy Folbre. 2001. "To Honor or Obey: The Patriarch as Residual Claimant." *Feminist Economics* 7, 1: 25–54.

Buss, David M. 1996. "Sexual Conflict: Evolutionary Insights into Feminism and the 'Battle of the Sexes.'" In David M. Buss and Neil M. Malamuth, eds., *Sex, Power, Conflict: Evolutionary and Feminist Perspectives,* 296–318. New York: Oxford University Press.

Chagnon, Napoleon. 1983. *Yanomamo: The Fierce People,* 3rd ed. New York: Holt, Rinehart, and Winston.

Cheung, Steven N.S. 1972. "The Enforcement of Property Rights in Children, and the Marriage Contract." *Economic Journal* 82, 326: 641–57.

Daly, Martin, and Margo Wilson. 1983. *Sex, Evolution, and Behavior,* 2nd ed. Belmont, CA: Wadsworth.

Dawkins, Richard. 1976. *The Selfish Gene.* New York: Oxford University Press.

Diamond, Jared. 1999. *Guns, Germs, and Steel: The Fates of Human Societies.* New York: W.W. Norton.

Dickemann, Mildred. 1979. "Female Infanticide, Reproductive Strategies, and Social Stratification: A Preliminary Model." In N.A. Chagnon and W. Iron, eds., *Evolutionary Biology and Human Social Behavior: An Anthropological Perspective,* 321–67. North Scituate, MA: Duxbury Press.

Euripedes. 2002. *Medea.* Trans. J. Michael Walton. London: Methuen Drama.

Fisher, Irving. 1930. *The Nature of Capital and Income.* New York: Macmillan.

Folbre, Nancy. 1994. *Who Pays for the Kids? Gender and the Structures of Constraint.* New York: Routledge.

Folbre, Nancy, and Thomas Weisskopf. 1998. "Did Father Know Best? Families, Markets and the Supply of Caring Labor." In Avner Ben-Ner and Louis Putterman, eds., *Economics, Values and Organization,* 171–205. Cambridge: Cambridge University Press.

Gintis, Herbert. 2000. *Game Theory Evolving.* Princeton, NJ: Princeton University Press.

Gowaty, Patricia Adair. 2003. "Power Asymmetries Between the Sexes, Mate Preferences, and Components of Fitness." In Cheryl Brown Travis, ed., *Evolution, Gender, and Rape,* 61–86. Cambridge, MA: MIT Press.

Gowaty, Patricia Adair. 1997. "Sexual Dialectics, Sexual Selection, and Variation in Reproductive Behavior." In Patricia Adair Gowaty, ed., *Feminism and Evolutionary Biology,* 351–384. New York: Chapman and Hall.

Hirshleifer, Jack. 2001. *The Dark Side of the Force: Economic Foundations of Conflict Theory.* New York: Cambridge University Press.

Hrdy, Sarah.1999. *Mother Nature: A History of Mothers, Infants, and Natural Selection.* New York: Pantheon.

Jones, Nicholas, G. Blurton, Frank W. Marlowe, Kristen Hawkes, and James F. O'Connell. 2000. "Paternal Investment and Hunter-Gatherer Divorce Rates." In Lee Cronk, Napoleon Chagnon, and William Irons, eds., *Adaptation and Human Behavior: An Anthropological Perspective,* 69–90. New York: Aldine de Gruyter.

Katz, Elizabeth. 1997. "The Intra-Household Economics of Voice and Exit." *Feminist Economics* 3, 3: 25–46.

Kendrick, John. 1976. *The Formation and Stocks of Total Capital.* New York: Columbia University Press.

Krebs, J.R., and N.B. Davies. 1981. *An Introduction to Behavioral Ecology.* Sunderland, MA: Sinauer Associates.

Lancaster, Jane B. 1991. "A Feminist and Evolutionary Biologist Looks at Women." *Yearbook of Physical Anthropology* 34: 1–11.

Lerner, Gerda. 1986. *The Creation of Patriarchy.* New York: Oxford University Press.

Lévi-Strauss, Claude. 1969. *The Elementary Structures of Kinship.* Boston: Beacon.

Low, Bobbi. 2000. *Why Sex Matters: A Darwinian Look at Human Behavior.* Princeton, NJ: Princeton University Press.

Lundberg, S., and R.A. Pollak. 1993. "Separate Spheres Bargaining and the Marriage Market." *Journal of Political Economy* 101, 6: 988–1010.

Mackie, Gerald. 1996. "Ending Footbinding and Infibulation: A Convention Account." *American Sociological Review* 61, 6: 999–1017.

McElroy, Marjorie B. 1990. "The Empirical Content of Nash-Bargained Household Behavior." *Journal of Human Resources* 25, 4: 559–83.

North, Douglas. 1981. *Structure and Change in Economic History.* New York: Norton.

Olson, Mancur. 1971. *The Logic of Collective Action: Public Goods and the Theory of Groups.* Cambridge, MA: Harvard University Press.

———. 1982. *The Rise and Decline of Nations. Economic Growth, Stagflation, and Social Rigidities.* New Haven: Yale University Press.

Pateman, Carole. 1988. *The Sexual Contract.* Stanford, CA: Stanford University Press.

Plutarch. 1992. *The Lives of the Noble Grecians and Romans.* Trans. John Dryden. New York: Modern Library.

Skaperdas, Stergios. 2002. "Restraining the Genuine *Homo Economicus:* Why the Economy Cannot Be Divorced from Its Governance." Paper prepared for the Mancur Olson Memorial Lecture Series, University of Maryland, College Park, February 8.

Skyrms, Brian. 1996. *Evolution of the Social Contract.* New York: Cambridge University Press.

Smith, J. Maynard 1982. *Evolution and the Theory of Games.* Cambridge: Cambridge University Press.

Smuts, Barbara. 1992. "Male Aggression Against Women: An Evolutionary Perspective." *Human Nature* 3: 1–44.

———. 1995. "The Evolutionary Origins of Patriarchy." *Human Nature* 6, 1: 1–32.

Sober, Elliot, and David Sloan Wilson. 1998. *Unto Others: The Evolution and Psychology of Unselfish Behavior.* Cambridge, MA: Harvard University Press.

Tavris, Carol. 1992. *The Mismeasure of Woman.* New York: Simon and Schuster.

Trivers, R. 1972 . "Parental Investment and Sexual Selection." In B. Campbell, ed., *Sexual Selection and the Descent of Man,* 136–179. Chicago: Aldine.

Willis, Robert. 1999. "A Theory of Out-of-Wedlock Child Rearing." *Journal of Political Economy* 107, 6: S33–64.

Wilson, Margo, Martin Daly, and Joanna E. Scheib. 1997. "Femicide: An Evolutionary Psychological Perspective." In Patricia Adair Gowaty, ed., *Feminism and Evolutionary Biology,* 431–65. New York: Chapman and Hall.

APPENDIX 25.1

The outcome of the game shifts even further if mothers derive an extra payoff y from devoting high effort themselves. In other words, they not only care more about making offspring better off but want to be the ones to do so, whether because this is more pleasurable to them (what Andreoni calls "warm glow" altruism) or more productive or both, as is the case with breast-feeding. I will term this situation the Parent Trap.

Figure 25.A   **The Parent Trap**

		Father	
		High effort	Low effort
Mother	High effort	$2 + x + y$, 2	$1 + x + y$, 3
	Low effort	$3 + x$, 1	$-x$, 0

In this case, if $x > 0$ and $y > 1$, mothers have a pure dominant strategy to provide high levels of effort whether fathers provide it or not. Fathers have a pure dominant strategy to provide only a low level of effort. Note that in this case mothers would prefer fathers to provide high effort but are unable to attain that result precisely because fathers can depend on them to provide high effort regardless.

CHAPTER 26

ECONOMIC DECISIONS IN THE PRIVATE HOUSEHOLD

ERICH KIRCHLER AND EVA HOFMANN

Knowledge of economic decisions is of importance to the economy, which is driven and perpetuated by consumers' decisions and actions. In this context, economic decisions in private households are especially of interest. These decisions take place in between the antagonists reasonableness and emotion and are investigated by sociologists, social psychologists, economic psychologists, economists, and consumer researchers. Research concentrates mainly on the dynamics and outcomes of spouses' disagreements about expenditures and savings as well as wealth and monetary management in the family. Researchers try to determine who prevails in disagreements, who decides in which situation, and which partner is influencing the other and how it is done.

In this essay findings in various disciplines are presented and discussed. The first part of the essay deals with definitions of economic decisions, close relationships, and everyday life, followed by a review of research methods for decisions in partnerships. In the second section, empirical findings about the relative influence of partners in decisions are reported on, as well as different determinants of influence. The third and last part treats decision outcomes and the effect on the partners themselves and their partnership.

ECONOMIC DECISIONS IN PRIVATE HOUSEHOLDS

Economic decisions are often classified by their context. Ferber (1973), for example, distinguishes between financial or economic and primarily nonfinancial decisions. Financial decisions cover monetary management, saving decisions, wealth and investment management, and expenditures. All other economic decisions in the private household are not denominated financially; they are primarily of the nonfinancial kind and include housework and job-related work, requirements of children, leisure activities, and the partners' relationship. Earlier empirical research concentrated mainly on financial decisions, especially purchase decisions; consequently the following paragraphs focus on that type.

Economists classify expenditure decisions by the kind of good that is up for purchase. Davis (1976), for instance, differentiates between purchase decisions of often-used goods and services, durable goods, and other economic decisions. Tschammer-Osten (1979) distinguishes between the purchase of products (e.g., food), services (e.g., attorney's services), and opportunities (e.g., stamps, shares), and object systems, which are combinations of these three types. Kotler (1982) presents a classification in which the period of use of the goods and the purchasing habits of consumers are of central interest. This means a differentiation between durable consumer goods (e.g., cars), everyday consumer goods (e.g., food), and services (e.g., attorney's services). Everyday consumer goods are products that are bought relatively often and are consumed rapidly (e.g., food). Decisions on them usually are abbreviated and psychologically automated. Durable consumer goods are representational and material too, but they can be used more than once, they are more expensive, and they are bought rarely. Purchase of these goods often requires a tedious decision process within the family. Services involve a purchase of activities or advantages, so-called intangible goods. The decision is very much influenced by the quality and credibility of the service provider.

Although the classification of decisions by their context is of practical importance, the psychological classification concentrates instead on the decision process. The psychological characteristics of decisions are the availability of cognitive scripts, the financial commitment, the social visibility of the good or service, and the changes that occur after the decision and their effects on family members (Kirchler 1988a; Ruhfus 1976). Cognitive scripts are usually applied if a good is purchased regularly and information for a satisfying decision is low or missing. Thus, inexpensive goods are often purchased by using these scripts, while differentiated scripts are much less often available for expensive goods. Family members usually think through and discuss purchases of expensive goods, because the necessary financial means are bounded. Also, the purchase of goods that have high added value besides the principal use has to be discussed. Because of the high additional use, the good is of importance to the family's prestige, thereby affecting all family members.

Generally a distinction is made between two types of purchase behaviors: unpremeditated or habitual buying and real purchase decisions. Which type of behavior consumers perform depends on several factors: (1) if there exist cognitive scripts for a purchase, (2) if the financial expenditures for a good to be purchased are high or low, (3) if this good is socially meaningful, and (4) if all or few family members are affected by the purchase. While habitual buying takes place often in private households, real decisions are of greater scientific interest, because they generate complex decision processes that are sustained and discussed by all family members.

From all conversations and discussions in families, about 10 percent can lead to conflicts because of different preferences of the family members (Kirchler et al. 2001). This essay explores how these different preferences affect the decision process and results as well as the harmony within the family.

Interaction in Close Relationships

There are several different definitions for close relationships. Close romantic relationships are long-lasting, and the partners are mutually bound to each other by means of their behavior, their emotions, and their cognitions (Kelley et al. 1983). Bierhoff and Grau (1999) define relationships in terms of two dimensions, width and depth. While width stands for the manifoldness of similarities, depth means the influence and the intimacy of partners. Close relationships are characterized by confident teamwork and the achievement of shared and also individual objectives. The process of achieving objectives is defined in terms of the acquisition of resources, such as money from occupational activity, different services in the household, and resources themselves (Winch and Gordon 1974). Objectives include reaching a preferred end as well as activities such as protection, emotional support, instrumental support, social support, and being helpful. The purpose of partnerships and families in private households is to supply all family members with love, status, information, money, goods, and services (Foa and Foa 1974) by means of the processes of acquiring, sourcing, production, and reproduction.

Living together in a household implies manifold interactions of partners. Depending on the partners' satisfaction with the partnership and on the relation of power, partners' behavior ranges from market-related exchanges to spontaneous altruistic behavior (Kirchler 1989). The degree of

Figure 26.1   **Interaction Principles in Close Relationships**

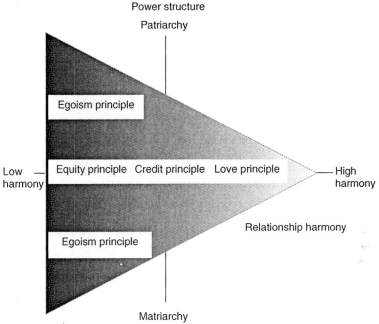

Source: Kirchler 1989, 119.

harmony between partners determines which behavioral principle partners display in interactions. In harmonious relationships, where it is not important if one of the partners is more powerful than the other, partners interact according to the "love principle." When satisfaction with the relationship decreases, the displayed behavior reveals characteristics of the "credit principle." The partners are considerate of each other and tend to gratify each other, but for every gratification they expect reciprocation over the shorter or longer run. If the quality of the relationship decreases further, behavior in interactions follows the "equity principle." In this principle of interaction the partners behave like two business partners and simply exchange resources. The more the quality of the relationship decreases, the more the degree of power is of interest. In disharmonious relationships the more powerful partner has the potential to control the barter business. In this case the interaction proceeds on the "egoism principle" (Figure 26.1).

For the observation of economic decisions in private households, the characteristics of the relationship and the emotions are also of major relevance (Park, Tansuhaj, and Kolbe 1991; Park et al. 1995). Park and colleagues (1995) find that love and empathy result in a higher consistency of preferences of the partners and in a lower disposition to conflict. Qualls and Jaffe (1992) show that the similarity of partners concerning their conceptions of sex roles, the structure of influences, and the importance of decisions correlate negatively with the disposition to conflict. Positive emotions suppress the use of certain conflict-resolution tactics such as punishment, threatening, and enforcement. In harmonious relationships the loving and empathizing partners accommodate each other and make sacrifices solely to organize their relationship more intensely (Van Lange et al. 1997).

Everyday Life

When economic decisions in private households are surveyed, the exploration of everyday life proves to be a challenge. Activities in everyday life are manifold and different. They range from going shopping to cleaning the house and arguing about which TV program to watch. Examining one activity alone proves to be very difficult because one single behavior is nearly impossible to isolate from all the others.

> Most relationships involve interactions of diverse types, and those interactions affect each other. Any marital therapist would agree not only that what goes on in bed affects what goes on at the breakfast table, but also that the atmosphere at the breakfast table affects that in bed. (Hinde 1997, 40)

Looking at the literature on economic decisions in private households in terms of the delimitation of different activities, occasions, and decisions in everyday life, there appears to be no consistent solution to the delimitation problem. Rather, researchers assume that decisions are natural and isolated units, but they might accept the decision stages concept of Davis and Rigaux (1974), who describe three stages of decisions: the initiating stage, the information-gathering stage, and the purchasing stage. In the first stage one of the partners expresses the wish to buy a certain good, in the second stage information about the good and the purchase is gathered, and in the third stage the actual purchase takes place. In reality, however, these three stages are difficult to distinguish.

According to Duck (1994), not only is everyday life a combination of several linked occasions and rapidly changing, but also the relationship itself is not stable. In this context Billig (1987) mentions the term "unfinished business," which refers to the permanent reinterpretation and reformulation of the relationship as new occasions arise. In a partnership daily incidents are subjectively reorganized in order to make them understandable for each partner and to delimit and distinguish everyday experiences so that they can be reported. During this process, categories of similar occasions are constituted and occasions are generalized so that in the end both partners describe in the same way how they usually make decisions.

Another aspect of economic decisions in private households that contributes to their complexity is the discrimination of implicit and explicit decisions (Sillars and Kalbflesch 1989). In close relationships decision are mostly made implicitly. Various factors facilitate the application of implicit decisions, such as the homogeneity of the partners and the development of an efficient communication style. The disproportion of resources, such as energy and time, and problem needs entail rapid decisions. The overlapping of decisions and other activities reduces attention, so decisions are impulsively made.

Methods to Survey Economic Decisions in Private Households

The investigation of everyday life is difficult for several reasons. First of all, the methods of survey themselves alter the decision process of partners. Normally, close relationships are protected from publicity, and in this shielded atmosphere partners cultivate a shared "language," which often seems abstruse to people outside the family. Some aspects of decision making are taboo, in that partners simply do not report them publicly. Finally, curious and sensitive questions can terminate the actual object of investigation.

Thus, observations and questionnaire studies often produce dramatic biases in surveys of close relationships. As a result of these biases, Duck (1991) and Kirchler (1989) recommend diaries to investigate decisions in private households. During the last decade several interesting instruments were generated (see, e.g., Almeida and Kessler 1998; Almeida, Wethington, and Chandler 1999; Bolger, DeLongis, Kessler, and Schilling 1989; Bolger, DeLongis, Kessler, and Wethington 1989; Diener and Larsen 1984; Downey et al. 1998; Laireiter et al. 1997; Larson and Almeida 1999; Larson and Csikszentmihalyi 1983; Pawlik and Buse 1982; Pervin 1976). Hormuth (1986), Stone, Kessler and Haythornthwaite (1991), and recently Bolger, Davis, and Rafaeli (2003) give a broad overview of the advantages and disadvantages of these different methods.

Diaries have been employed to investigate the usage of partners' time for some decades (Hornik 1982; Robinson et al. 1977; Vanek 1974). Larson and Bradney (1988) registered the current well-being of individuals in the presence of relatives and friends with diaries. Diaries have been also used to investigate the experiences of stress in everyday life and the spillover effect of occupation on the partnership (Almeida and Kessler 1998; Almeida, Wethington, and Chandler 1999; Bolger, DeLongis, Kessler, and Wethington 1989). While Laireiter and colleagues (1997) analyzed social networks using diaries, others (Auhagen 1987, 1991; Brandstätter and Wagner 1994; Duck 1991; Feger and Auhagen 1987; Kirchler 1988a, 1988b) investigated interaction processes between partners. Diaries are fruitful instruments to investigate close relationships, especially if both partners fill them in. This might be the reason why increasingly diaries are used for research on everyday experiences and well-being.

There are two types of diaries, which are used for investigation on an individual level. While in time-sample diaries participants journalize their experiences at a randomly chosen point in time, in event diaries they journalize experiences only when a specific event takes place. For example, Kirchler (1988a) modified Brandstätter's (1977) time-sample diary, so that women and men make their records independently but at the same time. Since Kirchler observes purchase decisions, event diaries are used, because purchase decisions take place too infrequently for time-sample diaries to be useful. The partners were instructed to journalize the day's purchase decisions every day in the evening. In Kirchler's (1988a) study the interval lasted one day; in other studies the interval lengths vary from days to weeks to months (Stone, Kessler, and Haythornthwaite 1991). The partners did not only report specifics about the purchase decisions, such as the product, the decision stage, and their interaction, but also answered questions about their relationship, such as about dominance, harmony, and relative contribution of resources. This event diary was enhanced and proved in follow-up studies, and finally in the Vienna Diary Study Kirchler and colleagues (2001) used the diary with forty sets of partners, who filled in the diary for one year. They journalized not only about their process of economic decision making but also about every other topic that caused arguments. This enabled the researchers to investigate not just economic decision making but the linkages with other topics.

Models of Economic Decisions in Everyday Life

Decisions have to be made to adjust an actual state to a target state, and the process of doing so can be described with several models. In general, researchers distinguish between normative and descriptive models to explain decision making. Normative models illustrate logical and rational processes of making decisions, while descriptive models describe how decisions are actually made in real life.

Normative models picture decisions as a number of singular operations that are successively undertaken and invariably produce a desirable result. This means that decision makers know exactly all the necessary criteria to make the decision. On the basis of these criteria they establish clear preferences and an obvious goal. Adjusting an actual state to a target state takes place through the execution of several sequential operations yielding a unique result. Normative models illustrate a rational decision process but not necessarily a reasonable decision result.

Although rational decision processes are often advantageous in everyday life, individuals' as well as groups' decision processes regularly deviate from the normative models. People frequently make rash decisions and do not take all of the necessary criteria into account because most subjects need to make decisions rapidly. However, these decisions are often rationalized ex post.

Descriptive models describe decisions as they are actually observed in everyday life. March and Shapira (1992), for example, illustrate decisions in organizations as a random concurrence of problems and solutions. Not only their model but also Braybrooke and Lindblom's (1963; Lindblom 1959, 1979) model can be used to explain decision making in private households. Although these two authors portray political decisions, their incremental decision process, which is often called "muddling through," can be applied to household decisions. The more complex tasks are, the lower the probability that decision makers use rational strategies. Since decisions in commerce, in politics, and in private households are mainly very complex, the scarcity of time leads to irrational decision processes and to the restriction to easily solvable subproblems as well as to the reproduction of solutions in a common context and to the renouncement of extensive analyses. According to Braybrooke and Lindblom (1963), making decisions is like a walk through a marsh. The decision maker takes little steps forward as long as the ground holds. As soon as undesired effects occur, the individual steps to the right, to the left, or even backward. The complex interactions of various impacting variables cannot be taken into account because the consequences cannot be foreseen, so decision makers act incrementally until a solution of the problem is found.

Park (1982) concentrated his research on decision making in the private household. He explains why such decisions do not follow normative models. Since decision makers' capacity for information processing is restricted, the partners are not capable of figuring out the important dimensions of a product for themselves and also for their partners. While it is difficult enough to figure out one's own preferences, it is nearly impossible to know about the partner's preferences and strategies for selecting a good. These facts imply that rational decision making does not take place in private households.

INFLUENCE IN ECONOMIC DECISIONS

Whenever marketing researchers are interested in economic decisions in private households, they ask family members about their relative influence in purchase decisions. They like to know who decides on the acquisition of which good. The following pages give a broad overview of the distribution of influence between partners as well as between parents and children. Additionally, determinants of influence, such as relative contribution of resources, relative interest in the result, and the subjective competence of partners, are discussed. This part of the essay concludes with the examination of decisions in private households, which are cross-linked with other events and other tasks in the family.

Protagonists and Social Norms

The target of investigating economic decisions in private households is the whole family; the protagonists are the wife, the husband, and the children. They all interact with each other according to different social norms and their relative contribution of resources.

Social Norms and Contribution of Resources

The comparative resource contribution theory postulates that in relationships the partner who is more highly educated, has a more prestigious occupation, has a better-paid job, and possesses in general more material and nonmaterial goods influences decisions in the household more than the other partner (Blood and Wolfe 1960; Lee and Beatty 2002). This theory is proven by life cycle research that points out that at the beginning of a partnership both partners have a say in economic decisions, but as the partnership continues each partner becomes responsible for certain areas in which he or she decides autonomously. As long as women have to care for infants their influence in economic decisions is usually minor compared to when they start working again. Robertson (1990) argues that this phenomenon results from providing reduced financial resources while caring for children. Nowadays, the comparative resource contribution theory cannot be proven in industrial countries (Kirchler 1989; Kirchler et al. 2001; Pross 1979). Other factors are much more responsible for the allocation of influence in private households.

Social norms are also responsible for the relation of influence (Blood and Wolfe 1960). Depending on societal moral concepts, the influence of partners ranges from the traditional role distribution, where the husband is responsible for financial decisions, to the liberal role distribution, where both partners are allowed the same competence in decisions. During recent decades societal moral concepts in industrial countries have changed, and partners have the same rights in former domains of decisions; they equilibrate their influences in different areas (Dutta 2000; Kirchler 1989; Snyder and Serafin 1985). Rodman (1967) argues that comparative resource contribution theory is valid in societies where the social norms are changing and therefore are ineffective, but that the theory is of no interest as soon as moral concepts are clearly established.

Wife and Husband

The influence of wife and husband on purchase decisions in private households has been surveyed for about fifty years. Anglo-American studies published between 1956 and 1988 show that wife and husband make about half of the decisions (53 percent) together. Twenty-four percent of the decisions are made by the husband on his own and the remaining 23 percent by the wife alone (Kirchler 1989).

Kirchler and colleagues (2001) illustrate in the Vienna Diary Study that the influences of wife and husband are nearly equal. The influence of the wife on economic and noneconomic decisions combined is 49 percent. In about 55 percent of conflicts the influence of both partners is evenly distributed. Cases where either the wife or the husband decides solely on her or his own are rare; wives make 2.3 percent of the decisions alone, compared to 1.2 percent for husbands. For economic decisions alone, the influence of wives declines to 46 percent. Generally, studies on purchase decisions show that influence is well balanced between the partners.

Parents and Children

The influence of children and adolescents in economic decisions in the family is not totally clear. On one hand, some researchers declare that the democratization in the family allows children co-determination (Labrecque and Ricard 2001; Lee and Beatty 2002; Lee and Collins 2000); on the other hand, others argue that their influence is negligible. Kirchler and Kirchler (1990) find that according to parents, adolescents scarcely influence economic decisions. Williams and Burns (2000) developed a scale to measure children's direct influence attempts to allow further research in this field.

For Ward and Wackman (1973) the influence of children depends on the type of good under consideration. Concerning cereals, snacks, sweets, and juices, mothers often accede to their children's wishes. When it comes to purchases of other edibles, such as bread and coffee, the influence of children is minor. Other authors (Gierl and Praxmarer 2001; Mauri 1996; Winter and Mayerhofer 1983a, 1983b) verify these findings: children's influence is important for purchases of toys, ice cream, sneakers, books, sweets, and lemonade, but not for pet food, clothes, and cameras.

Not only the type of good but also the children's age is of importance to their magnitude of influence. With increasing age children gain more influence concerning goods with which they are not directly concerned (Caron and Ward 1975; Jenkins 1979; Mehrotra and Torges 1977). Beatty and Talpade (1994) illustrate that teenagers influence important purchase decisions, especially if they are motivated by their interest in the usage of the goods. Researchers (Moschis 1987; Shim, Snyder, and Gehrt 1995) also found out that older and firstborn children influence buying decisions more than younger ones, especially if they live with just one parent (Ahuja and Stinson 1993).

Although the influence of children on their own is low, their influence as coalition partners of their parents is remarkable. If parents cannot agree upon a topic, they usually solve this disagreement with children's interventions or with the statement that the decision is important for the children. Kirchler and colleagues (2001) report that when one parent used coalition tactics to convince the other of their opinion, nearly always the children were present. According to Lee and Collins (2000), coalitions are mainly formed by fathers and elder daughters or by mothers and sons. Thus children and adolescents co-determine decisions indirectly while forming coalitions with their parents.

Decision Content

The influence of protagonists in economic decisions in private households does not depend only on social norms and individuals' position in the family. The type of goods, the type of money management, and the decision stage are also of importance.

Types of Goods. Traditionally, the influence of partners in economic decisions depended on the good and its characteristics. Women were responsible for purchases for the household, such as kitchen items, children's items, aesthetic items for the living room, toilet requisites, cosmetics, health care products, and items for the care of sick people. They also determined characteristics of goods, such as color and style. Men usually dealt with decisions outside the immediate household. Their responsibility concerned the buying of cars, insurance, tools, and technical equipment as well as characteristics such as the amount of expenditure, the mode of payment, and the place and time of purchase. Although partners' influence depends on the type and characteristics of goods, their influence over all decisions is balanced.

Some would expect that the traditional distribution of responsibilities between wife and husband has disappeared in recent years. Surprisingly, Mayerhofer (1994) finds that this is not the case. Women decide about the design of refrigerators, washing machines, and microwaves, while men decide about the technical performance parameters, the price, and the brand. It should be noted that this might be a biased result because the respondents might not be able to recall the decision processes exactly and fill in these gaps with traditional societal stereotypes.

Money Management, Saving, and Indebtedness. While purchase behavior is often investigated, the management of wealth and assets is rather neglected by researchers. Nevertheless, Meier,

Kirchler, and Hubert (1999) found out that men usually take care of wealth and asset management in partnerships; an exception are modern and egalitarian partnerships, where women co-determine. The partners' competence seems to be an important factor for this co-determination. While earlier studies (Ferber and Lee 1974) report that during the first period of a relationship couples decide jointly and then after a while the woman tends to decide, today this seems less common. Schaninger and Buss (1986), for example, state that women are more often given a say in partnerships that endure than in partnerships that eventually break apart. This would imply that both partners have the same knowledge about the family's financial situation. But Zagorsky (2003) reports that wives' and husbands' views differ. Wives usually state that the family receives less income and owes more debt than their husbands report.

Also, the topic of saving and indebtedness has not been sufficiently investigated (for an overview of studies on saving see Wärneryd 1999). Webley (1994) states that the demand for loans is increasing, and Engel, Blackwell, and Miniard (1993) observe that adolescents do not hesitate to borrow for new acquisitions, but the older the respondents the more they refuse to borrow. Although borrowing to build housing space is economically sensible and desirable, loans can lead private households into serious situations. Lea, Webley, and Levine (1993) demonstrate that indebtedness especially correlates with poverty. Individuals with low incomes are often more indebted than people with better earnings. Reasons for the indebtedness are mainly poverty and very seldom irresponsible expenditures and careless income budgeting.

Stages of Decisions. Decision processes can be divided into stages assuming that there is a beginning and an end to the processes. In the first stage the wish to purchase a good occurs. In the second stage the partners look for information about the good. The third stage is characterized by actual purchasing behavior. This straight sequence of the three stages can be interfered with by the recurrence of stages that have already been passed through. Decision processes do not have to be finished after the purchase; for example, partners might look for information after the purchase to justify the buying.

Davis and Rigaux (1974) survey the relation of influence between wife and husband during the decision process to buy a certain good. They identify four different types of decision processes, in which decisions are made autonomously by wives, autonomously by husbands, by both partners together, or alternately by the partners. Additionally, they distinguish between three stages of the decision process: the initiating stage, the information-gathering stage, and the purchasing stage. For further analysis they coded decisions in which men dominate with 1, decisions in which women dominate with 3, and decisions in which both partners decide together with 2. This coding allows for the design of a so-called roles triangle, which consists of four areas of decisions: (1) a decision is syncratic if more than 50 percent of all questioned couples respond that the influence of both partners is equal; (2) a decision is dominated by the woman if women have more influence; (3) a decision is dominated by the man if men have more influence, and (4) a decision is balanced if the influence of both partners is balanced (decisions are made alternately by the partners). A replication of the study is presented in Figure 26.2 (Kirchler and Kirchler 1990).

Relative Knowledge and Interest

Studies on influence in groups demonstrate that opponents cannot hold out against knowledge and the resultant informational pressure (Burnstein 1982). Discussants with more extended knowledge argue convincingly and win the argument over the others. This can also be applied to pur-

Figure 26.2 **Variation of Decision-Making Roles During the Three Stages of Purchase in Selected Product Categories**

The arrows indicate changes in decision-making roles from the initiating stage (represented by a circle) through the information-gathering stage (change of direction) to the purchasing stage (arrowhead).

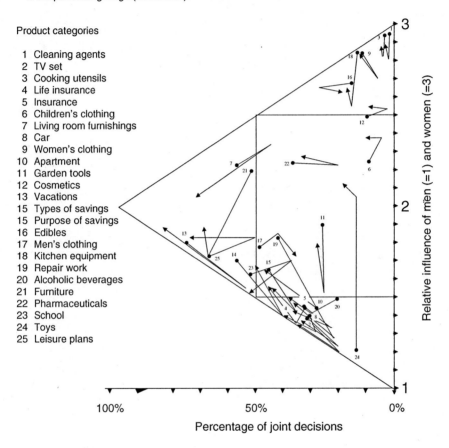

Product categories

1 Cleaning agents
2 TV set
3 Cooking utensils
4 Life insurance
5 Insurance
6 Children's clothing
7 Living room furnishings
8 Car
9 Women's clothing
10 Apartment
11 Garden tools
12 Cosmetics
13 Vacations
15 Types of savings
15 Purpose of savings
16 Edibles
17 Men's clothing
18 Kitchen equipment
19 Repair work
20 Alcoholic beverages
21 Furniture
22 Pharmaceuticals
23 School
24 Toys
25 Leisure plans

Relative influence of men (=1) and women (=3)

100%   50%   0%

Percentage of joint decisions

Source: Kirchler and Kirchler 1990

chase decisions in private households: the partner with broader knowledge dominates the decision (Burns 1976; Corfman 1987; Corfman and Lehman 1987; Davis 1972). But not only knowledge is of importance for purchase decisions; the interest in the purchase is also central. The more a partner is interested in a good, the more he or she collects information and looks for alternatives. Thus, interest and knowledge ensure influence (Seymour and Lessne 1984).

In the Vienna Diary Study fundamental analyses of disagreements in private households are undertaken (Kirchler et al. 2001). The partners journalize daily about whether they had an argument, who initiated the discussion, who had how much knowledge of the topic, and how important the discussion was for the wife and husband. Additionally, the discussion climate, the partners' ratios of influence, and the partners' subjective importance, interest, and competence were reported. It is shown that while for decisions concerning children subjective importance is more meaningful, for economic decisions partners with more knowledge have a greater say.

History of Decision Processes, or the Cross-Linking of Economic Decisions

An important characteristic of economic decisions in private households is the fact that they take place contemporaneously with other activities. Also, decision making often takes a long time and over this period can be further affected by other issues. Since partners have been living together and are going to live together for a reasonable time, it is obvious that earlier decisions have implications for current decisions. Thus, decision making has to be investigated in the context of former and future economic and noneconomic events.

Mental Accounting of Utility and Influence

Several studies of accounting (Brendl, Markman, and Higgins 1998; Heath and Soll 1996; Kahneman and Tversky 1984; Thaler 1980, 1985, 1994) illustrate that people categorize events and evaluate these categories separately. In the case of purchase decisions individuals establish different categories of certain goods and assign a particular budget to each category. As soon as the budget of a specific category is exhausted, people do not allow any further expenditures for goods of this kind, even if they are necessary. On the contrary, surplus funds in another category might be spent on goods that are in the long run unnecessary (Heath and Soll 1996).

Not only material values but also nonmaterial ones, such as influence in conflicts or personal utility, can be booked by partners. This implies that decision processes and outcomes also have to be balanced like economic accounts. Thus, the resistance of one partner in a purchase decision could stem not only from the purchase itself but also from unbalanced past decision processes and results. In a satisfying partnership both spouses expect a fair allocation of influence and utility. Partners can either categorize their decisions and balance them within the categories or have one single mental account for all decisions and balance this account over all decisions. Independently of which kind of mental accounting partners actually adopt, the investigation of mental accounting of nonmaterial goods is very difficult for several reasons. First, partners usually cannot exactly register the ratio of influence and utility. Second, different parameters have various weights in different situations. Third, a booking is never an exact entry but always an approximate retrospection that sometimes differs very much in the perspectives of the partners.

Temporal Cross-Linking

Decisions tie up with past decision processes and results and determine future processes. "A relationship is a historical process; time is the medium of relationship; change its constant. The dynamic temporal qualities of relationships are, at once, the most obvious and must frustrating aspects of relationship life with which researchers must cope" (Bochner, Ellis, and Tillman-Healy 1997, 313). A decision is often provocation for more decisions, dialogues, and arguments between the partners. A spouse may promise a certain behavior for forthcoming decisions to sustain an advantage in the present decision, but this determines prospective decisions. Furthermore, previous decisions are not forgotten; partners remember their interaction in earlier decision processes and refer to results of previous decisions in considering the current decision.

The concept of "utility debts" (Pollay 1968) demonstrates the importance of former experiences for the present dynamics of decision making. The partner whose wishes were fulfilled in the past has to redeem utility debts and balance the fictive utility account. If one partner decides in favor of the other, then the first one is privileged in the forthcoming decision.

Corfman and Lehman (1987; see also Corfman 1985, 1987) prove that partners' influence depends on the history of their decision processes, especially on the distribution of influence in previous decision processes. Additionally, they demonstrate that influence correlates positively with interest in a certain good and knowledge about it. Also, the quality of the relationship is a relevant determinant. The more important one partner thinks the improvement and stabilizing of the partnership is, the more indulgent he or she is. According to the authors, partners tend to balance their decisions. Once a partner has a greater say in one decision, the other partner has a greater say in another. But it is not the amount of influence that is important; what is of more importance is who has distinctly ruled the decision process, and whether the second partner has made advances to the first one. The partner who has had more of a say last time has to accommodate the other partner in the present conflict.

Kirchler and colleagues (2001) illustrate in the Vienna Diary Study that when surveying the balance of decision processes, a separation of economic conflicts and arguments about work, children, relationship, and leisure is necessary. Not only do the authors confirm the assumption that accounting and balance effects are of major importance in decision processes, they also find that not just the last but the three most recent decision processes and results determine the allocation of influence. Furthermore, they find that relative knowledge about the good affects the allocation as well.

Influence Tactics

Whenever partners disagree on a decision, they try to prevail without damaging the emotional climate between them. Their expectation of future interactions leads to the use of so-called soft influence tactics, which allow the influenced partner some latitude in accepting the employed tactics (Van Knippenberg and Steensma 2003). The partner agrees with the other's argument if the factual arguments are good and the emotions are not neglected (Barry and Oliver 1996). The partners usually use different tactics, such as clarifying, persuasion, and trading, to persuade each other; the tactic chosen depends on the context of the decisions as well as the quality of the relationship. Furthermore, cultural background is of importance for the selection of the tactic (Yukl, Fu, and McDonald 2003). Sometimes partners change the context by moving from one decision stage to another; for example, they might drift from the initiating stage into the information-gathering stage and back again. They do not only use factual arguments but also try to convince their partner by manipulation, blandishment, threats, or trade-offs. In the main, they try to interact in such a way that the other partner is induced to abandon his or her own position (Scanzoni and Polonko 1980; Szinovacz 1987).

An interesting aspect of the usage of tactics in partnerships is the investigation of the modification of attitudes. Brandstätter, Stocker-Kreichgauer, and Firchau (1980) present a balance model that visualizes a stepwise transformation from different viewpoints in discussions. The model allows one to picture the attitude of a person in a discussion process by calculating the weighted average of the processed information. During the discussion process the scale might change its direction either toward the person's own position or toward the converse opinion (see Figure 26.3).

The usage of certain tactics depends on the aim of the interaction (Seibold, Cantrill, and Meyers 1994). Usually partners aim for multiple goals in conflicts (Berger and Kellermann 1994; Dillard 1990). The dual concern model (Pruitt and Rubin 1986) maps out consequences of actions that stem from the importance of one's own goals and the importance of the partner's goals. It is often employed to describe the usage of tactics in conflicts in close relationships (Holmes and Murray 1996; Klein and Johnson 1997; Kurdek 1994; Spitzberg, Canary, and Cupach 1994). The tactical

Figure 26.3 **Symbolic Illustration of the Balance Model**

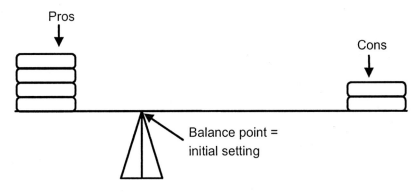

Source: Brandstätter, Stocker-Kreichgauer, and Firchau 1980

behavior of an individual in a conflict results from the individual's degree of concern with the discussed subject and the partner's degree of concern. Both factors can be represented by two orthogonal dimensions (Figure 26.4). According to this representation there are three different tactics that are used by partners: (1) if no partner is concerned, both are inactive; (2) if one partner is concerned but the other is not, then the concerned partner behaves competitively and aggressively while the other retreats; (3) if both are concerned, then they are very much interested in solving the problem and cooperatively discuss the matter.

Taxonomy of Tactics

Although some researchers have tried to create a universally valid set of tactics (Van de Vliert 1997), it seems to be impossible (Cody, Canary, and Smith 1994; Cody and McLaughlin 1990), because the type of tactic used depends on the situation (McLaughlin, Cody, and French 1990; Palan and Wilkes 1997). Kirchler and colleagues (Hölzl and Kirchler 1998; Kirchler 1993a, 1993b; Kirchler and Berti 1996; Kirchler et al. 2001; Zani and Kirchler 1993) investigate the usage of tactics in the context of purchase decisions. They have identified eighteen different tactics (Table 26.1) from other social psychological studies (Falbo and Peplau 1980; Howard, Blumstein, and Schwartz 1986; Nelson 1988; Sillars and Kalbflesch 1989; Sillars and Wilmot 1994) and an interview study with married couples (Kirchler 1990) who reported their behavior in purchase decisions.

Kirchler and colleagues (2001) distinguish four types of tactics: tactics to avoid conflicts, tactics to solve problems, tactics to persuade the partner, and tactics to negotiate. If partners use tactics to avoid conflicts (see Table 26.1, tactics 13, 14, and 15), they take over roles that emerge from segmentation in the family and determine who is responsible for which kind of decisions. The segmentation is a result of social stereotypes as well as expert knowledge and the possession of wealth (Davis 1976). These tactics avoid conflicts because it is already determined who is responsible, so the decisions are made automatically by the responsible family member without any discussion. Partners use the tactic to solve problems (see Table 26.1, tactic 18) if they agree about their basic aims but have to discuss the manner by which the objectives are achieved. This tactic includes tasks such as the collection of information and resembles tasks of individual decision processes. Tactics to persuade the partner (see Table 26.1, tactics 1 to 12) are used if there are divergences of values. These tactics include behaviors such as enforcement, pressure, threat, withdrawal of responsibility, and constant critique (Davis 1972, 1976). Additionally, joint pur-

Figure 26.4 **Dual Concern Model**

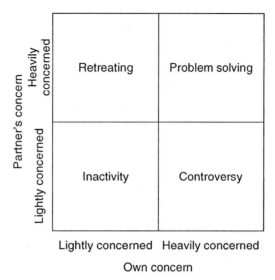

Source: Pruitt and Rubin 1986

chases as well as caring are tactics to persuade the partner. If partners have to decide about the allocation of resources and the appointment of costs, they usually use bargaining tactics (see Table 26.1, tactics 17 and 18).

Application of Tactics

The kind of tactic used by a partner depends very much on the emotional climate in the relationship, and in turn this emotional climate is determined by the kind of tactic used. If partners trust each other, they cooperate and maximize their joint utility. But if the relationship is characterized by mistrust, they compete and solely maximize their egoistic utility.

Kirchler (1993a) has investigated with a questionnaire study which tactics partners use in close relationships when discussing economic decisions. He presents the respondents with three different types of conflicts—conflicts about values, conflicts about achievement of objectives, and conflicts about allocation—and asks them which types of tactics they usually use. About 500 Italian (Zani and Kirchler 1993) and Austrian (Kirchler 1993b) participants filled in the questionnaire (for the results see Table 26.2). Generally, the results demonstrate that the usage of tactics depends on gender as well as on the kind of conflict. Women commonly use emotional tactics, while men tend to use factual and reasonable tactics.

DECISION RESULTS

In comparison with companies and committees, whose only aim is to gather information and accumulate money, partners in close relationships have multiple goals. On one hand, they want to employ their available resources as optimally as possible. On the other hand, they want to intensify their relationship. Although this might imply that decisions in good partnerships are made at

Table 26.1

Classification of Tactics

Context of tactics	Tactics	Examples
Emotions	1. Positive emotions	Manipulation, flattery, smiling, humor, seductive behavior
	2. Negative emotions	Threats, cynicism, ridicule, shouting
Physical force	3. Helplessness	Crying, showing weakness, acting ill
	4. Physical force	Forcing, injuring, violence, aggression
Resources	5. Offering resources	Performing services, being attentive
	6. Withdrawing resources	Withdrawing financial contributions, punishing
Presence	7. Insisting	Nagging, constantly returning to the subject, conversations designed to wear down opposition
	8. Withdrawal	Refusing to share responsibility, changing the subject, going away, leaving the scene
Information	9. Open presentation of facts	Asking for cooperation, presenting own needs, talking openly about importance/interest to self
	10. Presenting false facts	Suppressing relevant information, distorting information
Persons	11. Indirect coalitions	Referring to other people, emphasizing utility of purchase to children
	12. Direct coalitions	Discussing in the presence of others
Fact	13. Fait accompli	Buying autonomously, deciding without consulting partner
Role segmentation	14. Deciding according to roles	Deciding autonomously according to established role segmentation
	15. Yielding according to roles	Autonomous decision by partner according to role
Bargaining	16. Trade-offs	Offers of trade-offs, bookkeeping, reminders of past favors
	17. Integrative bargaining	Search for the best solution to satisfy all concerned
Reasoned argument	18. Reasoned argument	Presenting factual arguments, logical argument

Source: Kirchler 1989.
Note: Some studies of tactics take account of all 18 tactics. When only 15 tactics are discussed, tactics 13, 14, and 15 are omitted.

the expense of the preservation of the relationship, Jehn and Shah (1997) find that people in friendly relationships perform better in problem-solving tasks than acquaintances.

During the decision-making process partners look for satisficing problem solving. It has to be satisficing from both the economic and relationship points of view. Therefore the quality of the result depends both on whether partners are economical in resource use and on whether they perceive fairness and equitable allocation of outputs. In particular, fairness and equitable allocation influence future conflicts and decision processes because they are important determining factors of mutual trust and satisfaction in the relationship (Greenberg 1988).

Reasonableness and the Economic Application of Resources

Conflicts in partnerships arise if resources are not allocated reasonably, but rational decision processes and reasonable decision outcomes are not always possible. The intensifying of the

Table 26.2

Influence Tactics of 223 Italian and 252 Austrian Women and Men

	Reports of women		Reports of men	
Tactics	Italy	Austria	Italy	Austria
1. Positive emotions	3.30 (1.27)	3.46 (1.49)	3.19 (1.21)	3.40 (1.33)
2. Negative emotions	2.29 (.99)	2.17 (1.04)	2.30 (1.14)	2.19 (1.09)
3. Helplessness*	2.35 (1.20)	2.09 (1.20)	2.15 (1.08)	1.84 (.98)
4. Physical force	2.93 (1.36)	2.78 (1.29)	2.72 (1.45)	2.62 (1.32)
5. Offering resources*	2.34 (1.06)	2.87 (1.32)	2.36 (1.14)	3.09 (1.31)
6. Withdrawing of resources	1.86 (.90)	1.72 (.84)	1.87 (.94)	1.74 (.94)
7. Insisting	2.93 (1.37)	3.06 (1.44)	2.87 (1.34)	2.98 (1.37)
8. Withdrawal	4.04 (1.44)	3.88 (1.38)	3.82 (1.30)	3.60 (1.31)
9. Open presentation of facts*	5.52 (1.07)	4.99 (1.20)	5.17 (1.07)	4.84 (1.28)
10. Presenting false facts*	3.57 (1.26)	3.10 (1.19)	3.49 (1.38)	3.10 (1.30)
11. Indirect coalition*	3.68 (1.38)	4.25 (1.34)	3.63 (1.34)	4.26 (1.31)
12. Direct coalition	3.20 (1.69)	3.27 (1.67)	2.88 (1.58)	3.08 (1.68)
13. Fait accompli	1.96 (1.02)	1.92 (1.17)	2.19 (1.35)	2.36 (1.34)
14. Deciding according to roles	1.94 (1.03)	1.94 (1.15)	2.18 (1.34)	2.42 (1.44)
15. Yielding according roles	2.18 (1.24)	2.32 (1.41)	2.12 (1.20)	2.16 (1.18)
16. Trade-offs	3.03 (1.44)	3.10 (1.46)	2.70 (1.31)	2.86 (1.33)
17. Integrative bargaining	5.90 (.96)	5.71 (1.07)	5.60 (1.08)	5.46 (1.07)
18. Reasoned argument	5.37 (1.04)	5.33 (1.13)	5.33 (1.12)	5.50 (1.05)

Sources: Kirchler 1993a; Zani and Kirchler 1993.
Note: The displayed means (and standard deviations in parentheses) correspond to tasks of 7-point Likert scales from 1 = a tactic is definitely not applied to 7 = a tactic is definitely applied. The symbol * next to a tactic means that there are significant differences in application of the tactic between the Austrian and Italian participants.

relationship is also a goal, but actions such as anticipating the partner's every wish can lead to unreasonable expenditures. Happy and unhappy couples make about the same amount of expenditures, but their purchase behavior as well as the purchased goods are different—happy partners seem to buy fewer objects than unhappy ones (Schaninger and Buss 1986). This implies that happy couples buy expensive and indivisible goods and that unhappy ones anticipate a divorce and purchase divisible goods.

Since situations in which decisions have to be made are very often complex and unclear, the decision makers regularly deviate from normative models of decision behavior (Lindblom 1979). In particular, partners in close relationships have neither the time nor the capacity for synoptic decision processes. They often proceed incrementally and stepwise during the decision process. This can be a strategy to avoid unpleasant conflicts and discussions between partners.

Although we emphasized that incremental decisions are the best option in the given situation, Hill is of the opinion that the family is "a poor planning committee, an unwieldy play group and a group of uncertain congeniality. Its leadership is shared by two relatively inexperienced amateurs for most of their incumbency, new to the rules of spouse and parent" (Hill 1972, 14). Since purchase decisions and other decisions interact with each other, the decision makers of the family cannot pay full attention to the current decision task. They also might not look for an optimal decision, instead preferring to balance the dominance of the partners by repaying the utility debts. Additionally, a purchase can be necessary as a favor to the partner, not because it is the outcome of a reasonable decision. Also, Granbois and Summers (1975) show that women and men in a partnership realize more purchases than they would if they were separated from each other. Thus from an economic point of view individual decisions are cheaper than the decisions of couples. Nevertheless, sometimes it can be more strategic to agree with the partner's wishes, making an unreasonable purchase in order to maintain the current harmony in the relationship.

Fairness and Satisfaction

There are several prerequisites—such as taking care of the partner's wishes, factual communication, egalitarian relation of influence, disclosure of goals, prevention of indirect strategies of persuasion, and sufficient time—necessary to ensure that economically reasonable decisions are made and the detriment to the relationship is minimized (Klein and Hill 1979). Although economic efficiency and satisfaction could be antagonistic, Kourilsky and Murray (1981) confirm a positive correlation.

The Vienna Diary Study (Kirchler et al. 2001) provides information about perceived fairness during the decision process and in the decision result, and satisfaction with the decision result. According to this study, the choice of tactics interacts with perceived fairness and satisfaction in decisions. Decisions are perceived to be fair and satisfactory if the individual him- or herself applies tactics of offering resources (tactic 5) and factual argument (tactic 18) and if the partner also used the tactic of factual argument (tactic 18) but additionally employed the tactic of integrative bargaining (tactic 17). On the contrary, a decision result is perceived as unfair if the individual expresses negative emotions (tactic 2), appears helpless (tactic 3), insists (tactic 7), or withdraws (tactic 8), or if the partner does the same. Also, the partner's usage of the tactics of presenting falsehoods (tactic 10) and of flattery (tactic 1) lead to perceived unfairness.

Kirchler and colleagues (2001) also surveyed the influence of the allocation of partners' utility on the degree of perceived fairness. Research on justice revealed three types of rules of fair distribution: (1) the equity rule states that the distribution of resources depends on the contributions, (2) the equality rule says that resources are equally distributed between all individuals, and (3) the need rule stipulates that resources are distributed based on individuals' requirements. Clark and Chrisman (1994) give an overview of this research and reveal that all three rules are applied in close relationships. Some researchers (Hatfield and Traupmann 1981; Hatfield et al. 1985; Hatfield, Utne, and Traupmann 1979; Walster, Walster, and Berscheid 1978) support the idea that partners in close relationships behave according to the equity rule. Others (Clark and Mills 1979; Lujansky and Mikula 1983; Michaels, Acock, and Edwards 1986; Michaels, Edwards, and Acock 1984) maintain that the equity rule is not appropriate for romantic relationships. Some studies (Gray-Little and Burks 1983; Greenberg 1983; Pataki, Shapiro, and Clark 1992; Steil 1994) demonstrate that partners in close relationships follow the equality rule for the distribution of resources. Other authors (Deutsch 1975, 1985; Mills and Clark 1982; Lamm and Schwinger 1983; Clark, Mills, and Powell 1986) argue that resources are distributed according to the partners' requirements. Because of several scientific opinions on the distribution of utility, Kirchler and colleagues (2001) surveyed three different rules: (1) pure egoism—the more an individual benefits from a decision, the fairer he or she perceives it to be; (2) balance—the fairest decision is the one where both partners benefit exactly the same; and (3) requirement orientation—the distribution of utility is perceived to be fair if it is oriented to the partners' requirements. The results suggest that egoistic motives as well as balanced distribution influence the perception of fairness. Requirement orientation seems not to have any influence.

Kirchler and colleagues (2001) also investigate satisfaction with the result of a decision. Since partners have two goals in conflicts—they want to carry their point and at the same time do not want to do any harm to the relationship (Filley 1975; Ben-Yoav and Pruitt 1984; Kirchler 1989)—satisfaction depends also on the realization of these goals. A positive climate and distributive fairness encourage harmony and lead to satisfaction with the relationship. Prevailing in decisions is the other goal. The correlation with the satisfaction is not linear but U-shaped, because if the utility of one partner is too high, the achievement of harmony is interfered with. The results show that satisfaction with the decision increases if the decision process and the decision results are perceived to be fair, if the climate is good, if own utility is not too high, and if own influence on decision making increases. Perceived fairness and equable distribution of utility and influence are especially important in egalitarian partnerships.

CONCLUSION

This essay has discussed economic decisions in private households and demonstrated the complexity of decision-making processes in the everyday life of the family. Not only are several events, experiences, and earlier decisions cross-linked with current decisions but also family members have multiple goals—to decide satisficingly (from their point of view) and to maintain a harmonious relationship. This complicates observations of economic decisions and makes it difficult to use appropriate research methods. Nevertheless, Kirchler and colleagues (2001) refer to diaries as a promising technique to investigate decision making in families. With this method researchers seem to capture economic decisions in private households very well; however, further investigation is necessary.

The complexity of decision processes stems from several factors. They are influenced by social norms as well as the individuals' role in the family. Traditional families are more likely to have determined who is responsible for which type of decision. The responsibility for certain decisions, such as the purchase of furniture and cars, is strictly assigned either to the wife or to the husband. With respect to the purchase of certain goods, such as cereals and toys, children also influence the decision process. Although decision processes for several types of goods are already well investigated, research on the handling of money has been sparse and therefore is needed. The factors of individuals' interest and knowledge of the good and the purchase are also important to relative influence in the decision process. The higher an individual's interest and knowledge, the more say that person has. Another factor of substance is the history of earlier and current decision processes. Although from a normative point of view a decision can be easily made, earlier decision processes and results might be taken into account to preserve the harmony in the relationship and might lead to suboptimal choices in terms of rationality. The fact that family members apply different tactics in decisions to convince others of their opinion has also been of research interest (Kirchler et al. 2001) and furthermore explains partly the complexity of decision processes.

Earlier decision results, moreover, influence current decisions. In particular, the economic management of resources and the perceived fairness and satisfaction are important. Research on decision efficiency and on fairness and satisfaction has to be conducted to shed more light on the complexity of decision-making processes in private households.

REFERENCES

Ahuja, Roshan D., and Kandi M. Stinson. 1993. "Female-Headed Single Parent Families: An Explanatory Study of Children's Influence in Family Decision Making." *Advances in Consumer Research* 20: 469–74.

Almeida, David M., and Ronald C. Kessler. 1998. "Everyday Stressors and Gender Differences in Daily Distress." *Journal of Personality and Social Psychology* 75: 670–80.

Almeida, David M., Elaine Wethington, and Amy L. Chandler. 1999. "Daily Transmission of Tensions Between Marital Dyads and Parent-Child Dyads." *Journal of Marriage and the Family* 61: 49–61.

Auhagen, Ann Elisabeth. 1987. "A New Approach for the Study of Personal Relationships: The Double Diary Approach." *German Journal of Psychology* 11: 3–7.

———. 1991. *Freundschaft im Alltag. Eine Studie mit dem Doppeltagebuch.* Bern: Huber.

Barry, Bruce, and Richard L. Oliver. 1996. "Affect in Dyadic Negotiation: A Model and Propositions." *Organizational Behavior and Human Decision Processes* 67: 127–43.

Beatty, Sharon E., and Salil Talpade. 1994. "Adolescent Influence in Family Decision Making: A Replication with Extension." *Journal of Consumer Research* 21: 332–41.

Ben-Yoav, Orly, and Dean G. Pruitt. 1984. "Accountability to Constituents: A Two-Edged Sword." *Organizational Behavior and Human Performance* 34: 283–94.

Berger, Charles R., and Kathy Kellermann. 1994. "Acquiring Social Information." In John Augustine Daley and John Wiemann, eds., *Strategic Interpersonal Communication*, 1–31. Hillsdale, NJ: Lawrence Erlbaum.

Bierhoff, Hans W., and Ina Grau. 1999. *Romantische Beziehungen. Bindung, Liebe, Partnerschaft.* Bern: Huber.

Billig, Michael. 1987. *Arguing and Thinking: A Rhetorical Approach to Social Psychology.* Cambridge: Cambridge University Press.

Blood, Robert O., and Donald M. Wolfe. 1960. *Husbands and Wives: The Dynamics of Married Living.* Glencoe, IL: Free Press.

Bochner, Arthur P., Carolyn Ellis, and Lisa M. Tillman-Healy. 1997. "Relationships as Stories." In Steve Duck, ed., *Handbook of Personal Relationships: Theories, Research and Interventions*, 2nd ed., 307–24. Chichester, UK: Wiley.

Bolger, Niall, Angelina Davis, and Eshkol Rafaeli. 2003. "Diary Methods: Capturing Life as It Is Lived." *Annual Review of Psychology* 54: 579–616.

Bolger, Niall, Anita DeLongis, Ronald C. Kessler, and Elizabeth A. Schilling. 1989. "Effects of Daily Stress on Negative Mood." *Journal of Personality and Social Psychology* 57: 808–18.

Bolger, Niall, Anita DeLongis, Ronald C. Kessler, and Elaine Wethington. 1989. "The Contagion of Stress Across Multiple Roles." *Journal of Marriage and the Family* 51: 175–83.

Brandstätter, Hermann. 1977. "Wohlbefinden und Unbehagen." In Werner H. Tack, ed., *Bericht über den 30. Kongreß der deutschen Gesellschaft für Psychologie in Regensburg*, 2:60–62. Göttingen: Hogrefe.

Brandstätter, Hermann, Gisela Stocker-Kreichgauer, and Volker Firchau. 1980. "Wirkung von Freundlichkeit und Argumentgüte auf Leser eines Diskussionsprotokolls. Ein Prozessmodell." *Zeitschrift für Sozialpsychologie* 11: 152–67.

Brandstätter, Hermann, and Wolfgang Wagner. 1994. "Erwerbsarbeit der Frau und Alltagsbefinden von Ehepartnern im Zeitverlauf." *Zeitschrift für Sozialpsychologie* 25: 126–46.

Braybrooke, David, and Charles E. Lindblom. 1963. *A Strategy of Decision.* Glencoe, IL: Free Press.

Brendl, C. Miguel, Arthur B. Markman, and E. Tory Higgins. 1998. "Mentale Kontoführung als Selbstregulierung: Repräsentativität für zielgeleitete Kategorien." *Zeitschrift für Sozialpsychologie* 29: 89–104.

Burns, Alvin C. 1976. "Spousal Involvement and Empathy in Jointly-Resolved and Authoritatively-Resolved Purchase Subdecisions." *Advances in Consumer Research* 3: 199–207.

Burnstein, Eugene. 1982. "Persuasion as Argument Processing." In Hermann Brandstätter, James H. Davis, and Gisela Stocker-Kreichgauer, eds., *Group Decision Processes*, 103–24. London: Academic Press.

Caron, Andre, and Scott Ward. 1975. "Gift Decisions by Kids and Parents." *Journal of Advertising Research* 14: 15–20.

Clark, Margaret S., and Kathleen Chrisman. 1994. "Resource Allocation in Intimate Relationships: Trying to Make Sense of a Confusing Literature." In Melvin J. Lerner and Gerold Mikula, eds., *Entitlement and the Affectional Bond*, 65–88. New York: Plenum Press.

Clark, Margaret S., and Judson Mills. 1979. "Interpersonal Attraction in Exchange and Communal Relationships." *Journal of Personality and Social Psychology* 37: 12–24.

Clark, Margaret S., Judson Mills, and Martha C. Powell. 1986. "Keeping Track of Needs in Communal and Exchange Relationships." *Journal of Personality and Social Psychology* 51: 333–38.

Cody, Michael J., Daniel J. Canary, and Sandi W. Smith. 1994. "Compliance-Gaining Goals: An Inductive Analysis of Actor's Goal Types, Strategies and Successes." In John Augustine Daley and John M. Wiemann, eds., *Strategic Interpersonal Communication*, 33–90. Hillsdale, NJ: Lawrence Erlbaum.

Cody, Michael J., and Margaret L. McLaughlin, eds. 1990. *The Psychology of Tactical Communication.* Clevedon, UK: Multilingual Matters.

Corfman, Kim P. 1985. "Effects of the Cooperative Group Decision-Making Context on the Test-Retest Reliability of Preference Ratings." In Richard J. Lutz, ed., *Advances in Consumer Research,* 13:223–47. Provo, UT: Association for Consumer Research.

———. 1987. "Group Decision-Making and Relative Influence When Preferences Differ: A Conceptual Framework." In Jagdish N. Sheth and Elizabeth C. Hirschman, eds., *Research in Consumer Behavior,* 2:223–57. Greenwich, CT: JAI.

Corfman, Kim P., and Donald R. Lehman. 1987. "Models of Cooperative Group Decision-Making and Relative Influence: An Experimental Investigation of Family Purchase Decisions." *Journal of Consumer Research* 14: 1–13.

Davis, Harry L. 1972. "Determinants of Martial Roles in a Consumer Purchase Decision." Working paper no. 72–14, European Institute for Advanced Studies in Management, Brussels.

———. 1976. "Decision Making within the Household." *Journal of Consumer Research* 2: 241–60.

Davis, Harry L., and Benny P. Rigaux. 1974. "Perception of Marital Roles in Decision Processes." *Journal of Consumer Research* 1: 51–62.

Deutsch, Morton. 1975. "Equity, Equality and Need: What Determines Which Value Will Be Used as the Basis of Distributive Justice?" *Journal of Social Issues* 31: 137–48.

———. 1985. *Distributive Justice: A Social-Psychological Perspective.* New Haven, CT: Yale University Press.

Diener, Ed, and Randy J. Larsen. 1984. "Temporal Stability and Cross-Situational Consistency of Affective, Behavioral, and Cognitive Responses." *Journal of Personality and Social Psychology* 47: 871–83.

Dillard, James Price. 1990. "The Nature and Substance of Goals in Tactical Communication." In Michael J. Cody and Margaret L. McLaughlin, eds., *The Psychology of Tactical Communication,* 70–91. Clevedon, UK: Multilingual Matters.

Downey, Geraldine, Antonio L. Freitas, Benjamin Michaelis, and Hala Khouri. 1998. "The Self-Fulfilling Prophecy in Close Relationships: Rejection Sensitivity and Rejection by Romantic Partners." *Journal of Personality and Social Psychology* 75: 545–60.

Duck, Steve. 1991. "Diaries and Logs." In Barbara M. Montgomery and Steve Duck, eds., *Studying Interpersonal Interaction,* 141–61. New York: Guilford.

———. 1994. *Meaningful Relationships: Talking, Sense, and Relating.* Thousand Oaks, CA: Sage.

Dutta, Mousumee. 2000. "Women's Employment and Its Effects on Bengali Households of Shillong, India." *Journal of Comparative Family Studies* 31: 217–29.

Engel, James F., Roger D. Blackwell, and Paul W. Miniard. 1993. *Consumer Behavior.* Fort Worth, TX: Dryden Press.

Falbo, Toni, and Letitia A. Peplau. 1980. "Power Strategies in Intimate Relationships." *Journal of Personality and Social Psychology* 38: 618–28.

Feger, Hubert, and Ann E. Auhagen. 1987. "Unterstützende soziale Netzwerke: Sozialpsychologische Perspektiven." *Zeitschrift für klinische Psychologie* 86: 353–67.

Ferber, Robert. 1973. "Family Decision Making and Economic Behavior." In Eleanor Sheldon, ed., *Family Economic Behavior,* 29–61. Philadelphia: Lippincott.

Ferber, Robert, and Lucy Chao Lee. 1974. "Husband-Wife Influence in Family Purchasing Behavior." *Journal of Consumer Research* 1: 43–50.

Filley, Alan C. 1975. *Interpersonal Conflict Resolution.* Glenview, IL: Scott, Foresman.

Foa, Uriel G., and Edna B. Foa. 1974. *Societal Structures of the Mind.* Springfield, IL: Thomas.

Gierl, Heribert, and Sandra Praxmarer. 2001. "Einfluss von Kindern auf die Kaufentscheidungen ihrer Mütter." *Werbeforschung & Praxis* 1: 12–16.

Granbois, Donald H., and John O. Summers. 1975. "Primary and Secondary Validity of Consumer Purchase Probabilities." *Journal of Consumer Research* 1: 31–38.

Gray-Little, Bernadette, and Nancy Burks. 1983. "Power and Satisfaction in Marriage: A Review and Critique." *Psychological Bulletin* 93: 513–38.

Greenberg, Jerald. 1983. "Equity and Equality as Clues to the Relationship Between Exchange Participants." *European Journal of Social Psychology* 13: 195–96.

———. 1988. "Equity and Workplace Status: A Field Experiment." *Journal of Applied Psychology* 73: 606–13.

Hatfield, Elaine, and Jane Traupmann. 1981. "Intimate Relationships: A Perspective from Equity Theory." In Steve W. Duck and Robin Gilmour, eds., *Personal Relationships,* vol. 1: *Studying Personal Relationships,* 165–78. London: Academic Press.

Hatfield, Elaine, Jane Traupmann, Susan Sprecher, Mary Utne, and J. Hay. 1985. "Equity and Intimate

Relations: Recent Research." In William Ickes, ed., *Compatible and Incompatible Relationships,* 91–117. New York: Springer-Verlag.

Hatfield, Elaine, Mary K. Utne, and Jane Traupmann. 1979. "Equity Theory and Intimate Relationships." In Robert L. Burgess and Ted L. Huston, eds., *Social Exchange in Developing Relationships,* 99–133. New York: Academic Press.

Heath, Chip, and Jack B. Soll. 1996. "Mental Budgeting and Consumer Decisions." *Journal of Consumer Research* 23: 400–52.

Hill, Reuben. 1972. "Modern Systems Theory and the Family: A Confrontation." *Social Science Information* 10: 7–26.

Hinde, Robert A. 1997. *Relationships: A Dialectical Prospective.* Hove, East Sussex, UK: Psychology Press.

Holmes, John G., and Sandra L. Murray. 1996. "Conflict in Close Relationships." In Edward Tory Higgins and Arie W. Kruglanski, eds., *Social Psychology: Handbook of Basic Principles,* 622–52. New York: Guilford.

Hölzl, Erik, and Erich Kirchler. 1998. "Einflusstaktiken in partnerschaftlichen Kaufentscheidungen. Ein Beitrag zur Analyse von Aktions-Reaktions-Mustern." *Zeitschrift für Sozialpsychologie* 29: 105–16.

Hormuth, Stefan E. 1986. "The Sampling of Experiences in Situ." *Journal of Personality* 54: 262–93.

Hornik, Jacob. 1982. "Situational Effects on the Consumption of Time." *Journal of Marketing* 46: 44–55.

Howard, Judith A., Philip Blumstein, and Pepper Schwartz. 1986. "Sex, Power, and Influence Tactics in Intimate Relationships." *Journal of Personality and Social Psychology* 51: 102–9.

Jehn, Karen A., and Priti Pradhan Shah. 1997. "Interpersonal Relationships and Task Performance: An Examination of Mediating Processes in Friendship and Acquaintance Groups." *Journal of Personality and Social Psychology* 72: 775–90.

Jenkins, Roger L. 1979. "The Influence of Children in Family Decision-Making: Parents' Perception." *Advances in Consumer Research* 6: 413–18.

Kahneman, Daniel, and Amos Tversky. 1984. "Choices, Values, and Frames." *American Psychologist* 39: 341–50.

Kelley, Harold H., Ellen Berscheid, Andrew Christensen, John H. Harvey, Ted L. Huston, George Levinger, Evie MacClintock, Letitia Anne Peplau, and Donald R. Peterson. 1983. *Close Relationships.* New York: Freeman.

Kirchler, Erich. 1988a. "Household Economic Decision-Making." In Fred W. van Raaij, Gery M. van Veldhoven, Theo M.M. Verhallen, and Karl-Erik Wärneryd, eds., *Handbook of Economic Psychology,* 258–93. Amsterdam: North Holland.

———. 1988b. "Marital Happiness and Interaction in Everyday Surroundings: A Time-Sample Diary Approach for Couples." *Journal of Social and Personal Relationships* 5: 375–82.

———. 1989. *Kaufentscheidungen im privaten Haushalt. Eine sozialpsychologische Analyse des Familienalltages.* Göttingen: Hogrefe.

———. 1990. "Spouses' Influence Strategies in Purchase Decisions as Dependent on Conflict Type and Relationship Characteristics." *Journal of Economic Psychology* 11: 101–18.

———. 1993a. "Beeinflussungstaktiken von Eheleuten: Entwicklung und Erprobung eines Instrumentes zur Erfassung der Anwendungshäufigkeit verschiedener Beeinflussungstaktiken in familiären Kaufentscheidungen." *Zeitschrift für experimentelle und angewandte Psychologie* 40: 102–31.

———. 1993b. "Spouses' Joint Purchase Decisions: Determinants of Influence Strategies to Muddle Through the Process." *Journal of Economic Psychology* 14: 405–38.

Kirchler, Erich, and Chiara Berti. 1996. "Convincersi a vicenda nelle decisioni di coppia." *Giornale Italiano di Psicologia* 23: 675–98.

Kirchler, Erich M., and Erwin Kirchler. 1990. "Einflußmuster in familiären Kaufentscheidungen." *Planung und Analyse* 2: 49–54.

Kirchler, Erich, Christa Rodler, Erik Hölzl, and Katja Meier. 2001. *Conflict and Decision-Making in Close Relationships: Love, Money and Daily Routines.* East Sussex: Psychology Press.

Klein, David M., and Reuben Hill. 1979. "Determinants of Family Problem-Solving Effectiveness." In Wesley R. Burr, Reuben Hill, F. Ivan Nye, and Ira L. Reiss, eds., *Contemporary Theories About the Family: Research Bases Theories,* 1:493–548. New York: Free Press.

Klein, Renate C.A., and Michael P. Johnson. 1997. "Strategies of Couple Conflict." In Steve Duck, ed., *Handbook of Personal Relationships,* 2nd ed., 451–86. Chichester, UK: Wiley.

Kotler, Philip. 1982. *Marketing-Management. Analyse, Planung und Kontrolle.* Stuttgart: Poeschel.

Kourilsky, Marilyn, and Trudy Murray. 1981. "The Use of Economic Reasoning to Increase Satisfaction with Family Decision Making." *Journal of Consumer Research* 8: 183–88.

Kurdek, Lawrence A. 1994. "Conflict Resolution Styles in Gay, Lesbian, Heterosexual Nonparent and Heterosexual Parent Couples." *Journal of Marriage and the Family* 56: 705–22.

Labrecque, JoAnne, and Line Ricard. 2001. "Children's Influence on Family Decision-Making: A Restaurant Study." *Journal of Business Research* 54: 173–76.

Laireiter, Aanton-Rupert, Urs Baumann, Elisabeth Reisenzein, and Alois Untner. 1997. "A Diary Method for the Assessment of Interactive Social Networks: The Interval-Contingent Diary SONET-T." *Swiss Journal of Psychology* 56: 217–38.

Lamm, Helmut, and Thomas Schwinger.1983. "Need Consideration in Allocation Decisions: Is It Just?" *Journal of Social Psychology* 119: 205–9.

Larson, Reed W., and David M. Almeida. 1999. "Emotional Transmission in the Daily Lives of Families: A New Paradigm for Studying Family Process." *Journal of Marriage and the Family* 61: 5–20.

Larson, Reed W., and Nancy Bradney. 1988. "Precious Moment with Family Members and Friends." In Robert M. Milardo, ed., *Families and Social Networks,* 106–26. Newbury Park, CA: Sage.

Larson, Reed W., and Mihaly Csikszentmihalyi. 1983. "The Experience Sampling Method." In Harry Reis, ed., *New Directions for Naturalistic Methods in the Behavioral Sciences,* 41–56. San Francisco: Jossey-Bass.

Lea, Steven E.G., Paul Webley, and R. Mark Levine. 1993. "The Economic Psychology of Consumer Debt." *Journal of Economic Psychology* 14: 85–119.

Lee, Christina K.C., and Sharon E. Beatty. 2002. "Family Structure and Influence in Family Decision Making." *Journal of Consumer Marketing* 19: 24–41.

Lee, Christina K.C., and Brett A. Collins. 2000. "Family Decision Making and Coalition Patterns." *European Journal of Marketing* 34: 1181–98.

Lindblom, Charles E. 1959. "The Science of 'Muddling Through.'" *Public Administration Review* 19: 79–88.

———. 1979. "Still Muddling, Not Yet Through." *Public Administration Review* 39: 517–26.

Lujansky, Harald, and Gerold Mikula. 1983. "Can Equity Theory Explain the Quality and the Stability of Romantic Relationships." *British Journal of Social Psychology* 22: 101–12.

March, James G., and Zur Shapira. 1992. "Behavioral Decision Theory and Organizational Decision Theory." In Mary Zey, ed., *Decision Making: Alternatives to Rational Choice Models,* 273–303. Newbury Park, CA: Sage.

Mauri, Carlo. 1996. "L'influenza dei bambini sugli acquisti della famiglia." *Micro & Macro Marketing* 1: 39–57.

Mayerhofer, Wolfgang. 1994. "Kaufentscheidungsprozeß in Familien." *Werbeforschung & Praxis* 19: 126–27.

McLaughlin, Margaret L., Michael J. Cody, and Kathryn French. 1990. "Account-Giving and the Attribution of Responsibility: Impressions of Traffic Offenders." In Michael J. Cody and Margaret L. McLaughlin, eds., *The Psychology of Tactical Communication,* 244–67. Clevedon, UK: Multilingual Matters.

Mehrotra, Sunil, and Sandra Torges. 1977. "Determinants of Children's Influence on Mother's Buying Behavior." *Advances in Consumer Research* 4: 56–60.

Meier, Katja, Erich Kirchler, and Angela Hubert. 1999. "Savings and Investment Decisions Within Private Households: Spouses' Dominance in Decisions on Various Forms of Investment." *Journal of Economic Psychology* 20: 499–519.

Michaels, James W., Alan C. Acock, and John N. Edwards. 1986. "Social Exchange and Equity Determinants of Relationship Commitment." *Journal of Social and Personal Relationships* 3: 161–75.

Michaels, James W., John N. Edwards, and Alan C. Acock. 1984. "Satisfaction in Intimate Relationships as a Function of Inequality, Inequity, and Outcomes." *Social Psychology Quarterly* 47: 347–57.

Mills, Judson, and Margaret S. Clark. 1982. "Exchange and Communal Relationships." In Ladd Wheeler, ed., *Review of Personality and Social Psychology,* 3:121–44. Beverly Hills: Sage.

Moschis, George P. 1987. *Consumer Socialization: A Life-Cycle Perspective.* Lexington, MA: Lexington Books.

Nelson, Margaret C. 1988. "The Resolution of Conflict in Joint Purchase Decisions by Husbands and Wives: A Review and Empirical Test." *Advances in Consumer Research* 15: 436–41.

Palan, Kay M., and Robert E. Wilkes. 1997. "Adolescent-Parent Interaction in Family Decision Making." *Journal of Consumer Research* 24: 159–69.

Park, Jong, Patriya Tansuhaj, and Richard H. Kolbe. 1991. "The Role of Love, Affection, and Intimacy in Family Decision Research." *Advances in Consumer Research* 18: 651–56.

Park, Jong, Patriya Tansuhaj, Eric R. Spangenberg, and Jim McCullough. 1995. "An Emotion-Based Perspective of Family Purchase Decisions." *Advances in Consumer Research* 22: 723–28.

Park, Wahn C. 1982. "Joint Decisions in Home Purchasing. A Muddling-Through Process." *Journal of Consumer Research* 9: 151–62.

Pataki, Sherri, Cheryl Shapiro, and Margaret S. Clark. 1992. "Acquiring Distributive Justice Norms: Effects of Age and Relationship Type." *Journal of Social and Personal Relationships* 11: 427–42.

Pawlik, Kurt, and Lothar Buse. 1982. "Rechnergestützte Verhaltensregistrierung im Feld: Beschreibung und erste psychometrische Überprüfung einer neuen Erhebungsmethode." *Zeitschrift für Differentielle und Diagnostische Psychologie* 3: 101–18.

Pervin, Lawrence A. 1976. "A Free-Response Description Approach to the Analysis of Person-Situation Interaction." *Journal of Personality and Social Psychology* 34: 465–74.

Pollay, Richard W. 1968. "A Model of Family Decision Making." *British Journal of Marketing* 2: 206–16.

Pross, Helge. 1979. *Die Wirklichkeit der Hausfrau*. Reinbeck bei Hamburg: Rowohlt.

Pruitt, Dean G., and Jeffrey Z. Rubin. 1986. *Social Conflict: Escalation, Stalemate, Settlement*. New York: Random House.

Qualls, William J., and Francois Jaffe. 1992. "Measuring Conflict in Household Decision Behavior: Read My Lips and Read My Mind." *Advances in Consumer Research* 19: 522–31.

Robertson, Ann M. 1990. "Spousal Decision Processes for Financial/Professional Services." *Journal of Professional Services Marketing* 6: 119–35.

Robinson, John P., Janet Yerby, Margaret Fieweger, and Nancy Somerick. 1977. "Sex-Role Differences in Time Use." *Sex Roles* 3: 443–58.

Rodman, Hyman. 1967. "Marital Power in France, Greece, Yugoslavia, and the United States: A Cross-National Discussion." *Journal of Marriage and the Family* 29: 320–24.

Ruhfus, Rolf. 1976. *Kaufentscheidungen von Familien*. Wiesbaden: Gabler.

Scanzoni, John, and Karen Polonko. 1980. "A Conceptual Approach to Explicit Marital Negotiation." *Journal of Marriage and the Family* 42: 31–44.

Schaninger, Charles M., and W. Christian Buss. 1986. "A Longitudinal Comparison of Consumption and Finance Handling Between Happily Married and Divorced Couples." *Journal of Marriage and the Family* 48: 129–36.

Seibold, David R., James G. Cantrill, and Renee A. Meyers. 1994. "Communication and Interpersonal Influence." In Mark L. Knapp and Gerald R. Miller, eds., *Handbook of Interpersonal Communication,* 2nd ed., 542–88. Thousand Oaks, CA: Sage.

Seymour, Daniel, and Greg Lessne. 1984. "Spousal Conflict Arousal: Scale Development." *Journal of Consumer Research* 11: 810–21.

Shim, Soyeon, Lisa Snyder, and Kenneth C. Gehrt. 1995. "Parents' Perception Regarding Children's Use of Clothing Evaluative Criteria: An Exploratory Study from the Consumer Socialization Process Perspective." *Advances in Consumer Research* 22: 628–32.

Sillars, Alan L., and Pam J. Kalbflesch. 1989. "Implicit and Explicit Decision-Making Styles in Couples." In David Brinberg and James Jaccard, eds., *Dyadic Decision Making,* 179–215. New York: Springer.

Sillars, Alan L., and William W. Wilmot. 1994. "Communication Strategies in Conflict and Mediation." In John Augustine Daly and John M. Wiemann, *Strategic Interpersonal Communication,* 163–90. Hillsdale, NJ: Erlbaum.

Snyder, Jesse, and Raymond Serafin. 1985. "Auto Makers Set New ad Strategy to Reach Women." *Advertising Age,* September 23, 3.

Spitzberg, Brian H., Daniel J. Canary, and William R. Cupach. 1994. "A Competence Based Approach to the Study of Interpersonal Conflict." In Dudley D. Cahn, ed., *Conflict in Personal Relationships,* 183–202. Hillsdale, NJ: Erlbaum.

Steil, Janice M. 1994. "Equality and Entitlement in Marriage: Benefits and Barriers." In Melvin J. Lerner and Gerold Mikula, eds., *Entitlement and the Affectional Bond,* 229–58. New York: Plenum Press.

Stone, Arthur A., Ronald C. Kessler and Jennifer A. Haythornthwaite. 1991. "Measuring Daily Events and Experiences: Decisions for the Researcher." *Journal of Personality* 59: 575–607.

Szinovacz, Maximiliane E. 1987. "Family Power." In Marvin B. Sussman and Susanne K. Steinmetz, eds., *Handbook of Marriage and the Family,* 651–93. New York: Plenum.

Thaler, Richard H. 1980. "Toward a Positive Theory of Consumer Choice." *Journal of Economic Behavior and Organization* 1: 30–60.

———. 1985. "Mental Accounting and Consumer Choice." *Marketing Science,* 4: 119–214.

———. 1994. *Quasi Rational Economics*. New York: Sage.

Tschammer-Osten, Berndt. 1979. *Haushaltswissenschaft*. Stuttgart: Fischer.

Van de Vliert, Evert. 1997. *Complex Interpersonal Conflict Behavior*. East Sussex, UK: Psychology Press.

Vanek, Joann. 1974. "Time Spent in Housework." *Scientific American* 231: 116–20.

Van Knippenberg, Barbara, and Herman Steensma. 2003. "Future Interaction Expectation and the Use of Soft and Hard Influence Tactics." *Applied Psychology: An International Review* 52: 55–67.

Van Lange, Paul A. M., Caryl E. Rusbult, Steven M. Drigotas, Ximena B. Arriaga, and Betty S. Witcher. 1997. "Willingness to Sacrifice in Close Relationships." *Journal of Personality and Social Psychology* 72: 1373–95.

Walster, Elaine, G. William Walster, and Ellen Berscheid. 1978. *Equity: Theory and Research.* Boston: Allyn & Bacon.

Ward, Scott, and Daniel B. Wackman. 1973. "Children's Purchase Influence Attempts and Parental Yielding." In Harold H. Kassarjian and Thomas S. Robertson, eds., *Perspectives in Consumer Behavior,* 369–74. Glenview, IL: Scott, Foresman.

Wärneryd, Karl-Erik. 1999. *The Psychology of Saving: A Study on Economic Psychology.* Cheltenham, UK: Edward Elgar.

Webley, Paul. 1994. "The Role of Economic and Psychological Factors in Consumer Debt." Report 21, VSB-CentER Savings Project, Center for Economic Research, Tilburg University.

Williams, Laura A., and Alvin C. Burns. 2000. "Exploring the Dimensionality of Children's Direct Influence Attempts." *Advances in Consumer Research* 27: 64–71.

Winch, Robert F., and Margaret T. Gordon. 1974. *Family Structure and Function as Influence.* Lexington, MA: Lexington Books.

Winter, Mandfred, and Wolfgang Mayerhofer. 1983a. "Kind-Familie-Fernsehen-Werbung [I. Teil]." *WWG Information* 92: 38–44.

———. 1983b. "Kind-Familie-Fernsehen-Werbung [II. Teil–Empirische Studie. Die Effekte der Fernsehwerbung auf die Position des Kindes beim Kaufentscheidungsprozeß in der Familie.]." *WWG Information* 93: 79–84.

Yukl, Gary, Ping Ping Fu, and Robert McDonald. 2003. "Cross-Cultural Differences in Perceived Effectiveness of Influence Tactics for Initiation or Resisting Change." *Applied Psychology: An International Review* 52: 68–82.

Zagorsky, Jay L. 2003. "Husbands' and Wives' View of the Family Finances." *Journal of Socio-Economics* 32: 127–46.

Zani, Bruna, and Erich Kirchler. 1993. "Come influenzare il partner: Processi decisionali nelle relazioni di coppia." *Giornale Italiano di Psicologi* 20: 247–81.

PART 7

LIFE AND DEATH

CHAPTER 27

A PROLEGOMENON TO BEHAVIORAL
ECONOMIC STUDIES OF SUICIDE

BIJOU YANG AND DAVID LESTER

Suicide ranked as the eleventh leading cause of death in the United States in 2001. There were 30,622 suicides as compared to 20,308 murder victims. The suicide rate of 10.8 per 100,000 people per year was higher than the homicide rate of 7.1, and so people were 50 percent more likely to commit suicide than to be murdered. On the average, one person committed suicide in this country every 17.2 minutes (McIntosh 2003). However, compared to other countries, suicide mortality in the United States is not as dire as it may seem. According to the World Health Organization's *World Health Statistical Annual* (now online at www.who.int), in 2000 Lithuania, Belarus, and Russia had the highest suicide rates, almost four times that of the United States.[1]

If we use the years of life lost under the age of sixty-five to measure the significance of mortality, then suicide is ranked as the third most important contributor after heart disease and cancer (Congdon 1996). Thus suicide (and, we might add, nonfatal suicide attempts) is one of the major issues facing health and social service providers, especially given the recent trend of rapidly rising suicide rates among youths in many nations (Mathur and Freeman 2002; Freeman 1998; Willis et al. 2002; Middleton et al. 2003; Eckersley and Dear 2002; Micklewright and Stewart 1999; Birckmayer and Hemenway 2001; Al-Ansari et al. 2001; Christoffersen, Poulsen, and Nielsen 2003).

Unfortunately, scholars admit that suicide is still poorly understood despite numerous publications addressing the incidence and causes of suicide (Ruzicka 1995). This may be because suicide is a result of a "multidimensional malaise in a needful individual" (Shneidman 1985, 203), making the causes of suicide "complex and multifactorial" (Gunnell et al. 2003). While psychologists and psychiatrists try to understand suicide in individuals from a psychiatric or mental illness perspective (Lester 1988, 1991; Maris, Berman, and Silverman 2000), sociologists approach suicide from a societal perspective (Lester 1989), and epidemiologists focus on how different segments of the population are affected by suicide (Maris, Berman, and Silverman 2000).[2] Each of these approaches catches only one facet of the phenomenon, rather than the whole.[3]

Without a unified theory of suicide that deals with behavior at the individual level and social influences at the macroecological level, we cannot trace the mechanism of how individuals become suicidal at each stage of life. It is not surprising, therefore, that there are conflicting and inconsistent findings with respect to how socioeconomic factors impact on suicide. For example, according to Gunnell and colleagues (2003), higher unemployment and divorce rates are generally associated with higher suicide rates, but the evidence from time-series data is inconsistent (Platt 1984, 1986; Platt, Micciolo, and Tansella 1992; Pritchard 1988; Lester and Yang 1991a; Crawford and Prince 1999; Lester, Curran, and Yang 1991; Stack 1990).

Economics may provide a plausible avenue for the pursuit of a unified theory of suicide.

Rational choice theory has attracted a group of followers in sociology (e.g., Coleman 1990; Coleman and Fararo 1991; Bourdieu and Coleman 1991), partly due to Becker's pioneering application of the rational choice model to fertility, marriage, crime, and even addiction (Becker 1960, 1968, 1976; Becker and Murphy 1988). In fact, the same framework was applied to suicide in the 1970s (Hamermesh and Soss 1974), and subsequent research using this approach will be discussed in detail in the next section.

An economic approach can be useful in analyzing suicidal behavior for several reasons. First, suicide involves decision making. Second, economic factors are often found to be associated with suicide at the individual level and at the societal level. Third, suicides entail economic costs to the society. Lastly, economic policies can have both intended and unintended impacts on suicide rates, beneficial or detrimental.

Economics is the study of resource allocation. The amount of the resource of concern tends to be limited, and in order to achieve optimal allocation, certain choices have to be made. Thus, economics is about decision making and its consequences (Hicks 1979, 5). Suicidal behavior is a choice that can lead to death. During the process, besides deciding to end one's life, the individual has to choose a method, whether to write a suicide note, a location for the act, and so on. The process involves making decisions, a process that lies at the core of economic analysis.

It is well documented that economic factors can trigger the suicidal act and are correlated with suicide rates. At the individual level, poverty, business difficulties, or problems related to work are found in suicide notes (Lester et al. 2004; Volkonen and Martelin 1988; Shneidman and Farberow 1957; Fedden 1938).[4] At the macroecological level, income, GDP per capita, unemployment, economic growth, labor force participation, and income distribution/inequality have been found to correlate with the suicide rate (Neumayer 2003; Jungeilges and Kirchgassner 2002; Lester and Yang 1997, Lester 2001; Leenaars, Yang, and Lester 1993; Brainerd 2001; Platt, Micciolo, and Tansella 1992; Gunnell et al. 2003; Gerdtham and Johannesson 2003).

In addition, suicide entails an economic cost to the society and so raises public health and other public policy issues. First, the economic cost of suicide entails both direct and indirect costs. The former includes medical care and medico-legal costs; the latter refers to the earnings lost due to permanent disability or premature mortality. Specifically, direct medical care costs include hospital costs and inpatient physician costs for people who attempted suicide and are admitted to the hospital. Medico-legal costs for completed suicides include the cost of autopsies and legal investigations (Palmer et al. 1995). The indirect cost of suicide is based on both years of productive life lost and the corresponding estimated present value of lifetime earnings.[5]

While unemployment is the most common economic risk factor for adult suicides, promoting full employment, and thus job security (along with price stability), is one goal of the government in the United States, mandated by the Employment Act of 1946. The discretionary policy usually enacted is to reduce unemployment if cyclical unemployment is excessive. A successful countercyclical policy thus provides a beneficial externality that unintentionally may prevent suicide. Any other institutions or social networks that are established to promote or enhance physical or mental health can be considered as beneficial to the well-being of citizens and so help prevent suicide.

However, unintended detrimental impacts on suicide can be found in some segments of the population. For instance, one of the factors that appear to trigger rising suicide rates among African American adolescents results from restrictions on public assistance programs.[6] Specifically, a family with a male over the age of eighteen living in the household is disqualified from receiving public assistance. This restriction leads to the absence of the father and father figures from the home, leaving African American adolescents with fewer resources to help them cope with complex economic and social changes and, therefore, more vulnerable to suicide (Willis et al. 2002, 912).

Another detrimental impact from public policy may be the reversal of the policies that have protected older workers from the risk of suicide. In his study of twenty countries, Taylor (2003) found that among older workers, unemployment and suicide rates are found to be largely unrelated.[7] His explanation is that some countries have permitted older workers to retire early in recent decades via generously funded retirement benefits. In addition, disability and unemployment programs in many countries have offered early retirement benefits well before the official retirement age. However, these early retirement "pathways" are now under challenge in developed countries due to concerns over the aging population and related pension financing issues (Taylor 2003). Thus, it is very likely that policy makers will consider increasing the official retirement age, cutting down on pension benefits, or both. In doing so, not only would older workers lose the option of early retirement, they would also be forced to compete in an ever more disadvantageous labor market. The resulting psychological toll on older workers might make them more vulnerable to suicide (Taylor 2003).

There is one more possible impact of an aging population. As a growing aged population competes for national health care with the younger population, the quality of health care may suffer, especially for those who do not have private pensions or savings to supplement their Medicare coverage. Since research has showed that improved health care for older people is associated with a lower suicide rate (Gunnell et al. 2003), an impoverished health care service would not be helpful in preventing suicide in the elderly.[8]

Lastly, a better understanding of suicidal behavior may generate public policy suggestions to prevent suicide. For example, Yaniv (2001), after illustrating how the fear of hospitalization may deter suicide attempters from asking for help, makes several suggestions for preventing suicide, such as measures geared toward providing access to beneficial therapy and toward increasing public awareness about this access, and measures to reduce the fear of hospitalization.

Finally, all public policy has a broad impact on society. Thus, enactments of public policies, especially economic policies, should take into account their social impact as part of deciding their feasibility, a position long advocated by Yang and Lester (1995; Lester and Yang 2003).

In the distant past, economists interested in suicidal behavior focused primarily on estimating the costs of suicide due to legal and insurance concerns. The application of economic theories to understanding suicide began only thirty years ago. This chapter will review economic theories and concepts exploring suicide, including those developed by the present authors, with the intention of outlining a future research agenda for economists. A review of empirical studies is not within the scope of this chapter.

Attempted suicide is included in this chapter for two reasons. First, attempted suicide is more prevalent than completed suicide, especially among the young. Second, economists have developed some game-theoretical approaches to understanding attempted suicide (Yaniv 2001; Rosenthal 1993), which will be discussed in the following section. Even though there are no official American national data on attempted suicide, McIntosh (2003) has compiled the following estimates about suicide attempts in this country, which indicate that attempted suicide involves and has an impact on a greater segment of society than does completed suicide.

1. There are twenty-five attempts for every completed suicide in America, a ratio about 4:1 for the elderly and ranging from 100:1 to 200:1 for adolescents.
2. The annual number of suicide attempts is estimated to be about 765,000.
3. Five million living Americans are estimated to have attempted suicide.

4. Gender difference exist, with roughly three times more attempts made by females than by males.

The economic analysis of suicidal behavior, both completed and attempted, can be classified into two levels, namely, the micro/individual level and the macro/societal level. An example of the latter is the business cycle theory of suicide developed by Lester and Yang (1997), but since it is the mathematical reformulation of three sociological theories of suicide, it will not be included in this chapter.[9] The majority of economic analyses of suicidal behavior are based on individual behavior, and these will be discussed in the following section. They use either a conventional utilitarian framework based on rational choice concepts (Hamermesh and Soss 1974; Yeh and Lester 1987; Huang 1997; Dixit and Pindyck 1994; Marcotte 2003) or a behavioral approach (McCain 1997; Yaniv 2001; Rosenthal 1993). The behavioral approach to suicidal behavior is a recent development that incorporates emotions, ethics, and socialization (McCain 1997) or applies a game-theoretical approach (Yaniv 2001; Rosenthal 1993) to explore the minds of suicidal individuals.

ECONOMIC MODELS OF SUICIDAL BEHAVIOR AND SUICIDE PREVENTION

Economists do not judge whether suicide is wrong, immoral, or a deviant act. In most economic models for suicide, committing suicide is treated as a result of rational choice. Individuals are acting "rationally" if, given a choice between various alternatives, they select what seems to be the most desirable or the least undesirable alternative.

Up to the present time, economic analysis has been applied to explore several aspects of suicidal behavior: completed suicide, attempted suicide, suicide prevention, and the irrationality of suicide.

For completed suicide, the economic models include a cost-benefit analysis (Yeh and Lester 1987), a lifetime utility maximization framework (Hamermesh and Soss 1974), and the analogy of entering the labor force (Huang 1997). For attempted suicide, the models include an expanded lifetime utility maximization model (Marcotte 2003) and a game-theoretical framework to explore the incentive to attempt suicide without actually intending to die (Rosenthal 1993). For suicide prevention, Yeh and Lester (1987) used a basic demand-and-supply analysis to justify external intervention for suicide, while Yaniv (2001) applied a simple game-theoretical framework to estimate the role of help-seeking incentives in preventing suicide. Regarding the "irrationality" of suicide, Becker's (1962) notion of irrationality and its link to suicide was discussed by Lester and Yang (1991b).

Economic Approaches to Completed Suicide

Cost-Benefit Analysis

Yeh and Lester (1987) suggest that the decision to commit suicide depends upon the benefits and costs associated with suicide and with alternative actions. An individual will be less likely to commit suicide if the benefits from suicide decrease, the costs of suicide increase, the costs of alternative actions decrease, or the benefits from alternative activities increase.

The benefits from suicide include escape from physical or psychological pain (as in the suicide of someone dying from terminal cancer), the anticipation of the impact of the suicide's death on other people (as in someone who hopes to make the survivors feel guilty), or restoring one's public image (as in the suicide of Antigone in Sophocles's play of the same name). In addition, those who self-injure by cutting their wrists sometimes report that the act of cutting relieves built-up tension and that they feel no pain.

There are several costs in committing suicide. These include the money and effort spent in obtaining the information and equipment needed for the act of suicide, the pain involved in preparing to kill oneself and in the process of committing suicide, the expected loss as a result of committing suicide such as the expected punishment predicted by most of the major religions of the world, and the opportunity costs (that is, the net gain to be expected if alternative activities were chosen and life continued).

From this perspective, an individual will engage in suicidal behavior only if its benefits are greater than all of the costs mentioned above. Therefore, a cost-benefit economic model would suggest that suicide could be prevented by increasing its costs or by decreasing its benefits.

Lifetime Utility Maximization Model

The economic theory of suicide developed by Hamermesh and Soss (1974) is based on a lifetime utility function that is determined by the permanent income and the current age of the individual. The permanent income is the average income expected over a person's lifetime. Thus, the opportunity cost of committing suicide is the forgone earnings in the rest of one's life.

The permanent income and the current age of an individual determine the consumption level from which an individual will derive satisfaction. The current age also determines the cost of maintaining the day-to-day life of the individual, which is a negative attribute of the utility function.

A third element of the economic attributes of suicide is the taste for living or distaste for suicide, which is assumed to be a parameter normally distributed with a zero mean and constant variance. When the total discounted lifetime utility (which includes the taste for living) remaining to a person reaches zero, an individual will commit suicide.

This economic model of suicide contains the following assumptions: (1) the older the current age, the lower the total satisfaction, because the cost of day-to-day living increases with age; (2) the greater the permanent income, the higher the total satisfaction, since a higher income level warrants a higher consumption level. However, the additional satisfaction brought forth by additional income decreases with higher income.

Based on this lifetime maximization framework for suicide, several predictions can be derived. First, the suicide rate will increase with age. Since the marginal utility of lifetime income decreases with increased permanent income, the older an individual gets, the less additional satisfaction he is going to derive from consumption. This should increase the probability that the person will commit suicide.

Second, the suicide rate will be inversely related to permanent income. If an individual receives a greater amount of lifetime income, he is expected to have a greater amount of consumption and, therefore, a greater satisfaction from life. This should decrease the probability of committing suicide.

A later study by Crouch (1979) follows the same line as that of Hamermesh and Soss. Crouch began with the premise that an individual will commit suicide if the sum of his enjoyments from life (E) and his distaste for suicide (D) falls to or below zero, that is, when $E + D < 0$. Enjoyment for life depends upon the full income of the individual and loved ones and their living expenses that are a function of the individual's age. Several propositions are derived accordingly:

1. As the full income of the individual and/or his loved ones increases, the probability of suicide decreases and vice versa.
2. The higher the living expenses, the less the life enjoyment for the individual and so the greater the tendency to commit suicide.
3. The more religious the individual is, the more distasteful suicide will seem, and so the less likely he will be to commit suicide. (Crouch focused on the influence of Catholicism for his religious variable.)
4. Divorce (especially divorce that is opposed by the individual) and widowhood increase the likelihood of suicide because they decrease the full income of the family.

It can be seen that Crouch's formulation of suicidal behavior is based entirely on Hamermesh and Soss's idea of utility maximization, except that Crouch defines income differently than Hamermesh and Soss (but fails to give a complete definition) and includes income from the individual's loved ones.

A Labor-Force Entrance Analogy

Applying economic analyses of the decision to enter and leave the labor market to suicidal behavior, Huang (1997) conceptualized suicide as a decision to enter or leave the "life market." This decision to leave the life market will be based on utility maximization, where utility is derived from various aspects of the worth or value of life above and beyond income, such as love, health, fame, beauty, fun, adventure, prestige, respect, and security. This life income has to be earned, and it is a struggle to gain some of these rewards. Obtaining them requires a great deal of hard labor (L).

The opposite of work is leisure, including rest and relaxation (R), which entails letting go of pressure and responsibility. The ultimate maximum manifestation of leisure is complete and permanent rest—that is, death. In other words, labor measures the extent of effort and resolve to live while leisure measures its lack. Furthermore, the expected market rate wage (W) can be treated as the perceived opportunity or ability to earn life income for a unit of life effort.

Two solutions are possible. Most people will choose an interior solution, choosing to live with a varying amount of effort. Unfortunately, some will be unable to find an interior solution, and they may choose to drop out of the life market, that is, commit suicide, analogous to discouraged workers dropping out of the labor market.

What leads to the decision to terminate one's life? In this framework, people decide to drop out of the life market if the perceived obtainable wage in the life market falls short of some minimally acceptable level, perhaps as a result of a terminal disease, recurring depression, business fiasco, or public humiliation. Less likely, the decision to commit suicide can also be caused by an increase in the reservation wage. An individual, wealthy in the sense of life, may need more to keep life exciting and challenging. Having so much of everything, his utility from life diminishes, and he may become tired of life. Given a much higher reservation wage than the average person, and without a matched increase in perceived wage, the individual may find the corner solution desirable and choose to commit suicide.

Huang concluded that, in this perspective, suicide is not irrational. However, suicide may not be the correct solution, especially because there are uncertainties about many aspects of the future, and life market information is always incomplete and imperfect. In the model, W was the *perceived* expected wage from living, and the individual's perception may be erroneous owing to misinformation, misinterpretation, and/or miscalculation. Erroneous perceptions may lead to a suicide decision that is not totally rational.

There are some implications for suicide prevention here. During the decision-making process, the individual's decision to commit suicide may be reversed if he or she is given more objective information through proper counseling.

An Impulse-Filtering Model of Suicide

McCain (1997) proposed one of the few models of suicide that is based not on rational choice but rather on free-will economic choice.[10] The basic idea is that human choice behavior arises from "the interaction of a stream of impulses with a system of filters."[11] According to McCain, impulses generated in the brain can be random or not. Not all impulses are unpredictable; for example, some occur as predictable consequences of physiological events. These impulses then have to pass through a variety of filters, which determine whether the impulse is acted upon, suppressed, or transformed.

Filters are unique to the individual, are dependent upon one's experiences, and change as one gets older. The relative activity of filters varies with different circumstances, and these can be influenced by one's state of arousal and mood. Important filters include the filter of incremental utility, the cognitive filter, the emotional filter (including phobias and obsessive behavior), the ethical filter, and the filter of social conformity.

Among these, the cognitive filter stands out in its uniqueness and importance. First, it has the power to transform the action of other filters. Second, it is time-variant. As a result, memory plays a role in the filtering system. Third, the cognitive inventory tends to become reorganized in order to be more consistent in its interactions with the filter of social conformity.

A basic notion in rational choice theory is that people list various alternatives and rank them in order of preference in the current situation. One then chooses the most preferred alternative. In impulse-filtering theory, on the other hand, several competing impulses start out on the process toward shaping actions. Some impulses are permitted through the filters, while others are blocked. The result is that one impulse determines behavior and, had it not done so, no alternative impulse would have done so (without the mediation of the cognitive filter).

For suicide, therefore, the impulse of suicide may be blocked by any one of the filters (ethical, cognitive, social conformity, etc.). The impulse may be allowed through only if one or more of the blocking filters is modified. It should be noted that the suicidal act may appear impulsive, but it is not always a result of the sudden appearance of an impulse. The impulse may have been present for a long time but blocked by a filter. It is the sudden removal of the filter that leads to the sudden appearance of the behavior.

How easily may these filters be modified? Lester (1990) suggested that some changes might be easier than others. For example, depression has important concomitants (such as hopelessness and a distorted worldview). These cognitive components may change the cognitive filter such that it overrides the ethical filter, permitting the suicidal impulse through. Another example of a cognitive filter being modified comes from Jacobs (1982), who has documented how religious people who have hitherto viewed suicide as a sin change their religious views when suicidal in order to convince themselves that God will forgive them for sinning by killing themselves.

On the other hand, some filters may not be easily modified. Clarke and Lester (1989) have argued that many people will not choose another method for suicide if their preferred method is not available. This reluctance to consider alternative methods for suicide suggests that this filter may be resistant to pressures from the cognitive filter.

Economic Approaches to Suicide Attempts

Suicide Attempts as a Means to Improve Future Utility

Marcotte's (2003) focus on suicide attempts was stimulated by data from the National Comorbidity Survey that provided information about mental illness and suicidal behavior for a sample of 5,877 Americans. In his lifetime utility-maximizing framework, Marcotte proposed how suicide attempters can affect their future utility in two ways. First, future health and maintenance costs may be higher if the suicide attempt results in physical injury and permanent disability. Second, the suicide attempt may be used as a means of improving future consumption via eliciting more attention and care for oneself.

Thus Marcotte surmised that there are expected gains and risks associated with suicide attempts. While the gains arise from "modifications to the utility function" due to the attempt, the risk is due to a shift in the "probability of realizing future consumption." Thus the suicide is attempted if "the subsequent effect on utility exceeds the attempter's distaste for the attempt itself and the associate risk" (Marcotte 2003, 630).

Marcotte's formulation leads to several predictions. First, people with a higher expected income will be less inclined to attempt suicide. This prediction is consistent with Hamermesh and Soss's model. Second, a more novel implication is that the propensity to attempt suicide increases if the expected utility can be improved, such as if the act elicits "sympathy or resources" from others. Thus Marcotte proposed that if suicide attempts are used as a mechanism to enhance future utility via consumption, then people who attempt suicide and survive should fare better (for example, earn a higher income) than counterparts who contemplated suicide but never made an attempt (Marcotte 2003, 633).

Suicide as Investment Under Uncertainty

Dixit and Pindyck (1994) examined the nature of investment under conditions of uncertainty. Although their book focused on the investment decisions of firms, they noted that other decisions are made with the same conditions as investments: the decision is irreversible, there is uncertainty over the future rewards of the decision, and there is some leeway over the timing of the decision.

Dixit and Pindyck suggested that suicide fits these criteria. They noted that Hamermesh and Soss (1974) had proposed that individuals will commit suicide when the expected value of the utility of the rest of their life falls short of some benchmark (or down to zero). Dixit and Pindyck argued that Hamermesh and Soss failed to consider the option of staying alive. Suicide is irreversible, and the future is quite uncertain. Therefore, the option of waiting to see if the situation improves should be a likely choice. Even if the expected direction of life is downward, there may still be some nonzero positive probability that it will improve. Because of this consideration, Dixit and Pindyck's approach seems to fit attempted suicide better than completed suicide.

Dixit and Pindyck speculated that suicides project the bleak present into an equally bleak future. They ignore the uncertainty of the future and the option value of life. In this respect, Dixit and Pindyck saw suicides as irrational. They noted that religious and moral proscriptions against suicide compensate to some extent for this failure of rationality. These proscriptions raise the perceived cost of suicide and lower the threshold of the quality of life that precipitates suicide.

Suicide Attempts as a Signaling Game

Rosenthal (1993) focused on suicide attempts that have a chance of survival, that is, suicide attempts of moderate severity where the individual is "gambling" with the outcome. He suggested that the suicide attempt can be seen as a credible signal intended to manipulate the behavior of the receiver (spouse, psychiatrist, etc.) in a way favorable to the sender. As such, it resembles a game, even though the individuals in this model have "classical von Neuman-Morgenstern preference and are not risk-lovers" (Rosenthal 1993, 26).

In this perspective, the sender may be either depressed or normal, and it is assumed that the players know the respective probabilities of these two possibilities. The sender knows his type, while the receiver does not. The sender chooses an attempt (signal) strength that determines whether he or she survives. The receiver then chooses a sympathetic or unsympathetic response. If he could distinguish the types perfectly, the receiver would prefer to respond sympathetically to a depressed sender and unsympathetically to a normal sender. From senders' perspective, they would prefer a sympathetic response, but the preference is stronger in the depressed sender.

The signaling game employed by Rosenthal was a refined version of the Nash equilibrium concept, for the original one often generates several Nash equilibria that are for the most part unreasonable ones (Rosenthal 1993, 273). By using the refined Nash equilibrium concept, Rosenthal was able to draw two conclusions. First, gambling-type suicidal behavior would be less common if the suicidal individual strongly desires a sympathetic response. Second, if the receiver is very likely to give a sympathetic response, then depressed senders are less likely to engage in gambling-type suicidal behavior.

Economic Models of Suicide Prevention

A Demand-and-Supply Analysis of Suicide and Suicide Prevention

By treating suicide as a service that we purchase in the "market," Yang and Lester (Yeh and Lester 1987; Lester and Yang 1997) developed a demand-and-supply analysis of suicide. They concluded that suicide is a behavior with an unstable equilibrium, so if there is an external intervention, suicide can be prevented.

From a demand-side perspective, when we purchase a product, the price we pay for the product reflects the marginal benefits we expect to receive from consuming that product. In the "purchase" of suicide, the notion of its "price" is different from the ordinary price of a commodity. The benefit expected by a suicide is the relief of tremendous distress. Accordingly, we must use a scale of distress to measure the benefit expected by the suicidal individual. This benefit expected by the suicidal individual is reflected in the price he must pay for his suicide.

Accordingly, the demand curve is a relationship presumably indicating the probability of committing suicide as a function of the amount of distress felt by the individual. As the amount of distress increases, the probability of committing suicide increases. The demand for suicide is, therefore, an upward-sloping curve, which is quite different from the typical downward-sloping demand curve found in most economic analyses.

On the supply side, the probability of committing suicide is related to the cost of committing suicide. The cost of committing suicide includes the cost of losing one's life, collecting information about how to commit the act, purchasing the means for suicide, and so on. While the latter two items have a clear-cut scale of measurement, the cost of losing life is much harder to measure. It includes at least three components, namely, the psychological fear of death, the loss of income in the future that otherwise would have been earned by the suicide, and the loss of any enjoyment that would be experienced during the rest of one's normal life.

The higher the cost of committing suicide, the lower the probability that an individual will actually kill himself. Therefore, the supply curve should be a downward-sloping curve rather than the regular upward-sloping shape expected for most products.

It is important in such a demand-supply analysis of suicide to convert the psychological variables (level of distress and future pleasure) into measures comparable to monetary units, so that an equilibrium can be obtained through equating the demand and supply for suicide. One way to measure the level of distress is to operationalize it as the cost of the psychological services required to eliminate the distress that the suicidal person is experiencing.[12]

Since both the "price" and the "cost" of committing suicide are plotted against the probability of committing suicide, the demand curve is an upward-sloping curve and becomes vertical when the probability of committing suicide is equal to 1. The price level for committing suicide that corresponds to the point where the probability is equal to 1 refers to the threshold level of distress that an individual can no longer tolerate. In this situation, committing suicide becomes inevitable. The supply curve of the suicide intersects with horizontal axis at zero cost with certainty (a probability of 1).

At equilibrium, committing suicide is determined by the intersection of the supply and demand curves. Due to the peculiar nature of the demand and supply of suicide, the equilibrium so obtained is not a stable one. That is to say, any slight chance that the suicidal individual deviates from equilibrium could result in movement away from equilibrium. However, there is one situation that is more interesting from the suicide prevention perspective.

If the probability of committing suicide is initially at a level slightly lower than the equilibrium probability, this corresponds to a low level of distress from the demand-side perspective and a high cost of committing suicide from the supply-side perspective. As a result, the situation will lead to an even lower probability of committing suicide, and the individual will eventually withdraw from the suicidal situation.

Therefore, this demand-and-supply analysis of suicide implies that there is the opportunity for crisis intervention to be successful. Technically, this means shifting either the demand or the supply curve to the left or a combination of both. It turns out it is much easier to work on the supply-side factor.

Yeh and Lester examined some of the factors that contribute to the decision to commit suicide based on a review of the research on suicide by Lester (1983). They noted that most of the factors, such as psychiatric disturbance, gender, age, and dysfunctional family of origin, are reasonably stable characteristics. Thus, once the demand curve is formed, it will remain quite stable over time. Sudden shifts in the demand curve might be caused by events such as the sudden deaths of significant others, illness, or work difficulties, but the extent of the shifts may be quite limited.

Help-Seeking Incentives to Suicide Prevention

Suicide prevention is the primal goal of public health policy regarding suicide. There are four strategies to prevent suicide: (1) long-term treatment of individuals via medication (Roy 2001) or psychotherapy (Ellis 2001), (2) crisis intervention (Mishara and Daigle 2001), (3) restricting access to lethal methods (Clarke and Lester 1989), and (4) school education programs (Leenaars 2001). Each strategy competes for the society's resources in achieving the same goal.

The game-theoretical approach developed by Yaniv (2001) focuses on crisis intervention. In Yaniv's game-setting model, the suicide attempter (patient), contemplating the two outcomes (committing suicide or seeking last-minute help), interacts with a mental health practitioner (therapist) deciding between two options for preventing suicide (providing ambulatory crisis-intervention therapy or protective hospitalization). Yaniv made certain assumptions about the behavioral characteristics of the two players. When seeking last-minute help, suicide attempters may fear being hospitalized, while the mental health practitioner is a "cost-oriented social welfare agent" and may choose the less costly ambulatory crisis therapy over hospitalization. Thus the suicide attempter faces the risk of involuntary hospitalization, and the practitioner encounters the risk of the resulting suicide. Ultimately, the practitioner bases his decision on the likelihood of a genuine suicide threat in order to "minimize society's expected loss from suicide and suicide-prevention efforts" (Yaniv 2001, 464).

Yaniv derived two results from his model. First, if the hospitalization decision is exogenous to the patient's problem, then involuntary hospitalization constitutes an effective deterrent to seeking help by the suicide attempters. Second, when the model allows for therapist-patient interaction, the "disincentive role of the hospitalization subsides"(Yaniv 2001, 463). In other words, because either the ambulatory crisis therapy is highly successful or the fraction of genuinely suicidal patients and strategic therapists in the "market" is relatively small, the threat of involuntary hospitalization would cease to become an effective deterrent to seeking help. In addition, the patient becomes more inclined to ask for help when the probability of therapy success increases even though the therapist's tendency to hospitalize rises.

Some plausible suggestions for public policy to prevent suicide include measures geared toward successful therapy and increasing public awareness about it, plus measures to reduce the fear of hospitalization. Even though restricting the power of therapists may help ease the fear of hospitalization, legally enforcing it seems counterproductive in the practice of preventing suicide, especially considering that the condition of the patient may call for hospitalization. It might be against the ethical code of conduct on the part of therapists not to hospitalize an acutely suicidal patient.

Becker on Irrationality

Economists define rational behavior as maximizing some variable such as utility or profit. Irrational behaviors are the rare find among the subjects analyzed by economists. Becker (1962) defined two types of irrational behavior: random, erratic, and whimsical choices, and perseverative choices in which the person chooses what he or she has always chosen in the past. Lester and Yang (1991b) argued that these two types of irrational behavior parallel the major typology of suicidal behavior, in which suicidal behavior is seen as a time-limited impulsive crisis or as a chronic maladaptive pattern.

The vast empirical literature on suicide from the past hundred years has been reviewed by Lester (2000). The research most pertinent to the behavioral economics of suicide concerns the cognition of suicidal individuals—is the thinking rational or irrational? The thinking among those who survive attempts at suicide clearly has shown several distinctive features compared to that of nonsuicidal individuals. Suicide attempters tend to be rigid in their thinking, to think dichotomously (that is, in black-and-white terms, with polarized views of themselves, life, and death), and to be pessimistic and hopeless about the future (Hughes and Neimeyer 1990). These are the types of cognition that cognitive therapists label as irrational (Burns 1981). Thus cognitive therapists try to get their clients to monitor and challenge these irrational thoughts regularly and convert them to more rational thoughts.

It should be noted that irrational thinking differs from illogical reasoning. Thinking irrationally does not imply an inability to reason logically. Research has found no evidence that suicidal individuals have deficits in their ability to reason logically (Lester 2003). One component of irrational thinking concerns the validity of the premises (or assumptions) that individuals use in their reasoning, and there is a debate over whether the premises of suicidal individuals are rational. For example, if an individual who has been fired from a job says, "I will never be successful in my career," it can be argued that there is no evidence for that premise. The word *never* is too extreme. On the other hand, if an individual says, "My physical [or mental] pain is too great for me to tolerate," there is no evidence to refute such a premise because pain is subjective. Lester (2003) argued, therefore, that the decision to commit suicide can be rational, and he provided guidelines for individuals making such a decision.

CONCLUSION

There are several reasons why economic models will be useful in understanding suicide and in preventing suicide. First, suicide is a matter of choice. Second, suicidal behavior clearly incurs economic costs. Third, the economy has an impact on suicidal behavior, with economic downturns increasing the risk of suicidal behavior, at least in the wealthiest nations. Other economic factors, such as real income per capita, poverty, and income distribution, are also associated with the suicide rate.[13]

Fourth, established public policies have both positive and negative impacts on the social and economic environment that are related to the suicide rate. For instance, economic policies, including automatic stabilizers such as unemployment compensation and discretionary fiscal or monetary policies that are used to fine-tune the business cycle by lowering the unemployment rate, indirectly mitigate the hostile environment conducive to suicide. Early retirement programs, social security, or pension systems and disability programs that allow elderly workers to enjoy early retirement may help increase the well-being of the elderly, thereby reducing the detrimental factors that might trigger their suicidal behavior. Thus, when the financial crisis in the social security program due to the smaller number of workers supporting a larger generation of aging and elderly arrives, the problem might be solved by postponing the retirement age and reducing benefits. The detrimental impact of these changes in policy on the elderly should be reflected in their suicide rate.

Other public policies that have been documented that inadvertently create a fertile environment for suicide include the stipulation of restricting the presence of adult males in households in order to receive welfare assistance. This stipulation, which removed fathers and father figures from the home, was cited as one of many factors associated with the rising suicide rate among African American youth.

There are two further issues related to public policy. By understanding the motivation behind suicidal behavior, some suggestions can be made for policies that prevent suicide. For example, after illustrating how fear is behind the hesitation of suicide attempters asking for help at the last minute, Yaniv (2001) was able to offer suggestions for preventing suicide. The other issue concerns the enactment of public policy in that the social costs of any economic policy should be taken explicitly into account (Yang and Lester 1995; Lester and Yang 2003), be they positive or negative, so that there will be no unexpected impact on the community either at large or on certain segments of the population, as in the case of the restricting welfare policy on young African Americans.

This chapter has focused on economic analyses or models of suicide that have been developed since the 1970s. These include those based on the rational choice model and behavioral models, and they have addressed completed suicide, attempted suicide, and suicide prevention. Those models based on the rational choice model have limitations. They do not incorporate the interactions between the suicidal individuals and their families or the other actors in their life who are crucial to their decision of committing suicide, such as their therapists. The two behavioral models that used a game-theoretical approach do endogenize the interaction due to the nature of the approach—the game entails two players.

This suggests areas to which future research by economists may contribute. Suicide does not occur in a vacuum; it is the result of lifelong experiences, including interactions with other people. Therefore, social factors and social behavior should be a part of the unified model that captures the multifactorial nature of suicide. This is where sociology (which studies social networks, society, and culture) can come into play. The concept of social capital developed by Becker (1996) may be a good start for models based on rational choice. Another concept developed by sociologists that may be relevant to modern society and conducive to suicidal behavior is anomie. Anomie, according to Bulmahn (2000, 375), may be defined as a distinctive structural feature of modern societies whose destructive consequences are manifested by "growing alienation, increasing social isolation and rising suicidality." It would be interesting to conceptualize an economic model of suicide that captures the essence of anomie, which reflects the dark side of economic progress and development and can be destructive for some human beings.

Second, in pursuit of this multifactorial economic model, it would be useful to incorporate disciplines such as psychology. For instance, Mathur and Freeman (2002) developed an economic model of parental behavior based on the traditional utilitarian framework that incorporates a home production function of mental health as a way to explain how parents' employment might affect the mental health of their offspring. It is a fine model that is one of the first to incorporate the parent-offspring interaction, but unfortunately for our purposes it does not have great relevance for suicide. Since official data for youths are not available, we will use adult data as an illustration. According to results from the National Comorbidity Survey, 19.3 percent of the population has an affective disorder (depression) at some point in their life (Kessler et al. 1994). Among those depressed individuals, up to 15 percent eventually commit suicide (Achte 1986). If we use these two statistics, the link between depression and suicide will impact less than 1 percent of the total population. Thus, Mathur and Freeman's model is not adequate as a model of suicide, contrary to their assertion.

While rational choice models might incorporate social interactions into the framework, there are other behavioral dimensions that can be added. For instance, the notion of bounded rationality may have some relevance to the decision to commit suicide. If suicidal individuals are keenly aware of the possibility of disfigurement and permanent disability should the suicide attempt fail, would this affect their decision? Why does the fear of death not play a role in suicide while the loathing of life does? In other words, there are many emotions and desires that should be explored in explaining suicidal behavior, avenues that may enrich the behavioral economic approach to the study of suicide in the future.

NOTES

1. The suicides rates were 44.1 per 100,000 per year in Lithuania in 2000, 39.4 in Russia, and 34.9 in Belarus.

2. The discussion of epidemiological issues on suicides can be found in Maris, Berman, and Silverman 2000.

3. It should be noted that only three primary disciplines are referred to here in the study of suicide. Other disciplines, such as physiology, ethics, philosophy, and law, are important and are discussed in Maris, Berman, and Silverman 2000.

4. Studies have found a higher-than-average suicide rate among the poorest in the population. However, in his classic study, Durkheim (1951) argued that poverty protects people against suicide, while wealth makes people inclined to commit suicide because the rich believe that they have to depend on themselves alone (Ruzicka 1995, 96).

5. Palmer and colleagues (1995) reported three different measures of the impact of suicide: lives lost, years of life expectancy lost (YLL), and years of productive life lost (YPLL, defined as the expected number of years of life lost up to the age of 65). They provide data for the costs of suicide for 1980. Another indirect cost of suicide that is rarely taken into account in the scholarly literature is the lost production of survivors and their medical costs due to grieving. Survivors are family members and friends of a loved one who died from suicide. According to McIntosh (2003), every suicide is estimated to affect intimately at least six other people. Based on the roughly 742,000 suicides in the United States from 1977 through 2001, the total number of survivors is estimated to be 4.45 million. It might not be easy to estimate the economic cost incurred by the grieving process of these survivors, but the amount may be significant.

6. According to Gunnell and colleagues (2003, 608), there are general risk factors for suicide that underlie the recent rise of youth suicide, such as increases in unemployment, divorce (of their parents), and substance abuse. Some of these factors might act as "markers for more profound changes in the fabric of society that are affecting young people." For instance, Whitley and colleagues (1999) reported that the greatest rises in youth suicide occurred in the areas of Britain that had experienced the greatest increases in social fragmentation. While social fragmentation was also cited by Willis and colleagues (2002) as one factor making individuals more vulnerable to suicide, they claimed that "economic strain, the burgeoning drug trade and subsequent gun availability" (913) all have an impact on the suicide rates of African-American adolescents.

7. According to Taylor (2003), Japan and the United States are among the exceptions.

8. The other factors that Gunnell and colleagues (2003) found to be associated with elderly suicide in England and Wales include an increase in GDP and inadequate antidepressant prescribing.

9. The mathematical model for the business cycle theory of suicide can be found in Lester and Yang (1997) and Lester (2001). This model provides the theoretical foundation for a series of empirical studies that the authors have published in the field of suicidology, some of which are included in Lester and Yang (1997). The model establishes the basis for the inclusion of economic variables along with social variables in empirical studies of the suicide rate. One interesting finding from the reformation is the possibility of a natural rate of suicide, that is, the existence of a nonzero, positive suicide rate under normal economic conditions. We found that the natural rate of suicide in the United States based on 1980 and 1990 census data is about 6 per 100,000 people. Other researchers (e.g., Kunce and Anderson 2001–2) tested this hypothesis with various economic techniques and estimated that the natural rate of suicide was lower than 6 but still positive.

10. A detailed discussion of this idea can be found in McCain (1990).

11. McCain defined filters uniquely for his own analysis. A filter in cognitive psychology is typically defined as the selecting of some sensory experiences from a large set. For a discussion see, for example, Jahnke and Nowaczyk (1998).

12. This is complicated by the fact that mental health services are not always effective. Some people do not benefit from treatment. This could be taken into account by incorporating the probability of success of the treatment into the calculations as a multiplier of the cost of treatment. Converting future pleasure from life into monetary units is more difficult. One alternative could be to convert all of the components of the cost into subjective units, based on the ratings given by representative members of society.

13. There are numerous empirical studies that have documented the association between the suicide rate and these economic factors. Interestingly enough, one recent econometric study used fixed effect estimations to challenge the significance of socioeconomic factors (Kunce and Anderson 2002), while Neumayer (2003) refuted the association with empirical findings from both fixed and random effect estimations.

REFERENCES

Achte, K. 1986. "Depression and Suicide." *Psychopathology* 19, supp. 2: 210–14.
Al-Ansari, Ahmed M., Randah R. Hamadeh, Ali M. Matar, Huda Marhoon, Bana Y. Buzaboon, and Ahmed G. Raees. 2001. "Risk Factors Associated with Overdose Among Bahraini Youth." *Suicide and Life-Threatening Behavior* 31, 2: 197–206.

Becker, Gary S. 1960 "An Economic Analysis of Fertility." In Universities-National Bureau Committee for Economic Research, *Demographic and Economic Change in Developed Countries.* Princeton, NJ: Princeton University Press.
———. 1962. "Irrational Behavior and Economic Theory." *Journal of Political Economy* 70: 1–13.
———. 1968. "Crime and Punishment: An Economic Approach." *Journal of Political Economy* 76: 169–217.
———. 1976. *The Economic Approach to Human Behavior,* vol. 3. Chicago: University of Chicago Press.
———. 1996. *Accounting for Tastes.* Cambridge, MA: Harvard University Press.
Becker, Gary S., and Kevin Murphy. 1988. "A Theory of Rational Addiction." *Journal of Political Economy* 96: 675–700.
Birckmayer, Johanna, and David Hemenway. 2001. "Suicide and Firearm Prevalence: Are Youth Disproportionately Affected?" *Suicide and Life-Threatening Behavior* 31, 3: 303–10.
Bourdieu, P., and James S. Coleman. 1991. *Social Theory for a Changing Society.* New York: Russell Sage Foundation.
Brainerd, Elizabeth. 2001. "Economic Reform and Mortality in the Former Soviet Union: A Study of the Suicide Epidemic in the 1990s." *European Economic Review* 45: 1007–19.
Bulmahn, Thomas. 2000. "Modernity and Happiness: The Case of Germany." *Journal of Happiness Studies* 1: 375–400.
Burns, D. 1981. *Feeling Good.* New York: Signet.
Christoffersen, M.N., H.D. Poulsen, and A. Nielsen. 2003. "Attempted Suicide Among Young People: Risk Factors in a Prospective Register Based Study of Danish Children Born in 1966." *Acta Psychiatrica Scandinavica* 108: 350–58.
Clarke, Ronald V., and David Lester. 1989. *Suicide: Closing the Exits.* New York: Springer-Verlag.
Coleman, James, S. 1990. *Foundations of Social Theory.* Cambridge, MA: Harvard University Press.
Coleman, James, S., and T.J. Fararo. 1991. *Rational Choice Theory.* Newbury Park, CA: Sage.
Congdon, Peter. 1996. "Suicide and Parasuicide in London: A Small-Area Study." *Urban Studies* 33, 1: 137–58.
Crawford, M.J., and M. Prince. 1999. "Increasing Rates of Suicide in Young Men in England During the 1980s: The Importance of Social Context." *Social Science and Medicine* 49: 1419–23.
Crouch, R. 1979. *Human Behavior.* North Scituate, MA: Duxbury.
Dixit, A.K., and R.S. Pindyck. 1994. *Investment Under Uncertainty.* Princeton, NJ: Princeton University Press.
Durkheim, Emil. 1951. *Suicide: A Study in Sociology,* trans. J.A. Spaulding and G. Simpson. New York: Free Press.
Eckersley, Richard, and Keith Dear. 2002. "Cultural Correlates of Youth Suicide." *Social Science and Medicine* 55: 1891–904.
Ellis, Thomas. 2001. "Psychotherapy with Suicide Patients." In David Lester, ed., *Suicide Prevention: Resources for the Millennium,* 129–51. Philadelphia: Brunner-Routledge.
Fedden, H.S. 1938. *Suicide: A Social and Historical Study.* London: Peter Davies.
Freeman, Donald G. 1998. "Determinants of Youth Suicide: The Easterlin-Hollinger Cohort Hypothesis Reexamined." *American Journal of Economics and Sociology* 57: 183–99.
Gerdtham, Ulf-G., and Magnus Johannesson. 2003. "A Note on the Effect of Unemployment on Mortality." *Journal of Health Economics* 22: 505–18.
Gunnell, David, Nicos Middleton, Elise Whitley, Daniel Dorling, and Stephen Frankel. 2003. "Why Are Suicide Rates Rising in Young Men but Falling in the Elderly?—A Time-Series Analysis of Trends in England and Wales 1950–1998." *Social Science and Medicine* 57: 596–611.
Hamermesh, D.S., and N.M. Soss. 1974. "An Economic Theory of Suicide." *Journal of Political Economy* 82: 83–98.
Hicks, John. 1979. *Causality in Economics.* New York: Basic Books.
Huang, Wei-Chiao. 1997. "'Life Force' Participation Perspective of Suicide." In David Lester and Bijou Yang, eds., *The Economy and Suicide: Economic Perspectives on Suicide,* 81–89. Commack, NY: Nova Science.
Hughes, S.L., and R.A. Neimeyer. 1990. "A Cognitive Model of Suicidal Behavior." In D. Lester, ed., *Current Concepts of Suicide,* 1–28. Philadelphia: Charles Press.
Jacobs, J. 1982. *The Moral Justification of Suicide.* Springfield, IL: Charles Thomas.
Jahnke, John C., and Ronald H. Nowaczyk. 1998. *Cognition.* Upper Saddle River, NJ: Prentice Hall.
Jungeilges, Jochen, and Gebhard Kirchgassner. 2002. "Economic Welfare, Civil Liberty, and Suicide: An Empirical Investigation." *Journal of Socio-Economics* 31: 215–31.

Kessler, Ronald C., Katherine A. McGonagle, Shanyang Zhao, Christopher B. Nelson, Michael Hughes, Suzann Eshleman, Hans-Ulrich Wittchen, and Kenneth S. Kendler. 1994. "Lifetime and 12-Month Prevalence of DSM-III-R Psychiatric Disorders in the United States: Results from the National Comorbidity Survey." *Archives of General Psychiatry* 51: 8–19.

Kunce, Mitch, and April L. Anderson. 2001–2. "A Natural Rate of Suicide for the U.S., Revisited." *Omega* 44: 215–22.

———. 2002. "The Impact of Socioeconomic Factors on State Suicide Rates: A Methodological Note." *Urban Studies* 39, 1: 155–62.

Leenaars, Antoon A. 2001. "Suicide Prevention in Schools: Resources for the Millennium." In David Lester, ed., *Suicide Prevention: Resources for the Millennium,* 213–35. Philadelphia: Brunner-Routledge.

Leenaars, Antoon A., Bijou Yang, and David Lester. 1993. "The Effect of Domestic and Economic Stress on Suicide Rates in Canada and the United States." *Journal of Clinical Psychology* 49: 918–21.

Lester, Bijou Yang. 2001. "Learnings from Durkheim and Beyond." *Suicide and Life-Threatening-Behavior* 31: 15–31.

Lester, David. 1983. *Why People Kill Themselves.* Springfield, IL: Charles Thomas.

———. 1988. *Suicide from a Psychological Perspective.* Springfield, IL: Charles Thomas.

———. 1989. *Suicide from a Sociological Perspective.* Springfield, IL: Charles Thomas.

———. 1990. "An Economic Theory of Choice and Its Implications for Suicide." *Psychological Reports* 66: 1112–4.

———. 1991. *Psychotherapy for Suicide Clients.* Springfield, IL: Charles Thomas.

———. 2000. *Why People Kill Themselves,* 4th ed. Springfield, IL: Charles Thomas.

———. 2003. *Fixin' to Die.* Amityville, NY: Baywood.

Lester, David, Peter S. Curran, and Bijou Yang. 1991. "Time Series Regression Results of Suicide Rates by Social Correlates for the USA and Northern Ireland." *Irish Journal of Psychological Medicine* 8: 26–28.

Lester, David, Pricilla Wood, Christopher Williams, and Janet Haines. 2004. "Motives for Suicide: A Study of Australian Suicide Notes." *Crisis* 25: 33–34.

Lester, David, and Bijou Yang. 1991a. "The Relationship Between Divorce, Unemployment and Female Participation in the Labor Force and Suicide Rates in Australia and America." *Australian and New Zealand Journal of Psychiatry* 25: 519–23.

———. 1991b. "Suicidal Behavior and Becker's Definition of Irrationality." *Psychological Reports* 68: 655–56.

———, eds. 1997. *The Economy and Suicide: Economic Perspectives on Suicide.* Commack, NY: Nova Science.

———. 2003. "Unemployment and Suicidal Behavior: The Role of Economic Policy." *Journal of Epidemiology and Community Health* 57: 558–59.

Marcotte, Dave E. 2003. "The Economics of Suicide, Revisited." *Southern Economic Journal* 69: 628–43.

Maris, Ronald W., Alan L. Berman, and Morton M. Silverman. 2000. *Comprehensive Textbook of Suicidology.* New York: Guilford.

Mathur, Vijay K., and Donald G. Freeman. 2002. "A Theoretical Model of Adolescent Suicide and Some Evidence from U.S. Data." *Health Economics* 11: 695–708.

McCain, Roger A. 1990. "Impulse-Filtering: A New Model of Freely Willed Economic Choice." *Review of Social Economy* 48: 125–71.

———. 1997. "Impulse-Filtering and Regression Models of the Determination of the Rate of Suicide." In David Lester and Bijou Yang, eds., *The Economy and Suicide: Economic Perspectives on Suicide,* 67–80. Commack, NY: Nova Science.

McIntosh, John L. 2003. "Fact Sheet." American Association of Suicidology, http://www.suicidology.org. September 26.

Micklewright, John, and Kitty Stewart. 1999. "Is the Well-Being of Children Converging in the European Union?" *Economic Journal* 109: F692–F714.

Middleton, Nicos, David Gunnell, Stephen Frankel, Elise Whitley, and Daniel Dorling. 2003. "Urban-Rural Difference in Suicide Trends in Youth Adults: England and Wales, 1981–1998." *Social Science and Medicine* 57: 1183–94.

Mishara, Brian, and Marc Daigle. 2001. "Helplines and Crisis Interventions Services: Challenges for the Future." In David Lester, ed., *Suicide Prevention: Resources for the Millennium,* 153–71. Philadelphia: Brunner-Routledge.

Neumayer, Eric. 2003. "Socioeconomic Factors and Suicide Rates at Large-Unit Aggregate Levels: A Comment." *Urban Studies* 40: 2769–76.

Palmer, C.S., D.A. Revicki, M.T. Halpern, and E.J. Hatziandreu. 1995. "The Cost of Suicide and Suicide Attempts in the United States." *Clinical Neuropharmacology* 18, supp. 3: S25–S33.
Platt, Stephen D. 1984. "Unemployment and Suicidal Behavior." *Social Science and Medicine* 19: 93–115.
———. 1986. "Parasuicide and Unemployment." *British Journal of Psychiatry* 149: 401–5.
Platt, Stephen, Rocco Micciolo, and Michele Tansella. 1992. "Suicide and Unemployment in Italy: Description, Analysis and Interpretation of Recent Trends." *Social Science and Medicine* 34: 1191–201.
Pritchard, Collin.1988. "Suicide, Unemployment and Gender in the British Isles and European Economic Community (1974–1985)." *Social Psychiatry and Psychiatric Epidemiology* 23: 85–89.
Rosenthal, Robert W. 1993. "Suicide Attempts and Signalling Games." *Mathematical Social Sciences* 26: 25–33.
Roy, Alec. 2001. "Psychiatric Treatment in Suicide Prevention." In David Lester, ed., *Suicide Prevention: Resources for the Millennium,* 103–27. Philadelphia: Brunner-Routledge.
Ruzicka, Lado T. 1995. "Suicide Mortality in Developed Countries." In Alan D. Lopez, Graziella Caselli, and Tapani Valkonen, eds., *Adult Mortality in Developed Countries: From Description to Explanation,* 85–110. Oxford: Clarendon Press.
Shneidman, Edwin S. 1985. *Definition of Suicide.* New York: Wiley.
Shneidman, Edwin S., and Norman Farberow. 1957. *Clues to Suicide.* New York: McGraw-Hill.
Stack, Steven. 1990. "The Effect of Divorce on Suicide in Denmark, 1951–1980." *Sociological Quarterly* 31: 359–70.
Taylor, Philip. 2003. "Age, Labor Market Conditions and Male Suicide Rates in Selected Countries." *Aging and Society* 23: 25–40.
Volkonen, T., and T. Martelin. 1988. "Occupational Class and Suicide: An Example of the Elaboration of a Relationship." Research report no. 222, Department of Sociology, University of Helsinki.
Whitley, Elise, David Gunnel, Daniel Dorling, Nicos Middleton, and Stephen Frankel. 1999. "Ecological Study of Social Fragmentation, Poverty, and Suicide." *British Medical Journal* 319: 1034–37.
Willis, Leigh A., David W. Coombs, William C. Cockerham, and Sonja L. Frison. 2002. "Ready to Die: A Postmodern Interpretation of the Increase of African-American Adolescent Male Suicide." *Social Science and Medicine* 55: 907–20.
Yang, Bijou, and David Lester. 1995. "New Directions for Economics." *Journal of Socio-Economics* 24: 433–46.
Yaniv, Gideon. 2001. "Suicide Intention and Suicide Prevention: An Economic Perspective." *Journal of Socio-Economics* 30: 453–68.
Yeh, Bijou Y., and David Lester. 1987. "An Economic Model for Suicide." In David Lester, ed., *Suicide as a Learned Behavior,* 51–57. Springfield, IL: Charles Thomas.

CHAPTER 28

RATIONAL HEALTH-COMPROMISING BEHAVIOR AND ECONOMIC INTERVENTION

GIDEON YANIV

Health-compromising (HC) behaviors are behaviors practiced by people that undermine or harm their current or future health (Taylor 1995, ch. 6). Alcohol consumption, smoking, and use of psychoactive substances, all of which bear potential for dependency and addiction, are the most important HC behaviors, accounting for hundreds of thousands of deaths annually and billions of dollars in economic loss and treatment costs. Yet the range of HC behaviors is much wider, involving junk food consumption, excessive eating, insufficient sleep, driving at excessive speed, engaging in unsafe sex, lying in the sun on the beach, chatting on a cellular phone, delaying medical care, not adhering to doctors' orders, or attempting suicide. Although HC behaviors are traditionally considered to lie within the domain of psychologists, they have recently attracted the interest of economists, who have applied optimization techniques to show that HC behavior may be consistent with rational behavior, that is, that people may rationally choose to engage in activities that are harmful to their health. While psychologists stress treatment and reeducation as means of achieving behavioral changes, economists emphasize the role of incentives.

This essay surveys the growing economic literature on HC behaviors, highlighting the insights gained by economists with regard to their determinants and to possible economic interventions. The essay focuses on theoretical contributions only, placing special emphasis on the modeling of rational addiction, which has gained most of the attention in the literature. Other topics include rational harmful (excessive or cholesterol-rich) nonaddictive eating, rational engagement in unsafe sexual activity, rational delay in seeking medical diagnosis, and rational mental disorders (agoraphobia and insomnia). Because this handbook includes an essay on the economics of suicide (see Yang and Lester, this volume), the present survey abstains from reviewing this subject.

RATIONAL HARMFUL ADDICTION

Addiction to harmful goods such as drugs, tobacco, caffeine, or alcohol is undoubtedly the most researched topic of rational HC behavior. A review of EconLit reveals more than a hundred articles and a number of volumes on the subject. The seminal and most influential paper in this area is Becker and Murphy (1988), although related contributions had already appeared earlier or at the same time (e.g., Becker and Stigler 1977; Winston 1980; Iannaccone 1986; Michaels 1988; Lee 1988; Barthold and Hochman 1988; Leonard 1989). Most of the literature that followed has been devoted to empirical testing of the major theoretical prediction of Becker and Murphy's model, which is that even addicts negatively respond to a change in price (e.g., Chaloupka 1991; Becker, Grossman, and Murphy 1994; Waters and Sloan 1995; Olekalns and Bardsley 1996;

Grossman and Chaloupka 1998; Keeler 1999; Baltagi and Griffin 2002). Several contributions have interpreted, enriched, or offered simplified versions of the model (e.g., Becker, Grossman, and Murphy 1991; Orphanides and Zervos 1995; Skog 1999; Ferguson 2000; Gruber and Koszegi 2001), whereas others have suggested different theoretical approaches that highlight different aspects of addictive behavior (e.g., Frank 1996; Guth and Kliemt 1996; Suranovic, Goldfarb, and Leonard 1999; Jones 1999; Cameron 2000; Yuengert 2001; Boymal 2003).

This section reviews the two major approaches to modeling rational addiction in the economic literature: the reinforcement approach (introduced by Becker and Murphy 1988), which views the stimulating effect that past consumption has on current consumption as the key feature of addiction, and the withdrawal cost approach (introduced by Suranovic, Goldfarb, and Leonard 1999), which views as the key feature the discomforts and psychic effects experienced by addicts when attempting to reduce their addiction or quit altogether. Both approaches perceive addiction as the outcome of consumer choice. Both define addiction as rational if it involves forward-looking maximization (with stable preferences), that is, if in deciding on addictive consumption, a utility-maximizing consumer also considers the harmful consequences that current behavior might have on his or her future health (e.g., liver damage, lung cancer). Both seek to explain not just how addiction is initiated and sustained but also how it eventually ends.

The Reinforcement Approach

Becker and Murphy consider a consumer whose instantaneous utility function at time t is strictly concave with respect to three arguments:

$$U(t) = U[x(t), c(t), S(t)] \tag{1}$$

where $x(t)$ is the consumption of the (potentially) addictive good at time t, $c(t)$ is the consumption of a nonaddictive (composite) good, and $S(t)$ is the stock of "addictive capital," built up as a result of past consumption of the addictive good. The marginal utilities of x and c are assumed to be positive (i.e., $U_x > 0$ and $U_c > 0$), but the marginal utility of S is negative (i.e., $U_S < 0$), implying that greater past consumption of the addictive good lowers current utility. Becker and Murphy argue that this assumption captures the "tolerance" aspect of addiction, which means that given levels of current consumption are less satisfying the greater the level of past consumption. However, the negative impact of S on current utility may also reflect the recognition that addiction is harmful to the consumer's health.[1] The motion equation for addictive capital is

$$\dot{S}(t) = x(t) - \delta S(t) \tag{2}$$

where $\dot{S}(t)$ denotes the change in S at time t and δ is an instantaneous depreciation rate which measures the exogenous rate of disappearance of the mental and physical effects of past consumption. That is, the change in the capital stock at time t is the difference between current consumption and the exogenous depreciation on past consumption. Becker and Murphy also allow for expenditure on endogenous depreciation to reduce the stock of capital, which, for simplicity, is ignored here.

But addiction is not merely the accumulation of a harmful capital. Becker and Murphy's perception of addiction also involves the notion of "reinforcement," which means that greater past consumption increases the desire for current consumption. A necessary prerequisite for this behavior is that an increase in past consumption raises the marginal utility of current consumption (i.e. $U_{xS} > 0$). While this assumption is sufficient for reinforcing the current consumption of a myopic consumer, it is insufficient for doing so in the case of a *rational* consumer, who must also consider the future harmful consequences of his or her current behavior. For him or her, reinforcement requires that the positive effect of an increase in S on the marginal utility of x exceed the negative effect of greater x on future utility. Becker and Murphy seek conditions for the fulfillment of this requirement, which implies that even a rational consumer may become addicted.

Assuming a time-additive utility function, an infinite lifetime, and a constant rate of time preference, σ, the consumer is now allowed to maximize his or her lifetime utility function

$$V(0) = \int_0^\infty e^{-\sigma t} U[x(t),\ c(t),\ S(t)]dt \tag{3}$$

subject to the motion equation for addictive capital (equation 2) and the budget constraint (assuming perfect capital markets)

$$\int_0^\infty e^{-rt} [c(t) + p_x(t)x(t)]dt = Z(0) \tag{4}$$

where $c(t)$ is the numeraire with a constant price over time, $p_x(t)$ is the price of the addictive good at time t, r is a constant-over-time interest rate, and $Z(0)$ is the discounted value of the consumer's lifetime income and assets. Becker and Murphy assume that future earnings (which are part of Z) are negatively dependent on S, but this assumption has no qualitative implications in the model (it just gives rise to an additional adverse effect of current consumption on future well-being) and is therefore ignored here. Maximizing lifetime utility with respect to $x(t)$ and $c(t)$ yields the optimum conditions

$$U_x(t) = \mu p_x(t)e^{(\sigma - r)t} - \int_t^\infty e^{-(\sigma + \delta)(k - t)} U_S(k)dk = \Pi_x(t) \tag{5}$$

$$U_c(t) = \mu e^{(\sigma - r)t} \tag{6}$$

where μ is a Lagrange multiplier for the budget constraint (interpreted as the marginal utility of wealth). The term $\Pi_x(t)$ is the full price of the addictive good, consisting of two components: the market price of the good and the (discounted) future utility cost of consuming an additional unit of the good incurred due to the resulting increase in the addictive stock. Because $U_S(t)$ is negative, the full price of the addictive good is greater than its market price. Hence, a rational utility maximizer will consume less of the addictive good than he or she would if he or she were a myopic consumer who ignores the future consequences of his or her current behavior. As intuitively expected, the greater the rate of preference for the present (σ) or the depreciation rate on past consumption (δ), the lower the full price of the addictive good and the greater its consumption.

It is easily seen from optimum condition 5 that if addictive capital rises over time, reinforcement emerges only if the marginal utility of the addictive good rises more than its full price. Becker and Murphy now use a quadratic utility function (in x and S) to further investigate this requirement, showing (under the assumption of $\sigma = r$) that a necessary and sufficient condition for reinforcement is

$$(\sigma + 2\delta)U_{xS} > -U_{SS} \tag{7}$$

If condition 7 is satisfied, the consumer is said to be *potentially* addicted. This is so because actually becoming addicted requires a mechanism that triggers an increase in S. Clearly, $U_{xS} > 0$ is necessary to satisfy condition 7 if tolerance increases with S (i.e., if $U_{SS} < 0$). It also follows from condition 7 that the consumer is more likely to become potentially addicted the more heavily he or she discounts the future (i.e., has a higher σ) or the more rapidly addictive capital depreciates (i.e., has a larger δ). This is so because in the former case he or she is paying less attention to the future consequences of current behavior, whereas in the latter case current behavior has a smaller effect on the future.

Reinforcement implies that over time x varies in the same direction as S. However, the motion equation for addictive capital (equation 2) reveals that S may also remain steady over time. This will happen if $\dot{S} = 0$, or if current consumption of the addictive good, $x(t)$, equals the depreciation of past consumption, $\delta S(t)$. In this case, known as a steady (or a stationary) state, current consumption will remain constant as well. Figure 28.1 depicts the stationary locus of x and S (i.e., all combinations of x and S satisfying $x = \delta S$) as a straight line from the origin (with slope δ). Figure 28.1 also depicts the demand for current consumption (derived from the optimum conditions 5–6) as a function of addictive capital for a potentially addicted consumer with a cubic utility function (curve D_x^0). An intersection between the D_x^0 curve and the stationary locus reflects a steady-state choice, which may be stable or not. A quadratic utility function, under which condition 7 has been derived, would yield a linear demand curve that could only result in a single steady state. But Becker and Murphy use the quadratic utility function only as an approximation (near a steady state) to a higher-order utility function, such as the cubic utility function. The latter can be shown to generate a demand curve with decreasing marginal rates and consequently to produce two steady states, one stable (point a) and one unstable (point b).

Figure 28.1 may now be used to illustrate that whether or not a potentially addicted consumer actually becomes addicted depends on his or her initial stock of addictive capital and the position of his or her demand curve. Given the demand curve D_x^0, suppose first that the addictive stock is below S_b. Current consumption will then lie below the stationary line ($x = \delta S$), implying that $\dot{S} < 0$. Consequently, both S and x will decrease over time until the consumer fully abstains from consuming the addictive good. However, if the addictive stock is between S_b and S_a, current consumption will lie above the stationary line, exceeding the depreciation of the capital stock. Consequently, $\dot{S} > 0$, implying that both S and x will increase over time, converging eventually to a long-run equilibrium at point a. A rational consumer will therefore end up at the stable steady state where he or she keeps consuming sizable quantities of the addictive good.

But how does a rational consumer happen to accumulate an addictive stock greater than S_b? Becker and Murphy argue that stressful life events, acting like an exogenous shock, may help establish that level of addictive capital by temporarily raising the consumer's demand for current consumption. To understand this, suppose that the consumer is initially at S_m, where he or she entirely abstains from consuming the addictive good. Suppose further that following a stressful life event (e.g., the death of a loved one), the consumer's demand curve shifts upward from D_x^0 to

Figure 28.1   **Demand for Current Consumption and the Effect of a Fall in Price (or of a Stressful Life Event)**

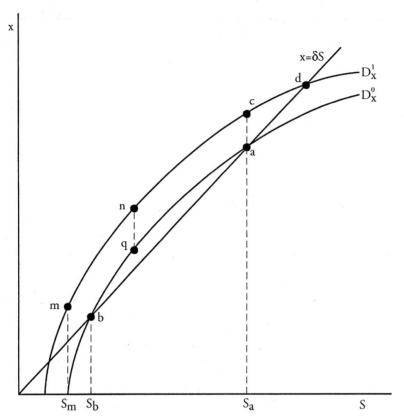

D_x^1. Consumption then rises abruptly to point *m,* which lies above the stationary line. As time progresses and stress continues, current consumption rises further, as the consumer moves upward along the D_x^1 curve. At some point *n* stress supposedly ceases. Consequently, consumption drops down to point *q* on the no-stress curve D_x^0. Unfortunately, the consumer has now accumulated addictive capital greater than S_b, sufficient to ensure his or her convergence to the stable steady state at point *a.*

Being hooked at the steady state for a while, suppose now that a favorable life event (e.g., finding a job) shifts the consumer's demand curve downward. If, by the time the temporary effects of the favorable event disappear and the demand curve shifts back to D_x^0, the addictive stock has fallen to a level between S_b and S_a, consumption will converge back to the steady state at point *a.* However, if the addictive stock has fallen to a level below S_b, the consumer will move away from the unstable steady state at point *b* toward abstention. Overall, he or she will move from being strongly addicted to quitting consumption altogether. If reinforcement is very powerful below S_b (i.e., if the demand curve is very steep at this interval) the consumer will quit his or her addiction cold turkey (laying off the addictive good abruptly). In fact, the model implies that strong addiction can only end cold turkey. Becker and Murphy view the unstable steady state as an important part of their analysis, because it helps explain why the same consumer is sometimes heavily addicted to a harmful good while at other times abstains completely.

The major predictions of the Becker and Murphy model concern the consumer's response to a change in the price of the addictive good. Suppose that the consumer is initially in a steady state equilibrium at point *a* and consider a permanent and unanticipated fall in p_x. This would shift the demand curve for *x* upward, from D_x^0 to D_x^1. Consequently, point *a* would no longer be an equilibrium point. Current consumption would first increase from point *a* to point *c*, and then, because point *c* lies above the stationary line, would grow further over time toward a new steady-state equilibrium at point *d*. Hence, a rational addict does respond to a change in price, and to a greater extent in the long run, because in the short run addictive capital is fixed. Furthermore, the steeper the demand curve, the greater the long-run response to a price change. Since reinforcement is stronger when the demand curve is steeper, strong addictions, contrary to intuition, do not imply weak price responses. These predictions of the Becker and Murphy model have been confirmed empirically over a wide range of addictive goods, suggesting that consumption can effectively be reduced, in both the short and long runs, through increasing the price of the addictive good via, for instance, the imposition of a consumption tax.

The Withdrawal Cost Approach

Contrary to Becker and Murphy, who entirely ignored the discomforts and psychic effects experienced by addicts when attempting to reduce their consumption or quit altogether, Suranovic, Goldfarb, and Leonard view the withdrawal effects as the key feature of addiction, arguing that repetitive (and even increasing) usage of a good over time is not sufficient to call its consumption an addiction. Rather, addiction requires that the consumer would wish to reduce or cease his or her habitual consumption but is unable to do so without a considerable cost. By explicitly recognizing the existence of withdrawal costs, Suranovic, Goldfarb, and Leonard seek to explain why addicts may wish to do one thing (quit their addiction) but choose another (remain addicted).

Suranovic, Goldfarb, and Leonard assume that the effects of addictive consumption at a given age can be decomposed into three additively separable components: current benefits (*B*), future losses (*L*), and withdrawal costs (*C*). Current benefits reflect relaxation and other pleasurable effects produced by consuming the addictive good, *x*, and are assumed to increase with *x* at a decreasing rate. That is, $B = B(x)$, where $B'(x) > 0$ and $B''(x) < 0$. Still, current consumption is detrimental to future health. Suranovic, Goldfarb, and Leonard assume that the harmful effects of addiction occur in the distant future and take the form of reduced life expectancy. Specifically, every unit of the addictive good (consumed at present or in the past) is assumed to reduce life expectancy by a fixed amount, α. Current consumption thus reduces life expectancy by αx. Future losses from current consumption are captured by the present value of the utility loss resulting from a shorter life expectancy, and are shown to increase with *x* at an increasing rate. That is, $L = L(x)$, where $L'(x) > 0$ and $L''(x) > 0$.

Withdrawal costs are assumed to arise if consumption is reduced below some habitual consumption level, x_h. They depend on past consumption history, *H*, and current consumption, *x*. There are no withdrawal costs when consumption is greater than (or equal to) the habitual level. That is, $C = C(x, H)$ for $x < x_h$, but $C = 0$ for $x \geq x_h$. The greater the fall in consumption below the habitual level, the greater the discomforts and psychic effects of withdrawal, hence $C_x < 0$. The sign of C_{xx} reflects the degree of addiction: if $C_{xx} > 0$, addiction is said to be weak, because a slight reduction in consumption below the habitual level will not hurt the consumer considerably; however, if $C_{xx} < 0$, addiction is said to be strong, because even a slight reduction in consumption will have painful effects.

Rather than following Becker and Murphy in assuming that the consumer chooses a consumption path over time to maximize his or her lifetime utility, Suranovic, Goldfarb, and Leonard allow the consumer to choose his or her current consumption only, releasing him or her from the duty of making "the superhuman calculations that are necessary to form a fully consistent lifetime consumption path." Subtracting L and C from B, the expected utility from current consumption of x is given by $U(x) = B(x) - L(x) - C(x)$. However, utility is also derived from the consumption of a composite good, z. The consumer is thus assumed to choose x and z so as to maximize his or her overall utility from both goods

$$W(x, z) = U(x) + V(z) \tag{8}$$

subject to the budget constraint

$$p_x x + p_z z = I \tag{9}$$

where p_x and p_z are the prices of x and z, respectively, and I is current income. The first-order conditions for utility maximization are

$$U'(x) - \mu p_x = 0 \tag{10}$$

$$V'(z) - \mu p_z = 0 \tag{11}$$

where μ is the Lagrange multiplier of the budget constraint (i.e., the marginal utility of income).

To induce consumption of the addictive good, the marginal utility, $U'(x)$, must be greater than the marginal cost, μp_x, at $x = 0$. This requires that $B'(x)$ be sufficiently large at this point. Suranovic, Goldfarb, and Leonard assume that some exogenous shock, such as sudden exposure to other users, initiates a new consumer's interest in experimenting with the addictive good and brings about a sufficiently large increase in current marginal benefits. Figure 28.2 depicts the new consumer's equilibrium at point a, where the marginal utility from consuming the addictive good (i.e., the slope of the utility curve U^1) equates the marginal cost. Contrary to the Becker and Murphy model, there is no reinforcement effect to increase the marginal utility of future consumption. However, as time goes by, the consumer establishes a consumption history, and withdrawal costs develop. This causes the utility curve to shift downward, from U^1 to U^2, for all consumption levels below x_h (there are no withdrawal costs above x_h), producing a kink at point a. Consequently, $U'(x) > \mu p_x$ at this point (evaluated from the left), which may help explain why the addictive good is habit-forming: a small increase in price will no longer reduce consumption, establishing x_h as the habitual consumption level.

Suranovic, Goldfarb, and Leonard now argue that as the consumer gets older, future losses increase, because the discount factor used to weight end-of-life utility rises as one approaches his or her terminal date. Assuming that the benefit and cost functions remain unchanged, the utility curve shifts downward for all x. This is shown to happen along with a reduction in slope at each consumption level. Figure 28.2 demonstrates that even if the utility curve falls as low as U^3, implying that the utility gained from consuming the addictive good is negative, optimum consumption may still be obtained at the habitual level, x_h, where the marginal utility, evaluated from the left of point b, exceeds the marginal cost (notice, on the other hand, that the optimum may also be zero consumption). However, when the utility curve shifts further down with age to U^4, the

Figure 28.2 **Consumer's Equilibrium Under Strong Addiction**

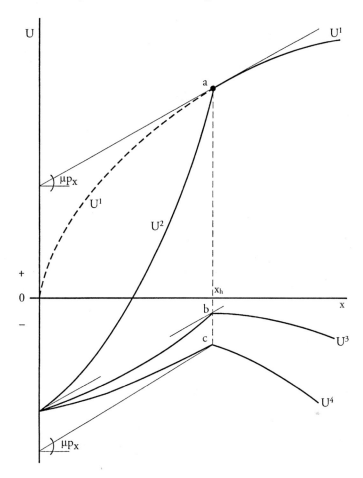

consumer will unhesitatingly move away from his or her habitual consumption at point c, terminating the addiction cold turkey.

Figure 28.2 is drawn under the assumption that addiction is strong (i.e., that $C_{xx} < 0$): since withdrawal costs rise rapidly for slight reductions in consumption below the habitual level, strong addiction results in a convex shape of U^2. As in the Becker and Murphy model, strong addiction is required to terminate an addiction cold turkey. However, contrary to the Becker and Murphy model, the Suranovic, Goldfarb, and Leonard model generates this result without relying on an exogenous shock. Rather, it occurs when future losses from consuming the addictive good, net of current benefits, become more painful than the discomforts associated with abrupt quitting. Suranovic, Goldfarb, and Leonard also show that for a weak addiction (i.e., for $C_{xx} > 0$), the U^2 curve has a concave shape, which leads to a gradual reduction of consumption over time, a result not captured by the Becker and Murphy model. Furthermore, as noted before, total utility from consuming the addictive good at the optimal level may become negative with age. This means that the consumer would have preferred to cease consumption and attain zero utility, but he or she is unable to do so without a considerable cost. Quitting addiction is worse than staying addicted, since it would result in an even lower utility level. Consequently, the utility-maximizing consumer becomes trapped in his or her own choices, continuing the addictive consumption while at the same time wishing he or she did not. Suranovic, Goldfarb, and Leonard point out that this consumer is an "unhappy addict," unlike the Becker and Murphy counterpart, who seems to be happy with the addiction. Becker and Murphy claim that this is not necessarily so because addiction may be triggered by unhappy life events, in which case the addict is clearly unhappy and would be even more so if he or she was prevented from consuming the addictive good. Still, the Suranovic, Goldfarb, and Leonard model does not require an exogenous shock to generate an unhappy addict; all it needs is explicit recognition in the role played by withdrawal costs.

How would a Suranovic, Goldfarb, and Leonard consumer respond to the imposition of a consumption tax? If the consumer has already established consumption history sufficient to develop withdrawal costs, a kink will emerge in his or her utility curve at the habitual level, x_h. Consequently, small increases in price may not affect his or her consumption. However, a consumer that has just begun consuming the addictive good (and has not yet developed quitting costs) may reduce consumption or quit altogether. A consumer who is just about to start (for whom $U'(0) \geq \mu p_x$) may not. A longtime consumer who is in the process of gradual quitting (in case of weak addiction) may reduce consumption more rapidly, and a longtime consumer who is about to quit cold turkey (in the case of strong addiction) may quit sooner. In the aggregate, the Suranovic, Goldfarb, and Leonard model thus predicts responsiveness to price changes (consistent with aggregate empirical results), even though some consumers may not respond at all.

RATIONAL HARMFUL EATING

Two recent papers, appearing approximately at the same time, address rational nonaddictive HC eating. Levy (2002a) considers the trade-off between satisfaction from overeating and the risk to life due to overweight. Yaniv (2002a) considers the trade-off between satisfaction from cholesterol-rich eating and the risk of heart attack due to artery narrowing. Both papers view the risk as emerging from deviating from some critical (healthful) value: physiologically optimal weight in the former case, and a prescribed low-cholesterol diet in the latter. Both papers apply an optimal control approach to the consumer's problem of selecting a consumption path that maximizes lifetime expected utility, showing that overweight or failure to adhere to a low-cholesterol diet may be the result of rational choice.

Overeating

Levy (2002a) considers a consumer whose utility, $U(t)$, at any instant of time, t, is a strictly concave function of food consumption, $c(t)$, perceived as a single homogenous argument. Hence $U(t) = U[c(t)]$, where $U_c > 0$ and $U_{cc} < 0$. Food consumption contributes to weight, $W(t)$, which may deviate from the physiologically optimal weight, W^*. The larger the deviation from the physiologically optimal weight, the higher the risk to life. Levy assumes that the cumulative probability of dying by the end of time t rises with the quadratic deviation of $W(t)$ from W^*, allowing for both overweight and underweight to be causes of death. Consequently, the probability of staying alive beyond time t, $\varphi(t)$, diminishes with $[W(t) - W^*]^2$. It is also assumed to be concave in this argument, which, together with the concavity of the utility function, is necessary to ensure the existence of an interior solution to the consumer's problem.

The consumer is assumed to choose a food consumption path over time that maximizes the present value of his or her lifetime expected utility

$$J = \int_0^T e^{-\rho t} \varphi \{[W(t) - W^*]^2 \} U[c(t)] dt \tag{12}$$

where ρ is a constant rate of time preference and T is an upper bound on life expectancy. The maximization problem is subject to the motion equation for weight

$$\dot{W}(t) = c(t) - \delta W(t) \tag{13}$$

where δ is a constant rate by which weight is reduced through burning calories in various activities and $\dot{W}(t)$ is the change in weight at time t, resulting from the opposing processes of gaining weight through consuming food and losing weight through burning calories.

Applying the optimal control technique, with λ as the shadow price of weight (in utility units), the solution for the consumer's problem involves the maximization of the Hamiltonian (omitting the time notation), $H = \varphi [(W-W^*)^2] U(c) + \lambda(c - \delta W)$. The necessary conditions for this maximization are $H_c = 0$ and $\dot{\lambda} = -H_W + \rho \lambda$, implying, respectively, that

$$\lambda = -\varphi[(W - W^*)^2] U_c \tag{14}$$

$$\dot{\lambda} = -\varphi_W[(W - W^*)^2] + (\rho + \delta)\lambda \tag{15}$$

where $\dot{\lambda}$ denotes the change in the shadow price over time, reflecting its evolution along the optimal consumption path. Because weight is assumed to be a bad, the shadow price, which is the subjective valuation that the consumer places on an additional unit of W, is negative. The necessary conditions for maximum lifetime expected utility also include the weight motion equation 13 and the transversality condition, $\lambda(T)W(T) = 0$, which requires that at the end of the planning horizon the shadow price of weight is zero.

Differentiating now equation 14 with respect to t, equating the result with equation 15 to cancel $\dot{\lambda}$ and substituting equation 14 for λ, the optimal food consumption and weight paths over time are found to satisfy

$$\frac{U_{cc}}{U_c} \dot{c} + \frac{\varphi_W}{\varphi} \left(\dot{W} - \frac{U}{U_c}\right) = \rho + \delta \tag{16}$$

At this point, Levy retreats to specific utility and probability functions, assuming $U = c^\beta$, where $0 < \beta < 1$, and $\varphi = \varphi_0 e^{-\mu(W-W^*)^2}$, where $0 < \varphi_0 < 1$ indicates the probability of surviving beyond time t if having the physiologically optimal weight ($W = W^*$) and $\mu > 0$ is the rate by which departure from W^* reduces the probability of survival. Substituting these functions and their derivatives into equation 16 and setting $\dot{c} = \dot{W} = 0$, the stationary values of c and W must satisfy $c(W-W^*) = (\rho + \delta)/2\mu$. Substituting now δW for c (since $\dot{c} = 0$) yields a quadratic equation in W, the solution of which reveals immediately that $W > W^*$. Hence, the rationally optimal weight at the steady state is greater than the physiologically optimal weight, the difference indicating the consumer's rationally optimal level of overweight. This level is shown to increase with β (i.e., the greater the satisfaction from eating) and with ρ (i.e., the smaller the concern for the future) and to fall with δ (i.e., the greater the rate of calories burning) and with μ (i.e., the greater the rate of decline in the probability of survival due to a marginal deviation from the physiologically optimal weight).

However, Levy shows that the stationary level of overweight is unstable: there is actually no convergence to the steady state but rather explosive oscillations around it, which is consistent with the observed phenomenon of binges followed by strict diets. Using a phase-plane diagram of food consumption and weight to graphically trace their optimal paths over time, he illustrates that there is also the possibility of a chronic decline in food consumption and weight in a late stage of life, which might lead to fatal underweight. Extending the model to the case where sociocultural norms of appearance exist, the stationary weight of a fat consumer is found to be lower and that of a thin consumer higher than would be the case in the absence of such norms.

Cholesterol-Rich Eating

Yaniv (2002) considers a consumer, who, at any instant of time, t, may spend his or her disposable income on the consumption of cholesterol-rich products, $c(t)$, and cholesterol-free products, $h(t)$, and whose instantaneous utility function, $U(t) = U[c(t), h(t)]$, diminishingly increases in both products (i.e., $U_c > 0$, $U_h > 0$, $U_{cc} < 0$, $U_{hh} < 0$). For any given allocation of income between the two products, the instantaneous marginal utility from cholesterol-rich products is assumed to exceed the instantaneous marginal utility from cholesterol-free products (i.e., $U_c > U_h$), implying that the former are more satisfying than the latter. Following, however, a blood test that reveals above-normal values of cholesterol in his or her blood, the consumer is advised by a physician to stick to a low-cholesterol diet under which cholesterol-rich products do not exceed a certain quantity, $\bar{c}$. Consuming cholesterol-rich products in excess of $\bar{c}$ bears the risk of suffering a heart attack in the future due to the narrowing of the arteries that supply blood to the heart. Let $F(t)$ represent the probability that an attack will occur by some time t in the future, and $\dot{F}(t)$ - the probability that an attack will occur exactly at time t. Suppose that the hazard rate, $\dot{F}(t) / [1 - F(t)]$, which is the probability of undergoing a heart attack at some time t in the future, *given that a heart attack has not occurred prior to that time,* is an increasing, convex function of high-cholesterol consumption and of a number of external risk factors, denoted by S, such as high blood pressure, diabetes, smoking, stress, genetic predisposition, etc. That is, $\dot{F}(t) / [1 - F(t)] = \lambda[c(t), S]$, where $\lambda_c > 0$ and $\lambda_S > 0$.[2] For simplicity, it is assumed that adhering to the prescribed diet eliminates the risk of a heart attack, hence $\lambda(c, S) = 0$ for $c \leq \bar{c}$.

If the consumer suffers a heart attack at some time t in the future, he or she is assumed to either die, with probability g, or receive lifesaving treatment and completely recover. Treatment costs, by assumption, are fully covered by health insurance, and loss of income during recovery is fully compensated by sick-pay benefits. Hence, the only major harm caused to the consumer if he or she does not die from an attack is the psychological shock accompanying the dreadful event (which involves hospitalization in a coronary care unit), K. Suppose, however, that the psychological shock is sufficiently intense to induce the consumer to strictly adhere to the prescribed diet, $\bar{c}$, thereafter.

The consumer must now decide whether or not to adhere to the prescribed diet, and if not, by how much to deviate from the physician's prescription. A rational consumer would decide on these questions through maximizing the present value of his or her expected lifetime utility stream from the consumption of cholesterol-rich and cholesterol-free products, taking into account the adverse effect of high cholesterol intake on the risk of a heart attack and its psychological and possibly deadly consequences. This may be viewed as a problem in optimal control, formulated as

$$\text{Max} \int_0^\infty e^{-\delta t} \{[1 - F(t)]U[c(t), h(t)] + F(t) (1 - \gamma)\bar{U} - \dot{F}(t) K\}dt \tag{17}$$

$$\text{subject to: } \dot{F}(t) = [1 - F(t)]\lambda [c(t), S] \tag{18}$$

$$\text{and: } h(t) = Y - c(t), \ c(t) \geq \bar{c} \tag{19}$$

where d is the discount rate of future utility, Y is disposable income, assumed to be constant over time, and $\bar{U} \equiv U(\bar{c}, Y - \bar{c})$ is the individual's postattack utility level. For simplicity it is assumed that the two products, c and h, have the same price, regardless of their cholesterol content, which is normalized to unity.[3]

Substituting equations 18 and 19 into equation 17 and letting q be the shadow price of the cumulative probability of suffering an attack, the solution for the consumer's problem involves the maximization of the Hamiltonian (omitting the time notation) $H = (1 - F)[U(c, Y - c) - \lambda(c, S)(K - q) + F(1 - \gamma)\bar{U}$. The necessary conditions for this maximization are $H_c = 0$ and $\dot{q} = -H_F + \delta q$, implying, respectively, that

$$U_c(c, Y - c) - U_h(c, Y - c) = \lambda_c(c, S)(K - q) \tag{20}$$

$$\dot{q} = U(c, Y - c) - \lambda (c, S) (K - q) - (1 - \gamma) \bar{U} + \delta q \tag{21}$$

where $\dot{q}$ denotes the change in the shadow price over time. Because the accumulation of risk is undesirable, the shadow price, which is the marginal value to the consumer of a slight increment to the overall risk, F, must be negative.

Kamien and Schwartz (1971) show that an optimal control problem as such, where the hazard rate is independent of past consumption and the planning horizon is infinite, is solved with a constant value of the shadow price. Setting $\dot{q} = 0$ in equation 21, substituting into equation 20, and rearranging yields the optimum condition

$$U_c - U_h = \lambda_c(c, S)\left[K + \frac{U - (1 - \gamma)\bar{U} - \lambda(c, S)K}{\delta + \lambda(c, S)}\right] \tag{22}$$

Condition 22 states that high cholesterol intake at any instant of time preceding an attack should be determined such that the marginal benefit from cholesterol-rich products (left-hand side) equates the marginal cost (right-hand side). The marginal benefit is captured through the positive marginal utility differential between cholesterol-rich and cholesterol-free products, reflecting the net marginal craving for cholesterol-rich products. The marginal cost is captured through the additional risk of suffering a heart attack emanating from consuming an additional unit of cholesterol-rich products. The increased risk involves not only the harm of suffering a psychological shock but also the discounted value of the future utility loss due to having to adhere, if surviving, to a low-cholesterol diet, net of the expected psychological shock of an attack that might occur even if the additional unit of cholesterol-rich products is avoided.

A sufficient condition for not adhering to the prescribed diet is that at $\bar{c}$ the marginal benefit from nonadherence exceeds the marginal cost. Because $\lambda(\bar{c}, S) = 0$, the marginal cost at this point is reduced to $\lambda_c(\bar{c}, S)(K + \gamma\bar{U} / \delta)$. Hence, an incentive for nonadherence is more likely to arise the lower the risk of suffering an attack due to a marginal deviation from the prescribed diet ($\lambda_c(\bar{c}, S)$), the lower the psychological shock accompanying the dreadful event (K), the lower the probability of dying from an attack (γ), the lower the utility derived from adhering to the prescribed diet if surviving an attack ($\bar{U}$), the greater the consumer's rate of preference for the present (δ), and the greater his or her net marginal craving for cholesterol-rich products when adhering to the prescribed diet ($U_c(\bar{c}, Y - \bar{c}) - U_h(\bar{c}, Y - \bar{c})$).

Given that the sufficient condition for nonadherence holds, the consumer will opt to deviate from the prescribed diet, raising the hazard rate to a level above zero. As nonadherence increases, the hazard rate will follow suit, shortening the expected time until a forthcoming attack. Consequently, the future must be discounted at a higher rate than the regular time preference factor, which increases with the level of nonadherence. As is evident from equation 22, this acts to moderate the marginal cost of nonadherence, stimulating a greater consumption of cholesterol-rich products. Hence, the hazard rate is not just a deterrent to nonadherence; it also imputes a lower value to future loss the greater the deviation from the prescribed diet, driving the consumer to behave less respectfully toward his or her future. This implies that an increase in any of the external risk factors, *S,* might *increase* consumption of high-cholesterol products, conforming with the fatalistic notion that if a person believes that his or her time is short, he or she will seek to increase the quality of the time still left, adhering to the old maxim "Eat, drink, and be merry, for tomorrow we die" (Isaiah 22:13) rather than to a low-cholesterol dietary regimen.

A major reason for the high mortality rates following heart attacks is the delay occurring in obtaining emergency treatment. The paper (Yaniv 2002) further allows the consumer to determine not only the extent of deviation from the prescribed diet but also the extent of involuntary delay in obtaining emergency treatment by subscribing to a private intensive care ambulance service or to an emergency call-in center, which provides round-the-clock cardiac diagnosis by phone. The probability of dying from a heart attack is now assumed to increase with the delay in obtaining emergency treatment, whereas the expenditure on reducing delay is assumed to be greater the shorter the desired delay. The analysis reveals that greater protection against the risk of dying from a heart attack does not necessarily give rise to a "moral hazard" effect in the form of stimulating HC behavior. That is, dietary adherence and self-protection may be complements in the sense that a fall in price, which induces the latter, enhances the former. It thus follows that public health intervention might be able to reduce both the risk of a heart attack and the risk of dying from an attack by subsidizing the price of private emergency services.

RATIONAL UNRESTRAINED SEXUAL ACTIVITY

Economists have shown considerable interest in AIDS-related issues, yet only a small number of contributions have addressed people's behavioral responses to AIDS (e.g., Philipson and Posner 1993; Ahituv, Holtz, and Philipson 1996; Kremer 1996; Levy 2002b). Out of this group, only Levy offers a dynamic utility-maximization model of engagement in unsafe sex that takes account of the trade-off between the additional satisfaction from this activity (over the satisfaction derived from safe sex) and the risk of contracting AIDS. Levy considers an individual who at any instant of time t allocates a given amount of time, normalized to unity, between risky (unrestrained by condoms) sexual activity, $x(t)$, and risk-free (restrained by condoms) sexual activity, $1 - x(t)$, and whose instantaneous utility function, $U(t)$, is linearly increasing in both risk-free and risky sexual activities. For any given allocation of time, the instantaneous marginal utility from risky sex is assumed to exceed the instantaneous marginal utility from risk-free sex, implying that risky sex is more satisfying than risk-free sex. Hence, $U(t) = \alpha x(t) + [1 - x(t)] = 1 + (\alpha - 1)x(t)$, where $\alpha - 1$ represents the positive marginal utility differential between risky and risk-free sex, referred to as the "inducement factor."

Unrestrained sex is risky because the individual might contract AIDS and die. The risk of dying from AIDS depends on the interaction between the individual's intensity of engagement in risky sex, $x(t)$, and the prevalence of AIDS in his or her (uncoordinated) group of potential sex partners. Denoting by $s(t)$ the proportion of this group infected by AIDS, the cumulative probability of dying from AIDS by the end of time t is assumed to be $\beta x(t)s(t)$, where $0 \le \beta \le 1$ is a risk-factor coefficient that may moderate the risk associated with unrestrained sex (e.g., the availability of drug cocktails). The probability of staying alive beyond time t is therefore $1 - \beta x(t)s(t)$.

The individual is now assumed to choose an intensity of engagement in risky sex over time that maximizes the present value of his or her lifetime expected utility

$$J = \int_0^T e^{-\rho t} [1 - \beta x(t)\, s(t)][1 + (\alpha - 1)x(t)]dt \tag{23}$$

where ρ is a constant rate of time preference and T is an upper bound on life expectancy. The maximization problem is subject to the motion equation for the prevalence of AIDS within the group of potential sex partners

$$\dot{s}(t) = \gamma x(t) - \delta\, s(t) \tag{24}$$

where $0 < \gamma < 1$ is the AIDS-transmission coefficient, $0 < \delta < 1$ is the AIDS-attrition coefficient, and $\dot{s}$ is the change in the proportion of the group infected with AIDS at time t. While the AIDS-infected proportion is reduced by attrition, it is also increased by the current transmission of AIDS to formerly unaffected members of the group who are currently engaged in unrestrained sexual activity. That is, risky sex not only is affected by the prevalence of AIDS in the group but also affects it. The transmission coefficient is proportional to the intensity of risky sex, viewing the individual as a representative member of his or her group.

Applying the optimal control technique, with λ as the shadow price for the prevalence of AIDS in the group, the solution for the individual's problem involves the maximization of the Hamiltonian (omitting the time notation), $H = (1 - \beta x s)[1 + (\alpha - 1)x] + \lambda(\gamma x - \delta s)$. The necessary conditions for this maximization are $H_x = 0$ and $\dot{\lambda} = -H_s + \rho\lambda$, implying, respectively, that

$$(\alpha - 1 - \beta s) - 2(\alpha - 1)\beta s x = -\lambda \gamma \tag{25}$$

$$\dot{\lambda} = \beta x + (\alpha - 1)\beta x^2 + \lambda(\rho + \delta) \tag{26}$$

where $\dot{\lambda}$ denotes the change in the shadow price over time. Because the contraction of AIDS is undesirable, the shadow price, which reflects the individual's discontent with the prevalence of AIDS in the group, must be negative.

Differentiating now equation 25 with respect to t, equating the result with equation 26 to cancel $\dot{\lambda}$, substituting from equation 25 for λ and from equation 24 for x, and setting $\dot{x} = 0 = \dot{s}$, the steady-state proportion of the group infected with AIDS is found to satisfy a quadratic equation, the solution for which is a complex mathematical expression involving the parameters α, β, γ, δ, and ρ. Therefore, Levy assesses the effects of the model parameters on the stationary prevalence of AIDS by numerical simulations. Setting $\beta = \gamma = \delta = 0.5$ and $\rho = 0.05$, he finds that even under a moderate inducement factor (i.e., $\alpha - 1$) of 20 percent, the stationary prevalence of AIDS and risky-sex intensity are considerably high ($s^* = x^* = 0.2304$). The simulation indicates that the stationary prevalence of AIDS largely rises with the inducement factor and converges to 1 when the inducement factor is 166 percent. Because the inducement factor is negatively related to the sensual quality of condoms, free-of-charge distribution of sensually improved condoms may considerably reduce the prevalence of AIDS. Indeed, the numerical simulation reveals that an improvement in the sensual quality of condoms that reduces the inducement factor from 20 percent to 10 percent will lower the stationary prevalence of AIDS by almost 51 percent. The simulation reveals further that the stationary prevalence of AIDS largely declines with the risk-factor coefficient (β), slightly rises with the AIDS-transmission coefficient (γ) and the rate of time preference (ρ), and slightly declines with the AIDS-attrition coefficient (δ).

Using a phase-plane diagram for the intensity of risky sex and the prevalence of AIDS, as well as the above numerical values for the parameters of the model, Levy shows that only two paths converge to the steady-state point: one for which the initial prevalence of AIDS is high and along which the prevalence of the disease declines over time even though the intensity of risky sex increases, and another for which the initial prevalence of AIDS is low and along which the prevalence of the disease increases over time even though the intensity of risky sex declines. Other paths may lead to spontaneous containment (i.e., without intervention) of the disease, whereas some paths, for which either the initial intensity of risky sex or the initial prevalence of AIDS is very high, are bound to lead (in the absence of effective intervention) to the extinction of the group of rational individuals.

RATIONAL DELAY OF MEDICAL DIAGNOSIS

The self-discovery of a suspicious physical or mental symptom often brings about an emotional turbulence: while recognizing the importance of having the symptom diagnosed promptly, individuals frequently delay diagnosis, seeking to avoid the pain or discomfort associated with the diagnostic process and fearing to hear that they are developing a serious illness.[4] Delaying diagnosis of suspicious symptoms has been extensively researched by health psychologists, who have attributed such behavior to irrational senses of invulnerability and fatalism. In a recent paper, Yaniv (2002b) proposes an economic-oriented approach to explaining individuals' delay behavior, perceiving delay as reflecting a rational weighing of the costs and benefits associated with this decision.

Consider an individual who at a certain point in time, denoted by 0, becomes aware of the presence of a suspicious physical or mental symptom, which, to the best of his or her knowledge, has the probability λ of indicating a serious illness. Suppose that λ is strictly positive and less than unity, so that the individual does not know for sure whether he or she is ill or not and must undergo a diagnosis to find this out. The diagnostic procedure is assumed to be perfectly accurate and thus perceived by the individual to bear the probability λ of yielding a positive result ($P \equiv$ ill), and the probability $1-\lambda$ of yielding a negative one ($N \equiv$ not ill). Suppose further that the individual's well-being is dependent upon knowing whether or not he or she is ill, and denote his or her utility levels at the alternative states of knowledge by v^P and v^N, respectively.

Because knowing that one is seriously ill is likely to result in lowered body image and self-esteem and to be accompanied by feelings of anxiety and depression (e.g., Rodin and Voshart 1986), Yaniv assumes that $v^N > v^P$. Not knowing for certain whether or not one is ill is assumed to be inferior to knowing for certain that one is not ill, but superior to knowing for certain that one is ill. Denoting the utility level attained at the initial state of uncertainty by v^0, assume therefore that $v^N > v^0 > v^P$.

Suppose that the suspicious symptom, while potentially life-threatening, is not too painful or incapacitating. The individual may thus consider the possibility of delaying diagnosis, fearing both the diagnostic process and finding out that he or she is actually ill, and hoping that the symptom will disappear by itself. Given that the symptom does not indicate severe illness, suppose that there is a differentiable cumulative probability distribution, $F(t)$, of the symptom disappearing by itself at or before time t. However, given that the symptom does indicate severe illness and that the individual avoids treatment, suppose that there is a differentiable cumulative probability distribution, $P(t)$, of dying at or before time t, and that after-death utility is zero. Suppose further that the functions $F(t)$ and $P(t)$, as well as their time derivatives, $\dot{F}(t)$ and $\dot{P}(t)$, are known to the individual.

If the symptom persists, the individual, at some point in time, θ (≥ 0), will seek a diagnosis. If the diagnosis is positive, the individual is assumed to follow doctors' orders concerning immediate and future treatment. Following doctors' orders ensures, by assumption, that the individual sustains his or her life. However, the longer the delay in diagnosis, the greater the irreversible damage to health incurred from not diagnosing the illness promptly. Specifically, suppose that the damage to health inflicted by the illness, $m(\theta)$, consists of a fixed component, g (≥ 0), reflecting damage that cannot be avoided by prompt diagnosis, and a self-induced, variable-with-delay component, $\mu(\theta)$. Hence, $m(\theta) = g + \mu(\theta)$, where $\mu'(\theta) > 0$ and $\mu''(\theta) > 0$. Suppose further that the greater the damage to health, the greater the intensity of treatment required constantly, at each time t following diagnosis, to sustain life, thus the greater the pain and discomfort involved in obtaining treatment. The pain and discomfort of treatment are assumed to be proportionate to the accumulated health damage, thus expressible as $sm(\theta)$, where $s > 0$ is a disutility coefficient. Diagnosing the symptom might inflict pain and discomfort as well, the disutility of which (henceforth the "psychic cost of diagnosis") is denoted by $z \geq 0$. The monetary costs of diagnosis and treatment are assumed to be covered by health insurance.

Denoting by δ (<1) the individual's time preference rate, he or she will apply for diagnosis at time θ^*, which maximizes the expected present value of his or her lifetime utility stream resulting from delayed diagnosis[5]

$$V = (1-\lambda)\{\int_0^\theta \dot{F}(t)[\int_0^t v^0 e^{-\delta\tau}d\tau + \int_t^\infty v^N e^{-\delta\tau}d\tau]\,dt$$

$$+ [1-F(\theta)][-ze^{-\delta\theta} + \int_0^\theta v^0 e^{-\delta t}dt + \int_\theta^\infty v^N e^{-\delta t}dt]\}$$

$$+ \lambda\{\int_0^\theta \dot{P}(t)\int_0^t v^0 e^{-\delta\tau}d\tau\,dt$$

$$+ [1-P(\theta)][-ze^{-\delta\theta} + \int_0^\theta v^0 e^{-\delta t}dt + \int_\theta^\infty (v^P - sm(\theta))e^{-\delta t}dt]\}$$

$$(27)$$

Table 28.1

Conditions Determining the Desirability of Delayed (D) and Prompt (M) Diagnosis

| | | Probability that the symptom indicates severe illness | | | |
		LOW	HIGH	LOW	HIGH
Damage to health incurred by a slight delay in diagnosis	LOW	M	D	D	D
	HIGH	M	M	D	M
		LOW		HIGH	
		Psychic cost of diagnosis			

Solving the maximization problem, the optimal time of applying for diagnosis, θ^*, is found to be that which balances, at the margin, the benefit from delaying diagnosis with the cost of doing so. On one hand, delaying diagnosis yields the benefit of not knowing for sure that one is actually ill as well as the opportunity to avoid painful or uncomfortable medical procedures. On the other hand, delaying diagnosis entails not only the loss of relief brought about by finding out that one is actually healthy, but also the risk of incurring increased health damage or dying before getting lifesaving treatment. Put differently, the optimal time of applying for diagnosis reflects a struggle between two opposing fears: fear of the diagnostic procedure and of finding out that one is actually ill (net of the hope that one is actually healthy) encourages further delay, at the risk of dying or of incurring increased health damage; fear of the consequences of further procrastination discourages further delay. Optimality is obtained at time θ^* (≥ 0) for which these opposing fears balance.

Table 28.1 summarizes the conditions on the parameters of the model, ensuring that $\theta^* > 0$, that is, that diagnosis delay (denoted by D) will be preferable to prompt diagnosis (denoted by M). The psychic cost associated with the diagnostic procedure plays a crucial role in determining the desirability of delay, which is due to the fact that this cost must be borne irrespective of the diagnostic result. While prompt diagnosis dominates the left-hand side of Table 28.1 (low psychic cost), delayed diagnosis dominates its right-hand side (high psychic cost). Still, prompt diagnosis will be desirable to the individual even if the diagnostic procedure entails considerable pain and discomfort, given that the probability of severe illness and the potential damage to health incurred by slightly delaying diagnosis are high as well. On the other hand, delay in diagnosis will be desirable even if the diagnostic procedure entails no pain or discomfort, given that the probability of illness is high but the potential damage to health from avoiding prompt treatment is low.

Table 28.1 provides a rational explanation for a variety of observed behavior concerning individuals' responses to the self-discovery of potentially life-threatening symptoms. Consider, for example, the "worried well," who frequently rush to emergency rooms upon the discovery of minor symptoms that "rational" individuals tend to ignore. Table 28.1 (left side, bottom row) suggests that if the perceived discomfort of being examined in an emergency room is negligible, it is perfectly rational to seek an immediate diagnosis even when suffering from minor chest pain, since standard cardiac diagnosis by means of an EKG is painless, whereas if the symptom does happen to indicate an impending heart attack, any delay might be crucial in physicians' ability to save the patient's life or prevent irreversible heart damage. On the other hand, Table 28.1 (right side, bottom row) suggests that it may also be rational for a senior executive, who following a stormy board meeting experiences extreme fatigue and dizziness, to delay summoning help, interpreting the symptoms as a mild disorder. Only if additional life-threatening symptoms appear that substantially increase the likelihood that he is developing a heart attack will the humiliation of being carried out of his office on a stretcher and undergoing emergency-room helplessness be justified. By the same token, Table 28.1 (left side, upper row) suggests that prior to the recent breakthroughs in combination drug therapy, it was very rational for people at risk of infection with AIDS to delay the simple and painless HIV antibody test, since being diagnosed as a carrier of the virus would adversely affect their well-being while having little or no effect on the progress of the disease. Those who do not belong to any of the groups at high risk for AIDS would normally not hesitate to take the HIV test upon the request of a new sex partner, anticipating an immediate sense of relief. However, if both the probability of illness and the damage incurred by a slight delay in diagnosis are high, as is the case with a sunburned construction worker who becomes aware of a change in color of a mole on his hand, Table 28.1 (right side, bottom row) suggests that avoiding prompt diagnosis is irrational, even if the psychic cost of diagnosis is high.

RATIONAL MENTAL DISORDER

HC behavior is detrimental not only to physical health. Two recent papers apply utility-maximization to the analysis of behaviors that might lead to the onset or exacerbation of mental disorders: agoraphobia (Yaniv 1998), which is the fear, and consequently the avoidance, of public places, and insomnia (Yaniv 2004), which is the inability to fall asleep or to stay asleep sufficiently long. In the former case, rational behavior may affect only the severity of an already existing disorder. In the latter case, rational behavior may also *initiate* the disorder. Unlike psychotic disorders (such as schizophrenia or paranoia), which are characterized by thought disturbances and misperceptions of reality, agoraphobia and insomnia do not involve a confusion of subjective impressions with external reality and must not interfere with the rationality premise.

Agoraphobia

Agoraphobia is the fear of being alone in public places from which escape might be difficult or in which help might not be available in case of sudden incapacitation, such as busy streets, crowded stores, closed-in spaces (tunnels, bridges, elevators), and closed-in vehicles (subways, buses, airplanes). Passing unaccompanied by friends or relatives through public places might provoke an episode of acute anxiety, associated with dramatic physiological, cognitive, and emotional symptoms, known as a panic attack. During an attack, agoraphobics often attempt to escape whatever situation they are in to seek help at home or in an emergency room. Recurrences of the frightening event, usually followed by prolonged physical exhaustion, may lead to a desire to avoid independent traveling through public places, resulting, in the more severe cases, in refusal to leave the house altogether. Time lost from work and the financial difficulties that arise due to loss of work are the major socioeconomic consequence of agoraphobia. While fear of an environment that is objectively safe is irrational, full or partial avoidance of this environment may be rational (i.e., resulting out of cost-benefit considerations) given that fear.

Consider the dilemma faced by an agoraphobic worker who, at the beginning of a given day, must make a binding commitment to her employer or clients regarding the number of her working hours, k, on that particular day. Suppose that the worker lives in the suburbs and works in the city, thus facing the risk of experiencing a panic attack on the way to/from work. Suppose further that the (subjective) probability of a panic attack occurring in either direction is identical. If, with probability $1 - p$, a panic attack does not occur on the way to work, the worker will successfully stand by her commitment, earning a total of $w(k)$ per day, where $w'(k) > 0$ and $w''(k) \leq 0$. If, with probability p, a panic attack does occur on the way to work, the worker is bound to return back home, where she will rest and recover for r hours. On that particular day, she will not attempt leaving for work again. Not only will she lose her daily earnings, but she will also incur additional costs of $z(k)$, where $z'(k) > 0$ and $z''(k) \geq 0$, for breaking her work commitment (e.g., damage to professional reputation, loss of clients, legal claims for compensation in case of substantial harm to clients). If, with probability $(1 - p)p$, the worker suffers an attack on her way *from* work, she will bear no financial loss, but will still need to recover at home (at the expense of leisure).

Suppose now that the worker's utility, U, is defined over daily income, I, and leisure hours, L, assumed to be spent at home after work. A decision to work thus gives rise to three possible outcomes (in utility terms): $U(I^p, L^p)$—if a panic attack occurs on the way *to* work, $U(I^q, L^q)$—if a panic attack occurs on the way *from* work, and $U(I^n, L^n)$—if a panic attack does not occur at all. Obviously, $I^q = I^n$. Suppose also that the utility function is strongly separable in income and hours of leisure, so that $U(I, L) = v(I) + \phi(L)$. Suppose further that the marginal utility of income is positive and strictly decreasing (i.e., $v'(I) > 0$, $v''(I) < 0$), so that the worker is risk-averse. Separability thus implies that risk aversion is independent of leisure consumption and that leisure is a normal good. Finally, suppose that the marginal utility of leisure is positive and strictly decreasing as well (i.e., $\phi'(L) > 0$, $\phi''(L) < 0$).

Assuming now that the worker has T waking hours to allocate between work and leisure, and an unearned income of size N, suppose that she chooses the volume of work commitment that maximizes her expected utility[6]

$$E(U) = (1 - p)[v(I^n) + (1 - p)\phi(L^n) + p\phi(L^q)] + p[v(I^p) + \phi(L^p)] \qquad (28)$$

where $I^n = N + w(k)$, $I^p = N - z(k)$, $L^n = T - k$, $L^p = T - r$, and $L^q = T - k - r$. When $p = 1$, equation 28 reduces to $v(I^p) + \phi(L^p)$, implying that expected utility is maximized at $k = 0$ (i.e., full work-avoidance). Assuming, however, that $0 < p < 1$ and maximizing equation 28 with respect to k yields the optimum condition

$$\Omega(k) \equiv w'(k)v'(I^n) - \phi'(L^n) = \frac{1}{1 - p}\{pz'(k)v'(I^p) + q[\phi'(L^q) - \phi'(L^n)]\} \qquad (29)$$

In the absence of agoraphobia ($p = q = 0$), $\Omega(k) = 0$ at the optimum, and the model collapses to the classical (deterministic) labor/leisure choice model. The worker's (normal) supply of labor, k^n, would then be determined at the point where the marginal rate of substitution between leisure and income ($\phi'(L^n) / v'(I^n)$) equals the marginal return to labor efforts ($w'(k^n)$). However, in the presence of agoraphobia, $\Omega(k) > 0$ at the optimum. Since $\Omega(k)$ varies inversely with k, it follows that agoraphobia results in the supply of less labor, k^*, than the normal level. The magnitude of deviation from normal work behavior, $k^n - k^*$, may thus serve as a measure for the severity of agoraphobia.

Condition 29 implies that the work-avoidance effect of agoraphobia increases with the probability of experiencing a panic attack on the way to/from work (p or q). It also increases with the size (absolute and marginal) of the financial loss borne by the worker in the case of not being able to stand by previous commitments ($z(k)$ and $z'(k)$), as well as with the time needed to recover after an attack (r). Notice that the work-avoidance effect is positive even if the financial loss due to the occurrence of an attack is zero or independent of the volume of work commitments (i.e., even if $z(k) = 0$ or $z'(k) = 0$). The possibility that recovery following an attack may be needed even if work has been successfully completed is sufficient to drive the supply of labor below its normal level, so as to ensure time for leisure activities that might involuntarily decrease.

A sufficient condition for the agoraphobic worker to avoid work altogether is that $d[E(U)]/dk \leq 0$ at $k = 0$. This yields

$$w'(0) \; \leq \; \frac{\phi'(T) \, + \, p[\phi'(T-r) \, - \, \phi'(T)]}{v'(N)} \; + \; \frac{p}{1-p} \, z'(0) \tag{30}$$

with the right-hand terms representing the worker's risk-adjusted reservation wage. Clearly, agoraphobia raises the worker's reservation wage above its normal level, $\phi'(T) \, / v'(N)$, the rise being an increasing function of p, r, and $z'(0)$. If the (subjective) probability of experiencing a panic attack on the way to work is too high, if the dread of an attack and the discomfort accompanying it are too intense, or if the marginal damage incurred for breaking her work commitment is too high, it will be worth the worker's while to stay at home and forgo the workday's earnings.

Assuming that psychiatric treatment may help reduce the (subjective) risk of experiencing a panic attack on the way to/from work, the paper (Yaniv 1998) proceeds to examine the effectiveness of psychotherapy in restoring normal work behavior, focusing on the role of costs (i.e., therapist's fee) in the psychotherapeutic process. The analysis reveals that psychotherapy costs generate two opposing income effects on work avoidance: on one hand, because leisure is a normal good, psychotherapy costs reduce leisure, driving the worker to increase her work efforts; on the other hand, psychotherapy costs make the worker less wealthy, which, given that (absolute) risk aversion decreases in income, discourages risk taking, therefore inducing a reduction in work effort. The analysis shows further that the costs of psychotherapy have a net favorable effect on work effort in severe cases of agoraphobia (particularly when the worker avoids work altogether) but might encourage work avoidance in less severe cases, counteracting the favorable effect of treatment per se. Costly psychotherapy might then aggravate the mental disorder, as measured by its work-avoidance effect. This suggests that mild cases of agoraphobia may be more effectively treated in public-funded community clinics or through corporate-financed mental health programs than by costly private practice.

The possible relationship between the cost of psychotherapy and its outcome has been a subject of interest to psychologists ever since Sigmund Freud (1913), who suggested that the payment of a fee to the therapist might contribute to the success of the treatment, since patients who pay a fee may try harder in order to justify their financial commitments. Empirical and experimental studies (e.g., Pope, Geller, and Wilkinson 1975; Yoken and Berman 1984), however, do not seem to support this hypothesis. Moreover, despite its popularity in the treatment of phobic disorders, there is little scientific evidence supporting the effectiveness of psychotherapy in these conditions (Griest, Jefferson, and Marks 1986), and much evidence pointing toward the effectiveness of noncostly self-administered behavior therapy. The discouraging effect that psychotherapy costs might have on the *tendency* to take risks may help explain why, despite reducing the risk of an attack, psychotherapy has proven less successful in the treatment of agoraphobia.

Insomnia

Insomnia is the inability to fall asleep or to stay asleep sufficiently long. While this phenomenon can be a symptom of various mental and physical illnesses, it is frequently diagnosed as a sleep disorder in its own right, caused often by stressful life events that occupy the individual's mind and lead to cognitive and emotional arousal when attempting to fall asleep. However, insomnia may also be triggered by desynchronization of the individual's biological sleep-wake cycle with the one she chooses to practice (Morin 1993). Because of irregular work schedules, late-night entertainment, or rapid crossing of several time zones, the individual's *desired* sleep-wake cycle may not be aligned with her biological cycle. Consequently, she might retire to bed earlier or later than her biological bedtime (which is the time she feels drowsy), thus experiencing difficulties falling asleep. Hence insomnia may also be the outcome of a rational choice: by choosing to deviate from her biological bedtime, the individual inflicts upon herself a disorder she finds too costly to avoid.

Consider an individual who intends to allocate her daily twenty-four hours between wakeful out-of-bed activities, A, and in-bed sleep, S. Suppose that the individual retires to bed at time θ every night and must wake up every morning at time θ^w to fulfill whatever obligations she may have (e.g., go to work, go to class, prepare her children for school, etc.). The number of hours she spends in wakeful activities will then be $A = \theta - \theta^w$, where θ is measured on a scale ranging from θ^w to $\theta^w + 24$. If the individual were able to fall asleep at the exact moment she retires to bed, the number of hours she spends sleeping would be given by $24 - A$. However, suppose that sleep is not guaranteed at any desired point in time, and so the individual's attempt to fall asleep right away might result in insomnia. The number of hours she spends in bed before falling asleep, I, may serve as a measure for the severity of her insomnia. It is positively related to the level of her psychological stress, R, and to the extent by which θ deviates from her biological bedtime, θ^b. Both R and $\theta - \theta^b$ may be viewed as inputs in an insomnia "production function," only the former is an exogenous factor, generated by the individual's attempt to cope with the challenges of daily life, whereas the latter is a decision variable, subject to the individual's choice. Formally, the insomnia production function is given by $I = I\,(\theta - \theta^b,\,R)$, where $I(0, 0) = 0$, $I_R > 0$, and $I_\theta \gtrless 0$ for $\theta \gtrless \theta^b$. Given the levels of A and I, the number of hours the individual will end up sleeping will be $S = 24 - A - I$, assuming that once she falls asleep her sleep is not interrupted until her alarm clock wakes her up at θ^w.

Suppose now that the individual derives utility from wakeful activities and sleep and suffers discomfort from not being able to fall asleep whenever she attempts to do so. Her utility function may thus be written as

$$V = U(A, S) - \psi(I) \tag{31}$$

which, by assumption, increases in both A and S at decreasing marginal rates (i.e., $U_A > 0$, $U_S > 0$, and $U_{AA} < 0$, $U_{SS} < 0$). The discomfort stemming from insomnia, $\psi(I)$, is assumed to increase in I at nondecreasing marginal rates (i.e., $\psi'(I) > 0$ and $\psi''(I) \geq 0$). Notice that insomnia adversely affects utility in two ways: it reduces hours of intended sleep and it generates direct discomfort.

The individual is assumed to choose θ^* so as to maximize her utility function subject to the insomnia production function. The optimum condition for utility maximization is

$$U_A = U_S + I_\theta(U_S + \psi') \tag{32}$$

implying that a solution to the individual's problem may be obtained at a positive, negative, or zero value of I_θ. Hence, the individual might find it optimal to retire to bed earlier than her biological bedtime (choose $\theta^* < \theta^b$), later than that (choose $\theta^* > \theta^b$), or exactly at her biological bedtime (choose $\theta^* = \theta^b$). Based on this choice, the individual is termed a sleep-advancer, a sleep-postponer, or a sleep-adherer, respectively. Condition 32 states that the optimal bedtime is determined at the point where the marginal benefit from delaying bedtime (U_A) equals the marginal cost of doing so [$U_S + I_\theta(U_S + \psi')$]. The marginal benefit is simply the utility derived from staying awake an additional hour, U_A. The marginal cost is composed, in contrast, of two elements: the first is the utility of sleep forgone because of staying awake an additional hour, U_S; the second involves the effect of bedtime delay on insomnia, I_θ, and varies with the individual's type. For a sleep-postponer the second element is positive, reflecting the utility forgone because of sleep deprivation and the discomfort caused by insomnia as a result of delaying bedtime beyond θ^b. For a sleep-advancer the second element is negative, reflecting the utility gain stemming from the reduction in insomnia due to delaying bedtime toward θ^b.

The model is first used to examine the effect of stress on optimal bedtime and the severity of insomnia, showing that a sleep-postponer will respond to stress by going to bed earlier than before, negatively adjusting her self-inflicted insomnia to the emergence of stress-induced insomnia. A sleep-adherer will go to bed earlier as well, only she will now be deviating from her biological bedtime, turning into a sleep-advancer and adding a self-inflicted element of insomnia to her stress-induced insomnia. A sleep-advancer might respond either way: going to bed closer to her biological bedtime or advancing her sleep even further.

Empirical evidence reveals that people suffering from insomnia tend to spend excessive amounts of time in bed (Spielman, Saskin, and Thorpy 1987). Unfortunately, excessive time awake in bed heightens arousal and undermines the discriminative properties of the stimuli (bed, bedtime, bedroom) previously associated with sleep. Therefore, the most significant component of the insomnia treatment is behavioral, aiming to curtail the time spent in bed so that it equals total sleep time, as well as to strengthen the association between sleep and stimulus conditions under which it typically occurs. However, patients often exhibit difficulties adhering to a bed restriction procedure, as its core recommendation appears to be counterintuitive. For many people with insomnia, a more plausible approach would involve *increasing* time in bed in an attempt to acquire more sleep (Riedel and Lichstein 2001). The model's results provide a rational support for such behavior. While sleep therapists aim at minimizing insomnia, patients may have a different objective in mind, such as utility maximization, which may justify an opposite strategy for coping with insomnia.

The model is finally applied to jet lag, which is a travel-induced sleep disorder that afflicts a healthy individual when, due to the crossing of several time zones in a short period of time, her internal clock becomes desynchronized with her external environment. More specifically, when the individual travels west, local clocks will be earlier than her internal clock, and when she travels east, local clocks will be later. The application shows that it is rational for the individual to postpone bedtime when traveling west and advance bedtime when traveling east. For a sleep-adherer, this response will trigger insomnia (irrespective of whether she travels west or east), which is the symptom of jet lag most frequently complained about. For a sleep-postponer, insomnia will be exacerbated when traveling west and weaken when traveling east, whereas for a sleep-advancer, the opposite will occur. Jet lag thus emerges as a rationally self-inflicted disorder that the individual finds too costly to avoid.

CONCLUSION

The present survey has reviewed a growing (yet still small) literature that applies an economic approach to the analysis of HC behaviors, traditionally researched by health/clinical psychologists. While psychologists stress weakness of will, absence of self-control, or irrational senses of invulnerability and fatalism as determinants of harmful and potentially self-destructive behavior, economists suggest that such behavior could be the outcome of rational choice and therefore respond to incentives. If addiction were an irrational behavior, a change in price would have little or no effect upon consumption. Yet a major conclusion of the rational addiction literature is that addictive consumption, like any other consumption, negatively responds to a change in price. Hence, imposing a sales tax on the addictive good is likely to reduce its consumption. While prices have not been explicitly incorporated into the nonaddictive harmful eating models, it is relatively easy to specify prices for cholesterol-rich and cholesterol-free products so as to show that an increase in the price of the former or a decrease in the price of the latter (which is often much higher) would enhance adherence to a low-cholesterol diet. Furthermore, the analysis shows that dietary adherence and self-protection through subscribing to private emergency services might be complements. Hence, subsidizing the price of such services could help reduce both the risk of a heart attack and the risk of dying from an attack. Similarly, subsidizing the price of sensually improved condoms is likely to discourage engagement in risky sexual activity and reduce the prevalence of AIDS, and subsidizing the cost of psychotherapy may reduce the severity of phobic disorders, contrary to the commonly held view that paying a high fee to the therapist is necessary for treatment success. Public health intervention often attempts to enhance good health behavior through community-wide health education programs. The present survey suggests that rather than trying to change people, public health intervention could try changing the costs they face.

NOTES

1. Chaloupka (1991) suggests a more basic formulation of the utility function that takes explicit account of the harmful effect of the addictive stock on the consumer's health and from which equation 1 can easily be derived. He formulates utility as a positive function of three arguments, $u(t) = u[H(t), R(t), c(t)]$, where H is health, R is the relaxation produced by consuming the addictive good, and c is a composite of other goods. Health is assumed to be positively related to a composite of medical care goods, m, but negatively related to the stock of addictive capital, S (i.e., $H(t) = H[m(t), S(t)]$, where $H_m > 0$, $H_S < 0$). Relaxation is assumed to be positively related to current consumption of the addictive good, x, but negatively related to the stock of addictive capital, S (i.e., $R(t) = R[x(t), S(t)]$, where $R_x > 0$, $R_S < 0$). Because H is a function of S and R is a function of x and S, utility can be expressed as in equation 1, incorporating m into c. The partial derivative signs of U now follow from the assumptions on the partial derivative signs of u, H, and R (for example, $U_S = u_R R_S + u_H H_S < 0$).

2. Notice that the hazard rate is defined on *current* consumption of high-cholesterol products rather than on *accumulated* consumption. Because a heart attack is caused by the accumulation of cholesterol deposits on the artery walls, one first tends to relate the hazard rate to the overall amount of past consumption. This, however, implies that the risk of suffering an attack continues to increase even if the individual restricts his or her high-cholesterol consumption to $\bar{c}$. Yet recent evidence suggests (e.g., Pickering 1997) that adhering to a low-cholesterol diet *reduces* the risk of an attack, because it acts to dissolve the cholesterol deposits and widen the diameter of the arteries. Even if cutting down on cholesterol consumption did not help dissolve cholesterol plaques, the important point in modeling nonadherence is how people *perceive* the risk of a heart attack. Casual observation suggests that people believe (either because this is what doctors are telling them so as to induce them to keep to a diet or because this is how they interpret doctors' orders) that the risk of an attack can be drastically lowered through reducing current consumption of cholesterol-rich products.

3. The integrand (equation 17) discounts the expected stream of lifetime utility over an infinite time horizon. At any given time t in the future, the individual faces the cumulative probability $1 - F(t)$ of not yet

suffering a heart attack, deriving the utility $U[c(t), h(t)]$ from consumption. However, with probability $F(t)$, he or she will suffer a heart attack by this time, which, with probability γ, will be fatal, resulting in his or her death (the utility of which is assumed to be zero). Given the probability $1 - \gamma$ of surviving the event, the individual will thereafter adhere to the recommended diet, deriving utility $\bar{U}$ from consumption. In addition, with probability $\dot{F}(t)$, a heart attack will occur exactly at time t, causing a psychological shock of size K.

4. Doherman (1977) found that patients experiencing myocardial infarction symptoms waited, on average, 4.5 hours before seeking medical treatment, which is one of the reasons for the high rates of mortality and disability following heart attacks. Antonovsky and Hartman (1974) concluded that at least three-fourth of cancer patients delayed visiting a physician for at least one month after first noticing a suspicious symptom, and that somewhere between 35 and 50 percent of patients delayed seeking treatment for over three months.

5. The expected present value of the lifetime utility stream comprises two major terms, one multiplied by $1 - \lambda$ and the other by λ. The former term relates to the possibility that the symptom does not indicate severe illness. In this case, the symptom either disappears, with probability $\dot{F}(t)$, at any time t preceding time θ, or, with probability $1 - F(\theta)$, remains intact until time θ when the individual applies for diagnosis. The latter term relates to the possibility that the symptom does indicate severe illness. In this case the individual either dies, with probability $\dot{P}(t)$, at any time t preceding time θ, or survives, with probability $1 - P(\theta)$, to apply for diagnosis at time θ. Expression 27 attaches the alternative utility levels, v^0, v^N, v^P, as well as the psychic costs of diagnosis and treatment, z and $sm(\theta)$, to the appropriate cases in accordance with the time of revelation.

6. Equation 28 states that if, with probability $1 - p$, the worker does not experience a panic attack on the way to work, he or she will gain utility $v(I^n)$ from income. The utility gained from leisure would then depend on whether or not a panic attack occurs on the way *from* work. If, with probability $1 - p$ it does not, the utility gained from leisure will be $\phi(L^n)$; if with probability p it does, utility from leisure will be $\phi(L^q)$. However, if, with probability p, the worker suffers a panic attack on the way to work, he or she will gain utility $v(I^P) + \phi(L^P)$ from income and leisure.

REFERENCES

Ahituv, Avner, Joseph V. Holtz, and Tomas Philipson. 1996. "The Responsiveness of the Demand for Condoms to the Local Prevalence of AIDS." *Journal of Human Resources* 31, 4: 869–97.

Antonovsky, Aaron, and Harriet Hartman. 1974. "Delay in the Detection of Cancer: A Review of the Literature." *Health Education Monographs* 2, 2: 98–128.

Baltagi, Badi H., and James M. Griffin. 2002. "Rational Addiction to Alcohol: Panel Data Analysis of Liquor Consumption." *Health Economics* 11, 2: 485–91.

Barthold, Thomas A., and Harold M. Hochman. 1988. "Addiction as Extreme-Seeking." *Economic Inquiry* 26, 1: 89–106.

Becker, Gary S., and Kevin M. Murphy. 1988. "A Theory of Rational Addiction." *Journal of Political Economy* 96, 4: 675–700.

Becker, Gary S., Michael Grossman, and Kevin M. Murphy. 1991. "Rational Addiction and the Effect of Price on Consumption." *American Economic Review* 81, 2: 237–41.

———. 1994. "An Empirical Analysis of Cigarette Addiction." *American Economic Review* 84, 3: 396–418.

Boymal, Jonathan. 2003. "Addiction and Interpersonal Externalities in the Labor Market." *Journal of Socio-Economics* 31, 6: 657–72.

Cameron, Samuel. 2000. "Nicotine Addiction and Cigarette Consumption: A Psycho-Economic Model." *Journal of Economic Behavior and Organization* 41, 3: 211–19.

Chaloupka, Frank. 1991. "Rational Addictive Behavior and Cigarette Smoking." *Journal of Political Economy* 99, 4: 722–42.

Doherman, Steven R. 1977. "Psychological Aspects of Recovery from Coronary Heart Disease: A Review." *Social Science and Medicine* 11, 199–218.

Ferguson, Brian S. 2000. "Interpreting the Rational Addiction Model." *Health Economics* 9, 7: 587–98.

Frank, Bjorn. 1996. "The Use of Internal Games: The Case of Addiction." *Journal of Economic Psychology* 17, 5: 651–60.

Freud, Sigmund. 1913. "On Beginning the Treatment: Further Recommendations on the Technique of Psycho-Analysis." In *The Standard Edition of the Complete Works of Sigmund Freud,* ed. James Strachey, 12:123–44. London: Hogarth Press, 1958.

Griest, John H., James W. Jefferson, and Isaac M. Marks. 1986. *Anxiety and Its Treatment.* Washington, DC: American Psychiatric Press.

Grossman, Michael, and Frank J. Chaloupka. 1998. "The Demand for Cocaine by Young Adults: A Rational Addiction Approach." *Journal of Health Economics* 17, 4: 427–74.

Gruber, Jonathan, and Botond Koszegi. 2001. "Is Addiction Rational? Theory and Evidence." *Quarterly Journal of Economics* 116, 4: 1261–303.

Guth, Werner, and Hartmut Kleimt. 1996. "One Person—Many Players? On Bjorn Frank's 'The Use of Internal Games: The Case of Addiction.'" *Journal of Economic Psychology* 17, 5: 661–68.

Iannaccone, Laurence R. 1986. "Addiction and Satiation." *Economics Letters* 21, 1: 95–99.

Jones, Andrew M. 1999. "Adjustment Costs, Withdrawal Effects, and Cigarette Addiction." *Journal of Health Economics* 18, 1: 125–37.

Kamien, Morton I., and Nancy L. Schwartz. 1971. "Limit Pricing and Uncertain Entry." *Econometrica* 39, 3: 441–54.

Keeler, Theodore E. 1999. "Rational Addiction and Smoking Cessation: An Empirical Study." *Journal of Socio-Economics* 28, 5: 633–43.

Kremer, Michael. 1996. "Integrating Behavioral Choice into Epidemiological Models of AIDS." *Quarterly Journal of Economics* 111, 2: 549–73.

Lee, Li-Way. 1988. "The Predator-Prey Theory of Addiction." *Journal of Behavioral Economics* 17, 4: 249–62.

Leonard, Daniel. 1989. "Market Behavior of Rational Addicts." *Journal of Economic Psychology* 10: 117–44.

Levy, Amnon. 2002a. "Rational Eating: Can It Lead to Overweightness or Underweightness?" *Journal of Health Economics* 21, 5: 887–99.

———. 2002b. "A Lifetime Portfolio of Risky and Risk-Free Sexual Behaviour and the Prevalence of AIDS." *Journal of Health Economics* 21, 6: 993–1007.

Michaels, Robert J. 1988. "Addiction, Compulsion, and the Technology of Consumption." *Economic Inquiry* 26, 1: 75–88.

Morin, Charles M. 1993. *Insomnia: Psychological Assessment and Management.* New York: Guilford Press.

Philipson, Tomas, and Richard Posner. 1993. *Private Choices and Public Health: The AIDS Epidemic in an Economic Perspective.* Cambridge, MA: Harvard University Press.

Pickering, Thomas. 1997. *Good News About High Blood Pressure.* New York: Simon and Schuster.

Pope, Kenneth S., Jesse D. Geller, and Leland Wilkinson. 1975. "Fee Assessment and Outpatient Psychotherapy." *Journal of Consulting and Clinical Psychology* 43, 6: 835–41.

Olekalns, Nills, and Peter Bardsley. 1996. "Rational Addiction to Caffeine: An Analysis of Coffee Consumption." *Journal of Political Economy* 104, 5: 1100–4.

Orphanides, Athanasios, and David Zervos. 1995. "Rational Addiction with Learning and Regret." *Journal of Political Economy* 103, 4: 739–58.

Riedel, Brant W, and Kenneth L. Lichstein. 2001. "Strategies for Evaluating Adherence to Sleep Restriction Treatment for Insomnia." *Behavioral Research Therapy* 39, 1: 201–12.

Rodin, Gary, and Karen Voshart. 1986. "Depression in the Medically Ill: An Overview." *American Journal of Psychiatry* 143, 6: 696–705.

Skog, Ole-Jørgen. 1999. "Rationality, Irrationality, and Addiction—Notes on Becker and Murphy's Theory of Addiction." In Jon Elster and Ole-Jørgen Skog, eds., *Getting Hooked,* 173–207. Cambridge: Cambridge University Press.

Spielman, Arthur J., Paul Saskin, and Michael J. Thorpy. 1987. "Treatment of Chronic Insomnia by Restriction of Time in Bed." *Sleep* 10, 1: 45–56.

Stigler, George J., and Gary S. Becker. 1977. "De Gustibus Non Est Disputandum." *American Economic Review* 67, 1: 76–90.

Suranovic, Steven M., Robert S. Goldfarb, and Thomas C. Leonard. 1999. "An Economic Theory of Cigarette Addiction." *Journal of Health Economics* 18, 1: 1–29.

Taylor, Shelley E. 1995. *Health Psychology.* New York: McGraw-Hill.

Waters, Teresa M., and Frank A. Sloan. 1995. "Why Do People Drink? Tests of the Rational Addiction Model." *Applied Economics* 27, 8: 727–36.

Winston, Gordon C. 1980. "Addiction and Backsliding: A Theory of Compulsive Consumption." *Journal of Economic Behavior and Organization* 1, 4: 295–324.

Yaniv, Gideon. 1998. "Phobic Disorder, Psychotherapy, and Risk-Taking: An Economic Perspective." *Journal of Health Economics* 17, 2: 229–44.

————. 2002a. "Nonadherence to a Low-Fat Diet: An Economic Perspective." *Journal of Economic Behavior and Organization* 48, 1: 93–104.

————. 2002b. "Rational Delay in Applying for Potentially Life-Saving Diagnosis." *Journal of Risk, Decision and Policy* 7, 2: 95–108.

————. 2004. "Insomnia, Biological Clock, and the Bedtime Decision: An Economic Perspective." *Health Economics* 13, 1: 1–8.

Yoken, Carol, and Jeffrey Berman. 1984. "Does Paying a Fee for Psychotherapy Alter the Effectiveness of Treatment?" *Journal of Consulting and Clinical Psychology* 52, 2: 254–60.

Yuengert, Andrew M. 2001. "Rational Choice with Passion: Virtue in a Model of Rational Addiction." *Review of Social Economy* 59, 1: 1–21.

PART 8

TAXATION, ETHICAL INVESTMENT, AND TIPPING

CHAPTER 29

TAXATION AND THE CONTRIBUTION OF BEHAVIORAL ECONOMICS

SIMON JAMES

Taxation has been the subject of a great deal of study in the tradition of neoclassical economics. By examining the rational self-interested response of individuals in different situations, mainstream economics has been able to provide a great deal of understanding of the effects of taxation in areas such as the supply of labor, saving, and enterprise. However, even in such clearly defined "economic" areas, behavioral economics can offer further insights and explanatory power beyond that provided by conventional economic theories. For example, even in modern times, labor market and household investment decisions might still be influenced by a range of social factors such as traditional gender roles (James 1992, 1995a, 1996).

In many areas of taxation—most notably tax compliance—behavioral economics has even more to offer in understanding taxpayer behavior and in developing appropriate policies and successful administrative strategies for their implementation. As an illustration of the importance of the behavioral contribution, this essay will concentrate on tax compliance. As will be shown, decisions about the extent to which taxpayers are willing to comply with the tax system can involve legal as well as illegal action. It also involves simple pecuniary incentives and disincentives as well as wider behavioral considerations regarding the fulfillment of obligations of various sorts.

The purposes of taxation are also relevant. Taxation is, of course, used to raise revenue, but it is also used to implement government policy by attempting to influence behavior through the use of tax concessions in some areas and additional taxation in others. Behavioral economics has a particular contribution to offer in assessing the likely effectiveness of such policies.

This essay begins with a brief history of the economics of taxation followed by a contrast between neoclassical and behavioral approaches to economics. The analysis then turns to the development of behavioral models and goes on to give an indication of the range of research methodology in the area. Behavioral economics is also examined specifically in the context of the purposes of taxation in order to show how the behavioral contribution might fit into a more general economic framework. It is clear from the study of behavioral economics that existing definitions of tax compliance are inadequate, and so a more relevant definition is developed. Revenue services have adopted behavioral models, and some of these applications of behavioral theory are summarized. Future possibilities for tax compliance research are outlined, and finally the essay presents some conclusions.

A BRIEF HISTORY OF THE ECONOMICS OF TAXATION

Taxation was extensively studied by the English classical economists such as Adam Smith. Many of them took account of behavioral factors as a matter of course. Indeed, Adam Smith's "four maxims" regarding taxation in general have become the starting point for many subsequent contributions over the years, and each of them has a behavioral dimension. The first two maxims relate to his view of the fairness of taxes and that taxes should be certain, not arbitrary. The third is that every tax "ought to be levied at the time, or in the manner, in which it is most likely to be convenient for the contributor to pay it." Finally, taxes "ought to be so contrived as both to take out and to keep out of the pockets of the people as little as possible over and above what it brings into the public treasury of the state" (Smith 1776, bk. V, ch. II, pt. II). Smith also indicates some of the psychological costs of taxation. In a memorable passage he says that "the odious examination of the tax gatherers" may cause taxpayers "much unnecessary trouble, vexation and oppression; and though vexation is not, strictly speaking, expense, it is certainly equivalent to the expense at which every man would be willing to redeem himself from it" (ibid.).

David Ricardo devoted ten chapters of his *Principles* to problems of taxation and was also well aware of the importance of behavioral factors. For example, he stated that taxation, whether it was levied on capital or on income, would be paid from income because of the "desire which every man has to keep his station in life, and to maintain his wealth at the height which it has once attained" (Ricardo 1821, ch. VIII).

As a further illustration, in his famous comparison between direct and indirect taxation, John Stuart Mill stated that in England there had long been a popular feeling opposed to direct taxation such as income tax. He went on to say that this feeling "is not grounded on the merits of the case, and is of a puerile kind. An Englishman dislikes, not so much the payment, as the act of paying. He dislikes seeing the face of the tax-collector, and being subject to his peremptory demand." Mill went on to suggest that if the level of taxation remained the same but indirect taxes were incorporated into direct taxation "an extreme dissatisfaction would certainly arise . . . while men's minds are so little guided by reason" (Mill 1848, bk. 5, ch. 6).

As economics came to replace the old discipline of political economy in the twentieth century, such wider aspects of behavior were not usually included in more "scientific" economic analysis of taxation. Neoclassical economics became more focused than the classical economists had been, and there seemed to be less concern with why individuals behaved the way they did; the assumption was simply that they had acted on rational economic and self-interested criteria narrowly defined.

NEOCLASSICAL THEORY AND BEHAVIORAL ECONOMICS

There are many formulations of neoclassical theory. For example, Edgeworth was quite clear that "economics investigates the arrangements between agents each tending to his own maximum utility" (Edgeworth 1881, 6). Furthermore, the "first principle of Economics is that every agent is actuated only by self-interest" (1881, 16). As Jevons remarked, the "fearless manner in which Mr Edgeworth applies the conceptions and methods of mathematical physics to illustrate, if not solve, the problems of hedonic science, is quite surprising" (1881, 581). Edgeworth went on to apply his approach to taxation, stating, for example, that the "science of taxation comprises two main subjects to which the character of pure theory may be ascribed; the laws of incidence and the principles of equal sacrifice" (Edgeworth 1925, 64).

The approach to the analysis of human behavior on the ground of self-interest narrowly defined has always attracted powerful criticism. For example, Veblen (1898) was scathing in his description of the hedonistic conception of man. According to Veblen, this conception envisaged an individual as a "lightning calculator of pleasure and pains, unaffected by experience with neither antecedent nor consequent"—in other words, a purely passive, isolated, and "self-contained globule of desire." The arguments have been repeated and developed ever since. Although there seem to be two separate approaches, mainstream and behavioral economics, they are in many ways two contributions to the same study. Edwin Cannan put it well in writing that there "is no precise line between economic and non-economic satisfactions, and therefore the province of economics cannot be marked out by a row of posts or a fence like political territory or a landed property" (1946, 4).

Tax compliance is a major issue in ensuring that countries can fund without excessive costs and difficulties the high levels of public expenditure required by modern societies. As Jean-Baptiste Colbert is reputed to have said in the seventeenth century, the art of taxation consists in so plucking the goose as to obtain the largest possible amount of feathers with the smallest possible amount of hissing.

There have been a number of surveys of the research literature relating to tax compliance, such as the recent one by Richardson and Sawyer (2001). As with other areas of economic study, it is easy to identify the two separate approaches to the study of compliance.

TAXPAYER COMPLIANCE AND ECONOMIC RATIONALITY

The neoclassical approach to tax compliance is based on a relatively narrow interpretation of economic rationality. It is supposed that totally amoral individuals maximize their utility by maximizing their income and wealth. They will evade tax if they consider that by doing so they can expect to increase their spending power. For example, according to Bernasconi, "evading tax is like gambling" and is perceived as an economic transaction like any other (1998, 123). Following this approach, compliance and noncompliance are simply explained by the money costs and benefits involved.

Allingham and Sandmo (1972) published a seminal and extensively quoted paper developing this approach, and there have been many refinements and developments of their model since. A particularly clear exposition of mainstream economic analysis of tax evasion was presented by Cowell (1985). This approach indicates a number of variables that are likely to be important in such a technical analysis of compliance. An important one is the tax structure— that is, the setting of tax rates—which may have a direct influence on compliance (Alm, Bahl, and Murray 1990; Clotfelter 1983). There has also been work on regressive taxes (Nayak 1978) and nonlinear tax schedules (Pencavel 1979). Other aspects that might affect the expected rate of return to noncompliance, such as uncertainty, have been examined (see, for example, Alm, Jackson, and McKee 1992).

There are also other obvious costs such as those of concealment (Cremer and Gahvari 1994). The chances of getting caught are important, so the probability of tax evasion being detected is relevant (Fischer, Wartick, and Mark 1992). So are the deterrent effects of auditing for noncompliance (Dubin and Wilde 1988) and the relative effects of different audit schemes (Alm, Cronshaw, and McKee 1993; Collins and Plumlee 1991). The analysis can, of course, be extended to other players in this game. Tax agents are important, so the whole approach can also be applied to them—for instance, the penalties that might be imposed on them (Cuccia 1994). Another such line of inquiry has focused on risk-averse tax collectors (Tzur and Kraizberg 1995). Finally, other related economic factors that might affect the decision-making process, such as inflation (Crane and Nourzad 1986), have also been studied.

The cost-benefit approach can also be extended to the possibility that compliance might be improved with pecuniary rewards to taxpayers (Falkinger and Walther 1991) as well as pecuniary punishments for noncompliance. After all, they are just two aspects of money incentives to conform.

However, this narrow "calculus of pleasure and pain," as described by Jevons (1871), does not seem to provide a full explanation of taxpayer behavior. For example, there is empirical evidence that many taxpayers are inherently honest and will disclose their financial affairs accurately regardless of the incentive to cheat (Erard and Feinstein 1994b; Gordon 1989). With respect to other taxpayers, deterrence theory suggests that there is a range of dimensions that influence behavior, apart from the risk of detection (Grasmick and Bursik 1990). A policy of treating the taxpayer as a social being rather than just an amoral fiscal gambler seems to justify more attention than perhaps it has received in policy areas to date. This is also important given the greater role self-assessment now plays in some tax systems (Barr, James, and Prest 1977; James 1995b).

THE DEVELOPMENT OF BEHAVIORAL MODELS

A behavioral approach to tax compliance has a great deal to offer in terms of supplementing and extending mainstream economic analysis. There are many contributions from different disciplines suggesting a range of other factors that might influence taxpayers' behavior. For instance, work in sociology has identified a number of relevant variables such as social support, social influence, attitudes, and certain background factors such as age, gender, race, and culture. Psychology reinforces this approach and has even created its own branch of "fiscal psychology" (Schmölders 1959; Lewis 1982). The contribution of psychology includes the finding that attitudes toward the state and revenue authorities as well as perceptions of equity are important factors in determining compliance decisions. Economic psychology also stresses the importance of attitudes, morals, values, and fiscal consciousness (Cullis and Lewis 1997). The roles of individuals in society and accepted norms of behavior have also been shown to have a strong influence (Wenzel 2001a, 2001b). Braithwaite (2003) examined such factors as the perception of justice and how social norms and laws can undermine each other.

The main theme of this approach is that individuals are not simply independent selfish utility maximizers (though this might be partly true); rather, they also interact with other human beings in ways that depend on different attitudes, beliefs, norms, and rules. It also means that as taxpayers, they normally can be expected to act as responsible citizens. That is, in normal circumstances, they should conform to reasonable obligations of the tax system without the extensive application of enforcement activity.

There are many detailed contributions to this approach, including some by economists. For example, Spicer and Lundstedt (1976) examined taxpayer norms and attitudes toward the tax system and tax offenders some time ago, and nonmaximizing behavior more recently (Spicer 1986). The importance of equity and fairness has also been a frequent theme (for example, Bordignon 1993 and Cowell 1992). Background factors such as cultural influence have been examined (Coleman and Freeman 1997), as have the implications of different political systems (Pommerehne, Hart, and Frey 1994). More direct contributions to policy in this area have come from a number of authors. For example, one is an appeal to taxpayers' conscience (Hasseldine and Kaplan 1992) and also to feelings of guilt and shame (Erard and Feinstein 1994a). Others have suggested more positive help for taxpayers (Hite 1989) and different methods of achieving this, such as the use of television to change taxpayers' attitudes toward fairness and compliance (Roberts 1994). It is also possible that taxpayers consider the benefits the community receives from government expenditures (Falkinger 1988). There may therefore be scope to improve compliance by drawing attention to the benefits of public spending.

Many more papers could have been cited, but this section gives an indication of the range of academic evidence that supports the behavioral approach.

RESEARCH METHODOLOGY

The main behavioral research methods used have been social surveys employing questionnaires and interviews—see, for example, the work of Williams (1966), Strümpel (1969), and Schmölders (1970). There are many examples specifically related to tax compliance. Yankelovich, Skelly, and White (1984) surveyed taxpayer attitudes. Christensen (1992) conducted a survey of tax clients and tax practitioners in order to compare their views of tax services. A third example is provided by Bain, Milliron, and Rupert (1997), who investigated the type of tax firm and the experience of the practitioner with respect to tax practitioner aggressiveness.

Experiments have also become increasingly used, for example, by Webley and colleagues (1991). A further example is that of Kaplan and colleagues (1988), who used an experimental study and found that experienced practitioners were not affected by variables such as the probability of audit, though inexperienced practitioners were. A notable contribution in this area was reported by Blumenthal, Christian, and Slemrod (2001) and Slemrod, Blumenthal, and Christian (2001). They describe a unique set of experiments conducted by the Minnesota Department of Revenue in the 1993 and 1994 tax year filing seasons, where actual Minnesota state taxpayers were issued with a normative appeal or a letter stating that their income tax returns would be "closely examined."

BEHAVIORAL ECONOMICS AND THE PURPOSES OF TAXATION

It is worth briefly discussing the purposes of taxation in order to identify the issues and also because it indicates—for example, in the discussion relating to Figure 29.1 below—how the behavioral contribution might fit into a more general economic framework. Following Musgrave (1959) and others, the economic justification for the public sector and the consequent requirement for taxation may be classified into three areas: the allocation branch, the distribution branch, and the stabilization branch. The allocation branch is concerned with inefficiencies in the market system in the allocation of economic resources. In an important sense this is the root of the economic rationality approach to tax compliance, although of course economic decisions may also be influenced by other factors. The distribution branch is concerned with the redistribution of income and wealth toward a scheme that society considers more equitable. It is in this branch that behavioral economics has a particularly important role to play. The third area is the stabilization branch, which might justify a role for government in trying to smooth out cyclical economic fluctuations and ensuring a high level of employment and price stability. There has been considerable debate and dispute about how effective the public sector can be in this matter (see, for example, James and Nobes 2003, ch. 6), but both mainstream and behavioral economics add to our understanding of such issues.

Musgrave's classification provides a useful general framework for attempting to integrate the contribution of behavioral economics to tax compliance, and this is shown graphically in Figure 29.1. The allocation branch is concerned with issues of efficiency in resource allocation, and this is conventionally analyzed by supposing that individuals act to maximize utility. Tax compliance is therefore also seen as a matter of economic rationality, with taxpayers as individuals who consider the pecuniary gains and losses from compliance or noncompliance. The distribution branch is concerned with issues of equity and incidence—how the effects of taxes are distributed. This would see taxation as an equity matter and might view the taxpayer in the more complex role of a member of society rather than simply a calculator of personal gains and losses. Both approaches offer explanations of compliance behavior and major contributions to the development of a compliance strategy.

Figure 29.1   **Different Economic Approaches to Tax Compliance**

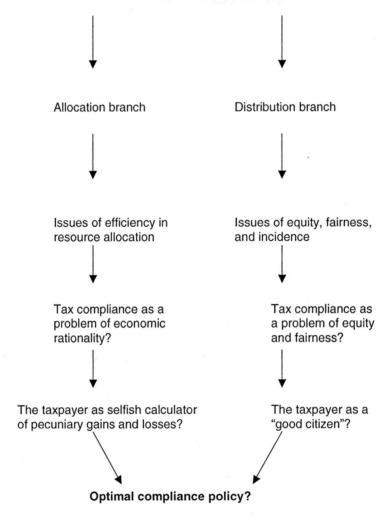

Rationale for Public Sector Expenditure and Taxation

Allocation branch

Distribution branch

Issues of efficiency in
resource allocation

Issues of equity, fairness,
and incidence

Tax compliance as a
problem of economic
rationality?

Tax compliance as
a problem of equity
and fairness?

The taxpayer as selfish calculator
of pecuniary gains and losses?

The taxpayer as a
"good citizen"?

Optimal compliance policy?

   The main question of interest is how to integrate them in designing an overall strategy by deriving what might be called an optimal compliance policy. While there is a wealth of literature on various aspects of compliance, there is relatively little on how these aspects might be optimally combined with others in order to develop an overall compliance policy. This could, however, be important even at a more detailed level. For instance, Klepper and Nagin (1989) point out that a policy innovation designed to reduce one form of noncompliance might result in taxpayers transferring their noncompliance activities to take advantage of a now superior alternative opportunity. Simply assessing only the direct impact of that measure might be inadequate and misleading. More generally, a full evaluation of any aspect of compliance policy should take account of its effects on each of the relevant areas. In order to do this it is helpful to use insights from behavioral economics to improve the definition of tax compliance.

THE BEHAVIORAL CONTRIBUTION TO THE DEFINITION OF TAX COMPLIANCE

It is clear from the study of behavioral economics that the definitions of tax compliance frequently used in the literature are too simplistic. A more comprehensive definition has been developed by James and Alley (1999). The most common previous approach has been to conceptualize compliance in terms of the "tax gap." This represents the difference between the actual revenue collected and the amount that would be collected if there were 100 percent compliance, though there are some variations. For example, and rather curiously, Brand (1996) refers to the "market share" of the Internal Revenue Service (IRS) in the United States. What Brand means by this is "the amount of the projected total tax base that the IRS actually collects." Andreoni, Erard, and Feinstein (1998) include a time dimension to compliance but are still mainly concerned with tax evasion as the central part of the tax gap definition. A more recent definition covers three distinct types of compliance: payment compliance, filing compliance, and reporting compliance—which Brown and Mazur (2003, 689) state are "three mutually exclusive and exhaustive measures."

However, such basic concepts are far too simplistic for practical policy purposes. Successful tax administration requires that taxpayers cooperate in the operation of a tax, rather than be forced to undertake every aspect of their obligations unwillingly. Tax law cannot cope with every eventuality and has to be supplemented with administrative procedures and decisions; just as important, in order to work it has to have a reasonable degree of willing compliance on the part of the taxpayers themselves.

One issue is whether "compliance" refers to voluntary or compulsory behavior. If taxpayers "comply" only because of dire threats or harassment or both, this would not appear to be full compliance, even if 100 percent of the tax was raised. Instead, it might be argued that proper compliance means that taxpayers meet their tax obligations willingly, without the need for inquiries, obtrusive investigations, reminders, or the threat or application of legal or administrative sanctions. A more appropriate definition could therefore include the degree of compliance with tax law and administration that can be achieved without the immediate threat or actual application of enforcement activity.

It is also too simplistic to suppose that there is some fixed tax revenue that would be collected if all taxpayers observed 100 percent obedience to the law. The level of potential tax revenue is determined by the level of economic activity. It is possible that an intrusive tax regime might reduce the willingness of taxpayers to earn more money or engage in commercial activity, not only because of the associated tax liability, but because that extra liability might involve inconvenient administrative requirements or the risk of a heavy-handed official response. There is also the "spite effect" described by Musgrave (1959, 240). It is not known how powerful any spite effects might be, but they could further affect the revenue potential. Paradoxically, the tax gap definition of noncompliance might then have been partly satisfied because there is less to collect.

Tax compliance may be seen in terms of tax avoidance and tax evasion. The two activities are conventionally distinguished in terms of legality, with *avoidance* referring to legal measures to reduce tax liability and *evasion* to illegal measures. Since taxation is not always precise, Seldon (1979) has also coined the term "tax avoision" to describe circumstances where the law might be unclear. However, some commentators see noncompliance only as a problem of evasion, which does not seem to capture the full policy implications of the issue. Clearly tax evasion is an extreme form of noncompliance. However, if law-abiding taxpayers go to inordinate lengths to reduce their liability, this could hardly be considered to be compliance either. Such activities might include engaging in artificial transactions to avoid tax, searching out every possible legitimate deduction, using delaying tactics and appeals wherever this might reduce the flow of tax payments, and so on. "Tax exiles" even seem to prefer to emigrate rather than fulfill their obligations as citizens—hardly an example of compliance. Even if such activities are within the letter of the law, they are clearly not within its spirit. Compliance might therefore be better defined in terms of complying with the spirit as well as the letter of the law.

The tax gap approach overlooks the possibility that some taxpayers pay more than their legal obligation. Not all taxpayers seek out every possible method of reducing their tax liability, and an unknown number do not claim their full entitlement to allowable deductions. For example, in a survey of nonfilers McCrae and Reinhart (2003) had one respondent who stated, "I pay too much tax, I'm just too lazy to claim it [a tax rebate]! But I'd rather have a decent health system and pay more."

A further complication, of course, is that taxation is used for many purposes other than simply raising revenue. As an instrument of economic and social policy, the purpose of taxation is often to influence behavior. It can therefore actually be the intention of the tax that it is avoided. For example, it has been argued that higher taxes on alcoholic drinks (Cook and Moore 1994; Irving and Sims 1993) and tobacco (Viscusi 1994) would reduce the consumption of those products and lead to improvements in the health of the population. Any such changes in behavior would constitute tax avoidance, but it would be in the spirit as well as the letter of the law and would fit the definition of compliance offered here, though not the tax gap definition. There have also been developments in other forms of "corrective taxation," referred to as environmental taxes (Smith 1992), green taxes (Oates 1995), and so on. The tax gap approach to compliance is clearly too simplistic and inappropriate with respect to compliance in such cases. Compliance in this context would appear to indicate compliance with government policy in a wider sense, rather than only compliance with the tax law, and therefore behavior that should be expected from a responsible citizen.

A definition that covers compliance with the spirit as well as the letter of the law also indicates the importance of the behavioral contribution to developing policies for promoting compliance.

APPLICATIONS OF BEHAVIORAL THEORY

Tax authorities in many countries, such as Canada, Sweden, the United Kingdom, and the United States, have attempted to improve communication with taxpayers and to increase their awareness of the tax system and how to meet their obligations. Furthermore, they have been doing so for some time (James, Lewis, and Allison 1987). In recent years the behavioral approach and specific compliance models have been adopted more explicitly as guides to compliance strategies.

One example is the model developed by Braithwaite and Braithwaite (2001), where the style of enforcement emphasized is to begin by taking account of the problems, motivations, and conditions behind noncompliance. Taxpayers are initially given the benefit of the doubt, and the revenue service's trust in their honesty is an important part of an initial regulatory encounter. Strong emphasis is placed on educating taxpayers regarding their tax obligations and assisting them to comply, while those aspects of administration that rely principally on threats and the automatic imposition of penalties are not emphasized. It is only when taxpayers continue to be uncooperative that more interventionist measures (for example, sanctions) are considered.

The Australian Tax Office and the New Zealand Inland Revenue Department have both used such a model to develop their tax compliance strategies, and it is illustrated in Figure 29.2.

The Internal Revenue Service (IRS) in the United States has also made considerable moves in similar directions, despite its reputation at times for considerable enthusiasm in rigorously administering the tax system (for example, see Payne 1993). The new approach was endorsed by then Vice President Al Gore and Treasury Secretary Robert E. Rubin (1998) with this straightfor-

Figure 29.2   **Compliance Model Used in Australia and New Zealand**

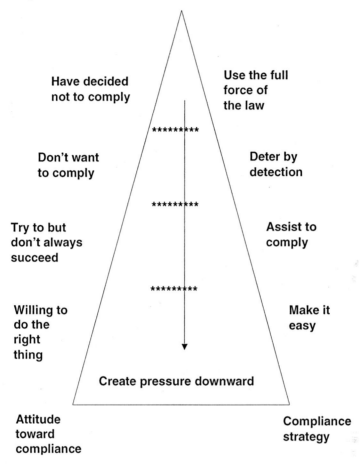

Source: Adapted from New Zealand Inland Revenue Department 2003, 6.

ward statement: "Our philosophy is simple: the taxpayers don't work for us, we work for them." However, the IRS has been developing this approach to promoting voluntary compliance for some years, as outlined in its forward-looking document *Compliance 2000* (U.S. Internal Revenue Service 1991). The strategy described in that document included behavioral issues such as proposals for more public education and inculcating in citizens a sense of responsibility toward taxes. The shift in the IRS's emphasis from enforcement to service to taxpayers is illustrated by Plumley and Steuerle (2003). In comparing the 1984 and 1998 IRS mission statements, they noted a change from "the purpose of the IRS is to collect the proper amount of tax *revenue* at the least cost to the public" (1984) to "provide America's taxpayers top quality *service*" (1998).

FUTURE RESEARCH

Behavioral economics is concerned with a wide range of factors—cultural, institutional, psychological, and social—that influence human decision making. Such factors vary over time, as does the tax system, and so future research seems to be limitless. Furthermore, the work on tax compliance could be extended to cover economic decisions in relation to compliance with many other obligations of one sort or another.

In terms of taxation, a particular line of future research relates to the development of e-commerce (Hickey 2000) and, indeed, e-taxation. Another is that most of the work so far is related to individual behavior, but there is also considerable scope to develop research relating to business behavior. In all areas there will be work for those with skills in compliance. As Edmund Burke (1780) put it: "Taxing is an easy business. Any projector can contrive new compositions; any bungler can add to the old."

CONCLUSION

There is no doubt that neoclassical economic analysis provides a great deal of insight into economic behavior. However, it is also clear that a wider behavioral approach can add considerably more to our understanding of economic activity. Individuals often do act in their own self-interest narrowly defined, but their behavior is also influenced by much wider considerations regarding their interactions with other individuals and society as a whole. Factors such as social norms, morals, perceptions of justice, various attitudes, and particular beliefs can influence the way people behave, even sometimes if their behavior is not in their own immediate self-interest. In the present context, behavioral economics adds enormously to our understanding of taxpayer behavior with respect to tax compliance—indeed, even in the development of a more comprehensive and appropriate definition of tax compliance itself. It has also enabled revenue services to develop a more sophisticated and appropriate strategy for promoting tax compliance.

REFERENCES

Allingham, Michael G., and Agnar Sandmo. 1972. "Income Tax Evasion: A Theoretical Analysis." *Journal of Public Economics* 1: 323–38.

Alm, James, Roy Bahl, and Matthew N. Murray. 1990. "Tax Structure and Tax Compliance." *Review of Economics and Statistics* 62: 603–13.

Alm, James, Mark B. Cronshaw, and Michael McKee. 1993. "Tax Compliance with Endogenous Audit Selection Rules." *Kyklos* 46: 27–45.

Alm, James, Betty Jackson, and Michael McKee. 1992. "Institutional Uncertainty and Taxpayer Compliance." *American Economic Review* 82, 4: 1018–26.

Andreoni, James, Brian Erard, and Jonathan Feinstein. 1998. "Tax Compliance." *Journal of Economic Literature* 36: 818–60.

Bain, C.E., V.C. Milliron, and T.J. Rupert. 1997. "The Effects of Firm Type and Experience on the Factors Influencing Tax Preparer Aggressiveness." *Journal of Business and Behavioral Sciences*, fall, 99–116.

Barr, N.A., S.R. James, and A.R. Prest. 1977. *Self-Assessment for Income Tax*, London: Heinemann.

Bernasconi, M. 1998. "Tax Evasion and Orders of Risk Aversion." *Journal of Public Economics* 67: 123–34.

Blumenthal, M., C. Christian, and J. Slemrod. 2001. "Do Normative Appeals Affect Tax Compliance? Evidence from a Controlled Experiment in Minnesota." *National Tax Journal* 54, 1: 125–36.

Bordignon, M. 1993. "A Fairness Approach to Income Tax Evasion." *Journal of Public Economics* 52: 345–62.

Braithwaite, Valerie, ed. 2003. *Taxing Democracy: Understanding Tax Avoidance and Evasion.* Aldershot, UK: Ashgate.

Braithwaite, V., and J. Braithwaite. 2001. "An Evolving Compliance Model for Tax Enforcement." In N. Shover and J.P. Wright, eds., *Crimes of Privilege.* New York: Oxford University Press.

Brand, Phil. 1996. "Compliance: A 21st Century Approach." *National Tax Journal* 49: 413–19.

Brown, Robert E., and Mark J. Mazur. 2003. "IRS's Comprehensive Approach to Compliance Measurement." *National Tax Journal* 61: 689–99.

Burke, Edmund. 1780. Speech in the House of Commons, 11 February. Cannan, Edwin. 1946. *Wealth: A Brief Explanation of the Causes of Economic Welfare,* London: Staples.

Christensen, A.L. 1992. "Evaluation of Tax Services: A Client and Preparer Perspective." *Journal of the American Tax Association* 14: 60–87.

Clotfelter, C.T. 1983. "Tax Evasion and Tax Rates: An Analysis of Individual Tax Returns." *Review of Economics and Statistics* 65: 363–73.

Coleman, Cynthia, and Lynne Freeman. 1997. "Cultural Foundations of Taxpayer Attitudes to Voluntary Compliance." *Australian Tax Forum* 13: 311–36.

Collins, J.H., and R.D. Plumlee. 1991. "The Taxpayer's Labour and Reporting Decision: The Effect of Audit Schemes." *Accounting Review* 66: 559–76.

Cook, P.J., and M.J. Moore. 1994. "This Tax Is for You: The Case for Higher Beer Taxes." *National Tax Journal* 47: 559–73.

Cowell, F.A. 1985. "The Economic Analysis of Tax Evasion." *Bulletin of Economic Research* 37: 163–93.

———. 1992. "Tax Evasion and Equity." *Journal of Economic Psychology* 13: 521–43.

Crane, Steven E., and Farrokh Nourzad. 1986. "Inflation and Tax Evasion: An Empirical Analysis." *Review of Economics and Statistics* 68: 217–23.

Cremer, Helmuth, and Firouz Gahvari. 1994. "Tax Evasion, Concealment and the Optimal Linear Income Tax." *Scandinavian Journal of Economics* 96: 219–39.

Cuccia, A.D. 1994. "The Effects of Increased Sanctions on Paid Tax Preparers: Integrating Economic and Psychological Factors." *Journal of the American Taxation Association* 16: 41–66.

Cullis, John G., and Alan Lewis. 1997. "Why People Pay Taxes: From a Conventional Economic Model to a Model of Social Convention." *Journal of Economic Psychology* 18: 305–21.

Dubin, Jeffrey A., and Louis L. Wilde. 1988. "An Empirical Analysis of Federal Income Tax Auditing and Compliance." *National Tax Journal* 41: 61–74.

Edgeworth, F.Y. 1881. *Mathematical Psychics.* London: Kegan Paul.

———. 1925. *Papers Relating to Political Economy.* London: Macmillan.

Erard, Brian, and Jonathan S. Feinstein. 1994a. "The Role of Moral Sentiments and Audit Perceptions in Tax Compliance." *Public Finance* 49 (supp.): 70–89.

———. 1994b."Honesty and Evasion in the Tax Compliance Game." *Rand Journal of Economics* 25, 1: 1–19.

Falkinger, J. 1988. "Tax Evasion and Equity: A Theoretical Analysis." *Public Finance* 43, 3: 388–95.

Falkinger, J., and W. Walther. 1991. "Rewards Versus Penalties: On a New Policy Against Tax Evasion." *Public Finance Quarterly* 19: 67–79.

Fischer, Carol M., Martha Wartick, and Melvin M. Mark. 1992. "Detection Probability and Taxpayer Compliance: A Review of the Literature." *Journal of Accounting Literature* 11: 1–46.

Gordon, J.P.F. 1989. "Individual Morality and Reputation Costs as Deterrents to Tax Evasion." *European Economic Review* 33: 797–805.

Gore, Al, and R.E. Rubin. 1998. *Reinventing Service at the IRS.* Washington, DC: Internal Revenue Service, Department of the Treasury.

Grasmick, H.G., and R.J. Bursik. 1990. "Conscience, Significant Others and Rational Choice: Extending the Deterrence Model." *Law and Society Review* 24: 837–61.

Hasseldine, D.J., and S.E. Kaplan. 1992. "The Effect of Different Sanction Communications on Hypothetical Taxpayer Compliance: Policy Implications from New Zealand." *Public Finance* 47: 45–60.

Hickey, Julian J.B. 2000. "The Fiscal Challenge of E-Commerce." *British Tax Review* 2: 91–105.

Hite, P.A. 1989. "A Positive Approach to Taxpayer Compliance." *Public Finance* 44: 249–67.

Irving, I.J., and W.A. Sims. 1993. "The Welfare Effects of Alcohol Taxation." *Journal of Public Economics* 52: 83–100.

James, Simon. 1992. "Taxation and Female Participation in the Labour Market." *Journal of Economic Psychology* 13: 715–34.

———. 1995a. "Female Labour Supply and the Division of Labour in Families." *Journal of Interdisciplinary Economics* 5: 273–90.

———. 1995b. *Self-Assessment and the UK Tax System.* London: Research Board of the Institute of Chartered Accountants in England and Wales.

———. 1996. "Female Household Investment Strategy in Human and Non-Human Capital with the Risk of Divorce." *Journal of Divorce and Remarriage* 25: 151–67.

James, Simon, and Clinton Alley. 1999. "Tax Compliance, Self-assessment and Administration in New Zealand—Is the Carrot or the Stick More Appropriate to Encourage Compliance?" *New Zealand Journal of Taxation Law and Policy* 5: 3–14.

James, Simon, Alan Lewis, and Frances Allison. 1987. *The Comprehensibility of Taxation: A Study of Taxation and Communications.* Aldershot: Avebury.

James, Simon, and Christopher Nobes. 2003. *The Economics of Taxation: Principles, Policy and Practice,* 7th ed. Harlow: Prentice Hall.

Jevons, William Stanley. 1871. *Theory of Political Economy.* London: Macmillan.

———. 1881. "Review of Edgeworth's *Mathematical Psychics.*" *Mind* 6: 581–83.

Kaplan, S.E., P.M.J. Reckers, S. West, and J. Boyd. 1988. "An Examination of Tax Reporting Recommendations of Professional Tax Preparers." *Journal of Economic Psychology* 9: 427–43.

Klepper, S., and D. Nagin. 1989. "Tax Compliance and Perceptions of the Risks of Detection and Criminal Prosecution." *Law and Society Review* 23: 209–39.

Lewis, Alan. 1982. *The Psychology of Taxation.* Oxford: Blackwell.

McCrae, J., and M. Reinhart. 2003. *Non-filers: What We Know.* Research Note 1. Canberra: Centre for Tax System Integrity, Australian National University.

Mill, John Stuart. 1848. *Principles of Political Economy.* London: Parker.

Musgrave, R.A. 1959. *The Theory of Public Finance: A Study in Political Economy.* New York: McGraw-Hill.

Nayak, P.B. 1978. "Optimal Income Tax Evasion and Regressive Taxes." *Public Finance* 33, 3: 358–66.

New Zealand Inland Revenue Department. 2003. *Report of the Inland Revenue Department for the Year Ended 30 June 2003.* Wellington: Inland Revenue.

Oates, Wallace E. 1995. "Green Taxes: Can We Protect the Environment and Improve the Tax System at the Same Time?" *Southern Economic Journal* 61: 915–22.

Payne, J.L. 1993. *Costly Returns: The Burdens of the US Tax System.* San Francisco: ICS Press.

Pencavel, J.H. 1979. "A Note on Income Tax Evasion, Labour Supply and Nonlinear Tax Schedules." *Journal of Public Economics* 12: 115–24.

Plumley, A., and E. Steuerle. 2003. "A Historical Look at the Mission of the Internal Revenue Service: What Is the Balance Between Revenue and Service?" In H. Aaron and J. Slemrod, eds., *The Crisis in Tax Administration.* Washington, DC: Brookings Institution.

Pommerehne, W.W., A. Hart, and B.S. Frey. 1994. "Tax Morale, Tax Evasion and the Choice of Policy Instruments in Different Political Systems." *Public Finance* 49 (supp.): 52–69.

Ricardo, David. 1821. *The Principles of Political Economy and Taxation,* 3rd ed. London: John Murray.

Richardson, M., and A.J. Sawyer. 2001. "A Taxonomy of the Tax Compliance Literature: Further Findings, Problems and Prospects." *Australian Tax Forum* 16: 137–320.

Roberts, M.L. 1994. "An Experimental Approach to Changing Taxpayers' Attitudes Towards Fairness and Compliance via Television." *Journal of the American Taxation Association* 16: 67–86.

Schmölders, G. 1959. "Fiscal Psychology: A New Branch of Public Finance." *National Tax Journal* 15: 184–93.

———. 1970. "Survey Research in Public Finance: A Behavioral Approach to Fiscal Policy." *Public Finance* 25: 300–6.

Seldon, Arthur. 1979. *Tax Avoision: The Economic, Legal and Moral Inter-Relationship between Avoidance and Evasion.* London: Institute of Economic Affairs.

Slemrod, J., M. Blumenthal, and C. Christian. 2001. "Taxpayer Response to an Increased Probability of Audit: Evidence from a Controlled Field Experiment in Minnesota." *Journal of Public Economics* 79, 3: 455–83.

Smith, Adam. 1776. *An Inquiry into the Nature and Causes of the Wealth of Nations.* Cannan ed. London: Methuen.

Smith, S. 1992. "Taxation and the Environment." *Fiscal Studies* 15: 19–43.

Spicer, M.W. 1986. "Civilization at a Discount: The Problem of Tax Evasion." *National Tax Journal* 39: 13–20.

Spicer, M.W., and S.B. Lundstedt. 1976. "Understanding Tax Evasion." *Public Finance* 31: 295–305.

Strümpel, B. 1969. "The Contribution of Survey Research to Public Finance." In A.T. Peacock, ed., *Quantitative Analysis in Public Finance.* New York: Praeger.

Tzur, J., and E. Kraizberg. 1995. "Tax Evasion and the Risk Averse Tax Collector." *Public Finance* 50: 153–65.

U.S. Internal Revenue Service. 1991. *Compliance 2000: Report to the Commissioner of Internal Revenues.* Washington, DC: Department of the Treasury.

Veblen, Thorstein. 1898. "Why Is Economics Not an Evolutionary Science?" In *The Place of Science in Modern Civilisation and Other Essays,* 73–74. New Brunswick, NJ: Transaction, 1961.

Viscusi, W.K. 1994. "Promoting Smokers' Welfare with Responsible Taxation." *National Tax Journal* 47: 547–58.

Webley, P., H. Robben, H. Elffers, and D. Hessing. 1991. *Tax Evasion: The Experimental Approach.* Cambridge: Cambridge University Press.

Wenzel, Michael. 2001a. "Misperceptions of Social Norms About Tax Compliance (1): A Pre-Study." Working paper no. 7. Canberra: Centre for Tax System Integrity, Australian National University.

———. 2001b. "Misperceptions of Social Norms About Tax Compliance (2): A Field-Experiment." Working paper no. 8. Canberra: Centre for Tax System Integrity, Australian National University.

Williams, Alan. 1966. *Tax Policy—Can Surveys Help?* London: Political and Economic Planning.

Yankelovich, Skelly, and White, Inc. 1984. *Taxpayer Attitudes Study: Final Report.* Washington, DC: Department of the Treasury, Internal Revenue Service, Public Affairs Division.

CHAPTER 30

ETHICAL INVESTING

Where Are We Now?

JOHN CULLIS, PHILIP JONES, AND ALAN LEWIS

In Allison Pearson's funny-sad best-selling novel *I Don't Know How She Does It,* the main character, Kate Reddy, a mother of two and an investment fund manager for the firm EMF, is assigned "a final [sales presentation] for a $300 million ethical pension fund account" in America. She is informed, "They want us to field a team that reflects EMF's commitment to diversity. . . . So I reckon that's gotta be you, Kate, and the Chinky (the newly appointed Momo) from research" (Pearson 2002, 123). Later, Kate tells the reader, "And of course I told Momo . . . how to compare screening criteria, and a dozen other things, but it was like asking a skate-boarder to dock a space station" (130). At the final a question is raised: "Ms. Reddy, New Jersey has recently signed up to the McMahon Principles. Would that be a problem for your asset collection?" (154). Kate has never heard of the principles. A would-be lover at the meeting comes to the rescue: "I think we can feel confident . . . that with Ms. Reddy's wide experience of ethical funds she would be up to speed with employment practices of companies in Ireland." Kate capitalizes on the situation, commenting: "As Mr. Abelhammer says, we have a team that screens for employment policies. On a personal note, I'd like to add I am fully behind the McMahon Principles, being Irish myself"—a half-truth (155).

A number of issues are encapsulated within these amusing interchanges: ethical investing is topical; it is big business; it may smack of faddish behavior; screens may be ambiguous; investment companies may respond to it in a cynical manner. The example illustrates a popular perception of ethical investment, but it is only one perception. Compare Allison Pearson's humorous account with a description of ethical investors based on analysis of questionnaire responses and interview studies in the United Kingdom:

> Compared to "ordinary" investors, more of them are in the caring professions—particularly health and education. Ethical investors are more frequently religious, active in pressure groups and supportive of "liberal" (and green) political stances. (Lewis 2002, 78)

Woodward (2000) also presents analysis of questionnaire responses. She describes the typical ethical investor as a well-educated, middle-aged manager or professional; more than half of the respondents in Woodward's sample claimed to be active in two or more cause-related movements (such as Greenpeace). Ethical investors may not be "saints," but in responses to questionnaires they appear to reveal a genuine commitment to "make a difference" (Lewis 2002, 97).

Comparisons of competing perceptions of ethical investing provide a natural springboard to deal with the main question in this essay: where are we now? In literature dealing with the economics of finance, financial investment appraisal is governed by analysis of mean and variance of expected financial returns (e.g., Copeland and Weston 1988). Analysis of ethical investment might embrace techniques employed in this literature, but it would appear that it does so with reference to a broader set of criteria. Hollis asks why some people refused to buy South African oranges "even when they were cheaper and juicier than their rivals"; the inference is that decisions are made with reference to "'ethical preferences' which appear to make sense of otherwise irrational behavior" (1992, 308). But to what extent have the criteria broadened? To what extent is ethical investing a fashion or a fad? To what extent does it reflect appraisal of investment against a broader set of criteria by investors hoping "to make a difference"?

This essay describes the establishment in the 1960s of ethical investing and of its growth thereafter. It presents background analysis to where we are now. Ethical mutual funds in the United States (called "ethical unit trusts" in the United Kingdom) screen companies to ensure that investment is directed toward companies deemed ethical and to divert investment from those deemed unethical. It considers the impact that screens might exert and the problems in defining ethicalness. As Kate Reddy notes, comparison of ethical screens is no easy matter—for some, assessing criteria is likely to prove almost as difficult as docking a space station. But if assessment of the impact of screening is so complex, are ethical investors really focused on changing social conditions? Are they really committed to the impact that ethical investment is intended to exert?

The complexity inherent in assessment of the final outcome of ethical investment is, in part, responsible for the persistence of quite disparate perceptions. Can ethical investors be so concerned about making a difference? Critics have claimed that "those who tout socially responsible investment have simply failed to do their homework" (Johnsen 2003, 219). If ethical investors are not able to explore all of the implications of reliance on screens, in what sense are they motivated by ethical considerations?

The essay also focuses on the individual's decision to invest ethically. Behavior often (always?) appears consistent with more than one motivation. The relevance of alternative motives is questioned. In this essay the relevance of different motivations is considered with reference to the pattern of growth and development of ethical investing. Is the pattern of growth of ethical investing consistent with instrumental motivation to make a difference?

Problems inherent in any assessment of ethical outcome and behavior consistent with competing motivations serve to sustain very different views of ethical investing. These are key issues that must be addressed to provide insight on where we are now and where we are going.

HISTORY, AUTHENTICITY, AND GROWTH OF "ETHICALS"

The somewhat cynical introduction to this essay is called into question immediately by reference to a case study of Friends Provident's "stewardship," the first U.K. ethical unit trust, founded in 1984 (Lewis 2002), Friends Provident was set up by two Quakers, Samuel Tuke and Joseph Rowntree, in 1832. No investments were to be made in arms, alcohol, tobacco, or gambling, in accordance with the beliefs of the Religious Society of Friends.

The Quakers were not alone in believing that morals matter in all aspects of life, including financial matters. John Wesley regularly preached, "Earn all you can; but not at the expense of conscience." From this Methodist tradition, Charles Jacob, a financial advisor in the Methodist Church, championed a proposal for a "stewardship" trust in 1973. Although initially stymied by the Department of Trade, on the grounds that restricting a portfolio on nonfinancial grounds would jeopardize the legal requirement of unit trusts to produce reasonable financial returns, a second proposal, in 1978, was successful.

The history of this ethical unit trust (the oldest and largest in the United Kingdom) suggests that initiators are genuine and are not simply engaged in marketing ploys (although the motives of the initiators are unlikely to be identical to those of the followers). The initiators are not appealing to fads and fashions: whether one is religious or not, it can surely be agreed that these labels trivialize religious belief and commitment. Its history also shows that the emergence of ethical funds is not the result of the efforts of one person in the wilderness. Mutual funds with exclusion criteria already existed in the United States. The successful stewardship application had the support of the then chairman of the stock exchange, Sir Nicholas Goodison, the Rowntree Trust Committee, and Friends Provident itself, uneasy about its increased secularization.

At the same time, analysis reveals that leading actors (movers and shakers) were aware of pent-up consumer demand. There was no product on the U.K. market in which people already conscious of their social responsibility could invest. The '70s and '80s witnessed a general increase in concern about ethical and environmental issues in the marketplace. Comprehension is enhanced by an appreciation of the interplay between religious tradition, the initiatives of the key players (institutions and individuals), and a changing environment.

The growth of the ethical investment movement has always attracted skepticism. The authenticity of ethical investors has been challenged, with Digby Anderson (1996), along with others, arguing that ethical investment has very little to do with ethics at all.

Friends Provident's stewardship can cite its association with the Ethical Investment Research and Information Service (EIRIS) and its committee of reference among its claims for authenticity. EIRIS was founded in 1983 following the plans of Trevor Jepson, chairman of Christian Concern for South Africa, with backing from not only the Quakers and Methodists but also the Church of England, the Presbyterian Church in Ireland and Wales, the Joseph Rowntree Trust, and Oxfam. EIRIS has charitable status and strives to provide objective information about investments across a wide range of criteria, which began with familiar religious exclusions and now include more secular concerns such as pollution, human rights, and animal testing. The Friends Provident committee of reference develops ethical policy based on evidence supplied by EIRIS and is aware of the ethical complexities: ethical criteria are not applied mechanically, and individual companies are occasionally discussed in some detail, especially if it is considered that the positive aspects of a company might outweigh some negative aspects.

The worldwide growth of ethical and socially responsible investing can be traced over the last twenty years, again suggesting that this form of investing is more than fad or fashion; it is perhaps better seen as a gathering social movement. In the United States today, it is estimated that there is some $2 trillion under investment in socially responsible investment (SRI) funds; this category includes 200 mutual funds, accounting for approximately 16 percent of total investment in the United States, according to the Social Investment Forum. In the United Kingdom there are approximately fifty ethical unit trusts with £4 billion under management, accounting for about 4 percent of total investments, according to EIRIS. In Europe approximately £11 billion has been invested ethically, and in Canada U.S. $300 billion has been invested by half a million investors (Schwartz 2003). It would be naive, however, to believe that all those investments are squeaky clean: the thoroughness of Friends Provident's stewardship is not mirrored throughout the industry, and some of the newer ethical and green funds do not use EIRIS and have no in-house researchers or advisory boards.

Twenty years ago (and since) financiers in the City of London shared the cynicism of the opening paragraphs of the current essay, describing these funds as "Brazil" funds because they were considered "nutty." These same financiers smirk less frequently these days, as the funds have mushroomed.

So what of the future? And can these investments make markets more moral? Many ethical investors believe they are doing more than merely salving their conscience; they believe that if there are enough "little voices" they will be heard, and companies that pollute or that employ child labor, for example, will have to change (Lewis 2002). Change is also engendered by the contemporary practices of ethical unit fund managers who are more likely than before to actively engage with companies to try to improve their behavior rather than merely withdrawing funds using avoidance criteria alone.

In the United Kingdom SRI funds have gained legitimacy through the actions of the current Labour government: as of July 2000, new legislation requires private sector pension funds to consider the social, environmental, and ethical aspects of their investments. This falls short of actually requiring funds to at least invest a portion of their portfolio ethically, but some commentators believe that this invitation could see ethical investing in the United Kingdom rising to £100 billion within a few years (Mackenzie 2000). There have been other relevant developments to fuel the fire as well, notably the launching of the FTSE4Good Index and the appointment of a minister for corporate social responsibility (CSR) in 2000.

The terms *ethical* and *socially responsible* (and, more commonly nowadays, *sustainable*) are labels regularly attached to a range of enterprises; it is important to ask what these terms mean (besides indicating that the activity is generally a good thing). *Social responsibility* is the favored term in the Labour government, the more troublesome label of *ethical* having been dropped. But could this legitimization of SRI as part of "third way" politics lead to a watering down of the ethical brew? CSR has formed a broad agenda where businesses are asked to improve their social, environmental, and local economic impact and consider how businesses affect society at large in terms of human rights, social cohesion, fair trade, and corruption. If anything, the notion of sustainability is even more vague and all-embracing.

In conclusion, it seems that the popularity of what we might now best refer to as SRI (the internationally most favored label) is set to continue to rise, given its increased visibility to institutional investors and because around 70 percent of individual investors feel they ought to be investing ethically even if they are not doing so at present, according to EIRIS.

ETHICAL SCREENS: ARE THEY ABLE TO MAKE A DIFFERENCE?

While actions by people of integrity have been evident, there has always been room for cynical comment. Whether investment is or is not ethical poses formidable philosophical questions that can be addressed only with reference to moral codes of conduct. But perhaps a more fundamental question is whether ethical investment is capable of making any difference at all. In questionnaire responses ethical investors insist that they strive to make a difference (i.e., to change outcome), but does such investment *really* make a difference? When asked about socially responsible investment, Nobel economics laureate Milton Friedman replied: "If people want to invest that way, that's their business. In most cases such investing is neither harmful nor helpful" (quoted in Laufer 2003, 165).

Ethical investment is defined in this essay with reference to the activity of ethical mutual funds that screen investment opportunities for more than just financial performance. Ethical funds screen companies with regard to "environmental performance, workplace practices, international business practices and product lines," and "certain industries, such as tobacco, gambling and weapons production are generally screened out" (Rivoli 2003, 271). The objective is to offer investors a portfolio that includes enterprises with good employer-employee relations, good environmental practices, socially acceptable products, and respect for human rights. Of course, ethical investment can also be defined with reference to other characteristics. It encompasses shareholder advocacy—the resolutions for social and environmental change tabled at shareholder meetings. It includes funds invested directly into community projects, such as low-income housing. However, by far the largest defining component of ethical investment is screened portfolio selection. Of a total of $2,159 billion in the United States in 1999, $1,232 billion was committed to investment reliant only on screening, $657 billion was committed to shareholder advocacy only, $265 billion was invested with screening and shareholder advocacy, and only $5.4 billion was assigned to direct community investing (Schueth 2003, 192). If ethical investment is to make a difference, screening must make an impact.

Comparisons of Financial Performance

If screening matters, surely this should be reflected in comparisons of the financial performance of restricted ethical portfolios and unrestricted investment portfolios. If ethical screening removes shares that would otherwise have been included in portfolios selected to maximize financial return, will the impact of ethical investing (to achieve changes in social conditions) be mirrored in lower financial rates of return received by ethical investors?

In questionnaire analysis, ethical investors report lower financial rates of return. In the United Kingdom, 42 percent of a sample of 1,146 ethical investors reported that they received a lower rate of return by investing ethically (Lewis 2002). However, in the same survey 41 percent believed that ethical investment yielded a similar return to that enjoyed by other portfolios. Nearly 14 percent believed that the rate of return was higher; 21 percent felt that ethical investment was less risky. Can it really be possible to gain financially and make a difference in social terms?

There are empirical studies of comparative financial performance that discover that ethical investors pay a price. Moskowitz (1992) reports underperformance of U.S. funds by 1 percent per annum; Tippet (2001) reports underperformance of Australian funds by 1.5 percent. Malkiel and Quandt (1971) estimated that ethical investors incurred a financial penalty of 3 percent per annum for applying noneconomic criteria when selecting investment. Analysis of the performance of "sin industries" (alcohol, tobacco, and gambling) in the 1980s and 1990s also suggests that ethical investors experienced lower financial returns; investment in sin industries outperformed the market on average (Luck and Tigrani 1994; Bloch and Lareau 1985).

By comparison, there are also studies that report risk-adjusted returns at least as high as returns on investment that is not socially responsible (Guerard 1997; Cummings 2000). Hayes (2000) and Hoyle (2000) claim that an ethical investor can expect a rate of return comparable to the market rate. Beckers (1989), Woodall (1989) and Gregory, Matatko, and Luther (1996) concluded that there was an insignificant difference in financial returns between ethical financial performance and market benchmarks.

But, perhaps more surprisingly, there are also studies that report financial premiums. Manchanda (1989), Marlin (1986), and Luther and Matatko (1994) suggest that ethical investment is capable of higher returns. Diltz (1995) found that the consequence of eleven different ethical screens and combinations of investment were largely neutral but that certain ethical screens might enhance performance. Cohen, Fenn, and Konar (1995) found no penalty for investing in a green portfolio and reported that in many cases a low-pollution portfolio might deliver better financial returns than an unconstrained portfolio.

Such different results may appear disconcerting, but it is important to realize that different

Date 1-6-07

M _____

Address _____

	Clerk	Reg. No.	Account Forward
1	Handbook of		75.-
2	Contemp Behav		
3	Economics		
4			
5			
6			
7	pd Visa		
8			
9			
10			
11			
12			
13	M.E. SHARPE, INC.		
14	80 Business Park Drive		
15	Armonk, NY 10504		75

results are possible depending on how comparisons are made and the definitions of ethical invest-ment and costs. For example, rates of return might be considered either before or after an allow-ance for ethical fund management costs. Munnell (1983), Rudd (1981), and Lamb (1991) believe that ethical investors incur a penalty due to management fees and the costs of assessing social data. Second, financial performance might be compared across quite different ethical portfolios. If screens focus on products (alcohol, tobacco, gambling), ethical investors are far more likely to pay a price than if screens are premised on business practices. If companies are screened to avoid those that pay excessive remuneration to their directors (or with reference to the financial inter-ests of directors beyond the company in question), ethical investment is more likely to enjoy better financial rates of return.

Comparisons also vary with respect to time horizons. If preferences of consumers in society are changing (moving away from products deemed unethical), then long-run financial perfor-mance by ethical investment is more likely to prove better than anticipated. Havemann and Webster (1999) refer to a recent Market and Opinion Research International (MORI) poll in the United Kingdom in which three in ten consumers reported that they had chosen (or boycotted) a com-pany for ethical reasons in the preceding twelve months. Klassen and McLaughlin (1996) found that companies that developed strong environmental programs are rewarded in the market, and note that companies involved in environmental disasters (for example, oil spills) experience a fall in company share price greater than can be explained simply in terms of direct cleanup costs.

When is it likely to achieve higher financial performance by investing ethically? Tippett (2001) argues that ethical investing is biased against large companies because the probability of being involved in at least one unacceptable practice is higher in larger companies. He sug-gests that there is a small-companies effect and argues that ethical investors' portfolios will include a larger share of smaller companies subject to higher returns. Moreover, ethical invest-ment is more likely to achieve higher returns when investment is located in companies that have been screened as honest (because monitoring costs for investors are lower). Havemann and Webster argue that "because they have fewer companies to invest in they know them better and are more focused on their activities . . . there will be less churn in the portfolio and hence lower trading costs" (1999, 12).

A combination of higher financial return and ethical investment is more likely when selection by ethical screens correlates with selection based only on financial criteria. Yach, Brinchman, and Bellet (2001) report the emergence of a perception in recent years that disinvestment in the tobacco industry is financially prudent. The industry has experienced many difficulties, including increased regulation and unprecedented litigation. The World Health Organization's Tobacco Free Initiative surveyed managers of ethical funds in the United States, Canada, and the United Kingdom, and the responses refer to strictly financial reasons for divesting from tobacco compa-nies. The authors conclude: "There is a movement toward disinvestment from tobacco for both ethical and financial reasons" (Yach, Brinchman, and Bellet 2001, 193). There are also cases in which investment in firms producing more healthy products also yield healthier financial returns.

Can Ethical Investment Exert Financial Pressure?

A second test of the efficacy of ethical investment focuses on potential to exert pressure on unethi-cal companies. Will ethical screening have any impact on high-profit/poor-social-performance firms? Will companies respond by changing their products and their business practices? If screen-ing is to exert pressure, it must reduce the share price for unethical firms. As the share price of an unethical company falls, costs of capital increase. The company is put under pressure to reconsider its product, marketing, and business practices. If ethical investment is to prove effective, screening must prove effective in capital markets.

In a perfectly competitive capital market, demand curves for individual equities will be infinitely price-elastic (horizontal). Investors will be able to buy, or sell, any amount of a firm's shares without affecting price (Rivoli 2003). In a perfect capital market investors are price takers. The value of the firm's equity is given by the present value of the cash flow generated by the firm; only events that change the present value of these cash flows will affect the share price.

Case studies call into question the proposition that companies' share price is affected by ethical screening. Teoh, Welch, and Wazzan (1999) identified seventeen U.S. firms with extensive presence in South Africa and examined whether share prices of these firms responded to an announcement by nine pension funds (on different dates) that firms with South African operations would be removed from their portfolios. They showed that, with only one exception, share prices did not drop significantly in response to this disinvestment announcement.

But case studies have been challenged (Rivoli 2003). More generally, the proposition that demand curves are infinitely elastic with respect to share price is tenuous and difficult to defend. Investors are unlikely to have the same information and to interpret it in the same way. If investors do not find close substitutes for shares of a particular firm, the demand curve for shares in a company is more likely to be downward-sloping (Chan and Lakonishok 1993). When transaction costs are related to the size of investors' positions, the demand curve is more likely to be downward-sloping (Loderer, Cooney, and Van Drunen 1991) Most importantly, Rivoli (2003) argues that if some stocks are unrestricted (i.e., held by both screened and unscreened funds), the price of such shares will be higher than the price of otherwise identical shares that do not appear in ethical funds. Ethical investors with a restricted portfolio (including only socially responsible companies) are likely to demand a higher risk premium. After surveying empirical studies, Rivoli concludes that "the available evidence is highly suggestive of finite price elasticities" (2003, 283).

Of course, the corollary is that ethical investment might prove even more potent if it were better targeted. Rivoli (2003) argues that ethical investing will exert greater pressure where (1) riskier firms are more responsive, (2) there are more unique firms (with fewer substitutes for the product), and (3) firms are trading in smaller, restricted markets. Yet while potency might be increased, the main conclusion is that ethical screening is able to exert pressure on unethical firms in capital markets. This potential increases as the percentage of ethical investing in capital markets increases.

If share price falls for unethical firms and the cost of capital increases, unethical firms face a dilemma. Heinkel, Kraus, and Zechner (2001) explore response to ethical investment in a risk-averse setting. Focusing on green investment, they demonstrate that polluting firms will become socially responsible as a consequence of exclusionary ethical investing, as long as the higher cost of capital more than exceeds the cost of business reform. Inevitably, firms must consider the costs of changing their product and practices. Bartlett and Preston (2000) identify difficulties inherent in making changes in a business culture that has been premised on pursuit of profit. It may take "sinners" some time to repent, but ethical screens are able to initiate the process.

Do Screens Ensure Anticipated Ethical Outcomes?

A third test of the ability to make a difference is set in terms of the extent to which ethical screens are likely to deliver the ethical outcomes that are anticipated. Ethical investment can both encourage ethical firms and exert pressure on unethical firms in capital markets. But, as noted previously, it is naive to assume that all screened investment generates the desired change. Ethical screens are pre-

Figure 30.1 **An Input-Output Taxonomy**

	Industry Output	
Company Input Processes	Ethical	Unethical
Ethical	1	2
Unethical	3	4

mised on very general criteria; there are many potential inconsistencies. Just as Kate Reddy, busy working mother of two, had no opportunity to investigate the McMahon Principles, so in a busy world ethical investors usually have little opportunity to explore all ramifications.

Consider screens that focus on products. Ethical mutual funds usually exclude investment in firms that produce weapons, tobacco, alcohol, and gambling. However, when screening against weapons, does it matter how the weapons might be used? Is there a difference, for example, between a firm that produces weapons used to resist tyranny and one whose products are used to maintain law and order? Does it matter that weapons are used for defense rather than for aggression? The impact of screening companies on ethical outcomes is far from obvious. Whether screens really deliver the desired ethical outcome is questionable.[1]

If a product is deemed unethical, does it matter that firms might be compliant in its production? Would a bank be unethical if it made loans to a firm that produced weapons? Would a steel company be unethical if it supplied munitions factories? Critics are concerned that ethical screens do not encompass all such considerations. Hoggett and Nhan (2002) note that Cussons (a British soap manufacturer) is deemed ethical by Hunter Hall (a highly regarded ethical fund) because Cussons does not test its products on animals. Hoggett and Nhan comment that a leading ingredient in Cussons soap is palm oil, and the production of palm oil is a major factor in the destruction of tropical rainforests.

A distinction can be made between product and production process. In Figure 30.1, a two-by-two taxonomy is presented, with case 4 clearly being lowest of the low. While boxes 2 and 3 might be considered somewhat gray, what would be the status of "bad" employers in "good" industries, or "good" employers in "bad" industries?

When ethical screens are premised on broadly acceptable principles they appear disarmingly simplistic. Schwartz argues that screens are "based on the fundamental moral principle of avoiding unnecessary harm and its ethical correlate, respect for an individual's moral right to health and safety." However, he continues by asking, "What if the individual is made fully aware of the risks [of a particular product] and still decides to use the product? . . . Can the individual be said to have legitimately waived [his or her] moral rights . . . ?" (2003, 202). The ethicalness of screens is called into question. Is it moral to deny choice to consumers when consumers are fully informed?

Fine lines must be drawn, but they imply a level of precision difficult to justify. Ethical mutual funds often rely on percentage limits—for example, Ethical Funds accepts that 20 percent of a firm's gross revenues can be derived from tobacco and military production (Schwartz 2003, 209). But, of course, there is more than one option; in the United Kingdom, ethical unit trusts operate with a similar restriction of 10 percent (Lewis 2002). In the United States, Total Social Impact (TSI) provides ratings of corporations based on business practices (socially responsible investment rating schemes are discussed in Dillenburg, Greene, and Erekson 2003). In some cases, reference has been made to "social and environmental metrics" (Laufer 2003, 163). Such fine-tuning appears neat and precise, but it begs important ethical questions. For some, the presentation of simplistic solutions is itself immoral (Anderson 1996).

Assessing the Scope for Mutual Ethical Funds to Make a Difference

Evidence assessed with reference to the tests described above indicates that ethical investment is capable of making a difference. Whether the impact exerted will ultimately accord with the intention of ethical voters is difficult to gauge, but in capital markets ethical mutual funds are able to exert pressure. There is growing recognition that ethical investment matters. However, when coupled with the awareness that ethical investors are unable to address all of the complexities inherent in reliance on screens, this raises important policy issues. Focusing on ethical mutual funds as financial agencies, Lewis and colleagues question their activity, which might be "as much an attempt to exploit a particular niche market in the unit trust sector, as . . . to promote more ethical business practice" (1998, 179).

Ethical mutual funds are unable to ignore investors' preferences. Lewis and McKenzie (2000) report that mutual ethical funds pursue objectives differently in the United Kingdom and in the United States. Questionnaire analysis in the United Kingdom reveals that investors prefer greater emphasis on passive signaling (boycotting shares of unethical companies) than on active engagement (shareholding activism to alter the behavior of unethical companies), and patterns of fund activity are consistent with this preference.

However, the extent to which agencies are responsive is another matter. Given complexities noted above, the extent to which investors' preferences act as a constraint has been questioned. There is growing concern that those who manage ethical funds are able to enjoy discretion, and this has resulted in increasing demands for codes of conduct to mandate disclosure requirements and to ensure a fair screening process (Schwartz 2003).

THE DECISION TO INVEST ETHICALLY: INFERRING MOTIVATION FROM BEHAVIOR

By any test, there is sufficient evidence that, collectively, ethical investment is capable of making a difference, and in questionnaires ethical investors insist that they intend to make a difference. But does this imply that each individual ethical investor is motivated simply to change social conditions, that is, to change outcome? Is this sufficient to explain the decision to invest ethically?

This section begins by focusing on instrumental motivation. There is no attempt to offer definitive normative assessment, that is, whether ethical investing is or is not altruistic. Ethical investing appears altruistic (personal sacrifice for the greater good), and altruism is not discounted. But analysis of altruism often produces examples of behavior better explained by self-interest.[2] Kaler (2000) explains why self-interested business managers often act ethically. At this stage, it is too early even to pose the question this way, that is, in terms of either altruism or self-interest. Margolis's (1982) analysis of a dual self (selfish *and* altruistic) appears a more plausible framework (Lewis 2002). Both altruism and self-interest may play a part in the analysis that follows, on the question of whether evidence proves consistent with the proposition that ethical investors are motivated purely by instrumental rationality.

Are Investors Motivated by Reward for Instrumental Action?

Neoclassical economic theory explains investment behavior with reference to instrumental pursuit of financial reward. The attraction is the rate of return that will be earned on funds invested. If this same analysis were equally relevant for ethical investment, individuals would be motivated by a rate of return that encompassed both financial and social change—a "social rate of return."

It is unlikely that ethical investors are especially sensitive to change in the social rate of return to their investment (i.e., to the prospect that their personal action will change social conditions). It is difficult enough to compare and forecast financial rates of return. The complexity of assessing an ethical rate of return to personal investment is daunting. It is unlikely that ethical investors incur the requisite decision-making costs.

The very success of ethical mutual funds (from the 1960s on) depended on the role that financial intermediaries played in reducing the costs of assessing ethical investment. Ethical screens offer low-cost symbols of what it means to invest ethically. In the absence of screens, socially conscious investors would be obliged to carry out their own evaluation of companies. Ethical screens provided the catalyst for pent-up social consciousness post-1960. Schueth argues: "The modern roots of social investing can be traced to the impassioned political climate of the 1960s." This "tumultuous decade" experienced "a series of themes from anti–Vietnam war movements to civil rights to concern about the cold war and equality for women" (Schueth 2003, 190). Lewis and Cullis refer to "the vitalization of what we term post-industrial values" and to "increased environmental consciousness" (1990, 403). Socially conscious individuals have responded to ethical screens, and there is no incentive for any individual to look beyond screens, to incur investigative costs in assessing the final effect of their action on social conditions. Financial rates of return can be compared on receipt of dividends; rates of return that encompass a social dimension are far more complex to assess.

Ethical investors typically hold small ethical portfolios. In the United Kingdom, 80 percent of ethical investors have "morally mixed" portfolios that include both ethical investment and unethical investment. From questionnaire evidence, the mean (average) amount invested ethically by those with morally mixed portfolios is 31 percent. The median holding is 21 percent; the most popular single amount is 10 percent (Lewis 2002). The portfolio of the typical ethical investor is too small to warrant the investigation.

So why do people have morally mixed portfolios? Interviews reveal that unethical investment is often inherited, and a certain amount of inertia sets in (Lewis 2002). There is little fungibility of assets; assets are allocated to different mental accounts (Thaler 1994). Yet investors with morally mixed portfolios take their ethical investments seriously and are relatively inelastic for losses, a result that has been replicated in questionnaire and computer simulations.

It is not just a matter of costs of information. Even if information were freely available and even if prospective social rates of return were demonstrably high, social rates of return would be unlikely to motivate investment. Change in social outcome is a public good. Some have argued that high social rates of return for those who act ethically will motivate action. Mueller (2003) argues that individuals incur costs in voting because, as ethical voters, they look to a payoff for society as a whole. If this analysis is applied to ethical investing, the return to any individual investor would appear substantial when social conditions are improved.

Following Mueller, the ethical investor, i, might be defined as maximizing the following objective function:

$$O_i = U_i + \Theta \, \Sigma U_j \ldots \qquad\qquad (30.1)$$

where: O_i = the objective of individual i;

U_i = the utility individual i derives from consuming goods and services;

ΣU_j = the sum of the utilities of other individuals in the community and Θ = a parameter.

If $\Theta = 0$ the individual is selfish and if $\Theta = 1$ the individual is altruistic. If $\Theta > 0$, the return to ethical investment appears very high because it includes ΣU_j (the happiness created for others).

There are two problems with this analysis. First, while the return (from changing social conditions) is high, the analysis does not focus directly on results that can be attributed to the individual's action. While there is a substantial social change (measured by ΣU_j), the relevant consideration to an instrumental individual is the extent to which his or her personal action has achieved this change (Plott 1987). Second, even if social return to personal investment were high, benefits are nonexcludable. Others (other altruists) are better off if ΣU_j is achieved. If altruists are instrumental, the rational strategy is to free-ride (to let others bear the costs). There is no motivation to invest even though investment would yield a high return (in terms of ΣU_j). In a different context, Olson remarks: "Even if the member of a large group were to neglect his own interests entirely, he still would not rationally contribute toward the provision of any collective or public good since his own contribution would not be perceptible" (1965, 64).

The proposition that ethical investors (even as altruists) are sensitive to prospective social rates of return and motivated to act instrumentally is tenuous.

Are Investors Motivated by the Intrinsic Value of Action?

Architects of utility theory were aware that utility might be derived from action. In the eighteenth century Jeremy Bentham (1789) argued that individuals derive satisfaction from action, quite distinct from utility derived from outcome contingent on action. Individuals signal self-worth, to themselves and to others, by action. Neoclassical theory focuses on instrumental action. Reflecting on Bentham's observations, Loewenstein argues that the "evolution of the utility concept during our century has been characterized by a progressive stripping away of psychology" (1999, 315). While ethical investors are relatively insensitive to the impact of personal action in terms of outcome, there is reason to anticipate greater sensitivity to perceptions of the intrinsic value of action, that is, the act of investing ethically.

Analysts of ethical investing highlight the relevance of perceptions of action. Rivoli (2003) argues that ethical investors derive utility by disassociating themselves from the behavior of unethical firms. Johnsen argues that "much of what passes as socially responsible investing (SRI) in many cases is nothing more than a panacea for those who want to rid themselves of . . . guilt" (2003, 219). Schueth suggests that there are two groups of ethical investors, one "more interested in the 'social change,'" the other motivated to "feel better about themselves" by taking action (2003, 190).

Ethical investors themselves express the importance of the act of ethical investment. Consider the following questionnaire response: "There are two reasons to invest ethically—to influence companies and to maintain integrity. Just because ethical investment was found to be ineffective would be no reason to withdraw one's funds" (Lewis 2002, 78). In questionnaires and experiments ethical investors are not sensitive to changes in financial rates of return. In one experiment participants who interacted with a virtual financial advisor on the World Wide Web "generally stayed 'loyal' to ethical investment even if it performed badly or was ethically ineffective" (Webley, Lewis, and Mackenzie 2001). Even when action was ethically ineffective it still appeared worth pursuing. Outcome is not the only concern. Inertia is evident in the adoption of a 10 percent ratio for ethical investing; widespread adoption of such a percentage appears more compatible with reliance on convention than with a purely instrumental cost-benefit evaluation of ethical portfolios.

For many (most?) ethical investors, participation in the process of ethical investment is likely to prove as important as the intention of changing social conditions. Perhaps like all activities, ethical investment can be thought of as generating two sources of utility. There is outcome (or result) utility generated by a social rate of return, and there is process (or participation) utility associated with the *act* of ethical investing in itself. The first is essentially an investment utility and the second a consumption utility.[3]

If the final or overall (expected) utility from ethical investing (U_{le}) requires the exploration of two terms whose weight in final utility is variable across individuals and over time,

$$U_{le} = \omega\, U(r_e - r^*) + (1 - \omega)\, U(P_e - P^*) \dots \tag{30.2}$$

where: ω = a weight such that $0 \leq \omega \leq 1$;

$\quad r_e$ = the return to ethical investing over a period;

$\quad r^*$ = the pecuniary return to investing independent of any ethical considerations over a period;

$\quad P_e$ = the process or participation payoff from ethical investing over a period;

$\quad P^*$ = the process or participation payoff from investing independent of any ethical considerations over a period.

Ethical investment reflects rational utility maximization if $U_{le} \geq 0$.

If $\omega = 1$ and $r_e > r^*$ then, at one extreme, the motivation is investment in outcome. On the other hand, if $\omega = 0$ and $P_e > P^*$ the motivation is pure participation. More generally, individual action can be expected to fall within a spectrum as the size of ω, r_e, r^*, P_e, and P^* alter as is likely, over time. Table 30.1 is indicative of how a taxonomy can be compiled.

Determinants of Intrinsic Motivation and the Growth of Ethical Investing: A Network Externalities Model

If the intrinsic value of action (of participation in process) is likely to play a role, what determines perceptions of the intrinsic value of action? An individual is said to be "intrinsically motivated to perform an activity when one receives no apparent reward except the activity itself" (Deci 1971, 105). Intrinsic motivation to perform an act (or duty) is based on moral and ethical considerations, but it is also affected by external intervention (e.g., Deci and Ryan 1980, 1985).[4] External intervention occurs when others acknowledge the value of action (see Frey 1997). One way of analyzing the determinants of perceptions of the intrinsic value of participation is via signals emitted by the behavior of others.

If intrinsic motivation is relevant, patterns of growth of ethical investing are likely to reflect response to behavior by others. To illustrate, consider a network externalities model. Network externalities occur when demand for (or utility an investor obtains from ethical in-

Table 30.1

A Taxonomy of Investors

$\omega = 1$
$r_e > r^*$ "outcome" ethical investor
$r_e < r^*$ "outcome" non-ethical investor

The multi-motivated investor
$0 \leq \omega \leq 1$
$r_e \leq r^*$
$r^* \leq r_e$
$P_e \leq P^*$
$P^* \leq P_e$

$\omega = 0$
$P_e > P^*$ "process" ethical investor
$P_e < P^*$ "process" non-ethical investor

vesting) depends on the number of other individuals who invest ethically. In some network externality models utility might decrease as others participate (e.g., in the case of conspicuous consumption). However, in the case of ethical investment the expectation is that the more that others engage, the more individuals identify intrinsic value in the act of participation.[5] As noted above, there is no necessity that this response be deemed altruistic. Ethical investing might be deemed altruistic; following Andreoni (1988), the "warm glow" from action increases as others acknowledge its significance. However, the motivation might simply be to win acceptability and respect, and in this context, the actions of others signal the significance of participation in a process.

If ethical investing is generally low-cost (e.g., $r_e - r^*$ is only marginally negative), then, other things being equal, the perception that others participate is likely to induce a critical mass of investors. If ethical investing were high-cost ($r_e - r^*$ noticeably negative), it is unlikely that the behavior of others would prove as important; a low participation equilibrium would be predicted.

Consider the situation if an investor has a stand-alone preference, s—utility that the investor would enjoy if she or he were the only (non-) ethical investor—but also enjoys a network externality, depending on the number of other investors who act in the same way. Suppose s is a positive preference for ethical investing. If the size of the ethical investing population is N_e, then utility can be represented as $U(s, N_e)$. (For those wishing to foster ethical investing the policy is clear they must take action to increase N_e over time.) If doing what others do matters, then the size of the non-ethically investing population (N_n) also matters ($U(N_n)$). If N_n is sufficiently large, then $U(N_n) > U(s, N_e)$ and those who have a preference for ethical investing will not be observed to demonstrate that preference. That is, $U(N_n - N_e) > U(s)$.

In Figure 30.2 (following Cabral 2000), the $U(s)$ and $-U(s)$ lines are the so-called absorbing barriers for a preference. As long as $U(N_n - N_e)$ (reduced to $N_n - N_e$ for convenience) is within that band, the individual will express the stand-alone preference. Outside the barriers, all choose the dominant choice irrespective of their own preference, and the process becomes self-reinforcing; the situation is one where individuals are locked into a process.

If ethical investing can be modeled in this path-dependent, sequential way, then a small num-

Figure 30.2   **Ethical Investing as Technology Choice with Network Externalities**

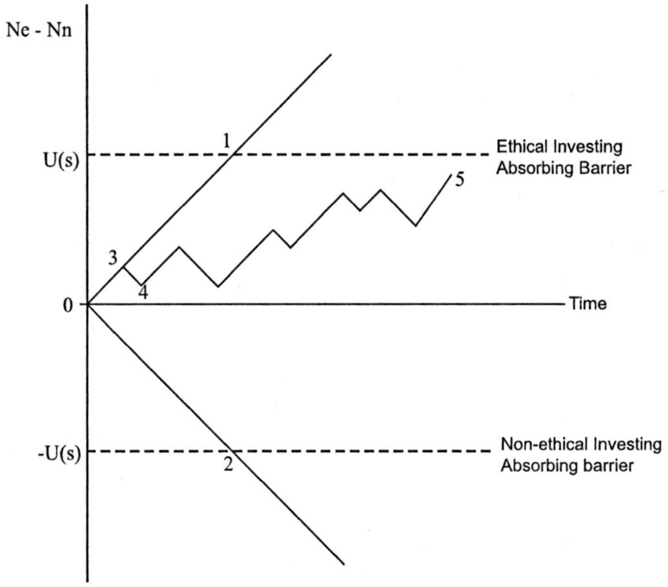

Source: Adapted from Cabral 2000.

ber of individuals with $U(s) > 0$ for ethical investing can have a large impact over time. (Unusually for economics, historical events matter, and this is where a psychological approach offers greater traction; it can model the actions of opinion formers and the like.)

In Figure 30.2 a single investor arrives each time period. If all investors were the same type (with the same stand-alone preference), then the absorbing barriers would be met very quickly, as indicted by the straight-line path of choices. If all have a preference for ethical investing, point 1 is reached, and if all have a preference for non-ethical investing, point 2 is reached. More realistically, investors will differ. In Figure 30.2 the first few to arrive (beginning at $t = 0$) are ethical investors, and a move toward the top absorbing barrier is made. However, at point 3 an individual arrives with the preference not to invest ethically and, as $N_e - N_n$ is within the absorbing barriers, that preference will be demonstrated. At point 4, several ethical investors arrive in sequence and $N_e - N_n$ increases, and so on.

As drawn, the model describes a growth of ethical investors as compared to non-ethical investors, but at point 5 the absorbing barrier has yet to be reached and not all investing will be ethical. As noted above, the first arrivals have an ability to set the process on an ethical investing path, which suggests a focus on the first individuals to advocate and choose ethical investing. The model illustrates how ethical investing might prove self-reinforcing behavior; rapid growth is possible. It also suggests that the development of ethical investing generally might vary from country to country.

Assessing the Importance of Instrumental and Intrinsic Motivations

Ethical investors hope to make a difference in social conditions, but in a busy life they have little incentive (little opportunity) to become sensitive to changes in the prospects of exerting an impact on outcome by additional ethical investment. Action is unlikely to be purely instrumental; the goal is nonexcludable. The proposition that only outcome motivates individual investment is tenuous. Motivation for the individual investor is likely to depend more heavily on perceptions of the intrinsic value of participation in process.

The more relevant the intrinsic value of action, the more the patterns of growth of ethical investing will reflect the existence of network externalities. The behavior of others can enhance (or demean) perceptions of the intrinsic value of action. A model of network externalities proves illustrative. Patterns of self-reinforcing growth are predicted when individuals are motivated by the intrinsic value of action and when perceptions of the intrinsic value of action depend on the involvement of others.

In practice, investors are unlikely to be as acutely aware of others (of precise numbers) in the way described. However, as Lewis comments, "if they do not always know each other [they] know *of* one another" (2002, 24).

ETHICAL INVESTING: SOME TESTABLE PREDICTIONS

In the introduction to this essay the typical ethical investor was described as middle-class, professional/managerial, and well educated. Recent questionnaire analysis was cited, but other questionnaire studies of ethical investors also emphasize levels of education. Rosen, Sandler, and Shani analyze responses from 4,000 investors in two mutual funds and note that "compared with other investors, socially responsible investors are younger and better educated" (1991, 201). Educated ethical investors are receptive to information that is reported in both the financial and popular press. Schueth emphasizes that "US investors are better educated and informed today than at any other time in history" (2003, 192).

Winnett and Lewis (2000) provide analysis of press coverage of ethical investment by identifying common themes. A key conclusion is that ethical investing attracts more than usual interest from journalists. As Lewis notes, "Financial journalists are paid to write, inform, and to some extent, entertain. The 'dismal science' of economics is not the easiest of topics to draw the crowds. Ethical investing helped because it is, at turns, exotic, quirky and ripe for investigation. . . . Financial journalists enthusiastically pick up the theme" (2003, 51–52).

In the United States 60 percent of socially conscious investors are women. Schueth emphasizes that women are increasingly engaged in the world of finance. He notes: "As they have worked their way up the ladder within large organizations, as they have started their own companies, as they have taken seats on boards of directors and assume roles as fiduciaries, women have brought a natural affinity to the concept of socially conscious investors" (2003, 192).

The action of those involved in shareholder advocacy also serves to signal the intrinsic value of ethical screening. Rivoli (2003) notes that, since the mid-1990s, approximately 250 to 300 shareholder resolutions related to social/ethical issues have been introduced each year in the United States. In 2000 the greatest number of proposals was associated with issues concerning the environment and energy. The success of resolutions, in terms of changing outcome, is moot. Rivoli notes that "none of the shareholder proposals introduced during the five-year period 1996–2000 garnered a majority of shareholders." However, it is also the case that proponents withdrew more than 27 percent of social policy shareholder resolutions introduced between 1997 and 2000, usually because a satisfactory agreement had been reached with management. The issue here is not so much success, in terms of impact on outcome, as visibility. Reports of shareholder advocacy reinforce perceptions that ethical investing has intrinsic merit.

The impact of social norms has been modeled in terms of response to the behavior of others (e.g., Myles and Naylor 1996). The more pervasive the low-cost signals, the stronger the perception of a social norm. Analysis of network externalities was premised on response to numbers.

Figure 30.3 **Stable Intermediate Norm**

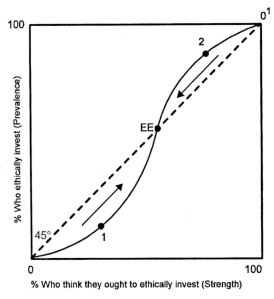

However, more generally, investors are responsive to dissemination of a social norm, that is, that individuals ought to invest ethically. Predictions formed with reference to the strength of social norms describe the same self-reinforcing pattern of growth.

Hargreaves-Heap (1992) argues that social movements are premised on self-supporting norms. Strength of norm can be defined as the proportion of investors who think they ought to ethically invest (whether they actually do or not). Prevalence of ethical investing depends positively on the strength of the norm of ethical investing. That is, the more individuals ethically invest, the greater the proportion in society who think they ought to ethically invest. When the strength of the norm exceeds the proportion actually conforming to the norm, more are induced to comply with the norm (and vice versa). Equilibrium occurs when the norm is self-supporting, that is, when the proportion who think they ought to conform with the norm equals the number who actually conform with the norm.

In Figures 30.3 to 30.7 the 45° line is the equilibrium line.

1. In Figure 30.3 the ethical investing equilibrium is EE. Below EE at point 1 the strength of the norm (S) exceeds the prevalence of the norm (P) and increased prevalence is induced ($\Delta P/\Delta S > 0$).[6] Above point EE, say at point 2, the strength of the norm (S) falls short of the prevalence of the norm (P) and prevalence is reduced ($\Delta P/\Delta S < 0$). Equilibrium EE is stable; any deviation from it will be self-correcting as $\Delta P/\Delta S > 1$ at EE.
2. In Figure 30.4, the equilibrium EEu is an unstable equilibrium; any deviation, or tremble, to points such as 1 and 2 from EEu induces feedback effects that make 0 and 0^1 the stable equilibria ($\Delta P/\Delta S < 1$ at EEu).
3. In Figures 30.5 and 30.6 there are multiple equilibria. Figure 30.5 is a low, or complete, stable equilibria ethical investing population. Figure 30.6 is a high, or zero, stable equilibria ethical investing population. Other patterns are clearly possible.

Figure 30.4   **Unstable to Extreme Norms**

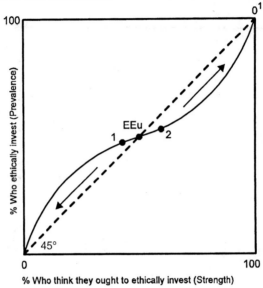

Figure 30.5   **Low and Complete Equilibria**

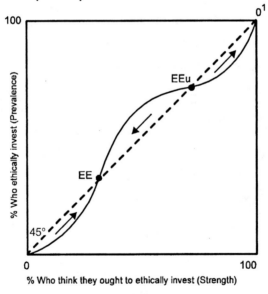

The key prediction is that the growth of ethical investing depends on the difference be-tween strength of social norm (the proportion of investors who think they ought to invest ethically) and prevalence of social norm (the proportion of investors who actually invest ethically). In June 1999 an EIRIS and National Opinion Poll survey of 493 representative

Figure 30.6 **High and Zero Equilibria**

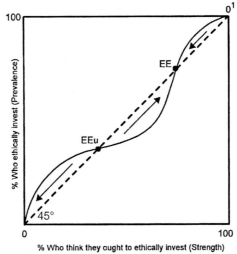

adults in Great Britain (see Havemann and Webster 1999) reported on strength of social norm in the United Kingdom:

1. Seventy-seven percent of respondents felt that their pension scheme should operate an ethical policy whenever it can do so without reducing financial return.
2. Thirty-seven percent would like to see a small part of their pension fund invested in businesses set up to promote social or environmental causes even if they offer a lower rate of return.
3. A majority (just over 50 percent in each case) wanted their pension fund (1) to invest in companies with a good employment record, (2) to exert influence on companies to limit pay deals for directors if a company had done badly, and (3) to divest from companies that broke environmental regulations.

It is clear that some 70 percent of investors are currently estimated to be interested in (or feel a need to be) socially responsible investors—but only some 4 percent presently do so. This point, labeled C, is plotted in Figure 30.7. Locating this observation in the southeast corner of the square-box figures (with norm strength far in excess of prevalence) permits prediction. It suggests rapid growth·of ethical investing, a prediction consistent with changes experienced in the recent past.[7]

To test predictions formed with reference to the difference between strength and prevalence of norm, consider the pattern of growth of ethical investing in the United Kingdom since the 1990s (EIRIS provides data since 1989). Evidence on size and growth of ethical investing are reported in Tables 30.2 and 30.3. In Table 30.2 the data relate to pooled ethically screened fund size (screened investments are those selected with reference to social, environmental, or other ethical criteria). The picture is one of steady, strong growth of pooled ethically screened funds, from under £200 million in 1989 to over £4 billion in 2001, an increase by a factor of twenty, with a lowest annual growth of some 11 percent.

As EIRIS notes, data must be interpreted carefully. Fund providers often provide estimated figures. Some individuals will be counted twice (if they have holdings in more than one fund); others (who are direct SRI investors or invest via other funds) are not counted at all. Even so, in

Figure 30.7   **Disequilibrium Indicating Fast Ethical Investment Growth**

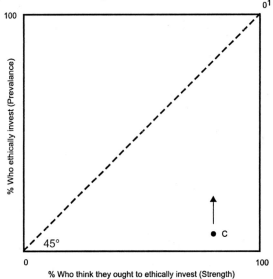

August 2001, 1.5 million investors in the United Kingdom subscribed to ethically screened funds, and the total value of investment was some £4 billion.

While questionnaire evidence regarding strength and prevalence of social norms is not as accessible in the United States, evidence of rapid growth in the United States suggests a similar situation, in which strength exceeds prevalence (Schueth 2003).

CONCLUSION

Kate Reddy, busy working mother of two, arrived at her "final" ill-prepared to deal with questions regarding the McMahon Principles. In a busy life, ethical investors fulfill a personal commitment while being less than fully informed of the final effectiveness of their action. But does this imply that ethical investing is simply a fad?

There is no inconsistency if investors intend to make a difference but are less than fully aware of the impact of action. The complexity of acquiring full information is daunting. Assessment of all ramifications would test an experienced financial analyst and dedicated philosopher. In a busy world, ethical investors are unable to make this level of commitment. However, in this they are no different from others in society. Statistical analysis reveals that donors to charities do not fully internalize all information that affects perceptions of the impact of action on outcome. In a study of the impact of indicators of accountability of charities (indicators that imply donations are more likely to affect outcome), statistical analysis revealed that such indicators exerted only "a weak impact on charities' ability to raise funds from the public"; such evidence suggested that "donors are concerned primarily with the donative act" (Berman and Davidson 2003, 428). The ability to assess impact of action on outcome differs for different decisions; there are situations in which it is more salient to rely more heavily on assessment of the intrinsic value of action.

Focusing on outcome, critics deny that ethical investment can make any difference at all. However, analysis with reference to different tests reveals that, collectively, ethical investment is able to exert an impact. There are some cases in which ethical investing, narrowly defined, can

Table 30.2

Pooled Ethically Screened Fund Size

Year	£ (millions)	Change over previous year	% change over previous year	Direction of growth rate
1989	199	—	—	—
1991	318	119	59.8	—
1992	372	54	17.0	↓
1993	448	76	20.4	↑
1994	672	224	50.0	↑
1995	792	120	17.9	↓
1996	1,008	296	37.4	↑
1997	1,465	377	34.7	↓
1998	2,198	733	50.0	↑
1999	2,447	249	11.3	↓
2000	3,296	849	34.7	↑
2001	4,025	729	22.1	↓

Source: Ethical Investment Research and Information Service.

Table 30.3

Number of Unit Holders/Policyholders in Pooled Ethically Screened Funds

Year	Number (thousands)	Change (thousands)	% change
September 1997	137	—	—
June 1998	304	167	121.8
June 1999	321	17	5.6 (↓)
June 2000	366	45	14.0 (↑)
June 2001	456	90	24.6 (↑)
August 2001	492	36	

Source: Ethical Investment Research and Information Service.

enjoy financial premiums. More generally, ethical investment is able to exert leverage on unethical firms in capital markets. The less competitive the capital market, the more that share prices (and cost of capital) respond to restricted investment. Demand for shares is likely to be less than infinitely price-elastic; ethical investment has the potential to effect change. With rapid growth (as a share of total investment), ethical investment has increasing potency.

As behavior is so often consistent with different motivations, critics question the incentive to invest ethically. In this essay, analysis has focused on the relevance of instrumental and intrinsic motivations (rather than on assessment of whether these are better described as self-interested or altruistic). Even though, collectively, ethical investment exerts an impact on outcome, the typical ethical investor is insensitive to the impact that she or he might exert on outcome. Comparisons of prospective financial rates of return are complex enough; there is little incentive for further analysis if outcome is nonexcludable (a public good). By comparison, low-cost signals that inform perceptions of the intrinsic value of action are easily accessed. The cohort in society that invests ethically is the cohort most likely to prove receptive to signals in the financial press and in the media generally. They are well-educated and middle-class; they are receptive to screens that serve as low-cost symbols of what is required to invest ethically.

Patterns of growth of ethical investment are consistent with the proposition that intrinsic motivation plays an important part in motivating ethical investment. A model of network externalities illustrates how the response to signals emitted by the behavior of others creates self-reinforcing growth of a social movement. More generally, predictions can be formed and tested with reference to the difference between strength and prevalence of social norms.

Ethical investing offers a case study of group action where individual motivation depends heavily on perceptions of the value of action but where the group collectively can exert an impact on outcome. In recent years the growth of ethical investing has been rapid in the United Kingdom and in the United States. Forecasts of future growth are optimistic (Mackenzie 2000). The encouragement by the Labour government in the United Kingdom to invest ethically provides yet another self-reinforcing signal. As the scene is now set, ethical investment has the potential to exert more influence the more that signals inform ethical investors that this is the right thing to do.

NOTES

1. Johnsen considers screening in the United States to avoid investment in firms that employ sweat-shop labor in South East Asia. He argues that U.S. investors would be dismayed to learn that "if sweat-shops were shut down many . . . young women might well be thrust into curb-side prostitution." He adds: "It is painfully obvious that US organized labor is the primary beneficiary of a policy that seeks to shut down sweat-shop labor" (2003, 220).

2. Charitable donation might be a response to fund-raising, that is, donors' desire to attend gala occasions, to purchase lottery tickets, etc. (Olson 1965). Individuals and firms give, to improve their reputation; politicians adopt altruistic postures to increase electoral support and prestige. Voluntary workers give time and effort to acquire on-the-job training experience and/or valuable personal contacts (Knapp, Koutsogeorgopoulou, and Davis Smith 1994 refers to personal investment gains). Workers give to charity to ease social pressure from supervisors to contribute to philanthropic schemes (Keating 1981; Keating, Pitts, and Appel 1981).

3. These motivations are readily captured in everyday colloquialisms: "Winners are grinners and losers can do what they like" and "Who cares who came in second" versus "It is not whether you won or lost but how you played the game" and "It is not the winning but the taking part."

4. Frey (1997) shows how the form of remuneration and form that government intervention takes (taxation, regulation, subsidy) impacts on intrinsic motivation.

5. In industrial economics this concept has obvious application to sectors such as mobile phone technologies, where the value of being on one system varies positively for any individual with the expected size of the membership of that network.

6. The curve EE is strictly convex ($f' > 0$ and $f'' > 0$), whereas beyond EE the curve is strictly concave ($f' > 0$ and $f'' < 0$).

7. It must be recognized, however, that of ethical investors only 20 percent claim "purity," with the remaining 80 percent having morally mixed portfolios of which around a fifth is ethically invested. Not only is there an apparent gap between norm strength and norm prevalence in the population, but it seems to be present within individuals as well.

REFERENCES

Anderson, Digby. 1996. "What Has Ethical Investing to Do with Ethics?" Research Report 21. Social Affairs Unit, London.
Andreoni, James. 1988. "Privately Provided Goods in a Large Economy: The Limits of Altruism." *Journal of Public Economics* 35: 57–73.
Bartlett, Andrew, and David Preston. 2000. "Can Ethical Behaviour Really Exist in Business?" *Journal of Business Ethics* 23: 199–209.

Beckers, Stan. 1989. "Ethical Investments in the UK: The EIRIS/BARRA Report." *BARRA International Newsletter,* 1st quarter, 1–4.

Bentham, Jeremy. 1789. *The Principles of Morals and Legislation.* New York: Macmillan, 1948.

Berman, Gabrielle, and Sinclair Davidson. 2003. "Do Donors Care? Some Australian Evidence." *Voluntas: International Journal of Voluntary and Nonprofit Organizations* 14: 421–429.

Bloch, H.R., and T. Lareau. 1985. "Should We Invest in 'Socially Responsible' Firms?" *Journal of Portfolio Management,* summer: 27–31.

Cabral, Luis M.B. 2000. *Introduction to Industrial Organisation.* Cambridge, MA: MIT Press.

Chan, Louis K.C., and Josef Lakonishok. 1993. "Institutional Trades and Intraday Stock Price Behaviour." *Journal of Financial Economics* 33: 173–99.

Cohen, Mark A., Scott A. Fenn, and Shameek Konar. 1995. "Environmental and Financial Performance: Are They Related?" Investor Responsibility Research Centre, Washington, DC, April.

Copeland, Thomas E., and J. Fred Weston. 1988. *Financial Theory and Corporate Policy,* 3rd ed. Reading, MA: Addison-Wesley.

Cummings, Lome S. 2000. "The Financial Performance of Ethical Investment Trusts: An Australian Perspective." *Journal of Business Ethics* 25: 79–92.

Deci, Edward L. 1971. "Effects of Externally Mediated Rewards on Intrinsic Motivation." *Journal of Personality and Social Psychology* 18: 105–15.

Deci, Edward L., and Richard M. Ryan. 1980. "The Empirical Exploration of Intrinsic Motivational Processes." *Advances in Experimental Social Psychology* 10: 39–80.

———. 1985. *Intrinsic Motivation and Self Determination in Human Behavior.* New York: Plenum Press.

Diltz, J. David. 1995. "The Private Cost of Socially Responsible Investing." *Applied Financial Economics* 5: 69–77.

Dillenburg, Stephen, Timothy Greene, and Homer Erekson. 2003. "Approaching Socially Responsible Investment with a Comprehensive Ratings System: Total Social Impact." *Journal of Business Ethics* 43: 167–77.

Frey, Bruno S. 1997. *Not Just for the Money: An Economic Theory of Personal Motivation.* Cheltenham: Edward Elgar.

Gregory, Allan, J. Matatko, and Robert Luther. 1996. "Ethical Unit Trust Financial Performance: Small Company Effects and Fund Size Effects." Working paper 96/6, Department of Accounting and Finance, University of Glasgow.

Guerard, John B. 1997. "Additional Evidence on the Cost of Being Socially Responsible in Investing." *Journal of Investing* 6: 31–35.

Hargreaves-Heap, Shaun. 1992. "Bandwagon Effects." In Shaun Hargreaves-Heap et al., eds., *The Theory of Choice: A Critical Guide,* 291–94. Oxford: Blackwell.

Havemann, Ross, and Peter Webster. 1999. "Does Ethical Investment Pay?" Ethical Investment Research Service, London, September.

Hayes, S. 2000. "The Greater Good: How Ethical Investment Pays Off." *Australian Financial Review,* 29–31.

Heinkel, Robert, Alan Kraus, and Josef Zechner. 2001. "The Effect of Green Investment on Corporate Behaviour." *Journal of Financial and Quantitative Analysis* 36: 431–49.

Hoggett, J., and M. Nhan. 2002. "Ethical Investment Grows in the United Kingdom." *Wall Street Journal,* June 19.

Hollis, Martin. 1992. "Ethical Preferences." In Shaun Hargreaves-Heap et al., eds., *The Theory of Choice: A Critical Guide,* 308–10. Oxford: Blackwell.

Hoyle, S. 2000. "Ethical Approach Catches on with Funds." *Australian Financial Review* 26–27.

Johnsen, D. Bruce. 2003. "Socially Responsible Investing: A Critical Appraisal." *Journal of Business Ethics* 43: 219–22.

Kaler, John. 2000. "Reasons to Be Ethical: Self Interest and Ethical Business." *Journal of Business Ethics* 27: 161–73.

Keating, Barry. 1981. "United Way Contributions: Anomalous Philanthropy." *Quarterly Review of Economics and Business* 21: 114–19.

Keating, Barry, Robert Pitts, and Dave Appel. 1981. "United Way Contributions: Coercion, Charity or Economic Self Interest?" *Southern Economic Journal* 47: 815–23.

Klassen, Robert D., and Curtis P. McLaughlin. 1996. "The Impact of Environmental Management on Firm Performance." *Management Science* 42: 1199–213.

Knapp, Marin, Vasiliki Koutsogeorgopoulou, and Justin Davis Smith. 1994. "The Economics of Volunteer-ing: Examining Participation Patterns and Levels in the UK." Department of Economics, University of Kent.

Lamb, D. 1991. "Morals and Money." *Money Management,* September, 39–46.

Laufer, William S. 2003. "Social Screening of Investments: An Introduction." *Journal of Business Ethics* 43: 163–65.

Lewis, Alan. 2002. *Morals, Markets and Money: Ethical, Green and Socially Responsible Investing.* Harlow, UK: Pearson.

Lewis, Alan, and John Cullis. 1990. "Ethical Investments: Preferences and Morality." *Journal of Behavioral Economics* 19: 395–411.

Lewis, Alan, and Craig Mackenzie. 2000. "Support for Investor Activism Among UK Ethical Investors." *Journal of Business Ethics* 24: 215–22.

Lewis, Alan, Paul Webley, Adrian Winnett, and Craig Mackenzie. 1998. "Morals and Markets: Some Theo-retical and Policy Implications of Ethical Investing." In Peter Taylor-Gooby, ed., *Choice and Public Policy: The Limits to Welfare Markets,* 164–83. London: Macmillan.

Loderer, Claudio, John W. Cooney, and Leonard D. Van Drunen. 1991. "The Price Elasticity of Demand for Common Stock." *Journal of Finance* 46: 21–51.

Loewenstein, George. 1999. "Because It Is There: The Challenge of Mountaineering for Utility Theory." *Kyklos* 52: 315–44.

Luck, Christopher, and Vida Tigrani. 1994. "Ethical Investment and the Returns to Sinful Industries." *BARRA Newsletter,* Spring: 1–4.

Luther, Robert, and J. Matatko. 1994. "The Performance of Ethical Unit Trusts: Choosing an Appropriate Benchmark." *British Accounting Review* 26: 77–89.

Mackenzie, Craig. 2000. "An Evolutionary Model." *Pensions Week,* March Supplement.

Malkiel, Burton, and Richard E. Quandt. 1971. "Moral Issues in Investment Policy." *Harvard Business Review* March-April, 37–47.

Manchanda, Vijay. 1989. "Ethical and Green Investing: The Fund Manager's View." *CNIM Articles, Local Government Chronicle,* October, 1–4.

Margolis, Howard. 1982. *Selfishness, Altruism and Rationality.* Cambridge: Cambridge University Press.

Marlin, Alice T. 1986. "Social Investing: Potent for Political Change." *Business and Society Review* 57:96–100.

Moskowitz, M. 1992. "When Your Conscience Needs a Guide." *Business and Society Review,* September-November: 71–75.

Mueller, Dennis C. 2003. *Public Choice III.* Cambridge: Cambridge University Press.

Munnell, A. 1983. "The Pitfalls of Social Investing." *New England Economic Review,* September/October, 20–37.

Myles, Gareth D., and Robin A. Naylor. 1996. "A Model of Tax Evasion with Group Conformity and Social Customs." *European Journal of Political Economy* 12: 49–66.

Olson, Mancur. 1965. *The Logic of Collective Action: Public Goods and the Theory of Groups.* Cambridge, MA: Harvard University Press.

Pearson, Allison. 2003. *I Don't Know How She Does It.* London: Vintage.

Plott, Charles R. 1987. "The Robustness of the Voting Paradox." In Charles K. Rowley, ed., *Democracy and Public Choice Essays in Honour of Gordon Tullock,* 100–2. Oxford: Basil Blackwell.

Rivoli, Pietra. 2003. "Making a Difference or Making a Statement? Finance Research and Socially Respon-sible Investment." *Business Ethics Quarterly* 13: 271–87.

Rosen, Barry N., Dennis M. Sandler, and David Shani. 1991. "Special Issue and Socially Responsible Investment Behavior: A Preliminary Empirical Investigation." *Journal of Consumer Affairs* 25: 221–34.

Rudd, Andrew. 1981. "Social Responsibility and Portfolio Performance." *California Management Review* 23: 55–61.

Schueth, Steve. 2003. "Socially Responsible Investing in the United States." *Journal of Business Ethics* 43: 189–94.

Schwartz, Mark S. 2003. "The Ethics of Ethical Investing." *Journal of Business Ethics* 43: 195–213.

Teoh, Siew H., Ivo Welch, and Christopher P. Wazzan. 1999. "The Effects of Socially Activist Investment Policy on the Financial Markets: Evidence from the South African Boycott." *Journal of Business* 72: 35–87.

Tippet, John. 2001. "Performance of Australia's Ethical Funds." *Australian Economic Review* 34: 170–78.

Webley, Paul, Alan Lewis, and Craig Mackenzie. 2001. "Commitment Among Ethical Investors: An Experimental Approach." *Journal of Economic Psychology* 22: 27–42.

Winnett, Adrian, and Alan Lewis. 2000. "'You'd Have to Be Green to Invest in This': Popular Economic Models, Financial Journalism and Ethical Investment." *Journal of Economic Psychology* 21: 319–39.

Woodall, A. 1989. "Ethical Investments in the UK: The EIRIS/BARRA Report." *BARRA International Newsletter,* 1st quarter.

Woodward, Teresa. 2000. *The Profile of Individual Ethical Investors and Their Choice of Investment Criteria.* Bournemouth: Bournemouth University Press.

Yach, Derek, Sissel Brinchman, and Suzanne Bellet. 2001. "Healthy Investments and Investing in Health." *Journal of Business Ethics,* 33: 191–98.

CHAPTER 31

TIPPING IN RESTAURANTS AND AROUND THE GLOBE

An Interdisciplinary Review

MICHAEL LYNN

On an average day, approximately 10 percent of the U.S. population eats at sit-down/family restaurants. In an average month, approximately 58 percent do so (Media Dynamics 2001). After completing their meals, almost all of these restaurant diners leave a voluntary gift of money (or tip) for the server who waited on them (Speer 1997). These tips, which amount to approximately $21 billion a year, are an important source of income for the nation's two million waiters (Lynn 2003b). In fact, tips sometimes represent 100 percent of waiters' take-home pay, because tax withholding eats up all of their hourly wages (Mason 2002).

Of course, tipping is not confined to restaurant servers or to the United States. In the United States, consumers also tip barbers, bartenders, beauticians, bellhops, casino croupiers, chambermaids, concierges, delivery people, doormen, golf caddies, limousine drivers, maître d's, massage therapists, parking attendants, pool attendants, porters, restaurant musicians, washroom attendants, shoeshine boys, taxicab drivers, and tour guides, among others (Star 1988). Although not as common as in the United States, tipping is also practiced in most countries around the world (Putzi 2002). In fact, national differences in tipping are a source of uncertainty for many international travelers, and local tipping practices are a topic covered in most travel guides.

Tipping is an interesting economic behavior, not only because it is widespread and practically important, but also because it is an expense that consumers are free to avoid. Although called for by social norms, tips are not legally required. Furthermore, since tips are not given until after services have been rendered, they are not necessary to get good service in establishments that are infrequently patronized. For this reason, many economists regard tipping as "mysterious" or "seemingly irrational" behavior (e.g., Ben-Zion and Karni 1977; Frank 1987; Landsburg 1993). The present essay explores this behavior and its implications for economic theory and public policy.

The essay is divided into four sections. The first two sections provide more detail about the phenomenon of tipping by summarizing and discussing the results of empirical research on the determinants and predictors of restaurant tipping and of national differences in tipping customs, respectively. Then economic theories about tipping are reviewed in light of the previously summarized empirical literature. Finally, the public welfare and policy issues raised by tipping are discussed.

DETERMINANTS AND PREDICTORS OF RESTAURANT TIPPING

Restaurant tips in the United States vary substantially across dining occasions, dining parties, servers, and restaurants. Numerous studies attempting to explain this variability in restaurant tipping have appeared in the psychology and hospitality management literatures, and a few such studies are beginning to appear in the economics literature (e.g., Bodvarsson and Gibson 1994; Bodvarsson, Luksetich, and McDermott 2003; Conlin, Lynn, and O'Donahue 2003; Lynn and McCall 2000a; McCrohan and Pearl 1991). This research has generally relied upon one or more of the following three methodologies:

1. Researchers have stood outside restaurants and conducted exit surveys of departing patrons about their just-completed service encounters and tipping behaviors.
2. Researchers have created panels of consumers who agreed to keep diaries of their restaurant dining experiences and tipping behavior.
3. Researchers have recruited restaurant servers to record information about their own behavior, their customers' characteristics, and the tips those customers leave.

Among the variables whose effects on restaurant tipping have been studied using these methodologies are bill size, payment method, dining party size, service quality, server friendliness, server sex, customer sex, customer patronage frequency, customer ethnicity, and various interactions between these variables. The results of this research are briefly reviewed in the paragraphs below.

Bill Size

Social norms in the United States call for tipping restaurant servers 15 to 20 percent of the bill, so it should not be surprising that dollar tip amounts are positively related to bill size. What may be surprising is how strong this relationship is. In a quantitative review of thirty-six studies involving 5,016 dining parties from over forty restaurants, Lynn and McCall (2000b) found that 69 percent of the average within-restaurant variability in dollar tip amounts can be explained by bill size alone. This suggests that bill size is twice as powerful as all other factors combined in determining dollar tip amounts within restaurants.

Of course, the effects of bill size are not invariant. Research suggests that bill size predicts dollar tip amounts better when the tipper is a regular patron of the restaurant (Lynn and Grassman 1990), the tipper has higher income and education (Lynn and Thomas-Haysbert 2003), and the tipper is Asian or white as opposed to black or Hispanic (Lynn and Thomas-Haysbert 2003). It is possible that these variables moderate the relationship between dollar tip amount and bill size because they reflect differences in awareness of the restaurant tipping norm. Supporting this possibility, one study found that blacks are half as likely as whites to know that the customary restaurant tip is 15 to 20 percent of the bill, and additional, unreported analyses of that study's data indicated that awareness of the norm increases with income and education (Lynn 2004b).

While dollar tips increase with bill size, percentage tips decrease with bill size (Green, Myerson, and Schneider 2003). This effect—known as the "magnitude effect in tipping"—is due to a positive intercept in the relationship between dollar tips and bill sizes rather than to a marginal decrease in the positive relationship between these two variables (Lynn and Sturman 2003). The positive intercept has been attributed to:

1. A tendency to leave a minimum tip when bill size is very small (Lynn and Bond 1992)
2. A tendency to add a constant amount for the mere presence of the server to the standard percentage tip (Green, Myerson, and Schneider 2003)
3. A tendency for some people to be "flat dollar tippers" while others are "percentage tippers" (Lynn and Sturman 2003)
4. A tendency to round up tip amounts (Azar 2003)

Of these explanations, however, only the "flat dollar tipper" explanation has received any empirical support. National surveys indicate that about 20 percent of restaurant tippers leave a flat dollar amount rather than a percentage of the bill (Paul 2001; Speer 1997), and a computer simulation by Lynn and Sturman (2003) demonstrated that this fact is sufficient to produce the magnitude effect in tipping.

Payment Method

Restaurant patrons paying with credit cards generally leave larger bill-adjusted or percentage tips than do those paying with cash (Feinberg 1986; Garrity and Degelman 1990; Lynn and Latane 1984; Lynn and Mynier 1993). These credit card effects on tipping could be due to:

1. The reduced psychological cost of delayed payments
2. Preexisting differences between cash and credit-card customers
3. Conditioned responses to credit-card stimuli (Feinberg 1986)

Consistent with the last of these explanations, McCall and Belmont (1996) found that people tipped more when the bill was presented on tip trays embossed with credit card insignia than when it was presented on plain tip trays and that this effect occurred even when people paid the bill with cash.

Dining Party Size

Large dining parties leave smaller percentage tips than do small dining parties (Freeman et al. 1975; Lynn and Latane 1984; May 1980). This effect has been attributed to:

1. A diffusion of the shared responsibility that each group member has for the server (Freeman et al. 1975)
2. An equitable adjustment for the smaller per-person effort involved in waiting on larger tables (Snyder 1976)
3. A cost-reducing adjustment for the larger bill sizes acquired by larger tables (Elman 1976)
4. A statistical artifact produced by a positive intercept in the relationship between dollar tips and bill sizes (Lynn and Bond 1992)

Of these explanations, only the statistical artifact explanation has been empirically supported (see Lynn and Bond 1992).

Service Quality

Dining parties that rate the service highly leave larger tips than those who rate the service less highly (Lynn and McCall 2000a). Furthermore, this relationship remains statistically significant even after controlling for customers' food ratings, customer patronage frequency, and many other variables (Conlin, Lynn, and O'Donahue 2003). The robustness of the effect after controlling for many potential confounds suggests that it is causal—that is, receiving better service causes people to leave larger tips. Despite its reliability and robustness, however, the service-tipping relationship is weak (see Bodvarsson and Gibson 1999; Bodvarsson, Luksetich, and McDermott 2003; Lynn 2000b, 2003a, 2004c). Customer service ratings account for only 1 to 5 percent of the within-restaurant variability between dining parties in tip percentages (Lynn and McCall 2000a). Similarly weak relationships between service and tipping have been observed at the server and restaurant levels of analysis (Lynn 2003b).

Several studies have examined potential moderators of the service-tipping relationship. A quantitative review of those studies testing the service by patronage frequency interaction found that the effects of service on tipping do not vary with the tipper's frequency of restaurant patronage (see Lynn and McCall 2000a). However, studies testing other interactions have found that the effect of service on tipping is moderated by customer ethnicity (Lynn and Thomas-Haysbert 2003) and day of the week (Conlin, Lynn, and O'Donahue 2003). Changes in service ratings are associated with larger changes in tip percentages among Asians and Hispanics than among blacks and whites. Changes in service ratings also have a bigger effect on weekday tip percentages than on weekend tip percentages. This latter effect may be attributable to the greater control over service delivery that servers have on weekdays (which are comparatively slow) than on weekends. Supporting this logic, Seligman and colleagues (1985) found that pizza delivery drivers received larger tips for faster deliveries, but only when the tipper believed the driver was personally responsible for the delivery time.

Server Friendliness

Although service ratings are only weakly related to tip percentages, server friendliness is a moderately strong predictor of tipping. Studies have typically found that servers' verbal and nonverbal signals of friendliness increase tip percentages by 20 to 40 percent or more (Lynn 1996, 2003b). For example, servers receive larger percentage tips when they:

1. Introduce themselves by name (Garrity and Degelman 1990)
2. Repeat customers' words when taking food orders (van Baaren et al. 2003)
3. Touch customers lightly on the arm, hand, or shoulder (Crusco and Wetzel 1984; Hornik 1992; Lynn, Le, and Sherwyn 1998; Stephen and Zweigenhaft 1986)
4. Give customers big, open-mouthed smiles (Tidd and Lockard 1978)
5. Squat down next to the table during interactions with customers (Davis et al. 1998; Lynn and Mynier 1993)
6. Entertain customers with games or jokes (Guéguen 2002; Rind and Strohmetz 2001b)
7. Draw smiley faces or other pictures on the back of checks (Guéguen and Legohérel 2000; Rind and Bordia 1996)
8. Write "thank you" or other messages on the backs of checks (Rind and Bordia 1995; Rind and Strohmetz 1998)
9. Call customer by name when returning credit card slips to be signed (Rodrigue 1999)

All of these studies involved random assignment of dining parties to the different treatments, so they provide fairly strong evidence that tipping is affected by servers' rapport with customers.

Server and Customer Sex

Men sometimes leave larger tips than do women (e.g., Crusco and Wetzel 1984; Lynn and Latane 1984), and waitresses sometimes receive larger tips than do waiters (e.g., Davis et al. 1998), but these sex effects on tipping are not always found (Lynn and Graves 1996; Lynn and Simons 2000). It appears that the effect of customer sex on tipping depends on server sex and vice versa. In an unpublished quantitative review of the tipping literature, Lynn and McCall (2000b) found that men tipped more than women in studies where the server was female, while women tipped more than men in studies where the server was male. Furthermore, Conlin, Lynn, and O'Donahue (2003) found a significant interaction between server and customer sex such that women tipped more than men when the server was male but not when the server was female. These findings suggest that tipping is affected by the dynamics of sexual attraction.

Customer Patronage Frequency

The regular patrons of a restaurant base their tips on bill size more than do new or infrequent patrons (Lynn and Grassman 1990; Lynn and McCall 2000b), perhaps because they are more familiar with the 15 to 20 percent restaurant tipping norm. They also tend to leave larger average tips than do infrequent patrons (Lynn and McCall 2000a). This latter effect remains significant even after controlling for customers' ratings of the food and service (Conlin, Lynn, and O'Donahue 2003; Lynn and Grassman 1990), so regular customers do not tip more merely because they perceive the food and service more positively than do infrequent customers. Instead, regular patrons may tip more because they are more likely to identify with servers or because they value servers' approval more than do infrequent patrons.

Customer Ethnicity

Black restaurant patrons are more likely than white patrons to tip a flat amount rather than a percentage of the bill. Blacks also leave smaller average restaurant tip percentages than do whites (Willis 2003). This latter effect remains sizable and statistically significant after controlling for education, income, and perceptions of service quality, so black-white differences in tipping are not due solely to socioeconomic differences or to discrimination in service delivery (Lynn and Thomas-Haysbert 2003; Lynn 2004a). Instead, they may be due to ethnic differences in familiarity with the restaurant tipping norm. Consistent with this possibility, Lynn (2004b) found that whites were twice as likely as blacks (71 versus 37 percent) to know that the customary restaurant tip in the United States is 15 to 20 percent of the bill amount.

Miscellaneous

Among the other variables positively related to bill-adjusted tip amounts in at least some studies are:

1. Alcohol consumption (Conlin, Lynn, and O'Donahue 2003; Lynn 1988; Sanchez 2002)
2. Sunny weather or forecasts of sunny weather (Cunningham 1979; Crusco and Wetzel 1984; Rind 1996; Rind and Strohmetz 2001a)
3. Metropolitan area size (Lynn and Thomas-Haysbert 2003; McCrohan and Pearl 1983, 1991)
4. Customer income (Lynn and Thomas-Haysbert 2003; McCrohan and Pearl 1983)

5. Customer youth (Conlin, Lynn, and O'Donahue 2003; Lynn and Thomas-Haysbert 2003; McCrohan and Pearl 1983)
6. Customer ratings of food quality (Lynn and McCall 2000a)
7. Server personality—i.e., self-monitoring (Lynn and Simons 2000)
8. Server physical attractiveness (Hornik 1992; Lynn and Simons 2000; May 1980)
9. Server adornment—i.e., wearing flowers in hair (Stillman and Hensley 1980)

PREDICTORS OF NATIONAL DIFFERENCES IN TIPPING NORMS

Tipping varies across nations in terms of whom it is customary to tip and how much it is customary to tip them. A handful of studies in the psychology and hospitality management literatures have attempted to measure these national differences in tipping norms and to examine their relationships with other variables. The most commonly studied measure of national tipping norms is the number of different service providers (out of a list of thirty-three) that it is customary to tip in a nation. I shall refer to this measure as the national prevalence of tipping. Two other measures of national tipping norms are the amounts—in percentages of the bill or fare—that it is customary to tip restaurant servers and taxicab drivers. I shall refer to these measures as national restaurant and taxicab tip rates, respectively. All of these measures of national tipping norms are based on content analyses of international tipping guidebooks.

Research on the predictors of these measures has generally focused on national character—that is, national values, motives, and personality traits. This focus rests on the assumption that tipping norms are primarily determined by consumers. Consumer acceptance of these norms is theorized to vary with the value that consumers place on the consequences or functions of tipping. Thus, researchers have examined the relationships between national tipping norms and national character traits relevant to those consequences and functions. The results of this research are briefly reviewed in the paragraphs below.

Achievement, Materialism, and Status

The national prevalence of tipping, the national restaurant tip rate, and the national taxicab tip rate all increase with Hofstede's (1983) measure of national commitment to traditionally masculine values such as achievement, materialism, and status over traditionally feminine values such as caring and relationships (Lynn and Lynn 2004; Lynn, Zinkhan, and Harris 1993). The national prevalence of tipping also increases with related measures such as national need for achievement, national value placed on recognition/status, and national extroversion (Lynn 1997, 2000a, 2000c). These findings are consistent with the idea that tipping functions as a reward for server performance and as a form of consumer status display (Shamir 1984).

Anxiety and Uncertainty Avoidance

The national prevalence of tipping and the national restaurant tip rate, but not the national taxicab tip rate, increase with Hofstede's (1983) measure of national desire to avoid uncertainty (Lynn and Lynn 2004; Lynn, Zinkhan, and Harris 1993). The national prevalence of tipping also increases with a national personality trait, called "neuroticism," that is associated with heightened anxiety and nervousness (Lynn 1994, 2000a). These findings are consistent with the idea that tipping functions as a guarantee of good and friendly service (Lynn and Lynn 2004). That uncertainty avoidance is unrelated to national taxicab tip rates may mean that people are less concerned about variability in the behavior of taxicab drivers than they are about variability in the behavior of waiters and other service providers.

Power

The national prevalence of tipping increases with McClelland's (1961) measure of national need for power (Lynn 2000c). This finding supports the idea that tipping is valued as a source of consumer power over servers (Hemenway 1993). On the other hand, national tipping customs are unrelated to Hofstede's (1983) measure of national acceptance of hierarchical power structures in analyses that statistically control for other national values (Lynn and Lynn 2004; Lynn, Zinkhan, and Harris 1993). These latter findings suggest that the power implications of tipping are not an impediment to its appeal among egalitarian-minded people. Perhaps the power over servers that tipping confers on consumers is seen by most people as benign or legitimate.

Individualism Versus Collectivism

National taxicab tip rates increase with Hofstede's (1983) measure of national emphasis on individual—as opposed to group—identity and motivation (Lynn and Lynn 2004). However, national prevalence of tipping and national restaurant tip rates are unrelated to national individualism after controlling for Hofstede's other values (Lynn and Lynn 2004; Lynn, Zinkhan, and Harris 1993). These inconsistent findings are difficult to explain, but the failure to find that communalistic nations tip more service providers or larger amounts than do individualistic nations is meaningful. It suggests that the communalistic benefits that tipping provides are not an important determinant of the development and spread of tipping norms (Levmore 2000).

Psychoticism

The national prevalence of tipping decreases with the average psychoticism score within nations (Lynn 2000a). Psychotic people tend to be aggressive, antisocial, and unempathetic, so this finding substantiates the idea that tipping norms are supported as a way to benefit or help servers.

Tax Burden

The national prevalence of tipping decreases with the percentage of national GDP collected in taxes (Schwartz and Cohen 1999). This relationship has been attributed to the lower disposable income associated with heavier tax burdens. However, this explanation assumes that higher national spending power leads to a greater prevalence of tipping and my own unpublished analysis indicates that the reverse is true. In a sample of thirty-two nations, I found that the national prevalence of tipping was negatively correlated with national purchasing power parity ($r = -.49, p < .004$).

Another potential explanation for the negative relationship between national tax burdens and tipping customs is that national attitude toward taxes affects both the tax burden and the support for norms, such as tipping, that facilitate tax evasion. However, an unpublished analysis I conducted does not support this explanation. I found that national attitudes toward tax evasion via underreporting of income was unrelated to both the national tax burden ($r = -.16, n = 17, p = .55$) and the national prevalence of tipping ($r = -.05, n = 16, p = .85$). Thus, additional explanations for the relationship between national tax burdens and tipping norms are needed.

ECONOMIC THEORIES OF TIPPING

The empirical literature on tipping reviewed above is dominated by psychologists. Only recently have economists begun to collect and analyze data on this phenomenon. However, tipping has intrigued economists for some time and has been the subject of several economic models, theories, and speculations, most of which address one of two questions: why rational individuals leave tips, and how the custom of tipping evolved. Economists' answers to these questions are critically reviewed in the paragraphs that follow.

Individual Motives for Tipping

Tipping is a voluntary activity. Although guided by social norms, compliance with those norms is not compulsory. This raises a question about why rational people leave tips. Economists have generated six different answers to this question. According to them, people tip in order to:

1. Buy future service from servers they will encounter again
2. Increase servers' incomes
3. Experience positive feelings such as pride or avoid negative feelings such as guilt
4. Receive social approval/status or avoid social disapproval
5. Build an honest character
6. Support the rule of tipping

Each of these explanations is critically evaluated in the paragraphs below.

Future Service

The hypothesized motive for tipping most consistent with traditional economic theory is that people tip in order to buy future service. This explanation retains the assumption of rational economic man who derives utility only from economic goods and services. The strong version of this explanation is that frequent patrons can ensure good future service by leaving tip amounts that are contingent on service quality (Ben-Zion and Karni 1977; Lynn and Grassman 1990). Servers who are aware of this contingency and want to improve their tip incomes will then be motivated to deliver good service. This reasoning is similar to that underlying the tit-for-tat strategy in iterated prisoner's dilemma games (Axelrod 1984), and it suggests that the relationship between service and tipping should be stronger for regular customers than for infrequent patrons. However, as mentioned earlier, tests of the service quality by patronage frequency interaction have failed to support this expectation. At the very least, these null results suggest that tippers are poor game theorists.

A weak form of the future service explanation is that frequent patrons can ensure good future service by tipping generously, because servers will be happier to wait on those known to be good tippers (Bodvarsson and Gibson 1994; Frank 1988; Sisk and Gallick 1985). This explanation preserves the traditional models of rational consumers, but assumes that servers have irrational desires to repay customers for past generosity by supplying good current service. This version of the future service explanation does have the advantage of predicting only a positive effect of patronage frequency rather than a service quality by patronage frequency interaction. As previously mentioned, researchers have found substantial evidence that regular customers do tip more than infrequent customers, so this weak version of the future service explanation is more consistent with the empirical literature than is the strong version. However, regular patrons may tip more than non-regular patrons for many reasons other than the desire for future service. Further-more, a national survey asking respondents for the best explanation of why they do or do not tip found that only 3 percent of respondents indicated that they tip for future service (Market Facts 1996). Thus this explanation for tipping needs additional testing.

Helping Servers

The traditional economic theory of consumer behavior cannot explain consumers' motives for tipping in restaurants that are infrequently patronized (Ben-Zion and Karni 1977). To explain tipping in this situation, several economists have expanded their assumptions about consumers' utility functions. One frequently considered idea is that consumers derive utility from increasing servers' incomes (Azar 2004b; Frank 1988; Schotter 1979). In other words, people tip out of feelings of empathy for servers. This idea is consistent with the previously reviewed findings that:

1. Tips increase with patronage frequency (because familiarity increases empathy)
2. Tips increase with server friendliness (because friendliness increases empathy)
3. The number of tipped service professions decreases with national psychoticism (because psychoticism decreases empathy)

It is also consistent with the results of a national survey in which 30 percent of respondents indicated that the main reason they tip is "because I feel people depend on the money to make a living" (Market Facts 1996).

Feelings of Pride and Guilt

Consumers' utility functions have also been broadened to include feelings of pride and guilt, which are theorized to accompany conformity and nonconformity with internalized tipping norms (Azar 2004a, 2004b; Bodvarsson and Gibson 1997; Conlin, Lynn, and O'Donahue 2003; Ruffle 1999). This idea is consistent with the previously reviewed findings that dollar tips increase with bill size and that percentage tips increase with service quality, because the restaurant tipping norm identifies these variables as important determinants of the appropriate tip amount. However, compliance with tipping norms is not evidence that those norms are internalized or that feelings of pride or guilt motivate compliance with those norms. Thus, more direct assessments of the relationships between tips and anticipated feelings of pride or guilt are needed to evaluate this explanation for tipping.

Social Approval and Status

Allowing consumers' utility functions to include social approval and status has also been sug-gested as a way to explain tipping (Azar 2004a, 2004b; Conlin, Lynn, and O'Donahue 2003; Ruffle 1999). Although sometimes lumped together with feelings of pride and guilt by econo-mists trying to explain tipping, the desire for social approval is distinct because it varies with the visibility of the tip and the characteristics of observers in a way that feelings of pride and guilt do not (see Azar 2004a; Bodvarsson and Gibson 1997). In fact, the previously reviewed findings that tips increase with patronage frequency, server friendliness, server physical attractiveness, and differences between the customers' and servers' sex provide support for the social approval expla-nation of tipping, because all these variables should increase the tippers' concern with the servers' approval. Also supporting this motivation for tipping are the previously reviewed effects on tipping customs of national values and personality traits associated with status seeking, because these national-level effects are difficult to explain if they do not stem from corresponding individual-level relationships. However, more direct assessments of the relationship between desire for social approval and tipping are needed to further test this explanation.

Character-Building Exercise

The most novel explanation for tipping advanced by an economist is that tipping is done as a character-building exercise. According to Robert Frank (1988), the motive behind tipping is "to maintain and strengthen the predisposition to behave honestly." He also suggests that cultivating an honest character is a choice that people make because others detect and reward those with an honest character. Although no empirical tests of this motivation for tipping currently exist, the novelty and creativity of the idea seem to argue against its validity. If the desire to cultivate an honest character truly motivates tipping, then it should have been apparent to others thinking and writing about tipping.

Support the Rule of Tipping

A final economic explanation for why individuals leave tips is based on game theory. Essentially, the argument is that one person's tipping or stiffing behavior causes others to behave likewise. Furthermore, an equilibrium in which everyone tips is preferable to an equilibrium in which no one tips because tipping improves service quality. Under these conditions, tipping is motivated by the desire to ensure a preferred equilibrium (Bodvarsson and Gibson 1997; Schotter 1979). As Bodvarsson and Gibson (1997) write: "The act of tipping . . . is irrational, but supporting the rule of tipping by leaving tips is rational." Unfortunately, this explanation of tipping is founded on an untenable assumption—namely, that an individual's behavior can influence the behavior of enough other people to affect the societal equilibrium. People can and do stiff servers without bringing down the whole custom of tipping (see Paul 2001), so "supporting the rule of tipping by leaving tips" is not rational from a self-interested perspective. Also undermining this explanation is the previously reviewed finding that the prevalence of tipping does not increase with national collectivism, because collectivists should be more inclined than individualists to contribute to public goods.

Social Functions of Tipping

Tipping is guided by social norms that specify whom and how much to tip. This raises a question about why tipping norms exist. This question is related, but not identical, to the question about why individual consumers tip. Some of the benefits that motivate individuals to leave tips may also induce societies to adopt tipping norms. For example, the desire for status probably affects individual tipping decisions and national tipping customs (see Lynn 1997). However, norms that induce many people to tip may provide benefits that no individual act of tipping can provide. In fact, economists' explanations for tipping norms have focused on this latter type of benefit. The specific benefits mentioned by economists are numerous but can be traced to just five basic consequences of tipping:

1. Tipping reduces the costs of monitoring and motivating server effort.
2. Tipping provides a nonlitigious means of addressing problems that arise from failures in service delivery (this is a version of the preceding consequence but is distinct enough to warrant separate discussion).

3. Tipping attracts good waiters to the restaurant industry.
4. Tipping facilitates tax evasion.
5. Tipping increases profits through price discrimination.

Each of these consequences of tipping is discussed below.

Efficient Incentive

The most common economic explanation for the custom of tipping is that it functions as an efficient means of monitoring and rewarding server effort (see Ben-Zion and Karni 1977; Bodvarsson and Gibson 1997; Conlin, Lynn, and O'Donahue 2003; Hemenway 1993; Jacob and Page 1980; Schotter 1979). The highly customized and intangible nature of services means that customers are in a much better position than managers to evaluate and reward server effort, so these tasks are given to consumers via the norm of tipping. This reasoning suggests that tipping reduces transaction costs, motivates servers to work hard, and enables restaurants to provide more customized levels of service (see economic models in Ben-Zion and Karni 1977 and Schotter 1979). The previously reviewed evidence that restaurant tips are positively related to service quality means that tipping has some elements of an efficient contract (Conlin, Lynn, and O'Donahue 2003). However, the fact that the service-tipping relationship is weaker on weekends than on weekdays and weaker for some ethnic groups than others means that tipping is not fully efficient (Conlin, Lynn, and O'Donahue 2003). More importantly, the average service-tipping relationship is smaller than the correlation of .3 that Cohen (1992) argued is "visible to the naked eye of a careful observer." This means that the relationship is too weak to be noticed by restaurant servers, so it seems doubtful that tipping can provide the hypothesized incentive for server effort (Lynn 2001; Lynn and McCall 2000a).

Enforcement Mechanism

Sisk and Gallick (1985) do not believe that tips are "used to reward marginal increments in service." Rather, they argue that tipping is an enforcement device that protects customers against pressures to eat and leave quickly and that protects restaurants from unscrupulous complaints about the service. The custom of tipping accomplishes this by allowing customers to withhold payment for inadequate service while still requiring those customers to pay for the meal (see Schotter 1979 for a similar argument). Thus, tipping acts like a guarantee and provides two benefits—it motivates servers to provide adequate service (Sisk and Gallick 1985) and it reduces the need for costly arguments and litigation when the service is inadequate (Schotter 1979). This explanation for tipping is supported by the previously reviewed relationships of tipping customs with national uncertainty avoidance and neuroticism, because neurotic and uncertainty-avoidant people should value guarantees of good treatment more than others (Lynn 2000a; Lynn and Lynn 2004).

Selection Device

Andrew Schotter (1979, 2000) argues that tipping is a selection device that separates good waiters from bad ones. He defines good waiters as those who can wait on many customers per work shift and poor waiters as those who can wait on only a few customers per work shift. Given this definition, the prospect of low tip income will keep poor waiters from deciding to work for tips. Thus,

Schotter claims that tipping disproportionately attracts good waiters to the restaurant industry and helps to solve the problem of adverse selection in employment that restaurant managers face. This explanation for tipping could easily be broadened to include more traditional definitions of good and poor waiters as long as customers give good servers more tips than they give poor servers. As previously mentioned, however, individual differences in servers' performance are only weakly related to their average tip percentages, so such a broadening of the explanation is not supported by the available data. Note that this weak empirical relationship is not inconsistent with Schotter's original explanation, because he assumes that good waiters earn larger dollar (not percentage) tips than do poor servers. That assumption has yet to be empirically tested.

Tax Evasion

Bodvarsson and Gibson (1997) argued that tipping is supported in part because it facilitates tax evasion. Tipping allows servers to pay lower income taxes because underreporting of tip income is more difficult for the government to catch than is underreporting of standard wages. In fact, a study by the Internal Revenue Service found that underreporting of tip income exceeds underreporting of income from all other legal sources (Internal Revenue Service 1990). In addition, tipping allows customers to pay lower sales taxes because (by lowering restaurants' labor costs) it reduces the prices restaurants charge for meals. Together, these tax evasion opportunities benefit customers, servers, and restaurateurs by reducing the costs of supplying services (Bodvarsson and Gibson 1997; Schwartz and Cohen 1999). However, the previously reviewed finding that tipping is more prevalent in countries with lower tax burdens casts doubt on the idea that tipping exists as a means of evading taxes. The motivation to evade taxes should be greater the higher those taxes, so if tipping customs are actively supported because they are a means of evading taxes, then tipping should be more (not less) prevalent the greater a nation's tax burden.

Price Discrimination

Finally, Zvi Schwartz (1997) developed a demand-supply model of tipping in segmented markets and showed that tipping increases firm profits under many (but not all) conditions. Basically, he argued that tipping is a form of price discrimination that allows restaurants to charge high prices for the food without losing business from price-sensitive customers as long as those customers are willing and able to reduce the total cost of eating out by leaving smaller tips. Unfortunately, no empirical data that could be used to test this model are currently available.

PUBLIC POLICY ISSUES CONCERNING TIPPING

Tipping is a private exchange between a customer and a service provider. Nevertheless, it raises important public policy issues. Among the tipping-related questions that public policy makers must address are the following: Should tipping be banned or not? How can underreporting of cash tip income be detected and/or reduced? Should mandated minimum wages be lower for tipped jobs than for nontipped jobs? Each of these questions is discussed in the paragraphs below.

Ban on Tipping

Tipping is widespread but is not universally loved. For over a hundred years, people in the United States have disliked the practice and tried to stop it (Azar 2004a). In the early 1900s, for example,

Arkansas, Mississippi, Iowa, South Carolina, Tennessee, and Washington state all passed laws prohibiting tipping (Segrave 1998). Although tipping is currently legal throughout the United States, one national survey indicates that 24 percent of U.S. adults still think the practice is unfair to consumers (Roper 2002), and another indicates that 34 percent of U.S. adults wish they were not expected to tip (Mills and Riehle 1987). Dissatisfaction with tipping also extends beyond the borders of the United States. Europeans have largely replaced tipping with automatic service charges (Segrave 1998), and the practice of tipping is actually illegal in Argentina and Vietnam (Magellan's 2003). This negative sentiment raises a question about whether tipping increases or decreases social welfare and, therefore, should be permitted or banned.

As described in the previous section, economists have argued that the institution of tipping provides numerous social benefits, such as increasing service quality, increasing profits, reducing transaction costs, reducing litigation, and reducing tax burdens. Economists have also argued that tipping must provide some individual benefits to consumers apart from avoidance of the guilt and social disapproval brought on by noncompliance with tipping norms (Azar 2004b; Schlicht 1998). Otherwise, they argue, self-interest would lead to slight undertipping, which would eventually erode the tipping norm itself. Social scientists in other disciplines have identified a number of candidates for those individual benefits—including a reduction of consumer anxiety about servers' envy of their customers (Foster 1972; Lynn 1994), a reduction of consumer guilt about the inequality between servers and customers (Shamir 1984), an increase in the consumer's social recognition and status (Lynn 1997; Paules 1991), an increase in the consumer's self-perceived freedom (Shamir 1984), and an increase in the consumer's psychological rewards from helping servers (Shamir 1984).

Balanced against the hypothesized benefits of tipping described above are several potential negative consequences of this custom. Tipping is thought to demean servers (Hemenway 1993; Segrave 1998), and it does increase the income uncertainty and role conflict experienced by servers (Butler and Skipper 1980; Shamir 1983). Tipping also encourages servers to rush customers in order to turn tables quickly, give customers food and drink items free of charge, spend little time or effort on customers considered poor tippers, and evade taxes by underreporting their tip incomes. More importantly, tipping norms put unwelcome social pressure on consumers to part with money they would rather keep (Crespi 1947; Segrave 1998).

Given the prevalence of tipping, it is tempting to assume that the benefits of this custom must outweigh its costs, but that assumption is not justified. Many of the hypothesized collective benefits of tipping have not been empirically demonstrated. In fact, the principal benefit attributed to tipping—that it increases service quality—is doubtful because tip amounts are only weakly related to service quality (Lynn and McCall 2000a). Of course, the previously reviewed relationships between tipping customs and national values and personality traits suggests that some of the hypothesized *psychological* benefits actually do contribute to the evolution and maintenance of tipping norms (see Lynn 2000a, 2000c; Lynn and Lynn 2004). However, it is possible that these benefits accrue to only a small subset of consumers and that most tippers unhappily follow the lead of this subset only to avoid social embarrassment. Thus, it is unclear if the benefits of tipping outweigh its costs; more theoretical and empirical work is needed to answer that question.

Undeclared Tip Income

The Internal Revenue Service (IRS) estimates that 50 percent of tip income is unreported, which results in the loss of tax revenue and a lowering of the perceived fairness of the income tax system (Internal Revenue Service 1990). In order to identify cheaters, tax auditors need accurate estimates of servers' actual tip incomes (McCrohan and Pearl 1991). Two approaches to this task have been analyzed in the economics literature and are briefly discussed below.

The approach to estimating tip income currently used by the IRS is to adjust the credit card tip rate in a restaurant by some amount and to apply that rate to a restaurant's and its servers' cash sales. This approach, known as the McQuatters formula, has been upheld by the courts (Newman 1988). However, Macnaughton and Veall (2001) have demonstrated that use of this formula can make the marginal tax rate on credit card tips exceed 100 percent, and they argue that this may undermine the formula's acceptability to the public. Furthermore, Newman (1988) suggests that estimating tip income on a restaurant by restaurant basis is cumbersome and that alternative approaches should be sought.

In the mid-1980s McCrohan and Pearl (1991) worked on such an alternative approach to predicting tip income. They used data from diaries kept by consumer panels to predict tipping rates from restaurant-level variables such as geographic location, metropolitan area size, restaurant practices, and restaurant type. They found that *"effective tipping rates were highest in Middle Atlantic and New England States and Lowest in North and South Central States; highest in large metropolitan areas; highest in restaurants that accept credit cards and lowest in those that do not accept credit cards, accept reservations, or serve alcoholic beverages; and highest (of major restaurant categories) in full menu and hotel restaurants and lowest in pizza restaurants"* (p. 230; italics mine). Their regression models represent one alternative approach to estimating tip income that tax authorities could use in auditing restaurants and servers (Newman 1988). Coming up with still more means of predicting tip income or of increasing tip reporting is one potentially fruitful direction for future economic research.

Tipped Minimum Wages

Tips represent taxable income in the United States and elsewhere. As a governmentally recognized part of income, tips raise a question about how much they should be counted toward legally mandated minimum wages. Not surprisingly, low-income workers tend to oppose the crediting of tips against minimum wage requirements (see MacKenzie and Snyder 2001). However, this is a complex issue whose merits rest on more than workers' preferences. For example, Wessels (1997) theorized that "the labor market for tipped restaurant servers is monopsonistic" and that the employment of these servers first increases and then decreases with a rise in the tipped minimum wage. The basic idea is that tipping constrains how many servers a restaurant can hire because more servers per customer mean fewer tips, and fewer tips must be offset with higher wages. Increasing the tipped minimum wage allows restaurants to improve service by hiring more servers even though it reduces servers' tip incomes because the higher wages compensate for the reduced tips. Of course, the benefits to restaurants of hiring more servers are marginally declining, so at some point further increasing the tipped minimum wage merely increases the costs of labor and reduces employment. Wessels tested this model with two different data sets and found strong support for it. Thus, a lowering of the tipped minimum wage by allowing tip credits can reduce employment over at least some range of minimum wages. This counterintuitive finding illustrates the complexity of the issues concerning tip credits and tipped minimum wages and, in so doing, illustrates the need for more theoretical and empirical work on these issues.

CONCLUSION

In conclusion, tipping is a widespread and practically important economic behavior. Moreover, it is a behavior that is difficult for neoclassical theory to explain. At the individual level of analysis, people leave tips even when they are infrequent patrons of a service establishment and are unlikely to encounter the same service worker again. Furthermore, individuals' decisions about how much to tip are affected by a host of variables unrelated to service levels. Thus, explanations for this behavior must go beyond the neoclassical idea that people base tips on service quality to ensure good service in the future. Adequately explaining individuals' tipping decisions requires a more behavioral approach—one that broadens the traditional consumer utility function to include desires to avoid guilt, obtain social approval, obtain status, treat others equitably, and help others as well as one that recognizes cognitive capacity, knowledge, mood, and cognitive processes as having a causal impact on economic decision making and behavior.

At an aggregate level of analysis, tipping norms vary across nations and appear to be affected by national variables unrelated to transaction costs or supply and demand for services. Thus, explanations for tipping norms must go beyond the idea that they are efficient means of monitoring and rewarding server performance. Adequately explaining tipping norms requires a behavioral perspective that encompasses national character and values as well as social learning and conformity.

Scholars in hospitality management and psychology have made numerous contributions to our understanding of tipping behavior, and a few economists have begun to explore this topic. However, more economists should study tipping because it promises to shed light on the content of consumers' utility functions, the role of social norms in the economy, and the evolution of economic institutions. Furthermore, economists should study tipping because it has an impact on important public policy issues of concern to economists. Rational or not, most economists leave tips; it is time they begin to study them as well.

REFERENCES

Axelrod, R.M. 1984. *The Evolution of Cooperation.* New York: Basic Books.
Azar, Ofer H. 2003. "The Social Norm of Tipping: A Review." Working paper, Department of Economics, Northwestern University, Evanston, IL.
———. 2004a. "The History of Tipping—from Sixteenth-Century England to United States in the 1910s." *Journal of Socio-Economics* 33: 745–64.
———. 2004b. "What Sustains Social Norms and How They Evolve? The Case of Tipping." *Journal of Economic Behavior and Organization* 54: 49–64.
Ben-Zion, Uri, and Edi Karni. 1977. "Tip Payments and the Quality of Service." In O.C. Ashenfelter and W.E. Oates, eds., *Essays in Labor Market Analysis,* 37–44. New York: John Wiley and Sons.
Bodvarsson, Orn, and William Gibson. 1994. "Gratuities and Customer Appraisal of Service: Evidence from Minnesota Restaurants." *Journal of Socio-Economics* 23, 3: 287–302.
———. 1997. "Economics and Restaurant Gratuities: Determining Tip Rates." *American Journal of Economics and Sociology* 56, 2: 187–203.
———. 1999. "An Economic Approach to Tips and Service Quality: Results of a Survey." *The Social Science Journal* 36, 1: 137–47.
Bodvarsson, Orn B., William A. Luksetich, and Sherry McDermott. 2003. "Why Do Diners Tip: Rule of Thumb or Valuation of Service?" *Applied Economics* 35: 1659–65.
Butler, Suellen, and James K. Skipper. 1980. "Waitressing, Vulnerability and Job Autonomy: The Case of the Risky Tip." *Sociology of Work and Occupations* 7, 4: 487–502.
Cohen, Jacob. 1992. "A Power Primer." *Psychological Bulletin* 112: 155–59.
Conlin, Michael, Michael Lynn, and Ted O'Donahue. 2003. "The Norm of Restaurant Tipping." *Journal of Economic Behavior and Organization* 52: 297–321.
Crespi, Leo P. 1947. "The Implications of Tipping in America." *Public Opinion Quarterly* 11: 424–35.
Crusco, April H., and Christopher G. Wetzel. 1984. "The Midas Touch: The Effects of Interpersonal Touch on Restaurant Tipping." *Personality and Social Psychology Bulletin* 10: 512–17.
Cunningham, Michael R. 1979. "Weather, Mood and Helping Behavior: Quasi Experiments with the Sunshine Samaritan." *Journal of Personality and Social Psychology* 37: 1947–56.

Davis, Stephen F., Brian Schrader, Tori R. Richardson, Jason P. Kring, and Jaime C. Kiefer. 1998. "Restaurant Servers Influence Tipping Behavior." *Psychological Reports* 83: 223–26.

Elman, D. 1976. "Why Is Tipping 'Cheaper by the Bunch': Diffusion or Just Desserts?" *Personality and Social Psychology Bulletin* 1: 584–87.

Feinberg, Richard A. 1986. "Credit Cards as Spending Facilitating Stimuli: A Conditioning Interpretation." *Journal of Consumer Research* 13: 348–56.

Foster, George M. 1972. "The Anatomy of Envy: A Study of Symbolic Behavior." *Current Anthropology* 13: 165–86.

Frank, Robert H. 1987. "If Homo Economicus Could Choose His Own Utility Function, Would He Want One with a Conscience?" *American Economic Review* 77: 593–604.

———. 1988. *Passions Within Reason*. New York: W.W. Norton.

Freeman, Stephen, Markus R. Walker, Richard Borden, and Bibb Latane. 1975. "Diffusion of Responsibility and Restaurant Tipping: Cheaper by the Bunch." *Personality and Social Psychology Bulletin* 1: 584–87.

Garrity, Kimberly, and Douglas Degelman. 1990. "Effect of Server Introduction on Restaurant Tipping." *Journal of Applied Social Psychology* 20: 168–72.

Green, Leonard, Joel Myerson, and Rachel Schneider. 2003. "Is There a Magnitude Effect in Tipping?" *Psychonomic Bulletin and Review* 10, 2: 381–86.

Guéguen, Nicolas. 2002. "The Effects of a Joke on Tipping When It Is Delivered at the Same Time as the Bill." *Journal of Applied Social Psychology* 32: 1955–63.

Guéguen, Nicolas, and Patrick Legohérel. 2000. "Effect on Tipping of Barman Drawing a Sun on the Bottom of Customers' Checks." *Psychological Reports* 87: 223–26.

Hemenway, David. 1993. *Prices and Choices: Microeconomic Vignettes*. Cambridge, MA: Ballinger.

Hofstede, Geert. 1983. "National Cultures in Four Dimensions: A Research Based Theory of Cultural Differences Among Nations." *International Studies of Management and Organization* 8: 46–74.

Hornik, Jacob. 1992. "Tactile Stimulation and Consumer Response." *Journal of Consumer Research* 19: 449–58.

Internal Revenue Service. 1990. "Tip Income Study." Department of the Treasury, Publication 1530 (8–90): Catalog Number 12482K.

Jacob, Nancy, and Alfred Page. 1980. "Production, Information Costs, and Economic Organization: The Buyer Monitoring Case." *American Economic Review* 70: 476–78.

Landsburg, Steven, E. 1993. *The Armchair Economist*. New York: Free Press.

Levmore, Saul. 2000. "Norms as Supplements." *Virginia Law Review* 86: 1989.

Lynn, Michael. 1988. "The Effects of Alcohol Consumption on Restaurant Tipping." *Personality and Social Psychology Bulletin* 14: 87–91.

———. 1994. "Neuroticism and the Prevalence of Tipping: A Cross-Country Study." *Personality and Individual Differences* 17, 1: 137–38.

———. 1996. "Seven Ways to Increase Server's Tips." *Cornell H.R.A. Quarterly*, June, 24–29.

———. 1997. "Tipping Customs and Status Seeking: A Cross-Country Study." *International Journal of Hospitality Management* 16, 2: 221–24.

———. 2000a. "National Personality and Tipping Customs." *Personality and Individual Differences* 28: 395–404.

———. 2000b. "The Relationship Between Tipping and Service Quality: A Comment on Bodvarsson and Gibson's Article." *Social Science Journal* 37: 131–35.

———. 2000c. "National Character and Tipping Customs: The Needs for Achievement, Affiliation, and Power as Predictors of the Prevalence of Tipping." *International Journal of Hospitality Management* 19: 205–10.

———. 2001. "Restaurant Tipping and Service Quality: A Tenuous Relationship." *Cornell H.R.A. Quarterly* (January): 14–20.

———. 2003a. "Restaurant Tips and Service Quality: A Weak Relationship or Just Weak Measurement?" *International Journal of Hospitality Management* 22: 321–25.

———. 2003b. "Tip Levels and Service: An Update, Extension and Reconciliation." *Cornell H.R.A. Quarterly*, December, 139–48.

———. 2004a. "Black-White Differences in Tipping of Various Service Providers." *Journal of Applied Social Psychology* 34, 11: 2261–71.

———. 2004b. "Ethnic Differences in Tipping: A Matter of Familiarity with Tipping Norms." *Cornell H.R.A. Quarterly*, January, 12–22.

———. 2004c. "Restaurant Tips and Service Quality: A Commentary on Bodvarsson, Luksetich and McDermott (2003)." *Applied Economics Letters* 11: 975–78.

Lynn, Michael, and Charles Bond. 1992. "Conceptual Meaning and Spuriousness in Ratio Correlations: The Case of Restaurant Tipping." *Journal of Applied Social Psychology* 22, 4: 327–41.

Lynn, Michael, and Andrea Grassman. 1990. "Restaurant Tipping: An Examination of Three 'Rational Explanations.'" *Journal of Economic Psychology* 11: 169–81.

Lynn, Michael, and Jeffrey Graves. 1996. "Tipping: An Incentive/Reward for Service?" *Hospitality Research Journal* 20, 1: 1–14.

Lynn, Michael, and Bibb Latane. 1984. "The Psychology of Restaurant Tipping." *Journal of Applied Social Psychology* 14: 551–63.

Lynn, Michael, Joseph-Mykal Le, and David S. Sherwyn. 1998. "Reach Out and Touch Your Customers." *Cornell H.R.A. Quarterly* 39 (June): 60–65.

Lynn, Michael, and Ann Lynn. 2004. "National Values and Tipping Customs: A Replication and Extension." *Journal of Hospitality and Tourism Research* 28, 3: 356–64.

Lynn, Michael, and Michael McCall. 2000a. "Gratitude and Gratuity: A Meta-Analysis of Research on the Service-Tipping Relationship." *Journal of Socio-Economics* 29: 203–14.

———. 2000b. "Beyond Gratitude and Gratuity: A Meta-Analytic Review of the Predictors of Restaurant Tipping." Working paper, School of Hotel Administration, Cornell University.

Lynn, Michael, and Kirby Mynier. 1993. "Effect of Server Posture on Restaurant Tipping." *Journal of Applied Social Psychology* 23, 8: 678–85.

Lynn, Michael, and Tony Simons. 2000. "Predictors of Male and Female Servers' Average Tip Earnings." *Journal of Applied Social Psychology* 30: 241–52.

Lynn, Michael, and Michael Sturman. 2003. "It's Simpler Than It Seems: An Alternative Explanation for the Magnitude Effect in Tipping." *International Journal of Hospitality Management* 22: 103–10.

Lynn, Michael, and Clorice Thomas-Haysbert. 2003. "Ethnic Differences in Tipping: Evidence, Explanations and Implications." *Journal of Applied Social Psychology* 33, 8: 747–1772.

Lynn, Michael, George M. Zinkhan, and Judy Harris. 1993. "Consumer Tipping: A Cross-Country Study." *Journal of Consumer Research* 20: 478–85.

MacKenzie, Michael, and Jo Snyder. 2001. "The Minimum Wage and a 'Tipping Wage.'" Report prepared for the Canadian Centre for Policy Alternatives-Manitoba. Available at www.policyalternatives.ca/manitoba/minwagereport.html.

Macnaughton, Alan, and Michael Veall. 2001. "Tipping and the McQuatters Formula." *Public Finance Review* 29, 2: 99–107.

Magellan's. 2003. "Worldwide Tipping Guide." Available at www.magellans.com/search/127149.JSP, November 8.

Market Facts. 1996. *American Demographics Tipping Study.* New York: Market Facts.

Mason, T.A. 2002. "Why Should You Tip?" Available at www.tip20.com.

May, Joanne M. 1980. "Looking for Tips: An Empirical Perspective on Restaurant Tipping." *Cornell H.R.A. Quarterly,* February, 6–13.

McCall, Michael, and Heather J. Belmont. 1996. "Credit Card Insignia and Restaurant Tipping: Evidence for an Associative Link." *Journal of Applied Psychology* 81, 5: 609–13.

McClelland, David. 1961. *The Achieving Society.* New York: Free Press.

McCrohan, Kevin, and Robert B. Pearl. 1983. "Tipping Practices of American Households: Consumer Based Estimates for 1979." 1983 Program and Abstracts Joint Statistical Meetings, Toronto, Canada. August 15–18.

———. 1991. "An Application of Commercial Panel Data for Public Policy Research: Estimates of Tip Earnings." *Journal of Economic and Social Measurement* 17: 217–31.

Media Dynamics. 2001. *Consumer Dimensions 2001.* New York: Media Dynamics.

Mills, Susan, and Hudson Riehle. 1987. "What Customers Think About Tips vs. Service Charges." *Restaurants USA,* October, 20–22.

Newman, Joel. 1988. "Waiter, There's an IRS Agent in My Soup." *Tax Notes,* August 22, 861–68.

Paul, Pamela. 2001. "The Tricky Topic of Tipping." *American Demographics,* May, 10–11.

Paules, Greta F. 1991. *Dishing It Out: Power and Resistance Among Waitresses in a New Jersey Restaurant.* Philadelphia: Temple University Press.

Putzi, S., ed. 2002. *Global Road Warrior,* version 3.0. Novato, CA: World Trade Press.

Rind, Bruce. 1996. "Effects of Beliefs About Weather Conditions on Tipping." *Journal of Applied Social Psychology* 26, 2: 137–47.

Rind, Bruce, and Prashant Bordia. 1995. "Effect of Server's 'Thank You' and Personalization on Restaurant Tipping." *Journal of Applied Social Psychology* 25, 9: 745–51.

———. 1996. "Effect on Restaurant Tipping of Male and Female Servers Drawing a Happy, Smiling Face on the Backs of Customers' Checks." *Journal of Applied Social Psychology* 26, 3: 218–25.

Rind, Bruce, and David Strohmetz. 1998. "Effect on Restaurant Tipping of a Helpful Message Written on the Back of Customers' Checks." *Journal of Applied Social Psychology* 29: 139–44.

———. 2001a. "Effects of Beliefs About Future Weather Conditions on Tipping." *Journal of Applied Social Psychology* 31, 2: 2160–4.

———. 2001b. "Effect on Restaurant Tipping of Presenting Customers with an Interesting Task and of Reciprocity." *Journal of Applied Social Psychology* 31: 1379–84.

Rodrigue, Karen M. 1999. "Tipping Tips: The Effects of Personalization on Restaurant Gratuity." Master's thesis, Division of Psychology and Special Education, Emporia State University, Emporia, KS.

Roper Organization. 2002. "Here's a Tip." *Public Perspective,* November/December, 52.

Ruffle, Bradley J. 1999. "Gift Giving with Emotions." *Journal of Economic Behavior and Organization* 39: 399–420.

Sanchez, Alfonso. 2002. "The Effect of Alcohol Consumption and Patronage Frequency on Restaurant Tipping." *Journal of Foodservice Business Research* 5, 3: 19–36.

Schlicht, Ekkehart. 1998. *On Custom in the Economy.* Oxford: Clarendon Press.

Schotter, Andrew. 1979. "The Economics of Tipping and Gratuities: An Essay in Institution Micro-Economics." Working Paper #79–19, C.V. Starr Center, New York University.

———. 2000. "Moral Hazard and Adverse Selection: Informational Market Failures." In *Microeconomics: A Modern Approach,* 3rd ed. Reading, MA: Addison-Wesley.

Schwartz, Zvi. 1997. "The Economics of Tipping: Tips, Profits and the Market's Demand-Supply Equilibrium." *Tourism Economics* 3, 3: 265–79.

Schwartz, Zvi, and Eli Cohen. 1999. "Tipping and the Nation's Tax Burden: A Cross-Country Study." *Anatolia, an International Journal of Tourism and Hospitality Research* 10, 2: 135–47.

Segrave, Kerry. 1998. *Tipping: An American History of Gratuities.* Jefferson, NC: McFarland and Company.

Seligman, Clive, Jean E. Finegan, J. Douglas Hazelwood, and Mark Wilkinson. 1985. "Manipulating Attributions for Profit: A Field Test of the Effects of Attributions on Behavior." *Social Cognition* 3: 313–21.

Shamir, Boas. 1983. "A Note on Tipping and Employee Perceptions and Attitudes." *Journal of Occupational Psychology* 56: 255–59.

———. 1984. "Between Gratitude and Gratuity: An Analysis of Tipping." *Annals of Tourism Research* 11: 59–78.

Sisk, David, and Edward Gallick. 1985. "Tips and Commissions: A Study in Economic Contracting." Working paper no. 125. Bureau of Economics, Federal Trade Commission. Washington, DC.

Snyder, Melvin L. 1976. "The Inverse Relationship Between Restaurant Party Size and Tip Percentage: Diffusion or Equity?" *Personality and Social Psychology Bulletin* 2: 308.

Speer, Tibbett. 1997. "The Give and Take of Tipping." *American Demographics,* February, 51–54.

Star, Nancy. 1988. *The International Guide to Tipping.* New York: Berkley Books.

Stephen, Renee, and Richard L. Zweigenhaft. 1986. "The Effect on Tipping of a Waitress Touching Male and Female Customers." *Journal of Social Psychology* 126: 141–42.

Stillman, JeriJane W., and Wayne E. Hensley. 1980. "She Wore a Flower in Her Hair: The Effect of Ornamentation on Non-Verbal Communication." *Journal of Applied Communication Research* 1: 31–39.

Tidd, Kathi L., and Joan S. Lockard. 1978. "Monetary Significance of the Affiliative Smile: A Case for Reciprocal Altruism." *Bulletin of the Psychonomic Society* 11: 344–46.

van Baaren, Rick, Rob Holland, Bregje Steenaert, and Ad van Knippenberg. 2003. "Mimicry for Money: Behavioral Consequences of Imitation." *Journal of Experimental Social Psychology* 39: 393–98.

Wessels, Walter John. 1997. "Minimum Wages and Tipped Servers." *Economic Inquiry* 35: 334–49.

Willis, Nicole G. 2003. "Discovering Research in a Restaurant: Hamburgers and a Hypothesis." *Perspectives on Social Work* 1, 1: 6–11.

PART 9

DEVELOPMENT, BEHAVIORAL LAW, AND MONEY

CHAPTER 32

ECONOMIC DEVELOPMENT, EQUALITY, INCOME DISTRIBUTION, AND ETHICS

ERIK THORBECKE

The essence and major objective of socioeconomic development is raising the standard of living of all individuals and particularly that of the poor.[1] It has become almost universally accepted that in the setting of low-income third world countries economic growth is a necessary condition for poverty reduction. A crucial issue in this context is whether a relatively unequal income distribution is also a precondition for growth to occur. This was the prevailing view under the classical framework, based on the argument that the rich (the capitalists) save a larger proportion of their income than the poor (the workers). Hence, for a given level of total income a more unequal income distribution would generate a larger flow of aggregate savings that could be channeled into investment to yield a higher growth rate of GDP.

In this sense the desirability of an unequal income distribution could be rationalized on economic grounds while clashing with the ethical concern for more equality, equity, and egalitarianism. More poverty today was a precondition to more economic growth and less poverty in the future. As the Cambridge school boldly put it, impoverishment of the masses is necessary for the accumulation of a surplus over present consumption.

In contrast, the modern approach to the political economy of development provides support for the contention that relative equality is consistent with growth—as demonstrated, for example, by the phenomenal growth performance of East Asia in the last half century. If indeed equality is conducive to growth, then it becomes a *means* toward economic development and future poverty alleviation, and the conflict between the ethical objective (norm) of egalitarianism and the economic conditions required for growth disappears. While it is clear that the relationship between inequality and growth is a very complex one, likely to be characterized by nonlinearities and threshold effects and strongly influenced by political economy factors and the prevailing institutional framework, a case can be made that under the proper conditions equality can be conducive to growth.

The essence of this paper is that if equality is a means to economic development, it converges with the ethical norm of egalitarianism. One important implication of this convergence is that policies and reforms targeted toward greater equality may become much more attractive and palatable to policy makers as the presumed trade-off between equity and efficiency tends to vanish.

It is important to clarify, at the outset, that by equality is meant here *relative* equality and that any reference to this concept should be interpreted in a relative sense. Even if one subscribes to the thesis that equality is consistent with future growth and development, it is clear that in a free-enterprise market economy incentives play a crucial role. Entrepreneurs are risk takers and expect to be rewarded for the creative destruction they perform.

Views regarding the optimal degree of equality (inequality) considered desirable in a given society to achieve the twin objectives of a fair (and just) society and the incentives and rewards required for growth differ significantly. At one extreme is Margaret Thatcher's belief (shared by her followers among the right wing) that "it is our job to glory in inequality and see that talent and abilities are given vent and expression for the benefit of all" (quoted in George 1997). At the other extreme would be the welfare state model long adopted by governments in Scandinavian countries and among developing countries by Sri Lanka, for example.

The determination of the optimal societal degree of equality (inequality) depends crucially on the specific norms prevailing in a specific society and the value it places on (1) present versus future equality and (2) the degree of inequality required to provide the necessary incentives to entrepreneurs. In principle one could derive the optimal degree of inequality consistent with those constraints through a computable general equilibrium model—an exercise that would go far beyond the scope of this paper.

EQUALITY AS AN ETHICAL END OR MEANS?

Over the ages the principle of equality was adopted by many cultures as an ethical end worthy of pursuing. Most religions advocate equality and poverty reduction—in one form or another—as desirable norms. Christianity emphasizes loving one's neighbors as oneself, which at the limit implies a high degree of altruism and equality, as individuals are expected to treat others as they treat themselves. This implies that interpersonal effects are given a high weight in each individual welfare (utility) function.

In advocating equality the key question is equality of what? The most likely candidate is the relative equality of human welfare—a highly multidimensional concept. It includes, among other components, the satisfaction of basic needs (particularly for food), as well as adequate education and health status. In addition, human welfare is enhanced in a society in which justice and fairness prevail. Equality of opportunity and "procedural justice" (Nozick) as opposed to "distributive justice" (Rawls) would be favored as alternative candidates by many people. However, equality of opportunity and procedural justice are greatly influenced by the prevailing distribution of income, wealth, and other, more intangible factors such as the distribution of power, knowledge, and information—all of which can be subsumed under the heading of human welfare.

Any attempt at measuring welfare is confronted with two major and intractable problems, first, how to make interpersonal welfare comparisons and, second, how to weigh each of the myriad of dimensions constituting welfare. However imperfect, the best proxy for human welfare is a person's income or wealth:

> A person's income may be a good proxy for his level of functioning, resource control, and opportunities: we do not claim it is the best one can do, but it is certainly one of the easiest characteristics of a person to measure, among those that might be appropriate for egalitarian concerns. (Putterman, Roemer, and Silvestre 1998, 866)

In this essay it is assumed that the distribution of income is an acceptable proxy for the distribution of human welfare and, in a more general sense, for equality as such. A more equal income distribution connotes a more equal distribution of human welfare and vice versa. One important qualification is that ideally one should focus on the secondary income distribution, that is, the primary income distribution after taxes corrected for the imputed value of public services (such as educational and health benefits) received by individuals.

How did equality evolve into and become a moral principle embraced by so many cultures and societies? Human beings are born with different genetic characteristics and intellectual potentials. They are also born in different settings and subject to a myriad of different environments as they grow up. Human beings seem to perceive from a very early age on how they differ from others physically, psychologically, and anthropologically.[2]

Traditional societies have tended to be organized on the basis of physical and moral differences among groups and individuals (e.g., serfs and lords, slaves and masters, castes, racial and ethnic groups). The segmentation into groups was internalized within societies. Could it be that at some stage the striving for equality was triggered by a reaction to the inequalities caused by segmenting individuals into ironclad categories that ruled out any intergroup mobility?

The perception of inequality among individuals does not appear to have prevailed in totally hierarchical societies such as that of the Incas and the feudal system in medieval Europe. In such hierarchical societies individuals accepted without questioning their predetermined socioeconomic status. The search for more equality would appear to come into play only after a society has reached a stage where a minimum degree of individualism and universalism prevails. As the rigid societal ordering starts to weaken, the demand for equality among the more deprived groups starts to express itself. Perhaps the prime historical example is the French Revolution, which called for "liberty, equality, and fraternity." This would suggest that the concept of equality is not innate but rather adopted to improve the functioning of a society. In this context one can hypothesize that those societies that embraced this norm functioned and survived better than those that did not. Cooperative behavior, in contrast with equality, would appear to be innate.

Whereas cooperative behavior brings with it a relatively more equal income distribution, if it goes too far it could conflict with the incentives needed for growth. In contrast, competitive behavior is typically associated with a more uneven income distribution that is called for to elicit innovations and investment, leading to growth. Too much equality and cooperative behavior can lead to stagnation, while too much inequality, fed by an overly competitive pattern of behavior, can lead to the breakdown of the social order.

So far the concept of equality has been considered and discussed as an end in itself. But, as pointed out in the first section, the modern approach to the political economy of development argues that an initial relatively equal income distribution is consistent with economic development. If this doctrine is correct, it implies that equality is also a *means* toward socioeconomic development, and the conflict vanishes between the desirability of egalitarianism on moral and ethical grounds and the (no longer valid) classical contention that the masses have to be impoverished in order to generate the flow of investment needed for growth. Furthermore, as is discussed in some detail in the next section, greater equality of the income distribution has beneficial effects on education, health, and political and social stability, and is a deterrent to crime. If equality is both an end and a means, we have a virtuous convergence.

INTERRELATIONSHIP BETWEEN EQUALITY (INEQUALITY) AND SOCIOECONOMIC VARIABLES

Inequality and Growth

The rejection of the Kuznets hypothesis of the inverted U-shaped relationship between growth and inequality (as per capita income increases) by a number of empirical studies provided much impetus to the new political economy literature that postulates that high initial inequality is detrimental to economic growth. The proponents of this approach, while rejecting the immutability of the Kuznets curve, would argue that growth patterns yielding more inequality in the income distribution would, in turn, engender lower future growth paths. Although country-specific evidence is quite limited and might not be generalizable to other settings, a recent study of the dynamics of inequality and growth in rural China based on the growth experience of villages found a robust statistically significant relationship between inequality and lower growth (Benjamin, Brandt, and Giles 2004). The authors suggested that the mechanism by which inequality exerts its negative effect was through its tilting of village economic activity away from higher-growth nonagricultural development and toward agriculture. It thereby impeded the structural transformation into nonagricultural activities.

The Channels Through Which Inequality Affects Growth

The new political economy theories linking greater inequality to reduced growth operate through a number of channels shown on Figure 32.1 (adapted from Thorbecke and Charumilind 2002). These channels are (1) unproductive rent-seeking activities that reduce the security of property; (2) the diffusion of political and social instability, leading to greater uncertainty and lower investment; (3) redistributive policies encouraged by income inequality that impose disincentives on the rich to invest and accumulate resources; (4) imperfect credit markets resulting in underinvestment by the poor—particularly in human capital; and (5) the strong positive effect of fertility of a relatively small income share accruing to the middle class (implying greater inequality), with, in turn, a significant and negative impact on growth.[3]

The nature of technological change is still another conduit through which inequality can affect growth. Changes in agricultural technology provide a good example of this link. The Green Revolution technology was developed in the public domain by international research institutions (e.g., the International Rice Research Institute and the International Maize and Wheat Research Institute). Foreign aid donors and foundations provided the funding for the public goods emanating from these institutions. Since the latter were not bound by the profit motive and property rights, they were able to develop high-yielding varieties that were scale-neutral and benefited small farmers as well as large farmers. In a sense, it could be argued that the secondary (as compared to the primary) world income distribution was made somewhat less unequal by the Green Revolution. The spread and diffusion of this technology was facilitated by being in the public domain and has led to a spectacular acceleration of food production in developing countries and a massive reduction in food crop prices and world hunger.

In contrast, the present biotechnology revolution is very much in the private domain. Issues of property rights and royalty payments present obstacles to the diffusion of this technology to small and poor farmers in the developing world, with the concomitant risk that the limited growth pattern that will result from adoption of that technology will be unevenly spread.

In addition to the above channels, some indirect paths (and more circuitous routes) are likely to exist through which inequality affects ultimately growth. Wide income and wealth disparities can impact on education, health, and crime through such manifestations as underinvestment in human capital, malnutrition leading to low worker productivity, and stress and anxiety, respectively. In turn, these manifestations may contribute to lower long-term growth. Both the above channels and additional indirect paths linking inequality to growth are discussed next in more detail.

We start by describing the causal mechanisms underlying the first two channels in Figure 32.1, since they are interrelated. The first argument is that a highly unequal distribution of income and wealth causes social tension and increases political instability (channel 2 in Figure 32.1). Greater instability creates more uncertainty, which discourages investment. The political instability, in turn, raises the risk of the government repudiating contracts and threatening the security of property rights, thereby discouraging capital accumulation still further. Moreover, when the gap be-

Figure 32.1   **Impact of Inequality on Growth**

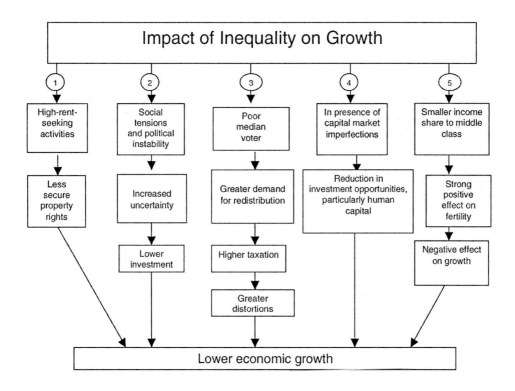

tween rich and poor widens, the latter presumably have a greater temptation to engage in rent-seeking or predatory activities at the expense of the former (channel 1). This increases the number of people who engage in illegal activities that pose a threat to property rights, thereby lowering economic growth (Benhabib and Rustichini 1991; Fay 1993). Poor countries may therefore fall into a vicious cycle of lower investment and reduced growth because they are more likely to be politically unstable (Alesina and Perotti 1996). Conversely, political stability, which is enhanced by the presence of a wealthy middle class, has a positive effect on growth.

The third channel linking inequality to lower economic growth is fiscal in nature and based on the work of Persson and Tabellini (1994), who construct a median-voter model where the political process and economic growth are endogenized. This channel is based on the effects of inequality on the demand for fiscal redistribution (Alesina and Rodrik 1994; Bertola 1993; Persson and Tabellini 1994), implying an inverse relation between inequality and investment in physical capital. An unequal income distribution implies that the median voter would tend to be poor. In turn, this would tend to cause a demand for fiscal redistribution financed by taxation. The taxes would be more distortionary in more unequal societies because the level of government expenditure and taxation results from a voting process in which income is the main determinant of a voter's preferences. In particular, in an unequal society, the poor see large gains from high taxation on the rich. Therefore, the poorer the median voter in relation to the voter with average income, the higher the equilibrium tax rate. This in turn leads to an inefficient tax system, distorts economic decisions, and discourages investment and therefore growth.

The fourth channel shown in Figure 32.1 reflects the tendency toward an underinvestment in education in the presence of imperfect credit markets. In the setting of a developing country, the poor, possessing little or no collateral, are practically sealed off from the formal credit market. Poor households are constrained for cash, and as they are unable to borrow, they have a hard time sending their children to school or keeping them there. These stylized conditions lead to a vicious cycle where initial inequality and poverty result in underinvestment in education among the poor, which further exacerbates inequality. Thus, a more equal income distribution not only would provide collateral to relatively low-income households but also tend to reduce credit market imperfections. Parents would have stronger incentives to send their children to school, and thus have a greater demand for more and higher-quality education. Their ability and willingness to pay for their children's education would rise, thereby resulting in a higher level of educational attainment in the population.

It has been argued that in a setting characterized by inequality and imperfect capital markets, low-income individuals would tend to underinvest in general, not just with respect to education. Though the poor and the rich are assumed to possess identical preferences, their savings and investment behavior may differ because they face different institutional constraints and, in particular, credit markets. Redistribution from rich to poor would stimulate growth (Aghion and Bolton 1997; Aghion and Howitt 1998) for the following reasons: (1) large sunk costs preclude the poor from investing in education and entrepreneurial projects, and (2) moral hazard occurs because the more the poor must borrow to undertake investment projects, the more they must share their returns with creditors. Incentives to supply the necessary effort to ensure a high return from the investment are therefore low. In this framework, redistribution toward borrowers would result in a favorable incentive effect and consequently a positive effect on growth.

The final and fifth channel depicted in Figure 32.1 is based on and reflects a demographic phenomenon (Perotti 1996). Lower-income households tend to have more children than higher-income households. Fertility rates are typically inversely related to household income. Hence, a society characterized by an uneven income distribution would tend to face a higher rate of growth of population than one marked by a more even income distribution. Expressed differently, it means that the smaller the income share accruing to the middle class, the greater its positive impact on fertility and negative impact on economic growth—resulting in a lower average per capita income.[4]

There is at least one more general channel through which inequality affects growth negatively. Since inequality is supposed to affect future growth and the future growth path, it also influences poverty. Cornia (2000) concludes that the widespread increase in inequality has been detrimental to the objective of poverty reduction, because large rises in inequality have stifled growth, and because, for any given growth rate of GDP, poverty falls less rapidly in the case of a more unequal distribution than in the case of a more equitable one. The obvious policy implication that follows from the above causal sequence is that successful poverty alleviation depends not only on favorable changes in average GDP per capita growth but also on favorable changes in income inequality. In short, the study reasserts the contention that the *pattern and structure* of economic growth and development, rather than the rate of growth per se, has significant effects on a country's future income distribution and poverty profile.[5]

IMPACT OF INEQUALITY ON EDUCATION, HEALTH, AND CRIME

Inequality can entail adverse effects on such socioeconomic variables as education, health, and crime and thus indirectly on growth and development. In addition to the previously discussed impact of inequality on underinvestment in human capital, there are other effects that deserve to be mentioned. The relationship between education and income equality is linked to the economic returns associated with education. Consider the present situation where the nature of technological change and the globalization trend are manifested by a rapidly increasing relative demand for technologically skilled workers. If the demand for unskilled labor is contracting, or growing at a slower rate than the demand for skilled labor, then wage inequalities will increase. The gap between rich and poor will start to widen. Income inequality will continue to grow until the supply of new college graduates depresses the return on schooling. Moreover, if there is a large disparity in the educational opportunities between the rich and the poor, the benefits of economic growth will be mainly captured by educated workers. This, in turn, would exacerbate income inequality.

Furthermore, as Birdsall points out:

> When the distribution of income is highly unequal, provision of subsidized basic education to a large segment of the school age population implies a relatively large tax burden on the rich. High-income families are likely to resist. One result can be the under-funding of education—and the decline in quality described above. A second result can be the channeling of public subsidies to higher-education institutions where the children of wealthier families are more likely to be the beneficiaries. (Birdsall 1999, 20)

There is a two-way interrelationship between inequality and health. Low income leads to malnutrition, low energy levels, low wages, and back to low income. This vicious circle dominates poor developing countries. There is overwhelming empirical evidence that poverty drives mortality. Income has a much bigger effect on health at lower rather than higher levels of income. As Deaton (2001) points out, "income inequality may make it more difficult for people to agree on the provision of public goods, such as health, water supply, waste disposal, education, and police." A highly skewed income distribution may reduce the provision of public goods and therefore worsen health.

Moreover, differential access to resources and services and unequal treatment between the rich and the poor may result in less effective preventive health care (e.g., childhood vaccinations) and more costly disease control (e.g., tuberculosis treatments). Wilkinson (2000) argues that psychosocial stress (level of depression, isolation, insecurity, and anxiety) is another pathway through which inequality affects health. For all the above reasons a reduction in deprivation (through, e.g., land ownership, democratic rights, women's agency) might therefore also lead to improved health in the population.

Next the impact of inequality on crime is explored. Conventional wisdom maintains that income inequality contributes to crime. However, the effects of income inequality on property crime should be distinguished from those on violent crime. The relationship between income inequality and crime can be described by three branches of theories: (1) Becker's (1968) economic theory of crime, (2) Merton's (1938) strain theory, and (3) Shaw and McKay's (1942) social disorganization theory. Property crime is well explained by Becker's economic theory of crime, while violent crime is explained more effectively by strain and social disorganization theories.

Becker's (1968) model was developed further by Ehrlich (1973); the latter argued that payoffs to crime, especially property crime, depend primarily on the "opportunities provided by potential victims of crime" (Ehrlich 1973, 538), as measured by the median income of families in a given community. In other words, the lower the level of legal income expected by an individual compared to the income level of potential victims, the higher the incentive to commit crimes, particularly crimes against property. Thus, for a given median income, income inequality can be an indication of the differential between the payoffs of legal and illegal activities.

Since incarceration entails loss of income, individuals with low earnings potential have a greater incentive to take the risk of committing burglary, a lower opportunity cost if caught, and a higher utility if successful (Chiu and Madden 1998). The net benefit of contemplated crime for an individual against another person can be modeled as proportional to the income difference between them (Deaton 2001). Moreover, this same model shows how low-income individuals' incentives to commit crime increase if the gap between the rich and the poor is greater.

Income inequality also reduces social capital, that is, the degree of trust and mutual support among individuals. In a poor developing country social capital is a crucial element in the functioning of a group and community. The community network constituted by friends (neighbors) and families provides a form of insurance against idiosyncratic shocks (e.g., illness, deaths, crop failure) that otherwise could be devastating to the affected households.

Finally, two sociological theories linking inequality to human welfare are worth mentioning: (1) relative deprivation and (2) role models. Relative deprivation theory holds that high levels of inequality make the poor feel worse off, increasing their alienation and stress (Jencks and Mayer 1990). One version of this hypothesis is that children feel deprived when they cannot have the same material possessions as other children in their school or neighborhood. Another version is that relative deprivation makes poorer parents feel stressed and alienated, lowering their expectations for their children or reducing the quality of their parenting (McLloyd 1990). The role model hypothesis holds that children model their behavior on the behavior of those around them. Inequality tends to exacerbate the impact of negative role models.

In summary, the various channels linking inequality to a worsening in human welfare discussed in some detail in this section of the paper imply strongly that a move toward greater equality would be conducive not only to an improvement in welfare today but also to socioeconomic growth and economic development in the future.

HOW UNEQUAL ARE GLOBAL AND NATIONAL INCOME DISTRIBUTIONS?

If inequality beyond a certain point worsens human welfare and if, as argued in the preceding section, welfare and economic development can be enhanced through greater equality, a key issue is to determine the actual degree of unevenness in the distribution of welfare. It is clear that welfare is a highly multidimensional concept and, as such, very difficult to measure. Hence income is used as an imperfect proxy for welfare. It will be seen that income is very unevenly distributed worldwide as well as within many countries.

At least three different concepts (types) of income inequality can be identified.[6] The first concept measures differences in mean incomes between countries (or regions). There is no population weighting, and every country counts the same. This concept is useful in determining the extent of convergence or divergence among countries or regions. The second concept takes mean national (or regional) incomes but weights them by countries' (or regions') populations. In this case the resulting income distributions will be strongly affected by large countries (e.g., China and India) and regions. The third concept measures interpersonal inequality at the global, national, or regional level. At the global level, this concept yields the world's income distribution.

A crucial question is whether the worldwide income distribution has become more or less even during the recent globalization era. According to concept 1 (national GDPs per capita with each country weighed equally), there has been an almost continuous and sharply rising divergence

Figure 32.2   **International Inequality: Unweighted (Concept 1) and Population-Weighted (Concept 2)**

Gini index of countries GDPs per capita

Source: Milosevic 2002b.

over the last half century, with the Gini coefficient rising from around .43 in 1950 to .53 in 2000. On the other hand, based on concept 2 (with each country's mean income weighed by population size), worldwide income distribution has become significantly more even, with the qualification that this trend is totally driven by China. The bottom graph in Figure 32.2 tracks the evolution of concept 1 since 1950, while the top panel captures the changes in concept 2. Figure 32.2 reveals clearly that estimates of between-countries inequality vary widely, depending on whether estimation is made on the basis of use of country weights (concept 1) or population weights (concept 2).[7] Note that both of these concepts ignore entirely the distribution of income within countries, and any change over time in those intracountry distributions.

The third concept captures the inequality across individuals of the world as it includes the within-country distributions derived from national income and expenditures surveys. In this sense, it is the best measure of world income inequality and its evolution over time. The various attempts to measure it are in general agreement that worldwide inequality is very high (according to Milanovic 2002, the global Gini coefficient amounted to 0.65 at the end of the nineties). It rose slightly up to the early nineties before falling marginally. The extent of inequality can be grasped when it is realized that the richest 1 percent of people in the world receive as much as the bottom

57 percent. Alternatively, the top 10 percent of the U.S. population enjoys an aggregate income equal to the total income of the poorest 43 percent in the world. Expressed differently, the total income of the richest 25 million Americans is equal to the total income of almost 2 billion poor (Milanovic 1999).

Next we explore inequality within countries. The degree of income inequality varies significantly from one country to another. Gini coefficients of intracountry income distributions range between 0.2 and 0.63 (World Bank 2001). The Slovak Republic, Belarus, Austria, and the Scandinavian countries have the most equal income distributions, with Gini coefficients ranging between 0.20 and 0.25. At the opposite end, Sierra Leone, South Africa, Brazil, Guatemala, and Paraguay display the highest Gini coefficients, between 0.60 and 0.65. The U.S. income distribution is relatively less even than in most Western European nations, with a Gini coefficient of 0.41.

In summary, the empirical evidence presented above suggests strongly that both the global income distribution and the within-country income distribution of many countries are very unequal and might thus be an obstacle to achieving the twin objectives of more equality on ethical grounds simultaneously with high growth rates of income. The bulk of world inequality is caused by between-countries inequality (about 70 percent of total global income inequality), with the share of within-country inequality amounting to the remaining 30 percent of the total. High and rising global inequality of income is likely to worsen intercountry conflicts and could affect global growth.

It is also relevant to note that between-countries inequality has fallen in the last decade because of the excellent growth performance of China and India, which together account for about one-third of the world's population. On the other hand, within-country inequality has increased in many countries—in particular within China and Eastern Europe. It appears that an important consequence of the globalization forces has been to stimulate the growth of the coastal provinces of China without having a significant impact on the inland provinces.

Finally, of all regions of the world Africa is by far the worst off in terms of overall incidence of poverty, extent of inequality, and stagnating growth and development. Of course, poor governance, corruption, geographical factors, and external conditions may be contributing to these three outcomes without necessarily implying any causal connection between inequality and growth. Yet the arguments presented in this essay provide some support for this link.

CONCLUSION

Equality is a fundamental ethical principle embraced by most cultures and religions. As such, it is a desirable norm to achieve and an end in itself. Equality is an all-encompassing concept that presumably can be interpreted as equality of human welfare. In turn, human welfare is multidimensional and very difficult to measure in any objective way. An imperfect yet acceptable and operationally useful proxy for human welfare is income. In this sense equality in terms of the degree of equality in the distribution of human welfare can be approximated by the distribution of income.

In the classical paradigm an unequal income distribution was considered a necessary precondition for growth, economic development, poverty reduction, and a more equitable income distribution in the future on the ground that the rich (capitalists) save a larger proportion of their income than the poor (workers). Hence a more unequal income distribution would generate a larger aggregate flow of savings and investment than a more equal one. This provided a rationale for an initial unequal distribution of income and wealth but created a conflict with the ethical norm of equality as a desirable end.

In contrast, the modern approach to the political economy of development identified many channels and paths through which an initially more equal income distribution is consistent with and contributes to growth and socioeconomic development. This essay discussed in some detail the positive impact of relative income equality on human welfare, in particular on political and social stability, education, health, and the deterrence of crime.

Under this new approach, equality was converted into a means toward development and poverty alleviation, removing the previous conflict between the desirability of egalitarianism on moral and ethical grounds and the classical view that the masses have to be impoverished in order to generate the flow of investment needed for growth. An important implication of the convergence of equality as both an end and a means is that policies and reforms targeted toward improving the education and health of the poor and, in general, reducing large inequities in income and wealth may become politically less difficult to implement.

Underlying a concern for equality is the presumption that income tends to be unequally distributed. The empirical evidence presented here showed how relatively unevenly world income is distributed and how pronounced the degree of inequality is within many countries. Hence a concern for more equality appears justified—particularly if it does not conflict significantly with efficiency. Clearly the striving for equality should not go so far as to act as a deterrent to the entrepreneurial incentives that are crucial to the functioning of a private enterprise system.

NOTES

1. This paper was prepared for an H. E. Babcock workshop on "Ethics, Globalization and Hunger" held at Cornell University on November 17–19, 2004. I owe a debt of gratitude to Alice Sindzingre for extremely useful suggestions in the process of writing of this paper. The paper also benefited from comments by two anonymous referees.

2. John Adams was reputed to have said, "Inequality of mind and body are so established in the constitution of human nature that no art or policy can ever plane them down to a level."

3. See Thorbecke and Charumilind (2002) for a detailed discussion of those channels. The rest of this section draws on this study.

4. Greater inequality does not necessarily have to imply higher fertility rates. That depends on where the increased dispersion in the income distribution occurs and where and how fast fertility rates change as one moves along the income distribution. For example, if one reduces inequality (but not mean incomes) in a very poor economy and fertility rates remain high until one reaches income levels twice the poverty line—both reasonable conjectures—then fertility would increase with a drop in inequality, not decrease. The basic point made above in the text is of course correct but needs to be qualified. I am grateful to a referee for this qualification.

5. For a more detailed discussion of the crucial importance of an appropriate pattern of growth and structural transformation on income distribution and the future growth path, see Nissanke and Thorbecke 2004.

6. The first three concepts listed here were defined by Milanovic (2004).

7. Estimates with use of country weights take each country as one observation, while those with population weights give people equal weights. The merits and demerits of using either method are discussed in detail in Ravallion 2004. He favors some hybrid weighting scheme as a best way of analyzing between-countries inequality.

REFERENCES

Aghion, Philippe, and Patrick Bolton. 1997. "A Theory of Trickle-Down Growth and Development." *Review of Economic Studies* 64, 1: 151–72.

Aghion, Philippe, and Peter Howitt. 1998. *Endogenous Growth Theory.* Cambridge, MA: MIT Press.

Alesina, Alberto, and Roberto Perotti. 1996. "Income Distribution, Political Instability, and Investment." *European Economic Review* 40, 6: 1203–28.

Alesina, Alberto, and Dani Rodrik. 1994. "Distributive Politics and Economic Growth." *Quarterly Journal of Economics* 109, 2: 465–90.

Becker, Gary S. 1968. "Crime and Punishment: An Economic Approach." *Journal of Political Economy* 76, 2: 169–217. Reprinted in G.J. Stigler, ed., *Chicago Studies in Political Economy*. Chicago: University of Chicago Press, 1988.

Benhabib, Jess, and Aldo Rustichini. 1991. "Social Conflict, Growth and Income Distribution." Department of Economics, New York University, New York.

Benjamin, Dwayne, Loren Brandt, and John Giles. 2004. "The Dynamics of Inequality and Growth in Rural China: Does Higher Inequality Impede Growth?" Paper presented at the conference "Inequality in China," Cornell University, October 2004.

Bertola, Giuseppe. 1993. "Market Structure and Income Distribution in Endogenous Growth Models." *American Economic Review* 83, 5: 1184–99.

Birdsall, Nancy. 1999. "Education: The People's Asset." Working Paper 5, Center on Social and Economic Dynamics, Washington DC, September 1999.

Chiu, W.H., and Paul Madden. 1998. "Burglary and Income Inequality." *Journal of Public Economics* 69, 1: 123–41.

Cornia, Giovanni Andrea. 2000. "Inequality and Poverty in the Era of Liberalisation and Globalisation." UNU/WIDER Discussion Paper, 2000. Published as chapter 1 in G. A. Cornia, ed., *Inequality, Growth, and Poverty in an Era of Liberalization and Globalization*. Oxford: Oxford University Press, 2004.

Deaton, Angus. 2001. "Health, Inequality, and Economic Development." Working Paper 8318, National Bureau of Economic Research, Cambridge, MA.

Ehrlich, Isaac. 1973. "Participation in Illegitimate Activities: A Theoretical and Empirical Investigation." *Journal of Political Economy* 81, 3: 521–65.

Fay, M. 1993. "Illegal Activities and Income Distribution: a Model of Envy." Department of Economics, Columbia University.

George, S. 1997. "How to Win the War on Ideas: Lessons from the Gramscian Right." *Dissent* 44, 3: 47–53.

Jencks, Christopher, and Susan E. Mayer. 1990. "The Social Consequences of Growing Up in a Poor Neighborhood." In Laurence Lynn and Michael McGeary, eds., *Inner-City Poverty in the United States*. Washington, DC: National Academy Press.

McLloyd, Vonnie. 1990. "The Impact of Economic Hardship on Black Families and Children: Psychological Distress, Parenting and Socio-Emotional Development." *Child Development* 61: 311–46.

Merton, Robert. 1938. "Social Structure and Anomie." *American Sociological Review* 3, 5: 672–82.

Milanovic, Branko. 1999. "True World Income Distribution, 1988 and 1993: First Calculation Based on Household Surveys Alone." Policy Research Working Papers Series No. 2244, November. Washington, DC: World Bank.

———. 2002. "Can We Discern the Effect of Globalisation on Income Distribution? Evidence from Household Budget Surveys." Policy Research Working Paper 2876, April. Washington, DC: World Bank.

———. 2004. "Half a World: Regional Inequality in Five Great Federations." Paper prepared for the World Bank and Carnegie Endowment for International Peace, Washington, DC.

Nissanke, Machiko, and Erik Thorbecke. 2004. "The Impact of Globalization on the World's Poor." Working paper, United Nations—World Institute for Development Economics Research, Helsinki.

Perotti, Roberto. 1996. "Growth, Income Distribution and Democracy: What the Data Say." *Journal of Economic Growth* 1, 2: 149–87.

Persson, Torsten, and Guido Tabellini. 1994. "Is Inequality Harmful for Growth." *American Economic Review* 84, 3: 600–21.

Putterman, Louis, John E. Roemer, and Joaquim Silvestre. 1998. "Does Egalitarianism Have a Future?" *Journal of Economic Literature* 36, 2: 861–902.

Ravallion, Martin. 2004. "Competing Concepts of Inequality in the Globalization Debate." Paper presented at the Brookings Trade Forum "Globalization, Poverty and Inequality," Washington, DC, May 13–14, 2004.

Shaw, Clifford, and Henry McKay. 1942. *Juvenile Delinquency and Urban Areas*. Chicago: University of Chicago Press.

Thorbecke, Erik, and Chutatong Charumilind. 2002. "Economic Inequality and Its Socioeconomic Impact." *World Development* 30, 9: 1477–95.

Wilkinson, Richard G. 2000. *Mind the Gap: Hierarchies, Health, and Human Evolution*. London: Weidenfeld and Nicolson.

World Bank. 2001. *World Development Report*. Washington, DC.

CHAPTER 33

INSUFFICIENT SOCIAL CAPITAL AND ECONOMIC UNDERDEVELOPMENT

HAMID HOSSEINI

Behavioral economists have leveled numerous objections to the narrow focus of neoclassical economics. Among these objections are (1) that conventional economic theory is not always consistent with the accumulated body of knowledge in disciplines such as psychology, sociology, anthropology, and organization theory, (2) that its assumptions are simplistic and unrealistic, in that it deduces its principles from features of human nature assumed to be constant and valid regardless of differences in time and space, rather than explaining economic phenomena on the basis of actual observed behavior, and (3) that it accepts the simplistic economic model of rational agents exhibiting optimizing behavior rather than more realistic behaviors such as the ones assumed by Simon's bounded rationality model (Hosseini 2003, 394).

In recent decades, behavioral economists have tried to make economics consistent with psychology. The granting of the Nobel Prize in economics to Herbert Simon in 1978 and to other behavioral economists more recently is an indication of their success in this effort. Behavioral economics (and thus economics as a whole) can benefit from the concept of social capital often used by sociologists and political scientists. In fact, various economists have already utilized social capital in their economic analysis during the last decade or so. Jeffrey Dayton-Johnson's 2003 paper in the *Journal of Socio-Economics* can even be regarded as an attempt to incorporate the concept of social capital into a behavioral economics model.

Defined by Robert Putnam as "features of social organization, such as trust, norms, and networks, that can improve the efficiency of society by facilitating coordinated action" (1993, 302), social capital has in fact a great deal of relevance to behavioral economics. With indirect roots in the works of Adam Smith and the institutionalists, social capital is a paradigm that is capable of bridging various social sciences. However, the utilization of social capital in economics, predictably, has been resisted by various economists, including Nobel laureates Kenneth Arrow and Robert Solow. While some economists have objected to it for the use of the capital metaphor, others have opposed it because of the difficulty of its measurement, and still others (i.e., neoclassical economists) have opposed its utilization altogether (finding it irrelevant to economics discourse).

In spite of these criticisms of social capital, and regardless of what we name it, I believe this concept can be useful in explaining economic behavior in both developed and less developed economies. I believe it is particularly useful and relevant in discussing the problem of underdevelopment, for development and its absence are closely linked to the behavior of individuals and the institutions human beings create. While both developed and less developed economies may lack an optimal amount of social capital, its deficiency is particularly pronounced in less advanced economies. Drastic changes in the less developed countries (LDCs) in the last century—

such as the breakdown of traditional social structures, the rise of excessive bureaucracy, and the emergence of unpopular and unaccountable governments—diminished traditional elements of social capital, and the replacement elements needed for modernization and economic development were not fully developed. The absence of needed elements of social capital in these countries helped to perpetuate poverty and underdevelopment. Assuming the relative deficiencies of markets and the government in achieving development in recent decades, I will argue that social capital can play two important roles in the process of development. On one hand, social capital can be explained as a complement of physical and human capital in the process of economic development. In this function, social capital, I will argue, can serve as a social glue complementing other forms of capital in the process of development. "The latest equipment and most innovative ideas in the hands or mind of the brightest, fittest person, however, will amount to little unless that person also has access to others to inform, correct, assist with, and disseminate work. Life at home, in the boardroom, or on the shop floor is both more rewarding and productive when suppliers, colleagues, and clients alike are able to combine their particular skills and resources in a spirit of trust, cooperation, and commitment to common objectives" (Woolcock 1998, 154). On the other hand, social capital can play a second role in the process of development: it can overcome the failures of markets and the government in the process of development, since the simultaneous failures of those institutions are, to a large extent, attributable to insufficient levels of social capital. A healthy dose of social capital can provide this missing link.

Before discussing these dual functions of social capital in the process of development, I will describe, as a critique of recent theory and practice of economic development, the evolution of the roles of physical and human capital in development economics. This critique requires a discussion of the shortcomings of the Harrod-Domar model (and similar models) of development that utilized human capital. While both physical and human capital are necessary, my contention is that policies based on these models alone are not sufficient to produce sustainable development. This section will be followed by a discussion of the use of social capital in economics, and the criticism leveled against it. Finally, after discussing the failures of both markets and governments in the process of development, I will discuss the use of social capital in overcoming the shortcomings of markets and governments. I will demonstrate that the absence or deficiency of the elements of social capital (such as trust among individuals and between individuals and agencies) is a major cause of economic backwardness in the less advanced countries. Assuming that the inadequacy of social capital in less developed economies is rooted in the undesirable policies of unaccountable (and often foreign-imposed) governments and the breakdown of traditional social structures and their replacement by weak and unstable social institutions and civil society, I believe social capital can be enhanced. The essay will end with a presentation of the ways social capital can be enhanced.

EXAGGERATING THE ROLE OF PHYSICAL CAPITAL IN EARLY DEVELOPMENT LITERATURE

Before World War II, the economics profession had ignored the less advanced economies, that is, the poor underdeveloped economies outside Europe and North America. Paul Rosenstein-Rodan's 1943 *Economic Journal* article, "Problems of Industrialization in Eastern and South-Eastern Europe," is said to be the first work dealing with underdevelopment but, as its title suggests, did not deal with poor non-Western societies. The extent of this neglect becomes obvious if one reads the 1938 League of Nations World Economic Survey. This report, prepared by the future Nobel Prize winner James Meade, had only one paragraph about Latin America and nothing whatsoever about

Asia and Africa (Arndt 1987, 33). Development economics is essentially a post–World War II phenomenon.

Influenced by Stalin's industrialization policy, the solutions provided for the Great Depression, and the Marshall Plan, early development economics essentially emphasized physical capital as the factor of production causing economic development. In doing so, these writers ignored the behavior of individuals and institutions in the less advanced countries. Early development economists had observed that the Marshall Plan, which financed the reconstruction of infrastructure and physical capital in Western Europe that had been destroyed by the Second World War, led to a quick recovery of Western European economies. "By analogy, it was assumed optimistically that, with decolonization, a similar injection of finance into developing countries would lead to their rapid economic development" (Adelman 1999, 3). In fact, the World Bank, the International Monetary Fund (IMF), and bilateral foreign assistance programs had all followed the proposition that, in these countries, physical capital was the only thing missing (ibid., 4), not realizing that physical capital needs to be complemented by both human and social forms of capital. This physical-capital-centered view was the basis of Rodan's big-push argument, and explains why Arthur Lewis wrote: "The central fact of economic development is rapid capital accumulation" (1954, 139). It is no wonder that many development approaches were predicated on the (investment-based) Harrod-Domar model, that Rostow's stage of takeoff (i.e., the stage requiring the most amount of physical capital/investment) received the most attention, that in the Sawan-Solow model growth reflects the use of physical capital and technology, and that human capital did not even play a role in these models. Interestingly enough, this one-dimensional notion of development continued for a long time. Development economists did not realize that a great gulf (that far exceeds the endowment of or access to physical capital, and which includes social capital) separated countries such as Germany and the poor LDCs.

The popularity of the Harrod-Domar model in the early years had to do with its simplicity, that is, the exaggerated role of physical capital (i.e., investment) in the process of development. In spite of its lack of success, that popularity did not end for many years. As William Easterly writes, "The Harrod-Domar growth model still lives in many international organizations. Over 90 percent of country desk economists at the World Bank use some version of this model in their projections" (1997, 12).

With the utilization of this model, many incorrect projections were made about the prospects of development in the LDCs. It is no wonder that Kamarck's 1967 book about African economic development, *The Economics of African Development*, was very optimistic about the prospects of economic development in sub-Sahara Africa. To him, the abundance of mineral resources in these countries provided them with the opportunity for high savings, investment, and development. Development economists such as Kamarck, while ignoring the roles of human and social capital, should at least have realized that there are serious absorptive capacity constraints to high investment in poor countries, and the injection of extra capital in those countries is subject to sharply diminishing returns.

HUMAN CAPITAL AND DEVELOPMENT ECONOMICS

The theory of human capital was developed by two Nobel laureates, Theodor Schultz and Gary Becker, in the 1960s and used by later development economists. However, it is interesting that the importance of what we now call human capital to economic development had been acknowledged previously by Simon Kuznets (another Nobel laureate in economics), who suggested that a nation's degree of growth (development?) requires not only physical capital but also "the body of knowledge amassed from tested findings and discoveries of empirical science, and the capacity and training of its population to use this knowledge effectively" (1955, 39).

According to Schultz, a society's endowment of educated, trained, and healthy workers determines and enhances the productivity of physical capital. This suggests that society should invest in its citizens through expenditures on education, training, and research. "Capital goods are always treated as produced means of production. But in general the concept of capital is restricted to material factors, thus excluding the skills and other capabilities of man that are augmented by investment in human capital. The acquired abilities of a people that are useful in their economic endeavor are obviously produced means of production and in this respect forms of capital, the supply of which can be augmented" (Schultz 1964). That is to say that education helps individuals fulfill and apply their abilities and talents. Education and training increase productivity. In fact, as argued by George Psacharopoulos and Maureen Woodhall, the average return on education and human capital is higher than that of physical capital in the LDCs (particularly for primary education) (1985, 21–22).

On the basis of the above, one can argue that low endowments of human capital would constitute a primary obstacle to economic development. In other words, human capital can help to realize the economies of scale inherent in the process of development/industrialization.

While Schultz and Becker developed the concept of human capital in economics, Chicago economist and Nobel laureate Robert Lucas applied it to growth and development. Lucas (1988) tried to argue that while physical capital by itself is subject to constant returns, it would be subject to increasing returns when it is combined with human capital. As Lucas (1988) and Romer (1994) have demonstrated, the productivities of both physical and (raw) labor would be magnified by a factor that reflects the level of human capital. They have demonstrated that when human capital and knowledge are low, economic growth too would be characterized by low degrees of economies of scale. To them, low human capital and knowledge are conductive to low productivity and growth rate (and a stationary state that leads to low per capita income levels). In contrast, however, if human capital and knowledge are high, economic growth would be subject to increasing returns to scale, which corresponds to high factor productivity and a high growth rate (and a stationary state that leads to high levels of per capita income). According to this line of thinking, investment in human capital and knowledge are therefore all that governments must do to propel developing countries from a low-growth trajectory to a high-growth one (Adelman 1999, 4).

Of course, human capital and knowledge, although necessary for productivity and growth, may require more to be effective in bringing about economies of scale than what is implied. For example, nonprice barriers (and an insufficient degree of social capital) might prevent the smooth transfer of resources necessary to take advantage of potential economies of scale, even if human capital is not in short supply. Insufficient social capital may also lead to missing markets, in particular for capital, preventing investment activities needed for the realization of potential scale economies.

SOCIAL CAPITAL AS CAPITAL

Social capital has been defined in different ways. As a result of this diversity of definitions, Joseph Stiglitz argues, it is "a concept with a short and already confused history" (2000, 59). A good definition is provided by Richard Rose: "social capital is defined as the stock of formal or informal social networks that individuals use to produce goods and services. In common with other definitions, this emphasizes that social capital is about recurring relationships about individuals" (2000, 149). Without using the term, Douglas North discusses the importance of social capital in economic history and economic development: "In the modern Western world, we think of life and the economy as being ordered by formal laws and property rights. Yet formal rules in even the most developed country make up a small (although very important) part of the sum of constraints that shape choices. In our daily interactions with others, whether within the family, in eternal social relations or in business activities, the governing structure is overwhelmingly defined by codes of conduct, norms of behavior, and conventions" (quoted in Rose 2000, 150).

Nobel laureate economist Robert Solow finds it misleading to use the term *capital* to refer to what is usually called *social capital,* because capital is typically identified with tangible, durable, and alienable objects, such as buildings and machines, whose accumulation can be estimated and whose worth can be assessed (Solow 1995, 2000). However, social capital more closely resembles knowledge and skills. So if, as the case of human capital suggests, economists have not "shied away from regarding knowledge and skills as forms of capital, we should not shy from its use in the case of social capital either" (Dasgupta 2003, 4). Kenneth Arrow (2000) urges the abandonment of the capital metaphor and thus the term *social capital,* emphasizing that the term *capital* implies a deliberate sacrifice in the present for future benefits that he claims is inappropriate to describe elements of social capital. I agree with Robison, Schmid, and Siles that "social capital may indeed involve a saving and investment today to obtain future benefits and Arrow's objection seems misplaced" (2002, 7). Baron and Hannon (1994) criticize the social capital metaphor, arguing that to qualify as capital an entity must possess an opportunity cost, something that social capital lacks. However, Robison, Schmid, and Siles argue that people can also make deliberate, hence costly, efforts to increase their social capital (2002, 8, referring to Woolcock 1998, 46). Even institutional economists find social capital problematic. "Institutional economists have long argued that social relationships involved in habit, custom, norms and law make a difference in the realization of the potential in physical goods and human skills. But a new name extending the capital metaphor is not needed to describe the institutions of collective action" (Schmid 2002, 747). Notwithstanding the merits of these arguments against the use of capital metaphor, it is perhaps too late to change it: "Arrow's recommendation that the term social capital be abandoned comes too late. The calves are out of the barn and into green pastures and not likely to return soon. The term social capital is now firmly entrenched in the language of social scientists" (Robison, Schmid, and Siles 2000, 7).

Many writers argue that several essential properties of physical capital also exist in social capital: transformation capacity, durability, flexibility, substitutability, decay, reliability, opportunities for investment, and alienability. According to Robison, Schmid, and Siles, "social capital," as they define it, "shares all of these essential capital-like properties" (2000, 9).

INSUFFICIENT SOCIAL CAPITAL: AN OBSTACLE TO DEVELOPMENT

Let us begin by providing a few concrete examples demonstrating that, as a result of the differences in the endowment of social capital, countries, regions, or cities that are similar in their endowments of physical and human capital can achieve very different levels of economic growth and development. In other words, social capital is an essential complement of the other two types of capital.

For example, on the basis of various papers published by the World Bank (Dasgupta and Serageldin 2000), and a 1996 paper by Joseph Stiglitz, we can attribute the economic success of East Asian countries partly to the abundance of social capital in those countries. As another example, after the 1991 fall of Somalia's government, civil disorder prevailed and income declined throughout the country, but the port city of Boosaaso was an exception—because of the efforts of community leaders and clan elders to bring about order, trade in the city flourished and income improved (Grootaert 1998, 1). Putnam (1993) demonstrates that the differences in the levels of development in northern Italy and southern Italy are due to differences in the endowments of social capital in those two regions. Putnam also discusses the case of Gujarat India, where community mobilization and joint efforts ended violent confrontations over the way forests (a source of export income) were managed, leading to the growth of income and the end of economic crisis for the residents of Gujarat.

Among the less advanced nations seeking development and industrialization, there are those that do not suffer from the absence or inadequacy of physical as well as human capital. However, in these countries the presence of even the abundance of these two forms of capital have not necessarily implied or led to development and industrialization. It is possible to argue that the presence or even abundance of physical and human capital will not necessarily amount to development if there is an insufficient degree of social capital. For example, economic development will not occur if there is no rule of law, or if trust among individuals, between individuals and organizations, and between the people and government does not exist. This suggests that elements of social capital behave as a complement to physical and human capital. A few decades ago, Kenneth Arrow and Gerald Debreu (1954) provided the proof of Adam Smith's conjecture two centuries earlier on the efficiency of invisible-hand allocations. But insufficient amounts of social capital imply failure of markets. As Bowles and Gintis argue, "The axioms required by the Fundamental Theorem of Welfare Economics were so stringent that Arrow stressed the importance of what would now be called social capital in coping with its failure" (2002, 423). What Bowles and Gintis had in mind was the following statement by Kenneth Arrow: "In the absence of trust . . . opportunities for mutually beneficial cooperation would have to be forgone . . . norms of social behavior [may be] . . . reactions of society to compensate for market failure" (Arrow 1971, 22). And Arrow relates economic backwardness to market failures caused by the absence of social capital: "Virtually every commercial transaction has within itself an element of trust, certainly any transaction conducted over a period of time. It can be plausibly argued that much of the economic backwardness in the world can be explained by the lack of mutual confidence" (1972: 357).

Markets will not give rise to the production and exchange of commodities unless individuals are connected through "social networks and the norms of reciprocity and trustworthiness that arise from them" (Putnam 2000, 19). In other words, if countries are to produce needed commodities and provide them through markets for exchange in an efficient manner (i.e., a way that can lead to development), we need to have a sufficient quantity of social capital—features of social organization such as trust and the norms of behavior and networks needed for the efficient production and exchange of these commodities.

In underdeveloped economies, insufficient amounts of social capital have implied the weakening of interpersonal networks, and thus an absence of trust among individuals and between individuals, organizations, and government agencies. In these countries, insufficient amounts of social capital cause numerous negative consequences (including the free rider problem). For example, absence of trust would prevent entrepreneurs from joining with other entrepreneurs in partnerships to organize new productive enterprises, banks from providing loans to those entrepreneurs, and individual companies and banks from accepting personal (or even small-company) checks unless endorsed by more credible/trustable individuals. Absence of trust in these societies leads to high transaction costs and to incomplete and even missing markets.

Trust is an important ingredient of social capital in the LDCs. It is related to the expectations individuals form about the actions of others that have a bearing on their choice of action when that action must be chosen before they can observe the actions of others (Dasgupta 2003, 8). Economically speaking, trust is important because its presence or absence can have a bearing on what we (as entrepreneurs, workers, consumers, etc.) choose to do, and in many cases what we can do. Thus, its absence can imply investments not made, needed goods and services not produced, workers not hired, or transactions not made.

Insufficient social capital also relates to government failures in the process of development. This is because sustainable economic development at least requires the rule of law; this is needed to protect property rights and to ensure the proper enforcement of agreements and contracts. Absence of social capital also leads to the absence of a sense of responsibility on the part of civil servants and members of the judiciary and law enforcement, which in turn would lead to corruption and red tape. Thus, in the LDCs, the prevalence of corruption and the absence of the sense of responsibility among these groups are not conducive to the upholding of the rule of law and thus to the fulfillment of the terms of contracts and economically related agreements. Corruption and the absence of responsible feeling imply unsuitable punishment for breaking (economic) agreements and contracts, for such behaviors would lead to people not acquiring the appropriate incentive to fulfill them. As a result, mutually beneficial economic agreements and contracts (starting companies, making new investments, or engaging in transactions) would not be initiated.

Trust, confidence, and other relevant aspects of social capital are interconnected. For example, if individuals lose trust or confidence in the legal system, they would not trust others to fulfill the terms of an agreement, and thus they may choose not to enter into agreements and contracts. The interconnectedness suggests that social capital (such as trust) "is riddled with beneficial externalities" (Dasgupta 2003). In fact, from a macroeconomic perspective, it is a public good that is necessary in the productive process.

MARKET VERSUS GOVERNMENT FAILURES IN DEVELOPMENT ECONOMICS LITERATURE

Conventional economics assumes the efficiency of the market mechanism in its ability to allocate goods, services, and factors of production. In a perfectly competitive economy, it is assumed that market forces ensure an optimal allocation of commodities and resources, both statically and dynamically. Even if the extra obstacles to the smooth functioning of the market mechanism in the LDCs are ignored, there are still limits to this presumed efficiency. In other words, there are cases where markets fail in achieving efficiency, even in the most advanced of nations. Obviously, the pressure of monopoly power, external economies, public goods, imperfect information, and asymmetry of information would prevent markets from working efficiently; neither would the market mechanism work efficiently if we are dealing with the cases of merit and orphan goods, or capital market myopia. For markets to bring about efficiency, prices must provide correct signals. However, prices may not provide right signals due to the distortions caused by any of the above distorting forces. Distortions in the market may cause labor or other factors of production to respond to price signals inadequately or even perversely. And, although ready to respond appropriately to correct price signals, factors of production may be immobile, unable to move quickly (as in the case of labor) or at all (in the case of land).

Going back to the early years of development economics during the 1940s and 1950s, most of its pioneers assumed market failures to be even more pervasive in the less developed countries. This point was in fact mentioned in Paul Rosenstein-Rodan's 1943 article, and it was elaborated by Tibor Scitovsky in his 1954 paper "Two Concepts of External Economies." Many development economists have emphasized that markets work even less well in the LDCs. Some development economists have gone as far as suggesting that a greater degree of market failure is the distinguishing characteristic of underdevelopment. An example is Hla Myint (1985), who argued that the nonexistence or segmentation of particular markets, caused by high transaction costs, forms a characteristic feature of underdevelopment. From this perspective, such economies fail since they are incapable of creating certain markets. Early development economists, because of their emphasis on the need for physical capital, emphasized the types of market failure that would prevent investment activity in productive enterprises and those in much-needed infrastructure. However, more recently, development economists have also discussed other types of market failure, in particular those that arise from the various facets of the learning process.

Because of the pervasiveness of market failures in the LDCs, many development economists of the early years found a strong government direction and participation as a necessary ingredient of economic development. It was as a result of the presumption of such failures of the market that early development economists proposed policy prescriptions such as the big push. Because of those market failures, as Rosenstein-Rodan argued, government has a great responsibility to make things ready for the takeoff: "there is a minimum level of resources that must be devoted to a development program if it is to have any chance of success. Launching a country into self-sustaining growth is a little like getting an airplane off the ground. There is a critical ground speed which must be passed before the craft can be airborne" (quoted in Hosseini 1999, 125).

Of course, to various conventional economists, market failures were not sufficient to warrant government intervention, in particular to the extent suggested by Rosenstein-Rodan's big-push policy. An early example was B.T. Bauer, who proposed a severely limited role for the government in LDCs, almost exclusively relying on markets including on world capital markets rather than foreign aid for external capital needs. Of course, not every conventional economist was as extreme as Bauer. Some conventional economists, while accepting the possibility of market failures in the LDCs, did not think that governments would necessarily be more successful. One such economist was the late Harry Johnson, who said, "The possibility of market failure is not sufficient to prove the certainty of government success" (quoted in Arndt 1985, 157). Arndt, paraphrasing Campos, explains this line of thinking as follows: "The price system with all its acknowledged defects, may yet, on balance, be the lesser evil, compared with the operation in practice of bureaucratic planning and control" (ibid.). More recently, Krueger has emphasized the case of government failure in the process of economic development: "Whether market failures had been present or not, most knowledgeable observers concluded that there had been colossal government failures. In many countries, there could be little question but that government failure significantly outweighed market failure" (1990, 9–10).

According to Krueger, there existed many government failures, involving both commission and omission. To her, government failures of commission included "exceptionally high-cost public enterprises, engaged in a variety of manufacturing and other economic activities not traditionally associated with the public sector." For failures of omission, Krueger mentions deterioration of transport and communication facilities (which raises costs for both public and private sector activities) and maintenance of fixed nominal exchange rates in the face of domestic inflation, among others. As a result of these government failures, large-scale and visible corruption emerges, and many programs whose objectives were to help the poor would end up benefiting the more affluent members of society (Krueger 1990, 10).

SOCIAL CAPITAL: A COMPLEMENT OF MARKETS AND GOVERNMENTS

As economists, we know that markets are important institutions. "Markets are attractive because of their ability to make use of private information. So where comprehensive contracts may be written and enforced at low costs, markets are often superior to other governance structures. Moreover, where residual claimancy and control rights can be closely aligned, market competition provides a decentralized and difficult to corrupt disciplining mechanism that punishes the inept and rewards high performances" (Bowles and Gintis 2002, 423).

The institution of the government too has its advantages; it is well suited for handling particular classes of problems. For example, it alone has the power and ability to provide and enforce the rules of the game that govern the interaction of private agents. Therefore, in cases "where an economic process will be effective only if participating is mandatory (e.g., participating in social insurance program, or paying for national defense) governments have an advantage" (Bowles and Gintis 2002, 424).

As stated in the previous section, there are also situations where both markets and governments fail, though these are not always acknowledged directly. For example, traditional supporters of laissez-faire and markets, by emphasizing "a thousand points of light" (President George H.W. Bush), "it takes a village" (Senator Hillary Rodham Clinton), and "faith-based initiatives" (President George W. Bush), have come to admit the failure of the market in providing certain public goods (and thus the need for social capital). Traditional and strong advocates of the role of the government, by admitting the shortcomings of five-year plans and the limits of government capacity and accountability, have come to the realization that social capital can help to overcome the failures of the government (ibid., 420). As suggested in the previous section, markets and governments have in particular failed in the less advanced countries. In these countries, because of high transaction costs, uncertainty, or insufficient information (not to mention the insufficiency of both physical and human capital), much-needed markets often did not come into existence. Even when they did, they were not strong enough to bring about development and industrialization. And governments, because of the insufficiency of information, lack of accountability, and the prevalence of corruption, were unable to correct the failures of the market in helping to bring about development and industrialization.

Obviously, to achieve industrialization and sustainable development, the less developed economies need both physical and human capital. Development and industrialization require infrastructure; they also need investments in various sectors of the economy, in particular in the manufacturing sector. As history has demonstrated, sustainable development also requires human capital (education, skills, knowledge), which requires investment in various levels of educational institutions. These various types of investments require the participation of markets (i.e., the private sector) and the government (the public sector). As argued before, in the process of development/industrialization, there are situations where both markets and governments fail and social capital is required as a remedy. It can be argued that even in the situations in which markets and governments can play their proper historical roles (including more advanced economies), social capital is still required. Endowment of trust, a sense of civic and social responsibility, and other elements of social capital not only complement the existence of physical and social capital but provide what markets and governments fail to provide. Trust and sense of civic and social responsibility and belonging in society set in motion various forces in society that allow the otherwise missing markets to appear, loans to be made, and investments to be undertaken; it can also remedy the failures of markets and governments. A society endowed with an adequate quantity of social capital can find it easier and cheaper to acquire certain types of needed information, types that might be expensive and hard to gather by firms, banks, and governments. Such a society gives rise to more cooperation and interaction among its members. This will lower the cost of acquiring knowledge about the behavior of other members and would increase the benefits of doing so. Such a society will minimize the free rider problem that is problematic in poor nations, impairing the sense of community and trust in these countries. A society endowed with social capital is motivated to punish free riders, which in essence implies the provision of a public good. By combining self-interest and non-self-interest, such a society can enhance the sense of cooperation and trust and reduce the type of corruption that leads to a reduction of service and productivity.

CONCLUSION

As argued before, the less advanced economies may or may not suffer from a shortage of physical and human forms of capital. However, these countries seem to be short in at least some aspects and elements of social capital. The insufficiency of social capital in these countries often results in a type of image among individual economic agents that can be characterized as zero-sum. Lack of trust among individuals and between individuals and agencies/firms leads to a lack of civic and social responsibility that will result in missing markets, inefficient and inadequate transactions, corruption, a substantial amount of free riding, and other problems. Such behaviors on the part of individuals, markets, firms, and governments constitute substantial obstacles to sustainable economic development and industrialization. These societies, I believe, need to make changes that would transform these zero-sum images to positive-sum perceptions. Obviously, this is a big task, requiring changes in various institutions as well as relations. These societies must create norms of individual behavior that advocate coordinated efforts. They must convince economic agents that by changing their less-than-cooperative or uncoordinated behavior, they will improve their benefits. Without such incentives, economic agents will not find changes in their behaviors advantageous.

Concerned policy makers in the LDCs, where elements of social capital are scarce, must encourage a climate of cooperation and trustworthiness, and promote norms of behavior that emphasize civic responsibility; these will enhance the endowment of social capital in their countries. In doing so, they must keep in mind the following. First, individuals and economic agents must become convinced that they alone will own the fruits of their efforts. They must have the confidence that they are the beneficiaries of their change of behavior—that is, the beneficiaries of more efficient productive enterprises, banks, and market exchange; better distribution of public goods; reduction of corruption, free riding, and red tape—and that the achievement of economic development will benefit all. Second, rule of law must be respected by individuals, organizations, civil servants, and those in the judiciary and law enforcement. This must be emphasized by policy makers and civic leaders alike. In a society in which the rule of law is emphasized, the efficiency of markets, firms, organizations, and government agencies will be enhanced, and the free rider problem, corruption, and harmful rent-seeking activity will be minimized. All of these factors are preconditions of development. Third, policy makers and civic and governmental leaders must emphasize equal treatment and nondiscrimination in government agencies, in firms, in the marketplace, and in all other organizations. This will build trust in various levels of society and bring greater economic efficiency. Fourth, free riding must end at the workplace, in particular in government agencies, where work effort is not always maximized. This, in addition to improving efficiency of various economic and governmental organizations, will enhance trust in government agencies (again, all prerequisites of economic development). Finally, government, civic, and economic leaders must build into the structure of social and economic relations opportunities for mutual monitoring, and punishment for noncooperative, corrupt, and free-riding behaviors. If all individuals have the sense of responsibility to monitor these unproductive behaviors, trust and efficiency would be perpetuated. Achieving these goals might not be easy (although education, political accountability, and a strong civil society would help in this effort), but these steps must be taken if the LDCs are to join the ranks of economically developed and industrialized countries.

REFERENCES

Adelman, Irma. 1999. "Fallacies in Development Theory and Their Implications for Policy." Paper presented at the 1999 conference of the Society for the Advancement of Behavioral Economics, June 13–14, San Diego.

Arndt, H.W. 1985. "The Origins of Structuralism." *World Development* 13, 2.

———. 1987. *Economic Development: The History of an Idea.* Chicago: University of Chicago Press.

———. 1988. "Market Failures and Development." *World Development* 16, 2: 219–29.

Arrow, K. 1971. "Political and Economic Evaluation of Social Effects and Externalities." In M.D. Intriligator, ed., *Frontiers of Quantitative Economics*, 3–23. Amsterdam: North Holland.

———. 1972. "Gifts and Exchanges." *Philosophy and Public Affairs* 1: 343–62.

———. 2000. "Observations on Social Capital." In Partha Dasgupta and Ismail Serageldin, eds., *Social Capital: A Multifaceted Perspective*, 3–5. Washington, DC: World Bank.

Arrow, K., and G. Debreu. 1954. "Existence of Equilibrium for a Competitive Economy." *Econometrica* 22: 265–90.

Baron, J., and M. Hannon. 1994. "The Impact of Economics on Contemporary Sociology." *Journal of Economic Literature* 32, 3: 1111–46.

Bowles, S., and H. Gintis. 2002. "Social Capital and Community Governance." *Economic Journal* 112: 419–36.

Dasgupta, P. 1988. "Trust as a Commodity." In D. Gambetta, ed., *Trust: Making and Breaking Cooperative Relations.* Oxford: Blackwell.

———. 2003. "Social Capital and Economic Performance." In E. Ostrom and T.K. Ahn, eds., *Foundations of Social Capital.* Northampton, MA: Edward Elgar.

Dasgupta, Partha, and Ismail Serageldin, eds. 2000. *Social Capital: A Multifaceted Perspective.* Washington, DC: World Bank.

Dayton-Johnson, J. 2003. "Knitted Warmth: The Simple Analytics of Social Cohesion." *Journal of Socio-Economics* 32: 623–45.

Easterly, W. 1997. "The Ghost of Financing Gap: How the Harrod-Domar Growth Model Still Haunts Development Economics." Available at http://www.worldbank.org/html/dec/Publications/Workpapers/WPS1800series/wps1807/wps1807.pdf.

Grootaert, C. 1998. "Social Capital: The Missing Link?" Social Capital Initiative working paper no. 3. Washington, DC: The World Bank.

Hosseini, H. 1999. "The State and the Market, Their Functions and Failures in the History of Economic Development Thought." *Managerial Finance* 25, 3–4: 19–38.

———. 2003. "The Arrival of Behavioral Economics: From Michigan or the Carnegie School." *Journal of Socio-Economics* 32: 391–409.

Kamarck, Andrew. 1967. *The Economics of African Development.* New York: Praeger.

Krueger, A. 1990. "Government Failures in Development." *Journal of Economic Perspectives* 4, 3: 9–25.

Kuznets, S. 1955. "Toward a Theory of Economic Growth." In Robert Lekachman, ed., *National Policy for Economic Welfare at Home and Abroad.* New York: Doubleday.

Lewis, Arthur. 1954. "Economic Development with Unlimited Supplies of Labor." *Manchester School* 22: 139–91.

Lucas, R. 1988. "On the Mechanics of Development Planning." *Journal of Monetary Economics* 22: 3–42.

Myint, H. 1985. "Organizational Dualism and Economic Development." *Asian Development Review* 3, 1: 24–42.

Psacharopoulos, George, and Maureen Woodhall. 1985. *An Analysis of Investment Choice.* New York: Oxford University Press.

Putnam, R.D. 1993. *Making Democracy Work: Civic Traditions in Modern Italy.* Princeton, NJ: Princeton University Press.

———. 2000. *Bowling Alone: The Collapse and Revival of American Community.* New York: Simon and Schuster.

Robison, L., A. Schmid, and M. Siles. 2002. "Is Social Capital Really Capital?" *Review of Social Economy* 60, 1: 1–21.

Romer, Paul. 1994. "The Origins of Economic Growth." *Journal of Economic Perspectives* 8: 3–22.

Rose, R. 2000. "Getting Things Done in an Antimodern Society: Social Capital Networks in Russia." In P. Dasgupta and I. Serageldin, eds., *Social Capital: A Multifaceted Perspective.* Washington, DC: World Bank.

Rosenstein-Rodan, P. 1943. "Problems of Industrialization in Eastern And South-Eastern Europe." *Economic Journal* 53: 202–211.

Schmid, A. 2002. "Using Motive to Distinguish Social Capital from ITS Outputs." *Journal of Economic Issues* 37, 3: 747–67.

Schultz, T. 1964. *Transforming Traditional Agriculture*. New Haven, CT: Yale University Press.

Scitovsky, Tibur. 1954. "Two Concepts of External Economies." *Journal of Political Economy* 62: 54–67.

Solow, Robert M. 2000. "Notes on Social Capital and Economic Performance." In Partha Dasgupta and Ismail Serageldin, eds., *Social Capital: A Multifaceted Perspective,* 6–12. Washington, DC: World Bank.

Stiglitz, Joseph. 1996. "Some Lessons from the East Asian Countries." *World Bank Research Observer* 11, 2: 151–77.

———. 2000. "Formal and Informal Institutions." In P. Dasgupta and I. Serageldin, eds., *Social Capital: A Multifaceted Perspective*. Washington, DC: World Bank.

Woolcock, M. 1998. "Social Capital and Economic Development: Toward a Theoretical Synthesis and Policy Framework." *Theory and Society* 27: 151–208.

CHAPTER 34

BEHAVIORAL LAW AND ECONOMICS

An Introduction

THOMAS S. ULEN

It is a commonplace in legal scholarship to note that law and economics (or the economic analysis of law) has been one of the most influential academic innovations of the twentieth century. For example, one might plausibly argue that in North America law and economics is the default method of scholarship for most areas of the law.[1] More realistically, perhaps, one might say that no one writing on legal topics today for a legal academic audience can afford to be unfamiliar with law and economics and expect his or her work to have an impact.

The great initial power of law and economics came from its use of the rational choice theory of microeconomics to examine legal decision making. That theory, on which I shall elaborate in the next section, provides a systematic method of explaining and predicting behavior. Its application to the decisions of all those whose behavior the law seeks to influence was spectacularly fruitful. Nonetheless, within the last decade or so there has appeared a literature that describes experimental results of real decision making that finds systematic deviations from the explanations and predictions of rational choice theory. The natural result is to question social scientific analyses of human decision making that fail to take adequate account of these experimental findings. So, a prediction regarding the likely response to a given legal command (such as that to take due care or be held liable for the consequences of failing to do so) that overlooks established and systematic human foibles in decision making is bound to be wrong.

Law and economics is slowly but certainly taking account of the behavioral literature's findings. In this chapter I shall give a brief introduction to the uses of behavioral research in the analysis of the law. I begin by giving a brief review of rational-choice-theory-based law and economics. Specifically, I shall lay out three traditional analyses of legal topics from a rational choice theory perspective. Then I shall give a very brief introduction to some behavioral issues before reexamining the three topics of the previous section from a behavioral perspective. In the penultimate section I want to sound several cautionary notes on the behavioral law and economics literature and the direction in which law and economics is headed.

RATIONAL CHOICE THEORY AND CONVENTIONAL LAW AND ECONOMICS

Rational choice theory (hereafter RCT) has been a tremendously powerful theory of decision making in the social sciences. Its strength lies in the paucity of its assumptions, the simplicity of its application, and the great success of its predictions. These strengths have been most evident in the investigation of explicitly economic decisions (Landsburg 1993, 2005; but also see Frank 2003 and Mullainathan and Thaler 2001), but there have also been successful applications of RCT in social sciences contiguous to economics, such as political science, sociology, international relations, anthropology, and, of course, law (Green and Shapiro 1994), It is this last series of applications on which I shall concentrate in this section. I shall first give a workable definition of RCT and then give three examples of its applicability to legal issues.

RCT Generally

While there is some disagreement about exactly what it is that RCT entails, for our purposes we might describe it as follows. RCT posits that human decision makers know the goals that they seek to achieve, such as happiness or well-being, and that they rationally pursue those goals. To do so, they are cognitively capable of identifying the alternative means of goal achievement open to them and of evaluating the relative worth of those means of reaching their ends. A rational decision maker has neither inconsistencies nor incoherencies in her preference orderings.

The strongest defense of this sparse theory of decision making is that it is economic in the sense of boiling down the great complexities of human decision making into a straightforward, easily mastered hypothesis with very wide applicability. Of course, none of these qualities, nor all of them together, is sufficient to justify accepting a theory (Kitcher 1993). The theory must also throw light on dark corners of the world; yield interesting and testable propositions about the world; be amenable to systematic inquiry, including hypothesis testing; and survive confrontations with data from the real world.[2] One also expects that there is some rough correspondence between the theory and the world, not just in the sense that the theory explains and predicts tolerably well but that it reasonably accurately describes the phenomena under consideration.[3] In brief, it is not generally thought to be enough that the theory is successful at prediction or explanation; it must resonate with those in the field as being "realistic." With respect to RCT, that means that we must see the gist of real human beings within the four corners of the theory.

There are two common criticisms that are made of RCT as an account of human decision making. The first is captured within the implied criticism of the previous paragraph: that many researchers do not recognize real human beings in the RCT model of humans. The rationally self-interested, coldly calculating decision makers of RCT sound more like automatons or robots than like flesh-and-blood human beings. Real people, the criticism holds, are fragile, prone to error, flighty, frequently irrational, and often in the grip of their emotions. They do not reach conclusions about how to behave or what to do on the basis of close reasoning about alternatives; rather, they often take decisions impulsively or because a friend or colleague dared them to do so. How, the critics argue, is this widely held view of fallible and fragile humans to be squared with the clear-eyed view of RCT?

The second common criticism of RCT is that it is meaningless because it is tautological and, therefore, irrefutable. To illustrate this criticism, recognize that RCT can be said to hold that whatever it is that people do must be rationally advancing their goals because otherwise they would have done something else. If, for example, I observe A hitting himself in the head with a block of wood, it must be because that enhances his well-being (assuming that is his goal).[4] The point is that RCT makes behavior that might otherwise seem to be irrational into rational conduct, however odd it might be.

RCT and Property Law

The most famous contention in law and economics is the Coase theorem (Coase 1960). Indeed, the article from which that theorem comes is the most heavily cited law review article of the twentieth century and the most frequently cited article in the law and economics literature.

The Coase theorem holds, in one version, that when transaction costs are zero (or very low), an efficient allocation of resources will obtain, regardless of the law, the context, or anything else (Cooter and Ulen 2004). The thrust of the theorem, for the law, is that the law matters for the efficient allocation of resources only when transaction costs impede bargaining. In all other circumstances bargaining between affected parties will achieve efficiency.

The implications of this theorem are far-reaching and have been commented upon so extensively that I will refer to only one possible application—the initial assignment of property interests to a valuable resource. Suppose that a valuable new resource appears and that, following the standard economic analysis, the law is eager to assign a property interest to the resource so that it is put to its highest and best use.[5] All other things being equal, the law would like to make the initial assignment of the property interest in this new resource to the party who places the higher value on it. One might argue that the costs of making that ex ante value determination are high, although not necessarily so. And one might further worry that the costs of making an inappropriate assignment are also high—if, for example, the resource is given to someone other than the highest-valuing owner, then additional resources might be exhausted in later transferring the resource from the initial assignee to the person who should have had it in the first place.

But, of course, none of these costs matters if the transaction costs among those who might want to possess the resource are zero. In that circumstance, the ownership will pass, costlessly, to the person who values it the most, and, thereafter, efficient use of the resource will occur. In this happy state of affairs there is no point in agonizing about the initial assignment or in worrying about any costs of subsequent transfer. Indeed, when transaction costs are zero, the best that the law can do is to assign the property interest as quickly as possible and in whatever manner suits the legal decision maker—for example, by a coin toss or by assigning it to the fifteenth person listed on the 173rd page of the local phone directory.

Naturally, a negative implication of the Coase theorem, with respect to initial property entitlements, is that when transaction costs are *not* zero, then the law needs to exercise some care in making the initial assignment. The error costs in putting the property into the hands of someone other than the highest-valuing user might be considerable. The resource could end up in the hands of someone who does not place a particularly high value on it and, because transaction costs are high, might remain inefficiently stuck in those hands. In order to avoid those social costs, it may make sense to incur the ex ante costs of making a determination of who is the highest-valuing user.

All this is fairly standard law and economics analysis. For the purposes of this introduction, the central point to which I want to draw attention is that this RCT-based analysis of the issue of the initial assignment to valuable property suggests that the *only* reason for legal interest in this initial assignment is the presence of high transaction costs that might prevent the resource from moving to its highest and best use.

RCT and Tort Law

The economic analysis of tort liability was one of the earliest uses of RCT to examine a legal issue (Calabresi 1970; Posner 1972; Brown 1974; Cooter and Ulen 2004; Shavell 2004). The insights that this application has gained have been numerous and important. We now tend to see exposure to tort liability principally in its deterrence role—that is, in its ability to minimize the social costs of accidents by inducing potential injurers and victims to take cost-justified precautions.

The gist of the theory is straightforward. Rationally self-interested decision makers will take the costs that their actions (or failures to act) might impose on others into account only rarely, choosing instead to focus on the costs and benefits that accrue to *them*. So, in deciding whether to drive safely, a rationally self-interested driver might focus, in the absence of exposure to liability for harm to others, only on the extent to which his driving decisions impinge on his own and his family's well-being and not on the extent to which it might confer benefits on others. Thus, he might drive within the posted speed limit only if doing so suits him and there are others around. He might replace his turn signal bulbs only if he gets around to it and believes that doing so will protect him from others.

The social task of tort liability is to induce people to take into account, in their decisions about what activities to pursue and how to pursue them, the external costs that their actions or failures to act might impose on strangers. Tort law seeks to induce this by holding out the possibility that causing an injury to another might result in their being financially responsible for the losses suffered by the victim.

How will this lead to taking care that would benefit others? Suppose that an injurer who fails to take cost-justified precaution—that is, precaution that costs less than the benefit it confers on others—will be held liable for the full extent of the victim's losses. For example, if an accident is likely to occur with a 2 percent probability and, if it occurs, to impose $10,000 in losses on the victim, then the expected cost of the accident is $0.02 \times \$10,000 = \$200$. If the injurer can prevent the accident from occurring by incurring an expenditure of $100, then he or she will do so on the ground that a $100 expenditure is less than a $200 expenditure (and recall that failing to take the expenditure will expose the injurer to a payment of $10,000). On this reading of the basis for tort liability, the system's task is to create the appropriate incentives for all parties, both victims and injurers, to take all cost-justified precaution.

One of the most important insights of the law and economics approach is its account of the differences between the efficiency aspects of the tort liability standards of strict liability and negligence. Although there are many nuances that could be painted regarding the tort liability standards that courts truly apply, let me focus on strict liability and negligence in the fiction that those are the only two options available to a court. I shall assume that potential injurers and potential victims are aware of their possible obligations under tort liability, that they understand the difference between negligence and strict liability and are confident that the court will apply the appropriate liability standard to any accident in which they are involved, that they know the various alternatives open to them for taking care and avoiding accidents, and that potential injurers and victims do not know one another or cannot bargain with one another prior to an accident.[6] Let us further assume that if there is an accident and if the defendant-injurer is deemed to be liable, then he must compensate the plaintiff-victim for the full extent of her compensable injuries. If, however, the defendant-injurer is not liable, then the plaintiff-victim must bear her own losses.[7]

Under these circumstances, and assuming for the time being that the applicable liability standard is negligence, how will a rational potential injurer decide what care to take?[8] He will reason as follows: "If I take all cost-justified precaution—that is, all the precaution whose cost is less than its expected benefit, then I cannot be held liable, even if there is an accident and I caused it. That being so, I'll take all cost-justified precaution."

A rational potential victim will reason in a similar fashion. She will recognize that a rational potential injurer will have taken all cost-justified precaution and will, therefore, not be liable for any injuries that she receives in the event of an accident. So she will have to bear her own accident losses. As a result, if there is any precaution that the potential victim can take and that costs less than the expected benefit that it confers on her, then she will have an incentive to take it.

The result of both of these rational calculations is that the exposure to negligence liability induces actions that minimize the social costs of accidents.[9]

To complete the analysis, let us distinguish the efficiency of strict liability from that of negligence. Notice that the negligence or fault standard imagines that *both* parties, the victim and the injurer (and assuming, contrary to fact, that the parties know which role they will fill if an accident occurs), can take action to reduce the probability and severity of an accident. This is a situation known in the literature as "bilateral precaution," and the literature's conclusion is that in circumstances of bilateral precaution, negligence liability is efficient in that it induces both parties to take all cost-justified precaution and thereby minimizes the (expected) social costs of accidents.

But what if only one of the parties can realistically take actions to reduce the probability and severity of an accident? What if everyone knows who the injurer will be, if there is an accident, and who the victim will be? In those circumstances, strict liability is the more efficient liability standard. Under strict liability the expected liability costs of the injurer are identical to the expected social costs of the accident. In taking that amount of precaution that minimizes his expected liability costs, the potential injurer is also minimizing the social costs of accidents. That leads to the potential injurer's taking exactly as much precaution as he would have taken if faced with the negligence standard. So what is the difference between the two standards? Recall that under negligence complying with the social-cost-minimizing level of precaution exonerates the defendant-injurer from liability for the victim's losses. But, unlike the fault standard, there is no exonerating level of care for the injurer under strict liability. The best that the injurer can do is to minimize his expected liability, not avoid it altogether.

The distinctive aspect of strict liability is that in its purest form it relieves the potential victim of any responsibility for taking care. Clearly this makes sense only if there is nothing meaningful that the potential victim can do to reduce the probability or severity of an accident. As a result, strict liability is the more efficient standard in settings of "unilateral precaution"— that is, circumstances in which only the potential injurer can take action to reduce the expected costs of an accident.[10]

There are, of course, many additional topics within the analysis of the tort liability system for which this rational choice account has great value. For instance, the view that the principal goal of exposure to tort liability is to deter wrongdoing by inducing rational actors to take care opens up a potentially fruitful line of inquiry into the possible substitutability between ex ante safety regulation and ex post regulation through the tort liability system as methods of efficiently achieving the social goal of minimizing the social costs of accidents (see Kolstad, Ulen, and Johnson 1990). And yet, as fruitful as the economic analysis of tort liability would seem to be, one might plausibly argue that the substantive impact of law and economics on tort law has been minimal. That judgment seems to me to be premature for at least two reasons. First, law and economics has not really altered the substantive conclusions of tort law. It has not, for instance, shown that tort law has been off the rails for many decades, and then provided a clear path for getting that area of law back on the rails. Rather, the principal task of law and economics, with respect to tort liability, seems to me to have been to provide an alternative and more satisfying basis on which to ground the entire tort liability system— namely, the minimization of the social costs of accidents. To illustrate one advantage of the economic analysis, previous theorists of tort law had not, as I indicated above, provided an entirely satisfactory account of the social functions of negligence and of strict liability. Law and economics has done so.

Second, law and economics has, despite its relative youth, given an important boost to empirical studies of legal issues, including of tort law issues. That empirical literature suggests that tort law really does induce precautionary behavior (as the economic analysis assumes) (Schwartz 1994; Dewees, Duff, and Trebilcock 1995). I do not want to oversell this conclusion because we are still at a very early stage of the empirical work. Nonetheless, I have no doubt whatsoever that had law and economics not provided an alternative basis for the analysis of tort law, there would have been no empirical work at all. Because I believe that empirical work is a vital part of the sensible formation of legal policy, I am happy to champion law and economics if only for the fact that it inevitably brings empirical work in its wake.

RCT and Criminal Law

In 1968 Gary Becker formalized a notion that had, perhaps, first been articulated by Jeremy Bentham in the late eighteenth century and others in the nineteenth century—that the decision to commit a crime is a choice amenable to the same rational calculation that attends all other choices (Becker 1968). So, a rationally self-interested criminal compares the expected costs and benefits of illegal activity and commits the crime if the expected benefit of doing so exceeds the expected cost, and refrains if the reverse is the case.

If decision makers decide whether to commit crime on this basis, then there is a clear implication for the goals of the criminal justice system. Society can deter crime by raising the criminal's expected cost of crime, by lowering the expected benefit of crime, or by some combination of those two policies.

The literature on this explanation of the decision to commit a crime is very large. It has now been a long enough period since Becker's original article that the heated contention that the hypothesis originally occasioned has given way to acceptance (often grudging). I am not asserting (and do not believe) that most students of crime subscribe to the Becker account in the sense that they believe that potential criminals reason in the manner that the theory suggests. Rather, I suspect that most scholars today subscribe to this implication of the hypothesis—that potential criminals are rational enough to be deterrable in many, if not most, circumstances.

There is still vigorous scholarly controversy about the extent to which deterrence works and the extent to which criminal justice system variables explain variations in crime rates.[11] Nonetheless, most scholars—and certainly all those familiar with and active in law and economics—accept the deterrence hypothesis. In fairness, I should say again that acceptance of this hypothesis is not the same thing as accepting the contention that all potential criminals are making decisions in the manner suggested by rational choice theory. Nonetheless, it seems to me that to subscribe to the deterrence hypothesis implies a subscription to some form—perhaps weak, perhaps strong—of rational behavior on the part of potential criminals.

BEHAVIORAL LAW AND ECONOMICS

Over the course of the last twenty years or so, a remarkable literature has appeared that demonstrates, among other things, that several crucial predictions of the rational choice theory are not borne out by experimental studies of human behavior.

In this section I shall first review the general findings of the behavioral literature. Then I shall turn to particular behavioral findings so as to illustrate how those particular findings might affect the three examples of rational choice law and economics surveyed in the previous section.[12]

Behavioralism Generally

Since the elaboration of rational choice theory in the 1950s and 1960s, there has been controversy about the descriptive accuracy of that theory. In a famous early articulation, Professor Milton Friedman contended that the worth of the theory arose from its predictive success, not from its descriptive fit (Friedman 1953). There were some powerful criticisms made of that point, but so long as the thrust of empirical studies was to support the predictions of rational choice theory, there was little incentive to debate the rational choice foundations of modern microeconomic theory.

Cognitive and social psychology, fields that themselves had a scholarly revival in the 1970s and 1980s, took up the challenge of examining the extent to which behavior mirrored the assumptions of rational choice theory. When, in the 1970s, 1980s, and 1990s, an increasing number of empirical results appeared that were not easily explainable using rational choice theory, that brought a new impetus to look at the foundations of rational choice (Kahneman, Slovic, and Tversky 1982) That reexamination continues today, but its promise to reshape microeconomic theory (and users of RCT generally) may be gauged by the fact that the psychologist Daniel Kahneman was one of the winners of the Nobel Prize in economic sciences in 2002, and Matthew Rabin of the Department of Economics at the University of California, Berkeley, won the John Bates Clark Medal in 2001.

The gist of the behavioral literature can be conveyed quickly. RCT holds, as we have seen, that human decision makers are close calculators of the costs and benefits of the options open to them; they do not make mistakes in choosing courses of action or goods and services that might maximize their well-being unless they have been systematically misled. The findings of the behavioral literature are that human beings make *systematic* mistakes in their decision making. These are not randomly distributed mistakes around a relatively constant mean but clear and persistent deviations away from the predictions of RCT. As we shall see, human beings seem to attach far more value to the way things are (to the status quo) than we would have expected to have been the case; they are far more optimistic about themselves, their talents, and their prospects for the future than experience or the facts warrant; they pay close attention to fixed costs, even though RCT says that they do not.

There is, so far, no coherent theory of human decision making that incorporates the well-established deviations from the predictions of RCT from the behavioral literature. Rather, we have a series of findings (Plous 1993). The future will, no doubt, generate that coherent theory.

No scientific community would lightly abandon a foundational assumption unless there was compelling evidence to do so (Kuhn 1996). And although there were anomalies in behavior that rational choice theory had difficulty explaining, there was no such compelling evidence. Moreover, rational choice theory can typically provide an explanation even of those anomalies.[13] As a result of all of these factors, rational choice theory retained its hold on the economics profession. And, as we have seen, rational choice theory, when applied to legal decision makers, proved to be remarkably fruitful.

Behavioral Considerations and the Coase Theorem

Above I outlined the connection between RCT and property law. Recall that the Coase theorem hypothesizes that when transaction costs are zero or very low, parties will bargain so that legal entitlements end up in the hands of those who value them the most. Put somewhat differently but equivalently, when transaction costs are zero, an efficient allocation of resources, including legal entitlements, will obtain, regardless of the initial assignment of those entitlements.

This Coasean view of the virtues of bargaining when transaction costs are low has been subjected to much empirical testing and generally found to be supported by that testing (Hoffman and Spitzer 1986). However, a recent behavioral finding has called the implications of the Coase theorem into question. That finding holds that people appear to place very different valuations on items depending on whether they have an entitlement to them or must acquire them. Specifically, it appears to be the case that people generally place a higher valuation on things, including entitlements, that they possess than they place on those same things if they do not have them (Korobkin 1998).

This difference is frequently referred to as the "bid-ask" spread, the "status quo bias," the "endowment effect," or the difference between the "willingness-to-pay price" and the "willingness-to-accept price." An example might be the following: if I have a particular model of laptop, I would not give it up for anything less than $2,000, but before I had the laptop I would not have paid more than $1,000 to acquire it.

One might say that if the difference I just hypothesized exists, it is easily explained: we tend to undervalue things about which we do not have personal experience; alternatively, we learn a great deal about our true valuation of some things through our experience with them. A laptop is a perfect example of the value of experience in teaching us our true valuation. My willingness to pay $1,000 to acquire a laptop when I do not have one makes sense in view of the fact that I have never had the experience of using a laptop. Once having had the experience, however, we shouldn't be surprised when I then say that I wouldn't accept less than $2,000 to give up the thing that I have now experienced.[14]

This makes perfect sense when there is something to be learned from actually possessing something. But the experiments that established the status quo bias or the bid-ask spread were done not with what might be called "experience goods" but with coffee mugs, candy bars, pens, and pencils. That is, people seem to attach a much higher value to *anything* that they possess than they would attach to that same thing if they did not possess it. Even though this spread was initially found for the sort of trivial goods mentioned above, it also appears to attach to legal entitlements.

The two-to-one spread that I have hypothesized as the difference between the willingness-to-pay price to acquire something and the willingness-to-accept price to sell something is not just for expositional simplicity. In fact, that is roughly the ratio that the behavioral experimenters have found to prevail. Generally speaking, the status quo bias leads people to place a valuation figure on something that they possess that is twice the valuation that they assign when they do not have that thing.

Assuming that there is a status quo bias and that it attaches to legal entitlements as well as to candy bars, what implications does this have for law and economics? One important implication is that legal entitlements may not change hands as easily as we might have thought to be the case. Legal entitlements may remain where they are assigned. That is, it may be more difficult to induce parties to exchange entitlements than one might have predicted.

Let us consider an example. Suppose that we imagine two people, A and B, either of whom might initially be assigned a particular legal entitlement. Let us assume that we know each party's willingness-to-pay price to acquire the entitlement and his or her willingness-to-accept price to sell the entitlement to someone else. We might summarize what we know in the following table:

	Willingness-to-pay price	Willingness-to-accept price
A	$500	$800
B	$400	$1,000

The table captures the gist of the status quo bias in that each person has a higher willingness-to-accept price than the willingness-to-pay price and the difference is roughly on the order of two to one.

The table further illustrates two ambiguities that this behavioral regularity creates for the law and economics of property. First, there is the ambiguity about what it means to "value something higher" than others do. (Remember that one goal of property law is to move resources into the hands of those who value those resources the most.) In maximizing value, should we strive to maximize willingness-to-pay price or willingness-to-accept price? The answer to that question is not obvious. Note that how we answer that question will determine whether we initially assign this legal entitlement to A or B. If we opt for maximizing willingness-to-pay, then we should assign the entitlement to A. If, however, we opt for maximizing willingness-to-accept, we should assign the entitlement to B. It is not at all clear to me which of these courses of action is the better one.

There is a second problem that the table illustrates. Regardless of how we initially assign the entitlement, that is where it is going to remain. There will be no exchange. Suppose that we initially assign the entitlement to A. We know from the table that the minimum price for which he would be willingness to give up the entitlement is $800. But the maximum price that B would be willing to pay to acquire the entitlement is $400. As a result, there is no cooperative surplus, no scope for a bargain. So the entitlement will remain with A.

But suppose that we were to choose to maximize willingness-to-accept price and on that ground we initially assigned the entitlement to B. From the table we know that the minimum price for which B would be willing to sell the entitlement is $1,000 but that the maximum price that A would be willing to pay to acquire the entitlement is $500. Again there is no scope for a bargain. So, the entitlement will remain with B.

The implication of this exercise is that the status quo bias causes us to be skeptical about the Coase theorem and its implications that bargaining will occur when transaction costs are zero or low. Because it appears that people systematically value something they possess more highly than that same thing when they do not possess it and that that fact may cause entitlements to remain where we initially assign them, we may want to be very careful how we assign legal entitlements. The possibility that bargaining would move an entitlement (or any other valuable resource) to its highest use leads to the implication that we did not need to scruple overly about initial assignments.

Let me draw one further implication. The second most commonly cited article in the law and economics literature is the famous article on remedies by Guido Calabresi and A. Douglas Melamed (1972). To make a very deep article and extensive literature simple, that article holds that the law should protect an entitlement by means of a property rule (that is, a rule that forbids interference with the legal entitlement unless there is explicit permission from the entitlement holder) when the transaction costs between the infringer and entitlement holder are low, and by means of a liability rule (that is, interference with the entitlement is allowed only at a price—called "compensatory money damages"—determined by the court in a "hypothetical bargain") when the transaction costs between the parties are high.[15]

If that suggestion is taken to heart, then when courts protect an entitlement by means of a property rule, which they do, we should find evidence of bargaining existing between some entitlement holders and infringers after the issuance of an injunction. But in a careful examination

of a number of cases in which courts issued injunctions, Ward Farnsworth (1999) found no instances of postinjunction bargaining. One possible explanation for this finding is that status quo
bias leads to the willingness-to-accept price of an entitlement holder always being higher than the
willingness-to-pay price of infringers.

Behavioral Considerations and Tort Law

Above I explained that law and economics perceives exposure to tort liability in terms of its
ability to induce efficient precaution—that is, precaution that minimizes the social costs of accidents. The RCT-based account that I gave of the thinking of potential injurers and victims may
have struck readers as far-fetched. While each of us reading this essay may recognize ourselves as
the close reasoner of the economic model, it is difficult to imagine that the model is an accurate
description of how most people reason about their tort responsibilities. How might we alter the
analysis of tort liability in light of some of the findings of the behavioral literature? For the
purposes of this essay let us focus on just one well-established bias in judgment, the overoptimism bias.

There is ample evidence that individuals are overoptimistic when it comes to assessing their
own abilities, their prospects, or other matters associated with themselves (Weinstein 1980; Plous
1993). For instance, researchers have asked those getting a marriage license to estimate the likelihood that their marriage will end in divorce, given that 50 percent of all U.S. marriages end in
divorce. Not surprisingly, the mean estimate is zero (Baker and Emery 1993).

Consider what this might mean for tort liability's ability to induce safe driving and thereby to
minimize the social costs of automobile accidents. Drivers—all drivers—are likely to be overoptimistic about their abilities to avoid an accident, to believe themselves to be above average in
their ability to drive safely, to drive defensively, and to obey all the relevant rules of the road. As
a result, they may not take actions, such as wearing a seat belt or repairing a burned-out turn
signal bulb, that would reduce the probability or severity of an accident. Or on a long trip they
may drive for a longer period than they ought in the belief that they are extremely skillful drivers.
In the limit they may not purchase enough first- or third-party insurance because they are so
confident in their driving abilities that they do not think it likely that they will ever injure or be
injured in an accident.

There is no obvious means of debiasing (as the phrase has it) drivers to give them a more
realistic view of their abilities.[16] For example, neither instituting a seat belt defense, under which
the victim is entitled to receive compensation from the injurer only for those injuries that he
would have suffered had he been wearing a seat belt, nor making not wearing a seat belt punish-
able by a fine is likely to have much effect on precautionary behavior.

If overconfidence is so pervasive that it makes most drivers impervious to the signals of the
tort liability system, what is to be done? One possible corrective is to substitute safety regulation
for exposure to tort liability. For instance, federal regulation might require all automobiles sold in
the United States to have certain safety features that some if not most drivers would not otherwise
purchase, such as collapsible steering wheels, shatterproof glass, and front and side airbags. In
addition, public officials might undertake to design roads differently, to pursue technological
means of making accidents less likely or less severe, or to increase their enforcement of the rules
of the road as a means of substituting for driver precaution.

One can imagine other cognitive biases (such as our inability to make probabilistic calculations well, unless closely trained) that affect potential injurers and victims and deflect them from
the precautionary behavior that tort liability seeks to encourage. My point here is to suggest that

real human beings have shared shortcomings that directly affect their ability to take the precautionary actions that RCT imagines all people take. I do not think that these cognitive biases and judgmental errors mean that tort liability is completely ineffectual. I believe, rather, that the law can make adjustments in its policies to take due account of these biases and errors. Let me go further and say that I do not think that those who study the law would have been able to make these knowing adjustments in legal doctrine and policy if law and economics, by assuming that RCT was the appropriate theory of human decision making, had not focused its attention on what the law might realistically achieve.

Behavioral Considerations and Criminal Law

The Beckerian theory of the decision to commit a crime imagines that rationally self-interested criminals commit a crime if the expected benefit of the crime exceeds the expected cost. The policy implications of this theory are that we can deter crime and thereby minimize the social costs of crime by increasing the expected cost of crime or lowering its expected benefit. Recognize that the expected cost of crime consists of the product of the probabilities of detection, arrest, and conviction and the sanction imposed upon conviction. So we could increase the expected cost of crime by taking steps to raise any or all of the probabilities involved, by raising the sanction, or by a combination of those steps. Because we are assuming that potential criminals are rationally self-interested, it does not matter how we go about increasing this expected cost: criminals will accurately compute the expected value whether we increase the probabilities or the sanction or both. That belief has another important implication: society can achieve any given level of deterrence by choosing whatever policy or policies lead to the appropriate level of expected cost. Thus, they can expend real resources in increasing the probabilities or seek to achieve the same result by simply increasing the sanction for guilt.

This RCT-based model of the decision to commit a crime has had a profound effect on criminal justice system scholarship and policy over the past thirty years. For example, during the 1980s and 1990s we adjusted criminal justice system policy to make sanctions more clear and certain than they had been. We increased the likelihood that, if convicted, a criminal would go to prison, with the result that the U.S. prison population increased fourfold, from less than 500,000 in the early 1980s to over 2 million in the early twenty-first century. And, arguably, this worked. Both nonviolent and violent crime rates have declined significantly since the early 1990s. (See Levitt 2004.)

Nonetheless, the Beckerian theory draws a picture of potential criminals that strikes many as being far removed from reality. True, high expected costs of crime may deter many potential criminals, but there are other factors, such as alcohol and drug abuse and dire economic prospects, that may impel crime but may not be so easily affected by criminal justice system policies. One might believe that potential criminals suffer from the same cognitive errors and judgmental shortcomings that we have already identified as being important in explaining other aspects of behavior that law seeks to affect. There is some evidence that they do (Wilson and Abrahamse 1992). And, as the recent scandals on wrongful convictions in Illinois show, there is some evidence that police and prosecutors also suffer from serious cognitive biases and judgmental errors (Turow 2003).

We can try to get a bearing on the relative worth of RCT-based and behavioral explanations by looking at some explanations for the remarkable decline in crime in the United States over the past ten years. Between 1991 and 2000 property crimes fell by 30 percent, and during the same period violent crimes fell by 40 percent. Homicide rates in the United States are at their lowest levels since the 1930s.

What explains these facts? I have already mentioned one possibility, so let me include it as the first entry in a list of possible explanations:

1. State and federal criminal sentencing grew more certain and severe during the 1980s and 1990s (and thereby deterred crime) by sentencing convicted criminals to longer prison terms and in larger and larger numbers.
2. Improvements in police practices, such as community policing and sprucing up public spaces through application of the "broken windows" policy (Wilson and Kelling 1982), have greatly curtailed the free rein that criminals had over certain neighborhoods in urban areas.[17]
3. The robust economic growth of the 1983–2001 period greatly increased the attraction of legitimate employment and raised the opportunity cost of criminal activity.
4. The waning of the crack cocaine trade in the early 1990s greatly reduced the violence that came from competition among illegal organizations for the lucrative crack cocaine trade.

These (and, as we shall see, other) explanations all sound plausible. More importantly for our purposes, each of them is consistent with an RCT-based theory of criminal behavior. But none of these theories seems to be as interesting or as powerful as an alternative theory that recently appeared.

In 1998 John Donohue, then at Stanford and now at Yale Law School, and Steve Levitt, of the Department of Economics of the University of Chicago, published a startling alternative explanation for the decline in crime—the legalization of abortion in the 1970s. Their article began from the observation that there just might be a causal connection between the U.S. Supreme Court decision *Roe v. Wade,* handed down in January 1973, that legalized abortion and the decline in violent crime that began exactly eighteen years later. In every society in the world about 50 percent of the crime is committed by eighteen-to-twenty-four-year-old males (Donohue and Levitt 2001). Could it possibly be the case that the legalization of abortion in 1973 led to a significantly smaller cohort of eighteen-year-old males in 1991? And if so, could this decline in the number of eighteen-year-old males in 1991 help to explain the decline in violent crime?

Donohue and Levitt are two of the most careful empirical scholars in the legal academy today, so their findings must be taken very, very seriously. Their exceptionally thorough study suggested that legalized abortion accounted for 50 percent of the decline in crime after 1991. Their study is largely sophisticated econometrics, but let me give you the flavor of this marvelous scholarship by citing six reasons for supporting their hypothesis:

1. The number of abortions rose dramatically throughout the 1970s, so by 1980 there were 1.6 million abortions per year—that is, one abortion per two live births. The effect was a significantly smaller population of eighteen-year-olds in the United States in the early 1990s as a percentage of the total population.
2. Five states legalized abortion in 1970 (three years before *Roe v. Wade*), and those states experienced a decline in crime before the rest of the country did.
3. "Higher rates of abortion in a state in the late 1970s and early 1980s are strongly linked to lower crime in that state for the period 1985 to 1997" (p. 382).
4. "There is no relationship between abortion rates in the mid-1970s and crime changes between 1972 and 1985" (p. 382).

5. Almost all the crime in the 1990s can be "attributed to reduction in crime among the cohorts born after abortion legalization; there is little change in crime among older cohorts over the last 30 years" (p. 382).
6. And finally, the decline in crime in the 1990s was nationwide, occurring in cities that had never had a crack cocaine epidemic nor had a reform of their policing practices and in rural areas where urban problems were unknown.

As if that were not startling enough, Donohue and Levitt went further. They identified two components of the effect of abortion on crime—the "cohort size" effect and the "cohort quality" effect. The cohort size effect arises from the fact that there were relatively fewer eighteen-to-twenty-four-year-old males in the U.S. population in the 1990s. But the cohort quality effect suggests that the cohort of young men who were born after the legalization of abortion in 1973 were less likely to commit crime than would a similar cohort that would have been born without abortion. The reason is that "women who have abortions are those most at risk to give birth to children who will engage in criminal activity—teenagers, unmarried women, and the economically disadvantaged" (p. 381).

Donohue and Levitt suggest that of the 50 percent of the decline in crime that legalized abortion can explain, half is attributable to the cohort size effect and half to the cohort quality effect.

These findings have not been effectively challenged yet, although they may be. They strongly suggest that the factors to which we confidently pointed in trying to explain the large declines in crime of the 1990s were slightly off the mark.[18]

Where does this survey leave us in explaining patterns of crime? My impression is that the RCT-based explanation of crime survives a confrontation with behavioral findings and is more robust than I would have predicted to be the case. There are, as the abortion literature suggests, some hidden currents in our society that are causing changes that we attribute to more easily observed currents. Nonetheless, deterrence theories of crime and the policies that they suggest are, by and large, surprisingly strong.

A CAUTIONARY NOTE

The previous section argued that behavioral law and economics has great promise for bringing law and economics closer to being an even more powerful tool for analyzing legal decision making. Here I want to sound a brief cautionary note on the use of the behavioral literature.

I suggested at the outset that law and economics has become the default method of doing legal scholarship in North America. I should also note that this success has excited much opposition and concern among those in the legal academy. There are multiple grounds for this opposition and concern, some of them to be taken seriously, some not. One of the concerns, more frequently whispered than given full voice, is that law and economics smuggles into legal analysis a conservative political ideology. Insofar as there is a nugget of truth to this criticism, it might be put this way: the economic analysis of law takes as its normative premise that law should further efficiency, while the traditional normative concern of law has always been justice or fairness. That is, law and economics is fundamentally at odds with the entire thrust of decades, if not centuries, of legal concerns.

This concern is one that is not so wide of the mark that we can dismiss it out of hand. I will not, however, elaborate on this point here—not because I think that it is an unimportant point, but because it is not closely enough related to the points that I want to stress about behavioral law and economics.

A closely related concern about the rise of law and economics in the legal academy is that it accelerates a trend that pushes legal education further away from its concern with professional education and its relationship with practitioners and closer to the socially isolated concerns of the academy. There is, too, some justice in this concern.

Now, having pointed out these two concerns with law and economics, I want to make the cautionary note that those who hold to these (and other) concerns about law and economics should not expect a great deal of comfort from the rise of behavioral law and economics. But let me begin at the beginning. Those who are skeptical of law and economics are likely to find behavioral law and economics attractive because it seems to undercut RCT and, in doing so, to undermine all of law and economics (most particularly the part that they believe to be wedded to a conservative political ideology). That view is, I believe, mistaken, and to hold to it is to miss a significant and fundamental point about law and economics and about behavioral law and economics. The central fallacy in this view is to believe that law and economics and RCT are inextricably entwined, so anything that undoes the latter must, as a logical necessity, undo the former. Law and economics is not a field of inquiry that exists to further RCT. Rather, its central focus is the effect of legal rules and institutions on real people and real problems. The main premise of the field is that law is a powerful method of organizing society to achieve collective aims and of encouraging individuals and organizations to align their desires with social desires. To that end law and economics is looking for any systematic analysis that can help us better understand how individuals and organizations respond to the directives contained in law.

The role of RCT in this analysis is that it is a comprehensive and well-articulated theory of decision making and, therefore, a plausible point from which to begin an analysis of how individuals and organizations respond to law. But because the ultimate goal is to find more effectual law and a better account of human decision making with respect to law, RCT will be helpful only to the extent that it is an accurate description of how people make legal decisions. As we have seen, there is now some compelling evidence that RCT is an imperfect guide to descriptions and predictions about these matters.

The fundamental point to be made here is that the scholarly investigation of legal issues is a dynamic and organic enterprise. It is not a settled body of learning that, like a completed edifice built on shaky foundations, will collapse when a few bricks in the lower stories are shown to be frangible. Rather, it is an edifice that is in the process of being built—we don't entirely know what it will look like; we are building up the body of learning slowly; and if there are adjustments that need to be made to improve the soundness of the enterprise, they will be made.

The findings from the behavioral literature are important adjustments in the scholarly construction of the law and economics edifice. But they are not the end of the adjustments. Those whose principal reason for taking an interest in the behavioral literature is to have a stout stick with which to beat RCT so as to bring down law and economics are bound to be disappointed. Behavioral law and economics represents an adjustment, not a tearing down of the entire body of learning. Think for a moment of the many things that we do not yet know about human behavior. To take but a few of those questions, consider how little we know about which cognitive biases are hardwired and, therefore, difficult to change and which are softwired and, therefore, capable of relatively easy debiasing (Jones 2001). Nor do we know how an individual's biases alter, if at all, over time or with circumstance; we assume that all individuals are subject to all biases all the time, but there may be variations by time of year, time of life, or by other identifiable context. And most importantly, I think that we need to be careful not to abandon RCT entirely. My strong suspicion is that further thinking and further empirical work will suggest that there is a strong place for RCT in our accounts of some human decision making. After all, RCT works tolerably well in explaining and describing much explicitly economic decision making. It breaks down as an explanation and predictor in some economic circumstances and has even greater difficulty in explaining choices outside of the economic sphere (Thaler 2001; Camerer et al., 2003).

There are numerous reasons why it should be the case that noneconomic choices, such as those about love, our work, whom to call a friend, and the like, should be more difficult than economic choices. One reason is that there is no clear metric for making noneconomic decisions and that, for better or worse, there is a monetary metric at work in the vast majority of economic decisions.[19] What this seems to signify for the future is that RCT will be useful in a more comprehensive account of human decision making when there are decisions involving mixed economic and noneconomic issues, such as a decision to accept a more lucrative and prestigious job but at a far remove from those one loves.

My point, again, is that we are not at the end of law and economics history, where it might be the case that we have a complete account of human decision making, either a theory *tout court* or one that serves well for legal decisions. Quite to the contrary, we are at an early stage of formal theorizing about the law generally (law and economics, the leader in that field of formalizing legal study, is only twenty-five years or so old), and behavioral insights are not yet widespread within economics.[20] Among many other changes that must occur is that those of us interested in behavioral theories must do a better job of learning psychology (Kahneman 2003). There is much work to be done, and I have no doubt at all that the many very bright people thinking and writing about these topics will produce insights of great significance in the coming decades. We know what great strides have been made in law and economics over the past twenty-five years, and I see no reason not to be optimistic that the next twenty-five years will bring equally astonishing insights.

CONCLUSION

Law and economics has become the default means for scholars in North America to investigate legal issues. That legal innovation began by importing the conventional theory of microeconomic decision making, rational choice theory, into the law and showing how the law might guide rational decision makers to make decisions that maximized both private and social well-being.

I have tried to demonstrate that bringing the insights of the behavioral economics literature to bear on the study of law has enriched the findings of the earlier law and economics literature that was based on rational choice theory. Although behavioral scientists have not yet provided a complete theory of human decision making to supplant rational choice theory, they have showed us that there are significant and systematic deviations from the descriptions and predictions of rational choice theory. Over the next several decades the theory of decision making and judgment will take on new dimensions and will become more complete and complex than it currently is. I take great heart from the fact that law and economics in its rational choice form spurred this marvelously interesting and rich inquiry into the effectiveness of the law. We should all look forward to the next steps in this ongoing scholarship.

NOTES

I am extremely grateful to Svet Minkov, Ted Ulen, and Ariel Yehezkel for their fine research assistance.

1. Some go further and suggest that the impact of law and economics on legal scholarship is likely to be much greater in the future than it has been so far. Among others I have made that claim (Ulen 2003, 2004).

2. There are additional characteristics that a successful scientific theory must have. For example, in his marvelous study of the process by which the Copernican conception of the universe supplanted the Ptolemaic conception, Thomas Kuhn stresses the elegance and economy with which a theory explains the same phenomena as an alternative theory (Kuhn 1990).

3. I do not mean this statement to apply to any field other than the social and behavioral sciences. No one, I suspect, would contend that string theory or quantum theory should or does correspond with our

"real" views of the universe or subatomic realms. The English astronomer Sir Arthur Eddington memorably said, "Not only is the universe stranger than we imagine; it is stranger than we can imagine."

4. In his famous article "Rational Fools" (1977), Amartya Sen criticizes RCT's paying no attention to the coherence of preferences by suggesting that an economist who comes upon a man sawing at the base of his toes with a dull knife would be led to give the man a sharp knife so as to assist him to achieve his ends more efficiently.

5. The theory would be that in the absence of a clear ownership claim the resource would be underutilized.

6. I could pile on some additional assumptions, such as that there is no first-party or liability insurance and that there is no regulatory policy other than or in addition to tort liability for minimizing the social costs of accidents. But let us leave those additional assumptions to one side and focus on how rational injurers and victims might behave when faced with exposure to tort liability. I shall relax these assumptions below.

7. For the sake of further simplicity, one could also say that what the court will do in determining liability is so clear that neither party will need to incur the costs of litigation.

8. In order to make the exposition straightforward, I assume that before an accident occurs, parties know whether they will be a victim or an injurer. It should be clear that if the parties were not certain whether in their next accident they were to be a victim or an injurer, the same analysis would hold.

9. The social costs of accidents are the sum of both parties' precaution costs and accident losses and the administrative costs of determining whom should bear the accident losses. I have given a rational choice analysis of negligence but could have given a very similar one for behavior under strict liability.

10. Consider, for instance, that there are circumstances when strict liability with contributory negligence (defined as the failure of the victim to take cost-justified precaution) is the most efficient standard.

11. For instance, the original literature finding a strong deterrent effect of the death penalty has given way to a widespread scholarly skepticism about our ability to ever demonstrate that deterrent effect conclusively. And there is controversy about whether the widespread availability of handguns increases or decreases crime. For a summary article on matters about which there is widespread scholarly agreement, see Levitt 2004.

12. Some of the material in this section draws on Korobkin and Ulen 2000.

13. Let me consider a brief example. Microeconomics teaches that rational decision makers do not let fixed costs influence their current actions, on the ground that "bygones are bygones." So, for example, someone who purchases a long-term health club membership and then feels compelled to go to the club from time to time on the ground that if he did not, the expenditure would have been wasteful, is violating the microeconomic teaching. But taking this reasoning one step further, one could argue that the person who reasons this way about his own proclivities *not* to work out at the health club unless he felt guilty about having made a wasteful expenditure is very cleverly using a rational technique to combat his own laziness.

14. Of course, there are other possibilities. Experience might teach that their prior valuation was too high or just right (not always, as I have seemed to apply, too low).

15. The gist of the argument is that when transaction costs are low, bargaining between the parties, which will be encouraged by a property rule, is the better means of determining whether the entitlement holder or the infringer values the entitlement more. When transaction costs are high, however, bargaining cannot answer that question of relative valuation. So the court must step in and perform a hypothetical market transaction by determining the minimum price for which the entitlement holder would have been willing to sell the infringer the right to interfere. For a more modern view of the issue see Kaplow and Shavell 1996.

16. To be more precise, there is no obvious way that the *law* can accomplish this debiasing. It is well known that people will receive a jolt to their overconfidence if someone they know has a serious automobile accident, on the theory that "if it could happen to her, it could happen to any of us."

17. The gist of the hypothesis is that unkempt public places are a signal to potential criminals that neither the police nor private individuals are much concerned with what goes on in the area, and so the area is a relatively safe neighborhood for criminals to victimize. It was said, for example, that the graffiti on New York's subway cars were a species of "broken windows" that invited potential wrongdoers to victimize people on the subway. So cleaning up the subway cars was a method of signaling that the police and others cared about the area and were on the lookout for criminal behavior.

18. But only slightly off the mark. For a full explanation of ten alternative factors, see Levitt 2004.

19. See Ulen 1998 for some additional factors that make non-economic decisions difficult.

20. I mentioned above in note 2 that only one microeconomic theory text, that of Robert H. Frank (2003), contains extensive material from the behavioral literature. See also Camerer 2003.

REFERENCES

Baker, Lynn A., and Robert E. Emery. 1993. "When Every Relationship Is Above Average: Perceptions and Expectations of Divorce at the Time of Marriage." *Law and Human Behavior* 17: 439.

Becker, Gary. 1968. "Crime and Punishment: An Economic Approach." *Journal of Political Economy* 76: 169.

Brown, John Prather. 1974. "Toward an Economic Theory of Liability." *Journal of Legal Studies* 2: 341.

Calabresi, Guido. 1970. *The Costs of Accidents: A Legal and Economic Analysis*. New Haven, CT: Yale University Press.

Calabresi, Guido, and A. Douglas Melamed. 1972. "Property Rules, Liability Rules, and Inalienability: One View of the Cathedral." *Harvard Law Review* 85: 1089.

Camerer, Colin. 2003. *Behavioral Game Theory*. New York: Russell Sage.

Camerer, Colin, Samuel Issacharoff, George Loewenstein, Ted O'Donoghue, and Matthew Rabin. 2003. "Regulation for Conservatives: Behavioral Economics and 'Asymmetric Paternalism.'" *University of Pennsylvania Law Review* 151: 1211.

Coase, Ronald A. 1960. "The Problem of Social Cost." *Journal of Law and Economics* 3: 1.

Cooter, Robert D., and Thomas S. Ulen. 2004. *Law and Economics*. 4th ed. Boston: Pearson Addison Wesley.

Dewees, Donald N., David Duff, and Michael Trebilcock. 1995. *Exploring the Domain of Accident Law: Taking the Facts Seriously*. New York: Oxford University Press.

Donohue, John J. III, and Steven D. Levitt. 2001. "The Impact of Legalized Abortion on Crime." *Quarterly Journal of Economics* 116: 379.

Farnsworth, Ward. 1999. "Do Parties to Nuisance Cases Bargain After Judgment? A Glimpse Inside the Cathedral." *University of Chicago Law Review* 66: 373.

Frank, Robert H. 2003. *Microeconomics and Behavior*. 5th ed. Boston: McGraw-Hill/Irwin.

Friedman, Milton. 1953. "The Methodology of Positive Economics." In *Essays in Positive Economics*. Chicago: University of Chicago Press.

Green, Donald, and Ian Shapiro. 1994. *Pathologies of Rational Choice Theory: A Critique of Applications in Political Science*. New Haven, CT: Yale University Press.

Hoffman, Elizabeth, and Matthew Spitzer. 1986. "Experimental Tests of the Coase Theorem with Large Bargaining Groups." *Journal of Legal Studies* 15: 149.

Jones, Owen D. 2001. "Time-Shifted Rationality and the Law of Law's Leverage: Behavioral Economics Meets Behavioral Biology." *Northwestern University Law Review* 95: 1114.

Kahneman, Daniel. 2003. "Maps of Bounded Rationality: Psychology for Behavioral Economics." *American Economics Review* 93: 1449.

Kahneman, Daniel, Paul Slovic, and Amos Tversky, eds. 1982. *Judgment Under Uncertainty: Heuristics and Biases*. Cambridge: Cambridge University Press.

Kaplow, Louis, and Steven Shavell. 1996. "Property Rules Versus Liability Rules: An Economic Analysis." *Harvard Law Review* 109: 715.

Kitcher, Philip. 1993. *The Advancement of Science: Science Without Legend, Objectivity Without Illusion*. New York: Oxford University Press.

Kolstad, Charles, Thomas S. Ulen, and Gary V. Johnson. 1990. "Ex Post Liability for Harm Versus Ex Ante Safety Regulation: Substitutes or Complements?" *American Economics Review* 80: 888.

Korobkin, Russell B. 1998. "The Status Quo Bias and Contract Default Rules." *Cornell Law Review* 83: 608.

Korobkin, Russell B., and Thomas S. Ulen. 2000. "Law and Behavioral Science: Removing the Rationality Assumption from Law and Economics." *California Law Review* 82: 1051.

Kuhn, Thomas S. 1990. *The Copernican Revolution: Planetary Astronomy in the Development of Western Thought*. Cambridge, MA: Harvard University Press.

———. 1996. *The Structure of Scientific Revolutions*. 3rd ed. Chicago: University of Chicago Press.

Landsburg, Stephen E. 1993. *The Armchair Economist: Economics and Everyday Life*. New York: Free Press.

———. 2005. *Price Theory and Applications*. 6th ed. Mason, OH: South-Western.

Levitt, Steven D. 2004. "Understanding Why Crime Fell in the 1990s: Four Factors That Explain the Decline and Six That Do Not." *Journal of Economic Perspectives* 18: 163.

Mullainathan, Sendil, and Richard J. Thaler. 2001. "Behavioral Economics." In *International Encyclopedia of the Social and Behavioral Sciences*. Amsterdam: Elsevier.

Plous, Scott. 1993. *The Psychology of Judgment and Decision-making*. New York: McGraw-Hill.

Posner, Richard A. 1972. "A Theory of Negligence." *Journal of Legal Studies* 1: 29.

Schwartz, Gary. 1994. "Reality in the Economic Analysis of Tort Law: Does Tort Law Really Deter?" *UCLA Law Review* 42: 377.

Sen, Amartya. 1977. "Rational Fools: A Critique of the Behavioral Foundations of Economic Theory," *Philosophy and Public Affairs* 6: 317.

Shavell, Steven. 2004. *Foundations of Economic Analysis of Law*. Cambridge, MA: Belknap.

Thaler, Richard. 2001. "Anomalies: Risk Aversion." *Journal of Economic Perspectives* 15: 219.

Turow, Scott. 2003. *Ultimate Punishment: A Lawyer's Reflections on Dealing with the Death Penalty*. New York: Farrar, Straus, and Giroux.

Ulen, Thomas S. 1998. "The Growing Pains of Behavioral Law and Economics" *Vanderbilt Law Review* 51: 1741.

———. 2003. "A Nobel Prize in Legal Science: Theory, Empirical Work, and the Scientific Method in Legal Scholarship." *University of Illinois Law Review,* 1037.

———. 2004. "The Unexpected Guest: Law and Economics, Law and Other Cognate Disciplines, and the Future of Legal Scholarship." *Chicago-Kent Law Review* 79: 403.

Weinstein, Neil. 1980. "Unrealistic Optimism About Future Life Events." *Journal of Personality and Social Psychology* 39: 806.

Wilson, James Q., and Alan Abrahamse. 1992. "Does Crime Pay?" *Justice Quarterly* 9: 359.

Wilson, James Q., and George Kelling. 1982. "Broken Windows: The Police and Neighborhood Safety." *The Atlantic,* March.

CHAPTER 35

ELEMENTS OF BEHAVIORAL
MONETARY ECONOMICS

TOBIAS F. RÖTHELI

Many surveys on behavioral economics start with a reference to Herbert Simon. Certainly Simon has been the single most important innovator in the field of behavioral economics, the approach to economics that takes into account the cognitive limitations (i.e., the bounded rationality) of human decision makers. However, monetary economics has obviously not been one of Simon's priorities.[1] This has very likely to do with the fact that monetary economics has always been a rather pragmatic mixture of deductive theorizing, on one hand, and rationalizations of empirical regularities (such as the relation between money growth and inflation), on the other (see Friedman and Hahn 1990). Although rarely explicitly tied to bounds of rationality, economic science traditionally links the raison d'être of money and the effects of money to various frictions in economic life, such as uncertainty and transaction costs. As a theorist who gave economic agents' judgment errors an important role in his analysis of monetary issues, Irving Fisher must be seen as one of the first behavioral monetary economists (see Fisher 1928; Thaler 1997).

The approach pursued in this essay is to describe elements of behavioral economics within monetary economics. Hence, the essay looks for insights concerning the functioning of monetary economies that have been gained by exploring the notion of less than perfect decision making. This does not mean that results based on the assumption of unbounded rationality will be excluded from the discussion. On the contrary, studies based on unbounded rationality have often preceded behavioral analyses and have thereby set a standard that proves to be useful as a benchmark. Thus, this text attempts an evaluation and an integration of contributions that start from different assumptions rather than a description of a new type (or school) of monetary economics. Along the way there will be several opportunities to point out open questions and possible extensions where the behavioral approach could yield further interesting insights into monetary economics.

Monetary economics deals with the medium of transactions of an economy. The field can be characterized by outlining its two major sets of issues. The first set of questions turns around the problem of why monetary exchange comes (or came) to replace barter arrangements and what good (or goods) plays the role of medium of exchange. The second set of issues deals with the effects of money in a monetized economy. Here the attention focuses on the effects variations in the supply of money have on nominal and real variables, the nominal variables being the price level, exchange rates, and the nominal interest rate. Among the real variables are relative prices, employment, the real rate of return, and output. While there are links between the two sets of issues in monetary economics, much theorizing and empirical work are based on the notion that the two sides can be analyzed separately.[2] A survey of studies in the two outlined subfields of monetary economics shows that the field addressing the more fundamental issue relating to reason and forms of monetization of an economy has so far generated fewer contributions that can be labeled "behavioral economics" as compared to the latter field, which deals with the effects of money. Hence, I will start by reviewing this more fundamental—and, from a behavioral viewpoint, less developed—field. Next I ask why and how money affects the economy. After that comes an analysis of the control of the money supply and monetary policy, followed by the conclusion.

WHY IS THERE MONETARY EXCHANGE AND WHAT FUNCTIONS AS MONEY?

The reason for monetary exchange is typically located in the difficulty of barter exchange to solve the problem of double coincidence of wants. This means that for a voluntary exchange of goods to take place, both potential trading partners have to want (i.e., value) the good the other side has to offer. Take the extreme example where goods perish quickly (i.e., where goods have very high storage costs). In this case exchanges would take place only between traders who want to *consume* the good the other part is offering. Under these circumstances the potential for trade would indeed be very limited. Fortunately, reality does not resemble this extreme example.

Commodity Money

In reality some goods both are durable and change hands at low (transaction) costs. Hence, these goods (or a subset of them) come to be accepted as a means of payment and are used not only for direct consumption. These goods are valued and accepted because people can use them in future exchanges to acquire the goods they want for consumption. The emergence and properties of commodity money (or many parallel commodity monies) have been studied and modeled by a succession of theorists such as Wicksell (1934) and Kiyotaki and Wright (1989), to name just a few (see Ostroy and Starr 1990 for a survey). The general insights from these models are that (1) monetary (i.e., indirect) exchange is likely to emerge and replace barter and (2) a change in the supply of commodity money (e.g., gold) affects relative prices in the economy. Hence, with commodity money there is no basis for analytically separating the monetary side of the economy from the real side. For the case of commodity money the classical dichotomy between real and nominal economic variables is thus at best a pragmatic simplification. In experimental studies predictions more specific than the two listed above of modern general equilibrium models of commodity money have fared rather poorly (see Duffy 1998 for a survey). It remains a matter of debate and ongoing research to settle whether these difficulties are due to the rationality assumptions underlying these models.

Comparing the system of barter trade with arrangements using one or several commodities serving as money, an argument based on limited computational power of agents is often made to motivate the step toward a unique exchange medium. Specifically, calculation costs have been referred to as one way to rationalize the transition from barter exchange (where potentially every good is exchanged for every other good) to a system where all exchanges are conducted against a single good, which is accepted as payment. The argument for a single medium of exchange is straightforward. With n goods there are $n(n-1)/2$ prices under a barter regime. Compare this to a monetized economy where only $n-1$ prices (all expressed in money terms) exist. Clearly, an agent attempting to maximize utility has to process a large number of comparisons and trade-offs. With prices of all goods expressed in one common unit, it becomes simpler to assess the optimality of consumption plans, for example, by comparing the marginal utility of one weight unit (or coin) of gold in different uses. This argument, however, is valid only in a world where only transactions in terms of money (i.e., the good serving as generally accepted medium of exchange) are costless. If all barter exchanges could be conducted without transaction costs, one could just as well pick any good (e.g., tomatoes) to economize on agents' computational resources.[3] Hence, the noted cognitive advantage of monetary exchange is the result of monetization rather than a reason for it.

Fiat Money

It is clearly a significant step for an economy to move from commodity money (e.g., gold) to a system with an intrinsically valueless medium of exchange such as paper money. Historically this development has taken time and has seen the government as a central player. In fact, the expression "fiat money" describes a medium of exchange that has no intrinsic value and exists by virtue of the state making it legal tender. Fiat money is related to but is not synonymous with paper money. In Europe banknotes were first issued in 1661 as a product of commercial activity: the Stockholm Bank in Sweden offered pieces of paper indicating the amount of copper deposited with the bank and thus created a light and mobile place holder for metal that was regularly used in transactions (see Weatherford 1997).

As Selgin (1994) and Dowd (2001) point out, fiat money has historically always emerged from convertible currency (or commodity money) and not directly from barter. Two elements have played key roles in the development of the modern paper money system. First, governments highly value the income that the supplier of the medium of exchange can generate (as emperors did controlling the supply of gold coins).[4] Second, the replacement of gold by paper money saves society the opportunity cost of gold, which can be used for nonmonetary purposes. These resource savings would be largest in a society running a system of paper money without it being backed by any gold (or other commodity) reserves at all. However, there is a substantial conflict between governments' need for revenue from money creation and the public's preference for stable money and hence a danger of overissue of money.[5] While modern monies are no longer convertible into gold, central banks still hold substantial amounts of gold reserves. This points toward an issue behavioral economics is only now beginning to address: the psychology of trust in institutions. It is remarkable to see the vague references to psychology by traditional economists when arguing that central banks should continue to hold gold reserves and to note the void of formal analysis by experts in bounded rationality.

WHY AND HOW DOES MONEY AFFECT THE ECONOMY?

It is common to divide the effects of changes in the supply of money into effects on nominal and real variables.[6] Among the nominal variables, the price level (and inflation, its rate of change) features prominently. In the sphere of international money, exchange rates (and their course over time) clearly are of concern. Among real variables, output, unemployment, relative prices, and the real interest rate are central. A set of classical propositions in monetary economics states that when all adjustments have run their course, a change in the supply of money leaves all real variables unchanged, whereas the price level and exchange rates change proportionally to the change in the money supply. These statements are called (1) the long-run neutrality proposition with respect to real variables, (2) the quantity theory of the price level, and (3) the purchasing power parity theory of the exchange rate, respectively.[7] In the short run the well-documented regularity that changes in the supply of money cause changes in real variables is due to the fact that prices and wages are sluggish (or sticky, to use the Keynesian term). The last thirty years have brought significant advances regarding the determinants of this sluggishness.

Dynamics of Wages and Prices

One side of the nominal sluggishness concerns the dynamics of wages. Fischer (1977) and Taylor (1979) presented models in which the type of staggering of wages empirically observed leads to nominal inertia and hence to real effects of monetary policy. From the point of view of behavioral economics it is interesting to note that the adjustment dynamics in these models is seen as depending on a comparison of currently set wages with wages that have been set in the immediate past. This indicates that sluggishness of wages is partially attributed to social comparisons and possibly considerations of fairness. Detailed empirical investigations of the implications of the staggered wage model have demonstrated that the initial model specifications by Fischer and Taylor have to be corrected. Fuhrer and Moore (1995) document that a model with a nominal wage setting where wage comparisons are made in real rather than nominal terms (contrasting with Fischer's and Taylor's assumption and also contrasting with approaches discussed below) significantly outperforms the older formulations in statistical tests. Moreover, Fuhrer and Moore's notion of wage dynamics generates empirically plausible effects of changes in monetary policy.

The other side of nominal sluggishness directly concerns goods' prices.[8] Here the incorporation of imperfect competition has furthered coherent modeling. The starting point of many approaches in this field is the insight that for price-setting firms, a change in their output price has only second-order (i.e., small) effects on profit (see Akerlof and Yellen 1985; Mankiw 1985). In Akerlof and Yellen's model some firms (termed near-rational) do not change their price (and wage), while some fully rational firms do. It turns out that the lack of optimal adjustment is not very costly for the sluggish actors, but output and employment react strongly (and for several periods) to a change in the money supply. In a more recent analysis Akerlof, Dickens, and Perry (2000) extend the near-rational behavior to the side of workers and their influence on wages. At low levels of inflation workers appear to be pressing less intensively for an inflation adjustment of wages. The interplay of rational firms, boundedly rational firms, and workers motivated to work harder by rising wages implies—even in the long run—a trade-off between inflation and employment. The econometric estimates by Akerlof, Dickens, and Perry (2000) seem to support their theoretical prediction: their model explains well the co-movement of inflation and unemployment (the so-called Phillips curve) in the United States over the period from 1954 to 1999.

The channel by which money affects real economic variables described by Akerlof, Dickens, and Perry (2000) is just one of several channels that have been proposed that originate in what is called *money illusion.* Money illusion (see Fisher 1928; Leontief 1936; Howitt 1989; Shafir, Diamond, and Tversky 1997) is present when economic agents decide differently when a higher nominal payoff is offered (e.g., for goods or labor services) but the general level of prices rises in proportion so as to make the payoff expressed in goods (i.e., in real terms) unchanged.[9] In experimental work Fehr and Tyran (2001) indicate that the magnitude of price sluggishness in a monopolistically competitive economy may strongly depend on agents' expectations that *others* are prone to money illusion. With some agents afflicted with money illusion, any change in the money stock necessitates a process in which decision makers iteratively recoordinate their expectations. Psychological reasons such as money illusion or concerns regarding fairness may also contribute to a downward rigidity of wages (see, e.g. Akerlof, Dickens, and Perry 1996). While sluggishness of wages (as discussed above) suggests that a high level of inflation should be corrected downward only gradually, downward rigidity of wages would imply that inflation should not be reduced to zero. I will return to this issue later, when the question of optimal long-run inflation will be addressed.

Inflation Expectations

An issue where behavioral economics has been particularly important is the study of inflation expectations. Before the advent of rational expectations, the formation of expectations was by theoretical necessity modeled as extrapolative or adaptive (see Nerlove 1958). After Muth (1961) introduced the rational expectations hypothesis the study of inflation expectations became one of the early and important fields for testing rationality of foresight. Figlewski and Wachtel (1981), Lovell (1986), and Bonham and Cohen (1995) used survey data to document that inflation expectations of a wide class of economic agents were not adequately explained by the rational expectations hypothesis. Instead, adaptive expectations seem to do more justice to the data. Inflation expectations are particularly relevant since they can play a crucial role in the transmission process determining the effects of monetary policy. In fact, the first generation of applications of rational expectations claimed that with rational inflation expectations, monetary policy would be without any effects on real variables. Not only has this claim been proven wrong (see Fischer 1977; Taylor 1979) but *deviations* from rational expectations have been documented as playing an important role in the effects of monetary policy on real variables (see Naish 1993; Ball and Croushore 1995; Roberts 1997; Rötheli 2000).

The International Side

Exchange rates connect the domestic economy to the international sphere. Behavioral modeling of exchange rate movements—in the light of difficulties of models based strictly on macroeconomic fundamentals and rational behavior—started in the 1980s. Frankel and Froot (1986) proposed the first model where chartists buy and sell currency alongside agents who base their actions on the analysis of fundamentals such as differentials in real output growth, interest rates, and money growth between countries. Pattern extrapolation by chartists has the potential to make the exchange rate deviate from its long-run (purchasing power) equilibrium value for extended periods. Empirically, such extrapolative or noise trading behavior seems to at least account for the slight tendencies of various currencies to exhibit bandwagon dynamics (see Rötheli 2004). Bandwagon dynamics arise when extrapolating traders induce the exchange rate (or another variable) to continue to change in a direction once taken (see also Hong and Stein 1999).

In recent years the behavioral modeling of exchange rates has also made use of tools developed in artificial intelligence. Following the analysis of closed-economy macroeconomic questions relating to rationality and learning by Marimon, McGrattan, and Sargent (1990) and Sargent (1993), researchers such as Arifovic (1996) and Lawrenz and Westerhoff (2003) have modeled decision makers (specifically traders on the foreign exchange market) as genetic algorithms (see Holland et al. 1986; Holland and Miller 1991). Such agents do not from the outset have perfect understanding of their market environment but rather learn in a hypothesis-evaluating and hypothesis-adapting way from their experience. Under certain conditions simulated markets populated by such trial-and-error learning agents converge in their functioning to markets populated by rational agents. However, many alternative outcomes are also possible, and the noise trader literature (see DeLong et al. 1991) has shown that market competition will not in general eliminate traders who stick to simple heuristics.

Transactions, Money Demand, and the Price Level

Much research on the effects of variations in the quantity of money on nominal and real variables has been conducted on the basis of a concept of money demand developed and extended over many years. In its Cambridge representation the demand for money balances is proportional to the level of transactions in an economy. The factor of proportionality (the so-called Cambridge k) was early on seen to depend on the customs and techniques of making payments in an economy. Hence, changes (e.g., innovations) in the payment system were understood to change the relation of the value of overall transactions to the money stock (also called the velocity of circulation). As operational factors influencing the demand for money, the rate of interest (suggested in Keynes 1936) and a number of other variables capturing in greater detail the opportunity costs and risk characteristics of money were proposed (see Baumol 1952; Friedman 1956; Tobin 1958; Goldfeld and Sichel 1990).

Over the last fifty years a great deal of intellectual effort has gone into developing theories that show money demand as the outcome of rational action and interaction of economic agents. In the process analysts have explored different notions that explain why the asset money that is dominated in return by other forms of wealth is actually held. One notion is to see money balances as yielding direct utility and hence being a variable belonging directly into the utility function of the consumer (see Patinkin 1950–51). Another approach sees money as a productive factor and hence gives money balances a place in the economic agent's production function (see Dornbusch and Frenkel 1973). Some economists (see Goodfriend and McCallum 1987; Wang and Yip 1992) have investigated under what conditions such modeling can be consistently linked to economizing behavior given the costs of transferring interest-bearing assets (such as bank accounts) into cash. While some of these theoretical developments have led to insights that have furthered the understanding of empirical observations, it seems fair to say that this process has neither led to an integrated theory of money demand nor provided a fully satisfactory empirical account of the relation between money balances and their suggested determinants. On the empirical level too many cases of "missing money" and "demand instability" keep intriguing analysts. On the theoretical level there is a widely felt unease with a metaphorical approach to monetary theory (see, e.g., Niehans 1978, 1). It is undoubtedly unsatisfactory for economic theory to treat the demand for money balances similarly to the demand for TV sets and automobiles. These are assets—just like money—that provide services some of the time, and holding them leads to opportunity costs. However, the analogy has its limits in that money provides its service only because it can be given away in return for a good.

Instead of studying the effects of money in models where a money demand function is stated as the building block, several researchers have chosen to build models with a different premise. These models start with the assumption that the economy under investigation is *fully monetized,* meaning that all goods are paid for in the general medium of exchange.[10] Examples of this type of analysis are, among others, Clower 1967; Niehans 1978, chs. 2–4; Krugman, Persson, and Svensson 1985; and Shubik 1990.[11] This type of analysis describes the distribution of goods among agents, their preferences, market forms, and conventions regarding the timing of market events. Shubik (1972, 1990) even proposes the use of model economies that are playable, that is, models in which actors, their roles, and institutions are so explicit that the economic processes captured can be enacted with subjects. I take up this suggestion here to illustrate how this type of modeling opens interesting possibilities for experimentally studying the role of agents' decision making in important issues of monetary economics. I use a new and simple playable monetized economy to analyze the determination of money prices and their relation to the stock of money as well as the role of uncertainty in this quantity theoretic framework.

Consider a world populated by two types of agents: A-types are assumed to be endowed every period with a fixed amount (100 units) of A goods, while B-types receive 100 units of B goods per period. While endowments are specialized, both types of agents have the desire to acquire the good that is not in their endowment. This desire is modeled by having each agent i produce a final (consumer) good called C with a production function:

$$C_i = \sqrt{A_i B_i} \,.$$

As indicated before, the model economy is a monetized economy. This means that agents buy and sell goods against money. Hence, an A-type wanting to acquire B-goods has to offer money, and the same holds for a B-type desiring A-goods. The transactions (goods against money) take place on *two* markets, and revenues from sales in one market cannot be allocated toward purchases in the other market within the same market period.[12] Each subject is endowed with an identical amount of cash: 100 cash units. In the basic setup the aggregate supply of money remains fixed over time. I simplify the selling and buying behavior by giving agents just one dimension for varying their behavior in each of these markets. The selling behavior is determined by agents deciding over the amount of their commodity endowment they want to sell in each period. The buying behavior is determined by agents deciding over the sum of money they are willing to spend on the good that is not yet in their possession.

An anonymous market mechanism then determines equilibrium prices and flows of goods and money. For any unit of good given away there is a quid pro quo in money. The equilibrium price in any market is determined on the assumption (also communicated to subjects) that the sum of money offered by them for purchases is understood as a unitary elastic individual demand function. This implies that the equilibrium price is the sum of all money amounts offered for a specific good divided by the total of all offered units of that good. The assumption is that goods are perishable, that is, they cannot be stored. In the experiment subjects are asked (and financially motivated) to maximize their cumulative output of the consumption good. Hence there is no discounting. A positive value of money in the final period of the experiment is ensured by offering to exchange the remaining cash against A- and B-goods in equal proportion at the average of the two prices in the final period. This ensures that (at the average price) subjects receive the maximum possible amount of C-goods for their remaining balances.[13]

This model has interesting theoretical features. First, it is obvious that the maximum output per period in this economy is 1,000 units of the consumption good in the aggregate, that is, an average of 50 units per subject. This maximum output can be reached only when the endowments are equally split among the agents. This happens when each agent offers 50 units of his good (i.e., keeps 50 units) and purchases 50 units of the other type of good. What trading strategy could possibly bring about this outcome? The answer is that very many strategies are capable of generating this outcome. All these strategies have in common that each subject offers 50 units of the good in the endowment. What makes them different is the sum of money offered for purchases. Any positive amount of money between 0 and 100 offered is a feasible strategy if every player offers this amount. Hence, the efficient output of 1,000 units of the final good can be produced and the necessary transactions carried out with very different amounts of money changing hands. The flip side is that in this economy, considering only situations where all agents offer 50 good units, the price level (i.e., the average of the two prices of the A-good and the B-good) can be anything larger than 0 and up to a value of 2.

So what is the rational agent to do? What amount of money should he offer? Here is the proposed equilibrium concept: it can be argued that a rational agent should (and will) offer 50 money units because every number between 0 and 100 is equally likely and 50 is thus the expected value. Under this strategy the prices of the two goods are both 1. If all agents follow this strategy, it can be shown that no subject has a motive to deviate from this strategy. More precisely, in this case the individual is indifferent between following this strategy or any other strategy that shares the feature that the sum of expenses for goods purchased and number of goods offered for sale is 100.[14] So much for the reasoning about rational behavior; we will see how human subjects decide in this setup.

Figure 35.1   **Different Price Level Paths for Different Groups of Subjects**

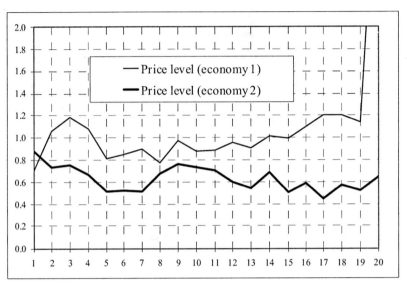

I enacted this playable economy as an experiment with students at the University of Erfurt who had studied (and successfully completed) economics courses at least one year previously. In an anonymous laboratory setting, an economy with ten A-type and ten B-type subjects was realized. Subjects were informed that they would receive one euro cent per consumption good. Once the experiment started, subjects had three minutes per market period to make their decisions. Before the actual experiment three trial periods were allowed in order to acquaint subjects with their task. After this learning phase the basic treatment was run. In this treatment no external changes impacted on the laboratory economy. The basic treatment was run with two different groups of subjects. Figure 35.1 shows the resulting two paths of the price level over twenty periods. It is evident that the two series differ systematically. Excluding the last period (for an apparent end-of-experiment effect in the second economy), the price level with the second group of subjects was on average 56 percent higher than with the first group of subjects. With the second set of subjects the price level does not significantly differ from a value of 1 (i.e., the level predicted on the assumption of rationality of all agents). With the first set of subjects, however, the price level is significantly below this value. While these results should not be overstated, the findings indicate that an experimental economy (and possibly actual economies as well) can operate on different price levels.

The second treatment for the two groups addresses two separate issues: for group one the supply of money was increased (by way of a transfer of 50 cash units to every subject) after the tenth market period. After this expansion the money stock remained on its elevated (by 50 percent) level for the rest of the experiment. Figure 35.2 shows the course of the price levels in the basic treatment (i.e., with a constant aggregate money supply) and in the treatment with the monetary expansion after the tenth period. It is obvious that the price level increases after the infusion of money. Tests indicate that the price levels for the two treatments during the first ten periods (i.e., with the same money supplies) do not differ significantly. However, after the money infusion the difference is statistically significant. The quantity theory of money would predict that for periods eleven to twenty the price level should be higher than in the first ten periods proportionally to the increase in the money stock (that is, by 50 percent higher). This theoretical prediction

Figure 35.2 **The Effect of a Monetary Expansion on the Price Level**

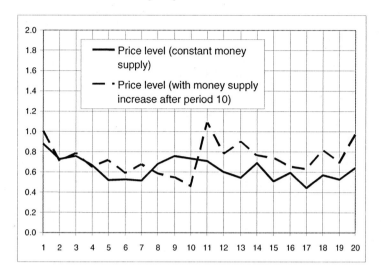

is statistically supported. This result is particularly interesting given the fact that for this group the price level paths in both treatments differ systematically from the prediction based on unbounded rationality. One interpretation of this result would suggest that the quantity theory of money may be one of the economic relationships that are robust to agents' deviations from perfect rationality. Another interpretation would point toward the fact that on average the price level with the increased money supply is only 38 percent higher, rather than the 50 percent that the quantity theory would predict. With a view to the policy issues to be taken up later, this deviation (while statistically insignificant) is substantial and should caution policy makers attempting to stabilize the price level (rather than the rate of inflation) by way of monetary control.

Let us turn now to studying the effect of endowment uncertainty. This was investigated with the second group of subjects, who had a different second treatment than group one. Here, subjects were exposed to randomly varying commodity endowments. Subjects were advised that their endowments would on average be 100 per period and that in any period this endowment (E_i) could fluctuate with a standard deviation of 10 units. In the experiment the endowments were selected such that there was no aggregate risk: that is, in any period the total endowment of A-goods and B-goods was 1,000 each. What can we expect to happen under these circumstances? Individually, in every period the rational agent should offer half of his good endowment (i.e., $E_i/2$). Moreover, expecting both prices to be one he should offer the same number of money units (also $E_i/2$) for the purchase of the other good. Therefore, given that the total endowments of goods do not fluctuate in the aggregate, nothing should change compared to the basic setup. However, it turns out the experimental evidence is at variance with this prediction. The data show that it takes time for subjects to adapt their behavior to the new environment. But once this adjustment has been made (about ten periods into the second run), the average sum of money offered for purchases is markedly lower in the stochastic environment as compared to the scenario with deterministic endowments. Hence, endowment risk appears to lead to a higher level of money balances not used up for transactions when—based on the assumption of rationality—we would not expect such extra (precautionary) money holdings. The counterpart of this effect can be seen in the course of the price level in the stochastic treatment. Figure 35.3 documents that the level of prices

Figure 35.3 **The Effect of Endowment Uncertainty on the Price Level**

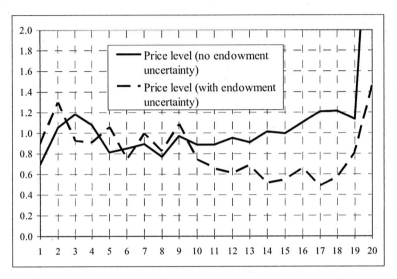

tends to be lower with endowment uncertainty. Again with a view to policy making, this effect indicates that shifts in the equilibrium price level can occur for reasons not accounted for by models based on perfectly rational decision making. The experimental setup developed here has the potential for further interesting analyses that are, however, beyond the limits of this essay.

MONEY SUPPLY AND MONETARY POLICY

In the analysis of the money supply process economists have traditionally given much attention to institutional detail, particularly on the financial side of the economy (for surveys, see Brunner and Meltzer 1990; Modigliani and Papademos 1990). Clearly, the assumption of economizing (or optimizing) behavior on the side of owners of assets (i.e., households and firms) and banks has always been an important tool for the analysis of the money supply process and related policy questions. However, the notion of substantive (i.e., unlimited) rationality of economic agents is more controversial here than in many other parts of economics. There is a tension between researchers who, acknowledging the present limited insight into the interplay of rationality and institutional settings, prefer not to be overly specific about rationality and those who would rather have only models in which rationality of behavior can be fully and clearly assessed. This tension is sometimes framed as a controversy between macroeconomics and micro-based modeling. However, such an assessment is very questionable: anyone who examines, for example, Brunner's and Meltzer's or Modigliani's work on the subject will acknowledge that their behavioral functions relating monetary and financial variables to policy variables (such as reserves and interest rates) are based on microeconomic reasoning. Hence, this critique of macroeconomics has no basis.

On substantive issues Brunner and Meltzer (1993, 173–82) question the relevance of many micro-based rational expectations models with much the same arguments that behavioral economists find important: the neglect of the costs of information acquisition, information heterogeneity, and the assumption that agents have a full understanding of policy rules. Moreover, these authors are deeply skeptical with respect to Lucas's (1976) demand that all policy recommendations should be based on empirical estimates of time-invariant parameters of tastes and technology. As Brunner and Meltzer (1993) point out, there is no basis to the belief that economics has as yet identified (or will ever be able to identify) these time-invariant parameters. Hence, monetary policy advice will very likely continue to be based on models that rely on regularities that do not depend on the assumption of perfect rationality: negatively sloped demand curves, diminishing marginal productivity, and the relation of money to output and the price level. Besides these general remarks three issues will be discussed in more detail: (1) the choice of instruments of monetary policy, (2) the debate of rules versus discretion, and (3) the question of the socially optimal long-run level of inflation. All three of these themes have a long history in monetary economics (for surveys, see Friedman 1990; Fischer 1990).

The Choice of Instruments of Monetary Policy

The analysis of the choice of the instrument of monetary policy has been much advanced by Poole's (1970) approach of framing the question as an optimization problem. When monetary policy attempts to minimize the variance of output, it turns out that the optimal instrument of policy (control of either the money stock or of an interest rate) depends in simple forms of this type of analysis on the relative magnitude of the unexplained variability of money demand (i.e., the variance of the error term of the LM curve) and aggregate goods demand (i.e., the variance of the error term of the IS curve). This approach in itself (as Poole suggested) can be seen as based on limited knowledge (or we could say bounded rationality), particularly on the side of policy makers: the fact that there are unpredictable changes in key macroeconomic relationships implies that the analyst and hence the policy maker have imperfect knowledge of the economy. On a more specific level the identification of the conditions favoring one instrument over the other or suggesting the precise form of their optimal combination (such as an interest rate rule with feedback from money growth) depends on empirical estimates. As Fair (1988) has shown, this assessment depends on assumptions regarding the rationality of private sector decision makers. When a macroeconomic model for the United States is estimated to serve as the basis for the assessment of rules in Poole's sense, it turns out that imposing rational expectations results in estimates of variances and co-variances that tend to favor money stock targeting as the optimal rule of policy. When, however, the hypothesis of adaptive expectations is entertained (alongside the hypothesis of rational expectations) it turns out that expectations in some markets are indeed formed adaptively and that an interest rate rule is superior to a money supply rule.

Rules Versus Discretion in Monetary Policy

Kydland and Prescott (1977) provided a new analytical basis for the debate of rules versus discretion. Their case for rule-based monetary policy rests on the phenomenon of time-inconsistency of optimal plans. Given that the policy maker and the public both value low inflation and a smooth path for output, it would be optimal to choose steady and moderate money growth. If, however, there is a short-run output (and employment) gain from engineering surprise inflation, the policy maker will be systematically tempted to increase money growth given the public's inflation expectation. This inconsistency of motives—policy favoring low inflation but then, given low expected inflation, preferring an increase in money growth—will affect the public's inflation outlook. Expected inflation and hence also actual inflation will be higher compared to a situation where the policy maker could commit himself to low and steady money growth. This is the loss associated with discretionary policy, since no output gains will come from this elevated level of inflation. The balancing of short- and long-run gains by monetary policy makers (i.e., policy makers having their reputation at stake) may under certain conditions solve this inefficiency, as Barro and Gordon (1983) have pointed out. However, a clear commitment in the form of an institutional (and possibly constitutional) restriction will be more likely to eliminate the inflationary bias. This argument for rules over discretion in monetary policy is analytically derived from the assumption of rational expectations of the public. It will be interesting to see how this result holds up when boundedly rational (and heterogeneous) expectations are considered. Future macroeconomic models in the tradition of behavioral economics should explore more behavioral and institutional detail and benefit from assessments by policy-experienced researchers such as Blinder (1999) and Poole (2000). Furthermore, new research will likely be done on the question of whether targets (like inflation targets) and central bank independence are effective enough as tools to eliminate the described inflation bias. Here behavioral economics can add insights in many ways. For example, it is an open question whether policy targets much affect the public's short- and medium-run expectations when a broad range of behaviorally plausible expectations schemes outperform the policy targets in forecasting accuracy (see Rötheli 1999).

The Optimal Long-Run Rate of Inflation

The question of the optimal steady-state level of inflation is linked to issues of wage stickiness and money illusion, as discussed earlier. If in fact institutional and behavioral restrictions on wage setting weigh as heavily as some believe (such as Akerlof, Dickens, and Perry 1996, 2000), it would be beneficial to accept a moderate level of inflation (say, around 3 percent per year) instead of aiming at zero inflation. This position for moderate secular inflation could be summarized as follows: if workers are happy with increasing wages as long as inflation is moderate, and if they are willing to work harder, then pushing inflation to zero is wrong because it diminishes output and welfare. A number of researchers are skeptical of this analysis (see Crawford and Harrison 1997, Smith 2000, and the positions reported in Kopcke, Little, and Tootell 2004). These observers see the possibility of downward real wage adjustments even with close to zero inflation (e.g., by labor accepting a wage freeze for some years into the future) and judge the costs of inflation to be too high (notably because of intertemporal distortions and accounting costs).

Instead of aiming for a certain level of inflation, some researchers have argued that monetary policy should stabilize the *price level*. Recently, Ball, Mankiw, and Reis (2005) have renewed this claim within a model where at least some agents slowly absorb macroeconomic information. However, the case for a price level target depends critically on monetary policy's ability to control the price level. Scores of studies questioning the stability of money demand and experimental analysis of the type proposed previously cast doubt on this assumption. Moreover, after, for example, a rise in the price level due to an unforeseen decrease in money demand, holding to a price level target would necessitate a phase of deflation. The alarms that went off when only the possibility of negative U.S. inflation rates was considered in 2003 indicate that the dangers of deflation have to be taken seriously (see Kumar et al. 2003). From this perspective, it seems unrealistic to propose price level targeting as a rule for monetary policy given the perceived dangers of deflation.

CONCLUSION

This essay documents that monetary economics has both a behavioral tradition and a behavioral future. Bounded rationality plays an important role in understanding monetary phenomena, and it also affects the design of optimal monetary policy. In particular, deviations from rational expectations are important for understanding the size and the persistence of real effects of monetary policy. These insights are important, for example, when assessing the possibilities of monetary stabilization policies and the cost of reducing inflation. Deviations from rationality are also important with regard to the choice of monetary instruments and targets. Notably, behavioral economics adds doubts to the proposal that monetary policy should target the price level rather than the rate of inflation: too many behavioral determinants of the equilibrium price level remain insufficiently understood and beyond the control of policy makers.

Based on the work presented here, it is safe to assume that behaviorally enriched analysis of monetary issues will continue to yield significant insights. A subject that is particularly likely to see extensions and revisions of results is the issue of rules versus discretion in monetary policy. Here, the assumption of rationality of foresight has so far played a dominant role in research. On one hand, the analysis of behaviorally more realistic models may well weaken the case for strict rules; on the other hand, it may lead to the design of new guidelines for policy intervention. Beyond the selective issues discussed here, it is possible that behavioral monetary economics will even make fundamental contributions to economic theory. Who would deny that a monetized market economy greatly helps to efficiently allocate cognitive resources such as attention, memory, and the capacity for reasoning?

NOTES

I would like to thank Morris Altman, Sean Flynn, and Mathias Zurlinden for comments.

1. Simon 1983, e.g., shows no reference to monetary economics at all.

2. Kiyotaki and Wright (1989, 1992), among others, attempt a joining of these issues.

3. The optimality of a consumption plan may then just as well be ensured by equating the marginal utility of one tomato exchanged directly for any other good. In reality, transaction costs in tomato barter trades vary depending on which good tomatoes are traded against. Hence, assessing optimality by comparing "tomato utilities" necessitates comparing utilities resulting from the least-cost barter sequences leading to the acquisition of any consumption good.

4. Ritter (1995) shows that the need for the government to raise income (seigniorage) by printing money can theoretically provide the basis for rational agents to support the transition from barter to fiat money. The promise not to overissue money receives its credibility from the self-interest of the government to raise revenue. From a behavioral perspective it appears that limited foresight would be both more realistic (historically considering the many cases of hyperinflation) and more robust. Even boundedly rational central banks are likely to be able to launch a fiat money when dealing with boundedly rational private agents.

5. I cannot treat here in any detail the interesting issue of whether a competitive supply of money (i.e., a system of paper money without government intervention) is feasible and desirable. White (1999, ch. 12) reviews and discusses the role of rationality of expectations in the highly controversial field of free banking.

6. I will not cover in any detail effects of changes in second moments of the money supply. This means that we are not dealing with changes in monetary regimes that change the risk characteristics of an economy, as analyzed in the work of Lucas (1982) and Helpman and Razin (1982). This sort of analysis dealing with behavior toward risk may be particularly sensitive to rationality assumptions. Rötheli 1997 experimentally documents that the effects of exchange rate risk are at variance with normative theory based on substantive rationality.

7. Moreover, when a variation in the rate of change of the money supply leaves real variables (notably the real interest rate as the difference between the nominal interest rate and expected inflation) unchanged, we speak of superneutrality of money (see Sidrauski 1967).

8. Blinder (1994) is an attempt to investigate the reasons for price sluggishness by way of interviewing firms. Saint-Paul (2005) offers an explanation of how sluggish nominal price adjustment emerges evolutionarily given price setters with bounded rationality.

9. Whether behavior of workers as modeled in Akerlof, Dickens, and Perry 2000 qualifies as an illusion in the common usage of the word is questionable. If workers are happier with a situation with modest wage increases (compared to a situation with no or lower wage increases) even when they understand that inflation erodes their purchasing power, the term *illusion* seems misplaced.

10. In my view Hicks (1969, 1989) gives some of the clearest historical and theoretical justifications why monetary models should start with descriptions and assumptions regarding the use of money rather than trying to incorporate explanations for the use of money.

11. This does not preclude that in some of these models payments can be deferred and that there exists credit.

12. One can think of these markets as operated in trading (or transactions) posts. There, the goods supplied and the money amounts offered are deposited. Once the equilibrium prices are determined, goods and money are distributed to the respective recipients. Clearly, this setup also takes care of the solvency requirement. That is, it guarantees that all contracts are honored.

13. Ensuring that money has a value in the final period of the game is an important aspect of experimental analyses of money (see Duffy 1998).

14. Call x the expenses for goods purchased and y the number of goods offered for sale. In this case the per-period level of consumption is $C = \sqrt{(100 - y)x} + (y - x)/2$ where the term $(y - x)/2$ is the value of the money balances exchanged into consumption goods at the end of the experiment. Optimizing consumption with respect to x and y leads to the condition $x + y = 100$. Hence, a strategy with $x = 50$ and $y = 50$ is just as good as one with $x = 0$ and $y = 100$, that is, a strategy where all endowments are sold and cash is accumulated to be exchanged for goods in the final period of the experiment.

REFERENCES

Akerlof, George, William T. Dickens, and George L. Perry. 1996. "The Macroeconomics of Low Inflation." *Brookings Papers on Economic Activity* 1996, 1: 1–59.

———. 2000. "Near-Rational Wage and Price Setting and the Long-Run Phillips Curve." *Brookings Papers on Economic Activity,* number 1, 1–44.

Akerlof, George A., and Janet L. Yellen. 1985. "A Near-Rational Model of the Business Cycle, with Wage and Price Inertia." *Quarterly Journal of Economics* 100, 5: 823–38.

Arifovic, Jasmina. 1996. "The Behavior of the Exchange Rate in the Genetic Algorithm and Experimental Economies." *Journal of Political Economy* 104, 3: 510–41.

Ball, Laurence, and Dean Croushore. 1995. "Expectations and the Effects of Monetary Policy." NBER working paper no. w5344. Cambridge, MA: National Bureau of Economic Research.

Ball, Laurence, N. Gregory Mankiw, and Ricardo Reis. 2005. "Monetary Policy for Inattentive Economies." *Journal of Monetary Economics* 52, 4: 703–25..

Barro, Robert J., and David B. Gordon. 1983. "Rules, Discretion and Reputation in a Model of Monetary Policy." *Journal of Monetary Economics* 12, 1: 101–21.

Baumol, William A. 1952. "The Transactions Demand for Cash: An Inventory Theoretic Approach." *Quarterly Journal of Economics* 66, 4: 545–56.

Blinder, Alan S. 1994. "On Sticky Prices: Academic Theories Meet the Real World." In N. Gregory Mankiw, ed., *Monetary Policy,* 117–50. Chicago: University of Chicago Press.

———. 1999. *Central Banking in Theory and Practice.* Cambridge, MA: MIT Press.

Bonham, Carl, and Richard Cohen. 1995. "Testing the Rationality of Price Forecasts: Comment." *American Economic Review* 85, 1: 284–89.

Brunner, Karl, and Alan H. Meltzer. 1990. "Money Supply." In Benjamin M. Friedman and Frank H. Hahn, eds., *Handbook of Monetary Economics,* 1:356–98. Amsterdam: Elsevier Science Publishers.

———. 1993. *Money and the Economy: Issues in Monetary Analysis.* Cambridge: Cambridge University Press.

Clower, Robert W. 1967. "A Reconsideration of the Microfoundations of Monetary Theory." *Western Economic Journal* 6, 1: 1–9.

Crawford, Allan, and Alan Harrison. 1997. "Testing for Downward Rigidity in Nominal Wage Rates." Paper presented at the Bank of Canada conference "Price Stability, Inflation Targets and Monetary Policy," May. Available at http://www.bank-banque-canada.ca/en/conference/con97/cn97-10.pdf.

DeLong, J. Bradford, Andrei Shleifer, Lawrence H. Summers, and Robert J. Waldmann. 1991. "The Survival of Noise Traders in Financial Markets." *Journal of Business* 64, 1: 1–19.

Dornbusch, Rudiger, and Jacob A. Frenkel. 1973. "Inflation and Growth: Alternative Approaches." *Journal of Money, Credit, and Banking* 5, 1: 141–56.

Dowd, Kevin. 2001. "The Emergence of Fiat Money: A Reconsideration." *Cato Journal* 20, 3: 467–76.

Duffy, John. 1998. "Monetary Theory in the Laboratory." *Federal Reserve Bank of St. Louis Review* 80, 5: 9–26.

Fair, Ray. 1988. "Optimal Choice of Monetary Policy Instruments in a Macroeconometric Model." *Journal of Monetary Economics* 22, 2: 301–15.

Fehr, Ernst, and Jean-Robert Tyran. 2001. "Does Money Illusion Matter?" *American Economic Review* 91, 5: 1239–62.

Figlewski, Stephen, and Paul Wachtel. 1981. "The Formation of Inflationary Expectations." *Review of Economics and Statistics* 63, 1: 1–10.

Fischer, Stanley. 1977. "Long-Term Contracts, Rational Expectations, and the Optimal Money Supply Rule." *Journal of Political Economy* 85, 1: 191–205.

———. 1990. "Rules Versus Discretion in Monetary Policy." In Benjamin M. Friedman and Frank H. Hahn, eds., *Handbook of Monetary Economics,* 2:1169–80. Amsterdam: Elsevier Science Publishers.

Fisher, Irving. 1928. *Money Illusion.* New York: Adelphi.

Frankel, Jeffrey A., and Kenneth Froot. 1986. "Understanding the U.S. Dollar in the Eighties: The Expectations of Chartists and Fundamentalists." *Economic Record,* December, 24–38.

Friedman, Benjamin M. 1990. "Targets and Instruments of Monetary Policy." In Benjamin M. Friedman and Frank H. Hahn, eds., *Handbook of Monetary Economics,* 2:1185–230. Amsterdam: Elsevier Science Publishers.

Friedman, Benjamin M., and Frank H. Hahn. 1990. "Preface to the Handbook." In Benjamin M. Friedman and Frank H. Hahn, eds., *Handbook of Monetary Economics,* 1:xi–xix. Amsterdam: Elsevier Science Publishers.

Friedman, Milton. 1956. "The Quantity Theory of Money—A Restatement." In Milton Friedman, ed., *Studies in the Quantity Theory of Money.* Chicago: University of Chicago Press.

Fuhrer, Jeffrey, and George Moore. 1995. "Inflation Persistence." *Quarterly Journal of Economics* 110, 1: 127–59.

Goldfeld, Stephen M., and Daniel E. Sichel. 1990. "The Demand for Money." In Benjamin M. Friedman and Frank H. Hahn, eds., *Handbook of Monetary Economics,* 1:299–356. Amsterdam: Elsevier Science Publishers.

Goodfriend, Marvin S., and Bennett T. McCallum. 1987. "Theoretical Analysis of the Demand for Money." In John Eatwell, Peter Newman, and Murray Milgate, eds., *The New Palgrave: A Dictionary of Economics.* London: Macmillan.

Helpman, Elhanan, and Assaf Razin. 1982. "A Comparison of Exchange Rate Regimes in the Presence of Imperfect Capital Markets." *International Economic Review* 23, 2: 365–88.

Holland, John H., Keith James Holyoak, Richard E. Nisbett, and Paul R. Thagard. 1986. *Induction: Processes of Inference, Learning, and Discovery.* Cambridge, MA: MIT Press.

Holland, John H., and John H. Miller. 1991. "Artificial Adaptive Agents in Economic Theory." *American Economic Review* 81, 2: 365–71.

Howitt, Peter. 1989. "Money Illusion." In John Eatwell, Murray Milgate, and Peter Newmann, eds., *Money* (New Palgrave), 244–47. New York: Norton.

Hicks, John. 1969. *A Theory of Economic History.* Oxford: Oxford University Press.

———. 1989. *A Market Theory of Money.* Oxford: Oxford University Press.

Hong, Harrison, and Jeremy C. Stein. 1999. "A Unified Theory of Underreaction, Momentum Trading, and Overreaction in Asset Markets." *Journal of Finance* 54, 6: 2143–84.

Keynes, John M. 1936. *The General Theory of Employment, Interest, and Money.* London: Macmillan.

Kiyotaki, Nobuhiro, and Randall Wright. 1989. "On Money as a Medium of Exchange." *Journal of the Political Economy* 97, 4: 927–54.

———. 1992. "Acceptability, Means of Payment, and Media of Exchange." In John Eatwell, Peter Newman, and Murray Milgate, eds., *The New Palgrave Dictionary of Money and Finance.* London: Macmillan.

Kopcke, Richard W., Jane S. Little, and Geoffrey M. B. Tootell. 2004. "How Humans Behave: Implications for Economics and Economic Policy." *New England Economic Review,* First Quarter, 3–35.

Krugman, Paul R., Torsten Persson, and Lars E.O. Svensson. 1985. "Inflation, Interest Rates, and Welfare." *Quarterly Journal of Economics* 100, 3: 677–95.

Kumar, Manmohan S., Taimur Baig, Jörg Decressin, Chris Faulkner-MacDonagh, and Tarhan Feydioglu. 2003. "Deflation Determinants, Risks, and Policy Options." IMF occasional paper no. 221. Washington, DC: International Monetary Fund.

Kydland, Finn E., and Edward C Prescott. 1977. "Rules Rather than Discretion: The Inconsistency of Optimal Plans." *Journal of Political Economy* 85, 3: 473–91.

Lawrenz, Claudia, and Frank Westerhoff. 2003. "Modeling Exchange Rate Behavior with a Genetic Algorithm." *Computational Economics* 21, 3: 209–29.

Leontief, Wassily. 1936. "The Fundamental Assumptions of Mr. Keynes' Monetary Theory of Unemployment." *Quarterly Journal of Economics* 5, 4: 192–97.

Lovell, Michael C. 1986. "Tests of the Rational Expectations Hypothesis." *American Economic Review* 76, 1: 110–24.

Lucas, Robert E. 1976. "Econometric Policy Evaluation: A Critique." *Carnegie Rochester Conference Series on Public Policy* 1: 19–46.

———. 1982. "Interest Rates and Currency Prices in a Two-Country World." *Journal of Monetary Economics* 10, 3: 335–59.

Mankiw, Gregory N. 1985. "Small Menu Costs and Large Business Cycles: A Macroeconomic Model of Monopoly." *Quarterly Journal of Economics* 100, 2: 529–37.

Marimon, Ramon, Ellen McGrattan, and Thomas J. Sargent. 1990. "Money as a Medium of Exchange in an Economy with Artificially Intelligent Agents." *Journal of Economic Dynamics and Control* 14, 2: 329–73.

Modigliani, Franco, and Lucas Papademos. 1990. "The Supply of Money and the Control of Nominal Income." In Benjamin M. Friedman and Frank H. Hahn, eds., *Handbook of Monetary Economics,* 1:399–494. Amsterdam: Elsevier Science Publishers.

Muth, John F. 1961. "Rational Expectations and the Theory of Price Movements." *Econometrica* 29, 3: 315–35.

Naish, Howard F. 1993. "The Near Optimality of Adaptive Expectations." *Journal of Economic Behavior and Organization* 20, 1: 3–22.

Nerlove, Marc. 1958 "Adaptive Expectations and Cobweb Phenomena." *Quarterly Journal of Economics* 73, 2: 227–40.

Niehans, Jürg. 1978. *The Theory of Money.* Baltimore: Johns Hopkins University Press.

Ostroy, Joseph M., and Ross M. Starr. 1990. "The Transactions Role of Money." In Benjamin M. Friedman and Frank H. Hahn, eds., *Handbook of Monetary Economics,* 1:3–62. Amsterdam: Elsevier Science Publishers.

Patinkin, Don. 1950–51. "A Reconsideration of the General Equilibrium Theory of Money." *Review of Economic Studies* 18, 1: 42–61.

Poole, William. 1970. "Optimal Choice of Monetary Policy Instruments in a Simple Stochastic Macro Model." *Quarterly Journal of Economics* 84, 2: 197–216.

———. 2000. "Monetary Aggregates and Monetary Policy in the Twenty-First Century." Paper presented at the conference "The Evolution of Monetary Policy and the Federal Reserve over the Past Thirty Years: A Conference in Honor of Frank E. Morris," October. Available at http://www.bos.frb.org/economic/conf/conf45/conf45c1.pdf.

Ritter, Joseph A. 1995. "The Transition from Barter to Fiat Money." *American Economic Review* 85, 1: 134–49.

Roberts, John M. 1997. "Is Inflation Sticky?" *Journal of Monetary Economics* 39, 2: 173–96.

Rötheli, Tobias. 1997. "International Investment and Exchange Rate Risk: An Experimental Analysis." *Jahrbücher für Nationalökonomie und Statistik* 216, 3: 347–60.

———. 1999. "Assessing Monetary Targeting with Models of Expectations Formation." *Journal of Policy Modeling* 21, 1: 139–51.

———. 2000. "Producers' Expectations: Their Role in the Monetary Transmission Mechanism." *Kyklos* 53, 1: 39–50.

———. 2004. "Bandwagon Effects and Run Patterns in Exchange Rates Once More." *Journal of International Financial Markets, Institutions and Money* 14, 1: 99–104.

Saint-Paul, Gilles. 2005. "Some Evolutionary Foundations of Price Level Rigidity." *American Economic Review* 95, 3: 765–79.

Sargent, Thomas J. 1993. *Bounded Rationality in Macroeconomics.* Oxford: Oxford University Press.

Selgin, George. 1994. "On Ensuring the Acceptability of a New Fiat Money." *Journal of Money, Credit and Banking* 26, 4: 808–26.

Shafir, Eldar, Peter Diamond, and Amos Tversky. 1997. "Money Illusion." *Quarterly Journal of Economics* 112, 2: 341–74.

Shubik, Martin. 1972. "On the Scope of Gaming." *Management Science* 18, 5: P20–36.

————. 1990. "A Game Theoretic Approach to the Theory of Money and Financial Institutions." In Benjamin M. Friedman and Frank H. Hahn, eds., *Handbook of Monetary Economics,* 1:171–219. Amsterdam: Elsevier Science Publishers.

Sidrauski, Miguel. 1967. "Rational Choice and Patterns of Growth in a Monetary Economy." *American Economy Review Papers and Proceedings* 57, 2: 534–44.

Simon, Herbert A. 1983. *Models of Bounded Rationality.* 2 vols. Cambridge, MA: MIT Press.

Smith, Jennifer C. 2000. "Nominal Wage Rigidity in the United Kingdom." *Economic Journal* 110, 462: 176–95.

Taylor, John B. 1979. "Estimation and Control of a Macroeconomic Model with Rational Expectations." *Econometrica* 47, 5: 1267–86.

Thaler, Richard H. 1997. "Irving Fisher: Modern Behavioral Economist." *American Economic Review* 87, 2: 439–41.

Tobin, James. 1958. "Liquidity Preference as Behavior Toward Risk." *Review of Economic Studies* 25, 2: 65–86.

Wang, Ping, and Chong K. Yip. 1992. "Alternative Approaches to Money and Growth." *Journal of Money, Credit and Banking* 24, 4: 553–62.

Weatherford, Jack. 1997. *The History of Money: From Sandstone to Cyberspace.* New York: Three Rivers Press.

White, Lawrence H. 1999. *The Theory of Monetary Institutions.* Oxford: Blackwell Publishers.

Wicksell, Knut. 1934. *Lectures on Political Economy.* Translated by E. Classen and Lionel Robins. London: Routledge.

CHAPTER 36

BEHAVIORAL FINANCE

TOMASZ ZALESKIEWICZ

Investors are rational, in the sense that they make decisions according to axioms of expected utility theory, they have stable preferences, and their forecasts about the future are unbiased. Financial markets are effective given that nobody is able to systematically beat the market, and security prices reflect only utilitarian characteristics (see Statman 1999a). These two assumptions of investors' rationality and market efficiency have dominated, like a charm, the standard theory of finance. Economic models of human behavior based on the two assumptions are simple and elegant, but more and more data show that they are incomplete or unrealistic. Results from the growing field of behavioral finance, which applies psychology to economic models, seem to indicate neither that investors are rational nor that markets are effective (at least in the sense of prices' rationality). The importance of psychosocial factors in economic interactions is also revealed in the experimental economists' work on financial markets. Smith showed, using experimental methods, that the behavior of individuals participating in trust games is sensitive to reciprocity (see Smith 2000 for a review). This means that traders tend to accept a reciprocal exchange even if this is not rational from an economic point of view.

According to Shefrin (2000), three topics that underlie behavioral finance are heuristic-driven biases in predicting future market tendencies, frame-dependent investors' preferences, and inefficient prices. Standard finance models assume a rational investor who is able to forecast prices in an unbiased fashion and who can make choices with respect to stable preferences toward risk. On the other hand, behavioral finance sketches a picture of a "normal" investor who is confused by cognitive errors, makes judgments that are guided by moods and affects, and is susceptible to different frames (Statman 1999a). Whereas the goal of traditional finance is to show the norm of rational investing, behavioral finance's ambition is to describe the real behavior of stock market agents.

Psychologists long have known that people have different cognitive biases. An example of how the pitfall of our intuition influences the judgment we make is shown in Figure 36.1.

Most people who are asked whether the lengths of the two lines presented in Figure 36.1 are equal answer that line B is longer than line A. However, perceived difference in the length of the two lines is only a visual illusion, as can be seen in Figure 36.2.

The reason for the error we make when comparing the length of the two lines is that they are presented in different contexts. As behavioral finance shows, making financial decisions is often similar to comparing the length of the two lines. Moreover, the sensitivity of financial judgments and choices to changes in context, also called frame dependence, sometimes becomes systematic. If many investors commit the same errors, they influence price changes and disturb market efficiency. In other words, stock prices start to deviate from fundamental values for long periods (see Shefrin 2000). Two examples indicate how cognitive errors committed by individual investors contribute to price changes on an aggregate market level. The first example refers to the departure

Figure 36.1   **The Comparison of the Length of Two Lines**

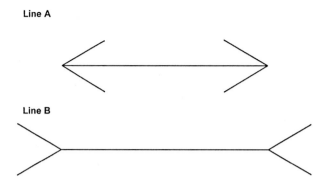

Figure 36.2   **The Visual Illusion**

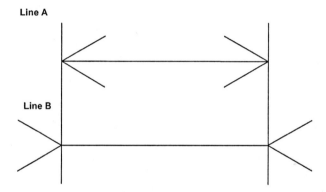

of stock prices from fundamentals, and the second example to price divergences between fundamentally identical securities.

Shiller (2000) compared actual prices and fundamental values of securities. Fundamental values are the hypothetical values of stocks for an investor with perfect foresight about the future value of dividends. If investors were rational, that is, if they were making financial choices with respect to fundamentals, no difference should be observed between actual stock price and the fundamental value. However, as can be seen in Figure 36.3, this difference is for some periods striking (see also Shefrin 2000).

Another example described by Froot and Dabora (1999) and Shleifer (2000) shows how fundamentally identical securities are differently priced. The example refers to the Royal Dutch/ Shell Group. The two companies are independently incorporated in the Netherlands and England. Royal Dutch is a part of the S&P 500 Index, and Shell is part of the Financial Times Stock Exchange Index. The former trades primarily in the United States and the latter primarily in the United Kingdom. The interests of both companies are merged on a 60/40 basis. If shares of Royal Dutch and Shell were traded by rational investors (arbitrageurs), they should trade in a 60-40 ratio (after adjusting for foreign exchange)—that is, the value of a Royal Dutch share should be equal to 1.5 times the value of a Shell share. However, as Figure 36.4 illustrates, one can observe

Figure 36.3   **Stock Price and Dividend Present Value**

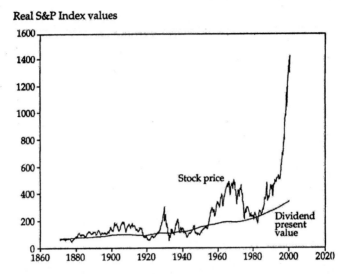

Source: Reprinted with permission from Robert J. Shiller, *Irrational Exuberance* (Princeton, NJ: Princeton University Press, 2000), 186. Copyright © 2000, Robert J. Shiller.

Figure 36.4   **Log Deviations from Royal Dutch/Shell Parity**

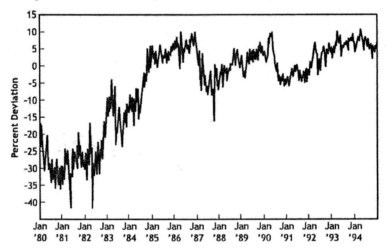

Source: Reprinted from K.A. Froot and E. Dabora, "How Are Stock Prices Affected by the Location of Trade," *Journal of Financial Economics* 53, 2 (1999): 189–216. Copyright © 1999, used with permission from Elsevier.

enormous deviations from Royal Dutch/Shell parity. The actual price ratio deviates from the expected price ratio by more than 35 percent.

In this essay I challenge the assumption of investors' rationality, showing how cognitive errors they commit are connected with the way securities are priced. In the first section I describe two pitfalls that influence forecasting of future price changes: overconfidence and unrealistic optimism. The second section explains the role experienced and anticipated emotions play in financial judgment and choice. I focus on three particular emotions: regret, hope, and fear. Section three presents the frame dependence of financial preferences. First, it shows how ambiguity aversion influences the evaluation of stocks. Second, it documents that loss aversion is a better description for preferences of individual investors than risk aversion. In this section I introduce the main assumptions of prospect theory and show an application of this theory to investors' buying and selling behavior and to the equity premium puzzle.

BIASED FORECASTS

Forecasting future price changes is one of the most important investment tasks. Standard finance argues that rational investors who possess limitless knowledge use different statistical tools correctly to make unbiased predictions. However, behavioral finance suggests that this is rarely the case. "Behavioral" investors process information in a heuristic way, using rules of thumb and mental shortcuts. Shefrin gives an example of a commonly used rule of thumb: "Past performance is the best predictor of future performance, so invest in a mutual fund having the best five-year record" (2000, 4). Using heuristics to process data can be an effective way to cope in the complex world of financial markets. On the other hand, it often results in committing errors because rules of thumb are generally imperfect, and heuristic-driven estimates are often inaccurate. Consider an example involving P/E ratios given by Fisher and Statman (2000).

Investors use P/E ratios to predict future stock returns. Many of them believe that using the P/E ratio can provide reliable forecasts of stock returns even in the short horizon. For instance, low P/E ratios are interpreted as forecasting high returns. Fisher and Statman studied the P/E ratios at the beginning of the 128 years from 1872 through 1999. They did not find a statistically significant relationship between P/E ratios at the beginning of a year and returns (real and nominal) during the following year (adjusted R-squared was lower than 0.01). A similar result was found when returns during the following two years were analyzed. The authors of the study also showed that the lowest one-year return following the six highest P/E ratios in the considered period was a 1.44 percent loss. The other five returns that followed extremely high P/E ratios were positive, with the highest a 28.58 percent gain. The data collected by Fisher and Statman indicated that information on the past P/E ratios record could not be used as a reliable tool to make unbiased predictions about future stock returns. Yet investors' belief that P/E ratios provide reliable forecasts of short-horizon returns is persistent. The authors argued that this persistence could be traced "to cognitive errors that underlie the illusion of validity" (Fisher and Statman 2000, 80). According to Kahneman and Tversky, the term "illusion of validity" means that "people are prone to experience much confidence in highly fallible judgment" (1973, 249). The rest of this essay will demonstrate examples of how biases connected with overconfidence and unrealistically high optimism can cause investors to be prone to the illusion of validity.[1]

Overconfidence in Market Forecasts

In one of the classic studies on human judgment, Lichtenstein and Fischhoff (1977) asked people to make difficult judgments and then to rate the probability that the judgments were correct. For example, people predicted future stock performance. At the beginning of the experiment they received market reports on twelve stocks and then predicted whether the stock would rise or fall. The authors found that participants' performance was slightly less than expected by chance: only 47 percent of the judgments were correct. However, the average confidence rating was 65 percent.

Similar results were found when people were asked to make other judgments: average confidence estimates exceeded performance accuracy.

Overconfidence means that people tend to overestimate their knowledge, even if (or especially if) they are experts in the field. Empirical evidence revealed that physicians who made diagnoses of pneumonia were very poorly calibrated, showing unwarranted certainty that patients had this disease. On the other hand, some experts (i.e., weather forecasters) were almost perfectly calibrated (Plous 1993). Dawes, Faust, and Meehl (1989) argued that this difference in predictions accuracy could be attributed to the various methods of judgment. The clinical method—used, for example, in medical judgments—involves collecting information existing in the expert's memory to make predictions for the future. In the actuarial method, by contrast, predictions are based on using external procedures, such as statistical rules or algorithms. Weather forecasting makes usage of the second method, which causes weather experts to be well calibrated in their judgments.

Do stock market forecasts implement clinical or actuarial methods? Tyszka and Zielonka (2002) argued that financial experts make use of clinical judgment or of a combination of clinical and actuarial methods, which may result in being highly confident and committing errors at the same time. In their study they asked financial analysts to forecast the value of the Warsaw Stock Exchange Index at the end of 2000, one and a half months in the future.[2] Additionally, the analysts' task was to rate on a 9-point scale their general confidence in their ability to correctly assess future stock returns and, in particular, the forecast of the Warsaw Stock Exchange Index they were asked to make. The results showed that, on average, financial analysts rated their knowledge as being relatively high. Mean self-evaluation was equal to 6 (on a 9-point scale). The average probability assessment was also found to be high and was equal to 58.03 percent. However, a positive self-evaluation and high confidence in the forecast was not reflected in the correctness of the stock exchange index prediction: only one-third of the analysts were correct in their forecasts.

In the second phase of this study, the participants were told of the correctness or incorrectness of their forecasts. They also completed a questionnaire consisting of a list of reasons why a prediction might fail. The authors reported that three justifications dominated in respondents' answers: (1) unexpected events occurred that changed the situation, (2) in a single prediction there is always chance of being wrong, and (3) the events in question are generally unpredictable. These justifications do not directly refer to probabilistic arguments. In other words, they do not reflect uncertainty connected with market predictions.

After respondents' justifications had been collected, the authors of the study asked them once more to make a self-evaluation of their ability to predict future returns. No statistically significant drop in the self-evaluation was found. Tyszka and Zielonka have argued that using justifications that do not refer to probabilistic arguments can be regarded as a psychological mechanism analysts use to defend their self-esteem. However, the authors showed that this self-protective strategy prevents financial experts from learning from experience.

An obvious question that one could ask here is whether overconfidence has an impact on investors' financial returns. Barber and Odean (2000) documented in their analysis that the more extreme the investor's overconfidence, the less she earns in the stock market. As they showed, the relation between overconfidence and earning is mediated by the variable of trade frequency. Overconfident investors believe more strongly in their judgments and choices. As a consequence of their high certainty, they trade more and their annual turnover is higher. To test the hypothesis concerning the relation between overconfidence reflected in trade frequency and annual portfolio returns, Barber and Odean examined information from a large discount brokerage firm on the trading decisions of 66,465 households from January 1991 through December 1996. In the first step, the level of trading for each individual investor was determined, and in the second step all investors were divided into five subgroups (quintiles) depending on trading frequency. The 20 percent of investors with the lowest turnover composed the first group, and the 20 percent of investors with the highest turnover composed the fifth group.

In general, Barber and Odean found that the average household turned over 75 percent annually, which means that households traded stocks quite frequently. However, large differences between five household groups were observed. Whereas the first subgroup had a turnover of 2.4 percent per year, the fifth subgroup had an annual turnover of over 250 percent per year. This difference appeared not to be related to households' average gross returns. All five subgroups had an annual gross return of about 18.7 percent. This suggests that frequent trading does not lead to better performance (in gross return). However, as all market participants are aware, trading costs are high. Barber and Odean stressed that "the average round-trip trade in excess of $1,000 costs three percent in commissions and one percent in bid-ask spread" (2000, 775). High trading costs cause net return to be much lower than gross return, especially for those investors who trade a lot. The two authors document that the households trading least frequently earned an annual net return of 18.5 percent, and households that traded most frequently earned an annual net return of 11.4 percent. At the same time the market returned 17.9 percent. The data collected by Barber and Odean show clearly that aggressive trading could not beat the market.

Trading frequency was related to two additional variables: gender and the system of investing (phone-based investing versus online-based investing). In one of the studies Barber and Odean (2001) analyzed the trading decisions of 37,664 individual investors (households) with accounts at a large discount brokerage between February 1991 and January 1997. All investors were classified into four groups depending on gender and marital status: single women, married women, married men, and single men. The authors examine differences between the four groups in the trade frequency. The investment folklore tells us that male investors tend to be more confident in their financial choices than female investors, because investing has traditionally been recognized as a masculine job, and men feel more competent than women in financial matters (Nofsinger 2001). Results collected by Barber and Odean (2001) confirm these assumptions. They show that trade frequency depends on both gender and marital status. The highest trade frequency is observed in the group of single men (an annual turnover of 85 percent) followed by married men (73 percent), married women (53 percent), and single women (51 percent). In general, male investors trade 45 percent more than female investors. The differences in trading behavior are reflected in the consequences of financial choices men and women make on the market buying and selling stocks. Although both women and men reduce their returns by trading, men's returns are reduced by 0.94 percentage points more a year than women's (2.65 percent versus 1.72 percent).

The second variable—the system of investing—is connected with the overconfidence phenomenon (Barber and Odean 2002). The authors examine the trading behavior of 1,607 investors that took place through a discount brokerage firm from January 1991 through December 1996. All investors whose decisions were analyzed switched from a phone-based trading system to an online-based trading system. In particular, the amounts of trading and annual portfolio returns were examined.

Barber and Odean find that switching to an Internet-based trading increased trading in a significant fashion. Before going online investors' average turnover was about 70 percent (similar to the turnover reported in Barber and Odean 2000). However, after going online trade frequency grew by up to 120 percent. In this study, as in many previous studies, an increase in trade frequency is followed by a decrease in portfolio performance. The authors of the analysis stressed that before going online investors performed well, beating the market by more than 2 percent annually. However, going online did not improve performance. Excessive Internet-based trading appeared to be not only more active but less profitable at the same time. After going online investors lagged the market by more than 3 percent annually. As Barber and Odean proved, the drop in portfolio performance after going online could be best explained by the bias of investors' overconfidence.

Positive Illusion in Market Forecasts

Another cognitive illusion closely connected with overconfidence that biases financial predictions is variously called overoptimism (Kahneman and Riepe 1998), desirability bias (Olsen 1997), and positive illusion (Moore et al. 1999). Psychologists have shown that most people tend to overestimate the likelihood of positive outcomes and underestimate the likelihood of negative outcomes. Optimistic individuals exaggerate their abilities and skills and believe that they are less likely than their peers to develop serious diseases (e.g., cancer or heart attack) (Kahneman and Riepe 1998), to be victims of crime, or to have automobile accidents (Moore et al. 1999). Assuming that individual investors are not exceptionally different from the rest of the population, one could expect them to be overly optimistic in their financial forecasts. As I will show, positive illusion in market predictions was documented both in computer-based investing simulations and in real forecasts of risk and return.

Moore and colleagues performed an experiment to examine whether business students estimate the past and the future performance of their own investments in an optimal or suboptimal (overly optimistic) manner. The authors of the research created a simulated market based on real data of large mutual funds and an S&P 500 index fund. The participants could invest money over a ten-year period and had the opportunity to make decisions about moving their money between funds. During the experiment people received information concerning the performance of the funds and the performance of the market. After each turn at the game the participants answered several questions on how satisfied they were with the performance of their investment, how they would estimate the increase in value of their investment in the next six months, and how they would estimate their performance relative to the average participant and relative to the market as a whole.

Moore and colleagues' analysis of the data shows that business students who participated in the simulation overestimated their own future performance relative both to the market and to other participants. Most participants forecasted that their investments would grow more than they actually did, indicating that the predictions were overly optimistic. The authors of the study also show that students overestimated the past performance of their portfolios despite having received information on the performance of market indices throughout the experiment. It is natural that the positive illusion found in the business students' judgments during the experiment could bias decisions made by real investors and analysts about real financial markets.

This assumption was confirmed in the research by De Bondt (1998), in which he recruited forty-five individual investors at a conference organized by the National Association of Investment Clubs. The investors made repeated weekly forecasts of the Dow Jones Industrial Average (DJIA) and of their main equity holdings. They made two kinds of forecasts: point forecasts and interval estimates. The interval estimates were based on investors' belief that there was a one-in-ten chance that the rated variable (the DJIA or investors' equity holdings) would turn out higher and a one-in-ten chance that it would turn out lower.

The results of this study showed clearly that individual investors were overly optimistic when making two-week and four-week return forecasts for their equity holdings. The predicted two-week returns were on average 0.64 percent too high, and the predicted four-week returns were on average 0.62 percent too high. The difference between perceived and actual returns for both periods was statistically significant. However, overly optimistic market predictions have not only statistical but also economic meaning, because they can lead investors to irrationally exuberant behavior (Shiller 2000).

The second part of the data analysis revealed that investors who participated in this study formed confidence intervals that were too narrow relative to the actual variability in equity prices.[3] This tendency was more severe for the four-week period than for the two-week period. This suggests that, especially for longer-term predictions, investors not only committed the error of overoptimism but also were overconfident. However, the phenomenon of positive illusion in financial forecasts was not observed when the participants were asked to predict the value of the DJIA. No statistically significant differences between perceived and actual returns for the DJIA were found. The lack of these differences means that investors are able to predict market indices correctly, but they are overly optimistic and too confident when forecasting returns for their own portfolios. A "behavioral" explanation that one can offer here is that investors tend to form overly optimistic forecasts when they are more emotionally involved. It is natural that predicting returns for the portfolio the investor holds is a much more involving task than trying to predict neutral values such as the market index. One could also argue that when forecasting returns for their equity holdings, investors experience a strong feeling of personal control that cause them to form more positive and unrealistic predictions.

The examples described above clearly demonstrate that individual investors tend to be overly confident and overly optimistic when making financial forecasts for the portfolios they hold. Overconfident market participants lower their returns by trading too much, especially when they go online. As Barber and Odean demonstrate, "those who trade most realize, by far, the worst performance" (2002, 459). Investors who have the bias of positive illusion hold unrealistic beliefs about the future returns of their equities and continuously overestimate the chances of success. Behavioral finance suggests that three psychological phenomena can be used to explain the errors of overconfidence and overoptimism: self-attribution bias, the illusion of knowledge, and the illusion of control (see Barber and Odean 2001, 2002; Shefrin 1999).

Self-attribution bias means that people manifest a tendency to ascribe their successes to their personal abilities and their failures to external factors such as decisions of other people or bad luck (Miller and Ross 1975). Investors who experienced recent success—for example, the prices of the shares they held went higher—were more likely to attribute it to their trading prowess. However, after experiencing a failure, they were more likely to attribute it to random processes that could not be forecasted. If this tendency is stable over time, it causes market participants to become increasingly overconfident about their personal skills and to trade more aggressively and more speculatively.

Investors have access to enormous quantities of financial data, especially if they trade online. It seems that receiving more information should improve the accuracy of economic forecasts. Psychology tells us, however, that this is not the case. Oskamp (1965) demonstrated in one study that when the amount of information increases, people are more confident in their decisions, but the choices themselves do not become more accurate. This phenomenon has been called the illusion of knowledge. It is obvious that the illusion of knowledge leads to overconfidence because, given more data, investors' confidence in financial forecasts increases faster than the accuracy of those forecasts.

Another pitfall investors face while making predictions on the stock market is the illusion of control. Langer (1975) showed in her classic study that people sometimes believe they are able to predict and control the outcomes of purely random events such as a coin toss. Langer argued that some factors could enhance the illusion of control. These are: task familiarity, choice, and active involvement. As Barber and Odean (2002) illustrated, investors who place their orders online

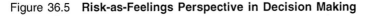

Figure 36.5   **Risk-as-Feelings Perspective in Decision Making**

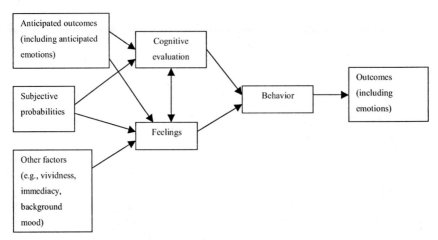

Source: G. F. Loewenstein et al., "Risk as Feelings," *Psychological Bulletin* 127, 2 (2001): 269–86. Copyright © 2001, American Psychological Association. Reprinted with permission.

experience a strong feeling of active involvement. They believe that they can better control the outcomes of their investment choices and that the chances of favorable outcomes are higher for themselves than for an average market participant. However, this often is only an illusion, because as some authors argue (see, for example, Malkiel 1996), the financial world is unpredictable (uncontrollable) and stock prices rise and fall in a random way.

EMOTIONS IN INVESTMENT JUDGMENT AND IN PORTFOLIO CHOICE

Traditional finance theory assumes that investment decision making involves rational Bayesian maximization of expected utility. Loewenstein and colleagues (2001) describe this assumption as a "consequentialist perspective." From this perspective decision making should be considered as a cognitive process, in which individuals estimate various actions and choose alternatives that maximize utility of their consequences. The consequentialist rational perspective also dominates in financial models such as portfolio theory (Markowitz 1952) and the capital asset pricing model (Sharpe 1964).

Recently, however, more and more empirical studies have shown that the consequentialist perspective does not reflect real decision-making behavior. The critiques of rational choice models have stressed that these models largely ignore the influence of emotions on the decision-making process (see Loewenstein et al. 2001 for a review). Thaler (2000) argues that economists' interest in how emotions determine financial decisions will increase in the future.

Loewenstein and colleagues (2001) developed the "risk-as-feelings" hypothesis that addresses the functions affect serves in choice under uncertainty. The idea of this new theoretical framework is presented in Figure 36.5.

The risk-as-feelings hypothesis postulates that risky decision making is influenced by emotions in different ways. First, feelings connected with the cognitive evaluation of the problem can be determined by the background moods. Second, anticipated emotions such as regret or disappointment influence both cognitive and emotional evaluation. Third, human reaction in a risky situation depends on direct (anticipatory) emotions such as worry, fear, dread, and anxiety. There is ample evidence that all three ways in which emotions determine the choice behavior are present in financial decision making. The next sections highlight the role played by mood and both antici- pated and anticipatory emotions in investment decisions.

BACKGROUND MOOD AND INVESTMENT CHOICE

The research from psychology shows that background mood plays an important role in the process of decision making. Some researchers argue that mood informs the judgments and choices we make. When we are in a positive mood we tend to use strategies that are less effort- intensive and to be more optimistic in our decisions. On the other hand, negative mood fosters more analytical thinking and more pessimistic decision making (see Isen 2000 for a review). There is evidence that background mood can influence decisions even if mood is unrelated to the actual decision problem. Research showed, for example, that people reported better life satisfaction on sunny days than on rainy days. Other researchers demonstrated that in good weather people became less skeptical, less depressed, and more generous (Dowling and Lucey 2005). The question is whether such attributes can also be observed in the behavior of traders on the stock market.

Several studies were performed to test the hypothesis that the changes in weather influence financial decisions on the stock market. Saunders (1993) examines the relation between the level of cloud cover in New York and the movement of the Dow Jones Industrial Index from 1927 to 1989 and the value-weighted and the equal-weighted NYSE/AMEX indices from 1962 to 1989. In general, Saunders finds that when the level of the cloud cover was high (100 percent) mean returns dropped significantly below average, but when the level of cloud cover was low (no more than 20 percent) mean returns were above average. These data suggest that investors' mood is influenced by weather conditions and greatly impacts the movement of equities.

Similar results were also obtained in other studies replicating Saunders's research. Hirshleifer and Shumway (2003) tested the correlation between the level of cloud cover and financial returns in twenty-six international equity markets. However, in contrast to previous research, instead of comparing returns for high cloudiness to returns for low cloudiness, the authors investigated the linear relationship between the level of cloud cover and financial returns across all levels of cloud cover. A negative relationship would mean that bad affective states caused by high cloudiness are connected with lower returns, and good moods resulting from sunny weather are associated with higher returns. A negative relationship between cloud cover and equity returns was found for eighteen of the twenty-six cities. In the case of four cities (Brussels, Milan, Sydney, and Vienna) the coefficient of the relationship was significant at the 5 percent level (two-tailed), and the value of the t-statistic for all cities was 4.49.

Other studies used different determinants of investors' mood to test the relationship with eq- uity returns, including temperature, seasonal affective disorder, daylight saving time changes, diurnal biorhythms, and lunar phases. Below some of the results described in the papers by Dowling and Lucey (2005) and by Nofsinger (2005) are listed:

- Low temperatures (below comfortable levels) are associated with above-average equity re- turns, and high temperatures are associated with below-average returns.
- Seasonal affective disorder affects returns such that from autumn to winter (when the length of night increases) returns are increasingly negative and from winter to spring (when the length of night decreases) returns are increasingly positive.
- Daylight saving time changes (in both spring and autumn), which disturb sleep patterns,

also influence equity returns—returns for Mondays following the time changes are lower than returns for other Mondays.

- A U-shaped pattern of return changes during the day (for Tuesday to Friday) can be explained by the variations in diurnal mood. The rising returns for Mondays can be attributed to the disappearance of depression throughout the day.
- Some investigations suggested the existence of association between returns and lunar phases in the way that returns in the days surrounding the new moon are higher than returns in the days surrounding the full moon.

Recently, Nofsinger (2005) has introduced the idea of "social mood," which affects the behavior of individual investors and financial managers. The core of this new concept is that changes in optimism and pessimism at the level of society create the background mood of an individual decision maker and influence her emotions. The social mood cycle introduced by the author suggests that increasing mood causes an increase in happiness, hope, and overconfidence and results in more optimistic financial decisions. On the other hand, declining mood connected with sadness, fear, and mistrust results in more pessimistic financial decisions. The mood changes in the minds of many individual investors impact aggregate investment, which one could use to forecast future financial and economic activity.

Expected Emotions in Financial Choices

Financial decisions have both economic and emotional consequences. From a financial point of view it is obvious that investors try to make choices that create gains and not losses. But the "emotional framework" also shows that when making decisions investors avoid options creating the feeling of regret and seek options creating the feeling of pride. "Regret is the emotion experienced for not having made the right decision. Regret is more than the pain of loss. It is the pain associated with feeling responsible for the loss" (Shefrin 2000, 30). People not only directly experience regret but also are able to predict that a particular course of action could lead to experiencing the feeling of regret when the consequences turn out to be negative.

Shefrin (2000) describes an example of how Harry Markowitz—the Nobel laureate and the developer of modern portfolio theory—made his personal allocation decision. Instead of seeking the optimum trade-off of risk and return, Markowitz chose a solution that minimized his future regret. The "emotionally optimal" solution was to split the contributions fairly between less risky bonds and riskier equities. Benartzi and Thaler (2001) showed that the behavior of individual investors often reflects the strategy Harry Markowitz used in making his allocation decision. They simply split their contributions between different investment forms equally. If, for example, two options would be available—riskier stocks and less risky bonds—investors could use the "$1/n$ heuristic" (also called naive diversification), that is, they could divide their contributions equally between these options.

Regret is an unpleasant emotion, so market participants take various actions to minimize it. Below I will give two examples that demonstrate how the avoidance of future regret leads investors to irrational financial behaviors. The first example is related to the use of dividends, whereas the second example introduces the phenomenon of disposition effect.

In an efficient market with no taxes, dividend policies are not important (see Modigliani and Miller 1958), but at least under the U.S. tax system dividends paid by companies are taxed at a higher rate than capital gains. Therefore, taxpaying shareholders would be better off if companies repurchased shares instead of paying cash dividends (Thaler 1999). However, on the real market companies pay dividends, and "behavioral investors" prefer cash dividends to homemade dividends, that is, dividends created by selling stocks. Consider the example of an investor who sold some shares of stocks to finance her consumer expenditures (e.g., to buy a washing machine), and afterward these stock shares soared. What would be the feeling experienced by the investor who realized that the choice to sell shares was wrong? Typically, the responsibility for an inappropriate choice brings considerable regret. Using dividends to finance consumer expenditures, instead of selling stocks, involves little regret. Hence, investors' demand for cash dividends can be caused by their tendency to avoid future regret.

Another example displaying how regret avoidance leads to suboptimal financial choices is illustrated in the disposition effect. Shefrin and Statman (1985) suggest that investors show a tendency to sell winners too early and to hold losers too long. Selling winning stock too early means that after it has been sold it continues to perform well. Holding a losing stock too long means, on the other hand, that its price continues to decline from the moment the investor considered selling it. Why is the disposition effect connected with seeking pride and avoiding regret? If a stock price rises, investors experience the temptation to sell it and make a quick profit. Winning a profit creates the feeling of pride. If the stock price goes down, selling it would create regret, because the investor would feel responsible for having chosen a losing stock in the past.

EXPERIENCED EMOTIONS IN THE JUDGMENT OF FINANCIAL RISK AND RETURN

The investment folklore tells us that two feelings that guide financial choices are greed and fear. However, psychologists have argued that this is only partly the case. According to Lopes (1987), the major emotions that influence risk-taking behavior are hope and fear. Experiencing hope means that a decision maker is focused on the most favorable outcomes and her behavior reflects the need for potential. The experience of fear induces an individual to focus more on outcomes that seem to be less favorable in order to satisfy the desire for security.

Experiencing positive and negative feelings not only influences choices under uncertainty but also interacts with the cognitive (rational) judgment of risk. The role of emotions in financial judgment becomes more important when the quantity of information is very large or very small. Under informational overload people tend to rely more on simple rules and heuristics that often weigh affective cues more heavily than fundamental data. Another example of how affective rating may become the main basis on which financial judgment is based is investors' evaluation of initial public offerings (IPOs). Typically, decision makers have very limited knowledge about the financial history of new companies, and they are not able to use technical indicators in making a financial judgment on those companies. Instead, when judging the overall worth of new offerings they tend to rely on emotion-based images that come to mind when they think about the company.

Two studies showed how investors use affective factors to estimate the value of securities (MacGregor et al. 1999; MacGregor et al. 2000). The goal of the first study was to investigate how affective ratings contribute to the overall judgment of financial risk and return across a domain of different investments. The second study was undertaken to test the role affect plays in financial forecasting. Below I describe the main results of both studies.

MacGregor and his colleagues (1999) presented a group of financial advisors and planners with a survey containing a set of several investments and the set of scales used to rate perceived risks and returns for these investments. Two stepwise multiple regression analyses were performed to examine the associations between different scales and the judgment of risk and the judgment of return. It appears that perceived risk was best predictable in terms of judgments of worry and volatility. Another variable that significantly contributed to the prediction of perceived risk was knowledge. The three variables accounted for an overall R-squared of 0.98. It means that an investment tends to be estimated as more risky when, among other things, an individual experiences more worry by investing in it.

Perceived return, on the other hand, was predictable in terms of the variables of volatility, performance predictability, and time horizon, for an overall R-squared of 0.96. In accordance with psychological theory (see Lopes 1987), the negative feeling of worry was strictly connected with the way decision makers estimated the financial riskiness of various investments.

The goal of the second study (MacGregor et al. 2000) was to test how affective judgments were used to evaluate a number of industry groups represented on the New York Stock Exchange. Participants' task was to estimate forty industry groups on several bipolar dimensions that reflected positive or negative affective evaluations of those groups. The dimensions used in this research were bad/good, boring/exciting, worthless/valuable, strong/weak, and passive/active. Additionally, people who participated in the study described the first three images that came into their minds when they thought about different industry groups and to judge whether those images were positive or negative. In the third part of the study, participants answered several questions in which they indicated their familiarity with companies in the industry group, rated returns of each group in the previous year (1994), predicted returns for the coming year (1995), and rated the likelihood that they would buy an IPO from the group. After all answers had been collected, the authors of the study were able to calculate relationships between affective evaluations of industry groups and participants' financial judgments and choices.

The results show that both imagery and affective judgments connected with industry groups were highly related to the likelihood of investing. As predicted, the more positive the evaluation of a group, the higher the probability that an investor would buy an IPO belonging to this group. Judgments of sectors' performance relative to the market were also highly associated with perceived affective qualities. Past and the future returns were estimated as higher when the industry group was perceived as good, strong, and valuable and when images connected with it were more positive. In general, stocks that were perceived better in affective terms were rated better in terms of their financial performance at the same time.

However, participants' judgments of financial performance appeared to be poorly or only moderately correlated with actual market performance. This means that if investors are not able to base their judgments on actual financial data, because they do not have access to it or the quantity of information is too large, they tend to base these judgments on more general and unstructured affective evaluations. Emotional judgments made in financial choices often are imperfect and can lead to committing cognitive errors. As MacGregor and colleagues argue, "a stock offering with a highly positive affective evaluation is likely to be seen as good in terms of a number of other specific attributes, such as the quality of its management or its prospects for long-term financial success. However, the basis for the affective evaluation may not be related to management quality or financial goodness, but rather to the association of the company with the exciting or glamorous qualities of its business sector" (2000, 104).

Emotions and the Portfolio Choice

Traditional portfolio theory (Markowitz 1952) teaches an investor that when choosing assets she should identify risk with the variance of returns, focus on the expected returns, and build the optimal portfolio as a whole, taking into account correlations between these assets. The idea of how an optimal risk variance portfolio is constructed is shown in Figure 36.6, on the left side.

Figure 36.6   The Idea of an Optimal Mean-Variance Portfolio and a Behavioral Portfolio

Mean–Variance Portfolio

Mean–variance portfolios are constructed as a whole, and only the expected return and the variance of the entire portfolio matter. Covariance between assets is crucial in determination of the variance of the portfolio.

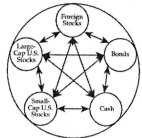

Behavioral Portfolio

Behavioral portfolios are constructed not as a whole but layer by layer, where each layer is associated with a goal and is filled with securities that correspond to that goal. Covariance between assets is overlooked.

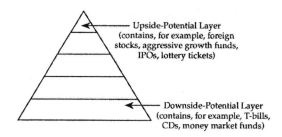

— Upside-Potential Layer (contains, for example, foreign stocks, aggressive growth funds, IPOs, lottery tickets)

— Downside-Potential Layer (contains, for example, T-bills, CDs, money market funds)

Source: Reproduced and republished from M. Statman, "Foreign Stocks in Behavioral Portfolios," *Financial Analysts Journal* March/April (1999): 12–16, with permission from CFA Institute. Copyright © 1999, CFA Institute. All rights reserved.

Mean-variance portfolio theory, based on Bernoulli's utility theory, assumes that investors are risk-averse, because the utility function is concave throughout. However, as some authors argued, deviations from general risk aversion can be observed, revealing that people display both risk-averse and risk-seeking behavior (Statman 2002). In psychological terms, this duality of behavior can be attributed to experiencing positive and negative emotions (see Lopes 1987). The negative emotion of fear strengthens the desire for security and motivates an investor to choose assets that are characterized by a low probability of loss. On the other hand, the positive feeling of hope strengthens the appetite for success and induces an investor to choose assets with a high probability of gain. Investors have different (higher or lower) aspiration levels, but they all want to avoid becoming poor and expect to become rich. Therefore, as Shefrin and Statman suggest, investors divide their current wealth into different mental accounts connected with specific financial goals. Focusing on negative and positive emotions at the same time causes investors to overlook covariance between assets and to construct behavioral portfolios as a layered pyramid (see Shefrin 2000; Shefrin and Statman 2000). The goal of the downside layer is to protect an investor against becoming poor, and the goal of the upside layer is to give her a chance to become rich. The idea of a behavioral portfolio is presented in Figure 36.6, on the right side.

One could argue that both the mean-variance portfolio and the behavioral portfolio are optimal, but that the meaning of optimality is different in each. The former is optimal in the sense of mathematical calculations of variance, expected returns, and covariance between risk and return. The latter is based on the search for an "emotional optimum," that is, the optimum of the positive emotion of hope and the negative emotion of fear. Shefrin (2000) argues that the balance between good and bad feelings and the level of aspiration influences, for example, the allocation between riskier stocks and less risky bonds. As shown in Figure 36.6, stocks are associated with the upside-potential layer and bonds are associated with the downside-potential layer.

The way in which emotions determine the selection of assets is reflected in the role foreign stocks play in behavioral portfolios (Statman 1999b). Because of the low correlation between foreign and domestic stocks, inclusion of the former in the portfolio can reduce its overall riskiness. However, investors typically overweight domestic stocks and underweight unfamiliar stocks in their portfolios, committing a "home bias" (French and Poterba 1991). Even the allocation to foreign stocks in model portfolios of mutual fund companies is much lower than the allocation prescribed by the optimal mean-variance theory. Statman argues that if some investors are ready to buy foreign stocks, they do this not because they want to have mean-variance-efficient portfolios but because they want to have more aggressive securities in the upside-potential layer.

Fisher and Statman (1997) show that model portfolios of mutual fund companies are not constructed within the mean-variance framework but rather within the behavioral framework of layered pyramids. Mutual fund companies offer prescriptions of how to match a portfolio with personal goals and individual attitudes toward risk. The authors give an example of advice given in the brochure of the Putnam mutual fund company: "The Investment Pyramid lists Putnam funds by investment category, e.g., tax-free income, growth and income, and growth. Putnam's income and tax-free funds offer lower reward potential with lower income risk. Growth and income funds provide greater reward potential with more risk. At the top of the pyramid are growth funds. These funds offer the greatest growth potential with the highest level of risk" (Fisher and Statman 1997, 15). The construction of the behavioral portfolio overlooks the fact that covariance between different funds is inconsistent with mean-variance optimization but satisfies investors' need for the balance between fear and hope.

PREFERENCES

Many assumptions about human behavior under uncertainty held in the standard finance model concern preferences. It is assumed that investors evaluate various prospects according to the axioms of expected utility theory (Von Neuman and Morgenstern 1947). The preferences of a rational agent are complete, transitive, continuous, and independent, and the agent takes actions to maximize general utility. Several principles formalized in the expected utility framework state, among other things, that decision weights do not depend on the origin of uncertainty and choices between options are independent of their description (see Thaler 1995 for a review of these principles and their criticism). However, empirical research has shown that people systematically violate the assumptions of expected utility theory when making decisions. Two demonstrations of these violations are aversion to ambiguity and frame dependence. In this section I will show how aversion to ambiguity and frame dependence influence financial choices and how they can be applied to the aggregate stock market.

Aversion to Ambiguity

In 1961 Ellsberg published a paper in which he demonstrated that people tend to dislike vague uncertainty; he labeled his finding "ambiguity aversion." Ellsberg performed an experimental study that required participants to make choices between two urns containing different proportions of red and blue balls. Urn 2 contained a total of 100 balls, 50 red and 50 blue, whereas Urn 1 also contained 100 balls, but the proportion of red and blue balls was unknown. In two experimental conditions participants could choose which urn they wanted to draw balls from to gain $100. In the first choice situation the blue ball needed to be drawn to get the payment, and in the second choice situation the red one needed to be drawn. Ellsberg found that in both conditions people avoided drawing from Urn 1, with the unknown proportion of blue and red balls. However, to be consistent with expected utility theory, participants should have drawn once from Urn 1 and once from Urn 2.[4] This suggests that people's choices were inconsistent with the utility theory but they were consistent with the tendency to avoid ambiguity—a situation in which people do not know what the probability distribution is.

Olsen and Troughton (2000, 25) summarized studies that test the phenomenon of ambiguity aversion and conclude that:

- Ambiguity influences selection.
- In general, decision makers are ambiguity-averse.
- Ambiguity causes more weight to be placed on negative information.
- Buyers pay lower prices for, and insurers require higher premiums on, objects or hazards subject to greater difficulty in estimation of value or probability of outcome.
- Risk aversion and ambiguity aversion do not appear to be highly correlated.

The same authors also carried out research with the goal of identifying the role of ambiguity in investment decision making. The participants in this study were professional money managers. It appears that managers use various risk attributes to evaluate stocks for which they know the company's name in a different way than they do for stocks without an associated company name. For example, the correlation between standard deviation and perceived risk was 0.05 for stocks without company names and 0.23 for stocks with company names. It seems that managers differently interpreted the meaning of quantitative risk attributes when they had or did not have knowledge about the name of the company. Only 33 percent of money managers who took part in Olsen and Troughton's study stated that they "would treat two securities with equivalent quantitative risk measures as equally risky" (2000, 27).

Another example of how aversion to ambiguity influences financial preferences is manifested by the phenomenon of home bias. As described in a previous section, home bias means that investors prefer well-known securities (e.g., domestic securities) to less well-known securities (e.g., foreign securities). The bias can be observed at different levels of the analysis, in both international and local investment.

French and Poterba (1991) showed that about 47 percent of the value of all stocks worldwide is represented by the stock market in the United States, about 26 percent by the market in Japan, and about 14 percent by the market in the United Kingdom. If the portfolios of individuals who invest in an international market were fully diversified, their allocations would reflect the proportions given above. However, as both authors demonstrate, they did not. Investors from the United States prefer U.S. stocks, investors from Japan prefer Japanese stocks, and investors from the United Kingdom prefer U.K. stocks. Because foreign stocks seem more ambiguous, investors tend to avoid them.

The home bias can also be observed when investors consider buying stocks of local companies or stocks of companies from other states. According to Huberman (2001), investors living in New York State prefer to allocate a higher percentage of their portfolios to New York companies (e.g., NYNEX), and investors from California prefer their local companies (e.g., Pacific Bell).

People not only like domestic and local stocks but also like stocks of companies they are employed in. Data presented by the Investment Company Institute show that company stock is the second highest asset allocation among 401(k) plans (see Montier 2002). Montier also gives an example of Coca-Cola employees who allocated no less than 76 percent of their contributions to the shares of their employer.

Frame Dependence

Empirically demonstrated violations of expected utility theory led to the construction of different nonexpected utility theories. According to Barberis and Thaler (2003), the theory from this set

Figure 36.7   **Value Function and Probability Weighting Function in Prospect Theory**

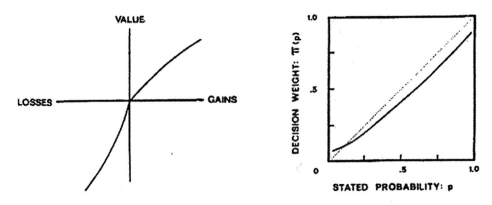

Source: Reprinted with permission from D. Kahneman and A. Tversky, "Prospect Theory: An Analysis of Decision Under Risk," *Econometrica* 47, 2 (1979): 263–91. Copyright © 1979, The Econometric Society.

that seems to be most promising for financial application is Kahneman and Tversky's prospect theory (see Kahneman and Tversky 1979, Tversky and Kahneman 1992). Whereas expected utility theory represents a normative approach to choices, prospect theory is a descriptive theory. It is concerned not with how decisions should be made but with how decisions are actually made.

The original version of prospect theory shows that when a person is faced with a gamble, in which outcome x can be reached with probability p and outcome y can be reached with probability q, she calculates its overall value as $\pi(p)v(x) + \pi(q)v(y)$, where π is a nonlinear probability-weighting function and v is a value function evaluated with respect to a particular reference point. Unlike in standard expected utility theory, in prospect theory probabilities are replaced by decision weights. From the point of view of prospect theory, people maximize a weighted sum of utilities. When people have to choose between several gambles, they decide in favor of the one with the highest overall value. The prospect theory's value function, as well as the probability weighting function, is shown in Figure 36.7.

Several features of prospect theory can be applied to financial choice. As can be seen in Figure 36.7, the utility function is concave over gains and convex over losses. This difference implies that people's preferences toward risk depend on whether they make choices in the domain of gains or in the domain of losses. Unlike expected utility theory, prospect theory reveals that people's decision behavior is influenced by the way the problem is framed. Hundreds of experiments (see Kahneman and Tversky 2000 for a review) have shown that decision makers avoid risk in the frame of gains but become risk-seeking in the domain of losses.

The curvature of the utility function also indicates that people are more sensitive to losses than to gains, because the value function is steeper for losses than for gains. The phenomenon is referred to as "loss aversion." For example, when people are presented with a gamble in which they can gain 110 or lose 100 with equal probabilities, they tend to reject it (see Barberis and Thaler 2003).

Another feature of prospect theory shows that the value function is evaluated with respect to a reference point that can be determined in many different ways. In financial choices investors can determine the reference point as the last known price of a share, the price for which a share was purchased, the level of financial aspiration, status quo, and so on. In this sense, the reference point is determined by aspects of the decision problem and by individual differences.

The probability weighting function shown in Figure 36.7 suggests that people overweight small probabilities. Kahneman and Tversky also found that people tended to perceive relatively unlikely outcomes as impossible (i.e., they assigned a weight of zero to them) and tended to perceive relatively certain outcomes as guaranteed (i.e., they assigned a weight of 1 to them).

Prospect theory proved to be successful in explaining many puzzles of the behavior of both individual and institutional investors (see, for example, De Bondt and Thaler 1995; Statman 1999a; Thaler 1999; Shefrin 2000). In the next two sections I show how prospect theory explains the phenomenon of the disposition effect and the equity premium puzzle.

Prospect Theory and Disposition Effect

The disposition effect is a label for investors' tendency to hold losers too long and to sell winners too early (Shefrin and Statman 1985). As I showed earlier, the behavior of rational investors who pay attention to tax consequences should reveal the opposite tendency. So why doesn't it? One possible answer is offered by prospect theory. Odean explains the relation between frame dependence and investment choices in this way: "Suppose an investor purchases a stock that she believes to have an expected return high enough to justify its risk. If the stock appreciates and the investor continues to use the purchase price as a reference point, the stock price will then be in a more concave, more risk-averse, part of the investor's value function. It may be that the stock's expected return continues to justify its risk. However, if the investor somewhat lowers her expectation of the stock's return, she will be likely to sell the stock. What if, instead of appreciating, the stock declines? Then its price is in the convex, risk-seeking part of the value function. Here the investor will continue to hold the stock even if its expected return falls lower than would have been necessary for her to justify its original purchase" (Odean 1998, 1777). In other words, investors sell winners because they tend to be risk-averse in the domain of gains and they hold losers because they tend to be risk-seeking in the domain of losses.

To test these expectations Odean (1998) performs an empirical analysis using data provided by a nationwide discount brokerage house. The data set includes almost 163,000 records of all trades made in 10,000 accounts from January 1987 through December 1993. Two ratios were computed: the proportion of gains realized (PGR) and the proportion of losses realized (PLR), where PGR is the number of realized gains divided by the number of realized gains plus the number of paper gains, and PLR is the number of realized losses divided by the number of realized losses plus the number of paper losses. Realized gain (loss) means that a stock that was in the portfolio at the beginning of the day was sold for a gain (loss). Paper gain (loss) means that a stock that was in the portfolio at the beginning of the day was not sold for a gain (loss). Both ratios were counted after all realized and paper gains and losses had been summed for each account and across accounts.

The hypothesis examined by Odean stated that the PGR ratio would be higher than the PLR ratio. The appearance of such a difference would indicate that investors' behavior revealed the disposition effect, that is, investors were more willing to sell winners than to sell losers. The analysis was made for all months in a year and for December separately. The reason for this distinction was that investors' tax-motivated willingness to sell becomes more intensive in the last month of the year.

Results obtained in Odean's study confirm all expectations described above. He finds that when the analysis was done for an entire year the aggregate PGR ratio exceeded the aggregate PLR ratio, and this difference was statistically significant (using the t-statistic test). In the words of Barber and Odean, "a stock whose value was up was more than 50 percent more likely to be sold from day to day than a stock whose value was down" (1999, 44). As expected, this tendency was not observed for December. These results indicate that, as suggested by prospect theory, investors are more prone to sell winners than to sell losers.

One could argue that this behavioral tendency can be explained by subsequent portfolio performance. Investors could simply assume that the losers they had kept in their portfolios would outperform the winners in the future, believing prices reflect mean reversion. However, Odean demonstrated that the disposition effect could not be explained by reversion to the mean. He compared average excess returns on winning stocks sold to average excess returns on paper losses.[5] It appears that returns on winners sold outperformed returns on paper losses by 3.4 percentage points over the first subsequent year and by 3.6 percentage points over the two subsequent years. Thus investors' tendency to sell winners and to hold losers is revealed to be suboptimal.

Weber and Camerer (1998) tested the disposition effect in an experimental study. Participants in this experiment were allowed to make decisions to buy and sell six risky assets whose prices were determined by a random process. The main hypothesis examined in the study stated that subjects would sell more shares when the price exceeded the purchase price than when the price was below the purchase price, the tendency suggested by disposition effect. Results collected by both authors confirm this hypothesis: "aggregating across all six shares, nearly 60% of the shares sold were winners; less than 40% were losers" (Weber and Camerer 1998, 175).

Prospect Theory and the Equity Premium Puzzle

One feature of financial preferences suggested in prospect theory is loss aversion, that is, the tendency to weigh losses much more heavily than gains. Prospect theory value function implies that losses are weighted about twice as much as gains (see Tversky and Kahneman 1992). Benartzi and Thaler (1995) used the phenomenon of loss aversion to explain one of the most intriguing puzzles of finance—the equity premium puzzle.

There is a huge difference between returns from less risky and more risky assets over time. A dollar invested in U.S. T-bills about seventy years ago would now be worth about $14. On the other hand, a dollar invested in large-cap U.S. stocks at the same time would now be worth more than $2,000. Stocks are riskier than T-bills, and risk is positively correlated with return, but, as shown by Mehra and Prescott (1985), the difference in returns described above (i.e., 7 percent a year) cannot be explained by risk aversion alone. Benartzi and Thaler (1995) argued that the reason is a psychological phenomenon of myopic loss aversion—a combination of weighting losses as more extreme than gains and investors' care for short-term gains and losses.

Myopic loss aversion can be explained using the results of an experimental study performed by Benartzi and Thaler (1999). The participants in this study were allowed to make a choice between two 100-trial gambles. Gamble A consisted of 100 repetitions of a lottery in which one could win 10 cents with a chance of 90 percent and lose 30 cents with a chance of 10 percent. Gamble B offered 100 plays in which there was a 10 percent probability to win 50 cents and a 90 percent probability to gain or lose nothing. A rational decision maker should choose gamble A, because it offers both a higher mean and a lower variance than gamble B. However, Benartzi and Thaler found that almost half of the participants preferred gamble B. The authors argued that subjects who decided in favor of gamble B behaved as if they were making choices between a single play of gamble A and a single play of gamble B, ignoring long-term gains offered by 100 trials of gamble A. Being loss-averse, they also rejected gamble A, which, unlike gamble B, included the possibility of losing some money in a single play.

How can the results of choices between simple lotteries be translated to decisions made on a real stock market? An investor with loss-averse preferences who often evaluates performance of her portfolio (e.g., every day) can easily overlook long-term returns offered by stocks, because she experiences daily falls of stock prices. Even if gains are also experienced on a daily basis, losses hurt more than gains yield pleasure. The myopic loss aversion will thus cause investors to be focused more on short-term losses than on long-term gains.

Benartzi and Thaler (1995) find that the length of the evaluation period that makes investors indifferent between more risky stocks and less risky bonds is about one year. In other words, for this evaluation period stocks and bonds seem to be equally attractive for investors. The authors used this result to analyze processes connected with retirement savings decisions (Benartzi and Thaler 1999). In an experimental study they presented university employees with two different distributions (charts) of returns for two hypothetical retirement funds. The distributions were derived from the actual distributions of stocks and bonds since 1926. One chart presented a distribution of one-year returns, and another chart showed a distribution of annual rates of return for a thirty-year investment, where years were drawn at random. It appeared that people from the two groups (i.e., groups observing two different distributions) made different investment choices. Those who observed annual returns invested 40 percent of their money in stocks. On the other hand, those who were shown rates of return for thirty-year investments invested 90 percent of their money in stocks. Benartzi and Thaler concluded that people from the second group could more easily see the attractiveness of long-term returns for stocks, whereas people from the first group revealed myopic loss aversion.

CONCLUSION

Statman (1999a) introduces two types of investors: "rational" investors and "normal" investors. The former can be found in traditional models from finance. They have stable preferences and are sensitive to quantitative parameters such as variance of returns and covariance between assets. The latter have limited cognitive capacities, tend to commit errors in market forecasts, and do not have stable preferences toward risk. In this essay I focused on the behavior of normal investors, introducing important concepts from the two growing fields of research: behavioral finance and the psychology of investing.

The first part of the essay revealed how knowledge from cognitive psychology can be used to explain errors investors commit in market predictions. I showed how investors tend to be overconfident and overly optimistic, especially when they predict returns for their own portfolios. Three psychological phenomena typically used to explain the positive illusion in market forecasts were described: self-serving bias in attribution, the illusion of knowledge, and the illusion of control.

The second part presented the role emotions play in the behavior of individual investors. I showed how experienced and anticipatory feelings influence financial judgments and portfolio choices. The idea of behavioral portfolio was also presented. The data collected in the psychology of emotions revealed how background moods created, for example, by weather changes cause people to behave in a more optimistic or more pessimistic manner. I showed that changes of weather are correlated with returns on the stock market. In this sense, different examples of investors' behavior that cannot be explained using traditional economic theories become clearer when we take moods and emotions into account.

The final part of this essay discussed investors' preferences toward risk and ambiguity. I showed how investors' tendency to avoid the unknown can be used to interpret the home bias, which often causes portfolios to be underdiversified. I also focused on Kahneman and Tversky's prospect theory—the descriptive theory of choice that seems to be most promising for financial applications. Two examples of such applications were presented: the disposition effect, which is the tendency to hold losers too long and to sell winners too early, and myopic loss aversion, which explains the well-known equity premium puzzle on the behavioral level.

Behavioral finance has been for many years perceived as a new and controversial field of research. Its ideas were used, first of all, to explain the so-called anomalies of investors' beliefs and choices. Today, as some authors (e.g., Thaler 1999) argue, behavioral finance has become more a norm than an extravagance. This means that the difference between the terms *finance* and *behavioral finance*—will disappear someday.

NOTES

1. Other cognitive errors that influence financial judgment are described in De Bondt and Thaler 1995; Kahneman and Riepe 1998; Montier 2002; Shefrin 2000.

2. The Warsaw Stock Exchange Index is the main index of the stock market in Poland.

3. Confidence intervals were calculated as (Phi–Plo) divided by the price level on the forecast date.

4. The choice of Urn 2 in the first condition implies a subjective probability that fewer than 50 percent of the balls in Urn 1 are winning (i.e., blue), while the choice of the same urn in the second condition implies the opposite (see Barberis and Thaler 2001).

5. Returns in excess of the CRSP value-weighted index.

REFERENCES

Barber, Brad M., and Terrance Odean. 1999. "The Courage of Misguided Convictions." *Financial Analysts Journal,* November/December, 41–55.

———. 2000. "Trading Is Hazardous to Your Wealth: The Common Stock Investment Performance of Individual Investors." *Journal of Finance* 55: 773–806.

———. 2001. "Boys Will Be Boys: Gender, Overconfidence, and Common Stock Investment." *Quarterly Journal of Economics* 116: 261–92.

———. 2002. "Online Investors: Do the Slow Die First?" *Review of Financial Studies* 15: 455–87.

Barberis, Nicolas, and Richard H. Thaler. 2003. "A Survey of Behavioral Finance." In George M. Constantinides, Milton Harris, and René Stultz, eds., *Handbook of the Economics of Finance,* 1053–123. Amsterdam: Elsevier Science.

Benartzi, Shlomo, and Richard R. Thaler. 1995. "Myopic Loss Aversion and the Equity Premium Puzzle." *Quarterly Journal of Economics* 110: 75–92.

———. 1999. "Risk Aversion or Myopia? Choices in Repeated Gambles and Retirement Investments." *Management Science* 45: 364–81.

———. 2001. "Naïve Diversification Strategies in Retirement Saving Plans." *American Economic Review* 91: 79–98.

Dawes, Robyn M., David Faust, and Paul E. Meehl. 1989. "Clinical Versus Actuarial Judgment." *Science* 243: 1668–74.

De Bondt, Werner F.M. 1998. "A Portrait of the Individual Investor." *European Economic Review* 42: 831–44.

De Bondt, Werner F.M., and Richard H. Thaler. 1995. "Financial Decision Making in Markets and Firms." In R. Jarrow, V. Maksimovich, and W.T. Ziemba, eds., *Finance, Series of Handbooks in Operations Research and Management Science,* 385–410. Amsterdam: Elsevier-Science.

Dowling, Michael, and Brian M. Lucey. 2005. "The Role of Feelings in Investor Decision-Making." *Journal of Economic Surveys* 19: 211–37.

Ellsberg, D. 1961. "Risk, Ambiguity, and the Savage Axioms." *Quarterly Journal of Economics* 75: 643–69.

Fisher, Kenneth L., and Meir Statman. 1997. "Investment Advice from Mutual Fund Companies." *Journal of Portfolio Management* 24 (fall): 9–26.

———. 2000. "Cognitive Biases in Market Forecasts." *Journal of Portfolio Management* 27: 72–82.

French, Kenneth. L., and James Poterba. 1991. "Investor Diversification and International Equity Markets." *American Economic Review* 81: 222–26.

Froot, Kenneth A., and Emil Dabora. 1999. "How Are Stock Prices Affected by the Location of Trade." *Journal of Financial Economics* 53: 189–216.

Hirshleifer, David, and Tyler Shumway. 2003. "Good Day Sunshine: Stock Returns and the Weather." *Journal of Finance* 58: 1009–32.

Huberman, Gur. 2001. "Familiarity Breeds Investment." *Review of Financial Studies* 14: 659–80.

Isen, Alice M. 2000. "Positive Affect and Decision Making." In Michael Lewis and Jeannette M. Haviland-Jones, eds., *Handbook of Emotions,* 417–35. New York: Guilford Press.

Kahneman, Daniel, and Mark W. Riepe. 1998. "Aspects of Investor Psychology." *Journal of Portfolio Management* 24 (summer): 52–65.

Kahneman, Daniel, and Amos Tversky. 1973. "On the Psychology of Prediction." *Psychological Review* 80: 237–51.

———. 1979. "Prospect Theory: An Analysis of Decision Under Risk." *Econometrica* 47: 263–91.

———. 2000. *Choices, Values, and Frames.* Cambridge: Cambridge University Press.

Langer, Ellen J. 1975. "The Illusion of Control." *Journal of Personality and Social Psychology* 32: 311–28.

Lichtenstein, Sarah, and Baruch Fischhoff. 1977. "Do Those Who Know More Also Know More About How Much They Know?" *Organizational Behavior and Human Performance* 20: 159–83.

Loewenstein, George F., Elke U. Weber, Christopher K. Hsee, and Ned Welch. 2001. "Risk as Feelings." *Psychological Bulletin* 127: 269–86.

Lopes, Lola L. 1987. "Between Hope and Fear: The Psychology of Risk." In L. Berkowitz, ed., *Advances in Experimental Social Psychology,* 255–95. San Diego, CA: Academic Press.

MacGregor, Donald G., Paul Slovic, Michael Berry, and Harold R. Evensky. 1999. "Perception of Financial Risk: A Survey of Advisors and Planners." *Journal of Financial Planning,* September, 68–86.

MacGregor, Donald G., Paul Slovic, David Dreman, and Michael Berry. 2000. "Imagery, Affect, and Financial Judgment." *Journal of Psychology and Financial Markets* 1: 104–10.

Malkiel, Burton G. 1996. *A Random Walk Down Wall Street.* New York: W.W. Norton & Company.

Markowitz, Harry M. 1952. "Portfolio Selection." *Journal of Finance* 7: 77–91.

Mehra, R., and Edward C. Prescott. 1985. "The Equity Premium: A Puzzle." *Journal of Monetary Economics* 15: 145–62.

Miller, Dale T., and Mike Ross. 1975. "Self-Serving Biases in Attribution of Causality: Fact or Fiction?" *Psychological Bulletin* 82: 213–25.

Modigliani, Franco, and Mertin H. Miller. 1958. "The Cost of Capital, Corporate Finance, and the Theory of Investment." *American Economic Review* 48: 655–69.

Montier, James. 2002. *Behavioural Finance: Insights into Irrational Minds and Markets.* Chichester, UK: John Wiley & Sons.

Moore, Don A., Terri R. Kurtzberg, Craig R. Fox, and Max H. Bazerman. 1999. "Positive Illusions and Forecasting Errors in Mutual Fund Investment Decisions." *Organizational Behavior and Human Decision Processes* 79: 95–114.

Nofsinger, John R. 2001. *Investment Madness. How Psychology Affects Your Investing.* London: Prentice Hall.

———. 2005. "Social Mood and Financial Economics." *Journal of Behavioral Finance* 6: 144–60.

Odean, Terrance. 1998. "Are Investors Reluctant to Realize Their Losses?" *Journal of Finance* 53: 1775–98.

Olsen, Robert A. 1997. "Desirability Bias Among Professional Investment Managers: Some Evidence from Experts." *Journal of Behavioral Decision Making* 10: 65–72.

Olsen, Robert A., and George H. Troughton. 2000. "Are Risk Premium Anomalies Caused by Ambiguity?" *Financial Analysts Journal,* March/April, 24–31.

Oskamp, Stuart A. 1965. "Overconfidence in Case-Study Judgments." *Journal of Consulting Psychology,* 29: 261–65.

Plous, Scott. 1997. *The Psychology of Judgment and Decision Making.* New York: McGraw–Hill.

Saunders, Laura. 1993. "Stock Prices and Wall Street Weather." *American Economic Review* 83: 1337–45.

Sharpe, William F. 1964. "Capital Asset Prices: A Theory of Market Equilibrium Under Conditions of Risk." *Journal of Finance* 19: 425–42.

Shefrin, Hersh. 1985. "The Disposition to Sell Winners Too Early and Ride Losers Too Long: Theory and Evidence." *Journal of Finance* 40: 777–90.

———. 2000. *Beyond Greed and Fear: Understanding Behavioral Finance and the Psychology of Investing.* Boston: Harvard Business School Press.

Shefrin, Hersh, and Meir Statman. 2000. "Behavioral Portfolio Theory." *Journal of Financial and Quantitative Analysis* 35: 127–52.

Shiller, Robert J. 2000. *Irrational Exuberance.* Princeton, NJ: Princeton University Press.

Shleifer, Andrei. 2000. *Inefficient Markets: An Introduction to Behavioral Finance.* New York: Oxford University Press.

Smith, Vernon L. 2000. *Bargaining and Market Behavior.* Cambridge: Cambridge University Press.

Statman, Meir. 1999a. "Behavioral Finance: Past Battles and Future Engagements." *Financial Analysts Journal,* November/December, 18–27.

———. 1999b. "Foreign Stocks in Behavioral Portfolios." *Financial Analysts Journal,* March/April, 12–16.

———. 2002. "Lottery Players/Stock Traders." *Financial Analysts Journal,* January/February, 14–21.

Thaler, Richard H. 1995. *Quasi Rational Economics.* New York: Russell Sage Foundation.

———. 1999. "The End of Behavioral Finance." *Financial Analysts Journal,* November/December, 12–17.

———. 2000. "From Homo Economicus to Homo Sapiens." *Journal of Economic Perspectives* 14: 133–41.

Tversky, Amos, and Daniel Kahneman. 1992. "Advances in Prospect Theory: Cumulative Representation of Uncertainty." *Journal of Risk and Uncertainty* 5: 297–323.

Tyszka, Tadeusz, and Piotr Zielonka. 2002. "Expert Judgments: Financial Analysts vs. Weather Forecasters." *Journal of Psychology and Financial Markets* 3: 152–60.

Von Neumann, John, and Oscar Morgenstern. 1947. *Theory of Games and Economic Behavior.* Princeton, NJ: Princeton University Press.

Weber, Martin, and Colin F. Camerer. 1998. "The Disposition Effect in Securities Trading: An Experimental Analysis." *Journal of Economic Behavior and Organization* 33: 167–84.

ABOUT THE EDITOR AND CONTRIBUTORS

Paul J. Albanese received his Ph.D. in economics from Harvard University. He has conducted research on personality and consumer behavior for the past twenty-five years and published a book in this area, *The Personality Continuum and Consumer Behavior* (2002). The Personality Continuum is an integrative framework for the interdisciplinary study of consumer behavior that looks at how qualitatively different levels of personality development are reflected in variations in basic patterns of consumer behavior. He is an associate professor of marketing at Kent State University and teaches courses on consumer behavior.

Morris Altman received his Ph.D. in economics from McGill University. He is a former visiting scholar at Cornell, Duke, Hebrew, and Stanford universities, is professor and head of the Department of Economics at the University of Saskatchewan, and is an elected fellow of the World Innovation Foundation (WIF). He is president of the Society for Advancement of Behavioral Economics (SABE) and is editor of the *Journal of Socio-Economics*. Altman has published more than seventy scholarly papers in behavioral economics, economic history, institutional economics, and empirical macroeconomics. He has also published *Human Agency and Material Welfare: Revisions in Microeconomics and Their Implications for Public Policy* (1996) and *Worker Satisfaction and Economic Performance* (2001) and is currently completing two other books, one related to behavioral labor and the other to behavioral growth theory. He is also currently writing on issues related to economics and ethics, choice behavior, human and labor rights and growth, and the methodologies underlying behavioral economics.

Gerrit Antonides is a professor of economics of consumers and households at Wageningen University, the Netherlands, and senior fellow of the Mansholt Graduate School. He has published in the areas of economic psychology, consumer behavior, and behavioral economics. In addition to publications in international journals, he has published *The Lifetime of a Durable Good* (1990) and *Psychology in Economics and Business* (1996), and co-authored *Consumer Behavior: A European Perspective* (1998) with W. Fred van Raaij. He serves as an associate editor of the *Journal of Economic Psychology* and as a board member of the Society for the Advancement of Behavioral Economics (SABE).

Nathan Berg, affiliated with School of Social Sciences, University of Texas-Dallas, and the Center for Adaptive Behavior and Cognition, Max Planck Institute for Human Development-Berlin, is an economist whose work in behavioral economics has shown that ignoring traditional prescriptions of normative decision theory can lead to enhanced human performance at both the individual and aggregate levels. Berg has shown that overconfident beliefs can improve market liquidity. He has shown that peer comparisons can induce increased risk taking and lead to higher levels of aggregate wealth. His work has also demonstrated that expected utility maximizers may adopt "coarse" or "informationally frugal" decision rules that ignore objectively predictive information, calling into question the normative status of Bayesian updating for the integration of newly arrived information. Berg's applied work on fuzziness in binary classification problems has provided methodological innovations for interpreting survey data on race, ethnicity, and sexual orientation and has been cited in *Business Week,* the *National Post,* the *Village Voice,* the *Advocate,* and the *Atlantic Monthly.*

Fergus Bolger holds a Ph.D. in cognitive psychology from the University of London and is currently a lecturer in decision science at Durham Business School. His current research interests are in judgment and decision making generally, but with specific reference to the nature of expectations regarding the likelihood of future events and their role in the choices made by consumers and other economic agents. He has published more than thirty articles and book chapters, including papers in the *British Journal of Psychology, Quarterly Journal of Experimental Psychology, Organizational Behavior and Human Decision Processes, International Journal of Forecasting, OMEGA,* and *Risk Analysis.*

Gerald A. Cory Jr. received his Ph.D. from Stanford University in 1974. He is senior fellow, Graduate Studies and Research, San Jose State University, where he also teaches business economics in the MBA program. He is past president (2004) of the Across Species Comparisons and Psychopathology Society, an international association of evolutionary psychiatrists and psychologists. He is the author of numerous books, papers, and articles. Recent books include *The Reciprocal Modular Brain in Economics and Politics* (1999), *The Evolutionary Neuroethology of Paul MacLean,* co-edited with R. Gardner (2002), and *The Consilient Brain: The Bioneurological Basis of Economics, Society, and Politics* (2004).

John Cullis is reader in economics and member of the Centre for Public Economics at the University of Bath. His research interests are in public sector economics in general and human resources in particular. He has held visiting posts at a number of North American universities. With Philip Jones, he is co-author of *Microeconomics and the Public Economy: Defending Leviathan* (1987) and *Public Finance and Public Choice: Analytical Perspectives,* 2nd edition (1998).

Alexander J. Field is the Michel and Mary Orradre Professor of Economics at Santa Clara University and the executive director of the Economic History Association. His research covers topics in macroeconomic theory and policy, American and European economic history, and the influence of evolutionary forces on human nature. His most recent publications include *Altruistically Inclined? The Behavioral Sciences, Evolutionary Theory, and the Origins of Reciprocity* (2001) and "The Most Technologically Progressive Decade of the Century," *American Economic Review* (2003). Professor Field received his A.B. from Harvard University (1970), his M.Sc. from the London School of Economics (1971), and his Ph.D. from the University of California, Berkeley (1974). He taught previously at Stanford University.

Nancy Folbre is professor of economics at the University of Massachusetts. Her research explores the interface between political economy and feminist theory, with a particular focus on care work. She recently co-edited *Family Time: The Social Organization of Care* (2004) with Michael Bittman, and is the author of *The Invisible Heart: Economics and Family Values* (2001) and *Who Pays for the Kids: Gender and the Structures of Constraint* (1994), as well as numerous journal articles. She served as co-chair of the MacArthur Foundation Research Network on the Family and the Economy for five years, and is a recipient of a five-year fellowship from the MacArthur Foundation. She is an associate editor of the journal *Feminist Economics.* For more information about her work see www-unix.oit.umass.edu/~folbre/folbre.

Roger Frantz is professor of economics at San Diego State University. He is a member of the editorial board of the *Journal of Socio-Economics* and a board member of the Society for the Advancement of Behavioral Economics. He is the editor of the forthcoming book *Renaissance in Behavioral Economics* and author of *X-Efficiency. Theory, Evidence, and Applications* and *Two Minds. Intuition and Analysis in the History of Economic Thought.* His work on intuition has also been published in the *Journal of Economic Psychology* and the *Journal of Socio-Economics.*

David George is professor of economics at La Salle University and is currently serving as president of the Association for Social Economics. Works currently in progress include an analysis of the impact of market values on higher education, the moral implications of higher-order preferences, and a critical examination of the capabilities approach to human welfare. Earlier writings include extended development of the welfare implications of higher-order preferences and studies of the rhetorical practices of economic textbooks. He is the author of *Preference Pollution: How Markets Create the Desires We Dislike* (2001).

Lonnie Golden is associate professor of economics and labor studies at Penn State University, Abington College. His research primarily focuses on the nature of and trends in working hours, work scheduling, workplace flexibility, overwork, overtime law and regulation, work-life balance, the non-standard work force, social and behavioral sources of labor supply, and labor productivity in the jobless recovery. He is co-editor of the books *Working Time: International Trends, Theory and Policy* (2001) and *Nonstandard Work: The Nature and Challenge of Changing Employment Arrangements* (2001). His Ph.D. is in economics from the University of Illinois at Urbana.

Werner Güth is presently director of the Max Planck Institute for Economics. His current research topics are the theory of bounded rationality, indirect evolution, and experimental economics. He has published in various economics journals but also in journals of neighboring disciplines.

Ralph Hertwig is a professor of applied cognitive science at the University of Basel. His previous positions include research scientist at the Max Planck Institute for Human Development and research scholar at Columbia University. His research focuses on the investigation of boundedly rational decision heuristics across diverse domains such as preferential choice, parental investment, and dietary decision making. He also studies how people sample and process information about risk and uncertainty, and how their understanding of probabilistic information can be improved. He has also written on the divergent experimental cultures in experimental economics and psychology.

Eva Hofmann is scientific assistant at the Faculty of Psychology, University of Vienna. She specializes in purchasing behavior, costumer commitment, psychology of money, and socially responsible investment behavior. Using several qualitative and quantitative research methods, she has written and published on topics such as gender differences and gender influences in purchasing decisions, and recently on motives and attitudes of socially responsible investors.

Hamid Hosseini is professor of international business (and economics), King's College. He received a Ph.D. in economics from the University of Oregon in 1977, an M.A. in economics from Michigan State University, and pursued further graduate studies at the University of California at Berkeley. He has two undergraduate degrees, in economics and engineering, from the University of Akron, 1968. He has had three sabbatical leaves at Harvard University, and one at the University of Chicago's Graduate School of Business. He is the author of over 100 publications, including numerous book chapters and refereed journal publications in journals such as *The History of Political Economy, Review of Social Economy, Journal of Economic Literature, Journal of Socio-Economics, American Journal of Economics and Sociology,* and many more.

Dr. Simon James is reader in economics at the School of Business and Economics, University of Exeter. He previously held a research post at the London School of Economics and is a visiting fellow at the Australian National University, a fellow of the Chartered Institute of Taxation, and a chartered tax adviser. Simon has five master's degrees: in economics, business administration, education, educational management, and law. The subject of his Ph.D. dissertation was taxation and economic decisions. He has published fifteen books and over forty research papers in leading journals. His current research interests include strategic management incorporating tax and other economic variables and tax compliance.

Philip Jones is professor of economics and member of the Centre for Public Economics at the University of Bath. His research interests are in public sector economics and public choice. Together with John Cullis, he has published papers on these topics in leading economics and politics journals.

Bruce E. Kaufman is professor of economics and senior associate of the W.T. Beebe Institute of Personnel and Employment Relations at Georgia State University. He has a Ph.D. in Economics from the University of Wisconsin at Madison and currently does research and teaching in labor economics, industrial relations, human resource management, and the history of thought. He is author or editor of fifteen books and several dozen scholarly articles, including *The Global Evolution of Industrial Relations* (2004) and *Theoretical Perspectives on Work and the Employment Relationship* (2004).

Erich Kirchler has been professor of economic psychology at the Faculty of Psychology, University of Vienna, since 1992, and head of the Department of Economic Psychology, Education, and Evaluation. He was president of the International Association for Research in Economic Psychology and president of the Austrian Association for Psychology. Apart from investigating decision making in the family, he focuses also on saving and credit decisions, tax compliance, and psychological aspects of the euro.

Jack L. Knetsch is professor emeritus at Simon Fraser University, where he has taught and carried out research in behavioral economics, environmental economics, and policy analysis for more than thirty years. He holds degrees in soil science, agricultural economics, and public administration, as well as a Ph.D. in economics from Harvard University. He has been with private and public organizations and agencies in the United States and Malaysia, and has accepted visiting appointments at universities in Europe, Australia, North America, and Asia, including currently a guest professorship at Nankai University. His behavioral economics research has focused on tests of people's valuations of gains and losses, the implications of the observed differences, judgments of fairness, and more recently on time preferences and measures of welfare change.

Stephen E.G. Lea took his degrees at the University of Cambridge and is now a professor of psychology at the University of Exeter. His research spans animal cognition, behavioral ecology, economic behavior, and human visual perception. He is one of the founders of economic psychology in Europe. He is best known for his research articles on pattern recognition in birds and for bringing together ecological, economic, and psychological approaches in the analysis of both human and animal behavior. His books include *The Individual in the Economy* (1987) and *The Economic Psychology of Everyday Life* (2001) as well as *The Descent of Mind* (1999), edited with Michael Corballis.

David Lester has doctoral degrees from Cambridge University in social and political science and Brandeis University in psychology. He has been president of the International Association for Suicide Prevention and has published extensively on suicide and murder.

Alan Lewis holds a personal chair in economic psychology at the University of Bath. His first book was titled *The Psychology of Taxation* (1982), and his most recent is *Morals, Markets and Money: Ethical, Green and Socially Responsible Investing* (2002). He was editor in chief of the *Journal of Economic Psychology* between 1996 and 2000.

Peter Lunt is a reader in social and economic psychology at University College London. His main areas of research interest are the psychology of consumption, media psychology, and the links between psychology and social theory. He has published two books in the area of economic psychology (*Mass Consumption and Personal Identity*, with Sonia Livingstone, and *Economic Socialization*, with Adrian Furnham). In addition, he has published academic journal articles on a range of issues related to the psychology of consumption. He is currently conducting research into the public understanding of financial service and communications regulation, funded by the Economic and Social Research Council, and is working on a book on the relation between social psychology and social theory.

Michael Lynn is an associate professor of consumer behavior and marketing in the School of Hotel Administration at Cornell University. A social psychologist with a Ph.D. from Ohio State University, his research interests center on consumer behavior—especially the use of goods, money, and services to satisfy needs for self-identity, social acceptance, and status. In addition to extensive research on tipping, he has conducted research on consumers' needs for uniqueness and the effects of scarcity on product desirability.

Gary D. Lynne is a professor (and former department head) in the Department of Agricultural Economics and the School of Natural Resources at the University of Nebraska at Lincoln. He has a long-standing interest in what motivates soil and water conservation behavior in farmers, while also examining other kinds of environmental behavior (e.g., recycling). More recently his work has been extended to issues in global climate change. He is currently teaching courses in ecological economics and behavioral economics. His "metaeconomics" suggests that a moral dimension be added to economics, going beyond the traditional focus on only self-interest.

Alan J. MacFadyen is associate professor of economics at the University of Calgary. His research interests lie in the areas of petroleum economics and behavioral economics. He was associate editor of the *Journal of Economic Psychology* for six years. With his psychologist wife, Heather, he edited and contributed to *Economic Psychology: Intersections in Theory and Application* (1986). This book examined factors determining economic behavior from the viewpoint of varying psychological perspectives, application of experimental methods in economics, and the psychological impact of changing economic conditions.

Shlomo Maital is the academic director of the Technion Institute of Management, Israel's leading executive leadership development institute, and a pioneer in action-learning methods. He was summer visiting professor for twenty years in the MIT Sloan School of Management's Management of Technology M.Sc. program, teaching over 1,000 R&D engineers from forty countries. He is the author, co-author, or editor of eight books, including *Executive Economics*, translated into seven languages, and the recent *Managing New Product Development and Innovation*. He is co-editor of a new journal, *International Journal for Technology Management and Innovation Education*. He was a pioneer in behavioral economics and co-founder of the Society for Advancement of Behavioral Economics, of which he is currently president-elect.

Ellen K. Nyhus is associate professor of marketing at Agder University College. Her research is concerned with economic socialization, psychological determinants of labor market success and female labor supply, intrahousehold decision making, and psychological determinants of saving and borrowing behavior.

Andreas Ortmann is a docent (associate professor) and senior researcher at CERGE-EI, a joint workplace of Charles University and the Academy of Sciences of the Czech Republic. His research interests focus on the origin and evolution of moral sentiments, conventions, and organizational forms. He has published in various economics and other social science journals.

Dr. Robert J. Oxoby is an assistant professor in the department of economics at the University of Calgary. He is the director of the University of Calgary's Behavioral and Experimental Economics Laboratory and a research fellow of the Institute for Advanced Policy Research at the University of Calgary. His research interests are in both theoretical and experimental economics on the ways in which individuals' incentives feedback on judgments and perceptions.

Mark Pingle is a professor of economics at the University of Nevada, Reno. He is an associate editor for the *Journal of Economic Behavior and Organization* and for the *Journal of Socio-Economics*. He is on the board of the Society for the Advancement of Behavioral Economics. He has published a series of behaviorally oriented articles on decision making. In particular, he has examined how imitation, submitting to authority, and other nonrational modes of decision behavior allow decision makers to effectively cope with the cost of solving a decision problem.

Jörg Rieskamp is a research scientist at the Max Planck Institute for Human Development, Berlin. After he received his Ph.D. in psychology at the Free University of Berlin he worked as a postdoctoral researcher in the Psychology Department of Indiana University. He studies cognitive models of judgment and decision making, particularly the adaptivity of people's reasoning processes in economic domains such as asset allocation. His work explores the extent to which people can improve their decisions when provided with substantial learning opportunity, and compares fundamentally different learning theories for predicting human learning.

Tobias F. Rötheli holds a doctorate in economics from the University of Bern. He has worked at the Swiss National Bank and has been a visiting scholar at the Federal Reserve Bank of St. Louis, Harvard University, and Stanford University. At present he is professor of macroeconomics at the University of Erfurt. His main research interest is the use of experiments and survey data for modeling expectations and decision making in micro- and macroeconomic models.

Hugh Schwartz received a Ph.D. from Yale University and is visiting professor of economics at the University of the Republic in Uruguay. He taught at the University of Kansas, Yale University, and Case Western Reserve University and worked for many years in the Inter-American Development Bank. Subsequently, he was a Fulbright lecturer and then visiting professor in Uruguay and Brazil and a visiting professor at the Technological Institute of Monterrey in Mexico. In addition to many articles, he edited two books and authored *Rationality Gone Awry? Decision Making Inconsistent with Economic and Financial Theory* (1998) and *Urban Renewal, Municipal Revitalization: The Case of Curitiba, Brazil* (2004).

Kevin Sontheimer is the director of the Economic Policy Institute at the University of Pittsburgh. His research work has spanned the areas of general equilibrium theory, the integration of monetary and general equilibrium theory, industrial organization and regulation, economics and ethics, and behavioral economics. His work has been published in various journals and monographs such as *Econometrica,* the *Journal of Economic Theory,* the *Journal of Money and Banking,* and the *Handbook of Behavioral Economics.*

Fang-Fang Tang is associate professor in the Department of Marketing, Faculty of Business Administration, Chinese University of Hong Kong. He holds a B.Sc. in applied mathematics from Chengdu University of Science and Technology, an M.Sc. in systems engineering from the Management School of Shanghai Jiaotong University, and a Ph.D. in quantitative economics and informatics from the University of Bonn. He has been doing game theory and experimental economics, in addition to Internet pricing. He was a visiting scholar at the Hebrew University for a year and taught in Singapore for four years before he moved to Hong Kong. He currently holds a special guest chair at Nankai University and serves as the external academic director of the Selten Laboratory of Experimental Economics in the International Business School of Nankai University.

Erik Thorbecke is the emeritus H.E. Babcock Professor of Economics and Food Economics and former director of the Program on Comparative Economic Development at Cornell University. He is presently a professor in the Graduate School there. His past positions include chairman of the Department of Economics at Cornell, a professorship at Iowa State University, and associate assistant administrator for program policy at the Agency for International Development. He was awarded an honorary doctorate by the University of Ghent in 1981. He has made contributions in the areas of economic and agricultural development, the measurement and analysis of poverty and malnutrition, the Social Accounting Matrix and general equilibrium modeling, and international economic policy. The Foster-Greer-Thorbecke poverty measure has been adopted as the standard poverty measure by the World Bank and practically all UN agencies, is used almost universally by researchers doing empirical work on poverty, and was recently incorporated in the Mexican constitution and used to allocate interregionally 14 billion pesos to educational, health, and nutritional programs benefiting the poor. Recent publications include *Taiwan's Development Experience: Lessons on Roles of Government and Market* with H. Wan (1999), *State, Market and Civil Organizations: New Theories, New Practices, and Their Implications for Rural Development* edited with A. de Janvry and E. Sadoulet (1995), *Intersectoral Linkages and Their Impact on Rural Poverty Alleviation: A Social Accounting Matrix Approach* (1995), and *Adjustment and Equity in Indonesia* with collaborators (1992). Earlier books include *The Theory and Design of Economic Development* with Irma Adelman (1968) and *The Role of Agriculture in Economic Development* (1968). He is the author or co-author of about 25 books and 200 articles. He has been an economic adviser to numerous U.S. and international agencies and foreign governments,

736   ABOUT THE EDITOR AND CONTRIBUTORS

including USAID, the Food and Agricultural Organization, the International Labor Organization, the World Bank, and the OECD.

Peter M. Todd received a Ph.D. in psychology from Stanford University in 1992, using neural network models to explore the evolution of learning. In 1995 he moved to Germany to help found the Center for Adaptive Behavior and Cognition, now at the Max Planck Institute for Human Development. His research interests have focused on modeling the interactions between decision making and decision environments, including how the two interact and co-evolve, and on exploring choices involving sequential search over time. The center's work on heuristic decision mechanisms led to the co-authored book *Simple Heuristics That Make Us Smart* (1999).

John F. Tomer is professor of economics at Manhattan College. Tomer is a founding member and active participant in the Society for the Advancement of Behavioral Economics; he was president from 1992 to 2003 and currently is executive director. Since 2002, he has served as co-editor of the *Journal of Socio-Economics.* He is the author of two books, *Organizational Capital: The Path to Higher Productivity and Well-being* (1987) and *The Human Firm: A Socio-Economic Analysis of Its Behavior and Potential in a New Economic Age* (1999). He has written over thirty-five articles, which have appeared in journals such as the *Eastern Economic Journal,* the *Journal of Economic Issues,* the *Review of Social Economy,* the *Journal of Socio-Economics, Human Relations,* the *Journal of Post Keynesian Economics,* and *Ecological Economics.* His family includes his wife, Doris, and sons, Russell and Jeffrey, now twenty-seven and twenty-three. He is an avid tennis player and skier.

Ger Trip is assistant professor of business economics at Wageningen University and fellow of the Mansholt Graduate School. He is team manager of VWO-Campus, an intermediary office between Wageningen University and secondary schools. He also holds the position of associate lector of agribusiness production chains at Inholland University. He has published in the areas of agricultural management and economics.

Thomas S. Ulen is Swanlund Chair, University of Illinois at Urbana-Champaign; professor of law, College of Law, University of Illinois at Urbana-Champaign; and director of the Illinois Program in Law and Economics. He received his bachelor's degree from Dartmouth College in 1968 and his Ph.D. in economics from Stanford University in 1979. He joined the faculty of the Department of Economics at the University of Illinois in 1977. Ulen is one of the pioneers in developing the field of law and economics. He has been a visiting professor at the University of California at Davis, Fudan University, Katholieke Universiteit (Leuven), the University of Ljubljana, the University of Bielefeld, the University of Hamburg, the Universidad Torcuato di Tella, and the University of Ghent. He has published three books on law and economics and more than seventy articles, essays, and book reviews. His textbook with Robert D. Cooter, *Law and Economics,* is now in its fourth edition and has been translated into Chinese, Japanese, Italian, Spanish, French, and Russian. Ulen has been recently working on the relationship between cognitive psychology and theories of human behavior as they apply to the law and have a book on that subject forthcoming from the University of Chicago Press with Russell Korobkin.

Paul Webley is professor of economic psychology and currently deputy vice chancellor at the University of Exeter. He was president of the International Association for Research in Economic Psychology from 1999 to 2001. His current research is concerned with the economic psychology of personal money management (saving, debt, investment), tax compliance, and children's economic behaviour. His books include *Tax Evasion: An Experimental Approach,* co-authored with H.S.J. Robben, H. Elffers, and D.J. Hessing (1991); *Children's Saving,* co-authored with E.J.S. Sonuga-Barke (1993); *The New Economic Mind,* co-authored with A. Lewis and A. Furnham (1995); and *The Economic Psychology of Everyday Life,* co-authored with C. Burgoyne, S.E.G. Lea, and B.M. Young (2001).

Bijou Yang Lester earned a M.A. and Ph.D. in economics from the University of Pennsylvania and an B.A. and M.A. in economics from National Taiwan University. She is professor of economics at Drexel University and has been treasurer of the Society for the Advancement of Behavioral Economics since 1992. She has published extensively on the economy and suicide, e-commerce, and neuroeconomics.

Gideon Yaniv is associate professor of economics at the Tel Aviv College of Management. He received his Ph.D. from the Hebrew University in 1978 and has since taught in most universities in Israel as well as held visiting positions at the University of California at Berkeley and Columbia University. For many years he directed the Economic Research Department at the National Insurance Institute in Jerusalem. His fields of interest are the economics of crime and law enforcement (in particular, tax evasion, welfare fraud, and minimum wage noncompliance) and the economics of health-compromising behavior, in which he has published extensively.

Tomasz Zaleskiewicz is associate professor at the Warsaw School of Social Psychology (Wroclaw Faculty). His research interests include behavioral finance, economic psychology, and behavioral decision theory. He is the author or co-author of four books on risk taking, risk perception, behavioral finance, and cognitive psychology. He has also published papers on risk taking and the psychology of investing in international journals, handbooks, and conference proceedings. His recent research focuses on an original theory of risk perception that introduces two categories of risk: instrumental risk and stimulating risk.

INDEX

Moral system, 8, 203
Morgenstern, Oskar, 212
MORI (Market and Opinion Research International), 607
Moscovici, Serge, 334–35
Motivation, 78, 83, 610–16
  arousal theory of, 184
  deep owner, 263
  for ethical investing, 610–16
  instrumental, 611–12, 615–16
  intrinsic, 612–16
  for self-interest, 36
  of workers, 262, 459
MRS (marginal rate of substitution), 480
Mullainathan, Sendhil, 188, 190
Müller-Lyer illusion, 222, 223
Müller-Peters, A., 292
Multiagent firms, x-efficiency in, 149–52
Multilevel selection, 169, 500. *See also* Group selection
Mundane realism, 447
Murphy, Kevin M., 561–65
Musgrave, R.A., 593, 595
Mutual funds, 603, 604, 610, 611
Myers, David G., 210, 211
Myint, Hya, 665–66

N

Narcissistic personality, 15
Narcissistic personality organization, 14–15. *See also* Primitive range
Nash equilibrium (demand game), 175, 411, 442, 462, 551
National Association of Investment Clubs, 712
National need for power, 632
National Opinion Poll survey, 618–19
National pride, 292
Natural selection, 174, 281, 284
  influence on behavior, 499
  and reproduction, 501
  for reproductive fitness, 500
Negotiators (labor), 460
Neoclassical economics, 8, 68, 146, 194
  behaviorism vs., 238–40
  concerns of, 239
  and decision making, 89
  desires in, 192
  efficiency in, 195
  and normality, 18
  to taxation, 590–92
  of tax compliance, 591
Neocortex, 25, 52
Neo-mammalian ("new") brain, 25
Network externalities model, 613–15
Neural architecture, 39–41
Neural circuitry, 24
Neural processes, 249–52
Neuroscience, 38, 102–3
Neuroticism, 631
Neurotic person, 9–10
Neurotic range (Personality Continuum), 9–11, 20–23
  self-control of person in, 10
  utility function at, 10–11

"New" (neo-mammalian) brain, 25
Newby-Clark, Ian R., 300
Newton, Isaac, 207
Newtonian physics, 60
New Zealand Inland Revenue Department, 596, 597
Nielson, Klaus, 258
Ninth-price Vickrey auctions, 431–33
Nixon, Richard, 210
Nofsinger, John R., 715–16
Noise, 231
Nonbehavioral choice theory, 341–42
Nonbehavioral rational choice theory, 343
Nonexponential discounting, 306
Nonkin, reciprocity among, 174
Nonoptimizer (behavioralist), 239
Nonoptimizing behavior, 239
Nonrationality, 212–13, 349
Norms. *See* Social norms
Normality, 4–5
Normal range (Personality Continuum), 4–9, 20–23
Normative beliefs, 185
Normative economics, 195–96, 521–22
North, D., 352
North, Douglas, 662–63
Nyhus, Ellen K., 301, 305, 307, 317

O

Objective circuits, 26
Objective expressions, 28
Object relations theory, 3
  concern in, 8
  stable behavior pattern determinants in, 5
Obsessive personality organization. *See* Neurotic range
Occam's razor, 212
Odean, Terrance, 710–11, 713, 723–24
Odyssey, 306–7
Oedipal situation, 5, 9
Offerman, T., 351
Offspring. *See* Child
O'Higgins, Eleanor R.E., 466
"Old" (paleo-mammalian) brain, 25
Omniscience, practical, 54, 55
One-shot prisoner's dilemma game, 173–75
Online investing, 711–12
On-site interview, 363
"On the Study of Statistical Institutions" (Kahneman and Tversky), 51
Opportunities, 190
Optimal behavior, 285
Optimal employment revenue, 140
Optimal foraging theory, 285, 287
Optimality, 281. *See also* Rationality
  Bellman's principle of, 347
  as biological term, 281
  in ecology, 281
Optimization, 244, 341, 500
Optimizer, 239
Optimizing decisions, 239
Optimizing operator, 347
Ordinal utility theory, 10, 17
Ordinary functioning, 9